Lecture Notes in Computer Science   8925

Commenced Publication in 1973
Founding and Former Series Editors:
Gerhard Goos, Juris Hartmanis, and Jan van Leeuwen

More information about this series at http://www.springer.com/series/7412

Lourdes Agapito · Michael M. Bronstein
Carsten Rother (Eds.)

Computer Vision –
ECCV 2014 Workshops

Zurich, Switzerland, September 6–7 and 12, 2014
Proceedings, Part I

 Springer

Editors
Lourdes Agapito
University College London
London
UK

Carsten Rother
Technische Universität Dresden
Dresden
Germany

Michael M. Bronstein
University of Lugano
Lugano
Switzerland

Videos to this book can be accessed at
http://www.springerimages.com/videos/978-3-319-16177-8

ISSN 0302-9743   ISSN 1611-3349   (electronic)
Lecture Notes in Computer Science
ISBN 978-3-319-16177-8   ISBN 978-3-319-16178-5   (eBook)
DOI 10.1007/978-3-319-16178-5

Library of Congress Control Number: 2015933663

LNCS Sublibrary: SL6 – Image Processing, Computer Vision, Pattern Recognition, and Graphics

Springer Cham Heidelberg New York Dordrecht London
© Springer International Publishing Switzerland 2015

Printed on acid-free paper

Springer International Publishing AG Switzerland is part of Springer Science+Business Media
(www.springer.com)

Foreword

Welcome to Zurich !

As you know, the European Conference on Computer Vision is one of the top conferences on computer vision. It was first held in 1990 in Antibes (France) with subsequent conferences in Santa Margherita Ligure (Italy) in 1992, Stockholm (Sweden) in 1994, Cambridge (UK) in 1996, Freiburg (Germany) in 1998, Dublin (Ireland) in 2000, Copenhagen (Denmark) in 2002, Prague (Czech Republic) in 2004, Graz (Austria) in 2006, Marseille (France) in 2008, Heraklion (Greece) in 2010, and Firenze (Italy) in 2012. Many people have worked hard to turn the 2014 edition into as great a success. We hope you will find this a mission accomplished.

The Chairs have decided to adhere to the classical single-track scheme. In terms of the time ordering, we have decided to largely follow the Firenze example (typically starting with poster sessions, followed by oral sessions), which offers a lot of flexibility to network and is more forgiving for the not-so-early-birds and hardcore gourmets.

A large conference like ECCV requires the help of many. They made sure you again get a full program including the main conference, tutorials, workshops, exhibits, demos, proceedings, video streaming/archive, and web descriptions. We want to cordially thank all those volunteers! Please have a look at the conference website to see their names (http://eccv2014.org/people/). We also thank our generous sponsors. You will see their logos around at several occasions during the week, and also prominently on the ECCV 2014 website (http://eccv2014.org/). Their support has been vital to keep prices low and to enrich the program. And it is good to see such level of industrial interest in what our community is doing!

Please do not forget to take advantage of your free travel pass. It allows you to crisscross our splendid city with its fabulous public transportation.

We hope you will enjoy ECCV 2014 to the full.

Also, willkommen in Zürich!

September 2014

Marc Pollefeys
Luc Van Gool

Preface

Welcome to the Workshop proceedings of the 13th European Conference on Computer Vision, held during September 6–12, 2014 in Zurich, Switzerland. We are delighted that the main ECCV 2014 was accompanied by 28 workshops.

We received 38 workshop proposals on diverse computer vision topics. The evaluation process was not easy because of the high quality of the submissions, and the final 28 selected workshops complemented the main conference program. Nearly all of the workshops were running for a full day, with the exception of two half-day workshops and one two-day workshop. In the end, the addressed workshop topics constituted a good mix between novel current trends and traditional issues, without forgetting to address the fundamentals of the computational vision area.

We would like to thank all the Workshop Organizers for their hard work and for making the workshop sessions a great success. We hope that participants enjoyed the workshops, together with the associated papers included in these volumes.

Kind regards / mit freundlichen Grüßen,

November 2014

Michael M. Bronstein
Lourdes Agapito
Carsten Rother

Organization

General Chairs

Luc Van Gool   ETH Zurich, Switzerland
Marc Pollefeys   ETH Zurich, Switzerland

Program Chairs

Tinne Tuytelaars   Katholieke Universiteit Leuven, Belgium
Bernt Schiele   MPI Informatics, Saarbrücken, Germany
Tomas Pajdla   Czech Technical University Prague,
                                    Czech Republic
David Fleet   University of Toronto, Canada

Local Arrangement Chairs

Konrad Schindler   ETH Zurich, Switzerland
Vittorio Ferrari   University of Edinburgh, UK

Workshop Chairs

Lourdes Agapito   University College London, UK
Carsten Rother   Technische Universität Dresden, Germany
Michael M. Bronstein   University of Lugano, Switzerland

Tutorial Chairs

Bastian Leibe   RWTH Aachen, Germany
Paolo Favaro   University of Bern, Switzerland
Christoph H. Lampert   IST, Austria

Poster Chair

Helmut Grabner   ETH Zurich, Switzerland

Publication Chairs

Mario Fritz   MPI Informatics, Saarbrücken, Germany
Michael Stark   MPI Informatics, Saarbrücken, Germany

Demo Chairs

Davide Scaramuzza   University of Zurich, Switzerland
Jan-Michael Frahm   University of North Carolina at Chapel Hill, USA

Exhibition Chair

Tamar Tolcachier   University of Zurich, Switzerland

Industrial Liason Chairs

Alexander Sorkine-Hornung   Disney Research Zurich, Switzerland
Fatih Porikli   ANU, Australia

Student Grant Chair

Seon Joo Kim   Yonsei University, Korea

Air Shelters Accommodation Chair

Maros Blaha   ETH Zurich, Switzerland

Website Chairs

Lorenz Meier   ETH Zurich, Switzerland
Bastien Jacquet   ETH Zurich, Switzerland

Internet Chair

Thorsten Steenbock   ETH Zurich, Switzerland

Student Volunteer Chairs

Andrea Cohen   ETH Zurich, Switzerland
Ralf Dragon   ETH Zurich, Switzerland
Laura Leal-Taixé   ETH Zurich, Switzerland

Finance Chair

Amael Delaunoy   ETH Zurich, Switzerland

Conference Coordinator

Susanne H. Keller   ETH Zurich, Switzerland

Workshop Organizers

W01 - Where Computer Vision Meets Art (VISART)

Gustavo Carneiro   The University of Adelaide, Australia
Alessio Del Bue   Italian Institute of Technology, Italy
Joao Paulo Costeira   Instituto Superior Tecnico, Lisbon, Portugal

W02 - Computer Vision in Vehicle Technology with Special Session on Micro Aerial Vehicles

David Geronimo   KTH, Sweden
Friedrich Fraundorfer   Technische Universität München
Davide Scaramuzza   University of Zurich, Switzerland

W03 - Spontaneous Facial Behavior Analysis

Guoying Zhao   University of Oulu, Finland
Stefanos Zafeiriou   Imperial College London, UK
Matti Pietikäinen   University of Oulu, Finland
Maja Pantic   Imperial College London, UK

W04 - Consumer Depth Cameras for Computer Vision

Andrea Fossati   ETH Zurich, Switzerland
Jürgen Gall   University of Bonn, Germany
Miles Hansard   Queen Mary University London, UK

W05 - ChaLearn Looking at People: Pose Recovery, Action/Interaction, Gesture Recognition

Sergio Escalera   Computer Vision Center, UAB and University
                                      of Barcelona, Catalonia, Spain
Jordi González   Universitat Autònoma de Barcelona and Computer
                                      Vision Center, Catalonia, Spain
Xavier Baró   Universitat Oberta de Catalunya and Computer
                                      Vision Center, Catalonia, Spain
Isabelle Guyon   Clopinet, Berkeley, California, USA
Jamie Shotton   Microsoft Research Cambridge, UK

W06 - Video Event Categorization, Tagging, and Retrieval toward Big Data

Thomas S. Huang	University of Illinois at Urbana-Champaign, USA
Tieniu Tan	Chinese Academy of Sciences, China
Yun Raymond Fu	Northeastern University, Boston, USA
Ling Shao	University of Sheffield, UK
Jianguo Zhang	University of Dundee, UK
Liang Wang	Chinese Academy of Sciences, China

W07 - Computer Vision with Local Binary Patterns Variants

Abdenour Hadid	University of Oulu, Finland
Stan Z. Li	Chinese Academy of Sciences, China
Jean-Luc Dugelay	Eurecom, France

W08 - Reconstruction Meets Recognition Challenge (RMRC)

Nathan Silberman	New York University, USA
Raquel Urtasun	University of Toronto, Canada
Andreas Geiger	MPI Intelligent Systems, Germany
Derek Hoiem	University of Illinois at Urbana-Champaign, USA
Sanja Fidler	University of Toronto, Canada
Antonio Torralba	Massachusetts Institute of Technology, USA
Rob Fergus	New York University, USA
Philip Lenz	Karlsruher Institut für Technologie, Germany
Jianxiong Xiao	Princeton, USA

W09 - Visual Object Tracking Challenge

Roman Pflugfelder	Austrian Institute of Technology, Austria
Matej Kristan	University of Ljubljana, Slovenia
Ales Leonardis	University of Birmingham, UK
Jiri Matas	Czech Technical University in Prague, Czech Republic

W10 - Computer Vision + ONTology Applied Cross-disciplinary Technologies (CONTACT)

Marco Cristani	University of Verona, Italy
Robert Ferrario	ISTC-CNR, Trento, Italy
Jason Corso	SUNY Buffalo, USA

W11 - Visual Perception of Affordances and Functional Visual Primitives for Scene Analysis

Karthik Mahesh Varadarajan   Technical University of Vienna, Austria
Alireza Fathi   Stanford University, USA
Jürgen Gall   University of Bon, Germany
Markus Vincze   Technical University of Vienna, Austria

W12 - Graphical Models in Computer Vision

Michael Yang   Leibniz University Hannover, Germany
Qinfeng (Javen) Shi   University of Adelaide, Australia
Sebastian Nowozin   Microsoft Research Cambridge, UK

W13 - Human-Machine Communication for Visual Recognition and Search

Adriana Kovashka   University of Texas at Austin, USA
Kristen Grauman   University of Texas at Austin, USA
Devi Parikh   Virginia Tech, USA

W14 - Light Fields for Computer Vision

Jingyi Yu   University of Delaware, USA
Bastian Goldluecke   Heidelberg University, Germany
Rick Szeliski   Microsoft Research, USA

W15 - Computer Vision for Road Scene Understanding and Autonomous Driving

Bart Nabbe   Toyota, USA
Raquel Urtasun   University of Toronto, Canada
Matthieu Salzman   NICTA, Australia
Lars Petersson   NICTA, Australia
Jose Alvarez   NICTA, Australia
Fatih Porikli   NICTA, Australia
Gary Overett   NICTA, Australia
Nick Barnes   NICTA, Australia

W16 - Soft Biometrics

Abdenour Hadid   University of Oulu, Finland
Paulo Lobato Correia   University of Lisbon, Portugal
Thomas Moeslund   Aalborg University, Denmark

W17 - THUMOS Challenge: Action Recognition with a Large Number of Classes

Jingen Liu	SRI International, USA
Yu-Gang Jiang	Fudan University, China
Amir Roshan Zamir	UCF, USA
George Toderici	Google, USA
Ivan Laptev	Inria, France
Mubarak Shah	UCF, USA
Rahul Sukthankar	Google Research, USA

W18 - Transferring and Adapting Source Knowledge (TASK) in Computer Vision (CV)

Antonio M. Lopez	Computer Vision Center and Universitat Autónoma de Barcelona, Spain
Kate Saenko	University of Massachusetts Lowell, USA
Francesco Orabona	Toyota Technological Institute Chicago, USA
José Antonio Rodríguez	Xerox Research EuroFrance
David Vázquez	Computer Vision Cente, Spain
Sebastian Ramos	Computer Vision Center and Universitat Autónoma de Barcelona, Spain
Jiaolong Xu	Computer Vision Center and Universitat Autónoma de Barcelona, Spain

W19 - Visual Surveillance and Re-identification

Shaogang Gong	Queen Mary University of London, UK
Steve Maybank	Birkbeck College, University of London, UK
James Orwell	Kingston University, UK
Marco Cristani	University of Verona, Italy
Kaiqi Huang	National Laboratory of Pattern Recognition, China
Shuicheng Yan	National University of Singapore, Singapore

W20 - Color and Photometry in Computer Vision

Theo Gevers	University of Amsterdam, The Netherlands
Arjan Gijsenij	Akzo Nobel, The Netherlands
Todd Zickler	Harvard University, USA
Jose M. Alvarez	NICTA, Australia

W21 - Storytelling with Images and Videos

Gunhee Kim	Disney Research, USA
Leonid Sigal	Disney, USA
Kristen Grauman	University of Texas at Austin, USA
Tamara Berg	University of North Carolina at Chapel Hill, USA

W22 - Assistive Computer Vision and Robotics

Giovanni Maria Farinella   University of Catania, Italy
Marco Leo   CNR- Institute of Optics, Italy
Gerard Medioni   USC, USA
Mohan Triverdi   UCSD, USA

W23 - Computer Vision Problems in Plant Phenotyping

Hanno Scharr   Forschungszentrum Jülich, Germany
Sotirios Tsaftaris   IMT Lucca, Italy

W24 - Human Behavior Understanding

Albert Ali Salah   Boğaziçi University, Turkey
Louis-Philippe Morency   University of Southern California, USA
Rita Cucchiara   University of Modena and Reggio Emilia, Italy

W25 - ImageNet Large-Scale Visual Recognition Challenge (ILSVRC2014)

Olga Russakovsky   Stanford University, USA
Jon Krause   Stanford University, USA
Jia Deng   University of Michigan, USA
Alex Berg   University of North Carolina at Chapel Hill, USA
Fei-Fei Li   Stanford University, USA

W26 - Non-Rigid Shape Analysis and Deformable Image Alignment

Alex Bronstein   Tel-Aviv University, Israel
Umberto Castellani   University of Verona, Italy
Maks Ovsjanikov   Ecole Polytechnique, France

W27 - Video Segmentation

Fabio Galasso   MPI Informatics Saarbrücken, Germany
Thomas Brox   University of Freiburg, Germany
Fuxin Li   Georgia Institute of Technology, Germany
James M. Rehg   Georgia Institute of Technology, USA
Bernt Schiele   MPI Informatics Saarbrücken, Germany

W28 - Parts and Attributes

Rogerio S. Feris   IBM, USA
Christoph H. Lampert   IST, Austria
Devi Parikh   Virginia Tech, USA

Contents – Part I

W02 - Computer Vision in Vehicle Technology

W03 - Spontaneous Facial Behavior Analysis

W04 - Consumer Depth Cameras for Computer Vision

**W05 - ChaLearn Looking at People: Pose Recovery, Action/Interaction,
Gesture Recognition**

W01 - Where Computer Vision Meets Art (VISART)

JenAesthetics Subjective Dataset: Analyzing Paintings by Subjective Scores

Seyed Ali Amirshahi[1,2]([✉]), Gregor Uwe Hayn-Leichsenring[2],
Joachim Denzler[1], and Christoph Redies[2]

[1] Computer Vision Group, Friedrich Schiller University Jena, Jena, Germany
{seyed-ali.amirshahi,joachim.denzler}@uni-jena.de
http://www.inf-cv.uni-jena.de
[2] Experimental Aesthetics Group, Institute of Anatomy I,
Jena University Hospital, Jena, Germany
{Gregor.Hayn-Leichsenring,christoph.redies}@med.uni-jena.de
http://www.anatomie1.uniklinikum-jena.de

Abstract. Over the last few years, researchers from the computer vision
and image processing community have joined other research groups in
searching for the bases of aesthetic judgment of paintings and photographs. One of the most important issues, which has hampered research
in the case of paintings compared to photographs, is the lack of subjective
datasets available for public use. This issue has not only been mentioned
in different publications, but was also widely discussed at different conferences and workshops. In the current work, we perform a subjective
test on a recently released dataset of aesthetic paintings. The subjective
test not only collects scores based on the subjective aesthetic quality, but
also on other properties that have been linked to aesthetic judgment.

Keywords: Computational aesthetics · Aesthetic · Beauty · Color ·
Content · Composition · Paintings · Subjective dataset · JenAesthetics
dataset

1 Introduction

In recent years, there has been a growing interest in the topic of aesthetic quality assessment of paintings and photographs in the computer vision and image
processing community. This interest has resulted in what is now known as computational aesthetics [12]. Numerous workshops, conferences and special sessions
dealing with this topic have attracted researchers in the past few years [2–10,17–
20,22–24,28–30,39]. Due to the nature of research in this field, further progress
depends on the availability of datasets for analysis.

Over the years, most research in this field has focused on proposing new
methods to evaluate different aesthetic properties [2–11,17,18,20,21,23,24,28–
30,38,39]. Although these methods reached interesting results, the lack of a
common dataset prevented different methods and approaches to be comparable
to one another.

© Springer International Publishing Switzerland 2015
L. Agapito et al. (Eds.): ECCV 2014 Workshops, Part I, LNCS 8925, pp. 3–19, 2015.
DOI: 10.1007/978-3-319-16178-5_1

Like in other fields of research that deal with quality assessment of stimuli, such as image and video quality assessment, subjective datasets [32–34, 36, 37] play an important role for research. Subjective datasets provide researchers with scores given by observers with regard to different properties of a stimuli. Thanks to the many photo-sharing websites nowadays used by professional and amateur photographers, several subjective datasets [8, 17, 19, 20, 22, 23] covering different types and styles of photographs have been introduced to the public. These websites provide the user with a large number of photographs that have been rated subjectively by the community of photographers. The procedure for collecting such datasets is inexpensive both in the sense of time consumption and financial cost. It should be mentioned that a drawback of these datasets is that the scoring of images is not done in a standardized format. This means that the subjective scores were likely given under various viewing condition using different displaying devices. To try to prevent such issues, in the field of image and video quality, subjective tests are normally collected using specific standards such as those described in [13]. Unfortunately, in the aesthetic quality assessment community, there is no specific standard agreed among different research groups with regard to how subjective tests should be performed as of yet.

Unlike for photographs, there has been no public dataset of paintings with subjective scores until recently. Last year, two small subjective datasets have been introduced to the community [2, 39]. However, these datasets fall short of corresponding to the needs of the community, which we will describe in the next section.

In this paper, we take advantage of the JenAesthetics dataset [1, 5, 15], which is available for public use, and perform a subjective test to evaluate different properties of the paintings in this dataset. The JenAesthetics dataset is one of the largest publicly available datasets and covers a wide range of different styles, art periods, and subject matters [1, 5]. The images in this dataset are colored oil paintings that are all on show in museums and were scanned at a high resolution. The present study will combine the objective data previously provided in [5] with different subjective scores.

The next sections of this article are as follow: Section 2 introduces the previous subjective datasets. Section 3 describes the JenAesthetics subjective dataset. Section 4 evaluates the subjective scores provided by the observers. Finally, Section 5 gives a short conclusion and proposes possible future work to extend this dataset.

2   Previous Work

Before the introduction of the two mentioned datasets [2, 39] (Sections 2.1 and 2.2, respectively), other researchers [4, 7, 10, 18, 21, 24, 28] have gathered their own datasets. This was done either by scanning high-quality art books, by ordering digital samples from museums, or by using their own personal collections. Unfortunately, there is no possibility to release these datasets to other research groups due to copyright restrictions, making different approaches incomparable to one another.

Table 1. Comparison of different properties between the JenAesthetics subjective dataset and the JenAestheticsβ [2] and the MART [39] subjective datasets. NA, not assessed.

Properties	JenAesthetics	JenAestheticsβ [2]	MART[39]
Number of images	1628	281	500
Number of observers per painting	19 - 21	49	20
Total number of observers	134	49	100
Scores of individual observers	yes	no	yes
Color images	yes	yes	majority
Average image size (pixels)	4583 × 4434	2489 × 2517	513 × 523
Number of properties evaluated	5	1 (beauty)	1 (emotion)
Rating scale	continuous, 1-100	ordinal, 1-4	ordinal, 1-7
Art periods/styles	11	NA	1
Number of subject matters	16	NA	1
Number of artists	410	36	78

In the following subsections, we will give a short summary on the two available subjective datasets [2,39]. Table 1 lists different properties of the available subjective datasets.

2.1 JenAestheticsβ [2]

This dataset, which was introduced in 2013, consists of 281 paintings of different subject matters and art styles. A positive aspect of this dataset is the high number of observers who rated the images. The subjective scoring in this dataset has been done based on a scale of 1-4. Subjective scores show that paintings with bluish or greenish colors are generally given higher subjective scores compared to paintings with brownish or dark colors [2]. This result confirms findings by Palmer and Schloss [25]. Compared to the JenAesthetics dataset [1,5,15], this dataset does not provide information on the art periods which the paintings belong to, and no subject matters are assigned to the paintings.

2.2 MART Dataset [39]

This subjective dataset of paintings consists of 500 abstract paintings produced between 1913 and 2008. The paintings were selected from the MART museum in Rovereto, Italy. The images in this dataset were divided into 5 subsets, each consisting of 100 images. 20 observers rated each subset based on a 7-point rating scale. The observers were mostly female (74 females, 26 males) and on average visited 5.5 museums per year. The observers were allowed to spend as much time as they wanted to see and observe a painting before giving a score, but they were advised to rate the paintings in the fastest possible manner. 11 images are in a monochrome format (Table 1). Also, the average pixel size of the images is relatively small compared to the JenAesthetics and the JenAestheticsβ [2] datasets. Unlike these two datasets, the paintings of the MART dataset belong to a single art period/style (i.e., abstract art).

3   JenAesthetics Subjective Dataset

In collecting the JenAesthetics dataset [1,5,15], Amirshahi et al. took advantage of the fact that the Google Art Project (http://www.googleartproject.com/) has released a large number of high-quality scanned versions of artworks for public use. Although the artworks in this dataset are mostly from famous painters, this does not guarantee that they will be ranked highly by non-expert observers. The non-expert observers who participated in our experiment were not familiar with most of the paintings and/or painters. The importance of familiarity in evaluating the quality of a photograph or painting has been noticed in different studies [8,18]. A painting is labelled as familiar in the JenAesthetics subjective dataset if the observer believes that he/she has previously seen the painting or if they know the painter. Moreover, as it will be discussed in Section 4, some famous paintings are not among paintings with the highest subjective scores. This implies that the observers are not necessarily biased towards famous paintings.

As mentioned previously, there is a lack of standards for subjective tests in the field of computational aesthetics. We believe that the following issues have to be taken into account when performing a subjective test of paintings.

1. Tests should be carried out under standard viewing conditions in a controlled environment. This will ensure that the observers are viewing all paintings under the same condition so that the scores are comparable.
2. The observers should not be familiar with the paintings. Different approaches have been taken to prevent the subjective scores from being biased towards a familiar painting. For example, Li et al. [18] removed scores given by observers when they expressed that they were familiar with the painting shown. In our work, we found that the observers were not familiar with the vast majority of paintings evaluated.
3. Multiple properties should be assessed and not just one. For example, if we evaluate the aesthetic quality as well as the observers' liking of the colors, composition, and content of the paintings, as done for the JenAesthetics subjective dataset in the present study, we can correlate each preference with the aesthetic scores given by the observer (see Section 4.2).
4. The visual ability of the observer should be taken into account. Results provided from observers with visual impairment should be treated differently compared to other observers.

In the following sections, we will first provide information on why specific questions/properties were evaluated by the observers (see Section 3.1). We will then describe the experimental procedure (see Section 3.2).

Table 2. Questions that the observers were asked for each property in the JenAesthetics subjective dataset. The two terms visible on the rating scale which correspond to the highest and lowest possible scores are also shown.

Property	Question asked	Left side	Right side
Aesthetic quality	How aesthetic is the image?	not aesthetic	aesthetic
Beauty	How beautiful is the image?	not beautiful	beautiful
Liking of color	Do you like the color of the image?	no	yes
Liking of content	Do you like the content of the image?	no	yes
Liking of composition	Do you like the composition of the image?	no	yes
Knowing the artist	Do you know the artist?	no	yes
Familiarity with the painting	Are you familiar with this painting?	no	yes

3.1 Properties Evaluated

Table 2 gives an overview on the properties evaluated in the JenAesthetics subjective dataset. The main goal for the dataset is to collect subjective scores related to the aesthetic quality of paintings. Previous works have taken different approaches to reach this goal. While in the case of the JenAestheticsβ dataset Amirshahi et al. [2] used beauty as their measure, Li et al. [19] asked their subjects to give their general opinion about the painting. For the MART dataset [39], the observers were asked to give a score with regard to their emotion towards the paintings. In this experiment, the lowest score represented the most negative emotion while the highest score represented the most positive emotion. In the JenAesthetics subjective dataset, we evaluate subjective scores with regard to both aesthetic quality and beauty. The two properties are compared in Section 4.2.

We also evaluated three other properties (i.e., the liking of color, composition and content of the paintings) and studied the relationship between these properties and the aesthetic and beauty scores (see Section 4.2). Previously, Amirshahi et al. [2] and Yanulevskaya et al. [39] used simple color features to predict the aesthetic quality of paintings with a high accuracy. Other works such as [25, 26, 31] have also focused on the importance of color when evaluating the aesthetic quality of images. The composition of an image (for example the rule of thirds) plays an important role in the aesthetic quality of paintings and photographs according to several studies [3, 8, 16, 18, 20, 35, 38]. Finally, it is well known that the content of a painting and/or photograph can influence the subjective rating of aesthetic quality. In the JenAesthetics dataset, the content of paintings is represented by the subject matter.

Table 3. Characteristics of the JenAesthetics subjective dataset.

Attribute	Value
Number of participants	134
Number of observers after removing clickers and people with color blindness	129
Number of observation sessions	190
Age range of the observers	19 to 42 years
Mean age	25.3 years
Male / female	70 / 59
Right / left-handed	119 / 10
With / without glasses	64 / 65
Interested / not interested in art	90 / 39
Nationality	15 different countries
Nationality represented most frequently	103 from Germany

To evaluate whether the subjective scores are in any way biased by being familiar with a painting, the observers' familiarity towards each painting was assessed. We also asked the observers whether he/she knew the painter. A similar approach was taken by Li et al. [18].

3.2 Experimental Procedure

Participants 134 participants attended this study; sixty-seven of them took part in two observation sessions (leading to a total of 201 sessions). Most of them were students, in particular of natural sciences, but other fields of studies and professions were reported also. However, no participant was a student of arts, art history, or any related field. All participants declared having normal or corrected-to-normal visual acuity and gave their written informed consent after receiving an explanation of the procedures. The consent allows us to use and share their subjective scores. Each participant was tested for color blindness using the Ishihara test [14]. Data from observers who were color blind were excluded from the analysis. See Table 3 for additional data on the participants.

Stimuli We used the 1628 art images from the JenAesthetics database [1] as stimuli. In every session, a subset of 163 images were rated. Works from 410 painters are available in this dataset. The dataset covers paintings from 11 art periods (Renaissance, Baroque, Classicism, Romanticism, Realism, Impressionism, etc.). Each painting in the dataset is tagged with up to three different subject matters. These subject matters (16 in total) include abstract, landscape, still life, portrait, nude, urban scene, and etc.

Procedure The experiment was performed using the PsychoPy [27] program (version 1.77.01) on a BenQ T221W widescreen monitor with a resolution of 1680×1050 pixels (WSXGA+). The monitors where calibrated with a colorimeter (X-Rite EODIS3 i1Display Pro) using the same calibration profile in order to create similar conditions for all observers.

For presentation, each image was scaled so that the longer side of the image was 800 pixels on the screen. The images were placed in the middle of the screen on a black background (see Figure 1). Images were presented with a size of 20.5 cm (longest side) on the computer screen, corresponding to about 19.4 degrees of visual angle (at a viewing distance about 60 cm).

First, twenty images from the dataset that were not used in the rating experiment were presented for three seconds each to get the observer used to the data.

Then, 163 images that were selected randomly from the dataset were presented to the observer in a random order. Careful attention was taken so that no two subsets where identical. In total, each painting was rated by 19 to 21 observers. The participants were asked to rate the images on seven properties using a sliding bar located on the bottom of the screen. Internally, the sliding bar was binned into 100 equal intervals. Accordingly, the ratings obtained (see Figures 3-8) ranged from 0 to 100. The rated properties were "Aesthetic quality", "Beauty", "Liking of color", "Liking of content", "Liking of composition", "Knowing the artist", and "Familiarity with the painting" (see Table 2 for details on the presented questions). As shown in Figure 1, the questions were presented above the sliding bar. The terms presented in Table 2 indicated the range for the rating at each end of the bar. The observers where instructed that the mentioned phrases on the scoring bar were to represent the two extreme cases for the scores and that their scores would not be treated on a binary scale. The participants had no time restrictions for answering each question. After rating, the next question appeared. The image was visible until the last rating was given. Participants who attended a second session were provided with a new randomly selected set of images that shared no images with the images shown in the first session, in which they participated.

4   Analysis of the Subjective Scores

The first step in analyzing the subjective scores gathered was to remove the scores that were provided by observers in an improper manner. These scores were mainly provided by what will be referred from here on as clickers. Clickers are observers who provide their results by randomly clicking the score bar, independent of the image content or the question asked. The random clicking of the score bar is mostly performed at a high speed resulting in short response times (Figure 2(a)). Also, clickers tend not to move their mouse for a few questions before moving their mouse to another position (Figure 2(b)). Subjective scores for each property were calculated after removing the scores provided by the clickers. After removing the clickers and the scores provided by people who were color blind, the total number of observers was 129.

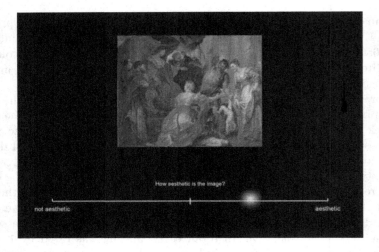

Fig. 1. Screen-shot from the subjective test for one of the assessed properties (aesthetic quality). The question regarding the assessed property is represented under the painting. Painting by Peter Paul Rubens, about 1617.

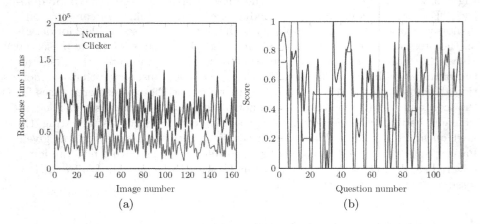

Fig. 2. Comparing results from a clicker and a normal observer. (a) Response time spent on each image. (b) Scores given to the seven properties for 17 paintings selected randomly for the same observers whose response times are shown in (a).

4.1   Calculating the Scores

After removing the clickers from the obtained data, the final step in producing a subjective datatest was to calculate a score for each property for each painting. Among the different options available, we decided that calculating the median value between the scores would be the best possible option. This is mainly to take into account the small chance that some scores are given in an incorrect way. For instance, the score might have been given by accidentally clicking the

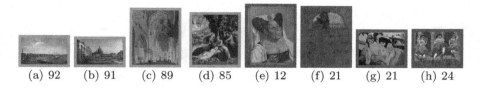

(a) 92   (b) 91   (c) 89   (d) 85   (e) 12   (f) 21   (g) 21   (h) 24

Fig. 3. The four paintings ranked highest for their aesthetic quality are marked by a green border ((a)-(d)) and the four paintings ranked lowest by a red border ((e)-(h)). The scores given to each painting is presented below each image. (a) Antonio Canaletto, 1738, (b) Antonio Canaletto, 1749, (c) Pieter Jansz Saenredam, 1648, (d) Dosso Dossi,1524, (e) Quentin Matsys, 1513, (f) Édouard Vuillard, 1900, (g) Ernst Kirchner, 1910, (h) Ernst Kirchner, 1920.

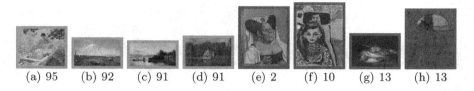

(a) 95   (b) 92   (c) 91   (d) 91   (e) 2   (f) 10   (g) 13   (h) 13

Fig. 4. The four paintings ranked highest for their beauty are marked by a green border ((a)-(d)) and the four paintings ranked lowest with a red border ((e)-(h)). The scores given to each painting is presented below each image. (a) Edmund C. Tarbell, 1892, (b) Antonio Canaletto, 1738, (c) Félix Ziem, 1850, (d) John Constable, 1816, (e) Quentin Matsys, 1513, (f) Ernst Kirchner, 1910, (g) Francisco Goya, 1812, (h) Édouard Vuillard, 1900.

score bar. Using the median scores provides us with a better chance to remove these outliers and achieve a more accurate score. Figures 3-7 represents the four highest rated paintings (marked by a green border) and the four lowest rated paintings (marked by a red border) for the first five properties introduced in Table 2. Figure 8 represents the distribution of the scores for each property. As shown in the figure, the median value of the subjective scores for all properties is around the mid-point of the score range. Note that the subjective scores cover a wide range of the score bar.

As mentioned before (Table 2), the observers were asked two more questions with regard to the familiarity of the paintings and the painter who created the painting. Results revealed that a majority of the paintings neither looked familiar nor did the observers know the painter (in both cases, 99% had a score of less than 10%). This finding suggests that the results for the other five properties cannot have been substantially influenced by familiarity of the observers with the paintings.

(a) 98   (b) 96   (c) 95   (d) 93   (e) 14   (f) 16   (g) 17   (h) 18

Fig. 5. The four paintings ranked highest for their liking of color are marked by a green border ((a)-(d)) and the four paintings ranked lowest with a red border ((e)-(h)). The scores given to each painting is presented below each image. (a) Edmund C. Tarbell, 1892, (b) P. C. Skovgaard, 1857, (c) Childe Hassam, 1913, (d) Antonio Canaletto, 1738, (e) Edgar Degas, 1890, (f) Isidre Nonell, 1903, (g) Pierre Puvis de Chavannes, 1881, (h) Ernst Kirchner, 1920.

(a) 95   (b) 95   (c) 94   (d) 93   (e) 11   (f) 13   (g) 13   (h) 14

Fig. 6. The four paintings ranked highest for their liking of composition are marked by a green border ((a)-(d)) and the four paintings ranked lowest with a red border ((e)-(h)). The scores given to each painting is presented below each image. (a) Antonio Canaletto, 1738, (b) Johan Christian Dahl, 1839, (c) Viktor Vasnetsov, 1881, (d) John Singleton Copley, 1765, (e) Émile Bernard, 1892, (f) Paul Cézanne, 1877, (g) Isidre Nonell, 1903, (h) Marcus Gheeraerts the Younger, 1591.

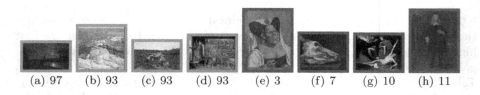

(a) 97   (b) 93   (c) 93   (d) 93   (e) 3   (f) 7   (g) 10   (h) 11

Fig. 7. The four paintings ranked highest for their liking of content are marked by a green border ((a)-(d)) and the four paintings ranked lowest with a red border ((e)-(h)). The scores given to each painting is presented below each image. (a) Johan Christian Dahl, 1839, (b) Childe Hassam, 1913, (c) Anton Mauve, 1887, (d) David Teniers the Younger, 1652, (e) Quentin Matsys, 1513, (f) Felice Boselli, 1690, (g) Jusepe de Ribera, 1621, (h) Abraham Staphorst, 1665.

4.2   Relationships Between Subjective Scores

Next, we investigated the relationships between the subjective scores of the different properties by calculating the Spearman correlation coefficient.

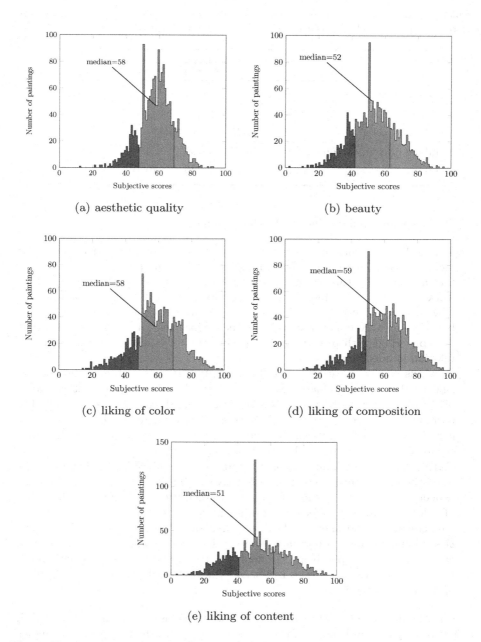

(a) aesthetic quality

(b) beauty

(c) liking of color

(d) liking of composition

(e) liking of content

Fig. 8. Histograms representing the score distribution of the median score for different properties evaluated in the JenAesthetics subjective dataset. Images defined as having high quality are shown in green and images defined as having low quality in red (see Section 4.2). The blue values represent intermediate values with the median value indicated.

Table 4. ρ values calculated for Spearman correlation between subjective scores for different properties. All values are significantly different from zero ($p < 0.01$).

Properties	Aesthetic quality	Beauty	Liking of color	Liking of composition	Liking of content
Aesthetic quality	1				
Beauty	.7802	1			
Liking of color	.6676	.7237	1		
Liking of composition	.7114	.7642	.6506	1	
Liking of content	.6216	.8110	.5945	.7010	1

The following findings deserve further comments:

- The highest correlation is seen between liking of content and beauty. The fact that the content and subject matter of a painting plays a crucial role for how an observer evaluates a painting was mentioned previously in [1]. Other works emphasize this fact for other stimuli, such as [16] for webpages.
- The second highest correlation is between subjective aesthetic quality and beauty scores. Keeping in mind that the Oxford dictionary defines aesthetic as "concerned with beauty or the appreciation of beauty", such a high correlation is not a surprise.
- Previous studies have related different composition techniques such as the rule of thirds, the golden ratio, etc. to the beauty and aesthetic quality of paintings and photographs [3,8,18,20,26,35,38]. In the present study, the correlation between the liking of composition and beauty is the third highest correlation, and the correlation between aesthetic quality and the liking of composition is the fifth highest correlation.
- With regard to the liking of color, studies such as [2,25,26,31] have emphasized the importance of color on subjective aesthetic and beauty scores. This aspect was also seen in the correlation between the scores given to the liking of color and ratings for beauty and aesthetic quality.
- The correlation between the beauty scores and the mentioned three properties (liking of color, content, and composition) are among the highest (fourth, third, and first, respectively). In contrast, the correlation for aesthetic quality with the three properties is not as high as that of beauty (seventh, fifth, and ninth, respectively).

We also implemented a five-fold cross validation classifier using a linear SVM. This was done to enable users of the dataset to compare the present performance of a classifier with their own classifiers based on the subjective scores provided in the present work.

For the each property in our classification, we divide the images into two groups (high quality and low quality). The assigning of the groups is done based on the subjective score for each image. If the image has a subjective score greater than $Median(allscores) + 10$, the image will be labelled as high quality and if the subjective score is lower than $Median(allscores) - 10$, it will be labelled as low quality. The other remaining properties are used as features in our classifier. Average recognition rates of this classification procedure are listed in Table 5 for different scenarios. From this table we can conclude that:

- High classification rates were found between subjective aesthetic quality and beauty scores and the other three properties. This finding was previously seen for the correlation rates (Table 4) and supports the notion that these properties (liking of color, composition and content) are closely related to the aesthetic quality and beauty judgement (see Section 3.1).
- Using the subjective scores provided for the liking of color and content together in our feature vector resulted in high recognition rates for beauty. As mentioned above, a close relation of color liking and beauty perception has been previously pointed out in the literature.
- Similar to the correlation rates shown in Table 4, the lowest classification rate is for the case in which either the liking of color or the liking of content is used as a feature to classify the other property. This result is not surprising since the two mentioned properties are usually not related to one another in paintings.

5   Discussion and Future Work

In this paper, we present subjective ratings of the previously introduced JenAesthetics dataset. We hope that such a public dataset of paintings along with their subjective scores will provide a significant contribution to the computational aesthetic community. The lack of a publicly available subjective dataset of paintings has been mentioned numerous times in different publications and/or meetings. The subjective dataset comprises scores for five different properties (aesthetic, beauty, and liking of color, composition, and content). The scores were gathered by performing 190 observation sessions by 129 observers. The results show that the properties assessed are highly correlated with one another. It was interesting to see that the subjective scores related to the liking of color, composition and content had a higher correlation with beauty scores than with aesthetic scores. This finding shows that a high aesthetic quality of a painting does not necessarily mean that the color, content, or composition are pleasing to the observer as well. The fact that the subjective scores for beauty and aesthetic quality were highly correlated confirms findings from previous studies [1–3, 8, 16, 18, 20, 25, 26, 31, 35, 38].

Compared to previous datasets, the JenAesthetics subjective dataset contains a larger number of paintings and covers a wider range of different subject matters, styles and art periods. It also evaluates different properties providing the user with many different scenarios to test and evaluate.

In the future, we will increase the number of images assessed in our subjective dataset. Also, we are planning to extract additional features from the images. Finding the relationship between scores provided in different subgroups, such as males and females, could be an interesting topic of investigation.

Table 5. Average classification rate of five-fold cross validation using different subjective scores as features in a linear SVM. In the first column, A corresponds to subjective scores for aesthetic quality, B for beauty, CL for liking of color, CM for liking of composition, and CN for liking of content.

Feature vector	Aesthetic	Beauty	Color	Composition	Content
A	–	76.37%	73.50%	74.09%	71.99%
B	76.53%	–	76.16%	78.10%	82.77%
CL	72.82%	76.40%	–	73.56%	70.19%
CM	74.59%	77.07%	73.77%	–	76.63%
CN	73.16%	79.80%	69.19%	73.87%	–
A, B	–	–	77.68%	80.63%	82.23%
A, CL	–	82.62%	–	76.19%	75.19%
A, CM	–	82.74%	74.73%	–	77.27%
A, CN	–	85.66%	74.61%	79.79%	–
B, CL	80.96%	–	–	80.02%	82.09%
B, CM	81.54%	–	77.81%	–	84.20%
B, CN	80.23%	–	77.62%	79.86%	–
CL, CM	78.60%	82.36%	–	–	78.13%
CL, CN	77.28%	86.11%	–	78.92%	–
CM, CN	76.46%	84.75%	73.28%	–	–
A, B,CL	–	–	–	80.47%	83.05%
A, B, CM	–	–	77.96%	–	84.76%
A, B, CN	–	–	77.68%	81.18%	–
A, CL, CM	–	85.04%	–	–	79.00%
A, CL, CN	–	88.30%	–	80.59%	–
A, CM, CN	–	87.90%	77.33%	–	–
B, CL, CM	81.56%	–	–	–	84.07%
B, CL, CN	81.03%	–	–	80.23%	–
B, CM, CN	81.59%	–	77.85%	–	–
CL, CM, CN	79.07%	87.42%	–	–	–
A, B, CL, CM	–	–	–	–	84.77%
A, B, CL, CN	–	–	–	81.35%	–
A, B, CM, CN	–	–	78.22%	–	–
A, CL, CM, CN	–	88.68%	–	–	–
B, CL, CM, CN	81.64%	–	–	–	–

References

1. Amirshahi, S.A., Denzler, J., Redies, C.: JenAesthetics-a public dataset of paintings for aesthetic research. Computer Vision Group, University of Jena Germany, Tech. rep. (2013)
2. Amirshahi, S.A., Hayn-Leichsenring, G.U., Denzler, J., Redies, C.: Color: A crucial factor for aesthetic quality assessment in a subjective database of paintings. In: 12th Congress of the International Colour Association (AIC). Newcastle, UK (July 2013)
3. Amirshahi, S.A., Hayn-Leichsenring, G.U., Denzler, J., Redies, C.: Evaluating the rule of thirds in photographs and paintings. Art & Perception 2(1–2), 163–182 (2014)
4. Amirshahi, S.A., Koch, M., Denzler, J., Redies, C.: PHOG analysis of self-similarity in aesthetic images. In: IS&T/SPIE Electronic Imaging, pp. 82911J–82911J. International Society for Optics and Photonics (2012)
5. Amirshahi, S.A., Redies, C., Denzler, J.: How self-similar are artworks at different levels of spatial resolution? In: Proceedings of the Symposium on Computational Aesthetics, pp. 93–100. ACM (2013)
6. Bhattacharya, S., Sukthankar, R., Shah, M.: A framework for photo-quality assessment and enhancement based on visual aesthetics. In: Proceedings of the International Conference on Multimedia, pp. 271–280. ACM (2010)
7. Condorovici, R.G., Florea, C., Vrânceanu, R., Vertan, C.: Perceptually-inspired artistic genre identification system in digitized painting collections. In: Kämäräinen, J.-K., Koskela, M. (eds.) SCIA 2013. LNCS, vol. 7944, pp. 687–696. Springer, Heidelberg (2013)
8. Datta, R., Joshi, D., Li, J., Wang, J.Z.: Studying aesthetics in photographic images using a computational approach. In: Leonardis, A., Bischof, H., Pinz, A. (eds.) ECCV 2006. LNCS, vol. 3953, pp. 288–301. Springer, Heidelberg (2006)
9. Datta, R., Li, J., Wang, J.Z.: Algorithmic inferencing of aesthetics and emotion in natural images: An exposition. In: IEEE 15th International Conference on Image Processing (ICIP), pp. 105–108. IEEE (2008)
10. Demetriou, M.L., Hardeberg, J.Y., Adelmann, G.: Computer-aided reclamation of lost art. In: Fusiello, A., Murino, V., Cucchiara, R. (eds.) ECCV 2012 Ws/Demos, Part I. LNCS, vol. 7583, pp. 551–560. Springer, Heidelberg (2012)
11. Deng, J., Dong, W., Socher, R., Li, L.J., Li, K., Fei-Fei, L.: Imagenet: A large-scale hierarchical image database. In: IEEE Conference on Computer Vision and Pattern Recognition (CVPR), pp. 248–255. IEEE (2009)
12. Hoenig, F.: Defining computational aesthetics. In: Proceedings of the First Eurographics Conference on Computational Aesthetics in Graphics, Visualization and Imaging, pp. 13–18. Eurographics Association (2005)
13. International Telecommunication Union: Recommendation ITU-R BT.500-11: Methodology for the subjective assessment of the quality of television pictures. Tech. rep., International Telecommunication Union/ITU Radiocommunication Sector (2009)
14. Ishihara, S.: Test for colour-blindness. Hongo Harukicho, Tokyo (1917)
15. JenAesthetics: JenAesthetics dataset (2013). http://www.inf-cv.uni-jena.de/en/jenaesthetics
16. Karvonen, K.: The beauty of simplicity. In: Proceedings on the 2000 Conference on Universal Usability, pp. 85–90. ACM (2000)

17. Ke, Y., Tang, X., Jing, F.: The design of high-level features for photo quality assessment. In: IEEE Computer Society Conference on Computer Vision and Pattern Recognition (CVPR), vol. 1, pp. 419–426. IEEE (2006)
18. Li, C., Chen, T.: Aesthetic visual quality assessment of paintings. IEEE Journal of Selected Topics in Signal Processing **3**(2), 236–252 (2009)
19. Luo, W., Wang, X., Tang, X.: Content-based photo quality assessment. In: IEEE International Conference on Computer Vision (ICCV), pp. 2206–2213. IEEE (2011)
20. Mai, L., Le, H., Niu, Y., Liu, F.: Rule of thirds detection from photograph. In: IEEE International Symposium on Multimedia (ISM), pp. 91–96. IEEE (2011)
21. Mallon, B., Redies, C., Hayn-Leichsenring, G.U.: Beauty in abstract paintings: Perceptual contrast and statistical properties. Frontiers in Human Neuroscience **8**(161) (2014)
22. Müller, H., Clough, P., Deselaers, T., Caputo, B. (eds.): Imageclef - Experimental evaluation in visual information retrieval, vol. 32. The Information Retrieval Series (2010)
23. Murray, N., Marchesotti, L., Perronnin, F.: Ava: A large-scale database for aesthetic visual analysis. In: IEEE Conference on Computer Vision and Pattern Recognition (CVPR), pp. 2408–2415. IEEE (2012)
24. Oncu, A.I., Deger, F., Hardeberg, J.Y.: Evaluation of digital inpainting quality in the context of artwork restoration. In: Fusiello, A., Murino, V., Cucchiara, R. (eds.) ECCV 2012 Ws/Demos, Part I. LNCS, vol. 7583, pp. 561–570. Springer, Heidelberg (2012)
25. Palmer, S.E., Schloss, K.B.: An ecological valence theory of human color preference. Proceedings of the National Academy of Sciences USA **107**(19), 8877–8882 (2010)
26. Palmer, S.E., Schloss, K.B., Sammartino, J.: Visual aesthetics and human preference. Annual Review of Psychology **64**, 77–107 (2013)
27. Peirce, J.W.: PsychoPy-Psychophysics software in Python. Journal of Neuroscience Methods **162**(1–2), 8–13 (2007). http://www.sciencedirect.com/science/article/pii/S0165027006005772
28. Redies, C., Amirshahi, S.A., Koch, M., Denzler, J.: PHOG-Derived aesthetic measures applied to color photographs of artworks, natural scenes and objects. In: Fusiello, A., Murino, V., Cucchiara, R. (eds.) ECCV 2012 Ws/Demos, Part I. LNCS, vol. 7583, pp. 522–531. Springer, Heidelberg (2012)
29. Redies, C., Hänisch, J., Blickhan, M., Denzler, J.: Artists portray human faces with the fourier statistics of complex natural scenes. Network: Computation in Neural Systems **18**(3), 235–248 (2007)
30. Redies, C., Hasenstein, J., Denzler, J., et al.: Fractal-like image statistics in visual art: similarity to natural scenes. Spatial Vision **21**(1–2), 137–148 (2007)
31. Schloss, K.B., Palmer, S.E.: An ecological valence theory of human color preferences. Journal of Vision **9**(8), 358–358 (2009)
32. Seshadrinathan, K., Soundararajan, R., Bovik, A.C., Cormack, L.K.: A subjective study to evaluate video quality assessment algorithms. In: IS&T/SPIE Electronic Imaging, pp. 75270H–75270H. International Society for Optics and Photonics (2010)
33. Seshadrinathan, K., Soundararajan, R., Bovik, A.C., Cormack, L.K.: Study of subjective and objective quality assessment of video. IEEE Transactions on Image Processing **19**(6), 1427–1441 (2010)
34. Sheikh, H.R., Sabir, M.F., Bovik, A.C.: A statistical evaluation of recent full reference image quality assessment algorithms. IEEE Transactions on Image Processing **15**(11), 3440–3451 (2006)

35. Svobodova, K., Sklenicka, P., Molnarova, K., Vojar, J.: Does the composition of landscape photographs affect visual preferences? The rule of the golden section and the position of the horizon. Journal of Environmental Psychology **38**, 143–152 (2014)
36. Wang, Z., Bovik, A.C., Sheikh, H.R., Simoncelli, E.P.: Image quality assessment: from error visibility to structural similarity. IEEE Transactions on Image Processing **13**(4), 600–612 (2004)
37. Liu, X., Pedersen, M., Hardeberg, J.Y.: CID:IQ – A New Image Quality Database. In: Elmoataz, A., Lezoray, O., Nouboud, F., Mammass, D. (eds.) ICISP 2014. LNCS, vol. 8509, pp. 193–202. Springer, Heidelberg (2014)
38. Xue, S.F., Lin, Q., Tretter, D.R., Lee, S., Pizlo, Z., Allebach, J.: Investigation of the role of aesthetics in differentiating between photographs taken by amateur and professional photographers. In: IS&T/SPIE Electronic Imaging, pp. 83020D–83020D. International Society for Optics and Photonics (2012)
39. Yanulevskaya, V., Uijlings, J., Bruni, E., Sartori, A., Zamboni, E., Bacci, F., Melcher, D., Sebe, N.: In the eye of the beholder: employing statistical analysis and eye tracking for analyzing abstract paintings. In: Proceedings of the 20th ACM International Conference on Multimedia, pp. 349–358. ACM (2012)

Relationship Between Visual Complexity and Aesthetics: Application to Beauty Prediction of Photos

Litian Sun[✉], Toshihiko Yamasaki, and Kiyoharu Aizawa

The University of Tokyo, Tokyo, Japan
{sun1101,yamasaki,aizawa}@hal.t.u-tokyo.ac.jp

Abstract. Automatic evaluation of visual content by its aesthetic merit is becoming exceedingly important as the available volume of such content is expanding rapidly. Complexity is believed to be an important indicator of aesthetic assessment and widely used. However, psychological theories concerning complexity are only verified on limited situations, and the relationship between complexity and aesthetic experience on extensive scope of application is not yet clear. To this end, we designed an experiment to test human perception on the complexity of various photos. Then we propose a set of visual complexity features and show that the complexity level calculated from the proposed features have a near-monotonic relationship with human beings' beauty expectation on thousands of photos. Further applications on beauty predication and quality assessment demonstrate the effectiveness of proposed method.

Keywords: Aesthetic assessment · Visual complexity · Beauty prediction

1 Introduction

The image processing and computer vision community has made great efforts to explore computational methods to make aesthetic decisions similar to human beings. Prediction of photograph aesthetic scores is an undoubtedly challenging problem. To understand how persons perceive visually pleasing stimuli, psychologists proposed many theories, in which complexity has been known to be an important indicator for aesthetic assessment.

Pioneers in computational aesthetics as D. E. Berlyne [3,4] suggested that the aesthetic appeal of a pattern seems to depend on the arousing and de-arousing influence of its collative or structural properties, and that arousing quality is a direct linear function of complexity, or the amount of information, whereas pleasantness is generally related to these determinants in an inverted-U manner. Specifically, aesthetic appeals increase with complexity until an optimal level of arousal is reached, and after this point, further increase in complexity would elicit a drop in preference level. Psychologists have conducted a lot of experiments to

© Springer International Publishing Switzerland 2015
L. Agapito et al. (Eds.): ECCV 2014 Workshops, Part I, LNCS 8925, pp. 20–34, 2015.
DOI: 10.1007/978-3-319-16178-5_2

verify or evaluate Berlyne's theory. Many have successfully observed an inverted-U function between complexity and aesthetic experience concerning architecture [1,13], while some only observes the ascending part of the curve [8], and some shows no support for an inverted U relation between preference and entropy [19].

The role that complexity plays in aesthetic preference prediction is also emphasized in the recent processing fluency theory [14,15] which goes further to explore the reason behind the relationship. It suggests that aesthetic experience is a function of the perceiver's processing dynamics: the more fluently the perceiver can process an image, the more positive is their aesthetic response. Fluency theory works well in predicting aesthetic effects due to many low-level features such as preferences for larger and more highly contrastive displays. However, fluency theory does not square well with the Berlyne's inverted-U results, in that it indicates a monotonic decrease in preference as a function of complexity.

Although complexity is regarded as an important indicator for aesthetic assessment, the relationship between complexity and aesthetic appeal is still debatable and further verification is necessary. The main difficulty in psychological experiments is the limitation of sample size, leading to the problem of insufficient complexity range. Empirical experiments would become time-costing for participants when the sample size numbered in thousands. Thus empirical experiments could not yield a general guideline for aesthetic assessment. Furthermore, the application scope of psychology theories is not clear, as complexity may vary greatly for intra and extra-category images.

Despite the lack of large-scale verification and compelling evidence in psychological theories, complexity has already been widely used for aesthetic classification for photo [18], art [6,17], and web-page design [20]. Mean gradient value is considered as measurement of complexity in some works [9,16,17]. Following a similar idea, features related to the file size of compressed image have been found to be a good approximation of judgements of visual complexity and efficient in aesthetic classification task [5,18], because compression algorithms such as JPEG and fractal compression generate good abstraction of lines, colors, repetition information of images. Nevertheless, previous complexity measurements did not take the other factors that may influence human sensation on complexity, such as curvature, object number, object size, pattern regularity, and pattern compositions.

In this work, we evaluate the role of complexity played in aesthetic assessment and intend to verify the Berlyne's inverted-U curve on thousands of photos through computational methods. We use the public database AVA (Aesthetic Visual Analysis) [12][1], which is derived from online phtograph challenges, with a rich variety of content. As the aesthetic preference of each image is voted 200 times averagely, the difference between individuals is greatly alleviated. AVA contains photos of 8 categories, with 5000 photos in each category. We first designed a small-scale preliminary experiment to test whether human sensation on complexity is congruous. Then we proposed a set of visual complexity features which is capable to summarize composition, statistical and distribution

---

[1] http://www.lucamarchesotti.com/ava/

information of patterns in a photo, and applied gradient boost trees regression on these features to set up the complexity model. After that we calculated complexity levels for large-scale photo database, and analysed the relationship between beauty expectation and complexity level. As application, we used the proposed visual complexity features to predict beauty scores using gradient boost trees regression, and to determine aesthetic quality using random forest as classifier.

The remainder of this article is organized as follows. The preliminary experiment is illustrated in Section 2. The visual complexity features are described in detail and used to train a complexity model in Section 3. The relationship between complexity and aesthetic experience is discussed in Section 4. The application of the proposed visual complexity features in beauty prediction is presented in Section 5. Finally, conclusions are given in Section 6.

2 Preliminary Experiment on Subjective Complexity

We selected 10 photos from 2500 training samples of each category from AVA dataset, making it 80 photos in all. The images were selected as evenly distributed along the aesthetic ratings ranges. Specifically, although in online photograph challenges photos could be aesthetically rated from 1 to 10, the average beauty scores of the 2500 photos in the training set of "Animal" category vary from 2.62 to 8.25. So we sampled photos with the beauty score interval as $(8.25 - 2.62)/10 \approx 0.56$. In this way we managed to collect photos of different aesthetic ratings from various categories.

Five participants (2 female and 3 male, aged from 23 to 28) attended this study. All were graduate students with normal or corrected-to-normal vision.

As depicted in Fig. 1, 10 images from the same category were shown at one time. And the participants were asked to choose a complexity level for these images from 5 options: 1 (very simple), 2 (simple), 3 (medium), 4 (complex) and 5 (very complex). Photos were shown by category in an alphabetic order: "Animal", "Architecture", "Cityscape", "Floral", "Fooddrink", "Portrait" and "Stilllife". Photos were arranged randomly to eliminate any possible pattern between complexity and aesthetic score.

For each image, we calculated the mean and standard deviation of complexity level provided by the five participants. The complexity levels of the 80 images averaged over 5 participants ranged from 1.4 to 5.0, and the standard deviation ranged from 0 to 1.33. As for the image that participants had most different ratings, at least two persons agreed with the same complexity level. This indicates that complexity is measurable for human beings. Fig. 2 shows example images labelled with different complexity levels.

To better understand how participants disagree on complexity levels, we show the distribution of standard deviation along the average complexity score in Fig. 3. Participants tend to agree with extreme complexity levels. The standard deviation is low for very simple or very complex images, while high for medium images.

Table 1 shows the average degree of disagreement of participants concerning different categories. People tend to agree with the complexity level of images

Fig. 1. Interface of complexity labelling experiment for the "Animal" category

Fig. 2. Example images of 5 complexity levels labelled by participants. The average complexity levels are rounded to integers, and from left to right they are 1(very simple), 2 (simple), 3 (medium), 4 (complex) and 5 (very complex). Images from the same column share the same averaged complexity level.

Table 1. Average of standard deviation value for different categories

Animal	Architecture	Cityscape	Floral	Fooddrink	Landscape	Portrait	Stilllife
0.7302	0.6931	0.4102	0.8260	0.6914	0.5871	0.5690	0.7694

from "Cityscape", "Landscape" and "Portrait" categories, while disagreement falls onto categories such as "Floral" and "Animal".

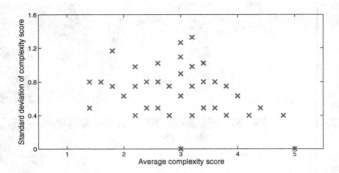

Fig. 3. Distribution of mean and standard deviation of complexity level labelled for 80 images

3   Visual Complexity Model

In this section we illustrate how the visual complexity features are extracted and trained to evaluate image complexity. Complexity is the degree of difficulty in reconstruction of description of an image. Visual complexity is correlated to factors like distribution of color, texture and edges, curvature, object number, object size, pattern regularity, pattern compositions, etc. We prepare low-level features like line segments, contour, and texture using the method of [2], sharpness using [21], and color information is represented in CIECAM02 color space. Then three categories of complexity information are extracted. Composition handles an image as a whole, and summarized the way in which the patterns are spatially distributed in the image. Statistics complexity treats an image as abstractions of object or texture patches. We count the number of objects and calculate the similarity between object and texture patches using mean and standard deviation values of certain information, such as curvature degree, texture regularity, etc. Distribution complexity regards an image as pixels, and measures the differences between distributions of a photo and a pure noise image using divergence. A total of 114-dimension feature is summarized in Table 2.

3.1   Composition

Composition is calculated using the orthogonal variant moments (OVM) method in [10], which is designed to be sensitive to specific perturbations such as transformation, and tolerant to certain extent of unexpected disturbance at the same time. As for an image $I(x, y)$, OVM generates a 5-D vector: $f_{ovm} = (A, L_x, L_y, D_x, D_y)$, where A is the average value of input. (L_x) and (L_y) are orthogonal components of the surface area. (D_x) and (D_y) represent the position of object in the image. Detailed calculation process is listed as below.

Table 2. Summary of complexity features

Category	Short Name	Dimension
Composition	Line segment	20
	Color	25
	Sharpness	5
	Relative color	10
Statistics	Eclipse fitness	10
	Object number	1
	Curvature	8
	Texture entropy	1
	Texture area	2
Distribution	Line orientation	10
	Texture orientation	10
	Color distribution	12

$$\eta = \frac{1}{height \times width} \qquad A = \eta \int\int I(x,y)dxdy \qquad (1)$$

$$L_x = \eta \int\int \sqrt{1 + \left(\frac{\partial I}{\partial x}\right)^2} \, dxdy \qquad L_y = \eta \int\int \sqrt{1 + \left(\frac{\partial I}{\partial y}\right)^2} \, dxdy \qquad (2)$$

$$D_x = \eta \int\int (x+dx)I(x,y)dxdy \qquad D_y = \eta \int\int (y+dy)I(x,y)dxdy \qquad (3)$$

To extract composition of a photo, we calculate OVM vectors from line segments, color, sharpness, and relative color information separately. The edge map generated by [2] is split into four parts using different thresholds. In this way, pattern displayed with different intensity or importance would be separated. Color information is divided into hue (including hue angle, hue eccentricity, hue composition), chroma, lightness. According to Moon-Spencer model [11], color harmony is closely related to the relative color. We focus on the surrounding region of contour lines. For each circular region with center point on the contour lines, the main relative hue and relative chroma is calculated as the difference between the most dominant color and the second most dominant color. To improve the computation efficiency, the contour lines are down sampled into center points. In this way, we obtain the relative information along the contour lines and its composition is summarized using OVM.

3.2 Statistics

To statistically measure visual complexity, we use contour information to count the number of objects, and to calculate characteristics of objects contour such as extent of fit to an ellipse, angular orientation, circularity, solidity, degree of curve and relative size compared with the whole picture. The circularity is represented by the ratio of the minor and major axes of the ellipses. Solidity is the ratio of contour area to its convex hull area. The degree of curve is measured as the ratio of the contour length to the perimeter of its minimum enclosing rectangular. These parameters of continuous lines in the contour map are summarized using mean and standard deviation values.

As curves are believed to be more complex than straight lines, we extract the curvature from contour using method in [7]. Granularity and regularity of texture is measured using area statistics and entropy.

3.3 Distribution

Another important measurement of visual complexity is distribution. Distribution information is represented as the combination of the histogram and its differences from histograms of templates $f_{db} = [H, D]$. Take the orientation of line segments for example, orientation ranged in [0,180) is cumulated and normalized into a histogram with 8 bins, $H = [h_1, h_2, ..., h_k]$, $k = 8$. The differences between the orientation histogram of line segments and those of the reference images, R, is measured using chi-square divergence. We choose two reference histograms. One with an averaged distribution in histogram represents the extreme noisy situation. And another reference histogram with only one bin valued 1 and all the other bins valued 0 represents the extreme regular situation. Divergence with the two reference histograms characterize the irregular or regular degree of orientation distribution. Detailed calculation is illustrated as following.

$$D = [d_1, d_2], \quad d_i = \sum_{j=1}^{k} (\frac{h_j}{r_{i,j}} - 1)^2 h_j \tag{4}$$

$$R_1 = [r_{1,1}, r_{1,2}, ..., r_{1,k}], \quad r_{1,i} = \frac{1}{k} \tag{5}$$

$$R_2 = [r_{2,1}, r_{2,2}, ..., r_{2,k}], \quad r_{2,i} = \begin{cases} 0, & \text{if } i \neq m \\ 1, & \text{if } i = m \end{cases}, \text{where } m = \arg\max_i h_i \tag{6}$$

The color distribution is summarized into complexity feature in a similar way. As the hue composition ranges from 0 to 400, we set the histogram with 10 bins.

3.4 Training the Complexity Model

As complexity is a continuous variable, a regression rather than classification would be a better choice to train complexity model from previously illustrated features. We employed gradient boosted trees for regression. Parameters such as the count of boosting iterations and maximal depth of each decision tree in the ensemble is optimized through 5-fold validation. Accuracy of regression is measured using root-mean-square error (RMSE).

To test and compare with other complexity features, we randomly select 10 out of the 80 photos labelled with complexity level in the experiment for testing and the left 70 photos are used for training. We conducted such training and testing 5 times. And the performance is measured by averaging the RMSEs in the 5-fold test.

We compare the proposed visual complexity features with compression file size related features proposed in [18] and sum of gradient features used in [16]. The average RMSE for the proposed feature in the random 5-fold test is 0.35/0.83 (training/testing), while it is 0.47/1.05 by [18], and 0.45/0.89 by [16]. The proposed features outperform the comparison methods in random 5-fold test.

In order to model the perceived complexity using the labelled complexity levels as accurate as possible, we split the 80 photos according to the standard deviation of complexity scores. The lower the standard deviation values, average complexity score is a better approximation of the actual visual complexity. So we only use photos with low rating disturbance for training, and expect the predicted complexity level is within the variance range of testing photos. We use the 70 photos with standard deviation less than 0.90 for training, and the left 10 photos with standard deviation vary from 0.90 to 1.33 for testing. The prediction accuracy and maximum absolute error are listed in Table 3.

Table 3. Comparison of visual complexity features in regression

Feature	Training		Testing	
	RMSE	Max err	RMSE	Max err
Human perception	0.63	0.89	1.09	1.33
Proposed visual complexity feature	0.31	0.82	**0.68**	**1.26**
Compression file size related feature [18]	0.60	1.58	0.73	1.75
Sum of gradient [16]	**0.29**	**0.80**	0.69	1.39

Complexity levels are in the range of [1,5].

The worst complexity prediction using proposed visual complexity features in testing has the absolute error of 1.26, which is less than the maximum standard deviation (1.33) of complexity level labelled by participants. And for the training set, the absolute error of the worst prediction is also lower than the maximum standard deviation (0.89). Thus, we prepare a visual complexity model that could model human beings' sensation of complexity very well.

4   Relationship between Complexity and Beauty

In this section we apply the visual complexity model obtained in Section 3 to the training sets in AVA dataset (each category has 2500 training photos), calculate the expectation of aesthetic score, and explore its relationship with complexity level.

We calculate the visual complexity level for photos from the training sets in AVA data. As illustrated in Table 1, participants tend to agree with the complexity for photos from "Cityscape" category, so we expect more accurate complexity evaluation on "Cityscape" category than other categories. Example photos from "Cityscape" category with different complexity levels are shown in Fig. 4.

Fig. 4. Example photos from "Cityscape" category of 5 complexity levels calculated by proposed visual complexity model. The two images from the same column share the same complexity level.

The complexity level calculated using our proposed method is rounded to integrate levels. We employ one-way analysis of variance (ANOVA) to compare the expectation of beauty experience along with complexity level. ANOVA results suggest that the beauty score distribution of at least one complexity level is significantly different from those of other complexity levels ($p < .05$ for each category), and box plots for all 8 categories are shown in the left of Fig. 5.

Due to the large variance ranges, the differences between the beauty score means of different complexity level is not clear. To further test the statistical significance of beauty score expectations, we conduct multiple comparison, group by group t-test, and show the results in the right part of Fig. 5. Beauty score expectations of the complexity level coloured as red are significantly different from the one coloured as blue.

Ascending trends could be observed on the right column of Fig. 5 in "Cityscape" and "Landscape" categories, and descending trends are shown in "Floral" and "Fooddrink" categories, while in the other categories only weak ascending or descending trends could be observed. In "Portarit" and "Architecture" categories, we could only observe the ascending trend for the middle 3 complexity levels. And in "Animal" category, the descending trend is not clear for complexity levels 4 and 5.

For "Cityscape" and "Landscape" categories, the ascending trends have clear statistical significance, except that aesthetic assessment expectations of photos with intermediate complexity levels may be easily confused with those of adjacent complexity level. Taking "Cityscape" category for example, mean beauty score of simple photos (complexity level 2) is significantly different from those of extreme simple, complex and extreme complex photos (complexity levels of 1, 4 and 5), while it is hard to tell mean beauty scores of simple photos from that of medium photos (complexity level 2 and 3).

We evaluate the relationship between aesthetic experience and complexity level on AVA dataset training photos (each category has 2500 training photos). Based on our results, we only observed ascending or descending parts of Berlyne's invert-U curve for different categories. As for the ascending trends in "Architecture", "Cityscape" and "Landscape", this is because buildings or landscape scenes are already complex considering the lines and components and few photographer would like to produce too complex photos in these categories. Thus the optimal complexity level in the Berlynes inverted-U curve may be not included in the photo, and the drop of aesthetic experience when complexity level is higher than the optimal level is not observed. As "Animal", "Floral" and "Fooddrink" categories in which most photos focus on single or small number of objects, the descending trends of beauty expectation is understandable. Too complex photo would lead to distraction and difficulty to focus onto the content of the photo. Simple photo is better to express the beauty of these categories. However "Portrait" and "Stilllife" categories are a little different, as photos convey more semantic meanings and are difficult to model by only low level features.

5   Application in Beauty Prediction

As verified in Section 5, visual complexity is closely related to aesthetic experience of photos. In this section we try to predict beauty scores for photos using visual complexity features.

Visual complexity features are first extracted as illustrated in Section 3. We employ gradient boosted tree to train the regression model. Parameters are optimized through 5-fold validation similar to Section 3.4. The regression accuracy is measured using RMSE, and the correlation coefficient between the predicted beauty score and the one labelled by human beings. As shown in Table 4, the proposed visual complexity features outperforms compression file size related features in [18] and sum of gradient used in [16]. Considering the fact that beauty scores range from 1 to 10 and the average error of the proposed method is 0.70 for the best case ("Landscape" category) and 0.97 for the worst case ("Animal" category), the proposed method is capable of giving a reasonable estimation of aesthetic experience with.

We also tested the visual complexity features under the high/low quality classification task. Photos are divided into high or quality class by introducing a threshold parameter δ. Photos with beauty scores higher than $5.5 + \delta$ is considered as of high quality, while photos with beauty scores lower than $5.5 - \delta$ is considered as of low quality. Higher δ leads to more unambiguous training samples making the classification easier, and when $\delta = 0$ the whole training set

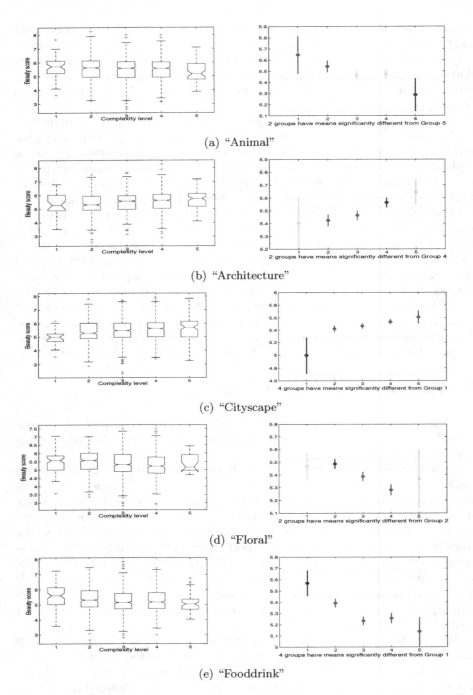

Fig. 5. Relationship between aesthetic experience and complexity level. Distribution of beauty experience along complexity level is represented by box plot in the left. And the difference significance is shown in the right.

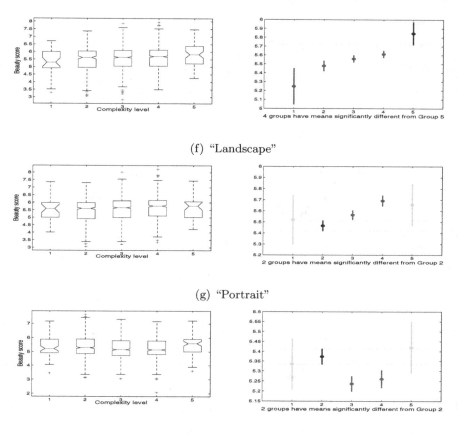

(f) "Landscape"

(g) "Portrait"

(h) "Stilllife"

Fig. 5. *(Continue)*

Table 4. Comparison of beauty prediction results

Category	Proposed method		Compression related [18]		Sum of Gradient [16]	
	RMSE	Correlation	RMSE	Correlation	RMSE	Correlation
Animal	0.97	0.16	**0.74**	**0.22**	1.05	0.04
Architecture	0.83	**0.21**	**0.71**	0.17	0.94	0.06
Cityscape	0.83	**0.30**	**0.82**	0.18	0.82	0.13
Floral	0.83	**0.21**	**0.77**	0.18	0.88	0.01
Fooddrink	**0.74**	**0.31**	0.80	0.20	0.83	0.04
Landscape	**0.70**	**0.38**	0.85	0.15	0.76	0.12
Portrait	**0.74**	**0.26**	0.78	0.15	0.84	0.07
Stilllife	0.78	0.23	**0.72**	**0.24**	0.83	0.04

Beauty scores are in the range of [1,10].

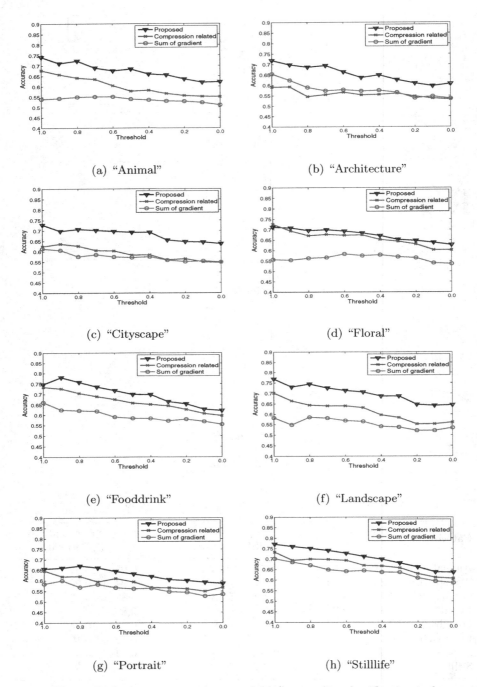

(a) "Animal"

(b) "Architecture"

(c) "Cityscape"

(d) "Floral"

(e) "Fooddrink"

(f) "Landscape"

(g) "Portrait"

(h) "Stilllife"

Fig. 6. Performance comparisons on high/low-quality classification task

is used. We employ random forests as classifier. The maximum tree depth is set as 5, and the maximum number of trees in the forest is set as 100.

We set the threshold δ as $[1.0, 0.9, ..., 0.1, 0.0]$. For $\delta = 1$, there are several hundreds of photos left for each category, which is large enough to test the proposed method. And the performance is shown in Fig. 6. These results are consistent with the performance in regression task. Visual complexity features have best performance for photos from "Landscape" category, and worst performance for "Portrait" category. This is because features indicating complexity in landscape photos mostly refer to more objects, and complex topographies and landforms could be easily summarized through composition and statistical features. On the contrary, the complexity of portrait photos which are mainly human faces is difficult to measure using only low-level features. Semantic interpretations are necessary, and familiarity may be a predominate factor in complexity detection.

The proposed visual complexity features averagely outperform 8.5% compression related features in [18] and 14.7% over sum of gradient in [16] for the "Landscape" category, and for the "Portrait" category 3.9% over compression related features in [18] and 6.8% over sum of gradient in [16].

6   Conclusions

Through a small-scale experiment[2], we found that human beings' judgement on complexity levels are congruous, hence complexity levels of photo is measurable. We proposed a set of visual complexity features and trained them into complexity model. And then we calculated complexity level for large-scale photo database to explore the relationship between beauty expectation and complexity level. Our analysis confirmed the ascending part of Berlyne's inverted-U curve and the importance of complexity in aesthetic assessment. The proposed visual complexity features are proved to be efficient in both beauty prediction and quality classification tasks.

In future work, we intend to enrich the definition of complexity to better model human beings' complexity sensation and include semantic features such as familiarity. To improve the accuracy of complexity model, we would collect complexity labels in a crowd-sourcing way. We would like to further explore the role that complexity played in aesthetic assessment and try to predict aesthetic ranks for photos.

References

1. Akalin, A., Yildirim, K., Wilson, C., Kilicoglu, O.: Architecture and engineering students' evaluations of house façades: Preference, complexity and impressiveness. Journal of Environmental Psychology **29**(1), 124–132 (2009)
2. Arbelaez, P., Maire, M., Fowlkes, C., Malik, J.: Contour detection and hierarchical image segmentation. IEEE Transactions on Pattern Analysis and Machine Intelligence **33**(5), 898–916 (2011)

---

[2] For further information about the photos used in the experiment and the collected complexity labellings, please contact sun1101@hal.t.u-tokyo.ac.jp

3. Berlyne, D.E.: Studies in the new experimental aesthetics: Steps toward an objective psychology of aesthetic appreciation. Hemisphere (1974)
4. Berlyne, D.: Aesthetics and psychobiology. Appleton-Century-Crofts, New York (1971)
5. Donderi, D.C.: Visual complexity: a review. Psychological Bulletin 132(1), 73 (2006)
6. Forsythe, A., Nadal, M., Sheehy, N., Cela-Conde, C.J., Sawey, M.: Predicting beauty: fractal dimension and visual complexity in art. British Journal of Psychology 102(1), 49–70 (2011)
7. He, X.C., Yung, N.H.: Curvature scale space corner detector with adaptive threshold and dynamic region of support. In: Proceedings of the 17th International Conference on Pattern Recognition, ICPR 2004, vol. 2, pp. 791–794. IEEE (2004)
8. Heath, T., Smith, S.G., Lim, B.: Tall buildings and the urban skyline the effect of visual complexity on preferences. Environment and Behavior 32(4), 541–556 (2000)
9. Mallon, B., Redies, C., Hayn-Leichsenring, G.U.: Beauty in abstract paintings: perceptual contrast and statistical properties. Frontiers in Human Neuroscience 8 (2014)
10. Martín H, J.A., Santos, M., de Lope, J.: Orthogonal variant moments features in image analysis. Information Sciences 180(6), 846–860 (2010)
11. Moon, P., Spencer, D.E.: Geometric formulation of classical color harmony. JOSA 34(1), 46–50 (1944)
12. Murray, N., Marchesotti, L., Perronnin, F.: Ava: A large-scale database for aesthetic visual analysis. In: 2012 IEEE Conference on Computer Vision and Pattern Recognition (CVPR), pp. 2408–2415. IEEE (2012)
13. Nasar, J.L.: What design for a presidential library? complexity, typicality, order, and historical significance. Empirical Studies of the Arts 20(1), 83–99 (2002)
14. Reber, R.: Processing fluency, aesthetic pleasure, and culturally shared taste. In: Aesthetic Science: Connecting Minds, Brains, and Experience, pp. 223–249 (2012)
15. Reber, R., Schwarz, N., Winkielman, P.: Processing fluency and aesthetic pleasure: is beauty in the perceiver's processing experience? Personality and Social Psychology Review 8(4), 364–382 (2004)
16. Redies, C., Amirshahi, S.A., Koch, M., Denzler, J.: PHOG-derived aesthetic measures applied to color photographs of artworks, natural scenes and objects. In: Fusiello, A., Murino, V., Cucchiara, R. (eds.) ECCV 2012 Ws/Demos, Part I. LNCS, vol. 7583, pp. 522–531. Springer, Heidelberg (2012)
17. Rigau, J., Feixas, M., Sbert, M.: Informational aesthetics measures. IEEE Computer Graphics and Applications 28(2), 24–34 (2008)
18. Romero, J., Machado, P., Carballal, A., Santos, A.: Using complexity estimates in aesthetic image classification. Journal of Mathematics and the Arts 6(2–3), 125–136 (2012)
19. Stamps III, A.E.: Entropy, visual diversity, and preference. The Journal of General Psychology 129(3), 300–320 (2002)
20. Tuch, A.N., Bargas-Avila, J.A., Opwis, K., Wilhelm, F.H.: Visual complexity of websites: Effects on users experience, physiology, performance, and memory. International Journal of Human-Computer Studies 67(9), 703–715 (2009)
21. Vu, C.T., Phan, T.D., Chandler, D.M.: A spectral and spatial measure of local perceived sharpness in natural images. IEEE Transactions on Image Processing 21(3), 934–945 (2012)

Computational Beauty: Aesthetic Judgment at the Intersection of Art and Science

Emily L. Spratt[1] and Ahmed Elgammal[2](✉)

[1] Department of Art and Archaeology, Princeton University, NJ, USA
espratt@princeton.edu
[2] Department of Computer Science, Rutgers University, NJ, USA
elgammal@cs.rutgers.edu

Abstract. In part one of the *Critique of Judgment*, Immanuel Kant wrote that "the judgment of taste ... is not a cognitive judgment, and so not logical, but is aesthetic [1]." While the condition of aesthetic discernment has long been the subject of philosophical discourse, the role of the arbiters of that judgment has more often been assumed than questioned. The art historian, critic, connoisseur, and curator have long held the esteemed position of the aesthetic judge, their training, instinct, and eye part of the inimitable subjective processes that Kant described as occurring upon artistic evaluation. Although the concept of intangible knowledge in regard to aesthetic theory has been much explored, little discussion has arisen in response to the development of new types of artificial intelligence as a challenge to the seemingly ineffable abilities of the human observer. This paper examines the developments in the field of computer vision analysis of paintings from canonical movements within the history of Western art and the reaction of art historians to the application of this technology in the field. Through an investigation of the ethical consequences of this innovative technology, the unquestioned authority of the art expert is challenged and the subjective nature of aesthetic judgment is brought to philosophical scrutiny once again.

Keywords: Computer Vision · Aesthetic Judgment · Aesthetic Theory · Critical Theory · Formalism

1 Aesthetics: Between Computer Science and Art History

Since the pioneering research on two-dimensional imaging for statistical pattern recognition that took place in the 1960s, when the computer was brought from a typewriting calculator to an image-processing machine, the field of computer vision science has developed into an independent field of study within the quickly evolving domain of artificial intelligence. While developments within computer vision have mainly derived from the impetus of defense technology, in the last twenty years the application of this research has been applied to the interpretation of two-dimensional images, creating a new branch of study. For example,

L. Agapito et al. (Eds.): ECCV 2014 Workshops, Part I, LNCS 8925, pp. 35–53, 2015.
DOI: 10.1007/978-3-319-16178-5_3

computer vision utilizes algorithms for different object recognition related problems including: instance recognition, categorization, scene recognition, and pose estimation. At this point in time, computers can examine an image and recognize distinct objects, and even categorize the scenes they occupy. Cultural and historical inferences about an image may slowly become determinable by computers, yet the complexities of these higher-level perceptions are currently possible only in the realm of human cognition.

On account of the significant advances in computer vision research in the analysis of art, we would like to suggest that the time has come to make an overall evaluation of the possibilities of aesthetic interpretation that the computer offers to date. While academics in the humanities have remained largely skeptical of the use of computer science to perform tasks that involve subjective interpretations of qualitative data, we seek to demonstrate how one intersection of the arts and sciences can be fruitfully navigated, that of computer vision and art history. Rather than relegating the aesthetic interpretation of art by computers solely to computer scientists, let us determine how machine-based analysis of art functions in comparison to human judgment by considering the voices of art historians and other representatives from the humanities. This collaborative approach thus heralds a reevaluation of the philosophy of aesthetic theory as it has been applied in art history in light of the scientific developments not only within computer vision but also in relation to neurobiology.[1]

Indeed, computer vision challenges the art historian's very conception of the processes of aesthetic judgment and what may be regarded as objective or subjective mental processes if a computer has the ability to perform similar tasks. Through examination of the innovations and histories of computer vision and aesthetics as a philosophical discourse that has been utilized in art history, we will question both how notions of authority in aesthetic judgment and the processes of aesthetic interpretation itself have been and are being constructed. While the art historian, critic, connoisseur, and curator have long held the esteemed position of aesthetic judge–their training, instinct, and eye, part of a seemingly inimitable cognitive process that occurs upon artistic evaluation–these new developments in computer science challenge the very tenets of aesthetic theory and call for their reevaluation. Similarly, this paper demands an accessible explanation from computer scientists as to how aesthetic judgments are being programmed into machines and to what end. Through a collaborative approach, we aim to begin to bridge the gap between computer science and art history, fostering research that will yield effective applications of computer vision in the analysis of art and theoretical reconsideration of aesthetic judgment given the newfound capabilities of machines.

In this paper, we will question the potential of a computer to make aesthetic judgments. We will consider the degree to which computers can aid specialists within art history and examine whether computer vision can offer unique insights to art historians regarding iconographic and stylistic influence. We also

---

[1] See, for instance, New York University's Center for Neural Science and the Visual Neuroscience Laboratory, http://www.cns.nyu.edu/.

will examine whether art historians would be open to using new technologies advanced by these developments in computer science and offer suggestions as to how to encourage collaboration between the fields. Through the initiation of a multidisciplinary discussion about these interrogations, this approach to two seemingly disparate fields, to our knowledge, is the first of its kind. The paper's structure is as follows: Sections two and three will review the research developments in computer vision regarding the analysis of art and examine the reaction of art historians to these developments. We explain the philosophical concept of aesthetic judgment and its implications in sections four and five. In the conclusion, we will discuss the present and future interaction between the fields of computer science and art history.

2   Computer-Based Stylistic Analysis of Art

The field of computer vision is focused on developing algorithms for understanding images and videos using computers and providing interpretations of them, essentially giving computers the ability to see. Given the context of the application, these interpretations have the capacity to yield highly variegated meanings, including the ability to recover three-dimensional forms of representations from a two-dimensional image, the recognition of objects in an image, and the analysis of human activities, gestures, facial expressions, and interactions.

In the last two decades, within the field of computer vision, there has been increasing interest in the area of computer-based analysis of art with some degree of collaboration with art historians. Earlier work in this area has focused on providing objective analysis tools, where computers are mainly used to quantify certain physical features of an artwork. These tools can provide art historians with measurements that are difficult to obtain by the human eye alone. For example, computer vision technology has been used to conduct extremely precise pigmentation analysis of a painting's color, quantify exacting statistical measures of brushstrokes, and provide detailed examinations of craquelure [2]. Computers also can provide tools to automate certain types of analysis that have long been performed manually by experts, particularly in the interpretation of perspective and lighting, and the decipherment of anamorphic images. An approachable review of the research in this area prior to 2009 was conducted by David Stork [2].

With the advances in computer vision and machine learning, computers now can make semantic-level predictions from images. For example, computers can now recognize object categories, human body postures, and activities in a scene. As a result, research on computer-based analysis of art has evolved and is now developing more sophisticated tasks, including the automatic classification of art to identify the hand of an artist, the ability to classify paintings according to style and to distinguish stylistically similar images of paintings, the quantification of the degree of artistic similarity found between paintings, and the capability to predict a painting's date of production. We collectively call these tasks computer-based stylistic analysis of art. At this point in time, computer vision has gone far beyond providing art historians with tools that are simply stylometric, or quantifiable physical measures. One trend in computer vision technology is the development of algorithms that encompass complex measures taken through a computer's visual analysis that are used to directly make predictions about a painting's attribution, date, authenticity, and style without the need of an art historian. In this section we review some of these new developments within computer science that approach the realm of aesthetic judgment through computer automation.

Most of the research concerning the classification of paintings utilizes low-level features or simple diagnostic measures, such as the appearance of color, shadow, texture, and edges. Researchers have extensively conducted computerized analysis of brushstrokes in images of paintings [3–9]. Brushstrokes, like fingerprints, provide what computer scientists call a signature that can help distinguish the hand of the artist. The analysis typically involves texture features that are assumed to encode the brushstroke signature of the artist. Recently, Li et al. proposed a method based on the integration of edge detection and image segmentation for brushstroke analysis [9]. Using these features they found that regularly shaped brushstrokes are tightly arranged, creating a repetitive and patterned impression that can represent, for example, Van Gogh's distinctive painting style, and help to distinguish his work from that of his contemporaries. This research group has analyzed forty-five digitized oil paintings of Van Gogh from museum collections.

T.E. Lombardi has presented a study of the capability of different types of low-level features extracted from paintings to identify artists [10]. Several features such as color, line, and texture were surveyed for their accuracy in classification of a given painting to identify the hand of an artist amongst a small data set of artists. Additionally, several machine learning techniques were used for classification, visualization, and evaluation. Through this research, the style of the painting was identified as a result of the computer's ability to recognize artistic authorship. For example, recognition that a painting was attributed to Claude Monet signaled an association with Impressionism. The idea of using color analysis for the identification of a painter has also been researched [11]. Bag of Words (BoW) (an approach originally used a decade ago for text classification and object recognition) was utilized by Khan et al. along with the fusion of color and shape information that could identify individual painters [12].

The problem of annotating digital images of art prints (painted copies of canonical paintings) was addressed by Carneiro et al.[13]. In that research, a reproduction was automatically annotated to one of seven themes (e.g., the Annunciation) as well as with the appearance of twenty-one specific symbols or objects (e.g., an angel, Christ, Mary). These computer scientists proposed that a graph-based learning algorithm, based on the assumption that visually similar paintings share the same types of annotation, would yield higher levels of accuracy in the identification of paintings. The data set they used contained reproductions from the fifteenth to the seventeenth century that were annotated by art historians and focused exclusively on religious themes. The analysis of art print images was later extended using a larger data set (PRINTART) with semantic annotation (e.g., Holy Family), localized object annotation, such as localizing a rectangle around the Christ Child, and simple body pose annotation, for instance locating the head and torso of Mary [14]. The research of Carneiro et al. demonstrated that the low-level texture and color features, typically exploited for photographic image analysis, are not effective because of inconsistent color and texture patterns describing the visual classes in artistic images [14]. In essence, the quality of painted reproductions greatly affects the ability of a computer to visually interpret a painting.

The research of Graham et al. examined the way we perceive two paintings as similar to each other [15]. The researchers collected painting similarity ratings from human observers and used statistical methods to find the factors most correlated with human ratings. They analyzed two sets of images, denoted as either scenes of landscapes or portraits and still lives. The analysis demonstrated that similarities between paintings could be interpreted in terms of basic image statistics. For landscape paintings, the image intensity statistics were shown to highly correlate with the similarity ratings; for portraits and still lives, the most important visual clues about their degree of similarity were determined to be semantic variables, such as the representation of people in a given composition.

The question of automatically ordering paintings according to their date of production was posed by Cabral et al.[16]. They formulated this problem by embedding paintings into a one-dimensional linear ordering and utilizing two different methods. In the first, they applied an unsupervised (without the use of annotation) dimensionality reduction (a technique used in machine learning to reduce the number of variables). To do so, they only needed to employ visual features to map paintings to points on a line. This approach, despite being fast and requiring no annotation, resulted in low accuracy. The second method took into account available partial ordering of paintings annotated by experts. This information was used as a constraint in order to find the proper embedding of a painting to a line, which was more chronologically accurate.

Unlike most of the previous research that focused on inferring the authorship of the artist from the painting, Arora et al. approached the problem of the classification of style in paintings into classes that are directly recognized in the history of art [17]. They defined a classification task between seven painting styles: Renaissance, Baroque, Impressionism, Cubism, Abstract, Expressionism, and Pop Art. In their research, they formulated a supervised classification problem (a machine learning paradigm where training data is assumed to have class labels annotated by experts). They presented a comparative study evaluating generative models versus discriminative models, as well as low- and intermediate-level versus semantic-level features. For the semantic-level description they used features called Classeme, which encode an image in terms of the output of a large number of classifiers [18]. Such classifiers are trained using images retrieved from Internet search engines, with an accompanying term list. The result was particularly interesting: the research found that the semantic-level discriminative model produced the best classification result with 65% style classification accuracy [17]. Indeed, the use of verbal descriptors that are associated with the visual

Fig. 1. A computer-recognized example of stylistic similarity, from Abe et al. is Frédéric Bazille's *Studio 9 Rue de la Condamine* (left), Norman Rockwell's *Shuffleton's Barber Shop* (right) [19].

content of a painting led to greater accuracy in classification compared to stylistic analysis alone. This result highlights the importance of encoding semantic information for the task of style classification and for the analysis of art in general.

The problem of discovering similarities between artists and inferring artistic influences was addressed by Abe et al. by defining similarity measures between artists over a data set of sixty-six artists and 1,710 paintings, ranging from the fifteenth to the twentieth century [19,20]. Based on the results of the research of Arora et al., they also used semantic-level features to encode the similarity of paintings [17]. Artist-to-artist similarity was encoded with variants of the Hausdorff distance (a regularly used geometric distance measure between two sets of points). This similarity measure was utilized to construct a directed graph of artists encoding both artist-to-artist similarity and temporal constraints, and that graph was used to discover potential influences. They evaluated their results by comparing the discovered potential influences against known influences cited in art historical sources. Figure 1 illustrates an example of two stylistically similar paintings detected by the approach of Abe et al., Frédéric Bazille's *Studio 9 Rue de la Condamine* (1870) and Norman Rockwell's *Shuffleton's Barber Shop* (1950) [19,20]. This type of comparison, however, would not be cited in art historical sources, as the connection between the paintings is purely formal and coincidental. The graph of artists was also used to achieve a visualization of artistic similarity (this is termed, map of artists).

Most of the aforementioned research uses computer vision analysis to perform tasks implicitly related to the domain of aesthetic judgment. There has also been recent research that has developed algorithms to make aesthetic judgments of a more explicit nature [21,22]. This research has used computer vision technology to predict how humans would score an image of a scene or an object according to its perceived beauty. For example, computer models can be trained to predict attributes of an image that beg aesthetic discernment, such as compositional strategies, the presence of particular objects, and even the way a sky is illuminated. The attributes are then used to predict aesthetic calculations for a given image [22]. This type of computer vision analysis narrows the concept of aesthetic judgment to a set of pre-defined objective rules.[2]

Given the progress in developing computer algorithms that are directly related to tasks regarding what humans would define as aesthetic judgments, a number of questions emerge regarding the implications of these applications. The ability of these computational models to perform aesthetic judgments in this capacity demonstrates that there is a difference in perception of the processes required for artistic evaluation in the arts versus the sciences. Currently, there is a trend in artificial intelligence and computer vision technology in using computational models inspired by the brain's complex neural network (known as deep networks); as the similarities between computer systems and neurobiology expand, the differences between aesthetic interpretation as it is understood in the humanities as opposed to the sciences will only widen if the questions this research poses are not adequately addressed. In the following sections we therefore explore the implications of these developments in computer vision technology.

3 Perspectives from the Field of Art History: Does Computer Vision Pose a Threat?

Unfortunately, these developments in computer vision are not widely known or fully understood in the humanities and thus indicate the disjuncture between the fields of art history and computer science, and a larger fracture between the arts and sciences. In order to gauge the current perceptions between these fields, we conducted two surveys that were distributed to computer scientists and art historians at Princeton University, Rutgers University, Cornell University, New York University, and the University of California at Los Angeles in August 2014.[3] The results revealed that while there has been some positive reception of the use of computer vision research in art history, it remains limited and often confined to the domain of art conservation and connoisseurship. Not only is there a general unfamiliarity with the developments of new technologies like those in computer vision and their potential use-value in the humanities, there is much concern about their implementation. While it is not surprising that the majority of computer scientists thought that the use of artificial intelligence technology in the humanities signals the beginning of a positive paradigm shift in academia whereas the majority of art historians thought it did not, we also discovered that computer scientists and art historians are, in fact, in agreement on key issues. For instance, both groups agreed that they should collaborate and that computer vision technology does not risk taking away an art historian's job.[4]

---

[2] Ethical consideration of the use of computer vision technology for these purposes is clearly needed and requires further investigation.

[3] For a complete analysis of our digital humanities survey see
https://sites.google.com/site/digitalhumanitiessurvey/

[4] Sensationalizing titles about computer vision research in the press may be inaccurate. See, Matthew Sparkes, "Could computers put art historians out of work?" [23].

Similar observations regarding the anxieties about the digital humanities project have been noted in regard to other specific applications.[5] Although art historians are generally skeptical of allowing computers to perform tasks that have been traditionally reserved for trained specialists and deemed capable for only human comprehension, to date there has been, to our knowledge, no exact measures of this implicit distrust in the sciences to produce knowledge of a subjective nature.[6]

Indeed, the key question in our survey, which inquired whether art historians would be willing to use computer vision to better understand paintings, aroused a strong territorial response from the field of art history. Given our empirical measures, which clearly demonstrate the divide between the fields, the authors of this paper have been trying to build a bridge between the disciplines that addresses the specific misunderstandings the survey results revealed. By investigating and analyzing the consequences that the use of artificial intelligence in domains that are traditionally understood to be reserved for humans pose, we hope to prevent further sequestration between the fields of art history and computer science.

What does it mean when an art historian, who is trained to evaluate art, or even a novice admirer of art, is faced with a machine that can perform a similar task? Since the very nature of our ability to aesthetically comprehend and judge beauty is the determining factor in what most people would describe as distinguishing us from machines, this type of computer science threatens our own conceptions of human identity [26]. While it is important to recognize these anxieties, we would like to propose that understanding some of the philosophical origins of how we have come to regard aesthetic judgment may offer a partial explanation as to why it is that persons not trained in computer science perceive these developments as a threat. Computer science, neither our friend, nor foe, presents to the humanities a challenge: is intangible, or sensory, knowledge really intangible if a computer can perform processes that manifest the same results that a human would produce?

4   Aesthetic Judgment: Between Philosophy and Art History

The concept of sensory knowledge derives from a long tradition in European theology, philosophy, and psychology, although it was not until the eighteenth century that this type of knowing began to be perceived in a positive light [27]. Predominantly on account of Alexander Gottlieb Baumgarten's *Aesthetica*, published in Latin in 1750, the notion that there was a type of knowledge distinct from that of logic or reason gained acceptance [28]. He termed this knowledge as *analogon rationis*, or analogue of reason, which had its own perfection distinct

---

[5]   These concerns are well expressed in, Stephen Marche, "Literature is not Data, Against Digital Humanities" [24].

[6]   See, for instance, Stanley Fish, "Mind Your P's and B's: The Digital Humanities and Interpretation" [25].

from logic. In consequence to this theory, it came to be argued that there should be two kinds of corresponding sciences of knowledge: that of logic and that of aesthetics. Baumgarten's philosophy thus provided the foundation for Immanuel Kant's theories on aesthetics and the background for the *Critique of Judgment*, published in 1790 [1,27].

The key to Kant's discourse was his rooting of the condition of aesthetic discernment in a subjective, non-logical process. Indeed, the philosophy of aesthetics from Baumgarten to Deleuze, not necessarily including the branch of philosophy that Hegel directed aesthetics, places aesthetic comprehension in the realm of subjectivity.[7] Kant articulated the conditions of this type of reasoning in the *Critique of Judgment*, locating aesthetic understanding in moral philosophy and the principles of universality [1]. In part one of the *Critique*, Kant explains the processes of analysis that is required for the interpretation of art. He writes:

> If we wish to discern whether anything is beautiful or not, we do not refer the representation of it to the Object by means of understanding with a view to cognition, but by means of the imagination (acting perhaps in conjunction with understanding) we refer the representation to the Subject and its feeling of pleasure or displeasure. The judgment of taste, therefore, is not a cognitive judgment, and so not logical, but is aesthetic-which means that it is one whose determining ground cannot be other than subjective. [8]

Despite the focus on the subjectivity of aesthetic interpretation through individual judgment, Kant goes on to explain that the judgment of taste is also universal. He considers this in regard to the knowledge of how things are, or their "theoretical knowledge," and to how things should be, or their "morality."[9] Kant argues that judging art is like judging the purposiveness of nature, as both can be examined in terms of beauty, either natural or artistic. While the philosophical relationship of nature and art remain outside the confines of this paper, it is important to take note that art was often evaluated in terms of its faithfulness to imitating nature until the modernist revolution led to the questioning of these values.

Just as nature was judged in terms of its purposiveness and its ability to manifest this quality in visual form, so too was art through its references. In this sense, Kant's perception of the quality of art is bound to the principles of the Romantic movement, as art historian Donald Preziosi notes, "the world being the Artifact of a divine Artificer [27]." Positioning himself against classical rationalism, that beauty is related to a singular inner truth in nature, Kant instead

---

[7] Hegel regarded art as "a secondary or surface phenomenon... thus harking back to pre-Baumgarten and pre-Kantian ideology which privileged the ideal or Thought by devalorizing visual knowledge." See Preziosi [27], *The Art of Art History*, 66-67.

[8] Kant, *Critique of Judgment* [1], 41.

[9] Ibid., this interpretation was facilitated by Donald Preziosi, see Preziosi [27], *The Art of Art History*, 66-67.

suggests that beauty is linked to the infinite quality of the human imagination yet grounded in the finiteness of being. In this sense, the universality of taste also relates to a type of collective consciousness that stems from God's universal creation. Kant further relates aesthetics and ethics, positing that beautiful objects inspire sensations like those produced in the mental state of moral judgment, thus genius and taste could be related to the moral character of an artist or viewer. How moral values can raise or lower the aesthetic value of art is, indeed, a subject of philosophical scrutiny, if not controversy, to this day [29].

The direction that Kant steered aesthetics has had a pervasive influence in philosophy into the contemporary period as Gilles Deleuze's conception of a transcendental empiricism demonstrates in its use of Kantian notions of sensibility. While art history has a tradition of intellectual borrowings for its theories and methodologies, its montage nature as a discipline, incorporating the perspectives of diverse fields in the humanities such as philosophy, comparative literature, anthropology, archaeology, and psychology, to name a few, has allowed for its inherent flexibility in critical interpretations that rarely produce a singular analysis of art. Indeed, parallel interpretations of a given object are implicitly understood to exist stemming from a wide range of theories and methodologies such as formal analysis, studies in iconography, conservation history, connoisseurship, Marxist theory, feminist theory, or social history, to list just several art historical perspectives, all of which may overlap or exclude each other.

Although the birth of art history is usually associated with the Renaissance and Giorgio Vasari's writing of the *Lives of the Most Excellent Painters, Sculptors, and Architects*, first published in 1550, how we define the origins of the discipline differs greatly according to the artistic tradition being considered, thus nuancing any standardization of what is meant by art historical analysis. In the West, Greek philosophers such as Plato and Aristotle could be credited with engaging in an early form of art history, commenting at length on the faculties of observation gained through sight and the physical drives associated with seeing [30]. Indeed, throughout the history of the discipline, art history has been directly influenced by the sciences to varying degrees over time and according to geography, yet never to the exclusion of philosophical approaches to the interpretation of art. For example, Carl Linnaeus (1707-1778), the founding father of modern taxonomy who drew heavily from Francis Bacon's (1561-1626) scientific method of empiricism, may be credited with establishing the foundations for the classification of artifacts in museums through his organization of natural history objects concurrently with philosophical developments in art history [31,32].

It wasn't until the nineteenth century, however, that the principles of connoisseurship that emerged from Vasari's legacy were reevaluated by Giovanni Morelli (1816-1891) [33]. While the period from the sixteenth century to the end of the nineteenth century witnessed many methodological developments in the history of art, these contributions were largely philosophical and less emulative of the direction taken by Linnaeus. Morelli's innovation was to focus on methods of connoisseurship that privileged direct engagement with a work of art that allowed for a very precise type of visual investigation. For instance, the rendering of a detail such as an ear could reveal the true authorship of a painting [34].

Morelli writes in a dialogue from *Italian Painters*, published in 1890, "Art connoisseurs say of art historians that they write about what they do not understand; art historians, on their side, disparage the connoisseurs, and only look upon them as the drudges who collect materials for them, but who personally have not the slightest knowledge of the physiology of art [35]." Morelli, and later the Vienna School of art history, which was heralded by Alois Riegl's (1858-1905) contributions on the history of ornament in terms of form (as opposed to history or philosophy), emphasized the strictly material interpretation that art history also accommodates. Not surprisingly, the theories of art espoused by Morelli and Riegl found immediate application to the world of connoisseurs, conservators, and museum associates. In the same vein, these types of materialist inquiries opened theoretical ground for philosophical consideration of the history of art measured through the development of form itself, devoid of its socio-historical constraints.

This brief review of some of the intersections between art history and the sciences, both in terms of the faculties of vision and aesthetic judgment along with the field's engagement with scientific methodologies, underscores the point that there has been a sustaining influence of science in the arts. Therefore, if we were better able to understand the capabilities of computer vision technology, why wouldn't art historians consider the philosophical implications of this modern-day science on aesthetic theory and visual perception?

5   The Implications of Aesthetic Philosophy on Human Perception and Art History

The machine's ability to make an aesthetic judgment about a painting, and then compare it stylistically to other paintings, demonstrates that logic is at work in the complicated algorithms that comprise the artificial intellegence system. These processes are all clearly imitative and objective at the point of the computer program training period; once the machine reaches the automaton level, the question of subjectivity enters. In this sense, are computer programmers like blind watchmakers, to use Richard Dawkins' famous metaphor of the evolution of the universe and the free will debate [36]? Are computers comparable to humans with genetic codes that predetermine outcomes, which are then shaped by the environment?

While structural similarities between the human brain and computer systems have already been well acknowledged in computer science and neurobiology, we are reminded of the origins of the field of computer science itself, which was initiated under the direction of a cognitive scientist and a neuroscientist. Fortunately, the intersections of these seemingly diverse areas of study are being specifically addressed in what some scholars are calling the field of *neuroaesthetics*, [37]. For example, we know that it is the orbitofrontal and insular cortices that are involved in aesthetic judgment and that this unique feature of our executive brain functioning may distinguish us from our primate ancestors [38]. By examining the biological functions of the visually perceiving brain, it is possible to calculate a much more accurate understanding of the processes involved in an act of aesthetic judgment.

The implications of these components of cognitive neuroscience on art and history are currently being addressed by David Freedberg in extension to his groundbreaking book on the psychological responses to art, *The Power of Images: Studies in the History and Theory of Response* (1989) [39]. Other inroads on this subject from within art history have been made by Michael Baxandall through his consideration of the notion of the historically constructed period eye and his interest in the processes of visual interpretation [40]. The history of biological inquiries on the interpretation of art have been well summarized by John Onians in his introduction to *Neuroarthistory* [37].

Interest in the psychology of seeing (in a broader sense), however, has a long history that may still be tied to Kant and the philosophical tradition. For instance, the Berlin School's theory of gestaltism that emerged in the 1890s posits that visual recognition occurs primarily on the level of whole forms as opposed to their parts. The application of gestalt psychology to art was most famously heralded by Rudolf Arnheim (1904-2007) in *Art and Visual Perception: A Psychology of the Creative Eye* (1954), which explored the concept of sensory knowledge through the act of seeing [41]. It is important to note that both psychologists and art historians grappling to understand the mechanisms of aesthetic interpretation have remained largely in dialogue with Kant's binary distinctions of the production knowledge.

Kant's interrogations thus still underlie basic questions about machine-based intelligence: if we are able to create artificial intelligence that performs types of reasoning that we have long considered subjective, we are either more machine-like than we admit, machines have more human potential than we estimate, or these processes are, in fact, tangibly measurable and objectively determined. In essence, the debate moves to the question of determinism and free will. While most people would agree that a computer, even one that has reached automaton status and has the ability to learn from its environment, is not free, we are less willing to concede the notion of human freedom when we too are ultimately bound by our genes and environment. For eighteenth-century philosophers, reasoning, particularly in the domain of subjectivity, was tied to God through morality and universality in terms of the decisions we are perceived to freely make. These philosophies are still debated today in different terms.

We would like to suggest that how we understand aesthetic judgment can still be tied to the eighteenth- and nineteenth-century philosophical tradition, yet we need to better interpret how these so-called subjective processes work, if they even are subjective, and integrate new scientific developments, such as those in neurobiology and computer science, into our conceptions of how knowledge is produced. Nonetheless, it is a paradox that developments in computer science could have pushed the humanities to reevaluate its most basic premises: for art

Fig. 2. *Wrapped Reichstag*, Berlin, 1971-95 Christo and Jeanne-Claude, Photo: Wolfgang Volz ©1995 Christo.

history, it is how we determine that something is beautiful and/or important, and how objects are interrelated. Have the advances in science not provided a platform in which we can begin to understand cognition, as it is applied to aesthetics, in a radically different way than eighteenth- and nineteenth-century philosophers conceived these processes? We easily discredit the idea of humors as ruling temperaments of the body but know that Kant considered them viable and one of them as an indication of the absence of temperament [42]. We still read Kant for his interpretations of physical and psychological states, yet not on his theory of the phlegmatic humor.

Science is obviously not the only domain from which to take direction. Let us heed caution from aesthetic critics such as Julius Meier-Graefe who, in 1904, explored the problem of the dominancy of paintings in the history of art in his response to modern art and the new mediums the movement favored [43]. That a machine has the ability to examine paintings does not mean that it has the capacity to understand sculpture, installation art, performance art, or land art. What would a computer make of the Christo and Jeanne-Claude installation, the *Wrapped Reichstag* (Figure 2)? Both three- and two- dimensional computer vision programs would be able to determine the sharp edges of the building and sense its occupation of a large amount of space, either in reality, or as it appears in a photo, yet how would the significance of the wrapping of such a canonical architectural form loaded with symbolism be readily understood and quantified for qualitative analysis by a machine? When computer scientists one day simulate the human brain, will the machine understand the Christo and Jeanne-Claude installation? Will machine aesthetic judgment be any different than human aesthetic judgment? Who shall we give the authority to make that judgment? These are important considerations to make in our society as it adapts to the advances in artificial intelligence. Norbert Wiener's famous remarks on the effects of what he termed cybernetics remain relevant today [44]. In 1950, he perceptively wrote that "the machine, which can learn and can make decisions on the basis of its learning, will in no way be obliged to make such decisions as we should have made, or will be acceptable to us. For the man who is not aware of this, to throw the problem of his responsibility on the machine, whether it can learn or not, is to cast his responsibility to the winds [44]."

6   Within the Limits of Probability: Computer Science and Art History Today

This paper has considered both the limitations of computer vision research and its potential for growth in regard to its application for art history. In conclusion, we would like to underscore the current concerns that this research poses for art historians in its immediate application. We have thus highlighted three main issues that demand further attention: the use of language between fields to describe global and specific concepts, the lack of uniformity in the interpretation of art, and the separate developments within computer science and art history regarding aesthetic interpretation.

Firstly, there is discomfort in the globalizing language that computer scientists use to describe their research. Rather than make claims about a computer's ability to analyze art at large, specificity as to what can be analyzed and what has been analyzed would assuage philosophical anxieties about the ontological nature of man versus the machine [45].[10] In this paper, we have been careful to describe computer analysis of what computer scientists call visual art, a term that is not readily utilized in art history, as an analysis of paintings from some of the canonical movements in art through history in the Western tradition. Instead of framing computer vision research in broad and global terms that are unsupportable (from the humanities' perspective), demonstrating the potential of this technology through specific examples allows art historians to consider its value in ways that don't interfere with their critical approach of analysis. If we can shift the onus of interpretation to the art historians, computer scientists would likely find art historians more willing to embrace computer vision technology.

While computer vision research has been instrumental in art conservation applications, it has not been utilized by art historians for more aesthetically based interpretations. Not surprisingly, our surveys further confirmed the apprehension in art history to the developments that computer vision offers in the realm of subjective interpretation. We would therefore like to propose that computer scientists collaborate with art historians on specific projects. Research that concerns the analysis of a multitude of images related to one artist or movement could be facilitated by the current capabilities of computer vision technology. The ability to compute perspective coherence, lighting and shading strategies, brushstrokes styles, and semantic points of similarity could, for example, aid the analysis of a large group of Italian drawings with unclear authorship. Similarly, the application of this technology for the identification of icon workshops that utilized the same iconographic templates in the context of Medieval, Byzantine,

---

[10] To this end, the first author presented a paper on this topic to archaeologists and art historians [45].

or Post-Byzantine devotional images would be extremely useful if a large data set of icons from diverse collections that are not readily accessible to the public could be brought together. Recent collaborations of this nature have already been initiated and should continue [9,46]. While this type of collaboration lies in the domain of connoisseurship more than what one would term art history, it seems clear that working within the realm of current capabilities in computer vision technology is the best way to build a collaboration between the fields that would eventually ignite a more philosophical understanding of these methods and their bearing on aesthetic theory.

The second issue regarding the immediate application of computer vision research in the domain of aesthetics concerns the way the social history of an object and the emotional engagement to art is calculated. In art history, the degree to which the context in which a work of art is produced should matter. How can a computer quantify the social history of a painting or the material means of its production? It is exactly this point that the critical theorists of art raised more than a century ago regarding the nature of art "both context-bound and yet also irreducible to its contextual conditions [47]." To quote the art historian Michael Podro, "Either the context-bound quality or the irreducibility of art may be elevated at the expense of the other. If a writer diminishes the sense of context in his concern for the irreducibility or autonomy of art, he moves towards formalism. If he diminishes the sense of irreducibility in order to keep a firm hand on extra-artistic facts, he runs the risk of treating art as if it were the trace or symptom of those other facts [47]." If art is treated autonomously, as having an independent progression in the realm of form, its history is purely stylistic. For the critical theorists, this extreme was considered an aesthetic failure, as judgment requires morality and thus is tied to value-based interpretations of art on the level of object analysis [47].

Furthermore, if our understanding of the history of art is related to the emotional response that an object elicits, how can a computer mimic human affect? On the other hand, the developments in computer vision technology and neurobiology suggest a new understanding of the very mechanisms of emotion. That what we have understood as subjective processes may in fact be objectively determined problematizes the argument that computers can never achieve the capacities beholden to the contemplative human mind. These issues have been addressed in the recent surge of philosophical research on creativity [48,49].

In essence, there is no singular correct interpretation of a work of art within art history, as multiple theories and methodologies place differing emphases on style, content, and context. To date, computer vision research offers predominantly stylistic interpretations of paintings that only recently have begun to include iconographic considerations. While these tools have allowed us to categorize paintings into broad genres and chronologies, computer science is currently unable to offer more immediate associations regarding the specific social history of an object and the degree to which these conditions influenced the final product. In the same vein, certain periods or genres are more amenable to some theoretical approaches than to others. For example, abstract expressionism, which is highly concerned with the role of form over content, naturally accommodates the high degree of stylistic interpretation that computer vision offers. Within modern art, computer vision research might have the potential to offer unexpected insights on the level of style.

Due to the use of broad data sets, it is not surprising that computer scientists have noticed some far-reaching stylistic influences. For instance, automatic influence detection demonstrated the ability to detect less overt connections between artists such as Eugene Delacroix's not-so-widely-known influence from El Greco both in terms of color and expressiveness [19]. While this observation highlights the remarkable subtleties of interpretation that computer vision is capable of generating, this type of analysis is of less use to an art historian than a more specific study, such as what an analysis of Kazimir Malevich's fairly uniform appearing Suprematist paintings might reveal in regard to style.

The last critical issue that emerges concerns the way we locate and attribute the onus of interpretation in computer vision analysis. To what degree can we ascribe the detection of influence or artistic merit to a machine when it was the computer scientists that wrote the programming that associated certain visual components with particular markers of identity? At what point in the process of training the program to make its own judgments does the machine develop autonomy, if ever? If computer scientists can be charged with owning the responsibility of artistic interpretation at the level of programming input, why wouldn't art historians be involved at this level of the research? While there is no question that at this stage of development within computer science that programs have demonstrated the ability to take on an autonomous quality based on what they have been taught, are these innovations so advanced at this point in time that we can consider them on par to human judgment? Unfortunately, aesthetic interpretation in computer science is developing in isolation from the aesthetic discourse in philosophy and art history. If the humanities were able to more clearly understand the use-value of computer vision research and art historians were able to collaborate with computer scientists as machine-based aesthetic interpretation develops, both fields would benefit.

That a computer is able to measure art aesthetically challenges the field of art history to reexamine its own aesthetic constructs. David Hume pontificated that "beauty is no quality in things themselves: it exists merely in the mind which contemplates them; and each mind perceives a different beauty [50]." If the interpretation of art lies in the eyes of the beholder and is thus a subjectively determined process that is associated with feeling, how can we understand the development of autonomous aesthetic evaluation from a computer without reevaluating the processes of human aesthetic judgment and emotion? Awareness of these concepts could equally steer the direction of computer vision in terms of its abilities to provide immediate practical applications to the field of art history rather than taking on the uncomfortable guise of a virtual art historian. Our survey confirmed that both computer scientists and art historians agree that the humanities should be more digitized; however, before art historians are willing to believe that it is possible to analyze art with a computer in terms of beauty, style, dating, and relative influence in the development of art through history, we must revisit the concept of aesthetic judgment.

References

1. Kant, I.: Critique of Aesthetic Judgment (Part One), from Critique of Judgment. Translated by James Creed Meredith. Clarendon Press, Oxford (1911)
2. Stork, D.G.: Computer vision and computer graphics analysis of paintings and drawings: An introduction to the literature. In: Jiang, X., Petkov, N. (eds.) CAIP 2009. LNCS, vol. 5702, pp. 9–24. Springer, Heidelberg (2009)
3. Sablatnig, R., Kammerer, P., Zolda, E.: Hierarchical classification of paintings using face- and brush stroke models. In: ICPR (1998)
4. Li, J., Wang, J.Z.: Studying digital imagery of ancient paintings by mixtures of stochastic models. IEEE Transactions on Image Processing 13(3), 340–353 (2004)
5. Lyu, S., Rockmore, D., Farid, H.: A digital technique for art authentication. Proceedings of the National Academy of Sciences of the United States of America 101(49), 17006–17010 (2004)
6. Johnson, C.R., Hendriks, E., Berezhnoy, I.J., Brevdo, E., Hughes, S.M., Daubechies, I., Li, J., Postma, E., Wang, J.Z.: Image processing for artist identification. IEEE Signal Processing Magazine 25(4), 37–48 (2008)
7. Berezhnoy, I.E., Postma, E.O., van den Herik, H.J.: Automatic extraction of brushstroke orientation from paintings. Machine Vision and Applications 20(1), 1–9 (2009)
8. Polatkan, G., Jafarpour, S., Brasoveanu, A., Hughes, S., Daubechies, I.: Detection of forgery in paintings using supervised learning. In: 2009 16th IEEE International Conference on Image Processing (ICIP), pp. 2921–2924 (2009)
9. Li, J., Yao, L., Hendriks, E., Wang, J.Z.: Rhythmic brushstrokes distinguish van gogh from his contemporaries: Findings via automated brushstroke extraction. IEEE Trans. Pattern Anal. Mach. Intell. (2012)
10. Lombardi, T.E.: The classification of style in fine-art painting. ETD Collection for Pace University. Paper AAI3189084 (2005)
11. Widjaja, I., Leow, W., Wu., F.: Identifying painters from color profiles of skin patches in painting images. In: ICIP (2003)
12. Khan, F.S., van de Weijer, J., Vanrell, M.: Who painted this painting? In: The CREATE 2010 Conference (2010)
13. Carneiro, G.: Graph-based methods for the automatic annotation and retrieval of art prints. In: ICMR (2011)
14. Carneiro, G., da Silva, N.P., Del Bue, A., Costeira, J.P.: Artistic image classification: An analysis on the PRINTART database. In: Fitzgibbon, A., Lazebnik, S., Perona, P., Sato, Y., Schmid, C. (eds.) ECCV 2012, Part IV. LNCS, vol. 7575, pp. 143–157. Springer, Heidelberg (2012)
15. Graham, D., Friedenberg, J., Rockmore, D.: Mapping the similarity space of paintings: image statistics and visual perception. Visual Cognition (2010)
16. Cabral, R.S., Costeira, J.P., De la Torre, F., Bernardino, A., Carneiro, G.: Time and order estimation of paintings based on visual features and expert priors. In: SPIE Electronic Imaging, Computer Vision and Image Analysis of Art II (2011)
17. Arora, R.S., Elgammal, A.M.: Towards automated classification of fine-art painting style: A comparative study. In: ICPR (2012)

18. Torresani, L., Szummer, M., Fitzgibbon, A.: Efficient object category recognition using classemes. In: Daniilidis, K., Maragos, P., Paragios, N. (eds.) ECCV 2010, Part I. LNCS, vol. 6311, pp. 776–789. Springer, Heidelberg (2010)
19. Abe, K., Saleh, B., Elgammal, A.: An early framework for determining artistic influence. In: 2nd International Workshop on Multimedia for Cultural Heritage (MM4CH) (2013)
20. Saleh, B., Abe, K., Arora, R.S., Elgammal, A.: Toward automated discovery of artistic influence. Multimedia Tools and Applications - Special Issue on Multimedia for Cultural Heritage (2014) (in press)
21. Datta, R., Joshi, D., Li, J., Wang, J.Z.: Studying aesthetics in photographic images using a computational approach. In: Leonardis, A., Bischof, H., Pinz, A. (eds.) ECCV 2006. LNCS, vol. 3953, pp. 288–301. Springer, Heidelberg (2006)
22. Dhar, S., Ordonez, V., Berg, T.L.: High level describable attributes for predicting aesthetics and interestingness. In: 2011 IEEE Conference on Computer Vision and Pattern Recognition (CVPR), pp. 1657–1664. IEEE (2011)
23. Sparkes, M.: Could Computers Put Art Historians Out of Work? The Telegraph (August 18, 2014). http://www.telegraph.co.uk/technology/news/11041814/Could-computers-put-art-historians-out-of-work.html?fb
24. Marche, S.: Literature is not Data, Against Digital Humanities. Los Angeles Review of Books (October 28, 2012). http://lareviewofbooks.org/essay/literature-is-not-data-against-digital-humanities
25. Fish, S.: Mind Your P's and B's: The Digital Humanities and Interpretation. The Opinion Pages, The New York Times (January 23, 2012)
26. Paul, E.S., Kaufman, S.B.: On philosophical interpretations of what makes us human. In: The Philosophy of Creativity: New Essays. Oxford University Press (2014)
27. Preziosi, D.: The Art of Art History: A Critical Anthology. Oxford University Press (1998)
28. Baumgarten, A.G.: Aesthetica. Georg Olms Publishing House (1961)
29. McMahon, J.A.: Art and Ethics in a Material World: Kant's Pragmatist Legacy. Routledge (2013)
30. Aristotle: Poetics. Translated by Joe Sachs. Focus Publishing, Newburyport (2006)
31. Zittel, C. (ed.): Philosophies of Technology: Francis Bacon and His Contemporaries. Brill, Leiden (2008)
32. Findlen, P.: Possessing Nature: Museums, Collecting, and Scientific Culture in Early Modern Italy (Studies on the History of Society and Culture). University of California Press, Berkeley (1994)
33. Fernie, E.: Art History and its Methods, a Critical Anthology. Phaidon Press Limited, Regent's Wharf (1995)
34. Morelli, G.: Kunstkritische Studien uber italienische Malerei: die Galerien Borghese und Doria Pamfilj in Rom. Leipzig (1890)
35. Morelli, G.: Principles and Methods in Italian Painters: Critical Studies of Their Works. Translated by C.J. Ffoulkes, London (1892)
36. Dawkins, R.: The Blind Watchmaker: Why the Evidence of Evolution Reveals a Universe Without Design. W. W. Norton & Company, New York (1996)
37. Onians, J.: Neuroarthistory: From Aristotle and Pliny to Baxandall and Zeki. Yale University Press, New Haven (2007)
38. Tsukiura, T., Cabeza, R.: Shared brain activity for aesthetic and moral judgments: implications for the beauty-is-good stereotype. Soc. Cogn. Affect. Neurosci. **6**(1), 138–148 (2011)

39. Freedberg, D.: The Power of Images: Studies in the History and Theory of Response. University of Chicago Press, Chicago (1989)
40. Baxandall, M.: Painting and Experience in Fifteenth Century Italy. Oxford University Press, Oxford (1972)
41. Arnheim, R.: Art and Visual Perception: A Psychology of the Creative Eye. University of California Press, Berkeley and Los Angeles (1954)
42. Louden, R.B.: Kant's Impure Ethics: From Rational Beings to Human Beings. Oxford University Press (2002)
43. Meier-Graefe, J.: Modern Art: Being a Contribution to a New System of Aesthetics. Translated by Florence Simmonds and George W. Chrystal. G.P. Putnam's Sons, New York and London (1908)
44. Wiener, N.: The Human Use of Human Beings: Cybernetics and Society. Da Capo Press, New York (1996)
45. Spratt, E.L.: Man versus Machine: Aesthetic Judgment in the Age of Artificial Intelligence. Presentation, Theoretical Archaeology Annual Group Meeting, University of Illinois at Urbana-Champaign (May 2014)
46. Hughes, J.M., Mao, D., Rockmore, D.N., Wang, Y., Wu, Q.: Empirical mode decomposition analysis for visual stylometry. IEEE Transactions on Pattern Analysis and Machine Intelligence $34(11)$, 2147–2157 (2012)
47. Podro, M.: The Critical Historians of Art. Yale University Press (1984)
48. Boden, M.A.: Creativity and artificial intelligence: A contradiction in terms? In: The Philosophy of Creativity: New Essays (2014)
49. Bohm, D.: On Creativity. Routledge, New York (1998)
50. Hume, D.: Of the standard of taste and other essays. In: Lenz, J.W. (ed.). Bobbs-Merrill, Indianapolis (1965)

In Search of Art

Elliot J. Crowley$^{(\boxtimes)}$ and Andrew Zisserman

Visual Geometry Group, Department of Engineering Science,
University of Oxford, Oxford, UK
`elliot@robots.ox.ac.uk`

Abstract. The objective of this work is to find objects in paintings by learning object-category classifiers from available sources of natural images. Finding such objects is of much benefit to the art history community as well as being a challenging problem in large-scale retrieval and domain adaptation.

We make the following contributions: (i) we show that object classifiers, learnt using Convolutional Neural Networks (CNNs) features computed from various natural image sources, can retrieve paintings containing these objects with great success; (ii) we develop a system that can learn object classifiers on-the-fly from Google images and use these to find a large variety of previously unfound objects in a dataset of 210,000 paintings; (iii) we combine object classifiers and detectors to align objects to allow for direct comparison; for example to illustrate how they have varied over time.

Keywords: Domain Adaptation · Object Classification · Computer Vision in Art

1 Introduction

"I do not search, I find." – Pablo Picasso.

Natural images (i.e. everyday photos taken with a camera) annotated with objects are everywhere – large numbers of annotated photos are readily available in curated datasets [20,23]; and, simply typing the name of an object into Google Image search will produce high quality images of that object. Unfortunately the same cannot be said of paintings; these are largely lacking in annotation. Art historians are often interested in determining when an object first appeared in a painting or how the portrayal of an object has evolved over time, to achieve this they have the unenviable task of finding paintings for study manually [11,29,46]. If they are instead provided with paintings annotated with objects they can conduct these studies far more easily.

In this paper, we provide this object annotation by using readily available natural images to learn object category classifiers able to find objects across hundreds of thousands of paintings. This is not a straightforward task; natural images and paintings can differ substantially in their low level statistics, and

© Springer International Publishing Switzerland 2015
L. Agapito et al. (Eds.): ECCV 2014 Workshops, Part I, LNCS 8925, pp. 54–70, 2015.
DOI: 10.1007/978-3-319-16178-5_4

paintings can exist in a number of depictive styles (e.g. impressionism, surrealism) where the very objects themselves can be warped like the clocks in Dali's 'Persistence of memory'. In addition to this, the objects themselves may have changed with time – photographs of planes will typically be of modern commercial jetliners whereas those in paintings can be more akin to Wright Flyers or Spitfires.

One of our contributions is to show that features generated using Convolutional Neural Networks (CNN) [33,34] are able to overcome much of this adversity. These networks have been shown to be effective for a variety of tasks [21,28,37,42], and we show that classifiers learnt with CNN features on natural images are very successful at retrieving objects in paintings, overcoming the problem of domain adaptation [19,32,43] and greatly outperforming classifiers learnt using Fisher Vectors [40,41] (section 3). We also compare the performance of curated datasets vs. images crawled from the internet to assess the suitability of the net as a training source.

We develop an on-the-fly system [8,15,39] (section 4) that learns classifiers for object categories in real-time by crawling Google images. These are then applied to a dataset of 210,000 oil paintings to retrieve paintings containing these object categories with high precision over many and disparate classes. The entirety of this process for a given query takes a matter of seconds.

Finally, inspired by the work of Lee *et al.* [35] we conduct longitudinal studies to examine how the portrayal of particular objects have varied over time by combining classifiers with Deformable-Parts based models (DPMs) (section 5) to produce mosaics of aligned objects; this benefits cultural historians as well as sating curiosity.

2 Datasets

In this section, the datasets of natural images and paintings used for evaluation (section 3) and large-scale object retrieval (section 4) are introduced.

2.1 Paintings

The publicly available 'Your Paintings' dataset [1] is utilized for this work. This dataset consists of over 210,000 oil paintings of medium resolution (the width is usually around 500 pixels). 10,000 of these have been annotated as part of the 'Tagger' project [7] whereby members of the public tag the paintings with the objects that they contain.

To quantitatively assess classifier performance a dataset of paintings with complete annotation in the PASCAL VOC [23] sense – that each painting has been annotated for the categories under consideration – is required for use as a test set. To satisfy this requirement we construct the **Paintings Dataset** as a subset of 'Your Paintings'. This subset is obtained by searching 'Your Paintings' for annotations and painting titles corresponding to the classes of VOC. With tags and

Table 1. The statistics for the datasets used for evaluation: the number of images containing an instance of a particular class are given, as well as the total number of training and validation images (where applicable). The `Paintings Dataset` is only ever used as a test set, whereas other datasets are used for training and validation.

Dataset	Split	Aero	Bird	Boat	Chair	Cow	Din	Dog	Horse	Sheep	Train	Total
`Paintings`	Total	200	805	2143	1202	625	1201	1145	1493	751	329	8629
VOC12	Train	327	395	260	566	151	269	632	237	171	273	3050
	Val	343	370	248	553	152	269	654	245	154	271	3028
	Total	670	765	508	1119	303	538	1286	482	325	544	6078
VOC12+	Train	769	1007	613	1428	419	659	1471	798	364	793	7812
	Val	343	370	248	553	152	269	654	245	154	271	3028
	Total	1112	1377	861	1981	571	928	2125	1043	518	1064	10840
`Net`	Train	252	264	254	267	254	278	269	272	258	260	2628
`Noisy`	Val	84	88	85	89	85	93	90	91	87	87	879
	Total	336	352	339	356	339	371	359	363	345	347	3507
`Net`	Train	203	192	173	197	149	254	220	192	216	222	2018
`Curated`	Val	68	64	58	66	50	85	74	64	72	74	675
	Total	271	256	231	263	199	339	294	256	288	296	2693

titles complete annotation is assumed as long as 'people' are ignored, as this particular class has a tendency of appearing frequently without being acknowledged. Thus, the 'person' class is not considered, and also we do not include classes that lack a sufficient number of tags (cat, bicycle, bus, car motorbike, bottle, potted plant, sofa, tv/monitor). Paintings are included for the remaining classes – aeroplane, bird, boat, chair, cow, dining-table, dog, horse, sheep, train. The statistics are given in table 1, and example class images are shown in figure 1. The URLs for the paintings in this dataset are provided at [6].

2.2 Natural Images

When learning classifiers from natural images there are two important factors to explore. The first of these is the number of images used for training; this factor will be explored by comparing two datasets: the first is the training and validation data of PASCAL VOC 2012 [24] for the 10 classes of the `Paintings Dataset` (hereby referred to as VOC12), the second is a larger dataset consisting of VOC12 plus all of the training, validation and test data of PASCAL VOC 2007 for the relevant classes (we refer to this as VOC12+).

The second factor to consider is the source of the training images, particularly the suitability of images obtained from the internet that may have label noise (as not all of the results from an online image search for an object will actually contain that object). For each of the classes in the `Paintings Dataset` the top 200 Google Image Search [5] results and top 200 Bing Image Search [2] results are collated for a search query of the class name to form the `Net Noisy` dataset (split randomly into training and validation); note that there are less than 400 images per class, this is because some links did not return an image. `Net Noisy`

Fig. 1. Example class images from the `Paintings Dataset`. From top to bottom row: dog, horse, train. Notice that the dataset is challenging: objects have a variety of sizes, poses and depictive styles, and can be partially occluded or truncated.

is then manually filtered to remove erroneous instances forming `Net Curated`. The statistics for all datasets are given in table 1.

3   Domain Transfer Experiments

In this section we evaluate the performance of object classifiers that have been learnt on natural images when they are applied to paintings. In all cases, the classifiers are applied to the `Paintings Dataset` which is used as a test set. Classifiers are learnt from four datasets of natural images as described in section 2 – VOC12, VOC12+, `Net Noisy` and `Net Curated` – to compare two factors: (i) the effect of increasing the number of training examples, (ii) the difference between learning from curated and extemporary datasets. Two different features are compared: (i) the Improved Fisher Vector (FV) [41], and (ii) features extracted from Convolutional Neural Networks (CNNs) over a number of training and testing augmentation strategies. The evaluation of these classifiers using Average Precision (AP) for each class and the mean of these (mAP) is given in section 3.1, and implementation details are given in section 3.2.

3.1   Evaluation

Average Precision (AP) is calculated for each class as well as the mean of these values (mAP), these measures are given in table 2.

In all instances mAP improves substantially when switching to CNNs from Fisher Vectors. For CNNs, using augmentation schemes causes mAP to increase

Table 2. Average Precision for Classification Performance on the **Paintings Dataset** for different training methods and sources. In the case of the CNN features, the type of training augmentation and testing pooling is indicated for each set.

Method	Dim	Train	Aero	Bird	Boat	Chair	Cow	Din	Dog	Horse	Sheep	Train	mAP
FV	84K	VOC12	32.3	18.7	74.2	35.5	21.7	34.1	23.9	42.8	19.6	64.0	36.7
(x,y)		VOC12+	32.3	20.9	73.1	33.6	19.8	33.5	25.0	46.7	26.8	69.1	38.1
		Net Noisy	28.2	15.6	68.9	24.4	11.1	23.9	22.8	38.2	21.2	51.8	30.6
		Net Cur	29.9	13.9	68.7	18.2	12.0	24.2	22.8	38.7	20.5	47.5	29.6
CNN	2K	VOC12	58.5	33.9	84.1	45.7	44.9	40.1	40.2	60.5	40.4	72.5	52.1
no aug		VOC12+	57.9	33.4	84.3	45.0	44.5	39.1	39.1	58.5	41.4	72.4	51.6
no pool		Net Noisy	49.4	35.8	82.1	34.5	23.2	38.2	32.3	59.3	31.4	71.2	45.7
		Net Cur	52.8	36.6	82.6	38.5	29.0	37.0	35.5	61.1	36.3	71.2	48.1
CNN	2K	VOC12	59.2	36.9	83.9	40.7	44.5	45.7	41.4	61.0	46.0	75.2	53.5
aug		VOC12+	59.9	37.1	85.6	41.6	44.7	43.3	40.3	61.2	47.3	76.4	53.7
max pool		Net Noisy	50.3	36.2	81.8	35.6	25.4	35.5	30.6	57.4	34.7	74.3	46.2
		Net Cur	52.0	37.5	82.3	38.2	31.5	33.8	36.0	61.8	35.2	71.1	47.9
CNN	2K	VOC12	59.4	37.2	84.6	42.0	44.9	46.1	41.5	61.2	48.0	75.9	54.1
aug		VOC12+	60.1	36.5	85.9	43.4	44.6	43.7	39.9	62.2	49.2	77.7	54.3
sum pool		Net Noisy	51.0	35.7	82.9	37.1	27.2	35.4	31.3	58.9	36.2	74.8	47.1
		Net Cur	52.6	37.9	83.0	40.0	33.3	34.0	36.7	62.8	36.2	72.0	48.8
CNN	2K	VOC12	59.5	35.0	84.7	45.6	46.9	40.2	42.5	61.6	42.7	74.5	53.3
no aug		VOC12+	59.9	35.0	86.0	45.7	45.9	40.5	41.3	59.4	43.8	75.1	53.3
sum pool		Net Noisy	52.7	37.8	84.0	37.2	23.7	39.0	32.7	61.2	34.2	74.4	47.7
		Net Cur	53.6	39.2	83.3	41.1	27.1	39.9	36.9	63.0	35.6	67.8	48.8
CNN	128	VOC12	57.8	33.2	85.4	48.8	41.9	44.5	39.3	60.2	45.3	75.6	53.2
aug		VOC12+	56.4	33.8	86.1	49.3	40.8	41.4	38.6	57.4	44.7	75.3	52.4
sum pool		Net Noisy	52.1	33.2	79.5	29.8	24.0	32.3	33.2	55.7	34.9	76.8	45.1
		Net Cur	53.2	37.7	81.9	35.9	32.2	31.4	34.6	58.4	34.1	73.9	47.3
CNN	1K	VOC12	60.2	38.9	85.5	40.4	45.5	46.6	41.4	61.5	48.3	75.7	54.4
aug		VOC12+	60.5	38.2	87.1	43.3	45.6	47.3	40.4	59.8	49.2	76.9	54.8
sum pool		Net Noisy	50.7	35.2	83.1	36.5	32.0	37.5	30.5	60.7	37.6	75.4	47.9
		Net Cur	53.0	37.2	83.4	36.3	37.3	39.2	35.6	64.3	36.8	72.1	49.5
CNN	4K	VOC12	54.5	35.4	84.2	40.7	42.4	50.2	39.4	56.2	43.3	73.8	52.0
aug		VOC12+	52.0	35.2	84.0	41.5	43.3	49.9	37.1	60.4	41.0	76.5	52.1
sum pool		Net Noisy	45.8	32.7	79.2	31.8	32.6	39.7	29.6	55.9	36.1	73.5	45.7
		Net Cur	47.5	33.7	77.5	42.0	31.9	38.6	35.1	55.2	35.6	68.1	46.5

by a small amount (typically ∼1–2%) relative to not using augmentation; the highest performance is obtained using augmented training data with sum-pooling of the augmented test data. Note that it takes around 0.3s to compute the features for a single frame of an image compared to 2.4s for augmented features; if time is of the essence the small improvement in performance is likely not worth the additional computation. The mAP is highest for 1024-D CNN features, although this performance is still very similar to that of other dimensions.

The benefits of augmentation differ by class; using 2K CNN features, the AP for bird using VOC12 with no augmentation is 33.9 whereas with training augmentation and sum pooling it rises to 37.2, sheep sees an even sharper rise from 40.4 to 48.0. This is likely because such objects can appear quite small (a bird from the distance, or a lone sheep on a hill) and can be missed if only a single central frame is extracted. Some objects (boat, cow) remain unaffected by augmentation. Sum pooling generally outperforms max pooling; sum pooling allows for a richer contextual description of each test painting; an exception to this is for chair, paintings for which can contain a lot of distracting clutter.

There is very little difference between the performance of VOC12 and VOC12+ despite VOC12+ having almost twice as many train-val images. This indicates that only a few hundred CNN training examples are required for a classifier to learn the important features for these classes. There is also minimal difference between the performance of Net Noisy and Net Curated; the classifier learning is robust to outliers being present in the training data. The important implication of this is that there is no real need to pre-filter images obtained from the internet.

Although there is a substantial mAP difference between training on VOC12 (or VOC12+) and Net images, some of the individual class APs are quite similar – notably bird and train.

In general, the most successful classifiers are those for boats, horses and trains. This is very likely because these objects are typically depicted similarly in both paintings and natural images. Conversely, furniture varies a lot between natural images and paintings (chairs and tables are of very different shapes and styles) leading to lower performance, though such classes are hard to classify even in the case of natural images [24].

3.2 Implementation Details

Fisher Vector Representation. For generating Fisher Vector features the pipeline of [13] is used with the implementation available from the website [4]: RootSIFT [9] features are extracted at multiple scales from each image. These are decorrelated and reduced using PCA to 80-D and augmented with the (x,y) co-ordinates of the extraction location. These features are used to learn a 512 component Gaussian Mixture Model (GMM). For each image, the mean and covariance of the distances between features and each GMM centre are recorded and stacked resulting in a $82 \times 2 \times 512 = 83{,}968$-D Fisher Vector.

CNN Representation. A deep CNN network similar to that of [47] is used [14] using the implementation available from the website [3]. It consists of 5 convolutional layers and 3 fully-connected layers. It is trained solely using ILSVRC-2012 using stochastic gradient descent as in [31].

To obtain a feature vector, a given image frame is passed through the network and the output of the penultimate layer is recorded. It has been shown previously that this output can be used as a powerful descriptor, readily applicable to other datasets [22]. Multiple networks are trained for various sizes of this layer to produce output vectors of different sizes (128-D, 1024-D, 2048-D and 4096-D).

For each training image, with no augmentation (no aug) each image is downsized so that its smallest dimension is 224 pixels and then a 224×224 frame is extracted from the centre, this frame is passed into the CNN producing a feature vector. When augmentation (aug) is used 10 frames are extracted from an image: the images are resized so the smallest dimension is 256 and then a

224 × 224 frame is extracted from the centre and four corners of each image and the left-right flip of these frames, these are passed in to the CNN resulting in 10 feature vectors. Each of these vectors is considered an independent training sample and one-vs-the-rest classifiers are learnt.

At test time different pooling schemes are utilized: there can be no pooling (no pool) where classifiers are applied to a single feature vector extracted from each test image (as in no aug above). Alternatively each test image is augmented and the classifiers are either applied to the mean of the 10 vectors extracted using the above augmentation scheme (sum pool) or they are applied to the vectors separately and the highest response is recorded (max pool).

Classification. Linear-SVM Classifiers are learnt using the training data per class in a one-vs-the-rest manner for a range of regularization parameters (C). The C that produces the highest mAP when the corresponding classifiers are applied to the validation set is recorded. The training and validation data are then combined to train classifiers using this C parameter, which are finally applied to the test data. For the Fisher Vector representation, a single feature vector is obtained for each image using the entirety of that image. For CNNs, augmentation and pooling schemes are incorporated at training and testing.

4 Finding Objects in Paintings on-the-fly

It is clear from section 2 that classifiers learnt from CNN features extracted from natural images are surprizingly successful at retrieving object categories from paintings. A further advantage is the speed of this process: extracting a frame from an image and producing a CNN feature takes ∼0.3s, training and applying a classifier takes only a fraction of a second because the features are sparse and of low dimensionality. In particular, the performance of Net Noisy indicates that the images crawled from a Google search are a suitable training source for a variety of classes without any pre-filtering, the natural extension being to obtain classifiers that are able to retrieve paintings for classes other than those in VOC.

With this is mind, we develop a live system similar to VISOR [15] thats crawls Google images in real-time for a given object query, downloads the images and learns a CNN-based classifier. This classifier is then applied to the entirety of 'Your Paintings' [1] (210K paintings) to produce a ranked list of paintings. We test this system for 200 different object queries across many categories and record the precision of the highest-ranked paintings (see section 4.1). A diagram of this process is given in figure 2 and the steps of the implementation are described below:

Features. 1024-D CNN features are used as these produced classifiers with the highest performance on the Paintings Dataset. As discussed in section 3.1 augmenting either the training and/or testing data improves performance at the cost of computation time. As such, for pre-processed features stored offline, sum-pooled feature vectors are used, whereas online where time is very important, features for positive training examples are computed without any augmentation.

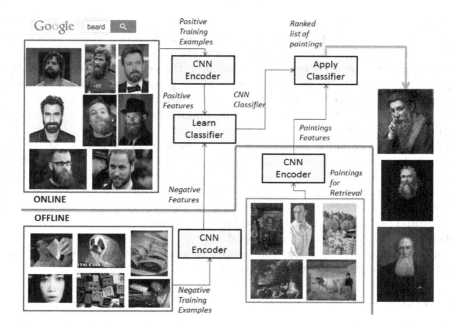

Fig. 2. A diagram of the on-the-fly system. The user types in a class query and positive training examples of that class are crawled from Google Images. These are then encoded using CNN features and used in conjunction with a pre-computed pool of negative features to learn a classifier in real time. This classifier then ranks hundreds of thousands of paintings for which the features are stored in memory before displaying the highest-ranked paintings. This entire process takes a matter of seconds.

Obtaining positive training images. To generate the positive training set for a given class, Google Image Search is queried with the class as a search term and the URLs for the top 200 images are recorded. These are then downloaded in parallel with a timeout of 1s to prevent the process from being too slow. CNN features are then computed in parallel over multiple cores from a single frame extracted from each image as in the 'no augmentation' scheme of section 3.2. For the Google Image search the photo filter is used; this may seem counter-intuitive as one would expect that without this filter paintings would appear which would benefit training, in actuality non-photo images tend to be clip-art that are even further in likeness from paintings than natural images are.

Negative training images. A fixed pool of negative training images is used to aid classification. This set consists of ~1000 images from the Google searches 'things' and 'photos'. The augmented CNN features of these images are pre-computed and stored in memory for immediate access. This only amounts to 40MB of memory.

Classification. Classifiers are learnt on a single core using the positive and negative features with a Linear-SVM. The classifier is then applied to all of 'Your Paintings' in a single matrix operation; the sum-pooled CNN features of 'Your Paintings' are pre-computed and stored in memory. This is the most memory intensive part of the process as all of 'Your Paintings' stored as 1024-D features with single precision amounts to 800MB.

Offline and Online Processing. In summary: the features for negative training images and all the paintings for retrieval are pre-computed offline. Online, i.e. at run time, the positive training images are downloaded and have their features computed; then the classifier is learnt, and finally the paintings are ranked on their classifier score.

Performance. Obtaining the 200 URLs for a search query typically takes 0.5s. The time taken to download the images at these URLs can vary by class but is often ∼2s. Across the 200 queries described below, the average number of images downloaded successfully is 177. Computing CNN features for the downloaded images takes ∼4.5s using 16 cores. Learning a classifier using the Liblinear [25] package and performing a matrix operation between the classifier and the dataset features only takes a fraction of a second.

In total, the entire process from typing in a search query to receiving the retrieved paintings takes roughly 7 seconds.

4.1   Evaluation

To evaluate how well the system works we test it for 200 different queries over a broad range of object categories. These include structures (arch, bridge, column, house), animals (bird, dog, fish), colours (red, blue, violet), vehicles (boat, car), items of clothing (cravat, gown, suit) as well as environments (forest, light, storm). The resulting classifier for each search term returns a ranked list of retrieved paintings, for each such list Precision-at-k (Prec@k) – the fraction of the top-k ranked results that are classified correctly – is recorded for the first 50 retrieved paintings. The highest ranked paintings for selected queries as well as the corresponding Prec@k curves are given in figure 3.

In general, the learnt classifiers are very successful and are able to retrieve paintings for a large variety of objects with high precision. The vast majority of the correctly retrieved paintings had not previously been tagged on 'Your Paintings', so these are new discoveries for those object classes.

In more detail, the classifiers that produce the highest precision are those for which objects in the training photos and paintings are portrayed in a similar manner. For example, for 'person' the vast majority of photos and paintings will be in portrait-style. The same can be said of animals such as 'horse' that are predominately captured from the side in a rigid pose. Conversely for certain smaller objects, particularly human body parts (arm, hand, eye) classifiers are not very successful. This is because of the drastic differences in depiction between the photos and paintings; in photos, the entire image will contain the object whereas in paintings the object is much smaller (in the case of eye, rarely more than a few pixels wide).

For objects with very simple shapes like circles (buttons, wheels) and rectangles (books, doors) results retrieved tend to be poor, simply consisting of paintings containing the shape rather than the object itself. Classifiers trained

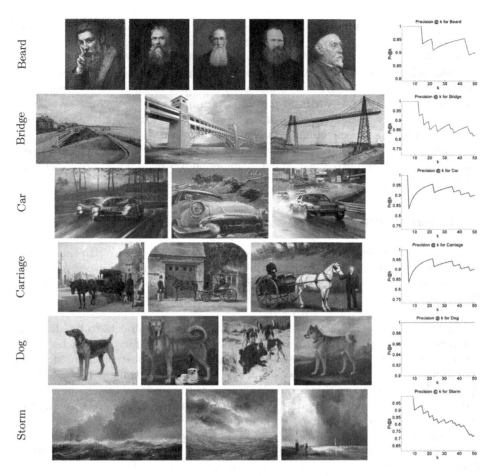

Fig. 3. Highest ranked paintings when classifiers are applied to 'Your Paintings' where the classifiers have been learnt from selected Google Image Search Queries as well as the Prec@k curve for the top 50 results.

on environments with no real fixed boundaries (winter, woodland) perform with great success, this is because paintings of these tend to be very realistic, mirroring nature. Also there is the added advantage that for environments the entire image is relevant rather than a smaller region; it is harder to inadvertently learn something else.

Colours are retrieved with high precision, something that is clearly not possible when using a handcrafted descriptor based around gradients (e.g. HOG [18] or SIFT [36]), CNNs are able to capture both gradient and colour information. This has a disadvantage for certain classes that are based around colours such as 'fire' and 'steam'; the paintings retrieved for these classes share colours (red, orange, yellow for 'fire', grey and black for 'steam') but not the classes themselves.

Vehicles are retrieved successfully despite the temporal depictive differences between vehicles in photos and paintings; of particular interest is 'car' – as addressed in section 2 very few paintings in 'Your Paintings' were known to contain cars, making this retrieval particularly impressive.

Unsurprizingly, classifiers trained on words afflicted with polysemy (those that can have multiple meanings – for example bow can be a weapon, a gesture, or a part of a ship) rarely retrieve any correct paintings because the positive training data is inherently noisy, this phenomenon has been noted previously by Schroff et al. [44].

5   Longitudinal Studies

In section 4 we have shown that it is possible to retrieve many paintings containing a given object in very little time with high precision. Inspired by the work of Lee et al. [35] we use these retrieved paintings to observe how the depiction of objects has varied over time. This is possible as many paintings in 'Your Paintings' are accompanied with a date.

To make these observations it is ideal for instances of objects to be aligned. For some classes objects are inherently aligned, such as for 'moustache'; the retrieved paintings are almost entirely portraits so the moustaches are side by side and easy to compare. A mosaic of moustaches over time is presented in figure 4. For most classes this is not the case: it is known from the classifier that the object is present but not its location. If an art historian were to compare objects between these paintings it would not be ideal to have to manually pick out, scale and align each of several hundred objects.

To find, scale and align objects automatically we employ the Deformable Part Model (DPM) [26,27] object category detector to find object locations in high-ranked paintings. This has the added benefit of depicting left/right facing objects in the same way (from the appropriate component response – see details below). Consider figure 6: the top half of the figure contains paintings from 'Your Paintings' that have been ranked highly for 'train' by a classifier learnt as in section 4; the trains are at different positions and scales, making comparison difficult. By applying a DPM a mosaic can be formed as in the bottom half of figure 6, allowing for much easier comparison.

Implementation Details. Classifiers are learnt using Google images as in section 4 to produce a ranked list of paintings. A DPM is learnt either (i) using PASCAL VOC 2012 bounding boxes or (ii) using the same positive and negative training instances used to learn the classifier. Note that for (ii) no bounding-box regions of interest (ROI) are provided so the entire image is taken to be an ROI. DPMs have been trained previously using the entire image as the ROI for scene classification [38]. The DPM has 3 mirrored components (for a total of 6) each comprising 8 parts. These are applied to the highest classified paintings for the class and the highest scoring detection windows are recorded. By left-right

Fig. 4. Moustaches through the ages. The nature of the object means the moustaches are aligned without the need for an object detector.

Fig. 5. Horses through the ages. These horses have been aligned using a DPM trained from Google Images.

Fig. 6. Train Alignment. The top half of this figure shows paintings that have been retrieved using a train classifier learnt using CNN features. Although all the images contain trains these are at different scales, positions and viewpoints. By utilizing a DPM, it is possible to obtain the location and orientation of each train as in the bottom half of the figure; this mosaic of aligned trains allows for much easier comparison.

flipping regions found by a mirrored component it is possible to display objects facing the same way as in figure 6.

DPM Discussion. In figure 6 the DPM used has been learnt using (i) (above), the results displayed are for the component corresponding to a train face. The aligned horses in figure 5 have been learnt using (ii). It is clear that alignment is better with correct ROIs but rough alignment is still achieved from a DPM learnt from entire images, allowing the objects to appear facing the same way.

Observations. The mosaics give us some insight into the nature of the objects throughout time. It is rather remarkable that the pencil moustache, typically associated with 20th Century actors like Errol Flynn appears in a portrait from 1565 (figure 4: top row). One can notice styles of particular times; several men around the late 19th Century have combined their moustaches with sideburns.

Consider the horses in figure 5, it can be seen that in later years there is a more prominent portrayal of muscles. The context is rather interesting; horses are accompanied largely by jockeys but there is an instance of a horse mounted by a solider in 1902. Later paintings tend to have the horse against a plain background rather than in the wild.

We can infer from the bottom half of figure 6 that trains first started to appear in paintings in the early 1900s. Seemingly artists prefer painting steam engines rather than their diesel or electric equivalents as these appear with the greatest frequency. Most of the trains have round faces; rectangular faced trains are most prevalent in 80s paintings.

6   Conclusions

In this paper we have demonstrated the benefit of using object classifiers learnt using CNN features from natural images to retrieve paintings containing an object for a large variety of objects. We have further shown that this process can be carried out in just seconds using our on-the-fly system.

Although this system works for many objects some prove elusive, particularly when there are large differences between the portrayal of the object in natural images and paintings. Several of these elusive objects are human body parts (eye, hand etc.); future work could use pose estimators to isolate areas in images (both natural and not) containing these objects, an area that has been partially investigated in the interesting study by Carneiro *et al.* [12].

Another difficulty is aligning objects in paintings using DPMs without image ROIs. This could be approached by utilizing discriminative regions [10,30,45] to isolate the object as in [17], allowing for better alignment. Query expansion [16] could also be explored: using retrieved paintings in conjunction with the initial training data to learn new classifiers that are able to find objects in paintings that previous classifiers have missed.

Acknowledgments. Funding for this research is provided by the EPSRC and ERC grant VisRec no. 228180. We are very grateful to Rachel Collings and Andy Ellis at the Public Catalogue Foundation and to Rob Cooper at BBC Research. We are thankful to Ken Chatfield and Karen Simonyan for providing their CNN and VISOR implementations and for help in their use.

References

1. BBC - Your Paintings. http://www.bbc.co.uk/arts/yourpaintings/
2. Bing image search. http://www.bing.com/images
3. Deepeval encoder. http://www.robots.ox.ac.uk/~vgg/software/deep_eval/
4. Encoding methods evaluation toolkit. http://www.robots.ox.ac.uk/~vgg/software/enceval_toolkit/
5. Google image search. http://www.google.com/images
6. The Paintings Dataset. http://www.robots.ox.ac.uk/~vgg/data/paintings/
7. Your Paintings tagger. http://tagger.thepcf.org.uk/
8. Arandjelović, R., Zisserman, A.: Multiple queries for large scale specific object retrieval. In: Proc. BMVC (2012)
9. Arandjelović, R., Zisserman, A.: Three things everyone should know to improve object retrieval. In: Proc. CVPR (2012)
10. Aubry, M., Russell, B., Sivic, J.: Painting-to-3D model alignment via discriminative visual elements. ACM Transactions of Graphics (2013)
11. Burke, J.: Nakedness and other peoples: Rethinking the italian renaissance nude. Art History **36**(4), 714–739 (2013)
12. Carneiro, G., da Silva, N.P., Del Bue, A., Costeira, J.P.: Artistic image classification: An analysis on the PRINTART database. In: Fitzgibbon, A., Lazebnik, S., Perona, P., Sato, Y., Schmid, C. (eds.) ECCV 2012, Part IV. LNCS, vol. 7575, pp. 143–157. Springer, Heidelberg (2012)
13. Chatfield, K., Lempitsky, V., Vedaldi, A., Zisserman, A.: The devil is in the details: An evaluation of recent feature encoding methods. In: Proc. BMVC (2011)
14. Chatfield, K., Simonyan, K., Vedaldi, A., Zisserman, A.: Return of the devil in the details: Delving deep into convolutional nets. In: Proc. BMVC (2014)
15. Chatfield, K., Zisserman, A.: VISOR: Towards on-the-fly large-scale object category retrieval. In: Lee, K.M., Matsushita, Y., Rehg, J.M., Hu, Z. (eds.) ACCV 2012, Part II. LNCS, vol. 7725, pp. 432–446. Springer, Heidelberg (2013)
16. Chum, O., Philbin, J., Sivic, J., Isard, M., Zisserman, A.: Total recall: Automatic query expansion with a generative feature model for object retrieval. In: Proc. ICCV (2007)
17. Crowley, E.J., Zisserman, A.: The state of the art: Object retrieval in paintings using discriminative regions. In: Proc. BMVC (2014)
18. Dalal, N., Triggs, B.: Histogram of oriented gradients for human detection. In: Proc. CVPR, vol. 2, pp. 886–893 (2005)
19. Daumé III, H., Marcu, D.: Domain adaptation for statistical classifiers. J. Artif. Intell. Res. (JAIR) **26**, 101–126 (2006)
20. Deng, J., Dong, W., Socher, R., Li, L.J., Li, K., Fei-Fei, L.: Imagenet: A large-scale hierarchical image database. In: Proc. CVPR (2009)
21. Donahue, J., Jia, Y., Vinyals, O., Hoffman, J., Zhang, N., Tzeng, E., Darrell, T.: Decaf: A deep convolutional activation feature for generic visual recognition. CoRR abs/1310.1531 (2013)
22. Donahue, J., Jia, Y., Vinyals, O., Hoffman, J., Zhang, N., Tzeng, E., Darrell, T.: Decaf: A deep convolutional activation feature for generic visualrecognition. arXiv preprint arXiv:1310.1531 (2013)

23. Everingham, M., Van Gool, L., Williams, C.K.I., Winn, J., Zisserman, A.: The PASCAL Visual Object Classes (VOC) challenge. IJCV **88**(2), 303–338 (2010)
24. Everingham, M., Van Gool, L., Williams, C.K.I., Winn, J., Zisserman, A.: The PASCAL Visual Object Classes Challenge 2012 (VOC 2012) (2012). http://www.pascal-network.org/challenges/VOC/voc2012/
25. Fan, R.E., Chang, K.W., Hsieh, C.J., Wang, X.R., Lin, C.J.: LIBLINEAR: A library for large linear classification. JMLR **9**, 1871–1874 (2008)
26. Felzenszwalb, P.F., Grishick, R.B., McAllester, D., Ramanan, D.: Object detection with discriminatively trained part based models. IEEE PAMI (2010)
27. Felzenszwalb, P.F., McAllester, D., Ramanan, D.: A discriminatively trained, multiscale, deformable part model. In: Proc. CVPR (2008)
28. Girshick, R.B., Donahue, J., Darrell, T., Malik, J.: Rich feature hierarchies for accurate object detection and semantic segmentation. In: Proc. CVPR (2014)
29. Juan, R.: The turn of the skull: Andreas Vesalius and the early modern memento mori. Art History **35**(5), 958–975 (2012)
30. Juneja, M., Vedaldi, A., Jawahar, C.V., Zisserman, A.: Blocks that shout: Distinctive parts for scene classification. In: Proc. CVPR (2013)
31. Krizhevsky, A., Sutskever, I., Hinton, G.E.: ImageNet classification with deep convolutional neural networks. In: NIPS, pp. 1106–1114 (2012)
32. Kulis, B., Saenko, K., Darrell, T.: What you saw is not what you get: Domain adaptation using asymmetric kernel transforms. In: CVPR (2011)
33. LeCun, Y., Boser, B., Denker, J.S., Henderson, D., Howard, R.E., Hubbard, W., Jackel, L.D.: Backpropagation applied to handwritten zip code recognition. Neural Computation **1**(4), 541–551 (1989)
34. LeCun, Y., Bottou, L., Bengio, Y., Haffner, P.: Gradient-based learning applied to document recognition. Proceedings of the IEEE **86**(11), 2278–2324 (1998)
35. Lee, Y., Efros, A., Hebert, M.: Style-aware mid-level representation for discovering visual connections in space and time. In: ICCV (2013)
36. Lowe, D.: Object recognition from local scale-invariant features. In: Proc. ICCV, pp. 1150–1157 (September 1999)
37. Oquab, M., Bottou, L., Laptev, I., Sivic, J.: Learning and transferring mid-level image representations using convolutional neural networks. In: Proc. CVPR (2014)
38. Pandey, M., Lazebnik, S.: Scene recognition and weakly supervised object localization with deformable part-based models. In: Proc. ICCV (2011)
39. Parkhi, O.M., Vedaldi, A., Zisserman, A.: On-the-fly specific person retrieval. In: International Workshop on Image Analysis for Multimedia Interactive Services. IEEE (2012)
40. Perronnin, F., Liu, Y., Sánchez, J., Poirier, H.: Large-scale image retrieval with compressed fisher vectors. In: Proc. CVPR (2010)
41. Perronnin, F., Sánchez, J., Mensink, T.: Improving the fisher kernel for large-scale image classification. In: Daniilidis, K., Maragos, P., Paragios, N. (eds.) ECCV 2010, Part IV. LNCS, vol. 6314, pp. 143–156. Springer, Heidelberg (2010)
42. Razavian, A., Azizpour, H., Sullivan, J., Carlsson, S.: CNN Features off-the-shelf: An Astounding Baseline for Recognition. CoRR abs/1403.6382 (2014)
43. Saenko, K., Kulis, B., Fritz, M., Darrell, T.: Adapting visual category models to new domains. In: Daniilidis, K., Maragos, P., Paragios, N. (eds.) ECCV 2010, Part IV. LNCS, vol. 6314, pp. 213–226. Springer, Heidelberg (2010)
44. Schroff, F., Criminisi, A., Zisserman, A.: Harvesting Image Databases from the Web. IEEE PAMI **33**(4), 754–766 (2011)

45. Singh, S., Gupta, A., Efros, A.A.: Unsupervised discovery of mid-level discriminative patches. In: Fitzgibbon, A., Lazebnik, S., Perona, P., Sato, Y., Schmid, C. (eds.) ECCV 2012, Part II. LNCS, vol. 7573, pp. 73–86. Springer, Heidelberg (2012)
46. Woodall, J.: Laying the table: The procedures of still life. Art History **35**(5), 976–1003 (2012)
47. Zeiler, M.D., Fergus, R.: Visualizing and understanding convolutional neuralnetworks. arXiv preprint arXiv:1311.2901 (2013)

Classification of Artistic Styles Using Binarized Features Derived from a Deep Neural Network

Yaniv Bar[⊠], Noga Levy, and Lior Wolf

The Blavatnik School of Computer Science, Tel Aviv University, Tel Aviv-Yafo, Israel
yaniv.bar@cs.tau.ac.il

Abstract. With the vast expansion of digital contemporary painting collections, automatic theme stylization has grown in demand in both academic and commercial fields. The recent interest in deep neural networks has provided powerful visual features that achieve state-of-the-art results in various visual classification tasks. In this work, we examine the perceptiveness of these features in identifying artistic styles in paintings, and suggest a compact binary representation of the paintings. Combined with the PiCoDes descriptors, these features show excellent classification results on a large scale collection of paintings.

1 Introduction

As digital acquisition of artistic images has advanced, vast digital libraries have been assembled over the Internet and in museums. With the development of recent automatic image analysis and machine vision techniques, the mission of artistic resource discovery is no longer left to the human expert. Automatic art identification and classification support the expert's mission of painting analysis, assist in organizing large collections of paintings and can be used for art recommendation systems.

Artistic visual styles such as impressionism, baroque and cubism have a set of distinctive properties which permits the grouping of artworks into related art movements. Therefore, every artwork has a visual style idiosyncratic "signature" which relates it to other works.

Style divisions are often identified and later defined by art experts and historians. This division is not a strict one; in many cases a style can span across many different painters where a single painter might span across several styles. Pablo Picasso, for example, painted in both surrealism and cubism styles. Some of these styles may be easily recognized by human art enthusiasts or experts while others are more subtle [2].

Visual style is not rigorously defined, but can be deduced from visual motifs present in a painting such as the choice of color palette, composition, scene, lighting, contours and brush strokes [21]. Yet, there has been little research in computer vision that explored style classification in recent years.

In this work, we investigate several known visual descriptors that attempt to extract these subtle artistic properties. These techniques serve as a benchmark

© Springer International Publishing Switzerland 2015
L. Agapito et al. (Eds.): ECCV 2014 Workshops, Part I, LNCS 8925, pp. 71–84, 2015.
DOI: 10.1007/978-3-319-16178-5_5

for our approach and include gradient histograms, color histograms, statistical methods [32], LBP [22], dictionary-based methods ([7], [26]) and pyramid based methods ([25], [19], [23], [29] [32]).

The "Picture Codes" (PiCoDes) [5] learns a compact binary code representation of an image optimized on a subset of ImageNet dataset [9], and is one of the leading methods tested.

Deep learning refers to generative machine learning models composed of multiple levels of non-linear operations, such as neural networks consisting of many layers. The deep architecture enables the generation of representations of mid-level and high-level abstractions obtained from raw data such as images.

Convolutional neural networks (CNNs) are feed-forward networks that can be learned efficiently, and recent results indicate that the generic descriptors extracted from CNN are very powerful and provide a breakthrough for recognition [28],[24].

In this work, we try to recognize the style of paintings using features extracted from a deep network, as well as PiCoDes and low-level descriptors. Combining features extracted from a deep network with PiCoDes yields a strong descriptor that outperforms all other tested descriptors while remaining compact.

The work that is most closely related to our work was done by Karayev et al. [16] on a variant of the artistic dataset we have used in this paper and using similar classes. However, in [16] small classes (less then 1000 images) are omitted, while we keep a more varying distribution. We use a low-dimensional binary descriptor, and analyze performance by average precision, average recall, F_1-score and classification accuracy. We combine different descriptors by concatenation or re-ranking based on the Borda count [25] and compare them to a broad set of methods.

An overview of the previous work is given in Section 2 , Section 3 describes the convolutional neural networks and our approach is explained in Section 4. Experimental setup is given in Section 5 followed by discussion on results in Section 6. Final conclusions are drawn in Section 7 .

2   Related Work

Readily available digitized art paintings data has been available for a few years, gaining more and more attention from researchers.

The related problem of artist identification within a specific style (Renaissance) was explored in [15] using the HOG descriptor. In [14], idiosyncratic characteristics of Van Gogh paintings were explored based on the artist's brush strokes. Stylization recognition is explored in [17] and [12] on smaller datasets with fewer classes compared to the dataset we use here. In [17], the dataset explored contains visually distinguishable artworks painted by a handful of painters. Each painter is associated with a different school or style. The dataset tested in [12] contains seven styles with less than a hundred images per style.

Comparative study of different classification methodologies for the task of fine-art style classification are covered in [32] and [1]. Several standard classifiers and features extraction techniques are explored in [32], inspired by visual cues in painting such as gradient and statistical measures. In [1], discriminative and generative classification models are covered using intermediate level features (Bag of Words) and Semantic-level features. The datasets tested in [32] and [1] covers only a handful of styles with less than a hundred images per style.

In [16], deep features from the CNN in [18] are applied on large scale datasets. The conclusion arising from the experiments is that features extracted from deep architecture networks produce excellent classification performance on several large-scale datasets, including a dataset of paintings.

2.1 Low-Level Descriptors

Edge texture information [32]. The relative frequency of edges within a painting can be very informative. While impressionism is characterized by blurry and subtle edges, in analytical cubism and pop art the edges are very pronounced. The edge descriptor of an image is computed as the number of pixels that are labelled as an edge relative to the total number of pixels, extracted by the Canny edge detector for different sensitivity thresholds (0.2, 0.3, 0.4 and 0.6). Consequently, strong edges would be present in the image for any threshold level, while the subtle transitions would only show up for lower thresholds.

Texture information descriptor based on Steerable Filter Decomposition (SPD) [32],[8]. Steerable Filter Decomposition approximates a matching set of Gabor filters with different frequencies and orientations. The descriptor is 28-dimensional, consisting of the mean and variance of a low pass filter, a high pass filter, and 12 sub-band filters from three scales and four orientation decompositions. The mean and variance roughly correspond to the sub-band energy and characterize the artist brush strokes. The code is available in http://live.ece.utexas.edu/research/quality.

Color histogram [32]. The color histogram is described by a concatenation of three normalized 8-bin histograms, one per each HSV channel.

Statistical measures [32]. A concatenation of the mean, variance, skewness and kurtosis for each HSV channel.

Local Binary Patterns (LBP) [22]. LBP texture features are known for effective face recognition that can assist in scene and image texture classification. LBP texture features also perform well for face detection and are helpful in distinguishing portrait and non-portrait images [13]. The descriptor is derived by (a) dividing the image into cells (16 × 16 pixels for each cell), (b) for each pixel in a cell, the 3 x 3 neighborhood surrounding the pixel is thresholded with the central pixel intensity value, treating the subsequent pattern of 8 bits as a binary number, (c) a histogram is computed over the values in each cell and (d) the concatenation of the histograms of all cells forms a descriptor.

Dictionary-based descriptors [7],[26]. The bag-of-words model is applied to image classification by treating image features as words. Initially, a dictionary of visual "words" based on local feature descriptors is constructed using k-means and later compared against visual "words" (local features) of an image.

The statistics of visual words occurrences are summarized in a sparse histogram. Typically, local features are obtained using SIFT [20]. Fisher vectors serve a similar purpose of summarizing statistics of visual words, with two distinctions – the dictionary is obtained by Gaussian Mixture Models (GMMs), and rather than storing only visual word occurrences, the difference between dictionary words against the pooled image visual words is stored.

GIST [23],[11]. GIST is known to perform well for retrieving images that are visually similar at a low resolution scale, and consequently can represent the composition of an image to some extent. The descriptor is derived by resizing an image to 128 x 128 and iterating over the different scales where for each scale the image is divided into 8×8 cells. For each cell, orientation (every 45 degrees), color and intensity histograms are extracted, and the descriptor is a concatenation of all histograms, for all scales and cells. The code is available at http://people.csail.mit.edu/torralba/code/spatialenvelope

PHOG [19],[6]. Histogram of Oriented Gradients (HOG) is used for the purpose of object detection by counting occurrences of gradient orientation in localized portions of an image. The image is first divided into cells and for each cell a histogram of gradient directions or edge orientations is extracted. Concatenating all histograms forms a HOG descriptor. When this process is done on different scales, it is called Pyramid Histogram of Oriented Gradients (PHOG) and is known to perform well for scene categorization, which is required for some of the styles considered in this work.

The code is available at http://www.robots.ox.ac.uk/~vgg/research/caltech/phog.html.

SSIM [29]. A method of extracting a "local self-similarity" (SSIM) descriptor is depicted in [29]. While many methods measure the similarity among images by using common underlying visual properties, a SSIM descriptor captures internal geometric, color, edges, repetitive patterns and complex textures in a single unified way while accounting for small local affine deformations. That is, the descriptor captures spatial similarities between regions of different texture and color. The code is available at http://www.robots.ox.ac.uk/~vgg/software/SelfSimilarity.

Color Quad Trees (CQT) [25]. A quad tree is a tree data structure. The root represents the entire image, the second level contains four nodes each representing one quadrant of the image and so on, until the final level of the tree. For each node, the mean is computed over the pixels intensity values connected to the node. Concatenating all measurements level by level forms the CQT descriptor. This descriptor can be used to represent the composition of an image such as an outdoor landscape or a portrait to some extent.

2.2   Binary Compact Image Representations

PiCoDes binary features [5],[31]. A compact binary vector that is optimized to yield good categorization accuracy. As a preliminary step, an offline transformation matrix is learned as a non-linear combination of classifiers over features such as Bag of SIFTs, GIST, PHOG, and SSIM. The PiCoDes binary image descriptor is computed by transforming the image data using the offline matrix such that the binary entries in the descriptor are thresholded projections of low-level visual features extracted from the image.

MC-Bit binary features [4],[31]. A descriptor learned as a non-linear combination of classifiers over the same bank of features is described for PiCoDes. While the classifiers of PiCoDes are jointly computed via an expensive iterative optimization that limits the actual number of classifiers (tested on a maximum of 2048 classifiers), the MC-bit classifiers are efficiently computed via recursive parallel optimization. Thus, the descriptor size can be scaled up.

VLG extractor was used for extracting both PiCoDes and MC-bit descriptors (http://vlg.cs.dartmouth.edu/picodes/PiCoDes/Home.html)

3 Deep Architecture Network

Deep neural networks have recently gained considerable interest due to the development of convolutional neural networks (CNN) that can be solved efficiently on large-scale datasets using limited computation capacity. The strength of deep networks is in learning multiple layers of concept representation, corresponding to different levels of abstraction. For visual datasets, the low levels of abstraction might describe edges in the image, while high layers in the network refer to object parts and even the category of the object viewed.

CNNs constitute a feed-forward family of deep networks, where intermediate layers receive as input the features generated by the former layer, and pass their outputs to the next layer.

Two popular choices are CNNs suggested by [18] and [27] for the Large Scale Visual Recognition Challenge of Imagenet [9], a large scale image database consisting of more than one million images categorized into 1000 classes. The features extracted from intermediate layers of these networks produce highly discriminative features that achieve state-of-the-art performance in visual classification tasks [28],[24].

The DeepFace architecture developed in [30] is another example of a successful CNN that achieves human accuracy in face recognition.

These CNNs are constructed of a few layers that learn convolutions, interleaved with non-linear and pooling operations, followed by locally or fully connected layers.

4 Our Approach

Our baseline descriptors are extracted from Decaf implementation [10] of a CNN trained on Imagenet, following the CNN in [18]. We use the notation of [10] to denote the activations of the nth hidden layer of the network as $Decaf_n$, and use the $Decaf_5$ and $Decaf_6$ features as well as the final output of 1000 predictions. $Decaf_5$ contains 9216 activations of the last convolutional layer, and $Decaf_6$ contains 4096 activations of the first fully-connected layer.

4.1   Encoding Scheme

Following PiCoDes ([5], [31]), we suggest a compact binary encoding over the baseline descriptors that is designed to distinguish among different categories. Given a dataset classified into k categories and represented by a d-dimensional descriptor, our algorithm learns a d'-dimensional representation, where $d >> d'$ and d' is a multiplicative of k, that is $d' = tk$.

The encoding algorithm works as follows:

First, a subset of the training set is generated by randomly choosing an equal number of examples per class (25 examples per class in our experiments).

This subset is used to learn k linear SVMs in a One-vs-All manner – the ith classifier is trained on m positive examples from class i and m negative examples randomly selected from all other classes ($m = 15$ in our experiments).

We learn t One-vs-All SVMs, that are each trained on different examples and generates k new binary classifiers. That is, we learn a total of d' binary classifiers with t classifiers per class.

For a new example x, define $p_i(x)$ as the binary decision of classifier i, $p_i(x) = \mathbb{1}\{w_i x - b_i\}$. The d'-dimensional encoding of x is $(p_1(x), \ldots, p_{d'}(x))$, the concatenation of the binary decisions of all classifiers on x.

Our dataset has 27 classes and we empirically set t to 15. Hence, the length of $Decaf_5$, for example, is reduced from 9216 dimensions to only 405 dimensions.

5   Experiments

Dataset. We use a subset of the WikiArt dataset which was collected from the visual art encyclopedia www.wikiart.org , a complete and well-structured online repository of fine art [3]. The collection describes 40,724 unique digitized paintings with variable resolution. Each painting is labelled with a subset of the following metadata, specifying the artist name and nationality, art movement (style), year of creation, material, technique, painting dimensions and the gallery it is presented at. Style label, however, is present in all paintings.

The collection covers over a thousand different artists and is categorized to 27 art styles. Figure 1 shows our dataset styles distribution. A small subset of less than 2% of the dataset is used to train the classifiers for the binary encoding, all other examples are used for multiclass classification.

Multiclass Classification. A three-folded cross validation was used. We applied popular machine learning classifiers – SVM, Adaboost, Nave Bayes and kNN and chose empirically the 5-NN classifier since it produced the best results among descriptors that were tested.

Accuracy Metrics. We measure the success of the multiclass classification by the following measures:

- Classification accuracy – the rate of correctly classified examples out of all examples.

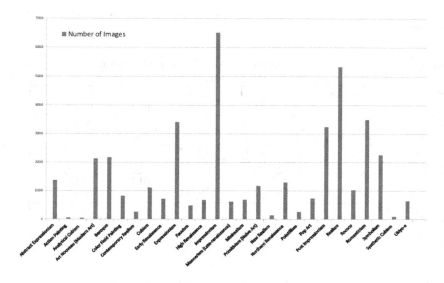

Fig. 1. Distribution of the image styles

- Precision and Recall – the precision of a class c is the proportion of images that are indeed in c out of the images predicted as c by the classifier, and recall is the proportion of images in c that are classified correctly. We report the average precision and recall over all classes. While accuracy is biased to larger classes, the average precision gives equal weight to all classes regardless of their size.
- F_1-score combines recall and precision, computed as $\frac{2 precision \times recall}{precision + recall}$.

Descriptors Fusion. We use two approaches to combine different descriptors. The early fusion method combines the different descriptors before applying classification. The late fusion refers to assembling classification results based on the different descriptors.

For early fusion, we simply concatenate the descriptors. Since the range of values of raw data varies widely, the values of each feature are normalized to zero mean and standardized to unit variance.

In the late fusion approach, the features of each descriptor are learned separately and their outputs are then merged. We adapt a re-ranking method based on a Borda count [25]. The Borda count is a single-winner election method in which voters rank options or candidates in order of preference. Once all votes are counted, the candidate that gained the highest number of points is the winner. In this work, the voters are the classifiers trained on different descriptors and the candidates are styles. For a given test image, kNN finds for each descriptor, the five closest images. We score the style results of those images in a descending order (5 to 1) and perform a maximum points scored vote based on the scores given by all descriptors.

Table 1. The performance of multiclass classification on the paintings dataset when using low-level descriptors

Descriptor	Dim.	Average Precision	Average Recall	F_1-Score	Accuracy
Edge texture information [32]	4	0.09	0.07	0.08	0.14
SPD [32],[8]	28	0.17	0.14	0.15	0.22
Color histogram [32]	24	0.14	0.11	0.12	0.20
Statistical measures [32]	12	0.09	0.07	0.08	0.14
LBP [22]	59	**0.18**	**0.15**	**0.16**	**0.23**
Bag Of Sifts [7]	500	0.17	0.13	0.15	0.22
Fisher Vectors [26]	1024	0.11	0.10	0.10	0.15
GIST [23],[11]	512	0.16	0.13	0.15	0.21
PHOG [19],[6]	336	0.13	0.10	0.11	0.19
SSIM [29]	1024	0.13	0.09	0.11	0.13
CQT [25]	1023	0.12	0.09	0.10	0.13

Code. The entire code was implemented in Matlab using VLFEAT framework www.vlfeat.org. The Decaf feature extraction part is obtained from Decaf CNN [10].

6 Results

Table 1 shows the performance of low-level descriptors. LBP, SPD and SIFT descriptors achieve the best performance in terms of accuracy. Empirically, descriptors that achieve the highest accuracy also achieve high scores in the other metrics. Therefore, we analyze the results based on accuracy and the other metrics are reported in the supporting tables. Table 2 shows PiCoDes with various dimensions and MC-bit descriptor. Not surprisingly, both descriptors outperform all low-level features since they are learned in an optimized way over a combination of powerful low-level descriptors.

In Table 3, the results of the Decaf CNN descriptors with and without binary encoding are presented. Similarly to the results in Table 2, the deep features outperform all low-level descriptors tested.

In Table 4, several forms of features fusion are examined, incorporating combinations of low-level descriptors, PiCoDes descriptors and Decaf CNN descriptors. Examining both early fusion (EF) and late fusion (LF) approaches, we reported only LF results as both of them gave similar results.

The best features fusion descriptor incorporates PiCoDes (2048-dimensionality) and $Decaf_6$ (4096-dimensionality), and has a 43% accuracy, a 6% increase over the best result of single descriptors.

Table 5 shows several forms of binary features fusion results that incorporates combinations of PiCoDes descriptors and encoded Decaf CNN descriptors. Each combination is reported for both early fusion and late fusion. All combinations

Table 2. The performance of multiclass classification on the paintings dataset when using binary compact image representations

Descriptor	Dim.	Sparsity Ratio	Average Precision	Average Recall	F_1-Score	Accuracy
PiCoDes [5]	128	0.44	0.21	0.16	0.18	0.24
PiCoDes [5]	1024	0.53	0.37	0.26	0.31	0.35
PiCoDes [5]	2048	0.45	**0.38**	**0.29**	**0.33**	**0.37**
MC-bit [4]	15232	0.70	0.31	0.25	0.28	0.32

Table 3. The performance of multiclass classification on the paintings dataset when using Decaf CNN and encoded Decaf CNN descriptors. The sparsity ratio is the average number of zero elements within the descriptor

Descriptor	Dim.	Type	Sparsity Ratio	Average Precision	Average Recall	F_1-Score	Accuracy
Decaf predictions [10]	1000	Real	0.26	0.19	0.15	0.16	0.21
$Decaf_6$ [10]	4096	Real	0.00	**0.38**	**0.31**	**0.34**	**0.37**
$Decaf_5$ [10]	9216	Real	0.72	0.42	0.26	0.32	0.35
Encoded $Decaf_6$	405	Binary	0.65	0.30	0.27	0.28	0.34
Encoded $Decaf_5$	405	Binary	0.54	0.27	0.23	0.25	0.31

Table 4. Multiclass classification performance results when using features fusion on the paintings dataset. All results for Late-Fusion approach. We use the following abbreviation: PD - PiCoDes

Descriptor	Dim.	Type	AP.	AR.	F_1.	Accuracy
HSV + LBP + SPD	111	Real	0.21	0.14	0.17	0.25
GIST + PHOG + SSIM + BOW	2372	Real	0.32	0.15	0.21	0.26
Decaf6 + LBP + SPD	4183	Real	0.42	0.25	0.31	0.35
Decaf6 + GIST	4608	Real	0.41	0.29	0.34	0.37
PD-2048 + LBP +SPD	2135	Real	0.43	0.24	0.31	0.35
PD-2048 + $Decaf_5$ + $Decaf_6$	15360	Real	**0.56**	0.32	**0.41**	0.39
PD-2048 + $Decaf_6$	6144	Real	0.48	**0.36**	**0.41**	**0.43**
PD-1024 + PD-2048 + $Decaf_6$	7168	Real	0.44	0.29	0.35	0.37
PD-1024 + PD-2048 + $Decaf_5$ + $Decaf_6$	16384	Real	0.50	0.34	**0.41**	0.42

show excellent results in terms of accuracy and descriptor compactness, matching or surpassing non-encoded features fusion results. The best features fusion descriptor incorporates PiCoDes (1024-dimensionality), PiCoDes (2048-dimensionality), encoded $Decaf_5$ (405-dimensionality) and encoded $Decaf_6$ (405-dimensionality) and matches the best (non-encoded) features fusion result using a binary descriptor with 63% compression.

A greater breakdown is illustrated in Figure 2 by showing the confusion matrix of our best features fusion.

Table 5. Multiclass classification performance results when using binary features fusion on the paintings dataset. We use the following abbreviations: EF - early fusion, LF - late fusion, PD - PiCoDes and Enc - encoded

Descriptor	Dim.	Fusion	Average Precision	Average Recall	F_1-Score	Accuracy
PD-2048 + Enc. $Decaf_6$	2453	EF	0.43	0.34	0.38	0.41
PD-2048 + Enc. $Decaf_6$	2453	LF	0.43	0.34	0.38	0.41
PD-2048 + Enc. $Decaf_5$ + Enc. $Decaf_6$	2858	EF	0.43	**0.36**	0.39	0.42
PD-2048 + Enc. $Decaf_5$ + Enc. $Decaf_6$	2858	LF	0.43	0.33	0.38	0.41
PD-1024 + Enc. PD-2048 + Enc. $Decaf_5$ + Enc. $Decaf_6$	2239	EF	0.42	**0.36**	0.39	0.42
PD-1024 + Enc. PD-2048 + Enc. $Decaf_5$ + Enc. $Decaf_6$	2239	LF	0.46	0.34	0.39	0.42
PD-1024 + PD-2048 + Enc. $Decaf_5$ + Enc. $Decaf_6$	3882	EF	0.42	**0.36**	0.39	0.42
PD-1024 + PD-2048 + Enc. $Decaf_5$ + Enc. $Decaf_6$	3882	LF	**0.47**	0.34	**0.40**	**0.43**

Different painting styles share similarities of color, composition and texture as well as sharing the object of the painting (e.g. still life, landscape, portraits etc.). Thus, misclassification between closely related styles occur quite often. A closer look in Figure 2 reveals the quality of classification. Confusion between relatively unrelated styles might occur. For example, Fauvism and Cubism are visually distinct as fauvism uses strong colors while cubism uses bland colors. In cubism objects are often reduced to their geometric form in a non-realistic way while fauvism is a more realistic simplified style. Cubism is precisely rendered while fauvism is loose and minimal. However, misclassification errors tend to occur significantly more frequently among closely related groups of styles, reflecting subtleties within these styles. Several examples are Renaissance styles (such as Early Renaissance, Late Renaissance, High Renaissance and Northern Renaissance) and Cubism related styles. Styles that are influenced by other styles in terms of visual motifs (continuation, branching out or reaction movement) also tend to get confused, such as Abstract Expressionism and Color Field Painting, Minimalism and Color Field Painting or Impressionism and Realism. For example, Color Field painting is referred as an extension of Abstract Expressionism paintings; both are abstract and express a dramatic use of colors. Figure 3 qualitatively demonstrates these relations through the confusion matrix, by rearranging the order of the styles so that groups of related styles are clustered together.

Experimentally, our best features fusion descriptor has the ability to find similarities within the style or even within the genre without over-tuning to a specific set of visual cues. For example, Portrait and landscape images appear in about half of the styles, yet performing a landscape/portrait image search of a specific style works well and landscape/portrait images of the same style are retrieved.

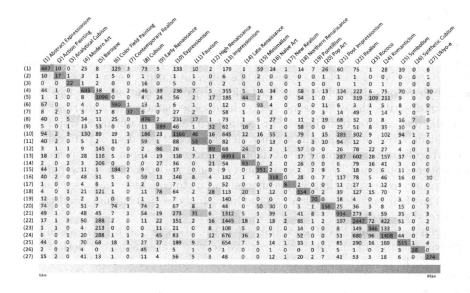

Fig. 2. The confusion matrix of our best features fusion representation: PiCoDes (1024-dim.), PiCoDes (2048-dim.), encoded $Decaf_5$ (405-dim.) and encoded $Decaf_6$ (405-dim.). Columns are color scaled from a minimum value of 0 (yellow) to a per-style maximum value (green). The main diagonal cells of the matrix, representing correct style classification is marked in green colors while off-diagonal cells, representing misclassification are marked in yellowish-light green colors. As described in Section 5, most of the off-diagonal cells that are marked in light-green colors represent misclassification between correlated styles

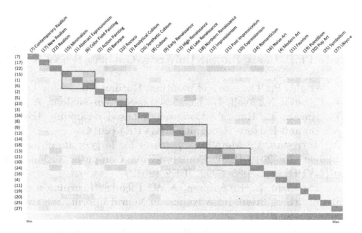

Fig. 3. The confusion matrix of our best features fusion representation: PiCoDes (1024-dim.), PiCoDes (2048-dim.), encoded $Decaf_5$ (405-dim.) and encoded $Decaf_6$ (405-dim.), rearranged by related styles. Each red box indicates the confusion within a family of styles

7 Conclusions

In this work, we suggest a representation of paintings that is both simple and efficient. We applied Decaf, a novel deep network trained on a comprehensive real-life ImageNet dataset to a problem of a different nature, known as art stylization. Style recognition differs from the task of object recognition, since two paintings can describe the same scene (e.g. a landscape painting of a marina) using very different artistic techniques. For example, a realistic painting as opposed to pointillism, a technique of painting in which small, distinct dots of pure color are applied to form a painting. For efficiency, we suggest an approach for encoding the features obtained by the Decaf convolutional network into a lower dimensional binary representation. Experiments lead us to conclude that deep features as well as their encoded version can distinguish styles better than hand-crafted low level descriptors.

When combining Decaf encoding with PiCoDes, a method of assembling low level features in an optimized way, we receive state-of-the-art performance results. A closer inspection of the misclassified examples indicate that this fused representation captures the subtle characteristics of styles and tends to mix up closely related styles, a reasonable confusion for the non-expert human observer.

There is still considerable room for improvement. One future direction is using a hierarchical style-based classification. A different direction is incorporating other deep neural network features known for good classification and detection results (e.g. OverFeat[28]). Examining the classification performance of our descriptor on other classification tasks – either art related (genre classification) or real life images, is also worth trying.

References

1. Arora, R.S.: Towards automated classification of fine-art painting style: A comparative study. Ph.D. thesis, Rutgers University-Graduate School-New Brunswick (2012)
2. Beckett, W., Wright, P.: The story of painting. Dorling Kindersley London (1994)
3. Ben-Shalom, I., Levy, N., Wolf, L., Dershowitz, N., Ben-Shalom, A., Shweka, R., Choueka, Y., Hazan, T., Bar, Y.: Congruency-based reranking. IEEE Conf. on Computer Vision and Pattern Recognition (CVPR) (2014)
4. Bergamo, A., Torresani, L.: Meta-class features for large-scale object categorization on a budget. In: 2012 IEEE Conference on Computer Vision and Pattern Recognition (CVPR), pp. 3085–3092. IEEE (2012)
5. Bergamo, A., Torresani, L., Fitzgibbon, A.W.: Picodes: Learning a compact code for novel-category recognition. In: Advances in Neural Information Processing Systems, pp. 2088–2096 (2011)
6. Bosch, A., Zisserman, A., Munoz, X.: Image classification using rois and multiple kernel learning. International Journal of Computer Vision **2008**, 1–25 (2008)
7. Csurka, G., Dance, C., Fan, L., Willamowski, J., Bray, C.: Visual categorization with bags of keypoints. Workshop on Statistical Learning in Computer Vision, ECCV **1**, 1–2 (2004)

8. Deac, A.I., van der Lubbe, J., Backer, E.: Feature Selection for Paintings Classification by Optimal Tree Pruning. In: Gunsel, B., Jain, A.K., Tekalp, A.M., Sankur, B. (eds.) MRCS 2006. LNCS, vol. 4105, pp. 354–361. Springer, Heidelberg (2006)
9. Deng, J., Dong, W., Socher, R., Li, L.J., Li, K., Fei-Fei, L.: Imagenet: A large-scale hierarchical image database. In: IEEE Conference on Computer Vision and Pattern Recognition, CVPR 2009, pp. 248–255. IEEE (2009)
10. Donahue, J., Jia, Y., Vinyals, O., Hoffman, J., Zhang, N., Tzeng, E., Darrell, T.: Decaf: A deep convolutional activation feature for generic visual recognition. arXiv preprint arXiv:1310.1531 (2013)
11. Douze, M., Jégou, H., Sandhawalia, H., Amsaleg, L., Schmid, C.: Evaluation of gist descriptors for web-scale image search. In: Proceedings of the ACM International Conference on Image and Video Retrieval. p. 19. ACM (2009)
12. Ivanova, K., Stanchev, P., Velikova, E., Vanhoof, K., Depaire, B., Kannan, R., Mitov, I., Markov, K.: Features for Art Painting Classification Based on Vector Quantization of MPEG-7 Descriptors. In: Kannan, R., Andres, F. (eds.) ICDEM 2010. LNCS, vol. 6411, pp. 146–153. Springer, Heidelberg (2012)
13. Jin, H., Liu, Q., Lu, H., Tong, X.: Face detection using improved lbp under bayesian framework. In: 2004 IEEE First Symposium on Multi-Agent Security and Survivability, pp. 306–309. IEEE (2004)
14. Johnson, C.R., Hendriks, E., Berezhnoy, I.J., Brevdo, E., Hughes, S.M., Daubechies, I., Li, J., Postma, E., Wang, J.Z.: Image processing for artist identification. IEEE Signal Processing Magazine 25(4), 37–48 (2008)
15. Jou, J., Agrawal, S.: Artist identification for renaissance paintings
16. Karayev, S., Hertzmann, A., Winnemoeller, H., Agarwala, A., Darrell, T.: Recognizing image style. arXiv preprint arXiv:1311.3715 (2013)
17. Keren, D.: Painter identification using local features and naive bayes. In: Proceedings of the 16th International Conference on Pattern Recognition, vol. 2, pp. 474–477. IEEE (2002)
18. Krizhevsky, A., Sutskever, I., Hinton, G.E.: Imagenet classification with deep convolutional neural networks. In: Advances in Neural Information Processing Systems. pp. 1097–1105 (2012)
19. Lazebnik, S., Schmid, C., Ponce, J.: Beyond bags of features: Spatial pyramid matching for recognizing natural scene categories. In: 2006 IEEE Computer Society Conference on Computer Vision and Pattern Recognition, vol. 2, pp. 2169–2178. IEEE (2006)
20. Lowe, D.G.: Distinctive image features from scale-invariant keypoints. International Journal of Computer Vision 60(2), 91–110 (2004)
21. Mishory, A.: Art history: an introduction. Open University of Israel (2000)
22. Ojala, T., Pietikäinen, M., Harwood, D.: A comparative study of texture measures with classification based on featured distributions. Pattern Recognition 29(1), 51–59 (1996)
23. Oliva, A., Torralba, A.: Modeling the shape of the scene: A holistic representation of the spatial envelope. International Journal of Computer Vision 42(3), 145–175 (2001)
24. Oquab, M., Bottou, L., Laptev, I., Sivic, J., et al.: Learning and transferring mid-level image representations using convolutional neural networks (2013)
25. Parker, J.R.: Algorithms for image processing and computer vision. John Wiley & Sons (2010)
26. Perronnin, F., Dance, C.: Fisher kernels on visual vocabularies for image categorization. In: IEEE Conference on Computer Vision and Pattern Recognition, CVPR 2007, pp. 1–8. IEEE (2007)

27. Sermanet, P., Eigen, D., Zhang, X., Mathieu, M., Fergus, R., LeCun, Y.: Overfeat: Integrated recognition, localization and detection using convolutional networks. arXiv preprint arXiv:1312.6229 (2013)
28. Sharif Razavian, A., Azizpour, H., Sullivan, J., Carlsson, S.: Cnn features off-the-shelf: an astounding baseline for recognition. arXiv preprint arXiv:1403.6382 (2014)
29. Shechtman, E., Irani, M.: Matching local self-similarities across images and videos. In: IEEE Conference on Computer Vision and Pattern Recognition, CVPR 2007, pp. 1–8. IEEE (2007)
30. Taigman, Y., Yang, M., Ranzato, M., Wolf, L.: Deepface: Closing the gap to human-level performance in face verification. In: IEEE CVPR (2014)
31. Torresani, L., Szummer, M., Fitzgibbon, A.: Efficient Object Category Recognition Using Classemes. In: Daniilidis, K., Maragos, P., Paragios, N. (eds.) ECCV 2010, Part I. LNCS, vol. 6311, pp. 776–789. Springer, Heidelberg (2010)
32. Zujovic, J., Gandy, L., Friedman, S., Pardo, B., Pappas, T.N.: Classifying paintings by artistic genre: An analysis of features & classifiers. In: IEEE International Workshop on Multimedia Signal Processing, MMSP 2009, pp. 1–5. IEEE (2009)

Re-presentations of Art Collections

Joon Son Chung[1], Relja Arandjelović[1]([✉]), Giles Bergel[2],
Alexandra Franklin[3], and Andrew Zisserman[1]

[1] Department of Engineering Science, University of Oxford, Oxford, UK
`relja@robots.ox.ac.uk`
[2] Faculty of English Language and Literature, University of Oxford, Oxford, UK
[3] Bodleian Libraries, University of Oxford, Oxford, UK

Abstract. The objective of this paper is to show how modern computer vision methods can be used to aid the art or book historian in analysing large digital art collections.

We make three contributions: first, we show that simple document processing methods in combination with accurate instance based retrieval methods can be used to automatically obtain all the illustrations from a collection of illustrated documents. Second, we show that image level descriptors can be used to automatically cluster collections of images based on their categories, and thereby represent a collection by its semantic content. Third, we show that instance matching can be used to identify illustrations from the same source, e.g. printed from the same woodblock, and thereby represent a collection in a manner suitable for temporal analysis of the printing process.

These contributions are demonstrated on a collection of illustrated English Ballad sheets.

1 Introduction

Art and book historians now have huge digital collections available for study [6, 7]. This offers an opportunity and a problem: subtle comparisons can potentially be carried out over far more data than was ever possible before, however, the manual analysis methods that have traditionally been used are simply inadequate for collections of this scale (or would take many years of effort by an art historian).

In this paper we show that standard computer vision methods are, fairly effortlessly, able to *re-present* images in art collections in a way that are suitable for manual analysis and to some extent, can automate some of this analysis. We consider two canonical problems: *semantic clustering* – re-presenting the data in clusters that are semantically related. This enables art historians to carry out longitudinal studies on how the depiction of a particular concept has changed over time; and *instance clustering* – re-presenting the data as clusters of exact copies. Analysis of exact copies is of interest in dating and time ordering collections.

We exemplify these two representations using a dataset of images of broadside ballad sheets [11]. These are cheap printed sheets containing lyrics of popular

© Springer International Publishing Switzerland 2015
L. Agapito et al. (Eds.): ECCV 2014 Workshops, Part I, LNCS 8925, pp. 85–100, 2015.
DOI: 10.1007/978-3-319-16178-5_6

(a) (b) (c) (d)

Fig. 1. Woodcut illustrations. The pair of illustrations on the left appear to be the same at first sight, but are printed from two different woodblocks. The pair on the right are printed from the same block, but there are small differences due to wear and tear.

songs (ballads), and woodblock printed illustrations. The sheets were printed from the sixteenth until the early twentieth centuries. The dataset, described in section 2, contains around 900 ballad sheets with many different 'concepts' illustrated (such as 'the devil' or 'death' or 'eating and drinking'). There are identical copies (printed from the same woodblock), near but not exact copies of woodblocks (so near but not exact illustrations, but semantically related) in which the differences in the features and the shapes of the illustrations are very subtle, and also different depictions of the same concept.

The task of matching the woodblocks presents many challenges – the large quantity of woodblocks and illustrations makes them very difficult to organise by hand, and a pair of illustrations such as Figures 1a and 1b that look identical to all but the most trained eye may in fact be from a close copy of a woodblock. Comparing illustrations from the same woodblock is no easier – small damages to the woodblock, such as a wormhole in Figure 1d that is not present in Figure 1c, are again not obvious to the eye. Such differences may be identified under close inspection when the set consists of a few images, but the task becomes completely infeasible in a set of thousands.

Paper outline: Section 3 describes how woodblock illustration regions can be determined automatically by first removing areas of text, based on their characteristic patterns, and then refined and verified by matching and comparing to regions of similar illustrations on other ballad sheets. Section 4 describes the semantic clustering where compact descriptors such as VLAD and GIST are utilised to compute similarities between the illustrations, and thereby cluster them into semantically similar groupings. Within each cluster of semantically similar images, further analysis based on exact instance matching (SIFT and spatial verification) is performed to find illustrations that come from the same woodblock (section 5). A number of features are generated from the difference between the images, and a Support Vector Machine (SVM) is trained to distinguish prints from the same block from those from a copy. Finally, differences exist even between prints from the same woodblock, many of which are the result of damage to the block. These visual damage cues can be used to find a temporal ordering of the sheets.

1.1 Related Work

The evolution and temporal ordering of illustrations is of great interest to art historians and bibliographers [3]. Monroy *et al.* [22] suggests that differences in the local image features can be used to visualise the temporal order in which the images were produced – *e.g.* the more times an illustration is copied, the more details that might differ from the original. Furthermore, Monroy *et al.* [21] notes that even closely traced copies of an artwork contain geometric distortions, and suggests grouping of deformations to reveal details about the process of copying the artwork.

For woodcuts, Hedges [13] discusses the correlation between wormholes in the centuries-old printed art and the history of the prints. The wormholes take a distinctive shape – small and round holes, around 1.4 to 2.3 mm in diameter – hence they are easily identifiable as the cues of relative age. The wormholes are not the only cues that can be used to order the illustrations. Hedges [12] gives useful insights into the cues one might use to order the woodcut illustrations.

There has been previous work on using instance (specific object) matching methods for Ballad images. In Bergel *et al.* [4] an image matching tool was developed to provide immediate matches of regions of interest within a collection of Ballad images. This used the standard bag of visual words method of [1, 25]. The paper only considered matching though, and there was no investigation of automated clustering, which is the goal of this submission.

2   The Ballads Dataset

Broadside ballads are cheap printed sheets carrying lyrics, illustrations and the names of popular tunes. They were sold, displayed, sung and read in the streets and alehouses of Britain from the 16th until the early 20th centuries [4, 11]. The dataset used here contains around 900 images of ballad sheets from four different collections. For some of the images, estimated print dates or date-ranges are given. No further description is provided with the photographed ballad sheets.

All of the images are photographed in a standard format as shown in Figure 2 – on black background, and with a ruler on one side to show the physical scale. The images are around 3K pixels on the longest dimension. Most of the ballad sheets contain around one to five woodcut illustrations. The woodblocks, which are of particular interest here, come in various sizes – the largest blocks are over 15cm along their longer dimension, whereas the smaller blocks can be around 3cm in width.

Fig. 2. Photographs of broadside ballad sheets

3 Automatic Cropping of Illustrations

In this section we outline the method of identifying and cropping candidate objects (woodblock illustrations) from images of the ballad sheets. There are two stages, first putative regions are obtained from areas that are *not* text on the sheet, second instance matching with other copies of the woodblock print with the collection is used to refine the regions and separate connected neighbouring objects into individual prints from different woodblocks.

3.1 Identifying Text Areas and Candidate Picture Regions

The main objects that appear in the broadside ballad sheets are text and pictures (woodblock illustrations). The vertical spacing of text is fairly regular – approximately 4 to 6 millimetres (8 to 12 pixels). As a result, if a horizontal sum of intensity values is taken over an area of text, it is possible to observe a regular pattern of intensities, as shown in Figure 3.

If a Fourier transform is taken over this signal, a sharp and distinctive peak is found at a frequency of around 0.1 (unit: per pixel), such as in the example shown in Figure 3a. However over any other area which does not contain text, no such peak is observed (Figure 3b). The process is repeated across the page with a moving window, and all areas showing a strong peak at such frequency are disregarded. Having removed the text, it is possible to search over the remaining

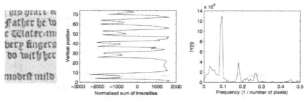

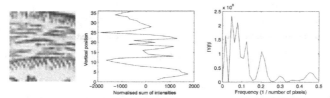

(a) An area of text – a distinctive peak is observed

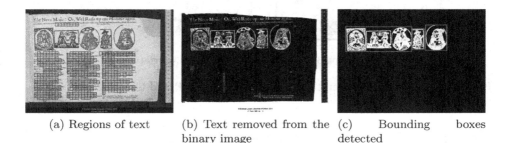

(b) An area of image – no distinctive peak is observed

Fig. 3. Fourier transform of horizontal sum

(a) Regions of text   (b) Text removed from the binary image   (c)   Bounding   boxes detected

Fig. 4. Text detection and removal, and candidate bounding boxes

area for candidate objects, given the known geometric constraints (for example, the illustrations must be greater than 3 cm in width and cannot lie on the page margin). The process is illustrated in figure 4.

Evaluation over a random set of 200 sheets shows good performance, with precision and recall of 98.5% and 99.1% respectively. There are examples where two neighbouring illustrations are erroneously proposed as one due to the illustrations being very close together. This is not considered an error at this point, and the problem is addressed in the following section.

3.2   Separation of Connected Neighbouring Objects

At this point, some illustrations that are in very close proximity (typically within a few pixels of each other) are often highlighted as one connected component. In this section we resolve this problem using a local implementation of the standard BoW retrieval system [25] by searching over *all* putative regions. (For the

(a) ImageMatch query from a sin-   (b) ImageMatch query from multiple images
gle image

Fig. 5. Estimation of the image boundary using ImageMatch

(a) Poor overlap (30%)   (b) Good overlap (95%)

Fig. 6. Overlap ratios between the original boundary (red) and the ImageMatch estimate (blue)

retrieval system in detail, we use affine-Hessian interest points [20], a vocabulary
of 100k vision words obtained using approximate k-means, and spatial re-ranking
of the top 200 tf-idf results using an affine transformation).

Given a query illustration, the BoW system returns a ranked list of similar images containing the illustration and the estimated positions of the ROIs.
For example, a query is generated from the image bound by the red rectangle
in Figure 5a, which generates the blue rectangles that represent the estimated
positions of similar images.

Now suppose that the queries are generated from many of the similar images
as shown in Figure 5b. Each of the queries will give an estimated position of the
matched image, which can be used as cues to determine the exact location.

Figure 6a shows a subsection of the starred image in Figure 5b. In the figure,
our original estimate of the image boundary is represented by the red rectangle. The blue rectangle represents an estimate given by an BoW ImageMatch
query. The overlap ratio between the blue and the red rectangles are calculated.
(The overlap ratio between areas A and B is defined as $\frac{A \cap B}{A \cup B}$.) In the example Figure 6a, the two rectangles show poor overlap (30%). The overlap ratios
between the red rectangle and all of the other estimates are calculated, which

Fig. 7. Separation of neighbouring illustrations. Blue boxes show all potential boundaries generated using ImageMatch. Green boxes show final separation of the illustrations.

mostly give poor ratios. This suggests a boundary refinement is necessary. However, if we suppose that the original image boundary is as shown in Figure 6b, the overlap ratio between the red rectangle and the BoW ImageMatch estimates would mostly show good overlap, which indicates that the original boundary is likely to be accurate.

The queries are generated from *all* of the illustrations detected in section 3.1, and the returned coordinates that overlap the ROI in question are noted as potential boundaries (Figure 7). This information is then used to cluster the boundaries of illustrations within the original candidate. First, the centre (x and y) and the size (height h and width w) of all blue boxes are calculated. Then, the boxes whose x and y values are furthest from the median are iteratively deleted until the standard deviation of the remaining boxes are within the threshold. The same is repeated for w and h values of the boxes that are not rejected in the previous step. The mean of the remaining boxes are taken as the new boundary. Where the resultant boundary does not cover most of the initial object (over 80%), the process is repeated using the remaining, unused ROIs, until the process returns no more estimates that do not overlap the new objects.

The green rectangles in Figure 7 show the final cropping result on the example image used throughout this chapter. On a test set of 200 pages, the method proved to be reliable for all examples where the new boundary is defined by averaging three or more BoW ImageMatch returns. As this process relies on majority voting on the cropping data from Section 3.1, it is necessary that a large majority of the illustrations are already correctly cropped as in the example Figure 7.

From the full set of 900 broadside ballad sheets, around 2,600 individual illustrations are detected and cropped. Selected results are shown in Figure 8.

4   Semantically Similar Illustrations

Having identified the woodblock illustrations in section 3, the main objective of this section is to automatically find and cluster the illustrations that are semantically similar to each other. Note, to avoid confusion, we are not trying to assign illustrations to manually curated classes defined by cataloguers, such as the Iconclass [14] system.

Fig. 8. Automatically detected boundaries of woodcut illustrations

Similarity of two illustrations is computed as a weighted sum of consistency between their aspect ratios and weighted similarities of three different image descriptors: VLAD, spatially pooled VLAD and GIST; which are described next.

GIST. The GIST [24] image descriptor provides a holistic description of the scene, capturing coarse image gradients, where local object information is not taken into account. Similarity of two illustrations is computed as the negative L2-distance between their GIST descriptors. While providing a good descriptor for the overall shape of a scene, GIST can be sensitive to cropping [9].

VLAD. The Vector of Locally Aggregated Descriptors (VLAD) [17] summarizes the distribution of local SIFT [19] descriptors in an image. It has gained popularity due to good performance in image retrieval tasks [2,8,15,18] while providing a compact image descriptor. Similarity between two illustrations is computed as the scalar product between their VLAD encodings.

Spatially pooled VLAD. Since VLAD does not encode any spatial information, we also compute VLAD for five predefined spatial tiles each spanning a quarter of the image area. The pooling regions are the four quadrants of the image and a region of equal size in the centre of the image. The similarity between two illustrations is computed as the weighted sum of scalar product between the spatially pooled VLAD's.

The weights are tuned manually over a small number of clusters and concepts, and then used for all further comparisons.

4.1 Clustering Similar Illustrations

Similarity is computed between all pairs of illustrations, which can be done efficiently due to using compact GIST and VLAD descriptors. For larger datasets, this step can be performed by approximate nearest neighbour search [23] or fast memory-efficient search by quantizing the descriptors [16]. The pairwise

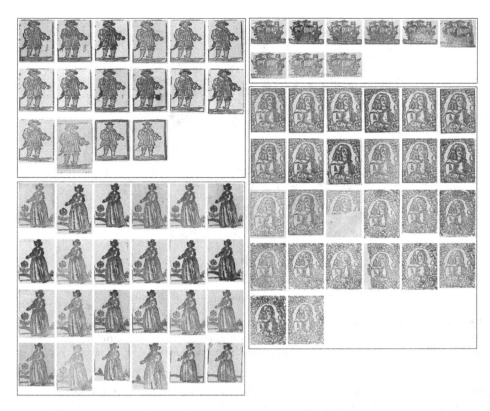

Fig. 9. Semantically similar images automatically detected and clustered

similarities are thresholded and a graph is formed such that nodes correspond
to illustrations and undirected edges connect nodes of sufficient semantic similarity. Clustering is then performed by extracting connected components from
the similarity graph. We then refine clusters with large intra-cluster variability
to alleviate cases where a weak erroneous link between two different clusters
causes undersegmentation. The refinement is performed by identifying clusters
with large variance of intra-cluster similarities, and removing edges by enforcing
a stricter similarity threshold, followed by recomputation of connected components. Some of the automatically obtained clusters are shown in figure 9.

5   Identifying Illustrations Printed from the Same Woodblock

The objective of this section is to automatically identify prints generated from
the same woodblock. This is of particular interest to cataloguers and art historians as tracking the use of a woodblock provides insights into the origin of
the printed material, such as the identity of the printer, the place of printing,

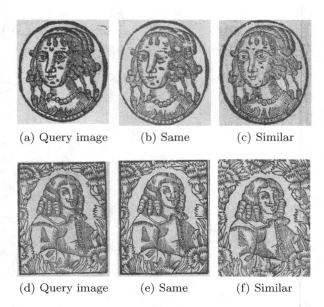

(a) Query image   (b) Same   (c) Similar

(d) Query image   (e) Same   (f) Similar

Fig. 10. Same vs similar pairs. In each row, the first two illustrations are printed from the same woodblock. The last illustration appears to be very similar, but comes from a different woodblock that is a copy of the original block.

or the sale or loan of a woodblock providing information about relationships between printers. Moreover, examining the changes in the condition of a woodblock, such as the development of wormholes, allows for automatic dating of the sheets [12,13].

Section 4 described a method for mining clusters containing similar illustrations, here we concentrate on finer clustering to only group illustrations printed from the same woodblock. Therefore, we examine all pairs of illustrations in a semantic cluster to determine if they come from the same woodblock. This is a challenging task as it was common practice to closely copy woodblocks therefore giving rise to sets of very similar illustrations (figure 10).

A linear SVM is trained to distinguish between a pair of *same* (i.e. printed from the same woodblock) and *similar* (i.e. printed from a similar and likely copied woodblock) illustrations, using features which assess geometric consistency of the illustrations. The use of geometry is motivated by the observation that, even though two similar illustrations look quite well aligned, it is unlikely that they are related with a very accurate global rigid transformation as a result of the geometrical errors accumulated during the copying process [22]. The geometry-based features are discussed next.

An affine transformation which aligns one illustration with the other is automatically estimated by forming a set of putative correspondences by matching SIFT [19] descriptors using the second nearest neighbour test [19], and finding the affine transformation which explains the largest number of the putative

(a) Inliers in a same pair   (b) Inliers in a similar pair

Fig. 11. Spatial distribution of inliers. Lines connect SIFT descriptors consistent with an affine transformation. The blue rectangles show the bounding boxes of spatially consistent descriptors.

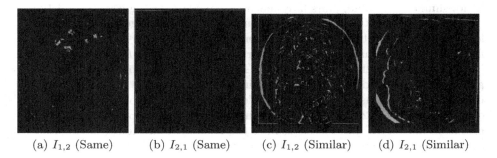

(a) $I_{1,2}$ (Same)   (b) $I_{2,1}$ (Same)   (c) $I_{1,2}$ (Similar)   (d) $I_{2,1}$ (Similar)

Fig. 12. Difference images for illustrations from same and similar woodblocks

correspondences using RANSAC [10]. Features which help determine the quality of the affine transformation are: i) the number of putative SIFT-based matches (n_p); ii) the ratio of number of matches spatially consistent with the best affine transformation, n_s, and n_p (n_s/n_p); and iii) the density of matches (n_s divided by illustration size).

We also observe that the spatial distribution of spatially consistent features is informative (figure 11) – a same pair has features matching across the entire illustration, while a similar pair often has only locally consistent matches. The spatial spread is measured as the proportion of the illustration area covered by the bounding box of spatially matched features. The bounding box is computed as the smallest axis aligned rectangle which contains the central 90% of features; this procedure ensures robustness by eliminating spurious matches which could affect the bounding box estimation.

Finally, we also include two features which capture fine level differences between the two illustrations. Let I_1 and I_2 be a pair of illustrations such that I_2 is automatically registered to I_1 using the aforementioned affine transformation, and both are binarized to 1 and 0 to indicate pixels which contain and don't

Table 1. Performance of same vs similar classification

	Precision	Recall	Precision	Recall
ImageMatch	78%	80%	69%	90%
RANSAC statistics	98%	80%	95%	90%
Our method	100%	80%	100%	90%

contain ink, respectively. From these, one can compute binary difference images $I_{i,j}$ which indicate pixels where image I_i contains ink and image I_j does not. As can be seen from figure 12, the difference images $I_{1,2}$ and $I_{2,1}$ can help discriminate between same and similar pairs of illustrations. This is because for a same pair, in an ideal scenario, an $I_{i,j}$ image will be completely empty (figure 12b) signifying that j was printed after i as all ink in I_j is present in I_i, i.e. ink could have only disappeared from I_i to I_j corresponding to potential damages to the woodblock (the disappeared ink is visible in image $I_{j,i}$, figure 12a). On the other hand, similar (not same) pairs have much less sparse $I_{i,j}$'s (figures 12c and 12d).

Let $|I_{i,j}|$ denote the number of ones in the difference image $I_{i,j}$, and without loss of generality let $I_{2,1}$ be the sparser image (i.e. $|I_{2,1}| \leq |I_{1,2}|$). The two features which summarize the above observations are $p_{min} = |I_{2,1}|/A$ and $p_{max} = |I_{1,2}|/A$, where A is the illustration area. Therefore, p_{min} is close to zero for same pairs (figure 12b) and large for similar pairs (figure 12d), while p_{max} also contains useful information as it should be smaller for same pairs compared to similar ones (figure 12a vs 12c). In practice, we first perform image opening with a small radius on images $I_{i,j}$ in order to remove the differences in the thickness of lines caused by varying amounts of ink on the woodblock.

To summarize, six features are used for classification into same versus similar illustration pairs – three capturing the counts and relative counts of putative and spatially consistent descriptor matches, one measuring the spatial distribution of spatially consistent matches, and two capturing pixel-wise differences in inking.

5.1   Evaluation Procedure and Results

Benchmark dataset. To evaluate the classification accuracy of the proposed method, we have manually labelled a random sample of 150 pairs of illustrations obtained from clusters in section 4, such that there is a roughly equal number of same vs similar pairs. This set was divided into 50% for training, 25% for validation and 25% for testing.

Baselines. We compare the proposed approach with two baselines. The first is a classifier based purely on the number of spatially verified matches obtained from ImageMatch (section 3.2), namely a pair of illustrations is deemed to be a same match if the number of matches in ImageMatch is larger than a threshold. The second is an SVM classifier trained only on the first three features of our method which capture the RANSAC-based statistics, i.e. n_p, n_s/n_p, and density of n_s.

Fig. 13. Clustering example. For the running example images our method finds two clusters, shown one per row.

Results. Table 1 shows the results of our method compared to the two baselines. It can be seen that ImageMatch is not as good as the other two methods as it only uses match count as a feature, as well as due to quantizing descriptors into visual words. The RANSAC statistics performs quite well, but our method which uses all six features significantly outperforms it, simultaneously achieving higher recall and precision, namely, our method gets 100% precision at 90% recall while RANSAC statistics achieves 98% precision at 80% recall, and only 95% precision and 90% recall.

We pick the operating point which achieves maximal recall for 100% precision (recall at this point is 90%) and cluster together illustrations which are deemed to be same matches. The final results on the running example are shown in figure 13, while figure 14 shows some further examples.

5.2 Application: Temporal Ordering of the Illustrations

The likely printer of a sheet can be identified if his identity is known for a sheet which shares an illustration belonging to the same cluster. In similar ways, one can also determine the place of printing or relationships between printers [5].

One interesting application is to automatically date a sheet – two sheets which contain an illustration printed from the same woodblock can be ordered temporally by examining fine-level changes in the impressions. This application is beyond the scope of this paper, but we give a brief sketch of the method. For example, from figures 12a and 12b, it is evident that illustration I_2 contains less ink that I_1 (as $I_{2,1}$, figure 12b, is empty) due to degradations of the woodblock (locations of which are apparent in $I_{1,2}$, figure 12a). Therefore, in this example it can be concluded that I_2 has been printed later than I_1. Using such automatically discovered temporal constraints[1], it is easy to order many sheets in terms of their

---

[1] Actually we have a more robust method than simply measuring the amount of ink difference in $I_{i,j}$, but it is beyond the scope of this paper.

Fig. 14. Illustrations from the same woodblock automatically detected and clustered

printing time. As dates of certain sheets are known, the temporal ordering can help narrow down the printing date of other sheets. Using this logic, it was possible to automatically assign dates or date-ranges to over 70 ballad sheets whose print dates were previously unknown.

6   Discussion

The three contributions of this paper: automatic cropping of illustrations, semantic clustering, and exact clustering (with applications to temporal ordering) have general applicability. For example, the cropping method could be applied to any collection that mixes text and repeated illustrations. The two types of clustering can be applied to any collection with some commonality in illustrations, e.g. those printed from woodblocks, such as medieval incunabula (e.g. 'The Book of Hours'), or collections with illustrations printed using engravings or lithography. All of these cases have the three aspects of illustrations from the same source, near copies and different depictions of concepts.

Acknowledgments. We are grateful for financial support from ERC grant VisRec no. 228180.

References

1. Arandjelović, R., Zisserman, A.: Three things everyone should know to improve object retrieval. In: Proc. CVPR (2012)
2. Arandjelović, R., Zisserman, A.: All about VLAD. In: Proc. CVPR (2013)
3. Barrow, T.: From 'The Easter Wedding' to 'The Frantick Lover': The repeated woodcut and its shifting roles. Studies in Ephemera: Text and Image in Eighteenth-Century Print (2013)
4. Bergel, G., Franklin, A., Heaney, M., Arandjelović, R., Zisserman, A., Funke, D.: Content-based image-recognition on printed broadside ballads: the Bodleian libraries' ImageMatch tool. In: IFLA World Library and Information Congress (2013)
5. Blayney, P.: The Stationers' Company and the Printers of London, 1501–1557 (2013)
6. British Library on Flickr. http://www.flickr.com/photos/britishlibrary/
7. British Printed Images to 1700: A digital library of prints and book illustrations from early modern Britain. http://www.bpi1700.org.uk/index.html/
8. Delhumeau, J., Gosselin, P.H., Jégou, H., Pérez, P.: Revisiting the VLAD image representation. In: Proc. ACMM (2013)
9. Douze, M., Jégou, H., Sandhawalia, H., Amsaleg, L., Schmid, C.: Evaluation of GIST descriptors for web-scale image search. In: Proc. CIVR (2009)
10. Fischler, M.A., Bolles, R.C.: Random sample consensus: A paradigm for model fitting with applications to image analysis and automated cartography. Comm. ACM **24**(6), 381–395 (1981)
11. Franklin, A.: The art of illustration in Bodleian Broadside Ballads before 1820. Bodleian Library Record **17**(5) (2002)
12. Hedges, B.: A method for dating early books and prints using image analysis. In: The Royal Society (2006)
13. Hedges, B.: Wormholes record species history in space and time. Biology Letters **9**(1), 20120926 (2013)
14. Iconclass. http://www.iconclass.nl/
15. Jégou, H., Chum, O.: Negative evidences and co-occurrences in image retrieval: the benefit of PCA and whitening. In: Proc. ECCV (2012)
16. Jégou, H., Douze, M., Schmid, C.: Product quantization for nearest neighbor search. IEEE PAMI (2011)
17. Jégou, H., Douze, M., Schmid, C., Pérez, P.: Aggregating local descriptors into a compact image representation. In: Proc. CVPR (2010)
18. Jégou, H., Perronnin, F., Douze, M., Sánchez, J., Pérez, P., Schmid, C.: Aggregating local images descriptors into compact codes. IEEE PAMI (2012)
19. Lowe, D.: Distinctive image features from scale-invariant keypoints. IJCV **60**(2), 91–110 (2004)
20. Mikolajczyk, K., Schmid, C.: Scale & affine invariant interest point detectors. IJCV **1**(60), 63–86 (2004)
21. Monroy, A., Bell, P., Ommer, B.: Shaping art with art: morphological analysis for investigating artistic reproductions. In: Proceedings of the International Conference on Multimedia (2012)

22. Monroy, A., Carqu, B., Ommer, B.: Reconstructing the drawing process of reproductions from medieval images. In: Macq, B., Schelkens, P. (eds.) ICIP, pp. 2917–2920. IEEE (2011)
23. Muja, M., Lowe, D.G.: Fast approximate nearest neighbors with automatic algorithmic configuration. In: Proc. VISAPP (2009)
24. Oliva, A., Torralba, A.: Modeling the shape of the scene: a holistic representation of the spatial envelope. IJCV (2001)
25. Philbin, J., Chum, O., Isard, M., Sivic, J., Zisserman, A.: Object retrieval with large vocabularies and fast spatial matching. In: Proc. CVPR (2007)

Detecting People in Cubist Art

Shiry Ginosar$^{(\boxtimes)}$, Daniel Haas, Timothy Brown, and Jitendra Malik

University of California Berkeley, Berkeley, USA
shiry@eecs.berkeley.edu

Abstract. Although the human visual system is surprisingly robust to extreme distortion when recognizing objects, most evaluations of computer object detection methods focus only on robustness to natural form deformations such as people's pose changes. To determine whether algorithms truly mirror the flexibility of human vision, they must be compared against human vision at its limits. For example, in Cubist abstract art, painted objects are distorted by object fragmentation and part-reorganization, sometimes to the point that human vision often fails to recognize them. In this paper, we evaluate existing object detection methods on these abstract renditions of objects, comparing human annotators to four state-of-the-art object detectors on a corpus of Picasso paintings. Our results demonstrate that while human perception significantly outperforms current methods, human perception and part-based models exhibit a similarly graceful degradation in object detection performance as the objects become increasingly abstract and fragmented, corroborating the theory of part-based object representation in the brain.

Keywords: Object detection · Perception · Abstract art · Cubism

1 Introduction

The human visual system is amazingly robust to abstractness of object representation. While we can recognize people in natural, realistic images such as camera snapshots, we are also easily able to identify human figures rendered in numerous forms of artistic depiction such as oil paintings, cartoons and line drawings, despite the fact that they frequently have little in common with a real human being in terms of texture, color and form. At the extreme, abstract artists intentionally push the envelope of human vision to the point at which objects are completely unrecognizable, yet we still find such distorted shapes reminiscent of the human form. Computer vision detection algorithms can also recognize objects outside the realm of natural images, though their models of the visual world may not always align with the human one [12]. Since algorithmic object detection in computer vision is usually compared against humans using natural images, such differences are seldom apparent. However, if we seek to design algorithms that achieve the power and flexibility of the human visual system by mimicking it, we should attempt to align the visual models of the detectors we train with the human model. Moreover, we must also evaluate their correspondence on images that stretch the limits of human vision.

© Springer International Publishing Switzerland 2015
L. Agapito et al. (Eds.): ECCV 2014 Workshops, Part I, LNCS 8925, pp. 101–116, 2015.
DOI: 10.1007/978-3-319-16178-5_7

In this paper, we employ the abstract depiction of objects in the Cubist paintings of Picasso as one such test corpus. Cubist paintings depict radically fragmented objects as if they were seen from many viewpoints at once, breaking them into medium sized cube-like parts that appear out of their natural ordering and do not conform to the rules of perspective [14]. Because the abstract objects present in Cubist art are not normally seen in nature, the human visual system must strain to recognize them. Since humans are usually still able to identify the depicted object, Cubism shows us that human perception does not rely on exact geometry and is tolerant to a rearrangement of mid-level object parts. However, findings from neuroscience show that this ability degrades as images become more scrambled or abstract [25][13]. We use the fragmentation and reordering of parts in Cubist paintings as an example of extreme conditions for the human visual system. Our claim is that if a method mimics human perceptual performance well, then it should behave similarly in these (as well as other) extreme conditions. We therefore aim to test whether there are existing detection methods that behave like human vision under these conditions. This stands in stark contrast to the common practice of evaluating computer vision models on datasets consisting only of camera snapshots and represents a novel contribution, as there is little research into how current systems perform on novel input.

We choose to focus on part-based detection methods that permit the rearrangement of medium-complexity parts, as they have been proven to do well at representing naturally occurring form deformations [7], and evaluate them in comparison to both human participants and object-level detection methods. Moreover, in order to chart the performance of the methods as human vision approaches its limit, we ask participants to divide the paintings into subsets according to the level of their abstractness and compare the performance of the humans and detection methods on each subset. Our results show that (1) existing part-based methods are relatively successful at detecting people even in abstract images, (2) that there is a natural correspondence between user ratings of image abstraction in the Cubist sense and part-based method performance, and (3) that these properties are not nearly as evident in non-part-based methods. By demonstrating that part-based methods mimic human performance, we both show that these methods are valuable for object recognition in non-traditional settings, and corroborate the theory of part-based object representation in the brain.

2   Related Work

Since in most tasks the human visual system serves as an upper bound benchmark for computer vision, some studies focus on characterizing its capabilities at the limit. For instance, Sinha and Torralba examined face detection capabilities in low resolution, contrast negated and inverted images [19]. In other cases, computational models are used to test the validity of theories from neuroscience [22]. We take inspiration from these studies and evaluate human object detection in man-made art in order to provide a less restrictive benchmark of robustness to form abstraction and deformation than natural images. By using this benchmark we hope to discover parallels between the characteristics of human and algorithmic object detection.

From research in neuroscience, we know that the human visual system can detect and recognize objects even when they are manipulated in various ways [15]. For instance, humans are able to recognize inverted objects, although their performance is degraded, especially when the objects are faces or words [21][19]. Similar results were obtained when comparing scrambled images to non-scrambled ones, leading to a theory of object-fragments rather than whole-object representations in the brain [11][23]. This theory is strengthened by recordings from neurons in the macaque middle face patch that indicate both part-based and holistic face detection strategies [8]. Thus, although humans are capable of recognizing images distorted by scrambling, they are less adept at doing so. By analogy, we might expect methods trained on natural images to suffer a similar degradation in the face of a reorganization of object parts.

Object detection is one of the prominent unsolved problems in computer vision. Traditionally, object detection methods were holistic and template-based [4], but recent successful detection methods such as Poselets [2][3] and deformable part-based models [7] have focused on identifying mid-level parts in an appropriate configuration to indicate the presence of objects. Other part-based methods discover mid-level discriminative patches in an unsupervised way [18][5], use visual features of intermediate complexity for classification [22], or rely on distinctive sparse fragments for recognition [1]. Finally, a model inspired by Cubism itself that assembles intermediate-level parts even more loosely has shown success in detecting objects [16]. Another approach to detection that has recently shown remarkable detection results is based on convolutional neural networks [9][17]. We discuss the methods that we have chosen to benchmark in Section 4.

3   Cubist 'Fragments of Perception'

While there are many kinds of visual deformation to which human vision is robust, we choose to focus on the object fragmentation and part-reorganization exhibited by Cubist paintings as it has an appealing correlation with the strengths of part-based detection methods. Cubism is an art movement that peaked in the early 20th century with the work of artists such as Picasso and Braque. Cubist painters moved away from the two-dimensional representation of perspective characteristic of realism [14]. Instead, they strove to capture the perceptual experience of viewing a three dimensional object from a close distance where in order to perceive an object, the viewer is forced to observe it part by part from different directions. Cubist painters collapsed these 'fragments of perception' onto one two-dimensional plane, distorting perspective so that the whole object can be viewed simultaneously. Despite the abstraction of form, the original object is often readily detectable by the viewer as the parts chosen to represent it are naturalistic enough and discriminative enough to allow for the recognition of the object as a whole. However, this becomes harder with the degree of departure from reality [13].

The fact that humans can detect non-figurative objects in Cubist paintings without prior training makes these paintings well-suited to benchmark robustness to abstractions of form in detection methods trained on natural images. In order to provide intuition that part-based models will be able to perform well on this task, we provide some initial evidence that computer vision methods can successfully identify key parts in the Cubist depictions of objects. We train an unsupervised discovery method of mid-level discriminative patches on the PASCAL 2010 "person" class images [18][5][6], and compare the part-detector activations on natural training images and Cubist paintings by Picasso in Figures 1 and 2. Despite the difference in low-level image statistics, the detectors are able to discover the patches that discriminate people from non-people in both image domains. In the rest of the paper, we build on these results to test whether part-based object models can use the detected parts in order to recognize the depicted objects as a whole.

Fig. 1. Heat maps showing the discriminative patches activations on a natural training image (Left) and "Girl Before a Mirror 1932", a Picasso Cubist painting (Right). The color palette correlates with confidence score and ranges from blue (lowest) to red (highest). In both cases the most discriminative patches for class person are parts of faces and upper bodies, suggesting that computer vision methods are able to identify the key parts of human figures even when they are split into 'fragments of perception' in Cubist paintings.

4   Object Detection Methods in Comparison

We chose four person detectors that represent the range of available approaches to test whether state-of-the-art detection methods mimic the human visual system at its limits. These are presented in the time ordering in which they were proposed: one holistic template-based method, one part-based model where the parts are learned automatically, one part-based model where the parts are learned from human annotations, and the most recent deep learning method. Here we discuss the details of each one.

Dalal and Triggs: Object appearance in images can be characterized by histograms of orientations of local edge gradients binned over a dense image grid (HOG) [4]. The Dalal and Triggs (D&T) method trains an object-level HOG template for detection using bounding box annotations. Since the features are binned, the detector is robust only to image deformation within the bins.

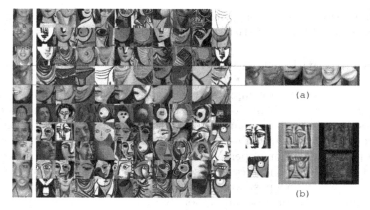

Fig. 2. Discriminative patch detectors trained on natural images are able to detect the parts that characterize person figures in Cubist paintings. (Left) Each row displays the top ten discriminative patches activations[1]. The leftmost column shows the top activation on the training data. Most of the detectors find corresponding face parts in the natural and painting images, although many are false positives. The fourth patch-detector from the top detects patches with little visual consistency on the paintings as well as the training data (a). Some false positive activations (b)(Bottom) seem more similar to true positives (b)(Top) in Hoggles space [24] (b)(Middle) than in HOG (b)(Right) or the original RGB (Left, marked in green) spaces.

Deformable Part Models: A holistic HOG template cannot recognize objects in the face of non-rigid deformations such as varied pose, which result in a rearrangement of the limbs versus the torso. Therefore, the deformable part-based models detection method (DPM) represents objects as collections of parts that can be arranged with respect to the root part [7]. In practice, the model trained on natural images often learns sub-part models (such as half a face).

Poselets: Poselets is a similar HOG-based part model that considers extra human supervision during training [2][3]. Here, parts are not discovered but learned from body-part annotations. Poselets do not necessarily correspond to anatomical body parts like limbs or torsos as these are often not the most salient features for visual recognition. In fact, a highly discriminative Poselet for person detection corresponds to "half of a frontal face and a left shoulder" [2].

R-CNN: R-CNN replaces the earlier rigid HOG features with features learned by a deep convolutional neural network [9][10]. While R-CNN does not have an explicit representation of parts, it is trained under a detection objective to be invariant to deformations of objects by using a large amount of data. Deep

---

[1] For each detector, the 10 most confident activations are presented by decreasing confidence, excluding lower confidence duplicates of 50% overlap or more. Detectors are sorted by the average score of their 20 top activations, excluding detectors where over 1/4 of activations are duplicates of activations from higher rated detectors.

methods outperform previous algorithms by a large margin on natural data. Here we test this state-of-the-art method on abstract paintings.

5   Experimental Setup

Since we are interested in comparing the above methods to human vision on data that approaches the limit of perception, we conduct two kinds of experiments. First, we study the human and algorithm performance on person detection over our full corpus of Cubist paintings. Second, we examine the degradation in performance of human perception and detectors as the paintings become more abstract. We conduct all comparisons using the PASCAL VOC evaluation mechanism, in which true positives are selected based on a 50% overlap between detection and ground truth bounding box [6].

5.1   Picasso Dataset

In the experiments described below we used as our test data a set of 218 Picasso paintings that have titles indicating that they depict people. These ranged from figurative portraits to abstract depictions of person figures as a collection of distorted parts. The set of paintings we used is highly biased in comparison to PASCAL person class images [6]. Given the nature of the art form, Cubist paintings usually depict people in full frontal or portrait views where most of the canvas area is devoted to the torso of a person. This results in higher average precision scores as a random detection that contains over 50% of the image would count as a true positive. This issue exists in any PASCAL VOC evaluation, but it is especially pronounced in this case.

5.2   Human Perception Study Setup

We conducted two experiments as part of our perception study. First, we recorded human detections of person figures in Cubist paintings. Second, we asked participants to bucket the paintings by their degree of abstraction compared to photorealistic depictions of people. For each painting, raters were asked to pick a classification on a 5-point Likert scale, where 1 corresponded to "*The figures in this painting are very lifelike*" and 5 corresponded to "*The figures in this painting are not at all lifelike*".

Participants. We recruited eighteen participants to partake in our perception study. Sixteen participants were undergraduate students at our institution, one was a graduate student and one a software engineering professional. Seventeen participants were male and one was female.

Mechanism. Participants completed the study on their personal laptops using an online graphical annotation tool we wrote for the purpose. Each participant spent an hour on the study and received a compensation of $15. Each participant annotated 146 randomly chosen paintings out of the total 218, so that every painting was annotated by 14 - 15 unique participants.

5.3   Detector Study Setup

We compare the human recognition performance we measured during the perception study to four object detection methods. We train all methods using the PASCAL 2010 "person" class training and validation images [6]. We train the methods using natural images so that they do not enjoy an advantage over humans by training on the paintings. However, some research suggests that human recognition in Cubist paintings does improve with repeated exposures [25]. We set all parameters in all four methods to the same settings used in the original papers, except for the Poselets detection score which we set to 0.2 based on cross validation on the training data.

5.4   Ground Truth

Because Picasso did not explicitly label the human figures in his paintings, there is no clear cut gold standard for human figure annotations in our image corpus. As a result, we rely on our human participants to form a ground truth annotation set. We do so by capturing the average rater annotation as follows. Since each painting might have more than one human figure, we use k-means clustering to group annotations by the human figure they correspond to. For each cluster, we obtain a ground truth bounding box by taking the median of each corner of the bounding boxes in that cluster along every dimension. This yields one ground truth bounding box per human figure per image, which we can now use to evaluate both human and detector annotations. For each human rater we withhold her annotations and construct a modified leave-one-out ground truth from the annotations of all other raters. When evaluating detectors, however, we include annotations from all human raters in the ground truth.

It is worth noting that since humans themselves are error-prone (especially when recognizing objects in more abstract paintings), our ground truth cannot be a perfect oracle. Rather, all evaluation is comparing performance to the average, imperfect human. From this perspective, our evaluation of human raters can be seen as a measure of their agreement, and our evaluation of detectors can be seen as a measure of similarity to the average human.

5.5   Evaluating Humans and Detectors

Unlike detectors, humans provide only one annotation per figure without confidence scores, so we cannot compute average precision. Our primary metric for humans is the F-measure (F1 score), which is the harmonic mean of precision and recall. In order to combine the F-measures of all participants, we consider both (qualitatively) the shape of the distribution of the scores, and (quantitatively) the mean F-measure.

To compare detectors with humans, we pick the point on the methods' precision-recall curve that optimizes F-measure, and return the precision, recall, and F-measure computed at this point. This is generous to the detectors but captures their performance if they were well tuned for this task.

6   Detection Performance on the Full Picasso Dataset

In the first part of the comparison we evaluate the performance of the humans and the four methods at detecting human figures in Picasso paintings.

6.1   Human Performance on the Full Picasso Dataset

First, we evaluate our human participants against the leave-one-out ground truth to determine how effective people are at recognizing human figures in Cubist art. Figure 3 displays the distribution of human F-measures for this task. Qualitatively, we see that humans perform quite well, as the distribution has its peak around 0.9, and there is little variance among the scores. It is worth noting the bump in the distribution around 0.6—there were a few raters whose annotations were significantly different from the ground truth annotation due to either a failure to recognize the images, or a misunderstanding of the annotation interface and instructions. Quantitatively, the first row of the table in Figure 7(Right) shows the mean human precision, recall, and F-measure. These numbers confirm our impressions of the distribution—humans tend to agree with each other on the location of person figures in the paintings.

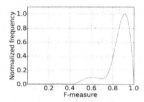

Fig. 3. Frequency distribution of human F-measure recognition scores in all 218 Cubist paintings against the leave-one-out ground truth bounding boxes. Due to the small number of participants, the curve has been smoothed for clarity.

6.2   Detector Performance on the Full Picasso Dataset

Qualitative Results. Part-based models trained purely on photographs performed surprisingly well when tested against the Picasso data. As can be seen in Figures 4 and Figure 5, Poselets and DPMs successfully produce bounding boxes for figures in the paintings, though they have their fair share of false positives and misses. The non-part-based methods do not perform as well, as is evident in Figure 6 where each row displays the top ten detections of a method over the entire painting dataset, sorted by each method's confidence score.

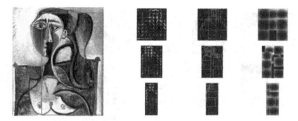

Fig. 4. (Left) DPM detects one of the two viewpoints of the split face, resulting in a shifted localization of the person as a whole. (Right) The DPM model trained on natural images learns sub-face parts in three different scales. This provides insight as to why DPM is able to detect a split-face patch resulting in the bounding box detection on the left.

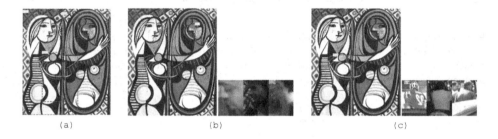

(a)   (b)   (c)

Fig. 5. The Poselets method is able to find person-parts in Cubist paintings and use them to detect person figures as a whole. (a) Bounding box detections in Picasso's "Girl Before a Mirror 1932" with a false positive detection in the center. (b) A true positive Poselet activation on the painting (Left) together with the corresponding activation on the training data (Right). In both image domains the Poselet detects a downward-angled face in profile. (c)(Left) The false positive activation that results in the incorrect bounding box detection in (a). Here the Poselet falsely detects an away-facing person in the painting (c)(Right).

Quantitative Results. Figure 7(Left) displays the precision-recall curves for each method when evaluated on all paintings. There is a clear ordering in accuracy: DPM performs the best by far, Poselets and RCNN come next, and Dalal and Triggs, though characterized by high recall, has extremely low precision, leading to terrible performance. In general, all of the methods achieve recall of up to 0.8, which implies that they are capable of recognizing most human figures in the image. However, DPM is the only method which can maintain a reasonable precision as recall increases, which explains its significantly greater AP. The table in Figure 7(Right) confirms these insights. DPM's performance on this task is quite encouraging, as its AP (0.38) is not too far off from its performance on photorealistic PASCAL 2010 photographs (0.41 without context rescoring) [10]. In practice this a favorable comparison as the PASCAL dataset, unlike ours, includes many images that do not contain people.

Fig. 6. Top ten detections for each method according to confidence from left to right. First row: DPM. Second row: Poselets. Third row: R-CNN. Fourth row: D&T. False positives are marked in blue. Qualitatively, it is evident that part-based models outperform the other approaches.

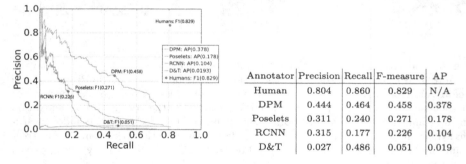

Annotator	Precision	Recall	F-measure	AP
Human	0.804	0.860	0.829	N/A
DPM	0.444	0.464	0.458	0.378
Poselets	0.311	0.240	0.271	0.178
RCNN	0.315	0.177	0.226	0.104
D&T	0.027	0.486	0.051	0.019

Fig. 7. Performance comparison via precision-recall curves (Left) and tabular data (Right). In both the plot and the table: for detectors, precision, recall, and F-measure are the maxima over the entire precision-recall curve. For humans, these numbers are averages across the raters. While DPM outperforms other methods, none of the methods reach human performance.

6.3   Comparing Human and Detector Performance

As is clear from the graphical and tabular data in Figure 7, a pair of humans are much better than a human and a detector at reaching an agreement about where the person figures are in Picasso paintings. The green dot in the upper right corner of the graph shows human precision and recall to be far higher than the orange dot of DPM, the highest-performing method.

6.4   Discussion of Performance on the Full Picasso Dataset

The comparison between the human participants and four methods on the task of detecting person figures in Picasso paintings demonstrates clearly that humans are highly skilled at this task, and that detectors are much less effective but can still achieve results within an order of magnitude of their detection performance on natural images. Among algorithms, part-based object detection methods perform better than object-level methods on images containing form abstraction. DPM and Poselets, our two part-based methods, demonstrate the best performance on the object detection task. This is likely due to the fact that part-based methods are able to recognize medium-level parts that remain intact even in Cubist paintings where standard human body parts are highly fragmented and rearranged. We emphasize the part-based approach here, as we have no reason to believe that the HOG features used by both DPM and Poselets carry any advantage over other image features organized in a part-based model.

Given its success in object detection on natural images, it is interesting that R-CNN does not perform well on this task. One reason for this could be that R-CNN is not a part-based model, however this is only partly true because the convolutional filters can be thought of as parts, and the max pooling as performing deformations. A second factor might be the fact that R-CNN over fits to the natural visual world and fails at adapting to the domain of paintings. There has been little research into how CNN-based networks perform on distorted images, but an initial investigation suggests that tiny changes to an image may cause drastic changes to their output [20].

7   Performance Degradation with Increased Abstraction

In the second part of the comparison we study the degradation of performance of humans and methods with increased painting abstractness.

7.1   Classifying Images by Degree of Abstraction

In our user study (described in Section 5.2), each rater labeled images on a scale from 1 (*The figures in this painting are very lifelike*) to 5 (*The figures in this painting are not at all lifelike*). By taking the rounded average of user labels for each image, we divide the images into five 'buckets of abstraction' in order to evaluate object detection performance as the abstraction of form increases. An example of a painting with an average rating of 1 is Picasso's "Seated Woman 1921", and an example of a painting with an average rating of 5 is Picasso's "Nude and Still Life 1931" (copyrighted paintings not reproduced). The number of images in each bucket is shown in Figure 8(Top Left).

7.2   Human Performance Degradation

Figure 8(Top Right) demonstrates the impact of abstraction of form on human object detection performance. As the images become more abstract, the distribution of human F-measures shifts clearly to the left. This indicates that human

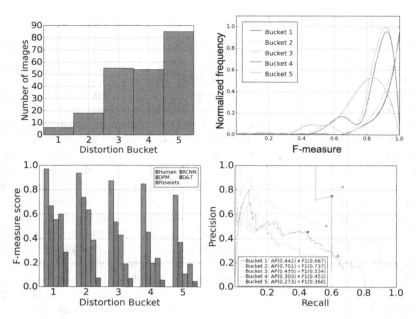

Fig. 8. Impact of increasing form abstraction on object detection performance. Bucket 1 contains images that appear most natural, and bucket 5 contains images that appear most abstract. (Top Left) A histogram showing the number of images per bucket. (Top Right) Human F-measure distributions by abstraction bucket. (Bottom Right) DPM precision-recall curves by bucket. (Bottom Left) Comparing humans and methods. Part-based models show a similar degradation behavior to human performance as the images become more abstract.

performance worsens on more scrambled human figures, which is consistent with previous results [21][19]. As noted in Section 6, there are a few annotators with low F-measures in each of the curves, which implies that these raters' errors are independent of image abstraction and are most likely due to a failure to follow the instructions rather than an inability to recognize objects.

7.3   Detector Performance Degradation

Qualitative Results. In Figure 9 we compare the top detections per method on paintings from bucket 2 versus bucket 5. The top discriminative-patches activations on these two buckets (Right) help visualize the difficulty in detecting meaningful mid-level parts as the paintings become more abstract.

Quantitative Results. Figure 8(Bottom Right) shows the precision recall curves for the DPM method with varying abstraction buckets. As with human performance, increasing the image abstraction of form causes a pronounced decrease in performance. The overlap between the curves for buckets 1 and 2 may be due to variance as a consequence of the low number of images in those two buckets.

Fig. 9. The degradation in performance with image difficulty. Top five detections per method (rows correspond to: DPM, Poselets, R-CNN, D&T) on images from bucket 2 (Left) and bucket 5 (Middle). False positives are marked in blue. This comparison shows that all detection methods perform worse on more abstract images. (Right) Degradation in performance is also evident in the detection of isolated parts. Top 10 discriminative patches activations for images of bucket 2 and bucket 5, with corresponding activations on PASCAL images. All activations on bucket 2 are true positives compared to only one from bucket 5 (in green).

7.4   Comparing Human and Detector Degradation

Figure 8(Bottom Left) compares the performance change of humans and detectors with varying abstraction buckets. As can be seen, the performance of all detectors degrades in a similar pattern to human performance as images become increasingly abstract, but the part-based methods follow the human pattern most closely. This matches our intuition about the similarities between part-based object detection and the human visual system. In contrast, the template-based Dalal and Triggs method abruptly breaks down after bucket 1.

7.5   Discussion of Degradation with Increased Abstraction

As we have demonstrated, part-based models for object detection show a smooth degradation in precision and recall as the images become more abstract. This is consistent with results from neuroscience, which indicate that humans are capable of detecting objects cut into parts, but that their ability degrades significantly when the parts are scrambled. The correspondence between human and computational method performance on this task suggests that a part-based object representation might be a good approximation for the mechanisms of object detection in the human brain. The ability to model these mechanisms computationally further corroborates the neuroscience theory of part-based object detection strategies. This is encouraging, even though current methods cannot yet perform at the level of human vision.

We note that the correspondence between part-based models and human perception is a somewhat surprising one. At their core, the methods we used are based on HOG features that we expected to be highly dependent on image statistics. It was pleasantly surprising to observe the correlation between these methods, trained on natural images, and human perception on Cubist paintings with completely different statistics. We believe that better performance could be achieved using part-based models that rely on higher level features than HOG.

8   Conclusions

Since computer vision aims to attain not only the performance of human vision but also its flexibility and robustness, we should characterize our algorithms' performance on novel and extreme inputs. In this paper, we have argued that object detection under abstraction of object form is an example of a challenging perception task that existing image benchmarks do not properly evaluate. We have proposed Cubist paintings as an additional corpus for object detection, as they contain rearranged object parts that are nevertheless recognizable to the human visual system as whole objects. Using this dataset, our evaluation comparing human performance to that of various object detection methods demonstrates that part-based models are a step in the right direction for modeling human robustness to part-rearrangement, since their performance degrades comparably to humans as the abstractness in images increases. By showing that these models can be trained on photographic data yet still perform on abstract data we demonstrate that they are less over-fit to the natural world than template-based and deep models.

Part-reorganization in Cubism is one example that pushes the envelope of human perception, but there are other artistic movements with characteristic abstractions, such as the use of blurring in Impressionism, that would provide rich grounds for study. Future work in the design of computer vision methods should be cognizant of the limitations of traditional camera snapshot datasets and look for complementary resources when evaluating computational methods. Ultimately, a plethora of such resources should not only be used for testing, but must be combined into rich training datasets when designing methods that truly mimic the wide range of human perception.

Acknowledgments. The authors would like to thank Mark Lescroart for his guidance and advice throughout this project, Bharath Hariharan, Carl Doersch, Katerina Fragkiadaki and Emily Spratt for their insightful comments and Sean Arietta for his code. This material is based upon work supported by the National Science Foundation Graduate Research Fellowship under Grant No. DGE 1106400.

References

1. Akselrod-Ballin, A., Ullman, S.: Distinctive and compact features. Image and Vision Computing **26**(9), 1269–1276 (2008)
2. Bourdev, L., Malik, J.: Poselets: body part detectors trained using 3D human pose annotations. In: Proceedings of the IEEE International Conference on Computer Vision (ICCV), pp. 1365–1372 (2009)

3. Bourdev, L., Maji, S., Brox, T., Malik, J.: Detecting people using mutually consistent poselet activations. In: Daniilidis, K., Maragos, P., Paragios, N. (eds.) ECCV 2010, Part VI. LNCS, vol. 6316, pp. 168–181. Springer, Heidelberg (2010)

4. Dalal, N., Triggs, B.: Histograms of oriented gradients for human detection. In: Proceedings of the IEEE Conference on Computer Vision and Pattern Recognition (CVPR), vol. 2, pp. 886–893 (2005)

5. Doersch, C., Singh, S., Gupta, A., Sivic, J., Efros, A.A.: What makes paris look like paris? ACM Transactions on Graphics (SIGGRAPH) 31(4), 101:1–101:9 (2012)

6. Everingham, M., Van Gool, L., Williams, C.K.I., Winn, J., Zisserman, A.: The Pascal Visual Object Classes (VOC) Challenge. International Journal of Computer Vision 88(2), 303–338 (2010). http://www.pascal-network.org/challenges/VOC/voc2010/workshop/index.html

7. Felzenszwalb, P., Girshick, R., McAllester, D., Ramanan, D.: Object detection with discriminatively trained part based models. Pattern Analysis and Machine Intelligence (PAMI) 32(9) (2010)

8. Freiwald, W.A., Tsao, D.Y., Livingstone, M.S.: A Face Feature Space in the Macaque Temporal Lobe. Nature Neuroscience 12(9), 1187–1196 (2009)

9. Girshick, R., Donahue, J., Darrell, T., Malik, J.: Rich feature hierarchies for accurate object detection and semantic segmentation. In: Proceedings of the IEEE Conference on Computer Vision and Pattern Recognition (CVPR) (2014)

10. Girshick, R.B., Felzenszwalb, P.F., McAllester, D.: Discriminatively trained deformable part models, release 5. http://people.cs.uchicago.edu/~rbg/latent-release5/

11. Grill-Spector, K., Kushnir, T., Hendler, T.: A sequence of object-processing stages revealed by fMRI in the human occipital lobe. Human Brain Mapping 6(4), 316–328 (1998)

12. Hsiao, E., Efros, A.A.: DPM superhuman, slides 43–51. http://www.cs.cmu.edu/~efros/courses/LBMV09/presentations/latent_presentation.pdf

13. Ishai, A., Fairhall, S.L., Pepperell, R.: Perception, memory and aesthetics of indeterminate art. Brain Research Bulletin 73(4–6), 319–324 (2007)

14. Laporte, P.M.: Cubism and science. The Journal of Aesthetics and Art Criticism 7(3), 243–256 (1949)

15. Lewis, M.B., Edmonds, A.J.: Face detection: Mapping human performance. Perception 32(8), 903–920 (2003)

16. Nelson, R.C., Selinger, A.: A cubist approach to object recognition. In: Proceedings of the IEEE International Conference on Computer Vision (ICCV), pp. 614–621 (1998)

17. Sermanet, P., Eigen, D., Zhang, X., Mathieu, M., Fergus, R., LeCun, Y.: Overfeat: integrated recognition, localization and detection using convolutional networks. In: International Conference on Learning Representations (ICLR 2014). CBLS (2014)

18. Singh, S., Gupta, A., Efros, A.A.: Unsupervised discovery of mid-level discriminative patches. In: Fitzgibbon, A., Lazebnik, S., Perona, P., Sato, Y., Schmid, C. (eds.) ECCV 2012, Part II. LNCS, vol. 7573, pp. 73–86. Springer, Heidelberg (2012)

19. Sinha, P., Torralba, A.: Detecting faces in impoverished images. Journal of Vision 2(7) (2002)

20. Szegedy, C., Zaremba, W., Sutskever, I., Bruna, J., Erhan, D., Goodfellow, I.J., Fergus, R.: Intriguing properties of neural networks. CoRR abs/1312.6199 (2013)

21. Tsao, D.Y., Livingstone, M.S.: Mechanisms of face perception. Annual Review of Neuroscience **31**, 411–437 (2008)
22. Ullman, S., Vidal-Naquet, M., Sali, E.: Visual features of intermediate complexity and their use in classification. Nature Neuroscience **5**(7), 682–687 (2002)
23. Vogels, R.: Effect of image scrambling on inferior temporal cortical responses. Neuroreport **10**(9), 1811–1816 (1999)
24. Vondrick, C., Khosla, A., Malisiewicz, T., Torralba, A.: HOGgles: visualizing object detection features. In: Proceedings of the IEEE International Conference on Computer Vision (ICCV) (2013)
25. Wiesmann, M., Ishai, A.: Training facilitates object recognition in cubist paintings. Frontiers in Human Neuroscience **4**, 11 (2010)

Artistic Image Analysis
Using the Composition of Human Figures

Qian Chen and Gustavo Carneiro[✉]

Australian Centre for Visual Technologies, University of Adelaide, Adelaide, Australia
gustavo.carneiro@adelaide.edu.au

Abstract. Artistic image understanding is an interdisciplinary research field of increasing importance for the computer vision and art history communities. One of the goals of this field is the implementation of a system that can automatically retrieve and annotate artistic images. The best approach in the field explores the artistic influence among different artistic images using graph-based learning methodologies that take into consideration appearance and label similarities, but the current state-of-the-art results indicate that there seems to be lots of room for improvements in terms of retrieval and annotation accuracy. In order to improve those results, we introduce novel human figure composition features that can compute the similarity between artistic images based on the location and number (i.e., composition) of human figures. Our main motivation for developing such features lies in the importance that composition (particularly the composition of human figures) has in the analysis of artistic images when defining the visual classes present in those images. We show that the introduction of such features in the current dominant methodology of the field improves significantly the state-of-the-art retrieval and annotation accuracies on the PRINTART database, which is a public database exclusively composed of artistic images.

Keywords: Artistic image analysis · Image feature · Image annotation and retrieval

1 Introduction

Artistic image understanding is a research area gaining increasing importance in the field of computer vision, as evidenced by the recent two editions of the workshop VISART, which have been held in conjunction with the European Conference on Computer Vision (ECCV) in 2012 and 2014, and also the two editions of the conference SPIE Computer Vision and Image Analysis of Art, held in 2010 and 2011. There are a large number of problems involved in artistic image understanding, but this paper is focused on the tasks of retrieving and annotating artistic images. These problems can be defined as follows [1]: 1) given an artistic keyword, retrieve un-annotated test images that are related to that keyword, and 2) given a test image, automatically produce relevant annotations represented by artistic keywords. The current dominant method in the field [1,2]

© Springer International Publishing Switzerland 2015
L. Agapito et al. (Eds.): ECCV 2014 Workshops, Part I, LNCS 8925, pp. 117–132, 2015.
DOI: 10.1007/978-3-319-16178-5_8

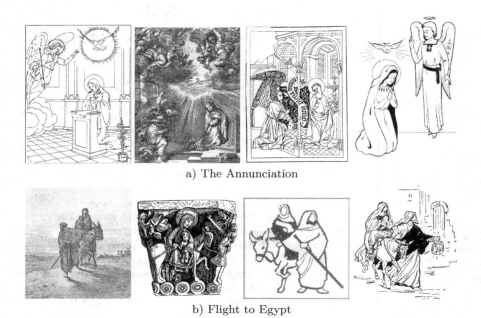

a) The Annunciation

b) Flight to Egypt

Fig. 1. Different artistic images depicting the theme "The Annunciation" (a) and "Flight to Egypt (b). Notice how the composition of human figures are quite similar among images of the same theme, where the "Annunciation" images show Angel Gabriel slightly elevated and Virgin Mary kneeling down at a relatively lower height; while the "Flight to Egypt" images show St. Joseph pulling a donkey, on which the Virgin Mary and baby Jesus are sitting. It is also worth noticing the low appearance similarity among artistic images of tha same theme (even though they have very similar annotations).

solves the two sub-problems above by exploring the artistic influence among different artistic prints with graph-based learning methodologies that take into consideration appearance and label similarities. However, the annotation and retrieval results reported show that there is quite a lot of room for improvement. For instance, the current retrieval and annotation results of this dominant method on the PRINTART database [1] show a mean average precision (MAP) of 0.18, an F1 score of 0.26 for class-based annotation, and an F1 score of 0.38 for example-based annotation.

In this paper we improve the retrieval and annotation accuracies of the methodology proposed by Carneiro et al. [1,2] with the use of a new type of feature that estimates the composition of human figures in the image. Our main motivation for exploring such feature lies in the fact that the composition of human figures of a scene depicted in an artistic image represents a powerful feature to be explored in its characterization. For instance, Figure 1 shows different prints of the same artistic themes ("The Annunciation" in (a) and "Flight to Egypt" in (b)), and although the texture of the images are quite different from each other (which makes the use of appearance similarity not quite useful), the composition of human figures are strikingly similar. The features that we propose explore different ways of representing the geometric distribution of human figures in the image, and we incorporate such features in the methodology by Carneiro et al. [1,2] when computing the similarity between images. We show that this new feature improves the retrieval and annotation accuracies of that methodology [1,2] on the PRINTART database [1]. Specifically, we show that the retrieval accuracy is improved by 44%, achieving an MAP of 0.26. In terms of class-based annotation, the results are improved by 46% for the average F1 score, which reaches the value of 0.38. Finally, the example-based annotation is improved by 32% in terms of the average F1 score, reaching 0.50.

2   Literature Review

The majority of works being published in computer vision on the topic of artistic image analysis annotation and retrieval is focused on the artistic identification problem with the goal of determining if a test image is an original work of art by a famous painter or is a fake [3–5]. Other works have also handled the problem of identifying stylistic patterns in paintings [6–8]. The automatic classification of Chinese paintings [9] and brushwork [10] also represent important contributions in this field. Nevertheless, most of these works can be regarded as successful adaptations of the content-based image retrieval systems [11] to these somewhat limited artistic image analysis problems, but a more deep interpretation of an artistic image, with the goal of annotating the image with global and local keywords [1], is still far from being possible.

One of the main reasons hindering the development in this area lies in the use of the aforementioned adaptations of systems developed for analyzing photos, but it is important to note that the analysis of photos and artistic image are intrinsically different problems. For example, the photo of a face has arguably fewer degrees of freedom when compared to an artistic representation of a face (drawing, printing), as exemplified in Figure 2. Specifically, notice how the face proportions and geometry are different among the artistic faces. Another compelling example presented by Carneiro [2] and reproduced here in Figure 3 is the variation in the representation of the visual class "sea" among different paintings. Simply building a classifier that identifies if a pixel (or an image patch) belongs to the visual class "sea" (similarly to what is done in typical computer vision analysis of photos [11]) cannot work in these examples due to lack of a consistent representation of the visual class "sea" among different works of art.

The examples in Figure 2-3 indicate that the analysis of artistic images must follow a different development path compared to the usual photo analysis. In particular, we believe that the analysis of artistic images must explore the influence between artistic works, which suffer small variations over the course of time. This idea has been explored by Carneiro et al. [1,2], by Abe et al. [12] and by

Fig. 2. Comparison between images of real faces (top row) and artistic representation of faces (bottom row). Notice that artistic faces have an arguably larger number of degrees of freedom in the sense that the face proportions and geometry can vary substantially among the artistic faces.

(a)   (b)   (c)   (d)

Fig. 3. Different paintings showing the visual class "sea" with different patterns of color and texture. In (a), we show Pieter Brueghel il Giovane's *Christ on the Storm on the Sea of Galilee*; in (b) we have Claude Monet's *Shadows on the Sea*";(c) shows August Renoir's *"Oarsmen Chatou"*; and (d) displays John Marin's *Sea Piece*. Figure from [2].

Graham et al. [6]. In the work by Carneiro et al. [1,2], they explore link analysis algorithms (a.k.a. graph-based learning methods) that compute the similarity between images using global image representation (based on bag of features) and expert annotation. On the other hand, Abe et al. [12] explores high and low-level image features and Graham et al. [6] proposes the use of several image statistics. Nevertheless, we also believe that the analysis of artistic images must also explore the composition of human figures in the image, which is a feature that has not been explored in the field, to the best of our knowledge.

3   Methodology

We first explain the database PRINTART [1] and the original image representation available with the database, then we present the new human figure compo-

Visitation (theme),	Judith (theme),	Holy Family (theme),
Mary, St. Elizabeth	Holofernes, Judith,	Christ-child, Mary
Zacharias	Maid servant	St. Joseph

Fig. 4. Example of global (text below the image) and face (red bounding box) annotations of the PRINTART images (from Artstor [13]) produced by an art historian. Note that the classes identified with '(theme)' in brackets represent the multi-class problems defined in Sec. 3.1.

sition features and how they are incorporated into the methodology developed by Carneiro et al. [1,2]. It is important to note that the detection of faces from artistic images is a relatively easier problem compared to the detection of human bodies, so hereafter we use faces as a proxy for the presence and location of human figures in an image.

3.1 Database PRINTART

The PRINTART database [1] contains 988 artistic images with global and face annotations (see Fig. 4). These images have been acquired from the Artstor digital image library [13] and annotated by art historians with global annotation keywords, representing one multi-class problem (theme with 27 classes) and 48 binary problems, and face annotations, representing the main characters relevant for the theme of the image.

The training set is defined with $\mathcal{D} = \{(\mathbf{x}_i, \mathbf{y}_i, \mathcal{P}_i)\}_{i=1}^{|\mathcal{D}|}$, where $\mathbf{x}_i \in \mathbb{R}^X$ represents the feature extracted from the image I_i, $\mathbf{y}_i$ denotes the global annotation of that image representing M multi-class and binary problems, and $\mathcal{P}_i$ represents the annotated faces in the image. Hence, $\mathbf{y}_i = [\mathbf{y}_i(1), ..., \mathbf{y}_i(M)] \in \{0,1\}^Y$, with each problem being denoted by $\mathbf{y}_i(k) \in \{0,1\}^{|\mathbf{y}_i(k)|}$ and $|\mathbf{y}_i(k)|$ representing the dimensionality of $\mathbf{y}_i(k)$ (i.e., $|\mathbf{y}_i(k)| = 1$ for binary problems, $|\mathbf{y}_i(k)| > 1$ with $\|\mathbf{y}_i\|_1 = 1$ for multi-class problems, $Y = 75$, and $M = 49$ with one multi-class problem (with 27 classes) and 48 binary problems). In other words, the binary problems are about the detection of a visual class (i.e., their presence or absence), and the multi-class problem (representing the image theme) considers the identification of which class is relevant in the image (assuming that one of the classes must be present). Finally, the set $\mathcal{P}_i = \{\mathbf{b}_{i,j}\}_{j=1}^{|\mathcal{P}_i|}$ denotes the face annotation in image I_i, where $\mathbf{b}_{i,j} \in \mathbb{R}^4$ denotes the bounding box (with two 2-D image coordinates) of the face j and $|\mathcal{P}_i|$ denotes the number of faces in image I_i. The test set is represented by $\mathcal{T} = \{(\widetilde{\mathbf{x}}_i, \widetilde{\mathbf{y}}_i, \widetilde{\mathcal{P}}_i)\}_{i=1}^{|\mathcal{T}|}$, with $\widetilde{\mathbf{x}}_i$ denoting the features of test image $\widetilde{I}_i$, $\widetilde{\mathbf{y}}_i$ representing the global annotation of the test image (available in order to compute the retrieval and annotation accuracies), and $\widetilde{\mathcal{P}}_i$ denoting the estimated faces. It it also important to note that there is no overlap between the training and test sets, which means that $\mathcal{D} \bigcap \mathcal{T} = \emptyset$. The union of $\mathcal{D}$ and $\mathcal{T}$ produces the full PRINTART dataset with 988 images (i.e., $|\mathcal{D} \bigcup \mathcal{T}| = 988$). The label cardinality of the database, computed as $LC = \frac{1}{|\mathcal{D}|+|\mathcal{T}|} \sum_{i=1}^{|\mathcal{D}|+|\mathcal{T}|} \|\mathbf{y}_i\|_1$, is 4.22, while the label density $LD = \frac{1}{(|\mathcal{D}|+|\mathcal{T}|)Y} \sum_{i=1}^{|\mathcal{D}|+|\mathcal{T}|} \|\mathbf{y}_i\|_1$, is 0.05.

The images in the PRINTART database use the standard bag of features (BoF) representation, which is publicly available from the PRINTART web site [1]. More specifically, 10000 SIFT descriptors [14] are extracted from a uniform grid over the image and scale spaces and a spatial pyramid [15] is used to form the image representation. The spatial pyramid representation is achieved by tiling the image in the following three levels, [16]: 1) the first level comprising the whole image, 2) the second level dividing the image into 2×2 regions, and 3) the third level breaking the image into 3×1 regions. Another important part of the BoF representation is the implementation of the visual vocabulary, which is built with the hierarchical clustering algorithm with three levels, where each node in the hierarchy has 10 descendants [17]. This means that the resulting directed tree has $1 + 10 + 100 + 1000 = 1111$ vertexes, and the image feature is formed by using each descriptor of the image to traverse the tree and record the path (note that each descriptor generates a path with 4 vertexes). Each SIFT descriptor from the image is then represented by four votes (weighted by the node entropy) in a histogram of the visited vertexes (containing 1111 bins). Using this hierarchical tree (with a total of 1111 vertexes) and the tiling described above (with 8 tiles), an image is represented with 8 histograms as in $\mathbf{x} \in \mathbb{R}^X$, where $X = 8 \times 1111$.

3.2   Human Figure Composition Features

In this section, we propose three different types of features that represent the human figure composition in an image. Note that to build these features, we assume that the faces detected from image I_i are represented with $\mathcal{P}_i = \{\mathbf{b}_{i,j}\}_{j=1}^{|\mathcal{P}_i|}$, as defined above.

Symmetry Robust Feature. It is important to notice that images annotated with the same theme (i.e., the multi-class problem in Sec. 3.1) present similar distribution of faces in the image (see Fig. 1), but it is also common to see a mirrored representation of the faces, such as the ones in Figure 5-(a). This is the motivation for the design of this feature, which is based on first, splitting the image into two halves (using the vertical line that divides the image into two halves) then sub-dividing each half into four regions, as shown in Fig. 5-(b). Finally, the feature is based on a histogram of five bins that represent the number of faces lying in each region and at the center of the image, but in order to

a) Mirrored versions of the same theme   b) Symmetry robust feature

Fig. 5. Mirrored distribution of human figures on images from the same theme (in this case, the theme is 'Holy Family') in (a) and the depiction of the symmetry robust feature representation (b).

make the feature robust to symmetric transformations, the symmetrically equivalent regions in both (vertical) halves have the same label, and are consequently represented by the same bin in the histogram (see vector $\mathbf{f}_i^{(1)}$ in Fig. 5-(b) that takes 0 faces from the centre, 1 face from R1 and 2 faces from R4). Assume that the histogram from this feature is represented by the vector $\mathbf{f}_i^{(1)} \in \mathbb{R}^5$, extracted with $\mathbf{f}_i^{(1)} = \phi_1(I_i, \mathcal{P}_i)$.

Relative Face Location Robust Feature. The number and relative location of faces with respect to one another is also a powerful representation of the composition of human figures in an image. For instance, consider the two images in Fig. 6, which shows two images from theme 'Magi'. Notice that even though the absolute location of faces are different in the two images, the number of human faces are the same and their relative locations are quite similar. Specifically in Fig. 6-(a), notice that there are always three faces at a relatively higher position, almost lying in a horizontal line (see the red-contour faces), and three faces at a lower position (see the yellow-contour faces). We propose the following algorithm to build a representation for this relative face location robust feature (Fig. 6-(b)): 1) select three faces in the image and draw a circle that pass through the center of the bounding box of all faces; 2) divide the circle into five regions and count the number of faces lying in each region (not only the three faces used to draw the circle); 3) repeat steps (1) and (2) for all sets of three faces and accumulate all results. In case only two faces are available, just draw a circle that passes through the center of the two faces, divide it in five regions and record the bins where the two faces reside (similarly to what is done for three faces - Fig. 6-(b)). Finally, for the case when only one face is available just build a vector with bin 1 equal to 1. Assume that the histogram from this feature is represented by the vector $\mathbf{f}_i^{(2)} \in \mathbb{R}^5$, extracted with $\mathbf{f}_i^{(2)} = \phi_2(I_i, \mathcal{P}_i)$.

a) Relative distribution of faces　　b) Relative face location robust feature

Fig. 6. Relative distribution of faces in images of the same theme ('Magi') in (a) and an example of one step of the algorithm to build the relative face location robust feature (b). Note that in this image, our proposed algorithm will run for four steps to get all sets of three faces in the image (i.e., 4 choose 3).

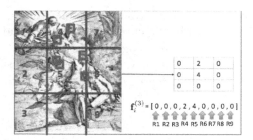

Fig. 7. Rule of thirds applied to the distribution of faces

Rule of Thirds Feature. The rule of thirds is a well-used composition technique that can also be applied to estimate the distribution of human figures in an artistic image. The technique is essentially about dividing the image into a 3×3 tiling and placing the important objects of the scene along these divisions. Our proposed representation consists of first dividing the image into a 3×3 tiling and then counting the number of faces lying in each one of these regions, as shown in Figure 7. Similarly to the features presented above, this feature is also represented by a histogram, where each bin contains the number of faces in each bin. Assume that the histogram from this feature is represented by the vector $\mathbf{f}_i^{(3)} \in \mathbb{R}^9$, extracted with $\mathbf{f}_i^{(3)} = \phi_3(I_i, \mathcal{P}_i)$.

3.3　Similarity Between Human Figure Distribution Features

The similarity between images I_i and I_k (with detected faces represented by the sets $\mathcal{P}_i$ and $\mathcal{P}_k$, respectively) with respect to the three human figure composition features defined above in Sec. 3.2 is computed with the following equation:

$$s_p(i, k) = \exp\left\{-\frac{1}{\lambda}\left(\alpha\|\mathbf{f}_i^{(1)} - \mathbf{f}_k^{(1)}\|_2^2 + \beta\|\mathbf{f}_i^{(2)} - \mathbf{f}_k^{(2)}\|_2^2 + \gamma\|\mathbf{f}_i^{(3)} - \mathbf{f}_k^{(3)}\|_2^2\right)\right\}, \quad (1)$$

where α, β, γ are the weights controlling the importance of each one of the features, λ is a weight controlling the slope of the function $s(.,.)$, and $\mathbf{f}_i^{(1)}, \mathbf{f}_i^{(2)}, \mathbf{f}_i^{(3)}$ are defined in Section 3.2. Also, assume that the similarity between a training image I_i, with face bounding boxes represented by $\mathcal{P}_i$, and a test image $\widetilde{I}$, with face bounding boxes $\widetilde{\mathcal{P}}$, is denoted by $s_p(i, \sim)$.

3.4 Incorporation of Human Figure Distribution Similarity

Following the notation by Carneiro [2], the annotation of a test image $\widetilde{I}$, represented by $(\widetilde{\mathbf{x}}, \widetilde{\mathcal{P}})$ from the test set $\mathcal{T}$ is achieved by finding $\widetilde{\mathbf{y}}^*$ that solves the following optimization problem:

$$\begin{aligned} &\text{maximize } p(\mathbf{y}|\widetilde{\mathbf{x}}, \widetilde{\mathcal{P}}) \\ &\text{subject to } \mathbf{y} = [\mathbf{y}(1), ..., \mathbf{y}(M)] \in \{0, 1\}^Y, \\ &\qquad \|\mathbf{y}(k)\|_1 = 1 \text{ for } \{k \in \{1, ..., M\}|\|\mathbf{y}(k)| > 1\}, \end{aligned} \quad (2)$$

where $p(\mathbf{y}|\widetilde{\mathbf{x}}, \widetilde{\mathcal{P}})$ is a probability function that computes the confidence of annotating the test image with a vector $\mathbf{y} \in \mathcal{Y}$ (with $\mathcal{Y}$ denoting the set of all possible annotations $\mathbf{y}$ in the training set). The retrieval problem is solved by building a set of test images that are relevant to a query $\mathbf{q} \in \{0, 1\}^Y$, as follows:

$$\mathcal{Q}(\mathbf{q}, \tau) = \{(\widetilde{\mathbf{x}}, \widetilde{\mathbf{y}}^*, \widetilde{\mathcal{P}})|(\widetilde{\mathbf{x}}, \widetilde{\mathcal{P}}) \in \mathcal{T}, (\mathbf{q}^\top\widetilde{\mathbf{y}}^*) > 0, p(\widetilde{\mathbf{y}}^*|\widetilde{\mathbf{x}}, \widetilde{\mathcal{P}}) > \tau\}, \quad (3)$$

where $\widetilde{\mathbf{y}}^*$ is obtained from (2), $\tau \in [0, 1]$ is a threshold, and $\mathcal{T}$ is the set of test images defined in Sec. 3.1.

We incorporate the similarity between human figure composition features (1) into the inverse label propagation framework [2], which basically takes a test image represented by $(\widetilde{\mathbf{x}}, \widetilde{\mathcal{P}})$ and ranks the most relevant training images $(\mathbf{x}, \mathbf{y}, \mathcal{P}) \in \mathcal{D}$ via a random walk process, which uses a graph $\mathcal{G} = (\mathcal{V}, \mathcal{E})$ built with the training set $\mathcal{D}$, where the nodes $\mathcal{V}$ represent the images and the weights of each edge in $\mathcal{E}$ are computed based on the appearance, label and human figure composition similarities between training images. Then given a test image in $\mathcal{T}$, represented by $(\widetilde{\mathbf{x}}, \widetilde{\mathcal{P}})$, we start a random walk process in this graph by taking into account the appearance and human figure composition similarities between the test image and training images. Carneiro [2] proposes three different ways to solve this process, and we follow the *combinatorial harmonics*, which shows the best performance among the proposed methods.

The random walk process based on the combinatory harmonics estimates the probability of first reaching each of the database samples $(\mathbf{x}_i, \mathbf{y}_i, \mathcal{P}_i) \in \mathcal{D}$ starting from the test image $(\widetilde{\mathbf{x}}, \widetilde{\mathcal{P}})$ [18], using the following adjacency matrix:
$\widetilde{\mathbf{W}} = \begin{bmatrix} \mathbf{W} & \widetilde{\mathbf{w}} \\ \widetilde{\mathbf{w}}^T & 0 \end{bmatrix}$, where $\widetilde{\mathbf{w}} = [s_x(\mathbf{x}_1, \widetilde{\mathbf{x}})s_p(1, \sim), ..., s_x(\mathbf{x}_{|\mathcal{D}|}, \widetilde{\mathbf{x}})s_p(\mathbf{x}_{|\mathcal{D}|}, \sim)]^\top$ (note that $s_p(1, \sim)$ is defined in (1)), and

$$\mathbf{W}(i, j) = s_y(\mathbf{y}_i, \mathbf{y}_j)s_x(\mathbf{x}_i, \mathbf{x}_j)s_p(i, j)s_x(\mathbf{x}_i, \widetilde{\mathbf{x}})s_p(i, \sim). \quad (4)$$

where the label similarity function is the Jaccard index defined by $s_y(\mathbf{y}_i, \mathbf{y}_j) = \frac{\mathbf{y}_i^\top \mathbf{y}_j}{\|\mathbf{y}_i\|^2 + \|\mathbf{y}_j\|^2 - \mathbf{y}_i^\top \mathbf{y}_j}$, and the feature similarity function is the histogram intersection defined as $s_x(\mathbf{x}_i, \mathbf{x}_j) = \sum_{d=1}^X \min(\mathbf{x}_i(d), \mathbf{x}_j(d))$ (i.e., this is the histogram intersection kernel over the spatial pyramid, where $\|\mathbf{x}\|_1 = 1$). The goal is then to find the distribution $\mathbf{g}^* \in \mathbb{R}^{|\mathcal{D}|}$ ($\|\mathbf{g}^*\|_1 = 1$), representing the probability of first reaching each of the training images in a random walk procedure, where the labeling matrix $\mathbf{G} = \mathbf{I}$ (i.e., an $|\mathcal{D}| \times |\mathcal{D}|$ identity matrix) denotes a problem with $|\mathcal{D}|$ classes, with each training image representing a separate class. The estimation of $\mathbf{g}^*$ is based on the minimization of the following function:

$$E([\mathbf{G}, \mathbf{g}]) = \frac{1}{2} \left\| [\mathbf{G}, \mathbf{g}] \widetilde{\mathbf{L}} \begin{bmatrix} \mathbf{G}^T \\ \mathbf{g}^T \end{bmatrix} \right\|_2^2, \tag{5}$$

where $\widetilde{\mathbf{L}} = \widetilde{\mathbf{D}} - \widetilde{\mathbf{W}}$ is the Laplacian matrix computed from the the adjacency matrix $\widetilde{\mathbf{W}}$, where $\widetilde{\mathbf{D}}$ is a matrix that has the sum of the rows in the diagonal (i.e., it is a diagonal matrix). This Laplacian matrix can be divided into blocks of the same sizes as in $\widetilde{\mathbf{W}}$, that is $\widetilde{\mathbf{L}} = \begin{bmatrix} \mathbf{L}_1 & \mathbf{B} \\ \mathbf{B}^T & \mathbf{L}_2 \end{bmatrix}$. Solving the following optimization problem produces $\mathbf{g}^*$ [18]:

$$\begin{aligned} & \text{minimize} \quad E([\mathbf{G}, \mathbf{g}]) \\ & \text{subject to} \quad \mathbf{G} = \mathbf{I}, \end{aligned} \tag{6}$$

which has the closed form solution [18]: $\mathbf{g}^* = (-\mathbf{L}_2^{-1}\mathbf{B}^T\mathbf{I})^\top$. Note that $\mathbf{g}^* \in [0, 1]^{|\mathcal{D}|}$ and $\|\mathbf{g}^*\|_1 = 1$.

The probability of annotation $\mathbf{y}$ is then computed from the test image with:

$$p(\mathbf{y}|\widetilde{\mathbf{x}}, \widetilde{\mathcal{P}}) = Z \sum_{i=1}^{|\mathcal{D}|} \mathbf{g}^*(i) p(\mathbf{y}|(\mathbf{x}_i, \mathbf{y}_i, \mathcal{P}_i)) \tag{7}$$

where $\mathbf{g}^*(i)$ is the ith component of the solution vector from (6), $p(\mathbf{y}|(\mathbf{x}_i, \mathbf{y}_i, \mathcal{P}_i)) = \frac{\delta(\|\mathbf{y} - \mathbf{y}_i\|_1)}{\sum_{j=1}^{|\mathcal{D}|} \delta(\|\mathbf{y} - \mathbf{y}_j\|_1)}$ [2] ($\delta(.)$ is the delta function), and Z is a normalization factor. In the experiments presented below in Sec. 4, this method is called 'FACGT' in case we use the manual face annotations and 'FAC++' or 'FACVJ' if we use the automated face detection Face++ [19] or Viola and Jones [20], respectively.

4   Experiments

Using the PRINTART database [1] and the setup described below, we measure the performance of the annotation methodologies with one type of retrieval and two types of annotation evaluations. The *retrieval* evaluation is based on the following precision and recall measures [21] computed with the first $Q \leq |\mathcal{T}|$

images retrieved with respect to query $\mathbf{q}$ (sorted by $p(\widetilde{\mathbf{y}}^*|\widetilde{\mathbf{x}}, \widetilde{\mathcal{P}})$ in (3) in descending order, where $\mathbf{q}^\top \widetilde{\mathbf{y}}^*) > 0$):

$$p_r(\mathbf{q}, Q) = \frac{\sum_{i=1}^Q \delta(\widetilde{\mathbf{y}}_i^\top \mathbf{q} - \mathbf{1}^\top \mathbf{q})}{Q}, \text{ and } r_r(\mathbf{q}, Q) = \frac{\sum_{i=1}^Q \delta(\widetilde{\mathbf{y}}_i^\top \mathbf{q} - \mathbf{1}^\top \mathbf{q})}{\sum_{j=1}^{|\mathcal{T}|} \delta(\widetilde{\mathbf{y}}_j^\top \mathbf{q} - \mathbf{1}^\top \mathbf{q})}, \quad (8)$$

where $\delta(.)$ is the delta function. The retrieval task is assessed with the mean average precision (MAP), which is defined as the average precision over all queries, at the ranks where recall changes.

The annotation of a test image, represented by $(\widetilde{\mathbf{x}}, \widetilde{\mathcal{P}})$, is computed by finding $\widetilde{\mathbf{y}}^*$ that solves the optimization problem (2). The first type of annotation evaluation, called *label-based* annotation [21], is computed for each class $y \in \{1, ..., Y\}$ with the respective precision, recall and F1 measures:

$$p_c(y) = \frac{\sum_{i=1}^{|\mathcal{T}|} (\pi_y \odot \widetilde{\mathbf{y}}_i^*)^\top \widetilde{\mathbf{y}}_i}{\sum_{i=1}^{|\mathcal{T}|} \pi_y^\top \widetilde{\mathbf{y}}_i^*}, \quad r_c(y) = \frac{\sum_{i=1}^{|\mathcal{T}|} (\pi_y \odot \widetilde{\mathbf{y}}_i^*)^\top \widetilde{\mathbf{y}}_i}{\sum_{i=1}^{|\mathcal{T}|} \pi_y^\top \widetilde{\mathbf{y}}_i}, \quad f_c(y) = \frac{2pga(y)rga(y)}{pga(y)+rga(y)}, \quad (9)$$

where $\pi_y \in \{0, 1\}^Y$ is one at the yth position and zero elsewhere, and $\odot$ represents the element-wise multiplication operator. The values of $pga(y)$, $rga(y)$ and $fga(y)$ are then averaged over the visual classes. The measure in (9) is called *label-based* because the result is assessed class by class, independently. On the other hand, the *example-based* annotation computes an image-based performance considering all labels jointly (i.e., a multi-label evaluation). Example-based annotation evaluation is computed for each test image and then averaged over the test set with respect to precision, recall, F1 and accuracy measures, which are respectively defined by [21]:

$$\begin{aligned} p_e &= \frac{1}{|\mathcal{T}|} \sum_{i=1}^{|\mathcal{T}|} \frac{(\widetilde{\mathbf{y}}_i^*)^\top \widetilde{\mathbf{y}}_i}{\|\widetilde{\mathbf{y}}_i^*\|_1}, & r_e &= \frac{1}{|\mathcal{T}|} \sum_{i=1}^{|\mathcal{T}|} \frac{(\widetilde{\mathbf{y}}_i^*)^\top \widetilde{\mathbf{y}}_i}{\|\widetilde{\mathbf{y}}_i\|_1}, \\ f_e &= \frac{1}{|\mathcal{T}|} \sum_{i=1}^{|\mathcal{T}|} \frac{2(\widetilde{\mathbf{y}}_i^*)^\top \widetilde{\mathbf{y}}_i}{\|\widetilde{\mathbf{y}}_i^*\|_1 + \|\widetilde{\mathbf{y}}_i\|_1}, & a_e &= \frac{1}{|\mathcal{T}|} \sum_{i=1}^{|\mathcal{T}|} \frac{(\widetilde{\mathbf{y}}_i^*)^\top \widetilde{\mathbf{y}}_i}{\|\min(1, \widetilde{\mathbf{y}}_i^* + \widetilde{\mathbf{y}}_i)\|_1}. \end{aligned} \quad (10)$$

We follow the same experimental setup proposed by Carneiro [2], with a 10-fold cross validation, where the PRINTART database is divided into a training set $\mathcal{D}$ with 90% of the database (i.e., $|\mathcal{D}| = 889$), and a test set $\mathcal{T}$ with the remaining 10% (i.e., $|\mathcal{T}| = 99$). We compute the retrieval and annotation evaluation measures (8)-(10) and display the results using the average and standard deviation in this 10-fold cross validation experiment. We use the same acronyms for the methodologies defined in [2], as follows: inverse label propagation (ILP), combinatorial harmonics (CH), stationary solution (SS), random walk (RW), bag of features (BoF), label propagation (LP), class label correlation (CC), matrix completion (MC), structural learning (SL), random (RND), and nearest neighbor (NN). In addition, the methods proposed in this paper are labeled 'FACGT' for the ones that uses the manual face annotations, and 'FAC++' or 'FACVJ' for the ones using automated face detection. Note that for the FAC++, we use the face detection 'Face++' [19] (available from http://www.faceplusplus.com/), which has produced state of the art face detection results in recent challenges. Essentially, Face++ is based on a multi-scale convolutional neural network methodology, and on the PRINTART database it produces an average precision of 0.75

a) Face++ [19]   b) Viola and Jones (OpenCV) [20]

Fig. 8. Example of face detection results from Face++ [19] (a) and Viola and Jones (OpenCV) [20] (b)

and recall 0.11 for the face detection problem (i.e., quite high precision, but relatively low recall - see Fig. 8-(a) for an example produced by the Face++ detector). For 'FACVJ', we use the classic Viola and Jones face detector [20] (available from OpenCV - http://opencv.org/), which has a relatively poor performance on PRINTART with a precision of 0.17 and recall also of 0.17 for the face detection problem (see Fig. 8-(b) for an example produced by the Viola and Jones detector).

Finally, the values of α, β, γ in (1) are estimated via the 10-fold cross validation experiment explained above, with $\alpha, \beta, \gamma \in [0, 1]$. Note that different values of α, β, γ are estimated for each one of the proposed methods FACGT, FAC++ and FACVJ. The value of λ in (1) is estimated as follows: $\lambda = \kappa(\alpha\sqrt{5} + \beta\sqrt{5} + \gamma\sqrt{9})$, where $\kappa \in [0, 1]$ is also estimated via cross validation and the constants $\sqrt{5}$ and $\sqrt{9}$ are related to the number of dimensions of the respective human figure composition features, defined in Sec. 3.2.

4.1 Results

Table 4.1 shows the retrieval and annotation results (8)-(10) for all methodologies from [2] and the methodologies FACGT, FAC++ and FACVJ proposed in this paper. Note that the methodology ILP-CH currently holds the state-of-the-art results for the PRINTART database. Figure 9 compares the annotation results between the proposed FACGT and ILP-CH, for cases where FACGT improves the results produced by the ILP-CH.

5   Discussion

According to the results in Sec. 4.1, we can conclude that for the database PRINTART used in this paper, the method that uses the manually annotated

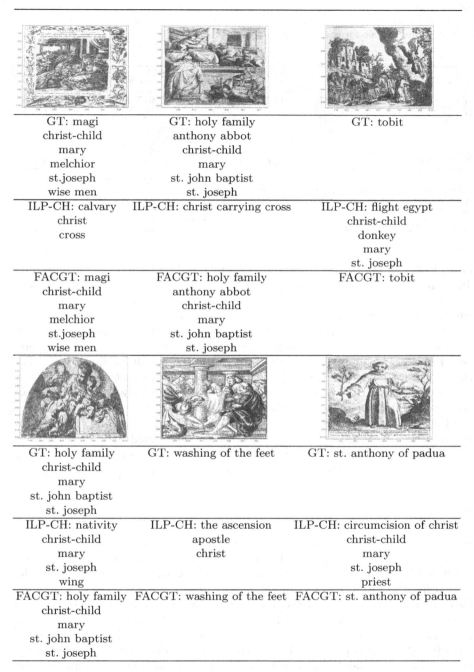

Fig. 9. Sample results on PRINTART showing the annotations from the ground truth (GT), the previously best method ILP-CH [2], and our proposed approach FACGT

Table 1. Retrieval, label-based and example-based results using the mean and standard deviation of the measures described in Sec. 4. The highlighted value in each column indicates the highest for each measure.

Models	Retrieval Label MAP	Label-based annotation			Example-based annotation			
		Average Precision	Average Recall	Average F1	Average Precision	Average Recall	Average F1	Average Accuracy
FACGT	**0.26 ± .03**	**0.39 ± .05**	**0.37 ± .06**	**0.38 ± .05**	**0.51 ± .04**	**0.50 ± .05**	**0.50 ± .04**	**0.45 ± .04**
FAC++	0.18 ± .03	0.25 ± .05	0.23 ± .03	0.24 ± .04	0.37 ± .03	0.37 ± .04	0.36 ± .03	0.31 ± .03
FACVJ	0.13 ± .02	0.16 ± .03	0.16 ± .04	0.16 ± .03	0.31 ± .03	0.31 ± .03	0.30 ± .03	0.25 ± .03
ILP-CH	0.18 ± .04	0.26 ± .05	0.26 ± .05	0.26 ± .05	0.39 ± .03	0.39 ± .04	0.38 ± .03	0.33 ± .03
ILP-SS	0.12 ± .01	0.15 ± .02	0.16 ± .05	0.15 ± .04	0.24 ± .04	0.24 ± .04	0.23 ± .04	0.20 ± .04
ILP-RW	0.10 ± .01	0.10 ± .03	0.13 ± .02	0.11 ± .03	0.33 ± .03	0.36 ± .03	0.34 ± .03	0.26 ± .03
BoF	0.12 ± .05	0.14 ± .11	0.10 ± .06	0.11 ± .08	0.47 ± .05	0.26 ± .08	0.30 ± .05	0.23 ± .05
LP	0.11 ± .01	0.12 ± .02	0.12 ± .02	0.12 ± .02	0.32 ± .03	0.28 ± .02	0.26 ± .02	0.19 ± .01
LP-CC	0.11 ± .01	0.13 ± .02	0.14 ± .02	0.13 ± .02	0.27 ± .03	0.26 ± .03	0.25 ± .03	0.18 ± .02
MC	0.17 ± .01	0.24 ± .03	0.11 ± .02	0.15 ± .02	0.47 ± .03	0.28 ± .02	0.32 ± .02	0.25 ± .02
SL	0.14 ± .01	0.20 ± .04	0.15 ± .03	0.17 ± .03	0.37 ± .04	0.32 ± .03	0.34 ± .03	0.28 ± .03
RND	0.08 ± .06	0.06 ± .01	0.07 ± .01	0.06 ± .01	0.26 ± .02	0.21 ± .01	0.22 ± .01	0.15 ± .01
NN	0.13 ± .01	0.17 ± .02	0.17 ± .04	0.17 ± .03	0.32 ± .04	0.32 ± .03	0.31 ± .03	0.26 ± .03

faces, FACGT, improves substantially the retrieval and annotation results produced by the previously best method ILP-CH. Thus we can conclude that there is enough evidence to accept the main hypothesis being tested by this paper, which is that the use of human figure composition improves the classification of artistic images. Nevertheless, when using actual face detection systems, the results are either comparable to ILP-CH (see the results for FAC++) or worse (see FAVJ). The main issue with these detectors lies in its quite low recall (below 0.2 for both detectors) and low precision (for the case of FACVJ). It is worth mentioning that we have tried most of the state-of-the-art face detectors that are publicly available, and these two are the ones with the best results on the PRINTART database. That relatively low perfomance can be explained by the fact that faces in artistic images are less constrained mainly in terms of geometric distribution of facial features (see Fig. 2), and consequently the generalization of current face detectors to this new domain is not straightforward.

6   Conclusion

In this paper we show that by exploring the composition of human figures in artistic prints, we can produce the currently best results on the PRINTART database. This shows empirically that this composition is in fact decisive for estimating the visual classes present in artistic images. Furthermore, we show that the current best face detectors in the field are not reliable enough to be used in this new domain of artistic image analysis. Therefore, there is plenty of room for improvement in this area of face detection from artistic images, where faces like the ones displayed in Fig. 2 can be reliably detected. We plan to adapt current face detectors by re-trainiing them using artistic images. Finally, given the positive results shown by the proposed composition of human figures, we also plan to explore other types of composition techniques, such as the rule of odds, composition of the eye gazing of human figures, and depth and pictorial cues (depth, illumination, depth, etc.) [22].

References

1. Carneiro, G., da Silva, N.P., Del Bue, A., Costeira, J.P.: Artistic image classification: an analysis on the PRINTART database. In: Fitzgibbon, A., Lazebnik, S., Perona, P., Sato, Y., Schmid, C. (eds.) ECCV 2012, Part IV. LNCS, vol. 7575, pp. 143–157. Springer, Heidelberg (2012)
2. Carneiro, G.: Artistic image analysis using graph-based learning approaches. IEEE Transactions on Image Processing **22**(8), 3168–3178 (2013)
3. Berezhnoy, I., Postma, E., van den Herik, H.: Computerized visual analysis of paintings. In: Int. Conf. Association for History and Computing, pp. 28–32 (2005)
4. Lyu, S., Rockmore, D., Farid, H.: A digital technique for art authentication. Proceedings of the National Academy of Sciences USA **101**(49), 17006–17010 (2004)
5. Polatkan, G., Jafarpour, S., Brasoveanu, A., Hughes, S., Daubechies, I.: Detection of forgery in paintings using supervised learning. In: International Conference on Image Processing (2009)
6. Graham, D., Friedenberg, J., Rockmore, D., Field, D.: Mapping the similarity space of paintings: image statistics and visual perception. Visual Cognition **18**(4), 559–573 (2010)
7. Hughes, J., Graham, D., Rockmore, D.: Stylometrics of artwork: uses and limitations. In: Proceedings of SPIE: Computer Vision and Image Analysis of Art (2010)
8. Jafarpour, S., Polatkan, G., Daubechies, I., Hughes, S., Brasoveanu, A.: Stylistic analysis of paintings using wavelets and machine learning. In: European Signal Processing Conference (2009)
9. Li, J., Wang, J.: Studying digital imagery of ancient paintings by mixtures of stochastic models. IEEE Trans. Image Processing **13**(3), 340–353 (2004)
10. Yelizaveta, M., Tat-Seng, C., Jain, R.: Semi-supervised annotation of brushwork in paintings domain using serial combinations of multiple experts. In: ACM Multimedia, pp. 529–538 (2006)
11. Datta, R., Joshi, D., Li, J., Wang, J.: Image retrieval: Ideas, influences, and trends of the new age. ACM Comput. Surv. **40**(2) (2008)
12. Abe, K., Saleh, B., Elgammal, A.: An early framework for determining artistic influence. In: Petrosino, A., Maddalena, L., Pala, P. (eds.) ICIAP 2013. LNCS, vol. 8158, pp. 198–207. Springer, Heidelberg (2013)
13. http://www.artstor.org
14. Lowe, D.: Distinctive image features from scale-invariant keypoints. International Journal of Computer Vision (2004). (paper accepted for publication)
15. Lazebnik, S., Schmid, C., Ponce, J.: Beyond bags of features, spatial pyramid matching for recognizing natural scene categories. In: CVPR (2006)
16. http://pascallin.ecs.soton.ac.uk/challenges/VOC/
17. Nistér, D., Stewénius, H.: Scalable recognition with a vocabulary tree. In: CVPR, pp. 2161–2168 (2006)
18. Grady, L.: Random walks for image segmentation. IEEE Trans. Pattern Anal. Mach. Intell. **28**(11), 1768–1783 (2006)
19. Fan, H., Cao, Z., Jiang, Y., Yin, Q., Doudou, C.: Learning deep face representation. arXiv preprint arXiv:1403.2802 (2014)

20. Viola, P., Jones, M.J.: Robust real-time face detection. International journal of computer vision **57**(2), 137–154 (2004)
21. Nowak, S., Lukashevich, H., Dunker, P., Rüger, S.: Performance measures for multilabel evaluation: a case study in the area of image classification. In: Multimedia Information Retrieval, pp. 35–44 (2010)
22. Arnheim, R.: Art and visual perception: A psychology of the creative eye. Univ. of California Press (1954)

Graph-Based Shape Similarity of Petroglyphs

Markus Seidl[1]([✉]), Ewald Wieser[1], Matthias Zeppelzauer[1],
Axel Pinz[2], and Christian Breiteneder[3]

[1] St. Pölten University of Applied Sciences, St Pölten, Austria
markus.seidl@fhstp.ac.at
[2] Graz University of Technology, Graz, Austria
[3] Vienna University of Technology, Vienna, Austria

Abstract. Petroglyphs can be found on rock panels all over the world. The possibilities of digital photography and more recently various 3D scanning methods opened a new stage for the documentation and analysis of petroglyphs. The existing work on petroglyph shape similarity has largely avoided the questions of articulation, merged petroglyphs and potentially missing parts of petroglyphs. We aim at contributing to close this gap by applying a novel petroglyph shape descriptor based on the skeletal graph. Our contribution is twofold: First, we provide a real-world dataset of petroglyph shapes. Second, we propose a graph-based shape descriptor for petroglyphs. Comprehensive evaluations show, that the combination of the proposed descriptor with existing ones improves the performance in petroglyph shape similarity modeling.

Keywords: Petroglyph similarity · Shape similarity · Graph matching · Graph edit distance · Graph embedding

1 Introduction

Petroglyphs have been pecked, scratched and carved in rock panels all over the world. The documentation with digital photography and more recently various 3D scanning methods enabled (semi-)automated analysis of petroglyphs and attracts research activity. In the past few years, works related to segmentation of petroglyph images [29], automated classification of petroglyph shapes [38][39][9][10] and digital presentation of rock art [30] have been published. The large number of single petroglyphs makes the usage of automated analysis methods attractive. In this paper, we contribute to the evaluation of shape similarity of petroglyphs. Our contribution is twofold: First, we provide a real-world dataset of petroglyph shapes that have been digitized from tracings of petroglyphs of the UNESCO world heritage site Valcamonica. The dataset further contains fine-grained expert annotations from archeologists. Second, we propose and evaluate a graph-matching approach for shape similarity of petroglyphs.

The motivation to investigate the skeletal graphs of petroglyphs for shape matching is with respect to our ultimate goal: The retrieval of possibly merged and unfinished or damaged (i.e. partial) petroglyphs from full rock panels. Hence,

© Springer International Publishing Switzerland 2015
L. Agapito et al. (Eds.): ECCV 2014 Workshops, Part I, LNCS 8925, pp. 133–148, 2015.
DOI: 10.1007/978-3-319-16178-5_9

we need a setup that not only requires invariance against affine transformations and articulations but also against partial shapes as well as merged shapes.

Merged or partial shapes pose two problems to shape descriptors and shape matching in general. First, the object boundaries have to be determined and second, the recognition of merged or partial shapes requires shape descriptors or matching methods that can recognize partial models. Existing state-of-the-art methods for petroglyph shape similarity approaches do not fulfill all these requirements. Therefore, we evaluate the discriminative performance of skeletal graphs of petroglyphs. This paper demonstrates, that skeletal graphs are a well-suited description for future part-based retrieval methods.

2 Related Work

Numerous surveys about shape analysis have been published, comprehensive and important in this field are the surveys by Pavlidis [26], Loncaric [21], Zhang and Lu [37] as well as by Yang et al. [35]. Classifications and taxonomies of shape descriptors have been proposed in the mentioned surveys in different variants. A widely used common denominator is the distinction between contour-based and region-based descriptors.

Latecki et al. compared several shape descriptors on the MPEG-7 CE-Shape-1 database [18]. The database contains only complete shapes with closed contours. They propose three main categories for shape descriptors: Contour-based descriptors, region-based descriptors and skeleton-based descriptors. They investigated robustness to scaling and rotation, similarity-based retrieval as well as motion and non-rigid deformations. The weakest performing descriptor in all cases was the skeleton-based approach, the most significant drawback is the lack of robustness against scaling and rotation. The authors assume, that none of the existing approaches to compute skeletons is robust enough. But, since the publishing of this paper in the year 2000, promising skeletonisation algorithms have been proposed and evaluated (e.g. [3]). We summarize region-based, contour-based and skeleton-based approaches that are relevant for our work and include petroglyph-related work where available.

2.1 Region-Based Descriptors

Zhu et al. propose the usage of a slight modification of the generalised Hough transform (GHT) for the mining of large petroglyph datasets [39]. The main arguments for GHT and against other shape similarity measures are the existence of petrogplyph images where a single petroglyph consists of several parts and the possibility of merged parts of petroglyphs that drastically change the topology of the petroglyphs. They extensively evaluate their approach and achieve good results. However, they mostly evaluate synthetic petroglyph shapes or simple petroglyph shapes drawn by humans rather than the more exact tracings based on peck marks which we use (see Section 3.1). Deufemia et al. use the radon transform of petroglyph images as shape descriptor for unsupervised recognition via self-organizing maps (SOM) [9]. In a second step, they use a fuzzy visual language parser to solve ambigous interpretations by incorporating archaeological knowledge. They evaluate the approach on a large dataset and achieve good results. However, Deufemia et al. as well as Zhu et al. do not consider partial or merged petroglyphs, i.e. part-based retrieval that is necessary for petroglyphs in real-world scenes.

Krish and Snyder propose the shape recognition approach SKS [15] which is based on the generalised Hough transform. They compare the performance of SKS with Hu moments, curvature scale space (CSS, see 2.2) matching and shape context (SC, see 2.2). Besides affine transformations, they evaluate partial shapes. The SKS feature performs good on partial shapes. But, the evaluation data set consists of 31 different shapes only and does not contain merged shapes.[1] Generally, region-based descriptors have the advantage that they do not need complete contours for descriptor extraction.

2.2   Contour-Based Descriptors

Mokhtarian et al. propose curvature scale space (CSS) image matching [25][23] [24]. They smooth a contour by convolution with a Gaussian kernel in different scales (i.e. different kernel sizes of the Gaussian kernel). Subsequently, they find the curvature zero crossings on the contour. The descriptor - the CSS image - consists of the zero crossings in a diagram where the size of the Gaussian kernel is on the y-axis and the normalized path length of the curve is on the x-axis. This CSS image is used to match shapes. Mai et al. use the CSS descriptors to acquire contour segments invariant to affine transformations [22]. They utilize the local maxima in the CSS image to locate the affine-invariant points and segment the contour at these points. They match the segments with a dynamic programming approach. They achieve very good experimental results. They outperform the dynamic programming approach by Petrakis et al. [27], who are utilizing contour segments as well. Belongie et al. propose the widely used shape context (SC) descriptor [6]. They sample points on the contour of an object. For each point, they compute the shape context based on the spatial distribution of the other points on the shape contour. They match two shapes by estimating the best transformation from one shape to the other and determining a dissimilarity based on shape context distance, appearance cost and transformation cost.

Deufemia et al. [10] propose a two stage classification of petroglyphs. They use shape context descriptors to provide an initial raw clustering with self-organizing maps. In the second step, they use an image deformation model to classify the petroglyph shapes. They evaluate their approach on a relatively small dataset (17 classes with 3 exemplars) that they enlarge by using 30 affine transformations of each image.

---

[1] The data set does not include petroglyphs.

Fig. 1. This figure shows a part of a tracing of a rock in Valcamonica (Coren di Redondo, Rock 1). ©Alberto Marretta, used with permission.

2.3   Skeleton-Based Descriptors

Siddiqi and Kimia propose a shock grammar for recognition [31]. Later, Siddiqi et al. propose the usage of shock graphs for shape matching [32]. Shocks are used to provide a structural description of 2D shapes. They are contour-based and deliver a medial axis of the shape, that has additional information for each part of the skeleton. The representation of the shape is a directed acyclic shock graph, which is used for shape matching.

Aslan Skeletons are coarse skeletons [1]. They are matched via tree edit distance and have been evaluated on different data sets with good results [5][12]. However, while they are insensitive to articulation and affine transformations, they can not be used for merged shapes, for shapes with holes and for shapes with large missing parts.

Ling and Jacobs propose the usage of the inner-distance, which is the shortest path between two landmark points (in this case contour points are used) of a shape [20]. Hence, they implicitly embed skeletal information in the descriptor. The distance between two contour points is the shortest path within the silhouette of the shape instead of the Euclidean distance between the two points. They use the idea for three approaches to shape description. First, they combine the inner-distance with multi-dimensonal scaling. Second, they utilize the inner-distance to build a new descriptor based on shape context, and third they extend the second approach with appearance information of the shapes along the inner-distance lines. They evaluate the approach on several datasets with good results. They state, that the proposed descriptors are invariant/insensitive to articulation and are capable to capture part structures.

Bai and Latecki introduce a skeleton-based approach that matches silhouettes based on skeleton paths, which are the geodesic paths between skeleton endpoints [2]. The shortest paths are represented by the radii of the maximum inscribed discs at skeleton points. They use DCE (Discrete Curve Evolution [17]) for the skeleton pruning. The descriptor is on two layers. First, the description of a skeleton endpoint is constructed from the shortest paths starting at this point, and second the similarity of two shapes is computed by matching the descriptors of the skeleton endpoints. They experimentally show, that the method is robust against articulations, stretching and contour deformations. Bai et al. combine contour features with skeletal features to improve shape classification [4]. They state, that contour-based approaches can represent detailed information well, and are up to a certain extent robust against partial and merged shapes but lack invariance against articulation and non-rigid deformation. In contrast to that, skeleton-based approaches are robust against non-rigid deformations. For the contour segments, they follow the ideas of Sun and Super [33], but use DCE to determine the segments. They achieve 96.6% classification rate on the MPEG-7 CE-Shape-1 [18] database. Xu et al. extend the skeleton path approach [2] by also considering junction points for the skeleton paths descriptor [34]. They call the junction points and end points of the skeleton graph critical points. They merge junction nodes based on the paths from the junction nodes to the end nodes. If the sum of path distances of two nodes normalised by the number of end nodes of the graph is below a set threshold the two nodes are merged. They achieve slightly better results than Bai and Latecki [2], and state, that the method is efficient even in the presence of articulation as well as partial and merged shapes. The line of work summarized in this paragraph is mostly built on the skeleton pruning algorithm based on DCE proposed by Bai et al.[3].

To our knowledge, there is no work on petroglyphs that utilizes skeletons or skeletal graphs. We aim at investigating the skeletal graph for petroglyph similarity modeling. In our approach, we use the the promising algorithm by Bai et al. [3] for skeletonisation and skeleton pruning. To investigate the distinctiveness of skeletal graphs, we model petroglyph similarity as graph similarity. In the following, we summarize works that use graph matching to model shape similarity and popular graph matching approaches. There are numerous approaches in shape matching that utilize graphs. Comparable to our approach are methods, that model shape similarity as similarity of the skeletal graph. Klein et al. use tree edit distance to match shapes described by their shock graphs [14]. Di Ruberto uses attributed skeletal graphs to model shape similarity [11]. Aslan skeletal graphs are matched with tree edit distance [5][12]. For our material (see Section 3.1), tree matching is not sufficient, as the skeletal graphs may contain cycles. Hence, we have to use graph matching. There is a long line of work in graph matching. A recent volume of workshop proceedings edited by Kropatsch et al. includes papers on many aspects of graph-based representations in pattern recognition [16].

Fig. 2. This figure shows examples of the petroglyph dataset that we investigate in this paper. Each column contains examples of one class. We observe, that some of the classes have high intra-class variance of shape. The petroglyphs are from various rocks in Valcamonica. ©CCSP - Centro Camuno di Studi Preistorici and Alberto Marretta, used with permission.

A popular and intuitive similarity measure for a pair of graphs A and B is the graph edit distance (GED). GED defines similarity of two graphs as the minimum number of edit operations (remove node, add node, remove edge, add edge) that are needed to transform graph A to graph B. The computation of the graph edit distance is NP-hard [36]. This problem is addressed in several ways. There are approximations for the GED, e.g. the widely used Hungarian algorithm, or A* beam search. Another way is to use graph spectra (e.g. [8]) or to embed node and edge attributes of graphs in vector spaces and subsequently use standard similarity measures and machine learning methods to match similarity (e.g. [13] or [19]).

3   Dataset and Approach

3.1   Benchmark Dataset

Manual tracing of petroglyphs on transparent material is the standard documentation technique for pecked rock art. See Figure 1 for a part of a tracing of a rock panel. To obtain such a tracing, the transparent material is placed on the rock panel and each peck mark is traced. We have access to digitized versions of numerous sheets. For this paper, we use a dataset of one hundred tracings of individual petroglyphs in ten classes. Figure 2 shows examples of our material.[2] Note the high intra-class variability not only in terms of affine transformations and articulations but also in general differences of the shapes in a class. Some classes are perceptually very close, e.g. classes two and three.

---

[2] The full dataset is available at http://ment.org/VISART14.

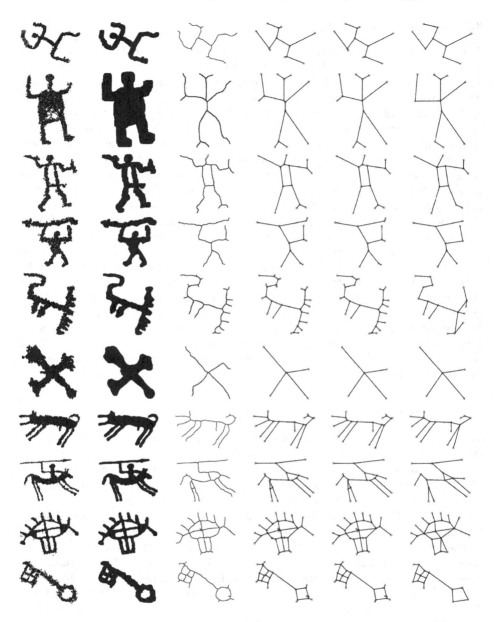

Fig. 3. This figure shows petroglyph tracings (column 1), pre-processed shapes (column 2), extracted skeletons (column 3) and the derived graphs with a pruning threshold of 2, 10 and 30px (columns 4-6). We observe, that the employed skeletonisation algorithm fails to extract details in some cases (heads in rows 1 and 4), while in other cases small details are covered well. Furthermore, we observe, that a high pruning threshold removes skeletal noise (rows 1, 2, 4, 6, 9 and 10), but may also discard relevant topological information (row 5).

3.2 Overview of our Approach

The literature review suggests, that a combination of contour-based and skeletal descriptors should yield optimum results. The existing petroglyph shape retrieval systems utilize region-based features [39][9] as well as contour-based features [10]. These methods are the baseline reference methods we compare our approach with. We concentrate on the investigation of skeletal features for the petroglyph shape recognition problem, because the petroglyph shapes are intuitively already skeletal shapes. Furthermore, we want to use the skeletons as basis for part-based matching in future. We propose to model similarity of petroglyphs as a skeletal graph matching problem. We derive the graphs from the skeletons of the petroglyph shapes. We use each end point and each junction point of a given petroglyph skeleton as nodes for our graph, and the skeleton branches connecting these points as edges. See Figure 3 for exemplary skeletons and derived graphs. We utilize the skeletal graph as descriptor that is invariant to affine transformations as well as articulations. Hence, we discard all spatial information, as we are only interested in topological information. We match the resulting undirected graphs following two strategies. First, we utilize the graph edit distance (GED) as pairwise similarity measure, and second, we use graph embedding (GE) to create a feature vector for each graph and match these feature vectors. We embed the graphs in feature vectors of a normed length by extracting several graph properties (see Table 1), and calculate pairwise distances with Euclidean distance. We classify using a k-NN classifier with an extension for intermediate descriptor fusion.

3.3 Descriptors

We compare the distinctiveness of contour-based as well as region-based shape descriptors with the distinctiveness of undirected skeletal graphs for the petroglyph classification problem. As baseline methods, we utilize a) Shape Context (SC) [6], which has been used by Deufemia et al. for petroglyph classification [10], b) Inner Distance Shape Context (IDSC) [20], as well as c) General Hough Transform (GHT) proposed by Zhu et al. for (GHT) proposed by Zhu et al. for petroglyph classification [39].[3] Our proposed petrogylph descriptor makes use of the skeletal graphs in two ways. First, we use the graphs directly as descriptors and measure the similarity with GED. We employ the A* algorithm with beam search and the Hungarian algorithm. Both variants tolerate cycles in the graphs.[4] Second, we utilize topology features of the undirected graphs for GE.[5] Please refer to Table 1 for the list of selected features for petroglyph description.

---

[3] For all three descriptors, implementations have been kindly provided by the respective authors.

[4] We use the implementation in the Graph Matching Framework kindly provided by Kaspar Riesen [28].

[5] We utilize the MIT strategic engineering tools for network analysis kindly provided by Bounova and de Weck [7]: http://strategic.mit.edu/downloads.php?page=matlab_networks.

We evaluate the distinctiveness of single topology features and of combinations of topology features. In order to be able to use skeletonisation and contour-based descriptors, we need to pre-process our material to achieve continuous boundaries. We use standard filters and morphological operations for this purpose. The resulting shape images are the input for SC, IDSC as well as for the skeletonisation for which we use the method by Bai et al. [3].[6] We normalize the width of the input petroglyph to 500px and prune the skeletons by joining nodes which have a spatial distance smaller than a threshold. GHT is computed on the original petroglyph images.[7]

Table 1. Topology based features extracted from the skeletal graphs. Each feature is a description of the whole graph. Please refer to [7] for more details.

id	Feature	Description
1	numNodes	Number of nodes
2	numEdges	Number of edges
3	numCycles	Number of independent cycles, also known as the cyclomatic number of a graph
4	linkDensity	Link density, i.e. ratio of existing links to maximum possible links
5	avgDegree	Average number of links over all nodes
6	numLeafs	Number of leafs, i.e. number of nodes with only one link
7 - 11	histDegrees	5 bin histogram of node degrees, i.e. counts of all nodes with 1,2...5 links. The maximum occurring degree in our dataset is 5
12	sMetric	Sum of degree products across all edges, i.e. for each edge, multiply the degrees of the two nodes connected by the edge and finally sum up the products
13	graphEnergy	Sum of the absolute values of real components of the eigenvalues
14	avgNeighDegree	Average of the average neighboring degrees of all nodes
15	avgCloseness	Average of closeness over all nodes
16	pearson	Pearson coefficient for the degree sequence of all edges of the graph
17	richClub	Rich club metric for all nodes with a degree larger than 1
18	algebConnect	Algebraic connectivity, i.e. the second smallest eigenvalue of the Laplacian
19	diameter	The longest shortest path between any two nodes in the graph
20	avgPathlength	Average shortest path
21	graphRadius	Minimum vertex eccentricity

---

[6] We thank Bai et al. for providing the implementation.

[7] We use resolutions of 10x10px, 20x20px and 30x30px. We report on the best performing resolution 10x10px.

3.4   Descriptor Fusion and Classification

Additionally to the performance of individual descriptors, we evaluate the performance of descriptor combinations. For SC, IDSC, GHT and GED we compute pairwise distances. For the feature vectors we obtain by GE, we calculate pairwise Euclidean distances. The combination of descriptors via the combination (i.e. unweighted summation) of distance matrices would require a normalization in all utilized feature spaces, which could only be provided by heuristically determined thresholds for the maximum dissimilarity that can occur for one specific descriptor. We want to avoid this step, and aim at preserving complementary distinctiveness as far as possible in the classification process. Instead of merging the similarity matrices, we employ single k-NN classifiers (k=5) for each individual feature. A straightforward approach would be to combine the classification results of all classifiers by majority voting. To obtain a richer and more expressive basis for making a decision, we refrain from this simple combination of classification results. Instead, we fuse the classifiers at an intermediate step. We use the class labels of the five nearest neighbors of each descriptor and concatenate these to a set of nearest neighbors which contains $5n$ class labels, with n being the number of descriptors combined. Subsequently, we classify according to the conventional rule of k-NN with a majority vote. This incorporates more information than a voting based on the classification results, as we implicitly include the probability of the classification result in form of the number of class members among the nearest neighbors. We validate our results of single descriptors as well as fused descriptors by leave-one-out-cross-validation (LOOCV). We employ accuracy as quality measure, i.e. the ratio of the number of correctly classified petroglyphs to the total number of classified petroglyphs.

4   Experimental Results

4.1   Graph Matching

Table 2 shows the results of GED employed on the unweighted undirected skeletal graphs. The maximum accuracy is 57%. Both employed methods achieve this result at a pruning threshold of 10px. We observe, that the results of both methods tend to decrease with an increasing pruning threshold larger than 10px. We assume, that the distinctiveness of the skeletal graphs first increases, as skeletal noise is pruned, and then decreases after a maximum of 10px as more and more topological distinctiveness is removed in the pruning process (see Figure 3). Furthermore, we observe, that for higher pruning thresholds, A* beam search outperforms the Hungarian algorithm.

   Table 3 summarizes the results of the evaluation of single topological features of GE. We observe, that feature 13 (graph energy) yields the best result with 47% accuracy given a pruning threshold of 10px. We achieve also the second and the third best results with a pruning threshold of 10px. This confirms the GED results (see Table 2), where a pruning threshold of 10px delivers the best results as well. Furthermore, we observe, that features 8,10 and 11 (bins 2,4

Table 2. Classification accuracy of GED in percent. We use LOOCV-validated 5-NN classification. The maximum number of open paths for the A* beam approximation is 6000.

	Pruning threshold					
	2	10	15	20	25	30
Hungarian	52	**57**	**57**	30	39	37
A* beam	51	**57**	49	47	47	47

and 5 of the degree histogram) perform around random (10%). We assume that this is due to the fact, that most graph nodes that are not leafs seem to be 3-connected (see Figure 3). Hence, the counts of 2, 4 and 5-connected nodes have weak discriminative capabilities.

Table 3. Classification accuracy (in percent) of GE utilizing single scalar topological features. We use LOOCV-validated 5-NN classification. p denotes the size of the pruning threshold. The three best values are emphasized. Please refer to Table 1 for the descriptions corresponding to the feature ids

	Feature id																					
p	1	2	3	4	5	6	7	8	9	10	11	12	13	14	15	16	17	18	19	20	21	Avg.
2	25	21	14	35	27	40	40	10	33	10	10	22	25	21	30	23	35	30	27	29	14	25
10	37	**44**	14	29	31	40	40	9	25	7	10	33	**47**	23	**43**	23	29	32	25	31	20	28
15	35	25	17	38	33	37	37	5	21	7	10	30	37	16	30	22	38	30	23	39	23	26
20	31	28	18	31	37	21	21	8	16	10	10	35	35	15	33	26	31	33	29	37	21	25
25	33	32	20	37	39	25	25	12	14	10	10	25	39	13	37	17	37	37	26	33	29	26
30	27	36	13	28	35	23	23	13	8	10	10	33	27	9	36	22	28	34	29	26	28	24
Avg.	31	31	16	33	34	31	31	10	20	9	10	30	35	16	35	22	33	33	27	33	23	

Table 4 reports the GE performance of the best feature combination of each dimension from 1 to 10. We employ brute-force feature selection for each number of feature dimensions, i.e. we evaluate all possible combinations for 1 to 10 out of the 21 single features (see Table 1). We observe, that feature combination strongly improves results. The maximum accuracy is 57%, as it is the case with GED as well.

4.2   Comparison with Baseline Descriptors and Descriptor Fusion

Table 5 contains the results of shape descriptors with which we compare our skeletal graph approach as well as combinations thereof. We observe, that SC and IDSC perform better than GE when employed as single descriptors. GE clearly outperforms the dedicated petroglyph descriptor GHT of [39]. Descriptor fusion generally improves results. The fusion of two or three shape descriptors improves the results slightly. The fusion of all four descriptors improves the results from 82% for the best single descriptor to 88%. This demonstrates, that the descriptors contain complementary information that is well preserved by using the proposed k-NN fusion method.

Table 4. Classification accuracy (in percent) of GE using combinations of 1 to 10 single topology features that perform best for each dimension. We use LOOCV-validated 5-NN classification with brute-force feature selection. The pruning threshold is 10px. The best values are emphasized. Please refer to Table 1 for the descriptions corresponding to the feature ids

Feature ids	Accuracy
13	47
2, 15	54
4, 6, 18	56
6, 7, 18, 20	**57**
6, 7, 15, 18, 20	**57**
4, 6, 7, 15, 18, 20	56
1, 2, 4, 6, 7, 15, 17	55
1, 2, 4, 6, 7, 13, 15, 17	55
1, 2, 4, 6, 7, 14, 15, 17, 20	53
1, 2, 4, 6, 7, 13, 14, 15, 17, 20	53

Table 5. Classification accuracy (in percent) of GE, SC, IDSC and GHT and combinations thereof. We use LOOCV-validated 5-NN classification for single shape features and the classifier fusion method described in Section 3.4

Descriptor	Single			Fused										
GE	x			x	x	x	x	x	x					x
IDSC		x		x			x	x		x	x	x		x
SC			x		x		x		x	x		x	x	x
GHT				x		x		x	x		x	x	x	x
Accuracy	57	81	82	39	80	78	54	86	84	83	84	81	86	81	88

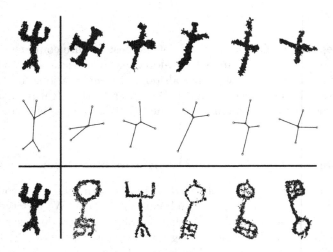

Fig. 4. This figure shows a sample which is misclassified with GED and GHT. The query image is on the left, and the five nearest neighbors on the right. The first two rows show the result for GED and the utilized graphs. The third row shows the result for GHT

To discuss the limitations of our approach and the weak performance of GHT on our dataset compared to the datasets employed by Zhu et al. [39], we present example query petroglyphs and their nearest neighbors. Figure 4 shows a query petroglyph, that is misclassified by GED as well as by GHT. We observe, that the skeletal graph of the query antrophomorph figure has a topology which is similar to the topology of a cross. Hence, the five nearest neighbors are crosses. The nearest neighbors computed by GHT also fail to determine the correct class for the query petroglyph. We observe, that the spatial distribution of the pixels in the query image is comparable to the nearest neighbors. Figure 5 shows a query petroglyph, that is correctly classified by GE and misclassified by GHT. We observe, that in the case of GE, the four nearest neighbors are topologically very close to the query graph. The fifth neighbor is different. But, we have to take into account, that GE matches with a set of features, that cannot necessarily be understood intuitively (see Table 4). The GHT nearest neighbors show comparable pixel distributions. We assume, that the less competitive performance of GHT on our dataset is related to the fact, that the test datasets used by Zhu et al. are manual transcriptions of petroglyph skeletons (or sometimes outlines, see [39] p95) which leads to simpler shapes than the detailed tracings of peck marks in our material.

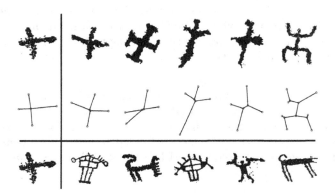

Fig. 5. This figure shows a sample which is correctly classified with GE and misclassified with GHT. The query image is on the left, and the five nearest neighbors on the right. The first two rows show the result for GE and the utilized graphs. The third row shows the result for GHT.

5   Conclusions

We present a novel petroglyph descriptor based on the skeletal graph topology and propose matching with graph edit distance (GED) and graph embedding (GE). For GE, we propose 21 different scalar topological features. We evaluate the descriptor and the matching on a petroglyph dataset containing 10 classes with 10 exemplars and compare the performance with other shape descriptors used in petroglyph classification.

Matching of the skeletal graphs with GE and with GED delivers comparable results. Both matching methods achieve 57% accuracy. GED is of high computational complexity, whereas GE has low computational demand due to low feature vector dimensionality. The two best performing combinations of topology features have only 4 and 5 feature dimensions. The contour-based features SC and IDSC outperform the region-based GHT and the skeletal graph-based GE and GED. GE and GED outperform the region-based GHT. The proposed descriptor fusion clearly improves results. In 5 of 7 descriptor combinations the usage of our descriptor improves results (see Table 5). The combination of our graph-based petroglyph descriptor with other descriptors yields a classification performance of 88% which is not achieved without the proposed skeletal descriptor. This shows that the skeletal features represent information not captured by the contour-based features and the region-based features. We conclude that descriptors derived from skeletons are valuable for petroglyph classification.

Future work will include improvement of our petroglyph descriptor based on the skeletal graph in two ways. First, we aim at improving pre-processing of the shapes as well as skeletonisation. Second, we will investigate the suitability of spatial features. In this paper, we investigated topological information of the skeletal graph, which is an highly invariant abstraction of the skeleton. In future, we will investigate, whether spatial relations of graph parts contain valuable information for our task, because our material has already undergone one step of abstraction by the artists, who created the petroglyphs. Finally, we will make use of our novel petroglyph shape descriptor in the task it was designed for and which it enables: part-based matching.

Acknowledgements. The images of petroglyph tracings used in this paper have been kindly provided by the CCSP - Centro Camuno di Studi Preistorici and by Alberto Marretta, who we thank. The work for this paper has been carried out in the project 3D-Pitoti which is funded from the European Community's Seventh Framework Programme (FP7/2007-2013) under grant agreement no 600545; 2013-2016.

References

1. Aslan, C., Erdem, A., Erdem, E., Tari, S.: Disconnected skeleton: shape at its absolute scale. IEEE Transactions on Pattern Analysis and Machine Intelligence 30(12), 2188–2203 (2008)
2. Bai, X., Latecki, L.: Path similarity skeleton graph matching. IEEE Transactions on Pattern Analysis and Machine Intelligence 30(7), 1282–1292 (2008)
3. Bai, X., Latecki, L., Liu, W.Y.: Skeleton pruning by contour partitioning with discrete curve evolution. IEEE Transactions on Pattern Analysis and Machine Intelligence 29(3), 449–462 (2007). 00228
4. Bai, X., Liu, W., Tu, Z.: Integrating contour and skeleton for shape classification. In: 2009 IEEE 12th International Conference on Computer Vision Workshops (ICCV Workshops), pp. 360–367. IEEE (2009)

5. Baseski, E., Erdem, A., Tari, S.: Dissimilarity between two skeletal trees in a context. Pattern Recognition **42**(3), 370–385 (2009)
6. Belongie, S., Malik, J., Puzicha, J.: Shape matching and object recognition using shape contexts. IEEE Transactions on Pattern Analysis and Machine Intelligence **24**(4), 509–522 (2002)
7. Bounova, G., de Weck, O.: Overview of metrics and their correlation patterns for multiple-metric topology analysis on heterogeneous graph ensembles. Phys. Rev. E **85**, 016117 (2012)
8. Demirci, M.F., van Leuken, R.H., Veltkamp, R.C.: Indexing through Laplacian spectra. Computer Vision and Image Understanding **110**(3), 312–325 (2008)
9. Deufemia, V., Paolino, L., de Lumley, H.: Petroglyph recognition using self-organizing maps and fuzzy visual language parsing. In: 2012 IEEE 24th International Conference on Tools with Artificial Intelligence (ICTAI), vol. 1, pp. 852–859 (2012)
10. Deufemia, V., Paolino, L.: Combining unsupervised clustering with a non-linear deformation model for efficient petroglyph recognition. In: Bebis, G., Boyle, R., Parvin, B., Koracin, D., Li, B., Porikli, F., Zordan, V., Klosowski, J., Coquillart, S., Luo, X., Chen, M., Gotz, D. (eds.) ISVC 2013, Part II. LNCS, vol. 8034, pp. 128–137. Springer, Heidelberg (2013)
11. Di Ruberto, C.: Recognition of shapes by attributed skeletal graphs. Pattern Recognition **37**(1), 21–31 (2004)
12. Erdem, A., Tari, S.: A similarity-based approach for shape classification using Aslan skeletons. Pattern Recognition Letters **31**(13), 2024–2032 (2010)
13. Gibert, J., Valveny, E., Bunke, H.: Graph embedding in vector spaces by node attribute statistics. Pattern Recogn. **45**(9), 3072–3083 (2012)
14. Klein, P.N., Sebastian, T.B., Kimia, B.B.: Shape matching using edit-distance: an implementation. In: Proceedings of the Twelfth Annual ACM-SIAM Symposium on Discrete Algorithms, SODA 2001, Society for Industrial and Applied Mathematics, Philadelphia, pp. 781–790 (2001)
15. Krish, K., Snyder, W.: A new accumulator-based approach to shape recognition. In: Bebis, G., Boyle, R., Parvin, B., Koracin, D., Remagnino, P., Porikli, F., Peters, J., Klosowski, J., Arns, L., Chun, Y.K., Rhyne, T.-M., Monroe, L. (eds.) ISVC 2008, Part II. LNCS, vol. 5359, pp. 157–169. Springer, Heidelberg (2008)
16. Kropatsch, W.G., et al. (eds.): GbRPR 2013. LNCS, vol. 7877. Springer, Heidelberg (2013)
17. Latecki, L.J., Lakamper, R.: Shape similarity measure based on correspondence of visual parts. IEEE Transactions on Pattern Analysis and Machine Intelligence **22**(10), 1185–1190 (2000)
18. Latecki, L.J., Lakamper, R., Eckhardt, T.: Shape descriptors for non-rigid shapes with a single closed contour. In: IEEE Conference on Computer Vision and Pattern Recognition, 2000, Proceedings, vol. 1, pp. 424–429. IEEE (2000)
19. Li, G., Semerci, M., Yener, B., Zaki, M.J.: Graph classification via topological and label attributes. In: 9th Workshop on Mining and Learning with Graphs (with SIGKDD) (August 2011) (2011). 00009
20. Ling, H., Jacobs, D.W.: Shape classification using the inner-distance. IEEE Transactions on Pattern Analysis and Machine Intelligence **29**(2), 286–299 (2007)
21. Loncaric, S.: A survey of shape analysis techniques. Pattern Recognition **31**(8), 983–1001 (1998)
22. Mai, F., Chang, C.Q., Hung, Y.S.: Affine-invariant shape matching and recognition under partial occlusion. In: 2010 17th IEEE International Conference on Image Processing (ICIP), pp. 4605–4608. IEEE (2010)

23. Mokhtarian, F.: Silhouette-based isolated object recognition through curvature scale space. IEEE Transactions on Pattern Analysis and Machine Intelligence **17**(5), 539–544 (1995)
24. Mokhtarian, F., Abbasi, S., Kittler, J., et al.: Efficient and robust retrieval by shape content through curvature scale space. Series on Software Engineering and Knowledge Engineering **8**, 51–58 (1997)
25. Mokhtarian, F., Mackworth, A.: Scale-based description and recognition of planar curves and two-dimensional shapes. IEEE Transactions on Pattern Analysis and Machine Intelligence **8**(1), 34–43 (1986)
26. Pavlidis, T.: A review of algorithms for shape analysis. Computer graphics and image processing **7**(2), 243–258 (1978)
27. Petrakis, E.G.M., Diplaros, A., Milios, E.: Matching and retrieval of distorted and occluded shapes using dynamic programming. IEEE Transactions on Pattern Analysis and Machine Intelligence **24**(11), 1501–1516 (2002)
28. Riesen, K., Emmenegger, S., Bunke, H.: A novel software toolkit for graph edit distance computation. In: Kropatsch, W.G., Artner, N.M., Haxhimusa, Y., Jiang, X. (eds.) GbRPR 2013. LNCS, vol. 7877, pp. 142–151. Springer, Heidelberg (2013)
29. Seidl, M., Breiteneder, C.: Automated petroglyph image segmentation with interactive classifier fusion. In: Proceedings of the Eighth Indian Conference on Computer Vision, Graphics and Image Processing (ICVGIP 2012) (2012)
30. Seidl, M., Judmaier, P., Baker, F., Chippindale, C., Egger, U., Jax, N., Weis, C., Grubinger, M., Seidl, G.: Multi-touch rocks: playing with tangible virtual heritage in the museum - first user tests. In: VAST11: The 12th International Symposium on Virtual Reality, Archaeology and Intelligent Cultural Heritage - Short Papers, pp. 73–76 (2011)
31. Siddiqi, K., Kimia, B.: A shock grammar for recognition. In: 1996 IEEE Computer Society Conference on Computer Vision and Pattern Recognition, 1996, Proceedings CVPR 1996, pp. 507–513 (1996)
32. Siddiqi, K., Shokoufandeh, A., Dickinson, S., Zucker, S.: Shock graphs and shape matching. International Journal of Computer Vision **35**(1), 13–32 (1999)
33. Sun, K.B., Super, B.J.: Classification of contour shapes using class segment sets. In: IEEE Computer Society Conference on Computer Vision and Pattern Recognition, 2005, CVPR 2005, vol. 2, pp. 727–733. IEEE (2005)
34. Xu, Y., Wang, B., Liu, W., Bai, X.: Skeleton graph matching based on critical points using path similarity. In: Zha, H., Taniguchi, R., Maybank, S. (eds.) ACCV 2009, Part III. LNCS, vol. 5996, pp. 456–465. Springer, Heidelberg (2010)
35. Yang, M., Kpalma, K., Ronsin, J.: A survey of shape feature extraction techniques. Pattern Recognition 43–90 (2008). 00163
36. Zeng, Z., Tung, A.K., Wang, J., Feng, J., Zhou, L.: Comparing stars: On approximating graph edit distance. Proceedings of the VLDB Endowment **2**(1), 25–36 (2009)
37. Zhang, D., Lu, G.: Review of shape representation and description techniques. Pattern Recognition **37**(1), 1–19 (2004)
38. Zhu, Q., Wang, X., Keogh, E., Lee, S.H.: Augmenting the generalized Hough transform to enable the mining of petroglyphs. In: Proceedings of the 15th ACM SIGKDD International Conference on Knowledge Discovery and Data Mining, KDD 2009, pp. 1057–1066. ACM, New York (2009)
39. Zhu, Q., Wang, X., Keogh, E., Lee, S.H.: An efficient and effective similarity measure to enable data mining of petroglyphs. Data Mining and Knowledge Discovery **23**(1), 91–127 (2011)

Improving Ancient Roman Coin Recognition with Alignment and Spatial Encoding

Jongpil Kim[(✉)] and Vladimir Pavlovic

Department of Computer Science, Rutgers University, Piscataway, NJ 08854, USA
jpkim@cs.rutgers.edu

Abstract. Roman coins play an important role to understand the Roman empire because they convey rich information about key historical events of the time. Moreover, as large amounts of coins are daily traded over the Internet, it becomes necessary to develop automatic coin recognition systems to prevent illegal trades. In this paper, we describe a new large annotated database of over 2800 Roman coin images and propose an effective automated system for recognition of coins that leverages this new coin image set. As the use of succinct spatial-appearance relationships is critical for accurate coin recognition, we suggest two competing methods, adapted for the coin domain, to accomplish this task.

Keywords: Recognition · Detection · Coin recognition

1 Introduction

A coin is usually a flat piece of metal issued by governmental authority as a medium of exchange. It has been produced in large quantities to facilitate trade from the ancient history to the present. Along with the trading purpose, the Roman empire knew how to effectively use the coin as their political propaganda. The ancient Roman coins were widely used to convey the achievements of Roman emperors to the public. They also served to spread messages of changing policies or merits through the empire. By engraving portraits on the coins, the Roman emperors also could show themselves to the entire empire. In short, the coins were the newspaper of the Roman empire. In this way, Roman coins are always connected to historical events and Roman imperial propaganda. Therefore, understanding the ancient Roman coins could serve as references to understand the Roman empire.

Because the coin market is very active, many coins are traded every day, mostly over the Internet [1]. But ancient coins are also becoming subject to a very large illicit trade [21]. The traditional way to detect illegal traffic of ancient coins is to manually search catalogues, dealers or internet by the authorities. But the manual process has limitations and is too slow to cover all trade. Therefore, there is a need to develop both reliable and automatic methods to recognize the coins.

© Springer International Publishing Switzerland 2015
L. Agapito et al. (Eds.): ECCV 2014 Workshops, Part I, LNCS 8925, pp. 149–164, 2015.
DOI: 10.1007/978-3-319-16178-5_10

(a) Vespasian   (b) Vitellius

Fig. 1. An example of Inter-class similarity in the ancient Roman coins. Vespasian looks similar to Vitellius.

There are tens of thousands of typologies that could be used to classify Roman coins [1][3]. Therefore those who do not have knowledge and experience cannot classify them without the help of experts or automatic classifiers. In this paper, we focus on the recognition of the Roman emperors on the Roman imperial coins. Specifically, for a given coin image, we propose an automatic method to recognize who is on the coin.

Inter-class similarity and intra-class similarity are two challenges to recognize the ancient Roman coins. For the inter-class similarity, different emperors share similar appearance as shown in Figure 1 and Figure 10. There are several reasons for the similar appearance: familiar relationship, engraver's lack of knowledge for the emperor's image or abstraction, or using the same template for different emperors. Another aspect of the coin recognition challenge is the intra-class dissimilarity as shown in Figure 2. There may exist a large variation within the same class. On a very basic level, the direction of the emperor's face varies over the coins: some emperors look left and the others look right without any specific rule as shown in Figure 2.

Several works [15], [16], [1], [9], [21], [22], [17] have proposed to recognize the coins using computer vision techniques. In general, they represent the coin image as low level visual features such as SIFT [14] and perform the recognition using the k-nearest neighbor method or the support vector machine. Among them, Arandjelović [1] introduces a new type of feature called directional kernel which captures geographical information between interest points. On the other hand, Zambanini et al. [17] employs the spatial pyramid models [13] to capture the structure of the coin. However, the previous approaches do not explicitly facilitate the use of the spatial structure of the coin such as the location of the face on the coin.

In this paper, we address the problem of automatically recognizing ancient Roman coins, while leveraging their spatial structure and without specifically focusing on the understanding of textual transcripts on coins. The ancient Roman coins have regular structure: the coin is round, the location of the emperor is roughly at the center of the coin and the emperors share common aspects across different coins. However, coins of the same emperor also exhibit large variations. Some of these variations are due to the differences in the coin material and

Fig. 2. The emperors on the five coins are the same, Nero. But there is variations on the shapes. In particular, one face looks left while the others look right.

diverse state of coin degradation. Others are due to the differences in which the same emperor was depicted by different coin creators. These intra-class variability aspects make the task of recognizing the coins very challenging. An additional challenge, as we demonstrate in this work, comes from the fact that the visual coin appearance gives rise to vastly different feature statistics compared to those of traditional face recognition tasks. To surmount these challenges we propose a framework to simultaneously leverage the consistencies in the coin structure and local appearance to improve the recognition accuracy.

To this end, we investigate two approaches: a method based on discriminative deformable part models (DPM) specifically adjusted to the coin domain through the use of polar coordinate representations and the Fisher vector with spatial-appearance encoding. The model using DPM first detects the face of the emperor on the coin and uses the detected location to build a spatial pyramid. The Fisher vector based model directly encodes the spatial information in its representation. The use of both representations allows the recovery of consistent patterns that characterize different Roman emperors despite the outlined intra-class differences. We use the support vector machine (SVM) to train the models. We also introduce a new large annotated database of Roman coins, consisting of over 2800 pieces made of different materials, depicting appearances of 15 Roman emperors. This new dataset allows us to establish the performance advantages of the proposed approaches compared with more traditional methods.

Contribution of this paper are twofold: 1) we have collected a new ancient Roman Imperial coin dataset where all the coins are annotated and consist of high-quality images; and 2) to leverage the new image set we introduce new baseline techniques for the coin classification using the deformable part model and the Fisher vector with spatial-appearance encoding. We believe that the baseline techniques will provide a benchmark for the future coin recognition problem.

This paper is organized as follows: Related work is summarized in Section 2. In Section 3, we explain our proposed method to recognize the ancient Roman coin. Then, we explain the coin dataset and show experimental results in Section 4. Lastly, we make conclusions in Section 5.

2   Related Work

Several methods have been proposed to recognize and analyze coins using computer vision techniques. Among those methods, gradient information based approaches [15], [16] and eigenspace decomposition based approaches [9] were proposed to recognize modern coins. But none of them are adequate for the ancient coin classification because the ancient coins are too often in very poor conditions, common recognition algorithms can easily fail [21]. Therefore, we do not consider those approaches in this paper. In [10], SIFT descriptors [14] are used to obtain 90% classification accuracy for 390 coin images where there are only 3 classes. A directional kernel to consider orientations of pixels was proposed in [1] for ancient Roman coin classification. However, we found that directional histograms used in [1] performed worse than the proposed method on our dataest. We will examine the results of the directional kernel method in Section 4.2.

Recently, a bag-of-words approach to coin recognition with standard spatial pyramid models was proposed in [17]. In [17], rectangular spatial tiling, log-polar spatial tiling and circular spatial tiling methods were used to recognize the ancient coins. However, they did not align the coin images. In this paper, we propose a new method to align the coin images by detecting the face on the coin. By comparing to the standard spatial pyramid model approach, we will show that the alignment is crucial to improve the recognition accuracy.

The coin recognition problem can be considered as the face recognition in terms of recognizing an Emperor's face on the coin. Many methods have been developed for the recognition of real face images. However, the use of such methods faces significant challenges when applied to ancient coins. In terms of its gradient/edge content, a typical critical feature used in face recognition, most ancient coins display vastly different statistics from photographed faces. This aspect is further aggregated by the fact that many coins are old, worn-out and damaged. For example, Figure 3 shows different HoG [4] distributions between the coins and the real faces. Please note that coins show random distributions while all the human faces share the common pattern.

Tzimiropoulos et al. [19] proposed a method to learn a subspace from image gradient orientations (IGO subspace learning) for appearance-based face recognition that was shown to be very robust to different types of image noise. The advantage of using the IGO subspace learning algorithm is that the cosine distance measure of the algorithm can cancel out outliers or noise caused by occlusion or illumination changes. However, the IGO-algorithm is very sensitive to the alignment, requiring exactly aligned images. We will examine the performance of the IGO-algorithm on the ancient Roman coin recognition problem in Section 4.

Coin recognition methods to read legends of Roman coin were proposed in [2] [11]. The legend provides rich contextual information about the coin such as issuer, mint date and emperor. Therefore, reading the legend means that we know almost everything about the coin including the identification of the emperor. In this sense, the coin recognition is different from the face recognition where there is no contextual information. However, because the letters in the legend are prone to be damaged as shown in Figure 1 and Figure 10, we can extract information from the legend only if we are given a very well-preserved coin. Therefore, we focus on the face of the emperor and implicitly use the legend as we extract features from the legend area without explicitly recognizing it.

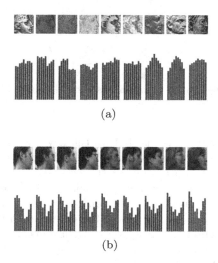

(a)

(b)

Fig. 3. HoG Distributions for coin and real face images. For each image, we extract the HoG descriptors with 9 bins and average them to build a histogram. TOP: 9 coin images. BOTTOM: 9 profile images. The real faces show regular patterns while the coins show different distributions.

3   A Spatial-Appearance Coin Recognition System

In this section, we explain ancient Roman coin recognition methods. First, we explain the standard bag-of-words approach with the spatial pyramid model. Second, we explain a new framework to recognize the ancient coin by employing the deformable part model [7] to locate the face of the emperor. Third, we introduce an alternative method for coin classification which directly encodes the spatial information based on the Fisher vector method.

3.1   Spatial Pyramid Model Approach

We use the bag-of-words (BoW) model to represent the coin images as visual histograms. In the BoW model, we select a set of key points on an input image, extract descriptors from the set of the points, quantize the descriptors to a visual codebook and represent the input image as a histogram of the codewords in the codebook.

Several strategies including dense regular grid [6] and difference-of-Gaussian (DoG) peaks [14] can be used to find the key points on the image. Among them, the dense grid sampling method shows better performance than the others so we choose it to find the key points in our system. On the grid points of the image, we extract SIFT descriptors [14] . k-means clustering method is then used to build the visual codebook and the image is represented as a histogram of the visual words from the codebook.

Fig. 4. An example of the spatial pyramid based on the polar coordinate system. An image is divided into 16 non-overlapping regions.

One problem of this approach is that all the key points are equally handled and the spatial locations of the points are ignored. Therefore, the dense sampling method makes no use of information of the coin structure. To overcome this limitation, we follow the spatial pyramid models widely used in computer vision area [13], [5]. As in [17], we use the polar coordinate system to take an advantage of round shapes of the coin and the face of the emperor. In the polar coordinate system, we place the center of the system at the mass center of the coin and an image is divided into 16 non-overlapping wedge shape regions as shown in Figure 4. The area of the outer circle is equal to the area of the coin and the radius of the inner circle is 60% of the radius of the outer circle.

But the polar system is also sensitive to the origin placement. In the next section, we employ the deformable part model to address the finding of the origin placement

3.2 Strongly-supervised Recognition using Deformable Part Model

In the ancient Roman coins, the shape of the face is a characteristic differentiating a Roman emperor from the other emperors. As coins are old and worn-out the location of the face varies across the coins as shown in Figure 5. In this paper, we employ the deformable part model (DPM) [7] to align the coin image by locating the face of the emperor.

To train DPM with the emperor's face, we define a bounding box of the face as depicted in Figure 5. Four outermost points to draw the bound box are as follows:

– "forehead": a point where the face and the hair meet
– "chin": a point where the chin and the neck meet
– "ear": the left most point of the ear
– "nose": the tip of the nose.

They are chosen so that the face areas inside the box agree all over the emperors. Negative images are collected from reverse images because they contain symbols without the face of the Roman emperor. After training, DPM will automatically detect the face location for a new coin image.

To align the coin image we place the center of the polar coordinate system onto the center of the detected face area by DPM. In this way, each region defined by the polar coordinate system contains consistent area of the coin. We then extract visual features on sub-regions of the polar coordinate system, build a histogram on each region and concatenate them to represent the image.

3.3   Coin Classification Using Fisher Vector

The coin recognition problem can be considered as the fine-grained classification problem as all the images belong to the same super class of 'coin' in this paper. In the fine-grained classification, the distribution of the gradients are often similar as the shapes of the coins look similar to each other. Therefore, Fisher vectors are able to describe the subtle changes in the gradients since they are designed to capture both the first order and the second order statistics of the gradient distribution [8].

Let each image patch be presented as $(\mathbf{x}, \mathbf{l})$ where $\mathbf{x}$ is a vector of visual descriptors of the patch and $\mathbf{l}$ the 2-D location of the patch. We assume that the visual descriptor and the location are independent from each other. We also assume that the patch is generated from a Gaussian mixture model (GMM). As in [12], we formulate the model as follows:

$$
\begin{aligned}
p(\mathbf{x}, \mathbf{l}) &= \sum_k \pi_k \cdot p(\mathbf{x}, \mathbf{l}; \Sigma_k^V, \Sigma_k^L, \mu_k^V, \mu_k^L) \\
&= \sum_k \pi_k \cdot p(\mathbf{x}; \Sigma_k^V, \mu_k^V) \cdot p(\mathbf{l}; \Sigma_k^L, \mu_k^L),
\end{aligned} \tag{1}
$$

π_k is a prior probability for the kth component, Σ_k^V, μ_k^V are means and covariances for the visual descriptors, Σ_k^L, μ_k^L mean and covariance for the location, and

$$
\begin{aligned}
p(\mathbf{x}; \Sigma_k^V, \mu_k^V) &\sim \mathcal{N}(\mathbf{x}; \Sigma_k^V, \mu_k^V) \tag{2} \\
p(\mathbf{l}; \Sigma_k^L, \mu_k^L) &\sim \mathcal{N}(\mathbf{l}; \Sigma_k^L, \mu_k^L). \tag{3}
\end{aligned}
$$

Then, the gradient of $\ln p(\mathbf{x}, \mathbf{l})$ with respect to all parameters becomes the Fisher vector to represent the patch $(\mathbf{x}, \mathbf{l})$. An image representation is obtained by averaging the gradients over all patches in the image. Let $I = \{\mathbf{f}_1, \ldots, \mathbf{f}_N\}$ be a set of D dimensional feature vectors extracted from an image where $\mathbf{f}^{D \times 1} = [\mathbf{x}^\top, \mathbf{l}^\top]^\top$. Then we have

$$
u_{jk} = \frac{1}{N\sqrt{\pi_k}} \sum_{i=1}^{N} q_{ik} \frac{f_{ji} - \mu_{jk}}{\sigma_j}, \tag{4}
$$

$$
v_{jk} = \frac{1}{N\sqrt{2\pi_k}} \sum_{i=1}^{N} q_{ik} \left[\left(\frac{f_{jk} - \mu_{jk}}{\sigma_{jk}} \right)^2 - 1 \right], \quad (j = 1, \ldots, D) \tag{5}
$$

where σ_{jk} is the jth diagonal entry of Σ_k and

$$
q_{ik} = \frac{p(\mathbf{f}_i; \Theta_k)}{\sum_t p(\mathbf{f}_i; \Theta_t)} \qquad \left(\Theta_k = \Sigma_k^V, \Sigma_k^L, \mu_k^V, \mu_k^L \right).
$$

The Fisher vector of the image I is the stacking of the vectors $\mathbf{u}_k$ and $\mathbf{v}_k$. Typically, the parameters Θ_k are trained by the Gaussian mixture model. In this paper, we use the implementation of [20] to represent the coin image as the Fisher vector.

4   Datasets and Experimentation Results

4.1   Coin Data Collection and Experimental Settings

We collect ancient Roman coin images from a numismatic web site. Each coin has a high resolution image (approximately 350×350 pixels jpeg image). Among the collected coin images, we found that some of the coins are hard to recognize because they are rusty and severely damaged. As we are dealing with the problem of recognizing the Roman emperors, a coin that is severely damaged or hard to recognize who is on the coin is discarded. After removing such worn-out coins, we select emperors who appeared more than 10 times in the dataset. Finally, we arrive at 2815 coins with 15 emperors. The sample images for the 15 emperors are depicted in Figure 10. All images in the dataset are ancient Roman Imperial coins dated from 27 BC to 355 AD. In this paper, we consider only the observe(front) of the Roman coin because the emperor is engraved in the observe and the reverse usually shows various non-face symbols.

The deformable part model (DPM) needs the bounding box information in the training procedure. Therefore, we manually annotate bounding boxes for randomly selected 500 coins. Because the coin has the regular structure, we found that 20% of the whole images is enough to train DPM and produce good detection results. As shown in Figure 5, four outermost points to define the bound box are "forehead", "chin", "ear" and "nose", all of which are easily determined by people.

The SIFT descriptor [14] is used to extract the visual descriptors on the grid points. The grid step size (spacing) is 4. Then we use k-means clustering to build the visual codebook, generating the histograms for the coin images using the visual codebook. In this paper, we set k to 200.

The multi-class SVM is used for training and prediction with the RBF-χ^2 kernel except for the Fisher vector based method. We use the linear SVM for the Fisher vector method because it is known that the Fisher vector performs well with simple linear classifiers [18]. All parameters are determined by the 5-fold cross validation. For the evaluation, we randomly partition the coin dataset into 5 equal size subgroups. Each subgroup keeps the same emperor ratio as the total coin dataset. Then, we use 4 subgroups as training data and 1 subgroup as test data. Experiments are repeated 5 times so that each of 5 subgroups becomes the test data, and we report the average of the 5 outputs as a final output. We calculate the average number of correctly classified test samples as the evaluation measure.

Fig. 5. Examples of DPM detection results. The red box represents the ground truth location of the face and and the blue box shows the detected face location by DPM. In most cases, DPM is able to detect the face area. The average accuracy of DPM is 87.18%.

4.2   Experimental Results

We first examine the performance of the deformable part model[1] on the coin dataset. Figure 5 depicts the results of DPM for randomly selected 4 coin images. The red box represents the manually annotated face area of the emperor and the detection area is given by the blue box. We can observe that DPM finds the face areas accurately. To quantitatively evaluate the performance, we use the number of overlapped pixels divided by the size of the ground truth face area as the evaluation measure. We average measured values over the testset and have 0.8718. The most difficult part to detect is the forehead point where the face and the hair meet as shown in the first image of Figure 5. We will use the detected face area in the next part to recognize the coin.

Next, we measure the performance of various method for the coin recognition. To set the baseline performance, we use the standard bag-of-words method without using the spatial pyramid model (`NoSpatial`). In the second method, similar to [17] we use the bag-of-words method with the polar coordinate system centered at the mass center of the coin (`Polar`). `Polar` presumes that the all the coin images are aligned along the mass center of the coin. Neither `NoSpatial` nor `Polar` takes the alignment of the coin into account while recognizing the coin. We also examined the performance of the standard spatial pyramid with the rectangular tiles and found that it performed worse than `Polar`. We believe that the polar coordinate system is more appropriate to capture the round shape of the coin than the rectangular tiles.

However, the location of the Roman emperor's face varies across the coin dataset. Therefore, we use the center of the face detected by DPM to align the coin images as many methods are sensitive to the alignment. To take the advantage of DPM, we construct the spatial pyramid model with the polar coordinate system centered at the center of the detected face by DPM (`DPM-Polar`).

The next method is based on the Fisher vector which encodes the spatial information as described in Section 3.3 (`FV`). Unlike `DPM-Polar`, FV does not need additional training procedure but facilitates the spatially local information in the framework of the Fisher vector approach. In this paper, we assume that

---

[1] We use the implementation available at http://people.cs.uchicago.edu/~rbg/latent-release5/.

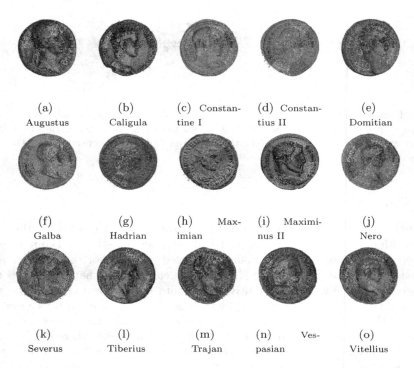

(a)   (b)   (c) Constan-   (d) Constan-   (e)
Augustus   Caligula   tine I   tius II   Domitian

(f)   (g)   (h) Max-   (i) Maximi-   (j)
Galba   Hadrian   imian   nus II   Nero

(k)   (l)   (m)   (n)   Ves-   (o)
Severus   Tiberius   Trajan   pasian   Vitellius

Fig. 6. Discriminative Regions for 15 emperors. Red for more discriminative and blue for less discriminative.

covariance matrix is the identity matrix and the mean vectors are generated by k-means clustering method because not only it is computationally efficient but also it shows better results than using means and covariance matrices from the Gaussian mixture model. We think that the Gaussian mixture model is rather over-fitted on the coin dataset. We do not use the Fisher vector representation with the spatial pyramid because it has not improved the recognition accuracy. In this paper, we set the number of mixtures in the Fisher vectors to 2000.

Then, we use the IGO subspace learning method [19] to examine how well the state-of-the art human face recognition method works for the coin recognition problem (IGO-PCA). We choose IGO-PCA because it was shown to be robust to different types of image noise, which often occur in the coin images. We align and crop the faces along the results of DPM to train IGO-PCA.

Regarding the previous coin classification method, we compare to the directional kernel approach [1](DK) which facilitates the spatial structure of the coin by considering the relationship of the gradient directions between two points on the coin.

The recognition accuracies are summarized in Table 1. NoSpatial shows worse performance than the others considering the spatial structure as it does not take the spatial information into account. On the other hand, Polar significantly

Table 1. Recognition accuracies for various methods

	NoSpatial	Polar	DPM-Polar	FV	IGO-PCA	DK [1]
Acc.	65.77%±1.24	83.48%±1.12	**85.93%± 0.64**	85.36%±0.72	67.42%±0.0097	33.0(±3.0)

improves the recognition accuracy over NoSpatial. The improvement implies that Polar is able to the advantage of the regular structure of the coin.

DPM-Polar shows the best performance among the competing methods because it facilitate the additional spatial information provided by DPM. FV performs comparable to DPM-Polar as it directly encodes the location information without defining spatial pyramids. This result implies that FV provides rich information about the structure of the coin.

IGO-PCA performs slightly better than NoSpatial and at least 16% worse than the others. The poor performance of IGO-PCA can be explained that that coin recognition is totally different from human face recognition and it is difficult to simply apply methods of human face recognition to the ancient Roman coin recognition problem.

DK shows the worst performance on our coin dataset. DK depends on the difference-of-Gaussian (DoG) sampling method to find a set of interest points on the coin image. To combine the visual feature (*e.g.*, SIFT) and the spatial information, it takes the orientation of the interest points into account to build the directional histogram. Therefore, DK becomes sensitive to the orientation of the pixel on the coin image. However, because not only coins in our dataset are old and sometimes damaged but also coin images are taken in different illumination conditions (this is typical in the coin images), it is likely that the orientations of the interest points mislead the classification, explaining the poor performance of DK. On the other hand, as the proposed method uses the uniform sampling on the grid and facilitates the location of the pixels instead of their orientations , it can reduce the effect of the noise of the coin image and therefore it is more robust than DK on the coin dataset.

Discriminative Region Analysis. To determine which area is more discriminative than the others in terms of the recognition, we use the Fisher vector representation described above. Because each component of the Gaussian mixture model (GMM) has the location information in the proposed method, we can project the component of GMM on the 2-D plane according to its location. Then, the importance of each component is determined by the weights derived from the linear SVM model. For the visualization of the discriminative region, we divide the coin area into 16 regions so that the sum of SVM weights of all components in a region represents the importance of the region.

Figure 6 depicts the experimental results. Red color represents more discriminative, blue less discriminative. In general, the upper head area is more discriminative than the other regions because it covers the hair style which is one of the important characteristics of the Roman Emperor as shown in Figure 10. On the other hand, upper right and lower left are less discriminative because they do not

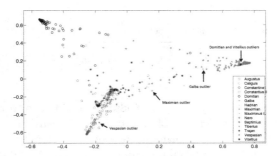

Fig. 7. Projection of the coin images on the 2-D plane using PCA. Each symbol corresponds to one image. A black arrow points an outlier which is far from the same class and/or close to another class.

contain the Emperor's face and the letters on those areas are not consistent over the coin dataset which we have collected. For the Emperors who have specific beard styles such as Maximian (h), Maximinus II (i) and Severus (k), **chin** and **neck** areas are discriminative. The analysis implies that the hair and beard style can provide guidance to discriminate the ancient Roman coins to those who do not have much knowledge on the ancient Roman coins.

Outlier Detection. To see outliers in the coin classification, we collect confidence values of the coin images by running the trained multi-class SVM. Therefore, each coin image is represented as a vector of the confidence values from SVM. Then, we study the manifold of this space of confidences. We do this by running the principal component analysis (PCA) on the confidence values and choose the top 2 principal components. This process allows us to map the coin images on the 2-D plane along the top 2 principal components so we can evaluate the relationship between two emperors with respect to the distance between them.

Figure 7 depicts the projection of the coin images on the 2-D plane. We can find that several emperors form groups together. Outliers can be determined based on the distance to the center of the group. In addition to identifying outliers, we can also judge which emperors are more similar to each other, which ones may be more difficult to distinguish. For evaluation, we select 5 images denoted by the black arrows in Figure 8.

Figure 8a (resp., Figure 8b) depicts Domitian (resp., Vitellius) which is far from the group of Domitian (resp., Vitellius) and close to Vespasian in the projection plane. Both images look like Vespasian in terms of the appearance. In Figure 8d, Galba which is closer to the group of Vespasian than the group of Galba looks like Vespasian as it loses details because of the damage on the coin. One can find that Maximian in Figure 8e looks very different from the ordinary appearance as shown in Figure 10h. Finally, because of the severe damage, Vespasian in Figure 8f is far from the others, making it the outlier.

(a)
Domi-
tian   (b) Vitel- (c)   Ves-   (d)   (e)   Max- (f)   Ves-
        lius   pasian   Galba   imian   pasian

Fig. 8. (a),(b): Outliers for Domitian and Vitellius which look similar to Vespasian (c). (d) Outlier for Galba which looks similar to Vespasian because of the damage on the coin. (e) Outlier for Maximian which looks totally different from the ordinary shape as shown in Figure (10h). (f) Outlier for Vespasian which is damaged and far from the other Vespasian images.

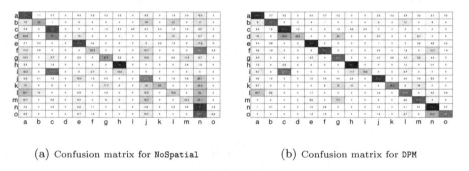

(a) Confusion matrix for NoSpatial   (b) Confusion matrix for DPM

Fig. 9. Confusion matrices for NoSpatial and DPM. DPM has improved the recognition accuracies across all the emperors. (Indices in the table correspond to indices in Figure 10).

Confusion Matrices. The confusion matrices for NoSpatial and DPM are depicted in Figure 9. One can find that DPM has improved the recognition accuracies across all the emperors. Constantius II (d) and Maximinus II (i) are not recognized using NoSpatial because the number of training samples for them is much smaller than the others. However, because of facilitating the spatial information to capture the characteristics of the emperors, DPM is able to improve the recognition accuracies for them.

Maximian (h) has the highest recognition accuracy because he has a distinct appearance from the others as shown in Figure 10. On the other hand, the most confused cases for DPM occurs between Constantine I(c) and Maximinus II (i) because they share very similar appearance as shown in Figure 10.

(a) Augustus   (b) Caligula   (c) Constantine I   (d) Constantius II   (e) Domitian

(f) Galba   (g) Hadrian   (h) Maximian   (i) Maximinus II   (j) Nero

(k) Severus   (l) Tiberius   (m) Trajan   (n) Vespasian

(o) Vitellius

Fig. 10. An example observe image of a coin for each of the 15 classes in the dataset

5   Conclusion

We proposed two automatic methods to recognize the ancient Roman coins. The first method employs the deformable part model to align the coin images to improve the recognition accuracy. The second method facilitates the spatial information of the coin by directly encoding the location information. As the first method takes the information of the face location into account, it performs slightly better than the second method. The experiments show that both methods outperform the other methods such as the standard spatial pyramid model and human face recognition method.

The contributions of the paper are collecting a new ancient Roman coin dataset and proposing an automatic framework to recognize the coins where we employ the state-of-the-art face recognition system and facilitate the spatial information of the coin to improve the recognition accuracy. The coin images are high-resolution (350-by-350 pixels) and the face locations are annotated. While the proposed coin recognition framework is based on the standard methods such as bag-of-words with spatial pyramids, Fisher vectors and DPM, we believe that their use in the context of the ancient coin recognition represents an interesting contribution.

References

1. Arandjelović, O.: Automatic attribution of ancient Roman imperial coins. In: IEEE Conference on Computer Vision and Pattern Recognition (CVPR) (2010)
2. Arandjelović, O.: Reading ancient coins: automatically identifying denarii using obverse legend seeded retrieval. In: Fitzgibbon, A., Lazebnik, S., Perona, P., Sato, Y., Schmid, C. (eds.) ECCV 2012, Part IV. LNCS, vol. 7575, pp. 317–330. Springer, Heidelberg (2012)
3. Cohen, H.: Description historique des monnaies frappées sous l'empire romain, vol. I-VIII, 2 edn. Paris, France (1880–1892)
4. Dalal, N., Triggs, B.: Histograms of oriented gradients for human detection. In: IEEE Conference on Computer Vision and Pattern Recognition (CVPR) (2005)
5. Dimitrovski, I., Kocev, D., Loskovska, S., Deroski, S.: Hierarchical annotation of medical images. Pattern Recognition **44**, 2436–2449 (2011)
6. Fei-Fei, L., Perona, P.: A bayesian hierarchical model for learning natural scene categories. In: IEEE Conference on Computer Vision and Pattern Recognition (CVPR) (2005)
7. Felzenszwalb, P.F., Girshick, R.B., McAllester, D., Ramanan, D.: Object detection with discriminatively trained part based models. IEEE Transactions on Pattern Analysis and Machine Intelligence **32**, 1627–1645 (2010)
8. Gavves, E., Fernando, B., Snoek, C.G.M., Smeulders, A.W.M., Tuytelaars, T.: Fine-grained categorization by alignments. In: International Conference on Computer Vision (ICCV) (2013)
9. Huber, R., Ramoser, H., Mayer, K., Penz, H., Rubik, M.: Classification of coins using an eigenspace approach. Pattern Recognition Letters (PATREC) **26**, 61–75 (2005)
10. Kampel, M., Zaharieva, M.: Recognizing ancient coins based on local features. In: Bebis, G., Boyle, R., Parvin, B., Koracin, D., Remagnino, P., Porikli, F., Peters, J., Klosowski, J., Arns, L., Chun, Y.K., Rhyne, T.-M., Monroe, L. (eds.) ISVC 2008, Part I. LNCS, vol. 5358, pp. 11–22. Springer, Heidelberg (2008)
11. Kavelar, A., Zambanini, S., Kampel, M.: Word detection applied to images of ancient Roman coins. In: International Conference on Virtual Systems and Multimedia (VSMM), pp. 577–580, September 2012
12. Krapac, J., Verbeek, J., Jurie, F.: Modeling Spatial Layout with Fisher Vectors for Image Categorization. International Journal of Computer Vision (IJCV) (2011)
13. Lazebnik, S., Schmid, C., Ponce, J.: Beyond bags of features: spatial pyramid matching for recognizing natural scene categories. In: IEEE Computer Vision and Pattern Recognition (CVPR) (2006)
14. Lowe, D.G.: Distinctive image features from scale-invariant keypoints. International Journal of Computer Vision (IJCV) **60**, 91–110 (2004)

15. van der Maaten, L.J.P., Boon, P.J.: Coin-o-matic: a fast system for reliable coin classification. In: MUSCLE CIS Coin Competition Workshop (2006)
16. Nölle, M., Penz, H., Rubik, M., Mayer, K., Hollaender, I., Granec, R.: Dagobert - a new coin recognition and sorting system. In: Conference on Digital Image Computing: Techniques and Applications (DICTA) (2003)
17. Piater, J., Rodríguez-Sánchez, A.: A Bag of Visual Words Approach for Symbols-Based Coarse-Grained Ancient Coin Classification. CoRR abs/1304.6, 1–8 (2013)
18. Sanchez, J., Perronnin, F., Mensink, T., Verbeek, J.: Image Classification with the Fisher Vector: Theory and Practice. International Journal of Computer Vision (IJCV) **105**, 222–245 (2013)
19. Tzimiropoulos, G., Zafeiriou, S., Pantic, M.: Subspace learning from image gradient orientations. IEEE Transactions on Pattern Analysis and Machine Intelligence (TPAMI) **34**, 2454–2466 (2012)
20. Vedaldi, A., Fulkerson, B.: VLFeat: An open and portable library of computer vision algorithms (2008). http://www.vlfeat.org/
21. Zaharieva, M., Kampel, M., Zambanini, S.: Image based recognition of ancient coins. In: Kropatsch, W.G., Kampel, M., Hanbury, A. (eds.) CAIP 2007. LNCS, vol. 4673, pp. 547–554. Springer, Heidelberg (2007)
22. Zambanini, S., Kampel, M.: Coarse-to-fine correspondence search for classifying ancient coins. In: Park, J.-I., Kim, J. (eds.) ACCV Workshops 2012, Part II. LNCS, vol. 7729, pp. 25–36. Springer, Heidelberg (2013)

W02 - Computer Vision in Vehicle Technology

Vision-Based Vehicle Localization Using a Visual Street Map with Embedded SURF Scale

David Wong[1]($\boxtimes$), Daisuke Deguchi[2], Ichiro Ide[1], and Hiroshi Murase[1]

[1] Graduate School of Information Science, Nagoya University, Nagoya, Japan
{davidw,ide,murase}@murase.m.is.nagoya-u.ac.jp
[2] Information and Communications Headquarters, Nagoya University, Nagoya, Japan
ddeguchi@nagoya-u.jp

Abstract. Accurate vehicle positioning is important not only for in-car navigation systems but is also a requirement for emerging autonomous driving methods. Consumer level GPS are inaccurate in a number of driving environments such as in tunnels or areas where tall buildings cause satellite shadowing. Current vision-based methods typically rely on the integration of multiple sensors or fundamental matrix calculation which can be unstable when the baseline is small.

In this paper we present a novel visual localization method which uses a visual street map and extracted SURF image features. By monitoring the difference in scale of features matched between input images and the visual street map within a Dynamic Time Warping framework, stable localization in the direction of motion is achieved without calculation of the fundamental or essential matrices.

We present the system performance in real traffic environments. By comparing localization results with a high accuracy GPS ground truth, we demonstrate that accurate vehicle positioning is achieved.

Keywords: Ego-localization · Monocular vision · Dynamic time warping · SURF · Vehicle navigation

1 Introduction

Vehicle ego-localization is an essential component of in-car navigation systems and a necessary step for many of the emerging driver assistance and obstacle avoidance methods. Standard GPS systems can be sensitive to the occlusions common in city driving situations, and rarely manage 5 m accuracy even in ideal environments. For tasks such as lane recognition and obstacle avoidance, higher precision in all environments is required.

For unrestrained motion in unfamiliar environments, Simultaneous Localization And Mapping (SLAM) [1] is an active area of research. Camera-based methods are popular [2], [3], [4]. For automotive navigation, the availability of *a-priori* information and the applicability of known constraints, such as a fixed ground plane, allow for simpler localization without the need for simultaneous map construction and loop closure detection. Therefore there are an increasing

© Springer International Publishing Switzerland 2015
L. Agapito et al. (Eds.): ECCV 2014 Workshops, Part I, LNCS 8925, pp. 167–179, 2015.
DOI: 10.1007/978-3-319-16178-5_11

number of methods that propose the use of cameras with a pre-constructed image database for vehicle positioning [5], [6], [7], [8], [9]. This configuration still has many challenges, including robust localization when lateral translation occurs (for example when a lane change takes place) and computational issues with the calculation of geometry such as the fundamental matrix between views.

In this paper we propose a method for ego-localization that makes use of the scale of Speeded Up Robust Features (SURF) [10] to match images, and show how the use of feature scale improves image match accuracy. A query image is localized by using the known position information of the closest match within a database, or image street map. Unlike other image feature-based localization techniques, no essential or fundamental matrix calculation is required, yet the advantages of feature-based methods including robustness to occlusions and lateral motion are retained. Our method consists of three main components:

1. A visual street map with embedded SURF and accurate position information for every image, constructed from high accuracy sensors including GPS, IMU and odometry
2. A weighted feature matching method which applies the constraints of typical road scenes to the matching of SURF points
3. A localization algorithm that monitors the scale difference between SURF features in the query and street map images within a Dynamic Time Warping (DTW) [11] algorithm to achieve stable localization

We demonstrate the performance of our system in a typical urban traffic environment, and show that using feature scale changes is a simple yet robust way to find the closest street map image and therefore localize the current image. We show how our method is capable of localization even when the traversed lane is different from the lane used for image street map construction.

This paper is organized as follows: In Sect. 2 we give a brief overview of related research. We describe the proposed method in more detail in Sect. 3 and experimental results are presented in Sect. 4. We discuss the results in Sect. 5 before concluding in Sect. 6.

2   Related Work

For automotive ego-localization, there are many visual methods which perform vehicle positioning by using a pre-constructed database [5], [8] or image databases such as Google Street View [9]. These systems perform complete localization relative to database images using structure from motion techniques. Such methods allow high accuracy, for example, up to 10 cm precision when combined with an IMU [5], but are also computationally intensive and therefore may barely run in real-time (Lategahn et al. [5] quote 3–10 Hz for their vision + IMU method). They also usually employ supporting sensors in the localization stage—either an IMU [5], or odometry information [9]. A simpler approach is to localize against the closest database image, of which location is known, using DTW [11] (or Dynamic Programming [12]) to remove temporal differences between query and database image streams [6], [13], or by using a low bit-rate image sequence instead of single images [14], which improves stability in varying lighting and weather conditions. The image similarity measure used for matching between sample images and those in the database can be based on average image intensity difference [14], or a kind of template matching [6], [13]. Lane changes and occlusions are not well handled by such methods because they cause a sustained difference in appearance of an appreciable portion of the image. Feature point-based methods are more robust to such changes. Kyutoku et al. [7] matched SIFT [15] features between images to calculate the position of the epipole as a DTW cost measure for comparing image capture positions. The epipole moves away from the vanishing point as the image capture positions become similar. While effective, this technique requires the calculation of the fundamental matrix so can be unstable when the baseline between the query and database images is small.

Vehicle ego-localization is similar to the localization component of the SLAM problem for robotic navigation [1]. There are a number of successful SLAM implementations using a single camera which typically employ structure from motion techniques to determine camera pose [2], [3], [4], [16]. SLAM methods do not easily scale to the large environments found in automotive environments; however the SLAM loop closure problem, where a robot must recognize when it has entered a previously mapped area, is similar to the map relative localization step of automotive ego-localization. State-of-the-art SLAM loop closure methods often use Bag of Features [4], [17], which are excellent at recognizing visually similar areas for loop closure but do not provide a solution for exact localization. They also require the construction of feature vocabularies, which can make scaling to very large environments challenging.

None of the methods mentioned above make use of the scale property of image features to determine image similarity. We show that by using scale differences between matched features as a cost measure for DTW, we can accurately match query images to an image map in an automotive setting. Our method does not require the calculation of feature vocabularies or reconstruction of scene geometry, and since it is feature-based, it continues to work well when partial occlusion or lane changes occur.

3   Proposed Ego-Localization Method

This section describes a method of ego-localization by comparing images captured from a vehicle-mounted camera and a pre-constructed visual street map. The street map is constructed using data captured from a vehicle equipped with cameras and accurate positioning hardware. Images captured in the localization step are compared to the street map images using DTW to compensate for speed differences in the two image streams. The process is described in more detail below. Sect. 3.1 describes the concept behind SURF scale matching, and Sect. 3.2 details the visual street map construction step. Sect. 3.3 describes the

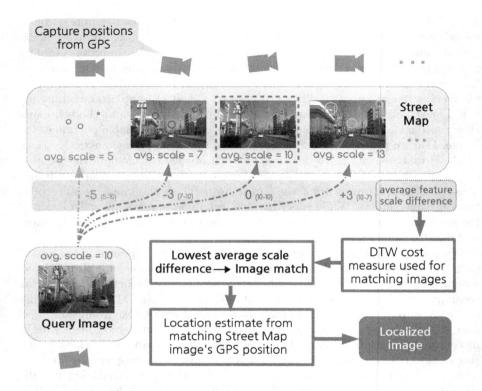

Fig. 1. A flow chart outlining the proposed method. The two main stages are the visual street map construction, and the ego-localization by DTW matching the query images from the vehicle to be localized to the street map.

localization of an input query image. An overview of the proposed system is presented in Fig. 1.

3.1   Concept: Image Matching Using SURF Scale

Scale invariant features such as SURF are commonly used for their robustness to changes in lighting and view orientation. One of the properties of SURF keypoints is their size, or scale. The method proposed in this paper is based around the use of the scale of these features for image matching and therefore localization. If two images have the same viewing direction, their corresponding SURF feature points will have a similar scale when the capture positions were spatially close. As the distance between the images increases, the difference in corresponding feature scales also increase. The proposed method makes use of this change to match images between the query image and the street map by averaging the scale change of the matched features. The street map image with the smallest average scale change from the query is selected as a match, therefore

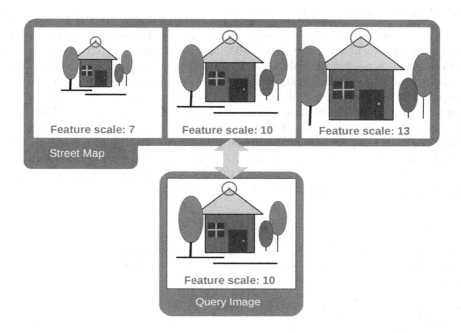

Fig. 2. A demonstration of scale change for image matching. The street map images are in the top row and the query image below. A sample feature matched across all views shows how the scale change is used to find the closest match.

localizing the query image in the direction of motion. In the context of DTW, features extracted from street map images behind the query image's location will have a smaller scale than the corresponding features of the query image; conversely, corresponding features from street map images from in front of the query image will have larger scale. Sequentially running through the street map images and finding where the feature scale changes are minimized leads to the spatially closest street map image for each query image, and because we know the location of each street map image in world co-ordinates, we can assign this position to the query image for localization. Only the scale change between the matched features is used, so there is no need to calculate fundamental matrices. This allows stable image matching even when the baseline between query and street map images is small, or zero. When lateral motion occurs, the average scale change remains constant so the method is also robust to changes in lane and road position when localizing in the direction of motion. Fig. 2 shows the concept of using feature scale change for image matching.

3.2   Visual Street Map Construction

The visual street map used by this method consists of a series of images with corresponding world locations and SURF feature points. The street map construction step is performed only once. In addition to one (or more) cameras for image capture, precise localization sensor hardware is required. For the results presented in this paper, the equipment used to construct the street map included several vehicle mounted cameras, a high accuracy GPS, and hub mounted odometry recording hardware. This hardware configuration allowed high accuracy positioning of each image frame in the visual street map. More information on the experimental setup is provided in Sect. 4. SURF features are extracted from each image in the visual street map, resulting in a series of images with corresponding camera positions and SURF keypoints with descriptors.

3.3   Localization

The localization step only requires the pre-constructed visual street map and query images from a vehicle-mounted camera. The process can be broken into two main steps:

1. SURF feature extraction and matching
2. Sequential image matching to the database images using average scale change of SURF points and DTW matching

The result is a position in world co-ordinates for the vehicle at the current image, corresponding to the closest street map image location.

SURF Feature Extraction and Matching. Extracted SURF features are matched to features from the series of the street map images, starting from the last matched image in the sequence. The proposed method relies quite heavily on a reasonable number of correct matches. To keep the localization step simple and efficient, RANSAC pruning of outlier feature matching is avoided. Instead, we propose a simple weighted matching cost which matches features based on known constraints. The views in both streams are forward looking and the camera heights are constant, so good image match candidates will have similar y pixel coordinates and a limited change in scale and feature response. Based on these properties, a weighted criteria is used for determining likely inlier matches. A spatial constraint is applied so that each potential match candidate is only searched for in a region with pixel values close to where the feature was located in the query image, particularly in the y direction of the image plane. The candidate features must also be from the same octave. Then the best match for the query image feature f_τ is calculated by finding the database image feature f_i within the set of N features $i = 1, 2, ..., N$ which minimizes the following equation:

$$m(i) = w_s |s(f_\tau) - s(f_i)| + w_r |r(f_\tau) - r(f_i)| \\ + w_d \mathrm{SSD}(f_\tau, f_i), \tag{1}$$

where $s(f)$ is the feature scale, $r(f)$ is the feature response, and $\text{SSD}(f_1, f_2)$ is the standard sum of squared differences of the feature descriptors. The weights w_s, w_d, w_r should be adjusted to give a strong inlier set while maintaining a high number of matched features.

DTW Matching. DTW is a popular for method for optimally aligning time-dependent sequences by using a local cost measure to compare sequence features [11]. In the proposed localization method, DTW computes the cost between the current query image and a sequence of street map images, and selects the minimum cost as an image match. The aim of the process is to find the most similar street map image for each query image, therefore removing temporal differences in the two image streams and allowing the query images to be localized relative to the image street map, as illustrated in the system overview in Fig. 1. We propose a cost measure based on the average scale change of matched SURF features. Matched SURF features that are extracted at the same octave [10] may vary in scale if there is a translation between the two cameras; we make use of the scale differences to match images which are closest to each other. For a set of street map images $I_1 = \{t \mid 0 \leq t \leq T_1\}$ and query images $I_2 = \{\tau \mid 0 \leq \tau \leq T_2\}$ we take the latest query image $I_2(\tau)$ for localization. A subset of the street map images, $\tilde{I} \subset I_1 \rightarrow \tilde{t} \in \tilde{I}$ is selected for cost minimization. This is done by calculating the query image feature matches with sequential street map images, starting with the previously matched street map image and continuing until the number of matched features falls below a threshold. Within the resulting subset of street map images, only the individual feature matches that are consistent throughout the whole subset are used. This results in a set of $N_{\tilde{t}, \tau}$ matched features f in each subset street map image $\tilde{I}(\tilde{t})$ and the query image $I_2(\tau)$. This step is important, because some street map images will have many more feature matches than others, and scale changes vary depending on overall feature size. By only considering features shared throughout the subset $\tilde{I}$, a fair comparison in relative scale change can be made. The number of features used is the same for each candidate feature street map match ($N_{\tilde{t}, \tau}$ is the same for all $\tilde{I}(\tilde{t})$), so as a cost measure for DTW, the absolute summed scale change is equivalent to the average scale difference. The cost of each image match $g(\tilde{t}, \tau)$ is therefore calculated by summing the absolute feature scale differences as follows:

$$g(\tilde{t}, \tau) = \sum_{i=0}^{N_{\tilde{t}, \tau}} |s(f_{\tilde{t}, i}) - s(f_{\tau, i})|, \qquad (2)$$

where $s(f)$ is the scale parameter extracted from the relevant SURF feature. The street map image which minimizes $g(\tilde{t}, \tau)$ is deemed to be the closest location to the query image, providing localization in the direction of motion.

4   Experiments

Testing of the proposed method was carried out in an urban environment which included a variety of buildings, traffic, lighting variations, and lane changes.

Rate

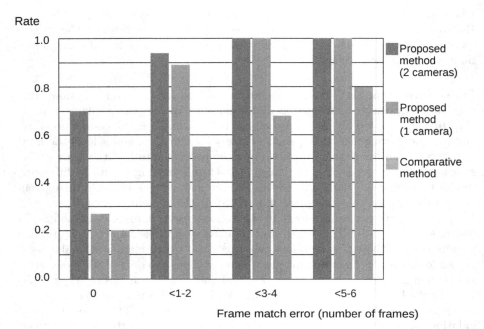

Frame match error (number of frames)

Fig. 3. Frame matching accuracy of the proposed method using one camera, two cameras, and the comparative method using the number of matched features.

4.1 Vehicle Configuration

The visual street map and query image streams were captured using a Mitsubishi Electric MMS-X320R Mobile Mapping System (MMS). This system incorporates three 5 megapixel cameras, three LASER scanners, GPS, and odometry hardware. The localization system of the MMS was used both for street map construction and also to supply a ground truth for the query image set for evaluation. Images from two forward facing cameras were used in both street map construction and localization performance testing. The MMS provides a claimed localization precision of greater than 6 cm (RMS), and the system provided an estimated average error of below 1 cm in the experiments we conducted.

For the purposes of evaluating the performance of the proposed method, two passes of the same road were made over a stretch of about 2 km. The two cameras captured frames at intervals of approximately 2 m, at vehicle speeds varying between 20 km/h and 50 km/h. The database pass was made in the left hand lane where the localization pass was made in the right hand lane.

4.2 Localization Performance

For feature matching, the weights w_s, w_d, w_r from (1) were selected by observing incorrect matches and modifying accordingly. The scale difference of correct

Table 1. Localization Results

Method	Average error (m)	Maximum error (m)
Proposed method (with SURF scale, one camera)	1.96	8.10
Proposed method (with SURF scale, two cameras)	1.56	6.00
Comparative method (without SURF scale, one camera)	8.45	16.12

matches was typically relatively small, so a w_s value of approximately ten times w_d and w_r (which were approximately equal) was found to be effective. This configuration still prioritized the SSD of feature descriptors for determining the best feature match.

Localization relative to the street map was performed using one camera and repeated with two cameras. For a comparative method that does not make use of feature scales, the inverse of the number of matched features was used for the DTW matching cost [18]. In the comparative method, the cost measure in (2) was replaced with the following:

$$g(\tilde{t}, \tau) = 1/N_{\tilde{t},\tau}. \tag{3}$$

If enough features are extracted and the same feature match filtering described by (1) is employed, the comparative method offers a reasonably effective way of identifying the general street map area of the current query image. However, the results we present below show how additionally monitoring the scale of the matched features allows a much more refined comparison of the input and street map images.

The localization accuracy for each method was evaluated by using the MMS localization data. The ground truth localization information associated with the query images was used to calculate the actual closest visual street map image, creating an image match ground truth. The match result of the query image relative to the street map was compared to the image match ground truth. The image matching results of the three methods are presented in Fig. 3.

The results show that the use of the scale of matched features gives a more robust distance measure between the query and street map images, even when the query images are captured in a different lane from the street map images. Comparison of the one and two camera results shows that wider field of view provided by two cameras increases the image matching performance of the method considerably. Fig. 4 shows a comparison of the street map images selected as matches and sample query images, for both the proposed method and the comparison method. The image matching performance of the proposed method is consistently good, with the GPS ground truth showing that the system finds the correct closest street map image for 70 % of the time, and is always within 3 frames of the correct match (when both cameras are used).

The cameras capture images at distance rather than time intervals, so there is a high accuracy penalty for each incorrectly matched image frame. An incorrect match results in a localization error of approximately 2 m or a multiple of 2 m because of the fixed frame capture separation of the MMS system. Despite of this, the average localization error of our system was less than 2 m, which is within one street map image interval, even when a single camera was used. The average localization accuracy results are presented in Table 1.

5   Discussion

Even though the street view map was constructed using a different lane from the query image views, successful localization was performed, illustrating the robustness of using feature scale for image matching when lateral change in viewpoint occurs. Because it is a feature-based localization method, it also demonstrated robust matching in the presence of occlusion. An example of successful matching in an occluded scene is shown in Fig. 5. Unlike most feature-based localization methods, no calculation of image geometry is required, so the method is simple. It also demonstrated good recovery from incorrect matches. In the dataset used for the experiments, the vehicle never came into a situation where localization was not possible within the spatial constraints applied by the DTW method. In the case where this could happen though, if the vehicle became lost, a regressive image matching method from a wider selection of the street map images may need to be performed.

There were a number of issues specific to the image capture method which limited the accuracy of the proposed method in our experiments. The 2 m capture interval of the camera meant that the metric localization error of individual image matches could only be evaluated in multiples of approximately 2 m. The accuracy of the system is highly dependent on the frame rate of capture and also visual street map image interval, so a higher frame rate would provide far superior results and more effective analysis of accuracy. The localization accuracy could also be potentially improved by applying a motion model and interpolating the query image position between the two closest matched street map images.

The use of both forward facing cameras improved the results, because of the wider field of view they enabled. The two cameras were not used as a stereo pair so a similar result could be achieved using a monocular camera and a lens providing a wide field of view.

The experiments in this method used the same vehicle and cameras for the street map construction and localization stages. This is quite a favorable configuration, so future work will include testing with images from a range of cameras and lens types as well as determining how differing camera heights and environmental conditions affect the stability of the system.

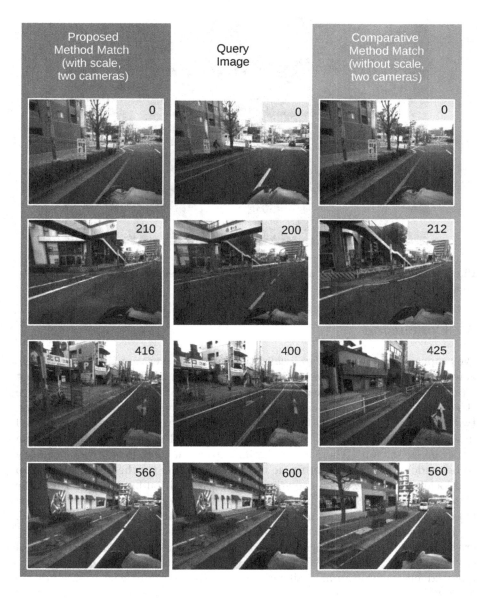

Fig. 4. Sample images showing DTW matching results. The central column is the query image, and the one on left the corresponding matched street map image using the proposed method. The column on the right shows the matched street map images using the comparative method. The numbers in the top right of the images are the sequence frame numbers, showing how DTW matching absorbs differences in vehicle speeds between the visual street map and query image sequences. Note that although results from using both cameras are displayed, only the left-hand camera image is shown for clarity.

Fig. 5. Example of successful image matching when occlusions occur in either the query image or street map image

6   Conclusion

We proposed a method for ego-localization using the average SURF scale change across matched features as a cost measure for sequential image matching against a pre-constructed visual street map. The experimental results show that effective street map image matching can be achieved with an average error of 1.56 m using two cameras. The system performs well even when the query images are captured in a different lane from the street map images, and is robust to occlusions in either image streams. There are potential improvements in localization accuracy to be made by using a higher frame rate image capture for the visual street map and localization stages. Interpolating the vehicle position between several of the closest matched street map images rather than taking the position of the single closest matched street map image is another potential extension to the method.

Future work will include the construction of a street map with a higher camera frame rate for greater localization accuracy, and testing in a larger variety of environmental conditions. We also plan to test the method with different cameras and lenses, for example a single camera with a wide angle lens configuration for a wide field of view to replace the two camera experimental setup presented in this paper.

Acknowledgments. Parts of this research were supported by JST CREST, JST COI, JSPS Grantin- Aid for Scientific Research, and the Japanese Ministry of Education, Culture, Sports, Science, and Technology (MEXT).

References

1. Durrant-Whyte, H.F., Bailey, T.: Simultaneous localization and mapping: Part I. IEEE Robotics and Automation Magazine **13**(2), 99–110 (2006)
2. Mouragnon, E., Lhuillier, M., Dhome, M., Dekeyser, F., Sayd, P.: Monocular vision based SLAM for mobile robots. In: Proc. 18th International Conference of Pattern Recognition (ICPR2006), vol. 3, pp. 1027–1031 (2006)
3. Davison, A.J., Reid, I.D., Molton, N.D., Stasse, O.: MonoSLAM: Real-time single camera SLAM. IEEE Trans. Pattern Analysis and Machine Intelligence **29**(6), 1052–1067 (2007)
4. Botterill, T., Mills, S., Green, R.D.: Bag-of-words-driven, single-camera simultaneous localization and mapping. Journal of Field Robotics **28**(2), 204–226 (2011)
5. Lategahn, H., Schreiber, M., Ziegler, J., Stiller, C.: Urban localization with camera and inertial measurement unit. In: Proc. 2013 IEEE Intelligent Vehicles Symposium (IV2013), pp. 719–724 (2013)
6. Uchiyama, H., Deguchi, D., Takahashi, T., Ide, I., Murase, H.: Ego-localization using streetscape image sequences from in-vehicle cameras. In: Proc. 2009 IEEE Intelligent Vehicles Symposium (IV2009), pp. 185–190 (2009)
7. Kyutoku, H., Takahashi, T., Mekada, Y., Ide, I., Murase, H.: On-road obstacle detection by comparing present and past in-vehicle camera images. In: Proc. 12th IAPR Conference on Machine Vision Applications (MVA2011), pp. 357–360 (2011)
8. Nedevschi, S., Popescu, V., Danescu, R., Marita, T., Oniga, F.: Accurate ego-vehicle global localization at intersections through alignment of visual data with digital map. IEEE Trans. Intelligent Transportation Systems **14**(2), 673–687 (2013)
9. Badino, H., Huber, D.F., Kanade, T.: Real-time topometric localization. In: Proc. 2012 IEEE International Conference on Robotics and Automation (ICRA2012), pp. 1635–1642 (2012)
10. Bay, H., Ess, A., Tuytelaars, T., Van Gool, L.: Speeded-Up Robust Features (SURF). Computer Vision and Image Understanding **110**(3), 346–359 (2008)
11. Muller, M.: Dynamic time warping. In: Information Retrieval for Music and Motion, pp. 69–84. Springer, Heidelberg (2007)
12. Wagner, D.B.: Dynamic programming. The Mathematica Journal **5**(4), 42–51 (1995)
13. Sato, J., Takahashi, T., Ide, I., Murase, H.: Change detection in streetscapes from GPS coordinated omni-directional image sequences. In: Proc. 18th International Conference of Pattern Recognition (ICPR2006), pp. 935–938 (2006)
14. Milford, M.: Visual route recognition with a handful of bits. In: Proc. 2012 Robotics: Science and Systems, pp. 297–304 (2012)
15. Lowe, D.: Distinctive image features from scale-invariant keypoints. International Journal of Computer Vision **60**(2), 91–110 (2004)
16. Se, S., Lowe, D., Little, J.: Vision-based mobile robot localization and mapping using scale-invariant features. In: Proc. 2001 IEEE International Conference on Robotics and Automation (ICRA2001), pp. 2051–2058 (2001)
17. Cummins, M., Newman, P.: Appearance-only SLAM at large scale with FAB-MAP 2.0. International Journal of Robotics Research **30**(9), 1–24 (2010)
18. Kameda, Y., Ohta, Y.: An implementation of pedestrian localization by first-person view camera in urban area (in Japanese). In: Proc. 13th Meeting on Image Recognition and Understanding (MIRU2010), pp. 364–369 (2010)

Approximated Relative Pose Solvers
for Efficient Camera Motion Estimation

Jonathan Ventura[1,2]([⊠]), Clemens Arth[2], and Vincent Lepetit[2]

[1] Department of Computer Science, University of Colorado Colorado Springs,
Colorado Springs, USA
jventura@uccs.edu
[2] Institute for Computer Graphics and Vision,
Graz University of Technology, Graz, Austria
{arth,lepetit}@icg.tugraz.at

Abstract. We propose simple and efficient methods for estimating the
camera motion between two images when this motion is small. While current solutions are still either slow, or unstable in case of small translation,
we show how to considerably speed up a recent stable but slow method.
The reasons for this speed-up are twofold. First, by approximating the
rotation matrix to first order, we obtain a smaller polynomial system to
be solved. Second, because of the small rotation assumption, we can use
linearization and truncation of higher-order terms to quickly obtain a
single solution. Our experiments show that our approach is both stable
and fast on challenging test sequences from vehicle-mounted cameras.

Keywords: Camera pose · Relative pose · Relative orientation · Five-pt
algorithm · Essential matrix · Gröbner basis

1 Introduction

Estimating the rotational and translational movement of a calibrated camera
between two images is a fundamental problem in computer vision, with many
applications such as visual odometry, structure-from-motion, and simultaneous
localization and mapping (SLAM). While many solutions to the relative pose
problem have been proposed in the past [3,4,9,12,13,15,17–20,22,23,25], existing solutions have still three critical issues. The first issue is numerical instability
when the translation is small with respect to the scene depth. A second issue
is multiplicity of solutions; even in the minimal case of five point correspondences, up to ten camera pose solutions are possible, and additional processing
is required to select the correct solution. Third, while recent work has shown
that the rotation can be estimated independently of the translation [13], thus

Electronic supplementary material The online version of this chapter (doi:10.
1007/978-3-319-16178-5_12) contains supplementary material, which is available to
authorized users. Videos can also be accessed at http://www.springerimages.com/
videos/978-3-319-16177-8.

L. Agapito et al. (Eds.): ECCV 2014 Workshops, Part I, LNCS 8925, pp. 180–193, 2015.
DOI: 10.1007/978-3-319-16178-5_12

avoiding the instability with small translation, this method is much slower than the state-of-the-art.

In this work, we introduce novel solution procedures for solving for the rotation independent of the translation. These solvers are as fast or faster than the state-of-the-art, and as accurate for small rotations. Our key observation is that, in many practical cases, the amount of rotation is small, and we can safely approximate the rotation matrix to the first-order. Using this approximation, we obtain a system of ten polynomial equations involving only the rotation parameters, which is a smaller system than the thirty equations required for the general case [13]. Once the rotation estimate is obtained, the translation can easily be estimated as well.

Our evaluations on synthetic and real datasets show that our solutions are as fast or faster than existing methods, without any significant loss in accuracy for small motions. The simplicity of our solvers are such that they are suitable for implementation in embedded hardware for ground vehicles or low-powered micro-aerial vehicles, or for application with high-speed cameras.

The remainder of the paper is structured as follows. We first review related work in Section 2. We then formalize the approximated relative pose problem in Section 3, and describe various solution procedures in Section 4. In Section 5, we compare our methods to state-of-the-art algorithms applied to visual odometry on two public datasets.

2   Related Work

The relative pose problem, the computation of the camera motion between two images from point correspondences, is an essential problem encountered in photogrammetry and computer vision with an eventful history. The first solution to the five-point problem was proposed by Kruppa [14], who proved that the problem has at most eleven solutions. Demazure [3], Faugeras [4], Maybank [20] and others improved upon this approach later. They showed that this problem has at most ten solutions in general, including complex ones, being the roots of a tenth-degree polynomial.

While Kruppa proposed an algorithm with little practical applicability, solutions in the context of modern Computer Vision based on eight and seven points were proposed by Longuet-Higgins [19] and Maybank [20]. A six-point solution was introduced by Philip [23], extracting the roots of a thirteen-degree polynomial. Nistér improved on this approach, solving a tenth-degree polynomial corresponding to the exact problem difficulty [22]. His solution is based on QR-factorization, Gauss-Jordan elimination on a 10×20 matrix, reduction to a single polynomial, and Sturm sequences for root-finding. From there on, algorithms based on five point correspondences, the minimal number of required correspondences, raised special interest for their application in a hypothesize-and-test framework [5].

A first solver based on Gröbner bases [2] was given by Stewénius et al. [24]. Alternative formulations also based on Gröbner bases were proposed by Kukelova *et al.* [15] and Kalantari *et al.* [9]. Li *et al.* proposed relatively simpler solutions for the five-point and six-points problem based on the hidden variable resultant [16,17]; however, this is less efficient.

More recently, Lim *et al.* proposed estimating the rotation and translation separately, relying on a special feature correspondence distribution [18]. Kneip *et al.* later proposed considering rotation and translation separately in the general case [13]. Their algorithm still exhibits instability in cases of negligible translational motion, which need to be explicitly detected. They parameterized the rotation with a 3×3 matrix, which requires adding twenty additional constraints which enforce the matrix to be orthogonal and have unit determinant. They then used the method of Gröbner bases to find up to twenty solutions for the rotation from a matrix of size 66×197 [13]. The authors also mention that they tried the Cayley rotation parameterization [1], which has the minimal three parameters, but leads to a larger and slower solution procedure. Kneip *et al.* later proposed an iterative solution which is more stable, but in practice requires using more than the minimal five correspondences in order to avoid local minima [12].

The work most closely related to ours is that of Stewenius et al. [25], who also use a first-order approximated rotation matrix. They briefly mention that it is possible to solve for the rotation independently of the translation, but then proceed to describe a method for instead computing the translation. This leads to a solver which is faster than Nistér's solver [22]. However, in this work we choose to solve for the rotation because it leads to an even faster solver based on linearization and truncation of higher-order terms.

3   Problem Statement

For the sake of completeness, we briefly describe here the method of Kneip *et al.* [13], which is our starting point. Let's consider two images of a rigid scene. The essential matrix E relates corresponding image locations u_i and v_i expressed in homogeneous coordinates, in the first and second images, respectively, by

$$v_i^T E u_i = 0 \, , \tag{1}$$

with $E = [t]_\times R$, where R and t are the rotation matrix and translation vector of the rigid motion of the camera between the two images. This can be re-arranged to isolate the rotation and translation parameters:

$$(u_i^T R^T [v_i]_\times) \cdot t = 0 \, . \tag{2}$$

Five point correspondences between the two images give five equations of the form of Eq. (2), which can be arrange into an equation system:

$$A(r) \cdot t = 0 \, , \tag{3}$$

where $A(r)$ is a 5×3 matrix and r are the parameters of the rotation. Since $A(r)$ has a null vector, it must be of at most rank two. Hence, all the 3×3 sub-determinants $|A_{ijk}|$ of $A(r)$ must be zero. This gives $\binom{5}{3} = 10$ equations which only involve the rotation parameters:

$$|A_{ijk}| = 0 \ \forall (i, j, k) \in \mathcal{S} \,, \tag{4}$$

with $\mathcal{S} = \{(1, 2, 3), (1, 2, 4), (1, 2, 5), (1, 3, 4), (1, 3, 5), (1, 4, 5), (2, 3, 4), (2, 3, 5), (2, 4, 5), (3, 4, 5)\}$.

Kneip *et al.* [13] solve these equations in the general case, which requires twenty additional constraints on the rotation matrix and results in a slow solver. We show below that under the assumption of a small motion, solving these equations becomes very simple.

4 Approach

In our approach, we first introduce an approximation of the rotation matrix, and use it to rewrite the system of equations (4). We then show how this system can be simplified, and very easily solved.

We assume that the motion between the two images is small. This allows us to replace the rotation matrix R by its first-order expansion:

$$\hat{R}(r) = I + [r]_\times \,, \tag{5}$$

where $r = [r_1, r_2, r_3]^T$ is a three-vector. The corresponding exact rotation matrix can be retrieved as $R(r) = \exp_{SO(3)}(r)$. This gives us a simple parameterization for the rotation matrix. Plugging it into the ten equations of (4) leads us to a system of ten cubic polynomials in twenty monomials:

$$M_{10 \times 20} \, x = 0 \,, \tag{6}$$

with

$$\begin{aligned} x = [&r_1^3, r_1^2 \, r_2, r_1 \, r_2^2, r_2^3, r_1^2 \, r_3, r_1 \, r_2 \, r_3, r_2^2 \, r_3, r_1 \, r_3^2, r_2 \, r_3^2, r_3^3, \\ &r_1^2, r_1 \, r_2, r_2^2, r_1 \, r_3, r_2 \, r_3, r_3^2, r_1, r_2, r_3, 1]^T . \end{aligned} \tag{7}$$

The following sections give three different solution procedures for solving this system of equations.

4.1 Reduction to a Single Polynomial

The system of equations given by Equation 6 has the same form as found in the five-point algorithm of Nistér [22], and thus can be solved in the same manner, namely, reduction to a single tenth-degree polynomial in r_3. The root-finding procedure leads to ten solutions for r_3; corresponding solutions for r_1 and r_2 are found by back-substitution.

Sturm sequences are used to bracket the roots, which are then quickly located exactly through bisectioning. In our case, we speed up the root-finding procedure by restricting our search to reasonable bounds on the rotation magnitude. In practice we assume that solutions for r_3 should lie within -15 and 15 degrees.

4.2 Neglecting the Cubic Terms and Solving by Linearization

Our assumption of a small motion implies that the components of the r vector are small. It follows that the higher-order terms in the equations (6) are negligible in comparison to lower order terms. Neglecting the cubic terms in Eq. (6) reduces the system to only ten quadratic equations in ten monomials, where

$$N_{10 \times 10}\, y = 0\,, \tag{8}$$

and

$$y = \left[\, r_1^2, r_1\, r_2, r_2^2, r_1\, r_3, r_2\, r_3, r_3^2, r_1, r_2, r_3, 1 \,\right]^T. \tag{9}$$

These monomials are the second half of the x vector defined in Eq. (7).

Eq. (8) is a polynomial system in the components of r. However, we noticed that in practice we can solve it by linearization [10], that is, we solve it as if it was a linear system. Since the last component of y is 1, we use the Cholesky decomposition method to find the other components, as it is the fastest method.

This method of solving is much faster than reduction to a single polynomial. It also produces a single solution instead of up to ten. However, this increased speed comes at the cost of decreased robustness to larger rotations, and greater sensitivity to noise.

4.3 Six-Point Least Squares Solution

If we build Eq. 4 using six point correspondences instead of five, we obtain $\binom{6}{3} = 20$ equations. This gives a system of twenty cubic equations in twenty monomials.

$$M_{20 \times 20}\, x = 0\,, \tag{10}$$

This system can also be solved as a linearized least-squares problem, this time without having to remove higher-order terms as we did for our five-point solution.

The speed of this method is roughly on par with the solution by reduction to a single polynomial, but it produces a single solution instead of ten. Because it avoids truncating the higher-order terms, it has better robustness to noise and larger rotations than the linearized five-point solver. However, it introduces a degeneracy when viewing a plane, because, in this case, the sixth correspondence is linearly dependent on the first five, meaning that the system is rank-deficient.

5 Evaluation

In the following we evaluate our approach in detail concerning different aspects. We demonstrate the accuracy of our methods for visual odometry on vehicle-mounted camera image sequences, and show its performance in terms of run-time.

We refer below to our novel algorithms using the following abbreviations: **Poly. 5pt.** is the solution by reduction to a single polynomial (Section 4.1), **Lin. 5pt.** is the truncated, linearized solution (Section 4.2), and **Lin. 6pt.** is the

Table 1. Average computation time for various solvers, in microseconds.

Method	Time (μs)
Poly. 5pt.	7.43
Lin. 5pt.	3.51
Lin. 6pt.	10.71
5 pt. (Nistér)	6.32
5 pt. (Stewénius)	61.50
5 pt. (Kneip 2012)	475.09
10 pt. (Kneip 2013)	100.74

linearized solution using six points (Section 4.3). We compare our methods against the following existing methods: **5 pt. (Nistér)** and **5 pt. (Stewénius)** refer to the essential matrix solvers of [22] and [25] respectively, **5 pt. (Kneip 2012)** is the direct rotation-only solution proposed by Kneip et al. [13], and **10 pt. (Kneip 2013)** is the iterative rotation-only method proposed by Kneip et al.[12]. The iterative method does not require ten correspondences, but this is the number recommended by Kneip et al. to avoid local minima. We use the reference implementations of **5 pt. (Stewénius)**, **5 pt. (Kneip 2012)**, **10 pt. (Kneip 2013)** from the *OpenGV* library [11], and we use the hand-optimized implementation of **5 pt. (Nistér)** provided by Richard Hartley[1].

5.1 Solver Computation Time

The average computation time for each solver is given in Table 1. The times were recorded using a *Apple Macbook Pro Late 2011* with a *2.5 GHz* i7 CPU. Each algorithm was run 10,000 times using randomly generated input data.

The fastest existing method is **5 pt. (Nistér)** which requires about 6 μs. Our **Poly. 5pt.** solver is only slightly slower, requiring about 7.5 μs. We believe the speed could be improved by using hand-optimization to build the constraint matrix, as was done for the **5 pt. (Nistér)** implementation.

Lin. 5pt., the truncated linearized five-point solver, is almost twice as fast as **5 pt. (Nistér)**. However, this speed comes at the cost of lower accuracy with greater rotation magnitudes, as will be seen in the following.

Lin. 6pt. is a bit slower than **5 pt. (Nistér)**, although again the speed could be improved by hand-optimizing the code to build the constraint matrix.

5.2 Accuracy with Increasing Rotation

We evaluated our solvers with respect to increasing amounts of rotation. We ran 10,000 trials on synthetic data to assess the angular error, given translational motion in either x, y or z direction and varying the overall rotation magnitude between 0 and 10 degrees.

The results are shown in Figure 1. As expected, on average the **Lin. 5pt.** gives a higher angular error for increasing amounts of rotation than the **Lin. 6pt.**

---

[1] http://users.cecs.anu.edu.au/~hartley/Software/5pt-6pt-Li-Hartley.zip

and the **Poly. 5pt.** solver, which give similar results. The median angular error is significantly lower for all solvers. This suggests that the mean is affected by outliers within all the results acquired. There is no significant difference comparing situations of translational motion along either the x, y or z axis. This indicates that our solvers don't exhibit any superior or inferior behavior for certain motion patterns (*i.e.* forward or sideward motion).

5.3   Image Sequences from Vehicle-Mounted Camera

We evaluated our approach on the KITTI visual odometry dataset [7]. It contains 11 sequences captured by a camera mounted on car driving around the streets of Karlsruhe, Germany. Ground truth trajectories were obtained using a combined GPS/IMU inertial navigation system. Stereo sequences are available, but we used the images from only one camera.

For each test sequence, feature tracks are obtained using the method of Geiger et al. [8]. To estimate the relative pose between successive frames, we used each solver in a *Preemptive RANSAC* [21] loop for robust estimation. In *Preemptive RANSAC*, a fixed number of hypotheses N is sampled, and then all correspondences are evaluated in blocks of size B. After each block is processed, the number of hypotheses is reduced by keeping only the best ones; this is repeated until all correspondences have been tested. This method is typically used in visual odometry applications, because it guarantees a fixed computation time for the robust estimation step and is thus ideal for embedded implementation [6]. For all methods we used $N = 200$ hypotheses and a block size of $B = 10$. Because the translation magnitude cannot be recovered directly from monocular motion, we scaled each resulting translation estimate to match the ground truth translation magnitude. This allows us to fairly compare all methods without having to choose between various visual odometry or SLAM multi-frame integration approaches.

In Figure 2, we plot the accuracy of the estimates against the time it takes to compute them, averaged over all the frames of the sequences from the KITTI dataset. We use the rotational error in degrees as our accuracy measure.

We considered the mean evaluation times both for single solver estimates and for the complete Preemptive RANSAC loop. **Lin. 5pt.** is the fastest method, but the accuracy averaged over all frames is slightly worse than **5 pt. (Nistér)**. The **Poly. 5pt.** and **Lin. 6pt.** methods are slightly slower than **5 pt. (Nistér)**, but have better average accuracy. These solutions all have an average RANSAC loop time of under ten milliseconds. While **5 pt. (Stewénius)** and **10 pt. (Kneip 2013)** have the best accuracy, their computational time is much higher. Finally, **5 pt. (Kneip 2012)** has worse average accuracy than our **Poly. 5pt.** solution and is also much slower.

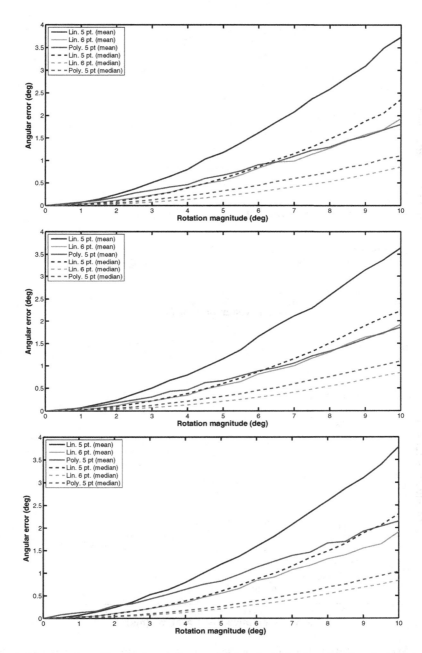

Fig. 1. Mean and median accuracy for translational motion in x (*top*), y (*middle*) and z (*bottom*) direction, respectively, for increasing magnitudes of rotation about a random axis

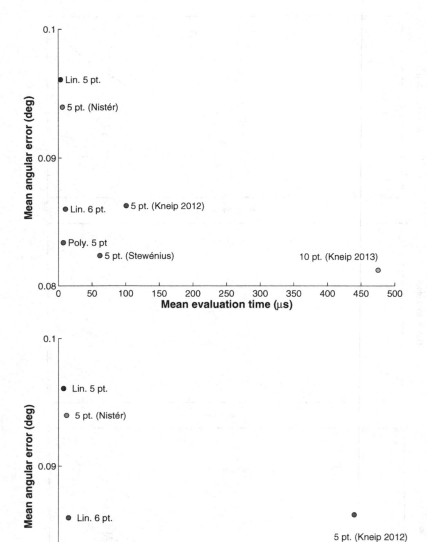

Fig. 2. Average rotational accuracy versus computation time, evaluated using the sequences from the KITTI dataset. Top: for a single evaluation and Bottom: for Preemptive RANSAC. Our **Lin. 5pt.** solver is faster than previous methods. Our **Poly. 5pt.** and **Lin. 6pt.** solvers are slightly slower than **5 pt. (Nistér)**, but more accurate.

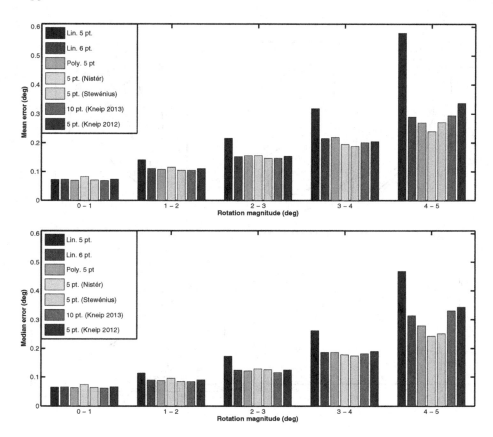

Fig. 3. Mean (top) and median (bottom) rotational accuracy for the KITTI sequences, aggregated by rotation magnitude. The error increases with the amount of rotation for all the solvers. Our **Lin. 5pt.** algorithm is more sensitive than the other ones, however after the final optimization step, it provides an accuracy similar to the other solvers up to four degrees, which seems enough in practice as shown in Figures 4 and 5.

5.4 Accuracy and Increasing Amounts of Rotation

We also assess the accuracy of the individual solutions with respect to increasing amounts of rotation as observed in the KITTI sequences. The results are shown in Figure 3.

All methods show a trend towards higher error with greater rotation magnitudes. This is likely due to the increasing inaccuracy of feature matching with greater intra-image motion. Our **Poly. 5pt.** and **Lin. 6pt.** solvers exhibit almost the same accuracy as the state-of-the-art methods across the range of rotations. **Lin. 5pt.** has the worst accuracy with increasing rotation, because of the truncated terms, and is only on par with the other solvers up to one degree of

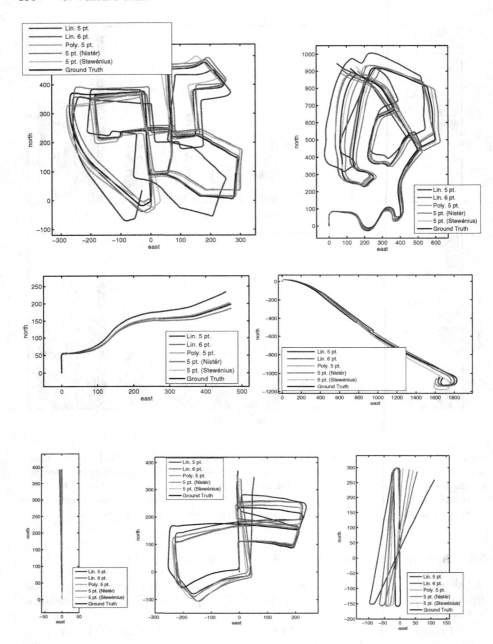

Fig. 4. Estimated trajectories for KITTI sequences with several solvers. Our solutions provide results similar to the existing solvers, while being as fast or faster to compute.

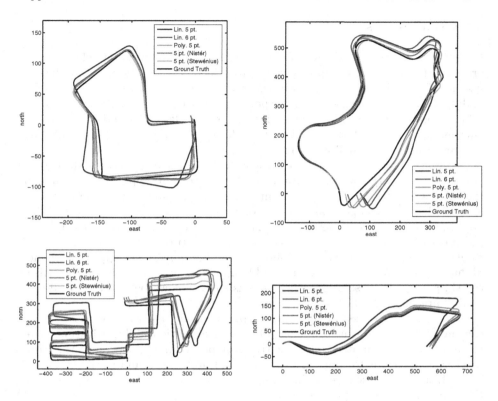

Fig. 5. Estimated trajectories for KITTI sequences with several solvers (cont.). Our solutions provide results similar to the existing solvers, while being as fast or faster to compute.

rotation. **10 pt. (Kneip 2013)** and **5 pt. (Kneip 2012)** also show slightly higher for the largest rotation range (four to five degrees).

Few sequential image pairs have rotation above five degrees in the sequences, indicating that this about the maximum expected for a car-mounted camera driving at city-street speeds. Furthermore, the camera was operated at 10 Hz, and with a faster camera rate, the maximum rotation observed would be even lower. This indicates that our solvers for approximated rotation are a reasonable choice for such an application.

The complete trajectories as estimated by each method on several sequences from KITTI are depicted in Figures 4 and 5. No non-linear optimization, bundle adjustment, or loop closure was applied to the trajectories; the trajectories were simply produced by integrating frame-to-frame motion estimates. Our **Poly. 5pt.** and **Lin. 6pt.** solvers give comparable results to the state-of-the-art. The **Lin. 5pt.** solver shows more severe errors accumulating over time. These come from the inaccurate estimates at image pairs observing larger rotations, while the majority of image pairs have correctly estimated relative pose.

6   Conclusions

In this work we presented several novel solutions to the five-point relative pose problem. By applying an approximated rotation representation, we produce a system of equations involving only the rotation terms that can be solved by finding the roots of a single univariate polynomial. We also explored two alternate solution procedures involving truncation of higher-order terms and linearization. Our methods are as fast or faster than the state-of-the-art, while exhibiting similar accuracy for small rotation magnitudes.

Evaluation on image sequences a from vehicle-mounted camera show that our solvers are very competitive and suitable for such an application. Although the solvers are, to varying degrees, limited in the amount of rotation they can handle, they are also generally as fast or faster than the state-of-the-art. This implies that they would permit a higher frame-rate camera to be used, since the processing time per-frame is reduced. This in turn reduces the amount of rotation which is expected to be observed, and so makes the approach viable. Manual optimization of the solvers would improve their speed even further. Also, the simplicity of the solution procedures is such that we believe they could be easily implemented on embedded hardware.

The approaches used in this work – approximating the rotation matrix, discarding polynomial terms of higher order, and resolution by linearization – are most certainly not limited to the relative pose problem. The success of this approach encourages us to consider other minimal problems found in the literature in the future, for which we could possibly create considerably improved solvers. Examples where this approach might also be applicable are the eight-point radial distortion problem, the six-point calibrated radial distortion problem or, more prominently, the four-point absolute pose problem with unknown focal length.

References

1. Cayley, A.: About the algebraic structure of the orthogonal group and the other classical groups in a field of characteristic zero or a prime characteristic, vol. 32. Reine Angewandte Mathematik (1846)
2. Cox, D.A., Little, J., O'Shea, D.: Ideals. Springer, Varieties and Algorithms (2006)
3. Demazure, M.: Sur deux problèmes de reconstruction. Tech. Rep. 882. INRIA, Rocquencourt, France (1988)
4. Faugeras, O.D., Maybank, S.: Motion from Point Matches: Multiplicity of Solutions. International Journal of Computer Vision 4(3), 225–246 (1990)
5. Fischler, M., Bolles, R.: Random Sample Consensus: A Paradigm for Model Fitting with Applications to Image Analysis and Automated Cartography. Communications of the ACM 24(6) (1981)
6. Fraundorfer, F., Scaramuzza, D.: Visual odometry: Part ii - matching, robustness, and applications. IEEE Robotics and Automation Magazine 19(2) (2012)
7. Geiger, A., Lenz, P., Stiller, C., Urtasun, R.: Vision meets Robotics: The KITTI Dataset. International Journal of Robotics Research (2013)
8. Geiger, A., Ziegler, J., Stiller, C.: StereoScan: Dense 3d reconstruction in real-time. In: IEEE Intelligent Vehicles Symposium (IV) (2011)

9. Kalantari, M., Jung, F., Guedon, J.P., Paparoditis, N.: The Five Points Pose Problem: A New and Accurate Solution Adapted to any Geometric Configuration. Advances in Image and Video Technology, pp. 215–226 (2009)
10. Kipnis, A., Shamir, A.: Advances in Cryptology, chap. Cryptanalysis of the HFE Public Key Cryptosystem by Relinearization, pp. 19–30. Springer, Berlin/Heidelberg (1999)
11. Kneip, L., Furgale, P.: OpenGV: A unified and generalized approach to real-time calibrated geometric vision. In: Proceedings of the IEEE International Conference on Robotics and Automation (2014)
12. Kneip, L., Lynen, S.: Direct optimization of frame-to-frame rotation. In: Proceedings of the IEEE International Conference on Computer Vision, December 2013
13. Kneip, L., Siegwart, R., Pollefeys, M.: Finding the exact rotation between two images independently of the translation. In: Fitzgibbon, A., Lazebnik, S., Perona, P., Sato, Y., Schmid, C. (eds.) ECCV 2012. LNCS, vol. 7577. Springer, Heidelberg (2012)
14. Kruppa, E.: Zur Ermittlung eines Objektes aus zwei Perspektiven mit innerer Orientierung. Sitzungsberichte der Mathematisch Naturwissenschaftlichen Kaiserlichen Akademie der Wissenschaften **122**, 1939–1948 (1913)
15. Kukelova, Z., Bujnak, M., Pajdla, T.: Polynomial Eigenvalue Solutions to Minimal Problems in Computer Vision. IEEE Transactions on Pattern Analysis and Machine Intelligence (2012)
16. Li, H.: A Simple Solution to the Six-Point Two-View Focal Length Problem. In: Proceedings of the European Conference on Computer Vision, pp. 200–213 (2006)
17. Li, H., Hartley, R.: Five-point motion estimation made easy. In: Proceedings of the IEEE International Conference on Pattern Recognition, pp. 630–633 (2006)
18. Lim, J., Barnes, N., Li, H.: Estimating Relative Camera Motion from the Antipodal-Epipolar Constraint. IEEE Transactions on Pattern Analysis and Machine Intelligence **32**(10), 1907–1914 (2010)
19. Longuet-Higgins, H.C.: A computer algorithm for reconstructing a scene from two projections. Nature 293(5828), 133–135, 9 September 1981
20. Maybank, S.: Theory of Reconstruction from Image Motion. Springer, New York (1992)
21. Nistér, D.: Preemptive RANSAC for Live Structure and Motion Estimation. Machine Vision and Applications **16**(5), 321–329 (2005)
22. Nistér, D.: An efficient solution to the five-point relative pose problem. In: Proceedings of the IEEE Conference on Computer Vision and Pattern Recognition (2003)
23. Philip, J.: A Non-Iterative Algorithm for Determining All Essential Matrices Corresponding to Five Point Pairs. The Photogrammetric Record **15**(88), 589–599 (1996)
24. Stewénius, H., Engels, C., Nistér, D.: Recent Developments on Direct Relative Orientation. ISPRS Journal of Photogrammetry and Remote Sensing **60**, 284–294 (Jun 2006)
25. Stewenius, H., Engels, C., Nistér, D.: An efficient minimal solution for infinitesimal camera motion. In: Proceedings of the IEEE Conference on Computer Vision and Pattern Recognition (2007)

Augmenting Vehicle Localization Accuracy with Cameras and 3D Road Infrastructure Database

Lijun Wei[✉], Bahman Soheilian, and Valérie Gouet-Brunet

IGN, SRIG, MATIS, Université Paris-Est, 73 Avenue de Paris,
94160 Saint Mandé, France
{lijun.wei,bahman.soheilian,valerie.gouet}@ign.fr

Abstract. Accurate and continuous vehicle localization in urban environments has been an important research problem in recent years. In this paper, we propose a landmark based localization method using road signs and road markings. The principle is to associate the online detections from onboard cameras with the landmarks in a pre-generated road infrastructure database, then to adjust the raw vehicle pose predicted by the inertial sensors. This method was evaluated with data sequences acquired in urban streets. The results prove the contribution of road signs and road markings for reducing the trajectory drift as absolute control points.

Keywords: Vehicle localization · Road infrastructure database · Road signs · Road markings

1 Introduction

To compensate the low performance of GPS receiver in dense urban environments caused by multi-path or building occlusions, dead-reckoning sensors like wheel encoder, inertial sensors, or visual odometry method have been integrated to continuously predict the vehicle movement. A main problem of the dead-reckoning methods is the pose error accumulation from point to point, thus a lot of methods have been proposed to alleviate the trajectory drift. *Personal Navigation Devices* use classic map matching method [1] to associate the vehicle location with a digital map of road networks. As the road network map usually well represent the topological relationship between different road segments, but lack of geometric accuracy, some other methods were proposed to generate an enhanced digital map with visual landmarks from onboard perception sensors. Visual landmarks are those static and recognizable objects in the environment. Several systems treat the reconstructed 3D points as landmarks [2][3][4]: interest points and descriptors (SIFT, SURF, HoG, etc.) are detected and extracted from multiple images and reconstructed into 3D point cloud by structure-from-motion with bundle adjustment. If the image sequence is already geo-referenced

© Springer International Publishing Switzerland 2015
L. Agapito et al. (Eds.): ECCV 2014 Workshops, Part I, LNCS 8925, pp. 194–208, 2015.
DOI: 10.1007/978-3-319-16178-5_13

by a localization device, each 3D point in the database is associated with its absolute 3D coordinates, and its 2D locations and visual appearance (descriptors) in the corresponding 2D images. The on-line localization step is then to associate the sensor perception with the landmarks in database, and to recover the current vehicle pose by n-point Direct Linear Transformation (DLT) minimization with RANSAC.

Instead of using the 3D points directly, in this work, we propose to use more semantic and more robust landmarks: a database of 3D road infrastructures, i.e., road signs and road markings, which was automatically generated from geo-referenced image sequences, as shown in Fig. 1. Compared with image points, the advantage of using road infrastructure objects is threefold: 1) volume of storage and matching: since the 3D point cloud contains millions of 3D points and corresponding image features, it requires large space for data storage and long time to access the sub point-clouds for landmarks association. As there are fewer road infrastructure objects than the sparse 3D points, it requires less volume for data storage and matching; 2) precision and robustness of landmarks: as the visual appearance of some image points might change during the day or in different seasons (e.g., trees), how to maintain an up-to-date point database is still an ongoing research. Visual landmarks of road infrastructures are more robust, static and precise in urban environments than the sparse points, and the road sign and road marking detection/reconstruction algorithms used can achieve sub-decimeter accuracy as reported in [5] [6]; 3) matching constraint: association of image points is done in multi-dimensional descriptor space and under multi-view geometric constraint, while road infrastructures are semantic visual landmarks with known visual appearance and geometric attributes; the matching step can be based on both geometric and semantic attributes to make it efficient.

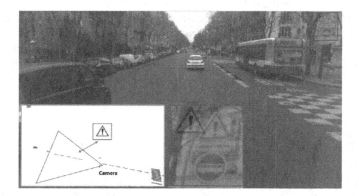

Fig. 1. Projection of 3D road sign and road marking landmarks on an image frame with raw camera pose (Left bottom: camera's field of view shown by blue triangle; middle bottom: zoomed view of the projected 3D road sign on image frame)

The most similar work to our study might be [7], in which a camera is used to detect the road markings and laser scanners are used to detect all the distinctive objects (traffic signs, trees, etc.). However, the explicit type and elevation information of the distinctive objects are not known. In [8], a map of curbs and road markings is generated from a stereo pair and used for vehicle localization in rural area. In [9], the authors also mentioned their road object map consisting of manually labeled and reconstructed static road objects like road crossings and road signs from a stereo pair. Their stored map objects are used for yielding an AR system by overlaying the objects on camera images. We use multi-cameras to automatically detect, recognize and reconstruct both the road markings and road signs. These map objects are then stored and used to improve the localization quality, especially in urban environments where GNSS performance is more challenging and the road occlusion is more frequent due to pedestrians and other vehicles. We currently assume that a rough initial vehicle position is provided by a GPS receiver at the beginning of a sequence.

In the remaining of this paper, we firstly introduce the method for generating a 3D road infrastructure database in Sec. 2; then, we present the localization method with 3D road infrastructure landmarks in Sec. 3; finally, some experimental results and discussions are respectively presented in Sec. 4 and Sec. 5.

2   Generation of a 3D Road Infrastructure Database

Road infrastructures include sidewalks, pedestrian crossings, road signs, traffic lights, etc. An accurate and up-to-date 3D database of road infrastructures is not only useful for infrastructure management and maintenance, it can also contribute to advanced driver assistance, like vehicle self-localization, lane keeping/alarming. An infrastructure database is usually manually surveyed and drawn by engineers with portable GPS, this procedure is time-consuming and expensive. This process can be largely accelerated by using ground mobile mapping system (MMS) [10] [11]. Road infrastructure objects are first automatically detected and identified from the acquired scene videos, and then triangulated into 3D with the vehicle poses from a high-precision geo-referencing device.

Fig. 2. (Left) One of the real images used for database generation; (Right) Reconstructed 3D road signs and road marking strips in the database

We follow the pipeline of road infrastructure database generation as in [12]: road markings, i.e. zebra crossings and dashed lines, are automatically detected and reconstructed from a calibrated front-view stereo pair [5]; and road signs are detected, recognized and reconstructed from a multi-camera system on the roof of the vehicle with a constrained multi-view reconstruction method as in [6]. The generated sign/marking database (Fig. 2) is composed of a list of 3D road signs/markings. Each road landmark is encoded with the following information:

(1) simple geometric shape: a road sign is encoded either as a 3D polygon, a triangle, or a circle (not discussed in this paper); a road marking strip is encoded as a parallelogram.

(2) coordinates of road landmark in sub-decimeter accuracy: as the positions of 2D detections are in sub-pixel precision, absolute coordinates (in Easting-Northing-Elevation format) of the corners of each landmark are in sub-decimeter accuracy. This database is also consistent with other geographic maps and environment models.

(3) type of a landmark: a road sign is encoded as "Indication", "Obligation", "Prohibition" or "Warning" type; a road marking strip is encoded as "zebra crossing", or dashed lines with specific types ("T2", "T3", "T'1" or "T'P").

(4) corresponding 2D images used for reconstruction are also listed.

Due to the occlusion by obstacles, it is possible that some road markings or road signs might not be visible in the image sequences used for data base generation. As the road surface of some urban streets is not covered by any markings, we did not use any model to fit or "interpolate" the missed road marking strips. Instead, we consider each road marking strip as a strip patch, which well defines the road marking plane in front of the vehicle.

3   Vehicle Localization with Road Infrastructure Database

In this section, we present the vehicle localization method using an IMU and the aforementioned road infrastructure database. Vehicle pose is firstly predicted by IMU in Sec. 3.1; then, road markings and signs are respectively detected from onboard cameras and associated with the database objects in Sec. 3.2; in addition to the attribute constraint, the Mahalanobis distance between two corresponding landmarks is discussed in Sec. 3.3.

3.1   Vehicle Pose Prediction

Like other visual landmarks based localization systems, we assume that all the sensors are rigidly installed on the experimental vehicle and well calibrated before the experiments. When initial state of the vehicle is given, the vehicle state can be continuously predicted by dead-reckoning systems. To facilitate the propagation of uncertainties between different vehicle positions, a pose-graph can be constructed [13] by considering each vehicle pose as a vertex and the displacement between two consecutive poses as an edge.

We use inertial sensors to provide accelerations and orientations of the vehicle in this work. Let $X_k = [X, Y, Z, \dot{X}, \dot{Y}, \dot{Z}]_k^T$ be the vehicle state at time k, where (X, Y, Z) are vehicle position and $(\dot{X}, \dot{Y}, \dot{Z})$ are vehicle velocities in navigation frame (Easting-Northing-Elevation). Assume that the vehicle acceleration a_k in navigation frame is constant between time step $(k-1)$ and k, the vehicle state at time k can be predicted by:

$$X_k = F_k X_{k-1} + G_k a_k \tag{1}$$

where $F_k = \begin{bmatrix} I_3 & (\Delta T)_{3\times3} \\ 0_{3\times3} & I_3 \end{bmatrix}$, I_3 is a 3×3 identity matrix, $G_k = \begin{bmatrix} (\frac{\Delta T^2}{2})_{3\times3} \\ (\Delta T)_{3\times3} \end{bmatrix}$, and $\Delta T = T_k - T_{k-1}$. a_k is the vehicle accelerations in navigation frame given by:

$$a_k = R_k a_k^b = R_k [a_x^b, a_y^b, a_z^b]^T = R(\gamma)R(\beta)R(\alpha)[a_x^b, a_y^b, a_z^b]^T \tag{2}$$

where $a_k^b(\in \mathbf{R}^3)$ is the vehicle accelerations in body frame reported by the IMU sensor, R_k is the vehicle attitude (transformation from vehicle body frame at time k to the navigation frame) represented by the vehicle Euler angles (roll α, pitch β and yaw γ) from gyroscope. Assume that the accelerations of vehicle in body frame are respectively perturbed by independent white noises with variance δa_x, δa_y, δa_z, the covariance matrix of a_k^b is written as $C_k = diag(\delta a_x^2, \delta a_y^2, \delta a_z^2)$. The covariance Qx_k of the vehicle pose at time k can be estimated by linearization of Eq. 1:

$$Qx_k = F_k Qx_{k-1} F_k^T + (G_k R_k) C_k (G_k R_k)^T \tag{3}$$

3.2   Matching Criteria between Two Road Landmarks

Meanwhile, road markings and signs are respectively detected using the same algorithm as in map generation stage, except that during the mapping stage, possible 2D road signs are matched over all image frames, while in localization stage, only the three front looking images captured at the same instant are used.

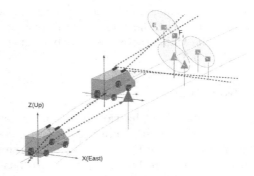

Fig. 3. Vehicle pose correction with visual landmarks (Database landmarks: in red color; online estimation: in green color)

The corresponding 2D detections are fed into the the constrained multi-view reconstruction algorithm as in the mapping stage.

For images at time t with multiple 2D detections S, these 2D detections are first reconstructed into 3D ($\mathcal{E}$) by constrained multi-view reconstruction algorithm, m landmarks can be reconstructed as: $\mathcal{E} = \{E_1, ..., E_i, ..., E_m\}$. Since matching of 2D detections is based on strict geometric and visual appearance constraints, the reconstruction step can help to remove some false positive detections. Then, with the m reconstructed landmarks $\mathcal{E}$, and n reference landmarks in the database: $\mathcal{F} = \{F_1, ..., F_j, ..., F_n\}$, we need to find all the hypotheses to associate each observation E_i with feature F_{j_i} [14]. If there is no matched landmark for E_i, this reconstruction will not be used.

The data association process of road signs and road markings is based on facing direction of landmark plane, Mahalanobis distance, landmarks type and uniqueness constraints, as illustrated in Fig. 3. The Mahalanobis distance is defined by considering both the noises of 3D reconstruction and pose transition process (Eq. 3). The association problem might become ambiguous when the IMU error is very large or the landmarks are densely distributed. If there are multiple candidate landmarks associations, the vehicle state track is split into multiple independent tracks, each within an EKF (Extended Kalman Filter) to correct the vehicle pose. If a GPS measurement is provided, it can be used as a measurement together with the road sign and road marking objects.

Matching Criteria between Two 3D Signs. A 3D road sign observation E_i is matched to a sign F_{j_i} in the database if the following criteria are satisfied:

1) two objects are identified as road signs in the same category;

2) facing directions of the two road sign planes are less than a threshold (set to 40° in our experiments);

3) Mahalanobis distance between two corresponding road signs is measured by their position difference in the camera frame, this distance should be less than a threshold defined by chi-squared distribution (will be detailed in Sec. 3.3 Eq. 4 to Eq. 6);

4) uniqueness constraint: when multiple road signs are reconstructed from the same image pair, they cannot be associated with the same landmark in the database at the same time.

Matching Criteria between Two Road Marking Objects. In the step of road sign detection/reconstruction, a 2D road sign detection is kept only if the whole sign is seen by the camera for the purpose of type identification. For road markings, this constraint is less strict. Due to the occlusion by obstacles in front of the vehicle, the camera might detect only a portion of a road strip. As the detected strip portion might be at any location inside the corresponding reference strip, a detection uncertainty is added to every strip in the database.

Let the local frame attached to a reference strip is with y axis collinear to the strip, the center of a marking strip reconstructed online might locate along the longitudinal axis, and its lateral position might locate along the lateral axis,

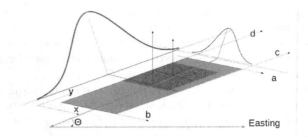

Fig. 4. Matching uncertainty between two strips (blue strip: reference)

as shown in Fig. 4. We set σ_x and σ_y respectively as the local uncertainties of this road strip, $\sigma_x = width/8$ ($width$ is the width of this strip), and σ_y is set as $1m$. The variances of this strip can be transformed into navigation frame with the strip slope θ, as $Q_l = \begin{bmatrix} cos(\theta) & -sin(\theta) \\ sin(\theta) & cos(\theta) \end{bmatrix} diag(\sigma_x^2, \sigma_y^2) \begin{bmatrix} cos(\theta) & -sin(\theta) \\ sin(\theta) & cos(\theta) \end{bmatrix}^T$.

3.3   Mahalanobis Distance between Corresponding Landmarks

Since our IMU can provide high accurate orientation measurement, vehicle orientation error is not considered in this work and only the noise of acceleration measurements were taken into account in error propagation. The same as other landmarks based localization system with EKF, several blocks of the process is introduced as follows:

1) **Measurement**: if m landmarks are reconstructed at time k, noted as $\mathcal{E}_k = \{E_1, ..., E_i, ..., E_m\}$, $E_i = (\Delta X_i, \Delta Y_i, \Delta Z_i)$ is the 3D position of the center of ith road landmark in current vehicle local frame, Q_{E_i} is the uncertainty of the reconstructed landmark.

2) **Observation**: let R be the attitude of current vehicle state, $F_j(x, y, z)$ be the center of a landmark in the database, the expected 3D position EM_j of the landmark F_j in current vehicle frame can be calculated with the vehicle position X_k and vehicle attitude R, as:

$$EM_j = R^{-1}(F_j - X_k) \tag{4}$$

The Jacobian matrix of EM_j with respect to X_K is $H = [-R^{-1} \; 0_{3 \times 3}]$.

3) **Innovation**: the difference between measurement landmark and the observation is: $vc_{ij} = E_i - EM_j$, with covariance:

$$S_{ij} = HQ_{x_k}H^T + R^{-1}Q_{F_j}R + Q_{E_i} \tag{5}$$

where Q_{F_j} is the position covariance of the reference landmarks in the database in navigation frame, and Q_{E_i} is the covariance of currently reconstructed landmark in local vehicle frame.

4) **Mahalanobis distance**: the Mahalanobis distance between the recon-structed landmark E_i and reference landmark F_j is written as:

$$dist(E_i, F_j) = vc_{ij}^T S_{ij}^{-1} vc_{ij} < \lambda \qquad (6)$$

If $dist(E_i, F_j)$ is less than a threshold $\lambda = \chi(0.05, 3)$ defined by χ^2 distribution table, landmark F_j is considered to be a possible correspondence of E_i. We might obtain a series of candidate correspondences for each landmark inside the confidence area.

5) **Joint compatibility**: when there are multiple landmarks being detected at the same time, instead of choosing the nearest neighbor of each landmark, the joint compatibility of all the road landmarks is taken into account. All the reconstructed landmarks E_i with at least one candidate correspondence are put into a single observation vector with uniqueness constraint, as:

$$\mathcal{E} = \{E_i\}^T = \{(\Delta X_i, \Delta Y_i, \Delta Z_i)\}^T, i \in 1, ..., m \qquad (7)$$

The observations from different corresponding landmarks are also concatenated as:

$$EM = \{R^{-1}(F_{j_i} - X_k)\}^T \qquad (8)$$

where F_{j_i} is the corresponding reference landmark of E_i. The Jacobian matrix of EM with respect to X_k is $H = - [R^{-1}, ..., R^{-1}]_k^T$. Difference between the mea-surement and observation vectors is: $vc = \mathcal{E} - EM$. Covariance S of the vector vc is calculated the same as in Eq. 5. If the Mahalanobis distance $dist(\mathcal{E}, F)$ is less than threshold $\lambda = \chi(0.05, 3k)$, k being the number of landmark correspon-dences under uniqueness constraint, this combination of landmark association is considered as an acceptable correspondence. All the possible combinations of correspondences inside the gating area are kept and the matching ambiguities will be resolved by sequential matching. Then, the vehicle track is split into mul-tiple tracks to maintain each landmarks association hypothesis with a parallel filter, as [15].

5) **Pose correction**: for each validated landmark association, the vehicle state in each track can be updated in parallel by Kalman gain: $K = track(i).Q_{x_k} H^T S^{-1}$ and $\bar{X}_k = X_k + K \times vc$, and the pose uncertainty is updated to: $Q_{x_k} = (I - KH)Q_{x_k}$. For the vehicle positions without any visual landmarks in view, pose-graph optimization can be used to distribute the final pose correction to other vehicle positions without LOS (Line of Sight) of the visual landmarks in a local bundle adjustment in the future.

4   Evaluation

Experiments were conducted to test the proposed pose correction method with acquired data sequences. As presented in section 2, a ground Mobile Mapping System was used for data collection (Paris). The vehicle was equipped with a high-quality geo-referencing device (GPS/INS/odometer) and 12 rigidly installed cameras on the roof of the vehicle, including a horizontal panoramic system of 8 cameras, 1 forward looking and 1 rear looking stereo pairs.

A data sequence of 2015 positions (about $12km$) was used to generate the landmarks database (orange trajectory in Fig. 5). As seen in Tab. 1 and Fig. 5, 120 road signs (yellow squares with red crosses) and 2116 road marking strips were generated with sub-decimeter accuracy. In average, at least one road sign exists for every 100 meters along the road. During the acquisition stage, the forward stereo pair can detect at least one road marking strip in front of the vehicle at about 50% locations. Road signs and road markings were respectively stored in a file of $351k$ and $890k$. The whole data volume per kilometer was $103k$.

Table 1. Statistic data of reference database

Images	Vehicle trajectory	Number of road signs	Number of marking strips
$2015 \times 12\ cameras$	12km	120 (351k)	2116 (890k)

We evaluated the contribution of road signs and road markings with another data sequence acquired by the same vehicle, but at different time. As the test path did not completely overlap with the reference sequence, we manually chose two portions of the test sequence which were long enough and the area of the path had been mapped in the previous stage (shown as cyan lines in Fig. 5).

Fig. 5. Road sign landmarks (yellow squares) and vehicle trajectories overlapped on Google Earth. The reference data sequence used for generating the landmarks database is shown in orange; the two test trajectories are shown in cyan.

Due to an occasional cable connection problem of the front looking stereo pair in the map generation stage, no road markings were generated for the area of the first segment (left bottom), thus this segments was with only road sign reference; the second segment was with both road signs and road markings. Pose ground-truth of the two segments were provided by GPS/INS/odometer post-processing software (though even this "ground-truth" might not be perfect, we will discuss this problem in the following experiments). Lengths of the two segments were respectively 1013m and 533m. The localization performance was evaluated using the number of true positive pose corrections, defined as:

- True positive (TP): landmarks were detected in images and associated with the corresponding database landmarks;
- False positive (FP): landmarks were detected in images, but associated with wrong database landmarks;
- True negative (TN): there was no corresponding landmark of a detection due to false detection or the incompleteness of the database;
- False negative (FN): landmarks were detected in images but not associated with the corresponding landmarks in database.

4.1 Localization Results of Segment 1

By assuming that the vehicle Euler angles were accurate and the vehicle initial position and velocity were known by GPS, the vehicle accelerations and rotations exported from the high-precision positioning system (with frequency of 100Hz) were used to predict the vehicle positions at first. Without any absolute measurements for pose correction, the vehicle trajectory drifts gradually, as seen in Fig. 6 (first row). Then, if a road sign is detected and associated, it is applied to adjust the vehicle trajectory, example is illustrated in Fig. 7; if there is no corresponding road landmark being detected for long period, the error ellipsoid of the vehicle position continues growing. Average linear distance between two

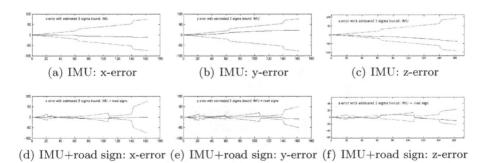

(a) IMU: x-error   (b) IMU: y-error   (c) IMU: z-error

(d) IMU+road sign: x-error (e) IMU+road sign: y-error (f) IMU+road sign: z-error

Fig. 6. Vehicle position error before (first row) and after (second row) incorporating road sign based correction. Blue curves: vehicle position error with respect to the ground truth; red curves: 3-sigma (3 times the standard deviation of the estimated position error)

detected road signs is 156m along the vehicle trajectory. As seen in Fig. 6 (second row), the position error after incorporating road sign based correction is in the form of sawtooth, and the average position error is reduced from 30m to 5.5m.

Fig. 7. Segment 1: Left: reference landmark overlapped on image frame with predicted vehicle pose; right: reference landmark overlapped on image frame after vehicle pose correction

Some statistic data of position correction with road landmarks is listed in Tab. 2. For segment 1, road signs were detected/reconstructed at 21 locations, 10 positions were adjusted by correctly associated road signs with the reference database, as shown in Fig. 8 (positions linked by red lines). Even with these limited information, the reference road landmarks still provide some useful corrections to the vehicle trajectories. 10 reconstruction were not associated with any landmarks and marked as true negative due to the incompleteness of reference database (3 reconstructions in this test as shown in Fig. 8 by yellow lines)

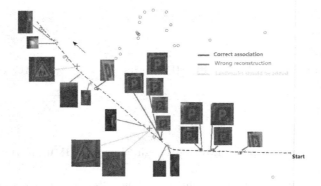

Fig. 8. Segment 1: landmarks association results (Red line: correct association; green line: wrong detection; yellow line: landmarks to be added into the database; red circles: reference road signs)

Table 2. Statistic data of position correction with road landmarks (Segment 1, with 165 vehicle positions in total; Segment 2: with 80 vehicle positions in total)

	Seg. 1	Seg. 2		
Landmarks	**Signs**	**Signs**	**Markings**	**Signs/Markings**
Locations with detections	21	15	50	59
TP (Correct association)	10	8	19	29
FP (Wrong association)	0	0	0	0
TN (No correspondence)	10	7	12	5
FN (Not associated with correspondence)	1	0	19	25

or wrong detection (7 reconstruction in this test as shown in Fig. 8 by green lines). But in reality, even though a road sign detection/recognition algorithm works perfect, as the road signs might be occluded by other vehicles along the street, it is difficult to obtain a complete landmark database by one acquisition.

4.2   Localization Results of Segment 2

For segment 2, we gradually added road signs and road markings for vehicle pose correction. When we displayed the onboard images of this segment using the poses provided by the GPS/INS/Odometer post-processing software, we observed that the images were consistent on horizontal dimensions, but did not overlap well in multiple runs on vertical dimension. Thus we only take use of the 2D positions as ground truth.

The vehicle positions predicted by accelerations were corrected by different landmarks. The position errors are compared in Fig. 9. As seen in Fig. 9, the average 2D position error of IMU based prediction was 6m, the error was 4.4m using IMU and road marking correction, the error was reduced to 2.46m using IMU and road sign correction. As road markings are more densely distributed in some area along the street, they can help to re-localize the vehicle more frequently, but also with more ambiguities especially on longitudinal direction. The

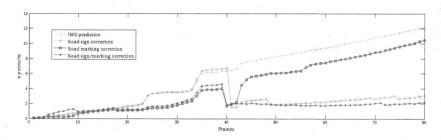

Fig. 9. Segment 2: Vehicle position error with IMU, IMU+road sign, IMU+road marking, IMU+road sign+road marking

distinctive road signs can help to improve the vehicle position precision on lateral and longitudinal directions. After incorporating road signs and road marking together, the error is further reduced to 1.81m. Although we don't have explicit ground truth of vehicle elevation, we noted some examples of elevation correction, like in Fig. 10, after incorporating the visual landmarks, image frames after vehicle pose correction are much more coherent with the database landmarks.

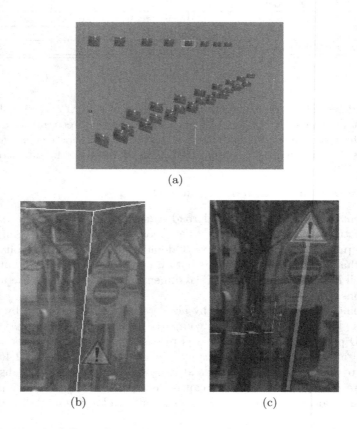

Fig. 10. Segment 2: a) From above to bottom: image frames predicted by IMU (in white box), GPS/IMU/Odometer software, IMU+road landmarks; b) Image frame predicted by GPS /INS /Odometer post-processing software; c) Corrected image frame after incorporating the road infrastructure objects

4.3 Complexity of the Method

The online localization processing is composed of pose prediction, landmarks (road signs/marking) detection/reconstruction, landmark association and vehicle pose correction steps. With current state-of-art techniques of landmark detection [16], it is possible to achieve real-time performance in the detection stage (the techniques of road sign and marking detection we employ can be easily optimized to be real-time). Because the data volume of the infrastructure database is much more smaller than the popularly used point cloud (as in [4] for example), it is also possible to achieve real-time performance in the stage of landmark association: typically on the segments tested during this step, matching of road signs/markings involves the comparison of about 20 simple features at maximum, while point-based approaches would involve the manipulation of several hundreds of thousands of multidimensional features.

5 Conclusion

In this paper, we presented a road infrastructure database based vehicle pose correction method. Road signs and road markings were detected from forward-looking cameras and associated with the corresponding landmarks in the infrastructure database to correct the predicted vehicle pose. The experiments results demonstrated that the detected road signs/markings can be used as absolute control points to periodically adjust the vehicle positions. Although the proposed method aims to augment the vehicle localization performance in urban environments, it might also be applicable on rural roads. As the robustness of the whole system is affected by: 1) robustness of the road landmark detection/recognition algorithm; 2) since the same type road landmarks look exactly the same, the ambiguity problem might not be solved by only one road visual landmark when the pose uncertainty is too large. After long period of being lost (without any pose correction), other global localization methods should be adopted to re-initialize the vehicle global position, like place recognition method (with ten meters of accuracy as reported in [17]), vehicle trajectory and road network based absolute localization method, etc. Besides, vehicle positions without road signs in view might be adjusted by pose-graph optimization or a bundle adjustment. IMU can be replaced by camera based estimation as the research on visual odometry or structure-from-motion is more and more mature now.

References

1. Quddus, M.A., Ochieng, W.Y., Noland, R.B.: Current map-matching algorithms for transport applications: State-of-the art and future research directions. Transportation Research Part C: Emerging Technologies **15**(5), 312–328 (2007)
2. Sattler, T., Leibe, B., Kobbelt, L.: Fast image-based localization using direct 2d-to-3d matching. In: ICCV, pp. 667–674 (2011)
3. Lategahn, H., Schreiber, M., Ziegler, J., Stiller, C.: Urban localization with camera and inertial measurement unit. In: Intelligent Vehicles Symposium, pp. 719–724 (2013)
4. Royer, E., Lhuillier, M., Dhome, M., Lavest, J.: Monocular vision for mobile robot localization and autonomous navigation. International Journal of Computer Vision **74**(3), 237–260 (2007)
5. Soheilian, B., Paparoditis, N., Boldo, D.: 3d road marking reconstruction from street-level calibrated stereo pairs. ISPRS Journal of Photogrammetry and Remote Sensing **65**, 347–359 (2010)

6. Soheilian, B., Paparoditis, N., Vallet, B.: Detection and 3d reconstruction of traffic signs from multiple view color images. ISPRS Journal of Photogrammetry and Remote Sensing **77**, 1–20 (2013)

7. Schindler, A.: Vehicle self-localization with high-precision digital maps. In: IEEE Intelligent Vehicles Symposium (IV), pp. 141–146, June 2013

8. Schreiber, M., Knoppel, C., Franke, U.: Laneloc: Lane marking based localization using highly accurate maps. In: IEEE Intelligent Vehicles Symposium (IV), pp. 449–454, June 2013

9. Lategahn, H., Stiller, C.: Vision only localization. IEEE Transactions on Intelligent Transportation Systems **15**(3), 1246–1257 (2014)

10. Maldonado-Bascon, S., Lafuente-Arroyo, S., Siegmann, P., Gomez-Moreno, H., Acevedo-Rodriguez, F.: Traffic sign recognition system for inventory purposes. In: IEEE Intelligent Vehicles Symposium, pp. 590–595 (2008)

11. Segvic, S., Brkic, K., Kalafatic, Z., Stanisavljevic, V., Sevrovic, M., Budimir, D., Dadic, I.: A computer vision assisted geoinformation inventory for traffic infrastructure. In: 13th International IEEE Conference on Intelligent Transportation Systems (ITSC), pp. 66–73 (2010)

12. Soheilian, B., Tournaire, O., Paparoditis, N., Vallet, B., Papelard, J.P.: Generation of an integrated 3d city model with visual landmarks for autonomous navigation in dense urban areas. In: IEEE Intelligent Vehicles Symposium (IV), pp. 304–309, June 2013

13. Olson, E., Leonard, J., Teller, S.: Fast iterative optimization of pose graphs with poor initial estimates. In: ICRA pp. 2262–2269 (2006)

14. Neira, J., Tardós, J.D.: Data association in stochastic mapping using the joint compatibility test. IEEE T. Robotics and Automation **17**(6), 890–897 (2001)

15. Nieto, J.I., Guivant, J.E., Nebot, E.M., Thrun, S.: Real time data association for fastslam. In: ICRA, pp. 412–418 (2003)

16. Houben, S., Stallkamp, J., Salmen, J., Schlipsing, M., Igel, C.: Detection of traffic signs in real-world images: The German Traffic Sign Detection Benchmark. In: International Joint Conference on Neural Networks. Number 1288 (2013)

17. Zamir, Amir Roshan, Shah, Mubarak: Accurate image localization based on google maps street view. In: Daniilidis, Kostas, Maragos, Petros, Paragios, Nikos (eds.) ECCV 2010, Part IV. LNCS, vol. 6314, pp. 255–268. Springer, Heidelberg (2010)

Autonomous Approach and Landing for a Low-Cost Quadrotor Using Monocular Cameras

Sergiu Dotenco[1]([✉]), Florian Gallwitz[1], and Elli Angelopoulou[2]

[1] Department of Computer Science,
Nuremberg Institute of Technology, Nuremberg, Germany
{sergiu.dotenco,florian.gallwitz}@ohm-university.eu
[2] Pattern Recognition Lab, Friedrich-Alexander-University Erlangen-Nürnberg,
Erlangen, Germany
elli@i5.cs.fau.de

Abstract. In this paper, we propose a monocular vision system for approach and landing using a low-cost micro aerial vehicle (MAV). The system enables an off-the-shelf Parrot AR.Drone 2.0 quadrotor MAV to autonomously detect a landpad, approach it, and land on it. Particularly, we exploit geometric properties of a circular landpad marker in order to estimate the exact flight distance between the quadrotor and the landing spot. We then employ monocular simultaneous localization and mapping (SLAM) to fly towards the landpad while accurately following a trajectory. Notably, our system does not require the landpad to be located directly underneath the MAV.

Keywords: Approach and landing · Ellipse detection · Conic sections · Pose estimation · MAV · PTAM · SLAM

1 Introduction

Approach and landing is one of the most fundamental maneuvers performed by aerial vehicles. The maneuver requires a considerable amount of precision in order to avoid any damage to the vehicle and its surroundings while the maneuver is executed. This is especially important in case an unmanned aerial vehicle (UAV) has to autonomously navigate in unknown, possibly GPS-denied environments. In this paper, we focus on this specific scenario.

In our method, we detect the landpad using a forward-facing camera mounted on the MAV. We use a heliport-like landpad marker of known size (see fig. 1) that is typically used to label helicopter landing sites. We estimate the distance between the quadrotor and the landpad, and employ a monocular SLAM framework to let the quadrotor follow a trajectory in an accurate manner. Since the monocular SLAM framework is subject to drift, we have to recover from possible trajectory deviations by centering the quadrotor over the landpad once the MAV has reached the landing spot. In this step we use the quadrotor's downward-facing camera. Once the quadrotor has stabilized its position, it performs the landing. We provide a video showing our system in action at http://youtu.be/Og3VZX2jE0A.

© Springer International Publishing Switzerland 2015
L. Agapito et al. (Eds.): ECCV 2014 Workshops, Part I, LNCS 8925, pp. 209–222, 2015.
DOI: 10.1007/978-3-319-16178-5_14

Fig. 1. In our method, we detect the circular landpad marker using the forward-facing camera, estimate the distance, and fly towards landing spot by employing monocular SLAM. Once the quadrotor has reached the target position, it tries to detect the landpad using the downward-facing camera, stabilize its position, and finally land.

In contrast to existing work, we do not assume the landpad to be located directly underneath the quadrotor. Instead, the quadrotor has to locate it using its forward-facing camera, fly towards it, and finally land on the marker. At the same time, we use a quadrotor platform with a fairly constrained camera setup rather than with cameras that are strategically positioned.

Our goals are, first of all, to demonstrate that autonomy can be achieved using constrained, inexpensive, off-the-shelf hardware. Also, we want to show that a (non-stereo) two-camera-setup can have an advantage over a setup where a single, downward-facing camera is used, since the two-camera-setup effectively extends the visibility range of the MAV. This allows the quadrotor to better perceive and eventually explore the environment [1].

As an MAV platform, we use Parrot AR.Drone 2.0, a low-cost quadrotor with a simple IMU and two monocular cameras. The quadrotor features 1 GHz ARM Cortex-A8 processor, 32-bit 800 MHz DSP, and 1 GB of DDR2 RAM 200 MHz. Computations, however, cannot be performed directly on-board. Instead, the quadrotor has to communicate with a ground station that receives sensory data, performs the computations, and generates steering commands. The steering commands are eventually sent back to the quadrotor through wireless LAN.

The MAV platform we use poses several challenges. Due to the very narrow vertical field of view of the forward-facing camera, the landpad has to be detected from an extremely oblique perspective. A blind spot between both cameras as shown in fig. 2 makes it impossible to track the position of the landpad while the quadrotor is flying towards it. There are also significant delays in the communication between the quadrotor and the ground station. Finally, the downward-facing camera of the quadrotor provides only low resolution images, and also features a very narrow field of view.

The remainder of the paper is organized as follows. In section 2 we present the related work. Section 3 provides an overview of our hardware platform.

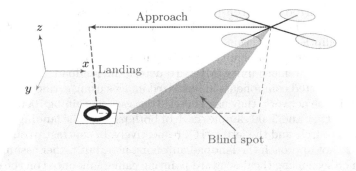

Fig. 2. Our experimental setup. The quadrotor has to locate the circular landpad using the forward-facing camera, estimate the distance, approach the landpad, and after recovering from possible drift using the downward-facing camera finally land on the marker.

Section 4 describes our approach, and in section 5 we discuss the experimental results. Finally, the conclusions are given in section 6.

2 Related Work

Most of the related work on monocular vision-based landing focuses on setups that use only a downward-facing camera for landing purposes. Lange et al. [2], for instance, presented a vision-based approach for autonomous landing and position control. In their work, they estimate the 3-dimensional position of the MAV relative to the landing pad. The velocity and position is stabilized using a dedicated optical flow sensor. As landing marker, they use a custom designed pattern consisting of four concentric white rings on black background. Each of the white rings has a unique ratio of its inner to outer border radii allowing fast detection. Lange et al. use the estimated center of the landpad to stabilize the quadrotor. Compared to our approach, they do not account for perspective projection, which shifts the center of the projected rings unevenly, and can possibly reduce the stabilization accuracy.

Eberli et al. [3] presented a similar approach. They used a downward-facing monocular camera mounted on the quadrotor to detect a marker consisting of two concentric circles. The detected marker is subsequently used for five degrees of freedom pose estimation and MAV set-point control. By using concentric circles it is possible to disambiguate between the inherently multiple camera poses determined from the projection of the circles. To stabilize the quadrotor, Eberli et al. use a linear-quadratic-Gaussian control with loop transfer recovery (LQG/LTR).

A fuzzy visual servoing approach for controlling an MAV was presented by Wendel et al. [4], which allows to perform takeoff, hovering, and landing without a marker. In their method, the forward-facing camera is used to obtain visual pose estimates using Parallel Tracking and Mapping (PTAM) based SLAM. In order to obtain the correct map scale, Wendel et al. use an ARToolKitPlus marker, which is placed into the scene during initialization.

Yang et al. [5] introduced an on-board monocular vision system for autonomous takeoff, hovering, and landing of an MAV. They estimate a five degrees of freedom pose from an elliptical projection of the circular pattern which encloses an "H". The remaining geometric ambiguity is resolved using the gravity vector estimated by an inertial measurement unit (IMU). To detect the landpad, Yang et al. find and classify connected components in binarized images using artificial neural networks. To train the network, they use a labeled data set containing 7000 samples of background clutter, and 3000 samples each of both parts of the landing pad corresponding to the circle and the letter "H", respectively. In contrast to our method, Yang et al. do not approach the landpad autonomously, but rather assume that it already can be seen using the downward pointing camera mounted on the quadrotor.

In a more recent work, Yang et al. [6] extended their system to actively search for, and land on an arbitrary landing site specified by a single reference image of unknown size. For autonomous navigation, they employ PTAM based monocular SLAM. A multi-scale ORB feature based detector is integrated into the SLAM framework for landing site detection. As opposed to our method, the navigation trajectory that determines the search path is predefined. To automatically initialize PTAM, they estimate the camera pose using a circular landing pad during the takeoff phase.

3   Hardware Platform

In our experimental setup, we use a stock Parrot AR.Drone 2.0 quadrotor MAV. Equipped with the indoor hull, the quadrotor weighs 420 g, and 380 g with the outdoor hull. With the indoor hull, the quadrotor measures 517 mm × 517 mm, and with the outdoor hull 451 mm × 451 mm.

3.1   Sensors

The quadrotor has two cameras, a 3-axis gyroscope, a 3-axis accelerometer, a 3-axis magnetometer, a sonar and a pressure altimeter. The MAV sends gyroscope measurements to the ground station at a rate of 200 Hz, and sonar measurements at 25 Hz.

The two cameras on the quadrotor are mounted perpendicularly to each other. One camera is pointing in the flight direction, and the other downwards. The forward-facing camera captures 30 frames per second with a resolution of 1280 × 720 pixels. The diagonal field of view of the forward-facing camera covers 92°. The downward-facing camera has a diagonal field of view of 64°, and captures video frames with a resolution of 320 × 240 pixels at a rate of 60 frames per second. The MAV on-board software uses the downward-facing camera mainly for velocity estimation, which however works reliably only if the quadrotor is flying above highly textured ground. The video streams of both cameras are compressed using H.264 baseline profile before they are sent to the ground station over wireless LAN. Due to a hardware limitation, the streams cannot be accessed simultaneously.

3.2   Control

The Parrot AR.Drone 2.0 on-board software uses the sensors to control the roll Φ, pitch Θ, the yaw rotational velocity $\dot{\Psi}$, and the vertical velocity $\dot{z}$ of the quadrotor according to a reference value [7]. The reference is set by sending a new control command $\boldsymbol{u} = (\tilde{\Phi}, \tilde{\Theta}, \tilde{\dot{\Psi}}, \tilde{\dot{z}}) \in [-1, 1]^4$ at least every 30 ms.

4   Our Method

In the proposed method, we first detect the landpad using the quadrotor's forward-facing camera. This is a particularly challenging task, since the land-pad is seen from an extremely oblique view angle. Then, we estimate the distance between the mounting position of the quadrotor's downward-facing camera and the center of the landpad. To accurately approach the landpad, we use a monocular simultaneous localization and mapping framework based on Parallel Tracking and Mapping (PTAM) [7]. Since the monocular SLAM framework can introduce drift over time, we have to recover from possible trajectory deviations once the quadrotor reached the landing spot. For this purpose, we switch to the downward-facing camera, and assume the landpad to be now approximately underneath the quadrotor. We then detect the landpad again, and center the quadrotor over the landpad by estimating the landpad pose. A PID controller is used for each of the axes to stabilize the quadrotor. The estimated landpad pose is used as reference.

4.1   Landpad Detection

In our setup, we use a heliport-like landpad marker. The landpad consists of the letter "H" enclosed by a circle. Under perspective projection, a circle is typically observed as an ellipse on the image plane. To detect the landpad, we first rectify the image using the camera intrinsic parameters in order to eliminate lens distortions, and correct the image aspect ratio such that the intrinsic parameters α_x, α_y that represent the focal length f in pixels along the x and y axes match. Then, we perform ellipse detection.

Ellipse Detection. To detect an ellipse, we modified the edge-grouping-based method of Nguyen et al. [8]. Their approach estimates ellipse parameters at curve level instead of inspecting individual edge points, which reduces the overall execution time. The algorithm consists of the following steps: (1) edge detection, (2) contour extraction, (3) line segmentation, (4) curve segmentation, (5) and curve grouping.

In the first step, we detect the edges in the image, and link the edge points into sequential lists. Edge contours with a length ℓ below 10 pixels are discarded. In order to reduce the number of edge points, the contours are segmented to lines. Instead of applying the line segmentation algorithm suggested by Nguyen et al., we use the Douglas-Peucker algorithm [9] with an approximation accuracy of

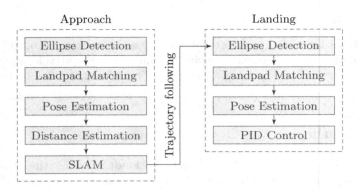

Fig. 3. The pipeline of our approach

$\epsilon = 1.5$, which produces more accurate curves at the expense of slightly higher computation time.

In a fairly cluttered scene, the extracted edge contours do not necessarily belong to a single ellipse. Rather, they could have resulted from several shapes merged together. Thus, the contours have to be partitioned into different curve segments, allowing curves that belong to a particular ellipse to be subsequently grouped. Under general observations, a curve belonging to an ellipse has to meet the following conditions. If one of the conditions is not met, the curve is segmented.

Curvature. A sequence of connected line segments traces an arc segment. The curvatures of these arcs should of the same sign throughout the sequence.

Length. The difference in the lengths of two neighboring line segments is small.

Angle. The difference between the gradients of tangents belonging to neighboring line segments is small.

Curve segmentation results in several arc segments. Arc segments that are not directly connected, but may belong to the same ellipse are now grouped. Two curves are grouped only if the end points are close to each other, and the difference between the gradient of the end point tangents is small.

Finally, we estimate ellipse parameters from the resulting set of curve points using a non-iterative least squares based geometric ellipse fitting [10] instead of the direct least squares based on an algebraic cost function as proposed by Nguyen et al. Only ellipses with a residual ρ below 0.075 are kept.

Landpad Matching. Once an ellipse is detected, we check whether it contains the letter "H". This is accomplished by first rectifying the ellipse. To achieve this, we first estimate the planar homography up to scale between each ellipse and the landpad reference by sampling four points on the ellipse and the circle in the reference image. Then, we rotate the rectified ellipse with respect to the angle of most dominant lines that were detected in the marker. This allows one to normalize the rotation of the letter "H". We use a voting scheme to determine the angle of most dominant lines, which should ideally correspond to the lines

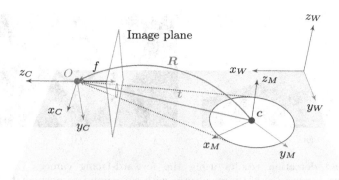

Fig. 4. The geometry of the scene. Three coordinate systems involved: a right-handed camera coordinate system (CCS), marker coordinate system (MCS), and world coordinate system (WCS). O denotes the center of projection, and $z = -f$ identifies the location of the corresponding image plane, f being the focal length. R denotes the rotation matrix that produces an oblique viewpoint, and t is the translation vector from the center of the circle c to the center of projection. The dotted lines contour the oblique elliptical cone.

belonging to the vertical bars of the "H". For this, let $(b_i)_{i=1,\ldots,n}$, be the bins of a histogram, where $b_i \subset \{\beta \in \mathbb{R} \mid 0 \leq \beta < \pi\}$, and $n = 18$, i.e., we use a bin width of $10°$. Let $0 \leq \alpha_j < \pi$ be the angles of the lines detected in the now circular image region. Each line angle α_j falls into a bin b_i. We select the bin with the most values b_k as the target angle candidate bin. The final rotation angle α is calculated as arithmetic mean $\alpha = \frac{1}{|b_k|} \sum_{a_j \in b_k} a_j$ over all the line angles in the candidate bin.

Finally, we apply Otsu's global thresholding [11] method to the circular image region, and use normalized cross-correlation as a match score between the landpad candidate and the reference image. The angle α is used as the yaw angle for pose estimation.

Pose Estimation. In order to estimate the landpad pose, we closely follow the method by Chen et al. [12]. In general, an ellipse is a type of conic section, i.e., a curve generated from an intersection of a cone with a plane. Considering a right-handed camera coordinate system with center of projection as origin and the optical axis as the z-axis, a conic section in the image domain can be described by the implicit second-order polynomial

$$Ax^2 + 2Bxy + Cy^2 + 2Dx + 2Ey + F = 0, \tag{1}$$

which can be defined in matrix form as

$$\boldsymbol{x}^\top \boldsymbol{C} \boldsymbol{x} = 0, \tag{2}$$

where $\boldsymbol{x} = \begin{bmatrix} x & y & 1 \end{bmatrix}^\top$. $\boldsymbol{C}$ is a nonzero real symmetric matrix given by

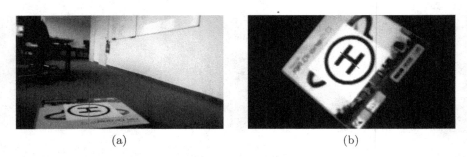

(a)   (b)

Fig. 5. Landpad detection results using the forward-facing camera (a) and the downward-facing camera (b) of the quadrotor with superimposed normals to the supporting plane of the landpad

$$C = \begin{bmatrix} A & B & D \\ B & C & E \\ D & E & F \end{bmatrix} \tag{3}$$

A bundle of straight lines passing through the center of projection and the ellipse defines an oblique elliptical cone. Assuming the focal length of the camera to be f, the corresponding image plane will be located at $z = -f$. The oblique elliptical cone can then be described by the points

$$p = k \begin{bmatrix} x & y & -f \end{bmatrix}^\top, \tag{4}$$

where k is a scale factor that defines the distance from the center of projection to p. From eqs. (3) and (4) follows

$$p^\top Q p = 0, \tag{5}$$

where

$$Q = \begin{bmatrix} A & B & -\frac{D}{f} \\ B & C & -\frac{E}{f} \\ -\frac{D}{f} & -\frac{E}{f} & \frac{F}{f^2} \end{bmatrix} \tag{6}$$

Here, similar to Kanatani et al. [13], we adapt the scale $\det Q = -1$, where $\det Q \neq 0$, in order to eliminate the scale indeterminacy of the cone.

Determining the 5 Degrees of Freedom Due to the cone's rotation invariance around the supporting plane normal, a circle pose can be determined only up to five degrees of freedom.

To determine the circle pose, let $\lambda_1, \lambda_2, \lambda_3$ be the ordered eigenvalues of Q, and v_1, v_2, v_3 its normalized eigenvectors. Then, Q can be expressed as

$$Q = V \Lambda V^\top, \tag{7}$$

where

$$\Lambda = \mathrm{diag}(\lambda_1, \lambda_2, \lambda_3), \quad V = \begin{bmatrix} v_1 & v_2 & v_3 \end{bmatrix} \tag{8}$$

Without loss of generality, we assume that

$$\lambda_1\lambda_2 > 0, \quad \lambda_1\lambda_3 < 0, \quad |\lambda_1| \geq |\lambda_2|, \tag{9}$$

i.e., the eigenvalues $\lambda_1, \lambda_2, \lambda_3$ are given in descending order, and Q has a signature of $(2, 1)$.

Now let r be the radius of the circle. The unit normal vector n of the circle plane described in camera coordinate system can be computed as

$$n = V \begin{bmatrix} S_2\sqrt{\frac{\lambda_1-\lambda_2}{\lambda_1-\lambda_3}} \\ 0 \\ -S_1\sqrt{\frac{\lambda_2-\lambda_3}{\lambda_1-\lambda_3}} \end{bmatrix}. \tag{10}$$

The center of the circle in the camera coordinate system is given by

$$c = z_0 V \begin{bmatrix} S_2\frac{\lambda_3}{\lambda_2}\sqrt{\frac{\lambda_1-\lambda_2}{\lambda_1-\lambda_3}} \\ 0 \\ -S_1\frac{\lambda_1}{\lambda_2}\sqrt{\frac{\lambda_2-\lambda_3}{\lambda_1-\lambda_3}} \end{bmatrix}, \tag{11}$$

where $S_1, S_2, S_3 \in \{-1, 1\}$ are undetermined signs, and

$$z_0 = S_3\frac{\lambda_3 r}{\sqrt{-\lambda_1\lambda_3}} \tag{12}$$

is the distance between the origin and the circle plane. This results in eight possible solutions for n and c. Since the normal to the supporting plane has two sides, we let it face the camera

$$n \cdot \begin{bmatrix} 0 & 0 & 1 \end{bmatrix}^\top > 0, \tag{13}$$

and require the center of the circle to be in front of the camera

$$c \cdot \begin{bmatrix} 0 & 0 & 1 \end{bmatrix}^\top < 0 \tag{14}$$

The visibility constraints from eqs. (13) and (14) allow us to determine two out of the three unknown signs.

Following eqs. (13) and (14), we end up with two sets of solutions: $(n_i, c_i)_{i=1,2}$. The preliminary pose estimates $(R_i, t_i)_{i=1,2}$ can then be computed as

$$R_i(\alpha) = \begin{bmatrix} g\cos\alpha & S_1 g\sin\alpha & S_2 h \\ \sin\alpha & -S_1\cos\alpha & 0 \\ S_1 S_2 h\cos\alpha & S_2 h\sin\alpha & -S_1 g \end{bmatrix}, \tag{15}$$

and

$$t_i(\alpha) = \begin{bmatrix} -S_2 S_3\sqrt{\frac{(\lambda_1-\lambda_2)(\lambda_2-\lambda_3)}{-\lambda_1\lambda_3}}r\cos\alpha \\ -S_1 S_2 S_3\sqrt{\frac{(\lambda_1-\lambda_2)(\lambda_2-\lambda_3)}{-\lambda_1\lambda_3}}r\sin\alpha \\ z_0 \end{bmatrix}, \tag{16}$$

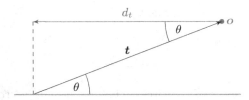

Fig. 6. Under the assumption that the quadrotor is flying parallel to the ground plane, the travel distance d_t can be computed using landpad's pitch angle θ and the translation t

where α is the yaw angle, z_0 as in eq. (12), and g, h are given by

$$g = \sqrt{\frac{\lambda_2 - \lambda_3}{\lambda_1 - \lambda_3}}, \quad h = \sqrt{\frac{\lambda_1 - \lambda_2}{\lambda_1 - \lambda_3}}. \tag{17}$$

t_i is the translation from the center of the circle to the optical center, while R_i is a rotation matrix that produces an oblique viewpoint. For exact details on these derivations refer to [12,13].

Resolving the Geometric Ambiguity. At this point we are left with two possible solutions for the pose estimates $(R_i, t_i)_{i=1,2}$, and thus have to determine which one is correct. Here, we assume the pinhole camera model and the camera calibration matrix K to be known. We now consider two separate cases in order to disambiguate the landpad pose.

In the first case, the landpad is observed using the forward-facing camera. The camera's optical axis is located perpendicularly to the landpad's normal, which is assumed to be lying on the ground and in front of the camera. Therefore, the corresponding pitch angle Θ, which can be computed by decomposing the rotation matrix R_i, cannot exceed 90°. The solution is thus *unique*.

In the second case, the landpad is observed using the downward-facing camera. Here, we follow the approach by Yang et al. [6] and compare the normals n_i with the gravity vector g, which is estimated using the IMU. The normal with the smallest angle with respect to g is used as the final pose estimate.

4.2   Distance Estimation

After detecting the landpad, we estimate the horizontal distance d_t between the mounting position of the downward-facing camera and the projection of the center of the landpad. Given θ is the pitch angle of the landpad's supporting plane (which can be determined from the rotation matrix R_i) with respect to the forward-facing camera, an estimate for the horizontal distance d_t, i.e., the distance along the optical axis as shown in fig. 6 can be computed as

$$d_t = \|t\|_2 \cos\theta + s, \tag{18}$$

where s is the displacement between the mounting position of the downward-facing and the forward-facing camera. We used a displacement value of $s = 25.7\,\text{cm}$, which was determined by measuring the distance between the tip of the forward-facing camera and the center of the downward-facing camera. Accounting for the displacement s allows to position the quadrotor (once it has reached the land-pad) in such a way that the landpad is in the field of view of the downward-facing camera.

Estimating the distance according to eq. (18) requires the quadrotor to be flying parallel to the ground. To ensure this, we account for the quadrotor's pitch angle Θ using gyroscope measurements by subtracting quadrotor's pitch angle Θ from θ.

4.3   Moving Towards the Landpad

Once we detected the landpad and estimated the flight distance d_t between the marker and the quadrotor, we employ the monocular SLAM framework introduced by Engel et al. [7] to accurately navigate towards the landpad.

The monocular SLAM framework consists of three main components:(1) a monocular SLAM system, (2) an extended Kalman filter (EKF) for data fusion and state estimation, (3) and PID control used to generate steering commands.

The monocular SLAM system is based on Parallel Tracking and Mapping (PTAM) combined with a closed-form solution for estimating the map scale. The EKF is used to fuse all the available data, and compensate for different time delays in the system that arise from the communication through wireless LAN and the computationally expensive visual tracking. The PID control is used in combination with the position and velocity estimates from the EKF to steer the quadrotor towards the desired location $q = \begin{bmatrix} \hat{x} & \hat{y} & \hat{z} & \hat{\psi} \end{bmatrix}^{\top} \in \mathbb{R}^4$ defined in a world coordinate system. For each of the four degrees of freedom, a separate PID controller is used with corresponding gains determined experimentally.

The scale of the visual map is estimated using both the visual SLAM and the metric sensors, such as the sonar altimeter, by minimizing the negative log-likelihood over pairs of samples that correspond to the traveled distance.

Steering the quadrotor towards the landing spot using the monocular SLAM framework can be summarized to two steps(1) adjusting the yaw angle, such that the quadrotor faces the center of the landpad, (2) and then estimating the target location p using quadrotor's current location and the travel distance d_t. Additionally, we increase the altitude of the quadrotor to 1 m while approaching the landpad to enlarge the field of view of the downward-facing camera.

4.4   Visual Position Control

Once the quadrotor has reached the landpad, it has to recover from possible trajectory deviations introduced by SLAM. At this stage we switch from the forward-facing camera to the downward-facing one. We perform the stabilization by first detecting the landpad again, this time using the downward-facing camera. Then, we estimate the pose of the landpad with respect to the pose of the quadrotor effectively aligning the corresponding coordinate systems in the

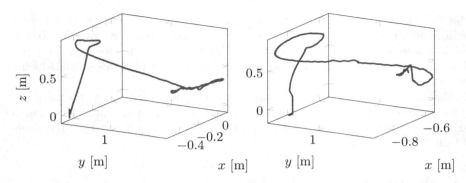

Fig. 7. Estimated trajectories of our approach and landing. Note that during the landing phase no visual observations are made by SLAM as only the downward-facing camera is active.

horizontal direction. To generate the steering commands, we use PID control with gains determined experimentally.

5   Experimental Results

We performed several runs of an experiment in indoor setting to evaluate the proposed method. In our experimental setup, we used a landpad with a radius of $r = 13.5$ cm. We initialized the map by manually steering the quadrotor in the test environment in order to get an accurate map scale estimate. Due to the very narrow vertical field of view of the forward-facing camera, we choose the origin of the quadrotor after the takeoff in a distance of approximately 1.20 m from the landing spot, at an altitude of about 50 cm. Positioning the quadrotor nearer or further away makes it impossible to detect the landpad as it either cannot be seen using the forward-facing camera anymore, or the perspective becomes extremely oblique. The landpad marker was placed on a box with a height of 14 cm.

All the computations were performed on a consumer laptop with an Intel Core i7 3610QM CPU and 8 GB RAM. The actual resolution of the frames that were captured by both cameras was 640×360 pixels. Depending on the complexity of the scene , i.e. the number of edges in the image, the landpad detection was running at a rate of 10 to 25 Hz, which can cause the quadrotor to drift while hovering over the landpad since the steering commands can not be sent fast enough. As seen in table 1, the computationally most expensive part of the landpad detection pipeline is the ellipse detection followed by landpad matching and image rectification. The computational cost for pose estimation is, however, negligible.

After initializing the map, we ran the experiment 12 times in a row. Once the quadrotor has landed, we manually measured the distance between the downward-facing camera and the landpad center. The average distance from the center after the landing was 15.7 cm with a standard deviation of 10.6 cm.

Table 1. Average runtime of individual landpad detection steps. Ellipse detection is computationally the most expensive part.

Step	Time [ms]
Rectification/aspect ratio correction	11.20
Ellipse detection	24.70
Landpad matching	11.33
Pose estimation	0.01
Total	47.24

As long as the map was properly initialized, the landing spot was reached by the quadrotor with just minor corrections performed by visual position control. In cases where the landpad has been missed by over 25 cm (measured from the land-pad center) after aproaching it, e.g. due to inaccurate map scale, or perturbances, no landing could be initiated as the landpad was not visible anymore. Further increasing the quadrotor's altitude while hovering over the landpad could be used as a strategy to overcome the limited range of the downward-facing camera.

6 Conclusions and Future Work

We presented a monocular vision system for approach and landing using an off-the-shelf Parrot AR.Drone 2.0 quadrotor MAV. In our method, we detect a circular landpad marker using the forward-facing camera by employing a contour-based ellipse detection method. We then estimate the distance between the quadrotor and the landpad, and use a PTAM based SLAM framework to fly towards the landing spot. Once the target position has been reached, we detect the landpad again, now using the downward-facing camera. To correct possible drift while approaching the landpad, the pose of the quadrotor with respect to the landpad is estimated and used to correct quadrotor's position.

We tested our method in an indoor setting where it has shown to work accurately by reaching the landing spot with an average deviation of 15.7 cm between the landpad center and the mounting position of the downward-facing camera. However, the accuracy of the method depends both on the quality of the map built by the PTAM based SLAM framework, and on the precision of the estimated map scale. In this work, we did not use a synchronization mechanism for landpad detection and pose estimation that compensates measurement delays between on-board and ground computers. Every video frame was processed instantly without storing and processing video frames that arrive in between. A synchronization mechanism, however, could improve the robustness of the system. In future work, we will integrate such a mechanism into our system. Our ultimate goal is to eliminate the use of a synthetic marker altogether, and use natural, on-line learned landmarks instead.

References

1. Fraundorfer, F., Heng, L., Honegger, D., Lee, G.H., Meier, L., Tanskanen, P., Pollefeys, M.: Vision-based autonomous mapping and exploration using a quadrotor MAV. In: IEEE/RSJ International Conference on Intelligent Robots and Systems, pp. 4557–4564. IEEE, October 2012
2. Lange, S., Sunderhauf, N., Protzel, P.: A vision based onboard approach for landing and position control of an autonomous multirotor UAV in GPS-denied environments. In: Proceedings of the IEEE International Conference on Advanced Robotics, pp. 1–6 (2009)
3. Eberli, D., Scaramuzza, D., Weiss, S., Siegwart, R.: Vision based position control for MAVs using one single circular landmark. Journal of Intelligent & Robotic Systems 61(1–4), 495–512 (January 2011)
4. Wendel, A., Maurer, M., Katusic, M., Bischof, H.: Fuzzy visual servoing for micro aerial vehicles. In: Proceedings of the Austrian Robotics Workshop (2012)
5. Yang, S., Scherer, S.A., Zell, A.: An onboard monocular vision system for autonomous takeoff, hovering and landing of a micro aerial vehicle. Journal of Intelligent & Robotic Systems 69(1–4), 499–515 (January 2013)
6. Yang, S., Scherer, S.A., Schauwecker, K., Zell, A.: Onboard monocular vision for landing of an MAV on a landing site specified by a single reference image. In: Proceedings of the International Conference on Unmanned Aircraft Systems, pp. 317–324 (2013)
7. Engel, J., Sturm, J., Cremers, D.: Camera-based navigation of a low-cost quadrocopter. In: Proceedings of the IEEE/RJS International Conference on Intelligent Robots and Systems, pp. 2815–2821, October 2012
8. Nguyen, T.M., Ahuja, S., Wu, Q.M.J.: A real-time ellipse detection based on edge grouping. In: Proceedings of the IEEE International Conference on Systems, Man and Cybernetics, pp. 3280–3286 (2009)
9. Douglas, D.H., Peucker, T.K.: Algorithms for the reduction of the number of points required to represent a digitized line or its caricature. Cartographica: The International Journal for Geographic Information and Geovisualization 10(2), 112–122 (October 1973)
10. Prasad, D.K., Leung, M.K.H., Quek, C.: ElliFit: An unconstrained, non-iterative, least squares based geometric ellipse fitting method. Pattern Recognition 46(5), 1449–1465 (2013)
11. Otsu, N.: A threshold selection method from gray-level histograms. IEEE Transactions on Systems Man Cybernetics 9(1), 62–66 (January 1979)
12. Chen, Q., Wu, H., Wada, T.: Camera calibration with two arbitrary coplanar circles. In: Pajdla, T., Matas, J.G. (eds.) ECCV 2004. LNCS, vol. 3023, pp. 521–532. Springer, Heidelberg (2004)
13. Kanatani, K., Liu, W.: 3D interpretation of conics and orthogonality. CVGIP: Image Understanding 58(3), 286–301 (1993)

A Low-Level Active Vision Framework
for Collaborative Unmanned Aircraft Systems

Martin Danelljan$^{(\boxtimes)}$, Fahad Shahbaz Khan, Michael Felsberg, Karl Granström,
Fredrik Heintz, Piotr Rudol, Mariusz Wzorek, Jonas Kvarnström,
and Patrick Doherty

Linköping University, Linköping, Sweden
`martin.danelljan@liu.se`

Abstract. Micro unmanned aerial vehicles are becoming increasingly interesting for aiding and collaborating with human agents in myriads of applications, but in particular they are useful for monitoring inaccessible or dangerous areas. In order to interact with and monitor humans, these systems need robust and real-time computer vision subsystems that allow to detect and follow persons.

In this work, we propose a low-level active vision framework to accomplish these challenging tasks. Based on the LinkQuad platform, we present a system study that implements the detection and tracking of people under fully autonomous flight conditions, keeping the vehicle within a certain distance of a person. The framework integrates state-of-the-art methods from visual detection and tracking, Bayesian filtering, and AI-based control. The results from our experiments clearly suggest that the proposed framework performs real-time detection and tracking of persons in complex scenarios.

Keywords: Visual tracking · Visual surveillance · Micro UAV · Active vision

1 Introduction

Micro unmanned aerial vehicles (micro UAVs) are becoming popular for aiding in numerous applications such as search and rescue, inspection, early warning, forest-fire reconnaissance and remote localization of hazardous radio-active materials. Generally these platforms have been remotely piloted with no active autonomous vision capabilities. However, in recent years significant amount of research has been done to develop active vision based functionalities for such platforms. The purpose of a vision component is to interpret the rich visual information captured by onboard cameras. In this paper, we propose a robust active vision framework for collaborative unmanned aircraft systems.

Several active vision frameworks for micro UAVs have been reported in recent years [21,23,27]. A vision based method for path planning of micro UAVs using a three-dimensional model of the surrounding environment is proposed in [23].

© Springer International Publishing Switzerland 2015
L. Agapito et al. (Eds.): ECCV 2014 Workshops, Part I, LNCS 8925, pp. 223–237, 2015.
DOI: 10.1007/978-3-319-16178-5_15

Yu et al. [27] propose a 3D vision system for estimating the UAV height over ground, used in the control loop of the helicopter. The work of [21] proposes a hardware and software system for micro UAVs that is capable of autonomous flight using onboard processing for computer vision. In this work, we tackle the challenging problem of developing an active vision framework for robust detection and tracking of persons in complex environments, which is necessary for stable virtual leashing, i.e. following a person at a predetermined distance.

Generally most approaches to object detection are based on the learning-from-examples paradigm [4,8,22]. In recent years, discriminative, part-based methods [8,28] have been shown to provide excellent performance for person detection. These methods rely on intensity information for image representation [4,18] and latent support vector machines for classification. A sliding window technique is then employed to scan an image at multiple scales. Contrary to the intensity based methods, Khan et al. [14] propose to use color information within the part-based framework of Felzenszwalb et al. [8]. The method employs color attributes for color representation while providing excellent detection performance on benchmark datasets. In our framework, we have the option to select both intensity and color based detection models for person detection.

Tracking of visual objects in an image sequence is a challenging computer vision problem. Typically methods employ either generative or discriminative approaches to tackle the visual tracking problem. The generative methods [1,16,17] work by searching for regions that are most similar to the target model. A template or subspace based model is usually employed. The discriminative approaches [9,11,29] work by differentiating the target from the background using machine learning techniques. Recently, Danelljan et al. [6] proposed an adaptive color attributes based tracking approach that outperforms state-of-the-art tracking methods while operating at real-time. In our framework, we incorporate this tracking approach due to its robustness and computational efficiency.

Multiple object tracking (MOT) is the processing of multiple detections from multiple objects such that reliable estimates of the number of objects, as well as each object's state, can be obtained. The Probability Hypothesis Density (PHD) filter is a computationally feasible first order approximation of the Bayesian multiple object tracking filter [19,20], and its output is a joint Bayesian estimate of the number of objects and their respective states. In comparison to classic MOT filters such as Joint Probabilistic Data Association Filter (JPDAF) or Multi-Hypothesis Tracker (MHT), see e.g. [2], the PHD filter does not require a solution to the data assocation problem. In our framework, we use a PHD filter to improve the tracking results obtained by the adaptive color based attributes based tracking.

In this work we propose a low-level active vision framework for unmanned aircraft systems based on the LinkQuad platform. Our framework employs state-of-the-art object detection, object tracking, Bayesian filtering and AI-based control approaches. Our experimental results clearly demonstrate that the proposed framework efficiently detects and tracks persons in both indoor and outdoor complex scenarios. Our framework can thus be used for stable virtual leashing.

Fig. 1. LinkQuad platform with the color camera sensor module

The rest of the paper is organized as follows. Section 2 describes the used Micro UAV platform. Section 3 presents our active vision framework. Experimental results are provided in Section 4. Finally, conclusions are provided in Section 5.

2   Active Vision Platform

The micro UAV platform used for the system evaluation is a LinkQuad, see Figure 1. It is a highly versatile autonomous UAV. The platform's airframe is characterized by a modular design which allows for easy reconfiguration to adopt to a variety of applications. Thanks to a compact design (below 70 centimeters tip-to-tip) the platform is suitable for both indoor and outdoor use. It is equipped with custom designed optimized propellers which contribute to an endurance of up to 30 minutes. Depending on the required flight time, one or two 2.7 Ah batteries can be placed inside an easily swappable battery module. The maximum take-off weight of the LinkQuad is 1.4 kilograms with up to 300 grams of payload.

The LinkQuad is equipped with in-house designed flight control board - the LinkBoard. The LinkBoard has a modular design that allows for adjusting the availabl computational power depending on mission requirements. Due to the available onboard computational power, it has been used for computationally demanding applications such as the implementation of an autonomous indoor vision-based navigation system with all computation performed on-board. In the full configuration, the LinkBoard weighs 30 grams, has very low power consumption and has a footprint smaller than a credit card. The system is based on two ARM-Cortex microcontrollers running at 72 MHz which implement the core flight functionalities and optionally, two Gumstix Overo boards for user software modules. The LinkBoard includes a three-axis accelerometer, three rate

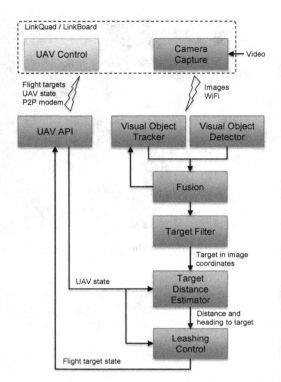

Fig. 2. Overview of the system components in our framework. Images captured by the camera are input to the object detection and tracking modules. The outputs of the two modules are combined in the fusion module. The results are further refined in the filtering component, which provides the image coordinate locations of the targets. The distance estimation component calculates the distance to the targets, which is used for leashing control.

gyroscopes, and absolute and differential pressure sensors for estimation of the altitude and the air speed, respectively. The LinkBoard features a number of interfaces which allow for easy extension and integration of additional equipment. It supports various external modules such as a laser range finder, analogue and digital cameras on a gimbal, a GPS receiver, and a magnetometer.

Experiments presented in this paper are performed using the LinkQuad UAV platform with a mounted FireFly MV color camera sensor manufactured by Point Grey Research Inc.[1]. The camera module also includes two servo mechanisms that allow for chaining the pan and tilt of the camera. The sensor is interfacing with the onboard Gumstix modules over the USB 2.0 interface.

3   Active Vision Components

The active vision framework consists of five main parts, namely object detection, visual tracking, target filtering, distance estimation and leashing control. Figure 2 depicts a logical schematics of the presented framework. Images captured onboard the UAV are distributed through a ROS topic by a *Camera Capture* ROS node. The node is running on a Gumstix module. The *Visual Object Tracker* and *Visual Object Detector* use this image stream as input. The object detector generates person detections in the images, while the visual tracker estimates the locations of visual object hypotheses in image coordinates. The results from these two components are fused at a later stage in the framework. In the target filtering component, the visual object estimates are further refined by modeling kinematics and detector noise. This component stabilizes the object identities and counters false detections. Image location estimates generated by the filtering component are then used to compute the distance and heading to the targets. This information is input to the leashing control module, which provides flight destinations to the UAV Control system.

3.1   Visual Object Detection

We implement two object detection methods, namely the HOG and Color-HOG based detectors. The former is the standard approach proposed by Dalal and Trigs [4]. It works by computing a feature representation using histogram of oriented gradients (HOG) on positive and negative samples of persons from the training set. A Support Vector Machine (SVM) classifier is then trained on these samples. Given a test image, the learned model is applied in a sliding window fashion to find potential detection responses. Our framework employs the HOG based classifier implemented in OpenCV.

As a second option, we use the Color-HOG detector proposed by Khan et al. [14]. The detector augments the standard HOG based method with color information. A late fusion scheme is employed to combine the color and shape information. We use color attributes [25] as an explicit color representation and fuse it with HOG features.

The visual object detector is implemented as a ROS node and runs in a separate thread. When the detections from a camera image are computed, the result is published. The detector then starts to process the latest available image from the camera.

3.2   Visual Object Tracking

We use the Adaptive Color Tracker (ACT) proposed recently by Danelljan et al. [6]. It has shown to achieve state-of-the-art performance on a large number of benchmark videos. The method is simple and computationally efficient, making it especially suitable for robotic applications. Here we use the ACT to track humans, but the method is generic and can be applied to track any visual object.

---

[1] http://ww2.ptgrey.com/USB2/fireflymv

The ACT works by learning a discriminative classifier on the target appearance. Its low computational cost is primarily due to two properties possessed by this tracking method. First, it assumes a periodic extension of the local image patch, which allows the usage of the fast Fourier transform (FFT) for the heavy computations. Second, the tracker applies a dynamically adaptive dimensionality reduction technique to reduce the number of features while preserving the important characteristics of the target appearance.

To update the tracker model at some frame n, a template t_n of size $M \times N$ centred around the target is first extracted. Danelljan et al. [6] suggests using a pixel dense representation of color name features [25] augmented with the usual grayscale values. These features are preprocessed by a normalization procedure followed by a windowing operation. The resulting template t_n is used to compute the kernelized auto-correlation $a_n(x, y)$ for all cyclic shifts x and y (in pixels) along the first and second coordinate respectively.

$$a_n(x, y) = \kappa(\tau_{x,y} P_n t_n, P_n t_n) \tag{1}$$

Here, κ is a Gaussian radial basis function kernel and $\tau_{x,y}$ is the cyclic shift operator. The projection operator P_n, that is computed by the dimensionality reduction technique, maps the pixel features onto a low-dimensional linear subspace. The desired output score y_n is set to a $M \times N$ sampled Gaussian function with a centred peak. The numerator $\hat{\alpha}_n$ and denominator $\hat{\beta}_n$ of the Fourier transformed classifier coefficients are updated with the new sample template using:

$$\hat{\alpha}_n = (1 - \gamma)\hat{\alpha}_{n-1} + \gamma \hat{y}_n \hat{a}_n \tag{2a}$$

$$\hat{\beta}_n = (1 - \gamma)\hat{\beta}_{n-1} + \gamma \hat{a}_n(\hat{a}_n + \lambda) \tag{2b}$$

Here, γ denotes a scalar learning rate parameter and λ is a scalar regularization parameter. The multiplication between signals is point-wise and $\hat{f}$ denotes the discrete Fourier transform (DFT) of a signal f. The tracker model also includes a template appearance u_n, which is updated as:

$$u_n = (1 - \gamma)u_{n-1} + \gamma t_n. \tag{3}$$

The tracking model is applied to a new image at time step n to locate the object by first extracting a $M \times N$ sample template v_n. This is done at the predicted target location and the extraction procedure is the same as for t_n. The kernelized cross-correlation between the sample template and the learned template appearance is given by:

$$b_n(x, y) = \kappa(\tau_{x,y} P_{n-1} v_n, P_{n-1} u_n) \tag{4}$$

The confidence scores s_n over the patch v_n are then computed as a convolution in the Fourier domain.

$$s_n = \mathscr{F}^{-1} \left\{ \frac{\hat{\alpha}_{n-1}\hat{b}_n}{\hat{\beta}_{n-1}} \right\} \tag{5}$$

Here $\mathscr{F}^{-1}$ denotes the inverse DFT operator. Henriques et al. [11] showed that the kernelized correlations a_n and b_n can be computed efficiently using the FFT.

The feature projection operator P_n is represented by a matrix that projects the feature vector of each pixel in a template onto a linear subspace. This projection matrix is obtained through an adaptive Principal Component Analysis proposed by [6]. A symmetric matrix $L_n = (1 - \eta)K_{n-1} + \eta C_n$ is computed as a linear combination between the feature covariance matrix C_n of the current template appearance u_n and a symmetric matrix K_n. Here, η is a scalar learning rate parameter. The matrix Q_n depends on the previously chosen projection matrices and is updated as $K_n = (1 - \eta)K_{n-1} + \eta P_n^T D_n P_n$ in each frame, where D_n is a diagonal weight matrix. This term ensures smoothness, which prevents the classifier coefficients to become outdated. The new projection matrix P_n is obtained by performing an eigenvalue decomposition on the matrix L_n and selecting the eigenvectors corresponding to the largest eigenvalues. This scheme for calculating the projection matrix minimizes a loss function formulated in [6], which regards both the current appearance and the set of previously selected feature spaces.

The visual tracking is implemented as a separate node in ROS in our framework. It processes all targets sequentially. All parameters of the ACT are set as suggested by the authors.

3.3 Combining Tracking and Detection

We use a separate component to fuse the tracking and detector results. It is implemented as a separate ROS node, and thus runs in a separate thread. When new tracking results are available for a visual object, the location and appearance model for this object is simply replaced with the ones returned by the tracker.

Person detections received by the detector component is used for the following puropses: to initialize new object candidates, verify existing object candidates, identify tracking failures and to correct the location and size of the visual object. A new object candidate is initialized when a detection is received that is not overlapping with any current objects or candidates. The image region that corresponds to this object candidate is then tracked until it is either verified or discarded. A candidate is verified if additional overlapping detections are received during the next-coming frames. If this occurs, the candidate is upgraded to a *known object*, otherwise it is discarded and removed.

To identify tracking failures, each known object must be verified with an overlapping detection within a certain number of frames. The object is identified as a tracking failure if no overlapping detection is received within the specified number of frames since the last verification. This leads to the removal of that object. To counter tracker drift, we also correct the target location and size with a partially overlapping detection if the overlap is less than a threshold.

3.4   Target Filtering

The target tracking module has three main parts: Bayesian estimation of

1. kinematics: velocity vectors are estimated for each target;
2. state uncertainty: full covariance matrices are estimated for each target state;
3. target ID: the visual tracking IDs are stabilized using the information contained in the estimated state vectors and covariance matrices.

The visual tracking output at time step k is a set $\mathbf{Z}_k = \{\mathbf{z}_k^{(j)}\}_{j=1}^{N_{z,k}}$, where each element $\mathbf{z}_k^{(j)} = (I_k^{(j)}, d_k^{(j)})$ consist of an ID $I_k^{(j)} \in \mathbb{N}$ a detection window $d_k^{(j)} \in \mathbb{R}^4$ that defines the position in the image and the windows width and height.

The purpose of the multiple object tracking (MOT) filter is to use the sets $\mathbf{Z}_k$ to estimate the object set $\mathbf{X}_k = \{\xi_k^{(i)}\}_{i=1}^{N_{x,k}}$, where both the number of objects $N_{x,k}$ and the object states $\xi_k^{(i)}$ are unknown. The object state at time step k is defined as $\xi_k^{(i)} = (\mathbf{x}_k^{(i)}, J_k^{(i)})$, where $J_k^{(i)}$ is the object's ID and $\mathbf{x}_k^{(i)}$ is the object state vector,

$$\mathbf{x}_k = \begin{bmatrix} p_k^x, p_k^y, v_k^x, v_k^y, w_k, h_k \end{bmatrix}^{\mathrm{T}} \tag{6}$$

where $[p_k^x, p_k^y]$ is the position, $[v_k^x, v_k^y]$ is the velocity, and w_k and h_k is the width and height of the detection window.

The process and detection models are

$$\mathbf{x}_{k+1} = F_{k+1}\mathbf{x}_k + \mathbf{w}_{k+1} = \begin{bmatrix} \mathbf{I}_2 & T_s\mathbf{I}_2 & \mathbf{0}_2 \\ \mathbf{0}_2 & \mathbf{I}_2 & \mathbf{0}_2 \\ \mathbf{0}_2 & \mathbf{0}_2 & \mathbf{I}_2 \end{bmatrix} \mathbf{x}_k + \mathbf{w}_{k+1} \tag{7}$$

$$\mathbf{z}_k = H_k\mathbf{x}_k + \mathbf{e}_k = \begin{bmatrix} \mathbf{I}_2 & \mathbf{0}_2 & \mathbf{0}_2 \end{bmatrix} \mathbf{x}_k + \mathbf{e}_k, \tag{8}$$

where $\mathbf{w}_{k+1}$ and $\mathbf{e}_k$ are zero-mean Gaussian noice processes with covariance matrices Q_{k+1} and R_k, respectively.

The visual tracking output is used as input in a Probability Hypothesis Density (PHD) filter [19,20]. Specifically we use a Gaussian mixture implementation [24] with a uniform distribution for the position component of the birth PHD intensity [3].

3.5   Distance Estimation

Controlling the UAV by leashing requires a distance estimate to the target. This is obtained by assuming a horizontal ground plane and a fixed person height h. Figure 3 contains a simple illustration of the scenario. The angle φ between the optical axis and the projection ray of the top of the target is calculated as

$$\varphi = \arctan\left(\frac{y}{f}\right) \tag{9}$$

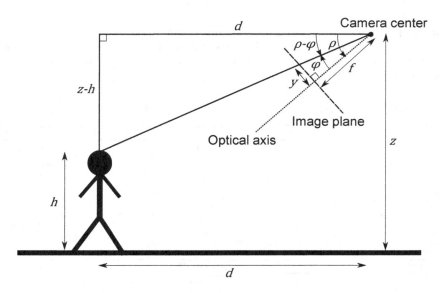

Fig. 3. To estimate the ground distance d between the UAV and the person, we assume a horizontal ground plane and a person height h. The angle φ is obtained from normalized image coordinate y of the upper edge of the bounding box and the effective focal length f. The UAV altitude z and camera pitch ρ are known. The distance is obtained using simple geometry by considering the larger triangle in the figure.

where y is the normalized image top-coordinate of the bounding box and f is the effective focal length. Using the known altitude z and camera pitch angle ρ, the distance d can be obtained from simple trigonometry.

$$d = \frac{z - h}{\tan(\rho - \varphi)} \tag{10}$$

Since we have a camera with a narrow field of view, a small yaw angle of the camera relative the target can be assumed. We therefore approximate the effective focal length to $f = 1$ m. We also assume that the UAV is flying approximately upright when extracting the top coordinate of the target. However, these assumptions have minimal impact due to other dominant model errors and measurement inaccuracies.

3.6   Leashing Control Module

The task of the *Leashing Control* module is to keep specified distance between the UAV and the target, and point the UAV towards the target. To achieve it the *Leashing Control* outputs the flight target state vector i.e. $[v_t^x, v_t^y, v_t^z, \psi_t]$, where $[v_t^x, v_t^y, v_t^z]$ are the target velocities, and ψ_t is the target heading.

The target state vector is used by the UAV velocity controller which in turn calculates target angle values used by the attitude stabilisation inner

Table 1. The results of the visual tracking evaluation. Six methods are compared on 12 benchmark sequences using center location error (a) and distance precision (b). The average frame-rate is also included in Table (b). The best and second best results are shown in red and blue respectively.

(a) Center location error

	CT	TLD	EDFT	Struck	LSHT	ACT
basketball	171	65.2	108	159	156	9.29
bolt	371	88	355	391	122	4.2
boy	32.1	4.09	2.34	3.35	32.6	4.39
couple	77.8	64.3	89.4	12.7	114	123
david	14.3	34.3	9.2	43.2	14.8	7.73
david3	68.5	136	6.46	107	53.7	9.11
human	428	110	5.77	5.36	6.59	7.25
singer1	15	10.6	16.6	12.4	21	9.21
skating1	184	104	199	82.3	82.3	7.95
trellis	51.1	55.9	59.6	15.3	61.2	20.8
walking	214	110	5.77	5.36	6.59	7.25
walking2	64.6	63.1	28.7	12.9	50.6	47.7
Average CLE	141	70.5	73.8	70.8	60.1	21.5

(b) Distance precision

	CT	TLD	EDFT	Struck	LSHT	ACT
basketball	4.14	51.3	30.5	11.6	5.1	99.9
bolt	2.57	32	2.57	2.86	37.4	100
boy	66.6	100	100	100	56.3	99.8
couple	30.7	31.4	21.4	83.6	10.7	10.7
david	79.2	65.8	100	32.7	76	100
david3	43.3	35.3	100	33.7	75	90.5
human	0.485	42.2	100	100	100	100
singer1	86.9	100	49.3	98.3	40.2	95.7
skating1	8.5	27	16.3	51	56	100
trellis	20.9	44.5	47.6	73.5	44.8	68.9
walking	12.1	42.2	100	100	100	100
walking2	40	37.6	40.2	85.6	39.8	42.4
Average DP	33	50.8	59	64.4	53.4	84
Average FPS	62	31.6	19	11.2	11.3	106

control loops. Flight target velocities i.e. $[v_t^x, v_t^y, v_t^z]$ are calculated in the following way. First, a new flight target position is calculated on a line which includes the current UAV position and the target position at a specified distance from the target. Then, the target velocities are proportional to the difference between the current UAV position and the new flight target's position.

Flight target heading ψ_t is calculated based on the UAV and target positions in the world coordinate frame.

Additionally the *Leashing Control* module implements a strategy for finding a target. This is done by commanding a sweeping motion using the heading target in order to increase chances of reacquiring a lost target or finding one in case it has not yet been found.

4   Experimental Evaluation

In this section we provide our experimental results. First, we evaluate the employed visual tracking method on benchmark videos and compare it to other state-of-the-art real-time visual tracking methods. Second, we show the impact of the target filtering component in our framework. Finally, we provide some fight test results.

4.1   Visual Tracking

We compare the ACT [6] with five other recent tracking methods from the literature with real-time performance, namely CT [29], TLD [12], EDFT [7], Struck [9] and LSHT [10]. We use the code and the suggested parameter settings provided by the respective authors. The recent evaluation protocol provided by

Wu et al. [26] is used.[2] From their dataset of 50 videos, we select the 12 videos of human or face tracking, where the setting is most similar to our application. The performance is measured in center location error (CLE) and distance precision (DP). CLE is defined as the average distance between the centroids of the tracked and ground truth bounding boxes, over the sequence. Distance precision is the relative number of frames in a sequence for which the distance between the centroids is less than 20 pixels. We also compare the frame rates of the different approaches. The experiments were performed on an Intel Xenon 2 core 2.66 GHz CPU with 16 GB RAM.

The results are shown in Table 1. ACT and Struck perform best on the same largest number of videos (five for CLE and six for DP). However, ACT obtains significantly better average performance, where it improves 23.6% in average distance precision over Struck. Moreover, the ACT is the fastest tracker in our evaluation, with almost ten times higher frame rate than Struck.

4.2 Target Filtering

The benefits of the target tracking module are most apparent in terms of stabilizing the tracking IDs. In ambiguous situations, such as when two or more targets pass each other in the image, the visual tracking IDs may become mixed up. Here the target tracking module uses the additional information contained in the kinematics and uncertainty estimates to maintain the target IDs correctly.

An example with two targets is given in Fig. 4. In the top left the two targets are approaching each other, with visual tracking/target IDs 14/2 (to the left, heading right) and 10/1 (to the right, heading left). During the crossing, shown in top right, the two targets overlap significantly. After the crossing, shown bottom left, both Visual tracker 14 and Visual tracker 10 have stuck to the target heading right in the image, and for the target heading left in the image a new Visual tracker with ID 15 has been initialized. However, the target tracking module has correctly fused the Visual tracking information with the estimated kinematics and uncertainty information, and the target IDs are correct. Shortly thereafter, shown bottom right, the Visual tracking has correctly deleted Visual tracker with ID 14.

4.3 System Evaluation

The presented system has been evaluated in a number of autonomous flights during which a micro UAV was following a person. A short description of a platform used for the flight tests is presented. Below follows a description of the experimental setup and the results of the flight tests.

---

[2] The evaluation code and benchmark image sequences are available at https://sites. google.com/site/trackerbenchmark/benchmarks/v10

Fig. 4. Example multiple object tracking results with two targets: one heading left and one heading right in the image. Shown are bounding boxes with IDs: visual tracking is indicated by red, multiple object tracking is indicated by green. During the crossing the targets overlap significantly, however the multiple target tracking maintains correct target IDs despite the visual tracking is associating erroneous IDs.

Experimental Setup. The presented system has been evaluated in a number of autonomous flights performed in a lab equipped with a motion capture system manufactured by Vicon Motion Systems company[3]. The system captures positions in a volume of $11 \times 11 \times 5$ meters and it was used both to provide a reference for the vision system performance evaluation and the state of the UAV used for the control (i.e. position and velocity in x, y, and z axes and heading). The state used for control was sent wirelessly and with an update rate of 10 Hz.

Figure 2 presents the interconnections and placement of the system components during the experimental flights.

Flight Test Results. During several flight tests the performance of the whole system was evaluated in terms of the accuracy of the vision-based distance estimation and the tracking performance of the control system.

Figure 5a presents the distance between the target and the UAV platform during a flight. The distance to keep was set to 5.5 meters and is depicted with the green line. The blue dotted curve shows the distance estimated based on vision as described in section 3. The red curve is the distance calculated using

---

[3] http://www.vicon.com/

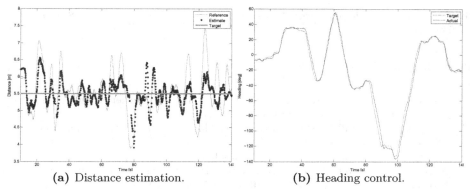

(a) Distance estimation.   (b) Heading control.

Fig. 5. The estimated relative distance of the target relative to UAV (a), target and actual heading (b) during the leashing experiment.

the Vicon reference system. As can be seen, during the flight the distance was kept with maximum error of 1.6 meters from the estimate and 1.9 meters from the reference.

Figure 5b presents the target heading ψ_t as described in Section 3.6 along with the actual heading during the leashing experiment. In case of slow changes in the target heading, our framework accurately tracks the target. For faster changes, the heading error increases due to the limited maximum allowed heading rate of the UAV. It is worthy to mention that it has little impact on the overall leashing performance.

In summary, our framework is able to perform the leashing control task using the active vision component described earlier. The accuracy of the distance estimation can be improved further by taking into account the size of the detection box. However, our results suggest that for the leashing task the simple distance estimation approach provides consistent results on several indoor scenarios. For most leashing applications, a small bias in the distance estimate is tolerable since the purpose of our framework is to follow a person at a roughly constant distance.

5 Conclusion

In this paper, we present a low-level active vision framework for unmanned aircraft systems. Our framework is implemented on the LinkQuad platform and employs state-of-the-art object detection, object tracking, Bayesian filtering and AI-based methods. It efficiently detects and tracks persons in real-time which is used for virtual leashing.

Future work involves improving the visual tracking by incorporating the Discriminative Scale Space Tracker (DSST) [5] into our framework since it has shown to outperform state-of-the-art methods [15]. The scale estimates obtained from the DSST can further improve the distance estimation and a removal of the ground plane assumption. Other potential research directions includes recognizing human actions [13] such as hand waiving, clapping etc. and to integrate efficient person re-identification techniques to tackle heavy occlusions and out-of-view scenarios.

References

1. Bao, C., Wu, Y., Ling, H., Ji, H.: Real time robust l1 tracker using accelerated proximal gradient approach. In: CVPR (2012)
2. Bar-Shalom, Y., Willett, P.K., Tian, X.: Tracking and data fusion, a handbook of algorithms. YBS (2011)
3. Beard, M., Vo, B., Vo, B.N., Arulampalam, S.: A partially uniform target birth model for Gaussian mixture PHD/CPHD filtering. IEEE Transactions on Aerospace and Electronic Systems 49(4), 2835–2844 (2013)
4. Dalal, N., Triggs, B.: Histograms of oriented gradients for human detection. In: CVPR (2005)
5. Danelljan, M., Häger, G., Shahbaz Khan, F., Felsberg, M.: Accurate scale estimation for robust visual tracking. In: BMVC (2014)
6. Danelljan, M., Shahbaz Khan, F., Felsberg, M., van de Weijer, J.: Adaptive color attributes for real-time visual tracking. In: CVPR (2014)
7. Felsberg, M.: Enhanced distribution field tracking using channel representations. In: ICCV Workshop (2013)
8. Felzenszwalb, P.F., Girshick, R.B., McAllester, D.A., Ramanan, D.: Object detection with discriminatively trained part-based models. PAMI 32(9), 1627–1645 (2010)
9. Hare, S., Saffari, A., Torr, P.: Struck: structured output tracking with kernels. In: ICCV (2011)
10. He, S., Yang, Q., Lau, R., Wang, J., Yang, M.H.: Visual tracking via locality sensitive histograms. In: CVPR (2013)
11. Henriques, J.F., Caseiro, R., Martins, P., Batista, J.: Exploiting the circulant structure of tracking-by-detection with kernels. In: Fitzgibbon, A., Lazebnik, S., Perona, P., Sato, Y., Schmid, C. (eds.) ECCV 2012, Part IV. LNCS, vol. 7575, pp. 702–715. Springer, Heidelberg (2012)
12. Kalal, Z., Matas, J., Mikolajczyk, K.: P-n learning: bootstrapping binary classifiers by structural constraints. In: CVPR (2010)
13. Khan, F.S., Anwer, R.M., van de Weijer, J., Bagdanov, A., Lopez, A., Felsberg, M.: Coloring action recognition in still images. IJCV 105(3), 205–221 (2013)
14. Khan, F.S., Anwer, R.M., van de Weijer, J., Bagdanov, A., Vanrell, M., Lopez, A.: Color attributes for object detection. In: CVPR (2012)
15. Kristan, M., et al.: The visual object tracking vot2014 challenge results. In: Bronstein, M., Agapito, L., Rother, C. (eds.) ECCV 2014 Workshops, Part II. LNCS, vol. 8926, pp. xx–yy. Springer, Heidelberg (2015)
16. Kwon, J., Lee, K.M.: Tracking by sampling trackers. In: ICCV (2011)
17. Liu, B., Huang, J., Yang, L., Kulikowski, C.: Robust tracking using local sparse appearance model and k-selection. In: CVPR (2011)
18. Lowe, D.G.: Distinctive image features from scale-invariant points. IJCV 60(2), 91–110 (2004)
19. Mahler, R.: Multitarget Bayes filtering via first-order multi target moments. IEEE Transactions on Aerospace and Electronic Systems 39(4), 1152–1178 (2003)
20. Mahler, R.: Statistical Multisource-Multitarget Information Fusion. Artech House, Norwood (2007)

21. Meier, L., Tanskanen, P., Fraundorfer, F., Pollefeys, M.: Pixhawk: A system for autonomous flight using onboard computer vision. In: ICRA (2011)
22. van de Sande, K., Uijlings, J.R.R., Gevers, T., Smeulders, A.W.M.: Segmentation as selective search for object recognition. In: ICCV (2011)
23. Sinopoli, B., Micheli, M., Donato, G., Koo, T.J.: Vision based navigation for an unmanned aerial vehicle. In: ICRA (2001)
24. Vo, B.N., Ma, W.K.: The Gaussian mixture probability hypothesis density filter. IEEE Transactions on Signal Processing **54**(11), 4091–4104 (2006)
25. van de Weijer, J., Schmid, C., Verbeek, J.J., Larlus, D.: Learning color names for real-world applications. TIP **18**(7), 1512–1524 (2009)
26. Wu, Y., Lim, J., Yang, M.H.: Online object tracking: a benchmark. In: CVPR (2013)
27. Yu, Z., Nonami, K., Shin, J., Celestino, D.: 3d vision based landing control of a small scale autonomous helicopter. International Journal of Advanced Robotic Systems **4**(1), 51–56 (2007)
28. Zhang, J., Huang, K., Yu, Y., Tan, T.: Boosted local structured hog-lbp for object localization. In: CVPR (2010)
29. Zhang, K., Zhang, L., Yang, M.-H.: Real-time compressive tracking. In: Fitzgibbon, A., Lazebnik, S., Perona, P., Sato, Y., Schmid, C. (eds.) ECCV 2012, Part III. LNCS, vol. 7574, pp. 864–877. Springer, Heidelberg (2012)

Online 3D Reconstruction and 6-DoF Pose Estimation for RGB-D Sensors

Hyon Lim[1]([✉]), Jongwoo Lim[2], and H. Jin Kim[1]

[1] Seoul National University, Seoul, Korea
{hyonlim,hjinkim}@snu.ac.kr
[2] Hanyang University, Seoul, Korea
jlim@hanyang.ac.kr

Abstract. In this paper, we propose an approach to Simultaneous Localization and Mapping (SLAM) for RGB-D sensors. Our system computes 6-DoF pose and sparse feature map of the environment. We propose a novel keyframe selection scheme based on the Fisher information, and new loop closing method that utilizes feature-to-landmark correspondences inspired by image-based localization. As a result, the system effectively mitigates drift that is frequently observed in visual odometry system. Our approach gives lowest relative pose error amongst any other approaches tested on public benchmark dataset. A set of 3D reconstruction results on publicly available RGB-D videos are presented.

Keywords: Simultaneous Localization and Mapping · RGB-D SLAM

1 Introduction

The goal of *online 3D reconstruction and 6-DoF pose estimation*, also known as Simultaneous Localization and Mapping (SLAM) is to incrementally build a 3D model of the surrounding environment while concurrently localizing the camera. This has been a key technology for autonomous navigation of robots and many useful applications [6,10–12,15,22,26]. To this end, selection of a keyframe and finding inter-keyframe geometric relationships, are one of the most important parts. However, most existing systems select keyframe based on heuristics, such as fixed time or distance intervals, and find geometric relation only between adjacent keyframes.

In this paper, we discuss two essential problems of online 3D reconstruction and camera tracking, which critically affect the quality and speed of the reconstruction[1]. The first problem is the online *keyframe selection*. The keyframes are

---

Electronic supplementary material The online version of this chapter (doi:10.1007/978-3-319-16178-5_16) contains supplementary material, which is available to authorized users. Videos can also be accessed at http://www.springerimages.com/videos/978-3-319-16177-8.

[1] A video of our method is available on http://youtu.be/gnbnFEjy8wU

© Springer International Publishing Switzerland 2015
L. Agapito et al. (Eds.): ECCV 2014 Workshops, Part I, LNCS 8925, pp. 238–254, 2015.
DOI: 10.1007/978-3-319-16178-5_16

Fig. 1. The 3D model of fr3/office reconstructed by the proposed method.
This reconstruction is obtained by registering the full point clouds of all keyframes
transformed according to their keyframe poses computed by the proposed method.
Position and orientation of keyframes are denoted by coordinate axis that is color
coded by red, green and blue (X-Y-Z order) in below four images.

the representative images of the scene chosen among the input frames, and they
are used in building the model and optimizing the structure [10, 22]. Since the
reconstruction is performed on top of the selected keyframes, selecting proper
keyframes is a critical task, but how to choose good keyframes has not been studied extensively so far. Several heuristic methods have been widely used, such as
using fixed time intervals or using fixed distance or rotation threshold. These
rule-of-thumb methods have introduced somewhat ad-hoc parameters, and they
tend to generate more than necessary keyframes to model the scene. Instead,
we propose an information theoretic approach to measure informativeness of
the current estimate to decide whether to put it as a keyframe or not. Detailed
method is described in Section 4.1.

The other problem we are tackling in this paper is the *loop closing*. The loop
closing is the task of finding new geometric relationships between keyframes,
which was not available from temporal incremental motion estimation. By closing
loops, the uncertainty of reconstruction can be reduced and the model quality can
be improved. However, the existing methods using visual features [4, 10, 11, 15, 22]
search only keyframe-to-keyframe loops. However, these existing approaches have
been overlooked normal frames between keyframes. As the number of normal
frames is significantly greater than the number of keyframes, finding a loop
on normal frames will increase the chance of finding of better loops. Other
approaches such as [10, 22] search metric loop closures by assuming some motion
prior to be available. However, such metric loop closure is less likely to be successful in most online 3D reconstruction scenarios due to the measurement noise
and pose drift.

To address the problems above, we propose a method which is not only
utilize an appearance-based method [3] but also bridges disconnected feature-
to-landmark relations inspired by image-based localization. The key distinction
of proposed method compared to the existing online 3D reconstruction methods
[4, 10, 11, 15, 22] is that we seek direct link between the 2D features and 3D landmarks at *every input image*, and add the image as a new keyframe on-the-fly
when a good match is found. Most existing methods ignores the non-keyframe
images (i.e., normal frames) mainly due to computational overhead, and only
utilized the keyframe-to-keyframe matching. However, we address this issue by

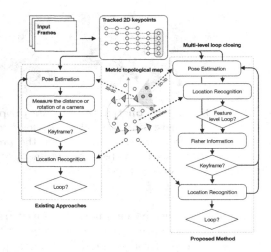

Fig. 2. The block diagram of the core steps in the existing methods (left side) and the proposed method (right side). Note that loop closure test is performed at every frame (while existing approaches perform at keyframe creation) and keyframe selection is based on the Fisher information in our method. Refer to the text for more detail.

distributing computational load by extracting specified number of descriptors on keypoints at each frame. This is inspired by work of real-time image-based localization [14]. The difference between the existing approaches and the proposed method is visualized in Fig. 2.

We developed a full 6-DoF online 3D reconstruction system with proposed methods to demonstrate the effectiveness of the proposed approaches. An example input and output of developed system is shown in Fig 1. We have evaluated our approach on public RGB-D datasets recorded in various environment [24]. We are able to achieve high quality of 3D reconstruction with less number of keyframes than existing keyframe selection scheme. Most of evaluation results show less than 10 cm in root mean square error (RMSE) of absolute trajectory error. To summarize, our key contributions are:

- A novel keyframe selection scheme based on Fisher information of the tracked camera pose. It measures informativeness of the given frame. As a result, a keyframe is added only if it has enough information, thus it can select keyframes adaptively and creates less number of keyframes to build similar quality reconstructions as compared in Section 5.
- A new loop closing strategy for online 3D reconstruction. This consists of two types of match. The one matching process seeks best similar view of current keyframe which only happens at keyframe creation process (keyframe-to-keyframe), while the another process searches best 3D landmarks in the 2D keypoints in an image (feature-to-landmark) at every input frame. The effectiveness of proposed method is tested our own built online 3D recon-

struction system with real experiments with ground truth comparison. We also evaluated the proposed approach with other method.

2 Related Work

2.1 Online 3D Reconstruction

The online 3D reconstruction is a task that reconstructs surrounding environments in 3D by utilizing input video sequences. A common components of online 3D reconstruction are feature point tracking, which takes care of the temporal keypoint relationship between frames, and bundle adjustment for accurate 3D reconstruction [25]. In the existing video-based reconstruction [11,12,26], the quality of frame-by-frame feature track seriously affects the quality of reconstruction. This is prone to image noise, object occlusions, illumination change, large-motion, which easily causes occasional feature dropout and distraction. If a feature track is interrupted by these disturbances, the existing methods create a new feature track even though it is a same physical point of lost feature. We argue that this non-consecutive track should be bridged correctly for accurate 3D reconstruction. However, most of approaches have no explicit answer to this question because it is not obvious how to insert this discontinuous track as observations. We will discuss this further in Section 4.3.

2.2 Keyframe Selection

Several selection schemes have been proposed to build a map with a smaller set of keyframes. The naïve choice is to choose every n-th frame. However, this will create unnecessary keyframes during stationary motion. Another popular option is to choose keyframe based on *distance or orientation change threshold* since last keyframe [10,11,15,22]. This method will sample Euclidean space evenly, but it does not consider sensor accuracy. For example, if a sensor quality is good enough to measure wide range of the environment, this method will create redundant keyframes. Henry *et al.* [6] selects keyframe based on the number of inliers during RANSAC procedure of current pose. But we observed that an information gain is different even when the same number of inliers is given. Snavely *et al.*[21] propose skeletal graphs to select informative frames. They solved *offline* problem by utilizing trace of translational covariance as an uncertainty measure. In offline problem, maximum and minimum boundaries of uncertainty are bounded in the problem as all the images are provided prior to run algorithm. However, our problem is *online 3D reconstruction and camera tracking*, and such boundary cannot be determined prior to run the system. Therefore, we consider Fisher information matrix and its summarized statistics to measure informativeness of the current frame and initialize the new keyframe based on this metric. Recently, similar work is proposed by Kerl et al [8]. They have utilized relative entropy that is somewhat heuristic method based on their observation, while ours utilized summarized statistics of Fisher information which represents theoretically lower bound of the variance of estimator. Furthermore, we show that simple thresholding works well as opposed to [8].

2.3   Image-Based Localization

Image-based localization in this paper is a problem of computing the 6-DoF location of given image with respect to existing set of images. In early period of research, only approximated location was obtained [20] by solving large-scale image retrieval approach [18]. Recently, a complete 6-DoF pose is obtained based on visual 3D maps built by structure from motion technique [7,13,19,26]. In [7, 26], synthesized views are created to group the set of features as same document in vocabulary tree [18]. Most relevant top-k views are considered for expensive SIFT [16] matching. In [13], prioritized 3D points are matched to input image using approximate nearest neighbor search. Unlike other approaches, it queries 3D point first rather than 2D features in an input image. In [19], direct 2D-3D matches are used to localize a frame. In [19] visual vocabulary-based prioritized search has been proposed to match the number of features required for geometric verification with less computation. We are particularly interested in direct 2D-3D match [14,19] with vocabulary tree [18] which introduces predictable amount of computation.

3   Problem Formulation

3.1   Metric-Topological Map Representation

The internal representation of the map can be *metric* or *topological*:

- The *metric representation* is the most common for robot navigation and considers a three-dimensional space in which it places the objects. The objects are placed with precise coordinates. This representation is very useful, but is sensitive to noise and it is difficult to close a loop because the location of all vertexes should be adjusted at the moment of the loop closure detection.
- The *topological representation* only considers relative relations between them. No exact global coordinates defined to describe the position of vertexes (i.e., keyframes). The map is then a graph, in which the vertexes corresponds to keyframes (or landmarks) and edges correspond to the relations (e.g., relative pose, image measurements).

The topological map can be transformed to metric map by compositing relative poses assigned on edges between vertexes. To this end, we search a topological graph starting from reference keyframe by breadth-first search (BFS). In many cases, current keyframe is set to origin and remaining keyframes pose are described based on the origin.

3.2   The Graph Representation of Topological Map

Keyframes and 3D points are represented as graph $\mathcal{G}$ consists of a set of keyframe vertexes $\mathcal{K}$, a set of homogeneous 3D points $\mathcal{M}$, and a set of edges represent the relative pose $\mathcal{P}$ between two keyframes or image projection $\mathcal{Z}$. Each keyframe

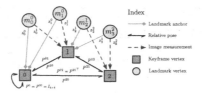

Fig. 3. A mini example of topological map. The i-th 3D point with anchor keyframe j is denoted by m_i^j. The anchor keyframe is a keyframe which observes a 3D point at first. The image measurement of m_i in j-th keyframe is defined z_i^j. The pose between keyframe i and j is denoted by P^{ij}.

vertex saves unique identification number, list of 3D points observed and normalized image coordinates of associated 3D points. Note that we do not save absolute pose in the keyframe vertexes.

Let $\mathcal{P} = \{p_{jk} \mid j, k \in [0, \ldots, m-1]\}$ be a set of m 6-DoF camera poses (i.e., keyframe poses) where each $p_{jk} \in SE(3)$ is a 6×1 vector contains orientation (i.e., angle-axis representation) and position that defines a 4×4 homogeneous transformation matrix $P^{jk} \in \mathbb{R}^{4 \times 4}$, a pose j defined in frame k. The transformation matrix P^{jk} and its inverse is defined as

$$P^{jk} = \left(P^{kj}\right)^{-1} = \begin{bmatrix} R^{jk} & T^{jk} \\ 0 & 1 \end{bmatrix} \in \mathbb{R}^{4 \times 4}, \quad \text{with } R \in SO(3), \quad T \in \mathbb{R}^3. \quad (1)$$

Let $\mathcal{M} = \{m_i^k \mid i \in [1, \ldots, n], k \in [0, \ldots, m-1]\}$ be a set of n landmarks described relative to anchor keyframe k. Each $m_i^k = [\bar{m}_i^k, 1]^\top = [\bar{m}_{i,1}^k, \bar{m}_{i,2}^k, \bar{m}_{i,3}^k, 1]^\top$ is a 4×1 homogeneous point where the bar notation selects the 3D component (See Fig. 3). A landmark m_i^k defined in keyframe k can be transformed to keyframe j by transformation matrix P^{jk} as Equation (2).

$$m_i^j = P^{jk} m_i^k = [R^{jk} \bar{m}_i^k + T^{jk}, 1]^\top = \begin{bmatrix} R^{jk} & T^{jk} \\ 0 & 1 \end{bmatrix} [\bar{m}_{i,1}^k, \bar{m}_{i,2}^k, \bar{m}_{i,3}^k, 1]^\top \quad (2)$$

In this paper, we assume that the camera is calibrated (i.e., intrinsic parameters are known a priori). Image projection using homogeneous coordinates $\pi : \mathbb{R}^4 \to \mathbb{R}^3$ is modeled as a pinhole camera:

$$\pi\left(P^{jk} m_i^k\right) = \left(\frac{\bar{m}_{i,1}^j f}{\bar{m}_{i,3}^j} + o_x, \quad \frac{\bar{m}_{i,2}^j f}{\bar{m}_{i,3}^j} + o_y, \quad 1\right)^\top, \quad (3)$$

where f is the focal length, $\mathbf{o} = [o_x, o_y]^\top$ is the principal point. The normalized image coordinates is defined by $\pi\left(P^{jk} m_i^k\right) / \|\pi\left(P^{jk} m_i^k\right)\|$. In a monocular camera, the observation of a 3D point m_i in keyframe j is denoted by (3) where $z_i^j \in \mathbb{R}^3$. In a binocular camera (e.g., stereo or RGBD camera), the observation is

$$z_i^j = \left[\pi(P^{jk} m_i^k), \quad f\frac{\bar{m}_{i,1}^j - b}{\bar{m}_{i,3}^j} + o_x\right]^\top \in \mathbb{R}^4, \quad (4)$$

Algorithm 1. Local bundle adjustment: Bundle adjust keyframes and landmarks within the sliding window w. Reference frame a_0 usually set to most recent frame.

```
    Input  : Reference keyframe a₀, Window size w
    Output : Bundle adjusted active keyframes A ∈ G and periphery keyframes A' ∈ G, A ≠ A'
 1  Initialize active keyframe set A, periphery keyframe set A' and active landmark set M_A as ∅;
 2  Perform metric embedding from a₀ only w number of frames. Insert embedded keyframes to A;
 3  // Construct active set A and periphery keyframe set A'
 4  forall the keyframe k ∈ A do
 5      L ⇐ All landmarks associated to a keyframe k ;
 6      forall the landmark m ∈ L do
 7          M_A ⇐ M_A ∪ {m};
 8          N ⇐ Set of keyframes that observed the landmark m;
 9          // Add periphery keyframes for pose optimization
10          forall the keyframe k' ∈ N do
11              if k' ∉ A then
12                  |  A' ⇐ A' ∪ {k'}
13              end
14          end
15      end
16  end
17  Perform bundle adjustment using cost function (5) with A, A', M_A;
18  // De-embedding : Update topological map using optimized poses
19  forall the Optimized keyframe i ∈ {A ∪ A'} do
20      P̄^{ia₀} ← Pose of the keyframe i with respect to a₀ ;          /* bundle adjusted pose */
21      N ← Find neighbor keyframes of i;
22      forall the neighbor keyframe j ∈ N do
23          P̄^{ja₀} ← Pose of the neighbor keyframe j with respect to a₀;
24          P^{ij} ← P̄^{ia₀} P̄^{ja₀⊤} ;                              /* Update an edge j → i */
25          P^{ji} ← P̄^{ja₀} P̄^{ia₀⊤} ;                              /* Update an edge i → j */
26      end
27  end
28  // Update landmark position in topological map
29  forall the Optimized landmark m̄_i^{a₀} ∈ M_A do
30      P̄^{ka₀} ← Pose of anchor keyframe k of a landmark m_i^{a₀} with respect to a₀;
31      m_i^k = P^{ka₀} m̄_i^{a₀} ;                                  /* m̄_i Bundle adjusted 3D point */
32  end
```

---

where b is the baseline between two cameras. All images are assumed to be undistorted and rectified.

3.3 Optimization of Pose Graph

In order to achieve constant-time operation, we define a sub set of keyframes $\mathcal{A}$ which is called *active keyframes* from set $\mathcal{K}$. The set $\mathcal{A}$ usually constructed with most recent-w keyframes from the current keyframe. The w is called window-size, typically 5 to 10 in our implementation. Local optimization is performed within the set $\mathcal{A}$.

As we preserve topological relations between map and poses, we further seek keyframes that are worthy of inclusion in the optimization. These keyframes are denoted $\mathcal{A}'$ which are selected based on the existence of covisible features between the set $\mathcal{A}$ and a neighbor keyframe set $\mathcal{N}$ of $\mathcal{A}$, but $\mathcal{N} \notin \mathcal{A}$. The original active keyframes include all measurement and poses to be optimized (i.e., poses and landmarks are optimized). However, only relative pose information of keyframes in $\mathcal{A}'$ are optimized (i.e., pose-to-pose only optimization). This approach is motivated by [22]. In contrast to [22] which used single global coordinates, our approach is purely based on relative formulation, so it shows better metric consistency in local window in large-scale loop closures. Therefore, our algorithm can handle complex multi level loop closures which will be described

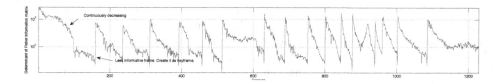

Fig. 4. Summarized statistics of Fisher information matrix. The time history of determinant of Fisher information matrix in FR2/SITTING_XYZ sequence. The sequence information is shown in Table. 1.

in detail in Section 4.3. Following cost function J is considered to optimize both 3D point and pose-to-pose constraint of local metric embeddings constructed by Algorithm 1:

$$J^2(\mathcal{G}, a_0) = \sum_{i \in \mathcal{M}_\mathcal{A}, j \in \mathcal{A}} v_{ij} \left(z_i^j - \pi \left(P^{ja_0} m_i^{a_0} \right) \right)^2 + \sum_{i,j \in \mathcal{A}'} v_{ij} \left(P^{ij\top} \Lambda_{ij} \left(P^{ia_0} P^{ja_0\top} \right) \right)$$

(5)

where $\mathcal{G}$ is a pose graph, a_0 is an reference frame of local window, v_{ij} $_{(i \neq j)}$ is a function where 1 if a direct path available in topological map, otherwise 0 and Λ_{ij} is a covariance matrix.

4 Proposed Method

4.1 Fisher Information for Uncertainty Measure

Current scheme to determine keyframe usually relies on a norm of translation or rotation part of the pose with respect to previous keyframe. This results uniform sample of poses and landmarks in the Euclidean space as proposed by existing approaches [10,11]. However, determination of this threshold is somewhat vague, also it is prone to pose estimation error or spiky motion. The distance or rotation threshold also depends on scene characteristic. For example, if a camera travels in a large outdoor environment, the same distance threshold as indoor environment will create keyframe too frequently. Therefore, we need a more intelligent metric to determine whether current frame should be registered as keyframe or not. In the following subsection, we describe detailed metric used for keyframe generation.

In [21], the uncertainty is modeled by a trace of covariance matrix. It is well suited for offline problem such as structure from motion (SfM) by calculation of uncertainty amount along given keyframe path. However, it is unclear to determine the threshold of trace of the covariance to represent uncertainty to be kept for the keyframe creation that is online process. To address this problem, we propose a novel keyframe selection scheme based on Fisher information matrix.

The Fisher information matrix can be approximated by the inverse of the covariance matrix of maximum-likelihood estimators [1]. As bundle adjustment is a maximum likelihood problem, estimators asymptotically have zero bias and the lowest-variance that any unbiased estimator can have [25]. Obtaining covariance is not straightforward, since the bundle adjustment problem is large. Filters like Kalman filter always keep covariance of the system, but they are not practical for such large problems.

Let pose $p^\star$ is a solution of maximum likelihood estimate of p obtained by bundle adjustment :

$$p^\star = \arg \min_p \|z - f(p)\|^2 \quad \text{where} \quad z = f(p), \tag{6}$$

where $f(\cdot)$ is a nonlinear measurement process (3) and z is a measurement. If measurement process $f(\cdot)$ is differentiable, the covariance matrix of pose p can be estimated by following equation:

$$\Sigma_{\mathbf{p}^\star} = (\mathrm{J}_{p^\star}^\top \Sigma_{\mathbf{z}} \mathrm{J}_{p^\star})^{-1} \tag{7}$$

where $\mathrm{J}_{p^\star}$ is Jacobian matrix evaluated at estimated pose $p^\star$, and $\Sigma_{\mathbf{z}}$ is covariance matrix of observations. We assume that the measurement process is independent and equal covariance which means that $\Sigma_{\mathbf{z}} = I$. The Fisher information matrix F is defined as

$$F = \Sigma_{\mathbf{p}^\star}^{-1}. \tag{8}$$

See Fig. 4 for F of FR2/SITTING_XYZ sequence. For online algorithm, computing the covariance of current frame with respect to all other existing keyframe is not feasible. As our representation separates global and local map, we only compute current pose uncertainty within active keyframes. This naturally models current frame uncertainty within a meaningful physical region. For example, if we consider whole pose graph to compute covariance, the distant keyframe might increase actual uncertainty we are interested in. In [21], only translational uncertainty was considered for offline structure from motion. However, the rotational uncertainty should be considered in online video-based reconstruction. We estimate full 6×6 covariances of 6-DoF pose with considering all landmarks currently observing and relative keyframes in pose graph.

4.2   Keyframe Selection Scheme

The Fisher information is inverse of covariance in our problem. We consider the determinant of Fisher information matrix τ_F:

$$\tau_F = \det(F) = \det \left(\Sigma_{\mathbf{p}^\star}^{-1} \right). \tag{9}$$

As the amount of variance can be approximated by determinant of covariance matrix, if estimator variance becomes large, proposed metric τ_F naturally converges to zero, but never reaches zero in theory. Fig. 4 shows actual value of proposed metric for RGB-D sequence FR2/XYZ along with time (See Table. 1 for details). Setting threshold of τ_F as moderately small number (e.g., 0.001 in our case) will adaptively selects keyframes based on surrounding environment and feature qualities. The proposed method creates keyframe based on uncertainty

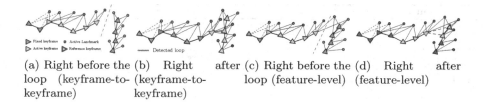

(a) Right before the loop (keyframe-to-keyframe) (b) Right after (keyframe-to-keyframe) (c) Right before the loop (feature-level) (d) Right after (feature-level)

Fig. 5. An illustrative example of two loop detection cases. (a) local bundle adjustment is performed past five frames. (b) If loop is found, corresponding relative pose and landmark observations are added to the bundle adjustment framework, then optimized. (c) Right before the loop, features in current frame and 3D landmarks are linked. (d) After the detection, pose links are registered.

bound of pose. Naturally it considers both position and rotational uncertainty in a single framework. In the previous approach, distance or rotation threshold was used to keep feasible problem size for optimization. In other words, the propose approach is naturally considers the quality of measurements which depends on scene size and the speed of moving camera. In summary, it creates even sample of keyframe in information wise, not heuristically determined distance threshold. Although a user still have to determine uncertainty boundary, however, the tuning parameter itself more informative. Tuning the threshold is easier than determination of $0.2\ m$ or 20 degrees which depends on scene characteristics for example.

4.3 Multi Level Loop Closing

Structure-from-motion or keyframe-based visual SLAM problem largely rely on the quality of feature tracking [27]. If feature tracks are disjointed caused by objects moving in an out of the view, or pure rotation motion, are not included as constraint in the bundle adjustment. Observing a 3D point in many views definitely helps to obtain accurate map and pose within bundle adjustment framework. We will call this constraint namely *feature-level loop* throughout this paper.

However, obtaining a feature-level loop is not a straightforward problem. In PTAM [10], they projected all 3D features in the map which are visible by the previous motion, to obtain non-consecutive feature-level loop. But, the PTAM requires strong motion prior to this end. Once a camera motion is lost, they compare small image patches of all keyframes to measure similarity then perform exhaustive matching that takes time. It is also prone to errors and not scalable. In [27], they proposed two-pass algorithm to find non-consecutive feature tracks which is the same as the feature-level loop. However, it is very slow and not an online algorithm.

In this paper, we propose feature-level loop closing motivated by recent development of image-based localization [7,19]. The main difference compared to image-based localization, we update database in real-time and utilize linked

Algorithm 2. Feature-level loop detection. $\tau = 0.7, \epsilon = 0.001$ in this paper.

```
Data: Vocabulary tree V, trained by using descriptors associated to 3D points.
Input  : SURF descriptors Q, of current input frame.
Output: Loop constraint P^{ka_0} between current frame a_0 and matched keyframes k.
1  M, K ← ∅ ;                                    /* Initialize M:2D-to-3D matches, K:votes */
2  W ← Find visual words of query descriptors Q using vocabulary tree V;
3  forall the visual word w ∈ W do
4  |    L ← Get landmark ids of w;
5  |    q ← Get SURF descriptor of w;
6  |    d_{first}, d_{second} = ∞;
7  |    forall the landmark l ∈ L do
8  |    |    q' ← Get SURF descriptor of a landmark l;
9  |    |    d ← Compute distance between descriptors q and q';
10 |    |    if d < d_{first} then
11 |    |    |    d_{second} = d_{first};
12 |    |    |    d_{first} = d ;
13 |    |    |    m ← A 2D feature related to the visual word w and a 3D landmark l are set as best match;
14 |    |    |    k ← Find anchor keyframe number of a landmark l_j;
15 |    |    end
16 |    end
17 |    if (d_{first})/(d_{second}) > τ then
18 |    |    M = M ∪ {m};
19 |    |    K = K ∪ {k};
20 |    end
21 end
22 Perform RANSAC with P3P using 2D-3D matches M;
23 /* Compute Fisher information and optimize pose. λ (= 15)                                  */
24 if the number of inliers > λ then
25 |    Optimize pose P using inliers. The determinant of Fisher information, J  is returned.;
26 |    if J > ε then
27 |    |    forall the voted keyframe k ∈ K do
28 |    |    |    Compute relative pose P^{ka_0} between current a_0 and target keyframe k;
29 |    |    |    Add relative pose constraint to the pose graph.
30 |    |    end
31 |    else
32 |    |    Create a new keyframe using current frame.
33 |    end
34 end
```

motion prior of the matched 3D landmark, to reject false positives. Also we use videos, not a discrete images as in [7,19], we utilize both temporal relationship among frames and feature-level loops. The two types of loop are shown in Fig. 5.

Keyframe-to-Keyframe Loop Closing. We first utilize existing keyframe-to-keyframe style loop closing. Our feature tracker will provide the most recent SURF descriptor tracked until the current frame. These descriptors are provided to vocabulary tree when keyframe is created. The SURF descriptors of a new keyframe are queried to the existing keyframes, and 2D-3D correspondences are obtained from query result. Further geometric verification is performed with RANSAC. Outliers will be removed during the RANSAC process. If enough inliers are found, nonlinear optimization minimizing reprojection error is performed to obtain accurate relative pose with respect to matched frame. We add this relative pose and 2D-3D observations to the graph, further local bundle adjustment will be performed.

Feature-Level Loop Closing. The majority of existing online 3D modeling or visual SLAM systems have been used keyframe-to-keyframe loop closure scheme [11,15,22] which seeks corresponding keyframe among existing keyframes. Loop closure operation (*i.e.*, querying current keyframe to the database) only happens

Table 1. Evaluation datasets. Evaluation sequences and its scene characteristics are shown. The length of camera traveled, duration, the number of images and keyframes reconstructed are listed. As you can see, relatively stationary motion shows low percentage of frames selected as keyframes.

Dataset	Travel Length [m]	Duration [s]	# images	# of keyframes	% of frames used
fr1/xyz	7.112	30.09	798	53	6.6
fr1/room	15.989	48.90	1362	138	10.1
fr1/desk	9.263	23.40	613	74	12.1
fr1/desk2	10.161	24.86	640	121	18.9
fr1/rpy	1.664	27.67	723	83	11.4
fr2/desk	18.880	99.36	2965	99	3.4
fr2/xyz	7.029	122.74	3669	53	1.5
fr3/office	21.455	87.09	2585	118	4.6
fr3/sitting_xyz	5.496	42.50	1261	17	1.4

Table 2. Comparisons to other approaches. We have compared our method to four different approaches. The nine sequences were evaluated. The reader should note that all the methods compared in this table are using pose estimation based on dense iterative closed point (ICP) using depth image. In contrast, our algorithm considers only a depth of each keypoint which is essentially same as a stereo camera. Without use of ICP algorithm as main pose estimator, we achieved few ($2.2cm$) difference compared to the state-of-the-art approaches in ATE. Furthermore, our approach has better performance in terms of relative pose error (RPE). This is due to the fact that our algorithm successfully close the loop which is a key of minimizing drift. We compared RPE with [23] because the RPE is only reported in [23].

	RMSE ATE in [m]					RMSE RPE in [m]	
Dataset	Ours	Stuckler et al.[23]	Bylow et al.[2]	Kinfu	RGB-D SLAM [5]	Ours	Stuckler et al.[23]
fr1/xyz	0.015	**0.013**	0.021	0.026	0.014	0.021	**0.02**
fr1/room	0.101	**0.069**	0.078	0.313	0.101	**0.056**	0.139
fr1/desk	0.059	0.043	0.046	0.057	**0.026**	**0.014**	0.075
fr1/desk2	0.108	**0.049**	0.069	0.420	0.059	**0.067**	0.09
fr1/rpy	0.031	0.027	0.042	0.133	**0.026**	**0.037**	0.04
Average	0.062	**0.040**	0.051	0.189	0.045	**0.032**	0.077
fr2/xyz	**0.013**	0.020	-	-	-	**0.002**	0.030
fr2/desk	0.072	0.052	-	-	-	**0.047**	0.099
fr3/office	**0.025**	-	0.039	0.064	-	0.011	-
fr3/sitting_xyz	0.017	-	-	-	-	0.005	-

when the keyframe insertion is performed. The existing approaches overlooked the fact that it is possible to have better loop closure from input frames between keyframes.

In this paper, we directly search 2D-3D correspondences efficiently to perform every-frame loop seeking by utilizing recent results of image-based localization [7,19]. In [4], similar view recognition is performed by using kd-trees. The system builds kd-tree incrementally, and all descriptors in current frame are queried to the database. They kept top-k views among registered views for geometric verification. However, this approach does not scale well due to the fact that the metric tree is required to store all descriptors on memory, also search time grows significantly as the number of features in the tree increases.

Instead computing pose from these 2D-3D matches directly, we create keyframe based on a pose between current and last keyframes that is most accurate pose in the graph. Then we add these 2D-3D matches to the keyframe. See Algorithm 2 in detail.

5   Experimental Result

The evaluation datasets are summarized in Table 1. For evaluation we chose 9 sequences across Freiburg1 to 3 (FR1-3) datasets that are especially recorded by handheld camera. Those datasets also have been used by several other authors for evaluation [2,5,9,23]. We have compared our approach with those authors (See Fig. 2). The experiments were performed on a laptop with an Intel Core i7 with 2.3 Ghz processor. But only single core is utilized for the proposed method to make the proposed method work on embedded system in the future.

We utilize the evaluation software that measures root mean square error (RMSE) of the translation drift (RPE) in m/s and absolute trajectory error (ATE) in meters. Detailed computation of those metrics is shown in [24].

(a) **fr1/xyz (left), fr2/xyz (right) sequences reconstructed.** Both sequences have a specific camera motion as shown in the figures (i.e., the camera was moved only in axial direction). The axial trajectory is clearly seen in the figures.

(b) **fr1/desk (left), fr1/desk2 (right) sequence reconstruction.** Two sequences were captured in the same physical place, but captured twice. Dense 3D point cloud model obtained by proposed method. Red, gree, red color bars mean X,Y,Z axes of the keyframes respectively.

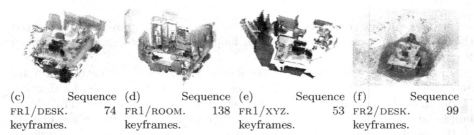

(c)   Sequence FR1/DESK. 74 keyframes.

(d)   Sequence FR1/ROOM. 138 keyframes.

(e)   Sequence FR1/XYZ. 53 keyframes.

(f)   Sequence FR2/DESK. 99 keyframes.

Fig. 6. Reconstruction results. Once all frames are processed, bundle adjustment with all keyframes is performed. Then the full-resolution depth image of each keyframes are projected by the assigned keyframe pose. Currently, colored points are rendered.

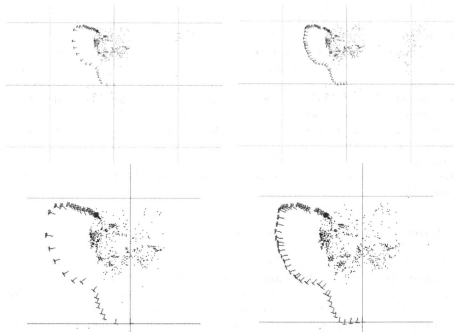

(a) PROPOSED KEYFRAME SELECTION SCHEME. The proposed method utilizes Fisher information matrix to select keyframe from 30fps video sequence. In fast or high angular velocity motion, our method automatically creates more dense keyframes compared to normal camera movement.

(b) EXISTING DISTANCE-BASED KEYFRAME SELECTION SCHEME. The keyframes are generated with 0.2m constant distance threshold with orientation norm 0.1 radian. This method creates regular sample of Euclidean 3D environment, but these keyframes are very redundant.

Fig. 7. Comparison between keyframe selection methods. The propose method and existing method are compared with same video sequence. Our method (left) adaptively creates sparse or dense keyframe compared to the right (distance-based approach).

Unlike existing RGB-D online mapping approaches which use all dense 3D point cloud to obtain relative pose between frames [5,17], we only utilize depths of tracked 2D features (usually 200 in a frame) and the relative pose is computed by P3P algorithm, essentially the same as stereo camera. Thus the RGB-D camera can be replaced with a stereo camera without changing the system.

We have compared our method with four other approaches: multi-resolution surfel maps (MRSMap) [23], KinectFusion [17], RGBD-SLAM [5] and Bylow *et al.*[2]. As shown in Table 2, our approach is superior in terms of relative pose error (RPE) as two types of loops are thoroughly considered. However, absolute trajectory error (ATE) is slightly inferior to existing approach (by less than a few centimeters). One of the main reasons is that we did not use dense depth map for motion estimation that is likely to be more accurate than image only pose estimation when the motion is slow. Another reason is that the ATE metric divides number of keyframes used. In most cases, our algorithm produces fewer numbers of keyframes than other approaches which used all frames as keyframe. The accuracy of our method can be shown by RPE as other approaches are less accurate despite they have used ICP and all frames. The reconstructed 3D environment map of evaluation sequences is shown in Fig. 6.

Fig. 7 shows the difference between the proposed and existing keyframe selection method. Our method creates keyframes adaptively as shown in the screenshot above according to the uncertainty amount of current pose computed with landmarks. A video of our method is available on http://youtu.be/gnbnFEjy8wU.

6   Conclusion and Future Work

We have proposed a novel and efficient framework for online 3D reconstruction and camera tracking. The information theoretic keyframe selection scheme can adaptively selects the keyframe, and the feature level loop detection successfully closes the loops with the same uncertainty metric. We demonstrated the proposed approach with ground truth, where it performs better than or at least as good as the state of the art methods. Considering that only sparse keyframes are used for reconstruction, the proposed algorithm has many benefits over the dense RGB-D reconstruction algorithms.

One interesting problem for the future work is to keep the number of keyframes and landmarks as sparse as possible while it preserves essential information of the environment. This is also connected to life-long visual mapping or skeletal graph construction. This would allow the map size to be proportional to the characteristics (e.g., size, a degree of clutter) of the environment not to the number of images taken in the environment.

Acknowledgments. This work was supported partly by the National Research Foundation of Korea (NRF) grant funded by the Korea government (MEST), ICT R&D programs of MSIP/IITP (No. 14-824-09-006 and No. 2014-10047078) and Defense Research Grant, funded by the Agency for Defense Development, under the contract UD120013JD.

References

1. Abt, M., Welch, W.J.: Fisher information and maximum-likelihood estimation of covariance parameters in gaussian stochastic processes. Canadian Journal of Statistics **26**(1), 127–137 (1998)
2. Bylow, E., Sturm, J., Kerl, C., Kahl, F., Cremers, D.: Real-time camera tracking and 3d reconstruction using signed distance functions. In: RSS (2013)

3. Cummins, M., Newman, P.: Fab-map: Probabilistic localization and mapping in the space of appearance. The International Journal of Robotics Research **27**(6), 647–665 (2008)
4. Eade, E., Fong, P., Munich, M.E.: Monocular graph slam with complexity reduction. In: IROS, pp. 3017–3024. IEEE (2010)
5. Endres, F., Hess, J., Engelhard, N., Sturm, J., Cremers, D., Burgard, W.: An evaluation of the rgb-d slam system. In: ICRA, pp. 1691–1696. IEEE (2012)
6. Henry, P., Krainin, M., Herbst, E., Ren, X., Fox, D.: Rgb-d mapping: Using kinect-style depth cameras for dense 3d modeling of indoor environments. The International Journal of Robotics Research **31**(5), 647–663 (2012)
7. Irschara, A., Zach, C., Frahm, J.M., Bischof, H.: From structure-from-motion point clouds to fast location recognition. In: CVPR, pp. 2599–2606. IEEE (2009)
8. Kerl, C., Sturm, J., Cremers, D.: Dense visual slam for rgb-d cameras. In: Proc. of the Int. Conf. on Intelligent Robot Systems (IROS) (2013)
9. Kerl, C., Sturm, J., Cremers, D.: Robust odometry estimation for rgb-d cameras. In: ICRA (2013)
10. Klein, G., Murray, D.: Parallel tracking and mapping for small ar workspaces. In: ISMAR, pp. 225–234. IEEE (2007)
11. Konolige, K., Agrawal, M.: Frameslam: From bundle adjustment to real-time visual mapping. IEEE Transactions on Robotics **24**(5), 1066–1077 (2008)
12. Konolige, K., Bowman, J.: Towards lifelong visual maps. In: IROS, pp. 1156–1163. IEEE (2009)
13. Li, Y., Snavely, N., Huttenlocher, D.P.: Location recognition using prioritized feature matching. In: Daniilidis, K., Maragos, P., Paragios, N. (eds.) ECCV 2010, Part II. LNCS, vol. 6312, pp. 791–804. Springer, Heidelberg (2010)
14. Lim, H., Sinha, S.N., Cohen, M.F., Uyttendaele, M.: Real-time image-based 6-dof localization in large-scale environments. In: CVPR, pp. 1043–1050. IEEE (2012)
15. Lim, J., Frahm, J.M., Pollefeys, M.: Online environment mapping. In: CVPR, pp. 3489–3496. IEEE (2011)
16. Lowe, D.G.: Object recognition from local scale-invariant features. In: ICCV, vol. 2, pp. 1150–1157. IEEE (1999)
17. Newcombe, R.A., Davison, A.J., Izadi, S., Kohli, P., Hilliges, O., Shotton, J., Molyneaux, D., Hodges, S., Kim, D., Fitzgibbon, A.: Kinectfusion: real-time dense surface mapping and tracking. In: ISMAR, pp. 127–136. IEEE (2011)
18. Nister, D., Stewenius, H.: Scalable recognition with a vocabulary tree. In: CVPR, vol. 2, pp. 2161–2168. IEEE (2006)
19. Sattler, T., Leibe, B., Kobbelt, L.: Fast image-based localization using direct 2d-to-3d matching. In: ICCV, pp. 667–674. IEEE (2011)
20. Schindler, G., Brown, M., Szeliski, R.: City-scale location recognition. In: CVPR, pp. 1–7. IEEE (2007)
21. Snavely, N., Seitz, S.M., Szeliski, R.: Skeletal graphs for efficient structure from motion. In: CVPR (2008)
22. Strasdat, H., Davison, A.J., Montiel, J., Konolige, K.: Double window optimisation for constant time visual slam. In: ICCV, pp. 2352–2359. IEEE (2011)
23. Stuckler, J., Behnke, S.: Integrating depth and color cues for dense multi-resolution scene mapping using rgb-d cameras. In: IEEE Conf. on Multisensor Fusion and Integration for Intelligent Systems, pp. 162–167. IEEE (2012)
24. Sturm, J., Engelhard, N., Endres, F., Burgard, W., Cremers, D.: A benchmark for the evaluation of rgb-d slam systems. In: IROS, October 2012

25. Triggs, B., McLauchlan, P.F., Hartley, R.I., Fitzgibbon, A.W.: Bundle adjustment – a modern synthesis. In: Triggs, B., Zisserman, A., Szeliski, R. (eds.) ICCV-WS 1999. LNCS, vol. 1883, pp. 298–372. Springer, Heidelberg (2000)
26. Wendel, A., Irschara, A., Bischof, H.: Natural landmark-based monocular localization for mavs. In: ICRA, pp. 5792–5799. IEEE (2011)
27. Zhang, G., Dong, Z., Jia, J., Wong, T.-T., Bao, H.: Efficient non-consecutive feature tracking for structure-from-motion. In: Daniilidis, K., Maragos, P., Paragios, N. (eds.) ECCV 2010, Part V. LNCS, vol. 6315, pp. 422–435. Springer, Heidelberg (2010)

Nature Conservation Drones for Automatic Localization and Counting of Animals

Jan C. van Gemert[1]([⊠]), Camiel R. Verschoor[2,3], Pascal Mettes[1],
Kitso Epema[2], Lian Pin Koh[4], and Serge Wich[5,6]

[1] Intelligent Systems Lab Amsterdam,
University of Amsterdam, Amsterdam, The Netherlands
{j.c.vanGemert,p.s.m.Mettes}@uva.nl
[2] Dutch Unmanned Aerial Solutions, Amsterdam, The Netherlands
{camielVerschoor,kitso.Epema,lianpinkoh,sergewich}@gmail.com
http://dutchuas.nl/
[3] IDI Snowmobile, Amsterdam, The Netherlands
http://idisnow.com
[4] Applied Ecology and Conservation Group,
University of Adelaide, Adelaide, Australia
[5] Institute for Biodiversity and Ecosystem Dynamics,
University of Amsterdam, Amsterdam, The Netherlands
[6] School of Natural Sciences and Psychology,
Liverpool John Moores University, Liverpool, UK

Abstract. This paper is concerned with nature conservation by automatically monitoring animal distribution and animal abundance. Typically, such conservation tasks are performed manually on foot or after an aerial recording from a manned aircraft. Such manual approaches are expensive, slow and labor intensive. In this paper, we investigate the combination of small unmanned aerial vehicles (UAVs or "drones") with automatic object recognition techniques as a viable solution to manual animal surveying. Since no controlled data is available, we record our own animal conservation dataset with a quadcopter drone. We evaluate two nature conservation tasks: (i) animal detection (ii) animal counting using three state-of-the-art generic object recognition methods that are particularly well-suited for on-board detection. Results show that object detection techniques for human-scale photographs do not directly translate to a drone perspective, but that light-weight automatic object detection techniques are promising for nature conservation tasks.

Keywords: Nature conservation · Micro UAVs · Object detection

1 Introduction

Accurate monitoring of the distribution and abundance of animal species over time is a key ingredient to successful nature conservation [3,4]. Successful conservation also requires data on possible threats to animals. Such threats can be

© Springer International Publishing Switzerland 2015
L. Agapito et al. (Eds.): ECCV 2014 Workshops, Part I, LNCS 8925, pp. 255–270, 2015.
DOI: 10.1007/978-3-319-16178-5_17

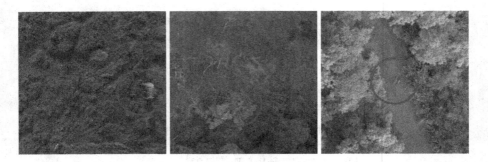

Fig. 1. Animal conservation images taken from a drone. From left to right: an elephant, an orangutan nest, and rhinos.

largely divided into habitat loss, disease and poaching. For some iconic species like the rhino, the elephant, and the tiger, poaching has reached proportions that places them at a high risk for local extinctions or even total extinction for some (sub)species as in the case of elephants [2,32].

Animal monitoring approaches typically involve both direct animal counts and indirect counting of animal signs such as nests, dung, and calls. Conventional ground surveys on foot can be time-consuming, costly, and nearly impossible to achieve in remote areas. For example, ground surveys of orangutan populations (Pongo spp.) in Sumatra, Indonesia can cost up to $250,000 for a three-year survey cycle. Due to this high cost, surveys are not conducted at the frequency required for proper statistical analysis of population trends. Furthermore, there remain many remote forested areas that have never been surveyed. Aerial surveys can overcome some of these constraints, although they have their own set of limitations, including the high cost of buying or renting small planes or helicopters, the lack of availability in remote areas, and the risks involved with flying low over landscapes in which landing is difficult, such as forests. There is thus a need for alternative methods for animal surveys.

Conservation workers have started using small unmanned aerial vehicles (UAVs, or "conservation drones") both for determining animal abundance and to obtain data on their threats [18,20]. Conservation drones are relatively inexpensive and easy to build, which makes drones accessible and affordable for many research teams in developing countries. These drones can fly fully autonomous missions to obtain high-resolution still images and videos. Recent studies have shown that the images from such drones can be used to detect not only large animal species (e.g. orangutans, elephants, rhinos, whales) and animal tracks (e.g. orang-utan nests, chimpanzee nests, turtle tracks), but also threats to animals (e.g. signs of human activity [16,21,26,35]). See Figure 1 for some examples of conservation images taken from a drone. Currently, most drone systems record data on board, which are then downloaded for manual visual inspection once the drone has landed. For animal abundance surveys, the amount of recorded data quickly grows to thousands of photos and hundreds of hours of video. Manually sieving through these data in search of animals is labor-intensive and inherently slow.

There is therefore a strong need to automate the detection of relevant objects on the still or video images. Recent efforts combining human labeling and automatic recognition seem promising [5], but this field is still in its infancy.

Another need for automated detection of objects comes from anti-poaching efforts. Ideally, drones would do on-board object detection and then only send the relevant images (i.e. those with a high probability of a positive identification) of the object of interest, e.g. *human, rhino, fire*, down to the ground station for a manual visual inspection by the rangers in order to take appropriate actions. This paper examines automatic object detection algorithms as a solution towards detecting animals and humans from images obtained from drones. The aim is to assess the potential of computer vision for surveys of animal abundance and anti-poaching efforts.

The field of computer vision has matured enough to automatically find objects in images with reasonable accuracy. Such methods are typically designed for and evaluated on general purpose objects by employing photographs from the Internet [22]. Thus, such methods are tuned towards human photographs, taken from a height of 1-2 meters with human-scale objects. Such objects can safely be assumed to consist of observable parts [11] or to be found by object-saliency methods (so called "object proposals"), tuned to human scale [1,15,17,31]. Yet, for drone imagery taken in high altitude (10-100m) the objects of interest are relatively small, questioning the suitability of current methods that use individual parts or object-saliency. Moreover, drone images are taken from above which results in a skewed vantage point, which changes influential surface and scene properties [8] when compared to normal human pictures. It can therefore not be taken for granted that current object detection methods for human-centered imagery find a one-to-one application in conservation drones.

In this paper we evaluate how current object detection techniques as developed for human-centered imagery scale to drone-centered nature conservation tasks. Because current object recognition methods make heavy use of object proposals, we first evaluate whether such proposals are capable of detecting animals in drone imagery. Next, we evaluate three light-weight object detection methods on two nature conservation tasks: i) animal detection in single images; ii) animal counting in video. We evaluate these two tasks on a novel fully annotated animal dataset recorded with a drone. The dataset consists of 18,356 frames containing 30 distinct animals. This work stems from a collaboration between conservation biologists, aerospace engineers and computer vision researchers. To facilitate a structured and repeatable evaluation we will make the dataset, annotations, code, and all our results publicly available.

2   Related Work

2.1   Drones for Nature Conservation

Drones are air vehicles that do not carry a pilot on board and are capable of flying autonomously. These vehicles follow flight plans based on GPS coordinates which are usually programmed before flight, but can also be changed during the flight. There are many types of drones, ranging in weight from a few grams to thousands of kilograms, varying in size from a few millimeters to tenths of meters with configurations according to normal aircrafts, helicopters, multi-rotors and flapping wings. The uses of these drones vary from the military to private consumers. The type of drones that are specifically useful for nature conservation are the modified model aircraft and multi-rotor. They are both affordable and easily converted into a drone with highly affordable open source autopilots like Ardupilot [20] or Paparazzi [13]. The modified model aircrafts yield long flying times and larger forward speed to cover more ground. In contrast, multi-rotor drones yield great control of the position and orientation of the camera as well as vertical take off and landing capabilities. Combine this with the birds eye view for the camera and these drones are perfect for conservation. Here we focus on the rotor-type drone.

Drones are currently already employed for conservation [20] for terrain mapping and classification of forest types [14,16,18,21,35]. These are examples of uses where no real time data analysis is needed [5]. For the protection of animals against poaching, real-time analysis is critical. This is recognized by the Wildlife Conservation UAV Challenge [38], which focuses on the on-board processing of data to find rhinos and humans. This is an international challenge (with almost 90 teams from all over the world) to create a cheap drone to help protect the rhino. The techniques to find animals and humans in real-time with limited computing power are not ready for real-world applications yet, validating our research on this topic.

2.2 Automatic Object Detection

The current state-of-the-art in automatic object detection is based on large convolutional neural networks [15,29]. Such "deep-learning" networks discriminatively learn image features from the bottom-up and proved hugely successful on global image classification [22]. The success of convolutional networks on full images spills over to the related task of object detection where in addition to the object class name, a detection bounding box around the object is required. The bounding box is obtained by elegant object-saliency methods that output a small set of only a few thousand bounding boxes that have a high likelihood to contain any type of object [1,31]. Such class-independent object-proposals serve as input to the convolutional network, yielding state-of-the-art accuracy. Such accuracy, however, relies heavily on modern computer hardware such as top of the line CPUs and massively parallel GPU implementations. The recognition times using modern hardware are reported as 53 sec/image by R-CNN [15] on a CPU and 13 sec/image on the GPU whereas OverFeat [29] operates at 2 sec/image on an heavy-weight GPU. These hardware requirements are not feasible in a light-weight drone, where every gram of weight reduces flight times. Since fast response time is essential for animal protection, convolutional networks are as of yet computationally too demanding for timely results on a drone.

Next to convolutional networks, other competitive object detection methods are based on the bag-of-words (BOW) model [31,33,34] or its Fisher vector

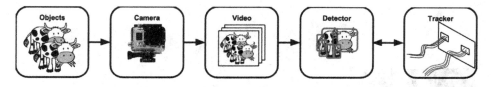

Fig. 2. Conservation evaluation pipeline. Animals are recorded on video or individual images. The animals are automatically detected, yielding a bounding box per animal per image. Individual detections are stitched together by tracking shared features to obtain an automatic estimate on the number of animals.

incarnation [6,28]. Such methods start with a limited set of object-proposals to reduce the search space. Each proposal is represented with a histogram of prototype counts of local features, e.g. sampled from interest points [9]. Larger prototype vocabularies typically yield best results, resulting in features sizes of over 170,000 [31] for BOW or over 300,000 for the Fisher vector [28] per bounding box. On a mobile drone the internal memory is limited making such large memory requirements of the BOW variants prohibitive.

Both the bag-of-words methods and the convolutional neural networks heavily rely on high quality object proposals. These proposals are tuned to a human scale, and we will first evaluate the suitability of object proposals for drone imagery. Successful low-memory and CPU-friendly object detection methods do not use object proposals but simple and fast image features combined with a classifier cascade. Such a cascade rejects obvious non-matching candidates early on; only allotting more computation time to promising candidates. An example of such an successful approach is the seminal Viola and Jones boosting method [36] used in embedded face detection algorithms for consumer cameras, phones and tablets. Other versions of a classifier cascade have been applied to a range of object detection methods with impressive speed-up results. The popular Deformable Part-based Model (DPM) of Felzenswalb et al. [11] models an object as a constellation of parts and a classifier cascade in combination with a coarse-to-fine search has successfully reduced computation time to 0.2 sec/image [10,27]. Similarly, the examplar SVM approach for object detection [25] can be sped up to 0.9 sec/image [23]. Cascade approaches are fast while retaining a reasonable accuracy and are thus most suitable for on a drone. Therefore we will focus our evaluation on the DPM and exemplar-based SVM methods.

3   Evaluating Nature Conservation

We evaluate two tasks for automatic nature conservation drones. i) animal detection and ii) animal counting. Automatically detecting animals gives insight in animal locations, which over time will reveal herd patterns and popular gathering places. Knowledge about the animal location will give the conservation worker valuable information about where to take anti-poaching measures. The second

Fig. 3. Recording the dataset. (a): the Pelican quadcoptor drone used to record the dataset (b): an example image from the train-set (c): an example image from the test-set. Note the slanted vantage point and tiny animals.

task, counting animals, will give abundance data over time, coupled to detection regions. This data gives the conservator a sense of the health of the animal population, and where and how many animals disappear, which warrants further investigation. The pipeline for the two evaluation tasks is visualized in Figure 2.

3.1   Recorded Dataset

Wildlife is notoriously hard to record in a controlled setting. To approximate a realistic conservation task, we used a quadcopter drone to record a dataset of domesticated farm animals. In figure 3(b,c) we show examples of the recordings. While the exact type of animal (cow), the lack of camouflage in the open fields and the presence of man-made structures is not common in the wild, this recording nevertheless retains important properties that match a realistic conservation scenario. Such realistic properties include the use of a quadcopter drone which is often used in the wild because of its maneuverable and its ability to take off from dense areas. Moreover, this type of drone gives us the opportunity to record under a wide variation of positions, heights, and orientations of the camera. Therefore, the recording setup matches closely as experienced in the wild. Furthermore, the animals are smaller and of a similar size and build as many conservation animals like the rhino or the elephant. The dataset provides an excellent first opportunity to evaluate nature conservation drone algorithms.

The dataset was recorded by the Ascending Technologies Pelican (quadcopter) with a mounted GoPro HERO 3: Black Edition action camera. In Figure 3(a) we show the drone in action. We manufactured a 3D printed custom-made mount to attach the camera to the drone. The mount is filled with foam to counter vibration of the camera during flight. The camera recorded videos at a quality of 1080p (1920 x 1080 pixels) having a medium field of view (55° vertical and 94.4° horizontal) with 60 frames per second.

We performed two separate flights to obtain a set for training and a disjoint set for testing. We manually annotated all animals in the dataset with vatic [37]. We removed large portions of the videos that do not contain any animals, which resulted in 6 videos obtained from the two seperate flights. We use the first 4 videos from the first flight for training, and the latter 2 videos from the second

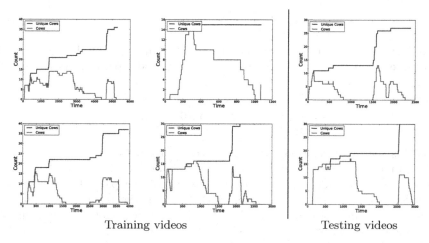

Training videos   Testing videos

Fig. 4. Number of animals per frame in each video, the green line shows the number of unique animals per frame, the blue line the cumulative total. The 2 left columns represent the training videos, the right column the test videos.

flight for testing. In total there are 12,673 frames in the training set and 5,683 frames in the test set. There are 30 unique animals present in the dataset. In figure 4 we visualize the appearance and disappearance of animals during the flight.

4   Object Detection Methods Suitable for Drones

4.1   Deformable Part-based Model

The deformable part-based model (DPM) of Felzenszwalb et al. [11] is a popular and successful object detection instantiation of the pictorial structure representation [12] where an object is modeled as a flexible constellation of parts. In addition to the gray-valued DPM, we also evaluate the color-DPM [19], where color information is added to the features.

In the DPM [11], an object consists of a collection of parts connected in a star-structure to a coarse root node. The parts and root node are represented by HOG features and the quality of a star model is the score of the root features at a given location plus the sum of the maximum over the part placements minus a deformation cost based on the deviation of the parts from its ideal location.

The DPM is trained on bounding box annotations around the whole object; where object-part locations are not labeled. To discriminatively train models in such a semi-supervised setup a latent SVM is used. From labeled bounding boxes $\{x_1, x_2, \ldots, x_n\}$ where each box has a class label y_i being either $+1$ or -1 a latent SVM allows training when the part-locations are unknown. A latent SVM scores an example x as

$$f_\beta(x) = \max_{z \in Z(x)} \beta \cdot \Phi(x, z), \tag{1}$$

where $\Phi(x, z)$ is a feature vector and the set $Z(x)$ has all possible latent variables (object configurations) and β is a vector of model parameters trained by minimizing the SVM hinge loss

$$L(\beta) = \frac{1}{2}||\beta||^2 + C \sum_{i=1}^{n} \max(0, 1 - y_i f_\beta(x_i)), \tag{2}$$

where C is the regularization parameter. See [11] for details.

A significant speed-up for the DPM can be obtained by a part-based cascade [10]. This cascade is based on an ordering of the parts hypotheses and prunes low scoring hypotheses, allowing the bulk of the computation time to be spent on promising candidates. Besides the cascade, another speed-up can be obtained by a hierarchical coarse-to-fine feature matching approach [27]. The speed-up is based on the observation that the computational cost of the DPM is dominated by the cost of matching each part to the image. The number of part matches can be significantly reduced by using a coarse-to-fine inference strategy. The combination of the cascade and the coarse-to-fine matching yields a speed-up of one up to two orders of magnitude resulting in detection rates of 0.2 sec/image [27]. Such speeds are acceptable for nature conservation applications on low-cost drone hardware.

4.2   Exemplar SVM

The ensemble of exemplar SVM object detection approach by Malisiewicz et al. [25] trains a parametric SVM for each positive exemplar in the dataset. This reaps the benefits of a non-parametric nearest neighbor search with training a parametric model. The parametric SVM can effectively deal with negative samples whereas the non-parametric approach retains the link between positively labeled training exemplars which allows knowledge transfer such as pose, geometry or layout from an exemplar to a new object. This approach is conceptually simple and yields good performance.

An exemplar SVM aims to separate each training example x_E from other examples in the set N_E that do not containing the object class by learning a weight vector w_E by optimizing

$$||w||^2 + C_1 h(w^T x_E + b) + C_2 \sum_{x \in N_E} h(-w^T x - b), \tag{3}$$

where $h(x) = \max(0, 1 - x)$ is the hinge loss and C_1 and C_2 are regularization parameters. Each individual exemplar SVM is trained on a unique set of negative examples which makes the output scores of the SVM's not necessarily comparable. To calibrate each SVM, a sigmoid function is fitted on hold-out data, resulting in comparable SVM output between 0 and 1. All exemplar models are applied on a test image by means of a sliding window, where exemplar co-occurences are used to obtain a detection.

To speed-up exemplar SVMs, Li et al. [23] use each exemplar as a weak classifier in a boosting approach. Boosting builds a strong classifier with a linear combination of weak classifiers. These weak classifiers are iteratively selected to optimize the mis-classification rate. The iterative approach of boosting performs feature selection, using only the best T weak classifiers. Feature selection drastically reduces the number of used exemplars where [23] need only 500 exemplars for state of the art performance. In addition to the feature selection, Li et al. [23] propose efficient feature-sharing across image pyramid scales resulting in a detection speed of 0.9 sec/image, which is similarly acceptable for on a drone.

5   Animal Counting

For counting animals, the algorithm needs to keep track of each unique animal to make sure a single animal is only counted once. This is a challenging task for several reasons. The animal detection algorithm may fail missing the animal completely or only in some frames in a video. It is also possible that the detection algorithm detects an animal where there is none which will inflate the amount of counted animals. Furthermore, because of the maneuverability of drone and possible pre-programmed flying paths, the same animal may appear and disappear from the drone camera completely.

The detection algorithms process every frame. To determine if two detections in subsequent frames belong to the same unique animal, the object detections have to be stitched together over time. We aim to track detections over multiple frames, even when one or a few detections are is missing. Thus, instead of basing our method on detection tracking which may be noisy, we track salient points which are more stable. For point tracking we use the KLT tracker [24] which uses optical flow to track sparse interest points for L frames, where L is a parameter. To determine whether two subsequent detection bounding boxes A and B belong to the same unique animal we use the intersection over union measure $\frac{A \cap B}{A \cup B} > 0.5$ of the set of point tracks through A and through B [7].

Note that animal counting is different from a spatio-temporal localization task, as e.g. proposed in [17,30]. In a localization task the objective is to carefully and completely identify what, when and where each object is in a video. In animal counting, the exact position is not as relevant to the conservation worker since she is interested in how many unique animals are correctly found.

6   Experiments

6.1   Experiment 1: Evaluating Proposal Quality

Object proposals significantly reduce the object detection search space by locating a modest collection of bounding boxes that with a high likelihood contain any type of object. We focus on the selective search object proposal algorithm of Uijlings et al. [31]because of its high-quality proposals. Selective search generates object proposals from an initial set of super-pixels obtained through an over-segmentation and merges super-pixels using a range of color, shape and other super-pixel similarity measures. We evaluate both the *fast* and *quality* settings of selective search [31].

Table 1. Statistics of object proposals on the drone dataset. Overlap between proposals A and ground-truth boxes B is measured as $\frac{A \cap B}{A \cup B}$. ABO (Average Best Overlap) is the best overlapping proposal per frame, averaged over all frames. Recall is measured as the fraction of ground truth boxes that have an overlap greater than 0.5.

Setting	ABO	Recall	Proposals / frame	Time / frame
Fast	0.635	0.873	ca. 18,369	ca. 31 sec.
Quality	0.740	0.976	ca. 64,547	ca. 140 sec.

In Table 1 we show an overview of the results achieved on a set of sampled video frames. As can clearly be seen in the Table above, the average best overlap scores and recall scores yielded on the dataset of this work do not meet the results reported in [31]. For the *fast* setting of selective search, only 87% of the cows can be found in the set of proposals, while the average best overlap (ABO) is a mere 63.5%. In contrast, on the Pascal VOC 2007, the same setting yields a mean ABO of 80.4%, while nearly all the objects can be found in the proposals. Similarly, the *quality* setting only yields an average best overlap of 74%. Besides a low detection and overlap rate, there is also a strong increase in the number of generated object proposals and the proposal generation time per frame. This is best shown for the *quality* setting, where it takes nearly two and a half minutes per frame to generate proposals resulting in more than 64,000 proposals.

As we are interested in lightweight solutions for drone imagery, the evaluation time of the selective search algorithm poses serious practical problems. Not only will it take at least 30 seconds to generate a set of proposals with an acceptable recall rate, after that, features have to be extracted and a classifier applied on tens of thousands of proposals. Thus, the proposals do not significantly reduce the search time and we conclude that object proposal-based detection systems are from a computational standpoint not suited for the problem at hand.

6.2 Experiment 2: Animal Detection

For the second experiment, the three high-speed object detection methods: DPM, color-DPM and exemplar SVM are evaluated on our dataset. In order to generate a final model for a specific object class, all three methods use a hard negative mining procedure. As such, a diverse set of negatives is required. To meet this requirement, the set-up of the Pascal VOC challenge is mimicked. More specifically, the images of the *cow* class in the Pascal VOC are replaced by randomly sampled images from the train and test video for resp. the train and test set. In this setup, the train images from the other 19 classes can be used for discriminative learning. These classes include people, animals (*cats, dogs, horses, sheep*),

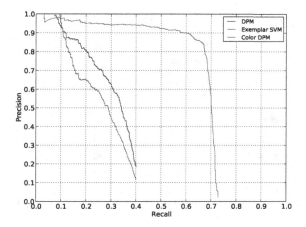

Fig. 5. Precision-recall curves for all three methods on the test images of the dataset

vehicles (*aeroplanes, bikes, boats, busses, cars, motorbikes, trains*), and indoor objects (*bottles, chairs, dining tables, potted plants, sofa's, tv's*).

The trained models are applied to all frames in the test set, containing a total of 1,227 ground truth bounding boxes. The result of this evaluation is a list of bounding box detections, ranked by their respective confidence value which is evaluated by precision and recall values.

In Figure 5, the precision-recall curves are shown for exemplar SVM, DPM, and color-DPM. As can be deduced from the Figure, exemplar SVM significantly outperforms both other methods in terms of precision (after a recall of 0.15) and recall. This holds similarly for the Average Precision scores; 0.66 for exemplar SVM, compared to 0.30 for DPM and 0.26 for color-DPM. These results are surprising when compared with reported results on standard object detection datasets. For example, Khan et al. [19] indicate that color-DPM is prefered over standard (grayscale) DPM, while DPM in turn reports better results than exemplar SVM [11].

A particular interesting aspect of the curves in Figure 5 is that both DPM models reach a final recall of roughly 0.4, while exemplar SVM reaches a final recall of roughly 0.72. A primary reason for this discrepancy lies in the total number of detected objects for the methods. While there are in total 1,227 positive instances of the object to be discovered, DPM detects 2,673 and color-DPM detects 4,156 bounding boxes. Exemplar SVM on the other hand, report a total of 40,654 bounding boxes. With such a high number of object detections, the final recall is bound to be higher.

The high number of object detections do however not explain the high precision of Exemplar SVM. The answer to this is two-fold. First, the use of a joint global and part-based model in DPM does not work favorably given the small scale of the animals in the drone images. As shown in Figure 6, individual

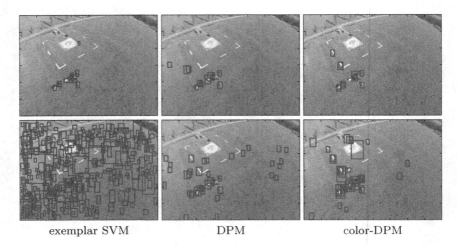

exemplar SVM	DPM	color-DPM

Fig. 6. Examples of detected bounding boxes for a test frame. The top row show the 10 highest ranked detections per method, while the bottom row shows all positive detections.

animals are generally tiny, due to the high altitude of the drones. When an animal is then visible e.g. in a window of 25 by 25 pixels, there is not enough gradient information for reliable global and part-based models. A second reason for the high results of exemplar SVM lies in the dataset. Since this evaluation is aimed at detecting cows, there is limited discrepancy between the instances to discover during training and testing. As we are in a practical scenario also interested in a limited range of wildlife animals, the use of animal exemplars for detection is beneficial.

In Figure 6, qualitative detection results are shown for a single test frame. For the top ranked detections (top row), the results of all methods look rather promising. When looking at all the positively detected bounding boxes however, the results become cluttered. For exemplar SVM, it is even unknown what the promising locations of the cows are. Nevertheless, the methods are capable of highly ranking the correct image locations, but also tend to fire on high contrast corner areas (such as the white lines or humans in Figure 6) and cluttered locations. Similar to the results of the first experiment, the results of this experiment indicate that results yielded on human-scale images are not be directly applicable to drone imagery.

6.3   Experiment 3: Animal Counting

In the third experiment we evaluate the quality of animal counting based on frame-based detections in combination with point tracks obtained by a KLT tracker [24]. To avoid counting the same animal multiple times for several frames, the frame-based object detections are either stitched to an existing group of detections or are seen as a new unique group of detections; where ideally each

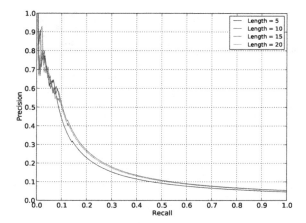

Fig. 7. Precision-recall curves for different point track sizes on the ground truth where bounding boxes are sampled every 5 frames from the annotations.

group of detections represents a single unique animal. The KLT algorithm generates point tracks of length L and we chose the values $L \in \{5, 10, 15, 20\}$ as a range of stable values.

Counting is evaluated by precision-recall curves, albeit with special considerations. The recall is defined as all unique animals. The precision is computed based on the correctness of a stitched group of detections. For counting, we consider a count correct only if it adheres to these three strict rules: i) there are no multiple animals within a single track; ii) all individual detections are animals and iii) the found animal is unique and has not been counted before. These strict criteria allow us to draw a precision-recall curve where we sort stitched frames based on the number of aggregated frames.

We first evaluate the quality of the tracking algorithm. To this end, we simulate a perfect detector by sampling ground truth boxes for every 5 frames in the video. The average precision is 0.216 and in Figure 7 we show the precision-recall curve. A track-length of $L = 15$ is performing best, although the difference is minimal.

Next, we evaluate the counting results using the automatically generated bounding box detection, using an empirically set threshold of -0.8 to discard false positives. In Figure 8 we show the corresponding precision-recall curves. Compared to the results of Figure 7, the curves are lower, while also not all animals are found. Similarly, the average precision score is lower, with a score of 0.193.

Based on the above yielded results, animal counting turns out to be a challenging problem. Even on ground truth detections, there is plenty of room for improvement, which we will focus on in future research.

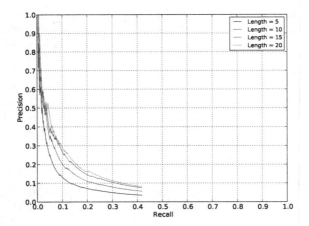

Fig. 8. Precision-recall curves for different point track sizes on the DPM detections with a threshold of -0.8.

7   Conclusion

We investigate if current automatic object detection methods as designed for human-centered objects are suitable for nature conservation on a drone, where objects are typically much smaller and observed from above. We define two task: i) animal detection and ii) animal counting. These tasks are important for monitoring animal distribution and animal abundance as typically required for successful nature conservation. To evaluate these tasks, we manually recorded and annotated a new dataset with a quad-copter drone. The animal detection task is benchmarked with three light-weight object detection algorithms that are suitable for on-board implementation since their potential detection speed is less than 1 second per image. We base the animal counting task on the detection task for which we define a suitable evaluation protocol. Results on counting show that this task is difficult, and as such an interesting research question. Results for object detection show that the performance of object detection methods as evaluated on images of human objects does not directly translate to drone imagery. According to the literature, the color-DPM should outperform the standard DPM, which in turn should outperform exemplar SVM. Our results are the exact opposite of this ordering. Nevertheless, detection results are promising, showing that automatic animal conservation with drones is a fruitful combination of biology, aircraft engineering and computer vision.

References

1. Alexe, B., Deselaers, T., Ferrari, V.: Measuring the objectness of image windows. IEEE Transactions on Pattern Analysis and Machine Intelligence **34**(11), 2189–2202 (2012)

2. Bouché, P., Renaud, P.C., Lejeune, P., Vermeulen, C., Froment, J.M., Bangara, A., Fiongai, O., Abdoulaye, A., Abakar, R., Fay, M.: Has the final countdown to wildlife extinction in northern central african republic begun? African Journal of Ecology **48**, 994–1003 (2010)
3. Buckland, S.T., Anderson, D.R., Burnham, K.P., Laake, J.L., Borchers, D.L., Thomas, L.: Introduction to Distance Sampling. Oxford University Press (2001)
4. Buckland, S.T., Anderson, D.R., Burnham, K.P., Laake, J.L., Borchers, D.L., Thomas, L.: Advanced Distance Sampling: Estimating Abundance of Biological Populations. Oxford University Press (2004)
5. Chen, Y., Shioi, H., Montesinos, C.F., Koh, L.P., Wich, S., Krause, A.: Active detection via adaptive submodularity. In: Proceedings of The 31st International Conference on Machine Learning, pp. 55–63 (2014)
6. Cinbis, R.G., Verbeek, J., Schmid, C.: Segmentation driven object detection with fisher vectors. In: International Conference on Computer Vision (ICCV) (2013)
7. Everingham, M., Sivic, J., Zisserman, A.: Taking the bite out of automated naming of characters in tv video. Image and Vision Computing **27**(5), 545–559 (2009)
8. Everts, I., van Gemert, J.C., Gevers, T.: Per-patch descriptor selection using surface and scene properties. In: Fitzgibbon, A., Lazebnik, S., Perona, P., Sato, Y., Schmid, C. (eds.) ECCV 2012, Part VI. LNCS, vol. 7577, pp. 172–186. Springer, Heidelberg (2012)
9. Everts, I., van Gemert, J.C., Gevers, T.: Evaluation of color spatio-temporal interest points for human action recognition. IEEE Transactions on Image Processing **23**(4), 1569–1580 (2014)
10. Felzenszwalb, P.F., Girshick, R.B., McAllester, D.: Cascade object detection with deformable part models. In: Computer Vision and Pattern Recognition (CVPR) (2010)
11. Felzenszwalb, P.F., Girshick, R.B., McAllester, D., Ramanan, D.: Object detection with discriminatively trained part-based models. IEEE Transactions on Pattern Analysis and Machine Intelligence **32**(9), 1627–1645 (2010)
12. Fischler, M.A., Elschlager, R.A.: The representation and matching of pictorial structures. IEEE Transactions on Computers **22**(1), 67–92 (1973)
13. Gati, B.: Open source autopilot for academic research - the paparazzi system. In: American Control Conference (ACC), pp. 1478–1481 (2013)
14. Getzin, S., Wiegand, K., Schöning, I.: Assessing biodiversity in forests using very high-resolution images and unmanned aerial vehicles. Methods in Ecology and Evolution **3**, 397–404 (2012)
15. Girshick, R., Donahue, J., Darrell, T., Malik, J.: Rich feature hierarchies for accurate object detection and semantic segmentation. In: Computer Vision and Pattern Recognition (CVPR) (2014)
16. Hodgson, A., Kelly, N., Peel, D.: Unmanned aerial vehicles (uavs) for surveying marine fauna: a dugong case study. PloS One **8** (2013)
17. Jain, M., van Gemert, J.C., Bouthemy, P., Jegou, H., Snoek, C.: Action localization by tubelets from motion. In: Computer Vision and Pattern Recognition (CVPR) (2014)
18. Jones IV, G.P., Pearlstine, L.G., Percival, H.F.: An assessment of small unmanned aerial vehicles for wildlife research. Wildlife Society Bulletin **34**, 750–758 (2006)
19. Khan, F.S., Anwer, R.M., van de Weijer, J., Bagdanov, A., Vanrell, M., Lopez, A.M.: Color attributes for object detection. In: Computer Vision and Pattern Recognition (CVPR) (2012)
20. Koh, L.P., Wich, S.A.: Dawn of drone ecology: low-cost autonomous aerial vehicles for conservation. Tropical Conservation Science **5**(2), 121–132 (2012)

21. Koski, W.R., Allen, T., Ireland, D., Buck, G., Smith, P.R., Macrander, A.M., Halick, M.A., Rushing, C., Sliwa, D.J., McDonald, T.L.: Evaluation of an unmanned airborne system for monitoring marine mammals. Aquatic Mammals **35**(347) (2009)

22. Krizhevsky, A., Sutskever, I., Hinton, G.E.: Imagenet classification with deep convolutional neural networks. In: Advances in Neural Information Processing Systems (NIPS), pp. 1097–1105 (2012)

23. Li, H., Lin, Z., Brandt, J., Shen, X., Hua, G.: Efficient boosted exemplar-based face detection. In: Computer Vision and Pattern Recognition (CVPR) (2014)

24. Lucas, B.D., Kanade, T., et al.: An iterative image registration technique with an application to stereo vision. In: International Joint Conference on Artificial Intelligence, vol. 81 (1981)

25. Malisiewicz, T., Gupta, A., Efros, A.A.: Ensemble of exemplar-svms for object detection and beyond. In: International Conference on Computer Vision (ICCV) (2011)

26. Mulero-Pázmány, M., Stolper, R., Essen, L.V., Negro, J.J., Sassen, T.: Remotely piloted aircraft systems as a rhinoceros anti-poaching tool in Africa. PloS One **9** (2014)

27. Pedersoli, M., Vedaldi, A., Gonzalez, J.: A coarse-to-fine approach for fast deformable object detection. In: Computer Vision and Pattern Recognition (CVPR) (2011)

28. van de Sande, K.E.A., Snoek, C.G.M., Smeulders, A.W.M.: Fisher and vlad with flair. In: Computer Vision and Pattern Recognition (CVPR) (2014)

29. Sermanet, P., Eigen, D., Zhang, X., Mathieu, M., Fergus, R., LeCun, Y.: Overfeat: integrated recognition, localization and detection using convolutional networks. In: International Conference on Learning Representations (2014)

30. Tian, Y., Sukthankar, R., Shah, M.: Spatiotemporal deformable part models for action detection. In: Computer Vision and Pattern Recognition (CVPR), pp. 2642–2649 (2013)

31. Uijlings, J.R., van de Sande, K.E., Gevers, T., Smeulders, A.W.: Selective search for object recognition. International Journal of Computer Vision **104**(2), 154–171 (2013)

32. UNEP: Elephants in the dust the african elephant crisis. a rapid response assessment (2013). www.grida.no, united Nations Environment Programme, GRID-Arendal

33. Van Gemert, J.C., Veenman, C.J., Geusebroek, J.M.: Episode-constrained cross-validation in video concept retrieval. IEEE Transactions on Multimedia **11**(4), 780–786 (2009)

34. Vedaldi, A., Gulshan, V., Varma, M., Zisserman, A.: Multiple kernels for object detection. In: International Conference on Computer Vision (ICCV) (2009)

35. Vermeulen, C., Lejeune, P., Lisein, J., Sawadogo, P., Bouché, P.: Unmanned aerial survey of elephants. PloS One **8** (2013)

36. Viola, P., Jones, M.: Rapid object detection using a boosted cascade of simple features. In: Computer Vision and Pattern Recognition (CVPR) (2001)

37. Vondrick, C., Patterson, D., Ramanan, D.: Efficiently scaling up crowdsourced video annotation. International Journal of Computer Vision, 1–21 (2012)

38. WCUAVC: Wildlife conservation uav challenge. http://www.wcuavc.com/

Real-Time Accurate Geo-Localization of a MAV with Omnidirectional Visual Odometry and GPS

Johannes Schneider[(⊠)] and Wolfgang Förstner

Department of Photogrammetry, University of Bonn, Nußallee 15,
53115 Bonn, Germany
johannes.schneider@uni-bonn.de, wf@ipb.uni-bonn.de

Abstract. This paper presents a system for direct geo-localization of a MAV in an unknown environment using visual odometry and precise real time kinematic (RTK) GPS information. Visual odometry is performed with a multi-camera system with four fisheye cameras that cover a wide field of view which leads to better constraints for localization due to long tracks and a better intersection geometry. Visual observations from the acquired image sequences are refined with a high accuracy on selected keyframes by an incremental bundle adjustment using the iSAM2 algorithm. The optional integration of GPS information yields long-time stability and provides a direct geo-referenced solution. Experiments show the high accuracy which is below 3 cm standard deviation in position.

Keywords: Visual odometry · Incremental bundle adjustment · Fisheye camera · Multi-camera system · Omnidirectional · MAV

1 Introduction

Micro aerial vehicles (MAVs) can operate from above in areas that are inaccessible from the ground such as hazardous environments. They become more and more important for example as low cost and flexible platforms for monitoring changes in agriculture, inspection of buildings and the wide field of surveillance purposes. In order to autonomously navigate in an unknown environment, the MAV must be able to perform self-localization. The position of the MAV is usually determined by a combination of GPS and IMU measurements, in which GPS maintains the long-term stability and provides geo-referencing. But an accurate position cannot be guaranteed e.g. when the GPS signal is obscured. In this case a fully autonomous operating MAV has to rely on alternative localization systems. Visual odometry has proven to be very effective on MAVs, as cameras are lightweight and the orientation and position can be recovered using the on-line acquired image sequence.

The MAV we use for our work in the research project *Mapping on Demand* [12] is based on a MikroKopter OktoXL assembly kit. The on-board sensing of a lightweight MAV has to be designed with regards to its limitation in size and weight, and the limited on-board processing power requires highly efficient algorithms. Our platform is equipped with a GPS unit, an IMU, a high resolution

© Springer International Publishing Switzerland 2015
L. Agapito et al. (Eds.): ECCV 2014 Workshops, Part I, LNCS 8925, pp. 271–282, 2015.
DOI: 10.1007/978-3-319-16178-5_18

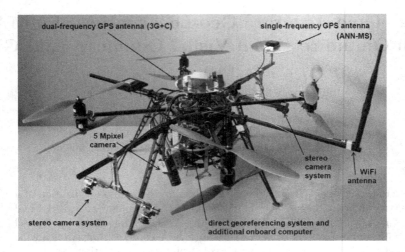

Fig. 1. The MAV based on the Okto XL frame set with its sensor and processing components setup

camera and four fisheye cameras, which are mounted as two stereo pairs, one looking ahead and one looking backwards, providing a large field of view at each time of exposure. Computation power is provided by an on-board computer (Intel Core i7, 8GB RAM) which is based on an EPI-QM77 embedded PC board. The arrangement of the components is shown in Fig. 1. The two cameras are used besides obstacle detection [17] together with the GPS-unit and IMU for ego-motion estimation. The RTK GPS and IMU is processed on-board in a direct geo-referencing unit described in [5]. Under favourable conditions it can provide the position and orientation of the MAV with an accuracy of under 2 cm and 1°, respectively. Our task is to fuse the geo-referenced ego motion with the visual odometry and to use it as an initial estimate for the orientation of the images of the high resolution camera, for near real-time surface reconstruction on a ground station, which is connected to the on-board computer through Wifi.

In contrast to single cameras and traditional stereo setups, an omnidirectional multi-camera setup covers a wider field of view, which leads to better constraints for localization. The four cameras with Lensagon BF2M15520 fisheye lenses with a field angle up to 185° capture four image sequences with a frame rate of 10 Hz in a synchronized way, see Fig. 2. The basis between the cameras of a stereo pair amounts to 20 cm providing highly overlapping views at each time of exposure. The monochromatic images have a resolution of 752×480 pixels.

Bundle adjustment is the work horse for orienting cameras and determining 3D points as it is statistically optimal and highly efficient in case sparse matrix operations are used. Factor graph based optimization frame works like g^2o have been shown to solve such problems efficiently by exploiting the characteristic structure [13]. Nevertheless, the computational expense rapidly grows with the number of involved images.

Fig. 2. Left: The omnidirectional multi-camera system as it is mounted on the MAV. Right: An example frame set consisting of four images taken with the four fisheye cameras.

Many visual odometry systems use PTAM [11] which runs in real-time by parallelizing the motion estimation and mapping task simultaneously and by using a keyframe-based bundle adjustment. However, it is not designed for large-scale outdoor environments and it is restricted to monocular and perspective cameras. To overcome the problem of continuously growing optimization problems, so called sliding window filters or local bundle adjustments are used that keep computational cost small enabling real-time applications [16],[6]. More recently the incremental optimization frame work iSAM2 has been released [10]. The incremental optimizer avoids periodical batch steps with recurring calculations by performing only calculations for entries of the information matrix, i.e. the normal equation matrix or inverse covariance matrix, that are actually effected by new measurements. Only a subset of all contained variables are relinearized and solved, which is realized by using the Bayes tree representation [9]. Fill-in is avoided through incrementally changing the variable ordering.

Multi-camera systems are regularly used for odometry, especially stereo camera systems, e.g. [15],[22] and more than two cameras e.g. in [14] or [8]. Fisheye-Cameras, see e.g. [1], catadioptric cameras, see e.g. [3] or omnidirectional cameras, see [23] ensure stable geometric positioning and full scene coverage due to their large field of view.

In this paper we treat the issue of visual odometry for real-time egomotion estimation using the synchronized images of the omnidirectional multi-camera system in a keyframe based fast incremental bundle adjustment using the iSAM2 algorithm [10]. To obtain longtime stability and to ensure the localization-system against sensor malfunctions, highly accurate GPS information can be integrated.

The paper is organized as follows. In the next section, we present our system for visual odometry. The image processing for data acquisition and reliable data association and the robust orientation of a set of frames taken in a synchronized way is presented. Further, we describe how the sparse non-linear incremental optimization algorithm iSAM2 is applied to avoid periodic batch bundle adjustment steps on sets of keyframes. The paper is based on previous work published in [19] where first results using the iSAM2 algorithm for visual odometry in a Matlab prototype are shown. In section 3 we present first results of the visual odometry and the integration of GPS. Finally, we conclude and give an outlook on our future work in section 4.

2   Concept for Visual Odometry

2.1   Overview

Visual odometry is the process of determining the pose of the cameras in real-time by using the associated image sequences. Our real-time system uses feature points and consists of several steps:

1. The data acquisition and association detects feature points, performs the matching and provides camera rays associated with the previous and the other camera images.
2. The fast orientation of individual frames provides a robust solution and approximate values for the subsequent bundle adjustment and allows to select keyframes.
3. The incremental bundle adjustment uses the new information at a keyframe and merges it optimally with the previous information and optionally with GPS/IMU processed pose information.

The last step uses all available data and is therefore the most costly one. To ensure real-time capability it needs to be efficient and the previous steps have to guarantee outlier free information. Therefore we chose for the third step the software package iSAM2 for "incremental smoothing and mapping" and aim at efficient and robust methods for reliable data association. The steps are now described in more detail.

2.2   Data Association

The data association in our visual odometry system is based on interest points, which are tracked simultaneously in the individual cameras by running four threads in parallel. We use the OpenCV implementation of the KLT tracker: Interest points are corners in the gradient image with a large smallest eigenvalue of the structure tensor [21], that are tracked using the Lucas-Kanade implementation with pyramids according to [4]. Fig. 2 shows an example of 50 extracted feature points in the four images of the fisheye cameras.

Each tracked feature point is converted into a ray direction, i.e. a normalized direction vector, that points to the observed scene point in the individual camera system. The fisheye lenses are modelled with the equidistant-model described in

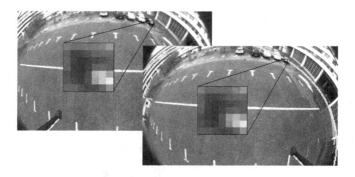

Fig. 3. Two frames taken in the left and right camera of a stereo pair. The extracted feature point in the left image on the rightmost car has the drawn epipolar line in the right image. The matching point in the right image lies on the indicated yellow line and the corresponding local image patches show a high correlation.

[1] which allows for ray directions that have a larger angle than $90°$ to the viewing direction. The interior orientation of each camera is determined by camera calibration according to [2] using Chebyshev polynomials. Using the equidistant-projection and applying all corrections to the feature points we obtain image points $^e x$. The spherically normalized ray direction $\mathbf{x}^s$ can be derived by using the radial distance $r = |^e x|$ that grows with the angle between the viewing direction and the camera ray. The uncertainty of each image point can be transformed to the uncertainty of the associated spherically normalized ray direction $\mathbf{x}^s$ via variance propagation yielding $\Sigma_{\mathbf{x}^s \mathbf{x}^s}$. Note that the covariance matrix of the camera rays is singular, as the normalized 3-vector only depends on two observed image coordinates.

Feature points in the overlapping images of a stereo camera pair are matched by using the correlation coefficients between the local 7×7 image patches at the feature points in the left and right images. The rotation R_1^2 and translation $\mathbf{t}_1^2$ from the left into the right camera of the respective stereo pair is determined in advance according to [18]. We can use this information to reduce the amount of possible correspondences to feature points lying close to the corresponding epipolar lines, see Fig. 3, by statistically testing the contradiction to the coplanarity constraint $[\mathbf{x}_1^s, R_1^2 \mathbf{t}_1^2, \mathbf{x}_2^s]$. We assume feature points with the highest correlation coefficient ρ_1 to match, if ρ_1 is above an absolute threshold, e.g. 0.8, and – if there is more than one candidate close to the epipolar line – the closest-to-second-closest-ratio $r = \rho_2/\rho_1$ with the second highest correlation coefficient ρ_2 is lower than an absolute threshold, e.g. 0.7. Finally, we counter-check if this criterion holds also for all feature points in the left image if there are more than one feature points fulfilling the coplanarity constraint. In some rare cases this procedure leads to wrong matches, which can be detected later with a third observing ray from another pose.

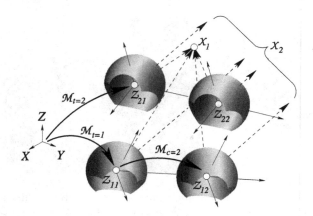

Fig. 4. A two-camera system with fisheye cameras $c = 1, 2$ with projection centers Z_{tc}, rigid motion M_c and time-varying motion M_t, having a field of view larger than $180°$ shown at two exposure times $t = 1, 2$ observing two points $X_i, i = 1, 2$, X_1 being close by and X_2 at infinity.

2.3 Localization of Each Frame

We use a map which consists in our context of a set of scene points $X = \{X_i, i = 1, ..., I\}$. The map is initialized on the initiating frame set by using the matched ray directions in a stereo pair.

The initiating frame set is chosen as the first keyframe with pose M_k. The index k denotes a motion of a set of keyframes $\mathcal{K}_k$ of all keyframe sets $\mathcal{K} = \{\mathcal{K}_k, k = 1, ..., K\} \subset \mathcal{T} = \{\mathcal{T}_t, t = 1, ..., T\}$, taken out of the set $\mathcal{T}$ of all frame sets $\mathcal{T}_t$, t being the index referring to the triggered time of exposure of a set of frames. If a pose from the direct georeferencing unit is available, it is used to define the coordinate system of the map. Otherwise the first keyframe is fixed with an an arbitrarily chosen pose M_k.

After initializing the map, robust estimates for the motion M_t of the MAV in the map are computed in a continuously running thread at each time of exposure t via simultaneous resection of all cameras. We use a generalized camera model with multiple projection centres $c = 1, ..., 4$ and known system calibration, described by the motion M_c of each single camera from the camera system. The measurement equation, which considers mutually fixed single view cameras, allows the single cameras to be omnidirectional and allows for far or ideal scene points, reads as

$$v_{itc} = J^\mathsf{T}(x_{itc})\mathsf{N}\left([I_3|0_3]\mathsf{M}_c^{-1}\mathsf{M}_t^{-1}X_i\right) \tag{1}$$

with the homogeneous scene point X_i, motion matrices M_t and M_c, and the observed and spherically ray direction x_{itc}^s and residual v_{itc} of scene point i in camera system k at time t, see Fig. 4, whereby $J(x) = \text{null}(x^\mathsf{T})$ and $\mathsf{N}(x) = x/|x|$.

We determine the solution for the six pose parameters of M_t by a robust iterative maximum likelihood-type estimation down weighting observations with large residuals by minimizing the robust Huber cost function [7]. The rigid motions $\mathcal{M}_c$ are determined in advance using a rigorous bundle adjustment estimating the system calibration [18]. We use the last determined pose $\mathcal{M}_{t-1}$ as the initial approximate value. The estimation of $\mathcal{M}_t$ then converges in most cases after 2-3 iterations. This procedure is very robust and time-effective, and allows to detect wrong data associations and to orientate with high frame rates. A track of observations getting a low weight is excluded from tracking and is not considered in the following frames any more.

2.4 Keyframe-Based Incremental Bundle Ajdustment

The applied bundle adjustment refers to sets of keyframes, which reduce the processing to some geometrically useful, tracked observations. A new keyframe set with motion $\mathcal{M}_k$ is initiated in case a geometric distance to the last keyframe set with motion $\mathcal{M}_{k-1}$ is exceeded, e.g. 1 m or 30°. In case a new keyframe set is initiated, the observations x_{ikc} are used to update and refine the scene points in $\mathcal{X}$ and poses in $\mathcal{K}$ in the incremental bundle adjustment, which runs then in a separated thread.

The tracked observations are classified into two sets, χ_1 and χ_2, where χ_1 are the observations of scene points that are already in the map and χ_2 denotes those observing new scene points. The map is continually expanded as a new keyframe set is added. Initial values for new tracked scene points are obtained by triangulation with observations χ_2. A new scene point has to be observed at least on three keyframe sets to get affiliated to the map. Its coordinates are determined using forward intersection. Care has to be taken with the sign: We assume the negative Z-coordinate of each camera system to be the viewing direction. The homogeneous representation of the scene points then need to have non-negative homogeneous coordinates $X_{i,4}$. In case of ideal points, we therefore need to distinguish the scene point $[\boldsymbol{X}_i; 0]$ and the scene point $[-\boldsymbol{X}_i; 0]$, which are points at infinity in opposite directions. Intersected scene points that show large residuals in the observations are put on the blacklist and deleted in the data association. Observations χ_2 are assumed to be revised from corrupted tracks via the former robust resection.

The map $\mathcal{X}$ and the set of poses in $\mathcal{K}$ are simultaneously refined using the bundle adjustment approach of [20]. The approach uses bundle of rays, allows for multi-camera systems and can numerically deal with points at infinity e.g. points at the horizon. The measurement equation reads as

$$\boldsymbol{v}_{ikc} = J^{\mathsf{T}}(\mathbf{x}'_{ikc})\mathsf{N}\left([I_3|\mathbf{0}_3]\mathsf{M}_c^{-1}\mathsf{M}_k^{-1}\mathbf{X}_i\right) \tag{2}$$

and is not linear in the scene points and pose parameters of $\mathbf{X}_i$ and M_k. The linearization of the non-linear model at the actual linearization points is shown in detail in [20]. We use the proposed model within the incremental solver iSAM2.

If available, pose information from the direct georeferencing unit for $\mathcal{M}_k$ are incorporated as direct observations of the pose parameters. For proper weighting the provided covariance information of the georeferencing unit is used. The

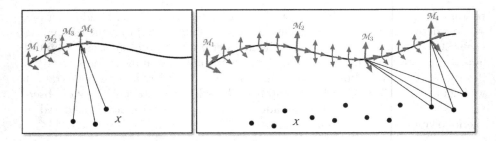

Fig. 5. On each acquired set of frames a new motion $\mathcal{M}_t$ (green) is determined by resection using the observed scene points in map $\mathcal{X}$. After a certain motion distance, e.g. 1 m or $30°$, a keyframe is initiated (red). At every keyframe, an incremental bundle adjustment step is performed to refine all keyframes $\mathcal{M}_k$ in $\mathcal{K}$ and scene points in map $\mathcal{X}$.

offset in rotation and translation between the camera system and the direct georeferencing unit is determined in advance by using GPS control points in a calibrating bundle adjustment. This way the offset has been determined with an accuracy of under 1 cm and 0.2°.

For our real-time application the processing of a new keyframe set $\mathcal{K}_k$ needs to be finished by the time the next keyframe set is added. For the first keyframe sets we use batch bundle adjustments as the map contains only a small number of scene points yet. After that the new information are incrementally merged with the previous information, yielding a fast optimal solution for the bundle adjustment using iSAM2 [10].

3   Experiments

Sensor data was recorded by the MAV during a 5 min flight in which a building was mapped with the high resolution camera. In this flight the visual odometry sets a new keyframe on average after 2 sec. The processing of a new keyframe needs on average 0.3 to 0.5 sec. In most cases this time is sufficient (1) to detect and track 200 feature points in each of the four cameras with a frame rate of 10 Hz, (2) to determine the spatial resections for each frame set, (3) to revise the tracks from outliers and (4) to execute the incremental bundle adjustment step.

The poses of the direct georeferencing unit are integrated as uncertain prior information on the keyframes to obtain long-term stability and a georeferenced ego-motion. Under favorable conditions the incremental bundle adjustment can determine a real-time standard deviation in the position of about 1–2 cm, see Fig. 6.

The theoretical a posteriori estimated uncertainties are in general too optimistic. Therefore we have determined the ego-motion with visual odometry without using prior information from GPS. Using a similarity transformation on the GPS positions we can determine deviations between the independently estimated trajectories. The deviations between the keyframe poses are shown in the histograms in Fig. 7. The histograms confirm the theoretical standard deviation from Fig. 6.

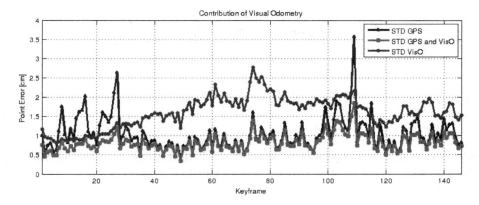

Fig. 6. Accuracy of the positions from GPS and from visual odometry, respectively shown as point errors $\sqrt{\sigma_X^2 + \sigma_Y^2 + \sigma_Z^2}$. The accuracy of the GPS measurements (black) and of the visual odometry which integrates the GPS measurements (red). The accuracy of pure visual odometry is derived from difference (blue): Apparently the visual odometry has a standard deviation below 3 cm and on an average is up to twice as uncertain as the GPS measurements, but temporarily it provides more accurate positions. The uncertainty of the integrated position is throughout less than 2 cm.

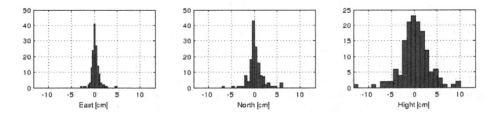

Fig. 7. The deviations between the keyframe positions from visual odometry, that were transformed on the GPS positions, to the GPS coordinates in the east, north and height component.

Figure 8 shows the cumulative percentage of the 2803 track lenghts. For this flight with 148 keyframes most track lengths contain eight keyframes, 5 % of the tracks contain 35 keyframes and at least twelve tracks contain 100 keyframes. As a consequence we obtain a high long-term stability for the orientation angles. The obtained real-time accuracy of the rotations is throughout in the order of about 0.05–0.1°. Especially scene points close to infinity, i.e. points that are far away relative to the motion of the observing camera system, can be observed for a long time, which increases the accuracy of the camera rotation as shown in [20].

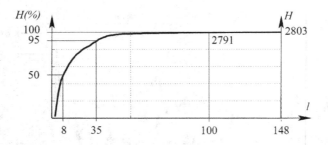

Fig. 8. Cumulative histogram $H(l)$ of the track lengths l of a flight with four fisheye cameras. The median and the 95-%-point is indicated.

The iSAM2 algorithm is very efficient as it relinearizes and solves only sub-problems that are actually influenced by the added observations. The optimization algorithm provides a solution which is in a statistical sense globally optimal. We compared the result with an offline batch bundle adjustment. The differences in the estimated pose parameters have been throughout in their estimated uncertainty.

4   Conclusions and Future Work

We presented our system for visual odometry performing a keyframe-based bundle adjustment for real-time structure and motion estimation in an unknown scene. Incremental bundle adjustment is performed by using the iSAM2 algorithm for sparse nonlinear incremental optimization in combination with a measurement equations that allows for multi-view cameras, omnidirectional cameras and scene points at infinity. The experiments show that a high accuracy level in the position can be obtained, which is in the order of RTK GPS. Long-time stability and a georeferenced position can be obtained by integrating GPS information. Using fisheye cameras and the inclusion of far points lead to stable poses. The inclusion of GPS is necessary in unknown environments for georeferencing. The visual odometry can bridge gaps due to interruption of the GPS signal with high accuracy.

Future work will focus on the issue of vibrations due to the rotors of the MAV on the mutual orientations of the multi-camera system. Further we have to solve the issue of estimating scene points which are at first near to the camera system and as the camera system moves away lying numerically at infinity.

Acknowledgments. This work was supported by the DFG-Project FOR 1505 Mapping on Demand. We thank CHRISTIAN ELING and LASSE KLINGBEIL for providing us the results of the direct georeferencing unit and we thank the anonymous reviewers for their valuable comments and suggestions on this work.

References

1. Abraham, S., Förstner, W.: Fish-eye-stereo calibration and epipolar rectification. ISPRS Journal of Photogrammetry and Remote Sensing (JPRS) **59**(5), 278–288 (August 2005)
2. Abraham, S., Hau, T.: Towards autonomous high-precision calibration of digital cameras. In: Proc. of SPIE Videometrics, vol. 3174, pp. 82–93, San Diego, USA, July 1997
3. Aliaga, D.: Accurate catadioptric calibration for real-time pose estimation of room-size environments. In: Proc. of the IEEE Intl. Conf. on Computer Vision (ICCV), pp. 127–134, Vancouver, Canada, July 2001
4. Bouguet, J.Y.: Pyramidal implementation of the lucas kanade feature tracker. Intel Corporation, Microprocessor Research Labs, Tech. rep. (2000)
5. Eling, C., Klingbeil, L., Wieland, M., Kuhlmann, H.: Direct georeferencing of micro aerial vehicles - system design, system calibration and first evaluation tests. Photogrammetrie - Fernerkundung - Geoinformation (PFG) (4), August 2014
6. Engels, C., Stewénius, H., Nistér, D.: Bundle adjustment rules. In: Proc. of the ISPRS Conference on Photogrammeric Computer Vision (PCV), Bonn, Germany, September 2006
7. Huber, P.: Robust Statistics. John Wiley, New York (1981)
8. Kaess, M., Dellaert, F.: Visual SLAM with a multi-camera rig. Tech. Rep. GIT-GVU-06-06, Georgia Institute of Technology, February 2006
9. Kaess, Michael, Ila, Viorela, Roberts, Richard, Dellaert, Frank: The Bayes tree: an algorithmic foundation for probabilistic Robot mapping. In: Hsu, David, Isler, Volkan, Latombe, Jean-Claude, Lin, Ming C. (eds.) Algorithmic Foundations of Robotics IX. STAR, vol. 68, pp. 157–173. Springer, Heidelberg (2010)
10. Kaess, M., Johannsson, H., Roberts, R., Ila, V., Leonard, J., Dellaert, F.: iSAM2: Incremental Smoothing and Mapping Using the Bayes Tree. Intl. Journal of Robotics Research (IJRR) **31**(2), 217–236 (February 2012)
11. Klein, G., Murray, D.: Parallel tracking and mapping for small ar workspaces. In: Proc. of the Intl. Symposium on Mixed and Augmented Reality (ISMAR), pp. 1–10, Nara, Japan, November 2007
12. Klingbeil, L., Nieuwenhuisen, M., Schneider, J., Eling, C., Dröschel, D., Holz, D., Läbe, T., Förstner, W., Behnke, S., Kuhlmann, H.: Towards autonomous navigation of an uav-based mobile mapping system. In: Proc. of the Intl. Conf. on Machine Control and Guidance (MCG), pp. 136–147, Brunswick, Germany, March 2014
13. Kümmerle, R., Grisetti, G., Strasdat, H., Konolige, K., Burgard, W.: G2o: A general framework for graph optimization. In: Proc. of the IEEE Intl. Conf. on Robotics & Automation (ICRA), pp. 3607–3613, Shanghai, China, May 2011
14. Maas, H.: Image sequence based automatic multi-camera system calibration techniques. ISPRS Journal of Photogrammetry and Remote Sensing (JPRS) **54**(5–6), 352–359 (December 1999)
15. Mostafa, M., Schwarz, K.: Digital image georeferencing from a multiple camera system by gps/ins. ISPRS Journal of Photogrammetry and Remote Sensing (JPRS) **56**(1), 1–12 (June 2001)
16. Mouragnon, E., Lhuillier, M., Dhome, M., Dekeyser, F., Sayd, P.: Generic and real-time structure from motion using local bundle adjustment. Elsevier Journal on Image and Vision Computing (IVC) **27**(8), 1178–1193 (July 2009)

17. Nieuwenhuisen, M., Dröschel, D., Schneider, J., Holz, D., Läbe, T., Behnke, S.: Multimodal obstacle detection and collision avoidance for micro aerial vehicles. In: Proc. of the European Conf. on Mobile Robotics (ECMR), pp. 7–12, Barcelona, Spain, September 2013

18. Schneider, J., Förstner, W.: Bundle adjustment and system calibration with points at infinity for omnidirectional camera systems. Photogrammetrie - Fernerkundung - Geoinformation (PFG) **4**, 309–321 (August 2013)

19. Schneider, J., Läbe, T., Förstner, W.: Incremental real-time bundle adjustment for multi-camera systems with points at infinity. In: ISPRS Archives of the Photogrammetry, Remote Sensing and Spatial Information Sciences, vol. XL-1/W2, pp. 355–360, Rostock, Germany, September 2013

20. Schneider, J., Schindler, F., Läbe, T., Förstner, W.: Bundle adjustment for multi-camera systems with points at infinity. In: ISPRS Annals of the Photogrammetry, Remote Sensing and Spatial Information Sciences, vol. I–3, pp. 75–80, Melbourne, Australia, August 2012

21. Shi, J., Tomasi, C.: Good features to track. In: Proc. of the IEEE Conf. on Computer Vision and Pattern Recognition (CVPR), pp. 593–600, Seattle, USA, June 1994

22. Strasdat, H., Montiel, J., Davison, A.: Visual slam: Why filter? Elsevier Journal on Image and Vision Computing (IVC) **30**(2), 65–77 (February 2012)

23. Tardif, J.P., Pavlidis, Y., Daniilidis, K.: Monocular visual odometry in urban environments using an omnidirectional camera. In: Proc. of the IEEE/RSJ Intl. Conf. on Intelligent Robots and Systems (IROS), pp. 2531–2538, Nice, France, September 2008

W03 - Spontaneous Facial Behavior Analysis

Statistically Learned Deformable Eye Models

Joan Alabort-i-Medina$^{(\boxtimes)}$, Bingqing Qu, and Stefanos Zafeiriou

Imperial College London, London, UK
{ja310,s.zafeiriou}@imperial.ac.uk, sylar.qu@gmail.com

Abstract. In this paper we study the feasibility of using standard deformable model fitting techniques to accurately track the deformation and motion of the human eye. To this end, we propose two highly detailed shape annotation schemes (open and close eyes), with +30 feature landmark points, high resolution eye images. We build extremely detailed Active Appearance Models (AAM), Constrained Local Models (CLM) and Supervised Descent Method (SDM) models of the human eye and report preliminary experiments comparing the relative performance of the previous techniques on the problem of eye alignment.

Keywords: Eye alignment · Eye tracking · Active appearance models · Constrained local models · Supervised descent method

1 Introduction

In recent years, the automatic analysis of facial images and video has attracted a lot of interest from the computer vision and machine learning research communities [18].

Within this context, eyes have proven to be among the most discriminative regions of the human face providing, for example, a reliable source of biometric information for face identification and recognition. On the same page, psychologist have reported strong evidence that the behaviour and movement of the eyes has strong connections with the brain cognitive processes [6] and offer important cues to understand the subtleness of facial behaviour [2]. On the other hand, gaze tracking is known to play an important role in the design of successful applications in human-computer interaction [10].

Consequently, the development of generic eye alignment algorithms capable of localizing and discriminating between different eye regions and capable of accurately describing the deformation and motion of the eyes is essential for the development of future human-centred-interfaces. For example, effective and reliable eye alignment is typically the first step in any deception and concealment-of-intent detection systems due to the proven correlation between eyelid movement and intentional deceit [5].

However, despite recent advances [10,11,14–16], accurate and robust eye alignment in unconstrained scenarios remains an extremely challenging task. The main difficulty arises from the very diverse appearance of eyes caused by both

© Springer International Publishing Switzerland 2015
L. Agapito et al. (Eds.): ECCV 2014 Workshops, Part I, LNCS 8925, pp. 285–295, 2015.
DOI: 10.1007/978-3-319-16178-5_19

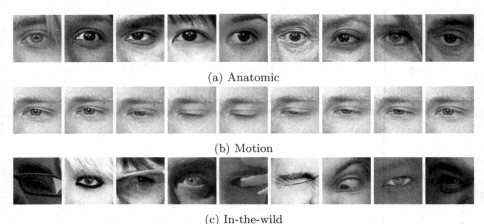

(a) Anatomic

(b) Motion

(c) In-the-wild

Fig. 1. Appearance variability of eyes

anatomical differences between individuals (Figure 1a) and the high deformability and fast movement of the different eye components (Figure 1b). Moreover, other factors such as different illumination conditions, head pose and partial occlusion contribute to increase the appearance variability of the eyes in in-the-wild images (Figure 1c).

In this paper, we study the feasibility of using standard deformable model fitting techniques, such as Active Appearance Models (AAM) [4,8] and Constrained Local Models (CLM) [13], as well as the recently proposed Supervised Descent Method (SDM) [17], to accurately track the deformation and motion of the human eye. To this end, we propose two highly detailed shape annotation schemes (open and close eyes), with +30 feature landmark points, for annotating high resolution eye images. Using the previous schemes, we build extremely detailed eye models and conduct a preliminary study comparing the performance of the previous three techniques on the problem of eye alignment.

The remainder of the paper is structured as follows. Section 2 reviews prior work on eye tracking. Our newly proposed annotation schemes for open and close eyes are describe in Section 3. Section 4 offers a quick overview of the different deformable model fitting techniques considered in the paper, i.e. AAM, CLM and SDM. Experimental results are presented in Section 5 and conclusions are drawn in Section 6

2   Prior Work

A largely diverse number of approaches, ranging from simple techniques based on the application of edge detectors and Hough transform [14,16] to more sophisticated model-based approaches [10,11], have been used to solve the eye alignment problem.

The two closest works to the approach present in this paper are the ones of Moriyama et al. [10] and Orozco et al. [11]. The authors of [10] propose a 2D handly-crafted parametrised generative eye shape model inspired by the anatomical structure of the human eye. Their approach requires manual initialization for the eye's texture. Fitting the previous eye model to a novel image is posed as an image alignment problem within the standard Lucas Kanade framework.

On the other hand, the authors of [11] propose an on-line appearance-based tracker that automatically adapts to changes in eye texture. They use a parametrised shape model based on a hand-crafted standard designed by the computer animation industry (Face Animation Parameters (FAP)). Fitting of their eye model is posed as a gradient descent optimization problem. Their approach requires careful manual initialization to ensure that the model gradually learns a useful representation of the eye texture.

Conversely, the models used in this paper make less assumption with respect to the shape and texture of the eyes since both of them are (either explicitly or implicitly) statistically learned from training data. Moreover, they can be automatically initialize using the coarse initialization provided by an off-the-shelf eye detector, removing the need for manual initialization. On the other hand, these thechniques rely on the availability of annotated training data.

3   Eye Model

Eyes are highly deformable organs that can be decomposed in several different parts [10] (Figure 3). Some of this parts might become partially or completely occluded by others due to the natural motion of the eyes. For example, on the open right eye images in Figure 1b all five different regions: upper lid, lower lid, sclera, iris and pupil are visible. In contrast, on the half-open and closed right eye images on the same figure, only the some of the previous parts are visible and the rest are naturally occluded.

In order to fit eyes using standard deformable model fitting techniques, one needs to define the shape of the object being modeled explicitly, as a set of feature landmark points. While this might be simple for some objects (e.g. frontal faces or rear cars), the self-occluding nature of the eyes produces drastic changes in their appearance making the definition of a single set of feature landmark points non trivial.

In this work, we propose to solve the previous problem by differentiating between full/half-open eyes and close eye and use two different sets of landmarks to describe the shape of the eyes in both of these states. Note that, although the open/half-open eye landmarks are adequate to describe most of the eye motion they cannot deal with the singularity that a close eye represents (it would be indeed very difficult to annotate close eye images using the set of landmark points describing the shape of full/half-open eyes).

A direct consequence of the previous decision is that all deformable model fitting techniques will need to differentiate between full/half-open eyes and close eyes. Hence, given a novel eye image this techniques will need to fit both full/half-open eye and close eye models to the image and evaluate the correctness of each model using a particular score metric. In this paper, we use a simple Support Vector Machine (SVM) classifier to determining the correctness of each model.

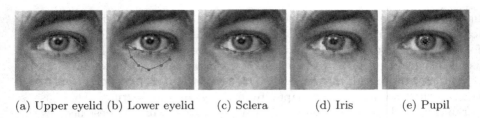

(a) Upper eyelid (b) Lower eyelid   (c) Sclera   (d) Iris   (e) Pupil

Fig. 2. A possible decomposition of eyes in different parts

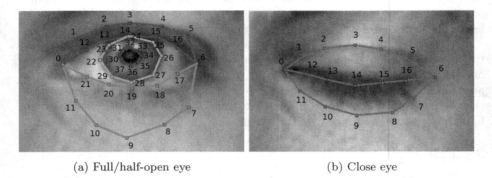

(a) Full/half-open eye   (b) Close eye

Fig. 3. Full/half-open and close eye feature landmarks points

Full/Half-Open Eye Model. The shape of full/half-open eyes is described by set of 38 feature landmarks points annotating the five different eye regions depict in Figure 3, i.e. (i) upper eyelid, (ii) lower eyelid, (iii) sclera, (iv) iris and, (v) pupil. A detailed diagram with the specific meaning of each landmark is shown in Figure 3a.

Close Eye Model. To describe the shape of close eyes 17 feature landmark points are used. Note that, the upper and lower eyelid are the only parts visible in this state. An annotated close eye is shown in Figure 3b.

4   Deformable Eye Fitting

This section reviews the three different deformable model fitting techniques used in this paper, i.e. AAM, CLM and SDM.

4.1   Active Appearance Models

Active Appearance Models (AAM) [4,8] are global deformable models that describe the shape and texture of a particular object as a linear combination of a set of bases. The shape model is built from a set of landmarks describing the shape of the object. These landmarks are first normalized with respect to a

2D global similarity transform and then Principal Component Analysis (PCA) is applied to obtained a set of linear shape bases. The previous basis are composed with a 2D global similarity transform that allows shapes to be arbitrarily positioned on the image coordinate system. The shape model can be mathematically expressed as:

$$\mathbf{s} = s\mathbf{R}(\bar{\mathbf{s}} + \mathbf{V}\mathbf{p}) + \mathbf{t}_{\mathbf{x},\mathbf{y}} \tag{1}$$

where $\bar{\mathbf{s}} \in \mathcal{R}^{2v \times 1}$ is the mean shape, and $\mathbf{V} \in \mathcal{R}^{2v \times n}$ and $\mathbf{p} \in \mathcal{R}^{n \times 1}$ denote the shape eigenvectors and shape parameters, respectively. Note that, s, $\mathbf{R}$ and $\mathbf{t}_{\mathbf{x},\mathbf{y}}$ contain the scale, rotation and translation parameters of the 2D global similarity transform.

The AAM's texture model is obtained by warping the texture information onto a common reference frame (generating the so called shape-free textures) and applying PCA to the vectorized warped textures. The texture model is defined by the following expression:

$$\mathbf{t} = \bar{\mathbf{t}} + \mathbf{U}\mathbf{c} \tag{2}$$

where $\mathbf{t} \in \mathcal{R}^{F \times 1}$ is the mean texture, and $\mathbf{U} \in \mathcal{R}^{F \times m}$ and $\mathbf{c} \in \mathcal{R}^{m \times 1}$ denote the texture eigenvectors and texture parameters, respectively.

Figure 4 and Figure 5 show the mean and first three principal components of a full/half-open open and a close eye intensity-based AAM using the annotation scheme described in the previous section.

Fitting Active Appearance Models (AAM). Fitting an AAM consists of minimizing the Sum of Squared Differences (SSD) between a vectorized warped image (given a first estimate of the shape, the image is warped onto the reference frame and then vectorized) and the linear texture model:

$$\mathbf{p}_o, \mathbf{c}_o = \arg\min_{\mathbf{p},\mathbf{c}} ||\mathbf{p}||^2_{\mathbf{\Lambda}^{-1}} + ||\mathbf{c}||^2_{\mathbf{\Sigma}^{-1}} + \frac{1}{\sigma^2}||\mathbf{i}[\mathbf{p}] - \bar{\mathbf{t}} + \mathbf{U}\mathbf{c}||^2 \tag{3}$$

Where $\mathbf{i}[\mathbf{p}] = \mathrm{vec}(\mathcal{I} \circ \mathcal{W}(\mathbf{p}))$ denotes the vectorized warped image, $\mathbf{\Lambda}$ and $\mathbf{\Sigma}$ are diagonal matrices containing the eigenvalues associated to the shape and texture eigenvectors $\mathbf{V}$ and $\mathbf{U}$ respectively, and σ^2 quantifies the estimated uncertainty about image.

There exist several algorithms to solve the previous optimization problem [1,4,8,12]. A concise review can be found in [9]. In these paper, we use the Alternating Inverse Compositional (AIC) algorithm proposed by the authors of [12]. For further details on AAM and the AIC algorithm the reader is referred to [12] and [9].

4.2   Constrained Local Models (CLM)

Constrained Local Models (CLM) [3,13] are parts-based deformable models that define the texture of a particular object as independent local image regions

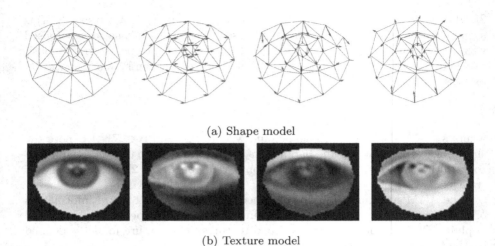

(a) Shape model

(b) Texture model

Fig. 4. Full/half-open eye Active Appearance Model

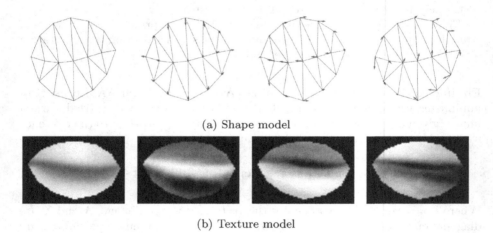

(a) Shape model

(b) Texture model

Fig. 5. Close eye Active Appearance Model

around each landmark. Their shape is represented using the same global PCA-based shape model used by AAM.

Even though generative approaches could be used to model local image regions, the usual approach is discriminative. For each landmark a classifier that quantifies the likelihood of the landmark being correctly aligned is learned based on the support of its local image region. The previous likelihood can be defined as:

$$\ell(l_i = 1 | \mathbf{x}_i, \mathcal{I}) = \frac{1}{1 + \exp\{l_i \, \mathcal{C}_i(\mathcal{I}, \mathbf{x}_i)\}} \tag{4}$$

where $\mathcal{C}_i$ denotes a linear classifier that discriminates between aligned and mis-aligned locations, i.e.:

$$\mathcal{C}_i(\mathcal{I}, \mathbf{x}_i) = \mathbf{w}_i \left[\mathcal{I}(\mathbf{y}_i), \cdots, \mathcal{I}(\mathbf{y}_m)\right] + b_i \tag{5}$$

and $\{\mathbf{y}_i\}_{i=1}^m \in \mathbf{\Omega}_{\mathbf{x}_i}$, i.e. the image patch around the current landmark estimate $\mathbf{x}_i$.

Fitting Constrained Local Models. Fitting Constrained Local Models involves solving the following optimization problem [13]:

$$\mathbf{p}_o = \arg\min_{\mathbf{p}} ||\mathbf{p}||_{\mathbf{\Lambda}^{-1}}^2 + \sum_{\mathbf{x}_i \in \mathbf{s}} \sum_{j=1}^K \frac{w_j}{\rho^2} ||\mathbf{x}_i - \mathbf{y}_j||^2 \tag{6}$$

where $w_j = \frac{1}{1+\exp\{l_i \, \mathcal{C}_j(\mathcal{I}, \mathbf{x}_j)\}}$ denotes the likelihood of each candidate landmark $\mathbf{y}_j$ in a particular local patch, $\mathbf{\Lambda}$ is a diagonal matrix containing the eigenvalues associated to the eigenvectors $\mathbf{V}$ of the shape model and ρ^2 quantifies the estimated uncertainty about shape.

The previous optimization problem can be solve using several strategies[3, 13]. See [13] for a detailed review. The most popular technique for solving the expression in Equation 6 is the Regularised Landmark Mean-Shift (RLMS) algorithm proposes by Saragih et al. in [13]. This is the approach used in this paper. For further details on CLM and the RLMS the reader is referred to [13].

4.3 Supervised Descent Method (SDM)

The Supervised Descent Method (SDM) [17] is a recently proposed techniques for solving general nonlinear optimisation problems in computer vision. This technique can be used to solve the deformable model fitting problem by defining a local appearance model around each landmark (similar to the one defined by CLM) and an implicit non-parametric shape model.

SDM is posed as the cascade regression problem in which the following expression is optimised at each level:

$$\mathbf{R}_o^k, \mathbf{b}_o^k = \arg\min_{\mathbf{R}^k, \mathbf{b}^k} \sum_{i=1}^N \sum_{j=1}^M ||\mathbf{s}_{i,*} - \mathbf{s}_{i,j}^k + \mathbf{R}^k \Phi(I_i, \mathbf{s}_{i,j}) + \mathbf{b}^k||_2^2 \tag{7}$$

Where N and M index the total number of images and perturbation respectively, $\mathbf{s}_{i,*} \in \mathcal{R}^{2v \times 1}$ denotes the correct position of the shape landmarks in a particular image I_i, $\mathbf{s}_{i,j}$ are the perturbed version of $\mathbf{s}_{i,*}$ that we wish to correct, $\Phi(I_i, \mathbf{s}_{i,j})$ denotes the vectorized features extracted at each local appearance region, and finally $\mathbf{R}_o^k$ and $\mathbf{b}_o^k$ are, respectively, the regression matrix and bias term that minimise the previous expression.

The solutions $\mathbf{R}_o^k$ and $\mathbf{b}_o^k$ are obtained in closed-form by solving a linear least squares problem at each cascade level. Once inferred, $\mathbf{R}_o^k$ and $\mathbf{b}_o^k$ are used

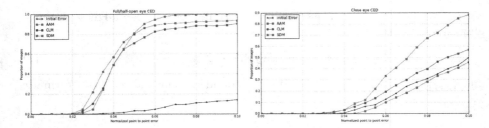

Fig. 6. CED curves for full/half-open and close eyes, respectively

to correct the position of $\mathbf{s}_{i,j}^{k}$ generating $\mathbf{s}_{i,j}^{k+1}$ and, with it, the next regression level of the cascade. In our implementation, this approach typically converges after 4 or 5 cascade levels. For more details on the SDM problem formulation for deformable object fitting and a more detailed explanation of its solution the reader is referred to [17].

5   Experiments

This section reports the performance of the previous three deformable model fitting techniques on the problems of eye alignment and eye tracking.

We report results for two different experiments. The first one compares, quantitatively, the accuracy of each technique, i.e. AAM, CLM, SDM. The second experiment shows qualitative results on the Helen [7] dataset, a recently proposed facial dataset containing high resolution in-the-wild images.

Note that, in order to save valuable space, all results are reported only for right eye models. We empirically verified that the results for right and left eye models are statistically equivalent (which is expected due to the obvious symmetry of the eyes).

5.1   Quantitative Eye Alignment Results

We start by evaluating the relative performance of each method on the problem of eye alignment.

For this experiment we collected and annotated two small dataset of 400 high resolution eye images each; one containing full/half-open eye images and the other close eye images. We randomly divide the available 400 annotated full/half-open eye images into equally sized training and testing sets. We train each model with the previous training set and report the accuracy their fitting accuracy on the testing set. The procedure is repeated for the available 400 annotated images containing closed eyes. Accuracy is reported using the error measure defined in [19], in which "face size" is simply replaced by the analogous "eye size". All methods are initialized by randomly perturbing the correct similarity transform and applying it to the mean shape of each model. Exemplar initializations obtained using the previous procedure are display in Figure 7.

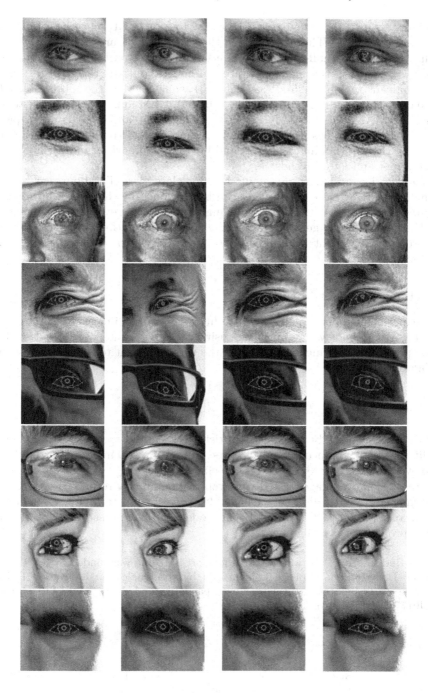

Fig. 7. Qualitative results on the Helen dataset. Columns for each subjects show: initialization, AAM result, CLM result and SDM result, respectively.

Figure 6 shows the Cumulative Error Distribution (CED) curves for full/half-open and close eyes. The results show that all methods are significantly more accurate fitting full/half-open eyes than close eyes. In particular, for full/half-open eyes, AAM is the most accurate method (it obtains the best results in the significant region $0.425 < err < 0.045$) while SDM is the most robust (it approaximatly fits all images with $err < 0.065$). CLM appear to be consistently inferior to AAM and SDM. It is worth noting, that all methods are capable of fitting the sclera, iris and pupil parts accurately and the reported errors are driven by the top (landmarks: [1-5]) and bottom landmarks (landmarks: [7-11]) of the upper and lower eyelids.

SDM is the most performant method for close eyes. The poor accuracy of all methods fitting close eyes images can be explained by the lack of meaningful features that can be extracted from the annotated close eye images, Figure 3b and Figure 5. This suggest that more contextual information (from the eyebrow or nose regions) might be necessary to accurately track close eyes using the previous methods.

5.2   Eye alignment in-the-wild

This experiment reports qualitative eye fitting results on images from the Helen dataset. All methods where initialized using the exact same procedure described in the previous experiment. Results for the three different techniques are shown in Figure 7.

6   Conclusions

In this paper we study the use of statistically learned models for deformable eye fitting. We introduce two novel shape annotation schemes, one for full/half-open eyes and another for close eyes, specifically designed to accurately annotate high resolution eye images. Finally, we report preliminary results comparing the performance of three different deformable model fitting techniques, i.e. Active Appearance Models, Constrained Local Models and Supervised Descent Method on the problem of eye alignment.

Acknowledgments. The work of Joan Alabort-i-Medina was funded by a DTA studentship from Imperial College London and by the Qualcomm Innovation Fellowship. The work of Stefanos Zafeiriou was partially funded by the EPSRC project EP/J017787/1 (4DFAB).

References

1. Amberg, B., Blake, A., Vetter, T.: On compositional image alignment, with an application to active appearance models. In: CVPR (2009)
2. Cohen, I., Sebe, N., Garg, A., Chen, L.S., Huang, T.S.: Facial expression recognition from video sequences: Temporal and static modeling. CVIU (2003)

3. Cootes, T.F., Taylor, C.J., Cooper, D.H., Graham, J.: Active shape models—their training and application. Computer Vision and Image Understanding (1995)
4. Cootes, T.F., Edwards, G.J., Taylor, C.J.: Active appearance models. IEEE Transactions on Pattern Analysis and Machine Intelligence (2001)
5. Fukuda, K.: Eye blinks: new indices for the detection of deception. International Journal of Psychophysiology (2001)
6. Stern, J.A., Walrath, L.C., Goldstein, R.: The endogenous eyeblink. Psychophysiology (1984)
7. Le, V., Brandt, J., Lin, Z., Bourdev, L., Huang, T.S.: Interactive facial feature localization. In: Fitzgibbon, A., Lazebnik, S., Perona, P., Sato, Y., Schmid, C. (eds.) ECCV 2012, Part III. LNCS, vol. 7574, pp. 679–692. Springer, Heidelberg (2012)
8. Matthews, I., Baker, S.: Active appearance models revisited. International Journal of Computer Vision (2004)
9. i Medina, J.A., Zafeiriou, S.: Bayesian active appearance models. In: CVPR (2014)
10. Moriyama, T., Kanade, T., Xiao, J., Cohn, J.F.: Meticulously detailed eye region model and its application to analysis of facial images. TPAMI (2006)
11. Orozco, J., Roca, X., Gonzlez, J.: Real-time gaze tracking with appearance-based models. Machine Vision and Applications (2009)
12. Papandreou, G., Maragos, P.: Adaptive and constrained algorithms for inverse compositional active appearance model fitting. In: CVPR (2008)
13. Saragih, J.M., Lucey, S., Cohn, J.F.: Deformable model fitting by regularized landmark mean-shift. International Journal of Computer Vision (2011)
14. Sirohey, S., Rosenfeld, A., Duric, Z.: A method of detecting and tracking irises and eyelids in video. Pattern Recognition (2002)
15. Tan, H., Zhang, Y.J.: Detecting eye blink states by tracking iris and eyelids (2006)
16. Wu, Y., Liu, H., Zha, H.: A new method of detecting human eyelids based on deformable templates. In: SMC (2004)
17. Xiong, X., De la Torre, F.: Supervised descent method and its application to face alignment. In: CVPR (2013)
18. Zeng, Z., Pantic, M., Roisman, G., Huang, T.: A survey of affect recognition methods: Audio, visual, and spontaneous expressions. TPAMI (2009)
19. Zhu, X., Ramanan, D.: Face detection, pose estimation, and landmark localization in the wild. In: CVPR (2012)

Quantifying Micro-expressions with Constraint Local Model and Local Binary Pattern

Wen-Jing Yan[1,2], Su-Jing Wang[1], Yu-Hsin Chen[1],
Guoying Zhao[3], and Xiaolan Fu[1(✉)]

[1] State Key Lab of Brain and Cognitive Science, Institute of Psychology,
Chinese Academy of Sciences, Beijing 100101, China
{yanwj,wangsujing,chenyouxin,fuxl}@psych.ac.cn,
yanwj@wzu.edu.cn
[2] College of Teacher Education, Wenzhou University, Wenzhou, China
[3] Center for Machine Vision Research, University of Oulu, Oulu, Finland
gyzhao@ee.oulu.fi

Abstract. Micro-expression may reveal genuine emotions that people try to conceal. However, it's difficult to measure it. We selected two feature extraction methods to analyze micro-expressions by assessing the dynamic information. The Constraint Local Model (CLM) algorithm is employed to detect faces and track feature points. Based on these points, the ROIs (Regions of Interest) on the face are drawn for further analysis. In addition, Local Binary Pattern (LBP) algorithm is employed to extract texture information from the ROIs and measure the differences between frames. The results from the proposed methods are compared with manual coding. These two proposed methods show good performance, with sensitivity and reliability. This is a pilot study on quantifying micro-expression movement for psychological research purpose. These methods would assist behavior researchers in measuring facial movements on various facets and at a deeper level.

Keywords: Quantification · Micro-expression · Dynamic information · Constraint Local Model (CLM) · Local Binary Pattern (LBP)

1 Introduction

Micro-expression is usually defined as a brief and subtle facial movement revealing an emotion that a person tries to conceal [32]. Such characteristics make it a potential cue for lie detection [28]. It was claimed that well-trained inspectors reached 80% accuracy in lie detection based on micro-expression [12], which seems to be much more effective than other nonverbal cues. Micro-expression possesses theoretical implications and have many practical applications [13][32], but very few scientific researches were conducted on its characteristics.

A key reason for the lack of research on micro-expression may be due to it's difficult analysis [13]. Up till now, FACS remains to be the most widely used method for analyzing facial movements and many recent works (such as [25][27]

© Springer International Publishing Switzerland 2015
L. Agapito et al. (Eds.): ECCV 2014 Workshops, Part I, LNCS 8925, pp. 296–305, 2015.
DOI: 10.1007/978-3-319-16178-5_20

continue to use FACS to quantify behaviors. However, when trying to apply FACS to manually analyzing micro-expressions, researchers may encounter the following problems.

First, micro-expression is featured not only by its short duration [9] but also low intensity [24][32][31], some of which doesn't even reach the lowest intensity (level A) stated by FACS. These two characteristics usually make micro-expressions imperceptible to the naked eyes. Even with frame-by-frame approach, FACS coders find it difficult to spot the onset frame, apex frame and offset frame for many micro-expressions. As for describing dynamic information, it is impractical to describe increasing intensity over time via manual coding. However, research has shown the importance of dynamic information in facial expression [16][1][15][18]. Further quantification of dynamic micro-expressions may lead to interest findings; however, researchers lack suitable tools to quantify them. Second, manual coding with FACS is "arduous", especially for subtle facial movements [5]. As for very subtle facial expressions (a facial expression with intensity lower than the lowest intensity level according to FACS), coding would be even more difficult. Third, the coders, especially from different research groups, may follow a slightly different coding criterion even when the same coding system is employed (e.g. FACS). For example, when coding the onset frame of a facial expression, in Yan et al.'s [32] and Porter et al.'s [24] studies, the coders considered the onset frame as the first frame in which a change has occurred from the baseline (also see [14]). In FACS investigator's guide [10], however, Ekman defined "the first frame (film) or field (video) when the AU was at all visible" as the onset. This definition is vague and heavily dependent upon the coders' subjective judgment. With different research groups, the onset and offset frame coding may be difficult to replicate.

1.1   Utilization of Feature Extraction Methods to Facial Expression Analysis

Considering the issues rising from the use of FACS through manual coding, computer scientists have been trying to develop tools to analyze facial movements [4][7][11][17][20][26]. Researchers in the field of computer vision have previously focused on accurately classifying different facial expressions [3][22] and AUs [6][20][29]. However, for behavioral researchers, it would be more meaningful to know how the facial movements change in detail. Since psychological researchers still debate over the existence of universal categories of emotional facial displays, for behavioral science research purposes it would be more useful to quantify facial movements and further study the patterns of facial movements, rather than just providing a classification. In the following, we will introduce Constraint Local Model (CLM), which is mainly a geometric feature-based method, and Local Binary Pattern (LBP), which is an appearance-based method. CLM is improved from the commonly used Active Appearance Model (AAM) and Active Shape Model (ASM), and LBP has been applied to extracting features for micro-expression recognition [23]. These two algorithms seem suitable to deal with micro-expression.

1.2   The Aim of This Work

In this study, we select and apply two feature extraction methods to quantify dynamic information of micro-expressions, which would be facilitate psychological studies on micro-expression. CLM is employed to automatically detect the facial feature points. Based on the points, the faces were aligned and the ROIs (Regions of Interest) on the face were drawn for texture feature extraction by LBP. These two methods were evaluated by testing the effectiveness on quantifying micro-expressions. This paper provides a brief introduction to these algorithms, the way of applying them to quantifying dynamic information and test their performance on analyzing spontaneous micro-expressions.

2   Methods

2.1   Materials

Fifty micro-expression samples from CASME2 were selected. CASME2 is a spontaneous micro-expression database which contains 247 samples at 200fps (the inter-frame duration is 0.05s) and with the spatial resolution at about 280x340 pixels on facial area [30]. For demonstration, two samples (Fig. 1) were used to show how these two methods were applied to analyzing micro-expressions.

2.2   Applying CLM to Quantifying Micro-expressions

CLM CLM is a type of point distribution model (PDM), which represents the geometry mean and some statistical modes of geometric variation inferred from a training set of shapes [8]. CLM typically involves an exhaustive local search for the best location of each PDM landmark that is then constrained to adhere to the PDM's parameterization. We tested the source codes from   [2], Jason Saragih's [1] and Yan Xiaoguang's [2], and found the Jason Saragih's tool performed best on CASME2. This algorithm trains 66 landmarks on the face. With the 66 landmarks detected on each frame, the coordinate of each landmark is generated. Since the facial movements may accompany some degree of head movements and even the slight head movement may blur or disrupt the targeted subtle facial movement, the coordinate of each landmark are subtracted by the coordinates of landmark 34, the nostril, which has a clear contour. Then we calculate the changes for each landmark. All video samples in CASME2 start with baseline (usually a neutral facial expression). To calculate the changes of each facial point, the corresponding coordinates of the 66 landmarks are subtracted by the pixel coordinates of the first frame. We get a graph depicting the changes of each landmark and form a "changing map" of the whole face, where the landmarks between 1 to 17 indicates the contour of the face, 18 to 27 indicates eye brows, and so on (see Figure 2).

---

[1] https://github.com/kylemcdonald/ofxFaceTracker
[2] https://sites.google.com/site/xgyanhome/home/projects/clm-implementation

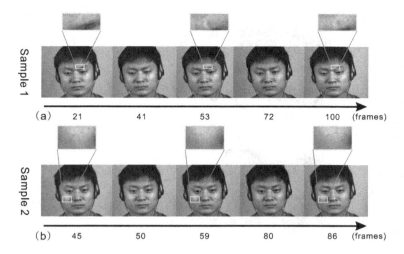

Fig. 1. The image-sequences of two samples from CASME2 that indicate the facial movements across time. (a) Zoomed-in images of the area of the left inner brow are shown in order to illustrate the movements. Frame 53 is the apex of the facial movement, while the frame 21 and frame 100 were taken as the baseline. The change is obvious for naked eyes. (b) Zoomed-in images of the area of the right cheek are to illustrate the movements. The apex frames are in 54-68 (too subtle to define), while frame 45 and 86 were taken as the baseline. The change is very subtle to detect, but better perceivable in video mode. Note: These samples were recorded by a 200fps camera, with an inter-frame duration 0.05s.

2.3   Applying LBP to Quantifying Micro-expressions

LBP For psychological research purpose, texture information of a certain region may be used to measure the change of the facial movements across time. Previous studies have shown that LBP is a powerful algorithm for texture description [21]. For a pixel C in the image, an LBP operator describes its local texture pattern by comparing and thresholding the gray values of its neighboring pixels against the gray value of pixel C. For the center pixel C with its P neighboring pixels sampled with the radius R, the LBP value is then calculated.

The source code are available here [3]. The following steps were carried out to quantify the aforementioned two samples (shown in Figure 1) of subtle facial movements with LBP. *Step 1.* Draw and select the region of interests (ROIs). Based on the landmarks detected by CLM, we draw the regions of interest (ROIs) for each frame. These ROIs were defined (partly) according to AUs. These regions includes the inner eyebrows (AU1, AU4), outer eyebrows (AU2), nose root (AU9), lower eyelid (AU7), cheeks (AU6), mouth corner (AU12, AU14, AU 15) and the regions at the side of the nose (AU 10), the jaw (AU17) and so on. The to-be-analyzed regions are selected by naked eyes. *Step 2.* Extract LBP for the ROI in each frame. *Step 3.* Calculate the change between the first frame

---

[3] http://www.cse.oulu.fi/CMV/Downloads/LBPMatlab

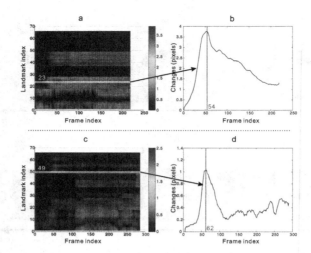

Fig. 2. The movements measured by calculating the changes of the landmarks across time. X-axis shows the frames of the video sample. (a) and (b) are for describing Sample 1, while (c) and (d) for Sample 2. In (a) and (c), y-axis indicates the numbered landmarks (from 1 to 66), and the color indicates the degree of change from the first frame. Landmarks 22 to 25 show great "activation" in (a), meaning that there is obvious change in the area of brows. The change of landmark 23 (left inner brow) is exhibited in (b), where y-axis means the location it changes.

and other frames for the ROIs. Similarity between two images is calculated by their correlation. And the rate of the texture change can be calculated by the difference between the first frame and the other frames. The correlation coefficient is calculated by:

$$d = \frac{\sum_{i=1}^{nBins} h_{1i} \times h_{2i}}{\sqrt{\sum_{i=1}^{nBins} h_{1i}^2 \times \sum_{i=1}^{nBins} h_{2i}^2}} \tag{1}$$

where h_1 indicates the gray-scale histogram of the first frame, h_2 the current frame. (1-d) indicates the rate of difference of the texture features in a ROI between these two frames. The peak of difference is found at frame 60 for sample 1, frame 59 for sample 2. The difference between the peak and first frame at left inner brow (sample 1) is about 0.018% and at right cheek is about 0.0025%. These values indicate the change of texture feature, which may serve as a measurement of intensity (Figure 3).

2.4 Data Analysis and Results

In the following, we compare the performance between the computer and manual coding in spotting the apex frames. It needs to be noted that the data obtained via manual coding don't necessarily represent the standard or correct answer as different people have different judgments.

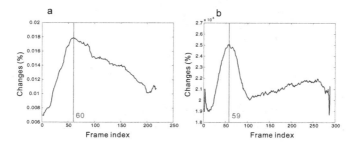

Fig. 3. The differences between the first frame and following frames across time for (a) Sample 1 (AU4, inner corner) and (b) Sample 2 (AU6, cheek)

CLM and LBP algorithms were tested on 50 samples of micro-expressions. Two coders coded the apex frame for each sample and the mean number of the two coded peaks was taken as the apex frame. To evaluate the performance of these two algorithms, the coded frame numbers by the proposed methods (CLM and LBP) and the manually coded on apex frame are compared (by subtracting the manually coded number). The result for CLM is: M=1.02, SE= 1.56; for LBP (subtracting manually coded number): M=0.31, SE=1.88. The difference (measured by frames) between the proposed methods and manual coding for each sample is demonstrated in Figure 4.

Analysis of variance (ANOVA) repeated-measures was conducted to test whether three coding methods, CLM, LBP and manual coding, are statistically different from each other (or whether from different population). Results show that the difference among these three methods is not significant, $F_{(2, 76)} = 0.273$, p $= 0.762$, which indicates that the performance of the proposed algorithms matches those of manual coding in terms of spotting apex frames.

The details about CLM and LBP coding for different areas are demonstrated in Table 1. CLM and LBP have their own advantages when quantifying different areas of the face. The CLM seems to be well suited for measuring the areas around the eyebrow. LBP seems to outperform CLM in quantifying the area around the mouth, where the movement such as pressing lips have obvious texture change but not necessarily shape change.

3   Discussion

In non-verbal behavior studies, manual coding usually have suffered from subjectivity and inaccurate quantification. To avoid the use of heuristic coding scheme in measuring micro-expressions, this paper introduced two feature extraction methods, CLM and LBP, to quantify dynamic facial movements. CLM detects the 66 landmarks on the face for each frame and the detected landmarks are also used for alignment (which can partly deal with head motion problem). The texture features of the aligned ROIs (which are based on the landmarks detected by CLM) were extracted by LBP. These methods could be adopted to analyze

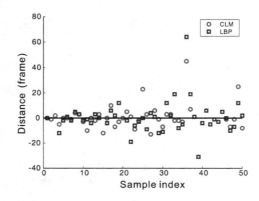

Fig. 4. The difference (in frames) between our proposed methods and manual coding on apex frame for each sample of micro-expression. The x-axis indicates sample No., and the y-axis indicates how many frames the proposed methods are off in comparison with the manual coding. The black line (y=0) represents the baseline (manual coding) and the blue squares and green circles represent the results of LBP and CLM respectively. Note: one frame is equivalent to 0.05 second in duration.

Table 1. The descriptive statistics for coding different areas with CLM and LBP

Area	Quantity	CLM			LBP		
		Reasonable	Mean	SE	Reasonable	Mean	SE
Eyebrow	16	16	3.31	2.99	14	3.00	4.92
Mouth	16	13	1.08	2.25	16	-4.38	2.85
Mix	5	3	5.00	10.1	5	8.00	3.02
Others	13	9	-4.22	1.89	12	0.08	1.38

micro-expression at a deeper level and reduce the amount of manual coding work. The following issues are some of the problems worth further discussion.

3.1   Sensitivity to Subtle Facial Movements

The values of the proposed methods for quantifying micro-expression mainly lies in its sensitivity and accuracy in quantifying the dynamic information of micro-expressions. CLM and LBP extract facial features with different approaches and each have their own advantages on different samples. CLM is sensitive to the eyebrow movement, which has a "clear" contour and thus CLM can accurately detect subtle movements near the eyebrow area. For LBP, the ROIs are initially drawn based on landmarks detected by CLM, the movement of the landmarks leads to the movement of ROIs (thus they are aligned). If the targeted areas don't show obvious texture change, the texture feature in these ROIs will not reveal changes as well. In contrast, for subtle movements such as a lip pressing, the landmarks of lip "corners" actually don't move too much, the gray-scale changes (texture changes) around the lip corner are obvious. The ROIs drawn based on by these landmarks are relatively steady, thus LBP is more suitable to measure these areas.

3.2   Measuring Dynamic (Temporal) Information

Dynamic information provides an abundance of information. Recently, researchers are paying more attention to dynamic facial expression instead of traditional static images of prototypical expressive patterns, since dynamic facial expressions are more ecologically valid [19]. With the advances of feature extraction methods, it is possible to measure and quantify the dynamic information such as moving distance, direction, velocity and texture feature, even on subtle facial movements. For CLM, the "changing map" of the facial movements (Figure 2) reveals the global characteristics which contain the information on the pattern of a facial expression. LBP doesn't show the direction but it can measure the global texture changes of the ROIs across time. These methods provide dynamic information that may reveal some specific patterns of facial expressions.

3.3   The Representative of Intensity

The strength of muscle contractions, acquired through electromyography, could be used to measure the intensity of a facial expression. For view-based analysis, however, the criteria for the intensity are difficult to define. In manual coding, coders define the intensity of a facial expression heuristically. For CLM, the intensity was calculated according to the displacement of the feature points across frames. For LBP, the intensity was represented by the texture (grayscale pixels) change of a certain ROI across frames. LBP may be better since it considers information in a region instead of simply the coordinates of the landmarks.

3.4   Limitations and Future Work

Though feature extraction methods have promising applications in analyzing micro-expressions, there are still several challenges. First, landmark detection on the face is not always accurate and steady, even though these algorithms have made a remarkable progress over the past decade. Second, we have not established criteria for defining the onset and offset frame of micro-expressions. To achieve automatic detection of onset and offset frames for a given facial movement, future research should focus on the indicators and criteria for determining these key frames.

Acknowledgments. This work was supported by grants from 973 Program (2011CB302201), the National Natural Science Foundation of China (61379095, 61375009, 61175023, 61472138), China Postdoctoral Science Foundation funded project (2012M520428, 2014T70133), the Beijing Natural Science Foundation (4152055), and the Open Projects Program of National Laboratory of Pattern Recognition (201306295). G. Z. was supported by the Academy of Finland and Infotech Oulu.

References

1. Ambadar, Z., Cohn, J.F., Reed, L.I.: All smiles are not created equal: Morphology and timing of smiles perceived as amused, polite, and embarrassed/nervous. Journal of Nonverbal Behavior **33**(1), 17–34 (2009)
2. Asthana, A., Zafeiriou, S., Cheng, S., Pantic, M.: Robust discriminative response map fitting with constrained local models. In: 2013 IEEE Conference on Computer Vision and Pattern Recognition (CVPR), pp. 3444–3451. IEEE (2013)
3. Bartlett, M., Littlewort, G., Whitehill, J., Vural, E., Wu, T., Lee, K., Eril, A., Cetin, M., Movellan, J.: Insights on spontaneous facial expressions from automatic expression measurement. Dynamic Faces: Insights from Experiments and Computation (2006)
4. Bartlett, M.S., Hager, J.C., Ekman, P., Sejnowski, T.J.: Measuring facial expressions by computer image analysis. Psychophysiology **36**(2), 253–263 (1999)
5. Bartlett, M., Littlewort, G., Frank, M., Lainscsek, C., Fasel, I., Movellan, J.: Automatic recognition of facial actions in spontaneous expressions. Journal of Multimedia **1**(6), 22–35 (2006)
6. Cohn, J.F., Sayette, M.A.: Spontaneous facial expression in a small group can be automatically measured: An initial demonstration. Behavior Research Methods **42**(4), 1079–1086 (2010)
7. Cohn, J.F., Zlochower, A.J., Lien, J., Kanade, T.: Automated face analysis by feature point tracking has high concurrent validity with manual facs coding. Psychophysiology **36**(1), 35–43 (1999)
8. Cristinacce, D., Cootes, T.F.: Feature detection and tracking with constrained local models (2006)
9. Ekman, P., Friesen, W.: Nonverbal leakage and clues to deception. Tech. rep., DTIC Document (1969)
10. Ekman, P., Friesen, W., Hager, J.: Facs investigator guide. A human face (2002)
11. Essa, I.A., Pentland, A.P.: Coding, analysis, interpretation, and recognition of facial expressions. IEEE Transactions on Pattern Analysis and Machine Intelligence **19**(7), 757–763 (1997)
12. Frank, M., Ekman, P.: The ability to detect deceit generalizes across different types of high-stake lies. Journal of Personality and Social Psychology **72**(6), 1429 (1997)
13. Frank, M., Maccario, C., Govindaraju, V.: Behavior and security, pp. 86–106. Greenwood Pub. Group, Santa Barbara (2009)
14. Hess, U., Kleck, R.: Differentiating emotion elicited and deliberate emotional facial expressions. European Journal of Social Psychology **20**(5), 369–385 (2006)
15. Hess, U., Kleck, R.E.: The cues decoders use in attempting to differentiate emotionelicited and posed facial expressions. European Journal of Social Psychology **24**(3), 367–381 (1994)
16. Kappas, A., Descteaux, J.: Of butterflies and roaring thunder: nonverbal communication in interaction and regulation of emotion. In: Nonverbal Behavior In Clinical Settings, pp. 45–74 (2003)

17. Koelstra, S., Pantic, M., Patras, I.: A dynamic texture-based approach to recognition of facial actions and their temporal models. IEEE Transactions on Pattern Analysis and Machine Intelligence **32**(11), 1940–1954 (2010)
18. Krumhuber, E., Kappas, A.: Moving smiles: The role of dynamic components for the perception of the genuineness of smiles. Journal of Nonverbal Behavior **29**(1), 3–24 (2005)
19. Krumhuber, E.G., Kappas, A., Manstead, A.S.: Effects of dynamic aspects of facial expressions: a review. Emotion Review **5**(1), 41–46 (2013)
20. Littlewort, G., Whitehill, J., Wu, T., Fasel, I., Frank, M., Movellan, J., Bartlett, M.: The computer expression recognition toolbox (cert). In: 2011 IEEE International Conference on Automatic Face & Gesture Recognition and Workshops (FG 2011), pp. 298–305. IEEE (2011)
21. Ojala, T., Pietikinen, M., Harwood, D.: A comparative study of texture measures with classification based on featured distributions. Pattern Recognition **29**(1), 51–59 (1996)
22. Pantic, M., Patras, I.: Dynamics of facial expression: recognition of facial actions and their temporal segments from face profile image sequences. IEEE Transactions on Systems, Man, and Cybernetics, Part B: Cybernetics **36**(2), 433–449 (2006)
23. Pfister, T., Li, X., Zhao, G., Pietikainen, M.: Recognising spontaneous facial microexpressions. In: 2011 IEEE International Conference on Computer Vision (ICCV), pp. 1449–1456. IEEE (2011)
24. Porter, S., ten Brinke, L.: Reading between the lies: Identifying concealed and falsified emotions in universal facial expressions. Psychological Science **19**(5), 508–514 (2008)
25. Rahu, M.A., Grap, M.J., Cohn, J.F., Munro, C.L., Lyon, D.E., Sessler, C.N.: Facial expression as an indicator of pain in critically ill intubated adults during endotracheal suctioning. American Journal of Critical Care **22**(5), 412–422 (2013)
26. Sebe, N., Lew, M.S., Sun, Y., Cohen, I., Gevers, T., Huang, T.S.: Authentic facial expression analysis. Image and Vision Computing **25**(12), 1856–1863 (2007)
27. Seidl, U., Lueken, U., Thomann, P.A., Kruse, A., Schrder, J.: Facial expression in Facial expression in alzheimers disease impact of cognitive deficits and neuropsychiatric symptoms disease impact of cognitive deficits and neuropsychiatric symptoms. American Journal of Alzheimer's Disease and Other Dementias **27**(2), 100–106 (2012)
28. Vrij, A.: Detecting lies and deceit: Pitfalls and opportunities. John Wiley & Sons Ltd., West Sussex (2008)
29. Wu, T., Butko, N.J., Ruvolo, P., Whitehill, J., Bartlett, M.S., Movellan, J.R.: Multilayer architectures for facial action unit recognition. IEEE Transactions on Systems, Man, and Cybernetics, Part B: Cybernetics **42**(4), 1027–1038 (2012)
30. Yan, W.J., Li, X., Wang, S.J., Zhao, G., Liu, Y.J., Chen, Y.H., Fu, X.: Casme: An improved spontaneous micro-expression database and the baseline evaluation. PLoS ONE (2014)
31. Yan, W.J., Wang, S.J., Liu, Y.J., Wu, Q., Fu, X.: For micro-expression recognition: Database and suggestions. Neurocomputing (2014)
32. Yan, W.J., Wu, Q., Liang, J., Chen, Y.H., Fu, X.: How fast are the leaked facial expressions: The duration of micro-expressions. Journal of Nonverbal Behavior, 1–14 (2013)

Audiovisual Conflict Detection in Political Debates

Yannis Panagakis[1](✉), Stefanos Zafeiriou[1], and Maja Pantic[1,2]

[1] Department of Computing, Imperial College London,
180 Queens Gate, London SW7 2AZ, UK
{i.panagakis,s.zafeiriou,m.pantic}@imperial.ac.uk
[2] EEMCS, University of Twente,
Drienerlolaan 5, 7522 NB Enschede, The Netherlands

Abstract. In this paper, the problem of conflict detection in audiovisual recordings of political debates is investigated. In contrast to the current state of the art in social signal processing, where only the audio modality is employed for analysing the human non-verbal behavior, we propose to use additionally visual features capturing certain facial behavioral cues such as head nodding, fidgeting, and frowning which are related to conflicts. To this end, a dataset with video excerpts from televised political debates, where conflicts naturally arise, is introduced. The prediction of conflict level (i.e., conflict/nonconflict) is performed by applying the linear support vector machine and the collaborative representation-based classifier onto audio, visual, and audiovisual features. The experimental results demonstrate that the fusion of audio and visual features, outperform the accuracy in conflict detection, obtained by features that resort to a single modality (i.e., either audio or video).

1 Introduction

Social signals and social behaviors are the expression of one's attitude towards social situation and interplay, and they are manifested through a multiplicity of non-verbal behavioral cues including facial expressions, body postures, gestures, and vocal outbursts like laughter. Social signals typically last for a short time (milliseconds, like turn taking, to minutes, like mirroring), compared to social behaviors that last longer (seconds, like agreement, to minutes, like politeness, to hours or days, like empathy) and are expressed as temporal patterns of non-verbal behavioral cues [1]. Since humans are predominantly social beings, the importance of social signals in everyday life situations is self-evident. In turn, multimedia data (e.g., television programs, movies, etc.) contain human social interactions and thus the automatic analysis and understanding of human social signals and social behaviors from audiovisual recordings is a cornerstone in the deployment of content-based multimedia indexing and retrieval systems, machine-mediated communication, state of the art human-computer interfaces, to mention but a few.

In spite of recent advances in social signal processing [1,2] and machine analysis of relevant behavioral cues such as blinks, smiles, head nods, laughter, and

L. Agapito et al. (Eds.): ECCV 2014 Workshops, Part I, LNCS 8925, pp. 306–314, 2015.
DOI: 10.1007/978-3-319-16178-5_21

similar [2–5], the research in machine analysis and understanding of more complex human social behaviors like interest, politeness, flirting, agreement, and conflict detection which this paper addresses, is still limited [1,2,6–8]. This can be, partly, attributed to both 1) an omnipresent neglect of the fact that observed behaviors may be influenced by those of an interlocutor and thus require analysis of both interactants at the same time, especially to measure such critically important patterns as mimicry, rapport, and disagreement, and 2) an overall lack of suitable annotated data that could be used to train the machine learning algorithms for recognition of relevant phenomena [1,2,6]. Recent efforts in machine analysis of social interactions were aimed at analysis of various social signals including social dominance [9], engagement and hot-spots [10], behavioral codes (e.g., acceptance and blame) [11], and the analysis of personality [12]. These approaches employed statistical models trained on various lexical, prosodic and conversational features.

Conflict is used to label a range of human experiences, from disagreement to stress and anger, occurring when the involved individuals act on incompatible goals, interests, or actions. Various research studies in human sciences argue that a "disagreement" does not have to result in a conflict; conflict describes a high level of disagreement, or "escalation of disagreement", where at least one of the involved interlocutors feels emotionally offended. However, while conflict has been extensively investigated in human sciences and recognized as one of the main dimensions along which an interaction is perceived and assessed [13], machine analysis of conflicts is limited to automatic agreement/disagreement detection [6,14–17] and is yet to be attempted based on audiovisual cues. To the best of our knowledge, the only work on the topic, and then based on audio cues only, is that by Kim *et al.* [7,8], who investigated the degree of conflict in broadcasted political debates by employing various prosodic/conversational features.

This paper addresses the problem of conflict detection in videos. As opposed to Kim *et al.* [7,8], the use of both audio and video modalities is investigated in conflict modeling and detection. Since, to the best of our knowledge, there are no available benchmarks datasets for audiovisual conflict detection, video excerpts from live political debates, where conflicts between participant naturally arise, are used. These videos have been extracted from more than 60 hours of live political debates, televised in between 2011 and 2012. In contrast with other benchmarks, political debates are real-world competitive multi-party conversations where participants do not act in a simulated context, but participate in an event that has a major impact on their real life (for example, in terms of results at the elections) [7]. Consequently, even if some constraints are imposed by the debate format, the participants have real motivations leading to real conflicts. From the entire dataset, 160 videos experts, with total duration 2h and 40 min, have been extracted. These videos have been annotated by 10 experts, in terms of continuous conflict intensity. The average annotation for each video is extracted by employing the Dynamic Probabilistic CCA [18]. Discrete labels (i.e., conflict/nonconflict here) are obtained next, by segmenting each video in non-overlapping conflict/nonconflict segments by applying an indicator function on the average annotation, resulting in 150 conflict (43 min) and 150 nonconflict (95 min) clips. The audio content of each video clip is parameterized in terms of prosodic and cepstral features, typically employed in affective computing [5]. Visually, the assessment of a conflict is highly related with the presence (or the absence) of certain facial behavioral cues such as head nodding, blinks, fidgeting and frowning [19]. To this end, the facial behavioral cues of each interactant are captured by tracking 66 facial points. The prediction of conflict level (i.e., conflict/nonconflict) is performed by applying a linear support vector machine (SVM) [20] and the collaborative representation-based classifier [21] onto feature vectors constructed by the audio modality, the video modality, and their combination. The experimental results indicate that the fusion of audio and video features outperforms the prediction accuracy obtained by features that resort to a single modality (i.e. either audio or video), yielding an accuracy of 85.59% when the collaborative representation-based classifier is employed in a two-class setting. Furthermore, the proposed method enables the modeling of conflict escalation and resolution.

The paper is organized as follows. In Section 2, the dataset and the annotation procedure is described. The audiovisual feature extraction process is outlined in Section 3. The experimental results are presented in Section 4. Conclusions are drawn in Section 5.

1.1 Dataset and Annotation Procedure

The dataset introduced in this paper for audiovisual conflict detection consists of video excerpts from televised political debates in Greek language. In particular, it consists of episodes of conflict escalation and resolution, which have been extracted from more than 60 hours of televised, live political debates aired as a part of the Anatropi Greek TV show[1]. Each debate includes at least two guests discussing under the moderation of the TV host.

From the entire dataset, 160 (140 min) non-overlapping dyadic episodes of conflict escalation have been manually extracted. For each episode of conflict, the database also contains an episode of conflict-free interaction of the two people in question. Each sample of the dataset is an audiovisual TV recording having both people involved in the dyadic episode in view. A sample frame from the dataset is depicted in Fig. 1. The episodes are of variable duration (i.e., 10 seconds to several minutes) and maybe noisy with a third party speaking in the background and people exhibiting large body movements.

The data have been annotated in terms of continuous conflict intensity by 10 expert annotators. The annotators assign a conflict intensity level, in the range [0, 1], at each video frame by employing a joystick-based annotation tool, while they are watching each video excerpt in real time. They have been advised to annotate the videos by considering the physical (related to the behavior being observed) and inferential (related to the the interpretation of the discussion) layer of the conversation [7]. The physical layer includes the behavioral cues

---

[1] http://www.megatv.com/anatropi/

Fig. 1. (a) A sample snapshot from the dataset depicting the TV host and the two guests in conflict. (b) Facial points extracted from each guest, capturing the facial characteristics of the interactants being in conflict.

observed during conflicts and include interruptions, overlapping speech, cues related to turn-organization in conversations as well as but head nodding, fidgeting and frowning [19]. The inferential layer is based on the perception of the competitive processes [15] where conflict is considered as a "mode of interaction" where "the attainment of the goal by one party precludes its attainment by the others". For instance, conflicting goals often lead to attempts of limiting, if not eliminating, the speaking opportunities of others in conversations.

To combine multiple annotators (Fig. 2(a)) subjective judgements, the Dynamic Probabilistic CCA with time warping [18] has been employed, yielding an average annotation for each video exert (Fig. 2(b)). The video excerpts are segmented next into non-overlapping conflict/nonconflict segments as follows: An indicator function assigns each frame the value 1 if the average annotation value is greater than its mean value and 0, otherwise. Segments corresponding to the discrete conflict/nonconflict sections of the video excerpt are depicted in Fig. 2(b). Finally, 150 conflict (43 min) and 150 nonconflict (95 min) clips, with discrete labels, have been selected. The annotated data are available at http://ibug.doc.ic.ac.uk/research.

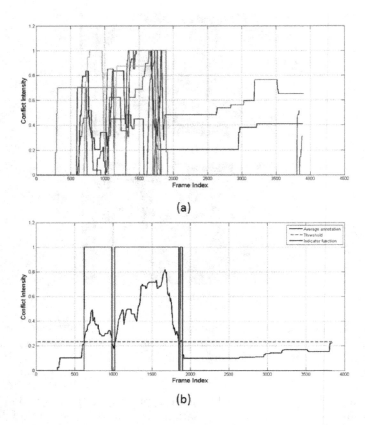

Fig. 2. (a) Conflict intensity as a continuous function of video frame index by various annotators. (b) Average continuous conflict intensity and segments corresponding to the discrete conflict/nonconflict sections of the video excerpt.

2   Feature Extraction

In this section, the procedure followed for audiovisual feature extraction from each video excerpt in the dataset is outlined.

2.1   Audio Features

The audio content of each episode in the dataset is parameterized in terms prosodic and spectral features, namely the pitch related feature [22], the mean and the RSM energy feature, as well as the Mel-frequency cepstral coefficients (MFCCs) [23] and the Delta (differential) MFCCs.

The MFCCs [23] encode the frequency content of the speech signal by parameterizing the rough shape of spectral envelope and they have been successfully applied in turn-taking analysis. Roughly speaking, the logarithm, which involved in the calculation of the MFCCs is a nonlinear transformation with additive property in the spectrum magnitude domain and thus the cepstral features can be consider as a superposition of latent variables, which are related to the speakers involved in the conversation. The MFCC calculation employs frames of duration 80 ms with a hop size of 40 ms, and a 42-band filter bank. The correlation between the frequency bands is reduced by applying the discrete cosine transform along the log-energies of the bands. The analysis yields a 23-dimensional vector of MFCCs for each video frame. This vector is appended with the Delta MFCCs, the 3 prosodic features, yielding an 49-dimensional audio feature vector for each video frame.

2.2 Visual Features

Cooper indicates that, facial behavioral cues related to conflict are head nodding, blinks, fidgeting, and frowning [19]. Consequently, the conflict can be visually captured by tracking the head pose, lips, eyebrows, eyelids, and related facial characteristics of the interactants in video sequences. To this end, the recently introduced persons' independent active appearance model, the so called active orientation model (AOM) [24] is employed for facial points tracking. In particular, the faces of the interactants are detected in the first frame of each video excerpt by the well-known Viola-Jones face detector [25]. Afterwards, the AOM is applied for tracking 66 2-dimensional facial points for each human throughout the video segment. As a result, for each video frame a 264-dimensional feature vector is obtained by stacking the points of each interactant. Facial points extracted from two interactants are depicted in Fig. 1 (b).

3 Experimental Results

In order to assess the performance of the proposed approach in conflict detection in political debates, experiments were conducted in the datset described in Section 2, by applying stratified 2-fold cross-validation.

To investigate the impact of each modality on conflict detection each video in the dataset is represented by three sequences of feature vectors. That is, by employing the 49-dimensional audio features, (audio modality), the 264-dimensional facial points (i.e., video modality) as well as the $264 + 49 = 313$-dimensional vector of audiovisual features. The latter feature vector is constructed by stacking the 49-dimensional audio on the top of the visual features for each video frame. Clearly, the length of the each feature sequence is equal to the number of the frames in video. The linear SVM [20] and the collaborative representation-based classifier (CRC) [21] are employed to assign each video frame into a class, namely to classify it as conflict or nonconflict. The classification results for frame level conflict detection are summarized in Table 1 for audio (A), video (V), and audiovisual features (AV). A single label for each video excerpt is obtained by averaging and rounding to the closest integer the

Table 1. Frame-level conflict detection accuracy (%). The number within the parenthesis indicate the standard deviation.

Features	SVM	CRC
A	73.54 (0.31)	73.54 (0.31)
V	74.99 (0.31)	73.36 (0.31)
AV	78.58 (1.92)	79.95 (0.98)

Table 2. Video excerpt-level conflict detection accuracy (%). The number within the parenthesis indicate the standard deviation.

Features	SVM	CRC
A	73.76 (1.06)	74.59 (1.21)
V	82.92 (8.31)	83.92 (5.12)
AV	84.30 (10.60)	85.59 (2.91)

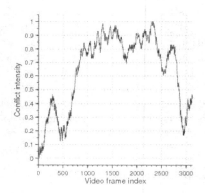

Fig. 3. (a) A sample snapshot from the dataset depicting the TV host and the two guests in conflict. (b) Conflict intensity as a function of video frame index.

predicted class labels of its frames. The classification results for video excerpt level conflict detection are summarized in Table 2.

By inspecting Table 1 and Table 2, it is clear that the fusion of audio with visual features provide more accurate conflict prediction. In particular, the audio-visual feature discriminate the video exerts in those which contain conflicts and those which not contain conflicts with an accuracy of 85.59%, which is a significant improvement compared to that obtained by the audio features (i.e., 74.59%). This can be attributed to the fact that the audio channel is often noisy since a third party is speaking in the background. In contrast the video modality contain clear information about the behavior of the interactants.

Finally, there are indications that the conflict escalation and resolution can be modeled following the proposed approach, that is by classifying audiovisual features by the CRC. This can be done by assigning to each test video frame the average of the class labels within a window of 50 frames (i.e., 2 sec in our case). This maps the conflict intensity onto the continuous space. A demonstration of this can be found online[2], where the normalized in $[0, 1]$ conflict intensity level is depicted as a function of the video frame index. A snapshot of this demonstration is depicted in Fig. 3.

4   Conclusions

In this paper, the problem of conflict detection in audiovisual recordings of political debated has been investigated. Audio and visual features have been demonstrated to detect the conflict more accurately than the features which resort to a single modality (i.e., either audio or video), when the CRC is employed.

In the future, the modeling of conflict escalation and resolution based on audiovisual and other features (e.g., conversational, lexical) will be investigated.

Acknowledgments. The work of Y. Panagakis was funded by the European Research Council under the FP7 Marie Curie Intra-European Fellowship. The work S. Zafeiriou was partially funded by the EPSRC project EP/J017787/1 (4DFAB). The work of M. Pantic was partially funded by the European Community 7th Framework Programme [FP7/2007-2013] under grant agreement no. 611153 (TERESA).

References

1. Pantic, M., Cowie, R., D'ericco, F., Heylen, D., Mehu, M., Pelachaud, C., Poggi, I., Schroder, M., Vinciarelli, A.: Social Signal Processing: The Research Agenda. Springer (2011)
2. Vinciarelli, A., Pantic, M., Heylen, D., Pelachaud, C., Poggi, I., D"Errico, F., Schroeder, M.: Bridging the gap between social animal and unsocial machine: A survey of social signal processing. IEEE Trans. Affective Computing **3**(1), 69–87 (2012)
3. Gunes, H., Pantic, M.: Automatic, dimensional and continuous emotion recognition. Int. J. Synthetic Emotion **1**(2), 68–99 (2010)
4. Pantic, M., Pentland, A., Nijholt, A., Huang, T.: Human-centred intelligent human-computer interaction (*hci2*): How far are we from attaining it? Int. J. Autonomous and Adaptive Communications Systems **1**(2), 168–187 (2008)
5. Zeng, Z., Pantic, M., Roisman, G.I., Huang, T.S.: A survey of affect recognition methods: Audio, visual, and spontaneous expressions. IEEE Trans. Pattern Analysis and Machine Intelligenc **31**(1) (2009) 39–58
6. Bousmalis, K., Morency, L., Pantic, M.: Modeling hidden dynamics of multimodal cues for spontaneous agreement and disagreement recognition. In: Proc. IEEE 2011 Int. Conf. Automatic Face and Gesture Recognition, pp. 746–752 (2011)
7. Kim, S., Valente, F., Vinciarelli, A.: Automatic detection of conflicts in spoken conversations: Ratings and analysis of broadcast political debates. In: Proc. 2012 IEEE Int. Conf. Audio, Speech and Signal Processing (2012)

---

[2] http://youtu.be/yC9wrOA3RB0

8. Kim, S., Yella, S.H., Valente, F.: Automatic detection of conflict escalation in spoken conversation. In: Proc. 13th Annual Conf. International Speech Communication Association (2012)

9. Jayagopi, D., Hung, H., Yeo, C., Gatica-Perez, D.: Modeling dominance in group conversations from non-verbal activity cues. IEEE Trans. Audio, Speech and Language Processing **17**(3), 501–513 (2009)

10. Wrede, D., Shriberg, E.: Spotting hotspots in meetings: Human judgments and prosodic cues. In: Proc. Eurospeech, pp. 2805–2808 (2003)

11. Black, M., Katsamanis, A., Lee, C.C., Lammert, A., Baucom, B., Christensen, A., Georgiou, P., Narayanan, S.: Automatic classification of married couples' behavior using audio features. In: Proc. InterSpeech (2010)

12. Pianesi, F., Mana, N., Cappelletti, A., Lepri, B., Zancanaro, M.: Multimodal recognition of personality traits in social interactions. In: Proc. 2008 Int. Conf. Multimodal Interfaces, pp. 253–260 (2008)

13. Levine, J.M., Moreland, R.L.: Small groups. Oxford University Press (1998)

14. Bousmalis, K., Mehu, M., Pantic, M.: Towards the automatic detection of spontaneous agreement and disagreement based on non-verbal behaviour: A survey of related cues, databases, and tools. Image and Vision Computing Journal **31**(2), 203–221 (2013)

15. M. Galley, K. McKeown, J.H., Shriberg, E.: Identifying agreement and disagreement in conversational speech: use of bayesian networks to model pragmatic dependencies. In: Proc. Meeting Association for Computational Linguistics, pp. 669–676 (2004)

16. Germesin, S., Wilson, T.: Agreement detection in multiparty conversation. In: Proc. Int. Conf. Multimodal Interfaces, pp. 7–14 (2009)

17. Hahn, S., Ladner, R., Ostendorf, M.: Agreement/disagreement classification: Exploiting unlabeled data using contrast classifiers. In: Proc. Human Language Technology Conf. of the NAACL, pp. 53–56 (2006)

18. Nicolaou, M.A., Pavlovic, V., Pantic, M.: Dynamic probabilistic cca for analysis of affective behaviour. In: Proc. 12th European Conference on Computer Vision, Florence, Italy, pp. 98–111, October 2012

19. Cooper, V.W.: Participant and observer attribution of affect in interpersonal conflict: an examination of noncontent verbal behavior. J. Nonverbal Behavior 10(2), 134–144 (1986)

20. Chang, C.C., Lin, C.J.: LIBSVM: A library for support vector machines. ACM Trans. Intell. Syst. Technol. **2**(3), 1–27 (2011)

21. Zhang, L., Yang, M., Feng, X.: Sparse representation or collaborative representation: Which helps face recognition? In: Proc. 2011 Int. Conference on Computer Vision, Washington, DC, USA, pp. 471–478 (2011)

22. Paul, B.: Accurate short-term analysis of the fundamental frequency and the harmonics-to-noise ratio of a sampled sound. In: Proc. of the Institute of Phonetic Sciences, pp. 97–110 (1993)

23. Mueller, M., Ellis, D., Klapuri, A., Richard, G.: Signal processing for music analysis. IEEE J. Sel. Topics in Sig. Process. 5(6), 1088–1110 (2011)

24. Tzimiropoulos, G., Alabort, J., Zaferiou, S., Pantic, M.: Generic active appearance models revisited. In: Proc. 11th Asian Conf. Computer Vision (2012)

25. Viola, P., Jones, M.J.: Robust real-time face detection. Int. J. Computer Vision **57**(2), 137–154 (2004)

Analysing User Visual Implicit Feedback in Enhanced TV Scenarios

Ioan Marius Bilasco[1], Adel Lablack[1](✉), Afifa Dahmane[1,2],
and Taner Danisman[1]

[1] Laboratoire d'Informatique Fondamentale de Lille, Université de Lille 1,
Villeneuve-d'Ascq, France
[2] Université des Sciences et Technologies Houari Boumediene, Algiers, Algeria
{marius.bilasco,adel.lablack,afifa.dahmane,taner.danisman}@lifl.fr

Abstract. In this paper, we report on user behaviors by analyzing visual clues while users are watching various TV broadcast in pilot settings. We detail the first results of the empathic analysis of viewers watching four distinct videos in dedicated recording sessions. Viewers are sitting in front of a TV set in unconstrained position (free postures, free head poses and free body movements) on a chair and recorded by a regular webcam at both low and high resolutions. We have extracted metrics related to: head and global movement, changes in head orientation and facial expressions (happy, angry, surprise). We have conducted preliminary studies about how the extracted metrics can be employed in order to detect the interest, the amusement or the distraction of a viewer.

Keywords: Facial expressions · Emotions · Moods · Global body movement · Head pose

1 Introduction

The explosion of available multimedia contents makes interesting the study of the behavior of users while they are accessing to these contents on their computers, tablets or smartphones. Thus, the use of webcams when the user is facing his access device allows identifying visual cues and constitute an implicit visual feedback in response to the access of multimedia content.

A lot of research is performed into systems that are able to offer a personalized content stream to media consumers taking into account user preferences and context. In order to offer a content suggestions experience to a user in a natural way, the sensed mood and state of mind of the user should be captured in real time. Thus, the user's bodily and behavioral reactions should be translated to indicators using reliable motion/emotion assessment techniques in order to propose an empathic system that incorporate the end-user behavior, reactions and responses to provide content.

The analysis of the user visual implicit feedback in enhanced TV scenarios to understand and respond to user intentions and emotions could improve the experience. It is performed using a set of metrics extracted from non-verbal cues such as facial expressions, body posture, head and hand gestures. Unfortunately, the

© Springer International Publishing Switzerland 2015
L. Agapito et al. (Eds.): ECCV 2014 Workshops, Part I, LNCS 8925, pp. 315–324, 2015.
DOI: 10.1007/978-3-319-16178-5_22

current available datasets might not generalize well to the real world situations in which such systems would be used [7].

2   Related Work and Background

Advancements in TV technology bring new interfaces and functionalities such as in smart and connected TVs. It allows people to watch various programs such as sports games, reality shows, movies, etc. This experience could be improved by taking into account the user visual implicit feedback. Most of the proposed systems focus on the recognition of emotional state of the user to trigger actions to enhance the user experience. In order to develop a video summarization tool, Joho et al. [5] have proposed an approach to detect personal highlights in video contents based on the analysis of facial activities of the viewer. Their analysis suggests that the motion vectors in the upper part of human face are more likely to be indicative of personal highlights than the lower part of the face. Abadi et al. [1] describes a multimodal approach to detect viewers' engagement through psychophysiological affective signals. This study aims to understand which channels and combinations thereof are effective for detecting a viewer's level of engagement. They notice that EEG and GSR responses seem to contribute similarly to the engagement classification task under study; moreover, Facial Motion features seem to provide complementary information and the psychophysiological features employed to assess the viewers' state of engagement seem to indicate high inter-subject variability. Soleymani et al. [9] have shown the feasibility of an approach to recognize emotion in response to videos. They have proposed a user-independent emotion recognition method using participants' EEG signals, gaze distance and pupillary response as affective feedbacks. Hanjalic and Xu [3] introduced "personalized content delivery" as a valuable tool in affective indexing and retrieval systems by selecting video and audio content features based on their relation to the valence-arousal space that was defined as an affect model.

Nowadays, there is a move away from the automatic inference of the basic emotions proposed by Ekman towards the inference of complex mental states such as attitudes, cognitive states, and intentions. This shift to incorporate complex mental states alongside basic emotions is necessary to build affect sensitive systems as part of an empathic technology. There is also a move towards analyzing natural expressions rather than posed ones since the Action Unit amplitudes and timings differ in spontaneous and acted expressions. These differences imply that recognition results reported on systems trained and tested on acted expressions could not be generalized to spontaneous ones. We focus on approaches used to analyze the behavior of people through an analysis of their mood which is generally highly correlated with their facial expressions and body movement in spontaneous expressions datasets.

3   Pilot Settings

We start by presenting the pilot settings since our analysis has been conducted according to these specific settings. Our Pilot videos have been recorded using regular cameras placed at the bottom of a TV screen which is distant from the user at approximately 2m. People sitting on a chair are following 4 fragments from "Everybody's Famous" series broadcasted by VRT. The fragments correspond to stories having different primary-intents (adrenaline: jumping in wingsuit, compassion and interest: prime minister's confidences, amusement: easter bunny, neutral: pupils on a school trip). The Figure 1 shows some screenshots from the video recorded as well as the overview of the scenario timing.

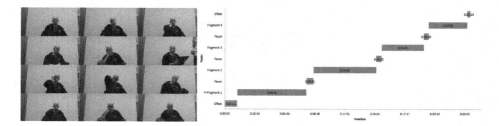

Fig. 1. Screenshots of a user watching TV and interacting during the recording session vs Video fragments and timeline in the recording sessions

During the pilot phase, we have captured 43 complete captures having an average of 22 minutes per session. We have recorded 37 high resolution videos (960 × 540) where the average face size is 107px and 6 in low resolution videos (320 × 240) where the average face size is 47px. The users were not instructed about how they should behave in order to be collaborative with the capturing system. They were informed that the capturing devices are on and that they will have to look at the TV and fill in a questionnaire at the end.

Hence, in the pilot analysis we are facing to big challenges : small faces and natural face and body poses as illustrated in Figure 1. The fact that the users were not especially collaborative yields to numerous occlusions (hand, hair) but also high pitch in faces orientation. In order to deal with these conditions we have selected a mix of local and global analysis solutions that track face expressions, but also movements. The analyzers are detailed in the following section.

4   The Architecture of the Analyzer

We present in Figure 2 an overview of the complete analyzing process. The first part of the process consists of locating the user within the scene and extracting basic information about the body and the face. At this point, we characterize the inner face movements and the global movements by exploring difference images and studying optical flow. Once the face is detected, we study the eyes region and extract specific eye movement patterns. The eye position is further used in order to normalize the face and estimating head orientation. We estimate metrics related to the level of interest and the positive (happy) / negative (anger) emotions in presence of frontal faces with limited pitch and pan, and eventually

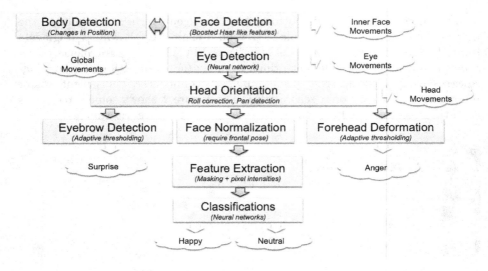

Fig. 2. Global architecture of the system

specific occlusions. We use continuous characterization for surprise and anger, and a discrete classifier for happy detection.

In the following, we detail the different metrics that we have extracted from the video streams. These metrics are then used to infer viewers mood that are actionable in a TV scenario.

4.1   Movement Based Analysis

This section evaluates the changes in the position and the global movements of the person. We take advantage of the scene configuration and we consider that globally all changes (except noise due to subtle illumination changes) reflect the user activity. However, we have reinforce the area of the study, by taking into account the head position (in case of a successful detection of face and/or eyes) in focusing the area of study in the neighboring regions (below and on sides). All metrics are normalized with regard to the region considered : whole image vs delimited region with regard to the head position.

We consider that there is a strong link between the generated metrics and the arousal of the person. However, we have to differentiate where the person keeps interest in viewing the TV (moving and still watching the TV set) or his engaged in actions not related to this activity (peeking up the tablet). Hence, in presence of body movements and the presence of continuous eye detection, we might infer that the person presents an arousal directly linked to the quantity of movement in the scene. Whereas in situations where the person lost eye contact with the screen (leaning forward for picking up the tablet), the body metric might not be directly correlated with the arousal metric.

In Figure 3, we present (on a scale of one to 100) the global body movement for a person while watching the second (on the left) and the third (on the right) segment of a viewing session.

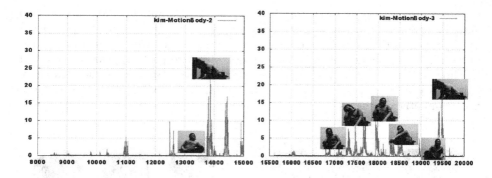

Fig. 3. Global movement analysis for the 2nd and 3rd segments

4.2   Preliminary Study on Face and Eye Detection

Considering the pilot conditions, most of the time the person is staying in the middle of the image. The spatial region containing the face can be inferred from the settings as well as personal characteristics. However, in order to have a more precise localization, we are using face detector from state of the art, such as, Boosted Haar classifiers. This kind of classifiers presents some drawbacks since they support only a limited set of head-poses and fail in case of strong occlusions. With the knowledge that the user is watching the video fragments, each frame of the video contains a single face and the absence of a detected face is a sign for either non supported head-poses (e.g. looking somewhere else) or partial occlusions. However, in order to distinguish between these two situations, we introduced a face tracker enhanced with eye location information.

As soon as a first face is detected, we use a dedicated neural network to detect the eye positions. In presence of small faces, we artificially increase their size to perform eye detection on high resolution images. Mean-shift trackers are then registered for each eye. In case of face lost, we take advantage of the tracked eye position in the following frames to infer the facial region. We have chosen the usage of eye tracker as eye regions are more specific with regard to the whole face and mean-shift trackers are more appropriate for this selection. In order to guarantee the coherency of the eye tracker, we observe the evolutions in terms of the Inter Pupillary Distance (IPD) and the associated roll angle. We also use this information in order to compute the position of a non-detected eye with regard to the position of the detected eye and the previous known IPD and roll angle values. When the regular face detector produces valid detections, the eye trackers are updated accordingly. This procedure allowed us to largely improve the face detection rate on the entire pilot data. We still keep the information about the faces missed by the regular face detector as an indicator of the user interest with the regard to the content.

Detected faces are then processed in order to analyze the head pose. We are using the eye positions in order to infer the roll. Then the roll is used in order to put the face in up-right position. On the latter image, we exploit the bilateral symmetry of the face in order to infer the yaw orientation class. We use the size and the orientation of the symmetrical area of the face to estimate yaw poses by the mean of Decision Tree model. As illustrated in Figure 4, when the face is in front of the camera, the symmetry between its two parts appears clearly and the line which passes between the two eyes and nose tip defines the symmetry axis. However, when the head performs a motion, for example, a yaw motion, this symmetry decreases.

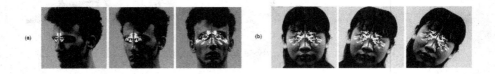

Fig. 4. (a) Variations in the size of the symmetrical region during yaw movement. (b) Variation in the angle of the symmetry axis during roll movement.

This approach doesn't require the location of interest points on the face and is robust to partial occlusions. The estimated pose is coarse but sufficient to infer general gaze direction. Symmetrical region is defined by analyzing pixels intensity. The intensity of one pixel on the right side of the face is more similar to its mirror pixel than another pixel in the image. An experiment has been conducted in [2] which indicate that the use of facial symmetry as a geometrical indicator for head pose is still reliable when local geometric features (such as eyes, nose or mouth) are missed due to occlusions or wrong detections.

At this stage, we are collecting the following information: is face detected or tracked? Are eyes detected or tracked? As well as, their positions and relative changes, is the face frontal or not? This latter information is used afterwards in order to guide and adapt the face expression analysis process, by filtering non frontal faces.

4.3   Face Expression Analysis

Our approach regardless of the emotion that we are seeking is divided into two stages. The first one consists in the different processing steps that allow extracting a normalized face from the input data. The second one consists in locating selected ROI from the face region and applying a specific filtering to each region to indicate the presence of an anger or surprise emotions, while happy emotion is extracted using a neural network.

Image Pre-Processing
This is an important step that aims to obtain images that have normalized intensity, are uniform in size and shape, and depict only the face region.

- Face and eye detection : As presented in the preliminary study of the face and eye detection, we have used the Boosted Haar like features method proposed by Viola and Jones [10] to detect the face. Then a neural network based approach is used to locate the positions of pupils. We derive only the eye detection code from the STASM library [8] which is variation of Active Shape Model of Coote's implementation that performs better on frontal upright faces with neutral expressions.
- Up-right face : We estimate the orientation of the face using the vertical positions of the two eyes and/or the facial symmetry. If the eyes are not in the same position, we compute the angle between these two pupil points and correct the orientation by setting the face center as origin point and we rotate the whole frame in opposite direction.
- Face normalization : We use histogram equalization to normalize image intensity by improving its contrast. It aims to eliminate light and illumination related defects from the facial area.

Emotion Extraction

Happiness detection is considered as a two-class classification problem where happiness is the positive class and the neutral is the negative class. We used MPLab GENKI-4K [4] dataset as a training set for happy/neutral classification. We used lower part of the normalized face which maximizes the accuracy for this particular classification problem. A backpropagation neural network having two hidden layers (20 and 15 neurons) used to train pixel intensity values obtained from the selected ROI. Input layer has 200 neurons and output layer has two neurons representing the happy and neutral classes.

In order to detect anger emotion, we focus on the ROI located in the upper part of the face and include the variations of AU4 of FACS where eyebrows are lowered and drawn together [6]. We apply Gabor filter to this region of face. In the literature, 2D Gabor filters have been used for texture analysis and classification. Gabor filters have both frequency and orientation selective properties. Therefore a 2D Gabor function is composed of a sinusoidal wave of specified radial frequency which is the spacing factor between the kernels in the frequency domain and orientation which is modulated by a 2D Gaussian. Gabor representation of a face image is computed by convolving the face image I (x, y) with the Gabor filter. Majority of AUs samples associated to anger emotion face images has vertical lines above the nasal root. So, we choose vertical orientation for the Gabor filter with a frequency of $\sqrt{1.3}$, Mu equal to 0, σ equal to π and Nu equal to 3 as Gabor parameters. Then real and imaginary responses are added together to find the magnitude response. After a binary thresholding, the sum of the total pixels in the magnitude response of the filter, just above the nasal root is examined by a threshold value to detect a negative emotion. Brighter pixels in the magnitude responses are used as an indicator of anger.

We use the same kind of approach used for anger detection to detect the emotion surprise. An adaptive thresholding is applied in the region of the face that includes the AU1 and AU2 to detect eyebrows movements.

5   Towards Inferring Viewers Moods

From a TV producer point of view, the scope of the analysis is not on measuring only the primary emotions expressed by the user, but also on moods that are actionable [11]. The primary emotion might be closely linked to the content (smile when watching a funny scene, disgust or fear when watching an horror scene) and not to the level of immersion of the user in the viewing experience. The moods targeted in this study are: bored, amused and interested. These moods were considered interesting since in their presence actions might be trigger in order to enhance the user experience. In presence of interest a complementary content could be proposed to the user. In presence of amusement an equivalent content might be proposed in order to keep the person active in watching. In presence of a bored user, the content presented might be changed by proposing to the user alternative contents.

We have tried to elaborate ad-hoc hypothesis for characterizing the mood of a user while watching a content that could convey various emotions (joy, sadness, etc.). We are lacking training corpuses for this context, as the annotation part is subjective and hard to collect. In addition, we are not able to leave the charge of recognizing moods to classifiers and other implicit solutions. In this work, we have proposed some explicit measurements that can be extracted and adapted to specific scenario requirements. These hypothesis were constructed taking into account the behavior exhibited by the user, as well, as the subjective evaluation of the content and the viewing experience done by the viewer itself at the end of the pilot.

In the following, we detail the hypothesis used for each of the moods and illustrate them using crossed-metrics situations where the moods addressed might be encountered. The common consideration of this entire hypothesis is that more importance is given to the global behavior of the user reflected by movement metrics. It allows to characterize the fact that the user is actively involved (amused, interest, frustrated) or passive (bored) in the experience. Then, we use the detected emotions to distinguish between moods having a similar level of involvement. For instance, bored persons (lacking of interest) might be subject to more frequent changes in the head pose (pan, pitch) and limited frontal poses as they might use secondary devices and often look aside. The global movement metric might be an indicator of whether we are in the presence of an active person to whom an alternative content might be proposed to get his attention.

High global movement metric, is not necessary a sign of lack of interest. For instance, in segment 3 (presented in Figure 5 - 17500 to 18500), the viewer moves a lot, but he maintains the eye contact with the TV. On the contrary, in the latter part of the segment (when he bends down for the tablet), we are in the presence of high movement metric, but the face and eye contact are lost frequently over an important time lapse denoting the lack of interest for the content displayed on the TV. In presence of viewer involvement, we explore the occurrences of positive expressions on the viewer face. We estimate that frequent occurrences with frequent movements are sign of amusement, whether the interest is signified by more calm viewing patterns although positive occurrences might arise.

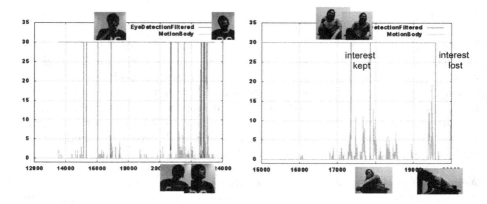

Fig. 5. Crossed Global movement and Eye Detection metrics to measure interests

In Figure 6, we present metrics measured over fragment 2 (left) and fragment 3 (right). In fragment 3 (frames 17500 to 18500), we can observe that the high arousal corresponds to frequent body movement (leaning forward and backward, covering face with hands, etc.), as well as, large intervals where the person is happy, can be considered as strong sign of amusement. The extracted metrics corresponding to segment 2 show moreover a calm viewing pattern, except the last part which corresponds to the person bending and taking the tablet. From time to time, the viewer exhibits some positive expressions sign of enjoyment of the content. For this latter case, the valence is not of major importance since we can observe the same pattern during negative experiences. What we underline here is the fact that in presence of calm viewing patterns, the observation of significant expressions distributed over time can reinforce the perceived interest.

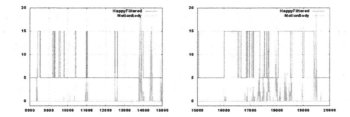

Fig. 6. Crossed Global movement metric and Happy detections to measure amusement

These hypothesis are applied to the pilot data by considering moving frame-windows. Mean values for various metrics are taken into account for the cross-metric analysis. For detecting amusement settings, we reinforce the analysis by considering the density of happy detection over larger time intervals.

6 Conclusion

In this paper, we have proposed ad-hoc metrics and rules for detecting action-able moods in a TV viewing scenario. We have employed both local and global approaches to deal with small resolutions, natural poses and occlusions. An anno-tation of the whole pilot corpus is performed in order to validate the inferring moods process, as well as, the precision of the proposed metrics. Further on, we will investigate deeply the fuzzy nature of the analyzers inputs in the inferring process. We have already made a first step in this direction by filtering faces that seem inappropriate for happy classification purposes.

Acknowledgments. This work was conducted in the context of the ITEA2 "Empathic Products" project, ITEA2 1105, and is supported by funding from the French Services, Industry and Competitivity General Direction.

References

1. Abadi, M.K., Staiano, J., Cappelletti, A., Zancanaro, M., Sebe, N.: Multimodal engagement classification for affective cinema. In: 5th Conference on Affective Computing and Intelligent Interaction (ACII) (2013)
2. Dahmane, A., Larabi, S., Djeraba, C., Bilasco, I.M.: Learning symmetrical model for head pose estimation. In: 21st International Conference on Pattern Recognition (ICPR), pp. 3614–3617 (2012)
3. Hanjalic, A., Li-Qun, X.: Affective video content representation and modeling. IEEE Transaction on Multimedia **7**(1), 143–154 (2005)
4. The MPLab GENKI Database, GENKI-4K Subset (2011)
5. Joho, H., Staiano, J., Sebe, N., Jose, J.M.: Looking at the viewer: analysing facial activity to detect personal highlights of multimedia contents. Multimedia Tools and Applications (MTAP) **51**(2), 505–523 (2011)
6. Lablack, A., Danisman, T., Bilasco, I.M., Djeraba, C.: A local approach for nega-tive emotion detection. In: 22nd International Conference on Pattern Recognition (ICPR) (2014)
7. Mahmoud, M., Baltrušaitis, T., Robinson, P., Riek, L.D.: 3D Corpus of Sponta-neous Complex Mental States. In: D'Mello, S., Graesser, A., Schuller, B., Martin, J.-C. (eds.) ACII 2011, Part I. LNCS, vol. 6974, pp. 205–214. Springer, Heidelberg (2011)
8. Milborrow, S., Nicolls, F.: Locating Facial Features with an Extended Active Shape Model. In: Forsyth, D., Torr, P., Zisserman, A. (eds.) ECCV 2008, Part IV. LNCS, vol. 5305, pp. 504–513. Springer, Heidelberg (2008)
9. Soleymani, M., Pantic, M., Pun, T.: Multimodal emotion recognition in response to videos. IEEE Transactions on Affective Computing (TAC) **3**(2), 211–223 (2012)
10. Viola, P., Jones, M.J.: Rapid object detection using a boosted cascade of simple features. In: International Conference on Computer Vision and Pattern Recognition (CVPR) (2001)
11. Willaert, K., Matton, M.: Empathic media personalization based on actionable moods. In: 1st Workshop on Empathic Television Experiences (EmpaTeX) (2014)

Micro-Expression Recognition Using Robust Principal Component Analysis and Local Spatiotemporal Directional Features

Su-Jing Wang[1,4](✉), Wen-Jing Yan[1,2], Guoying Zhao[3], Xiaolan Fu[1], and Chun-Guang Zhou[4]

[1] State Key Lab of Brain and Cognitive Science, Institute of Psychology, Chinese Academy of Sciences, Beijing 100101, China
{wangsujing,yanwj,fuxl}@psych.ac.cn
[2] College of Teacher Education, Wenzhou University, Wenzhou, China
[3] Center for Machine Vision Research, University of Oulu, Oulu, Finland
gyzhao@ee.oulu.fi
[4] College of Computer Science and Technology, Jilin University, Changchun 130012, China
cgzhou@jlu.edu.cn

Abstract. One of important cues of deception detection is micro-expression. It has three characteristics: short duration, low intensity and usually local movements. These characteristics imply that micro-expression is sparse. In this paper, we use the sparse part of Robust PCA (RPCA) to extract the subtle motion information of micro-expression. The local texture features of the information are extracted by Local Spatiotemporal Directional Features (LSTD). In order to extract more effective local features, 16 Regions of Interest (ROIs) are assigned based on the Facial Action Coding System (FACS). The experimental results on two micro-expression databases show the proposed method gain better performance. Moreover, the proposed method may further be used to extract other subtle motion information (such as lip-reading, the human pulse, and micro-gesture etc.) from video.

Keywords: Micro-expression recognition · Sparse representation · Dynamic features · Local binary pattern · Subtle motion extraction

1 Introduction

In our social life, deception is a reality. Its detection can be beneficial, not only to an individual but also to the whole society. Currently, the most widely used system is the polygraph which monitors uncontrolled changes in heart rate and electro-dermal response, as a result of the subject's arousal to deceit [12]. However, the polygraph is an overt system, which makes people realize that they are being monitored. As a result, some people may trick the machine by employing some anti-polygraph techniques, such as remaining calm and controlling their heart rate.

© Springer International Publishing Switzerland 2015
L. Agapito et al. (Eds.): ECCV 2014 Workshops, Part I, LNCS 8925, pp. 325–338, 2015.
DOI: 10.1007/978-3-319-16178-5_23

The recent studies [22][11][6][5] show that micro-expression can reveal an emotion that a person tries to conceal, especially in high-stake situations. Therefore, micro-expression might be treated as an effective cue for deception detection [5]. Compared with ordinary facial expressions, micro-expressions have three significant characteristics: short duration, low intensity and usually local movements (fragments of prototypical facial expressions).

Because of these characteristics, human beings are difficult to detect and recognize micro-expression. In order to improve the human's performance on recognizing micro-expression, Ekman [4] developed the Micro-Expression Training Tool (METT), which trains people to better recognize micro-expression. To better apply micro-expression as a cue to detect deception in practice, computer scientists try to train the computer to automatically recognize micro-expression.

Hitherto, there are just several papers on micro-expression recognition. Polikovsky *et al.* [16] used 3D-gradient descriptor for micro-expressions recognition. Wang *et al.* [19] treated a gray-scale video clip of micro-expression as a 3rd-order tensor and used Discriminant Tensor Subspace Analysis (DTSA) and Extreme Learning Machine (ELM) to recognize micro-expression. Pfister *et al.* [15] utilized a temporal interpolation model (TIM) [25] based on Laplacian matrix to normalize the frame numbers of micro-expression video clips. In addition, the LBP-TOP [23] was used to extract the motion and appearance features of micro-expressions and multiple kernel learning was used to classify the features.

We emphasize again the two important characteristics of micro-expression: short duration and low intensity, which makes that the micro-expression data are sparse in both temporal and spatial domains. The key problem is how to extract the sparse information. In this paper, the sparse information are extracted by Robust PCA (RPCA) [20]. RPCA is widely used for face recognition [18], video frame interpolation [2], brain imaging [8] and EEG signal processing [17] etc. RPCA leverage on the fact that the data are characterized by low-rank subspaces [3]. It decomposes the observed data matrix $\mathbf{D}$ into two parts:

$$\mathbf{D} = \mathbf{A} + \mathbf{E} \tag{1}$$

where $\mathbf{A}$ lies in a subspace of low rank and $\mathbf{E}$ is the error term. In many applications of RPCA, $\mathbf{A}$ is the deserved data and $\mathbf{E}$ is usually treated as noise and removed. In this paper, however, $\mathbf{E}$ includes the deserved subtle motion information of micro-expression. In the following, we use Local Spatiotemporal Directional Features (LSTD) [24] to extract local dynamic texture features of the subtle facial motion information from 16 Regions of Interest (ROIs) based on the Facial Action Coding System (FACS).

2   Extraction of Motion Information

In a micro-expression video clip, the subtle facial motion information is discriminant for recognizing micro-expression. Other information, such as identity information, is not useful for micro-expression recognition. This information accounts for the great proportion of whole information in a clip. Relatively, the subtle facial motion information is *sparse*. We aim to extract this sparse information.

Given a gray video clip $\mathcal{V} \in \mathbb{R}^{h \times w \times f}$ with h pixels height, w pixels width, and f frames. Each of its frame is vectorized as a column of matrix $\mathbf{D}$ with $h \times w$ rows and f columns. $\mathbf{D}$ consists of two parts: $\mathbf{D} = \mathbf{A} + \mathbf{E}$. Each column of $\mathbf{A}$ is the same with each other as possible. $\mathbf{E}$ includes the derived sparse subtle motion information. This may be formulated as follows:

$$\min_{\mathbf{A},\mathbf{E}} rank(\mathbf{A}) + \|\mathbf{E}\|_0 \qquad \text{subject to} \qquad \mathbf{D} = \mathbf{A} + \mathbf{E} \qquad (2)$$

where $rank(\cdot)$ denotes the rank of matrix and $\| \cdot \|_0$ denotes ℓ_0-norm, which counts the number of nonzero entries. This is a non-convex problem. RPCA [20] converted Eq.(2) into the following convex optimization problem:

$$\min_{\mathbf{A},\mathbf{E}} \|\mathbf{A}\|_* + \lambda \|\mathbf{E}\|_1 \qquad \text{subject to} \qquad \mathbf{D} = \mathbf{A} + \mathbf{E} \qquad (3)$$

where $\| \cdot \|_*$ denotes the nuclear norm, which is the sum of its singular values, and $\| \cdot \|_1$ denotes ℓ_1-norm, which is the sum of the absolute values of matrix entries. λ is a positive weighting parameter.

Eq.(3) involves minimizing a combination of both the ℓ_1-norm and the nuclear norm. In [20], the iterative thresholding technique is used. However, the iterative thresholding scheme converges extremely slowly. It can not be used to deal with the large-scale micro-expression video clips. Lin *et al.* [10] applied the method of augmented Lagrange multipliers (ALM) to solve Eq.(3) and improved the efficiency by more than five times of those in [20]. ALM is introduced for solving the following constrained optimization problem:

$$\min f(X) \qquad \text{subject to} \qquad h(X) = 0 \qquad (4)$$

where $f : \mathbb{R}^n \to \mathbb{R}$ and $h : \mathbb{R}^n \to \mathbb{R}^m$. The augmented Lagrangian function can be defined as follows:

$$L(X, Y, \mu) = f(X) + \langle Y, h(X) \rangle + \frac{\mu}{2} \|h(X)\|_F^2 \qquad (5)$$

Let X be $(\mathbf{A}, \mathbf{E})$, $f(X)$ be $\|\mathbf{A}\|_* + \lambda \|\mathbf{E}\|_1$, and $h(X)$ be $\mathbf{D} - \mathbf{A} - \mathbf{E}$. Eq. (5) is re-written:

$$L(\mathbf{A}, \mathbf{E}, Y, \mu) = \|\mathbf{A}\|_* + \lambda \|\mathbf{E}\|_1 + \langle Y, \mathbf{D} - \mathbf{A} - \mathbf{E} \rangle + \frac{\mu}{2} \|\mathbf{D} - \mathbf{A} - \mathbf{E}\|_F^2 \qquad (6)$$

In [10], Lin *et al.* proposed two algorithms: exact ALM and inexact ALM. A slight improvement over the exact ALM leads to the inexact ALM, which converges practically as fast as the exact ALM, but the required number of partial SVDs is significantly less. Here, we chose inexact ALM to extract the subtle facial motion information.

Fig. 1 shows several frames (Figs.1(a)-1(e)) of an micro-expression video clip and its corresponding subtle motion frames (Figs.1(f)-1(j)) of $\mathbf{E}$. It is difficult

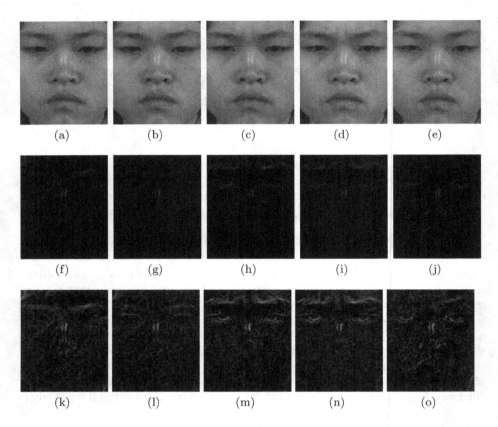

Fig. 1. An examples of extracting the subtle facial motion information. (a)-(e)indicate the original micro-expression frames sequence; (f)-(j)indicate the extracted subtle facial motion information; (k)-(o) indicates the enhanced display for (f)-(j) by multiplying each pixels with 4 (Considering some monitors may not well display the subtle facial motion information since the maximum gray value of (f)-(j) is less than 40)

for people to detect the subtle facial movement from Figs.1(a)-1(e). However, it is easy to detect the movement of eyebrows from Figs.1(f)-1(j). Moreover, there is very little identity information in Figs.1(f)-1(j). This may further improve subsequent classification accuracy.

It should be noticed that the frame numbers of micro-expression video clips are not the same. This leads to different sparse results for micro-expression with different frame numbers when setting the same λ. In order to address the problem, the frame numbers of all video clips are normalized by using linear interpolation.

3 Local Spatiotemporal Directional Features

In this section, we use Local Spatiotemporal Directional Features (LSTD) [24] to extract dynamic texture features of the subtle facial motion information. LSTD is built on the basis of the local binary pattern (LBP) [13].

In order to extract spatiotemporal texture, the local binary pattern from three orthogonal planes (LBP-TOP) [23] was proposed. With this approach the ordinary LBP for static images was extended to spatiotemporal domain. The LBP-TOP were developed for facial expression recognition [23] and micro-expression recognition [15].

Comparing with LBP-TOP, LSTD can extract more detailed spatiotemporal directional changes. In XY plane, there are mainly X and Y directions. Likewise, in XT and YT planes, there are X (Y) and T directions. The motion information changes in each direction further contributes to micro-expression recognition.

Fig. 2 shows a subtle motion video got in previous section and its images from the three planes. For each plane, we code it from two directions. Given a pixel, we can obtain a 3×3 neighboring area around it in each plane. For each row (column), a binary code is produced by thresholding its neighborhood with the value of the center pixel in this row (column). Fig. 2 shows the calculation for the X direction and Y direction in XY plane. Similarly, we can obtain the X direction and T direction in XT plane and Y direction and T direction in YT plane.

For each central pixel, we can get eight neighboring points and in total nine points in the calculation. The sampling distance of each direction can be changed. Fig. 3 shows that the sampling radius in X direction is three, the radius in Y direction is two, and the radius in T direction is four. So we can set R_x, R_y, and R_t with different values to represent the sampling radii in three directions. Then we could obtain $P_0, P_1, \ldots, P_8$ corresponding to, e.g. $I(x_c - R_x, y_c - R_y, t_c)$, $I(x_c, y_c - R_y, t_c)$, $I(x_c + Rx, y_c - Ry, tc)$, $I(x_c - Rx, y_c, t_c)$, $I(x_c, y_c, t_c)$, $I(x_c + R_x, y_c, t_c)$, $I(x_c - R_x, y_c + R_y, t_c)$, $I(x_c, y_c + R_y, t_c)$, $I(x_c + R_x, y_c + R_y, t_c)$ in XY plane, where R_x and R_y are sampling radii in X direction and Y direction, respectively. Similarly we can have R_t as sampling radius in T direction of XT and YT planes. From this area the local spatial-temporal feature is calculated for central pixel $P_4 = I(x_c, y_c, t_c)$.

The obtained neighboring area can be formulated as a 3×3 matrix

$$\mathbf{F} = \begin{bmatrix} P_0 & P_1 & P_2 \\ P_3 & P_4 & P_5 \\ P_6 & P_7 & P_8 \end{bmatrix} \tag{7}$$

We left-multiply $\mathbf{F}$ by $\mathbf{W}_l$:

$$\mathbf{W}_l = \begin{bmatrix} 1 & -1 & 0 \\ 0 & -1 & 1 \end{bmatrix}, \tag{8}$$

and obtain

$$\mathbf{W}_l\mathbf{F} = \begin{bmatrix} 1 & -1 & 0 \\ 0 & -1 & 1 \end{bmatrix} \begin{bmatrix} P_0 & P_1 & P_2 \\ P_3 & P_4 & P_5 \\ P_6 & P_7 & P_8 \end{bmatrix} = \begin{bmatrix} P_0 - P_3 & P_1 - P_4 & P_2 - P_5 \\ P_6 - P_3 & P_7 - P_4 & P_8 - P_5 \end{bmatrix}. \tag{9}$$

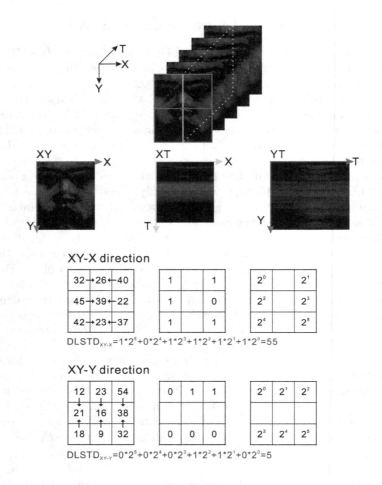

Fig. 2. Illustration of Local Spatiotemporal Directional Features

Here, we denote every entries of the obtained 2×3 matrix as

$$\begin{bmatrix} b_0 & b_1 & b_2 \\ b_3 & b_4 & b_5 \end{bmatrix}. \tag{10}$$

If the neighboring area matrix $\mathbf{F}$ comes from the XY plane, the code of LSTD in the $XY - Y$ direction is calculated by:

$$LSTD = \sum_{n=0}^{5} sign(b_n)2^n \tag{11}$$

where $sign(b)$ is 1 if $b \geq 0$ and 0 otherwise. Similarly, we can obtain the codes of LSTD in the $XT - T$ and $YT - Y$ directions.

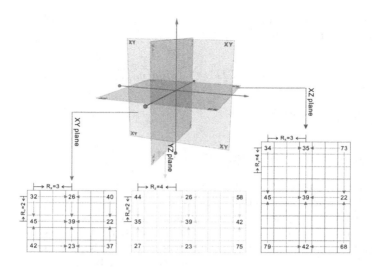

Fig. 3. Sampling in three planes with radius three in X direction, radius two in Y direction, and radius four in T direction

We right-multiply $\mathbf{F}$ by $\mathbf{W}_r$:

$$\mathbf{W}_r = \begin{bmatrix} 1 & 0 \\ -1 & -1 \\ 0 & 1 \end{bmatrix}, \tag{12}$$

we have

$$\mathbf{FW}_r = \begin{bmatrix} P_0 & P_1 & P_2 \\ P_3 & P_4 & P_5 \\ P_6 & P_7 & P_8 \end{bmatrix} \begin{bmatrix} 1 & 0 \\ -1 & -1 \\ 0 & 1 \end{bmatrix} = \begin{bmatrix} P_0 - P_1 & P_2 - P_1 \\ P_3 - P_4 & P_5 - P_4 \\ P_6 - P_7 & P_8 - P_7 \end{bmatrix}. \tag{13}$$

Here, we denote every entries of the obtained 3×2 matrix as

$$\begin{bmatrix} b_0 & b_1 \\ b_2 & b_3 \\ b_4 & b_5 \end{bmatrix}. \tag{14}$$

If the neighboring area matrix $\mathbf{F}$ comes from the XY plane, the code of LSTD in the $XY - X$ direction is calculated by Eq. (11). Similarly, we obtain the codes of LSTD in the $XT - X$ and $YT - T$ directions. Through the procedures above, six directions have been encoded. Since the coefficients of these directions are correlated, the coefficients should be decorrelated before quantization [14].

Assuming Gaussian distribution, independence can be achieved using a whitening transform:

$$\mathbf{g} = \mathbf{V}^T \begin{bmatrix} b_0 & b_1 & b_2 & b_3 & b_4 & b_5 \end{bmatrix}^T \tag{15}$$

where $\mathbf{V}$ is an orthonormal matrix derived from the Singular Value Decomposition (SVD) of the covariance matrix of the transform coefficient vector $\mathbf{b}$

and $\mathbf{V}$ can be solved in advance. For details, please refer to [14]. The code of Decorrelated LSTD (DLSTD) is calculated by:

$$DLSTD = \sum_{n=0}^{5} sign(g_n)2^n \tag{16}$$

where g_n are the elements of $\mathbf{g}$.

4   Action Unit and Region of Interest

For each micro-expression video clip $\mathcal{V} \in \mathbb{R}^{h \times w \times f}$ with h pixels height, w pixels width, and f frames, we used RPCA to extract its subtle motion information $\mathbf{E}$. The matrix $\mathbf{E}$ is reshaped as a 3 dimensional array $\mathcal{E} \in \mathbb{R}^{h \times w \times f}$. LSTD is used on $\mathcal{E}$ to extract texture feature. Similar to LBP, LSTD is also based on local texture feature. With LSTD, the object has to be divided into patches. For each patch, six directional histograms are calculated by LSTD. In this paper, we divided a face image into 16 Regions of Interest (ROIs) based on the Facial Action Coding System (FACS) [7]. Each ROI is a patch.

FACS is an objective method for quantifying facial movement based on a combination of 57 elementary components. These elementary components, known as action units (AUs) and action descriptors (ADs), can be seen as the *phonemes* of facial expressions: words are temporal combinations of phonemes. Similar to facial expressions, micro-expressions are spatial combinations of AUs. Each AU depicts a local facial movement. We selected a frontal neutral facial image as the template face and divided the template face into 16 ROIs. These ROIs do not exactly correspond to the AUs. Since there are overlaps between some AUs, the ROIs were modified to be more independent between each other.

The template face is used not only to draw ROIs but also to avoid the large variations in the spatial appearance of micro-expressions. All faces were normalized to a template face. First, the template face is marked with 68 landmarks ψ_M by using the Active Shape Model (ASM) [1]. Second, the first frame of a sample micro-expression clip was marked 68 landmarks ψ_{f1}, and estimated the 2D geometric transformation of the template face as $\psi_M = T\psi_{f1}$, where T is the transformation matrix. Third, the remaining frames are registered to the template face by applying the transformation T. Because there is little head movement in the video clip, the transformation T can be used to all the frames in the same video clip. The sizes of each frame of samples are normalized to 163×134 pixels.

Fig. 4 shows the template face, the 16 ROIs and their corresponding AUs. Fox example, ROI R_1 (or R_2) corresponds to AU1 and AU4 which represent the movements of inner eyebrows. Table 1 lists the 16 ROIs, the corresponding AUs and the facial movements. The ROIs are drawn to exclude some noises such as the nose tip and the eye ball movement.

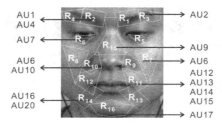

Fig. 4. The template face and 16 ROIs

5 Experiments

5.1 SMIC

Spontaneous MIcro-expression Corpus(SMIC) [9] consists of 164 samples from 16 participants. These micro-expressions were elicited by emotional video episodes in a lab situation, with the resolution of 640×480 pixels. SMIC includes 3 data sets: HS (recorded by a high speed camera), VIS (recorded by a normal visual camera), and NIR (recorded by a near-infrared camera). In the experiments, we use HS data set, which consists of 164 samples. These samples are labeled into 3 classes: positive (51 samples), negative (70 samples) and surprise (43 samples). Positive indicates happiness, while negative may include disgust, fear, sadness and anger. Fig. 5 illustrates an example from SMIC.

The frame numbers of all samples are normalized to 60 by using linear interpolation. The size of each frame is normalized to 163×134 pixels. Thus, each sample was normalized to a three dimensional array with the size of $163 \times 134 \times 60$. We used the leave-one-subject-out cross-validation in the experiments.

We conduct LBP-TOP, LSTD, and DLSTD on the micro-expression videos and the corresponding sparse subtle motion videos. When we use Eq.(3) to obtain

Table 1. ROIs, the corresponding AUs and the facial movements

ROIs	AUs	Facial Movements
R_1, R_2	AU1, AU4	inner eyebrows
R_3, R_4	AU2	outer eyebrows
R_5, R_6	AU7	lower eyelid
R_7, R_8	AU6	cheeks
R_9, R_{10}	AU6, AU10	side of the nose
R_{11}, R_{12}	AU12, AU13, AU14, AU15	mouth corner
R_{13}, R_{14}	AU16, AU20	side of the chin
R_{15}	AU9	nose root
R_{16}	AU17	chin

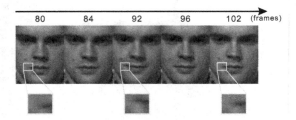

Fig. 5. A demonstration of the frame sequence in a micro-expression from SMIC. The apex frame presents at about 92 frames. The AUs for this micro-expression is 12. The three rectangles below the images show the lip corners (AU 12) in *zoom in* mode.

the sparse parts **E**, the parameter λ is set as 0.0017. For LBP-TOP, the number of neighboring points in the XY, XT and YT planes were all set as 4. The radius in axes X and Y were assigned various values from 1 to 4. To avoid too much combinations of parameters, we made $R_x = R_y$ and denoted as R_{xy}. The radii in axes T was assigned various values from 2 to 4. The results are listed in Table 2.

Table 2. Micro-expression recognition accuracies (%) of LBP-TOP, LSTD, and DLSTD on SMIC. +V means the algorithm is conducted on the original micro-expression videos. +S means the algorithm is conducted on the sparse subtle motion videos.

R_{xy}	R_t	LBP-TOP+V	LBP-TOP+S	LSTD+V	LSTD+S	DLSTD+V	DLSTD+S
	2	**67.0732**	54.8780	64.0244	52.4390	60.3659	55.4878
1	3	65.2439	53.0488	**71.3415**	53.0488	60.3659	57.3171
	4	63.4146	56.7073	**65.8537**	57.3171	60.3659	62.1951
	2	60.9756	**61.5854**	54.8780	58.5366	59.7561	60.3659
2	3	57.3171	59.7561	59.7561	59.7561	61.5854	**64.6341**
	4	61.5854	61.5854	57.3171	57.3171	60.9756	**67.6829**
	2	62.1951	59.7561	60.3659	63.4146	59.1463	**64.6341**
3	3	60.9756	61.5854	62.8049	62.8049	59.7561	**66.4634**
	4	60.9756	64.0244	60.9756	62.8049	59.7561	**67.6829**
	2	57.9268	**65.2439**	61.5854	64.0244	58.5366	63.4146
4	3	62.1951	**67.6829**	66.4634	65.2439	59.7561	67.0732
	4	59.7561	64.0244	64.0244	68.2927	59.7561	**68.2927**

In most cases, the algorithms on the sparse subtle motion videos overperform those on original videos. However, the performance of algorithms on the micro-expression videos are better than those on sparse videos when $R_{xy} = 1$. In other cases. This result may stem from the fact that there exists flickering light (because of the frame rate of the camera is higher than the frequency of the alternative current) in video samples in SMIC. From the table, we can also see

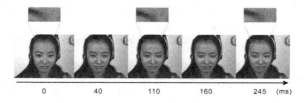

Fig. 6. A demonstration of the frame sequence in a micro-expression from CASME 2. The apex frame presents at about 110 ms. The AUs for this micro-expression is 4+9 (with AU 17 kept almost unchanged), which indicates disgust. The three rectangles above the images show the right inner brow (AU 4) in *zoom in* mode.

that the DLSTD on the sparse subtle motion videos has the best performance in many cases. The reason is that DLSTD decorrelates the coefficients of codes. The combination of the decorrelated codes gets better performance.

5.2   CASME 2

The CASME 2 [21] database includes 246 spontaneous facial micro-expressions recorded by a 200 fps camera. These samples were selected from more than 2,500 facial expressions. Compared with SMIC, the database is improved in increased sample size, fixed illumination, and higher resolution (both temporal and spatial). The selected micro-expressions in this database either had a total duration less than 500 ms or an onset duration (time from onset frame to apex frame) less than 250 ms. These samples are coded with the onset and offset frames, as well as tagged with AUs and emotions. Fig. 6 is an example. There are 5 classes of the micro-expressions in this database: happiness (32 samples), surprise (25 samples), disgust (60 samples), repression (27 samples) and tense (102 samples).

In these samples, the frame number of the shortest sample is 24 and that of the longest sample is 146. The frame numbers of all samples are normalized to 150 by using linear interpolation. The size of each frame is normalized to 163×134 pixels. So, each sample was normalized to a three dimensional array with the size of $163 \times 134 \times 150$. The parameter λ is set as 0.00095. Other experimental sets are the same with SMIC. The results are listed in Table 3.

From the table, we can see that the algorithms on the the sparse subtle motion videos obtain the best performance in every cases but $R_{xy} = 3$ and $R_t = 4$. In CASME 2, the illumination is fixed. So the 'sparse' processing can have a better effect. Moreover, this processing removes the identify information, which is considered noise for micro-expression recognition. From the table, we can also see that (D)LSTD is better than LBP-TOP. This also shows the code of six directions is better than the code of three planes.

Table 3. Micro-expression recognition accuracies (%) of LBP-TOP, LSTD, and DLSTD on CASME 2. +V means the algorithm is conducted on the original micro-expression videos. +S means the algorithm is conducted on the sparse subtle motion videos.

R_{xy}	R_t	LBP-TOP+V	LBP-TOP+S	LSTD+V	LSTD+S	DLSTD+V	DLSTD+S
	2	49.5935	55.2846	50.8130	58.5366	54.4715	**62.1951**
1	3	53.2520	**60.9756**	51.2195	57.7236	56.0976	**60.9756**
	4	54.4715	60.5691	52.4390	**60.9756**	56.0976	59.7561
	2	55.6911	59.3496	53.2520	59.7561	58.5366	**63.0081**
2	3	57.3171	**60.9756**	56.9106	56.5041	59.7561	60.1626
	4	58.1301	55.6911	56.5041	56.0976	60.5691	**63.0081**
	2	53.2520	59.3496	52.4390	60.9756	61.7886	**63.0081**
3	3	52.4390	60.5691	53.2520	60.9756	60.9756	**63.4146**
	4	52.8455	58.9431	53.6585	58.5366	**60.9756**	60.5691
	2	52.8455	57.7236	55.2846	**63.8211**	58.5366	62.1951
4	3	53.2520	61.3821	53.2520	**63.8211**	57.7236	63.4146
	4	54.8780	59.7561	53.6585	**65.4472**	58.5366	65.0407

6   Conclusions

In this paper, the subtle facial movement information of micro-expression is extracted by RPCA. RPCA decomposes the observed data into two parts: a low rank part and a sparse part. In general, the low rank part is the deserved data and the sparse part is considered as the error or noise and is removed. In this paper, however, we remove the low rank part consisting of the identity information and reserve the sparse part consisting of the the subtle facial movement information. Following, LSTD is used extracted the texture feature from 16 ROIs based on FACS. The results on two micro-expression databases show the proposed method get better performance.

In the further work, we will apply the proposed method on the subtle motion (such as lip-reading, the human pulse, and micro-gesture etc.) detection in surveillance.

Acknowledgments. This work was supported in part by grants from 973 Program (2011CB302201), the National Natural Science Foundation of China (61379095, 61375009, 61175023, 61472138), China Postdoctoral Science Foundation funded project (2012M520428, 2014T70133), the Beijing Natural Science Foundation (4152055), the Open Projects Program of National Laboratory of Pattern Recognition (201306295), the open project program (93K172013K04) of Key Laboratory of Symbolic Computation and Knowledge Engineering of Ministry of Education, Jilin University, and the Academy of Finland, and Infotech Oulu.

References

1. Cootes, T.F., Taylor, C.J., Cooper, D.H., Graham, J.: Active shape models-their training and application. Computer vision and image understanding **61**(1), 38–59 (1995)
2. Dao, M., Suo, Y., Chin, S., Tran, T.: Video frame interpolation via weighted robust principal component analysis. In: 2013 IEEE International Conference on Acoustics, Speech and Signal Processing (ICASSP), pp. 1404–1408. IEEE (2013)
3. Eckart, C., Young, G.: The approximation of one matrix by another of lower rank. Psychometrika **1**(3), 211–218 (1936)
4. Ekman, P.: Microexpression training tool (METT). University of California, San Francisco (2002)
5. Ekman, P.: Lie catching and microexpressions. The philosophy of deception pp. 118–133 (2009)
6. Ekman, P., Friesen, W.: Nonverbal leakage and clues to deception. Tech. rep, DTIC Document (1969)
7. Ekman, P., Friesen, W.V.: Facial action coding system: A technique for the measurement of facial movement, vol. 12. Consulting Psychologists Press, CA (1978)
8. Georgieva, P., De la Torre, F.: Robust principal component analysis for brain imaging. In: Mladenov, V., Koprinkova-Hristova, P., Palm, G., Villa, A.E.P., Appollini, B., Kasabov, N. (eds.) ICANN 2013. LNCS, vol. 8131, pp. 288–295. Springer, Heidelberg (2013)
9. Li, X., Pfister, T., Huang, X., Zhao, G., Pietikäinen, M.: A spontaneous micro-expression database: inducement, collection and baseline. In: IEEE International Conference on Automatic Face and Gesture Recognition and Workshops (2013)
10. Lin, Z., Liu, R., Su, Z.: Linearized alternating direction method with adaptive penalty for low-rank representation. In: Neural Information Processing Systems (NIPS) (2011)
11. Matsumoto, D., Hwang, H.: Evidence for training the ability to read microexpressions of emotion. Motivation and Emotion **35**(2), 181–191 (2011)
12. Michael, N., Dilsizian, M., Metaxas, D., Burgoon, J.K.: Motion profiles for deception detection using visual cues. In: Daniilidis, K., Maragos, P., Paragios, N. (eds.) ECCV 2010, Part VI. LNCS, vol. 6316, pp. 462–475. Springer, Heidelberg (2010)
13. Ojala, T., Pietikainen, M., Maenpaa, T.: Multiresolution gray-scale and rotation invariant texture classification with local binary patterns. IEEE Transactions on Pattern Analysis and Machine Intelligence **24**(7), 971–987 (2002)
14. Ojansivu, V., Heikkilä, J.: Blur Insensitive Texture Classification Using Local Phase Quantization. In: Elmoataz, A., Lezoray, O., Nouboud, F., Mammass, D. (eds.) ICISP 2008 2008. LNCS, vol. 5099, pp. 236–243. Springer, Heidelberg (2008)
15. Pfister, T., Li, X., Zhao, G., Pietikainen, M.: Recognising spontaneous facial micro-expressions. In: 12th IEEE International Conference on Computer Vision. pp. 1449–1456. IEEE (2011)
16. Polikovsky, S., Kameda, Y., Ohta, Y.: Facial micro-expressions recognition using high speed camera and 3D-gradient descriptor. In: 3rd International Conference on Crime Detection and Prevention. pp. 1–6. IET (2009)
17. Shi, L.C., Duan, R.N., Lu, B.L.: A robust principal component analysis algorithm for eeg-based vigilance estimation. In: 2013 35th Annual International Conference of the IEEE Engineering in Medicine and Biology Society (EMBC), pp. 6623–6626. IEEE (2013)

18. Wang, L., Cheng, H.: Robust principal component analysis for sparse face recognition. In: 2013 Fourth International Conference on Intelligent Control and Information Processing (ICICIP), pp. 171–176. IEEE (2013)
19. Wang, S.J., Chen, H.L., Yan, W.J., Chen, Y.H., Fu, X.: Face recognition and microexpression based on discriminant tensor subspace analysis plus extreme learning machine. Neural Processing Letters 39(1), 25–43 (2014)
20. Wright, J., Ganesh, A., Rao, S., Peng, Y., Ma, Y.: Robust principal component analysis: exact recovery of corrupted low-rank matrices via convex optimization. In: Advances in neural information processing systems, pp. 2080–2088 (2009)
21. Yan, W.J., Li, X., Wang, S.J., Zhao, G., Liu, Y.J., Chen, Y.H., Fu, X.: CASME II: An improved spontaneous micro-expression database and the baseline evaluation. PLoS ONE 9(1), e86041 (2014)
22. Yan, W.J., Wu, Q., Liang, J., Chen, Y.H., Fu, X.: How fast are the leaked facial expressions: The duration of micro-expressions. Journal of Nonverbal Behavior, pp. 1–14 (2013)
23. Zhao, G., Pietikainen, M.: Dynamic texture recognition using local binary patterns with an application to facial expressions. IEEE Transactions on Pattern Analysis and Machine Intelligence 29(6), 915–928 (2007)
24. Zhao, G., Pietikäinen, M.: Visual speaker identification with spatiotemporal directional features. In: Kamel, M., Campilho, A. (eds.) ICIAR 2013. LNCS, vol. 7950, pp. 1–10. Springer, Heidelberg (2013)
25. Zhou, Z., Zhao, G., Pietikainen, M.: Towards a practical lipreading system. In: 2011 IEEE Conference on Computer Vision and Pattern Recognition (CVPR), pp. 137–144. IEEE (2011)

W04 - Consumer Depth Cameras for Computer Vision

Exploiting Pose Information
for Gait Recognition from Depth Streams

Pratik Chattopadhyay[1]([✉]), Shamik Sural[1], and Jayanta Mukherjee[2]

[1] School of Information Technology, IIT Kharagpur, Kharagpur, India
{pratikc,shamik}@sit.iitkgp.ernet.in
[2] Department of Computer Science and Engineering, IIT Kharagpur,
Kharagpur, India
jay@cse.iitkgp.ernet.in

Abstract. A key-pose based gait recognition approach is proposed that utilizes the depth streams from Kinect. Narrow corridor-like places, such as the entry/ exit points of a security zone, are best suited for its application. Alignment of frontal silhouette sequences is done using coordinate system transformation, followed by a three dimensional voxel volume construction, from which an equivalent fronto-parallel silhouette is generated. A set of fronto-parallel view silhouettes is, henceforth, utilized in deriving a number of key poses. Next, correspondences between the frames of an input sequence and the set of derived key poses are determined using a sequence alignment algorithm. Finally, a gait feature is constructed from each key pose taking into account only those pixels that undergo significant position variation with respect to the silhouette center. Extensive evaluation on a test dataset demonstrates the potential applicability of the proposed method in real-life scenarios.

Keywords: Gait recognition · Depth camera · Key pose · Incomplete cycle sequences · Variance image

1 Introduction

Constant monitoring of subjects and identification of suspects are essential activities for providing public security inside crowded security zones. Human recognition using biometric identification mechanisms like finger print detection and iris scan cannot be employed in these congested places, since these methods require close interaction with subjects. Face recognition is also not convenient in such a scenario because highly detailed texture information in face images might be missing in surveillance videos, as they are usually captured from a distance. Gait is the only biometric which can possibly be applied to identify suspects in these congested security areas. Till date, a number of computer vision based gait recognition algorithms, corresponding to both the fronto-parallel [1–4] as well as the frontal views [5,6] have been developed, each of which has been shown to work effectively with low resolution gait video sequences.

© Springer International Publishing Switzerland 2015
L. Agapito et al. (Eds.): ECCV 2014 Workshops, Part I, LNCS 8925, pp. 341–355, 2015.
DOI: 10.1007/978-3-319-16178-5_24

Although it is known that gait video from the fronto-parallel view captures significant information about an individual's gait [7], in real-life, it is possible to encounter situations where surveillance needs to be carried out in narrow corridor-like places, such as the entry/ exit points of security zones. Due to the constricted field of view of a surveillance camera placed within a narrow region, it might not be able to capture sufficient number of frames of a walking sequence required for analyzing the gait characteristics of the concerned subject. On the other hand, a relatively higher percentage of frames can be recorded if the camera is positioned in a way so as to capture walking videos from the front view.

However, a drawback associated with frontal gait recognition is that, information about the important fronto-parallel component of gait [7] cannot be obtained from the silhouettes captured by an RGB camera from the frontal view. It appears that a substantial fronto-parallel information of the gait of a silhouette can be extracted even from the frontal view if the knowledge about its three dimensional pose is available. Gait videos collected using a depth camera like Microsoft Kinect [8] seems to be beneficial in this aspect. In this paper, we propose to carry out gait recognition using Kinect as a surveillance camera. The gait recognition scenario considered here is shown in Fig. 1. With reference to

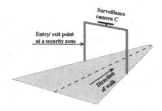

Fig. 1. Camera setup for gait recognition in a narrow security zone

the figure, the Kinect (C), used as a surveillance camera is installed at a certain height above a narrow pathway. As a subject walks through the pathway along the direction shown in the figure, C captures the depth information of the gait of the subject from the front view. This depth information is, henceforth, utilized in deriving an effective gait feature which preserves significant fronto-parallel information. Experimental results on an extensive dataset proves the efficacy of the proposed method in real-life scenarios.

The rest of the paper is organized as follows. Section 2 provides a brief background study on the recent research trend in frontal gait recognition using depth information. Construction of the gait feature and human recognition using the derived feature is explained in Section 3. A detailed description of the dataset along with experimental results is presented in Section 4. Section 5 concludes the paper and points out future scope of work.

2   Literature Survey

Early gait recognition approaches [1–4] use gait videos captured by RGB cameras and focus mostly on the fronto-parallel view of gait. Development of depth cameras like Kinect [8] has resulted in shifting of focus towards frontal gait recognition using depth information [5,6,9–11]. Among the existing depth cameras, Kinect [8], developed by Microsoft, has gained significant popularity in human tracking based research, primarily because of the useful human detection and skeleton tracking application [12] provided by the Kinect SDK. In the recent past, Kinect has been extensively used in deriving interesting frontal gait features that make use of both the skeleton streams [9–11] and the depth streams [5,6] obtained from its SDK. Each of these techniques has shown promising results, but a few assumptions inherent in these methods limit their applicability in real-life scenarios.

In [9], a gait feature using the skeleton joint coordinates is proposed by Kumar et al., in which the covariance of each joint trajectory over a complete gait cycle is used in recognition. Milovanovi et al., in [10], describe a recognition scheme where skeleton data of a gait cycle is mapped from the spatial domain to the spatio-temporal domain and content-based image retrieval techniques are applied for feature construction. Both these methods have been shown to work satisfactorily in the presence of complete gait cycles, but their performance in the absence of full cycle information is unclear. Chattopadhyay et al. propose a frontal gait recognition approach in [11], where a complete gait cycle is divided into a fixed number of key poses derived from the skeleton structure provided by Kinect SDK. The gait cycle partitioning scheme, as proposed in this work, has been shown to outperform [9] as well as a traditional binary silhouette based gait recognition scheme, namely, the technique using Gait Energy Image (GEI) [1]. Although gait recognition methods using the skeleton streams from Kinect have significantly fast response time, their effectiveness depends on the accuracy of the skeleton joints tracked by the SDK. Also, lack of complete silhouette shape/ depth information, because of using only the skeleton streams from Kinect, might have a negative impact on the accuracy of gait recognition.

Only a few approaches use solely the depth streams from Kinect to derive frontal gait features [5,6,13]. Hofmann et al. describe a gait recognition procedure in [13], where gradient histograms computed from the depth frames of a fronto-parallel view gait sequence are averaged over a gait cycle. The results presented in this work show that the use of depth information helps in achieving a higher recognition rate than GEI [1]. However, since no significant depth variation occurs in the fronto-parallel view gait sequences, it is unclear if the use of depth information has significant benefits for gait recognition from this view. The work by Sivapalan et al. in [5] provides an effective means of utilizing the depth streams from Kinect in carrying out gait recognition from the frontal view. The feature proposed in [5] is termed as Gait Energy Volume (GEV). It is derived by averaging the voxel volumes constructed from the corresponding point cloud sequences captured by Kinect over an entire gait cycle. But, as also explained in [2], such averaged information lacks intrinsic kinematic details about the gait of a subject. Hence, GEV fails to perform satisfactorily, if there exist a number of corrupted/ noisy silhouettes in the sequence, or if the Kinect fails to capture at least one complete gait cycle of the walking subject.

To overcome the limitations of GEV, a pose based feature termed as Pose Depth Volume (PDV) was proposed by Chattopadhyay et al. in [6]. Here, noisy depth silhouettes are initially smoothed by registering each depth frame with the corresponding RGB frame. PDV helps in preserving the dynamic component of gait at a higher resolution than GEV because the feature is derived at the granularity of key poses. However, the expensive voxel level computation in PDV and also the requirement of at least a complete gait cycle for its satisfactory performance, make it impractical for use in real-life situations.

It appears from the algorithms proposed in [2] (PEI) and [6] (PDV) that, carrying out gait recognition at the granularity of key poses significantly enhances the efficacy of recognition. This motivates us in proposing a key pose based gait recognition approach in order to carry out recognition in the scenario considered in the present paper (refer to Section 1, Fig. 1). In contrast to the existing frontal gait recognition techniques, the proposed method effectively preserves the important gait information corresponding to the fronto-parallel view by making use of the three dimensional depth information of the silhouette points provided by Kinect. Moreover, recognition from complete gait cycle information as considered in each of the techniques given in ([1,2,5,6,9–11]) cannot be regarded as a practical solution. Such constraint on the minimum length of a gait cycle is potentially eradicated in the present paper by carrying out subject identification using only the available key poses in a given sequence. This adds a higher degree of pertinency to the proposed approach as compared to the state-of-the-art gait recognition techniques in application sites similar to Fig. 1. The main contributions of the paper can be summarized as follows:

- Development of a frontal gait recognition technique when number of training samples is few and also when unconstrained data are captured with no restriction on the minimum length of the gait cycle,
- derivation of equivalent fronto-parallel view silhouettes by utilizing the depth information of the frontal surface of silhouettes recorded by Kinect and extraction of gait features from these silhouettes, thereby, preserving important gait information, and
- extensive experimental evaluation emphasizing the effectiveness of the proposed approach.

3   Proposed Approach

As described in Section 1, we propose a key pose based frontal gait recognition approach using Kinect captured datasets. Surveillance cameras inside a security zone, are usually mounted at a certain height facing downwards. The gait recognition scenario described in Section 1 also takes into account of a similar Kinect camera setup. Hence, the point cloud of a walking subject as captured by the

Kinect is inclined with respect to the Kinect coordinate system. The recognition procedure must be made invariant to the tilt angle since this angle may vary from one surveillance site to another.

3.1 Alignment of Silhouette Sequence and Construction of Voxel Volumes

Invariance to the camera tilt angle is achieved by applying a set of geometric transformation operations on each point cloud and also by aligning it with respect to a fixed coordinate system. The alignment operation is explained with the help of Fig. 2.

Coordinate System Transformation. The objective of this alignment procedure is to obtain an upright silhouette point cloud that will be perpendicular to the viewing direction. To achieve this, we determine transformed point cloud coordinates with respect to a different coordinate system (say, X', Y', Z'), such that, the $X'Y'$ plane of this coordinate system is parallel to the direction of orientation of the point cloud, and the Z' axis is along a direction normal to this plane. Without loss of generality, we consider that the origins of the Kinect coordinate system and the (X', Y', Z') coordinate system coincide. As seen

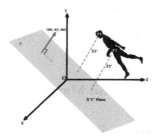

Fig. 2. Coordinate system transformation for silhouette alignment

in Fig. 2, initially linear regression [14] of the set of object points present in the Kinect captured point cloud is used in determining a plane $\mathcal{P}$ that passes through the origin of the Kinect coordinate system, and is closely parallel to the direction of alignment of the point cloud. Corresponding to each object point P_i with coordinates (X_i, Y_i, Z_i) (measured in the Kinect coordinate system), we determine its transformed coordinates P'_i (X'_i, Y'_i, Z'_i) with respect to the (X', Y', Z') coordinate system. Let the unit normal vector to the plane $\mathcal{P}$ constructed from the point set be given by (nx, ny, nz) (as shown in Fig. 2). If the equation of this plane is given by $Z = AX + BY$, the coordinates of P'_i in the (X', Y', Z') coordinate system are computed as follows:

$$Z_i' = \frac{AX_i + BY_i - Z_i}{\sqrt{A^2 + B^2 + 1}}, \quad X_i' = X_i - (Z_i')(nx), \quad Y_i' = Y_i - (Z_i')(ny).$$

$$(1)$$

Thus, the $X'Y'$ plane in the new $(X'Y'Z')$ coordinate system is actually the plane $\mathcal{P}$.

Volumetric Reconstruction from Point Cloud. The proposed key pose estimation and gait recognition procedures, as described in Sections 3.2 and 3.3, respectively, require the point cloud to be mapped to a three dimensional voxel volume V. This makes it convenient to extract the relevant features by raster scanning the three dimensional volume along the width, height and depth dimensions. The volume is constructed by mapping the (X', Y', Z') coordinates of each object point present in the aligned point cloud into appropriate voxel positions within the volume. Suppose, M, N, P, respectively represent the dimensions of the voxel volume V along its width, height and depth directions. Also, let $\mathcal{M}_x$ and m_x respectively denote the maximum and minimum X' coordinates of the object points present in the aligned point cloud. Similar notations are used to denote the magnitudes of the maximum and minimum object point coordinates corresponding to the Y' and Z' directions of the transformed coordinate system. The mapped coordinates $(X_{i_v}', Y_{i_v}', Z_{i_v}')$ within the volume corresponding to the ith object point (X_i', Y_i', Z_i') is then computed as:

$$X_{i_v}' = \frac{X_i' - m_x}{\mathcal{M}_x - m_x}(M-1), \, Y_{i_v}' = \frac{Y_i' - m_y}{\mathcal{M}_y - m_y}(N-1), \, Z_{i_v}' = \frac{Z_i' - m_z}{\mathcal{M}_z - m_z}(P-1).$$

$$(2)$$

Fig. 3(a) shows the plot of a three dimensional voxel volume constructed from an aligned point cloud.

3.2   Extraction of Key Poses and Mapping of a Gait Sequence into Key Poses

A sequence of key poses represents a human gait cycle [2,6,11] (refer to Fig. 5). A sufficiently large number of walking sequences would help in accurate estimation of these key poses. Here, we describe a procedure for deriving a fixed number (K) of key poses from the gait sequences of a large number of subjects. The voxel volume V consists of either object voxels or non-object voxels. Let us suppose that each of the object voxels has been assigned a value of '1', whereas, each non-object voxel is assigned a value of '0'. Since, the depth information provided by Kinect is inherently noisy, V also contains a significant amount of noise, as seen in Fig. 3(a). Deriving meaningful features for key pose extraction requires an effective mechanism for smoothing the noisy volume.

Distance transform [15] labels each voxel within a binary volume with the Euclidean distance to the nearest object pixel. In the present context, for smoothing the volume V, we use a variant of the distance transform operator. Suppose d_{max} is the maximum value within the distance transformed volume. Then the value assigned to a non-object voxel having a distance transformed value of d is $(1 - \frac{d}{d_{max}})$.

On application of the above operation, the value assigned to each non-object voxel in V lies within the range $(0, 1)$, so that a value closer to '1' indicates a smaller magnitude of d. On the other hand, the same value (i.e., '1') is retained corresponding to each of the object voxels. In addition to preserving the shape information, this step can effectively fill up all the noisy regions/ holes within the 3D aligned silhouette, thereby smoothing the volume. This helps in the extraction of robust features for key pose estimation as well as gait recognition, even if incorrect alignment occurs after the application of the alignment operation described in Section 3.1 due to noisy data. However, if the magnitude of d is high enough, then the voxel value in V is not altered. Fig. 3(b) shows the re-assigned values within the voxel volume V after applying the above noise removal procedure on Fig. 3(a).

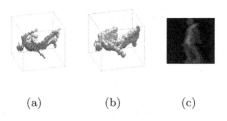

(a)   (b)   (c)

Fig. 3. (a) Aligned point cloud of a silhouette (b) Point cloud after noise removal and voxel filling (c) Average silhouette of the noise-free point cloud on the $Y'Z'$ plane

Since fronto-parallel view of gait contains the most informative gait features [7], we construct an equivalent fronto-parallel view silhouette frame using the depth information of the frontal surface of each silhouette captured by the Kinect. It is apparent from the above discussion that the $Y'Z'$ plane of the volume V provides information about the fronto-parallel view of a silhouette. In the present context, we propose to extract the feature vector for deriving key poses using a set of two dimensional silhouettes on the $Y'Z'$ plane. Each pixel within a two dimensional silhouette on the $Y'Z'$ plane is assigned a value equal to the mean of the values of all the voxel points whose projection on the $Y'Z'$ plane gets mapped to this pixel. Thus, if $(X'_{i_v}, Y'_{i_v}, Z'_{i_v})$ denotes the coordinates of a voxel point in the volume V and if $\mathcal{I}_{Y'Z'}$ denotes the projected frame on the $Y'Z'$ plane, then, the value assigned to the pixel (Y'_j, Z'_j) in the projected frame is given by:

$$\mathcal{I}_{Y'Z'}(Y'_j, Z'_j) = \frac{1}{M} \sum_{k=1}^{M} V(X'_{k_v}, Y'_{j_k}, Z'_{j_k}). \tag{3}$$

The silhouette thus obtained on the $Y'Z'$ plane after application of the above averaging operation is termed as the average silhouette. The average silhouette on the $Y'Z'$ plane derived from the point cloud of Fig. 3(b) is shown in Fig. 3(c).

The cluster centers obtained after clustering the silhouette sequence $\mathcal{I}_{Y'Z'}$ on the $Y'Z'$ plane are termed as the key poses in a gait cycle. In contrast to [2], where only binary silhouette sequences were used for key pose generation, the proposed method effectively captures the shape information of the fronto-parallel view as well as some dimensional information of the body parts corresponding to the frontal view. The value of K used in K-Means clustering is next determined from a rate distortion plot shown in Fig. 4. The plot shows the average distortion

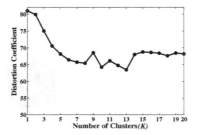

Fig. 4. Rate distortion curve for determining the appropriate number of key poses

of the clustering operation as a function of the number of key poses. The distortion coefficient is plotted as the sum of the Euclidean distances between each silhouette sequence vector $\mathcal{I}_{Y'Z'}$ from its nearest cluster center. It is seen from the figure that the curve attains a minimum value for $K = 13$ and remains stable after $K = 14$. Hence, selecting the value of K as 13 seems to be a good choice for the estimation of key poses. Fig. 5 shows the thirteen representative key poses in a gait cycle obtained after the application of constrained K-Means clustering on the fronto-parallel view silhouettes on the $Y'Z'$ plane. Given an input silhouette sequence, a local sequence alignment procedure based on dynamic programming [16] is used to find correspondences between the frames of the sequence and the set of derived key poses. As an initial step, the alignment operation requires determination of a similarity score value [2] between a frame and each of the derived key poses, which is accomplished by computing the Euclidean distance

Fig. 5. Thirteen key poses derived for representing a gait cycle

between these two. The state transition information used in the alignment procedure can be stated as follows: if a certain frame of a sequence corresponds to a key pose k, then its succeeding frame must be mapped to either of key pose k or key pose $((k+1)$ modulo $K)$, $k = 1, 2, 3, ..., K$.

3.3 Extraction of Gait Feature

Similar to the feature vector construction procedure for determining the key poses (refer to Section 3.2), extraction of the gait features is again done by considering the average silhouettes on the $Y'Z'$ plane. It may be noted that all the pixels belonging to a silhouette on this plane do not convey significant information about the gait of a subject. In most of the existing gait recognition literature [1,2,6], principal component analysis is used to reduce the feature vector length by eliminating redundant feature attributes. But this requires computation of the eigen silhouettes [2] corresponding to each frame of the sequence, which is time intensive.

It appears that pre-determination of the set of pixel coordinates carrying useful gait information can expedite the recognition procedure. This is accomplished by making use a variance image constructed from the aligned silhouette sequences corresponding to a large number of subjects on the $Y'Z'$ plane. The variance image is derived by computing pixel-wise variances of these sets of aligned silhouettes and is shown in Fig. 6(a). It is to be noted that the variance image actually preserves useful information about those pixel locations within an aligned silhouette frame which undergo significant change during walking. As seen in this figure, many pixels within the variance image have negligible

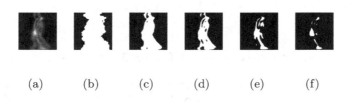

(a)   (b)   (c)   (d)   (e)   (f)

Fig. 6. (a) Variance image computed from the silhouette sequences of a large number of subjects (b), (c), (d), (e), and (f) Variance image binarization with $\beta = 0, 0.1, 0.2, 0.3,$ and 0.4, respectively

variance, indicating that the silhouette points corresponding to those locations do not undergo significant position variation with respect to the silhouette center during walking. It is evident that these pixels carry little gait information and leaving out these pixels during the gait feature vector construction does not adversely affect the accuracy of recognition. In order to select only a specific set of pixels with important gait information, we binarize the variance image using an experimentally determined threshold β, so that only pixels with variances greater than β are retained in the binarized image. Figs. 6(b), (c), (d), (e) and (f) show the binary images obtained after thresholding the variance image, where the β values are set to 0, 0.1, 0.2, 0.3 and 0.4, respectively. From the figure, it is seen that the silhouette shape information is preserved at a high resolution corresponding to β values of 0.1 and 0.2, and hence, features derived considering these values of β are expected to contain significant gait information. A β value of 0 provides useful gait information along with redundant information to a certain degree. However, β values greater than 0.2 misses pixels (or elements) with significant gait information and should not be considered for gait analysis. We denote this β thresholded binary image by $\mathcal{I}_\beta$.

Given an input silhouette sequence, and the mapping of each of its frames to the appropriate key poses, we next extract a gait feature vector corresponding to each of the K key poses. The final gait feature is the concatenation of the feature vectors derived for each key pose. Consider a total of $\mathcal{N}$ subjects in the dataset and suppose l frames, starting with frame index t up to frame index $t + l - 1$, namely, $F_{n,t}^k$, $F_{n,t+1}^k$, $F_{n,t+2}^k$, ..., $F_{n,t+l-1}^k$, of a gait sequence of the nth subject are mapped to a key pose k, where $n = 1, 2, 3, ..., \mathcal{N}$, and $k = 1, 2, 3, ..., K$. Let $\mathcal{F}_{n,t+j}^k$ denote the vector of the most informative pixel values extracted from the frame $F_{n,t+j}^k$, for each $j = 0, 1, 2, ..., l$-1. It may be noted that the vector $\mathcal{F}_{n,t+j}^k$ is constructed using information only from those pixel locations that undergo significant variation during walking, as depicted in $\mathcal{I}_\beta$. Thus, a lower value of β will cause $\mathcal{F}_{n,t+j}^k$ to have a higher dimension, and vice-versa.

Then, the gait feature vector $\mathcal{G}_n^k$ corresponding to the kth pose of the nth subject is derived as follows:

$$\mathcal{G}_n^k = \frac{1}{l} \sum_{j=0}^{l-1} \mathcal{F}_{n,t+j}^k, \quad n = 1, 2, 3, ..., \mathcal{N}, \quad k = 1, 2, 3, ..., K. \tag{4}$$

3.4 Recognition of a Test Subject Using the Proposed Feature

We denote the $\mathcal{N}$ subjects in the training set as S_1, S_2, S_3, ..., and $S_\mathcal{N}$. Let $\mathcal{G}_{n,tr}^k$ denote the feature vector corresponding to the kth pose of the nth training subject, where $n = 1, 2, 3, ..., \mathcal{N}$ and $k = 1, 2, 3, ..., K$. A similar notation $\mathcal{G}_{te}^k$ is used to denote the feature vector corresponding to the kth pose of an input test subject. For each of the $\mathcal{N}$ subjects in the training set, a measure of similarity is next computed which signifies the likelihood of the test subject to belong to the class of the current training subject. Suppose, out of the total number of K key poses, only p of them k_1, k_2, k_3, ..., k_p, are common for a given combination of training and test sequences. Initially, the feature vectors derived corresponding to this set of matching p key poses are concatenated to form a single vector. Thus, if $\mathcal{G}_{n,tr}$ and $\mathcal{G}_{te}$, respectively denote these concatenated feature vectors corresponding to the nth training subject and the given test subject, then:

$$\mathcal{G}_{n,tr} = [\mathcal{G}_{n,tr}^{k_1} \mathcal{G}_{n,tr}^{k_2} \mathcal{G}_{n,tr}^{k_3} ... \mathcal{G}_{n,tr}^{k_p}]^T \text{ and } \mathcal{G}_{te} = [\mathcal{G}_{te}^{k_1} \mathcal{G}_{te}^{k_2} \mathcal{G}_{te}^{k_3} ... \mathcal{G}_{te}^{k_p}]^T. \tag{5}$$

It is to be noted that each of $\mathcal{G}_{n,tr}$ and $\mathcal{G}_{te}$ might consist of missing attribute (null) values corresponding to the key poses those are absent in the training and the test sequences, respectively. Also reconstruction of the feature vectors by estimating these null attribute values is difficult because of the availability of insufficient number of sequences. Thus, the measure of similarity must be computed by comparing only the non-null attribute values common to both the vectors $\mathcal{G}_{n,tr}$ and $\mathcal{G}_{te}$. Since different pairs of training and test sequences will have different sets of non-null matching attributes, it is necessary to normalize the similarity metric to make it independent of the magnitudes of the individual attributes. The 'cosine' similarity metric is beneficial in such cases. The cosine similarity $\mathcal{D}_n$ between the vectors $\mathcal{G}_{n,tr}$ and $\mathcal{G}_{te}$ is computed as:

$$\mathcal{D}_n = 1 - cos(\alpha), \tag{6}$$

where, α is the angle included between the two vectors, given by:

$$\alpha = \frac{\mathcal{G}_{n,tr}^T \mathcal{G}_{te}}{||\mathcal{G}_{n,tr}||\,||\mathcal{G}_{te}||}. \tag{7}$$

The test subject is identified as S_r if:

$$\mathcal{D}_r \leq \mathcal{D}_n, \forall n = 1, 2, 3, ..., \mathcal{N}. \tag{8}$$

4   Experimental Evaluation

There is no existing database that provides the depth information of the gait of subjects using depth cameras like Kinect. Hence, to test the effectiveness of our approach, we construct a new dataset[1]. In the following sub-sections, we provide an elaborate description of the experimental setup, the testing protocol and, finally, an extensive evaluation of the proposed method using the captured dataset.

4.1   Dataset Description

A total of 29 subjects have been used in building our database. The experimental setup for recording both the training and the test sequences is made similar to the one shown in Fig. 1. A Kinect camera (K) in combination with the SDK provided by Microsoft is used for collecting the datasets. The camera is positioned at a height of 2.5 metres from the ground over a narrow pathway, facing downwards. The tilt angle of K is set to -23°. As a subject passes through this zone, the real-world X, Y and Z coordinates of the points on the frontal surface of the silhouette of each subject as tracked by K are recorded.

---

[1] Available on request.

For each subject, we record two distinct sequences *T1* and *T2*, which are used as training sets in our experiments. Test sets *T3* and *T4* for each subject are respectively collected under two different frame rates: 30 fps and 15 fps. Thus, in total, we have 116 distinct frontal sequences, containing four sequences corresponding to each subject. Due to a limitation on the maximum depth sensing range of Kinect, which is only 4 metres, many of these recorded sequences lack complete gait cycle information. Table 1 presents a statistics of the recorded training and test sets, showing the percentage of sequences that have missed k out of the K (= 13) key poses, $k = 1, 2, 3, ..., 13$.

Table 1. Percentage of key poses missed by various sequences

Dataset	Key Pose Indices													
	0	1	2	3	4	5	6	7	8	9	10	11	12	13
T1	17.24	24.14	06.89	03 45	06.89	03.45	13.79	20.70	03.45	00.00	00.00	00.00	00.00	00.00
T2	17.24	00.00	06.89	20 70	06.89	00.00	06.89	20.70	00.00	17.24	00.00	00.00	03.45	00.00
T3	10.34	17.24	06.89	06 89	06.89	03.45	20.70	27.60	00.00	00.00	00.00	00.00	00.00	00.00
T4	10.34	13.79	10.34	06 89	06.89	03.45	20.70	27.60	00.00	00.00	00.00	00.00	00.00	00.00

4.2   Testing Protocol and Results

Experiments are conducted in the context of biometric based identification where the gait feature derived from a test sequence is compared against a gallery of features derived from a number of training subjects. Implementation of the proposed algorithm is done in MatLab environment (version R2011a) on a system having 2.50 GHz Intel Core i5 processor and 4GB RAM.

First, we experimentally determine an optimal value of β required to binarize the variance image (refer to Fig. 6). For this, we plot cumulative match characteristic (CMC) curves corresponding to β values of 0, 0.1, 0.2, 0.3, 0.4 in Fig. 7(a), using only *T1* as the training set. The recorded response times for these different β values are plotted in Fig. 7(b). From Fig. 7(a), it is seen that the proposed method has a high recognition rate for $\beta \leq 0.2$, even in the presence of incomplete cycle sequences. But as observed from Fig. 7(b), the processing times required for $\beta = 0$ and $\beta = 0.1$ are significantly high. On the other hand, the response time corresponding to $\beta = 0.2$ is at most 3 seconds which is reasonably fast. Hence, the choice of the value of β as 0.2 can be considered as an effective balance between processing time and recognition accuracy. Each of the subsequent experiments conducted considers $\beta = 0.2$.

It is expected that an increased volume of training data will help in achieving higher accuracy during test cases. This is experimentally verified in Table 2. The table shows the recognition performance corresponding to the test sets *T3* and *T4*, recorded at 30 fps and 15 fps, respectively, and in presence of only *T1*, only *T2*, and both *T1* and *T2* (*T1+T2*) as training sets. Percentage accuracies are computed using two similarity measures: Cosine (*D1*) and Euclidean (*D2*).

The advantage of using a normalized similarity measure, such as the Cosine metric, in comparing feature vectors with missing attributes is evident from

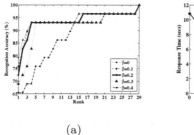 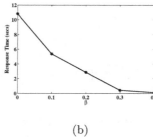

(a)   (b)

Fig. 7. (a) Cumulative match characteristic curves showing variation of recognition accuracy with rank for different values of β (b) Response times of the algorithm corresponding to these β values

Table 2. Variation of recognition accuracy with frame rate for different training data set combinations and for Cosine ($D1$) and Euclidean ($D2$) similarity measures

	$T3$		$T4$	
Training Set	$D1$	$D2$	$D1$	$D2$
$T1$	72.41	31.03	72.41	27.59
$T2$	55.17	13.79	51.72	13.79
$T1+T2$	86.21	41.38	79.31	37.93

the table. Moreover, from Tables 1 and 2, it is seen that there is no significant variation in recognition performance with reduction in frame rate, as long as the available key poses corresponding to the two frame rates closely match each other. In general, recognition rate is not remarkably high when only $T2$ is chosen as the training set. This is primarily because the gait sequences present in $T2$ contain a higher percentage of missing key poses (refer to Table 1).

To evaluate the effectiveness of an algorithm, it is often required to determine if its performance is satisfactory for a sufficiently small value of rank. A test subject is said to be perfectly classified at a given rank r, if the correct class of this subject is one of the top r predictions of the algorithm. We plot a rankwise improvement in classification performance of the proposed method in Fig. 8 corresponding to each of the training sets $T1$, $T2$ and $T1+T2$. It is seen from the figure that using both $T1$ and $T2$ as training sets, a recognition rate greater than 90% is achieved within a rank of 4, which highlights the efficacy of the proposed method in gait recognition setups similar to that shown in Fig. 1.

In each of the previous experiments, the value of K has been set to 13 (determined from the rate distortion plot of Fig. 4). However, a reader might be interested in studying the effect of change of the number of key poses (K) on the recognition rate. Hence, we plot the variation in percentage accuracy corresponding to K values of 7, 9, 11, 13, 15, 17, and 19 in Fig. 9. Training set for this experiment consists of only $T1$. It is seen from the figure that the curve initially has a non-decreasing trend for values of $K \geq 7$. It attains a peak value at $K =$

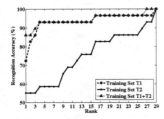

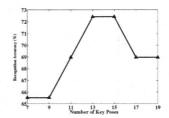

Fig. 8. CMC curves showing improvement in recognition rate with rank for the different training sets

Fig. 9. Variation of recognition accuracy with number of key poses using *T1* as the training set

13 and again decreases for values of $K > 15$. Thus, the choice of the value of K as 13 in each of the previous experiments is rightly justified. The reduction in recognition rate corresponding to $K \geq 7$ is due to the higher number of missing key poses in the gait sequences.

Finally a comparative performance analysis of the proposed method is made with existing work on frontal gait recognition using Kinect, namely, GEV [5], PDV [6], skeleton-covariance feature [9] and a pose based skeleton feature [11]. The effectiveness of the use of depth data in gait recognition is studied by comparing our approach with some of the traditional gait recognition methods which use RGB cameras for data collection, namely, GEI [1] and PEI [2]. Results are shown in Table 3 using only *T1* as the training set. It can be seen that the pro-

Table 3. Comparative performance of the proposed method with the existing literature

Gait Recognition Algorithms	Accuracy (%)	Time (in secs)
GEV [5]	27.59	2.58
PDV [6]	51.72	15.62
Skeleton Co-Variance Feature [9]	34.48	1.08
Skeleton Pose Based Feature [11]	51.72	2.23
GEI [1]	31.03	0.42
PEI [2]	44.83	1.34
Proposed feature	72.41	2.87

posed approach outperforms each of the state-of-the-art gait recognition techniques by more than 20%, which is remarkable. The slightly higher response time of our algorithm as compared to [1,2,5,9,11] can be sacrificed for achieving the significant improved recognition rate. This superior recognition performance together with a fast response time indicate the potentiality of this method in performing gait recognition from incomplete cycle sequences.

5   Conclusion and Future Scope

From the extensive set of experiments described in Section 4.2, it can be concluded that the proposed gait recognition procedure can be potentially applied in surveillance sites similar to Fig. 1. The pose based approach helps in preserving kinematic details in recognizing the gait of a subject from a given sequence. Evaluating the performance of the proposed algorithm in presence of a larger number of subjects and combining both back and front view sequences in the recognition procedure would be a direction for future research.

References

1. Han, J., Bhanu, B.: Individual Recognition Using Gait Energy Image. IEEE Transactions on Pattern Analysis and Machine Intelligence **28**(2), 316–322 (2006)
2. Roy, A., Sural, S., Mukherjee, J.: Gait Recognition Using Pose Kinematics and Pose Energy Image. Signal Processing **92**(3), 780–792 (2012)
3. Zhang, E., Zhao, Y., Xiong, W.: Active Energy Image Plus 2DLPP for Gait Recognition. Signal Processing **90**(7), 2295–2302 (2010)
4. Chen, C., Liang, J., Zhao, H., Hu, H., Tian, J.: Frame Difference Energy Image for Gait Recognition with Incomplete Silhouettes. Pattern Recognition Letters **30**(11), 977–984 (2009)
5. Sivapalan, S., Chen, D., Denman, S., Sridharan, S., Fookes, C.: Gait energy volumes and frontal gait recognition using depth images. In: International Joint Conference on Biometrics, pp. 1–6 (2011)
6. Chattopadhyay, P., Roy, A., Sural, S., Mukhopadhyay, J.: Pose Depth Volume Extraction from RGB-D Streams for Frontal Gait Recognition. Journal of Visual Communication and Image Representation **25**(1), 53–63 (2014)
7. Boulgouris, N.V., Hatzinakos, D., Plataniotis, K.N.: Gait recognition: A Challenging Signal Processing Technology for Biometrics Identification. IEEE Signal Processing Magazine **22**(6), 78–90 (2005)
8. Zhang, Z.: Microsoft Kinect Sensor and Its Effect. IEEE Multimedia **19**(2), 4–10 (2012)
9. Kumar, M.S.N., Babu, R.V.: Human gait recognition using depth camera: a covariance based approach. In: Proceedings of the 8th Indian Conference on Computer Vision, Graphics and Image Processing, article number 20. ACM, December 2012
10. Milovanovic, M., Minovic, M., Starcevic, D.: Walking in Colors: Human Gait Recognition Using Kinect and CBIR. IEEE Multimedia **20**(4), 28–36 (2013)
11. Chattopadhyay, P., Sural, S., Mukherjee, J.: Gait recognition from front and back view sequences captured using kinect. In: Maji, P., Ghosh, A., Murty, M.N., Ghosh, K., Pal, S.K. (eds.) PReMI 2013. LNCS, vol. 8251, pp. 196–203. Springer, Heidelberg (2013)
12. Shotton, J., Sharp, T., Kipman, A., Fitzgibbon, A., Finocchio, M., Blake, A., Cook, M., Moore, R.: Real-Time Human Pose Recognition in Parts from Single Depth Images. Communications of the ACM **56**(1), 116–124 (2013)
13. Hofmann, M., Bachmann, S., Rigoll, G.: 2.5D Gait biometrics using the depth gradient histogram energy image. In: 5th IEEE International Conference on Biometrics: Theory, Applications and Systems, pp. 399–403 (2012)
14. Montgomery, D.C., Peck, E.A., Vining, G.G.: Introduction to Linear Regression Analysis. John Wiley & Sons Inc, Hoboken (2012)
15. Wang, J., Makihara, Y., Yagi, Y.: Human tracking and segmentation supported by silhouette-based gait recognition. In: IEEE International Conference on Robotics and Automation, pp. 1698–1703 (2008)
16. Rabiner, L.R.: A Tutorial on Hidden Markov models and Selected Applications in Speech Recognition. Proceedings of the IEEE **77**, 257–286 (1989)

3D Hand Pose Detection
in Egocentric RGB-D Images

Grégory Rogez[1,2]([✉]), Maryam Khademi[1], J.S. Supančič III[1],
J.M.M. Montiel[2], and Deva Ramanan[1]

[1] Department of Computer Science, University of California, Irvine, USA
{grogez,mkhademi,supanci,dramanan}@ics.uci.edu
[2] Aragon Institute of Engineering Research (i3A), Universidad de Zaragoza,
Zaragoza, Spain
{grogez,josemari}@unizar.es

Abstract. We focus on the task of hand pose estimation from egocentric viewpoints. For this problem specification, we show that depth sensors are particularly informative for extracting near-field interactions of the camera wearer with his/her environment. Despite the recent advances in full-body pose estimation using Kinect-like sensors, reliable monocular hand pose estimation in RGB-D images is still an unsolved problem. The problem is exacerbated when considering a wearable sensor and a first-person camera viewpoint: the occlusions inherent to the particular camera view and the limitations in terms of field of view make the problem even more difficult. We propose to use task and viewpoint specific synthetic training exemplars in a discriminative detection framework. We also exploit the depth features for a sparser and faster detection. We evaluate our approach on a real-world annotated dataset and propose a novel annotation technique for accurate 3D hand labelling even in case of partial occlusions.

Keywords: Egocentric vision · Hand pose · Multi-class classifier · RGB-D sensor

1 Introduction

Much recent work has explored various applications of egocentric RGB cameras, spurred on in part by the availability of low-cost mobile sensors such as Google Glass, Microsoft SenseCam, and the GoPro camera. Many of these applications, such as life-logging [1], medical rehabilitation [2], and augmented reality [3],

---

This research was supported by the European Commission under FP7 Marie Curie IOF grant "Egovision4Health" (PIOF-GA-2012-328288).

Electronic supplementary material The online version of this chapter (doi:10. 1007/978-3-319-16178-5_25) contains supplementary material, which is available to authorized users. Videos can also be accessed at http://www.springerimages.com/videos/978-3-319-16177-8.

L. Agapito et al. (Eds.): ECCV 2014 Workshops, Part I, LNCS 8925, pp. 356–371, 2015.
DOI: 10.1007/978-3-319-16178-5_25

require inferring the interactions of the first-person observer with his/her environment. Towards that end, we specifically focus on the task of hand pose estimation from egocentric viewpoints. We show that depth-based cues, extracted from an *egocentric depth camera*, provides an extraordinarily helpful cue for egocentric hand-pose estimation.

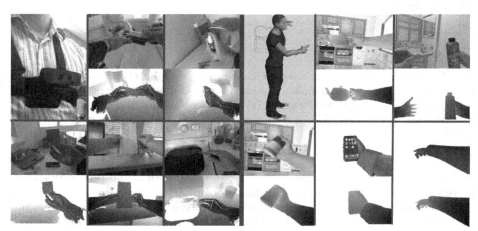

Real-world egocentric RGB-D video (test)   Synthetic egocentric RGB-D video (train)

Fig. 1. Testing (left) and training data (right). We show on the left hand side several examples of annotated training RGBD images captured with a chest-mounted Intel Creative camera. On the right, we present some examples of training images rendered using Poser.

One may hope that depth simply "solves" the problem, based on successful systems for real-time human pose estimation based on Kinect sensor [4] and prior work on articulated hand pose estimation for RGB-D sensors [5–7]. Recent approaches have also tried to exploit the 2.5D data from Kinect-like devices to understand complex scenarios such as object manipulation [6] or two interacting hands [5]. We show that various assumptions about visibility/occlusion and manual tracker initialization may not hold in an egocentric setting, making the problem still quite challenging.

Challenges: Most previous work has formulated the hand pose recognition task as a tracking problem given RGB or RGBD sequences with manual initialization. We would like a fully-automatic method that processes egocentric videos of daily activities, which is even more challenging for the following reasons. First, a limited field-of-view from an egocentric viewpoint causes hands to frequently move outside the camera view frustum, making it difficult to apply tracking models that rely on accurate estimates from previous frames. Second, fingers are often occluded by the hand (and possible other objects being manipulated) in

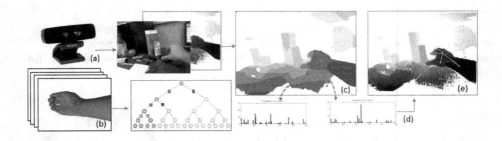

Fig. 2. System. (a) Chest-mounted RGB-D camera. (b) Synthetic egocentric hand exemplars are used to train a multi-class cascade classifier. The depth map is processed to select a sparse set of image locations (c) which are classified obtaining distributions over probable hand poses (d). An estimate is made e.g., by taking the max over these distributions (e).

first-person viewpoints, making hand detection and articulated pose estimation more challenging than the typically third-person viewpoint (see Fig. 2).

Our Approach: We describe a successful approach to hand-pose estimation that makes use of the following key observations. First, motivated by biological evidence [8], we show that **depth cues** provide an extraordinarily helpful signal for pose estimation in the near-field, first-person viewpoints. We find that time-of-flight depth cameras provide good depth estimates over a near-field workspace (0-70cm from the camera) while being easily mobile. Second, the egocentric setting provides a strong **viewpoint, shape, and interacting-object prior** over hand poses. We operationalize this prior by building parametric models over viewpoints of poses of a 3D, mesh-based hand model while interacting with common household objects. We then sample from this model (with an egocentric prior over viewpoint and hand shape) to generate large, synthetic depth data for training hand classifiers (see Fig. 2b). Third, **sparse, discriminative** classifiers allow us efficiently evaluate a large family of pose-specific classifiers. We classify global poses rather than local parts, which allows us to better reason about self-occlusions. Our classifiers process single frames, using a tracking-by-detection framework that avoids the need for manual initialization (see Fig. 2c-e).

Evaluation: Unlike human pose estimation, there exists no standard benchmarks for hand pose estimation, especially in egocentric videos. We believe that quantifiable performance is important for many broader applications such as health-care rehabilitation, for example. Thus, for the evaluation of our approach, we have collected and annotated (full 3D hand poses) our own benchmark dataset of real egocentric object manipulation scenes, which we will release to spur further research. It is surprisingly difficult to collect annotated datasets of hands performing real-world interactions; indeed, many prior work on hand pose estimation evaluate results on synthetically-generated data. We developed a semi-automatic labelling tool which allows to accurately annotate partially occluded hands and fingers in 3D, given real-world RGBD data. We compare to both commercial and academic approaches to hand pose estimation, and demonstrate that our method provides state-of-the-art performance for both hand detection and pose estimation.

2   Related Work

Egocentric Hand/Object Manipulation: Whereas third-person-view activity analysis is often driven by human full-body pose, egocentric activities are often defined by hand pose and the objects that the camera wearer interacts with. Previous work examined the problem of recognizing objects [9,10] and interpreting American Sign Language poses [11] from wearable cameras. Much work has also focused on hand tracking [12–15], finger tracking [16], and hand-eye tracking [17] from wearable cameras. Often, hand pose estimation is examined during active object manipulations [18–22]. One commonality behind such previous work is the use of RGB sensor input. Motivated in part by biological evidence [8], we show that depth cues considerably aids the processing of such near-field interactions.

Depth-Based Pose Estimation: Our technical approach is closely inspired by the Kinect system [4], which also makes use of synthetically generated depth maps for articulated pose estimation. Our approach differs in that we construct classifiers that classify entire poses rather than local landmarks or parts. We posit and verify that the numerous occlusions of articulated fingers from a wearable viewpoint requires a more global approach, since local information can be ambiguous due to occlusions. For this reason, temporal reasoning is also particularly attractive because one can use dynamics to resolve such ambiguities. Much prior work on hand-pose estimation takes this route [7,23,24]. Our approach differs from these approaches in that we focus on single-image hand pose estimation, which is required to avoid manual (re)initialization. A notable exception is the recent work of [25], who also process single images but focus on third-person views.

Egocentric RGB-D: Depth-based wearable cameras are attractive because depth cues can be used to better reason about occlusions arising from egocentric viewpoints. There has been surprisingly little prior work in this vein, with notable exceptions focusing on targeted applications such as navigation for the blind [26]. We posit that one limitation may be the need for small form-factors for wearable technology, while structured light sensors such as the Kinect often make use of large baselines. We show that time-of-flight depth cameras are an attractive alternative for wearable depth-sensing, since they do not require large baselines and so require smaller form-factors.

Features: Many methods based on RGB images rely on color-based skin detection and segmentation. Examples for hand tracking from a moving camera can be found in [27] or more recently [17]. Earlier algorithms for hand pose estimation based on RGB images can be found in [28]. Recent work has exploited Kinect-like depth sensors [25]. RGB and Time-of-Flight (ToF) cameras have also been combined for real-time 3D hand gesture interaction [3] or near-realtime detailed hand pose estimation [29].

Generative vs Discriminative: Generative model-based approaches have historically been more popular for hand pose estimation [30]. A detailed 3D model of the hand pose is usually employed for articulated pose tracking [5,31] and detailed 3D pose estimation [32]. Discriminative approaches [7,24] for hand pose estimation tend to require large datasets of training examples, synthetic, realistic or combined [7]. Learning formalisms include boosted classifier trees [33] and randomized decision forests[24], and regression forests [7]. We describe a discriminative approach based on [34], which uses a tree-structured multi-class cascade for pose estimation and detection. We specifically extend the work of [34] to use both RGB and Depth features.

3   Our Method

3.1   Setting and Choice of the Device

We use a chest-mounted Time-of-Flight camera, an Intel Creative (see Fig. 2a), which is particularly well-suited for short-range hand-object interactions.

TOF vs Structured Light: Much recent work on depth-processing has been driven by the consumer-grade PrimeSense sensor [35], which is based on structured light technology. At its core, this approach relies on two-view stereopsis (where correspondence estimation is made easier by active illumination). This may require large baselines between two views, which is undesirable for our egocentric application for two reasons; first, this requires larger form-factors, making the camera less mobile. Second, this produces occlusions for points in the scene that are not visible in both views. Time-of-flight depth sensing, while less popular, is based on a pulsed light emitter that can be placed arbitrarily close to the main camera, as no baseline is required. This produces smaller form factors and reduces occlusions in that camera view . Specifically, we make use of the consumer-grade TOF sensor from Creative [36].

3.2   Synthetic Training Exemplars

We represent a hand pose as a vector of joint angles of a kinematic skeleton θ. We use a hand-specific forward kinematic model to generate a 3D hand mesh given a particular θ. In addition to hand pose parameters θ, we also need to specify a camera vector ϕ that specifies both a viewpoint and position. We experimented with various priors and various rendering packages.

Floating Hands vs Full-Body Characters: Much work on hand pose estimation makes use of an isolated "floating" hand mesh model to generate synthetic training data. Popular software packages include the open-source `libhand` [37] and commercial Poser [38,39]. We posit that modeling a full character body, and specifically, the full arm, will provide important contextual cues for hand pose estimation. To generate egocentric data, we mount a synthetic camera on the chest of a virtual full-body character, naturally mimicking our physical data collection process. To generate data corresponding to different body and hand shapes, we make use of Poser's character library.

Viewpoint Prior: To specify a viewpoint prior for floating hands, we simply limited the azimuth ϕ_{az} to lie between 180 ± 30 (corresponding to rear viewpoints), elevation ϕ_{el} to lie between -30 and 10 (since hands tend to lie below the chest mount), and bank ϕ_b to lie between ± 30. We obtained these ranges by looking at a variety of collected data (not used for testing). For our full character models, we generate small perturbations of the virtual chest camera mount. This simulates camera viewpoint and body variation between individuals wearing egocentric cameras. We use forward kinematics of the arm to naturally limit hand poses to realistic viewpoints, another benefit of full-character egocentric modeling.

Pose Prior: Our hand model consists of 26 joint angles, $\theta \in [0, 2\pi]^{26}$. It is difficult to specify priors over such high-dimensional spaces. We take a nonparametric data-driven approach. We first obtain a training set of joint angles $\{\theta_i\}$ from a collection of grasping motion capture data [40]. We then augment this core set of poses with synthetic perturbations, making use of rejection sampling to remove invalid poses. Specifically, we first generate proposals by perturbing each original sample with Gaussian noise $\theta_i + \epsilon$, where $\epsilon \sim N(0, \sigma I)$ with $\sigma \in R^{26}$. The individual components within σ are evaluated by visual inspection. Notably, we also perturb the *entire arm* of the full character-body, which generates natural (egocentric) viewpoint variations of hand configurations. Note that we consider smaller perturbations for fingers to keep grasping poses reasonable. We remove those samples that result in poses that are self-intersecting or lie outside the field-of-view. Example poses are shown in Fig. 2b.

Interacting Objects: We wish to explore egocentric hand pose estimation in the context of natural, functional hand movement. This often involves interactions with the surrounding environment and manipulations of nearby objects. We posit that generating such contextual training data will be important for good test-time accuracy. However, modeling the space of hand grasps and the world of manipulable objects is itself a formidable challenge. We make use of the EveryDayHands animation library [41], which contains 50 canonical hand grasps and objects. This package was originally designed as a computer animation tool, but we find the library to cover a reasonable taxonomy of grasps and objects for egocentric recognition. Objects include general shapes such as balls and cylinders of varying size, as well as common everyday objects including utensils, phones, cups, etc. We apply our rejection-sampling technique to generate additional valid interacting object-hand grasp configurations, yielding a final dataset of 10,000 synthetic egocentric hand-object examples (see examples in Fig. 1).

3.3 Hierarchical Cascades (Past Work)

We would like a hand pose detector that simultaneously performs hand detection and pose estimation. We describe an approach based on the multi-class rejection-cascade classifiers of [34]. We review the basic formulation here, but refer the

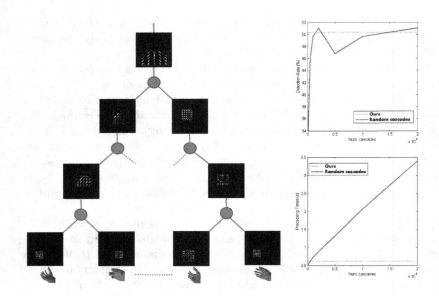

Fig. 3. (left) Hierarchical cascade of parts. (right) Detection rates and processing time varying the number of random cascades in the ensemble vs an exponential number of cascades. The hierarchy shows the coarse to fine detection, showing only one part per branch for clarity. We show on the upper right that our new detector is equivalent to an infinite number of Random Cascades (RC) from [34]. In the bottom right we show that the RC computational cost increases linearly with the number of cascades and that, when considering a very large number of cascades, our model is more efficient.

reader to [34] for further detail. From a high-level, both detection and pose estimation are treated as a K-way classification problem, with classes specifying one of K discrete poses or the background. The $K + 1$-way classifier is trained using an boosting-like algorithm where weak-classifiers are "parts" classifiers trained using linear SVMs defined on localized HOG features within a scanning-window coordinate frame. A multi-way classification strategy may require considerable amounts of training data and may be slow at test time, since K can be large. [34] describe an approach with three crucial properties that address these limitations, discussed below. We then describe various improvements that apply in our problem domain.

Coarse-to-Fine Sharing: Parts are *shared* across all K pose-classes through a hierarchical coarse-to-fine tree. Specifically, hierarchical K-means is used to cluster our set of training poses into K quantized pose classes, which are naturally arranged in a hierarchical tree with K leaves. The ith node in this tree represents a coarse pose class; a visualization is shown in Fig. 3. Given an image window x, a binary classifier tuned for coarse pose-class i is defined as:

$$f_i(x) = \prod_{j \in \text{ancestors}(i)} h_j(x) \quad \text{where} \quad h_j(x) = \mathbf{1}_{[w_j^T x > b_j]} \tag{1}$$

where the ancestors of node i include i, and $\mathbf{1}$ is the indicator function (evaluating to 1 or 0). Each binary "weak classifier" $h_j(x)$ is a thresholded linear function (trained with a linear SVM) that is defined on localized HOG features extracted from a subwindow of x. This allows us to interpret w_j as a zero-padded "part" template. Parts higher in the tree tend to be generic, and used across many pose classes. Parts lower in the tree, toward the leaves, tend to capture pose-specific details.

Rejection Cascades: At test time, the above set of hierarchical classifiers can naturally be implemented as a rejection cascade with a breadth-first search through the tree. This can be readily seen by rewriting (1) recursively as $f_i(x) = f_p(x)h_i(x)$, where p is the parent of i. We only need to evaluate the descendants of node i if $h_i(x)$ evaluates to 1. This means we can quickly prune away large portions of the pose-space when evaluating region x, making scanning-window evaluation at test-time quite efficient. Finally, a notable byproduct is that multiple leaf classes might fire in a given image region, each with a different leaf score. We generally report the highest-scoring pose as the final result, but show that alternate high-scoring hypotheses can still be useful (since they can be later refined using say, a tracker).

Ensembles of Cascades: To increase robustness, we would like to average predictions across an ensemble of classifiers. [34] describes an approach that makes use of a pool of weak part classifiers for each coarse-pose class (node) i:

$$h_i(x) \in H_i \quad \text{where} \quad |H_i| = M, i \in N \tag{2}$$

One can instantiate a tree by selecting a weak classifier (from its candidate pool H_i) for each node i in the tree. This allows one to define an exponential number of instantiations M^N, where N is the number of nodes (coarse pose-classes) in the tree and M is the size of each candidate pool. In practice, [34] found that averaging predictions from a small random subset of trees significantly improved results.

3.4 Joint Training of Exponential Ensembles

In this section, we present several improvements to [34] that apply in our problem domain. Because of local ambiguities due to self-occlusions, we expect individual part templates to be rather weak. This in turn may cause premature cascade rejections. We describe modifications for jointly training weak classifiers and averaging predictions over exponentially-large sets of cascade ensembles.

Sequential Training: Notably, [34] *independently* learned weak classifiers (w_i, b_i) by defining a positive/negative training set that is independent of other weak classifiers. That is, *all* training images corresponding to node (coarse pose-class) i are treated as positives, and *all* other poses are treated as negatives.

Instead, we use only the training examples that pass through the rejection cascade up to node i. This more accurately reflects the scenario at test-time. This requires classifiers to be trained in a sequential fashion, in a similar coarse-to-fine (breadth-first) search over nodes from the root to the leaves. This means weak learners are trained jointly rather than independently.,

Exponentially-Large Ensembles: Rogez et al. [34] average votes across a small number (around hundred) of explicitly-constructed trees. We now describe a simple procedure for exactly computing the average over the exponentially-large set of M^N. By averaging over a large set, we reduce the chance of a premature cascade rejection. Our insight is that one can compute an *implicit* summation (or average) over the set by caching partial summations. Assume nodes are numbered in breadth-first order, such that node 1 is the root. As before, we will iterate over nodes in a breadth-first, coarse-to-fine manner. We now apply *all* H_i weak classifiers and keep a record of the number that fire n_i:

$$t_i = t_p n_i \quad \text{where} \quad p = \text{parent}(i), \quad n_i = \sum_{h_i(x) \in H_i} h_i(x) \tag{3}$$

For any node i, the fraction of partial hierarchies (constructed from the root to node i) that vote for node i are given by the ratio $\frac{t_i}{M^{D(i)}}$, where $D(i)$ is the depth of node i. We omit the fairly straightforward proof due to lack of space. Hence the ratio for leaf nodes i yields the final set of (fine-scale) pose-class votes. Notably, once we reach an internal node for which no weak classifiers fire $n_i = 0$, then all of its descendants must generate votes $t_i = 0$, meaning that they need not be evaluated. This still allows for efficient run-time search (see Fig. 3).

Features: We experiment with two additional sets of features x. Rogez et al. [34] originally defined their model on oriented gradient histograms on RGB (HOG-RGB). We also evaluated oriented gradient histograms on depth images (HOG-D). While not as common, such a gradient-based depth descriptor can be shown to capture histograms of normal directions (since normals can be computed from the cross product of depth gradients) [42]. For depth we use 5x5 HOG blocks and 16 signed orientation bins.

3.5   Sparse Search

Two assumptions can be leveraged to effectively tackle egocentric hand detection in RGB-D images: 1) hands must lie in a valid range of depths, i.e., hands can not appear further away from the chest-mounted camera than physically possible and 2) hands tend to be of a canonical size s. These assumptions allow for a much sparser search compared to a classic scanning window, as only "valid windows" need be classified. A median filter is first applied to the depth map $d(x,y)$. Locations greater than arms length (75 cm) away are then pruned. Assuming a standard pinhole camera with focal length f, the expected image height of a hand at valid location (x,y) is given by $S_{map}(x,y) = \frac{s}{f} d(x,y)$. We apply our template classifier to valid positions on a search grid (16-pixel strides in x-y direction) and quantized scales given by S_{map}, visualized as red dots in Fig. 2c.

3rd-person hand detection 3rd-person finger tip detection Egocentric hand detection Egocentric finger tip detection

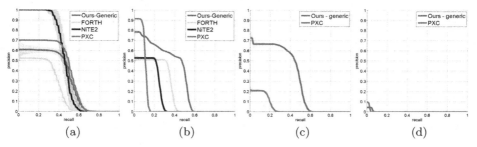

      (a)   (b)   (c)   (d)

Fig. 4. Numerical results for 3rd-person (a-b) and egocentric (c-d) sequences. We compare our method (tuned for generic priors) to state-of-the-art techniques from industry (NITE2 [43] and PXC [36]) and academia (FORTH [23]) in terms of (a) hand detection and (b) finger tips detection. We shade the 95% confidence interval obtained from the statistical bootstrap. We refer the reader to the main text for additional decription, but emphasize that (1) our method is competitive (or out-performs) prior art for detection and pose estimation and (2) pose estimation is considerably harder in egocentric views.

4   Experiments

Dataset: We have collected and annotated (full 3D hand poses) our own benchmark dataset of real egocentric object manipulation scenes, which we will release to spur further research [1]. We developed a semi-automatic labelling tool which allows to accurately annotate partially occluded hands and fingers in 3D. A few 2D joints are first manually labelled in the image and used to select the closest synthetic exemplars in the training set. A full hand pose is then created combining the manual labelling and the selected 3D exemplar. This pose is manually refined, leading to the selection of a new exemplar, and the creation of a new pose. This iterative process is followed until an acceptable labelling is achieved. We captured 4 sequences of 1000 frames each, which were annotated every 10 frames in both RGB and Depth. We use 2 different subjects (male/female) and 4 different indoor scenes. We invite the reader to view videos in our supplementary material.

    Evaluation: We present numerous evaluations for both hand detection and pose estimation. A candidate *detection* is deemed correct if it sufficiently overlaps the ground-truth bounding-box (in terms of area of intersection over union) by at least 50%. We evaluate pose estimation with *2D-RMS* re-projection error of keypoints. However, some baseline systems report the pose of only confident fingers. In such cases, we measure *finger-tip detection* accuracy as a proxy for pose estimation. For additional diagnosis, we categorize errors into detection failures, correct detections but incorrect viewpoint, and correct detection and viewpoint but incorrect articulated pose. Specifically, *viewpoint-consistent detections* are

---

[1] Please visit www.gregrogez.net/

VP Detection (PR)   2D RMSE (N candidates) VP Detection (N candidates)Cond 2D RMSE (N candidates)

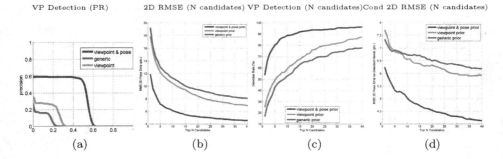

(a)   (b)   (c)   (d)

Fig. 5. Quantitative results for varying our priors evaluated with respect to (a) viewpoint-consistent hand detection (ROC curve), (b) 2D RMS error, (c) viewpoint-consistent detections and (d) 2D RMS error conditioned on viewpoint-consistent detections. Please see text for detailed description of our evaluation criteria and analysis. In general, egocentric-pose priors considerably improve performance, validating our egocentric-synthesis engine from Sec. 3.2. When tuned for $N = 10$ candidates per image, our system produces pose hypotheses that appear accurate enough to initialize a tracker.

detections for which the RMS error of all 2D joint positions falls below a coarse threshold (10 pixels). *Conditional 2D RMS* error is the reprojection error for well-detected (viewpoint-consistent) hands. Finally, we also plot accuracy as a function of the number of N *candidate detections* per image. With enough hypotheses, accuracy must max out at 100%, but we demonstrate that good accuracy is often achievable with a small number of candidates (which may layer be re-ranked, by say, a tracker).

Parameters: We train a cascade model trained with $K = 100$ classes, a hierarchy of 6 levels and $M = 3$ weak classifiers per branch. We synthesize 100 training images per class.

Third-Person vs Egocentric: We first evaluate our method (trained with a generic prior) for the tasks of third-person and egocentric hand analysis (Fig. 4). We compare against state of the art techniques from industry [36, 43] and academia [23]. Because a general prior span a larger range of viewpoints and poses, we train a model with $K = 800$ classes for this experiment. We only present egocentric results for our method and PXC, since the other baselines (FORTH and NITE2) are trackers that fail catastrophically on egocentric sequences where hands frequently leave the field-of-view. Moreover, because some baselines only report positions of confident fingers, we use finger-tip detection as a proxy for pose estimation. We conclude that (1) hand pose estimation is considerably harder in the egocentric setting and (2) our (generic-prior) pose estimation system is a state-of-the-art starting point for our subsequent analysis.

Pose+viewpoint Prior: In Fig. 5, we show that an egocentric-specific pose and viewpoint prior outperforms the generic prior from Fig. 4. In general, a viewpoint prior produces a marginal improvement, while a pose prior considerably improves accuracy in all cases. With a modest number of candidates ($N = 10$), our final system produces viewpoint-consistent detections in 90% of the test frames with an average 2D RMS error of 5 pixels. From a qualitative perspective, this performance appears accurate enough to initialize a tracker. Our results suggest that our synthesis procedure from Sec. 3.2 correctly models both viewpoint and pose priors arising in egocentric settings.

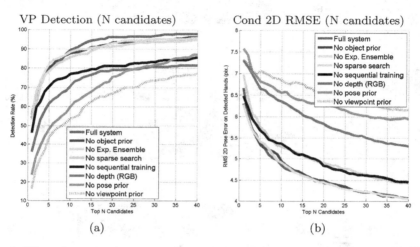

(a)   (b)

Fig. 6. We evaluate performance when turning off particular aspects of out system, considering both (a) viewpoint-consistent detections (b) 2D RMS error conditioned on well-detected hands. When turning off our exponentially-large ensemble or synthetic training, we use the default of 100 independently-trained cascades as in [34]. When turning off the depth feature, we use a classifier trained on aligned RGB images. Please see the text for further discussion of these results.

Ablative Analysis: To further analyze our system, we perform an ablative analysis that turns "off" different aspects of our system: sequential training, ensemble of cascades, depth feature, sparse search and different priors (viewpoint, pose, objects). Hand detection and conditional 2D hand RMS error are given in Fig. 6. Viewpoint prior, pose prior, depth HOG features and our new sequential training algorithm are key aspects in terms of performance. Turning these parameters off decreases the detection rate by a substantial amount (between 10 and 30%). Modeling objects produces better detections, particularly for larger numbers of candidates. In general, we find this additional prior helps more for those test frames with object manipulations.

Classifier Design: Our new sequential training of parts significantly outperforms the independent training of [34] by 10-15% (Fig. 6). Our exponentially-large ensemble of cascades and sparse search marginally improve accuracy but are much more efficient: in average, the exponentially-large ensemble is 2.5 times faster than an explicit search over a 100-element ensemble (as in [34]), while the

Reflective objects

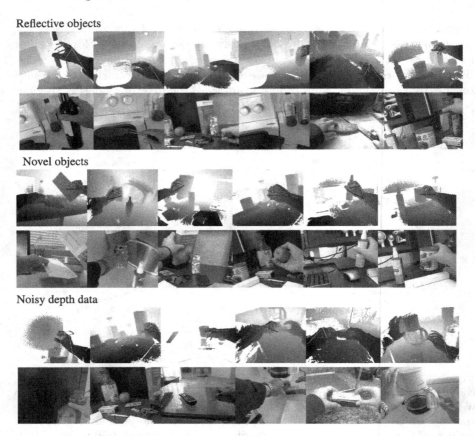

Novel objects

Noisy depth data

Fig. 7. Good detections. We show a sample of challenging frames where the hand is correctly detected by our system. Reflective objects (**top row:** wine bottle, pan, phone, knife and plastic bottle) produce incorrect depth maps due to interactions with our sensor's infrared illuminant. Novel objects (**middle row:** envelope, juice box, book, apple, spray and chocolate powder box) require generalization to objects not synthesized at train-time, while noisy depth data (**bottom row**) showcases the robustness of our system.

sparse search is 3.15 times faster than a dense grid. Hence our final classifier significantly improves upon the accuracy and speed of [34], which uses a default of 100 random, independently-trained cascades evaluated on a dense grid of RGB features.

Qualitative Results: We invite the reader to view our supplementary videos. We illustrate successes in difficult scenarios in Fig. 7 and analyze common failure modes in Fig. 8. Please see the figures for additional discussion.

noisy depth   reflective object (phone) novel object (keys) novel object (towel) truncated hand

Fig. 8. Hard cases. We show frames where the hand is not correctly detected by our system, even with 40 candidates. These hard cases include excessively-noisy depth data, hands manipulating reflective material (phone) or unseen/deformable objects that look considerably different from those in our training set (e.g. keys, towels), and truncated hands.

5   Conclusion

We have focused on the task of hand pose estimation from egocentric viewpoints. For this problem specification, we have shown that TOF depth sensors are particularly informative for extracting near-field interactions of the camera wearer with his/her environment. We have proposed to use task-specific synthetic training exemplars, trained with object interactions, in a discriminative detection framework. To do so efficiently, we have exploited a simple depth cue for fast detection. Finally, we have provided an insightful analysis of the performance of our algorithm on a new real-world annotated dataset of egocentric scenes.

References

1. Hodges, S., Williams, L., Berry, E., Izadi, S., Srinivasan, J., Butler, A., Smyth, G., Kapur, N., Wood, K.: SenseCam: a retrospective memory aid. In: Dourish, P., Friday, A. (eds.) UbiComp 2006. LNCS, vol. 4206, pp. 177–193. Springer, Heidelberg (2006)
2. Yang, R., Sarkar, S., Loeding, B.L.: Handling movement epenthesis and hand segmentation ambiguities in continuous sign language recognition using nested dynamic programming. PAMI **32**(3), 462–477 (2010)
3. den Bergh, M.V., Gool, L.J.V.: Combining rgb and tof cameras for real-time 3d hand gesture interaction. In: WACV, 66–72 (2011)
4. Shotton, J., Fitzgibbon, A.W., Cook, M., Sharp, T., Finocchio, M., Moore, R., Kipman, A., Blake, A.: Real-time human pose recognition in parts from single depth images. In: CVPR (2011)
5. Oikonomidis, I., Kyriazis, N., Argyros, A.A.: Tracking the articulated motion of two strongly interacting hands. In: CVPR (2012)
6. Romero, J., Kjellstrom, H., Ek, C.H., Kragic, D.: Non-parametric hand pose estimation with object context. Im. and Vision Comp. **31**(8), 555–564 (2013)

7. Tang, D., Kim, T.H.Y.T.K.: Real-time articulated hand pose estimation using semi-supervised transductive regression forests. In: ICCV (2013)
8. Sakata, H., Taira, M., Kusunoki, M., Murata, A., Tsutsui, K.I., Tanaka, Y., Shein, W.N., Miyashita, Y.: Neural representation of three-dimensional features of manipulation objects with stereopsis. Experimental Brain Research 128(1-2), 160–169 (1999)
9. Fathi, A., Ren, X., Rehg, J.: Learning to recognize objects in egocentric activities. In: CVPR (2011)
10. Pirsiavash, H., Ramanan, D.: Detecting activities of daily living in first-person camera views. In: CVPR (2012)
11. Starner, T., Schiele, B., Pentland, A.: Visual contextual awareness in wearable computing. In: International Symposium on Wearable Computing (1998)
12. Kurata, T., Kato, T., Kourogi, M., Jung, K., Endo, K.: A functionally-distributed hand tracking method for wearable visual interfaces and its applications. In: MVA, 84–89 (2002)
13. Kölsch, M., Turk, M.: Hand tracking with flocks of features. In: CVPR (2), 1187 (2005)
14. Kölsch, M.: An appearance-based prior for hand tracking. In: Blanc-Talon, J., Bone, D., Philips, W., Popescu, D., Scheunders, P. (eds.) ACIVS 2010, Part II. LNCS, vol. 6475, pp. 292–303. Springer, Heidelberg (2010)
15. Morerio, P., Marcenaro, L., Regazzoni, C.S.: Hand detection in first person vision. In: FUSION (2013)
16. Dominguez, S., Keaton, T., Sayed, A.: A robust finger tracking method for multimodal wearable computer interfacing. IEEE Transactions on Multimedia 8(5), 956–972 (2006)
17. Ryoo, M.S., Matthies, L.: First-person activity recognition: What are they doing to me?. In: CVPR (2013)
18. Mayol, W., Davison, A., Tordoff, B., Molton, N., Murray, D.: Interaction between hand and wearable camera in 2d and 3d environments. In: BMVC (2004)
19. Ren, X., Philipose, M.: Egocentric recognition of handled objects: Benchmark and analysis. In: IEEE Workshop on Egocentric Vision (2009)
20. Damen, D., Gee, A.P., Mayol-Cuevas, W.W., Calway, A.: Egocentric real-time workspace monitoring using an rgb-d camera. In: IROS (2012)
21. Ren, X., Gu, C.: Figure-ground segmentation improves handled object recognition in egocentric video. In: CVPR, pp. 3137–3144. IEEE (2010)
22. Fathi, A., Farhadi, A., Rehg, J.: Understanding egocentric activities. In: ICCV (2011)
23. Oikonomidis, I., Kyriazis, N., Argyros, A.: Efficient model-based 3d tracking of hand articulations using kinect. In: BMVC (2011)
24. Keskin, C., Kıraç, F., Kara, Y.E., Akarun, L.: Hand pose estimation and hand shape classification using multi-layered randomized decision forests. In: Fitzgibbon, A., Lazebnik, S., Perona, P., Sato, Y., Schmid, C. (eds.) ECCV 2012, Part VI. LNCS, vol. 7577, pp. 852–863. Springer, Heidelberg (2012)
25. Xu, C., Cheng, L.: Efficient hand pose estimation from a single depth image. In: ICCV (2013)
26. Mann, S., Huang, J., Janzen, R., Lo, R., Rampersad, V., Chen, A., Doha, T.: Blind navigation with a wearable range camera and vibrotactile helmet. In: ACM International Conf. on Multimedia. MM 2011 (2011)
27. Argyros, A.A., Lourakis, M.I.A.: Real-Time Tracking of Multiple Skin-Colored Objects with a Possibly Moving Camera. In: Pajdla, T., Matas, J.G. (eds.) ECCV 2004. LNCS, vol. 3023, pp. 368–379. Springer, Heidelberg (2004)

28. Erol, A., Bebis, G., Nicolescu, M., Boyle, R.D., Twombly, X.: Vision-based hand pose estimation: A review. CVIU **108**(1–2), 52–73 (2007)
29. Sridhar, S., Oulasvirta, A., Theobalt, C.: Interactive markerless articulated hand motion tracking using rgb and depth data. In: ICCV (2013)
30. Stenger, B., Thayananthan, A., Torr, P., Cipolla, R.: Model-based hand tracking using a hierarchical bayesian filter. PAMI **28**(9), 1372–1384 (2006)
31. Oikonomidis, I., Kyriazis, N., Argyros, A.A.: Full dof tracking of a hand interacting with an object by modeling occlusions and physical constraints. In: ICCV (2011)
32. de La Gorce, M., Fleet, D.J., Paragios, N.: Model-based 3d hand pose estimation from monocular video. IEEE PAMI **33**(9), 1793–1805 (2011)
33. Ong, E.J., Bowden, R.: A boosted classifier tree for hand shape detection. In: FGR (2004)
34. Rogez, G., Rihan, J., Orrite, C., Torr, P.H.S.: Fast human pose detection using randomized hierarchical cascades of rejectors. IJCV **99**(1), 25–52 (2012)
35. Sense, P.: The primesensortmreference design 1.08. Prime Sense (2011)
36. Intel: Perceptual computing sdk (2013)
37. Šarić, M.: Libhand: A library for hand articulation Version 0.9 (2011)
38. SmithMicro: Poser10 (2010) http://poser.smithmicro.com/
39. Shakhnarovich, G., Viola, P., Darrell, T.: Fast pose estimation with parameter-sensitive hashing. In: 2003 Proceedings of the Ninth IEEE International Conference on Computer Vision, pp. 750–757. IEEE (2003)
40. Romero, J., Feix, T., Kjellstrom, H., Kragic, D.: Spatio-temporal modeling of grasping actions. In: IROS (2010)
41. Daz3D: Every-hands pose library (2013). http://www.daz3d.com/everyday-hands-poses-for-v4-and-m4
42. Spinello, L., Arras, K.O.: People detection in rgb-d data. In: IROS (2011)
43. PrimeSense: Nite2 middleware (2013)

Assessing the Suitability of the Microsoft Kinect for Calculating Person Specific Body Segment Parameters

Sean Clarkson[✉], Jon Wheat, Ben Heller, and Simon Choppin

Centre for Sports Engineering Research, Sheffield Hallam University, Sheffield, UK
s.clarkson@shu.ac.uk

Abstract. Many biomechanical and medical analyses rely on the availability of reliable body segment parameter estimates. Current techniques typically take many manual measurements of the human body, in conjunction with geometric models or regression equations. However, such techniques are often criticised. 3D scanning offers many advantages, but current systems are prohibitively complex and costly. The recent interest in natural user interaction (NUI) has led to the development of low cost (~£200) sensors capable of 3D body scanning, however, there has been little consideration of their validity. A scanning system comprising four Microsoft Kinect sensors (a typical NUI sensor) was used to scan twelve living male participants three times. Volume estimates from the system were compared to those from a geometric modelling technique. Results demonstrated high reliability (ICC >0.7, TEM <1 %) and presence of a systematic measurement offset (0.001m^3), suggesting the system would be well received by healthcare and sports communities.

Keywords: Body segment parameters · BSP · Kinect · Depth camera · Measurement · Body scanning

1 Introduction

Within biomechanical and healthcare communities, reliable estimates of body segment parameters (BSPs) are desirable for a number of analyses [1]. For example, calculation of body volume index (BVI) is reliant on accurate measures of segment volume [2], whilst inverse dynamics models require estimates of segment mass to calculate joint force and power [3]. Accuracy is paramount [4], as small changes have been shown to greatly influence subsequent calculations [5–7].

Previous studies have used medical imaging and scanning systems (DEXA, MRI and CT) to obtain accurate subject specific BSP estimates [8–11]. However, the required investment [11], lengthy scan time of MRI [11], and health risks of DEXA and CT [9] have led to their criticism as viable methods.

Data tables [12] and regression equations based upon cadaver data [13],[14] have proven a popular method of estimating BSPs, owing to their quick, easy, and cost effective techniques. However, the use of models and historical data

© Springer International Publishing Switzerland 2015
L. Agapito et al. (Eds.): ECCV 2014 Workshops, Part I, LNCS 8925, pp. 372–385, 2015.
DOI: 10.1007/978-3-319-16178-5_26

results in BSPs of an inherently generic nature [15]. Such methods are also criticised as the data underpinning the models typically comes from small sample groups [16] that have a lack of gender and racial diversity [10], and is therefore unrepresentative of the wider population.

Geometric modelling techniques [17],[18] involve more measurements of the body, but typically offer significant accuracy improvements [19]. Wicke and Dumas [20] and Challis [19] suggested that limb segments can be reliably modelled using geometric shapes, but the trunk segment is difficult. For example, participants with a large stomach may not be well represented by the stadium solid shapes used in Yeadon's model [18], leading to an underestimation of volume. The complexity of approximating the trunk segment is further increased due to its likelihood of changing shape during the breathing cycle [19], leading to poor accuracy and reliability. These limitations have left researchers seeking alternative methods of estimating BSPs that are quicker, offer greater accuracy, and take into account the very specific nature of body segment shape.

Handheld laser scanners have previously been used to obtain subject specific BSPs within laboratory [1] and training environments [21]. Although offering high point accuracy [22] without associated health risks [23], their conventionally cited accuracy may be reduced when scanning living humans due to the possibility of involuntary movement over the lengthy scanning duration (~30 minutes). Full body scanners based on laser [24], and structured light [25] offer shorter scan times (<30 seconds), but are prohibitively expensive for the majority of sports and healthcare research laboratories [26].

The recent interest in natural user interaction (NUI) has led to the development of low cost (in the region of £200 [27]) sensors which use a combination of 3D structured light scanning [28] and computer vision techniques [29] to capture human motion in 3D [30]. 3D scan data is typically captured at a rate of 30Hz and can be accessed in raw point cloud form [31]: providing a low cost method of 3D scanning. Their launch has led to significant interest in a range of communities including: robotics [32], body scanning [30], healthcare [33], graphics [34] and apparel [35].

Despite this, there have been few studies investigating their validity. A number of recent studies [31,36,37] investigated the accuracy of typical NUI sensors, but mainly focussed on simple measurements such as Euclidian distances and plane fitting residuals. Only single sensors were investigated, whereas a body scanning system would typically comprise multiple sensors [30,38,39], possibly leading to a computing of error. A recent study by Clarkson et al [39] provides the most applicable assessment, using a scanning system comprising four Microsoft Kinect NUI sensors to take multiple scans of a machined cylinder representative of a large body segment. Circumference measurements were taken throughout the length of the cylinder and compared to gold standard measurements (± 0.01mm) taken with callipers. The results showed good reliability, and the presence of a systematic measurement overestimation. Nevertheless, suggesting potential for obtaining accurate and reliable BSPs of living human participants.

The purpose of this study was to compare two methods of obtaining first order BSP estimates (volume) of a living human participant's trunk segment. The trunk segment was chosen due to the well cited problems with modelling the trunk using geometric shapes. BSP estimates were obtained using a scanning system - comprising four NUI sensors - and with a geometric modelling technique. Intra participant reliability and the difference between methods was assessed. If the scanning system is able to produce comparable volume estimates and reliability then it could be used to replace current techniques, offering many advantages, and opening up numerous possibilities for the use of BSPs in a range of sports and health analysis environments.

2   Method

2.1   Scanning System

The Microsoft Kinect NUI sensor (Microsoft Corporation, Redmond, USA) was chosen for this study, owing to its low price point, support of a full software development kit (SDK), and the favourable results presented in previous studies [37–39].

The scanning system comprised four Microsoft Kinect sensors mounted in a vertical orientation (figure 1a). The vertical orientation increased the vertical field of view (figure 1b), allowing the Kinects to be positioned closer to object being scanned, and resulting in an increased point cloud resolution [40]. The Kinects were affixed to four tripods, and located 0.9m from the centre of a 0.4m x 0.4m x 1.1m calibrated volume. The experimental setup was determined from previous investigations, and known to be sufficient to contain a participant's trunk segment within the calibrated volume, without the outer extremities of the body becoming too close to the Kinect to prevent reliable resolution of depth.

A single computer running custom software (created using the Microsoft Kinect SDK- Microsoft Corporation, Redmond, USA) was used to control the Kinects, perform calibration, and capture scans. The software was used to switch the Kinect's infra-red (IR) projectors on and off during scanning to prevent interference between neighbouring sensors [38]. This resulted in a scan time of ˜1.5 seconds, simultaneously capturing 3D and colour data.

Previous research has shown the Kinect to exhibit significant distortion of the depth data [39]. Therefore a device specific calibration procedure was followed prior to collection [39], with the requisite calibration parameters used to correct the 3D data from each device.

The local coordinate system of each Kinect was aligned to a global frame using an initial calibration procedure [38]. A calibration object - comprising four spheres mounted on a vertical rod (figure 2a) - was placed in nine different positions within the capture volume. Point cloud scans and corresponding depth images were captured by each Kinect. Sphere centres were identified using a combination of Hough transforms [43] and a minimisation technique (figure 2c and 2e). A rigid body transformation algorithm [41] and RANSAC optimisation [38] used the sphere centre locations to calculate the requisite transformation matrices.

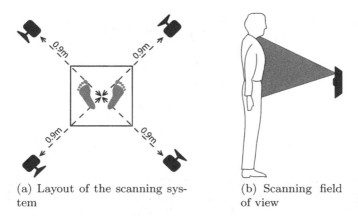

(a) Layout of the scanning system

(b) Scanning field of view

Fig. 1. Overview of the Kinect scanning system

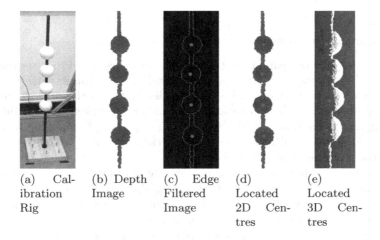

(a) Calibration Rig

(b) Depth Image

(c) Edge Filtered Image

(d) Located 2D Centres

(e) Located 3D Centres

Fig. 2. Global calibration procedure

2.2 Manual Measurement Protocol

After obtaining institutional ethics approval, twelve living male participants (aged 22 years $\pm$ 2, BMI 24 $\pm$ 3) were recruited for the study. Upon arrival, the height and weight of each participant was recorded using a stadiometer and digital scales to allow the classification of participants based upon BMI. Participants wore only a pair of close fitting lycra shorts throughout the duration of the study.

Trunk segment anatomical landmarks defined by Yeadon's model (figure 3) were located by an ISAK (International Society for the Advancement of Kinanthropometry) trained examiner, and palpated using 10mm diameter blue markers.

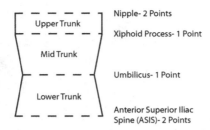

Fig. 3. Anatomical landmarks and segmentation process

Circumference measurements and breadths were taken at each segmentation level using anatomical tape and callipers respectively. The height of each segment was also recorded using a pair of callipers. Each measurement was repeated three times and an average value taken. These measurements were used in conjunction with Yeadon's formulae [18] to model the three segments and calculate the overall volume of the trunk.

2.3 Scanning Protocol

After measurement and palpation, the participants were asked to enter the scanning area. Each participant was scanned a total of three times, with one initial scan to allow the participant to become familiarised with the protocol and the data to be checked. Each scan took ˜1.5 seconds to complete, due to the delay in turning on/off the Kinect's IR projectors in sequence. A break of one minute was included between each scan, with the participants being asked to leave and re-enter the scanning area.

Footprints were placed in the centre of the capture volume to ensure the participants stood in the correct place, which also aided with improving inter scan measurement variability. The position of the footprints was determined with reference to Kirby et al [42] in order to maximise body stability.

Participants were asked to adopt a modified version of the anatomical pose defined by ISO 20685 [43] for the duration of the scan, with their arms externally rotated by 35° with reference to their trunk (figure 4). This ensured the underarm area of each participant was included in the scan, as these data were required to define the top of the upper trunk segment.

Hand supports were used to limit involuntary movement during scanning, which also aided participants in adopting the correct anatomical pose. Two tripods were used for this purpose, providing only light touch stabilisation of the index finger and not mechanical support [44–46]. Height and position of the supports were adjusted prior to scanning, with the aid of a goniometer to ensure the participant's arms were in the correct place.

Participants were asked to hold their breath at the end of the expiration cycle (end-tidal expiration) throughout the short scanning duration [21]. This ensured the diaphragm was empty, which limited shape change of the trunk between scans, and hence aided with scan reliability.

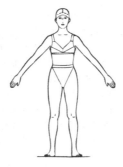

Fig. 4. The scanning pose (adapted from ISO 20685-1 [43])

2.4   Scan Post Processing and Volume Calculation

After collection, each 3D scan was manually digitised by a single operator using bespoke software (figure 5a). Unlike Yeadon's technique which models the trunk as three separate segments, the 3D scan includes a complete geometry of the trunk, and was therefore treated as a single object. Two markers were digitised on each scan, one of the ASIS markers, and one of the nipple markers: defining the top and bottom of the area of interest. For consistency, the participants right most markers were always digitised. Participants were assumed to be stood perpendicular to the global coordinate system whilst adopting the scanning pose, which allowed two segmentation planes to be constructed from the two digitised points (figure 5a).

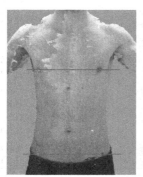

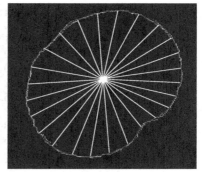

(a) Landmark digitisa-
tion

(b) Topological point cloud 'slice'.
Note. The spacing between triangles is exaggerated for illustration.

Fig. 5. The digitisation and segmentation technique

An automated technique was developed to calculate the enclosed volume of the region of interest. Firstly, the scan was constrained to only include the main cluster of points relating to the torso segment, removing outlying points-such as the arms. This was achieved by calculating the inter point distance, and removing any points with a distance greater than a pre-defined threshold.

Next, the valid scan points were split into 2 mm point 'slices' throughout the entire region of interest. A height of 2 mm was chosen as initial investigations showed this was the minimum permissible size to ensure features were accurately represented, whilst ensuring there was sufficient points to form a representative outer perimeter. Each slice was 'collapsed', creating a 2D topological representation (figure 5b). The area of each slice was calculated by creating triangles within the area contained by the points, about the centre of the slice (figure 5b). The area of each triangle was summed and multiplied by the slice height (2 mm) to calculate the volume of the slice. This process was repeated throughout the scan, and the volume of each slice summed to estimate the total segment volume.

3   Results

3.1   Agreement Between Methods

After post processing, volumes estimated from the three repeated 3D scans per participant were compared with those calculated using Yeadon's geometric model (table 1).

Table 1. Summary data for the 12 participants

Mean Difference Kinect vs Yeadon (%)	Kinect Standard Deviation	CoV (%)
6.90	0.83	0.78
10.19	1.04	0.94
10.46	1.25	1.13
-0.02	1.41	1.41
-0.51	1.02	1.03
4.23	0.39	0.37
7.19	0.32	0.30
10.15	0.26	0.24
0.79	0.38	0.38
4.09	0.93	0.90
11.51	1.40	1.25
9.92	0.59	0.54

Agreement between methods was assessed using limits of agreement (LOA) [50], allowing identification of systematic and random noise differences (figure 6).

Figure 6 shows the difference between the two methods to be greater than zero in all but two cases, suggesting presence of a fixed measurement bias ($0.001 m^3$). Figure 6 also suggests possibility of a proportional bias, with the trend of the

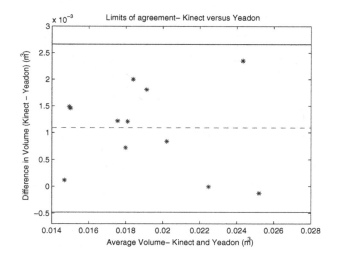

Fig. 6. Bland Altman plot of the difference between the two estimation techniques

difference between methods being reduced as mean volume increases. However, this cannot be reliably interpreted from the figure above.

To investigate further, ordinary least products regression (OLP) [51] was used to identify fixed and proportional measurement bias (figure 7), combined with an r^2 value to indicate random differences between the two techniques.

Fixed bias (a) = 0.002, 95% CI = 0.000 - 0.003
Proportional bias (b) = 0.970, 95% CI = 0.829 - 1.135
Random differences (r^2) = 0.95

The OLP analysis agrees with the previous Bland Altman plot, showing a $\approx$ 0, with a small confidence interval (0.003) whose lower limit is at a = 0. From this, we can be confident there is presence of a fixed measurement bias. Visual inspection of figure 7 also shows this to be the case, with the Kinect scanning system appearing to overestimate volume in comparison to Yeadon's geometric model. The OLP analysis suggests a lack of proportional bias (b $\approx$ 1), with visual inspection of figure 7 also agreeing. However, the confidence interval of b is wide (0.306) and has upper and lower bounds either side of one. Therefore, we cannot be confident in the findings of b, based upon the current dataset. Additional data is required as this should lead to a more reliable value of b, allowing conclusions to be formed. Ostensibly, high correlation is demonstrated between the two techniques (r^2 = 0.95), suggesting the presence of limited random noise.

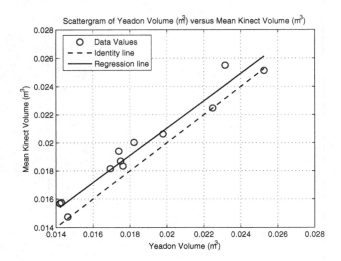

Fig. 7. Ordinary least products plot to compare the two measurement techniques

3.2   Reliability

The relative technical error of measurement (TEM) [52], [53] was calculated across the 3 repeated scans for all 12 participants and shown to be on average 0.88% (± 0.1).

Relative accuracy was quantified by calculating intraclass correlation coefficients (ICC). ICC for the 3 repeated scans across all 12 participants was calculated using a two way random effects model with single measures accuracy (ICC (2,1)) [54] and found equal to 0.997.

4   Discussion

This report compares trunk segment volume estimates of 12 living male participants obtained using a low cost 3D scanning system and conventional geometric modelling techniques. The motivation for this study was to develop a method of estimating volume of the human trunk segment that is quicker than current techniques, whilst demonstrating comparable accuracy and reliability. This would give wider access to such measurements within sports and healthcare environments, as current techniques are often prohibitively time consuming. Furthermore, it demonstrates the possibility to obtain additional measurements (such as centre of mass and moment of inertia) directly from the 3D data, rather than relying on generic assumptions or models.

Both the Bland Altman and OLP analysis clearly show presence of a systematic measurement offset between the two techniques. Results show the scanning system to on average overestimate volume when compared with Yeadon's geometric model. Previous research has shown such scanning systems to over-estimate shape [39], whilst the inability of Yeadon's model to accurately model some somatotypes is also well reported [19, 20]. For example, visual inspection of figure 6 shows there are some participants whose trunk volume is more closely comparable between both techniques. This could simply be related to random measurement errors in the 3D scans, or the manual measurements used in con-junction with Yeadon's model. Alternatively, it is more likely those participant's trunk segments are not well represented by a stadium solid shape, leading to overestimation of volume according to Yeadon's model, and hence a reduction in the seemingly systematic measurement offset. Future studies should look to investigate this further, grouping participants based on somatotypes or partic-ular body measurements, and analysing how the difference between the two techniques varies.

Results from the OLP analysis did not permit a reliable conclusion regarding the presence of proportional bias, largely due to the relatively small sample size. Additional data - particularly at the higher end of the volume spectrum - is required to enable a reliable conclusion to be formed.

The 3D scan data has the potential for a number of error sources, although the study was designed to limit these as much as possible. A significant assumption of the volume calculation method is that the participant's trunk segment is per-pendicular to the global coordinate system during scanning. Any misalignment would result in the segmentation planes being misaligned with the anatomical landmarks on the opposite side of the body to that was digitised. The potential for such errors was reduced by ensuring the supporting tripods were set at equivalent heights, thereby aiding the participant in adopting the correct position. However, the tripods were primarily intended to reduce involuntary movement during the scanning duration, which could otherwise introduce unwanted motion artefact in the 3D scans. Visual inspection of the 3D scans showed only slight presence of motion artefact in a limited number of scans. Another possible source of error, is in the manual digitisation of the anatomical markers on the colour rendered 3D scans. The 10mm coloured markers placed on anatomical landmarks can usually be digitised with ease, but can sometimes be occluded in areas where the scans overlap. For this reason, it may be better to digitise using the individual 2D colour images from each Kinect, and later convert to 3D via automated techniques. This suggests the potential for a further study, which compares both the accuracy and reliability of 2D and 3D digitisation techniques.

The steps introduced to limit such errors ensured intra participant reliability was high (table 1), which further suggests presence of a systematic measurement bias. Putting the results into context, ISAK state acceptable intra examiner relative TEMs of $\leq 1\%$ for a level 2 examiner taking body measurements (girths, lengths etc) [47]. The 12 participants in this study have an average TEM of 0.88% (0.10), suggesting the system presented here would be well received within sports and healthcare communities. A recent study by Outram et al [48] investigated the accuracy of trunk segment volume estimates using a slightly modified version of Yeadon's geometric model. ICC was used to assess reliability, which has been deemed appropriate for use in healthcare environments [49]. Average ICC across the trunk segment was shown to be 0.887, in comparison to an average ICC of 0.998 by the scanning system. Acceptable accuracy is typically deemed by an ICC $\geq$ 0.70 [50], again suggesting the system would be well received within sports and healthcare communities.

The system developed here is low cost ($\sim$£1500), easy to setup, calibrate, and use. The system is capable of obtaining BSP estimates much quicker than current techniques, increasing the availability of BSP estimates, and enabling their use in environments (such as sports training and competition) where current techniques are often prohibitively time consuming. Perhaps the biggest advantage of the system presented here is that all the measurements are directly calculated from the 3D scans, and are therefore specific to the person, and not reliant upon generic assumptions or models whose accuracy may vary with participant age, gender, or physique. In addition to the first order BSP presented here, the 3D scans allow the possibility of directly calculating higher order BSPs such as centre of mass and moment of inertia, as well as lower order anthropometrics such as circumferences, surface distances, and Euclidian distances. The ability to archive the 3D scans means additional measurements can be taken at any point in the future, also allowing historical scans to be overlaid on one another to compare changes in physique over time.

The high intra participant reliability, greater ICC than current techniques, adherence to ISAK reliability standards, and unique features offered by the system suggest it would be well received by sports and healthcare communities. The volume overestimation appears systematic throughout the scans, and the variable difference between techniques expected to be related to Yeadon's stadium solids and their ability to accurately model some somatotypes better than others. Whilst the system has demonstrated good performance when scanning the trunk segment, further work is required to determine equivalent metrics when scanning segments known to be better approximated by geometric shapes [19,20]: such as the arms and legs.

5   Conclusions

This study presents a simple, low cost 3D body scanning system ($\sim$£1500) which is able to calculate the volume of a living human's body segments using a semi-automated approach. The volume of 12 living male participants' trunk segments was estimated with the system, and compared to estimates obtained with Yeadon's geometric modelling technique. Results showed the 3D scanning system to systematically overestimate volume, in comparison to Yeadon's technique. Without gold standard data it is impossible to conclude whether this is a systematic measurement offset in the scanning system, or due to the well cited problems of modelling the trunk segment using geometric shapes. Reliability was high, within ISAK level 2 limits, and greater than that offered with Yeadon's geometric modelling techniques. Considering all these factors, and the unique advantages offered by the 3D scanning system, this study suggests great potential for use of the system within sports and healthcare environments to assess person specific BSPs: giving access to data which is currently infeasible due to prohibitively time consuming techniques.

Acknowledgements. The authors would like to acknowledge the assistance of Alice Bullas with the collection of anthropometric measurements in accordance with ISAK techniques.

References

1. Lerch, T., MacGillivray, M., Domina, T.: 3D Laser Scanning: A Model of Multidisciplinary Research. Journal of Textile and Apparel Technology and Management **5**(3), 1–22 (2006)
2. Robinson, A., Mccarthy, M., Brown, S., Evenden, A., Zou, L.: Improving the quality of measurements through the implementation of customised reference artefacts. In: 3D Body Scanning Technologies, pp. 235–246 Lugano (2012)
3. Piovesan, D., Pierobon, A., Dizio, P., Lackner, J.R.: Comparative analysis of methods for estimating arm segment parameters and joint torques from inverse dynamics. Journal of Biomechanical Engineering **133**(3), 31003(1)-31003(15) (March 2011)
4. Durkin, J.L., Dowling, J.J., Andrews, D.M.: The measurement of body segment inertial parameters using dual energy X-ray absorptiometry. Journal of Biomechanics **35**(12), 1575–1580 (2002)
5. Damavandi, M., Farahpour, N., Allard, P.: Determination of body segment masses and centers of mass using a force plate method in individuals of different morphology. Medical Engineering & Physics **31**(9), 1187–1194 (2009)
6. Pearsall, D.J., Costigan, P.A.: The effect of segment parameter error on gait analysis results. Gait & Posture **9**(3), 173–183 (1999)
7. Rao, G., Amarantini, D., Berton, E., Favier, D.: Influence of body segments' parameters estimation models on inverse dynamics solutions during gait. Journal of Biomechanics **39**(8), 1531–1536 (2006)
8. Bauer, J.J., Pavol, M.J., Snow, C.M., Hayes, W.C.: MRI-derived body segment parameters of children differ from age-based estimates derived using photogrammetry. Journal of Biomechanics **40**(13), 2904–2910 (2007)
9. Pearsall, D.J., Reid, J.G., Livingston, L.A.: Segmental inertial parameters of the human trunk as determined from computed tomography. Annuals of Biomedical Engineering **24**(2), 198–210 (1996)
10. Cheng, C.K., Chen, H.H., Chen, C.S., Chen, C.L., Chen, C.Y.: Segment inertial properties of Chinese adults determined from magnetic resonance imaging. Clinical Biomechanics **15**(8), 559–566 (2000)
11. Martin, P.E., Mungiole, M., Longhill, J.M.: The use of magnetic resonance imaging for measuring segment inertial properties. Journal of Biomechanics **22**(4), 367–376 (1989)
12. Dempster, W.: Space Requirements of the Seated Operator. Technical report, Michigan (1955)
13. Zatsiorsky, V.: The Mass and Inertia Characteristics of the Main Segments of the Human Body. Biomechanics VIII(B), 1152–1159 (1983)
14. Leva, P.D.: Adjustments to Zatsiorsky-Seluyanov's Segment Inertia Parameters. Journal of Biomechanics **29**(9), 1223–1230 (1996)

15. Gittoes, M.J.R., Kerwin, D.G.: Component inertia modelling of segmental wobbling and rigid masses. Journal of Applied Biomechanics **22**(2), 148–154 (2006)
16. Pearsall, D., Reid, J.: The Study of Human Body Segment Parameters in Biomechanics: A Historical Review and Current Status Report. Sports Medicine **18**(5), 126–140 (1994)
17. Hanavan, E.P.: A Mathematical Model of the Human Body. PhD thesis, USAF Institute of Technology, Ohio (1964)
18. Yeadon, M.R.: The simulation of aerial movement-II. A mathematical inertia model of the human body. Journal of Biomechanics **23**(1), 67–74 (1990)
19. Challis, J.H.: Precision of the Estimation of Human Limb Inertial Parameters. Journal of Applied Biomechanics **15**, 418–428 (1999)
20. Wicke, J., Dumas, G.A.: Influence of the Volume and Density Functions Within Geometric Models for Estimating Trunk Inertial Parameters. Journal of Applied Biomechanics **26**, 26–31 (2010)
21. Schranz, N., Tomkinson, G., Olds, T., Daniell, N.: Three-dimensional anthropometric analysis: differences between elite Australian rowers and the general population. Journal of sports sciences **28**(5), 459–469 (2010)
22. Nikon Corp: Metris D100 Laser Scanner (2011)
23. Henderson, R., Schulmeister, K.: Laser Safety. Taylor and Francis (2003)
24. Vitronic: Vitus 3D Body Scanner (2011)
25. TC2: TC2 NX-16 3D Body Scanner. Technical report, Cary, USA (2010)
26. Weiss, A., Hirshberg, D., Black, M.J.: Home 3D body scans from noisy image and range data. In: 13th International Conference on Computer Vision, Barcelona (2011)
27. Amazon: Kinect & Kinect Adventures for XBox 360 (2012)
28. Primesense Ltd: Three Dimensional Scanning using Speckle patterns (2009)
29. Shotton, J., Sharp, T., Fitzgibbon, A., Cook, M., Finocchio, M., Moore, R., Kipman, A., Blake, A.: Real-Time Human Pose Recognition in Parts from Single Depth Images. IEEE CVPR **3**, 1297–1304 (2011)
30. Boehm, J.: Natural user interface sensors for human body measurement. International Archives of the Photogrammetry, Remote Sensing and Spatial Information Sciences XXXIX(B3), 531–536 (2012)
31. Khoshelham, K.: Accuracy analysis of Kinect depth data. In: Lichti, D., Habib, A. (eds.) ISPRS Workshop Laser Scanning, Calgary, 1–6 (2010)
32. Henry, P., Krainin, M., Herbst, E., Ren, X., Fox, D.: RGB-D mapping: using kinect-style depth cameras for dense 3D modeling of indoor environments. The International Journal of Robotics Research **31**(5), 647–663 (2012)
33. Labelle, K.: Evaluation of Kinect joint tracking for clinical and in home stroke rehabilitation tools. PhD thesis, Notre Dame, Indiana (2011)
34. Izadi, S., Kim, D., Hilliges, O., Molyneaux, D., Newcombe, R., Kohli, P., Shotton, J., Hodges, S., Freeman, D., Davison, A., Fitzgibbon, A.: KinectFusion: Real-time 3D Reconstruction and Interaction Using a Moving Depth Camera. In: Symposium, U.I.S.T. (ed.) Santa, pp. 559–568. CA, Barbara (2011)
35. Stampfli, P., Rissiek, A., Trieb, R., Seidi, A.: SizeITALY - The Actual Italian Measurement Survey. In: 3D Body Scanning Technologies, Lugano, Switzerland (2012) 261–268
36. Boehm, J.: Accuracy Investigation for Natural User Interface Sensors. In: Low Cost 3D Sensors, Algorithms and Applications, Berlin (2011)
37. Menna, F., Remondino, F., Battisti, R., Nocerino, E.: Geometric investigation of a gaming active device. In: Proceedings of the SPIE 8085(XI) (2011) 80850G(1)-80850G(15)

38. Clarkson, S., Choppin, S., Hart, J., Heller, B., Wheat, J.: Calculating Body Segment Inertia Parameters from a Single Rapid Scan Using the Microsoft Kinect. In: Consulting, Hometrica (ed.) 3D Body Scanning Technologies, pp. 153–163, Lugano. Hometrica Consulting (2012)
39. Clarkson, S., Wheat, J., Heller, B., Webster, J., Choppin, S.: Distortion Correction of Depth Data from Consumer Depth Cameras. In: Consulting, Hometrica (ed.) 3D Body Scanning Technologies, pp. 426–437, Long Beach. Hometrica Consulting (2013)
40. Khoshelham, K., Elberink, S.O.: Accuracy and resolution of Kinect depth data for indoor mapping applications. Sensors 12(2), 1437–1454 (2012)
41. Soderkvist, I., Wedin, P.A.: Determining the movements of the skeleton using well configured markers. Journal of Biomechanics 26(12), 1473–1477 (1993)
42. Kirby, R., Price, N., MacLeod, D.: The Influence of Foot Position on Standing Balance. Journal of Biomechanics 20(4), 423–427 (1987)
43. International Standards Office: ISO 20685, 3-D Scanning Methodologies for Internationally Compatible Anthropometric Databases (2010)
44. Kouzaki, M., Masani, K.: Reduced postural sway during quiet standing by light touch is due to finger tactile feedback but not mechanical support. Experimental brain research 188(1), 153–158 (2008)
45. Lackner, J., Rabin, E., DiZio, P.: Stabilization of posture by precision touch of the index finger with rigid and flexible filaments. Experimental Brain Research 139(4), 454–464 (2001)
46. Schranz, N., Tomkinson, G., Olds, T., Petkov, J., Hahn, A.G.: Is three-dimensional anthropometric analysis as good as traditional anthropometric analysis in predicting junior rowing performance? Journal of sports sciences 30(12), 1241–1248 (2012)
47. Stewart, A., Sutton, L.: Body Composition in Sport, Exercise and Health, 1st edn. Routledge, Oxon (2012)
48. Outram, T., Domone, S., Wheat, J.: The reliability of trunk segment inertial parameter estimates made from geometric models. In: 30th Annual Conference of Biomechanics in Sports. Number 113, pp. 47–50 (2012)
49. Munro, B.: Statistical Methods for Health Care Research, 4th edn. Lippincott Williams and Wilkins, Philadelphia (2000)
50. de Vet, H.C.W., Terwee, C.B., Knol, D.L., Bouter, L.M.: When to use agreement versus reliability measures. Journal of clinical epidemiology 59(10), 1033–1039 (2006)

Visualization of Temperature Change Using RGB-D Camera and Thermal Camera

Wataru Nakagawa[1]([✉]), Kazuki Matsumoto[1], Francois de Sorbier[1],
Maki Sugimoto[1], Hideo Saito[1], Shuji Senda[2], Takashi Shibata[2],
and Akihiko Iketani[2]

[1] Keio University, Yokohama, Japan
nakagawa@hvrl.ics.keio.ac.jp
[2] NEC Corporation, Kawasaki, Japan

Abstract. In this paper, we present a system for visualizing temperature changes in a scene using an RGB-D camera coupled with a thermal camera. This system has applications in the context of maintenance of power equipments. We propose a two-stage approach made of with an offline and an online phases. During the first stage, after the calibration, we generate a 3D reconstruction of the scene with the color and the thermal data. We then apply the Viewpoint Generative Learning (VGL) method on the colored 3D model for creating a database of descriptors obtained from features robust to strong viewpoint changes. During the second online phase we compare the descriptors extracted from the current view against the ones in the database for estimating the pose of the camera. In this situation, we can display the current thermal data and compare it with the data saved during the offline phase.

1 Introduction

Usually, anomalies in power equipments or building structures are detected by looking for variations in the temperature which are difficult to be directly visualized. Such strong changes will often imply a malfunction or a future problem. A common way to evaluate the changes in the temperature state is to fix a camera and to compare the temperature at two different times. The resolution and the field of view of the thermal cameras is, however, quite small which makes difficult to monitor big size objects or large areas. Since the cost of such a device is also high, it makes it hard to use several cameras to cover a large surface.

We then propose a system for detecting abnormalities from temperature changes in wide areas with a thermal camera coupled with an RGB-D camera. Our approach is based on two precomputed 3D reconstructions of the target scene achieved with a RGB-D camera coupled with the thermal camera as shown in Fig. 1. The first reconstruction holds the color information, while the second one holds the thermal information. The colored 3D reconstruction is used with the Viewpoint Generative Learning (VGL) [11] algorithm to detect feature points robust to strong viewpoint changes. We then generate a database with the corresponding 3D positions and descriptors of these features. For comparing the

© Springer International Publishing Switzerland 2015
L. Agapito et al. (Eds.): ECCV 2014 Workshops, Part I, LNCS 8925, pp. 386–400, 2015.
DOI: 10.1007/978-3-319-16178-5_27

status of the temperature between the reconstruction and the current time, we accurately estimate the pose of the camera by finding keypoint correspondences between the current view and the database. Knowing the pose of the camera, we are then able to compare the thermal 3D reconstruction with the current status of the temperature from any viewpoint only with a hand-held camera.

Fig. 1. Our capture system is made of the Microsoft's KINECT and the optris PI160

Since the RGB-D camera and the thermal camera are two distinct devices, we need to estimate their relative pose. Here, we propose our own calibration board that makes easier the pose estimation of the thermal camera in reference to the RGB-D camera.

The remainder of the paper is organized as follow: After an overview of the components of our system, we describe our calibration process with the introduction of our calibration board. Section 4 will detail our reconstruction process based on Kinect Fusion, and in section 5 we will give a reminder about the VGL algorithm. After describing the online phase of our method, we finish by presenting the experiments.

In our system, Thermal information is projected onto the current color image, because that would makes easier to understand where we are looking at, and enhances our system [9]. In our knowledge, this is the first work to propose the visualization of temperature changes over middle sized areas.

2 Proposed Method

Our proposed method consists of two stages. During the first one, we precompute two 3D models of a scene, one with corresponding temperature distribution at the capture time and another with the color information. We will refer to this temperature map as the reference temperature. Kinect Fusion[5] is used to generate uncolored 3D Models. This offline phase thus requires a calibration that estimates the relative pose of the thermal camera in reference to the RGB-D camera. The thermal map will be used later for the comparison of the reference temperature with the current state. The colored model is the source of keypoints robust to strong viewpoint changes that will be used to create a database of descriptors and 3D points with the Viewpoint Generative Learning algorithm.

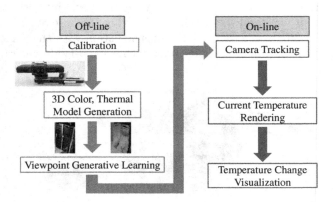

Fig. 2. System Overview

The database will then be available for the online phase for accurately estimating the pose camera.

During the second stage, we estimate the pose of the camera and use it to compare the current temperature state with the reference one. The pose of the camera is estimated by comparing the descriptors stored in the database with the ones extracted from the current view. At this time, we know the pose of the camera, the current state of the temperature, and the reference one stored in a 3D model. With the pose estimation we can then align the thermal 3D model with the current viewpoint. By combining these data, users are able to visualize thermal changes and can freely move the camera around the scene, but in the limits of the 3D model. An overview of our system is depicted in Fig. 2.

3   Calibration

3.1   Our Calibration Board

A traditional approach for calibration is to use a planar pattern like a chessboard that can be easily detected and matched from multiple cameras [12]. If this approach works well with standard color cameras, it remains difficult to directly apply it with images from a thermal camera since the temperature on the calibration board is uniform. A common solution is to heat the board using, for instance, a flood lamp as described by [3] or [8].

We extended this idea by proposing a special calibration board that is visible from both color and thermal cameras. Our board is made of two plastic plates generated with a 3D printer. The first one, the lower plate, is made of a planar surface covered of regular bumps corresponding to the black parts of the calibration pattern. The second plate is designed to plug onto the first one, It is thus

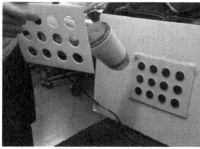
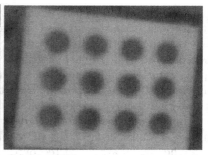

(a) The lower plate is heated while the upper one remains at ambient temperature

(b) The calibration board captured from the thermal camera

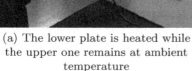

Fig. 3. The Board used for calibration the RGB-D and the thermal cameras

made of a planar surface with holes where the black parts of the calibration pattern should appear. At the end, combining both plates creates a flat calibration pattern like the ones commonly used. The plates can be observed in Fig. 3(a). To make it visible from the thermal camera, we simply heat the lower plate while the upper one remains at ambient temperature. This will provides enough contrasts in the resulting image to detect the calibration pattern as presented in Fig. 3(b). For our board, we preferred the use of a pattern made of black circles rather than a checkerboard for two reasons. First, a circle shape makes the plug of the two plates easier. Second, the detection of the center of the circles remains robust even if the captured images are blurred or if the heat from the lower plate propagates uniformly on the upper plate.

3.2 Estimation of Intrinsic Parameters

The intrinsic parameters of the thermal camera are evaluated using the Zhang's method [12]. We capture several views of our calibration board and evaluate the corresponding focal lengths, principal point and aspect ratio. The skew parameter is considered null. For better evaluation of the parameters and since the sensor is slightly different from the pinhole camera model, we start by fixing the principal point at the center of the image plane and refined it during the calibration process.

3.3 Estimation of Extrinsic Parameters

The goal of this calibration is to estimate the pose (rigid transformation) of the thermal camera with reference to the RGB-D camera. For this process, we take advantage of the 3D coordinates provided by the depth camera. For each circle's center from the calibration board, we can obtain the corresponding 3D position. By finding the corresponding pixels in the thermal image, we create a set of 3D/2D correspondences. We then apply the Efficient Perspective-n-Point algorithm to estimate the extrinsic parameters [6].

However, the depth map generated by the RGB-D camera suffers of noise. We then propose to fit the 3D coordinates extracted from the calibration board to a planar surface. The equation of this surface is found by first gathering several samples (∼400 3D points) from the target surface around the detected pixels. We then apply a singular value decomposition $U\Sigma V^*$ on the data and extract the singular vector from U describing the normal to the plane we are looking for. Finally, each of the 3D coordinates previously obtained from the center of the circles are projected onto the computed plane to accurately estimate their position. The resulting points are then used for the calibration of external parameters. Benefits of this approach will be demonstrated later in the experiment section.

4   Creation of the 3D Models

4.1   The 3D Models

Kinect Fusion[5] is used to generate uncolored 3D Model. This method estimates the pose of an RGB-D camera for each frame using a dense version of the Iterative Closest Point (ICP) algorithm on GPU [2], and integrating the depth information from each frame into a voxel grid using a Truncated Signed Distance Function(TSDF) [4].

While running Kinect Fusion for generating the uncolored 3D reconstruction of the scene, we also save the pose estimation of the camera and the corresponding color information. After finishing the reconstruction, we convert the voxel grid into two meshes. Using the pose estimation of the camera, we then map the color images on one mesh, and the thermal images on the other one. The field of view of the thermal camera is however smaller than the RGB-D camera' one and thermal data will not cover all the surface of the 3D model.

4.2   Resolution of Occlusions with the Thermal Images

As described in the previous subsection, we generate the colored 3D model and the thermal 3D model in similar ways. However, the RGB-D camera and the thermal camera are located at two slightly separate positions which implies that we need to apply the rigid transformation computed in Sec.3.3) to compensate this difference and correctly performing the mapping. Also, since the viewpoints are different, we need to deal with occlusions on the 3D reconstruction during the mapping stage as observed in Fig. 4(a).

Our solution is to perform a depth test by projecting depth and color pixels from the RGB-D camera onto the thermal image plane. First, the 3D points corresponding to the pixels from the depth image are projected onto the thermal image, and are discarded if the projection is outside of the thermal image plane. Since we are dealing with occlusions, a pixel of the thermal image can correspond

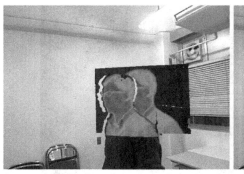 

(a) Before the processing   (b) After the occlusion removal

Fig. 4. Example of occlusion processing, almost all of the occlusion areas are removed by our depth test approach

to multiple depth/color values from the RGB-D image. Our goal is then to preserve the candidate with the smallest depth in the thermal image. This pixel will finally represent the surfaces visible from the thermal camera viewpoint.

At this point, several pixels of the thermal camera can still be incorrectly displayed in the color image, especially if the field of view of the cameras are strongly different. In our case, the RGB-D camera has a vertical fov of 45° while the thermal camera's field of view is 31°. So, when projecting a RGB-D pixel onto the thermal image, it will overlap multiple thermal pixels and not a single one. We resolved this issue by computing the average of the values inside of a 3×3 pixel area (empirically estimated) centered on the projected color pixel and by replacing the neighbors pixels with a strong absolute difference with average of this area.

Finally, for each pixel of the RGB-D image, we can find or not (in case of occlusions or if the projection is outside of the thermal image) a correspondence in the thermal image. An example of our occlusion removal process is presented in Fig. 4 (b).

5   Viewpoint Generative Learning for Tracking

During the online phase, in order to estimate the pose of the RGB-D camera with the scene captured for the 3D model, we need a tracking algorithm that can be robust against strong viewpoint changes and occlusions. Our solution is to use the Viewpoint Generative Learning (VGL) [11]. The first step requires, during the offline phase, to generate a database of descriptors from visual features with high repeatability. The idea is then to capture the reconstructed 3D model of the scene from several different views using the OpenGL rendering process as illustrated in Fig. 6. For each image obtained, we detect the features with SIFT [7]. We aggregate these features in the 3D space and conserve only the ones that can be detected over multiple views. We define these features with high repeatability

(a) The colored model   (b) The thermal model

Fig. 5. 3D models of a scene occupied by server machines

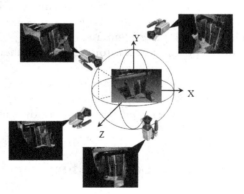

Fig. 6. Illustration of the multiple view rendering used in VGL

as stable keypoints and extract the corresponding descriptors. At this stage, however, the amount of data is too high for expecting a fast traversal of the database. We then decided to cluster the descriptors of a stable keypoints by applying k-means++ [1] on them. Finally, we store in the database the clustered descriptors and the 3D position of each stable keypoint.

6 Online Phase

6.1 Camera Tracking

During the online phase, we want to display the actual temperatures of the scene and make comparisons with the reference temperature mapped on the 3D thermal model. This means that we need to find correspondences between the pixels of the current view and the 3D coordinates and descriptors of the 3D model stored in the VGL database.

The tracking algorithm consists of two phase, the first one consists in initializing the pose of the camera by comparing the current view with the database. The second phase uses the initialization for performing a frame to frame tracking. This approach appears to be faster since requesting the database is slow. Also, we can only use descriptors stored in database, so if good features are detected in current frame, we end up discarding those if we don't have corresponding stable keypoints in database.

In the first frame, we start by detecting features in the current image captured by the RGB-D image and extract their descriptors. We look for the two most similar descriptors inside of the database using the Fast Library for Approximate Nearest Neighbors (FLANN) algorithm. We then evaluate the Euclidean distance ratio between the descriptors from the current view and these two nearest neighbors from the database. If the ratio is under a given threshold, we then verify the established correspondence, otherwise the correspondence is considered as incorrect. Using these results, we are able to generate a set of 3D/3D correspondences with the 3D position stored in the database and RGB-D current view. The pose of the RGB-D camera is finally deduced with a singular value decomposition associated to RANSAC for excluding wrong correspondences.

In the frame-to-frame tracking, we also extract descriptors from current RGB-D frame. We then searches in local neighborhood for correspondences with the feature from the previous frame assuming a small displacement. The matching pairs are evaluated based on Euclidean distance, and keep the closest one as matching pair. The pose is finally deduced with a singular value decomposition.

Fig. 7 shows an example of visualization of the reference temperature on the current captured view and of the current temperature.

6.2 Online Thermal Image Rendering

During the online processing, we project the thermal information from thermal camera onto the color image of the RGB-D camera using previously estimated intrinsic and extrinsic parameters of the camera. Occlusions are resolved in the same manner as the algorithm we mentioned in Sec.4.2, and applied on GPU with CUDA. The processing time will be presented in the experiment section.

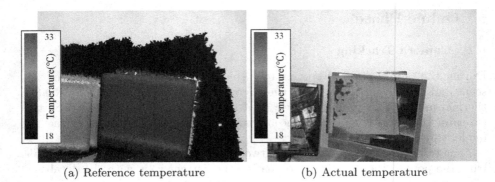

(a) Reference temperature   (b) Actual temperature

Fig. 7. Examples showing two different states of the temperature distribution of the scene

7   Experiment

7.1   Calibration Accuracy

In order to evaluate our calibration accuracy, we estimated the field of view of the thermal camera, which is calculated using intrinsic parameter from our calibration method, and compare it with the one written in technical description of thermal camera. We used two kinds of thermal camera in the experiment. One is NEC Aviofs Thermal Shot F30 with a resolution of 160×120 and a framerate 8 img/s. The other one is optris's PI160 with a resolution of 160×120 and a framerate 120 img/s. Vertical/Horizontal values of the field of view of the f30 is $31°/41°$. Vertical/Horizontal values of the field of view of the PI160 is $21°/28°$. We estimated those parameter of the F30 to $20.18°/27.56°$, and PI160 to $41.6396°/30.9459°$. We can safely say that our intrinsic parameters are correct while assuming that the principal point is close from the center of the image.

The accuracy of the extrinsic parameters are evaluated based on are-projection error computation. In this experiment, we compare the average of re-projection error with the planar approximation and without it. By using the extrinsic matrix and the intrinsic matrices of the RGB-D and thermal cameras, we projected the centers of the circle from our calibration pattern from the color image onto the thermal image that we define as the "projected point". We then compute the re-projection error as the sum of the distances between the projected points and the detected centers of the circles in thermal image. Table 1 depicts the accuracy of our calibration process with and without the planar fitting approach. This result demonstrates that the calibration process is more accurate when we use planar approximation for reducing the noise from the depth image. The Thermal Camera is the Thermal Shot F30 with a resolution of 160×120 and a framerate 8 img/s.

Table 1. Extrinsic Calibration Accuracy Comparison

Thermal Camera	Planer Approximation	Reprojection Error(pixel)
F30	Use	5.05
	Don't Use	5.46
PI160	Use	2.84
	Don't Use	2.92

7.2 Overall System Evaluation

In this experiment, we precomputed a two 3D models as shown in Fig. 8. In Scene1/Scene2, we demonstrate that proposed system is effectiveness against small/big objects. In scene1, we also compute the processing time. The system was executed on a PC with 16.0GB of Ram, a Core i7-4800MQ CPU and a Nvidia Geforce GTX 780M graphic card. The RGB-D camera is a Microsoft Kinect with a resolution 640 × 480 and a framerate of 30 img/s.

In scene1 we used the Thermo Shot F30, and scene2 we used optris PI160.

Processing Time. The processing time of our system is presented in Table 2. We computed the processing time on an average of 100 frames. We can observe 50% of the time is dedicated to the tracking. The reason is that we use SIFT [7] as local features, which is computationally expensive to extract. This might be improved by defining new descriptors which is a combination of local feature(computationally cheap one such as FAST [10]) and the depth information.

Table 2. Evaluation of Processing Time

	processing time(sec)
Tracking	0.110
Render on-line thermal image	0.008
Visualization	0.084
Total	0.202

Experiment with Small Objects. For this experiment, we used different small target objects such as a mannequin's head (manually heated), a laptop, a projector and an electric kettle. The objects can be seen in Fig. 9 with also the reference temperature and the current temperature states. We can visually notice that the thermal data match the 3D corresponding objects. For evaluating our system, we computed the average error between the depth values from the 3D model and the current captured depth map. We compared only pixels located in the area covered by the thermal data in the current view.

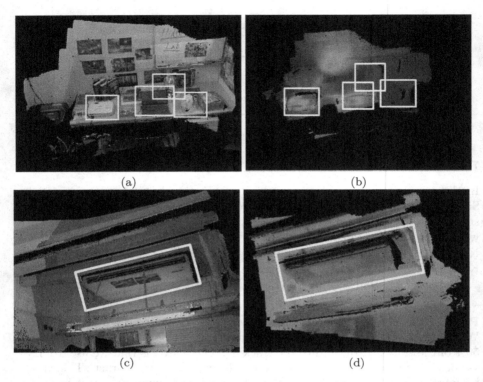

(a)   (b)

(c)   (d)

Fig. 8. 3D Color and Thermal Models used in experiment. The top row is a relatively small scene filled with several small target objects captured with NEC Avio's Thermo Shot F30. The bottom row is large scene which target object is air-conditioner captured with Optris PI 160. Target objects are emphasized with yellow lines.

In the left side of Table 3, we present the average error in terms of depth for each of our target objects. For objects with a relatively simple shape such as the projector, the error becomes less than 1cm. On the other hand, with more complex objects like the mannequin's head and the electric kettle, the error varies from 1cm to 3cm. However, with the laptop PC even if its shape is simple, the error is the largest one, because its material properties increase the noise in the depth map. By observing the results, we can then conclude that our system is stable to many kinds of small objects, and that the tracking and calibration are accurate enough for our purpose.

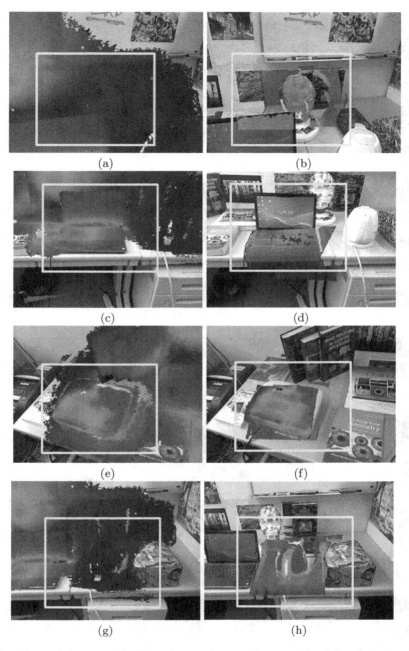

Fig. 9. Thermal image with the reference temperature on the left column and the current temperature state in the right column. Mannequin, notebook PC, projector, electric kettle from top to bottom The size of the thermal information is smaller in the right column because left one is generated by rendering precomputed 3D thermal model from the estimated camera pose.

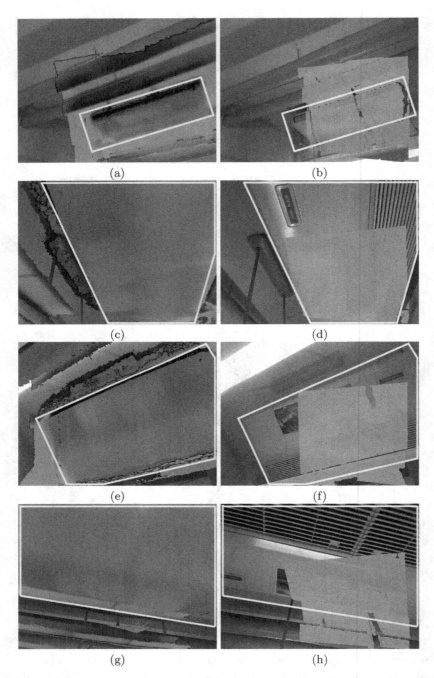

Fig. 10. Thermal image of normal state and abnormalities detecting time. Target object is air-conditioner and images are captured from front, side, under, behind against target object from top to bottom

Experiment with Large Object. For this experiment, we used an air-conditioner as a large target object. We evaluated in the same manner as for small objects. Accuracy is evaluated from different view points(front, side, under, behind). The result is shown in Fig. 10, and the right side of Table 3. We can visually notice that the thermal data match the 3D corresponding objects. Average of depth error from "Side", "Under", "Behind" viewpoints is under 3cm. We can then assume that the current view of the temperature is correctly projected on the reference model. Average of depth error from and "Front" viewpoint is over 4cm and is larger compared to the one from other viewpoints.

For "Front" viewpoint, images were captured from far, that is why camera tracking by matching descriptors would be a difficult task, and also depth accuracy with RGB-D camera would become low.

For these reasons, about result from "Front" viewpoint, we can say result is acceptable. We can then conclude that our system is robust to strong viewpoint changes and works for large object which we need to see temperature changes from many viewpoints to detect abnormalities. (For example, temperature change of outlet of cold air can only be seen from front viewpoint.)

Table 3. Overall System Evaluation

	Scene1		Scene2
Target Object	Average Error of Depth(mm)	Viewpoint	Average Error of Depth(mm)
Mannequin	13.63	Front	48.5208
Note-PC	43.88	Side	9.08713
Projector	6.39	Under	25.7105
Electric Kettle	23.48	Behind	26.9239

8 Conclusion

In this paper, we proposed a system for visualizing temperature changes of a given scene using a RGB-D camera coupled with a thermal camera. During an offline phase, we reconstruct a 3D model of the scene and save the poses of the camera with the corresponding color and thermal images. During the online phase, using the Viewpoint Generative Learning method applied on the 3D reconstruction of the scene, we are able to know the pose of the camera and compare the current status of the temperature compared with the reference one. With our experiments, we have shown that we can accurately calibrate our capture system and visualize the differences between current and reference temperatures. In future works, we would like to optimize the tracking by using new descriptors that could be a combination of local feature and depth information, and focus on single objects tracking rather than a whole scene.

References

1. Arthur, D., Vassilvitskii, S.: k-means++: the advantages of careful seeding. In: Proceedings of the 18th Annual ACM-SIAM Symposium on Discrete Algorithms, pp. 1027–1035 (2007)
2. Besl, P., McKay, N.D.: A method for registration of 3-d shapes. IEEE Transactions on Pattern Analysis and Machine Intelligence 14(2), 239–256 (1992)
3. Cheng, S., Park, S., Trivedi, M.: Multiperspective thermal ir and video arrays for 3d body tracking and driver activity analysis. In: IEEE Computer Society Conference on Computer Vision and Pattern Recognition - Workshops, 2005. CVPR Workshops, p. 3, June 2005
4. Curless, B., Levoy, M.: A volumetric method for building complex models from range images. In: Proceedings of the 23rd Annual Conference on Computer Graphics and Interactive Techniques, SIGGRAPH 1996, pp. 303–312 (1996)
5. Izadi, S., Newcombe, R.A., Kim, D., Hilliges, O., Molyneaux, D., Hodges, S., Kohli, P., Shotton, J., Davison, A.J., Fitzgibbon, A.: Kinectfusion: real-time dynamic 3d surface reconstruction and interaction. In: ACM SIGGRAPH 2011 Talks, SIGGRAPH 2011, pp. 23:1–23:1 (2011)
6. Lepetit, V., Moreno-Noguer, F., Fua, P.: Epnp: An accurate o(n) solution to the pnp problem. Int. J. Comput. Vision 81(2), 155–166 (2009)
7. Lowe, D.G.: Distinctive image features from scale-invariant keypoints. International Journal of Computer Vision, 91–110, November 2004
8. Prakash, S., Lee, P.Y., Caelli, T., Raupach, T.: Robust thermal camera calibration and 3d mapping of object surface temperatures. In: Proc. SPIE, vol. 6205, pp. 62050J-1–62050J-8 (2006)
9. Rosten, E., Drummond, T.W.: Machine learning for high-speed corner detection. In: Leonardis, A., Bischof, H., Pinz, A. (eds.) ECCV 2006, Part I. LNCS, vol. 3951, pp. 430–443. Springer, Heidelberg (2006)
10. Szabo, Z., Berg, S., Sjokvist, S., Gustafsson, T., Carleberg, P., Uppsall, M., Wren, J., Ahn, H., Smedby, O.: Real-time intraoperative visualization of myocardial circulation using augmented reality temperature display. International Journal of Cardiovascular Imaging, 521–528 (2012)
11. Thachasongtham, D., Yoshida, T., de Sorbier, F., Saito, H.: 3D object pose estimation using viewpoint generative learning. In: Kämäräinen, J.-K., Koskela, M. (eds.) SCIA 2013. LNCS, vol. 7944, pp. 512–521. Springer, Heidelberg (2013)
12. Zhang, Z., Zhang, Z.: A flexible new technique for camera calibration. IEEE Transactions on Pattern Analysis and Machine Intelligence 22, 1330–1334 (1998)

SlamDunk: Affordable Real-Time RGB-D SLAM

Nicola Fioraio$^{(\boxtimes)}$ and Luigi Di Stefano

CVLab - Department of Computer Science and Engineering, University of Bologna,
Viale Risorgimento, 2, 40135 Bologna, Italy
{nicola.fioraio,luigi.distefano}@unibo.it

Abstract. We propose an effective, real-time solution to the RGB-D SLAM problem dubbed SlamDunk. Our proposal features a multi-view camera tracking approach based on a dynamic local map of the workspace, enables metric loop closure seamlessly and preserves local consistency by means of relative bundle adjustment principles. Slam-Dunk requires a few threads, low memory consumption and runs at 30 Hz on a standard desktop computer without hardware acceleration by a GPGPU card. As such, it renders real-time dense SLAM affordable on commodity hardware. SlamDunk permits highly responsive interactive operation in a variety of workspaces and scenarios, such as scanning small objects or densely reconstructing large-scale environments. We provide quantitative and qualitative experiments in diverse settings to demonstrate the accuracy and robustness of the proposed approach.

Keywords: RGB-D SLAM · Real time SLAM · Relative bundle adjustment · Camera Tracking

1 Introduction

For many years, the Simultaneous Localization And Mapping (SLAM) problem has been addressed mainly by deploying either expensive and accurate 3D sensors, *e.g.* laser scanners, or monocular RGB cameras. Though impressive results dealing with laser measurements have been reported in literature [3,17], size, cost and computational issues limit the range of addressable applications significantly. On the other hand, though monocular SLAM has reached a considerable maturity [6,13], it still mandates dedicated hardware acceleration, *e.g.* by GPGPU processing, to attain dense 3D reconstruction in real-time [19].

Nowadays, consumer-grade RGB-D cameras capable of delivering color and depth in real-time, such as the Microsoft Kinect and Asus Xtion Pro Live, gain increasing interest as low-cost and low-power sensors suited to both robot platforms, *e.g.* in personal/service robotics, as well as user-operated systems. As for SLAM, real-time scanning based on GPGPU processing has been demonstrated by the well-known KinectFusion system [18], while most existing approaches deploying RGB-D cameras without any hardware acceleration run notably slower.

In this work we propose a novel SLAM system for RGB-D cameras designed to be accurate, robust and as efficient as to operate in real-time without any

© Springer International Publishing Switzerland 2015
L. Agapito et al. (Eds.): ECCV 2014 Workshops, Part I, LNCS 8925, pp. 401–414, 2015.
DOI: 10.1007/978-3-319-16178-5_28

Fig. 1. SlamDunk creates in real-time high quality point clouds in diverse settings, such as *e.g.* object scanning and reconstruction of indoor environments

kind of hardware acceleration. As illustrated in Fig. 1, the system can scan small objects as well as reconstruct large scale environments like a room or an entire apartment. The proposed approach creates a local map of the workspace which enables multi-view feature tracking. Scalability and real-time operation are achieved by smart feature selection and by avoiding global optimization through relative bundle adjustment [22]. However, unlike previous proposals [8, 10,14,24], we never marginalize point matches so to take advantage of all the available information for pose refinement. The code of our system will be soon made available under an open-source license and, to render usage as easy as possible, endowed with a clean interface to adjust only a few key parameters. We believe that our system will allow any user, equipped with an RGB-D sensor and commodity hardware, to scan and reconstruct in real-time indoor environments both effortlessly and effectively. Hence, we dub it SlamDunk.

The remainder of this paper is organized as follows. Next section reviews related publications and highlights similarities and differences with respect to our proposal. Sec. 3 presents the notation used throughout the paper. The proposed method is described in Sec. 4 and the experimental findings reported in Sec. 5. Finally, in Sec. 6 we outline some concluding remarks and potential research directions.

2 Related Work

Besides GPU-based approaches [5,18,26], a few other methods try to solve the SLAM problem for the specific case of RGB-D cameras. Two relevant approaches are RGB-D Mapping, introduced by Henry *et al.* [10], and the very similar RGB-D SLAM system, proposed by Endres *et al.* [8]. In both, visual features are extracted and matched to find correspondences between the current and previous frame (or previous keyframe). Then, 2D feature points are projected into the 3D space thanks to the available depth measurements and camera pose is estimated robustly by RANSAC-based Absolute Orientation [1]. We adopt the visual features approach alike, but within a multi-view matching scheme which provides more robust tracking especially when the previous frame is not informative enough. In RGB-D Mapping [10] camera pose estimation is further refined by

ICP-like alignment, which yields improvements mainly in rather dark or texture-less environments. Loop closure is explicitly addressed by separately matching a subset of previous frames (or keyframes) to the current one. Instead, our multi-view feature pool is built dynamically along with camera movement, thereby also handling metric loop closure inherently during camera tracking. Both the above mentioned systems, and ours alike, refine camera trajectory through pose graph relaxation [15]. However, inspired by [9], we consider all the relevant fea-ture matches instead of marginalizing to pose-pose constraints. Finally, RGB-D Mapping as well as RGB-D SLAM achieve real time operation only when using binary features [20] or GPU acceleration [27].

A different research line deals with dense estimation of the visual odometry between two consecutive RGB-D frames, as proposed by Steinbruecker *et al.* [23] and Kerl *et al.* [12]. However, their work is more focused on low-drift pairwise tracking rather than on development of a full-fledged SLAM system. Accord-ingly, they simply create a new keyframe every time the current frame can no longer be matched to the last keyframe, thus likely wasting memory in presence of a loopy trajectory. Furthermore, detection of a keyframe is followed by a loop closure detection which considers as candidates all camera poses within a cer-tain translation distance. As already mentioned, loop closure is instead handled inherently by our tracking proposal. Finally, [12,23] perform a pose-pose graph optimization similarly to [8,10].

More recently, two other real-time RGB-D SLAM systems running on a CPU have been proposed. Scherer and Zell [21] combine the well-known PTAM [13] with the relative bundle adjustment approach [22]. They select the best keyframe for tracking by feature re-projection, then a pairwise alignment based on sparse optical flow and RANSAC-based pose estimation is deployed. Instead, we pro-pose a multi-view tracking engine, so to attain higher accuracy on the same benchmark dataset.

Dryanovski *et al.* [7] have proposed a real-time visual odometry system based on an ICP-like registration between keypoints on the current frame and a sparse 3D landmark map. However, real-time operation is achieved with QVGA image resolution, while in this work we deploy full VGA images. Also, they update land-marks' positions using a Kalman filter, while we adopt local camera trajectory optimization.

It is worth pointing out that one of the main contributions of SlamDunk consists in the use of an active window of keyframes (see Sec. 4.1), which is both novel and key to our multi-view tracking approach. Indeed, other methods based on feature tracking, *e.g.* PTAM [13], cannot handle large workspaces due to the exceedingly large number of features that would be considered as candidates for tracking. On the other hand, proposals conceived to deal with long mapping paths, such as [22,24], find the active region following the existing connections between keyframes along the camera path; instead, by relying on the current camera position only, we foster the creation of links and, possibly, close short and medium size loops seamlessly.

3   Preliminaries

Throughout the paper we will assume to receive RGB-D frames from a camera, such as the Microsoft Kinect or the Asus Xtion Pro Live, so that at each time stamp i there exist a color image, C_i, and a depth map, D_i. Camera intrinsic parameters are known and the depth map is warped so to match the color image pixel-by-pixel. Thus, given the RGB camera matrix

$$K = \begin{pmatrix} f_x & 0 & c_x \\ 0 & f_y & c_y \\ 0 & 0 & 1 \end{pmatrix} \tag{1}$$

a pixel $\mathbf{m} = (u, v)$ in C_i can be back-projected into the 3D space by

$$\mathbf{p} = K^{-1} \begin{bmatrix} u \cdot D_i(\mathbf{m}) \\ v \cdot D_i(\mathbf{m}) \\ D_i(\mathbf{m}) \end{bmatrix}. \tag{2}$$

Then, the global coordinates of $\mathbf{p}$ are obtained by rotation and translation according to the estimated camera pose, generally written as a 3×3 rotation matrix R and a translation vector $t \in \mathbb{R}^3$. Hereinafter, we will denote the camera pose at time i as

$$T_i = \begin{pmatrix} R_i & t_i \\ \bar{\mathbf{0}} & 1 \end{pmatrix} \tag{3}$$

and the corresponding global coordinates of $\mathbf{p}_i$ as $T_i[\mathbf{p}]$.

4   The SlamDunk Algorithm

As depicted in Fig. 2, the proposed SLAM algorithm can be decoupled into three main modules, namely Local Mapping (Sec. 4.1), Camera Tracking (Sec. 4.2) and Local Optimization (Sec. 4.3).

As for the first module, we model the camera path as a collection of keyframes and store their poses within a quadtree data structure. However, as suggested by [22,24], to permit exploration of large workspaces we do not consider the whole path for tracking and mapping but, instead, dynamically select a subset of neighboring keyframes, referred to as *active keyframe window*, which creates a local map of the workspace that gets updated smoothly along with camera motion.

Following the pipeline in Fig. 2, each incoming RGB-D frame, made out of a color and depth image, is fed to the Camera Tracking module, which estimates the current camera pose. Purposely, visual features, such as SIFT [16] or SURF [2], are extracted from the color image and matched against the local map of the environment. More precisely, the features found in the current frame are matched into an indexing structure, referred to as *Feature Pool* in Fig. 2, which

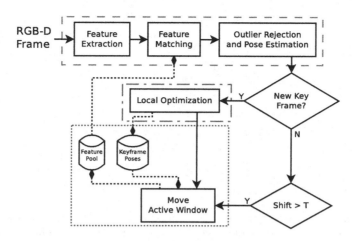

Fig. 2. The SlamDunk pipeline comprises three main modules: Local Mapping (blue dotted line), Camera Tracking (red dashed line) and Local Optimization (green dash-dot line)

stores all the features extracted from the color images of the frames belonging to the active keyframe window. Then, incorrect matches are filtered by means of a few RANSAC iterations and camera pose estimated from the inlier set.

Joint optimization of camera poses helps counteracting tracking errors and minimizing drift. As highlighted in Fig. 2, for the sake of efficiency SlamDunk optimizes poses *locally* and upon detection of a new keyframe rather than after tracking each incoming frame. Keyframe detection is based on the overlap between the current frame and the local map, thus effectively selecting those frames which contribute to better cover the explored environment. As executing a costly global optimization across all keyframes would hinder exploration of large workspaces, we rely on an efficient Local Optimization module which enforces consistency between a subset of keyframes linked to the newly spawned one. Our approach is particularly effective with very loopy trajectories, as when the camera comes back frequently to previously explored locations, we do not repeatedly spawn keyframes, as, *e.g.*, [8,23] would, but instead hook up to the known map. Moreover, as discussed in Sec. 4.4, by combining information from camera tracking and the local map, SlamDunk can infer loop closure and trigger a local optimization accordingly.

Finally, as with RGB-D cameras every color image is paired with a corresponding depth map, a complete, dense reconstruction of the environment is achieved by back projection and, possibly, raycasting into a 3D occupancy grid [11]. Accordingly, SlamDunk provides dense 3D reconstruction in real-time without any post-processing step.

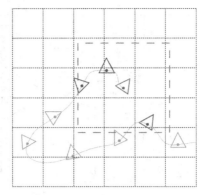

Fig. 3. Keyframe poses are indexed and retrieved within a quadtree structure. A squared window (red square) centered at a given pose (red triangle) is built and queried to get the active keyframes (blue triangles).

4.1 Local Mapping

Unlike [22,24], to select the subset of neighboring keyframes determining the local map of the workspace, we neither measure the distance between keyframes according to the estimated camera path nor we count the number of tracked features. Indeed, as illustrated in Fig. 3, we index two coordinates of the 3D translation vectors estimated for all keyframes into a quadtree approximately parallel to the ground floor. Then, to obtain the active keyframe window, *i.e.* the local map of the workspace, we just query the quadtree for a squared window of size W around a given camera pose. The choice of a quadtree data structure enables faster insertion and retrieval than more complex indexing approaches such as octrees or KD-Trees. The query to define a new active keyframe window is performed whenever a new keyframe is spawned and, more precisely, after the related Local Optimization (Sec. 4.3), so that the query is centered at the optimized pose of the newly created keyframe.

The visual features associated with active keyframes are gathered and indexed into a single KD-Tree structure, the *Feature Pool* in Fig. 2. Moreover, the number of indexed features is further reduced by considering the frustum of the camera pose placed at the center of the active window, so we accept a visual feature *iff* the corresponding 3D point lies inside that volume, *i.e.* it is actually visible from that viewpoint.

Finally, even though the current frame is not spawned as a keyframe, we might still need to move the active keyframe window. Indeed, if the camera moves back to an already well mapped location, there would be no need to create new keyframes; however, as the camera moves the overlap with the local map inevitably decreases so that, although useless and costly, a new keyframe is eventually created. This issue can be dealt with by having the active window follow camera movements. Though, in principle, the active window may be moved after every frame, such an approach usually implies a high computational effort and often small or no improvements at all. Therefore, a more efficient strategy consists in moving the active window only upon a significant camera shift with respect to the center of the local map. Accordingly, we compare the relative translation between the currently estimated pose and the active window center (referred to as "Shift" in Fig. 2): if this is found above a threshold T, we move the active window and recompute the feature pool.

4.2 Camera Tracking

Camera pose estimation is achieved through feature tracking across multiple views. Visual features [2,16] are extracted from the current RGB image and matched to the *Feature Pool*, *i.e.* the dynamic KD-Tree which stores the features associated with active keyframes (Sec. 4.1). We perform an approximate search with high confidence and a few threads (*e.g.* 4, as reported in Tab. 3) in order to reduce the overall complexity and thus search time. The KD-Tree search is the sole parallelized block of the entire pipeline.

The matching scheme is inspired by the *ratio* criterion described in [16]: given a threshold $\theta \in [0,1]$, we accept a match with Euclidean distance d_0 *iff* the next-closest feature provides a distance d_1 such that $\theta' = d_0/d_1 < \theta$. However, if a feature from the current frame has been also extracted from two different active keyframes, a correct matching step would return a ratio almost equal to 1, making it impossible to detect meaningful matches. Therefore, we compute such ratio looking for the next-closest feature *belonging to the same keyframe* as the closest one. Accordingly, we aim at the best matches from the most similar views.

It is worth pointing out that our multi-view matching scheme enables seamless recovery from tracking failures as long as the camera does not exit the current local map. Tracking failures may occur due to the camera being directed towards a featureless area of the scene or moved while temporarily occluded. In more general terms, a SLAM systems based on pairwise feature matching [8,10,23] is inherently prone to failure in case of no or low overlap between the current and previous frame (or previous keyframe). On the other hand, our multi-view approach may keep tracking even under these circumstances, as shown in the supplementary material.

As correspondences are sometimes incorrect, an outlier rejection strategy is employed after the feature matching phase. For each feature pair, we back project in 3D the associated pixels, thus obtaining 3D point correspondences between the current frame and the active window. Then, a standard RANSAC-based Absolute Orientation procedure [1] removes false correspondences and allows robust estimation of the current camera pose.

Once the pose of the current frame has been estimated, we decide upon keyframe spawning. This is a crucial step in every keyframe-based SLAM framework [13,24]: a fine sampling strategy would inevitably waste memory, while keeping too few frames may lead to a tracking failure. Our approach is to rely on the amount of overlap between the frame and the current local map. Accordingly, we coarsely divide the frame into $N \times M$ cells and count how many contain

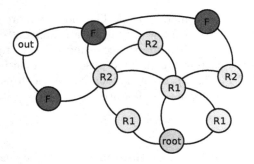

Fig. 4. Local mapping ($R = 3$). Starting from the selected root ("root" - blue), a breadth-first search reveals the first ("R1" - yellow), the second ("R2" - yellow) and the third ("F" - red) ring. The vertexes in the red ring are kept fixed. The white vertex ("out") does not contribute at all to the minimization problem.

more than F features successfully matched into the *Feature Pool*: if the count is smaller than a threshold τ, a new keyframe is created. Though very simple, we found this approach to provide good tracking quality under a variety of diverse circumstances.

4.3   Local Optimization

Keyframe detection brings in a vast amount of fresh information about the environment, sometimes even a loop closure. Hence, we refine our estimates and reduce relative mapping errors by means of camera pose optimization. Following Kümmerle *et al.* [15], we map the problem onto a general (hyper) graph, where vertexes represent the unknown 6DOF camera poses and edges encapsulate constraints to be satisfied. In particular, we minimize the following cost function

$$\mathbb{F}(T_0, \ldots, T_{n-1}) = \sum_{(\mathbf{m}_i, \mathbf{m}_j) \in \mathcal{C}} w_{ij} \|\mathbf{e}_{ij}\|^2 \qquad (4)$$

where $\{T_0, \ldots, T_{n-1}\}$ are the unknown poses, $\mathcal{C}$ is the set of feature matches between keyframes and $w_{ij} \|\mathbf{e}_{ij}\|^2$ is the cost associated to a feature match, with $w_{ij} \in [0, 1]$ representing a weight related to the degree of confidence of the match (*i.e.* $1 - \theta'_{ij}$, see Sec. 4.2). Exploiting the relationship between the RGB and Depth images, constraints between pixels, *i.e.* feature matches, are turned into constraints between 3D points (see Sec. 3). Thus, the $\mathbf{e}_{ij}$ term in Eq. (4) can be written as

$$\mathbf{e}_{ij} = \mathbf{p}_i - T_i^{-1} T_j [\mathbf{p}_j] \qquad (5)$$

where $(\mathbf{p}_i, \mathbf{p}_j)$ is the 3D point match associated to the feature match $(\mathbf{m}_i, \mathbf{m}_j) \in \mathcal{C}$ and (T_i, T_j) their respective camera poses.

Inspired by [22,24], instead of a time consuming global optimization, we devise a local optimization approach. As illustrated in Fig. 4, we pick the last detected keyframe as root for a breadth-first search into the optimization graph.

Then, all the vertexes found in the first R rings from the root are included into the optimization problem. However, those belonging to the outermost ring only provide constraints (edges) to the problem but are not subject to optimization, *i.e.* they are treated as constants rather than unknowns. This way, we ensure that the local pose configuration does not move w.r.t. the rest of the pose graph. If we find no camera poses in the Rth ring, then we fix the root in order to avoid gauge freedom. Thus, we dynamically adapt the optimization procedure to the local configuration, with just a small overhead as the map size increases and always preserving local consistency.

4.4 Metric Loop Closure

SlamDunk handles loop closure both implicitly as well as explicitly. As for the former modality, it is worth pointing out that the keyframes comprising the active window in Fig. 3 are spatially adjacent but not necessarily temporally close one to another along the camera path. This means that spatially adjacent keyframes gathered at distant times can contribute to the local map against which the camera is tracked: as such, tracking seamlessly deploys metric loops although no explicit detection is carried out. However, such implicit handling of loop closures would not trigger any pose optimization unless a new keyframe linking the two opposite endpoints of the loop is spawned, this event depending on the degree of overlap between the current frame and the local map, which is a criterion unrelated to loop closure detection. Therefore, we also explicitly detect metric loops by analysis of the pose graph. More precisely, upon successful tracking, if the overlap between the current frame and the local feature map does not legitimize the creation of a new keyframe, we still check whether at least a pair of keyframes matching the tracked frame would exhibit a shorter mutual distance on the pose graph because of the new links thus created. In such a case, we promote the tracked frame as a new keyframe and trigger a local optimization. In particular, given the list of matched keyframes, we measure the mutual shortest paths in the pose graph. If there exists a pair of such keyframes at a distance greater than a threshold, we insert the current frame in the map as a new keyframe, thus shortening their distance. We found a proper value for the threshold to coincide with the number of rings, R, used for the Relative Bundle Adjustment step of Sec. 4.3.

5 Experimental Results

In this section we evaluate our proposal both quantitatively and qualitatively. As for quantitative experiments, we use several sequences from the publicly available RGB-D benchmark dataset [25], which includes color and depth streams from a Microsoft Kinect and Asus Xtion Pro Live cameras, as well as ground truth data obtained by a motion capture system which tracks camera movements. Due to the complexity of the testing environment, the estimated ground truth is some-times not very accurate; nevertheless quantitative results are still meaningful

and useful to compare different SLAM systems. In particular, Tab. 1 reports
the results obtained by SlamDunk (SD) on four Kinect sequences together with
those published by the authors of a similar system based on visual features, *i.e.*
RGB-D SLAM [8]. As for SlamDunk, we test here three different variants, each
relying on a different state-of-the-art feature detector and descriptor, namely
SIFT (SD-SIFT) [16], SURF (SD-SURF64) and extended SURF (SD-SURF128)
[2], from the OpenCV implementation[4]. Throughout all the quantitative and
qualitative experiments described in this Section, the other parameters of our
method are set to the values reported in Tab. 3. The results reported in Tab. 1
vouch that SlamDunk is typically more accurate that RGB-D SLAM regardless
the adopted visual features. Moreover, SD-SIFT runs at 6/8 FPS, SD-SURF128
at 20/25 FPS (with a maximum of 30 FPS) and SD-SURF64 at 35/40 FPS.
Conversely, RGB-D SLAM achieves real-time operation only when using ORB
features [20] or GPU acceleration. On average, the feature matching and outlier
rejection steps take about 2 ms, while the feature pool update, which scales with
the size of the active window, usually requires from 4.8 to 14.6 ms. The local
optimization step could be the most time consuming, since it strongly depends
on the number of active camera poses and their corresponding matches. In our
experiments it required from 3.6 to 37.3 ms, though, being the optimization run
only upon keyframe creation, its impact on the overall performance is limited.

Table 1. RMSE of absolute trajectory error (meters) on four sequences from the
freiburg1 RGB-D SLAM benchmark dataset (Microsoft Kinect camera)

Sequence	SD-SIFT	SD-SURF64	SD-SURF128	RGB-D SLAM
fr1/xyz	0.017	**0.016**	**0.016**	0.021
fr1/360	0.111	0.101	**0.084**	0.103
fr1/desk	**0.022**	0.027	0.025	0.049
fr1/floor	0.044	0.052	**0.042**	0.055
AVERAGE	0.048	0.049	**0.042**	0.057

Table 2. RMSE and median of absolute trajectory error (meters) on three sequences
from the freiburg3 RGB-D SLAM benchmark dataset (Asus Xtion Pro Live camera)

Sequence		SD-SIFT	SD-SURF64	SD-SURF128
fr3/long office	RMSE	**0.023**	0.026	0.027
household	median	**0.021**	0.024	0.022
fr3/structure	RMSE	**0.012**	0.015	0.016
texture near	median	**0.007**	0.011	0.012
fr3/structure	RMSE	**0.024**	**0.024**	0.025
texture far	median	0.022	0.019	**0.015**
fr3/teddy	RMSE	**0.069**	0.095	0.089
	median	**0.033**	0.056	0.067
AVERAGE	RMSE	**0.032**	0.040	0.039
	median	**0.021**	0.028	0.029

Table 3. SlamDunk parameters used throughout the experiments

Number of Threads for KD-Tree Search	4
W	5m
T	$5\%W = 0.25$m
θ	0.8
N, M	4
F	1
τ	80%
R	3

Fig. 5. Details of the room shown on the right image of Fig. 1

Tab. 2 provides additional quantitative results on four sequences of the RGB-D benchmark dataset captured by an Asus Xtion Pro Live. To the best of our knowledge, the results achieved by RGB-D SLAM on these sequences are not available in any publication. Nonetheless, we report ours in Tab. 2, so to allow other researchers to compare quantitatively their methods to SlamDunk. Basically, these additional results on a different pool of sequences taken with a different camera confirm the good accuracy of our method. Between the three variants, SD-SIFT behaves consistently slightly better on the Asus Xtion sequences. However, the use of SURF features in SlamDunk provides overall the best trade-off between speed and accuracy. The Table reports also the median value of the absolute trajectory error, so to highlight how, in some cases, the median is significantly smaller than the RMSE, which is a symptom of a few larger errors within a trend of more accurate pose estimations than measured by the RMSE.

The effectiveness of our proposal can also be judged from qualitative results attained on sequences captured by an Asus Xtion Pro Live camera moved freely in the workspace. Purposely, we show qualitative results addressing three diverse scenarios: object scanning (Fig. 1), complete reconstruction of a room (Fig. 1 and Fig. 5) and robot navigation within an apartment (Fig. 6). Finally, we provide

Fig. 6. A simulated robot navigation through an apartment

additional qualitative results in the supplementary material. In particular, a video shows detailed navigation within the 3D reconstruction depicted in the right image of Fig. 1 and around the scanned object in the central image of Fig. 1. Moreover, we include a sequence that shows real-time 3D reconstruction of a Lab environment and demonstrates the ability of SlamDunk to recover from tracking failures due to the camera undergoing motion while the lens is temporarily occluded (as discussed in Sec. 4.2).

6   Final Remarks

We have presented SlamDunk, a novel real-time algorithm which allows for solving effectively the Visual SLAM problem with a few CPU-threads, small memory requirements and no hardware acceleration. Thanks to its peculiar traits, the approach described in this paper may represent a relevant step towards rendering real-time dense SLAM amenable to low-cost, low-power platforms, so to foster further research and pave the way for a host of new scenarios. In particular, the realm of mobile applications may soon become addressable, should the foreseeable advent of RGB-D sensing on off-the-shelf tablets and smartphones turn into reality [1]. Hence, we are currently working to create an implementation of SlamDunk suited to Android tablet devices.

---

[1] For example, the *Structure* sensor (http://structure.io/) as well as the Project Tango tablet by Google are scheduled for availability in 2014

References

1. Arun, K.S., Huang, T.S., Blostein, S.D.: Least-squares fitting of two 3-D point sets. IEEE Trans. on Pattern Analysis and Machine Intelligence (PAMI) **9**(5), 698–700 (1987)
2. Bay, H., Ess, A., Tuytelaars, T., Gool, L.V.: Speeded-up robust features (SURF). Computer Vision and Image Understanding **110**(3), 346–359 (2008)
3. Borrmann, D., Elseberg, J., Lingemann, K., Nüchter, A., Hertzberg, J.: Globally consistent 3D mapping with scan matching. Journal of Robotics and Autonomous Systems **56**, 130–142 (2008)
4. Bradski, G.: Dr. Dobb's Journal of Software Tools
5. Bylow, E., Sturm, J., Kerl, C., Kahl, F., Cremers, D.: Real-time camera tracking and 3D reconstruction using signed distance functions. In: Robotics: Science and Systems (RSS), Berlin, Germany (2013)
6. Davison, A., Reid, I.D., Molton, N.D., Stasse, O.: MonoSLAM: Real-time single camera SLAM. IEEE Trans. on Pattern Analysis and Machine Intelligence (PAMI) **29**(6), 1052–1067 (2007)
7. Dryanovski, I., Valenti, R., Xiao, J.: Fast visual odometry and mapping from RGB-D data. In: IEEE Int'l Conf. on Robotics and Automation (ICRA), pp. 2305–2310 (May 2013)
8. Endres, F., Hess, J., Engelhard, N., Sturm, J., Cremers, D., Burgard, W.: An evaluation of the RGB-D SLAM system. In: IEEE Int'l Conf. on Robotics and Automation (ICRA). St. Paul, MA (May 2012)
9. Fioraio, N., Konolige, K.: Realtime visual and point cloud SLAM. In: RSS Workshop on RGB-D: Advanced Reasoning with Depth Cameras, Los Angeles (CA), USA (2011)
10. Henry, P., Krainin, M., Herbst, E., Ren, X., Fox, D.: RGB-D mapping: Using kinect-style depth cameras for dense 3D modeling of indoor environments. The International Journal of Robotics Research **31**(5), 647–663 (2012)
11. Hornung, A., Wurm, K.M., Bennewitz, M., Stachniss, C., Burgard, W.: OctoMap: An efficient probabilistic 3D mapping framework based on octrees. Autonomous Robots (2013). http://octomap.github.com
12. Kerl, C., Sturm, J., Cremers, D.: Dense visual SLAM for RGB-D cameras. In: IEEE/RSJ Int'l Conf. on Intelligent Robots and Systems (2013)
13. Klein, G., Murray, D.: Parallel tracking and mapping for small AR workspaces. In: IEEE and ACM Int'l Symp on Mixed and Augmented Reality (ISMAR), pp. 225–234 (November 2007)
14. Konolige, K., Agrawal, M.: FrameSLAM: From bundle adjustment to real-time visual mapping. IEEE Transactions on Robotics **24**(5), 1066–1077 (2008)
15. Kümmerle, R., Grisetti, G., Strasdat, H., Konolige, K., Burgard, W.: g2o: A general framework for graph optimization. In: International Conference on Robotics and Automation (ICRA), Shanghai, China (May 2011)
16. Lowe, D.G.: Distinctive image features from scale-invariant keypoints. IJCV **60**(2), 91–119 (2004)
17. Montemerlo, M., Thrun, S.: Large-scale robotic 3-D mapping of urban structures. In: International Symposium on Experimental Robotics (ISER), Singapore (2004)
18. Newcombe, R., Izadi, S., Hilliges, O., Molyneaux, D., Kim, D., Davison, A., Kohli, P., Shotton, J., Hodges, S., Fitzgibbon, A.: KinectFusion: Real-time dense surface mapping and tracking. In: 10th IEEE International Symposium on Mixed and Augmented Reality (ISMAR), Washington, DC, USA, pp. 127–136 (2011)

19. Newcombe, R., Lovegrove, S., Davison, A.: DTAM: Dense tracking and mapping in real-time. In: International Conference on Computer Vision (ICCV), pp. 2320–2327 (November 2011)
20. Rublee, E., Rabaud, V., Konolige, K., Bradski, G.: Orb: An efficient alternative to sift or surf. In: IEEE Int'l Conf. on Computer Vision (ICCV), pp. 2564–2571 (November 2011)
21. Scherer, S., Zell, A.: Efficient onbard RGBD-SLAM for autonomous MAVs. In: 2013 IEEE/RSJ Int'l Conf. on Intelligent Robots and Systems (IROS), pp. 1062–1068 (November 2013)
22. Sibley, G., Mei, C., Reid, I., Newman, P.: Adaptive relative bundle adjustment. In: Robotics: Science and Systems (RSS), Seattle, USA (2009)
23. Steinbruecker, F., Kerl, C., Sturm, J., Cremers, D.: Large-scale multi-resolution surface reconstruction from RGB-D sequences. In: International Conference on Computer Vision, Sydney, Australia (2013)
24. Strasdat, H., Davison, A.J., Montiel, J., Konolige, K.: Double window optimisation for constant time visual SLAM. In: International Conference on Computer Vision (ICCV), Los Alamitos, CA, USA, pp. 2352–2359 (2011)
25. Sturm, J., Engelhard, N., Endres, F., Burgard, W., Cremers, D.: A benchmark for the evaluation of RGB-D SLAM systems. In: Proc. of the International Conference on Intelligent Robot Systems (IROS) (October 2012)
26. Whelan, T., Mcdonald, J., Kaess, M., Fallon, M., Johannsson, H., Leonard, J.: Kintinuous: Spatially extended KinectFusion. In: RSS Workshop on RGB-D: Advanced Reasoning with Depth Cameras, Sydney, Australia (2012)
27. Wu, C.: SiftGPU: A GPU implementation of scale invariant feature transform (SIFT) (2007). http://cs.unc.edu/ccwu/siftgpu

On Calibration of a Low-Cost Time-of-Flight Camera

Alina Kuznetsova[(✉)] and Bodo Rosenhahn

Institut für Informationsverarbeitung (TNT),
Leibniz University Hannover, Hannover, Germany
{kuznetso,rosenhahn}@tnt.uni-hannover.de

Abstract. Time-of-flight (ToF) cameras are becoming more and more popular in computer vision. In many applications 3D information delivered by a ToF camera is used, and it is very important to know the camera's extrinsic and intrinsic parameters, as well as precise depth information. A straightforward algorithm to calibrate a ToF camera is to use a standard color camera calibration procedure [12], on the amplitude images. However, depth information delivered by ToF cameras is known to contain complex bias due to several error sources [6]. Additionally, it is desirable in many cases to determine the pose of the ToF camera relative to the other sensors used.

In this work, we propose a method for joint color and ToF camera calibration, that determines extrinsic and intrinsic camera parameters and corrects depth bias. The calibration procedure requires a standard calibration board and around 20–30 images, as in case of a single color camera calibration. We evaluate the calibration quality in several experiments. The code for the calibration toolbox is made available online.

1 Introduction

The availability of three dimensional information is desirable in many areas of computer vision. Such information can be obtained using time-of-flight (ToF) sensors, which are becoming more and more affordable. However, ToF sensor measurements are subject to different sources of noise and systematic errors [6] (see Figure 1(a)), such as:

- Systematic errors due to simplification in distance calculation formulas and numerical imprecision.
- Intensity-related distance errors that depend on the reflectivity of different objects.
- External factors, such as lightning conditions, presence of other infra-red devices, etc.

As a consequence, precise calibration and sensor fusion become impossible without accounting for these errors, while good calibration quality is required in many computer vision problems, e.g. 3D reconstruction, or high-quality ground truth data acquisition.

© Springer International Publishing Switzerland 2015
L. Agapito et al. (Eds.): ECCV 2014 Workshops, Part I, LNCS 8925, pp. 415–427, 2015.
DOI: 10.1007/978-3-319-16178-5_29

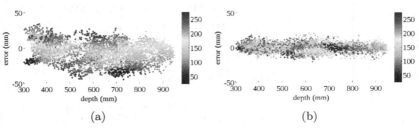

Fig. 1. 1(a) The dependency of the depth error measurement on the distance to the object and the horizontal image coordinate of the pixel is shown (horizontal coordinate is shown by color). The measurements are done using the Intel Creative Gesture Camera. 1(b) Corrected depth error: the clear structure of the error bias disappears and only the noise component is left.

1.1   Contribution

Several approaches for ToF camera calibration were proposed in [7,8]. However, they require knowing ground truth distance to the calibration object to correct the depth bias. Additionally, no approach was presented so far for simultaneous calibration of ToF and color sensors.

An algorithm for simultaneous calibration of a depth sensor and a color camera was presented in [3] for Microsoft Kinect, which exploits structured light technology to obtain depth image. In our experiments with ToF camera, however, the precision of the resulting calibration was not sufficient, due to noise and depth bias in ToF depth data.

In our work, we propose a novel calibration method for a ToF camera, along with its simultaneous calibration with a color camera or potentially other sensors. Our approach has several advantages:

- Ground truth depth measurement are not required to correct the depth bias.
- Only 20 − 30 images of a checkerboard pattern are needed for reliable calibration, which is the same amount of data as required for a single color camera calibration.

We employ sensor fusion to compensate for different sources of the calibration error, such as low resolution, depth systematic bias and noise (in Fig 1(b) the depth error is shown after running our algorithm; it can be seen, that the systematic component of the error disappeared).

We evaluate our approach using the Intel Creative Gesture Camera [4] in two experiments and show, that our calibration delivers better results then manufacturer-provided calibration for this camera.

2   Related Work

There exists an extensive literature on color camera calibration. The basic method is proposed in [12]: several images of a checker pattern are recorded, checkerboard corners are detected and then used to determine the intrinsic and extrinsic parameters through a non-linear optimization procedure.

Initially, ToF cameras were calibrated using amplitude images, delivered by most ToF cameras, as color images, and applying color camera calibration procedure [12]. This allows to obtain the intrinsic parameters of the camera. However, the resolution of ToF cameras is usually small (320 × 240 for the Intel sensor), therefore the obtained calibration is not very precise. Additionally, depth bias is not corrected in this case. In [5,7,8] it is shown that the bias is non-constant and shows high dependency on the distance to the camera. In the first two works it is proposed to correct it using ground truth distance measurements by fitting either a B-spline [7] to the measurement errors or creating a look-up-table [8]. Unfortunately, both methods rely on the ground truth data, which is not easy to obtain without a special setup. In [5], the bias is computed by fitting a 6-degree polynomial to the difference between the depth values, obtained through checkerboard-based calibration, and the measured depth values. However, the fact that the amplitude-based calibration is not itself accurate due to low resolution of the amplitude images is not taken into account.

Joint depth and color calibration method was proposed in [3] for another depth sensor, Microsoft Kinect, that does not provide amplitude images. In this method, 3D planes are used instead of checkerboard corners to find the parameters of the depth sensor, since the checkerboard corners are not visible in the depth image. The depth measurement bias, called depth distortion, is corrected on the basis of several images of a planar surface. However, in our experiments with the Intel Creative Gesture Camera, this method was inapplicable due to the imprecision and greater amount of noise in depth data.

Joint calibration of a system of several ToF and RGB cameras was proposed in [2]. There, projective alignment is used to find the mapping between different sensors. However, this method does not account for non-linear depth error and can only be used in case when a color camera is present.

Finally, in some applications depth bias is compensated after the calibration directly during the actual processing of 3D data, as in [1]. The 3D point cloud is computed initially using a standard corner-based calibration , and the bias is taken into account during 3D object reconstruction. However, this approach adds complexity in the data processing method and cannot be directly transferred to the problems other then 3D reconstruction.

We address the disadvantages of the approaches mentioned above by combining plane-based calibration [3] with the standard calibration procedure for the amplitude image, therefore compensating for the low resolution of the ToF images and depth inaccuracies. We also model depth bias, using a non-parametric kernel regression approach [9] for error estimation. The error is obtained by comparing the depth values measured by the ToF camera and the values obtained by the calibration procedure.

3   Calibration

For the ToF calibration, 20 to 30 images of a calibration board are required. The calibration board should consist of a black-and-white pattern (see Section 3.4 for further explanation) and sufficient space without this pattern (see Figure 3(a)).

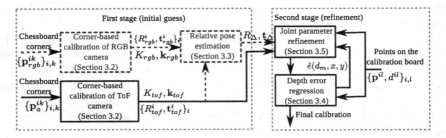

Fig. 2. Overview of the calibration procedure

We divide our algorithm in two stages (see Figure 2). In the first stage, we obtain the initial guess for the parameters of the ToF camera. In case there is also a color camera present, we initialize its parameters and its pose relative to the ToF camera. An initial guess for the ToF intrinsic parameters is obtained using corner-based calibration on the amplitude image (Section 3.2). Moreover, for each image the relative checkerboard position is obtained. The same procedure is done for the color camera and the corresponding parameters are determined. Then, the relative pose of color and ToF cameras can be obtained.

In the second stage, we iteratively refine the initial guess by subsequent re-estimation of the camera parameters and the depth bias:

1. Re-estimate the parameters of the cameras using joint optimization (Section 3.5).
2. Depth bias is estimated as described in Section 3.4.

3.1   Camera Model

We adopt the pinhole camera model to describe lens properties of both ToF and RGB cameras. Let $\boldsymbol{p} = (x, y)^T$ be image coordinates of a point and $(X, Y, Z)^T$ are its world coordinates. Then, the relation between these coordinates is given by:

$$
s \begin{pmatrix} x_n \\ y_n \\ 1 \end{pmatrix} = (R|t) \begin{pmatrix} X \\ Y \\ Z \\ 1 \end{pmatrix}
\tag{1}
$$

$$
\begin{pmatrix} x \\ y \end{pmatrix} = K \begin{pmatrix} x_n^d \\ y_n^d \\ 1 \end{pmatrix} = \begin{pmatrix} f_x & 0 & c_x \\ 0 & f_y & c_y \end{pmatrix} \begin{pmatrix} x_n^d \\ y_n^d \\ 1 \end{pmatrix},
\tag{2}
$$

where K is the projection matrix with unknown intrinsic parameters f_x, f_y, c_x, c_y, R, t is the transformation from world coordinate system to camera coordinate system (extrinsic parameters), s is a scale factor, and $x_n^d = x_n, y_n^d = y_n$ in case no lens distortion is assumed. Otherwise it can be modeled as:

$$r^2 = x_n^2 + y_n^2 \tag{3}$$

$$x_n^d = (1 + k_1 r^2 + k_2 r^4 + k_5 r^6) x_n + 2k_3 x_n y_n + k_4 (r^2 + 2x_n^2) \tag{4}$$

$$y_n^d = (1 + k_1 r^2 + k_2 r^4 + k_5 r^6) y_n + k_3 (r^2 + 2y_n^2) + 2k_4 x_n y_n, \tag{5}$$

where $\boldsymbol{k} = (k_1, k_2, \ldots, k_5)^T$ are distortion coefficients [3].

3.2 Corner-Based Calibration

To obtain an initial guess for the extrinsic and intrinsic parameters for RGB and ToF cameras, corner-based calibration, as described in [12], is used. As a pre-processing step, checkerboard corners $\boldsymbol{p}^{ik} = (x^{ik} \ y^{ik})^T, k = 1 \ldots K$ are extracted from each image with index $i = 1 \ldots I$. Intrinsic parameters are then initialized using image size. The relative position of the checkerboard with respect to the camera $\{R^i, \boldsymbol{t}^i\}_i$ is initialized using homographies. In the next step, parameter refinement is performed using a non-linear minimization of the following functional:

$$E_0 = \sum_i \sum_k \|\boldsymbol{p}^{ik} - \hat{\boldsymbol{p}}^{ik}\|^2 \tag{6}$$

where $\hat{\boldsymbol{p}}^{ik} = (\hat{x}^{ik}, \hat{y}^{ik})^T$ is the projection of each 3D point of the 3D checkerboard model from the world coordinate system to the image coordinate system, using equations (1)-(5).

After this step, the initial guess for the ToF camera parameters $K_{tof}, \boldsymbol{k}_{tof}$, $\{R^i_{tof}, \boldsymbol{t}^i_{tof}\}_i$ and color camera parameters $K_{rgb}, \boldsymbol{k}_{rgb}, \{R^i_{rgb}, \boldsymbol{t}^i_{rgb}\}_i$ is found.

3.3 ToF and RGB Relative Pose Estimation

In case a color camera is available, it can be used to further refine calibration. Furthermore, in many applications, knowing the relative pose between color and ToF camera is essential.

The relative pose is computed from the estimated relative poses of the planes $\{R^i_{tof}, \boldsymbol{t}^i_{tof}\}_i$ and $\{R^i_{rgb}, \boldsymbol{t}^i_{rgb}\}_i$ in each image. Firstly, plane parameterization is recomputed in the form of normal and offset from its relative pose to the camera. The parameters of the planes in ToF camera frame are denoted by $\boldsymbol{n}^i_{tof}, \theta^i_{tof}$ and the parameters in the color camera frame are denoted by $\boldsymbol{n}^i_{rgb}, \theta^i_{rgb}$. The normal vectors form the matrices $N_{tof} = (\boldsymbol{n}^1_{tof}, \boldsymbol{n}^2_{tof}, \ldots, \boldsymbol{n}^I_{tof})$ and $N_{rgb} = (\boldsymbol{n}^1_{rgb}, \boldsymbol{n}^2_{rgb}, \ldots, \boldsymbol{n}^I_{rgb})$ and the offsets — the row vectors $D_{tof} = (\theta^1_{tof}, \theta^2_{tof}, \ldots,$

θ^I_{tof}) and $\boldsymbol{D}_{rgb} = (\theta^1_{rgb}, \theta^2_{rgb}, \dots, \theta^I_{rgb})$. The relative rotation R_Δ is determined using the solution to the Procrustes problem to find the relative rotation [10]:

$$R_\Delta = VU^T \tag{7}$$

$$USV^T = N_{tof}N^T_{rgb}, \tag{8}$$

where (8) is SVD decomposition of the matrix $N_{tof}N^T_{rgb}$. The translation is found by minimizing the difference between the distances from the camera origin to each plane [11]:

$$\boldsymbol{t}_\Delta = (N_{rgb}N^T_{rgb})^{-1}N_{rgb}(\boldsymbol{D}_{rgb} - \boldsymbol{D}_{tof}) \tag{9}$$

The relative pose is then used to determine the plane position relative to the color camera as follows:

$$R^i_{rgb} = R_\Delta R^i_{tof} \tag{10}$$

$$\boldsymbol{t}^i_{rgb} = R_\Delta \boldsymbol{t}^i_{tof} + \boldsymbol{t}_\Delta \tag{11}$$

$R_\Delta, \boldsymbol{t}_\Delta$ are refined during joint optimization, as described in Section 3.5.

3.4 Depth Correction

We model depth measurements in the following way:

$$d_r = d_m + e + \xi, \tag{12}$$

where d_r corresponds to the real distance to the object, d_m is the depth measured by the camera, e is the bias specific for each camera, and $\xi \sim \mathcal{N}(0,\sigma)$ is the Gaussian noise.

In our experiments, we observed that e depends on three parameters: the real distance to the object d_r at a pixel (x,y), as well as pixel coordinates on the camera matrix, i.e. $e = e(d_r, x, y)$.

(a)   (b)   (c)

Fig. 3. 3(a) Three-color calibration pattern; 3(b) amplitude image: the black pattern is visible, while the color pattern is not; 3(c) depth image: the areas with black squares have invalid depth values.

Given that ground truth measurements are available, the dependence can be modeled by fitting a regression function to $e = d_r - d_m$. We use a non-parametric kernel regression with Gaussian kernel [9], as it is a fairly simple and fast approach.

In this case, $\hat{e}(d_r, x, y)$ is represented as follows:

$$\hat{e}(d_r, x, y) = \frac{\sum_j K(\boldsymbol{q}, \boldsymbol{q}_j) e_j}{\sum_j K(\boldsymbol{q}, \boldsymbol{q}_j)}, \quad \boldsymbol{q} = \begin{pmatrix} d_r \\ x \\ y \end{pmatrix}, \quad K(\boldsymbol{q}, \boldsymbol{q}_j) = e^{-\frac{1}{2h^2}\|\boldsymbol{q} - \boldsymbol{q}_j\|^2} \quad (13)$$

Here $(\boldsymbol{q}_j, e_j)$ are the points in the image, for which the error was measured; h is the bandwidth parameter, that is optimized using grid search. The regression result is shown in Figure 4(a).

However, obtaining ground truth measurements for each pixel is not a trivial task, which cannot be performed outside of a lab setup. We propose to avoid it by firstly calibrating extrinsic and intrinsic parameters of the camera without taking into account the depth bias and then using depth, predicted from the calibration, to determine $\hat{e}(d_r, x, y)$. Since d_r is not available at run-time, we estimate the bias as $\hat{e}(d_m, x, y)$, using $e_j = \hat{d}^{il} - d^{il}$, i.e. the difference between depth measurement d^{il} at pixel $\boldsymbol{p}^{il} = (x^{il}, y^{il})^T$ and the estimated depth $\hat{d}^{il}$ and $\boldsymbol{q}_j = (\hat{d}^{il}, x^{il}, y^{il})^T$.

To predict the expected depth value at a given pixel, we use the current estimates of the ToF camera parameters and render a plane onto each image. From the plane pose relative to the camera $R^i_{tof}, \boldsymbol{t}^i_{tof}$, the plane parameterization with normal $\boldsymbol{n}^i_{tof}$ and offset θ^i_{tof} can be computed. Then, the predicted depth value at pixel l, $\boldsymbol{p}^{il}$, is computed as:

$$\hat{d}^{il} = \frac{\theta^i_{tof}}{n^i_{tof,1} x^{il}_n + n^i_{tof,1} y^{il}_n + n^i_{tof,3}}, \quad (14)$$

where x^{il}_n, y^{il}_n are computed from $\boldsymbol{p}^{il}$ by first inverting (2) and then undistorting the normalized coordinates.

To be able to estimate the depth error reliably, however, it is required either to use a three-color pattern (see Figure 3(a)), or an additional space on the calibration board without any pattern on it. This is because the black checks, while visible on the amplitude image, produce unreliable depth data on the depth image, which is not usable for depth correction (see Figure 3(b),3(c)). The area, free of black-and-white squares, can be instead used to compare the measured distance and the distance predicted using estimated parameters of the camera and the plane pose.

The blue-and-white part of the pattern can be used to determine re-projection error from ToF image to color camera, for example, for calibration evaluation.

3.5   Joint Optimization

After the initial guess for the parameters is obtained, an iterative process is performed:

1. The parameters of the cameras $K_{tof}, \boldsymbol{k}_{tof}, \{R^i_{tof}, \boldsymbol{t}^i_{tof}\}_i$, and $K_{rgb}, \boldsymbol{k}_{rgb}$, $\{R^i_{rgb}, \boldsymbol{t}^i_{rgb}\}_i$, $R_\Delta, \boldsymbol{t}_\Delta$ in case of presence of a color camera, are jointly optimized.
2. Depth bias is estimated and corrected, as described in Section 3.4.

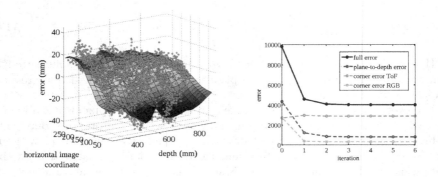

Fig. 4. 4(a)Depth error e measured relative to d_m and the x coordinate of the image (green dots); fitted regression surface $e(d_m, x)$. 4(b) Decrease of E_{full} depending on the iteration, as well as decrease in each of the sums of the error of E_{full}: depth-to-plane error (red), corner error for the amplitude images (green) and corner error on the rgb images (azure); as can be seen, 5 iterations are enough so that the algorithm converges.

The idea behind joint optimization of the parameters is the following. As mentioned above, corner-based calibration suffers from the low resolution of the ToF images and plane-based calibration from [3] gets confused by the systematic error and noise in depth measurements. We therefore fuse both approaches to compensate for their drawbacks.

Joint optimization of the parameters is performed by minimizing a corner-based error term and a plane-based error term together:

$$E_a = \sum_i \left(\underbrace{\sum_k \frac{\|\boldsymbol{p}^{ik}_a - \hat{\boldsymbol{p}}^{ik}_a\|^2}{\sigma^2_a}}_{\text{corner error ToF}} + \underbrace{\sum_l \frac{(d^{il} - \hat{d}^{il})^2}{\sigma^2_d}}_{\text{plane-to-depth error}} \right) \qquad (15)$$

Here, $\boldsymbol{p}^{ik}_a$ is the k-th checkerboard corner detected on image i, and $\hat{\boldsymbol{p}}^{ik}_a$ is the projection of the model's k-th corner using ToF camera distortion parameters and its projection matrix, $\hat{d}^{il}$ is depth prediction computed using (14) and d^{il} is the depth measurement delivered by the ToF camera. Each error term is normalized by the variance in the corresponding error: σ^2_a and σ^2_d, computed directly after the initialization step.

Plane-to-depth error estimation follows the idea described in [3]. Unlike [3], we use the same distortion model for the ToF camera as for the color camera, and not the reverse one.

In case of presence of a color camera, a new term is added to E_a:

$$E_{full} = \sum_i \left(\sum_k \frac{\|\boldsymbol{p}_a^{ik} - \hat{\boldsymbol{p}}_a^{ik}\|^2}{\sigma_a^2} + \underbrace{\sum_k \frac{\|\boldsymbol{p}_{rgb}^{ik} - \hat{\boldsymbol{p}}_{rgb}^{ik}\|^2}{\sigma_{rgb}^2}}_{\text{corner error RGB}} + \sum_l \frac{(d^{il} - \hat{d}^{il})^2}{\sigma_d^2} \right), \quad (16)$$

where $\boldsymbol{p}_{rgb}^{ik}$ is the k-th checkerboard corner detected in the corresponding color image i and $\hat{\boldsymbol{p}}_{rgb}^{ik}$ is the projection of the k-th corner into the color image using the relative checkerboard position from equations (10)-(11).

We show in Figure 4(b), that the error decreases when iterating between joint optimization and error regression, and in our experiments became stable after around 5 iterations. Note the slight increase of the corner error for the amplitude images: we attribute it to the fact that corner detection on the amplitude images is not very precise due to their low resolution.

4   Evaluation

To evaluate the presented calibration approach, we performed a series of experiments with Intel Creative Gesture Camera. The setup consists of both color and ToF sensors, the resolution of the ToF sensor is 320×240 and the admissible distance is from 100mm to 1000mm. In practice, however, the distances below 200mm and above ≈ 950mm are estimated very unreliably. The resolution of a color camera is 640×480 pixels.

To obtain the calibration, we recorded 25 images of the calibration board. For calibration quality it is important to cover most of the calibrated volume and to ensure that the poses are uniformly distributed in the volume, otherwise the calibration will be biased.

We evaluate the resulting calibration in two experiments. Firstly, we reconstruct 3D planes and compute the relative distance and the angular error between them.

Secondly, we evaluate the alignment between depth and color sensors by remapping depth images to RGB images using the obtained relative calibration. Note, that although the SDK [4], available for the camera, provided the capability to map a depth image onto a color image, the actual intrinsic parameters, relative pose and depth bias are not available. That makes it difficult to include additional sensors without completely re-calibrating the whole system.

The camera intrinsic parameters are presented in Table 1 and compared to the values provided by the manufacturer.

4.1   Reconstruction Quality

In this experiment, we measure the relative distance error and angular error between reconstructed planes to evaluate the quality of the calibration, and then compare it with the manufacturer's calibration.

Table 1. Intel Creative Gesture Camera intrinsic parameter estimation

	estimated	manufacturer
(f_x, f_y)	$(231.09, 231.16)$	$(224.50, 230.49)$
(c_x, c_y)	$(150.87, 118.22)$	$(160, 120)$
k	$(-0.14, -0.03, 0.00, 0.00, 0.23)$	-

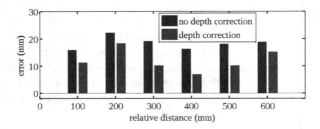

Fig. 5. Error in relative distance measurements with and without correction

Relative Distance Error. The distance between parallel planes is measured and compared with the ground truth value. In Figure 5, the average distance error is compared for several planes. As reference plane, a plane at the distance of 300mm from the camera was taken. As it can be seen, the correction allows to reduce the measurement error almost by a factor of 2 with respect to depth data without correction.

Angle Error. To measure the angle error, we recorded two perpendicular planes. Afterwards, they were reconstructed, and the angle between reconstructed planes was estimated as the angle between the normals to the planes. Results are presented in Table 2. They show that depth correction allows to improve the results in both experiments. Our calibration also allows to reduce angular error between planes. The relatively large deviation from 90 degrees can be explained by the fact, that most of the images contain planes, where one plane is almost perpendicular to the image plane (see Fig 6) or too close to the image boundary; this causes bigger normal estimation errors, for example, due to noise. In general, we

Fig. 6. Images of the two perpendicular planes, used for angle estimation; red polygons show the areas used to estimate plane normals

observed, that if the planes are placed in the middle of the scene, then the error for our calibration is less then 0.2 degrees, however, the closer they are moved to the side, the bigger the error gets.

Table 2. Estimation of the angle between two perpendicular planes. Comparison between manufacturer calibration, calibration without depth correction and calibration with depth correction.

	mean (degrees)	std. deviation (degrees)
manuf. calib.	83.42	3.72
calib. no. corr.	83.61	4.37
calib. with corr.	**85.08**	**2.88**

Table 3. Comparison between depth-color image alignment provided by manufacturer, our calibration without depth correction and with depth correction

	mean (px)	std. deviation (px)
manuf. calib.	2.6979	1.4864
calib. no. corr.	0.8642	0.5638
calib. with corr.	**0.8118**	**0.4391**

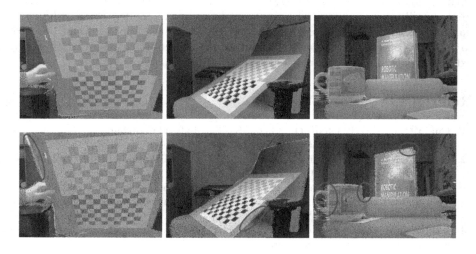

Fig. 7. Examples of the alignment between depth and RGB data for Intel Creative Gesture Camera, obtained using our calibration (top row) and the manufacturer calibration (bottom row); manufacturer calibration often does not give a perfect alignment between depth and rgb image

4.2 RGB-ToF Alignment

In this experiment, we evaluate the improvement in the relative pose estimation between depth and RGB camera.

In Table 3, the corner re-projection error is compared for the manufacturer-provided depth alignment, our relative calibration without depth correction and with depth correction. It can be seen that the alignment provided by our calibration is significantly better than the mapping provided by the manufacturer.

The results can also be confirmed visually. In Figure 7 the alignment achieved by our calibration is compared to the manufacturer-provided mapping. It can be seen, that the borders are preserved much better than in the case of manufacturer mapping.

5 Conclusion

In this work, we presented a calibration approach for a ToF camera, that can be used also to simultaneously calibrate it with a color camera. The proposed method does not require ground truth data to correct ToF camera depth bias and only uses $20 - 30$ images of a calibration board. We evaluated our approach for Intel Creative Gesture Camera in two experiments and compared the results with the manufacturer calibration, thus showing, that we are able to obtain more precise calibration results and provide explicit camera model. Due to the non-parametric nature of the depth bias representation, the approach can be used to calibrate other ToF cameras without additional effort. It also can be easily extended by adding additional sensors to the system.

References

1. Cui, Y., Schuon, S., Chan, D., Thrun, S., Theobalt, C.: 3d shape scanning with a time-of-flight camera. In: CVPR, pp. 1173–1180 (2010)
2. Hansard, M.E., Evangelidis, G., Horaud, R.: Cross-calibration of time-of-flight and colour cameras. CoRR 1401.8092 (2014)
3. Herrera, D., Kannala, J., Heikkila, J.: Joint depth and color camera calibration with distortion correction. IEEE Transactions on Pattern Analysis and Machine Intelligence **34**(10), 2058–2064 (2012)
4. Intel: Intel creative gesture camera. http://click.intel.com/creative-interactive-gesture-camera-developer-kit.html
5. Kim, Y.M., Chan, D., Theobalt, C., Thrun, S.: Design and calibration of a multi-view tof sensor fusion system. In: IEEE CVPR Workshop on Time-of-flight Computer Vision, pp. 1–7. IEEE, Anchorage (2008)
6. Schäfer, H., Lefloch, D., Nair, R., Lenzen, F., Streeter, L., Cree, M.J., Koch, R., Kolb, A.: Technical foundation and calibration methods for time-of-flight cameras. In: Grzegorzek, M., Theobalt, C., Koch, R., Kolb, A. (eds.) Time-of-Flight and Depth Imaging. LNCS, vol. 8200, pp. 3–24. Springer, Heidelberg (2013)
7. Lindner, M., Kolb, A.: Lateral and depth calibration of PMD-distance sensors. In: Bebis, G., et al. (eds.) ISVC 2006. LNCS, vol. 4292, pp. 524–533. Springer, Heidelberg (2006)

8. Lindner, M., Schiller, I., Kolb, A., Koch, R.: Time-of-flight sensor calibration for accurate range sensing. Comput. Vis. Image Underst. **114**(12), 1318–1328 (2010)
9. Nadaraya, E.A.: On estimating regression. Theory of Probability and its Applications **9**, 141–142 (1964)
10. Schnemann, P.: A generalized solution of the orthogonal procrustes problem. Psychometrika **31**(1), 1–10 (1966)
11. Unnikrishnan, R., Hebert, M.: Fast extrinsic calibration of a laser rangefinder to a camera. Tech. rep., Robotics Institute, Pittsburgh, PA, July 2005
12. Zhang, Z.: A flexible new technique for camera calibration. IEEE Trans. Pattern Anal. Mach. Intell. **22**(11), 1330–1334 (2000)

A Two-Stage Strategy for Real-Time Dense 3D Reconstruction of Large-Scale Scenes

Diego Thomas[1,2]($\boxtimes$) and Akihiro Sugimoto[1]

[1] National Institute of Informatics, Tokyo, Japan
{diego_thomas,sugimoto}@nii.ac.jp
[2] JFLI-CNRS, Tokyo, Japan

Abstract. The frame-to-global-model approach is widely used for accurate 3D modeling from sequences of RGB-D images. Because still no perfect camera tracking system exists, the accumulation of small errors generated when registering and integrating successive RGB-D images causes deformations of the 3D model being built up. In particular, the deformations become significant when the scale of the scene to model is large. To tackle this problem, we propose a two-stage strategy to build in details a large-scale 3D model with minimal deformations where the first stage creates accurate small-scale 3D scenes in real-time from short subsequences of RGB-D images while the second stage re-organises all the results from the first stage in a geometrically consistent manner to reduce deformations as much as possible. By employing planar patches as the 3D scene representation, our proposed method runs in real-time to build accurate 3D models with minimal deformations even for large-scale scenes. Our experiments using real data confirm the effectiveness of our proposed method.

1 Introduction

The ability to build an accurate 3D model of a large-scale indoor scene from an RGB-D image sequence is of great interest because of various potential applications in the industry. Such 3D models can be used for, for example, visualisation tasks, robot navigation, or space organisation. With the recent advent of consumer RGB-D sensors such as the Microsoft Kinect camera, the task of 3D scanning in indoor environments became easy and a number of techniques to map all acquired RGB-D data into a single 3D model have been proposed (*e.g.* KinectFusion and extensions ([11], [12], [13], [16])). As a consequence, the quality of generated 3D models has been remarkably improved for relatively small scenes (*e.g.* a space of a few square meters). Nevertheless, handling large-scale scenes still remains a challenging research area.

While early work such as KinectFusion [11] strives to build detailed small-scale 3D scenes from noisy RGB-D data in real-time, significant effort ([6], [15], [17]) has been recently devoted to allow detailed reconstruction of large-scale scenes by employing more compact yet accurate 3D scene representations. However, though fine details can be locally obtained, the 3D model as a whole becomes deformed

© Springer International Publishing Switzerland 2015
L. Agapito et al. (Eds.): ECCV 2014 Workshops, Part I, LNCS 8925, pp. 428–442, 2015.
DOI: 10.1007/978-3-319-16178-5_30

because of the accumulation of inevitable drift errors in camera pose estimation over a long sequence. To correct such deformations, elastic registration [19] between fragments of the whole scene can be used at the cost of significant computational overhead, which prevents from real-time application. On the other hand, for fast correction of deformations, graph optimisation [6] can be used where the scene is segmented into several (ideally) undeformed fragments that are connected to keyframes via visibility constraints. Keyframe pose constraints enforced over different keyframes are also used there. Once a loop is detected, the graph is optimised to re-position all fragments. Because one fragment is represented by a single vertex in the graph and the geometry of each fragment need not be modified, this process is executed quickly. By using visibility and keyframe pose constraints, drift errors are re-distributed uniformly (when all edges are weighted equally) along the estimated camera path to close the loop. However, this is not reasonable because the drift errors, in general, do not uniformly arise (parts of the scene with many features induce small errors while parts with less features do large errors).

In this paper, we also employ graph optimisation to correct deformations. One of our main contributions is the introduction to new geometric constraints for better geometrically consistent redistribution of drift errors. The new geometric constraints represent (ideally) exact relative positions in the real world between different objects in the scene. We reason that a 3D model is deformed when the relative positions between different objects that compose the scene do not match their exact relative positions. Therefore, to remove deformations from the 3D model, we strive to ensure that the relative positions of all objects in the 3D scene are as close as possible to their exact ones.

In order to generate such useful geometric constraints, two main difficulties arise: (a) how to ensure that each object itself is not deformed? And (b) how to obtain exact relative positions between different objects in the scene? One solution to reduce possible deformations is that we reconstruct each object in the scene from a short sequence of RGB-D images (as proposed in [19]). Multiple instances of a single object may then be generated for a long sequence, and how and when to merge them becomes crucial (as raised in [6]). We propose not to merge multiple instances of the same object but rather we introduce identity constraints that represent their relative positions. This allows more flexibility in re-positioning all objects in the 3D scene.

Overall, we propose a two-stage strategy for 3D modeling using RGB-D cameras where the 3D scene is represented using planar patches [15] for compact and structured, yet accurate, 3D modeling. The first stage, called local mapping, aims at generating, from short-time RGB-D image sequences, accurate small-scale structured 3D scenes with minimal deformations and geometric constraints in real-time. We here introduce a new model, called semi-global model, for tracking the camera pose and merging incoming RGB-D data in real-time with state-of-the-art accuracy. The second stage[1], called global mapping, on the other hand, aims at organising all the results obtained in the first stage to keep geometric consistency of the whole scene. To remove deformations from the

---

[1] The second stage runs in a parallel process to enable real-time 3D reconstruction.

global model as much as possible, we employ fragment registration and graph optimisation. Namely, we align an input local model to multiple rigid fragments of the global model, generate identity constraints between different instances of the same object and use the graph optimisation framework to satisfy geometric constraints, identity constraints, keyframe pose constraints and visibility constraints. Our proposed method enables us to (1) recover fine details of the scene thanks to employing the frame-to-global-model framework, (2) achieve real-time processing thanks to using our semi-global model for tracking and fusing RGB-D data, and (3) reconstruct large-scale indoor scenes without deformations thanks to the capability of re-positioning the different objects in the scene with respect to their exact relative positions.

2 Related Work

In the last few years, much work has been proposed to fuse input RGB-D data into a common single global 3D model.

Newcombe et al. [11] proposed KinectFusion: a system to build implicit 3D representations of a scene from an RGB-D camera at an interactive frame-rate. The implicit representation consists of a Truncated Signed Distance Function (TSDF) that is discretized into a volume covering the scene to be reconstructed. The TSDF is recorded into a regular voxel grid, which requires large amount of memory usage. This limits the practicability of the method for large-scale scenes. Then, much work has been done on extending the method for large-scale applications [13], [16]. On the other hand, the use of non-regular volumetric grid has been studied for compact TSDF representations. Zeng et al. [17] and Chen et al. [5] proposed an octree-based fusion method. Neibner et al. [10] proposed to use hash tables to achieve significant compression of the volumetric TSDF. However, because of the accumulation of errors generated when registering and integrating incoming RGB-D data, the global volumetric TSDF inevitably becomes deformed when applied to a large-scale scene. Moreover, correcting deformations in the volumetric TSDF is tedious and, in general, multiple passes over the whole sequence of RGB-D images are required. This becomes a critical limitation for large-scale applications.

Zhou et al. [18] proposed to use local volumes around points of interest, and Henry et al. [6] proposed to segment the scene into planar patches and to use 3D TSDF volumes around them to represent the 3D scene. In [6], a pose-graph optimisation for loop closure was proposed where each vertex of the graph is a planar patch connected to one or multiple keyframe(s). When a loop is detected, it gives constraints on the relationship between patches and keyframes. Optimising the graph to meet the constraints reduces deformations. When the 3D scene represented by old patches is deformed due to drift errors, however, the rigid alignment is not reliable anymore. Moreover, a critical question about when to merge overlapping patches in a loop is left open. Also, the processing time drops drastically due to procedures for maintaining planar patches. Thomas et al. [15], on the other hand, proposed a method that requires only three 2D images, called attributes, for each planar patch to model the scene, which allows more compact representation of the scene. Though they achieved significant compression of the 3D scene, no discussion was given about how to deal with deformations that arise when applied to large-scale scenes.

Meilland *et al.* [9] proposed a method to reconstruct large-scale scenes by using an image-based keyframe method. Multiple keyframes are recorded along the camera path and merged together to produce RGB-D images from any viewpoint along the camera path that can be used for robust camera tracking or visualisation. Once the whole image sequence is processed, a cloud of point or a mesh is generated by running a voxel-based reconstruction algorithm over the set of keyframes. Loops may be closed using keyframes, and drifts in the estimated camera pose can be corrected accordingly. However, uniformly redistributing drift errors over the camera path is not reasonable at large scale because the distribution of the errors is, in general, not uniform.

Zhou *et al.* [19] proposed to break the whole RGB-D image sequence into short-time subsequences. The KinectFusion algorithm is applied to each short-time subsequence and then local meshes of the scene are generated. After all subsequences are processed, they run an elastic registration algorithm that combines rigid alignment and non-rigid optimisation for accurate alignment and drift-error correction. This method achieves state-of-the-art accuracy in 3D reconstruction. However, the computational cost is expensive and the elastic registration is a post-process, which prevents the method from real-time applications.

Differently from the above methods, this paper uses graph optimisation framework with new geometric constraints built between planar patches representing different objects and identity constraints built between planar patches representing the same object to accurately and efficiently correct deformations of the global model.

3   Proposed Method

We break the whole sequence of RGB-D images into short subsequences (in our experiments we used subsequences of 100 frames) and take a two-stage strategy (Fig. 1), local mapping and global mapping, to build a large-scale 3D model.

We use planar patches [15] as the 3D scene representation. As shown in [15] and [6], however, using sets of planar patches in the frame-to-global-model framework significantly drops computational speed. In the local mapping, we thus introduce a new model, called semi-global model, for camera tracking and data integration. The attributes of all planar patches (*i.e.* Bump image (that represents local geometric disparity), Color image and Mask image (that represents confidence of measurements)) are then built on-line from the semi-global model. As we will show later, this allows us to keep real-time performance with state-of-the-art accuracy. Geometric constraints are generated from the first frame of each short subsequence. This is because the exact relative positions between different objects in the scene are reliably estimated only from a single image (deformations usually arise after merging multiple RGB-D images).

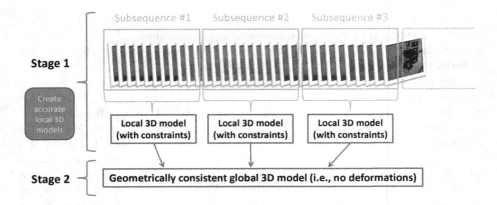

Fig. 1. Overview of our proposed strategy. The first stage generates local structured 3D models with geometric constraints from short subsequences of RGB-D images. The second stage organises all local 3D models into a single common global model in a geometrically consistent manner to minimise deformations.

In the global mapping, on the other hand, we build a graph where each vertex represents either a patch generated from the local mapping or a keyframe, and edges represent keyframe pose constrains [6], visibility constraints [6], our introduced geometric constraints, or identity constraints of patches over keyframes. Over the graph, we keep all similar planar patches (*i.e.* multiple instances of the same object) without merging, which allows more flexibility in re-positioning all the planar patches. Moreover, the geometric constraints enable us to redistribute errors more coherently with respect to the 3D geometry of the scene. This is crucial as in general, drift errors derived from camera tracking do not uniformly arise.

3.1   Local Mapping

To build local 3D models and generate their associated geometric constraints, two challenges exist: (1) how to build the structured 3D model in real-time and (2) how to generate "good" geometric constraints (*i.e.* constraints that represent the exact relative positions between all planar patches). We tackle these challenges with keeping in mind accuracy, real-time processing and minimal deformations. Fig. 2 illustrates the pipeline of the local mapping.

To tackle the first challenge, the frame-to-global-model framework has proven to be successful. However, the set of planar patches itself cannot be directly used as the global model. This is because (1) planar patches representation may not be as dense as the input RGB-D images (non co-planar parts of the scene are not represented), and (2) rendering all planar patches at every incoming frame is time consuming and unwise (as many points on a patch may disappear from the current viewing frustum and rendering such points is useless). Therefore, we need to employ another 3D model to perform accurate, robust and fast camera

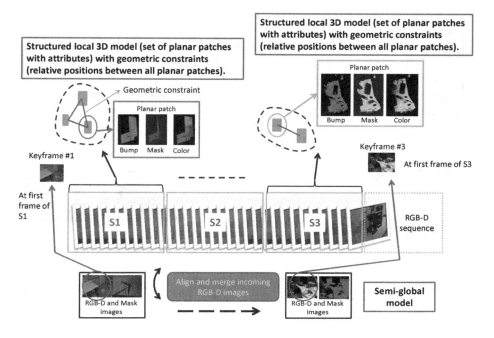

Fig. 2. Local mapping. A semi-global model is used for tracking the camera and merging incoming RGB-D images. Local 3D models are built dynamically by projecting (at every new incoming frame) the current semi-global model onto the attributes of different planar patches that are detected from the semi-global model at the first frame of each subsequence.

tracking and data integration. The standard TSDF volumetric representation is not good because it requires too much amount of GPU memory to update the attributes of all planar patches.

Semi-Global Model. Our semi-global model is defined as a pair of RGB-D and Mask images. The semi-global model is initialised with the first frame of the whole RGB-D image sequence. To generate predicted RGB-D and Mask images, we use OpenGL capability with the natural quadrangulation given by the organisation of points in the 2D image.

For each pixel $(u, v) \in [1 : n-1] \times [1 : m-1]$, a quad is created if Mask values of its 4-neighbor pixels are all positive and if the maximum Euclidean distance between all vertices at these pixels is less than a threshold (we used a threshold of 5cm in the experiments). We render the mesh three times with (1) depth information, (2) color information and (3) mask information, to generate the predicted RGB-D and Mask images. Fig. 3 illustrates how to obtain the predicted RGB-D and Mask images. The predicted RGB-D image is used to align the incoming RGB-D image using the technique described in [6], which combines both geometric and color information. The predicted Mask image is used to

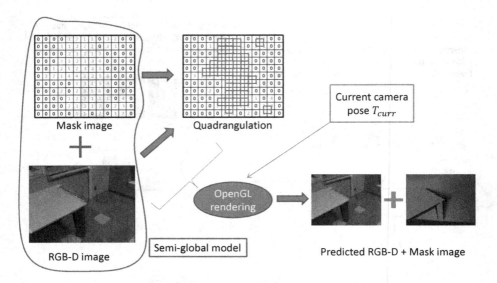

Fig. 3. Generating of predicted RGB-D and Mask images. We use OpenGL capacities to render RGB-D and mask images corresponding to the estimated current camera pose.

merge aligned data with a running average, as proposed in [15]. The semi-global model is then renewed to the newly obtained pair of merged RGB-D and Mask images. For every subsequence, the RGB-D image of the semi-global model at the first frame of the subsequence is selected as a keyframe and recorded on the hard drive.

Using the semi-global model enables us to keep real-time and accurate performance because it quickly generates high-quality dense predicted RGB-D images. Our proposed 3D model is semi-global in that all invisible points from the current viewing frustum of the camera are lost (but recorded in the set of planar patches that form the local 3D model).

As for the second challenge, a standard approach would be to incrementally build the local 3D model by adding new planar patches on the fly as they are being detected (as done in [15] or [6]) and to generate geometric constraints at the end of each subsequence by computing their relative positions. The relative positions (*i.e.* geometric constraints) between planar patches detected at different times can be significantly different from the exact relative positions due to drift errors. Therefore we propose to compute the geometric constraints only from a single RGB-D image (the first of each subsequence). This is justified by the fact that a single RGB-D image has few deformations and thus the relative positions between objects detected in a single image are close to the exact ones. We detect the set of planar patches from the first RGB-D image of each subsequence and fix it over the subsequence.

Local 3D Model. For each subsequence, we segment the first predicted RGB-D image into several planar patches (together with their attributes) that form our local 3D model. As proposed in [15], for each planar patch we use as its attributes three 2D images: a Bump image, a Color image and a Mask image. At every input frame, the attributes of each planar patch are updated using the semi-global model as follows.

Each point **p** of the semi-global model is projected into its corresponding planar patch. The values of Bump, Color and Mask images at the projected pixel are all replaced by those of **p** if the mask value of **p** is higher than that at the projected pixel (as explained in [15]).

Whenever all the process for a short subsequence of RGB-D images is finished, we record a generated local 3D model (*i.e.* the set of planar patches with their attributes), as well as the current keyframe (*i.e.* the first predicted RGB-D image) and geometric constraints on the planar patches.

3.2   Global Mapping

The objective of the second stage is to fuse all local 3D models generated in the first stage into a single geometrically consistent global 3D model with minimal deformations. The main problem here comes from the accumulation of registration errors. If the global model becomes deformed, the rigid alignment of new local 3D models to the (deformed) global model does not work. Moreover, merging planar patches representing the same object will drastically corrupt the global model. Even loop closure correction ([6]) does not work anymore, because planar patches themselves become deformed. Applying non-rigid alignment of local 3D models to the global model ([19]) is not good either, because of expensive computational cost.

Our main ideas for the global mapping are (1) to always align new local 3D models to undeformed subsets (called fragments) of the global model and (2) to introduce new constraints (called identity constraints) at each successful rigid alignment, rather than merging planar patches representing the same object. This allows more flexibility in re-organising the global model. An identity constraint represents the relative position between planar patches representing the same object in the scene that come from different local 3D models. A graph optimisation framework (namely, the g2o framework [4]) is then used to guarantee geometric consistency of the global model (thus reducing deformations). Note however that to obtain the final global 3D model in real-time, merging planar patches is executed separately depending on the object and updated on-line as the relative positions between all planar patches are being optimised.

Global Graph. We organise all planar patches and keyframes into a global graph that represents all constraints. Each vertex of the global graph represents either a planar patch or a keyframe, and each edge represents either a geometric constraint, an identity constraint, a keyframe pose constraint or a visibility constraint.

For each ith subsequence Seq_i, we denote by K_i the keyframe of Seq_i, by $Pset_i = \{P_j^i\}_{j \in [1:m_i]}$ the set of m_i planar patches built with Seq_i. For each planar patch P_j^i we denote by $BBox_j^i$ the projected 3D bounding box of the 3D points in P_j^i into the plane equation $(\mathbf{e}_1^{i,j}, \mathbf{e}_2^{i,j}, \mathbf{n}^{i,j}, d^{i,j})$ of P_j^i, where $\mathbf{n}^{i,j}$ is the normal of the plane, $d^{i,j}$ the distance of the plane from the origin and $(\mathbf{e}_1^{i,j}, \mathbf{e}_2^{i,j}, \mathbf{n}^{i,j})$ form an orthonormal basis. $\mathbf{pt}_j^i$ is the lower left corner of $BBox_j^i$. Each planar patch P_j^i is represented by a vertex in the graph to which a 3D transformation matrix V_j^i is assigned such that:

$$V_j^i = \begin{bmatrix} \mathbf{e}_1^{i,j} & \mathbf{e}_2^{i,j} & \mathbf{n}^{i,j} & \mathbf{pt}_j^i \\ 0 & 0 & 0 & 1 \end{bmatrix}.$$

Each keyframe K_i is represented by a vertex in the graph to which its pose (matrix) T_i (computed during the local mapping) is assigned.

To each edge $e = (a, b)$ that connects two vertices a and b, with transformation matrices T_a and T_b (respectively), we assign a 3D transformation matrix T_{edge} that defines the following constraint:

$$T_b T_a^{-1} T_{edge}^{-1} = \text{Id},$$

where Id is the 4×4 identity matrix. We detail in the following how to compute T_{edge} for each type of edges.

1. **Geometric constraints.** For each subsequence Seq_i we generate edges that connect all planar patches with each other. For each edge (P_j^i, P_k^i) we assign matrix $T_{i,j,k}^{Geo} = V_k^i (V_j^i)^{-1}$ (*i.e.* the relative position) that defines the geometric constraint between P_j^i and P_k^i.

2. **Identity constraints.** Identity constraints are defined by the relative positions between planar patches representing the same object in the scene (by abuse we will say that the planar patches are identical). Every time a set of patches $Pset_i$ is registered to another set of patches $Pset_j$, we generate edges that represent identity constraints. We first identify identical planar patches as follows. Two planar patches P_k^i and P_l^j are identical if and only if $\|d^{i,k} - d^{j,l}\| < \tau_1$, $\mathbf{n}^{i,k} \cdot \mathbf{n}^{j,l} > \tau_2$ and overlap$(P_k^i, P_l^j) > \tau_3$, where $\cdot$ is the scalar product, overlap(P_k^i, P_l^j) is a function that counts the number of overlapping pixels between P_k^i and P_l^j and τ_1, τ_2 and τ_3 are three thresholds (*e.g.* 10cm, 20° and 3000 points respectively in the experiments). For every pair of identical planar patches (P_k^i, P_l^j) we generate an edge, and assign to it matrix $T_{i,k,j,l}^{Id} = V_l^i (V_j^j)^{-1}$ that defines the identity constraint.

3. **Keyframe pose constraints [6].** For every two successive subsequences Seq_i and Seq_{i+1}, we generate an edge (K_i, K_{i+1}), and assign to it matrix $T_{i,i+1}^{Key} = T_{i+1} T_i^{-1}$ that defines the keyframe pose constraint between K_i and K_{i+1}.

4. **Visibility constraints [6].** For each subsequence Seq_i we generate edges so that K_i is connected with any planar patch in $Pset_i$. To each edge (K_i, P_j^i),

we assign to it matrix $T_{i,j}^{Vis} = V_j^i T_i^{-1}$ that defines the visibility constraint between P_j^i and K_i.

On-line Update of Global Graph. The global graph grows every time a local 3D model is generated. Once a local model $Pset_i$ comes, we first add vertices for each planar patch P_j^i and a vertex for the keyframe K_i. We then add edges so that K_i and K_{i-1} (if $i > 1$) are connected, K_i and any entry in $Pset_i$ are connected and all planar patches in $Pset_i$ are connected with each other (they represent the keyframe pose constraint, visibility constraint and geometric constraint, respectively).

Second, we perform fragment registration of $Pset_i$ with multiple fragments of the global graph to include $Pset_i$ into the global model while minimising deformations as much as possible. We first identify a set of keyframes each of which is sufficiently close to K_i, and divide the set into fragments so that each fragment consists of only successive keyframes.

We define the set S_i of the neighboring keyframes of K_i in the global graph as follows:

$$S_i = \{K_j \mid d(K_i, K_j) < \tau_d \text{ and } \alpha(K_i, K_j) < \tau_\alpha\},$$

where $d(K_i, K_j)$ and $\alpha(K_i, K_j)$ are the Euclidean distance between the centres of two cameras, and the angle between the two viewing directions of the two cameras (respectively) for the ith and j^{th} keyframes (in the experiments, we set $\tau_d = 3\text{m}$ and $\tau_\alpha = 45°$).

We then break the set S_i into p fragments: $S_i = \{F_i^1, F_i^2, ..., F_i^p\} = \{\{K_{s_1}, K_{s_1+1}, K_{s_1+2}, ..., K_{s_1+t_1}\}, ..., \{K_{s_p}, K_{s_p+1}, K_{s_p+2}, ..., K_{s_p+t_p}\}\}$ where for all $j \in [1 : p-1]$, $s_{j+1} > s_j + t_j + 1$. We reason that the local 3D models corresponding to successive keyframes are registered together in a sufficiently correct (*i.e.* undeformed) manner to perform rigid alignment with $Pset_i$. This is not the case if the set of keyframes contains non-successive keyframes.

We then align $Pset_i$ with each of $\{F_i^j\}_{j \in [1:p]}$. We align $Pset_i$ with a fragment F_i^j ($j \in [1 : p]$) as follows. Let us denote by $Pset_i^j$ the set of all planar patches connected to a keyframe in F_i^j.

We first initialise the transformation by using matches of SIFT features [8] between K_i and K_{s_j}. We use the RANSAC strategy here to have a set of matched features. If the number of matched features is greater than a threshold (we used a threshold of 30 in our experiments), then the transformation is initialised by the matched features, it is set to the identity transformation otherwise.

After the initialisation, we applied the GICP algorithm [14] to align $Pset_i$ and $Pset_i^j$. Because of millions of points in $Pset_i^j$, searching for the closest points in a standard manner (using k-d trees for example) is not practical at all. Instead, we borrow the idea of the projective data association algorithm [3], which can be run efficiently on the GPU. Namely, for each planar patch $P_l \in Pset_i$ and for each pixel (u, v) in the Bump image of P_l, we project the 3D point $\mathbf{pt}(u, v)$ into all planar patches in $Pset_i^j$. We then identify the closest point of $\mathbf{pt}(u, v)$

as the point at the projected location with the minimum Euclidean distance to
$\mathbf{pt}(u, v)$ and with angle between the two normals sufficiently small (we used a
threshold of 40° in the experiments). If the minimum distance is greater than a
threshold (we used a threshold of 5cm in the experiments), then we regard that
$\mathbf{pt}(u, v)$ has no match.

After aligning $Pset_i$ with $Pset_i^j$ as seen above, we generate edges that represent the identity constraints, and then optimise the global graph using the g2o
framework [4]. We fix the poses of all planar patches in $Pset_i$ and those of all
planar patches in $Pset_{s_j}$. We also fix those of K_{s_j} and K_i. The poses of the other
vertices are then optimised with respect to all constraints before proceeding to
align $Pset_i$ with the next fragment (if there is one). After each optimisation, all
planar patches are positioned such that (1) the relative positions between the
planar patches in the same local model are close to the exact ones (this reduces
the deformations between different objects in the scene), and (2) the relative
positions between planar patches representing the same object in the scene are
close to the relative positions obtained with fragment registration (this reduces
the deformations within each object in the scene).

4   Experiments

We evaluated our proposed method in several situations using real data. All
scenes were captured at 30 fps. We used a resolution of 0.4cm for attribute
images in all cases. The CPU we used was an Intel Xeon processor with 3.47
GHz and the GPU was a NVIDIA GeForce GTX 580. Our method runs at about
28 fps with a live stream from a Kinect camera.

Figure 4 (a) shows results obtained by our method using data RGBD_DATASET
_FREIBURG3_LONG_OFFICE_HOUSEHOLD [2]. In this data-set, captured with a
Kinect camera, the camera turns around a small scale scene, which requires loop-
closure operations for 3D reconstruction. We compared results by our method
with those shown in [19]. Note that we used the mocap camera trajectory in
Fig. 4 (b) [7] as the ground truth. The circled parts on the the right side of
Fig. 4 (a) and on the left side of Fig. 4 (b) focus on the corner of the central
wall to attest the ability of each method to correct deformations. In the squared
boxes, we zoomed in a smooth surface (blue box) and thin details (red box) to
attest the capability of each method to generate fine details of the 3D scene.

Figure 4 (a) shows that our method succeeded in building a geometrically
consistent and accurate 3D model. As we can see in the circled parts, our method
significantly outperformed in accuracy the Extended KinectFusion method [13]:
to the part where there is only one corner, two corners of the wall are incorrectly
reconstructed by [13] while ours reconstructed it as one corner. This is because
[13] does not employ any loop closure. In the squared boxes, we can observe that
the amount of noise (spiky effects in the blue box) obtained by our method is
similar to that by [18] or the ground truth (the mocap trajectory). On the other
hand, [19] achieved better accuracy than ours: the surface is smoother on the
wall (blue box). Note that due to employing planar patches representation, our

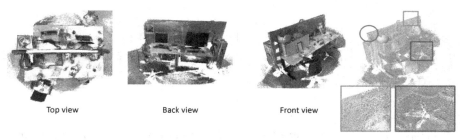

Top view   Back view   Front view

(a) Results obtained with our method with real-time performance

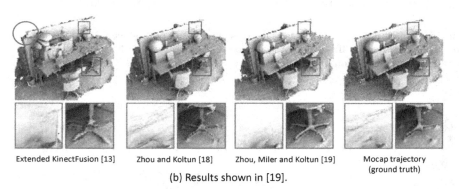

Extended KinectFusion [13]   Zhou and Koltun [18]   Zhou, Miler and Koltun [19]   Mocap trajectory
(ground truth)

(b) Results shown in [19].

Fig. 4. Results obtained with data LONG_OFFICE_HOUSEHOLD. The circled areas show the advantage of using loop-closure algorithms. Without loop-closure, the scene was deformed. The blue boxes show smoothness of the reconstructed surface. The image should be uniformly white when illuminated (spiky effects comes from noise). The red boxes show ability to reconstruct thin details. Unfortunately, when using planar patches representation, some details were lost.

method generated a 3D model that is less dense than that obtained by [18] or [19]: parts of the chair in the red box are missing with our method. We remark that, the results by [18] or [19] are off-line while ours are on-line.

Figure 5 (a) shows results obtained by our method using data COPYROOM and data LOUNGE (captured with an Xtion Pro Live camera) available at [1]. We compared the results obtained by our method with the state-of-the-art results [19] on these two datasets. The dataset COPYROOM consists of 5490 RGB-D images and contains a loop while the dataset LOUNGE consists of 3000 RGB-D images and does not contain any loop. We displayed top-views of the obtained 3D models to attest the amount of deformations of the reconstructed scenes. From these results we can see that our method was able to reconstruct the 3D models in details at large scale without deformations, similarly as in [19]. We remark that our results were produced on-line, while those by [19] were off-line. Moreover, with our method we could generate textured 3D models while texture is not available in the results by [19].

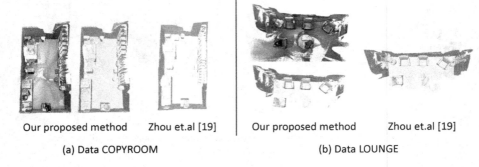

Our proposed method   Zhou et.al [19] | Our proposed method   Zhou et.al [19]

(a) Data COPYROOM   (b) Data LOUNGE

Fig. 5. Top views of two reconstructed scenes. Our method can build geometrical consistent large-scale 3D scenes in real-time. Our proposed method also allowed us to obtain color information of the 3D scene.

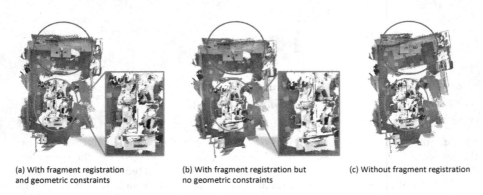

(a) With fragment registration   (b) With fragment registration but   (c) Without fragment registration
and geometric constraints   no geometric constraints

Fig. 6. Comparative results obtained with data OFFICE. The improvement of the obtained results using geometric constraints for the fragment registration is significant, as shown in the circled parts.

We scanned an indoor scene of 10m by 5m, called OFFICE, with a Kinect camera. The dataset contains 8500 images. This scene is challenging in that deformations become evident at some parts (inside the green circle) in the middle of the scene due to unconnected objects (*e.g.* opposite faces of the central wall), in addition to complex camera motion. As a consequence, deformations of the generated 3D model can be easily observed, and thus the advantage of introducing geometric constraints can be highlighted. Fig. 6 shows the results by our method with/without using geometric constraints ((a) v.s. (b)) and with/without applying fragment registration ((a), (b) v.s. (c)). The improvement of the obtained results using our geometric constraints for the fragment registration is significant, as shown in the circled parts. Fig. 6 (c) shows that, without handling deformations (*i.e.* without fragment registration), results are catastrophic.

5 Conclusion

We proposed a two-stage strategy, local mapping and global mapping, to build in details large-scale 3D models with minimal deformations in real time from RGB-D image sequences. The local mapping creates accurate structured local 3D models from short subsequences while the global mapping organises all the local 3D models into a global model in an undeformed way using fragment registration in the graph optimization framework. Introducing geometric and identity constraints facilitates repositioning planar patches to remove deformations as much as possible. Our method produces 3D models of high quality, without deformations and in real-time, even for large-scale scenes.

References

1. 3D Scene Dataset: http://www.stanford.edu/~qianyizh/projects/scenedata.html
2. RGB-D SLAM Dataset and Benchmark. http://vision.in.tum.de/data/datasets/rgbd-dataset
3. Blais, G., Levine, M.D.: Registering multi vie range data to create 3D computer objects. IEEE Trans. on PAMI **17**(8), 820–824 (1995)
4. Cameral, R., Grisetti, G., Strasdat, H., Konolige, K., Burgard, W.: g2o: A general framework for graph optimisation. In: Proc. of ICRA (2011)
5. Chen, J., Bautembach, D., Izadi, S.: Scalable real-time volumetric surface reconstruction. ACM Transactions on Graphics **32**(4), 113:1–113:16 (2013)
6. Henry, P., Fox, D., Bhowmik, A., Mongia, R.: Patch volumes: segmentation-based consistent mapping with RGB-D cameras. In: Proc. of 3DV 2013 (2013)
7. Henry, P., Krainin, M., Herbst, E., Ren, X., Fox, D.: RGB-D mapping: Using Kinect-style depth cameras for dense 3D modelling of indoor environments. International Journal of Robotics Research **31**(5), 647–663 (2012)
8. Lowe, D.G.: Object recognition from local scale-invariant features. In: Proc. of ICCV, pp. 1150–1157 (1999)
9. Meilland, M., Comport, A.: On unifying key-frame and voxel-based dense visual SLAM at large scales. In: Proc. of IROS (2013)
10. Neibner, M., Zollhofer, M., Izadi, S., Stamminger, M.: Real-time 3D reconstruction at scale using voxel hashing. ACM Transactions on Graphics **32**(6), 169:1–169:11 (2013)
11. Newcombe, R., Izadi, S., Hilliges, O., Molyneaux, D., Kim, D., Davison, A., Kohli, P., Shotton, J., Hodges, S., Fitzgibbon, A.: Kinectfusion: real-time dense surface mapping and tracking. In: Proc. of ISMAR 2011, pp. 127–136 (2011)
12. Nguyen, C., Izadi, S., Lovell, D.: Modeling kinect sensor noise for improved 3D reconstruction and tracking. In: Proc. of 3DIM/PVT 2012, pp. 524–530 (2012)
13. Roth, H., Vona, M.: Moving volume kinectfusion. In: Proc. of BMVC (2012)
14. Segal, A., Haehnel, D., Thrun, S.: Generalized-ICP. Robotics: Science and Systems (2009)
15. Thomas, D., Sugimoto, A.: A flexible scene representation for 3D reconstruction using an RGB-D camera. In: Proc. of ICCV (2013)
16. Whelan, T., McDonald, J., Kaess, M., Fallon, M., Johansson, H., Leonard, J.: Kintinuous: Spatially extended kinectfusion. Advanced Reasoning with Depth Camera. In: Proc. of RSS Workshop on RGB-D (2012)

17. Zeng, M., Zhao, F., Zheng, J., Liu, X.: Octree-based fusion for realtime 3D reconstruction. Transaction of Graphical Models **75**(3), 126–136 (2013)
18. Zhou, Q.-Y., Koltun, V.: Dense scene reconstruction with points of interest. ACM Transaction on Graphics **32**(4), 112:1–112:8 (2013)
19. Zhou, Q.-Y., Miller, S., Koltun, V.: Elastic fragments for dense scene reconstruction. In: Proc. of ICCV (2013)

An Active Patch Model for Real World Appearance Reconstruction

Farhad Bazyari$^{(\boxtimes)}$ and Yorgos Tzimiropoulos

Department of Computer Science, University of Lincoln, Lincoln LN6 7TS, UK
{fbazyari,gtzimiropoulos}@lincoln.ac.uk

Abstract. Dense mapping has been a very active field of research in recent years, promising various new application in computer vision, computer graphics, robotics, etc. Most of the work done on dense mapping use low-level features, such as occupancy grid, with some very recent work using high-level features, such as objects. In our work we use an active patch model to learn the prominent, primitive shapes commonly found in indoor environments. This model is then fitted to coming data to reconstruct the 3D scene. We use Gauss-Newton method to jointly optimize for appearance reconstruction error and geometric transformation differences. Finally we compare our results with Kinect Fusion [6].

Keywords: Dense mapping · Deformable patches · Gauss-Newton optimization

1 Introduction

Structure from motion and mapping has been studied intensively for a long time in computer vision society both in terms of theory and application. But scarcity of computational power in older systems meant that most systems had to work with sparse, feature-point based maps. However with recent advancements in processing units (both CPU and GPU) and easy access to commodity depth sensor such as Microsoft Kinect, we have seen some breakthroughs in dense mapping systems which in return have paved the path for many new applications in robotics and manipulation, computer graphics and augmented reality and so on which was simply not possible using traditional sparse representations.

Different representations are available for 3D maps such as 3D mesh, which has the appeal that can be readily used by rendering mechanisms (e.g. OpenGL). However there has been growing interest in using non-parametric representations, such as Truncated Sign Distance Function (TSDF) [1] due to their constant complexity which is independent from the complexity of the scene/map they are representing. This characteristic is particularly appealing in on-line applications where fixed complexity means constant operation time and more robustness to motion, etc.

TSDF has been embraced by most dense mapping systems and very promising results have been demonstrated [6,7]. However it is a very low-level representation, storing information at the voxel level only (equivalent to pixels in 2D

© Springer International Publishing Switzerland 2015
L. Agapito et al. (Eds.): ECCV 2014 Workshops, Part I, LNCS 8925, pp. 443–456, 2015.
DOI: 10.1007/978-3-319-16178-5_31

images). On the other hand, there has been a few very recent works that try to make use of higher-level information that might be available to the system such as type of objects to expect in the map [8]. This type of information is problem specific and is only useful in very controlled environments.

In this work we propose the use of mid-level features which while providing better quality maps and more compact representation, are very common in almost any man-made environment and hence are not problem specific. We use deformable 3D patches to learn the most common primitive shapes from training dataset. Loosely speaking these primitive shapes are equivalent to small planar surfaces, sharp corners, etc. and our generative model will later on be able to produce any random 3D map from these building blocks. After model is trained, it can be fitted to new test data to produce a higher quality map. We optimize for appearance and geometric transformation (3D rigid-body transformation in our case) simultaneously. This separation of appearance and geometric transformation will allow for a much simpler model (in terms of number of components) and leads to better results. Optimization is based on Gauss-Newton method and is done iteratively. Finally we make comparison between our results and one of the state-of-the-art dense mapping systems.

2   Related Work

While SLAM systems have been around for more than a decade now [2,4,5], it has been only recently that true dense mapping has been considered in SLAM systems mostly due to the availability of computational power (especially GP-GPUs) and also because of advancements and availability of commodity depth sensors such as Microsoft Kinect.

Kinect Fusion [6] is one of the first practical systems that uses Kinect sensor and returns dense map in form of a TSDF structure. It is a full SLAM system closing the loop between tracking and mapping while sensor pose tracking is done using Iterative Closest Point algorithm [11].

In order to overcome the limitations that active sensors impose, Newcombe at al. introduced DTAM [7] which is in many ways similar to KinectFusion, but it uses a single monocular camera. Hence it can work in much wider scale range and can scan objects much farther away from sensor. Also passive sensing means it has smaller energy requirements and can be used with a wide range of sensors.

In a recent work, SLAM++ [8] have put the object detection directly inside tracking and mapping loop. This will increase the map quality, because noise free model is already available. Also it helps the tracker to track against the correct model hence improving stability. It also provide the possibility of presenting the map in a much more compact form. The problem with this method is that it only works in very controlled environment where we have very good knowledge about the type of objects that can be found in there.

In their work on face pose detection, Tzimiropoulos et al. [9,10] model the variance in different faces in 2D images in terms of shape and appearance variations. Then they train their linear model on real world samples and take an iterative optimization approach for fitting their model to new test data. While quite different in application, their optimization technique is very similar to the one we use in this work.

Probably the closest work to ours is of Zhu et al. [12] who try to learn small 2D patches from a set of high resolution images. These trained patches are later on used to increase the quality of low resolution test images. They jointly train their model for high resolution/low resolution patch dictionary and also for deformation of their patches at fitting stage, to minimize the reconstruction error while making best use of prior knowledge.

Finally we like to mention the related work of Hejrati and Ramanan [3] who focus on object recognition and 3D reconstruction at the same time. They use a simple part based model to reconstruct the object in a way that best agrees with visual evidence while also trying to do recognition and making use of prior information.

3 Method

In this section we will first briefly mention data preparation step, then we explain our model and also how Gauss-Newton optimization is used to fit model to (noisy) data.

3.1 Preparing Data

We use TSDF (Truncated SDF) to store and work with 3D structures (this is also used in Kinect Fusion and many other mapping systems). TSDF in its most basic form, divides the working volume into a regular grid of same size voxels. Each voxel stores two numbers ; *value* that indicates shortest distance from center of the voxel to closest surface, and *weight* which is an indicator of our certainty in *value*. By convention; a positive *value* means the voxel is in front of surface (in empty space outside objects) and a negative *value* indicates voxel being located behind a surface (or inside watertight objects) and hence being occluded. True surface is then extracted by (bilinear) interpolation and is marked as zero-set of this 3D scalar volume. The confidence measure (weights) are used in this interpolation step for extracting the zero set.

Figure 1 illustrates SDF in 2D and 3D, in this paper we will visualize only the zero-level of TSDFs and patches which correspond to surfaces in real world. However it is important to remember that our patches are cubes in 3D and when running optimization/fitting, we are dealing with all the information stored in 3D patches and not only information on the zero-level set.

The aforementioned patches are small parts of original TSDF structure in the form of n-by-n-by-n grid. Each patch is in fact a miniature TSDF structure itself and we hope to form a vocabulary of these patches that captures commonly occurring primitive 3D shapes. Figure 2.

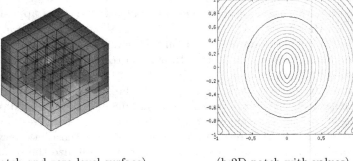

(a:3D patch and zero level surface)   (b:2D patch with values)

Fig. 1. Signed Distance Function is positive outside surface and negative behind surfaces (inside object) with values linearly proportional to distance to closest surface

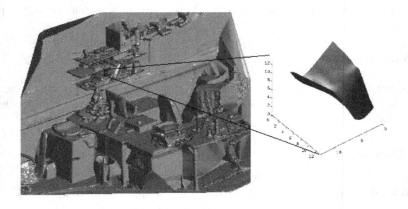

Fig. 2. On left we see extracted surfaces (zero-level set of TSDF structure). And on right, one sample *patch* ($12 \times 12 \times 12$ voxels) is enlarged

3.2   Formation of Patches

In training phase, we have a number of TSDF structures which represent random but noise free data. These data are gathered from indoor environments. In order to be able to recognize the pattern in these data, each of these TSDF structures have to be broken down into smaller patches. Also in the fitting phase, new data comes to us in the shape of a large point cloud (e.g. from a depth sensor) and again we need to break this down into patches that we can work on. So patch formation has to be done both for training and fitting.

Let us consider that we already have a large TSDF structure. We also have a sensor pose for that TSDF. So by performing ray-tracing we can form a large point cloud that sit on the zero-level set (figure 3). (If we were in fitting phase, incoming data was already in form of point cloud and this step was unnecessary, but the rest applies unchanged.) We are only interested in patches that fall on the surfaces. so a random point in this point cloud is chosen and a partition around this point is taken as a candidate for the patch (red wire-frame cube in figure 3a). Then all these points are concatenated and using Singular Value Decomposition 3 momentum of this cloud is found.

$$[U, S, V] = SVD(\text{point cloud}) \tag{1}$$

momentums are stored as columns of V. Next, point cloud is rotated around its center so that these momentums are aligned with x-y-z axis (optionally we rotate them by $\pi/4$ radian around z axis so that dominant momentums are diagonal. This only makes visualization and code easier) figure 3c. Aligning patches is important because one can imagine that many instances of same 3D structure can occur with different poses. Each of these segments are similar to each other up to a rigid body transformation. By aligning their momentums with x-y-z axis, dependency on point of view is largely eliminated. Now new, and modified, patch is formed around this new point cloud. to do so we form a delaunay triangulation on the point cloud and then perform ray-tracing along the axes with weakest momentum (z-axes in figure 3d), filling the patch while doing so.

3.3   Training the Model and Fitting Data

Training. Our aim is to form a small set of primitive 3D shapes (or eigen-shapes) which can later be combined to give a good estimated reconstruction of any arbitrary scene. For that, we take K random patches from our dataset. Each of these patches consist of n^3 smaller voxels (from underlying TSDF structure). By concatenating these voxels each patch will be deformed into an array of size n^3. If we assume our sample pool is large enough to contain all major primitive structural shape, we can use Principal Component Analysis (PCA) to find a lower dimensional representation for our sample pool.

In order to have a representative set of samples, we can either apply PCA on a very large number of patches, or we can separate the variation in our data to shape variations and appearance variations. Latter approach will save us a lot of computational expense as well as giving a far more compact set. Here appearance is referred to the readings, or *values*, from TSDF while shape variations refer to rigid body transformation. We plan to study the affect of scale variation as well as affine transformation in future work.

So by applying PCA on the appearance space, we can find A_0 which is the average patch, and also we have m shapes (m much smaller than number of samples and also size of sample n^3) that linearly form the m-dimensional appearance space. Matrix A is formed by concatenating these eigen-shapes in its rows. Vector c controls the linear combination of eigen-shapes.

$$\hat{Y} = A_0 + Ac, \quad c = A^T(Y - A_0) \tag{2}$$

Where Y is the patch we are trying to fit the model to and $\hat{Y}$ is reconstructed patch.

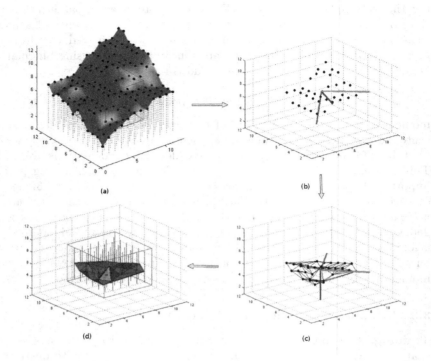

Fig. 3. Starting from top-left and moving clock-wise; (a) TSDF structure that we want to take a sample patch from. Point cloud is formed by ray-tracing. (b) Points that fall into patch are separated and their momentum calculated using SVD. (c) The momentums are aligned with x-y-z axis and delaunay triangulation is formed on them. (d) New, modified, patch is formed by interpolation and ray-tracing.

In the same way, we can linearize the shape space. As mentioned before, in this work we only deal with rigid-body transformation in 3D space. So mean shape, s_0 is a zero vector and 6 eigen-vectors that form matrix S span the 6 dimensional space of rotation and translation in 3D.

$$\hat{s} = s_0 + Sp, \quad p = S^T(s - s_0) \tag{3}$$

More details about this transformation is given in section 3.4.

Fitting. Now having all above, when the new reading arrives, we try to minimize the reconstruction error by solving for both appearance and shape simultaneously.

$$\arg \min_{p,c} ||Y(S(x;p)) - A_0 - Ac||^2. \tag{4}$$

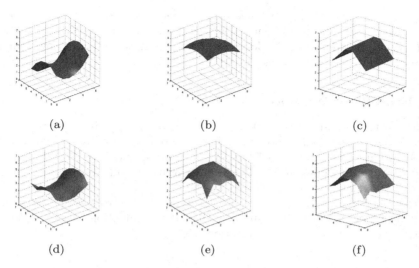

(a)　　　　　　　　　　(b)　　　　　　　　　　(c)

(d)　　　　　　　　　　(e)　　　　　　　　　　(f)

Fig. 4. To illustrate that trained model is capable of reproducing some random and common shapes in 3D, we gave our system 3 random shapes (top row) and model has reproduced the (bottom row).

Where $S(x; p)$ governs the 3D transformation of patch-cube as decided by parameters p, and $Y(S(x; p))$ is the values read from TSDF structure associated to this patch.

from 2 and 3 and by replacing them in 4 we get

$$\arg\min_{\Delta p, \Delta c} ||Y - A_0 + J_0 \Delta p - \sum_{i=1}^{m} (c_i + \Delta c_i)(A_i + J_i \Delta p)||^2. \tag{5}$$

Where J_i is the $N \times n$ Jacobian built as follows: $[A_{i,x}(k) \ A_{i,y}(k) \ A_{i,y}(k)]$ $\frac{\delta S(x_k; p)}{\delta p}$. And $A_{i,x}(k)$ and $A_{i,y}(k)$ and $A_{i,z}(k)$ are the x and y and z gradients of A_i. ($\frac{\delta S}{\delta p}$ is explained in detail in section 3.4). All above are defined in the model coordinate system, hence $p_0 = 0$. with some abuse of notation we set $J_i = [A_{i,x} \ A_{i,y} \ A_{i,z}]\frac{\delta S}{\delta p}$.

By omitting the higher order terms from 5 we get:

$$\arg\min_{\Delta p, \Delta c} ||Y - A_0 - Ac - A\Delta c - J\Delta p||^2. \tag{6}$$

Now we can solve for appearance and shape parameters simultaneously, using Gauss-Newton method;

$$[\Delta p; \Delta c] = H_{final}^{-1} J_{final}^T (Y - A_0 - A_c) \tag{7}$$

where $J_{final} = [A; J] \in R^{N \times (m+n)}$ and $H_{final} = J_{final}^T J_{final}$ are final Jacobian and Hessian respectively.

Please note that shape parameters p are used in taking the sample from incoming data, and the dependency of sample Y on p is data dependent and non-linear, hence the step above is done iteratively along with taking new samples and calculating jacobians at each iteration.

3.4   Rigid Body Transformation Formulae

In this work, we assume geometric deforming of the patches (referred to as shape change in section 3.3 and denoted as S) is only rigid body transformation. Namely we are dealing with 6 DOF (3 for rotation and 3 for translation). In future work, we are aiming at including scale variations and affine transformation into our optimization too.

Rotation is presented by Rodriguez formula. That is rotation in 3D is presented by a vector which has unit length and the direction of vector defines rotations axis (right hand rule). Rotation angle is θ.

$$R(w, \theta) = I_3 + \hat{w} sin(\theta) + \hat{w}^2 (1 - cos(\theta)),$$

$$\hat{w} = \begin{bmatrix} 0 & -w_z & w_y \\ w_z & 0 & -w_x \\ -w_y & w_x & 0 \end{bmatrix} \tag{8}$$

Where rotation vector is unit length $[w_x, w_y, w_z]$.
For small θ and by omitting higher order term of $\hat{w}$ we have:

$$R(w, \theta) \approx I_3 + \hat{w}\theta \tag{9}$$

For small changes in rotation, increments are integrated like so;

$$P' = R(w)P_i + T_i \tag{10}$$

Where T is translation in 3D and $P_i = [X_i, Y_i, Z_i]^T$.
By linearizing the system for each of the 6 DOF, we can write the rigid body transformation in a linear system. So above can be re-written as:

$$P_i' = \begin{bmatrix} 0 & Z_i & -Y_i & 1 & 0 & 0 \\ -Z_i & 0 & X_i & 0 & 1 & 0 \\ Y_i & -X_i & 0 & 0 & 0 & 1 \end{bmatrix} q, \tag{11}$$

Where $q = [w_x, w_y, w_z, t_x, t_y, t_z]^T$ is the 6-by-1 vector containing 3 rotation parameters and 3 translation parameters.

Obviously the above is done for a single point in 3D, but we have a regular grid to work with. So naturally the same structure extends.

$$S = \begin{bmatrix} 0 & S_z^1 & -S_y^1 & 1\,0\,0 \\ \vdots & \vdots & \vdots & \vdots\,\vdots\,\vdots \\ 0 & S_z^{n^3} & -S_y^{n^3} & 1\,0\,0 \\ -S_z^1 & 0 & S_x^1 & 0\,1\,0 \\ \vdots & \vdots & \vdots & \vdots\,\vdots\,\vdots \\ -S_z^{n^3} & 0 & S_x^{n^3} & 0\,1\,0 \\ S_y^1 & -S_x^1 & 0 & 0\,0\,1 \\ \vdots & \vdots & \vdots & \vdots\,\vdots\,\vdots \\ S_y^{n^3} & -S_x^{n^3} & 0 & 0\,0\,1 \end{bmatrix} \tag{12}$$

This is S mentioned in 3.

3.5   Global Consistency

So far we have discussed how the new readings from sensor will be broken down to smaller pieces, same size as our patches, and then a reconstructed version of these patches will replace them in the TSDF structure. This means all operations are done locally. But one thing that has not been taken into consideration is that there is correlation between neighboring patches. Therefore we need some sort of mechanism to enforce global consistency.

We take a simple yet effective approach here, and that is while breaking down the TSDF structure into small patches, we allow a significant overlap between neighboring patches. So if a patch has already been replaced by its reconstruction, when we are reading its neighboring patch a part of our reading is coming from what we have already processed (TSDF is update in real-time). So when this new patch is being reconstructed, it naturally tends to adjust itself to reconstruction done for its neighbors. This way global consistency is achieved. In future work we plan to look into more sophisticated ways of imposing global consistency, namely we will make a graph of all the patches and apply some graph optimization techniques.

4   Experiment

4.1   Preparing Training Data with Alignment

Kinect Fusion provides us with a 3D TSDF structure that can be easily broken down to smaller pieces for learning the primitive shapes. In the training set, we take a number of TSDF structures from indoor (office) environment. Each TSDF is produced by running Kinect Fusion for 500 frames. The area reconstructed in each TSDF structure is constrained to a cube of 3-by-3-by-3 m^3 and resolution is 512 voxels in each direction. We found this setting suitable both in terms of level of details reconstructed in final model, and also in terms of memory and computational requirements. Each voxel has a volume of 6-by-6-by-6 mm^3 and this is a theoretical limit on the resolution of the final model. In practice however, we saw that system is capable of capturing details a lot smaller than that size, up to 3mm in width.

4.2   Learning Phase

Once we have prepared all the sample patches, it is time to learn the more frequent shapes among them. We use Principal Component Analysis for this as explained earlier, 3.3. In our experiments we use patches of 6-by-6-by-6 voxels. Around 400,000 patches are used for training. We keep only a small subset of eigen-shapes, 10 in our case. We saw that on the train-set, keeping only 10 eigen shapes introduces an error of less than 5%. Table 1 shows the top 20 eigen-value, one can see that eigen values drop very rapidly, indicating the presence of structure in patch appearance.

Attention needs to be paid to choosing the right number of eigen-shapes (size of matrix A in 2). By using higher number of eigen-shapes, we give our model more flexibility. This flexibility will allow the model to match the (noisy) data better but that does not necessarily translate to better approximation of noise-free structure. On the other hand, by giving too few eigen-shapes to the model, it will fail to reconstruct the more difficult structure that may be present in the scene. Choice of number of eigen-shapes to keep depends very much on size of patches, sensor noise and other problem specific factors. Our choice was made based on experimentation.

Table 1. Top 20 eigen values of training set

Number	1	2	3	4	5	6	7	8	9	10
Eigen Value	19.21	8.93	6.10	5.08	3.56	2.73	2.33	1.96	1.89	1.58
Number	11	12	13	14	15	16	17	18	19	20
Eigen Value	1.42	1.21	1.17	1.07	1.01	0.92	0.81	0.76	0.73	0.67

4.3   Fitting

In this phase we use Kinect Fusion again for obtaining test data. But only the first frame reading from the sensor is considered and Kinect Fusion stops, after receiving this first frame. We used fixed number of 10 iteration in the iterative optimization phase, However we also observed that because of the pre-alignment there is very little transformation correction needed and Convergence is very quick. Algorithm 1 outlines the systems flow.

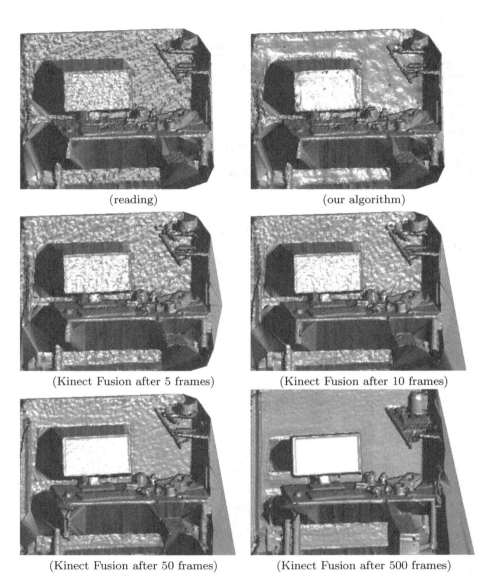

(reading)   (our algorithm)

(Kinect Fusion after 5 frames)   (Kinect Fusion after 10 frames)

(Kinect Fusion after 50 frames)   (Kinect Fusion after 500 frames)

Fig. 5. Top left is the original reading, top right is the output of our algorithm. Row 2 and 3; shows the output of kinect fusion after fusing data from 5,10, 50 and 500 frames

initialization;
if *training is needed* **then**

> read training data;
> pre-processing;
> form a big matrix and apply PCA;
> trim the eigen-shapes (A) and calculate the jacobian for corresponding A;

end
load eigen-shapes and jacobians;
read new test data;
break TSDF down into small patches;
pre-process;
for *each patch in test set* **do**

> project the reading into space span by A;
> **for** *10 iterations* **do**
>
>> correct for rigid-body transformation;
>> project into space span by A;
>> update parameters p and c;
>
> **end**
> integrate the reconstructed data back into original TSDF;

end

Algorithm 1: Pseudocode of our algorithm

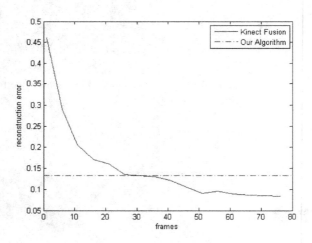

Fig. 6. Reduction of reconstruction error due to merging more frames together in Kinect Fusion (blue), or applying our method to one frame only (red).

4.4   Evaluation

Figure 5 shows the results of a test TSDF, and the reconstructed map. One can see visually that while 3D map has been denoised, most of 3D structure has been preserved. Output of our algorithm is compared with output from Kinect Fusion after 5, 10 and 50 frames.

Also figure 6 demonstrates the reduction in reconstruction error when different number of frames have been used in Kinect Fusion, (steps of 5 frames). Measure of error used here is the root-mean-square between difference of ground truth and reconstructed patch.

In our experiment denoising achieved by 'projection alone' was equal to fusing data from around 8 frames. This might be useful if one has to sacrifice the optimization step in the interest of time or computational power available. But by adding 10 iteration in 'optimization step' reduction in error is equivalent to 28 frames combined using Kinect Fusion. Figure 6.

5   Conclusion

In this work we introduced a generative model for dense 3D maps, based on deformable 3D patches. Our model is capable of learning prominent spatial structure in man-made environments in an unsupervised manner. We also introduced a fitting strategy which jointly optimizes for 3D appearance and geometric transformation using robust Gauss-Newton method. We showed that significant noise reduction and compactness can be achieved using our method. We plan to integrate our method directly inside a SLAM loop and also employ better global optimization methods in our future work.

References

1. Curless, B., Levoy., M.: A volumetric method for building complex models from range images. In: Proceedings of the 23rd Annual Conference on Computer Graphics and Interactive Techniques (ACM) (1996)
2. Davison, A.J., Reid, I.D., Molton, N.D., Stasse, O.: Monoslam: Real-time single camera slam. IEEE Transactions on Pattern Analysis and Machine Intelligence **29**(6), 1052–1067
3. Hejrati, M., Ramanan, D.: Analysis by synthesis: 3d object reconstruction by object reconstruction. In: Computer Vision and Pattern Recognition (CVPR) (2014)
4. Klein, G., Murray, D.: Parallel tracking and mapping for small ar workspaces. In: 6th IEEE and ACM International Symposium on Mixed and Augmented Reality, ISMAR (2007)
5. Montemerlo, M., Thrun, S., Koller, D., Wegbreit, B.: FastSLAM: A factored solution to the simultaneous localization and mapping problem. In: Proceedings of the AAAI National Conference on Artificial Intelligence, AAAI, Edmonton, Canada (2002)
6. Newcombe, R.A., Izadi, S., Hilliges, O., Molyneaux, D., Kim, D., Davison, A.J., Kohi, P., Shotton, J., Hodges, S., Fitzgibbon, A.: Kinectfusion: real-time dense surface mapping and tracking. In: 2011 10th IEEE International Symposium on Mixed and Augmented Reality (ISMAR), pp. 127–136, October 2011
7. Newcombe, R.A., Lovegrove, S., Davison, A.: Dtam: dense tracking and mapping in real-time. In: 2011 IEEE International Conference on Computer Vision (ICCV), pp. 2320–2327, November 2011

8. Salas-Moreno, R., Newcombe, R., Strasdat, H., Kelly, P., Davison, A.: Slam++: Simultaneous localisation and mapping at the level of objects. In: 2013 IEEE Conference on Computer Vision and Pattern Recognition (CVPR), pp. 1352–1359, June 2013
9. Tzimiropoulos, G., Pantic, M.: Optimization problems for fast aam fitting in-the-wild. In: 2013 IEEE International Conference on Computer Vision (ICCV), pp. 593–600. IEEE (2013)
10. Tzimiropoulos, G., Pantic, M.: Gauss-newton deformable part models for face alignment in-the-wild. In: Proceedings of the IEEE Conference on Computer Vision and Pattern Recognition, pp. 1851–1858 (2014)
11. Zhang, Z.: Iterative point matching for registration of free-form curves and surfaces. International Journal of Computer Vision **13**(2), 119–152 (1994)
12. Zhu, Y., Zhang, Y., Yuille, A.L.: Single image super-resolution using deformable patches. In: IEEE Conference on Computer Vision and Pattern Recognition (CVPR) (2014)

W05 - <u>ChaLearn</u> Looking at People: Pose Recovery, Action/Interaction, Gesture Recognition

ChaLearn Looking at People Challenge 2014: Dataset and Results

Sergio Escalera[1,2,3]($\boxtimes$), Xavier Baró[1,4], Jordi Gonzàlez[1,5],
Miguel A. Bautista[1,2], Meysam Madadi[1,2], Miguel Reyes[1,2],
Víctor Ponce-López[1,2,4], Hugo J. Escalante[3,6], Jamie Shotton[7],
and Isabelle Guyon[3]

[1] Computer Vision Center, Campus UAB, Barcelona, Spain
sergio@maia.ub.es
[2] Department of Mathematics, University of Barcelona, Barcelona, Spain
[3] ChaLearn, Berkeley, California
[4] EIMT/IN3 at the Open University of Catalonia, Barcelona, Spain
[5] Department of Computer Science, Univ. Autònoma de Barcelona, Barcelona, Spain
[6] INAOE, Puebla, Mexico
[7] Microsoft Research, Cambridge, UK

Abstract. This paper summarizes the ChaLearn Looking at People 2014 challenge data and the results obtained by the participants. The competition was split into three independent tracks: human pose recovery from RGB data, action and interaction recognition from RGB data sequences, and multi-modal gesture recognition from RGB-Depth sequences. For all the tracks, the goal was to perform user-independent recognition in sequences of continuous images using the overlapping Jaccard index as the evaluation measure. In this edition of the ChaLearn challenge, two large novel data sets were made publicly available and the Microsoft Codalab platform were used to manage the competition. Outstanding results were achieved in the three challenge tracks, with accuracy results of 0.20, 0.50, and 0.85 for pose recovery, action/interaction recognition, and multi-modal gesture recognition, respectively.

Keywords: Human pose recovery · Behavior analysis · Action and interactions · Multi-modal gestures · Recognition

1 Introduction

The automatic, computational analysis of the human body in image sequences, referred to as Looking at People (LAP) in [11], keeps making rapid progress with the constant improvement of (i) new published methods that constantly push the state-of-the-art, and (ii) the recent availability of inexpensive 3D video sensors such as Kinect. Applications are countless, like HCI, surveillance, communication, entertainment, safety, e-commerce and sports, thus having an important social impact in assisting technologies for the handicapped and the elderly, for example.

© Springer International Publishing Switzerland 2015
L. Agapito et al. (Eds.): ECCV 2014 Workshops, Part I, LNCS 8925, pp. 459–473, 2015.
DOI: 10.1007/978-3-319-16178-5_32

In 2011 and 2012, ChaLearn[1] organized a challenge on single user one-shot-learning gesture recognition with data recorded with Kinect. In 2013, 54 teams participated in the ChaLearn challenge which was devoted to Multimodal Gesture Recognition. In that edition, we proposed a user-independent gesture recognition task in visual data recorded with Kinect and containing a large set of continuously performed Italian gestures.

In the edition of 2014, we have organized a second round of the same gesture recognition task including a finer begin-end labeling of gestures with the objective of performing gesture recognition. Additionally, for the 2014 edition, we have organized two competitions for human pose recovery and action recognition in RGB data. One goal of the challenge, inspired by the previous 2005-2012 Pascal VOC image recognition challenges on Human Layout Analysis successfully organized by Everingham et al. [6], was also to automatically recognize human limbs from RGB data. Another goal was to run a competition for human action and interaction recognition on RGB data.

In this paper we detail how the ChaLearn LAP 2014 challenge was organized, the data sets, the results achieved by almost 200 participants that joined the competition, and the main characteristics of the winning methods.

2 Challenge Tracks and Schedule

The ChaLearn LAP 2014 challenge featured three quantitative evaluations: automatic human pose recovery on RGB data, action/interaction recognition on RGB data, and gesture recognition from a multi-modal dataset recorded with Kinect. The characteristics of each competition track are the following:

• Track 1: Human Pose Recovery: a novel data set containing 120K+ manually annotated limbs for 8K+ frames showing actors performing natural motion was provided for automatic body limb detection.

• Track 2: Action/Interaction recognition: in total, 235 action samples performed by 17 actors were provided. The selected actions involved the motion of most of the limbs and included interactions among various actors.

• Track 3: Multi-modal gesture recognition: The RGBD data contains nearly 14K manually labeled (beginning and ending frame) gesture performances in continuous video sequences, with a vocabulary of 20 Italian gesture categories. This third track focused on multi-modal automatic learning of a set of gestures with the aim of performing user independent continuous gesture recognition.

The challenge was managed using the Microsoft Codalab platform[2]. The schedule of the competition was as follows.

February 9, 2014: Beginning of the quantitative competition, release of development and validation data.

April 24, 2014: Beginning of the registration procedure for accessing to the final evaluation data.

---

[1] http://gesture.chalearn.org/
[2] https://www.codalab.org/competitions/

May 1, 2014: Release of the encrypted final evaluation data and validation labels. Participants started training their methods with the whole data set.

May 20, 2014: Release of the decryption key for the final evaluation data. Participants started predicting the results on the final evaluation labels. This date was the deadline for code submission as well.

May 28, 2014: End of the quantitative competition. Deadline for submitting the predictions over the final evaluation data. The organizers started the code verification by running it on the final evaluation data.

June 1, 2014: Deadline for submitting the fact sheets.

June 10, 2014: Publication of the competition results.

3   Competition Data

In the next subsections we describe the data sets and their characteristics provided for the three challenge tracks[3].

3.1   Track 1: Human Pose Recovery Data Set

Publicly available datasets for human pose recovery lack of refined labeling or contain a very reduced number of samples per limb (e.g. *Buffy Stickmen V*3.01, *Leeds Sports* and *Hollywood Human Actions* [7,9,10]). In addition, large datasets often use synthetic samples or capture human limbs with sensor technologies such as *MoCap* in very controled environments [3].

Being aware of this lack of public available datasets for multi-limb human pose detection, we presented a novel fully limb labeled dataset, the Human Pose Recovery and Behavior Analysis *HuPBA* 8$k+$ dataset [13]. This dataset is formed by more than 8000 frames where 14 limbs are labeled at pixel precision, thus providing 124, 761 annotated human limbs. The characteristics of the data set are:

- The images are obtained from 9 videos (RGB sequences) and a total of 14 different actors appear in the sequences. The image sequences have been recorded using a stationary camera with the same static background.
- Each video (RGB sequence) was recorded at 15 fps rate, and each RGB image was stored with resolution 480 × 360 in BMP file format.
- For each actor present in an image 14 limbs (if not occluded) were manually tagged: Head, Torso, R-L Upper-arm, R-L Lower-arm, R-L Hand, R-L Upper-leg, R-L Lower-leg, and R-L Foot.
- Limbs are manually labeled using binary masks and the minimum bounding box containing each subject is defined.
- The actors appear in a wide range of different poses and performing different actions/gestures which vary the visual appearance of human limbs. So there is a large variability of human poses, self-occlusions and many variations in clothing and skin color.

A list of data attributes for this first track data set is described in Table 1. Examples of images of the data set are shown in Figure 1.

---

[3] Data sets are available at http://sunai.uoc.edu/chalearnLAP/

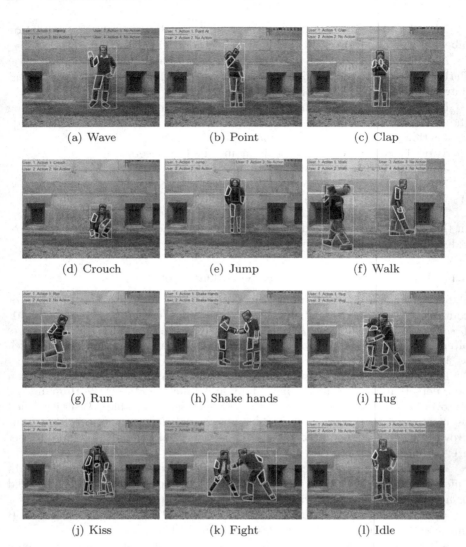

Fig. 1. Key frames of the *HuPBA* 8K+ dataset used in the tracks 1 and 2, showing actions ((a) to (g)), interactions ((h) to (k)) and the idle pose (l).

Table 1. Human pose recovery data characteristics

Training frames	Validation frames	Test frames	Sequence duration	FPS
4,000	2,000	2,236	1-2 min	15
Modalities	Num. of users	Limbs per body	Labeled frames	Labeled limbs
RGB	14	14	8,234	124,761

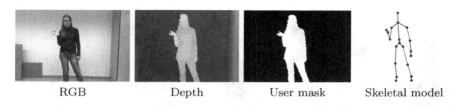

RGB   Depth   User mask   Skeletal model

Fig. 2. Different modalities of the data set used in track 3

Table 2. Action and interaction data characteristics

Training actions	Validation actions	Test actions	Sequence duration	FPS
150	90	95	9× 1-2 min	15

Modalities	Num. of users	Action categories	interaction categories	Labeled sequences
RGB	14	7	4	235

3.2   Track 2: Action/Interaction Data Set

In addition to human-limb labelling, in the *HuPBA 8K+* dataset we also annotated the beginning and ending frames of actions and interactions. A key frame
example for each gesture/action category is also shown in Figure 1. The challenges the participants had to deal with for this new competition are:

• 235 action/interaction samples performed by 14 actors.

• Large difference in length about the performed actions and interactions.
Several distractor actions out of the 11 categories are also present.

• 11 action categories, containing isolated and collaborative actions: Wave,
Point, Clap, Crouch, Jump, Walk, Run, Shake Hands, Hug, Kiss, Fight. There
is a high intra-class variability among action samples.

Table 2 summarizes the data set attributes for this second track.

3.3   Track 3: Multi-Modal Gesture Data Set

This track is based on an Italian gesture data set, called *Montalbano gesture
dataset*, an enhanced version of the ChaLearn 2013 multi-modal gesture recognition challenge [4,5] with more ground-truth annotations. In all the sequences,
a single user is recorded in front of a Kinect, performing natural communica-
tive gestures and speaking in fluent Italian. Examples of the different visual
modalities are shown in Figure 2. In ChaLearn LAP 2014 we have focused on
the user-independent automatic recognition of a vocabulary of 20 Italian cul-
tural/anthropological signs in image sequences, see Figure 3.

The main characteristics of the database are:

• Largest data set in the literature, with a large duration of each individual
performance showing no resting poses and self-occlusions.

• There is no information about the number of gestures to spot within each
sequence, and several distractor gestures (out of the vocabulary) are present.

• High intra-class variability of gesture samples and low inter-class variability
for some gesture categories.

Fig. 3. The *Montalbano* gesture dataset

Table 3. Main characteristics of the *Montalbano* gesture dataset

Training seq.	Validation seq.	Test seq.	Sequence duration	FPS
393 (7,754 gestures)	287 (3,362 gestures)	276 (2,742 gestures)	1-2 min	20
Modalities	Num. of users	Gesture categories	Labeled sequences	Labeled frames
RGB, Depth, User mask, Skeleton	27	20	13,858	1,720,800

Table 4. Comparison of public dataset characteristics

	Labeling at pixel precision	Number of limbs	Number of labeled limbs	Number of frames	Full body	Limb annotation	Gesture-action annotation	Number of gestures-actions	Number of gest-act. samples
Montalbano[5]	No	16	27 532 800	1 720 800	Yes	Yes	Yes	20	13 858
HuPBA 8K+ [13]	Yes	14	124 761	8 234	Yes	Yes	Yes	11	235
LEEDS SPORTS[9]	No	14	28 000	2 000	Yes	Yes	No	-	-
UIUC people[16]	No	14	18 186	1 299	Yes	Yes	No	-	-
Pascal VOC[6]	Yes	5	8 500	1 218	Yes	Yes	No	-	-
BUFFY[7]	No	6	4 488	748	No	Yes	No	-	-
PARSE[12]	No	10	3 050	305	Yes	Yes	No	-	-
MPII Pose[1]	Yes	14	-	40 522	Yes	Yes	Yes	20	491
FLIC[14]	No	29	-	5 003	No	No	No	-	-
H3D[2]	No	19	-	2 000	No	No	No	-	-
Actions[15]	No	-	-	-	Yes	No	Yes	6	600
HW[10]	-	-	-	-	-	No	Yes	8	430

A list of data attributes for data set used in track 3 is described in Table 3.

In Table 4 we compare the *HuPBA 8K+* and *Montalbano* datasets used in the ChaLearn LAP 2014 with other publicly available datasets. These datasets are chosen taking into account the variability of limbs and gestures/actions. Considering limb labelling, the *HuPBA 8K+* dataset contains the highest number of annotated limbs at pixel precision. When compared with other action datasets, the number of action instances are similar. On the other hand, the *Montalbano* database contains many more samples and much more variety of gestures than any proposed dataset up to this date.

4   Protocol and Evaluation

The evaluation metrics used to evaluate the participants for the three tracks, based on the Jaccard Index, are detailed in the following subsections.

4.1   Evaluation Procedure for Track 1

For all the $n \leq 14$ limbs labeled for each subject at each frame, the Jaccard Index is defined as:

$$J_{i,n} = \frac{A_{i,n} \bigcap B_{i,n}}{A_{i,n} \bigcup B_{i,n}}, \tag{1}$$

where $A_{i,n}$ is the ground truth of limb n, and $B_{i,n}$ is the prediction for the same limb at image i. For the *HuPBA 8K+* dataset used in this track, both $A_{i,n}$ and $B_{i,n}$ are binary images where pixels with value 1 denote the region in which the n-th limb is predicted, 0 otherwise. Particularly, since $A_{i,n}$ (ground truth) is a binary image and 1-pixels indicate the region of the $n-$th limb, this positive region does not necessarily need to be square. However, in all cases the positive region is a polyhedron defined by four points. Thus, the numerator in Eq. (1) is the number of 1-pixels that intersects in both images $A_{i,n}$ and $B_{i,n}$, and the denominator is the number of union 1-pixels after applying the logical *OR* operator.

The participants' methods were evaluated based on Hit Rate ($H_{i,n}$) accuracy for for each limb n at each image i. In essence, a hit is computed if $J_{i,n} \geq 0.5$.

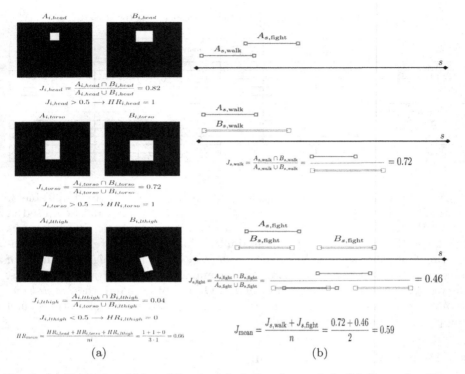

(a)   (b)

Fig. 4. (a) Example of Mean hit rate calculation for track 1. (b) Example of mean Jaccard Index calculation for tracks 2 and 3.

Then, the mean hit rate among all limbs for all images was computed (where all limb detections had the same weight) and the participant with the highest mean hit rate won the challenge.

$$H_{i,n} = \begin{cases} 1 & \text{if } \frac{A_n \bigcap B_n}{A_n \bigcup B_n} \geq 0.5 \\ 0 & \text{otherwise} \end{cases} \tag{2}$$

In the case of false positives (e.g. predicting a limb that is not on the ground truth because of being occluded), the prediction did not affect the mean Hit Rate calculation. In that case where $n < 14$, participants do not need to provide any prediction for that particular limb. In other words, n is computed as the intersection of the limb categories in the ground truth and the predictions.

An example of the mean hit rate calculation for an example of $n = 3$ limbs and $i = 1$ image is show in Figure 4(a). In the top part of the image the Jaccard Index for the head limb is computed. As it is greater than 0.5 then it is counted as a hit for image i and the head limb. Similarly, for the torso limb the Jaccard Index obtained is 0.72 (center part of the image) which also computes as a hit for torso limb. In addition, in the bottom of the image the Jaccard Index obtained for the left thigh limb is shown, which does not count as a hit since $0.04 < 0.5$. Finally, the mean hit rate is shown for the three limbs.

4.2 Evaluation Procedure for Tracks 2 and 3

To evaluate the accuracy of action/interaction recognition, we use the Jaccard Index as in track 1, the higher the better. Thus, for the n action, interaction, and gesture categories labeled for a RGB/RGBD sequence s, the Jaccard Index is defined as:

$$J_{s,n} = \frac{A_{s,n} \bigcap B_{s,n}}{A_{s,n} \bigcup B_{s,n}}, \tag{3}$$

where $A_{s,n}$ is the ground truth of action/interaction/gesture n at sequence s, and $B_{s,n}$ is the prediction for such an action at sequence s. $A_{s,n}$ and $B_{s,n}$ are binary vectors where 1-values correspond to frames in which the $n-$th action is being performed. The participants were evaluated based on the mean Jaccard Index among all categories for all sequences, where motion categories are independent but not mutually exclusive (in a certain frame more than one action, interaction, gesture class can be active).

In the case of false positives (e.g. inferring an action, interaction or gesture not labeled in the ground truth), the Jaccard Index is 0 for that particular prediction, and it will not count in the mean Jaccard Index computation. In other words n is equal to the intersection of action/interaction/gesture categories appearing in the ground truth and in the predictions.

An example of the calculation for two actions is shown in Figure 4(b). Note that in the case of recognition, the ground truth annotations of different categories can overlap (appear at the same time within the sequence). Also, although different actors appear within the sequence at the same time, actions/ interactions/gestures are labeled in the corresponding periods of time (that may overlap), there is no need to identify the actors in the scene.

The example in Figure 4(b) shows the mean Jaccard Index calculation for different instances of actions categories in a sequence (single red lines denote ground truth annotations and double red lines denote predictions). In the top part of the image one can see the ground truth annotations for actions walk and fight at sequence s. In the center part of the image a prediction is evaluated obtaining a Jaccard Index of 0.72. In the bottom part of the image the same procedure is performed with the action fight and the obtained Jaccard Index is 0.46. Finally, the mean Jaccard Index is computed obtaining a value of 0.59.

5   Challenge Results and Methods

In this section we summarize the methods proposed by the participants and the winning methods. For the three tracks, 2 (track 1), 6 (track 2) and 17 (track 3) teams submitted their code and predictions for the test sets. Tables 5, 6 and 7 summarize the approaches of the participants who uploaded their models.

Team	Accuracy	Rank position	Features	Pose model
ZJU	0.194144	1	HOG	tree structure
Seawolf Vision	0.182097	2	HOG	tree structure

Table 5. Track 1 Pose Recovery results.

Team name	Accuracy	Rank	Features	Dimension reduction	Clustering	Classifier	Temporal coherence	Gesture representation
CUHK-SWJTU	0.507173	1	Improved trajectories [17]	PCA	-	SVM	Sliding windows	Fisher Vector
ADSC	0.501164	2	Improved trajectories [17]	-	-	SVM	Sliding windows	-
SBUVIS	0.441405	3	Improved trajectories [17]	-	-	SVM	Sliding windows	-
DonkeyBurger	0.342192	4	MHI, STIP	-	Kmeans	Sparse code	Sliding windows	-
UC-T2	0.121565	5	Improved trajectories [17]	PCA	-	Kmeans	Sliding windows	Fisher Vector
MindLAB	0.008383	6	MBF	-	Kmeans	RF	Sliding windows	BoW

Table 6. Track 2 action/interaction recognition results. MHI: Motion History Image; STIP: Spatio-Temporal interest points; MBF: Multiscale Blob Features; BoW: Bag of Visual Words; RF: Random Forest.

Team	Accuracy	Rank	Modalities	Features	Fusion	Temp. segmentation	Dimension reduction	Gesture representation	Classifier
LIRIS	0.849987	1	SK, Depth, RGB	RAW, SK joints	Early	Joints motion	-	-	DNN
CraSPN	0.833904	2	SK, Depth, RGB	HOG, SK	Early	Sliding windows	-	BoW	Adaboost
JY	0.826799	3	SK, RGB	SK, HOG	Late	-	PCA	-	MRF, KNN
CUHK-SWJTU	0.791933	4	RGB	Improved trajectories [17]	-	Joints motion	MRF	Fisher Vector, VLAD	SVM
Lpigou	0.788804	5	Depth, RGB	RAW, SK joints	Early	Sliding windows	PCA	-	CNN
stevenwudi	0.787310	6	Depth	RAW	Late	Sliding windows	Max-pooling CNN	-	HMM, DNN
Ismar	0.746632	7	SK	SK	-	Sliding windows	-	-	RF
Quads	0.745449	8	SK	SK quads	-	Sliding windows	-	Fisher Vector	SVM
Telepoints	0.688778	9	SK, Depth, RGB	STIPS, SK	Late	Joints motion	-	-	SVM
TUM-fortiss	0.648979	10	SK, Depth, RGB	STIPS	Late	Joints motion	-	-	RF, SVM
CSU-SCM	0.597177	11	Skeleton, Depth, mask	HOG, Skeleton	Late	Sliding windows	-	2DMTM	SVM, HMM
iva.mm	0.556251	12	Skeleton, RGB, depth	Skeleton, HOG	Late	Sliding windows	-	BoW	SVM, HMM
Terrier	0.539025	13	Skeleton	Skeleton	-	Sliding windows	-	-	RF
Team Netherlands	0.430709	14	Skeleton, Depth, RGB	MHI	Early	DTW	-	-	SVM, RT
VecsRel	0.408012	15	Skeleton, Depth, RGB	RAW, skeleton joints	Late	DTW	-	-	DNN
Samgest	0.391613	16	Skeleton, Depth, RGB, mask	Skeleton, blobs, moments	Late	Sliding windows	-	-	HMM
YNL	0.270600	17	Skeleton	Skeleton	-	Sliding windows	-	Fisher Vector	HMM, SVM

Table 7. Track 3 Multi-modal gesture recognition results. SK: Skeleton; DNN: Deep Neural Network; RF: Ranfom Forest; 2DMTM: 2D motion trail model; RT: Regression Tree.

5.1   Track 1: RGB Pose Recovery Results

For the first track, as shown in Table 5, both winner participants applied a similar approach based on [18]. Basically, both methods estimate human pose based on static images employing a mixture of templates for each part. This method incorporates the co-occurrence relations, appearance and deformation into a model represented by an objective function of pose configurations. When co-occurrence and spatial relations are tree-structured, optimization can be efficiently conducted via dynamic programming. Inference is conducted via maximizing the objective function with respect to the most probable configuration.

5.2   Track 2: RGB Action/Interaction Recognition Results

Table 6 summarizes the methods of the six participants that participated on the test set of track 2. One can see that most methods are based on similar approaches. In particular, alternative representations to classical BoW were considered, as Fisher Vector and VLAD [8]. Most methods perform sliding windows and SVM classification. In addition, to refine the tracking of interest points, 4 participants used improved trajectories [17]. Next, we describe the main characteristics of the three winning methods.

First Place: The method was composed of two parts: video representation and temporal segmentation. For the representation of video clip, the authors first extracted improved dense trajectories with HOG, HOF, MBHx, and MBHy descriptors. Then, for each kind of descriptor, the participants trained a GMM and used Fisher vector to transform these descriptors into a high dimensional super vector space. Finally, sum pooling was used to aggregate these codes in the whole video clip and normalize them with power L2 norm. For the temporal recognition, the authors resorted to a temporal sliding method along the time dimension. To speed up the processing of detection, the authors designed a temporal integration histogram of Fisher Vector, with which the pooled Fisher Vector was efficiently evaluated at any temporal window. For each sliding window, the authors used the pooled Fisher Vector as representation and fed it into the SVM classifier for action recognition.

Second Place: a human action detection framework called "mixture of heterogeneous attribute analyzer" was proposed. This framework integrated heterogeneous attributes learned from various types of video features including static and dynamic, local and global features, to boost the action detection accuracy. The authors first detected a human from the input video by SVM-HOG detector and performed forward-backward tracking. Multiple local human tracks are linked into long trajectories by spatial-temporal graph based matching. Human key poses and local dense motion trajectories were then extracted within the tracked human bounding box sequences. Second, the authors proposed a mining method that learned discriminative attributes from three feature modalities: human trajectory, key pose and local motion trajectory features. The mining framework was based on the exemplar-SVM discriminative middle level feature detection approach. The learned discriminative attributes from the three types of visual features were then mixed in a max-margin learning algorithm which also explores the combined discriminative capability of heterogeneous feature modalities. The learned mixed analyzer was then applied to the input video sequence for action detection.

Third Place: The framework for detecting actions in video is based on improved dense trajectories applied on a sliding windows fashion. Authors independently trained 11 one-versus-all kernel SVMs on the labeled training set for 11 different actions. The feature and feature descriptions used are improved dense trajectories, HOG, HOF, MBHx and MBHy. During training, for each action, a temporal sliding window is applied without overlapping. For every action, a segment was labeled 0 (negative) for a certain action only if there is no frame in this segment labeled 1. The feature coding method was bag-of-features. For a certain action, the features associated with those frames which are labeled 0 (negative) are not counted when we code the features of the action for the positive segments with bag-of-features. On the basis of the labeled segments and their features, a kernel SVM was trained for each action. During testing, non-overlap sliding window was applied for feature coding of the video. Every frame in a segment was consistently labeled as the output of SVM for each action. The kernel type, sliding window size and penalty of SVMs were selected during validation. When building the bag-of-features, the clustering method was K-means and the vocabulary size is 4000. For one trajectory feature in one frame, all the descriptors were connected to form one description vector. The bag-of-features were built upon this vector.

5.3   Track 3: Multi-Modal Gesture Recognition Recognition Results

Table 7 summarizes the methods of the 17 participants that contributed to the test set of track 3. Although DTW and HMM (and variants) were in the last edition of the ChaLearn Multi-Modal Gesture competition [4,5], random forest has been widely applied in this 2014 edition. Also, three participants used deep learning architectures. Next, we describe the main characteristics of the three winning methods.

First Place: The proposed method was based on a deep learning architecture that iteratively learned and integrated discriminative data representations from individual channels, modeling cross-modality correlations and short- and long-term temporal dependencies. This framework combined three data modalities: depth information, grayscale video and skeleton stream ("articulated pose"). Articulated pose served an efficient representation of large-scale body motion of the upper body and arms, while depth and video streams contained complementary information about more subtle hand articulation. The articulated pose was formulated as a set of joint angles and normalized distances between upper-body joints, augmented with additional information reflecting speed and acceleration of each joint. For the depth and video streams, the authors did not rely on hand-crafted descriptors, but on discriminatively learning joint depth-intensity data representations with a set of convolutional neural layers. Iterative fusion of data channels was performed at output layers of the neural architecture. The idea of learning at multiple scales was also applied to the temporal dimension, such that a gesture was considered as an ordered set of characteristic motion impulses, or dynamic poses. Additional skeleton-based binary classifier was applied for accurate gesture localization. Fusing multiple modalities at several spatial and temporal scales led to a significant increase in recognition rates, allowing the model to compensate for errors of the individual classifiers as well as noise in the separate channels.

Second Place: The approach combined a sliding-window gesture detector with multi-modal features drawn from skeleton data, color imagery, and depth data produced by a first-generation Kinect sensor. The gesture detector consisted of a set of boosted classifiers, each tuned to a specific gesture or gesture mode. Each classifier was trained independently on labeled training data, employing bootstrapping to collect hard examples. At run-time, the gesture classifiers were evaluated in a one-vs-all manner across a sliding window. Features were extracted at multiple temporal scales to enable recognition of variable-length gestures. Extracted features included descriptive statistics of normalized skeleton joint positions, rotations, and velocities, as well as HOG descriptors of the hands. The full set of gesture detectors was trained in under two hours on a single machine, and was extremely efficient at runtime, operating at 1700 fps using skeletal data.

Third Place: The proposed method was based on four features: skeletal joint position feature, skeletal joint distance feature, and histogram of oriented gradients (HOG) features corresponding to left and right hands. Under the naïve Bayes assumption, likelihood functions were independently defined for every feature. Such likelihood functions were non-parametrically constructed from the training data by using kernel density estimation (KDE). For computational efficiency, k-nearest neighbor (kNN) approximation to the exact density estimator was proposed. Constructed likelihood functions were combined to the multi-modal likelihood and this serves as a unary term for our pairwise Markov random field (MRF) model. For enhancing temporal coherence, a pairwise term was additionally incorporated to the MRF model. Final gesture labels were obtained via 1D MRF inference efficiently achieved by dynamic programming.

6   Discussion

This paper has described the main characteristics of the ChaLearn Looking at People 2014 Challenge which included competitions on (i) RGB human pose recovery, (ii) RGB action/interaction recognition, and (iii) multi-modal gesture recognition. Two large data sets (*HuPBA8K* and *Montalbano* datasets) were designed, manually-labelled, and made publicly available to the participants for a fair comparison in the performance results. Analysing the methods used by the 25 teams that finally participated in the test set and uploaded their models, several conclusions can be drawn.

For the case of pose recovery, tree-structure models were mainly applied. Both participants used pictorial structures for inferring best configuration of body parts. The winner achieved almost 0.2 of accuracy.

In the case of action/interaction RGB data sequences, methods for refining the tracking process of visual landmarks while considering alternatives to the classical BoW feature representation have been used. So the general trend was to compute a quantification of visual words present in the image and performing sliding windows classification using discriminative classifiers. Most top ranked participants used SVMs, although random forests were also considered. It has been proven that removing incoherent visual words based on a background motion estimation before performing vector quantification was useful to improve the final recognition score. The winner achieved an accuracy of over 0.5.

In the case of multi-modal gesture recognition, and following current trends in the computer vision literature, a deep learning architecture achieved the first position, with an accuracy score of almost 0.85. Most approaches were based on skeleton joint information and several state-of-the-art descriptors were jointly used by the participants without showing a generic common trend. Temporal segmentation was usually considered by sliding windows or skeleton motion information. As in our previous ChaLearn gesture recognition challenges, SVM, RF, HMM, and DTW algorithms were widely considered.

Interestingly, as said before, it is the first time that participants used deep learning architectures such as Convolutional Neural Networks, which exhibited high recognition rates. In particular, the winner of the competition used all the modalities and information of the human joints to segment gesture candidates. As expected, the code of the participants took a lot more time for training than the rest of approaches.

As a conclusion, there are still much ways for improvement in the two RGB domains considered, namely human pose recovery and action/interaction recognition from RGB data. On the other hand, for multi-modal gesture recognition, there is still room for improvement in the precise begin-end frame level segmentation of gestures, a challenging task to perform even by humans.

Future trends in Looking at People may include group interactions and cultural event classification, where context also places an important role, while including the analysis of social signals, affective computing, and face analysis.

Acknowledgments. We sincerely thank all the teams who participated in ChaLearn LAP 2014 for their interest and for having contributed to improve the challenge with their comments and suggestions. Special thanks to Pau Rodríguez for his time in annotating part of the gestures in the *Montalbano* dataset. We also thank the Microsoft Codalab submission website for their timely support, together with the researchers who joined the program committee and reviewed for the ChaLearn LAP 2014 workshop. This work was also partially supported by Spanish projects TIN2009-14501-C02-02, TIN2012-39051, and TIN2012-38187-C03-02.

References

1. Andriluka, M., Pishchulin, L., Gehler, P., Schiele, B.: Human pose estimation: new benchmark and state of the art analysis. In: CCVPR, IEEE (2014)
2. Bourdev, L., Malik, J.: Poselets: body part detectors trained using 3d human pose annotations. In: ICCV, pp. 1365–1372. IEEE (2009)
3. De la Torre, F., Hodgins, J.K., Montano, J., Valcarcel, S.: Detailed human data acquisition of kitchen activities: the CMU-multimodal activity database (CMU-MMAC). Tech. rep., RI-TR-08-22h, CMU (2008)
4. Escalera, S., Gonzàlez, J., Baró, X., Reyes, M., Guyon, I., Athitsos, V., Escalante, H.J., Sigal, L., Argyros, A., Sminchisescu, C., Bowden, R., Sclaroff, S.: Chalearn multi-modal gesture recognition 2013: grand challenge and workshop summary. In: 15th ACM International Conference on Multimodal Interaction, pp. 365–368 (2013)
5. Escalera, S., Gonzàlez, J., Baró, X., Reyes, M., Lopes, O., Guyon, I., Athitsos, V., Escalante, H.J.: Multi-modal gesture recognition challenge 2013: Dataset and results. In: ChaLearn Multi-modal Gesture Recognition Grand Challenge and Workshop (ICMI), pp. 445–452 (2013)
6. Everingham, M., Gool, L.V., Williams, C., Winn, J., Zisserman, A.: The pascal visual object classes (VOC) challenge. IJCV **88**(2), 303–338 (2010)
7. Ferrari, V., Marin-Jimenez, M., Zisserman, A.: Progressive search space reduction for human pose estimation. In: CVPR (2008)
8. Jegou, H., Perronnin, F., Douze, M., Sanchez, J., Perez, P., Schmid, C.: Aggregating local image descriptors into compact codes. IEEE TPAMI **34**(9), 1704–1716 (2012)
9. Johnson, S., Everingham, M.: Clustered pose and nonlinear appearance models for human pose estimation. In: BMVC (2010). doi:10.5244/C.24.12
10. Laptev, I., Marszalek, M., Schmid, C., Rozenfeld, B.: Learning realistic human actions from movies. In: CVPR, pp. 1–8 (2008)
11. Moeslund, T., Hilton, A., Krueger, V., Sigal, L. (eds.): Visual Analysis of Humans: Looking at People. Springer, The Netherlands (2011)
12. Ramanan, D.: Learning to parse images of articulated bodies. In: NIPS, pp. 1129–1136 (2006)
13. Sánchez, D., Bautista, M.A., Escalera, S.: HuPBA 8k+: Dataset and ECOC-graphcut based segmentation of human limbs. Neurocomputing (2014)
14. Sapp, B., Taskar, B.: Modec: Multimodal decomposable models for human pose estimation. In: CVPR, IEEE (2013)
15. Schuldt, C., Laptev, I., Caputo, B.: Recognizing human actions: a local SVM approach. ICPR **3**, 32–36 (2004)
16. Tran, D., Forsyth, D.: Improved human parsing with a full relational model. In: Daniilidis, K., Maragos, P., Paragios, N. (eds.) ECCV 2010, Part IV. LNCS, vol. 6314, pp. 227–240. Springer, Heidelberg (2010)
17. Wang, H., Schmid, C.: Action recognition with improved trajectories. In: ICCV (2013)
18. Yang, Y., Ramanan, D.: Articulated human detection with flexible mixtures of parts. IEEE TPAMI (2013)

Multi-scale Deep Learning for Gesture Detection and Localization

Natalia Neverova[1,2]([⊠]), Christian Wolf[1,2], Graham W. Taylor[3], and Florian Nebout[4]

[1] Université de Lyon, CNRS, Lyon, France
{natalia.neverova,christian.wolf}@liris.cnrs.fr
[2] INSA-Lyon, LIRIS, UMR5205, 69621 Villeurbanne cedex, France
[3] University of Guelph, Guelph, Canada
gwtaylor@uoguelph.ca
[4] Awabot, Lyon, France
florian.nebout@awabot.com

Abstract. We present a method for gesture detection and localization based on multi-scale and multi-modal deep learning. Each visual modality captures spatial information at a particular spatial scale (such as motion of the upper body or a hand), and the whole system operates at two temporal scales. Key to our technique is a training strategy which exploits i) careful initialization of individual modalities; and ii) gradual fusion of modalities from strongest to weakest cross-modality structure. We present experiments on the *ChaLearn 2014 Looking at People Challenge* gesture recognition track, in which we placed first out of 17 teams.

Keywords: Gesture recognition · Multi-modal systems · Deep learning

1 Introduction

Visual gesture recognition is one of the central problems in the rapidly growing fields of human-computer and human-robot interaction. Effective gesture detection and classification is challenging due to several factors: cultural and individual differences in tempos and styles of articulation, variable observation conditions, the small size of fingers in images taken in typical acquisition conditions, noise in camera channels, infinitely many kinds of out-of-vocabulary motion, and real-time performance constraints.

Recently, the field of deep learning has matured and made a tremendous impact in computer vision, demonstrating previously unattainable performance on the tasks of object detection, localization [1,2], recognition [3] and image segmentation [4,5]. Convolutional neural networks (ConvNets) [6] have excelled on several scientific competitions such as ILSVRC [3], Emotion Recognition in the Wild (EmotiW 2013) [7], Kaggle Dogs vs. Cats [2] and Galaxy Zoo. Taigman et al. [8] recently claimed to have reached human-level performance using ConvNets for face recognition. On the other hand, extending these models to problems involving the understanding of *video* content is still in its infancy, this idea

© Springer International Publishing Switzerland 2015
L. Agapito et al. (Eds.): ECCV 2014 Workshops, Part I, LNCS 8925, pp. 474–490, 2015.
DOI: 10.1007/978-3-319-16178-5_33

having been explored only in a small number of recent works [9–11]. It can be partially explained by lack of sufficiently large datasets and the high cost of data labeling in many practical areas, as well as increased modeling complexity brought about the additional temporal dimension and the interdependencies it implies.

The first gesture-oriented dataset containing a sufficient amount of training samples for deep learning methods was proposed for the the *ChaLearn 2013 Challenge on Multi-modal gesture recognition*. The deep learning method we describe here placed first in the 2014 version of this competition [12].

A core aspect of our approach is employing a multi-modal convolutional neural network for classification of so-called dynamic poses of varying durations (i.e. temporal scales). The best single scale configuration corresponding to a certain formulation of the dynamic pose alone places first (see Section 5 for more details), while introducing parallel multi-scale paths leads to an additional gain in performance. Finally, we find it interesting to provide a comparison of the proposed approach with a baseline model employing a popular ensemble method. The performance of a hybrid solution, leading to another small gain, is reported for a reference.

Data modalities integrated by our algorithm include intensity and depth video, as well as articulated pose information extracted from depth maps. We make use of different data channels to decompose each gesture at multiple scales not only temporally, but also spatially, to provide context for upper-body body motion and more fine-grained hand/finger articulation. We pay special attention to developing an effective learning algorithm since learning large-scale multi-modal networks like the one we train on a limited labeled dataset is a formidable challenge.

Our classification model outputs prediction updates in real-time in frame-wise manner. Nevertheless, since temporal integration is involved, the classification model suffers from a certain degree of inertia. Furthermore, due to high similarity between gesture classes on pre-stroke and post-stroke phases, frame-wise classification at that time is often uncertain and therefore erroneous. To compensate for these negative effects, an additional module is introduced for filtering, denoising and more accurate gesture localization.

The major contributions of the present work are the following: (i) we develop a deep learning-based multi-modal and multi-scale framework for gesture detection, localization and recognition; and (ii) propose a progressive learning procedure enabling our method to scale to a higher number of data modalities.

2 Related Work

Gesture Recognition — Traditional approaches to action and distant gesture recognition from video typically include sparse or dense extraction of spatial or spatio-temporal engineered descriptors followed by classification [13–18].

Near-range applications may require more accurate reconstruction of hand shapes. In this case, fitting a 3D hand model, as well as appearance-based algorithms provide more appropriate solutions. A group of recent works is dedicated to inferring the hand pose through pixel-wise hand segmentation and estimating the positions of hand joints in a bottom-up fashion [19–22]. In parallel, tracking-based approaches are advancing quickly [23,24]. Finally, graphical models, exploring spatial relationships between body and hand parts, have recently attracted close attention from the vision community [25,26].

Multi-modal aspects are of relevance in this domain. In [27], a combination of skeletal features and local occupancy patterns (LOP) are calculated from depth maps to describe hand joints. In [28], the skeletal information is integrated in two ways for extracting HoG features from RGB and depth images: either from global bounding boxes containing a whole body or from regions containing an arm, a torso and a head. Similarly, [29] fuse skeletal information with HoG features extracted from the RGB channel, while [30] propose a combination of a covariance descriptor representing skeletal joint data with spatio-temporal interest points extracted from the RGB modality augmented with audio features.

Representation Learning — Various fundamental architectures have been proposed in the context of motion analysis for *learning* (as opposed to handcrafting) representations directly from data, either in a supervised or unsupervised way. Independent subspace analysis (ISA) [31] as well as autoencoders [9,32] are examples of efficient unsupervised methods for learning hierarchies of invariant spatio-temporal features. Space-time deep belief networks [33] produce high-level representations of video sequences using convolutional RBMs.

Vanilla supervised convolutional networks have also been explored in this context. A method proposed in [34] is based on low level preprocessing of the video input and employs a 3D convolutional network for learning of mid-level spatio-temporal representations and classification. Recently, Karpathy et al. [10] have proposed a convolutional architecture for general purpose large-scale video classification operating at two spatial resolutions (a fovea stream and a context stream).

A number of deep architectures have recently been proposed specifically for multi-modal data. Ngiam et al. [35] employ sparse RBMs and bimodal deep antoencoders for learning cross-modality correlations in the context of audio-visual speech classification of isolated letters and digits. Srivastava et al. [36] use a multi-modal deep Boltzmann machine in a generative fashion to tackle the problem of integrating image data and text annotations. Kahou et al. [7] won the 2013 Emotion Recognition in the Wild Challenge by building two convolutional architectures on several modalities, such as facial expressions from video frames, audio signal, scene context and features extracted around mouth regions. Finally, in [37] the authors propose a multi-modal convolutional network for gesture detection and classification from a combination of depth, skeletons and audio.

3   Gesture Classification

On a dataset such as *ChaLearn 2014*, we face several key challenges: learning representations at multiple spatial and temporal scales, integrating the various modalities, and training a complex model when the number of labeled examples

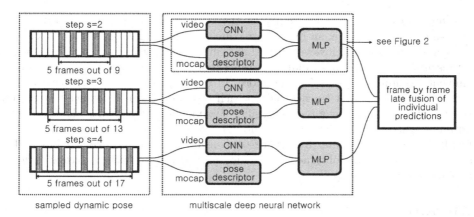

sampled dynamic pose   multiscale deep neural network

Fig. 1. The deep convolutional multi-modal architecture operating at 3 temporal scales corresponding to dynamic poses of 3 different durations

is not at *web-scale* like static image datasets (e.g. [3]). We start by describing how the first two challenges are overcome at an architectural level. Our training strategy to overcome the last challenge is described in Sec. 3.4.

Our proposed multi-scale deep neural model consists of a combination of single-scale paths connected in a parallel way (see Fig. 1). Each path independently learns a representation and performs gesture classification at its own temporal scale given input from RGB-D video and articulated pose descriptors. Predictions from all paths are then aggregated through additive late fusion. This strategy allows us to first extract the most salient (in a discriminative sense) motions at a fine temporal resolution and, at the same time, consider them in the context of global gesture structure, smoothing and compensating for per-block errors typical for a given gesture class.

To differentiate among temporal scales, a notion of dynamic pose is introduced. By *dynamic pose* we mean a sequence of video frames, synchronized across modalities, sampled at a given temporal step s and concatenated to form a spatio-temporal 3d volume. Varying the value of s allows the model to leverage multiple temporal scales for prediction, thereby accommodating differences in tempos and styles of articulation of different users. Our model is therefore different from the one proposed in [4], where by "multi-scale" the authors imply a multi-resolution spatial pyramid rather than a fusion of temporal sampling strategies. Regardless of the step s, we use the same number of frames (5) at each scale. Fig. 1 shows the three such paths used in this work (with $s = 2 \ldots 4$). At each scale and for each dynamic pose, the classifier outputs a per-class score.

All available modalities, such as depth, gray scale video, and articulated pose, contribute to the network's prediction. Global appearance of each gesture instance is captured by the skeleton descriptor, while video streams convey additional information about hand shapes and their dynamics which are crucial for discriminating between gesture classes performed in similar body poses.

Due to the high dimensionality of the data and the non-linear nature of cross-modality structure, an immediate concatenation of raw skeleton and video signals is sub-optimal. However, initial discriminative learning of individual data representations from each isolated channel followed by fusion has proven to be efficient in similar tasks [35]. Therefore, in our approach, discriminative data representations are first learned within each separate channel, followed by joint fine tuning and fusion by a meta-classifier (independently at each scale, for more details see Sec. 3.4). A shared set of hidden layers is employed at different levels for, first, fusing "similar by nature" gray scale and depth video streams and, second, combining the obtained joint video representation with the transformed articulated pose descriptor.

3.1   Articulated Pose

We formulate a pose descriptor, consisting of 7 logical subsets, and allow the classifier to perform online feature selection. The descriptor is calculated based on 11 upper body joints, relevant to the task, whose raw, i.e. pre-normalization, positions in a 3D coordinate system associated with the depth sensor are denoted as $\mathbf{p}_{\mathrm{raw}}^{(i)} = \{x^{(i)}, y^{(i)}, z^{(i)}\}$, $i = 0...10$ ($i = 0$ corresponds to the *HipCenter* joint).

Following the procedure proposed in [38], we first calculate normalized joint positions, as well as their velocities and accelerations, and then augment the descriptor with a set of characteristic angles and pairwise distances.

Joint positions. The skeleton is represented as a tree structure with the *HipCenter* joint playing the role of a root node. Its coordinates are subtracted from the rest of the vectors $\mathbf{p}_{\mathrm{raw}}$ to eliminate the influence of position of the body in space. To compensate for differences in body sizes, proportions and shapes, we start from the top of the tree and iteratively normalize each skeleton segment to a corresponding average "bone" length estimated from all available training data. It is done in the way that absolute joint positions are corrected while corresponding orientations remain unchanged:

$$\mathbf{p}^{(i)}(t) = \mathbf{p}_{\mathrm{raw}}^{(i-1)}(t) + \frac{\mathbf{p}_{\mathrm{raw}}^{(i)}(t) - \mathbf{p}_{\mathrm{raw}}^{(i-1)}(t)}{||\mathbf{p}_{\mathrm{raw}}^{(i)}(t) - \mathbf{p}_{\mathrm{raw}}^{(i-1)}(t)||} b^{(i-1,i)} - \mathbf{p}_{\mathrm{raw}}^{(0)}(t), \qquad (1)$$

where $\mathbf{p}_{\mathrm{raw}}^{(i)}$ is a current joint, $\mathbf{p}_{\mathrm{raw}}^{(i-1)}$ is its direct predecessor in the tree, $b^{(i-1,i)}$, $i = 1 \dots 10$ is a set of estimated average lengths of "bones" and $\mathbf{p}$ are corresponding normalized joints. Once the normalized joint positions are obtained, we perform Gaussian smoothing along the temporal dimension ($\sigma = 1$, filter size 5×1) to decrease the influence of skeleton jitter.

Joint velocities are calculated as first derivatives of normalized joint positions: $\delta \mathbf{p}^{(i)}(t) \approx \mathbf{p}^{(i)}(t+1) - \mathbf{p}^{(i)}(t-1)$.

Joint accelerations correspond to the second derivatives of the same positions: $\delta^2 \mathbf{p}^{(i)}(t) \approx \mathbf{p}^{(i)}(t+2) + \mathbf{p}^{(i)}(t-2) - 2\mathbf{p}^{(i)}(t)$.

Inclination angles are formed by all triples of anatomically connected joints (i, j, k), plus two "virtual" angles (Right,Left)*Elbow*-(Right,Left)*Hand*-*HipCenter*:

$$\alpha^{(i,j,k)} = \arccos \frac{(\mathbf{p}^{(k)} - \mathbf{p}^{(j)})(\mathbf{p}^{(i)} - \mathbf{p}^{(j)})}{||\mathbf{p}^{(k)} - \mathbf{p}^{(j)}|| \cdot ||\mathbf{p}^{(i)} - \mathbf{p}^{(j)}||} \tag{2}$$

Azimuth angles β provide additional information about the pose in the coordinate space associated with the body. We apply PCA on the positions of 6 torso joints (*HipCenter, HipLeft, HipRight, ShoulderCenter, ShoulderLeft, ShoulderRight*) to obtain 3 vectors forming the basis: $\{\mathbf{u}_x, \mathbf{u}_y, \mathbf{u}_z\}$, where $\mathbf{u}_x$ is approximately parallel to the shoulder line, $\mathbf{u}_y$ is aligned with the spine and $\mathbf{u}_z$ is perpendicular to the torso.

Then for each pair of connected bones, β are angles between projections of the second bone ($\mathbf{v}_2$) and the vector $\mathbf{u}_x$ ($\mathbf{v}_1$) on the plane perpendicular to the orientation of the first bone. As in the previous case of inclination angles, we also include two virtual "bones" (Right,Left)*Hand-HipCenter*.

$$\mathbf{v}_1 = \mathbf{u}_x - (\mathbf{p}^{(j)} - \mathbf{p}^{(i)}) \frac{\mathbf{u}_x \cdot (\mathbf{p}^{(j)} - \mathbf{p}^{(i)})}{||\mathbf{p}^{(j)} - \mathbf{p}^{(i)}||^2}$$
$$\mathbf{v}_2 = (\mathbf{p}^{(k)} - \mathbf{p}^{(j)}) - (\mathbf{p}^{(j)} - \mathbf{p}^{(i)}) \frac{(\mathbf{p}^{(k)} - \mathbf{p}^{(j)}) \cdot (\mathbf{p}^{(j)} - \mathbf{p}^{(i)})}{||\mathbf{p}^{(j)} - \mathbf{p}^{(i)}||^2} \tag{3}$$
$$\beta^{(i,j,k)} = \arccos \frac{\mathbf{v}_1 \cdot \mathbf{v}_2}{||\mathbf{v}_1|| ||\mathbf{v}_1||}$$

Bending angles γ are a set of angles between a basis vector $\mathbf{u}_z$, perpendicular to the torso, and normalized joint positions:

$$\gamma^{(i)} = \arccos \frac{\mathbf{u}_z \cdot \mathbf{p}^{(i)}}{||\mathbf{p}^{(i)}||} \tag{4}$$

Pairwise distances. Finally, we calculate pairwise distances between all normalized joint positions: $\rho^{(i,j)} = ||\mathbf{p}_n^{(i)} - \mathbf{p}_n^{(j)}||$.

Combined together, this produces a 183-dimensional pose descriptor for each video frame: $\mathbf{D} = [\mathbf{p}, \delta\mathbf{p}, \delta^2\mathbf{p}, \alpha, \beta, \gamma, \rho]^T$. Finally, each feature is normalized to zero mean and unit variance.

A set of consequent 5 frame descriptors sampled at a given step s are concatenated to form a 915-dimensional dynamic pose descriptor which is further used for gesture classification. The two subsets of features involving derivatives contain dynamic information and for dense sampling may be partially redundant as several occurrences of same frames are stacked when a dynamic pose descriptor is formulated. Although theoretically unnecessary, this is beneficial in the context of a limited amount of training data.

3.2   Depth and Intensity Video: Convolutional Learning

In our approach, two video streams serve as a source of information about hand pose and finger articulation. Bounding boxes containing images of hands are cropped around positions of the *RightHand* and *LeftHand* joints. Within each set of frames forming a dynamic pose, hand position is stabilized by minimizing

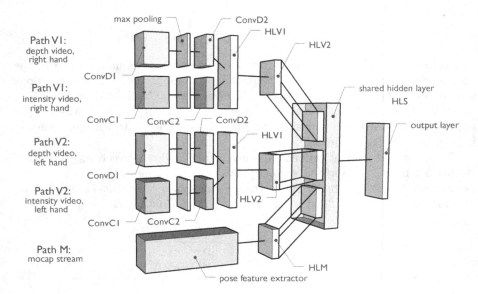

Fig. 2. Single-scale deep architecture. Individual classifiers are pre-trained for each data modality (paths V1, V2, M) and then fused using a 2-layer shared fully connected network initialized in a specific way (see Sec. 3.4). The first layers perform 3D convolutions followed by 3D max pooling shrinking the temporal dimension. The second layers are exclusively spatial. Weights are shared across V1 and V2 paths.

inter-frame square-root distances calculated as a sum over all pixels, and corresponding frames are concatenated to form a single spatio-temporal volume. The color stream is converted to gray scale, and both depth and intensity frames are normalized to zero mean and unit variance. Left hand videos are flipped about the vertical axis and combined with right hand instances in a single training set.

During pre-training, video pathways are adapted to produce predictions for each hand, rather than for the whole gesture. Therefore, we introduce an additional step to eliminate possible noise associated with switching from one active hand to another. For one-handed gesture classes, we estimate the motion trajectory length of each hand using the respective joints provided by the skeleton stream (summing lengths of hand trajectories projected to the x and y axes):

$$\Delta = \sum_{t=2}^{5}(|x(t) - x(t-1)| + |y(t) - y(t-1)|), \tag{5}$$

where $x(t)$ is the x-coordinate of a hand joint (either left or right) and $y(t)$ is its y-coordinate. Finally, the hand with a greater value of Δ gets assigned to the label class, while the second one is assigned the zero-class label.

For each channel and each hand, we perform 2-stage convolutional learning of data representations independently (first in 3D, then in 2D space, see Fig. 2) and then fuse the two streams with a set of fully connected hidden layers. Parameters of the convolutional and fully-connected layers at this step are shared between the right hand and left hand pathways. Our experiments have demonstrated that relatively early fusion of depth and intensity features leads to a significant increase in performance, even though the quality of predictions obtained from each channel alone is unsatisfactory.

3.3   Fusion

Once individual single-scale predictions are obtained, we employ a simple voting strategy for fusion with a single weight per model. We note here that introducing additional per-class per-model weights and training meta-classifiers (such as an MLP) on this step quickly leads to overfitting.

At each given frame t per-class network outputs o_k are obtained via per-frame aggregation and temporal filtering of predictions at each scale with corresponding weights μ_s defined empirically through cross-validation on a validation set:

$$o_k(t) = \sum_{s=2}^{4} \mu_s \sum_{j=-4s}^{0} o_{s,k}(t + j), \tag{6}$$

where $o_{s,k}(t + j)$ is the score of class k obtained for a spatio-temporal block sampled starting from the frame $t + j$ at step s. Finally, the frame is assigned the class label $l(t)$ having the maximum score: $l(t) = \arg\min_k o_k(t)$.

3.4   Training

With an increasing number of data modalities, efficient training of large-scale deep architectures becomes one of the most practically important issues in domains such as gesture understanding. Due to an exploding number of parameters, direct modeling of joint data distributions from all available data sources is not always possible. The problem becomes even more crucial if we aim on simultaneous data fusion and modeling temporal sequences. In this work we used several strategies, such as pre-training of individual classifiers on separate channels and iterative fusion process of all modalities.

Recall Fig. 2 illustrating a one scale deep multi-modal convolutional network. Initially it has 5 separate pathways: depth and intensity video channels for right (V1) and left hands (V2), and a mocap stream (M).

We start with transforming of each data input to the form which is discriminative for the given classification task by passing the data through a modality-specific 3-step convolutional neural network (ConvD1-ConvD2 in the case of depth data and ConvC1-ConvC2 in the case of intensity video) or by manual feature extraction (in the case of mocap data, as it was described in Sec. 3.1).

From our observations, inter-modality fusion is effective at early stages if both channels have the same nature and convey overlapping information. On the other hand, mixing modalities which are weekly correlated, is rarely beneficial until

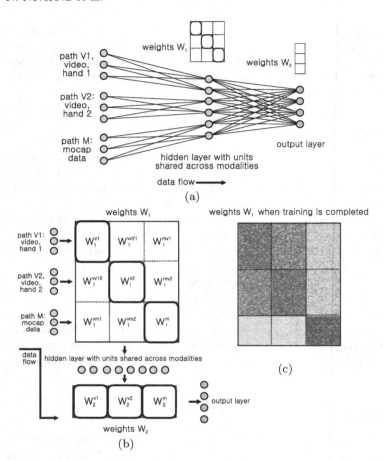

Fig. 3. (a) Architecture of shared hidden and output layers. Output hidden units on each path are first connected to a subset of neurons of the shared layer; (b) Structure of parameters of shared hidden and output layers (corresponds to the architecture above); (c) Energy structure of weights W1 after training. Diagonal blocks are dominated by individual modalities, off-diagonal elements reflect cross-modality correlations.

the final stage. Accordingly, in our architecture two video channels corresponding to the same hand are fused immediately after feature extraction (hidden layers HLV1 and HLV2), while exploring cross-modality correlations of complementary skeleton motion and hand articulation is postponed by two layers (the fusion is performed only at a shared layer HLS).

Furthermore, proper initialization of the shared layer HLS before data fusion is important. Direct fully-connected wiring of pre-trained paths to the shared layer with randomly initialized weights leads to quick degradation of pre-trained connections and as a result, our experience suggests that the joint representation performs worse than a linear combination of the predictions of individual classifiers. This may be related to the fact that the amount of data at our disposal is still not sufficient for straightforward training of such large-scale architectures.

To address this issue, one possible strategy would be to train a classifier on data that is arranged in a specific meaningful order, starting from clean samples that are easy to classify and proceeding to the most complex ones, allowing the network to learn more and more sophisticated concepts (as it is done, for example, in curriculum learning [39]). This approach has shown to yield better generalization in less time. We employ a similar but alternative strategy, changing the network itself in an iterative way, evolving from a weak prediction model to increasingly more complex prediction models. The network is divided into meaningful parts that are pre-trained separately and then combined. We begin training by presenting modality-specific parts of the network with samples where only one modality is present. In this way, we pre-train initial sets of modality-specific layers that extract features from each data channel and create more meaningful and compact data representations.

Once pre-training is completed, we proceed with integrating all channels, one by one, in an iterative manner (see Fig. 3). We choose the order of modalities in a specific way to first combine the data where the strongest cross-modality structure is expected. This permits the model to gradually and effectively learn a joint distribution, focusing representational power on where it is most effective, while keeping the input compact and the number of parameters relatively small. In the task of multi-modal gesture recognition, the video stream and articulated pose alone convey sufficient information about the gesture, i.e. recognition can be performed reasonably well from each channel independently. However, data in the two depth channels, representing the articulation of each of the two hands, is complementary and can improve accuracy.

To ensure that the joint model is meaningful, both the shared representation layer and output layer are first configured to produce an optimal weighted sum of individual modalities. The network parameters are further optimized starting from this initialization. We start the fusion procedure by integrating two highly dependent video channels (V1 and V2) with shared parameters, then add the third visual modality (articulated pose, path M) (see Fig. 3).

4   Gesture Localization

With increasing duration of a dynamic pose, recognition rates of the classifier increase at a cost of loss in precision in gesture localization. Using wider sliding windows leads to noisy predictions at pre-stroke and post-stroke phases, in some cases overlapping several gesture instances at once. On the other hand, too short dynamic poses are not discriminative either as most gesture classes at their initial and final stages have a similar appearance (e.g. raising or lowering hands).

To address this issue, we introduce an additional binary classifier to distinguish resting moments from periods of activity. Trained on dynamic poses at the finest temporal resolution $s = 1$, this classifier is able to precisely localize starting and ending points of each gesture.

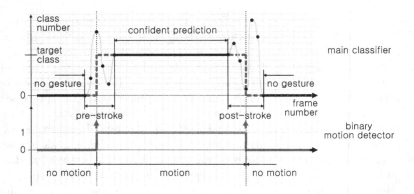

Fig. 4. Gesture localization. Top: output predictions of the main classifier; Bottom: output of the binary motion detector. Noise at pre-stroke and post-stroke phases in the first case is due to high similarity between gesture classes at these time periods and temporal inertia of the classifier.

The module is implemented based on the same articulated pose descriptor input to the MLP. All training frames labeled with some gesture class are used as positive examples, while a set of frames right before and after such gesture are considered as negatives. This strategy allows us to assign each frame with a label "motion" or "no motion" with accuracy of 98%.

To combine the classification and localization modules, frame-wise gesture class predictions are first obtained as described in Section 3.3. Output predictions at the beginning and at the end of each gesture are typically noisy (see the top curve at Fig. 4). For each spotted gesture, its boundaries are extended or shrunk towards the closest switching point produced by the binary classifier.

5   Experiments

The *Chalearn 2014 Looking at People Challenge (track 3)* dataset consists of 13,858 instances of Italian conversational gestures performed by different people and recorded with a consumer RGB-D sensor. It includes color, depth video and articulated pose streams. The gestures are drawn from a large vocabulary, from which 20 categories are identified to detect and recognize [12]. Training data is accompanied by a ground truth label for each gesture, as well as information about its starting and ending points. The corpus is split into development, validation and test set, where the test data has been released after code submission.

5.1   Experimental Setup

The hyperparameters used for the convolutional nets are provided in Table 1. They were constant across temporal scales. Gesture localization was performed with an MLP with 300 hidden units. All hidden units of both modules (framewise

Table 1. Hyperparameters chosen for the deep learning models

Layer	Parameters	Layer	Parameters
Convolutional layer ConvD1	25×5×5×3	Hidden layer HLV1	900
Convolutional layer ConvD2	25×5×5	Hidden layer HLV2	450
Convolutional layer ConvC1	25×5×5×3	Hidden layer HLM	300
Convolutional layer ConvC2	25×5×5	Hidden layer HLS	63
Max pooling, steps	2×2×3	Output layer	21

Table 2. *ChaLearn 2014 "Looking at people Challenge (track 3)"* results (top 10)

Rank	Team	Score	Rank	Team	Score
1	**Ours**	**0.8500**	6	Wu [40]	0.7873
2	Monnier et al. [41]	0.8339	7	Camgoz et al. [42]	0.7466
3	Chang [43]	0.8268	8	Evangelidis et al. [44]	0.7454
4	Peng et al. [45]	0.7919	9	Undisclosed authors	0.6888
5	Pigou et al. [46]	0.7888	10	Chen et al. [47]	0.6490

classification and following localization) had rectified linear (ReLU) activations. Hyperparameters were optimized on the validation data. Early stopping based on a validation set was employed to prevent the models from overfitting. Optimal fusion weights for the different temporal scales were found to be: $\mu_{s=2} = 0.26$, $\mu_{s=3} = 1.02$, $\mu_{s=4} = 2.20$ and the weight of the baseline model (see Section 5.2) was set to $\mu_{\text{ERT}} = 1$.

We followed the evaluation procedure proposed by the challenge organizers and adopted the Jaccard Index to quantify model performance:

$$J_{s,n} = \frac{A_{s,n} \cap B_{s,n}}{A_{s,n} \cup B_{s,n}}, \tag{7}$$

where $A_{s,n}$ is the ground truth label of gesture n in sequence s, and $B_{s,n}$ is the obtained prediction for the given gesture class in the same sequence. Here $A_{s,n}$ and $B_{s,n}$ are binary vectors where the frames in which the given gesture is being performed are marked with 1 and the rest with 0. Overall performance was calculated as the mean Jaccard index among all gesture categories and all sequences, with equal weights for all gesture classes.

5.2   Baseline Model

In addition to the main pipeline, we have created a baseline model based on an ensemble classifier trained in a similar iterative fashion but on purely handcrafted descriptors. It was done to explore relative advantages (and disadvantages) of using learned representations and also the nuances of fusion. In addition, due to differences in feature formulation as well as in the nature of classifiers, we found it beneficial to combine the proposed deep network with the baseline method in a hybrid model as separately two models make different errors (see Table 4).

We use depth and intensity hand images and extract three sets of features. HoG features describe the hand pose in the image plane, and histograms of depths describe pose along the third spatial dimension. The third set reflects temporal dynamics of the hand shape.

HoG features from intensity images. First, we make use zero-mean and unit variance-normalized intensity images to extract HoG features h_{int} [48] at 9 orientations from a 2-level spatial pyramid [49], i.e. from the whole image and a magnified version of it containing 3×3 cells.

Histograms of depths. 9-bin depth histograms h_{dep} are extracted on two scales from depth maps of both hands: from a whole map and from each quarter of its upsampled version (by a factor of 2).

Derivatives of histograms. First derivatives of HoGs and depth histograms are calculated: $\delta h(t) \approx h(t+1) - h(t-1)$, where h can stand for both h_{int} and h_{dep}. Combined together, these three sets of features form a 270-dimensional descriptor $[h_{int}, h_{dep}, \delta h_{int}, \delta h_{dep}]$ for each frame and, consequently, a descriptor of dimension of 1350 for the dynamic pose of each hand.

Extremely randomized trees (ERT) [50] are adopted for data fusion and gesture classification. Ensemble methods of this sort have generally proven to be especially effective in conjunction with handcrafted features. During training, we followed the same iterative strategy as in the case of the neural architecture. First, three ERT classifiers are trained independently on (i) skeleton descriptors (the same as described in Section 3.1)), (ii) video features for the right hand and (iii) video features for the left hand. Once training is completed, features from all modalities with importance above the mean value are selected and once again fused for training a new, general ERT classifier. Feature importance is calculated as mean decrease in impurity (i.e. total decrease in node impurity weighted by proportion of samples reaching that node and averaged over all trees [51]).

At each step, ERT classifiers are trained with 300 estimators, an information gain criterion, no restrictions in depth and $\sqrt{N_f}$ features considered at each step (where N_f is the total number of features).

5.3   Results and Discussion

The top 10 scores of the challenge are reported in Table 2. Our winning entry corresponding to a hybrid model (i.e. a combination of the proposed deep neural architecture and a baseline model (see Section 5.2)) surpasses the second best score by a margin of 1.61 percentage points. We also note that the multi-scale neural architecture still demonstrates the best performance, as well as the top one-scale neural model alone (see Tables 3 and 4).

Detailed information on the performance of neural architectures at each scale is provided in Table 3, including the multi-modal setting and per-modality tests. Interestingly, the discriminative power of articulated pose strongly depends on the sampling step and achieves a maximum value in the case of large sliding windows. On the other hand, video streams, containing information about hand shape and articulation, seem to be less sensitive to this parameter and demonstrate very good performance even for short spatio-temporal blocks. This signifies

Table 3. Performance at different temporal scales (deep learning + binary motion detector). All numbers reported in the table are the Jaccard Index.

Step	Articulated pose	Video	All
2	0.6938	0.7862	0.8188
3	0.7734	0.7926	0.8255
4	0.7891	0.7990	0.8449
all	**0.8080**	**0.8096**	**0.8488**

Table 4. Performance of different architectures (Jaccard Index)

Model	W. motion detector	W/o motion detector	(Rank)
Deep learning (proposed)	0.8118	**0.8488**	(1)
ERT (baseline)	0.7278	0.7811	(6)
Deep learning + ERT (hybrid)	0.8143	**0.8500**	(1)

that in the context of this dataset, a body pose is interesting exclusively in terms of its dynamics, while hand postures are fairly discriminative alone, even in nearly static mode. The overall highest performance is nevertheless obtained in the case of a dynamic pose with duration roughly corresponding to the length of an average gesture (s=4, i.e. 17 frames).

The comparative performances of the baseline and hybrid models are reported in Table 4. In spite of low scores of the isolated ERT baseline model, fusing its outputs with the ones provided by the neural architecture is still slightly beneficial, mostly due to differences in feature formulation in the video channel (adding ERT to mocap alone did not result in a significant gain).

For each combination, we also provide results obtained with a classification module alone (without additional gesture localization) and coupled with the binary motion detector. The experiments have shown that the localization module contributes significantly to overall performance.

The deep learning architecture is implemented with the Theano library. A single scale predictor operates at frame rates close to real time (24 fps on GPU).

6   Conclusion

We have presented a general method for gesture and near-range action detection from a combination of depth and intensity video and articulated pose data. The model can be extended by adding alternative sensory pathways without significant changes in the architecture. It can elegantly cope with more spatial or temporal scales. Beyond scaling, an interesting direction for future work is a deeper exploration into the dynamics of cross-modality dependencies. Considering full signal reconstruction (similar to [35]), or explicit feedback connections as in the case of Deep Boltzmann Machines [36] would be helpful in the case when the input from one or more modalities is missing or noisy.

Acknowledgments. This work was partially funded by a French grant INTERABOT, call "Investissements d'Avenir / Briques Génériques du Logiciel Embarqué", and by a French region "Rhônes Alpes" through the ARC6 research council.

References

1. Girshick, R., Donahue, J., Darrell, T., Malik, J.: Rich feature hierarchies for accurate object detection and semantic segmentation. In: CVPR (2014)
2. Sermanet, P., Eigen, D., Zhang, X., Mathieu, M., Fergus, R., LeCun, Y.: OverFeat: Integrated Recognition, Localization and Detection using Convolutional Networks. In: ICLR (2014)
3. Krizhevsky, A., Sutskever, I., Hinton, G.: ImageNet Classification with Deep Convolutional Neural Networks. In: NIPS (2012)
4. Farabet, C., Couprie, C., Najman, L., LeCun, Y.: Learning Hierarchical Features for Scene Labeling. PAMI **35**(8), 1915–1929 (2013)
5. Couprie, C., Clment, F., Najman, L., LeCun, Y.: Indoor Semantic Segmentation using depth information. In: ICLR (2014)
6. LeCun, Y., Bottou, L., Bengio, Y., Haffner, P.: Gradient-based learning applied to document recognition. Proceedings of the IEEE **86**(11), 2278–2324 (1998)
7. Kahou, S.E., Pal, C., Bouthillier, X., Froumenty, P., Gülçehre, C., Memisevic, R., Vincent, P., Courville, A., Bengio, Y.: Combining modality specific deep neural networks for emotion recognition in video. In: ICMI (2013)
8. aigman, Y., Yang, M., Ranzato, M.A., Wolf, L.: DeepFace: Closing the Gap to Human-Level Performance in Face Verification. In: CVPR (2014)
9. Baccouche, M., Mamalet, F., Wolf, C., Garcia, C., Baskurt, A.: Spatio-Temporal Convolutional Sparse Auto-Encoder for Sequence Classification. In: BMVC (2012)
10. Karpathy, A., Toderici, G., Shetty, S., Leung, T., Sukthankar, R., Li, F.F.: Large-scale Video Classification with Convolutional Neural Networks. In: CVPR (2014)
11. Simonyan, K., Zisserman, A.: Two-Stream Convolutional Networks for Action Recognition in Videos. In: arXiv preprint arXiv:1406.2199v1 (2014)
12. Escalera, S., Baró, X., Gonzàlez, J., Bautista, M.A., Madadi, M., Reyes, M., Ponce, V., Escalante, H.J., Shotton, J., Guyon, I.: ChaLearn Looking at People Challenge 2014: Dataset and Results. In: ECCV ChaLearn Workshop on Looking at People (2014)
13. Wang, H., Kläser, A., Schmid, C., Liu, C.L.: Dense trajectories and motion boundary descriptors for action recognition. IJCV **103**(1), 60–79 (2013)
14. Wang, H., Ullah, M.M., Klaser, A., Laptev, I., Schmid, C.: Evaluation of local spatio-temporal features for action recognition. BMVC **124**(1-124), 11 (2009)
15. Dollár, P., Rabaud, V., Cottrell, G., Belongie, S.: Behavior Recognition via Sparse Spatio-Temporal Features. In: 2nd Joint IEEE International Workshop on Visual Surveillance and Performance Evaluation of Tracking and Surveillance (2005)
16. Laptev, I., Marszałek, M., Schmid, C., Rozenfeld, B.: Learning realistic human actions from movies. In: CVPR (2008)
17. Kläser, A., Marszałek, M., Schmid, C.: A spatio-temporal descriptor based on 3D-gradients. In: BMVC (2008)
18. Willems, G., Tuytelaars, T., Van Gool, L.: An Efficient Dense and Scale-Invariant Spatio-Temporal Interest Point Detector. In: Forsyth, D., Torr, P., Zisserman, A. (eds.) ECCV 2008, Part II. LNCS, vol. 5303, pp. 650–663. Springer, Heidelberg (2008)

19. Keskin, C., Kiraç, F., Kara, Y., Akarun, L.: Real time hand pose estimation using depth sensors. In: ICCV Workshop on Consumer Depth Cameras. IEEE (2011)
20. Półrola, M., Wojciechowski, A.: Real-Time Hand Pose Estimation Using Classifiers. In: Bolc, L., Tadeusiewicz, R., Chmielewski, L.J., Wojciechowski, K. (eds.) ICCVG 2012. LNCS, vol. 7594, pp. 573–580. Springer, Heidelberg (2012)
21. Tang, D., Yu, T.H., Kim, T.K.: Real-time Articulated Hand Pose Estimation using Semi-supervised Transductive Regression Forests. In: ICCV (2013)
22. Tompson, J., Stein, M., LeCun, Y., Perlin, K.: Real-Time Continuous Pose Recovery of Human Hands Using Convolutional Networks. ACM Transaction on Graphics (2014)
23. Oikonomidis, I., Kyriazis, N., Argyros, A.: Efficient model-based 3D tracking of hand articulations using Kinect. BMVC 101(1–101), 11 (2011)
24. Qian, C., Sun, X., Wei, Y., Tang, X., Sun, J.: Realtime and Robust Hand Tracking from Depth. In: CVPR (2014)
25. Wang, F., Li, Y.: Beyond Physical Connections: Tree Models in Human Pose Estimation. In: CVPR (2013)
26. Tang, D., Chang, H.J., Tejani, A., Kim, T.K.: Latent Regression Forest: Structured Estimation of 3D Articulated Hand Posture. In: CVPR (2014)
27. Wang, J., Liu, Z., Wu, Y., Yuan, J.: Mining actionlet ensemble for action recognition with depth cameras. In: CVPR (2012)
28. Sung, J., Ponce, C., Selman, B., Saxena, A.: Unstructured Human Activity Detection from RGBD Images. In: ICRA (2012)
29. Chen, X., Koskela, M.: Online RGB-D gesture recognition with extreme learning machines. In: ICMI (2013)
30. Nandakumar, K., Wah, W.K., Alice, C.S.M., Terence, N.W.Z., Gang, W.J., Yun, Y.W.: A Multi-modal Gesture Recognition System Using Audio, Video, and Skeletal Joint Data Categories and Subject Descriptors. In: 2013 Multi-modal Challenge Workshop in Conjunction with ICMI (2013)
31. Le, Q.V., Zou, W.Y., Yeung, S.Y., Ng, A.Y.: Learning hierarchical invariant spatio-temporal features for action recognition with independent subspace analysis. In: CVPR, pp. 3361–3368 (2011)
32. Ranzato, M., Huang, F.J., Boureau, Y.L., LeCun, Y.: Unsupervised Learning of Invariant Feature Hierarchies with Applications to Object Recognition. In: CVPR (2007)
33. Chen, B., Ting, J.A., Marlin, B., de Freitas, N.: Deep learning of invariant Spatio-Temporal Features from Video. In: NIPS Workshop on Deep Learning and Unsupervised Feature Learning (2010)
34. Ji, S., Xu, W., Yang, M., Yu, K.: 3D Convolutional Neural Networks for Human Action Recognition. PAMI 35(1), 221–231 (2013)
35. Ngiam, J., Khosla, A., Kin, M., Nam, J., Lee, H., Ng, A.Y.: Multimodal deep learning. In: ICML (2011)
36. Srivastava, N., Salakhutdinov, R.: Multimodal learning with Deep Boltzmann Machines. In: NIPS (2013)
37. Neverova, N., Wolf, C., Paci, G., Sommavilla, G., Taylor, G.W., Nebout, F.: A multi-scale approach to gesture detection and recognition. In: ICCV Workshop on Understanding Human Activities: Context and Interactions (HACI) (2013)
38. Zanfir, M., Leordeanu, M., Sminchisescu, C.: The Moving Pose: An Efficient 3D Kinematics Descriptor for Low-Latency Action Recognition and Detection. In: ICCV (2013)
39. Bengio, Y., Louradour, J., Collobert, R., Weston, J.: Curriculum learning. In: ICMIL (2009)

40. Wu, D.: Deep Dynamic Neural Networks for Gesture Segmentation and Recognition. In: ECCV ChaLearn Workshop on Looking at People (2014)
41. Monnier, C., German, S., Ost, A.: A Multi-scale Boosted Detector for Efficient and Robust Gesture Recognition. In: ECCV ChaLearn Workshop on Looking at People (2014)
42. Camgoz, N.C., Kindiroglu, A.A., Akarun, L.: Gesture Recognition using Template Based Random Forest Classifiers. In: ECCV ChaLearn Workshop on Looking at People (2014)
43. Chang, J.Y.: Nonparametric Gesture Labeling from Multi-modal Data. In: ECCV ChaLearn Workshop on Looking at People (2014)
44. Evangelidis, G., Singh, G., Horaud, R.: Continuous gesture recognition from articulated poses. In: ECCV ChaLearn Workshop on Looking at People (2014)
45. Peng, X., Wang, L., Cai, Z.: Action and Gesture Temporal Spotting with Super Vector Representation. In: ECCV ChaLearn Workshop on Looking at People (2014)
46. Pigou, L., Dieleman, S., Kindermans, P.J.: Sign Language Recognition Using Convolutional Neural Networks. In: ECCV ChaLearn Workshop on Looking at People (2014)
47. Chen, G., Clarke, D., Giuliani, M., Weikersdorfer, D., Knoll, A.: Multi-modality Gesture Detection and Recognition With Un-supervision, Randomization and Discrimination. In: ECCV ChaLearn Workshop on Looking at People (2014)
48. Dalal, N., Triggs, B.: Histograms of Oriented Gradients for Human Detection. In: CVPR (2005)
49. Lazebnik, S., Schmid, C., Ponce, J.: Beyond Bags of Features: Spatial Pyramid Matching for Recognizing Natural Scene Categories. In: CVPR (2006)
50. Geurts, P., Ernst, D., Wehenkel, L.: Extremely randomized trees. Machine Learning **63**(1), 3–42 (2006)
51. Breiman, L., Friedman, J., Stone, C.J., Olshen, R.A.: Classification and regression trees (1984)

A Multi-scale Boosted Detector for Efficient and Robust Gesture Recognition

Camille Monnier[✉], Stan German, and Andrey Ost

Charles River Analytics, Cambridge, MA, USA
cmonnier@cra.com

Abstract. We present an approach to detecting and recognizing gestures in a stream of multi-modal data. Our approach combines a sliding-window gesture detector with features drawn from skeleton data, color imagery, and depth data produced by a first-generation Kinect sensor. The detector consists of a set of one-versus-all boosted classifiers, each tuned to a specific gesture. Features are extracted at multiple temporal scales, and include descriptive statistics of normalized skeleton joint positions, angles, and velocities, as well as image-based hand descriptors. The full set of gesture detectors may be trained in under two hours on a single machine, and is extremely efficient at runtime, operating at 1700fps using only skeletal data, or at 100fps using fused skeleton and image features. Our method achieved a Jaccard Index score of 0.834 on the ChaLearn-2014 Gesture Recognition Test dataset, and was ranked 2nd overall in the competition.

Keywords: Gesture recognition · Boosting methods · One-vs-all · Multimodal fusion · Feature pooling

1 Introduction

Automated gesture recognition has many desirable applications, including home entertainment, American Sign Language (ASL) translation, human-robot interaction (HRI), and security and surveillance. The area has been a focus of extensive research and development in the past decade, and while significant advances in sensor technologies and algorithmic methods have been made, current systems remain far from capable of human-level recognition accuracy for most real-world applications. The problem of recognizing gestures in a stream of data comprises multiple challenges, including noisy or missing data, non-uniform temporal variation in gesture execution, variability across individuals, and significant volumes of data. In this paper, we present an efficient and highly-competitive approach to detecting and recognizing gestures in a stream of multi-modal (skeleton pose, color, and depth) data. Our proposed method achieved a Jaccard Index score of 0.834 on the ChaLearn-2014 Gesture Recognition Test dataset, and was ranked 2nd overall in the competition.

© Springer International Publishing Switzerland 2015
L. Agapito et al. (Eds.): ECCV 2014 Workshops, Part I, LNCS 8925, pp. 491–502, 2015.
DOI: 10.1007/978-3-319-16178-5_34

1.1 Related Work

Vision-based pose and gesture recognition technologies have been developed for three general categories of sensors: monocular cameras, stereo cameras, and fused color/active ranging sensors such as the Microsoft Kinect. Monocular (single-camera) methods offer an advantage in terms of cost and flexibility of application, but represent a significant challenge from an algorithmic perspective as depth, segmentation and pose data are not easily obtained. Much of the foundational work in pose and gesture recognition addresses monocular imagery [1,2], and this continues to be an active area of research [3–5]. Stereo cameras, which provide depth information in addition to color imagery and function equally indoors and outdoors, have recently been applied to the problem of recognizing gestures in real-world applications such as gesture recognition for robot control [6,7].

The Kinect series of sensors, which provides built-in skeleton tracking data along with high-resolution depth and co-registered color imagery, has been applied to a wide variety of tasks involving gesture recognition, including entertainment, human-robot control [8], and virtual telepresence [9]. While the technology is restricted to indoor use, the rich data produced by the Kinect is particularly well-suited to the task of recognizing complex human gestures such as american sign language (ASL), as well as culturally significant gestures and body language.

Researchers have developed a variety of approaches to extracting features suitable for representing complex gestures or gesture elements, including bag-of-words representations [10], poselets [11,12], and hierarchical representations [13,14]. Significant effort has been aimed at developing methods capable of discriminating between complex temporal sequences. Popular models reported in the gesture recognition literature typically derive from sequence-learning methods such as Hidden Markov Models (HMM) and Conditional Random Fields (CRF) [15]. Song *et al.*[13] propose a hierarchical sequence summarization (HSS) approach to recognizing gestures based on CRFs. The winners of the 2013 ChaLearn competition combine an HMM audio classifier with a dynamic time warping (DTW) based pose sequence classifier [16].

So-called "non-temporal" models that operate on fixed-length sequences, such as Support Vector Machines (SVM) [17], Random Decision Forests (RDF) [18], and boosting methods [19] have been successfully applied to the problem of gesture and action recognition[14,20], but are often passed over in favor of models that are expected to implicitly handle complex temporal structures, such as HMM and CRF [13,21]. In this paper, we demonstrate that non-temporal methods such as Adaboost can indeed yield highly-competitive results for gesture detection when combined with appropriate multi-scale feature representations.

2 Proposed Method

We propose an approach to gesture recognition that combines a sliding-window detector with multi-modal features drawn from skeleton, color, and depth data produced by a first-generation Kinect sensor. The gesture detector consists of a set of boosted classifiers, each tuned to a specific gesture. Each classifier is trained independently on labeled training data, employing bootstrapping to collect hard examples. At run-time, the gesture classifiers are evaluated in a one-vs-all manner across a sliding window. Fig. 1 illustrates our multi-scale approach to feature extraction and gesture classification. We describe the dataset, features, and classifiers in the following sections.

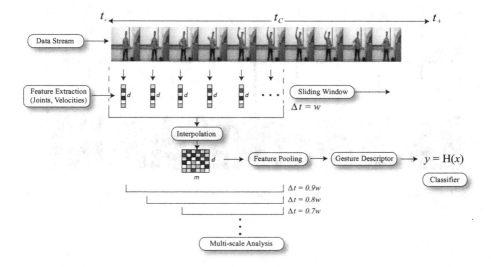

Fig. 1. Overview of our sliding-window approach. Local features are extracted on a frame-by-frame basis, and interpolated to a fixed-size feature matrix. Following a pooling step, the resulting descriptor is processed by a previously trained classifier. The process is repeated at multiple scales and offsets in the data stream.

Table 1. ChaLearn 2014 Gesture Dataset Statistics

Dataset	Labeled Instances	Length (min)
Development	7,754	∼470
Validation	3,362	∼230
Test	2,742	∼240

3   Dataset

We report methods and results developed on the ChaLearn 2014 Gesture Recognition challenge dataset. The challenge dataset consists of *Development*, *Validation*, and *Testing* sets used throughout different stages of the competition. Each dataset respectively contains 470, 230, and 240 minute-long sequences of culturally-relevant gestures performed by multiple individuals. Fig. 1 describes statistics for each dataset. The challenge focuses on a specific set of 20 labeled Italian gestures, but includes multiple unlabeled gestures as confusers. Data products include color and depth video, segmentation masks, and skeleton joint data produced by a first-generation Kinect sensor. Fig. 2 illustrates sample data for a single gesture sequence.

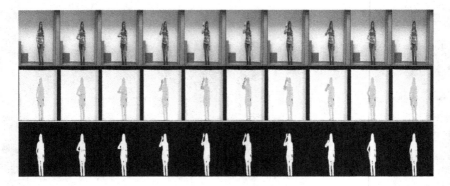

Fig. 2. Example color, depth, and segmentation data corresponding to a single gesture instance

4   Features

We extract features including normalized skeleton joint positions, rotations, and velocities, as well as HOG descriptors of the hands. Features are extracted at multiple temporal scales to enable recognition of variable-length gestures. Features including skeleton pose and hand shape are extracted from each frame of video to produce a corresponding sequence of d-dimensional descriptors. These descriptors are interpolated to produce a fixed-width $m \times d$ sequence describing the sequence, where m is the expected minimum duration, in frames, of a single gesture. Features in this sequence are then pooled to produce a final descriptor that may be processed by a gesture classifier. This process is repeated at multiple time scales, to account for temporal variation between gesture types and across individuals.

4.1   Skeleton Features

We extract multiple features from the skeleton data produced by the Kinect, including the normalized positions of the 9 major joints in the upper body, relative positions of these joints, joint angles, and instantaneous derivatives (velocities) of each feature. To reduce variability across subjects, joint positions x^i_j for each subject i are first normalized according to the length of an individual's torso s_i, following

$$x_{i,j} = \frac{x_{i,j} - x_{i,hip}}{s_i} \qquad (1)$$

Where s_i is measured as the distance between the hips and the base of the neck. Following normalization, four types of features are extracted: normalized joint positions x_j; joint quaternion angles q_j; Euclidean distances between specific joints; and directed distances between pairs of joints, based on the features proposed by Yao *et al.* [22]. This latter feature consists of the distance from one joint to another along the normal vector defined by the source joint and the its parent. The features corresponding to joint positions and angles account for $9 \times 3 \times 2 = 54$ dimensions. We compute joint-pair features between all joints with a parent node (8 joints, excluding the hip), yielding an additional $8 \times 8 = 64$ dimensions, for a total of 110 static pose features. Finally, first-order derivatives are computed across adjacent frames, for all skeletal features, bringing the total feature vector size to 220 dimensions describing the skeleton's pose and instantaneous motion in a single frame of data.

4.2   Hand Features

While many of the gestures contained in the ChaLearn-2014 dataset may be differentiated by examining the positions and movements of large joints such as the elbows and wrists, a number of gestures differ primarily in hand pose, as well as in slight differences in positioning relative to the body or face. Fig. 3 illustrates a typical set of similar gesture pairs. The first-generation Kinect provides tracking data for large joints, but does not provide tracking information for the fingers necessary to differentiate between gestures such as these.

G11
"Ok"

G15
"Non ce ne piu"

G4
"E un furbo"

G18
"Buonissimo"

Fig. 3. Examples of gestures that differ primarily in hand pose

We employ a straightforward approach to describing hand shape. First, a square image chip is extracted around each hand, using the position information provided by the Kinect. As the scale of the subject's hand in the image is unknown, we estimate the dimensions of each hand chip based on the known scale of a body part that is parallel to the image plane. For simplicity, we again use the torso as a reference, as the gestures are performed by upright subjects who are typically far enough from the camera for perspective effects to be negligible.

Explicitly, image dimensions for a subject's hand are computed as:

$$w_{i,h} = \frac{\|x_{i,wrist} - x_{i,elbow}\|}{s_i} s_i' \tag{2}$$

where s_i' is the length of the subject's torso as measured in image space. This approach produces an image chip scaled to the length of the subject's forearm, which is sufficient for capturing a fully-extended hand. Extracted hand images are then rescaled to 64x64 using bilinear interpolation.

To reduce the inclusion of background in the hand shape descriptor, we conduct an additional masking step using the associated depth image. Depth data is extracted using the same approach as for color images, producing a 64x64 depth image for each hand. Foreground masks are then computed by eliminating pixels whose depth deviates by more than a threshold T_d from the median depth of the image. In our experiments, T_d was computed empirically as the mean extent of well-segmented hands (i.e., hands held away from the body) in the dataset. Fig. 4 illustrates the process for producing masked hand images.

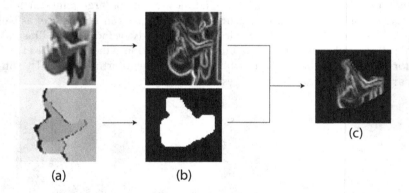

Fig. 4. Hand segmentation process. Color and depth images centered around the hand are extracted (a) using known skeleton joint positions. Depth is smoothed, thresholded to remove background, and expanded using dilation to produce a segmentation mask, and a gradient image is computed from the color image (b). The mask is applied to the gradient image (c), from which HOG features are extracted.

We compute a masked histogram of oriented gradients (HOG) descriptor [23] for each hand, using the extracted color images and depth masks. HOG features are computed for 9 orientation bins across 16x16 non-overlapping blocks, resulting in shape descriptors of dimensionality $d_{HOG} = 144$ for each hand.

4.3   Feature Pooling

Following the extraction of skeleton and hand features at each frame, features within the time window to be classified are collected and linearly interpolated to a fixed-length sequence of size $m \times d$. To reduce sensitivity to translation and minimize noise, we perform mean pooling at multiple overlapping intervals of varying length. To capture high-level information related to gesture periodicity or complexity, we compute the variance of each feature within the same intervals used for mean pooling. Fig. 5 illustrates the pooling process. The pooled features are then combined into the final feature vector used in classification, resulting in a feature vector of dimensionality $d = 20746$.

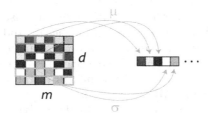

Fig. 5. Notional illustration of feature pooling. The raw feature vector is oversampled using multiple overlapping regions in which mean and variance are computed. Mean pooling is achieved using intervals and step sizes of length 2,4, and 8. Variance is computed over intervals of length 6,12 and a step size of 4. In our experiments, we define $m = 24$.

5   Classification

As sliding-window methods must typically analyze many windows at various scales, we apply an efficient boosted classifier cascade [24] to the task of recognizing individual gestures. This type of classifier provides a significant advantage in run-time efficiency over "monolithic" methods such as nonlinear SVMs, because the cascade structure enables partial evaluation (and thereby partial feature extraction) on the majority of negative samples. Each gesture is independently learned by a single boosted classifier using a one-versus-all (OVA) approach [25]. We use boosted classifiers comprising 1000 depth-2 decision trees in our experiments. During training, each classifier is initialized using the full set of labeled positive gesture examples, along with a subset of randomly sampled negative gestures and non-gestural examples. The initial gesture detector is then applied to the training data to collect hard examples, and the classifier subsequently retrained, in a process commonly referred to as bootstrapping [26,27]. The full set of gesture classifiers require approximately 2 hours to train on modern laptop, with 4 rounds of bootstrapping.

At runtime, the set of classifiers is applied to each time window, and the maximum response stored. As many overlapping windows and time scales are considered, multiple detections are typically produced in the vicinity of gestures or gesture-like sequences. To resolve conflicting detections, we apply non-maximal suppression (NMS) using the PASCAL overlap criterion [28].

6   Experimental Results

In this section, we discuss the performance of variations in our proposed method within the context of the ChaLearn competition, and provide a more detailed analysis of the top-scoring method using standard measures of detector performance.

The ChaLearn competition evaluated methods using the Jaccard Index $J \in \{0, 1\}$, which measures detection accuracy as the fractional overlap between a detection window and ground truth. Overall performance is summarized using the mean of the Jaccard Index for all truthed gesture instances. False positives are included in this statistic, and contribute a Jaccard Index value of $J = 0$.

We evaluated the performance of our proposed method using four feature sets, progressively combining: normalized skeleton joints and velocities (SK); joint angles and angular velocities (JA); joint-pair distances and velocities (JP); and hand HOG descriptors (HH). Classifiers were trained on the *Development* data, and evaluated on the reserved *Validation* data. To ensure a fair comparison across feature sets, classifier thresholds were chosen to achieve a constant rate of 1 false positive per minute (fppm). In all cases, the system was evaluated over windows computed at 30 scales, using a step size of 2 frames. Table 2 illustrates the Jaccard Index score for each variant. The baseline feature set (SK) yields a competitive score of 0.742, which is improved slightly by the inclusion of joint angle data (SK+JA). A more significant improvement is apparent from the inclusion of joint-pair features (SK+JA+JP), which likely reflects the importance of fine interactions between the various moving parts of the body, including the face and hands.

Table 2. Jaccard Index scores for detectors trained on the four feature sets. Classifiers were trained on *Development* and evaluated on *Validation* datasets

Feature set	JI Score
SK	0.742
SK+JA	0.755
SK+JA+JP	0.791
SK+JA+JP+HH	0.822

An analysis of the confusion matrix for the skeleton-only detector reveals that skeleton data is sufficient to accurately differentiate between the majority of the labeled gestures in the ChaLearn dataset, and is even sufficient to discriminate between most instances of visually similar gestures such as those illustrated in 3. The addition of hand-specific descriptors (SK+JA+JP+HH) significantly reduces error rates on these gestures, and yields our strongest detector with $J = 0.834$ on the *Test* dataset. Despite the introduction of additional unlabeled gestures in the *Test* dataset, the detector achieved higher accuracy than on the *Validation* dataset; this may be explained by the fact that the final detector was trained on a larger dataset consisting of both *Development* and *Validation* data, and may therefore be expected to exhibit better generalization properties. The full 20-gesture detector is highly efficient, exceeding 100fps on the ChaLearn data on a single-core modern laptop. Using skeleton features only (SK+JA+JP), our detector is capable of processing over a minute of data per second, equivalent to 1700fps.

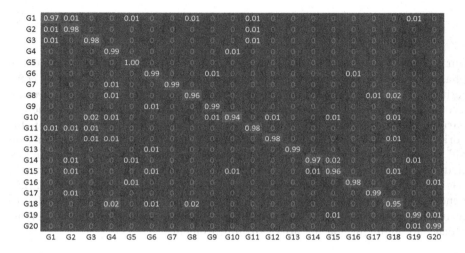

	G1	G2	G3	G4	G5	G6	G7	G8	G9	G10	G11	G12	G13	G14	G15	G16	G17	G18	G19	G20
G1	0.97	0.01			0.01			0.01			0.01							0.01		
G2	0.01	0.98									0.01									
G3	0.01		0.98								0.01									
G4				0.99					0.01											
G5					1.00															
G6						0.99			0.01							0.01				
G7			0.01				0.99													
G8			0.01					0.96								0.01	0.02			
G9					0.01				0.99											
G10			0.02	0.01					0.01	0.94		0.01			0.01			0.01		
G11	0.01	0.01	0.01								0.98									
G12			0.01	0.01								0.98						0.01		
G13						0.01							0.99							
G14		0.01			0.01									0.97	0.02				0.01	
G15		0.01				0.01				0.01				0.01	0.96			0.01		
G16				0.01												0.98				0.01
G17		0.01															0.99			
G18			0.02		0.01		0.02											0.95		
G19															0.01				0.99	0.01
G20																			0.01	0.99

Fig. 6. Confusion matrix for the 20 hand labeled gestures in the ChaLearn-2014 *Test* dataset, produced by the SK+JA+JP+HH detector. Results are computed for detections that overlap ground truth according to the PASCAL criterion

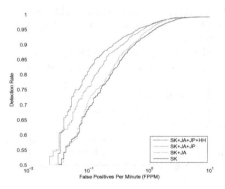

Fig. 7. Detection/false-positive tradeoff (ROC) curves for the four detectors. Although detection accuracy converges near 1 fppm, measurable differences in Jaccard Index are apparent. This difference is likely explained by the use of the PASCAL criterion in computing ROC curves, which require only 50% overlap to be considered a match.

Figure 6 illustrates the confusion matrix for the final detector on the *Test* data, computed at a 1 fppm. Recognition rates across gestures is generally consistent - detected gestures are classified with mean accuracy 97.9 ± 1.61%, with a single gesture (G10) falling below 95% recognition rate. The remaining source of error in our experiments is generally attributed to false positives caused by unlabeled confusers in the *Test* data. Figure 7 illustrates the tradeoff between detection and false-positive rates.

7   Conclusions

Our approach to gesture detection achieves highly competitive results on the ChaLearn 2014 gesture recognition dataset, ranking 2nd in the overall competition. The proposed method deviates from many recently developed gesture recognition systems in its use of a boosted classifier cascade rather than sequence-learning methods such as HMM and CRF. A message from the outcome of this work is a reminder that simple methods based on effective feature construction will frequently outperform more sophisticated models that incorporate inadequate feature data. While our approach performed well on the ChaLearn dataset, it is likely that other types of gestures, such as ASL, will provide more complex structures that will pose a more significant challenge. In future work, we plan to evaluate our approach on a wider set of gesture lexicons and application areas, which may highlight specific areas for improvement.

References

1. Poppe, R.: A survey on vision-based human action recognition. Image and Vision Computing **28**(6), 976–990 (2010)
2. Andriluka, M., Roth, S., Schiele, B.: Monocular 3d pose estimation and tracking by detection. In: 2010 IEEE Conference on Computer Vision and Pattern Recognition (CVPR), pp. 623–630 (2010)
3. Wang, H., Kläser, A., Schmid, C., Liu, C.L.: Dense trajectories and motion boundary descriptors for action recognition. International Journal of Computer Vision **103**(1), 60–79 (2013)
4. Cherian, A., Mairal, J., Alahari, K., Schmid, C., et al.: Mixing body-part sequences for human pose estimation. In: CVPR 2014-IEEE Conference on Computer Vision & Pattern Recognition (2014)
5. Yu, T.H., Kim, T.K., Cipolla, R.: Unconstrained monocular 3d human pose estimation by action detection and cross-modality regression forest. In: 2013 IEEE Conference on Computer Vision and Pattern Recognition (CVPR) pp. 3642–3649. IEEE (2013)
6. Nickel, K., Stiefelhagen, R.: Visual recognition of pointing gestures for human-robot interaction. Image and Vision Computing **25**(12), 1875–1884 (2007)
7. Song, Y., Demirdjian, D., Davis, R.: Continuous body and hand gesture recognition for natural human-computer interaction. ACM Transactions on Interactive Intelligent Systems (TiiS) 2(1), 5 (2012)

8. Van den Bergh, M., Carton, D., De Nijs, R., Mitsou, N., Landsiedel, C., Kuehnlenz, K., Wollherr, D., Van Gool, L., Buss, M.: Real-time 3d hand gesture interaction with a robot for understanding directions from humans. In: RO-MAN, 2011 IEEE, pp. 357–362. IEEE (2011)
9. Zhang, Z.: Microsoft kinect sensor and its effect. IEEE MultiMedia 19(2), 4–10 (2012)
10. Laptev, I., Marszalek, M., Schmid, C., Rozenfeld, B.: Learning realistic human actions from movies. In: IEEE Conference on Computer Vision and Pattern Recognition, CVPR 2008, pp. 1–8. IEEE (2008)
11. Bourdev, L., Malik, J.: Poselets: Body part detectors trained using 3d human pose annotations. In: 2009 IEEE 12th International Conference on Computer Vision, pp. 1365–1372. IEEE (2009)
12. Holt, B., Ong, E.J., Cooper, H., Bowden, R.: Putting the pieces together: Connected poselets for human pose estimation. In: 2011 IEEE International Conference on Computer Vision Workshops (ICCV Workshops), pp. 1196–1201. IEEE (2011)
13. Song, Y., Morency, L.P., Davis, R.: Action recognition by hierarchical sequence summarization. In: 2013 IEEE Conference on Computer Vision and Pattern Recognition (CVPR), pp. 3562–3569. IEEE (2013)
14. Wang, J., Chen, Z., Wu, Y.: Action recognition with multiscale spatio-temporal contexts. In: 2011 IEEE Conference on Computer Vision and Pattern Recognition (CVPR), pp. 3185–3192. IEEE (2011)
15. Mitra, S., Acharya, T.: Gesture recognition: A survey. IEEE Transactions on Systems, Man, and Cybernetics, Part C: Applications and Reviews 37(3), 311–324 (2007)
16. Wu, J., Cheng, J., Zhao, C., Lu, H.: Fusing multi-modal features for gesture recognition. In: Proceedings of the 15th ACM on International Conference on Multimodal Interaction, pp. 453–460. ACM (2013)
17. Vapnik, V.N., Vapnik, V.: Statistical learning theory. vol. 2. Wiley, New York (1998)
18. Breiman, L.: Random forests. Machine Learning 45(1), 5–32 (2001)
19. Freund, Y., Schapire, R., Abe, N.: A short introduction to boosting. Journal-Japanese Society For Artificial Intelligence 14(771–780), 1612 (1999)
20. Gall, J., Yao, A., Razavi, N., Van Gool, L., Lempitsky, V.: Hough forests for object detection, tracking, and action recognition. IEEE Transactions on Pattern Analysis and Machine Intelligence 33(11), 2188–2202 (2011)
21. Tang, K., Fei-Fei, L., Koller, D.: Learning latent temporal structure for complex event detection. In: 2012 IEEE Conference on Computer Vision and Pattern Recognition (CVPR), pp. 1250–1257. IEEE (2012)
22. Yao, A., Gall, J., Fanelli, G., Van Gool, L.J.: Does human action recognition benefit from pose estimation?. In: BMVC, vol. 3, p. 6 (2011)
23. Dalal, N., Triggs, B.: Histograms of oriented gradients for human detection. In: IEEE Computer Society Conference on Computer Vision and Pattern Recognition, CVPR 2005, vol. 1, pp. 886–893. IEEE (2005)
24. Bourdev, L., Brandt, J.: Robust object detection via soft cascade. In: IEEE Computer Society Conference on Computer Vision and Pattern Recognition, CVPR 2005, vol. 2, pp. 236–243. IEEE (2005)
25. Rifkin, R., Klautau, A.: In defense of one-vs-all classification. The Journal of Machine Learning Research 5, 101–141 (2004)

26. Dollar, P., Wojek, C., Schiele, B., Perona, P.: Pedestrian detection: An evaluation of the state of the art. IEEE Transactions on Pattern Analysis and Machine Intelligence **34**(4), 743–761 (2012)
27. Walk, S., Majer, N., Schindler, K., Schiele, B.: New features and insights for pedestrian detection. In: 2010 IEEE Conference on Computer Vision and Pattern Recognition (CVPR), pp. 1030–1037. IEEE (2010)
28. Everingham, M., Van Gool, L., Williams, C.K., Winn, J., Zisserman, A.: The pascal visual object classes (voc) challenge. International Journal of Computer Vision **88**(2), 303–338 (2010)

Nonparametric Gesture Labeling from Multi-modal Data

Ju Yong Chang[✉]

Electronics and Telecommunications Research Institute,
Daejeon 305-700, Korea
juyong.chang@etri.re.kr

Abstract. We present a new gesture recognition method using multi-modal data. Our approach solves a labeling problem, which means that gesture categories and their temporal ranges are determined at the same time. For that purpose, a generative probabilistic model is formalized and it is constructed by nonparametrically estimating multi-modal densities from a training dataset. In addition to the conventional skeletal joint based features, appearance information near the active hand in the RGB image is exploited to capture the detailed motion of fingers. The estimated log-likelihood function is used as the unary term for our Markov random field (MRF) model. The smoothness term is also incorporated to enforce temporal coherence of our model. The labeling results can then be obtained by the efficient dynamic programming technique. Experimental results demonstrate that our method provides effective gesture labeling results for the large-scale gesture dataset. Our method scores 0.8268 in the mean Jaccard index and is ranked 3rd in the gesture recognition track of the ChaLearn Looking at People (LAP) Challenge in 2014.

Keywords: Gesture recognition · Nonparametric estimation · Multimodal data

1 Introduction

Human activity recognition is one of the important problems in computer vision and it has various applications such as human-computer interaction, visual surveillance, and intelligent robot. The goal of human activity recognition is to automatically understand human behavior from input data sequence.

Until now, a large amount of research has been conducted for human activity recognition. There are several excellent surveys for RGB image/video based activity recognition [1]. Recently, research based on depth data attracts great attention [2]. The use of depth data enables us to overcome several difficulties of traditional RGB based methods such as appearance variation, illumination change, and loss of 3D information. Moreover, 3D human pose can be efficiently estimated from depth data [3]. According to the recent interesting study [4], such intermediate high-level pose features result in better recognition performance than low/mid-level features such as dense trajectories [5], histograms of oriented gradients [6], and histograms of optical flow [7].

© Springer International Publishing Switzerland 2015
L. Agapito et al. (Eds.): ECCV 2014 Workshops, Part I, LNCS 8925, pp. 503–517, 2015.
DOI: 10.1007/978-3-319-16178-5_35

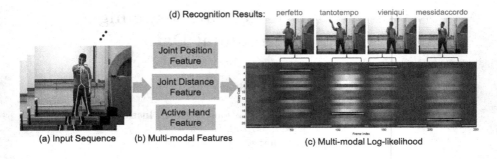

Fig. 1. Overview of the proposed method is illustrated. From the input test sequence (a), multiple features in (b) are computed. They are used to construct the log-likelihood matrix in (c). The x and y-axes denote the frame index and gesture class, respectively. Dark pixels represent the high likelihood region. By using this as the unary term, our MRF model produces the gesture labeling results, that are denoted by the yellow lines. Final recognized gestures are shown in (d).

However, the structure of the estimated 3D pose sometimes lacks enough complexity for certain activity recognition problems. For example, many human gestures contain finger motion, but it is not easy to estimate the 3D pose of the articulated hand model unless close range. In that case, it is necessary to simultaneously consider both the rough information of 3D pose and the detailed appearance of the image. Therefore, in this paper, we focus on human gesture recognition based on multi-modal data, especially using the 3D pose information and the RGB image.

Recently, the Looking at People (LAP) Challenge[1] was held for solving the human gesture recognition problem from multi-modal data [8]. The challenge focused on *multiple instance, user independent spotting* of gestures. Its dataset and goal have the following features. First, it includes a large amount of data, specifically 13,858 gesture instances. Target gestures are defined by twenty Italian cultural and anthropological signs and they are composed of simple atomic motions with both hands. Unlike the setting in many existing gesture/action recognition works, the detection problem should be solved rather than the classification problem where the input video sequence is assumed to be pre-segmented. This means the starting and ending points of the gesture should be also estimated together with its category in this challenge.

In this paper, we present a novel gesture recognition method using multi-modal data. Our proposed method is based on the labeling problem, where a gesture category label should be inferred for every frame in a video. To solve the labeling problem, we basically take a simple classification approach for each frame. Specifically, a multi-class classification problem should be solved to assign every frame in a video one of the multiple labels corresponding to known gesture categories. This is a very simple formulation that does not explicitly assume any temporal or hierarchical modeling of human gestures or actions.

---
[1] http://gesture.chalearn.org

The proposed method utilizes following features: skeletal joint position feature, skeletal joint distance feature, and appearance features corresponding to left and right hands. Under the naive Bayes assumption, likelihood functions are independently defined for every feature. Such likelihood functions are nonparametrically constructed from the training data by using kernel density estimation (KDE). For computational efficiency, k-nearest neighbor (kNN) approximation to the exact density estimator is proposed. Constructed likelihood functions are combined to the multi-modal likelihood and this serves as the unary term for our pairwise Markov random field (MRF) model. For enhancing temporal coherence, the smoothness term is additionally incorporated to the MRF model. Final gesture labels can be obtained via 1D MRF inference and this can be efficiently done by dynamic programming. The overview of our method is illustrated in Fig. 1.

2 Related Works

There is extensive literature on action recognition research. In this section, we only review the methods relevant to our approach, especially ones based on depth data. According to the recent surveys [1,2], action recognition researches can be classified into two categories: sequential approaches and space-time approaches. *Sequential approaches* have traditionally focused on how to model the temporal dynamics of the target actions or gestures. They are usually based on a hidden Markov model (HMM) [9,10], a conditional random field (CRF) [11], or a graphical model (GM) with more complex structures [12]. These models generally assume the target actions to be represented by the dynamic changes of states and such dynamic patterns are automatically learned from the training data. Our method is also based on the MRF, a kind of GM, and it looks similar to the sequential approaches at first glance. However, our method does not explicitly model the temporal dynamics and the labels of our MRF model represent the gesture categories rather than the intermediate states.

In the dynamic time warping (DTW) based approaches [13,14], the input test sequence to be recognized is aligned with known sequences of the dataset to produce the alignment-based distances, which are used to determine the action category by finding the best matches. These approaches can be viewed as a nonparametric version of the sequential approaches. Our method is also based on the nonparametric matching process between the input data and the dataset. However, the distance measure in our method is defined as the simple Euclidean distance without the time-consuming alignment step. Therefore, our approach is computationally more efficient than the DTW-based methods and applicable to the large-scale gesture recognition datasets like the LAP multi-modal gesture dataset [8].

Space-time approaches usually take a space-time volume and extract local or global features inside it. The extracted features and the ground-truth action categories of the training dataset are used to discriminatively learn parametric models by using support vector machines (SVM) [15,16], structural SVM [17], etc. Such discriminative approaches require a learning step and the performance of the learned model generally depends on the size of the training dataset. Therefore, most of the discriminative approaches suffer from a heavy computational burden for training with the large-scale dataset.

We next investigate nonparametric space-time approaches most relevant to our method. The authors in [18] proposed a nonparametric action recognition method based on the skeletal joint information. In their work, the EigenJoints descriptor is developed and the Naive-Bayes-Nearest-Neighbor (NBNN) classifier is adopted to solve the gesture classification problem. Three features including posture, motion, and offset features are computed from the skeletal joint information. They are then concatenated into one feature vector and principal component analysis (PCA) is used to construct the EigenJoint feature. Their method applies the Naive Bayes (NB) assumption to the EigenJoint features obtained for all frames in a given data sequence. On the other hand, our method utilizes the multi-modal features and assume the NB assumption for the multi-modal features in each frame. While their approach assumes segmented video input for classification, our approach combines the nonparametric model with the MRF to simultaneously solve both classification and segmentation.

In [19], the Moving Pose (MP) descriptor that captures not only the skeletal joint position features but also differential properties like the speed and acceleration of the joints was proposed. The discriminative key frames for each action class are learned from the training dataset and they are used to produce the matching scores between the test sequence and the action classes by using the modified kNN classifier. Moreover, it is applied to all frames according to the sliding window strategy for action detection in unsegmented sequences. However, the labeling problem is locally solved for each frame and temporal coherence between subsequent frames is not enforced. On the other hand, our method adopts the pairwise MRF with the smoothness term, so temporally coherent solutions can be obtained. While the MP descriptor is developed only for the skeletal joint features, our approach can handle the multi-modal data by probabilistic fusion of the nonparametrically estimated likelihood functions.

3   Proposed Method

Suppose we are given a training dataset and each frame in a training sequence is labeled a gesture category $g^{(i)} \in \mathcal{G}$, where i and $\mathcal{G}$ denote the frame index and the set of all gesture labels, respectively. In this paper, each sequence can have multiple gesture categories without overlapping, that is, each frame in a sequence is constrained to be labeled only with one gesture category. Now the objective is to solve the *labeling problem*, where each frame of a test sequence should be assigned a gesture category label.

3.1   Generative Probabilistic Model

We basically approach to the gesture labeling problem by solving the classification problem, where temporal positions or dynamics are not considered at all and the gesture should be independently classified for each frame. This is an extremely simple assumption compared to the general HMM or CRF based approaches that usually introduce the intermediate states and model gestures by the temporal dynamics of the states. Now the generative probabilistic model for gesture classification can be simply formalized as follows. Hidden random variables G generate M multi-modal observations $X_j, j \in \{1, \ldots, M\}$. Here the observed feature X_j is computed from the multi-modal data in the several frames near the current frame. Under the naive Bayes assumption, the multi-modal features are conditionally independent of each other given the gesture category. Therefore, the multi-modal likelihood can be defined by

$$p(X_1, \ldots, X_M | G) = p(X_1 | G) \cdots p(X_M | G). \tag{1}$$

Now we present the multi-modal features and how to estimate their corresponding likelihoods.

3.2   Multi-modal Features

In this paper, the skeletal joint data and RGB images are assumed to be the multi-modal input to our proposed method. It is well known that the skeletal joint features can be efficiently and robustly estimated from the depth image [3]. From the skeletal joints, we only consider K joints belonging to the upper body. Let $x_j, j = 1, \ldots, K$ denote the 3D coordinates of such joints. We then define the normalized joint coordinates $\bar{x}_j, j = 1, \ldots, K$ by taking the differences between x_j and the reference joint x_p, that is assumed to be the *neck* joint in this paper. To increase the discriminability, we concatenate the normalized joint coordinates from L_P frames near the current frame to construct the *skeletal joint position feature* $\mathbf{x}_P$. The resultant $\mathbf{x}_P$ is a $L_P \cdot 3 \cdot K$ dimensional vector and it holistically describes the motion dynamics of the upper body near the current frame.

Despite the normalization process, the skeletal joint position feature is not viewpoint invariant. As a viewpoint invariant feature, we utilize the Euclidean distance $\|x_j - x_k\|$ between joint j and k. The *skeletal joint distance feature* $\mathbf{x}_D$ is then defined by concatenating all such distances for L_D frames. Note that the dimensionality of $\mathbf{x}_D$ is $L_D \cdot \frac{K(K-1)}{2}$. This is a kind of the relational pose feature [20], describing geometric relations between specific joints in a short sequence of frames.

We additionally consider the RGB image to exploit the details not captured by the skeletal joint features. For that purpose, the 3D joints of left and right hands are first projected to the RGB image. Histogram of oriented gradients (HOG) descriptors are then computed for the windows centered on the projected points. We concatenate the HOG descriptors of L_L frames near the current frame to construct our *appearance feature* $\mathbf{x}_L$ for the left hand. The appearance feature for the right hand $\mathbf{x}_R$ is similarly defined from the HOG descriptors corresponding to the right hand.

Because our features are constructed from several frames, their dimensionality is generally very high, especially for the appearance features. Therefore, we use the PCA to reduce the computational complexity of our method. We also apply the standardization process to compensate the different scales of the multi-modal features. As a result, each multi-modal feature will have zero-mean and unit-variance.

3.3   Active Hand Approach

In general, gestures including the motion of hands often express the information with just one hand and which hand to use is not important. For gestures based on both hands, their motions are usually similar to each other. Based on these observations, we propose to select the main hand and to use its appearance feature for gesture representation. For that purpose, we introduce a new deterministic variable $a^{(i)}$ for each frame i:

$$a^{(i)} = \begin{cases} 0, \text{ if } \|x_l^{(i+1)} - x_l^{(i)}\| > \|x_r^{(i+1)} - x_r^{(i)}\|; \\ 1, \text{ otherwise}, \end{cases} \tag{2}$$

where $x_l^{(i)}$ and $x_r^{(i)}$ denote the 3D joint coordinates of left and right hands, respectively. The variable $a^{(i)}$ can be intuitively understood as an indicator of which hand is more active at i-th frame. Now our hypothesis is that the active hand is the main hand and using only the feature of the main hand is helpful for gesture classification. We finally define the *appearance feature for the active hand* $\mathbf{x}_A$ by $\mathbf{x}_L$ if the left hand is active ($a = 0$) and by $\mathbf{x}_R$ if the right hand is active ($a = 1$). In this paper, this active hand feature $\mathbf{x}_A$ is adopted instead of the left and right hand features $\mathbf{x}_L$ and $\mathbf{x}_R$.

3.4   Nonparametric Estimation of Multi-modal Likelihood

Now we present how to estimate the likelihood function for each feature from the training dataset. Let $\mathbf{x}_1^g, \ldots \mathbf{x}_N^g$ denote all the features labeled a gesture category class g from all the training sequences. Then the kernel density estimator of the likelihood function is:

$$\hat{p}(\mathbf{x}|g) = \frac{1}{N} \sum_{j=1}^{N} K(\mathbf{x} - \mathbf{x}_j^g), \tag{3}$$

where $K(\mathbf{x})$ is the kernel function, which should be non-negative and integrate to one. In this paper, the spherical Gaussian function is used for the kernel function $K(\mathbf{x}) = (2\pi)^{-D/2}\sigma^{-D} \exp(-\frac{1}{2\sigma^2}\|\mathbf{x}\|^2)$, where D and σ denote the dimensionality of the feature vector and the bandwidth parameter, respectively.

In general, N (i.e., the number of training samples belonging to each gesture class) is very large, so computing the likelihood in (3) is computationally very expensive. Therefore we approximate it by considering only the largest term in the summation (3). Because the Gaussian kernel is assumed, this term corresponds to the nearest neighbor of the feature vector $\mathbf{x}$ within $\mathbf{x}_1^g, \ldots \mathbf{x}_N^g$, and the likelihood function (3) can be rewritten as:

$$p^{\text{NN}}(\mathbf{x}|g) \propto \exp(-\frac{1}{2\sigma^2}\|\mathbf{x} - \mathbf{x}_{\text{NN}}^g\|^2), \tag{4}$$

where $\mathbf{x}^g_{\text{NN}}$ denotes the nearest neighbor vector. This nearest neighbor vector can be efficiently found by using the randomized kd-trees [21]. In general, we can consider the k-nearest neighbors ($k \geq 2$), but empirically this improves the performance very little.

We apply the above estimation process to all multi-modal features, and obtain their corresponding approximate likelihoods. They are then combined to the multi-modal likelihood and its negative log-likelihood can be written as

$$L(\mathbf{x}|g) = \sum_{j=1}^{M} \frac{1}{2\sigma_j^2} \|\mathbf{x}_j - \mathbf{x}^g_{j,\text{NN}}\|^2, \tag{5}$$

where σ_j is the bandwidth for the j-th multi-modal feature and $\mathbf{x}^g_{j,\text{NN}}$ denotes the nearest neighbor of the multi-modal feature $\mathbf{x}_j$ within the training samples of the gesture class g. Note that the bandwidth parameters $\sigma_j, j \in \{1, \ldots, M\}$ control the relative importance between the multi-modal features. They can be decided based on several approaches such as maximum likelihood criterion [22], discriminative method with the hinge loss [23], etc. In this paper, we simply use the cross-validation. This requires us to search a 2D parameter space of $(\frac{\sigma_D}{\sigma_P}, \frac{\sigma_A}{\sigma_P})$, which is feasible.

3.5   MRF Model with Temporal Coherence

Now let us assume that the test sequence is given and its multi-modal features are $\mathbf{x}^{(i)} = (\mathbf{x}_1^{(i)}, \ldots, \mathbf{x}_M^{(i)})$, $i = 1, \ldots, T$, where T is the length of the test sequence. We can then locally perform gesture labeling for the test sequence by using the negative log-likelihood in (5). Specifically, for each frame i of the test sequence, the optimal gesture class $g^{(i)*}$ can be found by minimizing the negative log-likelihood:

$$g^{(i)*} = \arg \min_{g^{(i)}} L(\mathbf{x}^{(i)}|g^{(i)}). \tag{6}$$

However, this locally optimized solution may lack the temporal coherence. Therefore, we formulate the following MRF model to enhance the temporal coherence of the solution:

$$E(\mathbf{g}) = \sum_{i=1}^{T} E_{\text{unary}}(\mathbf{x}^{(i)}, g^{(i)}) + \lambda \sum_{i=1}^{T-1} E_{\text{pairwise}}(g^{(i)}, g^{(i+1)}), \tag{7}$$

where $\mathbf{g} = (g^{(1)}, \ldots, g^{(T)})$ denotes the gesture label vector. The unary term is defined as the negative log-likelihood ratio:

$$E_{\text{unary}}(\mathbf{x}^{(i)}, g^{(i)}) = L(\mathbf{x}^{(i)}|g^{(i)}) - \min_{g \in \bar{g}^{(i)}} L(\mathbf{x}^{(i)}|g), \tag{8}$$

where $\bar{g}^{(i)}$ denotes the set of all gesture classes excluding $g^{(i)}$. This slightly improves the performance rather than using the negative log-likelihood. And the pairwise term is defined as the simple smoothness constraint:

$$E_{\text{pairwise}}(g^{(i)}, g^{(i+1)}) = \begin{cases} 0, & \text{if } g^{(i)} = g^{(i+1)}; \\ 1, & \text{otherwise.} \end{cases} \tag{9}$$

The parameter λ controls the strength of the smoothness constraint and it is determined by the cross-validation. Now the final gesture label vector $\mathbf{g}$ can be obtained by minimizing the MRF energy in (7). Because our model is 1D MRF, its optimal solution can be very efficiently computed by using the dynamic programming.

4   Experimental Results

4.1   Dataset and Evaluation Metric

To evaluate the performance of the proposed gesture labeling method, we use the gesture dataset [8] introduced in ChaLearn LAP Challenge. It is composed of total 940 sequences (470 training, 230 validation, and 240 test sequences) and each sequence contains RGB, depth data, skeleton information extracted from the depth data by [3], and manually annotated gesture labels. Target gestures are twenty Italian cultural/anthropological signs performed by many subjects. Specifically, there are total 13,858 gesture instances (7,754 training, 3,362 validation, and 2,742 test instances) and this is one of the largest-known datasets for gesture recognition.

Let $A_{(s,n)}$ and $B_{(s,n)}$ denote the ground-truth of gesture n at sequence s and its prediction result, where both $A_{(s,n)}$ and $B_{(s,n)}$ are sets including frames at which the n-th gesture is being performed in the s-th sequence. The Jaccard index can then be defined as

$$J_{(s,n)} = \frac{|A_{(s,n)} \cap B_{(s,n)}|}{|A_{(s,n)} \cup B_{(s,n)}|}, \tag{10}$$

which represents the similarity between two sets. The Jaccard index $J_{(s,n)}$ is averaged over all gesture classes and all sequences to produce the *mean Jaccard index*. We use this mean Jaccard index as the main evaluation criterion. We also compute the *precision* and *recall* to evaluate the detection performance of our method. For that purpose, we need to judge whether the detected gesture interval is the true/false positive. Similarly to the object detection research [24], the detection result is considered to be correct if the overlap ratio r between the ground-truth interval I_{gt} and the predicted interval I_p exceeds 0.5:

$$r = \frac{\text{length}(I_{gt} \cap I_p)}{\text{length}(I_{gt} \cup I_p)}, \tag{11}$$

where $I_{gt} \cap I_p$ represents the intersection of the ground-truth and predicted intervals and $I_{gt} \cup I_p$ their union.

4.2   Implementation Details

Each frame of the dataset sequence is labeled one of the twenty gesture categories, but there are also many frames containing no meaningful gestures. We

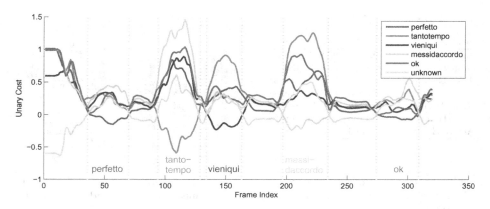

Fig. 2. Unary costs for one of the test sequences (sample index 701) are illustrated in this figure. Colored texts and gray dotted lines denote the ground-truth gesture classes and their starting/ending frames, respectively.

simply regard it as the twenty-first gesture category in our gesture labeling framework. However, note that it is excluded from computing the evaluation metrics such as the Jaccard index, precision, and recall.

For the skeletal joint position and distance features, $K = 10$ joints in the upper body are utilized. The RGB images of both hands are resized to 128×128 images, and their HOG descriptors are computed with 16×16 cell size and 9 orientations. The size of the temporal window for constructing our features are $L_P = 14$, $L_D = 14$, and $L_A = 2$, respectively. We then apply the PCA to each feature for dimensionality reduction. The variance thresholds of the PCA are 0.99 for the skeletal joint position and distance features, and 0.85 for the appearance feature of the active hand. Remaining parameters are the bandwidth parameters σ_P, σ_D, σ_A, and the smoothness parameter λ. They are determined by the cross-validation. Finally, the open source VLFeat library [25] is used to compute the HOG descriptors and to perform the fast nearest neighbor search with the randomized kd-trees.

4.3   Performance Analysis

From now, we present the evaluation results of the proposed gesture labeling method. First, to investigate the feasibility of our method, we only consider the skeletal joint position feature. Fig. 2 shows the unary costs for a test sample with the annotated ground-truth. We can see that the unary costs provide the strong cues for gesture labeling. The value of the unary cost (i.e., negative log-likelihood ratio) for the ground-truth gesture class is lowest among all the gesture classes except the *ok* gesture in Fig. 2. Therefore, the proposed method can produce satisfactory results without considering the coherence between the neighboring frames. It is well illustrated in Fig. 3, where the evaluation results of our method

Feature	mJ	mP	mR
Joint Pos. (Local)	0.7547	0.7891	0.8556
Joint Position	0.7816	0.8653	0.8754
Joint Distance	0.7536	0.8403	0.8496
Left Hand	0.3613	0.6505	0.4421
Right Hand	0.6412	0.8270	0.7396
Both Hands	0.7136	0.9013	0.8494
Active Hand	0.7504	0.8885	0.8822

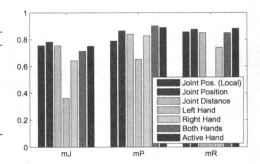

Fig. 3. Performance of the proposed method based on a single feature is illustrated. mJ, mP, and mR denote the mean Jaccard index, mean precision, and mean recall, respectively.

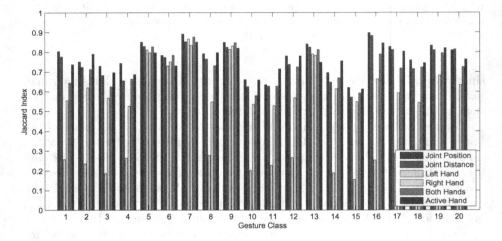

Fig. 4. Jaccard index scores are illustrated for each gesture category

with and without the smoothness term can be found. The mean Jaccard index of our results based on the local approach (6) is 0.7547. We then adopt the smoothness term in (9) and globally optimize the MRF energy in (7), which results in 0.7816. Note that the local approach achieves a reasonable performance and the global version further improves it.

We next examine the performance of the proposed method based on a single feature. Fig. 3 shows the evaluation results corresponding to the various features introduced in Section 3.2 and 3.3. Note that the right hand based appearance feature results in better performance than the left hand based one. This is because the right hand is more frequently used in many gesture instances of the dataset. Both hands are then simultaneously utilized and this outperforms the single hand cases as expected. Finally, the active hand feature defined in Section 3.3 is evaluated, which produces better results than using the both hands. Note that

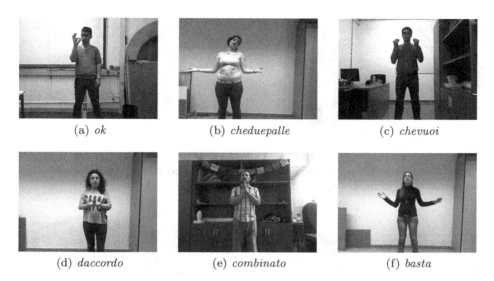

(a) *ok*   (b) *cheduepalle*   (c) *chevuoi*

(d) *daccordo*   (e) *combinato*   (f) *basta*

Fig. 5. The pose of fingers plays an important role in recognizing the *ok* gesture in (a). The gestures based on the motions of both hands are illustrated in (b)-(f).

only half the amount of information is required to represent the active hand feature compared to the both hands.

For detailed analysis, the Jaccard index scores are computed for each gesture category and they are illustrated in Fig. 4, where the numbers of x-axis denote the following twenty gesture classes: *vattene, vieniqui, perfetto, furbo, cheduepalle, chevuoi, daccordo, seipazzo, combinato, freganiente, ok, cosatifarei, basta, prendere, noncenepiu, fame, tantotempo, buonissimo, messidaccordo,* and *sonostufo*. We can see that the active hand based approach significantly outperforms the others especially for the gesture category 11, i.e., *ok*. This is reasonable because the specific configuration of fingers is an important characteristic to distinguish the *ok* from the other gestures. It is also noticeable that the left hand based method achieves comparable results with the right hand for the gesture classes 5, 6, 7, 9, 13, i.e., *cheduepalle, chevuoi, daccordo, combinato,* and *basta*. All these gestures are composed of the same motions of both hands. See Fig. 5 that illustrates the above mentioned gestures.

We then investigate the performance of our multi-modal approach. Let us consider the joint position $\mathbf{x}_P$, joint distance $\mathbf{x}_D$, and active hand $\mathbf{x}_A$ based features. To exploit the multiple features, their bandwidth parameters σ_P, σ_D, and σ_A should be decided. We set σ_P to 1.0 and then optimize σ_D and σ_A by the brute-force search. The smoothness parameter λ is similarly determined. Fig. 6 illustrates the results of this cross-validation process with the validation dataset. Fig. 7 shows that the mean Jaccard index score is slightly improved by optimizing the bandwidth parameters. Note that the simple feature combination with equal

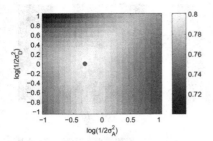 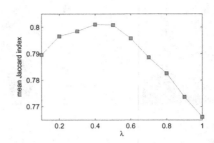

Fig. 6. The bandwidth parameters and the smoothness coefficient are determined by the simple brute-force search

Feature	mJ	mP	mR
P	0.7816	0.8653	0.8754
P+D	0.7948	0.8962	0.8824
P+L+R	0.8110	0.9254	0.9157
P+A	0.8244	0.8950	0.9191
P+D+A (NoCV)	0.8247	**0.9258**	**0.9204**
P+D+A	**0.8268**	0.9199	0.9158

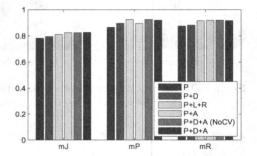

Fig. 7. Performance of the proposed method based on multiple features is illustrated. P, D, L, R, and A denote the joint position, joint distance, left hand, right hand, and active hand based features, respectively. NoCV denotes that cross-validation is not used and all bandwidth parameters are equally set to 1.0.

bandwidth produces the comparable result 0.8247 with the optimal case 0.8268 thanks to the standardization process between the multi-modal features.

Fig. 7 and 8 show the evaluation results by using various combinations of multiple features. We can see that the use of multiple features significantly improves the recognition performance. Specifically, by using the joint position, joint distance, and active hand features together, the proposed method scores 0.8268 in the mean Jaccard index and this result is a 3rd place in the gesture recognition track of the ChaLearn LAP Challenge. The top 10 results of the challenge are reported in Table 1.

We finally examine the computational complexity of the proposed method. Our algorithm can be roughly divided into two parts: (1) the training process including feature pre-processing and kd-tree construction, (2) the testing process including nearest neighbor search with the kd-trees and MRF optimization by dynamic programming. The training part uses the training and validation datasets, whereas the testing part runs on the test dataset. The run-time results of them are 1191.7 and 474.1 seconds respectively, as measured on a 12 core

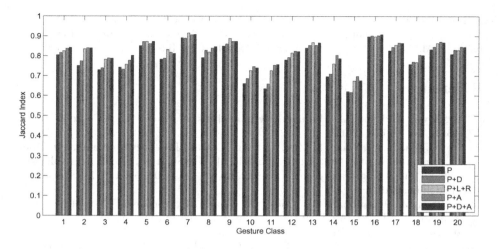

Fig. 8. Jaccard index scores are illustrated for each gesture category

CPU machine. Specifically, it takes 1.4 milliseconds per frame to perform the gesture labeling of a test sequence, which shows the efficiency of our approach.

Table 1. Results of ChaLearn LAP Challenge (track 3) are illustrated

Rank	Team	Score	Rank	Team	Score
1	Neverova et al. [26]	0.8500	6	Wu [27]	0.7873
2	Monnier et al. [28]	0.8339	7	Camgoz et al. [29]	0.7466
3	**Ours**	**0.8268**	8	Evangelidis et al. [30]	0.7454
4	Peng et al. [31]	0.7919	9	Undisclosed authors	0.6888
5	Pigou et al. [32]	0.7888	10	Chen et al. [33]	0.6490

5   Conclusions

We have proposed a novel gesture recognition method based on the nonparametric density estimation of the multi-modal features. Our approach can produce gesture category labels for all frames of the test sequence, which allows not only gesture classification but also accurate localization. Experimental results demonstrate that the proposed method achieves a convincing performance in terms of the mean Jaccard index criterion. In our method, the bandwidth parameters and the smoothness coefficient are determined by the simple cross-validation. The computational complexity of this brute-force search grows exponentially with the number of features. In the future, we aim to estimate these parameters by using a more sophisticated learning process.

Acknowledgments. This work was supported by the ICT R&D program of MSIP/ IITP. [2014(APP0120130417001), Development of High Accuracy Mobile and Omnidirectional Multi-user Gesture Recognition Technology for Interaction with Content]

References

1. Aggarwal, J., Ryoo, M.: Human activity analysis: A review. ACM Comput. Surv. **43**(3), 16:1–16:43 (2011)
2. Ye, M., Zhang, Q., Wang, L., Zhu, J., Yang, R., Gall, J.: A survey on human motion analysis from depth data. In: Grzegorzek, M., Theobalt, C., Koch, R., Kolb, A. (eds.) Time-of-Flight and Depth Imaging. LNCS, vol. 8200, pp. 149–187. Springer, Heidelberg (2013)
3. Shotton, J., Fitzgibbon, A., Cook, M., Sharp, T., Finocchio, M., Moore, R., Kipman, A., Blake, A.: Real-time human pose recognition in parts from single depth images. In: CVPR, pp. 1297–1304 (2011)
4. Jhuang, H., Gall, J., Zuffi, S., Schmid, C., Black, M.J.: Towards understanding action recognition. In: ICCV, pp. 3192–3199 (2013)
5. Wang, H., Klser, A., Schmid, C., Liu, C.L.: Dense trajectories and motion boundary descriptors for action recognition. International Journal of Computer Vision **103**(1), 60–79 (2013)
6. Dalal, N., Triggs, B.: Histograms of oriented gradients for human detection. In: CVPR, vol. 1, pp. 886–893 (2005)
7. Laptev, I., Marszalek, M., Schmid, C., Rozenfeld, B.: Learning realistic human actions from movies. In: CVPR, pp. 1–8 (2008)
8. Escalera, S., Baró, X., Gonzàlez, J., Bautista, M.A., Madadi, M., Reyes, M., Ponce, V., Escalante, H.J., Shotton, J., Guyon, I.: Chalearn looking at people challenge 2014: dataset and results. In: ECCV Workshops (2014)
9. Jalal, A., Uddin, M.Z., Kim, J.T., Kim, T.S.: Recognition of human home activities via depth silhouettes and r transformation for smart homes. Indoor and Built Environment, 1–7 (2011)
10. Xia, L., Chen, C.C., Aggarwal, J.: View invariant human action recognition using histograms of 3d joints. In: CVPR Workshops, pp. 20–27 (2012)
11. Sminchisescu, C., Kanaujia, A., Li, Z., Metaxas, D.: Conditional models for contextual human motion recognition. In: ICCV, vol. 2, pp. 1808–1815 (2005)
12. Sung, J., Ponce, C., Selman, B., Saxena, A.: Unstructured human activity detection from rgbd images. In: IEEE International Conference on Robotics and Automation (ICRA), pp. 842–849 (2012)
13. Lin, Z., Jiang, Z., Davis, L.S.: Recognizing actions by shape-motion prototype trees. In: ICCV, pp. 444–451 (2009)
14. Wang, J., Wu, Y.: Learning maximum margin temporal warping for action recognition. In: ICCV, pp. 2688–2695 (2013)
15. Wang, J., Liu, Z., Wu, Y., Yuan, J.: Mining actionlet ensemble for action recognition with depth cameras. In: CVPR, pp. 1290–1297 (2012)
16. Oreifej, O., Liu, Z.: Hon4d: histogram of oriented 4d normals for activity recognition from depth sequences. In: CVPR, pp. 716–723 (2013)
17. Wei, P., Zheng, N., Zhao, Y., Zhu, S.C.: Concurrent action detection with structural prediction. In: ICCV, pp. 3136–3143 (2013)
18. Yang, X., Tian, Y.: Eigenjoints-based action recognition using naïve-bayes-nearest-neighbor. In: CVPR Workshops, pp. 14–19 (2012)

19. Zanfir, M., Leordeanu, M., Sminchisescu, C.: The moving pose: an efficient 3d kinematics descriptor for low-latency action recognition and detection. In: ICCV, pp. 2752–2759 (2013)
20. Müller, M., Röder, T., Clausen, M.: Efficient content-based retrieval of motion capture data. ACM Transactions on Graphics (TOG) **24**(3), 677–685 (2005)
21. Muja, M., Lowe, D.G.: Fast approximate nearest neighbors with automatic algorithm configuration. In: International Conference on Computer Vision Theory and Application (VISAPP), pp. 331–340 (2009)
22. Murillo, J.M.L., Rodríguez, A.A.: Algorithms for gaussian bandwidth selection in kernel density estimators. Neural Inf. Proc. Systems (2008)
23. Behmo, R., Marcombes, P., Dalalyan, A., Prinet, V.: Towards optimal naive bayes nearest neighbor. In: Daniilidis, K., Maragos, P., Paragios, N. (eds.) ECCV 2010, Part IV. LNCS, vol. 6314, pp. 171–184. Springer, Heidelberg (2010)
24. Everingham, M., Van Gool, L., Williams, C.K., Winn, J., Zisserman, A.: The pascal visual object classes (voc) challenge. International Journal of Computer Vision **88**(2), 303–338 (2010)
25. Vedaldi, A., Fulkerson, B.: VLFeat: An open and portable library of computer vision algorithms (2008). http://www.vlfeat.org/
26. Neverova, N., Wolf, C., Taylor, G., Nebout, F.: Multi-scale deep learning for gesture detection and localization. In: ECCV Workshops (2014)
27. Wu, D.: Deep dynamic neural networks for gesture segmentation and recognition. In: ECCV Workshops (2014)
28. Monnier, C., German, S., Ost, A.: A multi-scale boosted detector for efficient and robust gesture recognition. In: ECCV Workshops (2014)
29. Camgoz, N.C., Kindiroglu, A.A., Akarun, L.: Gesture recognition using template based random forest classifiers. In: ECCV Workshops (2014)
30. Evangelidis, G., Singh, G., Horaud, R.: Continuous gesture recognition from articulated poses. In: ECCV Workshops (2014)
31. Peng, X., Wang, L., Cai, Z.: Action and gesture temporal spotting with super vector representation. In: ECCV Workshops (2014)
32. Pigou, L., Dieleman, S., Kindermans, P.J.: Sign language recognition using convolutional neural networks. In: ECCV Workshops (2014)
33. Chen, G., Clarke, D., Giuliani, M., Weikersdorfer, D., Knoll, A.: Multi-modality gesture detection and recognition with un-supervision, randomization and discrimination. In: ECCV Workshops (2014)

Action and Gesture Temporal Spotting with Super Vector Representation

Xiaojiang Peng[1,3]($\boxtimes$), Limin Wang[2,3], Zhuowei Cai[3], and Yu Qiao[3]

[1] Southwest Jiaotong University, Chengdu, China
xiaojiangp@gmail.com
[2] Department of Information Engineering, The Chinese University of Hong Kong,
Hong Kong, China
[3] Shenzhen Key Lab of CVPR, Shenzhen Institutes of Advanced Technology,
CAS, Shenzhen, China

Abstract. This paper focuses on describing our method designed for both track 2 and track 3 at Looking at People (LAP) challenging [1]. We propose an action and gesture spotting system, which is mainly composed of three steps: (i) temporal segmentation, (ii) clip classification, and (iii) post processing. For track 2, we resort to a simple sliding window method to divide each video sequence into clips, while for track 3, we design a segmentation method based on the motion analysis of human hands. Then, for each clip, we choose a kind of super vector representation with dense features. Based on this representation, we train a linear SVM to conduct action and gesture recognition. Finally, we use some post processing techniques to void the detection of false positives. We demonstrate the effectiveness of our proposed method by participating the contests of both track 2 and track 3. We obtain the best performance on track 2 and rank 4th on track 3, which indicates that the designed system is effective for action and gesture recognition.

Keywords: Action recognition · Gesture recognition · Temporal spotting · Super vector

1 Introduction

Action and gesture recognition [2,3] for a short video clip has become an important area in computer vision, whose aim is to classify the ongoing action or gesture into a predefined category. It has wide applications in our daily life such as human computer interaction, content based video retrieval, and sports video analysis. However, most of the existing research works focus on the action and gesture dataset, where the videos have been manually trimmed to bound the action interest, such as HMDB51 [4] and UCF101 [5]. These datasets have a limitation in measuring the effectiveness of proposed method in practical settings. Instead, in this paper, we try to address a more difficult problem, namely *temporal spotting* of action and gesture. We are given a continuous video stream and we need to recognize and temporally localize the ongoing action in the video sequence simultaneously.

© Springer International Publishing Switzerland 2015
L. Agapito et al. (Eds.): ECCV 2014 Workshops, Part I, LNCS 8925, pp. 518–527, 2015.
DOI: 10.1007/978-3-319-16178-5_36

(a) Track 2: Action/Interaction Recognition

(b) Track 3: Gesture Recognition

Fig. 1. Some examples of track 2 and track 3 of Looking at People Challenging. For track 2, we show several action instances such as waving, walk, and fight. For track 3, we show the different modalities provided for gesture recognition. From left to right: RGB information, depth information, user segmentation mask, and skeleton. Note that both figures are from the contest webpage.

We mainly describe our method designed for Track 2 and Track 3 of Looking at People (LAP) challenge [1] organized by ChaLearn in conjunction with the ECCV 2014 conference. Track 2 focuses on action (interaction) recognition from RGB data, with 11 action classes, such as wave, point, clap, and couch [6]. Track 3 is about the gesture recognition from multi-modal data, including: color, depth, skeleton, and user mask [7]. This competition task aims to learn a vocabulary of gestures corresponding to 20 Italian cultural signs, such as vattene, vieniqui, perfettor, and ok. Some video examples of both tracks are shown in Figure 1. It is worth noting that, in test phase of both tracks, we are given a temporally untrimmed video which may contain multiple action and gesture instances. Our method need to temporally localize and recognize these ongoing instances.

As shown in Figure 2, our method is mainly composed of three steps: (i) temporal segmentation, (ii) clip classification, and (iii) post processing. Firstly, we temporally divide the untrimmed video sequence into several clips. We resort to a simple sliding window scheme for track 2 of action recognition, while we design a temporal segmentation method based on hand motion for track 3 of gesture recognition. Then, for each short video clip, we extract dense trajectories with four kinds of descriptors: HOG, HOF, MBHx, and MBHy [8]. We choose the Fisher Vector [9] as encoding method to obtain the global representation for each video clip and train a linear SVM for classification. Finally, we use some post-processing techniques to eliminate the false positive detections. For example, during our training phase, we train a classifier for the background class. This background classifier will enable us to eliminate some detections corresponding to the background class.

We will provide a detailed description about our method for both Track 2 and Track 3 in Section 2. Then, we will report the performance of our method on both Tracks in Section 3. Finally, we conclude our paper in Section 4.

2   Method

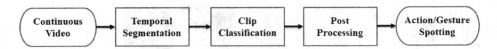

Fig. 2. The pipeline of our method for action and gesture temporal spotting. We firstly conduct video temporal segmentation. Then for each video clip, we extract super vector representation and perform clip classification. Finally, we use post processing techniques to eliminate the false detections.

We propose an temporal spotting system for the Track 2 and Track 3 of Looking at People (LAP) challenge as shown in Figure 2. Our system is mainly composed of three steps: (i) temporal segmentation, (ii) clip classification, and (iii) post processing. We will give a detailed description of these steps in the remainder of this section.

2.1   Temporal Segmentation

In this section, we mainly describe the method of dividing a continuous video into short clips, each of which may contain the action and gesture of interest. We design two different methods for track 2 of action recognition and track 3 of gesture recognition respectively.

Action Recognition. For the track 2 of action (interaction) recognition, it gives a continuous video stream, which contains a sequence of action instances. We need to firstly localize these instances and then recognize their corresponding action classes. We resort to a temporal sliding scheme to conduct action localization. Based on the observation on training dataset, we set the window length as 15-frames and scanning step as 5-frames. To speed up the sliding window process, we firstly extract the low-level features and encode these descriptors as described in the next section. Then we design a temporal integration histogram, with which we can efficiently calculate the feature histogram for the sub-window of any location and any length.

Gesture Recognition. Unlike Track 2, the track 3 of gesture recognition provides several data modalities such as RGB information, depth information, user mask, and skeleton information. We observe that the motion trajectory of human hand is an important cue for gesture spotting in a continuous video stream. With a reasonable assumption that the hands of an actor are almost in the same

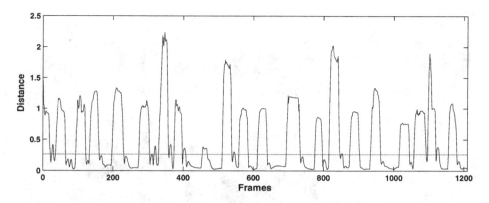

Fig. 3. A example of temporal segmentation for gesture recognition based on hand motion analysis

position when he is not performing a gesture, we propose temporal segmentation method based the analysis of hand trajectory.

We firstly estimate the position of actor hands when he is not performing a gesture. With the given pose information, we use a 2D histogram of 100×100 cells overlapped with a pixel grid to estimate the spatial distribution of hand position in the whole video. Then we choose the cell with highest frequency as the static hand position. Based on the static hand position, for each frame, we calculate the distance of current hand position to the static position. Finally, according to this distance, we use a single threshold τ to determine whether the actor is performing a gesture or not. An example of temporal segmentation is shown in Figure 3. With this simple yet effective method, we split a untrimmed video into several clips, each of which can be used for gesture recognition in the next section.

2.2   Clip Classification

In this section, we give a detailed description of video clip representation and classification. Note that, for both track 2 and track 3, we resort to the same video representation, and we just use the RGB modality for gesture recognition of track 3.

The key element of clip classification is the visual representation of video data. Following the success of Dense Trajectories (IDTs) [1] in action recognition on the wild videos [8], we choose the IDTs as our low-level features of RGB data. Specifically, we use the public code released on the project page. We set the length of trajectory as 9 and extract four kinds of descriptors, namely HOG, HOF, MBHx, and MBHy. Some examples of extracted dense trajectories are shown in Figure 4. From these examples, we observe that these extracted dense

---

[1] https://lear.inrialpes.fr/people/wang/dense_trajectories

Fig. 4. Examples of extracted dense trajectories for videos from both Track 2 of action recognition and Track 3 of gesture recognition

trajectories focus on the foreground regions with high motion saliency. The four kinds of descriptors correspond to different views of video data such as static appearance, dynamic motion, and motion boundary. These different aspects are of importance for action and gesture recognition.

With these low-level descriptors, we adopt the Bag of Visual Words [10] model to obtain the global representation. According to the recent study works [11,12], super vector based encoding methods are very effective by aggregating different order statistics in a high-dimensional feature representation. Specifically, we choose Fisher Vector [9] as the encoding method using the implementation of vlfeat [13]. Given a set of local descriptors $\mathbf{F} = [\mathbf{f}_1, \cdots, \mathbf{f}_N] \in \mathbb{R}^{M \times N}$, we first use the PCA and Whiten technique to remove the correlations among different dimensions and normalize the variance. Then, based on the transformed feature descriptors $\mathbf{X} = [\mathbf{x}_1, \cdots, \mathbf{x}_N] \in \mathbb{R}^{D \times N}$ where $\mathbf{x}_i = \Lambda \mathbf{f}_i$ and $\Lambda \in \mathbb{R}^{D \times M}$ is the transform matrix of PCA and Whiten processing, we learn a generative Gaussian Mixture Model (GMM):

$$p(\mathbf{x}; \theta) = \sum_{k=1}^{K} \pi_k \mathcal{N}(\mathbf{x}; \mu_k, \Sigma_k), \qquad (1)$$

where K is mixture number, and $\theta = \{\pi_1, \mu_1, \Sigma_1, \cdots, \pi_K, \mu_K, \Sigma_K\}$ are model parameters. $\mathcal{N}(\mathbf{x}; \mu_k, \Sigma_k)$ is D-dimensional Gaussian distribution.

With some reasonable assumptions that the posterior probability is sharply peaked on a single value of k for any descriptor $\mathbf{x}$, the Fisher Information Matrix (FIM) is a diagonal matrix [9]. Then Fisher vector is derived from Fisher Kernel [14] as follows:

$$\mathcal{G}_{\pi_k}^{\mathbf{X}} = \frac{1}{\sqrt{\pi_k}} \sum_{i=1}^{N} (\gamma_k(\mathbf{x}_i) - \pi_k), \qquad (2)$$

$$\mathcal{G}_{\mu_k}^{\mathbf{X}} = \frac{1}{\sqrt{\pi_k}} \sum_{i=1}^{N} \gamma_k(\mathbf{x}_i) \left(\frac{\mathbf{x}_i - \mu_k}{\sigma_k} \right), \tag{3}$$

$$\mathcal{G}_{\sigma_k}^{\mathbf{X}} = \frac{1}{\sqrt{2\pi_k}} \sum_{i=1}^{N} \gamma_k(\mathbf{x}_i) \left[\frac{(\mathbf{x}_i - \mu_k)^2}{\sigma_k^2} - 1 \right], \tag{4}$$

where $\gamma_k(\mathbf{x})$ is the posteriori probability of local descriptor $\mathbf{x}$ assigned to k^{th} Gaussian Mixture:

$$\gamma_k(\mathbf{x}) = \frac{\pi_k \mathcal{N}(\mathbf{x}; \mu_k, \Sigma_k)}{\sum_{i=1}^{K} \pi_i \mathcal{N}(\mathbf{x}; \mu_i, \Sigma_i)}. \tag{5}$$

In our current implementation, we choose the first order and second order super vector with power ℓ_2-normalization ($\alpha = 0.5$) as our super vector representation $\mathcal{S}$:

$$\mathcal{S} = [\mathcal{G}_{\mu_1}^{\mathbf{X}}, \mathcal{G}_{\sigma_1}^{\mathbf{X}}, \cdots, \mathcal{G}_{\mu_K}^{\mathbf{X}}, \mathcal{G}_{\sigma_K}^{\mathbf{X}}], \quad \mathcal{S} = \frac{\text{sign}(\mathcal{S})\sqrt{|\mathcal{S}|}}{\|\sqrt{\mathcal{S}}\|_2}. \tag{6}$$

It is worth noting that we separately construct super vector representation $\mathcal{S}_i$ for the ith kind of descriptor according to the above description. We then concatenate the four kind of super vector representation as a whole one $\mathcal{S} = [\mathcal{S}_1, \mathcal{S}_2, \mathcal{S}_3, \mathcal{S}_4]$. Using this concatenated representation, we train a linear SVM for each action and gesture class using the implementation of LIBSVM [15]. For multiclass classification, we use the one-vs-all training scheme and choose the prediction with the highest score as its predicted label.

2.3   Post Processing

In order to avoid the false detections, which may correspond to the irrelevant background action classes, we design a post processing technique. Firstly, during training phase of action and gesture recognition, we mine some instances of static background or noisy motion. We then use these instances to train a classifier which represents the background class. During test phase, if a video sub-window or clip is predicted as the background class, we will remove this detection. Secondly, we use a single threshold -0.8 to eliminate those detections with low confidence score. In our evaluation, we find this post processing step is very effective for removing those false positive detections and improving the performance of action and gesture spotting.

3   Evaluation

In this section, we present the experimental results for track 2 of action recognition and track 3 of gesture recognition at Looking at People (LAP) challenge [1]. For both tracks, we set the number of GMM mixture as 256.

Dataset and Evaluation Measurement. For track 2 of action recognition, it has 11 action categories such as wave, point, clap and so on. For training data,

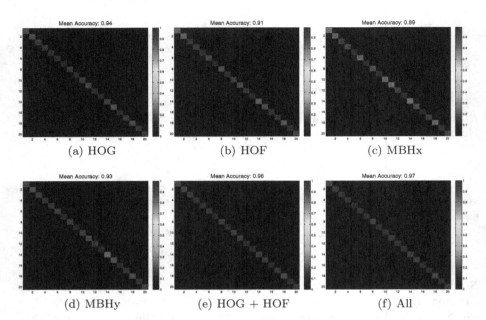

Fig. 5. Results of different descriptors (HOG, HOF, MBHx, and MBHy) and their combinations (HOG+HOF, All) on the gesture recognition

it has 5 video sequences, containing 135 action instances in total. For validation data, there are 2 video sequences including 44 action instances. There are 2 video sequences with 52 action instances for final evaluation in test phase. We firstly train our model on the training dataset and adjust the parameters according to its performance on the validation dataset. Finally, in order to increase the training data, we retrain our model on both the training and validation dataset, and verify its performance on the testing dataset.

For track 3 of gesture recognition, there are totally 20 gesture categories of Italian signs. For training dataset, there are 470 video sequences, corresponding to 6, 830 gesture instances. For validation dataset, it has 230 video sequences and 3, 454 gesture instances. For final evaluation, there are 240 video sequences for testing.

Regarding the evaluation measurement, for both track 2 and track 3, it uses the **Jaccard Index** to evaluate the performance of action and gesture spotting. Specifically, the Jaccard Index is defined as follows:

$$J_{s,n} = \frac{A_{s,n} \cap B_{s,n}}{A_{s,n} \cup B_{s,n}}, \tag{7}$$

where $A_{s,n}$ is the ground truth of action (or gesture) n at sequence s, and $B_{s,n}$ is the prediction for such action (or gesture) at sequence s. For final evaluation, our method is evaluated based on the mean Jaccard Index among all action (or gesture) classes. For track 2, the number of action classes is 12, and there are 20 gesture classes for track 3.

Gesture Recognition. As the clip representation using iDTs with Fisher Vector are adapted from the action recognition tasks [12], we firstly conduct an exploration experiment to verify its performance on gesture recognition. Specifically, we use the 6, 830 gesture instances from the training dataset for SVM training. We demonstrate the effectiveness of this representation on the 3, 454 gesture instances from the validation dataset. The experimental results are shown in Figure 5 and we observe that this representation is very effective for capturing the visual information of gesture. Combining all the descriptors, we obtain a mean accuracy of 0.97 on the validation dataset.

Contest Result. We report the action and gesture spotting performance for both track 2 and track 3 of Looking at People (LAP) challenge, and the results are shown in Table 1 and Table 2. Our spotting system obtains the best performance for track 2 and ranks the 4th for track 3. It is worth noting that our system only use the modality of RGB for gesture recognition, while other top performers use other modalities such as skeleton and depth. The top performance on both tracks demonstrate that our designed temporal spotting system is very effective for action and gesture recognition.

Table 1. Contest results for track 2 of action recognition

Rank	Team	Score
1	**Ours**	0.507173
2	Pei et al. [16]	0.501164
3	Shu [17]	0.441405

Table 2. Contest results for track 3 of gesture recognition

Rank	Team	Modalities	Score
1	Neverova et al. [18]	Skeleton, depth, RGB	0.849987
2	Monnier et al. [19]	Skeleton, depth, RGB	0.833904
3	Chang [20]	Skeleton, RGB	0.826799
4	**Ours**	RGB	0.791933

4   Conclusion

We have presented our method designed for the contests of track 2 and track 3 at Looking at People (LAP) challenge. We firstly segment each video sequence into clips and then use a super vector representation to describe the clip visual content. The performance on both tracks demonstrate that our method is effective for action and gesture recognition. In the future, we may consider using more modalities to further improve the our spotting performance for gesture recognition.

Acknowledgments. This work is partly supported by Natural Science Foundation of China (91320101, 61036008, 60972111), Shenzhen Basic Research Program (JC20100 5270350A, JCYJ20120903092050890, JCYJ20120617114614438), 100 Talents Program of CAS, Guangdong Innovative Research Team Program (201001D0104648280).

References

1. Escalera, S., et al.: Chalearn looking at people challenge 2014: dataset and results. In: Bronstein, M., Agapito, L., Rother, C. (eds.) Computer Vision - ECCV 2014 Workshops. LNCS, vol. 8925, pp. 459–473. Springer, Heidelberg (2015)
2. Aggarwal, J.K., Ryoo, M.S.: Human activity analysis: A review. ACM Comput. Surv. **43**(3), 16 (2011)
3. Mitra, S., Acharya, T.: Gesture recognition: A survey. IEEE Transactions on Systems, Man, and Cybernetics, Part C **37**(3), 311–324 (2007)
4. Kuehne, H., Jhuang, H., Garrote, E., Poggio, T., Serre, T.: HMDB: a large video database for human motion recognition. In: ICCV, pp. 2556–2563 (2011)
5. Soomro, K., Zamir, A.R., Shah, M.: UCF101: A dataset of 101 human actions classes from videos in the wild. CoRR abs/1212.0402 (2012)
6. Sanchez, D., Bautista, M., Escalera, S.: Hupab 8k+: Dataset and ecoc-graphcut based segmentation of human limbs. Neurocomputing (2014)
7. Escalera, S., Gonzàlez, J., Baró, X., Reyes, M., Lopes, O., Guyon, I., Athitsos, V., Escalante, H.J.: Multi-modal gesture recognition challenge 2013: dataset and results. In: ICMI, pp. 445–452 (2013)
8. Wang, H., Kläser, A., Schmid, C., Liu, C.L.: Dense trajectories and motion boundary descriptors for action recognition. International Journal of Computer Vision **103**(1), 60–79 (2013)
9. Perronnin, F., Sánchez, J., Mensink, T.: Improving the fisher kernel for large-scale image classification. In: Daniilidis, K., Maragos, P., Paragios, N. (eds.) ECCV 2010, Part IV. LNCS, vol. 6314, pp. 143–156. Springer, Heidelberg (2010)
10. Sivic, J., Zisserman, A.: Video google: a text retrieval approach to object matching in videos. In: ICCV, pp. 1470–1477 (2003)
11. Wang, X., Wang, L.M., Qiao, Y.: A comparative study of encoding, pooling and normalization methods for action recognition. In: Lee, K.M., Matsushita, Y., Rehg, J.M., Hu, Z. (eds.) ACCV 2012, Part III. LNCS, vol. 7726, pp. 572–585. Springer, Heidelberg (2013)
12. Peng, X., Wang, L., Wang, X., Qiao, Y.: Bag of visual words and fusion methods for action recognition: Comprehensive study and good practice. CoRR abs/1405.4506 (2014)
13. Vedaldi, A., Fulkerson, B.: VLFeat: An open and portable library of computer vision algorithms (2008). http://www.vlfeat.org/
14. Jaakkola, T., Haussler, D.: Exploiting generative models in discriminative classifiers. In: NIPS, pp. 487–493 (1998)
15. Chang, C.C., Lin, C.J.: LIBSVM: A library for support vector machines. ACM TIST **2**(3), 27 (2011)

16. Yong, P., Bingbing, N., Indriyati, A.: Mixture of heterogeneous attribute analyzers for human action detection. In: Bronstein, M., Agapito, L., Rother, C. (eds.) Computer Vision - ECCV 2014 Workshops. LNCS, vol. 8925, pp. 528–540. Springer, Heidelberg (2015)

17. Shu, Z., Yun, K., Samaras, D.: Action detection with improved dense trajectories and sliding window. In: Bronstein, M., Agapito, L., Rother, C. (eds.) Computer Vision - ECCV 2014 Workshops. LNCS, vol. 8925, pp. 541–551. Springer, Heidelberg (2015)

18. Neverova, N., Wolf, C., Taylor, G.W., Nebout, F.: Multi-scale deep learning for gesture detection and localization. Computer Vision - ECCV 2014 Workshops. LNCS, vol. 8925, pp. 474–490. Springer, Heidelberg (2015)

19. Monnier, C., German, S., Ost, A.: A multi-scale boosted detector for efficient and robust gesture recognition. In: Bronstein, M., Agapito, L., Rother, C. (eds.) Computer Vision - ECCV 2014 Workshops. LNCS, vol. 8925, pp. 491–502. Springer, Heidelberg (2015)

20. Chang, J.Y.: Nonparametric gesture labeling from multi-modal data. In: Bronstein, M., Agapito, L., Rother, C. (eds.) Computer Vision - ECCV 2014 Workshops. LNCS, vol. 8925, pp. 503–517. Springer, Heidelberg (2015)

Mixture of Heterogeneous Attribute Analyzers for Human Action Detection

Yong Pei, Bingbing Ni$^{(\boxtimes)}$, and Indriyati Atmosukarto

Advanced Digital Sciences Center, Singapore, Singapore
{pei.yong,bingbing.ni,indria}@adsc.com.sg

Abstract. We propose a human action detection framework called "mixture of heterogeneous attribute analyzer". This framework integrates heterogeneous attributes learned from static and dynamic, local and global video features, to boost the action detection performance. To this end, we first detect and track multiple people by SVM-HOG detector and tracklet generation. Multiple short human tracklets are then linked into long trajectories by spatio-temporal matching. Human key poses and local dense motion trajectories are then extracted within the tracked human bounding box sequences. Second, we propose a mining method to learn discriminative attributes from these three feature modalities: human bounding box trajectory, key pose and local dense motion trajectories. Finally, the learned discriminative attributes are integrated in a latent structural max-margin learning framework which also explores the spatio-temporal relationship between heterogeneous feature attributes. Experiments on the ChaLearn 2014 human action dataset demonstrate the superior detection performance of the proposed framework.

Keywords: Human trajectory · Key pose · Local dense trajectories · Discriminative mining · Latent structural max-margin learning

1 Introduction

Video-based human action detection has drawn significant research attention in recent years because of its promising applications including smart video surveillance, assisted living, and video-based human computer interaction (HCI). However, human action detection is very difficult given that realistic video sequence contains significant variations of people in posture, motion and clothing, camera motion, view angle changes, illumination changes, occlusions, self-occlusions, and background clutter.

In literature, various types of visual features have been proposed to address this research challenge. Among them, the most popular ones are spatio-temporal motion features, such as spatio-temporal interest points (STIPs) [1] [2] [3] [4] [5] and dense motion trajectories [6] [7]. These features have shown reasonable performance in action recognition. Typically, spatio-temporal motion features are extracted densely over the entire video sequence, and the occurrences of the

© Springer International Publishing Switzerland 2015
L. Agapito et al. (Eds.): ECCV 2014 Workshops, Part I, LNCS 8925, pp. 528–540, 2015.
DOI: 10.1007/978-3-319-16178-5_37

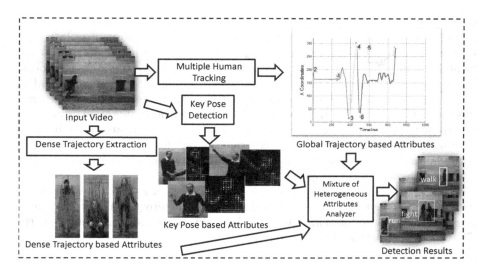

Fig. 1. Overview of the proposed mixture of heterogeneous attribute analyzers scheme for action detection

encoded motion features are accumulated to form the action representation, known as bag-of-words method. Local feature selection are sometimes performed. Wang et al. [8] used a latent structural model for adaptively selecting discriminative local features and their contextual information for action recognition. Ryoo and Aggarwal [9] used a spatio-temporal graph model for selecting and matching $3D$ local interest points and their relationship.

Human key pose information has also been considered for action recognition. Yamato et al. [10] proposed a HMM based method for action recognition by matching frame-wise image features. Lv and Nevatia [11] proposed an action recognition method by key pose matching and Viterbi path searching. In Vahdat et al. [12], sequence of key poses are used for recognizing human interactions. In particular, single human key pose sequences and interactions between two humans key poses are modeled in a graphical model for action recognition. The work by Raptis and Sigal [13] (i.e., which is contemporary with our proposed method) attempts to represent an action with several key frames based on poselet [14] representation.

However, as the problem of action detection is very challenging, previous methods which utilize only one types of visual features might not perform optimally. It is obvious that by combining various types of visual features (heterogeneous features) we can obtain complementary discriminative information and achieve better detection performance. For example, local dense motion trajectories are capable of representing some body part's movement, e.g., hand waving; human key pose is very useful in distinguishing those actions with obvious posture, e.g., two persons in shaking hands; also, human global motion trajectory can tell us whether the person is walking, running or standing still. Motivated by these observations, in this work we propose a novel framework that integrates heterogeneous attributes learned from static and dynamic, local and global video features, to boost the action detection performance. In particular, we first detect and track multiple people and extract human key poses and local dense motion trajectories features. Second, we propose a mining method to learn discriminative attributes from three feature modalities: human bounding box trajectory, key pose and local dense motion trajectories. Finally, the learned discriminative attributes are integrated in a latent structural max-margin learning framework which also explores the spatio-temporal relationship between heterogeneous feature attributes. Experiments on the ChaLearn 2014 human action dataset: http://gesture.chalearn.org/[15] demonstrate the superior detection performance of the proposed framework.

The rest of this paper is organized as follows. Section 2 presents some related works. Section 3 presents the proposed mixture of heterogeneous attribute analyzers framework for action detection. Extensive experimental results on the ChaLearn 2014 action detection dataset are given in Section 4. Section 5 concludes the paper.

2   Related Work

Previous works integrate human motion and object appearance as well as human interaction information for action recognition. Gupta and Davis [16] proposed a HMM-like Bayesian graphical model to jointly recognize objects and three types of simple movements including *reaching*, *grasping* and *manipulating*. Escorcia and Niebles [17] proposed to represent dynamics of spatio-temporal human interactions using relative object location and size with respect to the human, as well as overlap between human and object, based on pairs of human and object tracks. Prest et al. [18] explored similar idea of modeling the interaction between human and object trajectories, and they proposed a robust human and object tracking method. Different from these works, we proposed to integrate heterogeneous visual feature attributes including local and global, dynamic and static information for action recognition.

3   Methodology

An overview of the proposed mixture of heterogenous feature analyzer based action detection framework is illustrated in Figure 1. Our contributions are as follows. First, we propose a multiple human tracking method and we develop a set of trajectory based visual attributes which can facilitate action recognition. Second, we propose a discriminative key pose mining method to learn informative pose attributes for action representation. Third, we learn dense motion trajectory based attributes to discover discriminative human body part's movement. Finally, we propose a latent structural learning model which integrates heterogeneous visual attributes along with their spatio-temporal relationship for action detection. Details of various components of the proposed framework are elaborated as follows.

3.1   Global Motion Feature: Human Trajectory

We adopt a tracking-by-detection method for tracking human trajectories locally, i.e., to generate short human tracklets. Human bounding boxes are first detected by HOG-SVM detector [19]. Manually labeled human bounding boxes from the training data are used to train the human detector. We use about 3000 training instances and we randomly select a set of negative (non-human) bounding boxes three times of the number of human samples. The bounding box sizes of the training samples are normalized. A scanning window is applied to each video frame to detect the human, and several scales and aspect ratios are used. To improve the human detection accuracy, we iteratively add hard negative samples (i.e., negative samples with high detection scores) detected from the training frames and re-train the model.

We then temporally track the detected human bounding boxes across frames into short segments, i.e., tracklets, based on pairwise matching of human detections over consecutive frames. To do this, we establish all the human detection matches between frame i and $i + 1$. To match two detections in consecutive frames, the weighted ℓ_2 distance between their HOG representations and X-Y center coordinates is calculated. We impose that for any detection in frame i, there can be at most one candidate match in frame $i + 1$. Those matches which have the length of at least $L_{\min}$ (e.g., 5) frames form human tracklets. To cope with occlusions and missed detections during tracking, we apply an average temporal filter to smooth positions and sizes of the sequence of detected windows, and linear interpolate to fill missed frames.

After we obtain a set of short trajectory segments (tracklets), we spatio-temporally link them into multiple long trajectories for multiple humans in the video. To do this, we first establish the matching between tracklets, using the weighted ℓ_2 distance between their HOG representations and X-Y-T center coordinates between the bounding boxes of the head/tail frames from a pair of tracklets. With n tracklets, we can constructed a $n \times n$ matching graph. We then apply the Hungarian algorithm [20] to obtain the tracked long trajectories.

We then define a set of attributes from the above obtained human bounding box trajectories. Assume each attribute is calculated from a t to $t + T$ temporal window. The attributes defined on a single trajectory include: 1) trajectory length; 2) X-axis moving distance; 3) Y-axis moving distance; 4) mean speed; 5) X-direction mean speed; 6) Y-direction mean speed. The attributes defined on a pair of trajectories include: 1) relative displacement; 2) relative X-axis displacement; 3) relative Y-axis displacement; 4) mean relative speed; 5) mean relative X-direction speed; 6) mean relative Y-direction speed. The final attribute values are obtain by binarizing these values using thresholds: $\phi(x) = I(x > \tau)$, where x denotes one of the above defined values and τ is the empirical threshold value estimated from the training data for each type of attribute (i.e., the threshold value is set by maximizing the class separability). All the threshold values can be found from our published code. [1] We denote the vector of the global human trajectory based attributes as ϕ_G.

---

[1] Our code will be released upon the publication of this work.

3.2   Static Feature: Human Key Pose

As shown in previous works [11–13], human key pose information can be very helpful in distinguishing different actions, since some actions are associated with some distinctive postures. Inspired by the middle level discriminative mining framework proposed in [21], we develop a discriminative key pose discovery method which contains *seeding*, *re-training* and *selection* phases. This method is described as follows.

Seeding. We obtain the seed key poses using the following pipeline. Training samples are annotated with different aspect ratios and sizes. We first perform a *super-clustering* based on K-means according to the aspect ratios of the annotated samples to divide all training samples into several super clusters. The number of super clusters is typically set as 3. Within each super cluster, we normalize sample size and cluster all training samples into different pose clusters according to their HOG features using K-means. We set the initial number of key pose types K to a large number, i.e., $K = 1000$, since we will select discriminative ones in the later processing step. Each cluster is associated with about 3 to 10 samples. We normalize the average aspect ratio for each cluster and train the linear HOG-SVM model associated with this cluster using the one-*vs*-all scheme. Note that although the same pose type can be shared among multiple action categories, in most cases each cluster only contains instances from the same action class due to the fine granularity being used. The obtained K detection models are regarded as seed key pose types.

Re-training. The purpose of the re-training phase is to consolidate the detection model for each candidate key pose. To do this, we iteratively perform the following steps. We use sliding windows of a key pose detector on the training images to obtain candidate bounding boxes. We then add the top ranked (based on the SVM output score) new instances detected from the images of the related classes to the positive training set and those top ranked new instances from the unrelated classed to the negative training sets (as *hard negative*). We then re-train the HOG-SVM detector. This iteration is performed 10 times (i.e., our empirical study shows 10 is enough).

Selection. Finally we use the entropy which was defined in [21] to select distinctive key pose models. In practice, for each action, we retain the top $K = 3$ to $K = 5$ key pose models.

The key pose attributes are defined as $\phi_P(\mathbf{x}) = [\phi^1(\mathbf{x}), \phi^2(\mathbf{x}), \cdots, \phi^K(\mathbf{x})]^T$, where each $\phi^k(\mathbf{x})$ is a linear detection output. $\mathbf{x}$ denotes the HOG features.

3.3   Local Motion Feature: Dense Trajectory

Dense trajectory has shown its great potential in action recognition [7] [22]. We follow the method in [23] to learn discriminative attributes from the bag-of-words representation. The dictionary size is set as 2000. Max pooling is used. For dense trajectory extraction and descriptor computation, we use the toolbox provided in [7] [22]. Besides the learned dense trajectory attributes, based on video observations, two types of additional visual attributes are defined for dense trajectories. These attributes include: 1) normalized trajectory length compared to the human bounding box; and 2) principle orientation of trajectory. Details are provided as follows.

Normalized trajectory length. This attribute is useful for describing the magnitude of movement. For example, small movement during the action *Wave Hands* generates relatively short trajectories, while the action *Crouch Down* and *Jump* generate relatively long trajectories. Mathematically, assuming a trajectory is represented by a series of 2D points $\{(x_t, y_t)\}_{i=1,\cdots,T}$ (i.e., T denotes the number of frames), this attribute is defined as $\sum_{i=2}^{T} \sqrt{(x_i - x_{i-1})^2 + (y_i - y_{i-1})^2}$ /h_{bbox}, where h_{bbox} denotes the height of the detected human bounding box.

Principle orientation of trajectory. Different actions produce different orientated trajectories. For example, actions such as *Wave Hands* and *Clap Hands* mainly produce horizontal orientated trajectories, while *Crouch* and *Jump* will most probably generate vertical ones. The mathematical definition for this attribute is given as: $\sum_{i=2}^{T} |y_i - y_{i-1}|/h_{\text{bbox}}$. Large value means vertical orientated trajectory, and vice versa.

A single trajectory can only provide weak information. Therefore we aggregate the effect of the trajectories in a pooling window, i.e., the number of trajectories with a certain attribute is used for representation. In this work, instead of using a fixed location/scale pooling window, we propose to use a variable pooling window which is shown in Figure 3.

We also design another attribute called **histogram of trajectory points**. As different actions involve different body parts, the densities of trajectories at different positions of the human body varies significantly. Therefore, it is meaningful to use the distribution of dense trajectories for action description. A 3×3 or 5×3 grid on the bounding box of human detection is used to calculate the trajectory point spatial distribution, which is a 9/15-dimensional vector as illustrated in Figure 2. We denote the dense trajectory based attribute vector as ϕ_D.

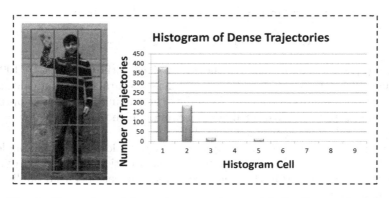

Fig. 2. Illustration of the trajectory point spatial distribution feature

3.4   Heterogeneous Attributes Integration

The above feature extraction step provides us with a set of heterogeneous attributes which contain dynamic and static, local and global visual features. The next step is to seamlessly integrate these attributes for action representation and detection. To this end, we propose a latent structural model for attributes combination. This model not only reflects the discriminative capability of individual attributes, but also encodes the spatio-temporal relationship between different attributes. The model is defined as follows:

$$S(\mathbf{w}, \mathbf{p}, \mathbf{h}) = \mathbf{w}_G^T \boldsymbol{\phi}_G + \mathbf{w}_P^T \boldsymbol{\phi}_P(\mathbf{p}) + \mathbf{w}_D^T \boldsymbol{\phi}_D(\mathbf{h}) + \mathbf{w}_T^T \boldsymbol{\psi}_T(\mathbf{p}) + \mathbf{w}_S^T \boldsymbol{\psi}_S(\mathbf{h}). \quad (1)$$

Each term is explained as follows. $\boldsymbol{\phi}_G$ is the human global trajectory based attribute vector. $\boldsymbol{\phi}_P(\mathbf{p})$ denotes the concatenated HOG key pose representations sampled according to the temporal indices specified by the hidden vector $\mathbf{p}$, i.e., $\mathbf{p} = [t_1; t_2; \cdots; t_K]$ assuming K key poses are selected. $\boldsymbol{\phi}_D(\mathbf{h})$ is the pooled dense motion trajectory based attribute representation and the pooling window is specified by $\mathbf{h}$, i.e., $\mathbf{h} = [dx, dy, dw, dh]$ where (dx, dy) denotes the center offset of the pooling window with reference to the human bounding box and (dw, dh) is the relative width and height of the pooling window with respect to the human bounding box. $\boldsymbol{\psi}_T(\mathbf{p}) = [t_1; t_1^2; t_2; t_2^2; \cdots; t_K; t_K^2]$ measures the temporal configuration of the key poses. $\boldsymbol{\psi}_S(\mathbf{h}) = [dx; dx^2; dy; dy^2; dw; dw^2; dh; dh^2]$ measures the spatial configuration of the dense trajectory attribute pooling window. Please refer to Figure 3 for illustration. The model weights to be learned are defined as $\mathbf{w} = [\mathbf{w}_G; \mathbf{w}_P; \mathbf{w}_D; \mathbf{w}_T; \mathbf{w}_S]$.

The objective function can be rewritten as the linear model $S(\mathbf{w}, \mathbf{p}, \mathbf{h}) = \mathbf{w}^T \boldsymbol{\varphi}(\mathbf{p}, \mathbf{h})$, where $\boldsymbol{\varphi}(\mathbf{p}, \mathbf{h}) = [\boldsymbol{\phi}_G; \boldsymbol{\phi}_P(\mathbf{p}); \boldsymbol{\phi}_D(\mathbf{h}); \boldsymbol{\psi}_T(\mathbf{p}); \boldsymbol{\psi}_S(\mathbf{h})]$. Assume we have N labeled training samples and y^t the corresponding action label for sample t. The model learning problem is formulated as:

$$\min_{\mathbf{w}, \boldsymbol{\xi}} \frac{1}{2} \|\mathbf{w}\|_2^2 + \mathcal{C} \sum_{t=1}^{N} \xi_t,$$
$$s.t. \ \max_{\mathbf{h}, \mathbf{p}} \ \mathbf{w}^T \boldsymbol{\varphi}(\mathbf{p}, \mathbf{h}) \geq 1 - \xi_t, \text{if } \mathbf{y}^t = 1, \xi_t \geq 0, \forall t,$$
$$\mathbf{w}^T \boldsymbol{\varphi}(\hat{\mathbf{p}}, \hat{\mathbf{h}}) \leq -1 + \xi_t, \ \forall \hat{\mathbf{h}}, \hat{\mathbf{p}}, \text{if } \mathbf{y}^t = -1, \xi_t \geq 0, \forall t. \quad (2)$$

Here $\boldsymbol{\xi} = (\xi_1, \xi_2, \cdots, \xi_N)^T$ denotes the set of slack variables and $\mathcal{C} = 1000$ the weighting factor for the constraints. This latent structural SVM model leads to a non-convex optimization problem. We follow the cutting plane based optimization scheme proposed in [24] for model learning, which has been widely used in latent structural learning problems [25] [8].

For action detection, we run temporal sliding windows with variable length (i.e., fixed set of lengths) and optimize the configuration $\mathbf{h}$ and $\mathbf{p}$ by dynamic programming. For detection efficiency, we use a fixed set of spatial pooling window configurations.

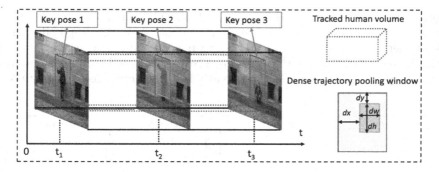

Fig. 3. Illustration of the spatio-temporal relationship encoding used in our proposed latent structural learning formulation. Note that dx, dy, dw, dh are scaled with respect to the human detection bounding box (red).

4   Experiment

In this section, we will provide systematic evaluations on the effectiveness of our proposed attribute learning modules, as well as the entire framework for action detection.

4.1   Dataset

The dataset used for evaluation is the ChaLearn 2014 Track 2 action recognition dataset, which focuses on action/interaction recognition on RGB data. The dataset contains a labeled database of 235 action performances from 17 users. It includes 11 action categories: *Wave, Point, Clap, Crouch, Jump, Walk, Run, Shake Hands, Hug, Kiss,* and *Fight*. Seven sequences are used for training (five training sequences and two validation sequences) and two sequences are used for testing. The training set contains 150 manually labeled action performances as well as a validation dataset with 90 labeled action performances. The final evaluation data (testing set) contains 95 performances.

The evaluation metric used for the Chalearn 2014 dataset is based on the Jaccard Index. Readers who are interested in the details of the metric please refer to the ChaLearn 2014 data description website: http://gesture.chalearn. org/mmdata.

4.2   Heterogenous Attribute Extraction Results

We first show the results of feature extraction for various types (heterogeneous) of visual features including global human trajectory, key pose and dense motion trajectory. Figure 4 visualizes several examples of the tracked multiple human global moving trajectories from the ChaLearn 2014 dataset. Left images (w.r.t the dash line) show the tracked short trajectories and right ones show the linked long trajectories. We annotate different tracklets with different numbers. From

Figure 4 we note that although the proposed multiple human tracking module is very simple, the tracking results are quite reasonable. Also, the proposed tracklet linking method is quite effective and it can remove spurious tracklets. We will see in the rest of the section that the global trajectory based attributes obtained using this proposed tracking method greatly help the action recognition task.

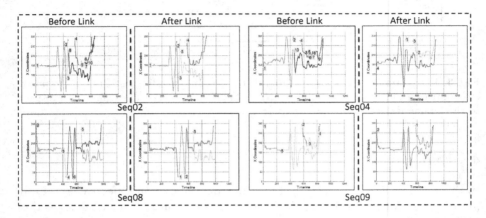

Fig. 4. Examples of the multiple people tracking results in terms of the X direction movement. Images on the left of the dash line show the short tracklets using our human detection and tracking method; images on the right of the dash line show the linked long trajectories of multiple persons using our tracklet matching method.

In Figure 5, we illustrate several examples of the learned discriminative key poses with high entropy values (each column corresponds to the instances belonging to one key pose) using our proposed mining algorithm. We see that these mined key poses are quite consistent within each cluster and they are representative poses for certain actions. For example, the key pose 1, 2, 3,4 well correspond to the action *Kiss/Hug*, *Point*, *Crouch* and *Shake Hands*, respectively. Note that a learned key pose can be shared by more than one action category. We will show in the later experiments that these learned discriminative key poses play an important role in action recognition.

In Figure 6, we show the temporal distributions of several example attributes based on dense motion trajectories on Sequences 04 of the ChaLearn 2014 dataset. X-axis represents the time line and the Y-axis value denotes the number of dense trajectories that possess the concerned attribute. Note that the peaks of attribute 1 and 2 in the left figure correspond to the action *Crouch* and *Sit up* respectively, while the peak of attribute 3 in the right figure corresponds to the action *Jump*. This result shows that extracted dense trajectory based attributes reflect discriminative information.

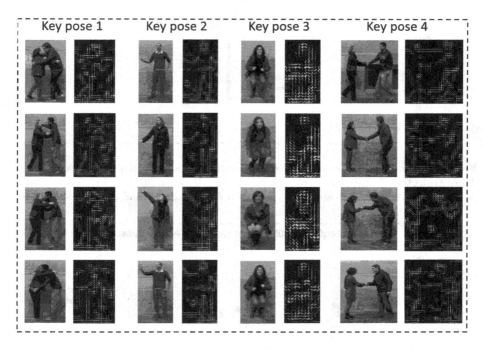

Fig. 5. Examples of the learned discriminative key poses

4.3   Action Detection Results

We compare our method with the state-of-the-art action recognition method, i.e., the dense trajectory method [7] [22]. We use the implementation and the default parameter settings provided by the authors [7] [22]. We do not compare with the recently proposed improved dense trajectory method [26] since on the ChaLearn 2014 dataset, the background motion is ignorable therefore the original dense trajectory method can perform equally well as the improved dense trajectory method. The action recognition comparison result is shown in Figure 7. We note from Figure 7 that the proposed mixture of heterogeneous analyzers method greatly outperforms the dense trajectory based method. This is because that the proposed method seamlessly combines heterogeneous features such as global motion, local dense trajectory and static key pose feature, which explores the complementary nature among all these types of visual features and boosts the recognition performance. On the contrary, using dense trajectory only is not optimal in dealing with some action classes. As can be seen from Figure 7, key pose information is a more discriminative cue for recognizing the action *Hug* and *Shake Hands* as these two classes do not contain rich dense trajectory features. In general, combining various visual feature attributes achieves the best action detection performance. Our final evaluation score on the testing data of ChaLearn 2014 action dataset is 0.501164.

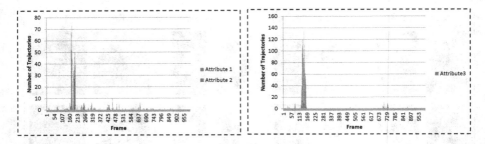

Fig. 6. Temporal distribution (histogram) for three example attributes based on the dense trajectory features on Sequence 04 of the ChaLearn 2014 action dataset. The peaks of distributions correspond to the action *Crouch*, *Sit up* and *Jump*, respectively.

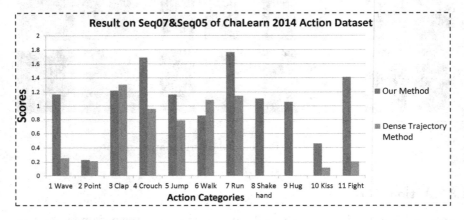

Fig. 7. Per class action recognition performance comparison on the ChaLearn 2014 dataset (testing set). Our final evaluation score on the testing data of ChaLearn 2014 action dataset is 0.501164.

To further unveil the working mechanism of the proposed mixture of heterogeneous analyzers scheme, we conduct a study to evaluate the effectiveness of different components (attributes) of our method including: global human trajectory based attribute, key pose based attribute and dense trajectory based attribute. Namely, for detecting some actions, we disable some types of attributes and evaluate the detection performance drop. The comparison results are shown in Table 1. From Table 1, we note that in general, combining different types of visual attributes achieves much better action recognition performance. For some actions such as *Hug*, key pose based attributes possess discriminative capabilities since almost every two people have the similar way of performing *Hug*. For actions such as *Wave*, dense motion trajectories play an important role in classification. This is because different persons have different ways of pointing with different poses and the more important cue is the local movement induced by hand motion.

Table 1. Action detection performances using different combinations of heterogeneous attributes

Sequence No.	Action	Method	Recall	Accuracy	Score
07	Hug	global trajectory	0.6452	0.2985	0.2564
		global trajectory + key pose	0.6452	1.0000	0.6452
05	Wave	key pose	0.3600	1.0000	0.3600
		key pose + dense trajectory	1.0000	0.8333	0.8333
05	Point	key pose	0.8333	0.1005	0.0985
		key pose + global trajectory	0.8333	0.2500	0.2381

5   Conclusion

We have proposed a mixture of heterogenous feature analyzers scheme that integrates various types of visual features including static and dynamic, local and global features and explores their spatio-temporal relationship, for discriminative action representation. Extensive experiment on the ChaLearn 2014 action datasets demonstrates the effectiveness of the proposed heterogeneous feature integration framework.

Acknowledgments. The study is supported by a research grant for the Human Sixth Sense Programme at the Advanced Digital Sciences Center from Singapore's Agency for Science, Technology and Research(A*STAR).

References

1. Dollar, P., Rabaud, V., Cottrell, G., Belongie, S.: Behavior recognition via sparse spatio-temporal features. In: VS-PETS (2005)
2. Klaser, A., Marszalek, M., Schmid, C.: A spatio-temporal descriptor based on 3d gradients. In: British Machine Vision Conference (2008)
3. Laptev, I., Lindeberg, T.: Space-time interest points. In: International Conference on Computer Vision (2003)
4. Niebles, J.C., Chen, C.-W., Fei-Fei, L.: Modeling temporal structure of decomposable motion segments for activity classification. In: Daniilidis, K., Maragos, P., Paragios, N. (eds.) ECCV 2010, Part II. LNCS, vol. 6312, pp. 392–405. Springer, Heidelberg (2010)
5. Tang, K., Fei-Fei, L., Koller, D.: Learning latent temporal structure for complex event detection. In: International Conference on Computer Vision and Pattern Recognition (2012)
6. Raptis, M., Kokkinos, I., Soatto, S.: Discovering discriminative action parts from mid-level video representations. In: International Conference on Computer Vision and Pattern Recognition (2012)
7. Wang, H., Kläser, A., Schmid, C., Cheng-Lin, L.: Action recognition by dense trajectories. In: International Conference on Computer Vision and Pattern Recognition, pp. 3169–3176 (2011)
8. Wang, Y., Mori, G.: Hidden part models for human action recognition: Probabilistic versus max margin. IEEE Transactions on Pattern Analysis and Machine Intelligence **33**(7), 1310–1323 (2011)

9. Ryoo, M.S., Aggarwal, J.: Spatio-temporal relationship match: video structure comparison for recognition of complex human activities. In: International Conference on Computer Vision, pp. 1593–1600 (2009)
10. Yamato, J., Ohya, J., Ishii, K.: Recognizing human action in time-sequential images using hidden markov model. In: International Conference on Computer Vision and Pattern Recognition, pp. 379–385 (1992)
11. Lv, F., Nevatia, R.: Single view human action recognition using key pose matching and viterbi path searching. In: International Conference Computer Vision and Pattern Recognition (2007)
12. Vahdat, A., Gao, B., Ranjbar, M., Mori, G.: A discriminative key pose sequence model for recognizing human interactions. In: ICCV Workshop, pp. 1729–1736 (2011)
13. Raptis, M., Sigal, L.: Poselet key-framing: A model for human activity recognition. In: International Conference on Computer Vision and Pattern Recognition, pp. 2650–2657 (2013)
14. Bourdev, L., Malik, J.: Poselets: body part detectors trained using 3d human pose annotations. In: International Conference on Computer Vision (2009)
15. Snchez, D., Bautista, M., Escalera, S.: Hupba 8k+: Dataset and ecoc-graphcut based segmentation of human limbs. Neurocomputing (2014)
16. Gupta, A., Davis, L.: Objects in action: an approach for combining action understanding and object perception. In: IEEE Conference on Computer Vision and Pattern Recognition (2007)
17. Escorcia, V., Niebles, J.: Spatio-temporal human-object interactions for action recognition in videos. In: IEEE International Conference on Computer Vision Workshops (ICCVW), pp. 508–514 (2013)
18. Prest, A., Ferrari, V., Schmid, C.: Explicit modeling of human-object interactions in realistic videos. IEEE Transactions on Pattern Analysis and Machine Intelligence 35(4), 835–848 (2013)
19. Dalal, N., Triggs, B.: Histograms of oriented gradients for human detection. In: International Conference on Computer Vision and Pattern Recognition, pp. 886–893 (2005)
20. Kuhn, H.W.: The hungarian method for the assignment problem. Naval Research Logistics Quarterly 2, 83–97 (1955)
21. Juneja, M., Vedaldi, A., Jawahar, C.V., Zisserman, A.: Blocks that shout: distinctive parts for scene classification. In: IEEE Conference on Computer Vision and Pattern Recognition (2013)
22. Wang, H., Kläser, A., Schmid, C., Liu, C.L.: Dense trajectories and motion boundary descriptors for action recognition. International Journal of Computer Vision 103(1), 60–79 (2013)
23. Liu, J., Kuipers, B., Savarese, S.: Recognizing human actions by attributes. In: IEEE Conference on Computer Vision and Pattern Recognition, pp. 3337–3344 (2011)
24. Joachims, T., Finley, T., Yu, C.N.J.: Cutting-plane training of structural svms. Machine Learning 77(1), 27–59 (2009)
25. Felzenszwalb, P.F., Girshick, R.B., McAllester, D., Ramanan, D.: Object detection with discriminatively trained part based models. IEEE Transactions on Pattern Analysis and Machine Intelligence 32(9), 1627–1645 (2010)
26. Wang, H., Schmid, C.: Action recognition with improved trajectories. In: International Conference on Computer Vision (2013)

Action Detection with Improved Dense Trajectories and Sliding Window

Zhixin Shu[(✉)], Kiwon Yun, and Dimitris Samaras

Stony Brook University, Stony Brook, NY 11794, USA
{zhshu,kyun,samaras}@cs.stonybrook.edu

Abstract. In this paper we describe an action/interaction detection system based on improved dense trajectories [19], multiple visual descriptors and bag-of-features representation. Given that the actions/interactions are not mutual exclusive, we train a binary classifier for every predefined action/interaction. We rely on a non-overlapped temporal sliding window to enable the temporal localization. We have tested our system in ChaLearn Looking at People Challenge 2014 Track 2 dataset [1,2]. We obtained 0.4226 average overlap, which is the 3rd place in the track of the challenge. Finally, we provide an extensive analysis of the performance of this system on different actions and provide possible ways to improve a general action detection system.

Keywords: Video analysis · Action recognition · Action detection · Dense trajectories

1 Introduction

Human activity analysis has received considerable attention over the last two decades [3,4]. It is important in many computer vision applications, including video surveillance, content-based video retrieval, human computer interactions, etc. Early attempts on this problem focused on simple actions performed by a single person (e.g. walking, waving and hopping) [5–8]. However, most recent research has been extended to more complex activities such as actions in daily life [9,10], and interactions between multiple persons or objects [11–14]. Much of the state-of-the-art work in action recognition is based on local spatiotemporal features [15,16], trajectories [17–20] or mid-level features [21–23] (e.g. pose and parts).

The ChaLearn Looking at People (LAP) Challenge 2014 [1] is designed to encourage researchers to evaluate and optimize most recent techniques from three different tracks such as human body pose recovery, action and interaction recognition, and gesture recognition. This work is our participation of the Track 2 - action/interaction recognition on RGB data. The Challenge provides videos of 235 action performances from 17 users corresponding to 11 action categories including both natural isolated activities performed by a single person (e.g. waving, pointing, walking, etc.) and interactions between multiple persons

© Springer International Publishing Switzerland 2015
L. Agapito et al. (Eds.): ECCV 2014 Workshops, Part I, LNCS 8925, pp. 541–551, 2015.
DOI: 10.1007/978-3-319-16178-5_38

(e.g. shaking-hands, hugging, fighting, etc.). The goal of the challenge is to recognize the performing action in videos by labeling each frame as an action category. To achieve this goal, we used improved dense trajectory features proposed by Wang and Schmid [19], and applied a sliding window fashion. Even though improved dense trajectory features provide the state-of-the-art performance on a variety of datasets for action classification [19,23,24], applying the feature for temporal localization using a sliding window is not well explored. We show this simple approach can perform well in the ChaLearn LAP dataset. The average Jaccard index obtained on the testing set is 0.4226, which we achieved 3rd place in the challenge.

2   Detecting Actions in Video with Improved Trajectories

In this section, we describe the framework and method of the system that we use for action detection. On the basis of trajectory features, feature descriptors and bag-of-features coding method, we train a binary SVM for every action that is previously defined. All the classifiers are trained independently. A sliding window is applied for the purpose of localizing actions.

2.1   System Framework

The framework of the system is illustrated in Fig.1. In both training and testing stage, we apply a temporal sliding window on the video data to generate video segments. The training data are human-labeled videos where the labels are the actions/interactions in the video and the exact time when it takes place. From the training set, we extract and process the visual features, according to which binary classifier is independently trained for each action. At the stage of testing, the same process of sliding window and feature extraction is applied on the unlabeled video. The trained classifiers are used to detect the existence of every action in each video segment.

2.2   Visual Features

Video data is usually in large size and contains redundant information. Most information in the image sequences is background and noise. To recognize human actions in videos, we shall use compact and efficient features to represent the information that we are interested in.

Videos are essentially image sequences which can be seen as pixels aligned in 3D space, which consists of 2 dimensions in the image and a third dimension of time. The space-time interest points[16] is a natural generalization of the local image feature of interest points from 2D to the 3D space. The basic idea is to make use of the idea from 2D interest points like Harris[25] corners and generalize it to 3D case. Laptev[16] showed that STIP features can capture some interesting events in spatial-temporal spaces that can be used for a compact representation of video data as well as for interpretation of spatio-temporal events.

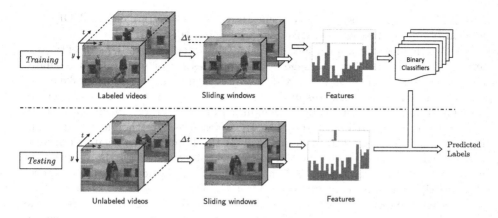

Fig. 1. The framework for action detection

Another successful feature for video representation is dense trajectory[18] proposed by Wang et al. In this approach, dense points are sampled from each frame in videos and tracked on a dense optical flow field. Dense trajectory features are able to cover most of the motion features of a video and therefore can be used as a tool to capture the motion patterns and the local features of motions together with local image features. A main problem about trajectory-based features is that trajectories also capture the camera motion. The trajectories generated by actions or events will be severely affected by the camera motion trajectories. There are works trying to separate the trajectories from action in the video with the trajectories brought by camera movement. On the basis of dense trajectory, Jain et al.[26] proposed a variation by decomposing visual motion into dominant and residual motions. Wang's improved dense trajectories[19] provided a SURF feature based camera motion compensation method to address the problem.

In our system, we use the improved dense trajectories[19] as visual features for action classification. The type of feature we used is selected experimentally. We have tested STIP features, dense trajectories and improved dense trajectories on the ChaLearn LAP dataset, and the improved dense trajectories perform better than other features. The camera is mostly static in ChaLearn LAP dataset where the trajectory features generally performs better than STIP features on capturing actions. Few video clips in the dataset contain camera shake. Comparing to the original dense trajectories, the improved trajectories compensate on camera movement, which aids in the suppression of camera shake artifacts.

2.3   Action Representation

Features like space-time interest points or trajectories contain the information of events or motion patterns in videos. However, in order to use such feature information for the task of classification, we should find a way to describe the features. Similar to previous works[18][19][26], the visual descriptors used in our system, including Histogram of gradient(HOG)[27], histogram of flow(HOF)[28], motion boundary histograms(MBH)[29] and dense trajectories[19].

HOG encodes the appearance by using the intensity gradient orientations and magnitudes. HOG is an image appearance descriptor which is not formally used as motion description in the video. However, it is also useful to make a distinction of local image features in the video since the descriptor is based on the position of features. Moreover, for human action recognition, most features are located at the human body area. The HOG features are, therefore, capturing human appearances in the frame as well as the human pose related information, which is also a strong cue for action classification. HOF is a statistical description of the orientation and magnitude of the optical flow field. Hence, this descriptor mainly captures the motion information between frames. MBH is designed to capture the gradient of horizontal and vertical components of the flow. The motion boundary encodes the relative pixel motion and, therefore, suppresses camera motion. In the trajectory based method, the trajectory itself plays a significant role which encodes the shape of the trajectory represented by normalized relative coordinates of the successive points forming the trajectory. This description depends on the dense flow used for tracking points.

Feature coding is the final step of action representation in our system, which unifies the form of the representations by building statistics upon the descriptors. Bag-of-features representation is widely used in the context of action detection in computer vision. It is originated from the natural language processing field that they use bag-of-words to represent documents. On the basis of visual descriptors computed from the training set, we constructed the bag-of-features codebook with k-means clustering. There are two ways to build bag-of-features from multiple descriptors. One is building separate codebook for every descriptor and concatenate the coding result for every video segment to form the representation. The other way is to concatenate the descriptors of a feature as one big descriptor and build the codebook upon that. By experimental comparisons between two methods with different vocabulary size, we decide to use the second way to construct bag-of-features and the size of the feature dictionary is determined to be 4096.

2.4   From Recognition to Detection

The action detection is built upon an action classification procedure that not only predicts the labels of actions in videos but also their time and duration. In the system, we use a non-overlapped sliding window to locate the time of actions in video. A video, as shown in Fig.1, can be seen as a 3D image volume. The sliding window is applied on the time direction to segment out a series of video segments of length Δt. We train classifiers on the video segments generated from training data. During testing, we predict on the same length of video segments. Therefore, $1/\Delta t$ can be seen as the temporal resolution of the system. Since the unit represents a temporal position in the video, it will be included as a part of the detection results which tells us when does the actions/interactions take place.

There are two problems about the sliding window approach: 1) how to decide the size of window, and 2) how to label the video segments.

The size of the sliding window Δt is related to the temporal scale of the temporal feature that we extracted. In trajectory features, it is associated with the length of the trajectories. However, the length of trajectories is upper bounded but not necessarily fixed. Therefore, the choice of Δt is made in the validation stage as a model parameter. On the other hand, different actions entail different motion patterns and the model for every action is trained independently, so the optimal Δt for every action is not necessarily the same.

The bag-of-features representation is a feature statistic constructed on a video segment of length Δt. However, in training data, the actions are not labeled with a fixed length. The length of continuous frame sequences labeled as one action varies from 7 to more than 40. In our system, we do not align the video segments to action labels because the start and end of actions are unknown in testing data.

The training and prediction of every action is conducted independently. For an action A and a video segment V, where V_i represents the ith frame of V such that $1 \leq i \leq \Delta t$. The video segment V is labeled $+1$ for action A if there exists i such that V_i is labeled $+1$ for action A. Otherwise V is labeled -1 for action A. During training, we build a bag-of-features representation for every action in every video segment. If V is labeled -1 for action A, the BoF representation is the statistics of feature descriptions from all the trajectories in all frames V_i where $1 \leq i \leq \Delta t$. If V is labeled $+1$, the BoF representation is the statistics of feature descriptions from the frames which are labeled $+1$. During testing, since no label is given, we build the BoF of a video segment with the descriptors in all frames. The classifiers will predict a video segment with a single label, either positive or negative, for every action. We assign the predicted label of the video segment to every frame in it as the result of detection.

3 Experiments

In this section, we show the experimental result of our system on ChaLearn LAP dataset[2].

3.1 Dataset

The data consists of 9 videos, each of which is approximately 60 seconds long. 7 videos are used for training and 2 are used for testing. In these videos, 235 performances from 17 users corresponding to 11 action/interactions categories are recorded and manually labeled. The categories include *Wave, Point, Clap, Crouch, Jump, Walk, Run, Shake Hands, Hug, Kiss,* and *Fight*. Actions are performed by one or more actors at the same time, meaning that the vocabulary of 11 actions is formed by either single actor or multiple actor actions.

3.2   Result and Analysis

The evaluation method is Jaccard index which is defined as

$$J_i = \frac{T_i \cap P_i}{T_i \cup P_i} \tag{1}$$

For the ith action, the Jaccard of our detection system J_i is the overlap of the human labeled ground truth T_i and system prediction P_i in the test video sequences. The average Jaccard index is the algebraic average of J_i of all actions. In the ChaLearn dataset, the chance of overlap is around 0.06.

Kernel SVMs are used as classifiers for the system. Since the actions are not mutually exclusive, we train classifiers for each action in a one vs. all fashion. There are 11 actions in this dataset, therefore, we train 11 SVMs for each of the actions independently. The BoF statistics of every labeled video segments are normalized and used to train the SVMs. The kernel used is RBF-χ^2 kernel and the regularization as well as the window size is determined by validation data. We choose $\Delta t = 15$ and $C = 100$ in SVM for all actions.

The average Jaccard index obtained from our system on the testing set (Seq05 and Seq07) of ChaLearn LAP data is 0.4226. Table 1 shows the Jaccard value we obtained for all actions and their average.

Table 1. Detection results by Jaccard index. While shake-hands, crouch, jump and walk have higher accuracy, kiss, hug, point have lower accuracy.

Wave	Point	Clap	Crouch	Jump	Walk
0.4691	0.2907	0.3267	0.5441	0.5224	0.5064
Run	Shake hands	Hug	Kiss	Fight	**Average**
0.4886	0.5610	0.2883	0.1616	0.4892	**0.4226**

Examples of detection results of our system on test data can be found in Fig. 2 (correct detections) and Fig. 3 (incorrect detections). In our observations, *point* is one of the most difficult action category to detect among all 11 actions given in the data set. For example, in Fig 3-(4), no label is returned when the actor is *pointing*. In Fig 3-(7), *point* is detected as both *wave* and *point*. In Fig 3-(2), *wave* is detected as both *wave* and *point*. The interaction *kissing* is also a difficult case. In Fig. 3-(8) *kiss* is detected as *hug*. There are two reasons why some pairs of actions are confused each other. The first is the motion patterns of these actions are very similar to each other, but our features are based on motion tracking. The other reason is there exists some confusion between actions similar on human pose. For example, *point* and *wave* are more similar to each other on human pose than any other actions. Similarly, *hug* and *kiss* are similar on pose. In our system, the pose information captured by local image descriptors (HOG) also plays an important role in classifying actions.

Another interesting incorrect detection result is between *walk* and *run*. These two actions are rarely confused with other actions but often detected at the same

Fig. 2. Correct detection results. The blue labels at the left of the frame are the human labeled ground truth provided in the dataset. At the right side, the red labels reflect the detection result computed by our system.

time, as showed in Fig. 3-(3). Intuitively, *walk* and *run* have a similar motion pattern. The main difference between them is on the velocity of motion and pose. The poses of *walk* and *run* are more closer to each other compared with other actions. This observation tells us that the trajectory-like features might be strong in differentiating *walk* and *run* with other actions but not between these two. It might be helpful to build a hierarchy of classifiers or make use of other features to classify between *walk* and *run*. Considering the objective actions/iterations we are handling in this system, two actions can be performed at the same time, meaning that some actions/interactions are not mutually-exclusive. For example,

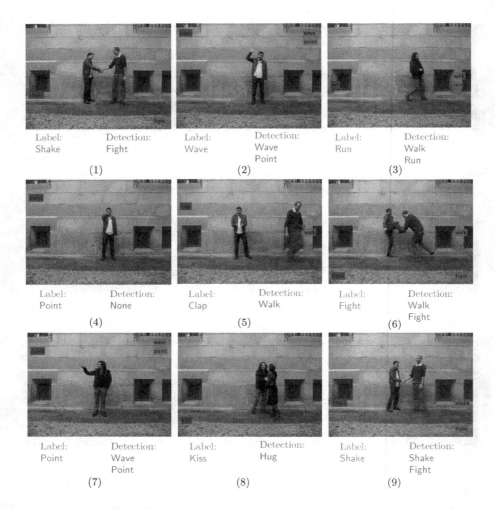

Fig. 3. Incorrect detection results. The blue labels at the left of the frame are the human labeled ground truth provided in the dataset. At the right side, the red labels reflect the detection result computed by our system.

as shown in Fig. 2-(2), two people are *walking* and *shaking* at the same time. That is why we use 11 binary classifiers instead of one multi-class classifier in our system. However, some actions/interactions are very unlikely to appear together. For example, for a single person, it is very unusual to walk and run at the same time. This is a human experience imposed prior. Practically, we can include this prior to the system, but it also will be interesting to automatically discover the exclusiveness of actions from data and build the detection system with a hierarchical structure. We will leave this as a future work.

In Fig. 3-(5), we show a result where the action was labeled with *clap* but detected as *walk*. However, as we can see from the frame, one person is *clapping* and the other is *walking* in the scene. We should notice that even the human labeling is not perfect, but still this is a failure case in our system because the *clap* is not detected. In our system, we take the statistics related to all the motions detected, which does not depend on the number or location of objects in the scene. When the scene contains more than one action, it might be useful to make use of a human detection system to improve performance.

4   Conclusion

We implement a supervised action/interaction detection system to participate in the 2014 ChaLearn LAP challenge. Our framework for detecting actions in videos is improved dense trajectories-based action classification applied on a sliding window fashion. We independently trained 11 one-versus-all kernel SVMs on the labeled training set for 11 different actions. The feature and feature descriptions we used are improved dense trajectories, HOG, HOF, MBHx and MBHy.

We have discussed two possible directions for future work in the last section where we suggest that it will be interesting to automatically discover the dependencies of actions and make use of human detectors to improve the performance. Besides that, future work could be on understanding the actions not only using motion but also many other properties of the action. For example, people can recognize actions from single image without motion information, which indicates that the human posture and the image background are strong cues for humans to understand actions. On the other hand, the detection of action from video data does not necessarily rely on a sliding window. There are researchers[30] show work on detect a sparse key frames from video and uses them to represent video events.

Acknowledgments. The implementation of kernel SVMs that we use is Krzysztof Sopylas chi-square kernel implementation[1] which is build on the basis of libsvm[2]. For the computation of features and feature descriptions, we directly use the code of improved dense trajectories from Heng Wang [3].

This work was partially supported by NSF IIS-1161876, IIS-1111047, NIH R21 DA034954 and the DIGITEO Institute, France.

References

1. Escalera, S., et al.: ChaLearn looking at people challenge 2014: dataset and results. In: Bronstein, M., Agapito, L., Rother, C. (eds.) Computer Vision - ECCV 2014 Workshops. LNCS, vol. 8925, pp. 459–473. Springer, Heidelberg (2015)

---

[1] http://wmii.uwm.edu.pl/~ksopyla/projects/libsvm-with-chi-squared-kernel/
[2] http://www.csie.ntu.edu.tw/~cjlin/libsvm
[3] https://lear.inrialpes.fr/people/wang/improved_trajectories

2. Snchez, D., Bautista, M., Escalera, S.: HuPBA 8k+: Dataset and ECOC-GraphCut based Segmentation of Human Limbs. Neurocomputing (2014)
3. Poppe, R.: A survey on vision-based human action recognition. Image and Vision Computing **28**(6), 976–990 (2010)
4. Aggarwal, J., Ryoo, M.: Human activity analysis: A review. ACM Comput. Surv. **43**(3), 16:1–16:43 (2011)
5. Blank, M., Gorelick, L., Shechtman, E., Irani, M., Basri, R.: Actions as space-time shapes. In: Proceedings of the International Conference On Computer Vision, ICCV (2005)
6. Dollár, P., Rabaud, V., Cottrell, G., Belongie, S.: Behavior recognition via sparse spatio-temporal features. In: 2nd Joint IEEE International Workshop on Visual Surveillance and Performance Evaluation of Tracking and Surveillance, PETS (2005)
7. Niebles, J., Wang, H., Fei-Fei, L.: Unsupervised learning of human action categories using spatial-temporal words. International Journal of Computer Vision **79**(3), 299–318 (2008)
8. Schuldt, C., Laptev, I., Caputo, B.: Recognizing human actions: a local svm approach. In: Proceedings of the 17th International Conference on Pattern Recognition, ICPR (2004)
9. Messing, R., Pal, C., Kautz, H.: Activity recognition using the velocity histories of tracked keypoints. In: Proceedings of the International Conference On Computer Vision, ICCV (2009)
10. Kuehne, H., Jhuang, H., Garrote, E., Poggio, T., Serre, T.: Hmdb: a large video database for human motion recognition. In: Proceedings of the International Conference On Computer Vision, ICCV (2011)
11. Ayazoglu, M., Yilmaz, B., Sznaier, M., Camps, O.: Finding causal interactions in video sequences. In: Proceedings of the International Conference On Computer Vision, ICCV (2013)
12. Ryoo, M.S., Aggarwal, J.K.: Spatio-temporal relationship match: video structure comparison for recognition of complex human activities. In: Proceedings of the International Conference On Computer Vision, ICCV (2009)
13. Yun, K., Honorio, J., Chattopadhyay, D., Berg, T.L., Samaras, D.: Two-person interaction detection using body-pose features and multiple instance learning. In: IEEE Conference on Computer Vision and Pattern Recognition Workshops, CVPRW (2012)
14. Yao, B., Fei-Fei, L.: Modeling mutual context of object and human pose in human-object interaction activities. In: IEEE Conference on Computer Vision and Pattern Recognition, CVPR (2010)
15. Wang, H., Ullah, M.M., Kläser, A., Laptev, I., Schmid, C.: Evaluation of local spatio-temporal features for action recognition. In: British Machine Vision Conference, BMVC (2009)
16. Laptev, I.: On space-time interest points. International Journal of Computer Vision **64**(2-3), 107–123 (2005)
17. Ali, S., Basharat, A., Shah, M.: Chaotic invariants for human action recognition. In: Proceedings of the International Conference On Computer Vision, ICCV (2007)
18. Wang, H., Kläser, A., Schmid, C., Liu, C.L.: Action recognition by dense trajectories. In: IEEE Conference on Computer Vision and Pattern Recognition, CVPR (2011)
19. Wang, H., Schmid, C.: Action recognition with improved trajectories. In: Proceedings of the International Conference On Computer Vision, ICCV (2013)

20. Fathi, A., Mori, G.: Action recognition by learning mid-level motion features. In: IEEE Conference on Computer Vision and Pattern Recognition, CVPR (2008)
21. Raptis, M., Kokkinos, I., Soatto, S.: Discovering discriminative action parts from mid-level video representations. In: IEEE Conference on Computer Vision and Pattern Recognition, CVPR (2012)
22. Zhang, W., Zhu, M., Derpanis, K.: From actemes to action: a strongly-supervised representation for detailed action understanding. In: Proceedings of the International Conference On Computer Vision, ICCV (2013)
23. Oneata, D., Verbeek, J., Schmid, C.: Efficient action localization with approximately normalized fisher vectors. In: IEEE Conference on Computer Vision and Pattern Recognition, CVPR (2014)
24. Simonyan, K., Zisserman, A.: Two-Stream Convolutional Networks for Action Recognition in Videos. arXiv:1406.2199v1 (2014)
25. Harris, C., Stephens, M.: A combined corner and edge detector. In: Alvey Vision Conference, vol. 15, p. 50 (1988)
26. Jain, M., Jgou, H., Bouthemy, P.: Better exploiting motion for better action recognition. In: IEEE Conference on Computer Vision and Pattern Recognition, CVPR (2013)
27. Dalal, N., Triggs, B.: Histograms of oriented gradients for human detection. In: IEEE Conference on Computer Vision and Pattern Recognition, CVPR (2005)
28. Laptev, I., Marszaek, M., Schmid, C., Rozenfeld, B.: Learning realistic human actions from movies. In: IEEE Conference on Computer Vision and Pattern Recognition, CVPR (2008)
29. Dalal, N., Triggs, B., Schmid, C.: Human detection using oriented histograms of flow and appearance. In: Leonardis, A., Bischof, H., Pinz, A. (eds.) ECCV 2006. LNCS, vol. 3952, pp. 428–441. Springer, Heidelberg (2006)
30. Raptis, M., Sigal, L.: Poselet key-framing: a model for human activity recognition. In: IEEE Conference on Computer Vision and Pattern Recognition, CVPR (2013)

Deep Dynamic Neural Networks
for Gesture Segmentation and Recognition

Di Wu$^{(\boxtimes)}$ and Ling Shao

The University of Sheffield, Sheffield, UK
stevenwudi@gmail.com, ling.shao@ieee.org

Abstract. The purpose of this paper is to describe a novel method called Deep Dynamic Neural Networks *(DDNN)* for the Track 3 of the Chalearn Looking at People 2014 challenge [1]. A generalised semi-supervised hierarchical dynamic framework is proposed for simultaneous gesture segmentation and recognition taking both skeleton and depth images as input modules. First, Deep Belief Networks *(DBN)* and 3D Convolutional Neural Networks *(3DCNN)* are adopted for skeletal and depth data accordingly to extract high level spatio-temporal features. Then the learned representations are used for estimating emission probabilities of the Hidden Markov Models to infer an action sequence. The framework can be easily extended by including an ergodic state to segment and recognise video sequences by a frame-to-frame mechanism, rendering it possible for online segmentation and recognition for diverse input modules. Some normalisation details pertaining to preprocessing raw features are also discussed. This purely data-driven approach achieves *0.8162* score in this gesture spotting challenge. The performance is on par with a variety of the state-of-the-art hand-tuned-feature approaches and other learning-based methods, opening the doors for using deep learning techniques to explore time series multimodal data.

Keywords: Deep Belief Networks · 3D Convolutional Neural Networks · Gesture recognition · ChaLearn

1 Introduction

In recent years, human action recognition has drawn increasing attention of researchers, primarily due to its growing potential in areas such as video surveillance, robotics, human-computer interaction, user interface design, and multimedia video retrieval.

Previous works on video-based motion recognition focused on adapting handcrafted features and low-level hand-designed features [2–4] have been heavily employed with much success. These methods usually have two stages: an optional feature detection stage followed by a feature description stage. Well-known feature detection methods ("interest point detectors") are Harris3D [5], Cuboids [6] and Hessian3D [7]. For descriptors, popular methods are Cuboids [8], HOG/HOF [5], HOG3D [9] and Extended SURF [7]. In a recent work of Wang *et*

© Springer International Publishing Switzerland 2015
L. Agapito et al. (Eds.): ECCV 2014 Workshops, Part I, LNCS 8925, pp. 552–571, 2015.
DOI: 10.1007/978-3-319-16178-5_39

al. [10], dense trajectories with improved motion-based descriptors epitomized the pinnacle of handcrafted features and achieved state-of-the-art results on a variety of "in the wild" datasets. Given the current trends, challenges and interests in action recognition, this list would probably continue to spread out extensively. The very high-dimensional dense-trajectory features usually require advanced dimensionality reduction techniques [11,12] to make them applicable.

In the evaluation paper of Wang *et al.* [13], one interesting finding is that there is no universally best hand-engineered feature for all datasets, suggesting that learning features directly from the dataset itself may be more advantageous. Albeit the dominant methodology for visual recognition from images and videos relies on hand-crafted features, there has been a growing interest in methods that learn low-level and mid-level features, either in supervised, unsupervised, or semi-supervised settings [14–16].

With the recent resurgence of neural networks invoked by Hinton and others [17], deep neural architectures have been proposed as an effective solution for extracting high level features from data. Deep artificial neural networks (including the family of recurrent neural networks) have won numerous contests in pattern recognition and representation learning. Schmidhuber [18] compiled a historical survey compactly summarising relevant works with more than 850 entries of credited works. Such models have been successfully applied to a plethora of different domains: the GPU-based cuda-convnet [19] classifies 1.2 million high-resolution images into 1000 different classes; multi-column Deep Neural Networks [20] achieve near-human performance on the handwritten digits and traffic signs recognition benchmarks; 3D Convolutional Neural Networks [21,22] recognize human actions in surveillance videos; Deep Belief Networks combining with Hidden Markov Models [23,24] for acoustic and skeletal joints modeling outperform the decade-dominating paradigm of Gaussian Mixture Models+Hidden Markov Models. In these fields, deep architectures have shown great capacity to discover and extract higher level relevant features.

However, direct and unconstrained learning of complex problems is difficult, since (i) the amount of required training data increases steeply with the complexity of the prediction model and (ii) training highly complex models with very general learning algorithms is extremely difficult. It is therefore common practice to restrain the complexity of the model and this is generally done by operating on small patches to reduce the input dimension and diversity [16], or by training the model in an unsupervised manner [15], or by forcing the model parameters to be identical for different input locations (as in convolutional neural networks [19–21]).

With the immense popularity of Kinect [25,26], there has been renewed interest in developing methods for human gesture and action recognition from 3D skeletal data and depth images. A number of new datasets [27–30] have provided researchers with the opportunity to design novel representations and algorithms and test them on a much larger number of sequences. It may seem that the task of action recognition given 3D joint positions is trivial, but this is not the case, largely due to the high dimensionality of the pose space. Furthermore, to achieve continuous action recognition, the sequence need to be segmented into contiguous action segments; such segmentation is as important as recognition itself and is often neglected in action recognition research.

In this paper, a data driven framework is proposed, focusing on analysis of acyclic video sequence labeling problems, *i.e.*, video sequences are non-repetitive as opposed to longer repetitive activities, *e.g.*, jogging, walking and running.

2   Experiments and Analysis

2.1   Chalearn LAP Dataset and Evaluation Metrics

This dataset[1] is on "multiple instance, user independent learning and continuous gesture spotting" [27] of gestures. And in the 3 track, there are more than 14,000 gestures are drawn from a vocabulary of 20 Italian cultural/anthropological sign gesture categories with 700 sample sequences for training and validation and 240 sample sequences for testing.

The evaluation criteria for this track is the *Jaccard* index (overlap) on a frame-to-frame basis.

$$J(A, B) = \frac{A \bigcap B}{A \bigcup B}$$

2.2   Model Architecture: Deep Dynamic Neural Networks

Inspired by the framework successfully applied to the speech recognition [23], the proposed model borrows the idea of a data driven learning system, relying on a pure learning approach in which all the knowledge in the model comes from the data without sophisticated pre-processing or dimensionality reduction. The proposed Deep Dynamic Neural Networks *(DDNN)* can be seen as an extension to [24] in that instead of only using the Restricted Boltzmann Machines to model human motion, various connectivity layers, *e.g.*, fully connected layers, convolutional layers, *etc.*, are stacked together to learn higher level features justified by a variational bound [17] from different input modules.

A continuous-observation HMM with discrete hidden states is adopted for modelling higher level temporal relationships. At each time step t, we have one random observation variable X_t. Additionally we have an unobserved variable H_t taking values of a finite set $\mathcal{H} = (\bigcup_{a \in \mathcal{A}} \mathcal{H}_a)$, where $\mathcal{H}_a$ is a set of states associated to an individual action $\boldsymbol{a}$ by force-alignment scheme defined in Sec. 2.4. The intuition motivating this construction is that an action is composed of a sequence of poses where the relative duration of each pose may vary. This variance is captured by allowing flexible forward transitions within the chain. With this definitions, the full probability model is now specified as HMM:

$$p(H_{1:T}, X_{1:T}) = p(H_1)p(X_1|H_1) \prod_{t=2}^{T} p(X_t|H_t)p(H_t|H_{t-1}), \tag{1}$$

---

[1] http://gesture.chalearn.org/homewebsourcereferrals

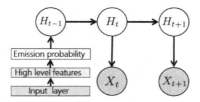

Fig. 1. Per-action model: a forward-linked chain. Inputs (skeletal features or depth image features) are first passed through Deep Neural Nets (Deep Belief Networks for skeletal modality or 3D Convolutional Neural Networks for depth modality) to extract high level features. The outputs are the emission probabilities of the hidden states.

where $p(H_1)$ is the prior on the first hidden state; $p(H_t|H_{t-1})$ is the transition dynamics model and $p(X_t|H_t)$ is the emission probability modelled by the deep neural nets.

The motivation for using deep neural nets to model marginal distribution is that by constructing multi-layer networks, semantically meaningful high level features will be extracted whilst learning the parametric prior of human pose from mass pool of data. In the recent work of [31], a non-parametric bayesian network is adopted for human pose prior estimation, whereas in the proposed framework, the parametric networks are incorporated. The graphical representation of a per-action model is shown as Fig. 1.

2.3   *ES-HMM*: Simultaneous Segmentation and Recognition

The aforementioned framework can be easily adapted for simultaneous action segmentation and recognition by adding an ergodic states-$\mathcal{ES}$ which resembles the silence state for speech recognition. Hence, the unobserved variable H_t takes an extra finite set $\mathcal{H} = (\bigcup_{a\in\mathcal{A}} \mathcal{H}_a)\bigcup \mathcal{ES}$, where $\mathcal{ES}$ is the ergodic state as the resting position between actions and we refer the model as *ES-HMM*.

Since our goal is to capture the variation in speed of performing gestures, we set the transitions in the following way: when being in a particular node n in time t, moving to time $t+1$, we can either stay in the same node (slower performance), move to node $n+1$ (the same speed of performance), or move to node $n+2$ (faster performance). From the $\mathcal{ES}$ we can move to the first three nodes of any gesture class, and from the last three nodes of any gesture class we can move to the $\mathcal{ES}$ as shown in Fig. 2. The *ES-HMM* framework differs from the Firing Hidden Markov Model of [32] in that we strictly follow the temporal independent assumption, forbidding inter-states transverse, preconditioned that a non-repetitive sequence would maintain its unique states throughout its performing cycle.

The emission probability of the trained model is represented as a matrix of size $N_{TC} \times N_{\mathcal{F}}$ where $N_{\mathcal{F}}$ is the number of frames in a test sequence and output target class $N_{TC} = N_{\mathcal{A}} \times N_{\mathcal{H}_a} + 1$ where $N_{\mathcal{A}}$ is the number of action class and $N_{\mathcal{H}_a}$ is the number of states associated to an individual action a and one $\mathcal{ES}$ state. Once we have the trained model, we can use the normal online

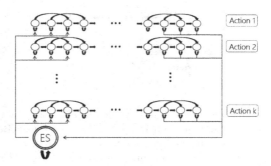

Fig. 2. State diagram of the *ES-HMM* model for low-latency action segmentation and recognition. An ergodic states (ES) shows the resting position between action sequence. Each node represents a single frame and each row represents a single action model. The arrows indicate possible transitions between states.

or offline smoothing, inferring the hidden marginal distributions $p(H_t|X_t)$ of every node (frame) of the test video. Because the graph for the Hidden Markov Model is a directed tree, this problem can be solved exactly using the max-sum algorithm. The number of possible paths through the lattice grows exponentially with the length of the chain. The Viterbi algorithm searches this space of paths efficiently to find the most probable path with a computational cost that grows only linearly with the length of the chain [33]. We can infer the action presence in a new sequence by Viterbi decoding as:

$$V_{t,\mathcal{H}} = P(H_t|X_t) + \log(\max_{\mathcal{H}\in\mathcal{H}_a}(V_{t-1,\mathcal{H}})) \qquad (2)$$

where initial state $V_{1,\mathcal{H}} = \log(P(H_1|X_1))$. From the inference results, we define the probability of an action $a \in \mathcal{A}$ as $p(y_t = a|x_{1:t}) = V_{T,\mathcal{H}}$. Result of the Viterbi algorithm is a path–sequence of nodes which correspond to hidden states of gesture classes. From this path we can infer the class of the gesture (*c.f.* Fig. 10). The overall algorithm for training and testing are presented in Algorithm 1 and 4.

2.4 Experimental Setups

For input sequences, there are three modalities, *i.e.* skeleton, RGB and depth (with user segmentation) provided. However, only skeletal modality and the depth modality are considered(*c.f.* Fig. 3). In the following experiments, the first 650 sample sequences are used for training, 50 for validation and the rest 240 for testing where each sequence contains around 20 gestures with some noisy non-meaningful vocabulary tokens.

Hidden states (H_t)**:**   Force alignment is used to extract the hidden states, *i.e.*, if a gesture token is 100 frames, the first 10 frames are assigned as hidden state *1* and the 10-20 frames are assigned as hidden state *2* and so on and so forth.

Algorithm 1. Multimodal Deep Dynamic Networks – training

Data:

$\mathbf{X}^1 = \{\mathbf{x}_i^1\}_{i \in [1...t]}$ - raw input(skeletal) feature sequence.

$\mathbf{X}^2 = \{\mathbf{x}_i^2\}_{i \in [1...t]}$ - raw input(depth) feature sequence in the form of $M_1 \times M_2 \times T$, where M_1, M_2 are the height and width of the input image and T is the number of contiguous frames of the spatio-temporal cuboid.

<small>Note that the GPU library *cuda-convnet* [19] used requires square size images and T is a multiple of 4.</small>

$\mathbf{Y} = \{\mathbf{y}_i\}_{i \in [1...t]}$ - frame based local label (achieved by semi-supervised forced-aligment),

where $\mathbf{y}_i \in \{C * S + \boldsymbol{1}\}$ with C is the number of class, S is the number of hidden states for each class, $\boldsymbol{1}$ as ergodic state.

1 **for** $m \leftarrow 1$ *to* 2 **do**
2   **if** m *is* 1 **then**
3   Preprocessing the data $\mathbf{X}^1$ as in Eq.3.
4   Normalizing(zero mean, unit variance per dimension) the above features and feed to to Eq.5.
5   Pre-training the networks using *Contrastive Divergence*.
6   Supervised fine-tuning the Deep Belief Networks using $\mathbf{Y}$ by standard mini-batch *SGD* backpropagation.
7   **else**
8   Preprocessing the data $\mathbf{X}^2$ (normalizing, median filtering the depth data) Algo.2 or Algo.3.
9   Feeding the above features to Eq.8.
10   Supervised fine-tuning the Deep 3D Convolutional Neural Networks using $\mathbf{Y}$ by standard mini-batch *SGD* Backpropagation.

Result:

GDBN - a gaussian bernoulli visible layer Deep Belief Network to generate the emission probabilities for hidden markov model.

3DCNN - a 3D Deep Convolutional Neural Networks to generate the emission probabilities for hidden markov model.

$\mathbf{p(H_1)}$ - prior probability for $\mathbf{Y}$.

$\mathbf{p(H_t|H_{t-1})}$ - transition probability for $\mathbf{Y}$, enforcing the beginning and ending of a sequence can only start from the first or the last state.

Ergodic states: Neutral frames are extracted as 5 frames before or after a gesture tokens labelled by ground truth.

2.5 Skeleton Module and DBN Training

Only upper body joints are relevant to the discriminative gesture recognition tasks. Therefore, only the 11 upper body joints are considered. The 11 upper body joints used are *"ElbowLeft, WristLeft, ShoulderLeft, HandLeft, ElbowRight, WristRight, ShoulderRight, HandRight, Head, Spine, HipCenter"*.

The 3D coordinates of N joints of frame c are given as: $X_c = \{x_1^c, x_2^c, \dots, x_N^c\}$. 3D positional pairwise differences of joints [24] are deployed for observation

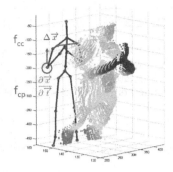

Fig. 3. Point cloud projection of depth image and the 3D positional features

domain $\mathcal{X}$. They capture posture features, motion features by direction concatenation: $\mathcal{X} = [f_{cc}, f_{cp}]$ as demonstrated in Eq 3. Note that offset features f_{ci} used in [24] depend on the first frame, if the initialization fails which is a very common scenario, the feature descriptor will be generally very noisy. Hence, the offset features f_{ci} are discarded and only the two more robust features $[f_{cc}, f_{cp}]$ (as shown in Fig. 3) are kept:

$$f_{cc} = \{x_i^c - x_j^c | i, j = 1, 2, \ldots, N; i \neq j\} \tag{3}$$

$$f_{cp} = \{x_i^c - x_j^p | x_i^c \in X_c; x_j^p \in X_p\} \tag{4}$$

This results in a raw dimension of $N_{\mathcal{X}} = N_{joints} * (N_{joints} - 1)/2 + N_{joints}^2) * 3$ where N_{joints} is the number of joints used. Therefore, in the experiment with $N_{joints} = 11, N_{\mathcal{X}} = 528$. Admittedly, we do not completely neglect human prior knowledge about information extraction for relevant static postures, velocity and offset overall dynamics of motion data. Nevertheless, the aforementioned three attributes are all very crude pairwise features without any tweak into the dataset or handpicking the most relevant pairwise, triple wise, *etc.* , designed features [32,34–36]. A similar data driven approach has been adopted in [28] where random forest classifiers were adapted to the problem of recognizing gestures using a bundle of 35 frames. These sets of feature extraction processes resemble the *Mel Frequency Cepstral Coefficients (MFCCs)* for the speech recognition community [23].

Gaussian Bernoulli Restricted Boltzmann Machines. Because input skeletal features($a.k.a.$observation domain $\mathcal{X}$) are continuous instead of binomial features, we use the Gaussian RBM ($GRBM$) to model the energy term of first visible layer:

$$E(v, h; \theta) = -\sum_{i=1}^{D} \frac{(v_i - b_i)^2}{2\sigma_i^2} - \sum_{i=1}^{D} \sum_{j=1}^{F} W_{ij} h_j \frac{v_i}{\sigma_i} - \sum_{j=1}^{F} a_j h_j \tag{5}$$

The conditional distributions needed for inference and generation are given by:

$$P(h_{j=1}|\mathbf{v}) = g(\sum_i W_{ij}v_i + a_j));\qquad(6)$$

$$P(v_{i=1}|\mathbf{h}) = \quad (v_i|\mu_i, \sigma_i^2).\qquad(7)$$

where $\mu_i = b_i + \sigma_i^2 \sum_j W_{ij}h_j$ and   is normal distribution. In general, we normalize the data (mean substraction and standard deviation division) in the preprocessing phase. Hence, in practice, instead of learning σ_i^2, one would typically use a fixed, predetermined unit value *1* for σ_i^2.

For high level skeleton feature extraction, two network architectures, *i.e.*, a smaller one and a larger one were experimented: $[N_\chi, 1000, 1000, 500, N_{TC}]$ and $[N_\chi, 2000, 2000, 1000, N_{TC}]$, where $N_\chi = 528$ is the observation domain dimension; N_{TC} is the output target class. Because in all our experiments the number of states associated to an individual action $N_{\mathcal{H}_a}$ is chosen as 10 for modeling the states of an action class, therefore $N_{TC} = 20 + 1 = 201$.

In the training set, there are in total 400, 117 frames. During the training of *DBN*, 90% is used for training, 8% for validation (for the purpose of early stopping) 2% is used for test evaluation. The feed forward networks are pre-trained with a fixed recipe using stochastic gradient decent with a mini-batch size of 200 training cases. Unsupervised initializations tend to avoid local minima and increase the networks performance stability and we have run 100 epochs for unsupervised pre-training. For Gaussian-binary RBMs, learning rate is fixed at 0.001 while for binary-binary RBMs as 0.01 (note in generally training *GRBM* requires smaller learning rate). For fine-tuning, the learning rate starts at 1 with 0.99999 mini-batch scaling. Maximum number of fine-tuning epoch is 500 with early stopping strategy and during the experiments, early stopping occurs around 440 epoch. Optimization complete with best validation score (the frame based prediction error rate) of 38.19%, with test performance 38.11%.

Though we believe further carefully choosing network architecture would lead to more competitive results, in order not to "creeping overfitting", as algorithms over time become too adapted to the dataset, essentially memorizing all its idiosyncrasies, and losing ability to generalize [37], we would like to treat the model as the aforementioned more generic approach. Since a completely new approach will initially have a hard time competing against established, carefully fine-tuned methods. More fundamentally, it may be that the right way to treat dataset performance numbers is not as a competition for the top place. This way, fundamentally new approaches will not be forced to compete for top performance right away, but will have a chance to develop and mature.

The performance of skeleton module is shown in Tab 1. And it can be seen that larger net (Net2) will generally perform better than smaller net (Net1), averaging multi-column nets almost will certainly further improve the performance [20]. Hence, in the following experiments, only the multi-column averaging results are reported.

Algorithm 2. Normalization scheme 1: template matching

Data:

T - exemplary template with original scale of size 320 × 320,
(Sample0003 is chosen as the exemplary template, shown in 4a).

$\mathbf{R_{depth}}$ - reference depth, fixed to **1941** (acquired from the above
exemplary template **T**).

$\hat{\mathbf{T}}$ - test image, as shown in 4b.

M - user foreground segmented mask.

1 Apply a 5 × 5 aperture median filter to test depth frame $\hat{\mathbf{T}}$ as in [39] to reduce the salt and pepper noise.

2 Multiply test depth frame $\hat{\mathbf{T}}$ with the user segmented mask **M**: $\hat{\mathbf{T}} = \hat{\mathbf{T}} \times \mathbf{M}$.

3 Template matching test image $\hat{\mathbf{T}}$ with **T** using normalized cross-correlation [40], the response score **R** is shown in 4c.

4 Shift the image according to the maximum response **R** to its centre applying affine transformation [41].

5 Scale the image according to reference depth $\mathbf{R_{depth}}$ and the median depth of a bounding box in the centre of the image with 25 × 25 size as shown as the green boundingp box in 4d.

6 Resize the image from 320 × 320 to 90 × 90.

Result:

$\tilde{\mathbf{T}}$ - Resize-normalized image shown in the yellow bounding box of 4d.

2.6   Depth 3D Module

Preprocessing and Normalizing: Shifting, Scaling and Resizing. Working directly with raw input Kinect recorded data frames, which are 480 × 640 pixel images, can be computationally demanding. Deepmind technology [38] presented the first deep learning model to successfully learn control policies directly from high-dimensional sensory input using deep reinforcement learning. Similarly, basic preprocessing steps are adopted aimed at reducing the input dimensionality from the original 480 × 640 pixels to 90 × 90 pixels. The square-sized of the final image is required because the used GPU implementation from [19] expects square inputs and the input channel should be in the set of $[1, 3, 4x]$. There are two normalization schemes implemented as 2 using depth template matching method and 3 using skeletal joins as assistant normalization. Note that the scheme 2 depends heavily on the provided maximum depth from the recording scene and scheme 3 depends on the accurate detection of skeleton joins, and both scheme require the performer remains a roughly static position (though the max pooling scheme in 3DCNN to some extend overcome the problem of position shifting). Generally, scheme 3 is more robust than scheme 2 because the provided maximum depth can sometimes be very noisy, *e.g.*, Sample0671, Sample0692, Sample0699, *etc.* After the normalization and resizing, a cuboid of 4 frames, hence, size 90 × 90 × 4, is extracted as a spatio-temporal unit.

Algorithm 3. Normalization scheme 2: skeleton normalization

Data:

$\mathbf{S_{spine}}$ - Skeleton Spine joints pixel coordinates.

$\mathbf{S_{shoulder}}$ - Skeleton Shoulder joints pixel coordinates.

$\hat{\mathbf{T}}$ - test image.

$\mathbf{M}$ - user foreground segmented mask.

$\mathbf{R_{length}}$ - reference length of shoulder to spine, fixed to **100** (1 meter).

1 Apply a 5×5 aperture median filter to test depth frame $\hat{\mathbf{T}}$.

2 Multiply test depth frame $\hat{\mathbf{T}}$ with the user segmented mask $\mathbf{M}$.

3 Shift the image according to the centroid of Spine joint $\mathbf{S_{spine}}$.

4 Scale the image according to the $\mathbf{R_{length}}/(\mathbf{S_{spine}} - \mathbf{S_{shoulder}})$.

Result:

$\tilde{\mathbf{T}}$ - Resize the shifted-scaledp image to 90×90 .

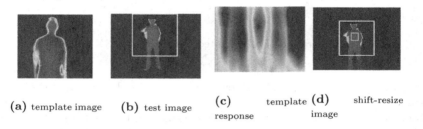

(a) template image   (b) test image   (c) template response   (d) shift-resize image

Fig. 4. Illustration of normalization scheme 1: template matching

3DCNN Architecture and Details of Learning. The 3D convolution is achieved by convolving a 3D kernel to the cuboid formed by stacking multiple contiguous frames together. We follow the nomenclature as in [22]. However, instead of using $tanh$ unit as in [22], the Rectified Linear Units ($ReLUs$) [19] were adopted where trainings are several times faster than their equivalents with $tanh$ units. Formally, the value of a unit at position (x, y, z) (z here corresponds the time-axis) in the jth feature map in the ith layer, denoted as v_{ij}^{xyz}, is given by:

$$v_{ij}^{xyz} = max(0, (b_{ij} + \sum_{m} \sum_{p=0}^{P_i-1} \sum_{q=0}^{Q_i-1} \sum_{r=0}^{R_i-1} w_{ijm}^{pqr} v_{(i-1)m}^{(x+p)(y+q)(t+r)})) \qquad (8)$$

The 3DCNN architecture is depicted as Fig. 5: the input contextual frames are stacked as size $90 \times 90 \times 4$ substracting the mean activity over the training set from each pixel, the first layer contains 16 maps of $7 \times 7 \times 4$ 3D kernel followed by local response normalization layer [19] and stride 2 max pooling; the second convolutional layers has 32 maps of 5×5 kernel followed by local response normalization layer and stride 2 max pooling; the third convolution layer is composed of 32 maps of 6×6 kernel followed by max pooling; then we have one fully connected layer of size 1000; the output layer N_{TC} is of size

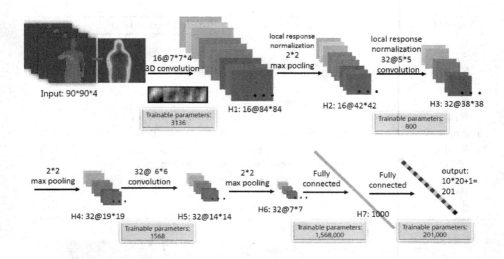

Fig. 5. An illustration of the architecture of the 3DCNN architecture.

$201 = 10 \times 20 + 1$ (number of hidden states for each class× number of classes plus one ergodic state).

The training set is roughly of 400,000 frames and is divided into 33 mini-batches with first 30 batches for training and the rest 3 batches for validation. Standard *SGD* is run for the first 100 epochs with learning rate of 0.1 and the weight learning rate as 0.001 and weight bias learning rate 0.002 both momentum are fixed as 0.9, weight decay is fixed to 0.0005, the next 100 epochs with 0.1× learning rate. Another network trained by randomly cropping 82×82 pixels on the flight as [19] is also implemented to enhance the model's robustness. During the test time, the centre part and other 4 corner parts are averaged to obtain the final score, *c.f.* Fig 6c. Due to the time constraint, only 150 epochs are trained with the learning rate reduced to one tenth at the 92th epoch. The training frame based classification error for the aforementioned two networks are shown in 6a and 6b. One interesting observation is that for the network with uncropped input, reducing the learning rate at 100 epoch, the frame-based classification rate reduces drastically whereas for the network with cropped input, reducing the learning rate results in a spike increase of frame-based classification error rate. The reason for this discrepancy worths further investigation. The performance of depth module is shown in Tab 1.

Looking into the Networks-visualization of Filter Banks. The weight filters of the first *conv1* layer are illustrated in Fig 7 and it can be seen that both shape pattern filters and motion filters are learnt effectively and the filters/weights of the cropped input trained networks are smoother then the uncropped one. Interestingly, the 3DCNN is able to learn the most informative motion part of the body effectively (highest response parts are the arms/hands areas), albeit no signal was

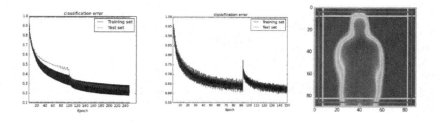

(a) Frame based classification error uncropped input.

(b) Frame based classification error with cropped input.

(c) Cropped images to enhance model's robustness.

Fig. 6. Visualization of the first filters and training statistics for 3DCNN

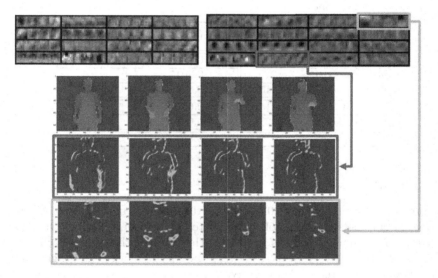

Fig. 7. Top left: the *conv1* weights of the 3DCNN learnt with uncropped input; top right: the *conv1* weights of the 3DCNN learnt with cropped input. It can be seen that filters/weights of the cropped input trained networks are smoother. Bottom: visualization of sample frames after *conv1* layer (Sample0654, 264-296 frames, sampled every 8 frames). It can be seen that the filters of the first convolutional layer are able to learn both shape pattern(red bounding box) and motion(yellow bounding box). Also note that the high response maps correspond to the most informative part of the body, even though during the training process, all local patches are learned indiscriminately regardless of its location.

explicitly given during training instructing which body parts the gesture recognition tasks should focus on.

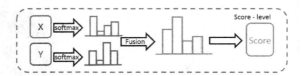

Fig. 8. Illustration of descriptor fusion

Table 1. Comparison of results in terms of Jaccard index between different network structures and various modules. DBDN Net1 corresponds to network structure of [528, 1000, 1000, 500, 201] and DBDN Net2 [528, 2000, 2000, 1000, 201], DBDN Multi-Net is the average of 3 Nets (2 Net1 and 1 Net2 with different initializations). It can be seen that larger net has better performance and multi-column net will further improve the classification rate. Norm1 corresponds to the normalization scheme 2 and Norm2 corresponds to the scheme 3.

Evaluation Set / Module	Validation	Test
Skeleton–DBDN Net1	0.7468	-
Skeleton–DBDN Net2	0.8017	-
Skeleton–DBDN MultiNet	0.8236	0.7873
Depth–3DCNN Norm1 2	0.6378	-
Depth–3DCNN Norm2 3	0.6924	0.6371
Score Fusion	0.8045	*0.8162*

2.7 Post-Processing

The predicted token less than 20 frames are discarded as noisy tokens. Note that there are many noisy gesture tokens predicted by viterbi decoding. One way to sift through the noisy tokens is to discard the token path log probability small than certain threshold. However, because the metric of this challenge: *Jaccard index* strongly penalizes false negatives, experiments show that it's better to have more false positives than to miss true positives. Effective ways to detect false positives should be an interesting aspect of future works.

2.8 Score Fusion

To fuse the dual model prediction, the strategy shown as Fig 8 is adopted. The complementary properties of both modules can be seen from the Viterbi path decoding plot in Fig 10. Note that the skeleton module generally performs better than the depth module, one reason could be that the skeleton joints learnt from [25] lie in success of utilizing huge and highly varied training data: from both realistic and synthetic depth images, a total number of 1 million images were used to train the deep randomized decision forest classifier in order to avoid overfitting. Hence skeleton data are more robust.

2.9 Computational Complexity

Though learning the Deep Neural Networks using stochastic gradient descent is tediously lengthy, once the model finishes training, with a low inference cost, our framework can perform real-time video sequence labeling. Specifically, a single feed forward neural network incurs trivial computational time ($\mathcal{O}(T)$) and is fast because it requires only matrix products and convolution operations. The complexity of Viterbi algorithm is $\mathcal{O}(T * |S|^2)$ with number of frames T and state number S.

3 Conclusion and Discussion

Hand-engineered, task-specific features are often less adaptive and time-consuming to design. This difficulty is more pronounced with multimodal data as the features have to relate multiple data sources. In this paper, we presented a novel Deep Dynamic Neural Networks(DDNN) framework that utilizes Deep Belief Networks and 3D Convolutional Neural Networks for learning contextual frame-level representations and modeling emission probabilities for Markov Field. The heterogeneous inputs from skeletal joints and depth images require different feature learning methods and the late fusion scheme is adopted at the score level. The experimental results on bi-modal time series data show that the multimodal DDNN framework can learn a good model of the joint space of multiple sensory inputs, and is consistently as good as/better than the unimodal input, opening the door for exploring the complementary representation among multimodal inputs. It also suggests that learning features directly from data is a very important research direction and with more and more data and flops-free computational power, the learning-based methods are not only more generalizable to many domains, but also are powerful in combining with other well-studied probabilistic graphical models for modeling and reasoning dynamic sequences. Future works include learning the share representation amongst the heterogeneous inputs at the penultimate layer and backpropagating the gradient in the share space in a unified representation.

4 Supplementary Materials

4.1 Deep Learning Library: Theano and Cuda-convnet

Theano. The Deep Belief Network library used in this section is **_Theano_** [42] [2] which is a Python library that allows you to define, optimize, and evaluate mathematical expressions involving multi-dimensional arrays efficiently.

Cuda-convnet. The GPU enabled blazing fast Convolutional Neural Network library used in this section is **_cuda-convnet_** [19] [3] which is a fast C++/CUDA implementation of convolutional (or more generally, feed-forward) neural

---

[2] http://deeplearning.net/software/theano/
[3] https://code.google.com/p/cuda-convnet/

networks. It can model arbitrary layer connectivity and network depth. Any directed acyclic graph of layers will do. Training is done using the back-propagation algorithm.

4.2   Details of the Code

Deep Belief Dynamic Networks. The python project for "Leveraging Hierarchical Parametric Network for Skeletal Joints Action Segmentation and Recognition" can be found at:
https://github.com/stevenwudi/CVPR_2014_code

Deep 3D Convolutional Dynamic Networks. The python project, C++/CUDA backend for Deep 3D Convolutional Dynamic Network can be found at:
https://github.com/stevenwudi/3DCNN_HMM

4.3   Extra Figures for Illustration

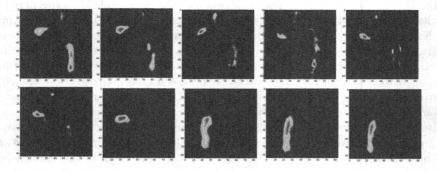

Fig. 9. More illustrations of the middle level features from the activation images after first convolutional layer. High response arms and hands areas are learnt automatically without explicit learning signal in term of location information.

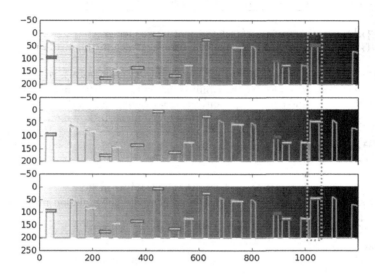

Fig. 10. Viterbi decoding of two modules and their fusion result of sample sequence 704. Top to bottom: skeleton, depth, score fusion with x-axis representing the time and y-axis representing the hidden states of all the classes with the ergodic state at the bottom. Red lines are the ground truth label, cyan lines are the viterbi shortest path and yellow lines are the predicted label. There are some complementary information of the two modules and generally skeletal module outperforms the depth module. The fusion of the two could exploit the uncertainty, *e.g.* light green dashed box indicates that depth module makes the correct prediction whereas the skeletal module fails, the combined module is still making the correct prediction.

Algorithm 4. Multimodal Deep Dynamic Networks – testing

Data:
$\mathbf{X}^1 = \{\mathbf{x}_i^1\}_{i \in [1...t]}$ - raw input(skeletal) feature sequence.
$\mathbf{X}^2 = \{\mathbf{x}_i^2\}_{i \in [1...t]}$ - raw input(depth) feature sequence in the form of
$\qquad M \times M \times T$.
GDBN - a gaussian bernoulli visible layer Deep Belief Network to
$\qquad$ generate the emission probabilities for hidden markov model.
3DCNN - the trained 3D Deep Convolutional Neural Networks to
$\qquad$ generate the emission probabilities for hidden markov model.
$\mathbf{p}(\mathbf{H}_1)$ - prior probability for $\mathbf{Y}$.
$\mathbf{p}(\mathbf{H}_t|\mathbf{H}_{t-1})$ - transition probability for $\mathbf{Y}$.

1   **for** $m \leftarrow 1$ *to* 2 **do**
2   **if** m *is* 1 **then**
3   Preprocessing and normalizing the data $\mathbf{X}^1$ as in Eq.3.
4   Feedforwarding network **GDBN** to generate the emission probability
$\qquad\qquad \mathbf{p}(\mathbf{X}_t|\mathbf{H}_t)$ in Eq.1.
5   Generating the score probability matrix $\mathbf{S}^1 = \mathbf{p}(\mathbf{H}_{1:T}, \mathbf{X}_{1:T})$.
6   **else**
7   Preprocessing the data $\mathbf{X}^2$ (normalizing, median filtering the depth
$\qquad\qquad$ data) Algo.2 or Algo.3.
8   Feedforwarding **3DCNN** to generate the emission probability
$\qquad\qquad \mathbf{S}^2 = \mathbf{p}(\mathbf{X}_t|\mathbf{H}_t)$ in Eq.1.
9   Generating the score probability matrix $\mathbf{S}^2 = \mathbf{p}(\mathbf{H}_{1:T}, \mathbf{X}_{1:T})$.
10   Fusing the score matrix $\mathbf{S} = \mathbf{S}^1 + \mathbf{S}^2$.
11   Finding the best path $\mathbf{V}_{t,\mathcal{H}}$ using $\mathbf{S}$ by Viterbi decoding as in Eq.2.

Result:
$\mathbf{Y} = \{\mathbf{y}_i\}_{i \in [1...t]}$ - frame based local label
$\qquad$ where $\mathbf{y}_i \in \{C * S + \boldsymbol{1}\}$ with C is the number of class, S is the
$\qquad$ number of hidden states for each class, $\boldsymbol{1}$ as ergodic state.
$\mathbf{C}$ - global label, the anchor point is chosen as the middle state frame.

References

1. Escalera, S., Bar, X., Gonzlez, J., Bautista, M., Madadi, M., Reyes, M., Ponce, V., Escalante, H., Shotton, J., Guyon, I.: Chalearn looking at people challenge 2014: dataset and results. In: European Conference on Computer Vision workshop (2014)
2. Liu, L., Shao, L., Zheng, F., Li, X.: Realistic action recognition via sparsely-constructed gaussian processes. Pattern Recognition (2014). doi:10.1016/j.patcog.2014.07.006
3. Shao, L., Zhen, X., Li, X.: Spatio-temporal laplacian pyramid coding for action recognition. IEEE Transactions on Cybernetics **44**(6), 817–827 (2014)
4. Wu, D., Shao, L.: Silhouette analysis-based action recognition via exploiting human poses. IEEE Transactions on Circuits and Systems for Video Technology **23**(2), 236–243 (2013)
5. Laptev, I.: On space-time interest points. International Journal of Computer Vision (2005)
6. Dollár, P., Rabaud, V., Cottrell, G., Belongie, S.: Behavior recognition via sparse spatio-temporal features. In: Visual Surveillance and Performance Evaluation of Tracking and Surveillance. IEEE (2005)
7. Willems, G., Tuytelaars, T., Van Gool, L.: An efficient dense and scale-invariant spatio-temporal interest point detector. In: Forsyth, D., Torr, P., Zisserman, A. (eds.) ECCV 2008, Part II. LNCS, vol. 5303, pp. 650–663. Springer, Heidelberg (2008)
8. Scovanner, P., Ali, S., Shah, M.: A 3-dimensional sift descriptor and its application to action recognition. In: International Conference on Multimedia. ACM (2007)
9. Klaser, A., Marszalek, M., Schmid, C.: A Spatio-temporal descriptor based on 3D-gradients. In: British Machine Vision Conference (2008)
10. Wang, H., Kläser, A., Schmid, C., Liu, C.L.: Dense trajectories and motion boundary descriptors for action recognition. International Journal of Computer Vision (2013)
11. Zhou, T., Tao, D.: Double shrinking sparse dimension reduction. IEEE Transactions on Image Processing **22**(1), 244–257 (2013)
12. Xu, C., Tao, D.: Large-margin multi-view information bottleneck. IEEE Trans. Pattern Anal. Mach. Intell. **36**(8), 1559–1572 (2014)
13. Wang, H., Ullah, M.M., Klaser, A., Laptev, I., Schmid, C., et al.: Evaluation of local spatio-temporal features for action recognition. In: British Machine Vision Conference (2009)
14. Yuan, J., Bae, E., Tai, X.-C., Boykov, Y.: A continuous max-flow approach to potts model. In: Daniilidis, K., Maragos, P., Paragios, N. (eds.) ECCV 2010, Part VI. LNCS, vol. 6316, pp. 379–392. Springer, Heidelberg (2010)
15. Le, Q.V., Zou, W.Y., Yeung, S.Y., Ng, A.Y.: Learning hierarchical invariant spatio-temporal features for action recognition with independent subspace analysis. In: IEEE Conference on Computer Vision and Pattern Recognition (2011)
16. Baccouche, M., Mamalet, F., Wolf, C., Garcia, C., Baskurt, A.: Spatio-temporal convolutional sparse auto-encoder for sequence classification. In: British Machine Vision Conference (2012)
17. Hinton, G.E., Osindero, S., Teh, Y.W.: A fast learning algorithm for deep belief nets. Neural Computation (2006)
18. Schmidhuber, J.: Deep learning in neural networks: An overview (2014). arXiv preprint arXiv:1404.7828

19. Krizhevsky, A., Sutskever, I., Hinton, G.E.: Imagenet classification with deep convolutional neural networks. In: Neural Information Processing Systems (2012)
20. Ciresan, D., Meier, U., Schmidhuber, J.: Multi-column deep neural networks for image classification. In: IEEE Conference on Computer Vision and Pattern Recognition (2012)
21. Shuiwang Ji, Wei Xu, M.Y., Yu, K.: 3d convolutional neural networks for human action recognition. In: International Conference on Machine Learning. IEEE (2010)
22. Ji, S., Xu, W., Yang, M., Yu, K.: 3d convolutional neural networks for human action recognition. IEEE Transactions on Pattern Analysis and Machine Intelligence (2013)
23. Mohamed, A., Dahl, G.E., Hinton, G.: Acoustic modeling using deep belief networks. IEEE Transactions on Speech, and Language Processing, Audio (2012)
24. Wu, D., Shao, L.: Leveraging hierarchical parametric networks for skeletal joints based action segmentation and recognition. In: IEEE Conference on Computer Vision and Pattern Recognition (2014)
25. Shotton, J., Fitzgibbon, A., Cook, M., Sharp, T., Finocchio, M., Moore, R., Kipman, A., Blake, A.: Real-time human pose recognition in parts from single depth images. In: IEEE Conference on Computer Vision and Pattern Recognition (2011)
26. Han, J., Shao, L., Shotton, J.: Enhanced computer vision with microsoft kinect sensor: a review. IEEE Transactions on Cybernetics 43(5), 1317–1333 (2013)
27. Escalera, S., Gonzlez, J., Bar, X., Reyes, M., Lops, O., Guyon, I., Athitsos, V., Escalante, H.J.: Multi-modal gesture recognition challenge 2013: dataset and results. In: ACM ChaLearn Multi-Modal Gesture Recognition Grand Challenge and Workshop (2013)
28. Fothergill, S., Mentis, H.M., Kohli, P., Nowozin, S.: Instructing people for training gestural interactive systems. In: ACM Computer Human Interaction (2012)
29. Guyon, I., Athitsos, V., Jangyodsuk, P., Hamner, B., Escalante, H.J.: Chalearn gesture challenge: design and first results. In: IEEE Conference on Computer Vision and Pattern Recognition Workshops (2012)
30. Wang, J., Liu, Z., Wu, Y., Yuan, J.: Mining actionlet ensemble for action recognition with depth cameras. In: IEEE Conference on Computer Vision and Pattern Recognition (2012)
31. Lehrmann, A., Gehler, P., Nowozin, S.: A non-parametric bayesian network prior of human pose. In: International Conference on Computer Vision (2013)
32. Nowozin, S., Shotton, J.: Action points: A representation for low-latency online human action recognition. Technical report (2012)
33. Bishop, C.: Pattern recognition and machine learning. Springer (2006)
34. Chaudhry, R., Ofli, F., Kurillo, G., Bajcsy, R., Vidal, R.: Bio-inspired dynamic 3d discriminative skeletal features for human action recognition. In: IEEE Conference on Computer Vision and Pattern Recognition Workshops (2013)
35. Müller, M., Röder, T.: Motion templates for automatic classification and retrieval of motion capture data. In: SIGGRAPH/Eurographics Symposium on Computer Animation, Eurographics Association (2006)
36. Ofli, F., Chaudhry, R., Kurillo, G., Vidal, R., Bajcsy, R.: Sequence of the most informative joints (smij): A new representation for human skeletal action recognition. Journal of Visual Communication and Image Representation (2013)
37. Torralba, A., Efros, A.A.: Unbiased look at dataset bias. In: IEEE Conference on Computer Vision and Pattern Recognition (2011)

38. Mnih, V., Kavukcuoglu, K., Silver, D., Graves, A., Antonoglou, I., Wierstra, D., Riedmiller, M.: Playing atari with deep reinforcement learning (2013). arXiv preprint arXiv:1312.5602
39. Wu, D., Zhu, F., Shao, L.: One shot learning gesture recognition from RGBD images. In: International Conference on Computer Vision and Pattern Recognition Workshops (2012)
40. Lewis, J.: Fast normalized cross-correlation. Vision Interface **10**, 120–123 (1995)
41. Bradski, G. Dr. Dobb's Journal of Software Tools
42. Bergstra, J., Breuleux, O., Bastien, F., Lamblin, P., Pascanu, R., Desjardins, G., Turian, J., Warde-Farley, D., Bengio, Y.: Theano: a CPU and GPU math expression compiler. In: Proceedings of the Python for Scientific Computing Conference (SciPy) (2010)

Sign Language Recognition Using Convolutional Neural Networks

Lionel Pigou[✉], Sander Dieleman, Pieter-Jan Kindermans,
and Benjamin Schrauwen

ELIS, Ghent University, Ghent, Belgium
lionelpigou@gmail.com

Abstract. There is an undeniable communication problem between the Deaf community and the hearing majority. Innovations in automatic sign language recognition try to tear down this communication barrier. Our contribution considers a recognition system using the Microsoft Kinect, convolutional neural networks (CNNs) and GPU acceleration. Instead of constructing complex handcrafted features, CNNs are able to automate the process of feature construction. We are able to recognize 20 Italian gestures with high accuracy. The predictive model is able to generalize on users and surroundings not occurring during training with a cross-validation accuracy of 91.7%. Our model achieves a mean Jaccard Index of 0.789 in the ChaLearn 2014 Looking at People gesture spotting competition.

Keywords: Convolutional neural network · Deep learning · Gesture recognition · Sign language recognition

1 Introduction

Very few people understand sign language. Moreover, contrary to popular belief, it is not an international language. Obviously, this further complicates communication between the Deaf community and the hearing majority. The alternative of written communication is cumbersome, because the Deaf community is generally less skilled in writing a spoken language [17]. Furthermore, this type of communication is impersonal and slow in face-to-face conversations. For example, when an accident occurs, it is often necessary to communicate quickly with the emergency physician where written communication is not always possible.

The purpose of this work is to contribute to the field of automatic sign language recognition. We focus on the recognition of the signs or gestures. There are two main steps in building an automated recognition system for human actions in spatio-temporal data [15]. The first step is to extract features from the frame sequences. This will result in a representation consisting of one or more feature vectors, also called descriptors. This representation will aid the computer to distinguish between the possible classes of actions. The second step is the classification of the action. A classifier will use these representations to discriminate between the different actions (or signs). In our work, the feature extraction is automated by using convolutional neural networks (CNNs). An artificial neural network (ANN) is used for classification.

© Springer International Publishing Switzerland 2015
L. Agapito et al. (Eds.): ECCV 2014 Workshops, Part I, LNCS 8925, pp. 572–578, 2015.
DOI: 10.1007/978-3-319-16178-5_40

2 Related Work

In our work, we build on the results of Roel Verschaeren [18]. He proposes a CNN model that recognizes a set of 50 different signs in the Flemish Sign Language with an error of 2.5%, using the Microsoft Kinect. Unfortunately, this work is limited in the sense that it considers only a single person in a fixed environment.

In [19] an American Language recognition system is presented with a vocabulary of 30 words. They constructed appearance-based representations and a hand tracking system to be classified with a hidden Markov model (HMM). An error rate of 10.91% is achieved on the RWTH-BOSTON-50 database.

The approach in [4] uses the Microsoft Kinect to extract appearance-based hand features and track the position in 2D and 3D. The classification results are obtained by comparing a hidden Markov model (HMM) approach with sequential pattern boosting (SP-boosting). This resulted in an accuracy of 99.9% on 20 different isolated gestures on their specifically constructed data set and 85.1% on a more realistic one with 40 gestures.

The Microsoft Kinect is also used in [2] that proposes a recognition system for 239 words of the Chinese Sign Language (CSL). Here, the 3D movement trajectory of the hands are used besides a language model to construct sentences. This trajectory is aligned and matched with a gallery of known trajectories. The top-1 and top-5 recognition rates are 83.51% and 96.32% respectively.

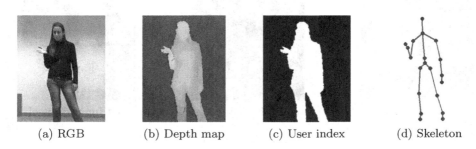

(a) RGB   (b) Depth map   (c) User index   (d) Skeleton

Fig. 1. Data set for the CLAP14 gesture spotting challenge [5]

3 Methodology

3.1 Data

We use the data set from the *ChaLearn Looking at People 2014* [5] (CLAP14) challenge in this work. More specifically, *Track 3: Gesture Spotting*. This dataset consists of 20 different Italian gestures, performed by 27 users with variations in surroundings, clothing, lighting and gesture movement. The videos are recorded with a Microsoft Kinect. As a result, we have access to the depth map, user index (location of the user in the depth map) and the joint positions (Figure 1).

We use 6600 gestures in the development set of CLAP14 for our experiments: 4600 for the training set and 2000 for the validation set. The test set of CLAP14 is also considered as the test set for this work and consists of 3543 samples. The users and backgrounds in the validation set are *not* contained in the training set. The users and backgrounds in the test set *can* occur in the training and the validation set.

3.2   Preprocessing

Our first step in the preprocessing stage is cropping the highest hand and the upper body using the given joint information. We discovered that the highest hand is the most interesting. If both hands are used, they perform the same (mirrored) movement. If one hand is used, it is always the highest one. If the left hand is used, the videos are mirrored. This way, the model only needs to learn one side.

The preprocessing results in four video samples (hand and body with depth and gray-scale) of resolution 64x64x32 (32 frames of size 64x64). Furthermore, the noise in the depth maps is reduced with thresholding, background removal using the user index, and median filtering. The outcome is shown in Figure 2.

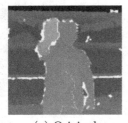      

    (a) Original   (b) Noise reduction   (c) 4 Input channels

Fig. 2. Preprocessing

3.3   Convolutional Neural Network (CNN)

CNNs (based on [13]) are feature extraction models in deep learning that recently have proven to be to be very successful at image recognition [12], [3], [20], [7]. As of now, the models are in use by various industry leaders like Google, Facebook and Amazon. And recently, researchers at Google applied CNNs on video data [11].

CNNs are inspired by the visual cortex of the human brain. The artificial neurons in a CNN will connect to a local region of the visual field, called a receptive field. This is accomplished by performing discrete convolutions on the image with filter values as trainable weights. Multiple filters are applied for each channel, and together with the activation functions of the neurons, they form feature maps. This is followed by a pooling scheme, where only the interesting information of the feature maps are pooled together. These techniques are performed in multiple layers as shown in Figure 3.

3.4 Proposed Architecture

For the pooling method, we use max-pooling: only the maximum value in a local neighborhood of the feature map remains. To accommodate video data, the max-pooling is performed in three dimensions. However, using 2D convolutions resulted in a better validation accuracy than 3D convolutions.

The architecture of the model consists of two CNNs, one for extracting hand features and one for extracting upper body features. Each CNN is three layers deep. A classical ANN with one hidden layer provides classification after concatenating the outcomes of both CNNs. Also, local contrast normalization (LCN) as in [10] is applied in the first two layers and all artificial neurons are rectified linear units (ReLUs [14], [6]). An illustration of the architecture is depicted in Figure 3.

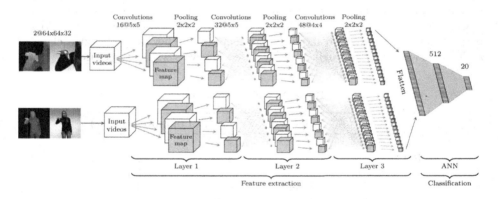

Fig. 3. The architecture of the deep learning model

3.5 Generalization and Training

During training, dropout [9] and data augmentation are used as main approaches to reduce overfitting. The data augmentation is performed in real time on the CPU during the training phase whiles the model trains on the GPU as in [12]. This consists of zooming up to 10%, rotations up to (-)3°, spatial translations up to (-)5 pixels in the x and y direction, and temporal translations up to (-)4 frames.

We use Nesterov's accelerated gradient descent (NAG) [16] with a fixed momentum-coefficient of 0.9 and mini-batches of size 20. The learning rate is initialized at 0.003 with a 5% decrease after each epoch. The weights of the CNNs are randomly initialized with a normal distribution with $\mu = 0$ and $\sigma = 0.04$, and $\sigma = 0.02$ for the weights of the ANN. The biases of the CNNs are initialized at 0.2 and the biases of the ANN at 0.1.

Experiments are conducted on one machine with a hexa-core processor (Intel Core i7-3930K), 32GB SDRAM and a NVIDIA GeForce GTX 680 GPU with 4096MB of memory . The models are implemented using the Python libraries Theano [1], and PyLearn2 [8] for the fast implementation of 2D convolutions by Alex Krizhevsky [12].

3.6   Temporal Segmentation

The CLAP14 challenge consists of spotting gestures in video samples. Each video sample is an unedited recording of a user signing 10 to 20 gestures, including *noise* movements that are not part of the 20 Italian gestures. The goal of the temporal segmentation method is to predict the begin and end frames of every gesture in the video samples.

We use the sliding windows technique, where each possible interval of 32 frames is evaluated with the trained model (as previously described). Consecutive intervals with identical classes and sufficiently high classification probability (thresholding) are considered as a gesture segment. The validation set of CLAP14 is used to optimize the thresholding parameters. Furthermore, an extra class is added to the classifier to help identify video intervals without gesture.

Table 1. Validation results

	Error rate (%)	Improvement (%)
Tanh units	18.90	
ReLU	14.40	**23.8**
+ dropout	11.90	17.4
+ LCN (first 2 layers)	10.30	13.4
+ data augmentation	**8.30**	19.4

4   Results

Our most notable experiments are the models with ReLUs, dropout, LCN and data augmentation. The validation results of these experiments are shown in Table 1. We observe a validation accuracy of 91.70% (8.30% error rate) for our best model. Furthermore, ReLUs prove to be very effective with an improvement of 23.8% with respect to tanh units.

The accuracy on the test set is 95.68% and we observe a 4.13% false positive rate, caused by the noise movements. Note that the test result is higher than the validation result, because the validation set doesn't contain users and backgrounds in the training set.

The final score for the CLAP14 competition is the mean Jaccard Index of each gesture and video sample. The Jaccard Index is a measure for overlapping frames between prediction and ground truth. The validation score of our best model is 0.789675 and the final score is 0.788804, which ranks us fifth of the 17 qualified teams.

5 Conclusion

This work shows that convolutional neural networks can be used to accurately recognize different signs of a sign language, with users and surroundings not included in the training set. This generalization capacity of CNNs in spatio-temporal data can contribute to the broader research field on automatic sign language recognition.

References

1. Bergstra, J., Breuleux, O., Bastien, F., Lamblin, P., Pascanu, R., Desjardins, G., Turian, J., Warde-Farley, D., Bengio, Y.: Theano: a CPU and GPU math expression compiler. In: Proceedings of the Python for Scientific Computing Conference (SciPy), June 2010, oral Presentation
2. Chai, X., Li, G., Lin, Y., Xu, Z., Tang, Y., Chen, X., Zhou, M.: Sign Language Recognition and Translation with Kinect (2013). Language Recognition and Translation with Kinect.pdf. http://vipl.ict.ac.cn/sites/default/files/papers/files/2013_FG_xjchai_Sign
3. Cireşan, D., Meier, U., Schmidhuber, J.: Multi-column deep neural networks for image classification. In: IEEE Conference on Computer Vision and Pattern Recognition (CVPR), pp. 3642–3649. IEEE (2012)
4. Cooper, H., Ong, E.J., Pugeault, N., Bowden, R.: Sign language recognition using sub-units. The Journal of Machine Learning Research 13(1), 2205–2231 (2012)
5. Escalera, S., Bar, X., Gonzlez, J., Bautista, M.A., Madadi, M., Reyes, M., Ponce, V., Escalante, H.J., Shotton, J., Guyon, I.: Chalearn looking at people challenge 2014: Dataset and results. In: ECCV Workshop (2014)
6. Glorot, X., Bordes, A., Bengio, Y.: Deep sparse rectifier networks. In: Proceedings of the 14th International Conference on Artificial Intelligence and Statistics 15, pp. 315–323 (2011). http://eprints.pascal-network.org/archive/00008596/
7. Goodfellow, I.J., Bulatov, Y., Ibarz, J., Arnoud, S., Shet, V.: Multi-digit number recognition from street view imagery using deep convolutional neural networks (2013). arXiv preprint arXiv:1312.6082
8. Goodfellow, I.J., Warde-Farley, D., Lamblin, P., Dumoulin, V., Mirza, M., Pascanu, R., Bergstra, J., Bastien, F., Bengio, Y.: Pylearn2: a machine learning research library (2013). arXiv preprint arXiv:1308.4214. http://arxiv.org/abs/1308.4214
9. Hinton, G.E., Srivastava, N., Krizhevsky, A., Sutskever, I., Salakhutdinov, R.R.: Improving neural networks by preventing co-adaptation of feature detectors (2012). arXiv preprint arXiv:1207.0580
10. Jarrett, K., Kavukcuoglu, K.: What is the best multi-stage architecture for object recognition?. In: IEEE 12th International Conference on Computer Vision, pp. 2146–2153 (2009). http://ieeexplore.ieee.org/xpls/abs_all.jsp?arnumber=5459469

11. Karpathy, A., Toderici, G., Shetty, S., Leung, T. Sukthankar, R., Fei-Fei, L.: Large-scale video classification with convolutional neural networks. In: CVPR (2014)
12. Krizhevsky, A., Sutskever, I., Hinton, G.: Imagenet classification with deep convolutional neural networks. Advances in Neural Information, 1–9 (2012). http://books.nips.cc/papers/files/nips25/NIPS2012_0534.pdf
13. Lecun, Y., Bottou, L., Bengio, Y., Haffner, P.: Gradient-based learning applied to document recognition. Proceedings of the IEEE 86(11) (1998)
14. Nair, V., Hinton, G.E.: Rectified linear units improve restricted boltzmann machines. In: Proceedings of the 27th International Conference on Machine Learning (ICML 2010), pp. 807–814 (2010)
15. Poppe, R.: A survey on vision-based human action recognition. Image and Vision Computing 28(6), 976–990 (2010)
16. Sutskever, I., Martens, J., Dahl, G., Hinton, G.: On the importance of initialization and momentum in deep learning. In: Proceedings of the 30th International Conference on Machine Learning (ICML 2013), pp. 1139–1147 (2013)
17. Van Herreweghe, M.: Prelinguaal dove jongeren en nederlands: een syntactisch onderzoek. Universiteit Gent, Faculteit Letteren en Wijsbegeerte (1996)
18. Verschaeren, R.: Automatische herkenning van gebaren met de microsoft kinect (2012)
19. Zaki, M.M., Shaheen, S.I.: Sign language recognition using a combination of new vision based features. Pattern Recognition Letters 32(4), 572–577 (2011)
20. Zeiler, M.D., Fergus, R.: Visualizing and understanding convolutional neural networks (2013). arXiv preprint arXiv:1311.2901

Gesture Recognition Using Template Based Random Forest Classifiers

Necati Cihan Camgöz$^{(\boxtimes)}$, Ahmet Alp Kindiroglu, and Lale Akarun

Computer Engineering Department, Bogazici University, Istanbul, Turkey
{cihan.camgoz,alp.kindiroglu,akarun}@boun.edu.tr

Abstract. This paper presents a framework for spotting and recognizing continuous human gestures. Skeleton based features are extracted from normalized human body coordinates to represent gestures. These features are then used to construct spatio-temporal template based Random Decision Forest models. Finally, predictions from different models are fused at decision-level to improve overall recognition performance. Our method has shown competitive results on the ChaLearn 2014 Looking at People: Gesture Recognition dataset. Trained on a dataset of 20 gesture vocabulary and 7754 gesture samples, our method achieved a Jaccard Index of 0.74663 on the test set, reaching 7th place among contenders. Among methods that exclusively used skeleton based features, our method obtained the highest recognition performance.

Keywords: Template based learning · Random Decision Forest · Gesture recognition

1 Introduction

Gestures are natural and expressive tools of human communication. As computers take a greater role in daily life, creating natural human computer interaction methods, such as gesture interfaces, has become a necessity. Especially hand and arm gestures, which people commonly use to communicate with each other, have now become commonly used human computer interaction methods [12]. However, there are still limitations in sensing, detecting and modelling gestures. Recent developments such as the emergence of consumer depth cameras and the availability of large annotated corpora have turned automatic gesture recognition to a competitive and active research field.

Automatic Gesture Recognition aims to spot and distinguish gestures from a gesture vocabulary given a sensory input. However, imperfect human pose detection and recognition coupled with spatio-temporal variability of the gestures makes distinguishing between gestures a challenging task [20].

Many state-of-the-art gesture recognition systems use depth cameras to capture gestures [25]. Video-based gesture recognition deals with challenging tasks, such as the difficulty of locating hands in the presence of rapid arm movements and lighting changes [7,12]. Depth cameras alleviate some of these difficulties as

© Springer International Publishing Switzerland 2015
L. Agapito et al. (Eds.): ECCV 2014 Workshops, Part I, LNCS 8925, pp. 579–594, 2015.
DOI: 10.1007/978-3-319-16178-5_41

they are able to operate under difficult lighting conditions where RGB cameras fail [27].

In the literature, video-based gesture recognition methods differ according to two criteria: gesture cues and learning methods for training gesture recognition systems.

Once a gesture has been sensed, it is described via meaningful mathematical features. The chosen features often depend on the elements of the gesture being detected. In a typical gesture learning module, features like joint locations, angles between joints, hand locations, trajectories and hand shape parameters are used. These features can be obtained from modalities such as motion, color and depth. In conjunction with statistical learning methods, these features are then used to distinguish classes of gestures from each other.

Classification of human gestures relies on learning temporal information as well as spatial information. Due to the spatio-temporal nature of gestures, learning the temporal structure of human actions is crucial in building successful gesture recognition models. In the literature, three common approaches are used to learn the temporal structure of models [18]:

The first of these approaches omits temporal dependencies and models gestures using either individual key frames or histogram of feature sequences. In vocabularies where the temporal aspect of gestures is static (meaning there is not much variation in appearance during the gesture), using a single representative image may be sufficient. In [26], Carlsson and Sullivan use differences in edge templates to classify key frame images. Likewise, using features of multiple frames in a histogram setting, such as the temporal bag of words approach [21], builds effective classifiers by modelling the frequencies of different features. However, such models fail to distinguish among similar gestures with different temporal ordering.

A more popular approach to temporal modelling is using action grammars. In these approaches, features are grouped into certain configurations, such as states. Changes among these states are modelled using graphical models. Hidden Markov Models [19] are the most popular representation among these probabilistic methods. Since the works of Starner and Pentland [24] in recognizing American Sign Language letters and Yamato et al. [29] in recognizing tennis gestures, they have been used extensively for gesture learning. Other approaches, such as Conditional Random Fields [14] or Autoregressive Models [1] have also been used.

Another approach to temporal modelling is by using gesture templates. Instead of modelling frame features into clusters and representing the interactions of these clusters, these models deal with learning static sequential groups of features called templates. Models for these approaches are often constructed by either stacking a sequence of features together or by stacking a sequence of images together to learn features in the spatio-temporal domain. Techniques such as motion history images [3] are popular approaches of this technique.

While these approaches model blocks of features over a temporal domain, they have no mechanism for detecting temporal changes such as slower execution of a gesture. To handle such changes, the model should be trained with either temporally similar samples or temporally normalized samples using approaches, such as Dynamic Time Warping [22].

Since templates are obtained by concatenating spatial features onto fixed sized vectors, non-temporal machine learning techniques, such as support vector machines, nearest neighbour methods or ensemble methods can be used to learn such representations [2].

In this paper, we present a continuous gesture recognition framework for recognizing continuous Italian gestures [8]. We extract skeleton based features from human body part annotations provided for the ChaLearn 2014 Looking at People Competition [8]. We use template based Random Decision Forest [4] methods for continuous per-frame gesture recognition. We concatenate a temporal sequence of features to form our template; and experiment with different sampling strategies. In Section 2, we outline the ChaLearn competition dataset. In Section 3, we describe our gesture recognition methodology. Then we present our experimental setup and results in Section 4 and share our conclusions in Section 5.

2   ChaLearn 2014 Italian Gestures Dataset

The Italian Gestures dataset [8], featured by ChaLearn 2014, was designed to evaluate user independent continuous Gesture Recognition performance. The dataset consists of 13,858 gestures from a vocabulary of 20 Italian cultural/ anthropological signs performed by 27 unique users. The list of Italian gestures in the dataset can be seen in Table 1.

Table 1. List of Italian Gestures in the dataset

Italian Gestures			
vattene	ok	vieniqui	cosatifarei
perfetto	basta	furbo	prendere
cheduepalle	noncenepiu	chevuoi	fame
daccordo	tantotempo	seipazzo	buonissimo
combinato	messidaccordo	freganiente	sonostufo

The dataset was recorded by Microsoft Kinect sensors, and it includes skeleton model [23], user mask, RGB and depth images. A visualization of dataset modalities can be seen in Figure 1. The dataset consists of 450 development, 250 validation, and 240 test videos in which there are a total of 7754, 3362, and 2742 individual gestures, respectively.

The dataset was featured by ChaLearn 2014 Looking at People competition's Track 3: Gesture Recognition. The emphasis of the gesture recognition track was on multi-modal automatic learning of a set of 20 gestures performed by several different users, with the aim of performing user independent continuous gesture spotting.

Fig. 1. Data modalities of the dataset. From left to right: RGB Images, Depth Images, User Mask and Skeleton Model

3   Method

Our gesture recognition method takes the skeleton model of gesticulating users as input. These models were provided by the dataset and contain 2.5D joint coordinates and their rotations. Given a skeleton model as input, our method goes through the following five stages:

1. Joint coordinates are normalized.
2. Gestures are represented by the skeleton based features that are extracted from the set of normalized coordinates and joint rotations.
3. Gesture Templates are constructed to incorporate temporal information for spatial machine learning methods.
4. Gesture representations are then given to Random Desicion Forests to perform gesture spotting and gesture classification.
5. Decision-level fusion is used to combine predictions of multiple classification models.

The block diagram of our framework can be seen in Figure 2.

3.1   Joint Coordinate Normalization

The skeleton model provided by the dataset contains joint world coordinates, joint pixel coordinates and their rotations in each frame of a video. World coordinates represent the global position of a tracked joint in 2.5D space.

We normalize the world coordinates to obtain comparable and user invariant joint coordinates. To do so, we move the hip center to $(0 \quad 0 \quad 0)^T$ in $3D$ space and the shoulder center to $(0 \quad 1 \quad 0)^T$ in all frames. Then, a rotation of the body around the y axis is performed in order to bring the left shoulder to the z=0 plane, thus making all users turn straight towards the camera. Visualization of these preprocessing steps can be seen in Figure 3.

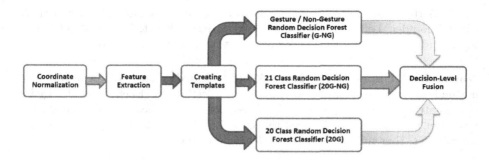

Fig. 2. Our Gesture Recognition Framework

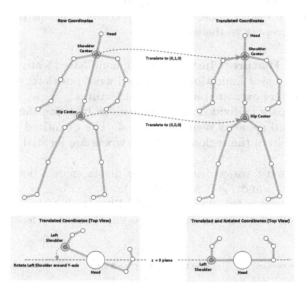

Fig. 3. World Coordinate Normalization

3.2 Gesture Representation

A total of six groups of features were extracted from the skeleton model for each frame. The features we have used to represent gestures are as following:

Upper Body Joint World Coordinates: The world coordinates represent the global position of a tracked joint in 2.5D space. Each joint coordinate is represented by C_x, C_y, C_z components of the subject's global position in milimeters [8].

From the upper body joints, we have used Head, Shoulder Center, Left & Right Shoulder, Left & Right Elbow, Left & Right Wrist, Left & Right Hand, Spine and Hip Center's world coordinates, thus making 36 features in total.

Normalized Upper Body Joint World Coordinates: We have obtained normalized world coordinates as explained in Section 3.1. Each normalized joint coordinate is represented by N_x, N_y, N_z components of the subject's global position after normalization. We used the same 12 joints from the unprocessed joint coordinates, thus making another 36 features in total.

Upper Body Joint Rotations: The world rotation contains the orientation of skeleton bones in terms of absolute transformations. Each joint orientation is represented with four quaternion values $\theta_w, \theta_x, \vartheta_y, \theta_z$. The orientation of a bone is relative to the previous bone, and the hip center contains the orientation of the subject with respect to the sensor.

Skeleton Based Features: Instead of using hand based features, which can be unreliable due to sensor limitations, quantized wrist positions, wrist movements and trajectories were extracted as additional features.

The gesture space is divided into nine regions by using the middle point of shoulder bones and spine as seen in Figure 4. The quantized positions, representing the centroid of the region where the wrists are located, are the features W_R and W_L.

Additionally, wrist trajectories and their displacements between frames are used as features (T_R and T_L & M_R and M_L).

Since the gestures in this dataset mainly differ in shoulder, elbow, and wrist positions; bone orientations are also used as supplementary features ($B_{1:4}$).

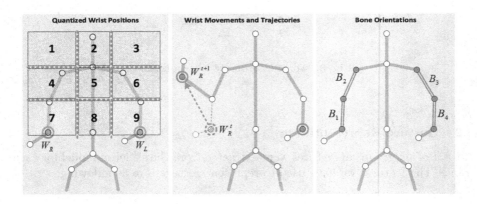

Fig. 4. Skeleton Based Features

3.3   Constructing Gesture Templates

As mentioned in Section 3.2, our feature vector belonging to frame at time t (F_t) consists of the features in Equation 1.

$$F_t = <C_x, C_y, C_z, N_x, N_y, N_z, \theta_w, \theta_x, \theta_y, \theta_z, W_R, W_L, T_R, T_L, M_R, M_L, B_{1:4} > \tag{1}$$

Due to their lack of temporal mechanisms, spatial machine learning methods such as Support Vector Machines and Random Decision Forests are not suitable for recognizing gestures. In order to use powerful spatial classifiers, such as ensemble methods with temporal data, temporal features need to be of fixed sizes. In our framework, this is achieved through padding per-frame features (F_t) together in fixed k sized structures called **templates** (T_t) as in Equation 2.

$$T_t = <F_{t-\frac{k-1}{2}}, ..., F_{t-1}, F_t, F_{t+1}, ..., F_{t+\frac{k-1}{2}} > \tag{2}$$

In template based gesture recognition, increasing template size enhances temporal representation. However, memory and computational power restrictions of development systems limit the feature vector size. To overcome this, selection methods of frames for templates can be altered. We have experimented with the original rate videos, 2x downsampled videos and 3x downsampled videos as shown in Figure 5.

t-8	...	t-4	t-3	t-2	t-1	t	t+1	t+2	t+3	t+4	...	t+8	(1)
t-16	...	t-8	t-6	t-4	t-2	t	t+2	t+4	t+6	t+8	...	t+16	(2)
t-24	...	t-12	t-9	t-6	t-3	t	t+3	t+6	t+9	t+12	...	t+24	(3)

Fig. 5. Frame selection for original rate (1), 2x downsampled (2) and 3x downsampled (3) videos with the template size of 17.

3.4   Gesture Recognition with Random Desicion Forests

Random Decision Forest (RDF) is a supervised classification and regression technique that has become widely used due to its efficiency and simplicity. RDF's are an ensemble of random decision trees (RDT) [4]. Each tree is trained on a randomly sampled subset of the training data. This reduces overfitting in comparison to training RDTs on the entire dataset; therefore increasing stability and accuracy.

During training, a tree learns to split the original problem into smaller ones. At each non-leaf node, tests are generated through randomly selected subsets of features and thresholds. The tests are scored using the decrease in entropy, and best splits are chosen, and used for each node [4]. Based on these tests, bone leaf nodes separate the data into their left and right child nodes. At a leaf node, only samples that belong to the same class remain.

Classification of a frame is performed by starting at the root node and assigning the pixel either to the left or to the right child recursively until a leaf node is reached. Majority voting is used on prediction of all decision trees to decide on the final class of the gesture.

3.5   Decision-Level Fusion

In order to explore the effect of decision-level fusion, four different fusion strategies were used on the dataset.

These methods were used to fuse the predictions from three different models. To predict the label of a frame given its features, a 21-class classifier was used. However, as reported by Kuznetsova et al. [10], we have observed that random forest classifiers perform better when a lower number of classes are classified in a hierarchy. For this reason, the task of separating gestures from non-gestures and separating gestures among each other were handled by training different RDF classifiers.

Three RDF models were trained using the same development dataset: the 2 class Gesture/Non-Gesture (G-NG) model, the 20 class Gesture only model (20G) and the 21 class combined model (20G-NG).

1. **Non-Gesture Suppression:** Using the G-NG and 20G-NG models, all non-gesture frame predictions from G-NG model were imposed on the 20G-NG model's predictions. Remaining class labels were untouched.
2. **Median Filtering:** In addition to Non-Gesture Suppression, median filter of length three was used to suppress single frame anomalies.
3. **Majority Filtering Based Gesture Prediction:** Using the G-NG and 20G-NG models, gesture predictions from the 20G-NG model were replaced using a majority filtering approach. For each frame labeled as gesture by G-NG class, a majority filter of size M was applied on the 20G-NG predictions and the most frequently occuring gesture label in an M size neighborhood was assigned to that frame.
4. **20G Model Based Gesture Prediction:** An additional 20G model was used in conjuction with 20G-NG and G-NG models to perform better fusion. Each frame that was labeled as a gesture by G-NG and as a non-gesture by 20G-NG was assigned the value indicated by the 20G model.

4   Experiments and Results

To verify the effectiveness of the proposed approach, we have used the ChaLearn 2014 Gesture Recognition dataset. We performed our parameter optimization using the validation set, and reported test results on the test set with our best validation parameters.

All RDF models were trained with 134K features, where 134 is the number of features we have used and K is the template window size. At each node, these features were sampled with replacement from the training set and M features were selected, where $M = \sqrt{134K}$. A total of 100 trees were trained with each model. These values were determined through experimentations with the validation set.

In all the experiments, we use the Jaccard Index as our evaluation metric. Jaccard Index is a commonly used success criterion for the evaluation of gesture spotting. It is preferred in situations where penalizing false positives is considered as important as rewarding true positives. In this sense, for each frame belonging to one of the $n = 20$ gesture categories, Jaccard Index is defined as:

$$J_{s,n} = \frac{A_{s,n} \bigcap B_{s,n}}{A_{s,n} \bigcup B_{s,n}} \tag{3}$$

$A_{s,n}$ is the ground truth of gesture n at sequence s, and $B_{s,n}$ is the prediction for such a gesture at sequence s. $A_{s,n}$ and $B_{s,n}$ are vectors where entries denote frames in which the nth gesture is being performed [8].

Performance is evaluated based on the mean Jaccard Index among all gesture categories for all sequences, where all gesture categories are independent. In addition, when computing the mean Jaccard Index, all gesture categories have the same importance as indicated by the performance criteria of the ChaLearn 2014 Challenge [8].

Using the Jaccard Index, we have tested our system with several parameters such as template size, template selection strategy and fusion methods.

Template Size Optimization: The size and selection criterion of the temporal gesture templates were crucial parameters of the designed system. After obtaining per-frame spatial features, templates for each frame were formed by stacking features belonging to consecutive frames. We have experimented with template sizes from 1 to 21 while incrementing template size by four at each experiment.

Experiments showed that increasing the template size increased overall recognition performance. While 0.369 Jaccard Index was obtained by using single frame templates, templates formed by the concatenation of 21 consecutive frames yielded the best score as 0.76. The effects of changing the size of the templates for the 20G-NG classification can be seen in Table 2 and Figure 6.

Due to large memory and computation time requirements, further experimentation with templates larger than 17 frames was not feasible. However, the results displayed a positive correlation between recognition performance and the length of represented temporal interval. To represent larger intervals without exceeding the memory limitations, template sampling (or in other words, video downsampling) strategies were applied.

Table 2. Evaluation of Different Template Sizes

Template Size:	1	5	9	13	17	21
Jaccard Index:	0.369	0.413	0.702	0.730	0.748	0.760

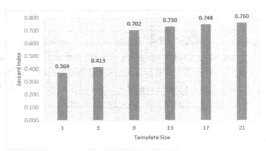

Fig. 6. Evaluation of Different Template Sizes

We have experimented with original rate videos, 2x downsampled videos and 3x downsampled videos. By adding every 2 and 3 consecutive frames, temporal intervals of length 33 and 49 were presented as 17 frame templates. Compared to the 0.748 Jaccard Index obtained without downsampling, adding 2x downsampling yielded a higher Jaccard Index of 0.773. The results can be seen in Table 3.

Table 3. Evaluation of Using Downsampled Videos

Downsampling rate:	none	2	3
Represented Interval Size:	17	33	49
Jaccard Index:	0.7483	0.7734	0.7724

Decision-Level Fusion: In order to explore the effects of decision-level fusion, four different fusion strategies were used on the dataset. Experiments were performed by training three separate models on the development set using different sets of labels. These are:

- 2 class G-NG model
- 20 class 20G model
- 21 class 20G-NG model

To decide on the fusion strategy, baseline performances were obtained using a template size of 17 with no downsampling. The G-NG method was the most accurate with a 2 class per-frame accuracy (not Jaccard Index) of 93%. The 20G-NG model had a 21 class accuracy of 88% with a hugely imbalanced class distribution favouring non-gestures. The 20G achieved the lowest accuracy with 80% performance. As co-articulation from non-gesture frames aid in the detection of gestures, the lack of non-gesture samples in training may have resulted in the lower performance of the 20G model.

As a result, in order to boost our performance on 21 class prediction of frame labels, the G-NG and 20G methods were used to boost the recognition performance of the 20G-NG classifier using different decision-level fusion approaches.

Experimental results showed that 21 sized templates cumulatively using non-gesture suppression, median filtering and majority filtering based gesture prediction approaches achieved 0.776 Jaccard Index. The results of different fusion methods based on this strategy can be seen in Figure 7 and Table 4.

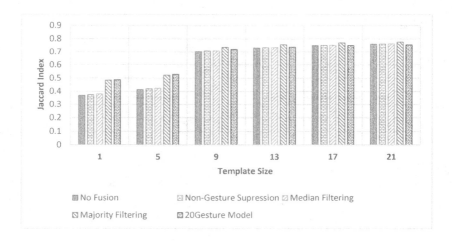

Fig. 7. Evaluation of Fusion Methods with Different Template Sizes

The effectiveness of the fusion methods on eliminating Gesture-Non-gesture misclassifications can be seen by examining the confusion matrices in Figure 8.

Combination of Fusion and Downsampling: By combining four different fusion methods with 3 different downsampling strategies, we have obtained the best results of our method on the validation set. Using 2x downsampling with non-gesture suppression, median filtering and majority filtering based gesture prediction, we have achieved 0.7875 Jaccard Index compared to the 0.7483 Jaccard Index of our baseline method. The results of these models are presented in Figure 9 and Table 5.

Table 4. Evaluation of Fusion Methods with Different Template Sizes

Method:	No Fusion	NG Supp.	Median Filt.	Majority Filt.	20G Model
Template Size: 1	0.369	0.375	0.380	0.484	0.486
Template Size: 5	0.413	0.419	0.423	0.522	0.528
Template Size: 9	0.702	0.707	0.707	0.736	0.719
Template Size: 13	0.730	0.733	0.734	0.756	0.738
Template Size: 17	0.748	0.750	0.751	0.769	0.748
Template Size: 21	0.760	0.761	0.762	**0.776**	0.754

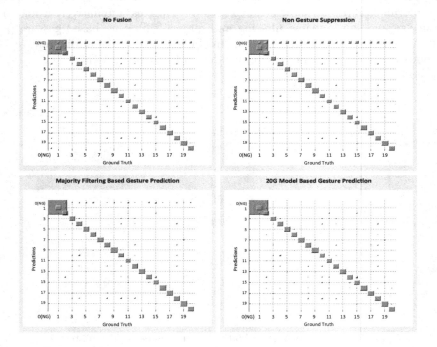

Fig. 8. Confusion matrices for different fusion methods: No Fusion (Top Left), Non-Gesture Suppression (Top Right), Majority Filtering Based Gesture Prediction (Bottom Left), 20G Model Based Gesture Prediction (Bottom Right). Large boxes on top left corner represents the prolific non-gesture class.

Table 5. Evaluation of Combining Decision-Level Fusion with Downsampling

Fusion Method:	No Fusion	NG Supp.	Median Flt.	Majority Flt.	20G Mod.
No downsampling:	0.7483	0.7504	0.7512	0.7691	0.7481
2x Downsampling:	0.7734	0.7715	0.7740	**0.7875**	0.7635
3x Downsampling:	0.7724	0.7707	0.7729	0.7869	0.7627

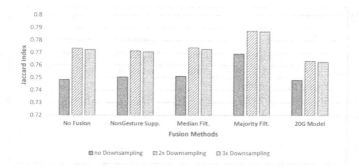

Fig. 9. Evaluation of Combining Decision-Level Fusion with Downsampling

Comparison of Test Results with other Methods: The overall performance evaluation and comparison of the system was done using the evaluation framework of the ChaLearn competition [8]. Due to timing and complexity considerations, we have submitted our template based random forest (**tbRF**) method results with no downsampling and template size 17. A summary of the challenge results can be seen in Table 6.

Table 6. Comparison of Our System with other ChaLearn [8] Competitors

Method	J.Index	Modality	Features	Classifier
[15]	0.8499	rgb depth skeleton	Raw Skeleton Joints	DeepNN
[13]	0.8339	rgb depth skeleton	HOG skeleton	Adaboost
[5]	0.8267	rgb skeleton	HOG skeleton	MRF KNN
[16]	0.7919	rgb	HOG HOF VLAD	SVM
[17]	0.7880	rgb depth	Raw Skeleton Joints	CNN
[28]	0.7873	depth skeleton	Raw	HMM DeepNN
tbRF	**0.7466**	**skeleton**	Skeleton Based	RDF
[9]	0.7454	skeleton	Skeleton / Fisher Vector	SVM
[6]	0.6489	rgb depth skeleton	STIPS	RDF
[11]	0.5971	mask depth skeleton	HOG Skeleton	SVMHMM

Looking at the results, we can claim that we obtain the best results among the papers that only use skeleton based features. Observation of the close performance of [9] in Table 6 may suggest the limits of skeleton based features. However, we were able to show that performance was increased through the exploitation of the temporal characteristics.

5   Conclusions

The paper has described a system for the visual recognition of gestures. The system takes body coordinates extracted by Microsoft Kinect, and performs feature normalization and template based Random Decision Forest learning to automatically recognize gestures.

We have achieved a 0.7875 Jaccard Index on the evaluation dataset using 2x downsampled video based templates, and 0.769 with original rate video based templates. These results were justified as we achieved a final Jaccard Index of 0.746 on the ChaLearn 2014 challenge test set using original rate video based templates. This score placed our team at the 7th place among 17 contenders in the third track of the competition. From the submitted fact sheets, it appears that the method presented in this paper was the highest performing among other methods that exclusively used features based on skeleton data. We also note that the 0.746 Jaccard Index on the test set did not include downsampling approaches as these methods were not implemented before the challenge deadline.

Furthermore, the recognition models were only trained on the training set. We were unable to increase the size of our development set with validation samples, as the 31GB memory required by the Random Decision Forest algorithm made training impractical. While we were able to verify that expanding the template size to 21 frames improved overall recognition performance, we were unable to perform additional experiments due to computational limitations. Therefore, reducing the memory requirements through better memory management or more efficient feature representations may allow the method to achieve even higher results.

Possible future works to improve continuous recognition performance include changing Random Decision Forest feature sampling strategies and incorporating depth/color based features to increase the discriminative power of the gesture representation methods. Furthermore, using transfer learning methods to increase user independence may also benefit overall recognition performance.

References

1. Agarwal, A., Triggs, B.: Tracking articulated motion using a mixture of autoregressive models. In: Pajdla, T., Matas, J.G. (eds.) ECCV 2004. LNCS, vol. 3023, pp. 54–65. Springer, Heidelberg (2004)
2. Bishop, C.M.: Pattern Recognition and Machine Learning (Information Science and Statistics). Springer, New York (2006)
3. Bobick, A.F., Davis, J.W.: The recognition of human movement using temporal templates. IEEE Transactions on Pattern Analysis and Machine Intelligence **23**(3), 257–267 (2001)
4. Breiman, L.: Random forests. Machine Learning **45**(1), 5–32 (2001)
5. Chang, J.Y.: Nonparametric gesture labeling from multi-modal data. In: European Conference on Computer Vision (ECCV) 2014 ChaLearn Workshop, Zurich (2014)
6. Chen, G., Clarke, D., Weikersdorfer, D., Giuliani, M.: Multi-modality gesture detection and recognition with un-supervision randomization and discrimination. In: European Conference on Computer Vision (ECCV) 2014 ChaLearn Workshop, Zurich (2014)

7. Erol, A., Bebis, G., Nicolescu, M., Boyle, R.D., Twombly, X.: Vision-based hand pose estimation: A review. Computer Vision and Image Understanding **108**(1–2), 52–73 (2007)
8. Escalera, S., Baró, X., Gonzàlez, J., Bautista, M.A., Madadi, M., Reyes, M., Ponce, V., Escalante, H.J., Shotton, J., Guyon, I.: ChaLearn looking at people challenge 2014: dataset and results. In: ECCV Workshop, Zurich (2014)
9. Evangelidis; G., Singh; G., Horaud, R.: Continuous gesture recognition from articulated poses. In: European Conference on Computer Vision (ECCV) 2014 ChaLearn Workshop, Zurich (2014)
10. Kuznetsova, A., Leal-Taixe, L., Rosenhahn, B.: Real-time sign language recognition using a consumer depth camera. In: ICCV 2013 (2013)
11. Liang, B., Zheng, L.: Multi-modal gesture recognition using skeletal joints and motion trail model. In: European Conference on Computer Vision (ECCV) 2014 ChaLearn Workshop, Zurich, pp. 1–16 (2014)
12. Mitra, S., Acharya, T.: Gesture Recognition: A Survey. IEEE Transactions on Systems, Man and Cybernetics, Part C (Applications and Reviews) **37**(3), 311–324 (2007)
13. Monnier, C., German, S., Ost, A.: A multi-scale boosted detector for efficient and robust gesture recognition. In: European Conference on Computer Vision (ECCV) 2014 ChaLearn Workshop (2014)
14. Mori, G.: Max-margin hidden conditional random fields for human action recognition. In: 2009 IEEE Conference on Computer Vision and Pattern Recognition, pp. 872–879. IEEE (2009)
15. Neverova, N., Wolf, C., Taylor, G.W., Nebout, F.: Multi-scale deep learning for gesture detection and localization. In: European Conference on Computer Vision (ECCV) 2014 ChaLearn Workshop, Zurich (2014)
16. Peng, X., Wang, L.: Action and gesture temporal spotting with. In: European Conference on Computer Vision (ECCV) 2014 ChaLearn Workshop (2014)
17. Pigou, L., Dieleman, S., Kindermans, P.J., Schrauwen, B.: Sign language recognition using convolutional neural networks. In: European Conference on Computer Vision (ECCV) 2014 ChaLearn Workshop, Zurich (2014)
18. Poppe, R.: A survey on vision-based human action recognition. Image and Vision Computing **28**(6), 976–990 (2010)
19. Rabiner, L., Juang, B.: An introduction to hidden Markov models. IEEE ASSP Magazine (1986)
20. Rautaray, S.S., Agrawal, A.: Vision based hand gesture recognition for human computer interaction: a survey (2012)
21. Schuldt, C., Laptev, I., Caputo, B.: Recognizing human actions: a local svm approach. In: Proceedings of the 17th International Conference on Pattern Recognition, ICPR 2004, vol. 3, pp. 32–36, August 2004
22. Sempena, S., Maulidevi, N.U., Aryan, P.R.: Human action recognition using Dynamic Time Warping. In: Proceedings of the 2011 International Conference on Electrical Engineering and Informatics, pp. 1–5 (2011)
23. Shotton, J., Fitzgibbon, A., Cook, M., Sharp, T., Finocchio, M., Moore, R., Kipman, A., Blake, A.: Real-time human pose recognition in parts from single depth images. In: CVPR, vol. 2 (2011)
24. Starner, T., Pentland, A.: Real-time American sign language recognition from video using hidden Markov models. In: Proceedings of Computer Vision (1995)
25. Suarez, J., Murphy, R.R.: Hand gesture recognition with depth images: a review. In: Proceedings - IEEE International Workshop on Robot and Human Interactive Communication, pp. 411–417 (2012)

26. Sullivan, J., Carlsson, S.: Recognizing and tracking human action. In: Heyden, A., Sparr, G., Nielsen, M., Johansen, P. (eds.) ECCV 2002, Part I. LNCS, vol. 2350, pp. 629–644. Springer, Heidelberg (2002)
27. Wachs, J.P., Kölsch, M., Stern, H., Edan, Y.: Vision-based hand-gesture applications (2011)
28. Wu, D., Shao, L.: Deep dynamic neural networks for gesture segmentation and recognition. In: European Conference on Computer Vision (ECCV) 2014 ChaLearn Workshop, Zurich (2014)
29. Yamato, J., Ohya, J., Ishii, K.: Recognizing human action in time-sequential images using hidden Markov model. In: Proceedings CVPR 1992, IEEE Computer Society Conference on Computer Vision and Pattern Recognition, pp. 379–385 (1992)

Continuous Gesture Recognition
from Articulated Poses

Georgios D. Evangelidis[1]([⊠]), Gurkirt Singh[2], and Radu Horaud[1]

[1] INRIA Grenoble Rhône-Alpes, Grenoble, France
{georgios.evangelidis,radu.horaud}@inria.fr
[2] Siemens RTC-ICV, Bangalore, India
gurkirt.singh@siemens.com

Abstract. This paper addresses the problem of continuous gesture recognition from articulated poses. Unlike the common isolated recognition scenario, the gesture boundaries are here unknown, and one has to solve two problems: segmentation and recognition. This is cast into a labeling framework, namely every site (frame) must be assigned a label (gesture ID). The inherent constraint for a piece-wise constant labeling is satisfied by solving a global optimization problem with a smoothness term. For efficiency reasons, we suggest a dynamic programming (DP) solver that seeks the optimal path in a recursive manner. To quantify the consistency between the labels and the observations, we build on a recent method that encodes sequences of articulated poses into Fisher vectors using short skeletal descriptors. A sliding window allows to frame-wise build such Fisher vectors that are then classified by a multi-class SVM, whereby each label is assigned to each frame at some cost. The evaluation in the ChalearnLAP-2014 challenge shows that the method outperforms other participants that rely only on skeleton data. We also show that the proposed method competes with the top-ranking methods when colour and skeleton features are jointly used.

1 Introduction

Gesture and human action recognition from visual information is an active topic with many potential applications in human-computer interaction. The recent release of depth sensors (e.g., Kinect) led to the development of recognition methods based on depth or RGB-D data. Moreover, recent advances on human pose recognition from depth data [23] made the human skeleton extraction possible, so that three information sources are at one's disposal: color, depth, and skeleton. The latter has been proved very effective for human action recognition when used either alone [7, 26] or in conjunction with color/depth features [17, 35].

The majority of gesture (or action) recognition methods consider known boundaries of individual gestures and solve the isolated gesture recognition problem as a single-label assignment (1-of-L) problem, e.g., by invoking a multi-class

Support from the European Research Council (ERC) through the Advanced Grant VHIA (#340113) is greatly acknowledged.

© Springer International Publishing Switzerland 2015
L. Agapito et al. (Eds.): ECCV 2014 Workshops, Part I, LNCS 8925, pp. 595–607, 2015.
DOI: 10.1007/978-3-319-16178-5_42

classfier. However, the continuous case is mostly met in practice, i.e., a video may contain a sequence of gestures in an unknown order and with unknown gesture boundaries. Therefore, one has to solve both the segmentation and the classification problem in order to answer the question: *which* gesture and *when* is performed?

In this paper, we address the above problem within an energy minimization framework, that is, we formulate it as a frame-wise labeling problem under the constraint for a piece-wise constant solution. We build on a recent isolated action recognition method [7] and extend it to the continuous case for gesture recognition. Unlike [7], we use a reduced set of the proposed skeletal descriptors per pose in order to describe the position of the hands with respect to the body. Based on a sliding window, we build frame-wise Fisher vectors that encode the poses of a video segment. Then, a multi-class SVM allows us to assign each label to each frame at some cost, while a binary classifier estimates costs for a "no-gesture" class. All these costs, summarized in a table, are finally exploited by a dynamic programming method that estimates the piece-wise constant labeling which minimizes the total energy. Fig. 1 illustrates the proposed pipeline. We test our method on the ChalearnLAP-2014 dataset [5] and we compare our method with other challenge participants. Note that our primary goal is to first extensively investigate the potential of the skeleton information in a continuous recognition framework, before combining skeletal data with other modalities.

The remainder of the paper is organised as follows. We summarise the related work in Sec. 2 and we present the skeleton-based representation in Sec. 3. Sec. 4 presents the energy minimization framework, while our method is tested on public datasets in Sec. 5. Finally, Sec. 6 concludes this work.

2   Related Work

Regardless of the continuous nature of the recognition problem,[1] one initially has to extract features from the available modalities in order to encode the footage. While the potential of color information to provide informative features in a recognition scenario has been extensively studied [30], the release of depth sensors led to the development of depth descriptors, e.g, local occupancy patterns [27,31] and histogram of spatio-temporal surface normals [18,37]. More interstingly, the articulated human pose estimation from depth data [23] inspired many researchers to use skeleton as third modality along with RGB-D data, thus building several skeletal descriptors: joint position differences [31,36], joint angles [3], joint motion characteristics [38], poses of spatio-temporal joint groups [29], relative positions of joint quadruples [7], relative position of joint edges [26], joint angle trajectories [17]. The benefit of combing features from multiple visual sources has been also illustrated [17,31,35].

The features are typically translated into a single vector, e.g. Bag-of-Words (BoW) histograms [35] or Fisher vectors [7], while a classifier, e.g. SVM, does

---

[1] we do not distinguish the problems of human action and gesture recognition, since the latter can be roughly seen as the former when the upper-body part is used

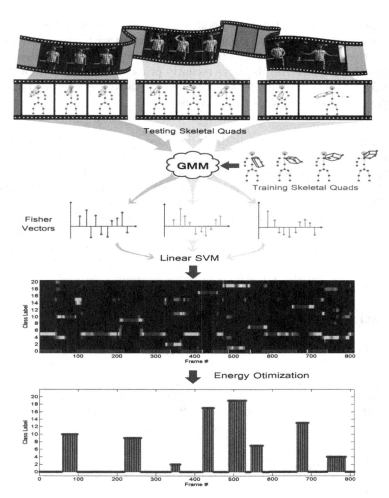

Fig. 1. A Gaussian Mixture Model (GMM), learnt on training data, is supposed to generate skeletal quads. Based on the GMM parameters, the skeletal quads of a gesture segment are encoded into a Fisher vector, and a multi-class SVM assigns a cost per label. A global energy minimizer uses these costs to provide a piece-wise constant labeling.

the 1–of–L label assignment in isolated case. Such a strategy is only locally applicable in a continuous recognition scenario and one has to deal with the temporal nature of the labeling, like in speech recognition. The latter inspired people to develop continuous gesture/action recognition models.

The first continuous sign-language recognizers used hidden Markov models (HMM) [25,28] for both modeling and recognition. CRF models [24,32] have been also proposed to avoid HMM's narrow temporal dependencies. Dynamic programming (DP) constitutes a standard framework as well, either in one-pass or two-pass mode, while it can be used in conjunction with either generative or discriminative classifiers [9,14,22]. In the DP context, action templates (temporal models that replace HMMs) were recently proposed to be used in a dynamic warping framework [11]. We refer the reader to the latter for a detailed discussion about the pros and cons of all the above models.

ChalearnLAP-2014: Several methods have been proposed in the context of the ChalearnLAP-2014 challenge [5] for the continuous gesture recognition problem. The majority of the methods exploit features from both RGB and depth data [2,4,13,15,16,21,33], while [1] and [19] rely on single modalities, i.e., skeleton and RGB respectively. The silence-based pre-segmentation of sequences is proposed by [4,13], while the rest of the methods simultaneously solve the segmentation and recognition problems, e.g., with the help of a temporal model [2,33]. A deep learning framework that employs convolutional neural networks obtained the best results in the challenge [16]. We refer the reader to [5] for a detailed categorization of the above methods in terms of several features.

3   Gesture Representation

We rely on [7] in order to encode a set of articulated poses into an informative vector. This approach uses skeletal features, referred to as skeletal quads, to describe a sequence for isolated action recognition. A set of skeletal features is then encoded as a Fisher vector with the help of a trained GMM that explains the generation of any feature set. We briefly discuss these two steps below, that are slightly modified for a gesture recognition scenario.

3.1   Skeletal Quads

In order to describe a gesture instance, and in particular the hand pose with respect to the body, we use the skeletal quad [7]. This descriptor encodes the geometric relation of joint quadruples thus leading to a low-dimensional descriptor (see Fig 2). This idea originates in [12], while it has been successfully adopted to video synchronisation [6,8]. In short, if $(\mathbf{x}_1\ \mathbf{x}_2\ \mathbf{x}_3\ \mathbf{x}_4)$ is an ordered set of four joints, i.e., $\mathbf{x}_i \in \mathbb{R}^3$, it is encoded as $\mathbf{q} = [\mathcal{S}(\mathbf{x}_3); \mathcal{S}(\mathbf{x}_4)]$,[2] with $\mathbf{q} \in \mathbb{R}^6$, where

$$\mathcal{S}(\mathbf{x}_i) = s\mathbf{R}[\mathbf{x}_i - \mathbf{x}_1], \quad i = 1\ldots4, \tag{1}$$

and s, $\mathbf{R}$ are the scale and rotation respectively, such that $\mathcal{S}(\mathbf{x}_1) = [0,0,0]^\top$ and $\mathcal{S}(\mathbf{x}_2) = [1,1,1]^\top$. In other words, a similarity normalization is applied to the quadruple, whereby a gesture descriptor is obtained. When the actor looks at the camera (e.g., ChalearnLAP dataset), the above scheme is sufficient. When the camera viewpoint or the body orientation drastically change, any rotation

---

[2] the notation $[\cdot\,;\cdot]$ denotes vertical vector concatenation

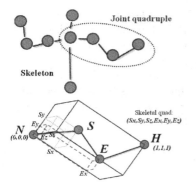

x_1	x_2	x_3	x_4
HipCenter	Head	HandLeft	HandRight
HipCenter	Head	HandRight	HandLeft
HipCenter	ShoulderCenter	ElbowRight	ElbowLeft
HipCenter	ShoulderCenter	ElbowLeft	ElbowRight
HipCenter	ShoulderCenter	ElbowRight	HandRight
HipCenter	ShoulderCenter	ElbowLeft	HandLeft
Spine	ShoulderLeft	HandLeft	ElbowLeft
Spine	ShoulderRight	HandRight	ElbowRight
ShoulderRight	ShoulderLeft	HandRight	HandLeft
ShoulderRight	ShoulderLeft	HandLeft	HandRight
ShoulderRight	HandRight	WristRight	ElbowRight
ShoulderLeft	HandLeft	WristLeft	ElbowLeft
ShoulderRight	HandRight	ElbowLeft	HandLeft
ShoulderLeft	HandLeft	ElbowRight	HandRight

Fig. 2. (*Left:*) A sketch from [7] that illustrates the coding when (x_1 x_2 x_3 x_4) correspond to the joints {Neck, Hand, Shoulder, Elbow}; the quad descriptor is $q = [S_x, S_y, S_z, E_x, E_y, E_z]^\top$. (*Right:*) The 14 joint quadruples whose quads are locally describe the upper-body pose.

around the local axis $x_1 x_2$ (axis NH in Fig. 2) must be also normalised, i.e., **R** should account for this further rotation as well. This would lead to a fully view-invariant code with less discriminability in principle.

Unlike [7] that enables all possible quads, we choose 14 specific quads based on the upper-body joints, as shown in Fig. 2 (right). Note that this list is not cross-validated based on some data-sets, but it intuitively describes the relation among upper-body joints, by taking into account the body symmetry. For example, the first quad encodes the coordinates of the two hands when the origin is the Hip-Center and the Head coincides with the point $[1, 1, 1]^\top$.

3.2   Gesture Encoding

Fisher vectors have been proved more discriminative than the the popular BoW representation in a recognition context [20]. We adopt this representation in order to describe a gesture sequence as a set of gesture instances. Note that the low dimension of the skeletal quads compensates for the large inherent dimensionality associated with Fisher vectors.

If statistical independence is assumed, a set of M skeletal quads, $Q = \{q_i, 1 \le i \le M\}$, can be modelled by a K-component Gaussian mixture model (GMM), i.e.,

$$p(Q|\theta) = \prod_{i=1}^{M} \sum_{k=1}^{K} w_k \mathcal{N}(q_i | \mu_k, \sigma_k), \qquad (2)$$

where $\theta = \{w_k, \mu_k, \sigma_k\}_{k=1}^{K}$ is the set of the mixture parameters with mixing coefficients w_k, means $\mu_k \in \mathbb{R}^6$ and *diagonal* covariance matrices, represented here as vectors, i.e., $\sigma_k \in \mathbb{R}^{6 \times 1}$. Once the GMM parameters are estimated, e.g., via the standard EM algorithm, any set Q may be described by its Fisher score [10], namely the gradient of the log-probability with respect to the GMM parameters, $J_\theta^Q = \nabla_\theta \log p(Q|\theta)$. The quadratic form of two such gradient vectors and the inverse information matrix defines the Fisher kernel, which can be written as a linear kernel of the so called Fisher vectors (FV), denoted here as $\mathcal{J}$. The reader is referred to [10] for a detailed analysis.

By considering the gradients with respect to $\boldsymbol{\mu}_k$ and $\boldsymbol{\sigma}_k$, the FV consists of the concatenation of two vectors $\mathcal{J}_{\boldsymbol{\mu}_k}^Q$ and $\mathcal{J}_{\boldsymbol{\sigma}_k}^Q$. One can easily show (see [20]) that the $(6k - 6 + j)$-th element of the above vectors ($1 \leq j \leq 6$, $1 \leq k \leq K$), that is the j-th entry for the k-th block, is given by

$$\mathcal{J}_{\boldsymbol{\mu}_k}^Q(j) = \frac{1}{M\sqrt{\pi_k}} \sum_{i=1}^{M} \gamma_{k,i} \frac{q_i^j - \mu_k^j}{\sigma_k^j},$$

$$\mathcal{J}_{\boldsymbol{\sigma}_k}^Q(j) = \frac{1}{M\sqrt{2\pi_k}} \sum_{i=1}^{M} \gamma_{k,i} \left(\left(\frac{q_i^j - \mu_k^j}{\sigma_k^j} \right)^2 - 1 \right), \tag{3}$$

where $\gamma_{k,i}$ is the posterior probability that $\mathbf{q}_i$ belongs to kth cluster conditioned by Q. The normalization by M is added to avoid dependence on the Q's cardinality. Since quads live in $\mathbb{R}^6$, the Fisher vectors are reasonably long, i.e., of dimension $12K$. Once the FV is computed, we apply a power-normalisation step, i.e., each vector element x is transformed to $sgn(x) * |x|^\alpha$ ($0 < \alpha < 1$), and the resulting vector is further normalized by its l_2 norm. Note that the power-normalization eliminates the inherent sparseness of the FV; the benefit is discussed in detail in [20].

Unlike [7], we do not use a temporal pyramid since we are going to describe the gestures locally. As a consequence, it is only the following energy minimization scheme that takes into account the temporal nature of gestures towards a continuous labelling.

4   Continuous Gesture Recognition

We formulate the continuous gesture recognition problem as a labeling problem. In particular, every frame $t \in \{1, ..., T\}$ must be assigned a label $f_t \in \mathcal{L}$ that denotes the gesture ID the frame belongs to. As a consequence, the goal is to find the frame-wise labeling $f = \{f_1, ..., f_t, ..., f_T\}$ subject to: i) f is consistent with the observations, ii) f is *piece-wise constant*. Note that a frame-wise labeling direclty answers the question "which gesture and when is performed?".

Such a *global* labeling problem can be cast into an energy minimization framework, that is, one estimates the labeling f that minimizes the energy

$$E(f) = E_D(f) + E_S(f), \tag{4}$$

where $E_D(f)$ (the data term) measures the dissimilarity between f and observations and $E_S(f)$ (the smoothness term) penalizes labelings that are not piece-wise constant.

The data-term is typically defined as $E_D(f) = \sum_{t=1}^{T} D_t(f_t)$, where $D_t(f_t)$ measures how appropriate the label f_t is for t-th frame. Here, we use a mutli-class SVM classifier to evaluate this appropriateness. Note that the framework of [34] allows one to compute an empirical probability of assigning a label to an input. We train a multi-class SVM in a one-versus-all manner using FVs of isolated gesture examples. During testing, FVs are built based on a sliding temporal window centered at each frame. Instead of a fully varying window size, we suggest the use of three windows: a narrow, a mid-size and a wide window. By denoting as $p_t(f_t)$ the probability of assigning the label f_t to frame t, the above appropriateness is computed by the following convex combination

$$D_t(f_t) = 1 - \sum_{j=1}^{3} w_j p_t^j(f_t) \tag{5}$$

where j stands for different windows and w_j can balance their contribution.

The smoothness term penalizes the assignment of different labels to successive frames. If we consider that each frame interacts with its immediate neighbors (first-order Markov assumption), the smoothness term can be written as a summation of pairwise potentials

$$E_S(f) = \sum_{t=1}^{T-1} V(f_t, f_{t+1}). \tag{6}$$

Since we seek a piece-wise constant labeling, we define the potential function

$$V(f_t, f_{t+1}) = \begin{cases} 0 & \text{if } f_t = f_{t+1} \\ \beta & \text{otherwise.} \end{cases} \tag{7}$$

To efficiently solve the global optimization problem

$$\min_f E(f), \tag{8}$$

we use a dynamic programming approach, while we leave more sophisticated solutions for a future paper. If $C_t[f_t]$ denotes the minimum labeling cost for the first t frames provided that the t-th frame has label f_t, the following recursive equation (t is increasing) fills in a table C of size $|\mathcal{L}| \times T$:

$$\begin{aligned} C_1[f_1] &= D_1(f_1) \\ C_t[f_t] &= D_t(f_t) + \min_{f_{t-1}}(C_{t-1}[f_{t-1}] + V(f_{t-1}, f_t)). \end{aligned} \tag{9}$$

Once the table is filled, the optimal solution can be obtained by first finding the label of the last frame, i.e., $f_T^* = \arg\min_f C_T[f]$, and then by tracing back in order of decreasing t:

$$f_t^* = \arg\min_{f_i} \left(C_t[f_t]) + V(f_t, f_{t+1}^*) \right). \tag{10}$$

In order to take into account the silent part of a gesture sequence, we train a binary classifier based on silent and non-silent parts of a sufficient number of training examples (see details in Sec. 5). This leads to an extra row in table C that corresponds to a "no-gesture" class. Note that this does not imply a pre-segmentation, but rather, we let the energy minimizer decide which frames are silent or no.

Note that if one wants to solve the isolated recognition problem, dynamic programming is not required (C reduces to a vector). In such a case, the single label is directly obtained by $f^* = \arg\max_f p(f)$.

5   Experiments

5.1   MSR-Action3D Dataset

Although we focus on the continuous recognition problem, it is important to show that our gesture representation is quite discriminative in the isolated recognition scenario. Our method reduces to [7] for isolated case, being the only difference the few quads that are considered here. We refer the reader to [7] for a performance analysis of the method in isolated case. Here, we just present an updated comparison table based on the widely used MSR-Action3D dataset, by including very recent methods that are missed in [7].

We skip the details of the dataset (see [7]). We just notice that 20 actions are performed by 10 actors and that a cross-subject splitting is considered, i.e. five actors for training and five actors for testing. FVs are built based on 128-component GMM, while they are power-normalized with $\alpha = 0.3$. Instead of all possible joint quadruples (4845) in [7], only 44 meaningful quads are used; they relate hand and leg joints with the body.[3] Note that this leads to a more efficient recognition since the running time of building FVs is reduced by a factor of 100.

Table 1 shows the performance of various methods for this dataset. We do not observe significant loss in performance when using fewer quads. Our method achieves similar performance with the state-of-the-art methods that count on skeleton joints, while it competes with the best-performing methods that use multi-modal features.

5.2   Multi-modal Gesture Dataset 2014

The Multi-modal Gesture dataset was released for the ChalearnLAP-2014 challenge (Track3) [5]. More than $14,000$ gestures drawn from a vocabulary of 20 Italian sign gesture categories were performed by several actors. Each actor, being captured by a Kinect camera, performed a non-fixed number of gestures. Multi-modal data are available, i.e., skeleton (20 joints), RGB and depth image sequences.

The dataset is divided into three parts, development data ($7,754$ manually labeled gestures), validation data ($3,362$ labelled gestures) and evaluation data (2742 gestures). Training and parameter cross-validation was done on development and validation data respectively; testing was done on the evaluation data. In particular, the GMM and the linear multi-class SVM[4] were learned on the

---

[3] We used the code provided by https://team.inria.fr/perception/research/skeletalquads/

[4] The scikit-learn Python package was used

Table 1. Recognition accuracy on MSRAction3D datasets.

Modality	Methods	Average Accuracy
	EigenJoints [36]	82.33%
	Joint Angles [17]	83.53%
	FV of skeletal quads (**less quads**)	89.07%
Skeleton	Skeleton Lie group [26]	89.45%
	FV of skeletal quads [7]	89.86%
	Pose Set [29]*	90.22%
	Moving pose [38]	**91.70%**
	Joints+Actionlets [31]	88.20%
	HON4D [18]*	88.89%
Skeleton, RGB-D	Joints + Depth Cuboids [35]	89.30%
	Super Normal vectors [37]	93.09%
	Joints+STIP [39]*	94.30%
	Joint Angles+MaxMin+HOG^2 [17]*	**94.84%**

*different cross-subject splitting

development data while the parameter β of the smoothness term was cross-validated on the validation set; best performance was obtained with $\beta = 3$. As mentioned, 14 quads were invoked (see Fig. 2). We used a GMM with 128 components that led to 1536D Fisher vectors, which were power-normalized with $\alpha = 0.5$. While we observed that less components lead to a lower performance in validation set, we did not test more components to avoid very long FVs. The size of the three sliding windows were 15, 37 and 51, while equal weights ($w_j = 1/3$) were used to compute the cost of assigning each label per frame. There was no significant difference in the performance when changing the window size and the weights. As with the multi-class classifier, the cost of assigning a "no-gesture" label is the average cost obtained from three classifications of short windows, i.e., with 5, 7 and 9 frames. We used 50 videos of the development data for this training, by considering each FV of a window as an example. The performance of the recognition was quantified by the average Jaccard index.

Table 2 summarizes the Jaccard indices of the participants in the challenge. We first sort out the methods that count on skeleton data, and then the methods that combine different modalities. The proposed method and Camgoz et al. [1] achieve the best performance when only skeleton joints are used (almost same index). Note that the Jaccard index 0.745 corresponds to the performance of the software version submitted to the challenge. A fixed bug led to a higher index, i.e., 0.768. As previously, the best performing methods use multi-modal features. Neverova et al. [16] exploit all the modalities, thus obtaining the highest Jaccard index (0.850). Note that Peng et al. [19] performs quite well by using only RGB data.

We also report the performance of our method when skeletal features are combined with color features, i.e., histograms of flows (HOF) [30]. We reduce the dimensionality of HOF feature from 108 to 48 using PCA, and then, we learn another GMM with 64 components which led to 6144D Fisher vector. An early

Table 2. Results of the ChalearnLAP-2014 challenge (Track 3) [5]

Team	Modality	Jaccard index
Camgoz et al. [1]	Skeleton	0.746
FV of quads (**this work**)	Skeleton	0.745 (0.768*)
Team-13 (Terrier)	Skeleton	0.539
Team-17 (YNL)	Skeleton	0.271
Neverova et al. [16]	Skeleton, Depth, RGB	**0.850**
Monnier et al. [15]	Depth, RGB	0.834
Ju Yong Chang [2]	Skeleton, RGB	0.827
FV of quads+HOF (**this work**)	Skeleton, RGB,	0.816
Peng et al. [19]	RGB	0.792
Pigou et al. [21]	Depth, RGB	0.789
Di Wu and Ling Shao [33]	Skeleton, Depth	0.787
Team-9 (TelePoints)	Skeleton, Depth, RGB	0.689
Chen et al. [4]	Skeleton, Depth, RGB	0.649
Bin Liang and Lihong Zheng [13]	Skeleton, Depth	0.597
Team-12 (Iva.mm)	Skeleton, Depth, RGB	0.556
Team-14 (Netherlands)	Skeleton, Depth, RGB	0.431
Team-16 (vecsrel)	Skeleton, Depth, RGB	0.408

*A fixed software bug led to a higher index

fusion is performed, i.e., the two FVs are concatenated into a single input to be classified. This leads to a higher index (0.816) and makes the proposed method comparable with the top-ranking methods. Note that we did not investigate what is the best color feature to be combined with the quads. It is worth noticing that the performance when using only HOF features is 0.693. Apparently, the combination of skeletal quads with more sophisticated features [30] would lead to a higher index.

Fig. 3 depicts the confusion matrices for the continuous case when each frame is considered as an example (the reader should not confuse these numbers with the Jaccard indices of Table 2). We also show the confusion matrices that correspond to the isolated recognition scenario, i.e. when the gesture boundaries are known. The accuracy of our method in the isolated case is 90%, 86% and 94% when using skeleton, HOF and both features, respectively. The proposed representation is quite discriminative in either case. However, quite similar gestures like "Le vuoi prendere" (id 14) and "Non ce ne piu" (id 15) may be confused without finger joints. The confusion matrix in the continuous case is more sparse since the confusions are concentrated in the column of the no-gesture class (label 00), owing to the frame-wise labeling. It is important to note that the recognition accuracy of this class, i.e., 89%, 86% and 91%, is based on the final global labeling, as with any other class. Apparently, the use of color features improves the discrimination and the matrices tend to be more diagonal. Note that the percentages do not sum up to 100 since we keep the integer part of the numbers.

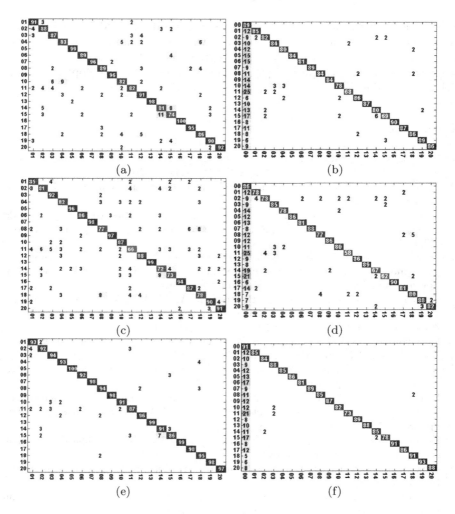

Fig. 3. Confusion matrices of our recognition method for Multi-modal gesture dataset when using skeletal quads (a,b), HOF (c,d), skeletal quads + HOF (e,f) in isolated (left) and continuous recognition scenario (right).

6   Conclusions

We dealt with the continuous gesture recognition problem from series of articulated poses. The problem was cast into a labeling framework and it was solved as a global energy minimization problem. We proposed a dynamic programming solver that exploits the outputs of multiple SVMs and provides a piece-wise constant labeling. We mainly tested our method on the Multi-model Gesture dataset, released for the ChalearnLAP-2014 challenge purposes. Despite the use of the skeleton information only, the proposed method achieved high recognition scores, while its performance was boosted when extra modalities, e.g. colour data, were used. Future work consists of extending Fisher vectors to deal with the temporal nature of a pose sequence, and of investigating the optimal fusion with other modalities.

References

1. Camgoz, N.C., Kindiroglu, A.A., Akarun, L.: Gesture recognition using template based random forest classifiers. In: ECCV Workshops (2014)
2. Chang, J.Y.: Nonparametric gesture labeling from multi-modal data. In: ECCV Workshops (2014)
3. Chaudhry, R., Ofli, F., Kurillo, G., Bajcsy, R., Vidal, R.: Bio-inspired dynamic 3d discriminative skeletal features for human action recognition. In: CVPR Workshops (CVPRW) (2013)
4. Chen, G., Clarke, D., Weikersdorfer, D., Giuliani, M., Gaschler, A., Knoll, A.: Multi-modality gesture detection and recognition with un-supervision, randomization and discrimination. In: ECCV Workshops (2014)
5. Escalera, S., Bar, X., Gonzlez, J., Bautista, M.A., Madadi, M., Reyes, M., Ponce, V., Escalante, H.J., Shotton, J., Guyon, I.: Chalearn looking at people challenge 2014: Dataset and results. In: ECCV Workshops (2014)
6. Evangelidis, G., Bauckhage, C.: Efficient subframe video alignment using short descriptors. IEEE T PAMI **35**, 2371–2386 (2013)
7. Evangelidis, G., Singh, G., Horaud, R., et al.: Skeletal quads: Human action recognition using joint quadruples. In: ICPR (2014)
8. Evangelidis, G.D., Bauckhage, C.: Efficient and robust alignment of unsynchronized video sequences. In: Mester, R., Felsberg, M. (eds.) DAGM 2011. LNCS, vol. 6835, pp. 286–295. Springer, Heidelberg (2011)
9. Hoai, M., Lan, Z.Z., De la Torre, F.: Joint segmentation and classification of human actions in video. In: CVPR (2011)
10. Jaakola, T., Haussler, D.: Exploiting generative models in discriminative classifiers. In: NIPS (1999)
11. Kulkarni, K., Evangelidis, G., Cech, J., Horaud, R.: Continuous action recognition based on sequence alignment. IJCV (2014) (preprint)
12. Lang, D., Hogg, D.W., Mierle, K., Blanton, M., Roweis, S.: Astrometry.net: Blind astrometric calibration of arbitrary astronomical images. The Astronomical Journal **137**, 1782–2800 (2010)
13. Liang, B., Zheng, L.: Multi-modal gesture recognition using skeletal joints and motion trail model. In: ECCV Workshops (2014)
14. Lv, F., Nevatia, R.: Recognition and segmentation of 3-D human action using HMM and multi-class adaboost. In: Leonardis, A., Bischof, H., Pinz, A. (eds.) ECCV 2006. LNCS, vol. 3954, pp. 359–372. Springer, Heidelberg (2006)
15. Monnier, C., German, S., Ost, A.: A multi-scale boosted detector for efficient and robust gesture recognition. In: ECCV Workshops (2014)
16. Neverova, N., Wolf, C., Taylor, G.W., Nebout, F.: Multi-scale deep learning for gesture detection and localization. In: ECCV Workshops (2014)
17. Ohn-Bar, E., Trivedi, M.M.: Joint angles similiarities and hog^2 for action recognition. In: Computer Vision and Pattern Recognition Workshops (CVPRW) (2013)

18. Oreifej, O., Liu, Z.: Hon4d: Histogram of oriented 4d normals for activity recognition from depth sequences. In: CVPR (2013)
19. Peng, X., Wang, L., Cai, Z.: Action and gesture temporal spotting with super vector representation. In: ECCV Workshops (2014)
20. Perronnin, F., Sánchez, J., Mensink, T.: Improving the fisher kernel for large-scale image classification. In: Daniilidis, K., Maragos, P., Paragios, N. (eds.) ECCV 2010, Part IV. LNCS, vol. 6314, pp. 143–156. Springer, Heidelberg (2010)
21. Pigou, L., Dieleman, S., Kindermans, P.J., Schrauwen, B.: Sign language recognition using convolutional neural networks. In: ECCV Workshops (2014)
22. Shi, Q., Cheng, L., Wang, L., Smola, A.: Human action segmentation and recognition using discriminative semi-markov models. IJCV **93**(1), 22–32 (2011)
23. Shotton, J., Fitzgibbon, A., Cook, M., Sharp, T., Finocchio, M., Moore, R., Kipman, A., Blake, A.: Real-time human pose recognition in parts from single depth images. In: CVPR (2011)
24. Sminchisescu, C., Kanaujia, A., Metaxas, D.: Conditional models for contextual human motion recognition. CVIU **104**(2), 210–220 (2006)
25. Starner, T., Weaver, J., Pentland, A.: Real-time american sign language recognition using desk and wearable computer based video. IEEE T PAMI **20**(12), 1371–1375 (1998)
26. Vemulapalli, R., Arrate, F., Chellappa, R.: Human action recognition by representing 3d skeletons as points in a lie group. In: CVPR (2014)
27. Vieira, A.W., Nascimento, E.R., Oliveira, G.L., Liu, Z., Campos, M.F.: On the improvement of human action recognition from depth map sequences using spacetime occupancy patterns. Pattern Recognition Letters **36**, 221–227 (2014)
28. Vogler, C., Metaxas, D.: ASL recognition based on a coupling between HMMs and 3D motion analysis. In: ICCV (1998)
29. Wang, C., Wang, Y., Yuille, A.L.: An approach to pose-based action recognition. In: CVPR (2013)
30. Wang, H., Schmid, C.: Action recognition with improved trajectories. In: ICCV (2013)
31. Wang, J., Liu, Z., Wu, Y., Yuan, J.: Mining actionlet ensemble for action recognition with depth cameras. In: CVPR (2012)
32. Wang, S.B., Quattoni, A., Morency, L., Demirdjian, D., Darrell, T.: Hidden conditional random fields for gesture recognition. In: CVPR (2006)
33. Wu, D., Shao, L.: Deep dynamic neural networks for gesture segmentation and recognition. In: ECCV Workshops (2014)
34. Wu, T.F., Lin, C.J., Weng, R.C.: Probability estimates for multi-class classification by pairwise coupling. The Journal of Machine Learning Research **5**, 975–1005 (2004)
35. Xia, L., Aggarwal, J.: Spatio-temporal depth cuboid similarity feature for activity recognition using depth camera. In: CVPR (2013)
36. Yang, X., Tian, Y.: Eigenjoints-based action recognition using naive-bayes-nearest-neighbor. In: CVPR Workshops (CVPRW) (2012)
37. Yang, X., Tian, Y.: Super normal vector for activity recognition using depth sequences. In: CVPR (2014)
38. Zanfir, M., Leordeanu, M., Sminchisescu, C.: The moving pose: An efficient 3d kinematics descriptor for low-latency action recognition and detection. In: ICCV, pp. 2752–2759 (2013)
39. Zhu, Y., Chen, W., Guo, G.: Fusing spatiotemporal features and joints for 3d action recognition. In: CVPR Workshops (CVPRW), pp. 486–491 (2013)

Multi-modality Gesture Detection and Recognition with Un-supervision, Randomization and Discrimination

Guang Chen[1,2(✉)], Daniel Clarke[2], Manuel Giuliani[2], Andre Gaschler[2], Di Wu[3], David Weikersdorfer[2], and Alois Knoll[1]

[1] Technische Universität München, Garching bei München, Germany
chenhnu@gmail.com
[2] fortiss GmbH, Guerickestr. 25, 80805 Munich, Germany
[3] University of Sheffield, Sheffield, UK

Abstract. We describe in this paper our gesture detection and recognition system for the 2014 ChaLearn Looking at People (Track 3: Gesture Recognition) organized by ChaLearn in conjunction with the ECCV 2014 conference. The competition's task was to learn a vacabulary of 20 types of Italian gestures and detect them in sequences. Our system adopts a multi-modality approach for detecting as well as recognizing the gestures. The goal of our approach is to identify semantically meaningful contents from dense sampling spatio-temporal feature space for gesture recognition. To achieve this, we develop three concepts under the random forest framework: un-supervision; discrimination; and randomization. Un-supervision learns spatio-temporal features from two channels (grayscale and depth) of RGB-D video in an unsupervised way. Discrimination extracts the information in dense sampling spatio-temporal space effectively. Randomization explores the dense sampling spatio-temporal feature space efficiently. An evaluation of our approach shows that we achieve a mean Jaccard Index of 0.6489, and a mean average accuracy of 90.3 % over the test dataset.

Keywords: Multi-modality gesture · Unsupervised learning · Random forest · Discriminative training

1 Introduction

Gesture detection and recognition refers to detecting and classifying meaningful motions executed by human. It has become a popular research field in recent years due to the low-cost sensors and its promising application prospects in human-computer interaction.

During the past decades, approaches of gesture recognition were controller-based, in which users had to wear human motion capture systems. The interfaces of users and devices are traditional command line and graphic user interfaces [13]. Recently, vision-based gesture recognition has become the mainstream of

© Springer International Publishing Switzerland 2015
L. Agapito et al. (Eds.): ECCV 2014 Workshops, Part I, LNCS 8925, pp. 608–622, 2015.
DOI: 10.1007/978-3-319-16178-5_43

the research due to the abilities which enable the controller-free and natural user interactions (NUI) [6,9]. NUI are based on natural interaction (e.g., gestures) that people use to communicate with the smart objects (e.g., smartphones). Therefore, NUI have better user experience compared to a more traditional graphic user interface. Kinect, the motion sensing input device developed by Microsoft corporation, features a RGB camera, a depth sensor and a multi-array microphone. With all these features, Kinect serves as an ideal experimental platform for developing new NUI systems of multi-modality gesture detection and recognition.

The primary objective of the 2014 ChaLearn Looking at People (Track 3: Gesture Recognition) [7,8] was to evaluate the performance of computational methods on gesture recognition. Track 3 of the challenge aims at the recognition of continuous, natural human gestures with the multi-modality nature of the visual cues, as well as technical limitations such as spatial and temporal resolution and unreliable depth cues.

The dataset of this competition is captured by Kinect. More than 14000 gestures are drawn from a vocabulary of 20 Italian sign gesture categories. However, the input samples may include other unrecognized gestures that are not included in the vocabulary. During the development phase, a large database of 7754 manually labeled gestures is available (referred to as the development dataset) and another dataset of 3,362 labeled gestures is provided for algorithm validation (referred to as the validation dataset). The challenge is to make predictions on the evaluation data of 3579 gestures (referred to as the testing dataset) revealed at the final evaluation phase. The evaluation is based on the Jaccard Index. For each one of the $n \leq 20$ gesture categories labelled for each sequence s, the Jaccard Index is defined as follows: $J_{s,n} = (A_{s,n} \cap B_{s,n})/(A_{s,n} \cup B_{s,n})$ where $A_{s,n}$ is the ground truth of action n at sequence s, and $B_{s,n}$ is the prediction for such a gesture at sequence s. $A_{s,n}$ and $B_{s,n}$ are binary vectors where 1-value entries denote frames in which the n-th gesture is being performed.

This paper presents an overview of our approach and gives technical details. In Section 2, we describe the overall architecture of the proposed system. In Section 3, we provide the details of the individual modules that constitute our gesture recognition system. In Section 4, we discuss the results achieved by our system. Finally, we present our conclusions in Section 5.

2   System Architecture

The architecture of the proposed multi-modality gesture detection and recognition system starts with the multi-modality input data. Each input sample in the 2014 ChaLearn Looking at People (Track 3: Gesture Recognition) contains a sequence of gestures performed by a subject and these gestures are typically separated by pauses in between. However, some of the gestures in the input sample are consecutive. Some of input samples include unrecognized gestures except for the gestures corresponding to one of the 20 gestures in the pre-defined gesture vocabulary. The first task of our approach is to detect the candidate gestures and temporally segment them by identifying their start and end frames. We use the skeletal joint data for gesture detection and segmentation. We assign each frame of the input sample a label: *gesture* or *non-gesture*, and train a Support Vector Machine model for each input sample. Within the prediction labels of the test sample, we segment the sample into several candidate gestures.

Once the given input sample is broken down into candidate gesture segments, the next task is to provide a suitable representation of the candidate gesture contained within each segment. We utilize spatio-temporal features extracted from the RGB-D video data to represent the gesture. In contrast to previous work [10,11,14,15], we extracted the spatio-temporal features using an unsupervised learning approach. At the heart of unsupervised learning approach is the extension of Independent Subspace Analysis algorithm [3–5,12] for the use of RGB-D video data. To effectively model the motion patterns of the gestures for the classification, we approach this problem from the perspective of mining a large number of video blocks with arbitrary shapes. spatio-temporal sizes, or locations that carry discriminative gesture video statistics. However, this approach poses a fundamental challenge: without any feature selection, even a modestly sized video will yield millions of video blocks. In addition, as large number of the blocks overlap significantly, these blocks are highly correlated and introduce significant redundancy among these features. To address this issue, we propose a random forest with discriminative decision trees approach to mine video blocks that are highly discriminative for the gesture classification tasks. Unlike traditional decision trees [1], our approach uses a SVM classifier at each node and integrates information at different depths of the tree to effectively mine a very dense sampling space of the video data. The final predicted label for a candidate gesture is assigned to the class which maximizes the average of the posterior probability from the leaf node of each tree.

3   Gesture Detection and Segmentation

We train SVM models to classify a fixed length time window of each input sample and then use a sliding window on the test sample to obtain a probability distribution over time for each window. The predicted labels for the test sample with likelihood scores average the prediction confidence of all the SVM models trained on the training samples. According to the predicted labels of the test sample, we segment the sample into several candidate gestures. A new SVM model is trained to tackle the problem of consecutive gestures in the input sample.

3.1   Segmentation Based on Skeletal Joints

We analyze the skeletal joint data stream from the Kinect sensor to identify the start frame and end frame of each gesture within an input sample. We approach this problem as two-class classification task: classify each frame of the input sample as *gesture* frame or *non-gesture* frame. We only focus on the joints above waist level reducing the number of joints from 20 to 12.

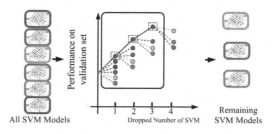

Fig. 1. Illustration of the process of greedy SVM model selection: Left: initial number T of the SVM model ($T = 6$ in this figure). Middle: greedy SVM model selection process (the number of dropped SVM model is $n = 3$). Right: the remaining $T - n$ SVM model that maximize validation performance ($T - n = 3$)

Skeletal Feature Engineering. We extract the skeletal feature from the skeletal joint data. The 3D coordinates of these joints are, however, not invariant to the position of the subject. Therefore we align the skeletal joints of each frame for each sample so that the hip centers of all frames overlap each other. 3D position differences of joints are employed to characterize gesture information including motion feature f_c and hand-based feature f_h. Features $f_{c,t}$ and $f_{h,t}$ are extrated from a 13-frame-long sliding window s_t where the frame t is at the center of this sliding window.

Let $p_{j,t} \in \mathbb{R}^3$ be the 3D world position $(x_{j,t}, y_{j,t}, z_{j,t})$ of joint j at frame t. J represent the 12 joints used in our approach. The motion features $f_{c,t}$ of frame t are defined as the joints differences within the sliding window s_t:

$$f_{c,t} = \{max(p_{j,i} - p_{j,t}) \mid \forall j \in J\}, i \in [t - 6, t + 6]; i \neq t \qquad (1)$$

We designed the hand-based feature f_h to pay attention to hand motion signals as all the gestures are performed by the hands. In particular, we consider only the y-coordinate of the hand joint locations and hip joint locations. We first compute the y-coordinate differences between hand joint and hip joint:

$$\delta_{hh,i} = max(\mid y_{jr,i} - y_{jh,i} \mid, \mid y_{jl,i} - y_{jh,i} \mid) \qquad (2)$$

where jr, jl, jh represent the right hand joint, left hand joints, and hip joint, respectively. As the same gesture can be performed by either right hand or left hand, Equation 2 is able to achieve the invariance under different hand performances. To capture the motion property of the hand joints, the hand-based features $f_{h,t}$ of frame t are defined as y-coordinate differences between hand joint and hip joint of each frame within the sliding window s_t:

$$f_{h,t} = \{\delta_{hh,i} \mid i \in [t - 6, t + 6]\} \qquad (3)$$

Skeletal Feature Classifier. We extract the motion feature f_c and hand-based feature f_h from each frame of the input sample. In our implementation, each frame is represented by 13-frame-long sliding window where the frame is at

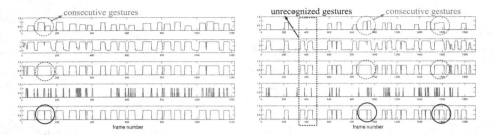

Fig. 2. Segmentation result of Sample 701 (left side) and Sample 707 (right side) in the testing dataset. From top to down: ground truth label of the samples; the labeled results of the SVM models; initial segmentation results; the labeled results of the SVM models for dealing with the consecutive gestures; final segmentation results of the samples

the center of the window. We annotate each frame with a label, either *gesture* frame or *non-gesture* frame according to the annotation labels provided by the training dataset. However, as the unrecognized gestures in the training dataset were mislabled as *non-gesture* frames, we choose the y-coordinate differences $\mid y_{jr,i} - y_{jl,i} \mid$ between right hand joint jr and left hand joint jl to filter out the false *non-gesture* frames. Any *non-gesture* frame which has the y-coordinate differences $\mid y_{jr,i} - y_{jl,i} \mid$ above a specified threshold are removed from the training data. To eliminate the effect of different sizes of the performers, we train a two-class SVM model for each input sample of the training dataset and validation dataset, in total, having 700 SVM models. Finally, we select a subset of SVM models to maxmize the performance of the validation dataset by following a greedy SVM model selection procedure (see Fig. 1).

3.2 Dealing with Consecutive Gestures

Normally, each sample includes between 10 and 20 candidate gestures. Most of them are typically separated by *long-pauses* (e.g., the *long-pause* contains tens of *nongesture* frames), but some of them are consecutive gestures (e.g., separated by *short-pause* containing less than 2 frames, which is indicated by the blue dash circles in Fig. 2). The above SVM models may classify the *non-gesture* frames of *short-pause* as *gesture* frames (indicated by the red circles in Fig. 2). To tackle this problem, we train a new SVM model to classify the frames of candidate gestures as *consecutive frame* or *nonconsecutive frame*. To get the training data of the new model, we scan all the samples in the training and validation dataset and find the consecutive gestures where two adjacent gestures are separated by a *short-pause*. We manually annotate the frames in the *short-pause* as *nonconsecutive frame* and the frames in the adjacent gestures as *consecutive frame*. We then train the SVM model based on the labeled training data. For the frames in the candidate gesture, if two consecutive frames are labeled as *consecutive frames* by the new SVM model, we divide the candidate gesture into another two candidate gestures further (indicated by the black circles in Fig. 2). Fig. 2 shows the segmentation results of Sample 701 and 707 in the testing dataset.

4   Gesture Classification

The segmentation results cannot separate the pre-defined gestures from the unrecognized gestures (indicated by the black rectangles in Fig. 2). Thus, during the gesture classification phase, we will perform the classification of 21 classes of gestures (20 pre-defined gestures plus unrecognized gesture) instead of 20 classes of pre-defined gestures. We first explore a 3D dense representation of each candidate gesture. Dense features have shown the advantages in classifying human activities [17]. Inspired from [17], we combine discriminative training and randomization to obtain an effective classifier with good generalizability. This allows us explore a richer feature set efficiently as well as identifies semantically meaningful video blocks that closely match human intuition.

4.1   Spatio-Temporal Feature Extraction

We extract spatio-temporal features from two channels (grayscale and depth) of RGB-D video data by using Independent Subspace Analysis (ISA) algorithm [12]. ISA is a popular unsupervised learning algorithm that learns spatio-temporal features from unlabeled video data. An ISA network [12] is described as a two-layer neural network, with square and square-root nonlinearities in the first and second layers respectively. We start with any input subvolume $x^t \in \mathbb{R}^n$ (each subvolume is a sequence of image patches). The activation of each second layer unit is

$$p_i(x^t; W, V) = \sqrt{\sum_{k=1}^{m} V_{ik} \left(\sum_{j=1}^{n} W_{kj} x_j^t \right)^2} \qquad (4)$$

where i is the indicator of the activation of the second layer unit; $j = 1, ..., n$; $k = 1, ..., m$; n and m are the dimension of input unit x^t and the number of units in the second layer, respectively.

ISA learns the parameters W by finding sparse feature representations in the second layer, by solving

$$\min_W \sum_{t=1}^{T} \sum_{i=1}^{m} p_i(x^t; W, V) \\ s.t.\ WW^T = \mathbf{I} \qquad (5)$$

Here, $W \in \mathbb{R}^{u \times n}$ denotes the weights connecting the input units to the first layer units (u denotes the number of units in the first layer); $V \in \mathbb{R}^{m \times u}$ denotes the weights connecting the first layer units to the second layer units (V is typically fixed to represent the subspace structure of the neurons in the first layer); T is the number of the input units x^t. The orthonormal constraint is to ensure the features are sufficiently diverse.

One advantage of unsupervised feature learning is that it readily applies to novel data, such as grayscale and gradient magnitude video data from an RGBD-camera. We learn spatio-temporal features up to two channels of RGB-D video

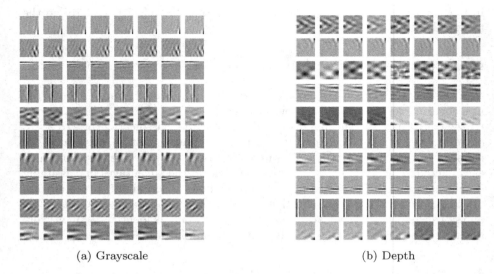

(a) Grayscale   (b) Depth

Fig. 3. Visualization of randomly selected spatio-temporal features learned from two channels of the RGB-D video data - from left to right, grayscale and depth. Each row of the figure indicates a spatio-temporal feature

data: grayscale and depth. The learned features are visualized in Fig. 3. These features are interesting to look at and share some similarities. For example, the learned feature (each row of the sub-figure) is able to assign similar patterns into a group, and has sharper edges like Gabor filters.

4.2   Dense Sampling Spatio-Temporal Space

Our approach aims to identify discriminative spatio-temporal blocks that are useful for the gesture classification. For example, in order to recognize whether a human is performing the gesture "*Ok*", we want to use the spatio-temporal blocks surrounding the human hands that are closely related to the gesture "*Ok*". We need to identify not only the spatial position of this kind of blocks (the image coordinate of the blocks) but the temporal position of the blocks (the start and end timestamps of the blocks). An algorithm that can reliably locate such regions is expected to achieve high classification accuracy. We achieve this goal by searching over spatio-temporal blocks with arbitrary spatial size, temporal size, and the 3D position of the blocks. We refer to this extensive set of spatio-temporal blocks as the *dense sampling spatio-temporal space*. Considering blocks with arbitrary spatial and temporal sizes, the actual density of spatio-tempral blocks is significantly higher. Richer feature indeed provide enough information for the classification task, however, many spatio-temporal blocks are not discriminative for distinguishing different gesture classes. Additionally, dense sampling introduces many overlapped spatio-temporal blocks which introduces significant redundancy. Therefore, it is challenging to explore this 3D dimensional, noisy and redundant feature space. In this work, we address this problem using the idea of combining discrimination and randomization.

4.3 Discriminative Random Forest Framework

In order to explore the 3D dense sampling feature space for the gesture classification, we combine two ideas: 1) Discriminative training to extract the information in the spatio-temporal blocks effectively; 2) Randomization to explore the 3D dense feature space efficiently. Specifically, we adopt a random forest framework [2,17] where each tree node is a SVM classifier that is trained on one spatio-temporal block.

Introduction of Random Forest Framework. A random forest is a multi-class classifier consisting of an ensemble of decision trees where each tree is constructed via some randomization. As illustrated in Fig. 4, the leaf nodes of each tree encode a distribution over the gesture classes. All internal nodes contain a binary classifier that splits the data into two parts and sends the two parts to its children nodes. The splitting is stopped when a leaf node is encountered. A candidate gesture is classified by descending each tree and combining the leaf distributions from all the trees of the forest. This method allows the flexibility to explore a rich feature space effectively because it only considers a small subset of features (e.g., several hundreds of spatio-temporal blocks sampled from the video data) in every tree node.

Each tree returns the posterior probability of a test example belonging to the given classes. The posterior probability of a particular class at each leaf node is learned as the proportion of the training videos (each training video contains one gesture) belonging to that class at the given leaf node. The posterior probability of class c_m at leaf l of tree t is denoted as $P_{t,l}^m(c_m)$, where m means the type of the modality used in the representation of video data. Thus, a test candidate gesture can be classified by averaging the posterior probability from all the trees of the forest:

$$\hat{c}_m = \arg \min_{c_m} \frac{1}{T} \sum_{t=1}^{T} P_{t,l_f}^m(c_m) \tag{6}$$

where $\hat{c}_m$ is the predicted labeled using the modality data m, T is the number of the trees of the forest, and l_f is the leaf node that the testing video falls into.

Sampling the Dense Spatio-temporal Feature. As shown in Fig. 4, each internal node in the decision tree corresponds to a set of spatio-temporal video blocks that are sampled from the 3D dense sampling space (Section 4.2), where the spatio-temporal blocks can have many possible spatio-temporal size and spatio-temporal positions. In order to sample candidate spatio-temporal blocks, we first normalize all videos to unit width, height and temporal dimension, and then randomly sample (x_l, y_l), (x_r, y_r) and (t_s, t_e) from a uniform distribution $U([0,1])$. The coordinates (x_l, y_l) and (x_r, y_r) specify two diagonally opposite

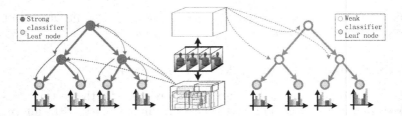

Fig. 4. Comparison of our discriminative decision tree (Left side of the figure) with conventional random decision tree (Right side of the figure). Conventional decision trees use information from the entire video data at each node, which encodes no spatio-temporal information. Our decision trees sample the spatio-temporal blocks from the dense sampling space. The histograms below the leaf nodes illustrate the posterior probability distribution. Our approach use strong classifiers (SVM) in each node, while the conventional method uses weak classifiers.

vertices of the spatial region of the block. The coordinates (t_s, t_e) specify the start and end position along the temporal dimension of the block. Such blocks could correspond to small area of the gesture segment or even the complete gesture segment. This allows the method to capture both the global and local information in the video.

In our approach, each saptio-temporal block is represented by a histogram of spatio-temporal features. The features are augmented with the decision value $w^T f$ (described in Equation 7) of this video segment from its parent node (indicated by the red lines in Fig. 4). Therefore, the feature representation combines the information of all upstream tree nodes that the corresponding video segment has descended from.

Learning the Binary Classifier of the Tree Node. We describe the process of learning the binary splits of the data using SVM. This is achieved in two steps: 1) Randomly assigning all segments from each class to a binary label; 2) Using SVM to learn a binary split of the data. Assume that we have C classes of gesture segments at a given node. We uniformly sample C binary variables. We then assign all sampled blocks of a particular class c_i a binary class label. As each node performs a binary split of the data, this allows us to learn a simple binary SVM at each node. Using the feature representation f of an spatio-temporal block, we find a binary split of the data:

$$score = w^T f, \begin{cases} score \leq 0, & go\ to\ left\ child \\ score > 0, & go\ the\ right\ child \end{cases} \tag{7}$$

where w is the set of weights learned from a linear SVM. We evaluate each binary split that corresponds to a spatio-temporal blocks with the information gain criteria [1], which is computed from the complete training video segments that fall at the current tree node. The splits that maximize the information gain are selected and the splitting processing is repeated with the new splits of the data. The tree splitting stops if a pre-defined tree depth or a minimum number of samples in the current node has been reached, or the information gain of the current node is larger than a specified threshold.

4.4   Pre-processing and Implementation Details

Pre-processing of the RGB-D Video Data. It is our observation that gestures only relate to upper body movement of the performers. Within the performance of the gestures of each sample, there is little movement of the lower part of the body, especially the foot movement. Therefore, we cut out part of the video data containing only the upper body of the performers from the entire video data. During the gesture classification phase, we extract spatio-temporal features from this partial video instead of the complete video in each sample. We resize this partial video to a fixed spatial size video of 200×200. For the learning of the binary split of the tree node, the randomly sampled spatio-temporal blocks of different gesture segments should have the same spatio-temporal size and spatio-temporal positions. However, the temporal dimension of gesture segments is different. We therefore employed time normalization for the temporal alignment of all gesture segments. We apply the max pooling along the temporal dimension of the dense sampling feature space of the gesture segments. All the gesture segments are normalized to have a fixed temporal size.

Implementation Details. We densely extract two types of ISA features (Gray-ISA and Depth-ISA) on each gesture segment with a spatial spacing of 2 pixels and a temporal spacing of 2 frames. Using k-means clustering, we construct a vocabulary of codewords for each modality. Then we use Locality-constrained Linear Coding [16] to assign the spatio-temporal features to codewords. A bag-of-words histogram representation of the spatio-temporal blocks is used if the spatial size and temporal size of the blocks are smaller than 0.2, while a 2-level spatial pyramid is used if the spatial size of the block is between 0.2 and 0.9. We limit the maximum spatial size and temporal size to 0.9 and 0.8 respectively. For each tree of the forest, we sample 150 spatio-temporal blocks in the root node and the first level nodes respectively, and sample 200 spatio-temporal blocks in all other nodes. Sampling a smaller number of blocks in the root can reduce the correlation between the resulting trees. In total, we have trained 100 trees for each type of ISA features.

5   Results and Discussion

In this section, we present the experimental results to evaluate the performance of our approach. We use the training set and validation set as the final training dataset, and the testing set as the final testing dataset. To best understand the classification performance of our approach, we use the ground truth labels to segment the testing dataset instead of the predicted gesture segmentations.

Table 1. Mean average precision (map) and classification accuracy (acc) on the testing dataset. The Gray-ISA-Drf and Depth-ISA-Drf models were represented by Gray and Depth in this table, respectively. Each column shows the results obtained from one model. The last row of the table shows the mean results of the 20 pre-defined gesture classes. The best result is highlighted in bold

Gesture	Gray		Depth	
	map	acc	map	acc
vattene	**90.1**	**76.4**	88.2	73.6
vieniqui	**92.1**	**85.7**	87.6	79.1
perfetto	**94.7**	**94.4**	92.7	89.3
furbo	**97.8**	90.4	91.5	**92.7**
cheduepalle	**99.6**	**97.7**	**99.6**	**97.7**
chevuoi	96.1	**89.9**	96.4	85.9
daccordo	**99.3**	**99.4**	99.2	97.5
seipazzo	**97.5**	**96.2**	96.8	92.4
combinato	**99.0**	**98.3**	97.3	97.3
freganiente	**92.7**	**88.2**	87.4	75.9
ok	**88.4**	**74.1**	81.5	60.9
cosatifarei	**96.4**	**92.0**	95.9	90.4
basta	99.8	98.3	**99.8**	**99.4**
prendere	**93.1**	**82.1**	89.5	81.5
noncenepiu	**83.8**	68.6	75.2	**70.9**
fame	**99.0**	**97.8**	**99.0**	**97.8**
tantotempo	**99.0**	**96.5**	96.9	95.4
buonissimo	**94.0**	**92.1**	85.7	77.5
messidaccordo	96.8	94.4	**97.4**	**95.6**
sonostufo	98.0	93.7	**98.8**	**93.7**
	95.3	**90.3**	92.8	87.2

We train our models on 10000 gesture segments of the training dataset, and perform the classification task of 21 gesture classes (20 pre-defined gesture classes and one unrecognized gesture class) on 3579 gesture segments in the testing dataset. However, we only show the results of the 20 pre-defined gesture classes, because the ground truth of testing dataset only provide the annotation of the 20 pre-defined gestures. We used two channels (grayscale and depth) of the RGB-D video data to train the spatio-temporal features and the discriminative random forest models. Finally, we use two types of spatio-temporal features (Gray-ISA and Depth-ISA), and two RF models (Gray-ISA-Drf and Depth-ISA-Drf) where each model contains 100 decision trees. We also utilize a fusion model which uses a simple late fusion strategy by combining the likelihood scores of the above two RF models.

The classification results measured by mean average precision (map) and average accuracy (acc) are shown in Table 1. The Gray-ISA-Drf model achieves the best result on the average map (95.3%) and acc (90.3%) of 20 gesture classes. Note that we achieved this accuracy using very-low resolution videos

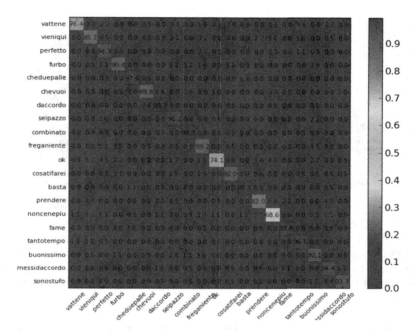

Fig. 5. The fusion matrice on the testing dataset using the the Gray-ISA-Drf model. Rows represent the actual gesture classes, and columns represent predicted classes (best viewed in color)

(200 *pixels* × 200 *pixels*). In detail, the Gray-ISA-Drf model and fusion model achieve the best result on seven and 16 out of 20 classes respectively. While the performance based on the Gray-ISA-Drf model is promising, the accuracy of the Depth-ISA-Drf model is relative low. This is probably because the process of down-sampling depth video to a lower resolution loses some important information of depth data. It is expected to achieve a better performance by investigating different fusion strategies (e.g., different combination of single models, fusion before training the random forest model). Fig. 5 is the visualization of confusion matrix of the Gray-ISA-Drf model. We can see that 12 out of 20 gesture classes achieved a result of > 90% accuracy. This is a good performance considering that we use single spatio-temporal feature, without using any hand-engineering spatio-temporal features or skeleton-based feature (for classification task).

In Fig. 6, we visualize the 2D heat maps of the dominant positions of the first 40 gesture segments in the testing dataset. The 2D heat maps show the distribution of the discriminative positions discovered by our approach for the specific gesture segment. These maps are obtained by aggregating the spatial regions of the spatio-temporal blocks of all the tree nodes in the random forest weighted by the probability of the corresponding gesture class. We can see the difference of distributions for different gesture classes. We observe that they show semantically meaningful locations of where we would expect the discriminative regions

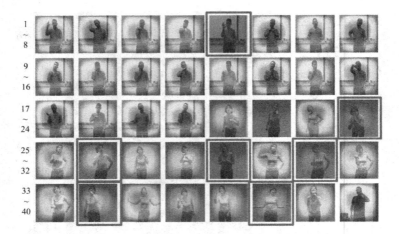

Fig. 6. The 2D heat maps of the dominant positions of the first 40 gesture segments in the testing dataset. Red rectangles mean the mis-classified gesture segments. Red indicates high frequency and blue indicates low frequence.(best viewed in color)

of subjects performing different gestures to occur. For example, the regions of corresponding to the hand joint of the human body are usually highlighted. We can also see that the regions corresponding to background or irrelevant joints (e.g., head, hip center) are not frequently selected.

6   Conclusion

Gesture detection and recognition has a wide variety of applications and the *2014 ChaLearn Looking at People* Challenge serves as an important benchmark of the state-of-the-art in this field. We present our multi-modality gesture detection and recognition system in this paper. Our system utilizes the random forest framework with discriminative decision trees to discover spatio-temporal blocks that are highly discriminative for gesture recognition tasks. We show that our method identifies semantically meaningful spatio-temporal blocks that closely match human intuition. Though the proposed system achieves fairly good performance as indicated by the Jaccard Index of 0.6489 in the final evaluation phase, this performance is still far from what was achieved by the top-ranked team in the challenge. We also observe that the good classification performance (a 90.3% accuracy) of our system failed to bring a high Jaccard Index score. We have identified a few areas of improvement in future, especially in the case of designing better features for gesture detection, in the case of mining mid-level information from the gesture segments and in the case of rejecting unrecognized gestures. We expect that the implementation of these changes will improve the accuracy of our system substantially.

References

1. Bosch, A., Zisserman, A., Muoz, X.: Image classification using random forests and ferns. In: IEEE 11th International Conference on Computer Vision, ICCV 2007, pp. 1–8, October 2007
2. Breiman, L.: Random forests. Machine Learning **45**(1), 5–32 (2001)
3. Chen, G., Clarke, D., Giuliani, M., Gaschler, A., Knoll, A.: Combining unsupervised learning and discrimination for 3d action recognition. Signal Processing (2014)
4. Chen, G., Clarke, D., Knoll, A.: Learning weighted joint-based features for action recognition using depth camera. In: International Conference on Computer Vision Theory and Applications (2014)
5. Chen, G., Giuliani, M., Clarke, D., Knoll, A.: Action recognition using ensemble weighted multi-instance learning. In: IEEE International Conference on Robotics and Automation (2014)
6. Chen, G., Zhang, F., Giuliani, M., Buckl, C., Knoll, A.: Unsupervised learning spatio-temporal features for human activity recognition from RGB-D video data. In: Herrmann, G., Pearson, M.J., Lenz, A., Bremner, P., Spiers, A., Leonards, U. (eds.) ICSR 2013. LNCS, vol. 8239, pp. 341–350. Springer, Heidelberg (2013)
7. Escalera, S., Bar, X., Gonzlez, J., Bautista, M.A., Madadi, M., Reyes, M., Ponce, V., Escalante, H.J., Shotton, J., Guyon, I.: Chalearn looking at people challenge 2014: dataset and results. In: Proceedings of the ChaLearn Looking at People 2014 Workshop, ECCV 2014 (2014)
8. Escalera, S., Gonzlez, J., Bar, X., Reyes, M., Lops, O., Guyon, I., Athitsos, V., Escalante, H.J.: Multi-modal gesture recognition challenge 2013: dataset and results. In: Chalearn Multi-Modal Gesture Recognition Workshop, International Conference on Multimodal Interaction (2013)
9. Gaschler, A., Huth, K., Giuliani, M., Kessler, I., de Ruiter, J., Knoll, A.: Modelling state of interaction from head poses for social Human-Robot Interaction. In: ACM/IEEE HCI Conference on Gaze in Human-Robot Interaction Workshop (2012)
10. Hadfield, S., Bowden, R.: Hollywood 3d: recognizing actions in 3d natural scenes. In: IEEE Conference on Computer Vision and Pattern Recognition, pp. 3398–3405 (2013)
11. Laptex, I.: On space-time interest points. International Journal of Computer Vision **64**, 107–123 (2005)
12. Le, Q., Zou, W., Yeung, S., Ng, A.: Learning hierarchical invariant spatio-temporal features for action recognition with independent subspace analysis. In: IEEE Conference on Computer Vision and Pattern Recognition, pp. 3361–3368 (2011)
13. Lu, D.V., Pileggi, A., Smart, W.D.: Multi-person motion capture dataset for analyzing human interaction. In: RSS 2011 Workshop on Human-Robot Interaction. RSS, Los Angeles, California, July 2011
14. Wang, J., Liu, Z., Chorowski, J., Chen, Z., Wu, Y.: Robust 3D action recognition with random occupancy patterns. In: Fitzgibbon, A., Lazebnik, S., Perona, P., Sato, Y., Schmid, C. (eds.) ECCV 2012, Part II. LNCS, vol. 7573, pp. 872–885. Springer, Heidelberg (2012)

15. Wang, J., Liu, Z., Wu, Y., Yuan, J.: Mining actionlet ensemble for action recognition with depth cameras. In: IEEE Conference on Computer Vision and Pattern Recognition, pp. 1290–1297 (2012)
16. Wang, J., Yang, J., Yu, K., Lv, F., Huang, T., Gong, Y.: Locality-constrained linear coding for image classification. In: 2010 IEEE Conference on Computer Vision and Pattern Recognition (CVPR), pp. 3360–3367, June 2010
17. Yao, B., Khosla, A., Fei-Fei, L.: Combining randomization and discrimination for fine-grained image categorization. In: IEEE Conference on Computer Vision and Pattern Recognition (CVPR), June 2011

Multi-modal Gesture Recognition Using Skeletal Joints and Motion Trail Model

Bin Liang$^{(\boxtimes)}$ and Lihong Zheng

Charles Sturt Universtiy, Wagga Wagga, Australia
{bliang,lzheng}@csu.edu.au

Abstract. This paper proposes a novel approach to multi-modal gesture recognition by using skeletal joints and motion trail model. The approach includes two modules, *i.e.* spotting and recognition. In the spotting module, a continuous gesture sequence is segmented into individual gesture intervals based on hand joint positions within a sliding window. In the recognition module, three models are combined to classify each gesture interval into one gesture category. For skeletal model, Hidden Markov Models (HMM) and Support Vector Machines (SVM) are adopted for classifying skeleton features. For depth maps and user masks, we employ 2D Motion Trail Model (2DMTM) for gesture representation to capture motion region information. SVM is then used to classify Pyramid Histograms of Oriented Gradient (PHOG) features from 2DMTM. These three models are complementary to each other. Finally, a fusion scheme incorporates the probability weights of each classifier for gesture recognition. The proposed approach is evaluated on the 2014 ChaLearn Multi-modal Gesture Recognition Challenge dataset. Experimental results demonstrate that the proposed approach using combined models outperforms single-modal approaches, and the recognition module can perform effectively on user-independent gesture recognition.

Keywords: Gesture recognition · Skeletal joints · HMM · SVM · 2DMTM · PHOG

1 Introduction

Human gesture recognition has been a very active research topic in the area of computer vision. It has been widely applied in a large variety of practical applications in real world, *e.g.* human-computer interaction, video surveillance, health-care and content-based video retrieval [9]. However, it is still a challenging problem owing to the large intra-class variability and inter-class similarity of gestures, cluttered background, motion blurring and illumination changes.

In the past decades, research on human gesture recognition mainly concentrates on recognizing human actions and gestures from video sequences captured by ordinary RGB cameras [1]. The difficulties of gesture recognition based on RGB video sequences come from several aspects. Human gestures captured by ordinary RGB cameras can only encode the information induced by the lateral

© Springer International Publishing Switzerland 2015
L. Agapito et al. (Eds.): ECCV 2014 Workshops, Part I, LNCS 8925, pp. 623–638, 2015.
DOI: 10.1007/978-3-319-16178-5_44

movement of the scene parallel to the image plane. Gesture motion information performed in a high dimensional space may be lost.

Recently, the launch of cost-effective depth cameras (*e.g.* Kinect) provides possibilities to alleviate the difficulties mentioned above. Depth information has long been regarded as an essential part of successful gesture recognition [11]. Using depth cameras, depth information can be obtained simultaneously with the RGB video. In addition, the positions of skeletal joints can also be predicted effectively from the depth data [22]. As a result, the depth maps and skeletal joints provide more information than RGB data. Thus, recent research has been motivated to explore more efficient multi-modal gesture recognition methods [2,5,17,28]. Furthermore, how to recognize human gestures using multimodal information in an efficient way is still a hot topic.

In order to promote the research advance in gesture recognition, ChaLearn organized a challenge called "2014 Looking at People Challenge" [7] including three parallel challenge tracks. Track 3 (Gesture Recognition) is focused on multiple instances, user independent gesture spotting and learning. The dataset of the competition is recorded with a Microsoft Kinect camera, containing RGB videos, depth videos, user mask videos and skeleton data. Fig. 1 shows an example of different data sources available. The gesture vocabulary used in this dataset consists of 20 Italian cultural/anthropological signs. The most challenging points are that there are no obvious resting positions and the gestures are performed in continuous sequences. In addition, sequences may contain distracter gestures, which are not annotated since they are not included in the main vocabulary of 20 gestures [8].

Fig. 1. An example from the dataset: RGB video, depth video, user mask video and skeleton data (left to right)

In this paper, we propose to use multi-modal data for gesture recognition. Specifically, a novel approach using skeletal joints and motion trail model [16] is proposed for multi-modal gesture recognition. The general framework of the proposed approach is illustrated in Fig. 2. In the gesture spotting module, within sliding windows we calculate the vertical difference of hand positions to divide one continuous gesture sequence into several gesture intervals. Three models, *i.e.* skeletal joints, depth maps and user masks, are then used to classify each gesture interval into one gesture category. For skeletal joints, *pairwise joints distance* and *bone orientation features* are extracted as skeleton features to encode 3D space information of the gesture. A concatenated classifier, HMM-SVM, is employed for skeleton features classification in time-domain. Furthermore, an RBF-SVM

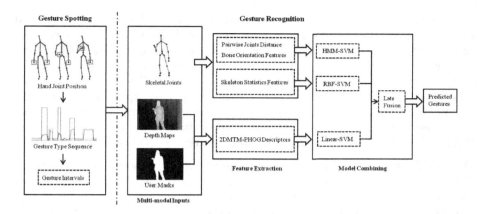

Fig. 2. The general framework of the proposed approach

classifier is used to classify *skeleton statistics features*. Meanwhile, depth maps and user masks are also used in our work, since skeleton data only encode joint information of human, ignoring the motion region information. Specifically, gesture regions are segmented by combining depth maps and user masks. 2D motion trail model (2DMTM) is performed on gesture regions for gesture representation, since 2DMTM is able to represent gesture motion information along with static posture information in 2D space to encode the motion region information of human gestures [16]. Then Pyramid Histograms of Oriented Gradient (PHOG) descriptors are extracted from 2DMTM. 2DMTM-PHOG descriptors are classified by linear-SVM. These models are complementary to each other. Finally, the probability scores from classifiers are fused for the final recognition. We evaluate our approach on 2014 Chalearn Multi-modal Gesture Recognition Challenge dataset [7] and further explain why the combination of the models achieves far better results than the single model.

The remainder of this paper is organized as follows. Section 2 reviews four categories of existing methods in the area of gesture recognition. In section 3, we provide a detailed procedure of our proposed approach based on skeletal joints and motion trail model. Experimental results and discussions are presented in section 4. At last, we give a conclusion of the paper and outline the future work in section 5.

2   Related Work

According to the data inputs, the existing methods of gesture recognition or action recognition can be roughly divided into four categories: *RGB video based, depth video based, skeleton data based* and *multi-modal data based*.

RGB video based methods. In video sequences captured by RGB cameras, the spatio-temporal interest points (STIPs) [13] are widely used in gesture recognition, as human gestures are showing spatio-temporal patterns. These methods first detect interesting points and then extract features based on the detected local motion volumes. These features are then combined to model different gestures. In the literature, many spatio-temporal feature detectors [6,12,13,18] and features [14,21,26,27] have been proposed and shown promising performance for gesture recognition in RGB videos. Bobick and Davis [3] propose Motion History Image (MHI) and Motion Energy Image (MEI) to explicitly record shape changes for template matching. Tian *et al.* [23] employ Harris detector and local HOG descriptor on MHI to perform action recognition and detection. The core of these approaches is the detection and representation of spatio-temporal volumes.

Depth video based methods. With the release of depth cameras, there are many representative works for gesture recognition based on depth information. Li *et al.* [15] propose a bag of 3D points model for action recognition. A set of representative 3D points from the original depth data is sampled to characterize the action posture in each frame. The 3D points are then retrieved in depth maps according to the contour points. To address issues of noise and occlusions in the depth maps, Vieira *et al.* [24] present a novel feature descriptor, named Space-Time Occupancy Patterns (STOP). Yang *et al.* [31] develop Depth Motion Maps (DMM) to capture the aggregated temporal motion energies. The depth map is projected onto three pre-defined orthogonal Cartesian planes and then normalized. Oreifej and Liu [19] describe the depth sequence using a histogram capturing the distribution of the surface normal orientation in the 4D space of time (HON4D), depth, and spatial coordinates. Inspired by the great success of silhouette based methods developed for visual data, Jalal *et al.* [10] extract depth silhouettes to construct feature vectors. HMM is then utilized for recognition. More recently, Liang and Zheng [16] propose a three dimensional motion trail model (3D-MTM) to explicitly represent the dynamics and statics of gestures in 3D space using depth images. Specifically, depth images are projected onto two other planes to encode additional gesture information in 3D space. Evaluations on the MSR Action3D dataset [15] show a good performance.

Skeleton data based methods. Furthermore, motivated by the joints estimation of Kinect and associated SDK, there have been many different approaches relying on joint points for action recognition. In [25], the joints of the skeleton are used as interest points. In this way, the shapes of the area surrounding the joint along with the joint location information are captured using a local occupancy pattern feature and a pairwise distance feature, respectively. Xia *et al.* [29] propose a compact representation of postures named HOJ3D using the 3D skeletal joint locations from Kinect depth maps. They transfer skeleton joints into a spherical coordinate to achieve view-invariance. A more general method has been proposed by Yao *et al.* [32] where skeleton is encoded by relation pose features. These features describe geometric relations between specific joints in a single pose or a short sequence of poses. Yang *et al.* [30] propose a type of features by adopting the differences of joints. EigenJoints are then obtained by PCA for classification.

Multi-modal data based methods. Instead of using a single model, gesture recognition methods based on multi-modal data have been explored widely in recent years. Zhu *et al.* [33] propose to recognize human actions based on a feature-level fusion of spatio-temporal features and skeleton joints. The random forest method is then applied to perform feature fusion, selection, and action classification together. Wu *et al.* [28], the winner team of the 2013 Multi-modal Gesture Recognition Challenge [8], propose a novel multi-modal continuous gesture recognition framework, which makes full exploration of both audio and skeleton data. A multi-modal gesture recognition system is developed in [17] for detecting as well as recognizing the gestures. The system adopts audio, RGB video, and skeleton joint models. Bayer and Silbermann [2] present an algorithm to recognize gestures by combining two data sources (audio and video) through weighted averaging, and demonstrate that the approach of combining information from two difference sources boosts the models performance significantly.

3   The Proposed Approach

We propose a multi-modal gesture recognition approach based on skeletal joints and motion trail model [16]. The framework consists of gesture spotting module and gesture recognition module. In gesture spotting module, each continuous gesture sequence is divided into gesture intervals using hand joint positions and sliding windows. After gesture spotting, classifiers based on skeleton features and 2DMTM-PHOG descriptors are constructed separately and then combined together to generate the final recognition result. In this section, we present the proposed approach in detail.

3.1   Gesture Spotting

The process of identifying the start and end points of continuous gesture sequences is called *Gesture Spotting*. We only focus on the positions of the hand joint to do gesture spotting, since all the gestures from the dataset are mainly performed using a single hand or two hands. The spotting method of work [17] is extended in our work by adding adaptive thresholds and sliding windows. The basic idea is that joint positions of two hands along vertical direction are varying while gesture is performing. Thus, the peaks of the hand joints position sequences indicate the presence of gesture performance, as shown in Fig. 3. In this way, a continuous gesture sequence can be segmented into individual gesture intervals according to the y-coordinates of hand joints. More specifically, the aim is to transform a continuous hand joint position sequence into a sequence of gesture types: left-hand dominant, right-hand dominant, two-hands dominant and neutral position. Therefore, the start and end points of gesture intervals would be the gesture boundaries in the gesture type sequence.

The gesture spotting in our approach consists of three steps. In the first step, single hand dominant gestures (left-hand dominant and right-hand dominant) are detected. A gesture type filter g is designed to transform hand joint position sequence to gesture type sequence. Let T be the total number of frames in a gesture sequence. Let $y(t)$ be the y-coordinate of a joint position in the tth

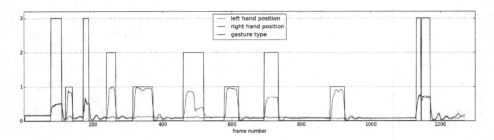

Fig. 3. Hand joint position and gesture type sequence

$(t = 1, 2, \ldots T)$ frame. In order to avoid the noise in the hand position sequence, a sliding window of size w is added here. Thus, a vector of a single joint position can be defined as $Y(t) = [y(t), \; y(t+1), \; \ldots, \; y(t+w-1)]$ to represent joint locations within a sliding window. The average joint position $\bar{Y}(t) = \|Y(t)\|_1 / w$ can be obtained using L_1-norm. Therefore, the value of the filter g for the tth frame is defined as follows:

$$g(t) = \begin{cases} 1, & \text{if } \bar{Y}_l(t) - \bar{Y}_r(t) > \eta_1 \\ 2, & \text{if } \bar{Y}_l(t) - \bar{Y}_r(t) < -\eta_1 \\ 0, & \text{otherwise} \end{cases} \tag{1}$$

where $\bar{Y}_l(t)$ and $\bar{Y}_r(t)$ are the average joint positions of left hand and right hand within the sliding window, respectively. $\eta_1 = d/5$ is an adaptive threshold, where d is the average distance between "shoulder center" and "hip center" within the sliding window. The filter value of 1 indicates left-hand dominant gesture, and the filter value of 2 indicates right-hand dominant gesture. If the value of the filter is 0, the gesture type could be either two-hands dominant or neutral position.

The second step is to identify the boundaries of two-hands dominant gestures. This is done by comparing the distance between hands position and hip position. If the distance is greater than the adaptive threshold $\eta_2 = d/10$, it is assumed that a two-hands dominant gesture is present. In this case, the filter value for that frame is changed to 3.

The last step of segmentation is to check the duration of the candidate gesture intervals. If the duration of a gesture is extremely short, the "gesture" will be discarded because noisy data could result in impulse intervals. On the other hand, if the duration is two times longer than the average duration, the "gesture" will be divided into two gestures. In general, this step is to discard "short-interval gestures" and separate "long-interval gestures". Fig. 3 shows the hand position sequences and the corresponding gesture type sequence after filtering. In the figure, hand joint positions are normalized to range $[0, 1]$. For gesture type sequence, the value of 1 indicates the left-hand dominant gesture, the value of 2 indicates the right-hand dominant gesture, the value of 3 indicates two-hands dominant gesture, and the value of 0 indicates neutral position.

3.2   Recognition based on Skeletal Joints

The spatial information of gestures is important for gesture recognition. Provided that the human skeleton joints can be estimated efficiently [22], we use pairwise joints distance and bone orientation features to complete the spatio-temporal features. The skeletal joints data provide 3D joint positions and bone orientations. Specifically, within frame t, skeleton data of each joint i is encoded using three coordinates: *world position* $s_{i,w}(t) = (x_{i,w}(t),\ y_{i,w}(t),\ z_{i,w}(t))$ representing the real-world position of a tracked joint, *pixel position* $s_{i,p}(t) = (x_{i,p}(t),\ y_{i,p}(t))$ with respect to the mapped pixel position over RGB maps, and *bone rotation* $s_{i,r}(t) = (w_{i,r}(t),\ x_{i,r}(t),\ y_{i,r}(t),\ z_{i,r}(t))$ in the form of a quaternion related to the bone rotation.

The skeleton positions of the joints are, however, not invariant to the gesture movements. Therefore, before extracting any features, all the 3D joint coordinates are transformed from the world coordinate system to a person centric coordinate system by placing the hip center at the origin. Inspired by the work of Wang *et al.* [25], we use pairwise joints distance as skeleton features. Furthermore, to eliminate the effect of variant sizes of the subjects, the transformed skeletons are then normalized by the sum of the pairwise distances of all selected skeletons. To characterize the posture information of the frame t, we compute the pairwise joints distances within that frame as follows:

$$f_w(t) = \left\{ \frac{\|s_{i,w}(t) - s_{j,w}(t)\|_2}{\sum \|s_{i,w}(t) - s_{j,w}(t)\|_2} \ \middle| \ i,j = 1, 2, \ldots N; i \neq j \right\} \qquad (2)$$

where N is the number of selected joints. To capture the corresponding mapped posture information $f_p(t)$, the mapped pairwise joints distances within the frame t can be extracted in the similar way.

In addition, joint orientation information is essential for gesture movement. The orientation information is provided in form of quaternions. To encode the bone rotation features, we normalize the quaternion of joint i by its magnitude $\|s_{i,r}(t)\|_2$. According to our observation, most of the gestures are performed by upper-body movements, so we only extract 12 skeletal joints of upper-body from all 20 skeletal joints available: the head, shoulder center, spine, hip center, shoulders, elbows, wrists and the hands. Pairwise joints distance and bone orientation features are then concatenated together as the final skeleton features.

For classification task, we first use HMM [20] to construct a model for each gesture category. After forming the models for each category, we take a gesture interval and calculate its probability of all the 20 models. Then 20 probability scores are obtained. Usually the gesture is classified as one category which has the highest probability score, but we continue to use the obtained 20 scores as a new feature vector for the gesture, and adopt SVM [4] as a concatenated HMM-SVM classifier. The performance on validation data demonstrate that the concatenated HMM-SVM classifier performs better than the single HMM classifier.

The skeleton features mentioned above are extracted within each frame, and the holistic information (*e.g.* repeat movements, high-frequency motion regions and the range of gesture movements) of gestures may be lost. Therefore, in order to capture the holistic information of skeleton features, another 4 statistics (variance, mean, minimum and maximum) are used to aggregate the skeleton features of each frame over a gesture interval. Then an RBF-SVM classifier is trained to classify the skeleton statistics features. In this way, gestures can be disriminated from each other.

3.3   Recognition based on Motion Trail Model

To capture gesture regions information, the 2D motion trail model (2DMTM) [16] is adopted in our approach. It employs four templates along the front view, $i.e.$ depth motion history image (D-MHI$_f$), average motion image (AMI$_f$), static posture history image (SHI$_f$), and average static posture image (ASI$_f$). 2DMTM is able to represent the motion information and static posture information of human gestures in a compact and discriminative way.

In order to alleviate the influence of noisy background, we need to segment gesture regions from the original depth maps. Since user mask videos are available for each gesture sample, we propose to segment the gesture regions using depth videos and mask videos. Additionally, median filter is applied to remove the noise in the videos. We assume a binary user mask at frame t is M_t, and the corresponding depth map is D_t. Then gesture regions can be segmented by aligning these two maps to find their intersection $R_t = M_t \cap D_t$, as shown in Fig. 4

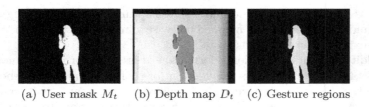

(a) User mask M_t (b) Depth map D_t (c) Gesture regions

Fig. 4. Gesture regions segmentation

Then the 2DMTM is performed on the segmented gesture region sequence. The motion update function $\Psi_M(x, y, t)$ and static posture update function $\Psi_S(x, y, t)$ are defined to represent the regions of motion and static posture with gesture performing. They are called for every frame analyzed in the gesture interval:

$$\Psi_M(x, y, t) = \begin{cases} 1 & \text{if } K_t > \varsigma_M, \\ 0 & \text{otherwise.} \end{cases} \qquad (3)$$

$$\Psi_S(x, y, t) = \begin{cases} 1 & \text{if } R_t - K_t > \varsigma_S, \\ 0 & \text{otherwise.} \end{cases} \qquad (4)$$

where x, y represent pixel position and t is time. $R_t = (R_1, R_2, \ldots, R_T)$ is a segmented gesture region sequence, and $K_t = (K_1, K_2, K_3, \ldots, K_T)$ is a difference image sequence indicating the absolute difference of depth value. In addition, these two update functions need thresholds ς_M and ς_S for motion and static information within consecutive frames.

Therefore, the depth motion history image (D-MHI) $H_M(x, y, t)$ can be obtained by using motion update function $\Psi_M(x, y, t)$:

$$H_M(x, y, t) = \begin{cases} T & \text{if } \Psi_M(x, y, t) = 1 \\ H_M(x, y, t-1) - 1 & \text{otherwise} \end{cases} \tag{5}$$

where T is the total number of frames in the gesture sequence. Additionally, static posture history image (SHI) $H_S(x, y, t)$ can be generated utilizing the static posture update function $\Psi_S(x, y, t)$ to compensate for static regions over the whole action sequence, which can be obtained in the similar way as D-MHI:

$$H_S(x, y, t) = \begin{cases} T & \text{if } \Psi_S(x, y, t) = 1 \\ H_S(x, y, t-1) - 1 & \text{otherwise} \end{cases} \tag{6}$$

In order to cover the information of repetitive movements and repetitive static postures over the whole gesture interval, average motion image AMI and average static posture image ASI are employed. The summation of all motion information $\Psi_M(x, y, t)$ or static information $\Psi_S(x, y, t)$ and normalization of the pixel values define the AMI and ASI:

$$A_M = \frac{1}{T} \sum_{t=1}^{T} \Psi_M(x, y, t), \quad A_S = \frac{1}{T} \sum_{t=1}^{T} \Psi_S(x, y, t) \tag{7}$$

Fig. 5 shows the motion trial model (2DMTM) of one gesture example. D-MHI and SHI present more recent moving regions and static regions brighter, respectively. AMI and ASI capture the average motion regions and average static regions information. Therefore, the 2DMTM gesture representation is able to characterize the accumulated motion and static regions distribution, meanwhile significantly reduces considerable data of depth maps to just four 2D gray-scale images.

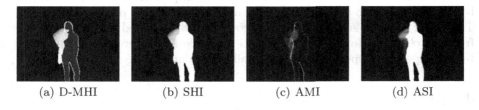

(a) D-MHI   (b) SHI   (c) AMI   (d) ASI

Fig. 5. 2DMTM of one gesture example

For feature extraction from 2DMTM, we apply PHOG [16] on 2DMTM to characterize local shapes at different spatial scales for gesture recognition.

Specifically, the 2DMTM-PHOG descriptor is extracted from the calculation of gradients in a dense grid of the 2DMTM to encode human gesture representation. It is directly performed on the four templates from the 2DMTM, which requires no edge or interesting regions extraction. In 2DMTM-PHOG, each template is divided into small spatial grids in a pyramid way at different pyramid levels. Each gradient orientation is quantized into B bins. Gradients over all the pixels within a grid are accumulated to form a local B bins 1-D histogram. Therefore, each template from 2DMTM at level l is represented by a $B \times 2^l \times 2^l$ dimension vector. Since there are four templates in 2DMTM, we concatenate the four PHOG vectors as the 2DMTM-PHOG descriptor. The obtained feature vector, $V \in \mathbb{R}^d$ $(d = 4 \times B \times \sum_{l=1}^{L} (2^l \times 2^l))$, is the 2DMTM-PHOG descriptor of the 2DMTM. In our experiment, we choose $B = 9$ bins and $L = 3$ levels empirically. Finally, linear-SVM is adopted to classify 2DMTM-PHOG descriptors.

3.4   Combining Skeleton and Motion Trail Model

In the above, three classifiers have been constructed for recognition: the spatio-temporal skeleton features based concatenated HMM-SVM classifier, skeleton statistics features based RBF-SVM classifier, and 2DMTM-PHOG descriptor based linear-SVM classifier. We have used LIBSVM [4] for all of our SVM implementations. LIBSVM has implemented an extension to SVM to provide probability estimates in addition to the decision values. Thus, each classifier is able to predict a probability score for each gesture category, indicating the confidence of prediction.

Table 1. Weights used for combining classifiers

Features	Classifier	Weight
Pairwise Joints Distance+Bone Orientation Features	HMM-SVM	0.35
Skeleton Statistics Features	RBF-SVM	0.45
2DMTM-PHOG Descriptors	Linear-SVM	0.20

We examine the influence of each classifier on performance and conclude a late fusion scheme to combine three classifiers based on their probability weights. Therefore, a fusion scheme is used to combine the weighted probability scores from the classifiers for the final recognition (Table 1). The weights are obtained by the experiments performed on the validation data.

4   Experimental Results

The proposed approach has been evaluated on the 2014 Chalearn Multi-modal Gesture Recognition Challenge dataset [7]. We extensively compare the proposed multi-modal approach with the single-modal approaches using mean Jaccard Index. In order to investigate the recognition module performance of the proposed approach, we further use truth start and end points to do gesture spotting, and then evaluate gesture recognition using the proposed approach in terms of accuracy.

4.1 Dataset and Experimental settings

The 2014 Chalearn Multi-modal Gesture Recognition Challenge dataset is focused on "multiple instances, user independent learning" of gestures. There are 20 Italian sign categories, *e.g.*, *vattene*, *vieniqui*, and *perfetto*. Several features make this dataset extremely challenging, including the continuous sequences, the presence of distracter gestures, the relatively large number of categories, the length of the gestures sequences, and the variety of users [8]. Therefore, the dataset provides several models to attack such a difficult task, including RGB, depth videos, user mask videos, and skeletal model.

The dataset is split into three parts: training data, validation data, and test data. We use all the gesture sequences from training data for learning our models. Validation data is used for parameters optimization. The size of sliding window is 5 frames, and the number of hidden states in HMM is 15 in our work. Besides, the optimal parameters of SVMs are obtained by 5-fold cross-validation. At last, the proposed approach is evaluated on test data.

4.2 Evaluation Metric

For each unlabeled video sequence, the gesture category, corresponding start and end points are predicted using the proposed approach. Recognition performance is evaluated using the Jaccard Index. Therefore, for each one of the 20 gesture categories labeled for each gesture sequence, the Jaccard Index is defined as follows:

$$J_{s,n} = \frac{A_{s,n} \cap B_{s,n}}{A_{s,n} \cup B_{s,n}} \qquad (8)$$

where $A_{s,n}$ is the ground truth of gesture n in sequence s, and $B_{s,n}$ is the prediction for the corresponding gesture in sequence s. The proposed approach is evaluated upon mean Jaccard Index among all the gesture categories for all sequences. The mean Jaccard Index not only indicates the performance of recognition, but also the performance of gesture boundaries identification. Thus, higher mean Jaccard Index means better performance of the approach.

4.3 Comparison of Single-modal and Multi-modal Performance

In order to evaluate the performance of the proposed approach, we compare the experimental results by using single-modal and multi-modal approaches. Continuous gesture sequences are first divided into individual gesture intervals using hand joints positions and sliding windows. Then we perform experiments using single-model and multi-modal approaches, and compare the results. For skeleton joints, pairwise joints distance and bone orientation features are classified by concatenated HMM-SVM classifier, and skeleton statistics features are classified by an RBF-SVM classifier. Additionally, depth maps and user masks are used to segment gesture regions, and 2DMTM is employed for gesture representation. To capture the gesture regions information, 2DMTM-PHOG descriptors are adopted and a linear-SVM is trained for classification.

Table 2. Comparison of single-modal and multi-modal performance

Model	Classifier	Jaccard Index Score
Skeleton	HMM-SVM	0.453989
Skeleton	RBF-SVM	0.519499
Depth+Mask	Linear-SVM	0.462335
Skeleton+Depth+Mask	Multi-Modal	**0.597177**

The experimental results are shown in Table 2. From the results, we can see that the Jaccard Index scores are 0.453989, 0.519499 and 0.462335 using only HMM-SVM, RBF-SVM and linear-SVM, respectively. The RBF-SVM using skeleton statistics features has a higher score than other single-modal classifiers. It is probably because holistic skeleton information are user-independent, which means that the skeleton statistics features of the same gestures performed by different users are similar. In order to compensate the temporal information of skeleton joints, HMM-SVM is used to encode spatio-temporal skeleton features. Using our fusion scheme, the Jaccard Index score is improved to 0.597177, which is our final score for the competition.

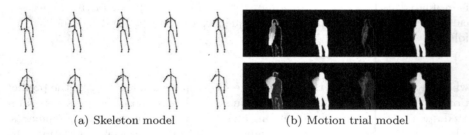

(a) Skeleton model   (b) Motion trial model

Fig. 6. Gesture samples with similar skeleton models

It is obvious that multi-modal recognition improves the performance significantly. Our analysis indicates that theses models are complementary to each other. Specifically, some skeleton joint positions are not very accurate in some cases. In addition, it is hard to differentiate two gestures when their skeleton models are very similar, but gesture representation using 2DMTM can provide discriminative information in this case. For example, as shown in Fig. 6(a), the two gesture samples have similar skeleton model, so the classifiers using skeleton model could fail to recognize them as two different categories. However, motion trail model provides complementary motion region information

of the gestures, which can help to complete recognition task in a better way
(Fig. 6(b)). Therefore, the proposed multi-modal approach improves performance than single-modal approaches. According to the final ranking results
released by the competition organizers, our team is ranked 11/17 in the final
evaluation phase.

4.4 Recognition using Truth Spotting Labels

Gestures in the dataset are continuous and some of them are distracter gestures,
so gesture spotting and distracter gestures rejection need to be considered in the
competition. Thus, the performance of gesture spotting and distracter gestures
rejection have a great effect on the final recognition results. In order to investigate
how our approach impacts the final result, we first evaluate the performance of
gesture spotting module using mean Jaccard Index, and the score is 0.819643.
To investigate the performance of recognition module, we use the truth labels
of start and end points provided by the dataset to do the spotting, and then
recognize the gesture intervals using the multi-modal approach. In this way, only
the performance of recognition module of multi-modal approach is evaluated,
and compared with other single-modal approaches. Since we use truth labels to
divide continuous gestures, the performance of recognition module is evaluated
in terms of accuracy. The experimental results are shown in Table 3.

Table 3. Comparison of recognition using truth spotting labels

Model	Classifier	Accuracy
Skeleton	HMM-SVM	77.47%
Skeleton	RBF-SVM	83.02%
Depth+Mask	Linear-SVM	76.99%
Skeleton+Depth+Mask	Multi-Modal	**92.80%**

From the Table 3, we can see that the multi-modal approach also outperforms
other single-modal approaches in recognition performance. The final recognition
accuracy over the whole test data reaches **92.80%**, which is a relatively high
score in "user independent" gesture recognition. Furthermore, the visualization
of confusion matrix is illustrated in Fig. 7. From the confusion matrix, we can see
that the highest accuracy is 100% for category 5 (*cheduepalle*), and the lowest
accuracy is 85% for category 14 (*prendere*). Based on the results in section 4.3
and this section, we deduce that the spotting module remains to be improved
to increase the overall performance of the proposed approach. In addition, we
observe the test data and find out that the skeleton data of some gestures are
missing, which causes some gestures are mis-discarded when performing gesture spotting. Therefore, only skeleton data might not be enough for a better
gesture spotting, and combining other models could improve the performance.

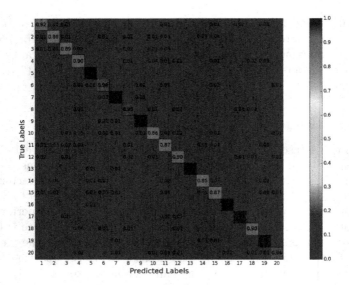

Fig. 7. Confusion matrix

5   Conclusion

We have presented a novel approach to multi-modal gesture recognition. The framework consists of gesture spotting module and gesture recognition module. In gesture spotting module, the start and end points of continuous gesture sequences are identified using hand joint positions within a sliding window. In gesture recognition module, the skeleton features characterize the spatio-temporal skeletal joints positions and holistic skeleton information while the 2DMTM-PHOG descriptors capture the motion regions information during a gesture performance. Three different classifiers, *i.e.* HMM-SVM, RBF-SVM and Linear-SVM, are then combined based on the late fusion scheme. We have conducted experiments on the 2014 Chalearn Multi-modal Gesture Recognition Challenge dataset, and shown that our proposed approach outperforms single-modal approaches. We further investigate the performance of recognition module in our approach, and get a relatively high accuracy of 92.80%. This demonstrates the good performance of recognition module. For the future work, we will combine more models to further improve the performance of gesture spotting under our proposed multi-modal framework.

References

1. Aggarwal, J., Ryoo, M.S.: Human activity analysis: A review. ACM Computing Surveys (CSUR) **43**(3), 16 (2011)
2. Bayer, I., Silbermann, T.: A multi modal approach to gesture recognition from audio and video data. In: Proceedings of the 15th ACM on International Conference on Multimodal Interaction, pp. 461–466. ACM (2013)

3. Bobick, A.F., Davis, J.W.: The recognition of human movement using temporal templates. IEEE Transactions on Pattern Analysis and Machine Intelligence **23**(3), 257–267 (2001)
4. Chang, C.C., Lin, C.J.: LIBSVM: A library for support vector machines. ACM Transactions on Intelligent Systems and Technology **2**, 27:1–27:27 (2011). http://www.csie.ntu.edu.tw/cjlin/libsvm
5. Chen, X., Koskela, M.: Online rgb-d gesture recognition with extreme learning machines. In: Proceedings of the 15th ACM on International Conference On Multimodal Interaction, pp. 467–474. ACM (2013)
6. Dollár, P., Rabaud, V., Cottrell, G., Belongie, S.: Behavior recognition via sparse spatio-temporal features. In: 2nd Joint IEEE International Workshop on Visual Surveillance and Performance Evaluation of Tracking and Surveillance 2005, pp. 65–72. IEEE (2005)
7. Escalera, S., Bar, X., Gonzlez, J., Bautista, M.A., Madadi, M., Reyes, M., Ponce, V., Escalante, H.J., Shotton, J., Guyon, I.: Chalearn looking at people challenge 2014: Dataset and results. In: European Conference on Computer Vision Workshops (ECCVW) (2014)
8. Escalera, S., Gonzàlez, J., Baró, X., Reyes, M., Lopes, O., Guyon, I., Athitsos, V., Escalante, H.: Multi-modal gesture recognition challenge 2013: Dataset and results. In: Proceedings of the 15th ACM on International Conference On Multimodal Interaction, pp. 445–452. ACM (2013)
9. Jaimes, A., Sebe, N.: Multimodal human-computer interaction: A survey. Computer Vision and Image Understanding **108**(1), 116–134 (2007)
10. Jalal, A., Uddin, M.Z., Kim, J.T., Kim, T.S.: Recognition of human home activities via depth silhouettes and transformation for smart homes. In: Indoor and Built Environment, p. 1420326X11423163 (2011)
11. Janoch, A., Karayev, S., Jia, Y., Barron, J.T., Fritz, M., Saenko, K., Darrell, T.: A category-level 3d object dataset: Putting the kinect to work. In: Consumer Depth Cameras for Computer Vision, pp. 141–165. Springer (2013)
12. Jhuang, H., Serre, T., Wolf, L., Poggio, T.: A biologically inspired system for action recognition. In: IEEE 11th International Conference on Computer Vision, ICCV 2007, pp. 1–8. IEEE (2007)
13. Laptev, I.: On space-time interest points. International Journal of Computer Vision **64**(2–3), 107–123 (2005)
14. Laptev, I., Lindeberg, T.: Local descriptors for spatio-temporal recognition. In: MacLean, W.J. (ed.) SCVMA 2004. LNCS, vol. 3667, pp. 91–103. Springer, Heidelberg (2006)
15. Li, W., Zhang, Z., Liu, Z.: Action recognition based on a bag of 3d points. In: 2010 IEEE Computer Society Conference on Computer Vision and Pattern Recognition Workshops (CVPRW), pp. 9–14. IEEE (2010)
16. Liang, B., Zheng, L.: Three dimensional motion trail model for gesture recognition. In: 2013 IEEE International Conference on Computer Vision Workshops (ICCVW), pp. 684–691 (December 2013)
17. Nandakumar, K., Wan, K.W., Chan, S.M.A., Ng, W.Z.T., Wang, J.G., Yau, W.Y.: A multi-modal gesture recognition system using audio, video, and skeletal joint data. In: Proceedings of the 15th ACM on International Conference on Multimodal Interaction, pp. 475–482. ACM (2013)
18. Oikonomopoulos, A., Patras, I., Pantic, M.: Spatiotemporal salient points for visual recognition of human actions. IEEE Transactions on Systems, Man, and Cybernetics, Part B: Cybernetics **36**(3), 710–719 (2005)

19. Oreifej, O., Liu, Z.: Hon4d: Histogram of oriented 4d normals for activity recognition from depth sequences. In: 2013 IEEE Conference on Computer Vision and Pattern Recognition (CVPR), pp. 716–723. IEEE (2013)

20. Rabiner, L.: A tutorial on hidden markov models and selected applications in speech recognition. Proceedings of the IEEE **77**(2), 257–286 (1989)

21. Scovanner, P., Ali, S., Shah, M.: A 3-dimensional sift descriptor and its application to action recognition. In: Proceedings of the 15th International Conference on Multimedia, pp. 357–360. ACM (2007)

22. Shotton, J., Sharp, T., Kipman, A., Fitzgibbon, A., Finocchio, M., Blake, A., Cook, M., Moore, R.: Real-time human pose recognition in parts from single depth images. Communications of the ACM **56**(1), 116–124 (2013)

23. Tian, Y., Cao, L., Liu, Z., Zhang, Z.: Hierarchical filtered motion for action recognition in crowded videos. IEEE Transactions on Systems, Man, and Cybernetics, Part C: Applications and Reviews **42**(3), 313–323 (2012)

24. Vieira, A.W., Nascimento, E.R., Oliveira, G.L., Liu, Z., Campos, M.F.M.: STOP: space-time occupancy patterns for 3d action recognition from depth map sequences. In: Alvarez, L., Mejail, M., Gomez, L., Jacobo, J. (eds.) CIARP 2012. LNCS, vol. 7441, pp. 252–259. Springer, Heidelberg (2012)

25. Wang, J., Liu, Z., Wu, Y., Yuan, J.: Mining actionlet ensemble for action recognition with depth cameras. In: 2012 IEEE Conference on Computer Vision and Pattern Recognition (CVPR), pp. 1290–1297. IEEE (2012)

26. Willems, G., Tuytelaars, T., Van Gool, L.: An efficient dense and scale-invariant spatio-temporal interest point detector. In: Forsyth, D., Torr, P., Zisserman, A. (eds.) ECCV 2008, Part II. LNCS, vol. 5303, pp. 650–663. Springer, Heidelberg (2008)

27. Wong, K.Y.K., Cipolla, R.: Extracting spatiotemporal interest points using global information. In: IEEE 11th International Conference on Computer Vision, ICCV 2007, pp. 1–8. IEEE (2007)

28. Wu, J., Cheng, J., Zhao, C., Lu, H.: Fusing multi-modal features for gesture recognition. In: Proceedings of the 15th ACM on International Conference On Multimodal Interaction, pp. 453–460. ACM (2013)

29. Xia, L., Chen, C.C., Aggarwal, J.: View invariant human action recognition using histograms of 3d joints. In: 2012 IEEE Computer Society Conference on Computer Vision and Pattern Recognition Workshops (CVPRW), pp. 20–27. IEEE (2012)

30. Yang, X., Tian, Y.: Eigenjoints-based action recognition using naive-bayes-nearest-neighbor. In: 2012 IEEE Computer Society Conference on Computer Vision and Pattern Recognition Workshops (CVPRW), pp. 14–19. IEEE (2012)

31. Yang, X., Zhang, C., Tian, Y.: Recognizing actions using depth motion maps-based histograms of oriented gradients. In: Proceedings of the 20th ACM International Conference on Multimedia. pp. 1057–1060. ACM (2012)

32. Yao, A., Gall, J., Van Gool, L.: Coupled action recognition and pose estimation from multiple views. International Journal of Computer Vision **100**(1), 16–37 (2012)

33. Zhu, Y., Chen, W., Guo, G.: Fusing spatiotemporal features and joints for 3d action recognition. In: 2013 IEEE Conference on Computer Vision and Pattern Recognition Workshops (CVPRW), pp. 486–491 (June 2013)

Increasing 3D Resolution of Kinect Faces

Stefano Berretti$^{(\boxtimes)}$, Pietro Pala, and Alberto del Bimbo

University of Florence, Florence, Italy
stefano.berretti@unifi.it

Abstract. Performing face recognition across 3D scans of different resolution is now attracting an increasing interest thanks to the introduction of a new generation of depth cameras, capable of acquiring color/depth images over time. However, these devices have still a much lower resolution than the 3D high-resolution scanners typically used for face recognition applications. Due to this, comparing low- and high-resolution scans can be misleading. Based on these considerations, in this paper we define an approach for reconstructing a higher-resolution 3D face model from a sequence of low-resolution 3D scans. The proposed solution uses the scaled ICP algorithm to align the low-resolution scans with each other, and estimates the value of the high-resolution 3D model through a 2D Box-spline approximation. The approach is evaluated on the *The Florence face* dataset that collects high- and low-resolution data for about 50 subjects. Measures of the quality of the reconstructed models with respect to high-resolution scans and in comparison with two alternative techniques, demonstrate the viability of the proposed solution.

Keywords: Kinect camera · 3D super-resolution · 2D box-splines

1 Introduction

Person identity recognition by the analysis of 3D face scans is attracting an increasing interest, with several challenging issues successfully investigated, such as 3D face recognition in the presence of non-neutral facial expressions, occlusions, and missing data [1,2]. Existing solutions have been evaluated following well defined protocols on consolidated benchmark datasets, which provide a reasonable coverage of the many different traits of the human face, including variations in terms of gender, age, ethnicity, occlusions due to hair or external accessories. The resolution at which 3D face scans are acquired changes across different datasets, but it is typically the same within one dataset. Due to this, the difficulties posed by considering 3D face scans with different resolutions and their impact on the recognition accuracy have not been explicitly addressed in the past. Nevertheless, there is an increasing interest for methods capable of performing recognition across scans acquired with different resolutions. This is mainly motivated by the availability of a new generation of low-cost, low-resolution 4D scanning devices (i.e., 3D plus time), such as Microsoft Kinect or Asus Xtion PRO LIVE. In fact, these devices are capable of a combined

© Springer International Publishing Switzerland 2015
L. Agapito et al. (Eds.): ECCV 2014 Workshops, Part I, LNCS 8925, pp. 639–653, 2015.
DOI: 10.1007/978-3-319-16178-5_45

color-depth (RGB-D) acquisition at about 30fps, with a resolution of 18ppi at a distance of about $80cm$ from the sensor. The spatial resolution of such devices is lower than that of high-resolution 3D scanners, but these latter are also costly, bulky and highly demanding for computational resources. Despite the lower resolution, the advantages in terms of cost and applicability of consumer cameras motivated some preliminary works performing face detection [3], continuous authentication [4] and recognition [5–7] directly from the depth frames of the Kinect camera. However, based on the opposite characteristics evidenced by 4D low-resolution and 3D high-resolution scanners, new applicative scenarios can be devised, where high-resolution scans are likely to be part of gallery acquisitions, whereas probes are expected to be of lower resolution and potentially acquired with 4D cameras.

In this context, reducing the impact on the recognition accuracy due to the match of low-resolution probes against high-resolution gallery scans is relevant, but an even more challenging task with potentially wider applications is given by the reconstruction of one super-resolved face model out of a sequence of low-resolution depth frames acquired by a 4D scanner. In fact, this could open the way to more versatile 3D face recognition methods deployable in contexts where the acquisition of high resolution 3D scans is not convenient or even possible. Based on these premises, in this work we aim to provide an effective approach specifically tailored to reconstruct a higher-resolution face model from a sequence of low-resolution depth frames, thus capable of reducing the gap between low- and high-resolution acquisitions.

1.1   Related Work

Methods to recover one high-resolution image from a set of low-resolution images possibly altered by noise, blurring or geometric warping, have been formerly introduced for 2D still images [8–12], and go under the term of super-resolution.

Super-resolution techniques have been also applied to 3D generic data [13, 14]. Previous work that focus in particular on super-resolution of 3D faces are reported in [15, 16]. In [15], high resolution 3D face models are used to learn the mapping between low-res data and high-res data. Given a new low-res face model the learned mapping is used to compute the high-res face model. Differently, in [16] the super-resolution process is modeled as a progressive resolution chain, whose features are computed as the solution to a MAP problem. However, in both the cases, the framework is validated just on synthetic data.

Methods in [17, 18] and [19] approach the problem of noise reduction in depth data by fusing the observations of multiple scans to construct one denoised scan. In [17], the Kinect Fusion system is presented, which takes live depth data from a moving Kinect camera and creates a high-quality 3D model for a static scene object. Later, dynamic interaction has been added to the system in [20], where camera tracking is performed on a static background scene and the foreground object is tracked independently of camera tracking. Aligning all depth points to the complete scene from a large environment (e.g., a room) provides very accurate tracking of the camera pose and mapping [17]. However, this approach is targeted to generic objects in internal environments, rather than to faces. In [18], a 3D face model with an improved quality is obtained by a user moving in front of a low resolution depth camera. The model is initialized with the first depth image, and then each subsequent cloud of 3D points is registered to the reference one using a GPU implementation of the ICP algorithm. This approach is used in [19] to investigate whether a system that uses reconstructed 3D face models performs better than a system that uses the individual raw depth frames considered for the reconstruction. To this end, authors present different 3D face recognition strategies in terms of the used probes and gallery. The reported analysis shows that the scenarios where a reconstructed 3D face model is compared against a gallery of reconstructed 3D face models, and where one frame (1F) is compared against multiple frames in the gallery (NF), provide better results compared to the baseline 1F-1F approach. Although the method is not conceived to increase the resolution of the reconstructed model with respect to the individual frames, it supports the idea that aggregating multiple observations enhances the signal to noise ratio, thus increasing the recognition results with respect to the solution where a single frame is used. In [21], a method to increase the resolution of the face scans acquired with a Kinect is proposed. The method is based on ICP registration on the first frame of the sequence and subsequent points approximation, but results are quite preliminary and no evidence that the approach is indeed capable of producing a super-resolution is provided.

1.2 Our Method and Contribution

In this paper, we present an original solution to derive one super-resolution 3D face model from the low-resolution depth frames of a sequence acquired through a Kinect camera. In the proposed approach, first, the region containing the face is automatically detected and cropped in each depth frame; then, the face of the first frame is used as reference and all the faces from the other frames are aligned to the reference; finally, the aggregated data of these multiple aligned observations are resampled at a higher resolution and approximated using 2D-Box splines. The proposed approach has been evaluated on the *The Florence face* dataset, which includes, for each individual, one Kinect depth sequence and one high-resolution face scan acquired through a 3dMD scanner. In summary, the main contributions of this paper are:

- A complete approach to reconstruct a super-resolved 3D face model from a sequence of low-resolution depth frames of the face, with the proof the proposed approach is capable of producing a super-resolved 3D model rather than just a denoised one;
- An evaluation demonstrating the accuracy of the reconstructed super-resolved models with respect to the high-resolution scans, and in comparison to two alternative solutions.

The rest of the paper is organized as follows: The problem statement and the basic notation are defined in Sect. 2; The super-resolution approach based on facial data approximation is described and validated in Sect. 3. Experimental results are reported and discussed in Sect. 4. Finally, discussion and conclusions are given in Sect. 5.

2   Problem Statement

In this work, we aim to reconstruct a *depth image* of the face (*image* for short), which shows both super-resolution and denoising, starting from a sequence of low-resolution *depth frames* (*frames* in the following). In particular, low-resolution frames are acquired by a Kinect camera placed in front of a sitting subject, while s/he is slightly rotating the head to the left and right side. In Fig. 1(a), a sample depth frame is shown. The face region is cropped in each frame by using the *Face Tracking* function available in the device SDK, as shown in Fig. 1(b).

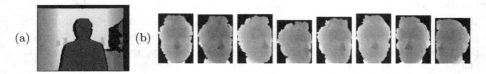

Fig. 1. (a) Sample depth frame acquired by the Kinect; (b) Some cropped frames from the sequence, with the pose of the face varying from frontal to right and left side

To simplify the notation and without loss of generality, we assume that each frame is defined on a regular low-resolution grid $\Omega = [1,\ldots,N] \times [1,\ldots,N]$. The high-resolution image is defined on a regular high-resolution grid $\Sigma = [1,\ldots,M] \times [1,\ldots,M]$, being $\zeta = M/N$ the *resolution gain*. The forward degradation model, describing the formation of low-resolution frames from a high-resolution image can be formalized as follows:

$$X_L^{(k)} = P_k(X_H), \quad k = 1,\ldots,K , \tag{1}$$

being $\{X_L^{(k)}\}$ the set of K low-resolution frames, X_H the high-resolution image, and P_k the operator that maps the high-resolution image onto the coordinate system and sampling grid of the k-th low-resolution frame. The mapping operated by P_k accounts mainly for the geometric transformation of X_H to the coordinates of the k-th low-resolution frame $X_L^{(k)}$, the blurring effect induced by the atmosphere and camera lens, down-sampling, and additive noise. In particular, we note the coordinate system of the high-resolution image X_H is aligned to the coordinate system of the first low-resolution frame $X_L^{(1)}$ of the sequence, which is used as *reference*. The geometric transformation that maps the coordinate systems of subsequent low-resolution frames to the first frame of the sequence is computed with a variant of the ICP algorithm, which jointly estimates the 3D rotation and translation parameters as well as the scaling one [22] (this operation is applied just to the cropped region of the face). The data cumulated by this process represent a cloud of points in the 3D space, and these points are regarded as observations of the value of the high-resolution image X_H.

Let $\mathbf{x}_i^{(k)}$ be the 3D coordinates (x, y and the depth value z) of the i-th facial point in the k-th frame $X_L^{(k)}$. Registration of facial data represented in $X_L^{(k)}$ to data represented in the reference frame $X_L^{(1)}$ is obtained by computing the translation, rotation and scaling transformation that best aligns the data:

$$\min_{\mathbf{R},\mathbf{S},\mathbf{t},p} \sum_{i=1}^{\left|X_L^{(k)}\right|} \left\| \mathbf{R} \cdot \mathbf{S} \cdot \mathbf{x}_i^{(k)} + \mathbf{t} - \mathbf{x}_{p(i)}^{(1)} \right\| , \qquad (2)$$

being $\mathbf{R}$ an orthogonal matrix, $\mathbf{S}$ a diagonal scale matrix, $\mathbf{t}$ a translation vector, $|.|$ the cardinality of a set, and $p : \left\{ 1, \ldots, \left|X_L^{(k)}\right| \right\} \mapsto \left\{ 1, \ldots, \left|X_L^{(1)}\right| \right\}$ a function that maps indexes of facial points across the k-th and the 1-st frames. The solution of Eq. (2), namely $\mathbf{R}^k, \mathbf{S}^k, \mathbf{t}^k$, is computed according to the procedure described in [22].

The ICP algorithm usually requires an appropriate initialization to avoid convergence to local minima. For this purpose, alignment of the generic frame $X_L^{(k)}$ to the reference frame $X_L^{(1)}$ is obtained by first applying to $X_L^{(k)}$ the transformation computed for the previous frame $X_L^{(k-1)}$. In this way, the transformation of the $(k-1)$-th frame is used to predict the transformation of the k-th frame, and ICP is then used for fine registration.

3 Increasing the Face Resolution

Based on the procedure described so far, data points of the frames $X_L^{(k)}$, $k = 2, \ldots, K$ are aligned to the data in the first frame $X_L^{(1)}$, used as reference. The set of all these scattered data points $\left\{ \mathbf{P}^{(j)} \right\}_{j=1}^{J} = \left\{ (P_x^{(j)}, P_y^{(j)}, P_z^{(j)}) \right\}_{j=1}^{J}$ represent the observed samples of the underlying face surface, which is approximated through a function $\Gamma(x, y)$. This function is defined on a high resolution uniform grid Φ compared to the low resolution uniform grid Ω of the reference frame $X_L^{(1)}$. It should be noticed that, under the effect of Eq. (2), data points are scattered and distributed irregularly with respect to both the high and low resolution grids Φ and Ω. The approximation model acts as a function $\Gamma(x, y)$ that given the set of scattered points $\left\{ \mathbf{P}^{(j)} \right\}_{j=1}^{J}$ that are expected to sample the 2D facial surface in the 3D space, projects them onto a reference plane Π (the (x, y) plane of the first frame) and then estimates the *height* of the surface for a generic point $p \in \Pi$ within the convex hull of the projected set of points (see Fig. 2). In this way, given the super-resolution uniformly spaced grid Φ in Π,

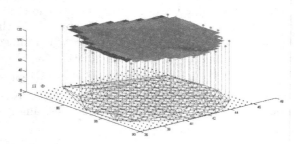

Fig. 2. The projection of points of frames in a sequence onto the reference plane associated to the first frame distribute irregularly. Estimation of values of the underlying surface (shown in gray) on a regular grid (blue points) is obtained by computing one approximating function that fits the data.

it is possible to estimate the value of the 2D facial surface for each point of Φ enclosed within the convex hull of the projection of the scattered points onto Π.

To estimate the approximating function, the 2D Box-splines model is used [23]. Accordingly, the approximating function $\Gamma(x, y)$ is expressed as a weighted sum of Box splines originated by translation of a 2D base function $B_{0,0}(x, y)$ with local support. Given a 1D lattice $\{x_{-n}, \ldots, x_{-1}, x_0, x_1, \ldots, x_n\}$, the 1D first degree ($C^0$ continuity) base function $b_0(t)$ is defined as:

$$
b_0(t) = \begin{cases}
0 & if\ t \in (-\infty, x_{-1}] \\
\frac{t - x_{-1}}{x_0 - x_{-1}} & if\ t \in (x_{-1}, x_0] \\
\frac{x_1 - t}{x_1 - x_0} & if\ t \in (x_0, x_1] \\
0 & if\ t \in (x_1, \infty)\,.
\end{cases}
\tag{3}
$$

The translated copy of the base function, centered on the generic node x_i of the lattice is computed as $b_i(t) = b_0(t - x_i)$. Extension of this framework to the 2D case is possible by considering a 2D lattice $\{x_{i,j}\}$ and the 2D base function $B_{0,0}(x, y)$ computed as the tensor product of the 1D base function:

$$
B_{0,0}(x, y) = b_0(x)b_0(y)\,.
\tag{4}
$$

The translated copy of the base function, centered on the generic node $x_{i,j}$ of the lattice is computed as $B_{i,j}(x, y) = b_i(x)b_j(y)$. Functions $B_{i,j}(x, y)$ are continuous and with local support, being zero for all points (x, y) not included in any of the rectangular cells with one vertex on $x_{i,j}$. The function $\Gamma(x, y)$ is expressed as:

$$
\Gamma(x, y) = \sum_{i,j} w_{i,j} B_{i,j}(x, y)\,,
\tag{5}
$$

being $w_{i,j}$ the set of weights that yield the best approximation to the points cloud. In order to determine the values of these weights, two types of constraints are considered targeting the fit of $\Gamma(x,y)$ to the data points and the regularity of $\Gamma(x,y)$, in terms of continuity and derivability. In the ideal case, $\Gamma(x,y)$ would fit all the data points. This constraint is expressed by K equations of the form:

$$\Gamma(P_x^{(k)}, P_y^{(k)}) = P_z^{(k)} \quad k = 1, \ldots, K \ . \tag{6}$$

Due to the form of the basis functions (Eqs. (3)-(4)), $\Gamma(x,y)$ is continuous everywhere. Since $\Gamma(x,y)$ is not derivable in correspondence to the points of the lattice $\{x_{i,j}\}$, its smoothness is forced by the following set of equations:

$$\left. \frac{\partial^+ \Gamma(x,y)}{\partial x} \right|_{x_{ij}} = \left. \frac{\partial^- \Gamma(x,y)}{\partial x} \right|_{x_{ij}} \tag{7}$$

$$\left. \frac{\partial^+ \Gamma(x,y)}{\partial y} \right|_{x_{ij}} = \left. \frac{\partial^- \Gamma(x,y)}{\partial y} \right|_{x_{ij}} \quad i, j = -n, \ldots, n \ .$$

The left and right partial derivatives of Eq. (7) can be obtained analytically, and combined with Eq. (6) represent a system of $K + n^2$ linear equations in the n^2 variables $w_{i,j}$. Values of the variables $w_{i,j}$ are computed by resolving a least-squares fit, which minimizes the sum of the squares of the deviations of the data from the model.

3.1   Resolution Gain

The proposed solution results in a face surface with an increased resolution, rather than just in a surface denoising. This can be shown considering the reference frame of a sample sequence in Fig. 3(a), and the reconstruction obtained from the depth sequence of the same face at different resolutions, namely, 104×157, 207×313 and 413×625, as reported in Fig. 3(b)-(d), respectively.

Although, in theory, the resolution gain can be set arbitrarily, the interest lies in the identification of the highest value of the *real* resolution gain, beyond which the amount of information encoded in the reconstructed surface does not change: two reconstructions of a surface at two different resolutions encode the same information if the reconstruction at the higher resolution can be obtained by resampling and interpolation of the reconstruction at the lower resolution. For this purpose, we compare results of the proposed super-resolution approach with those obtained through resampling and interpolation of data at the original resolution. Assuming $\Omega = [1, \ldots, N] \times [1, \ldots, N]$ be the original sampling grid and $\Sigma = [1, \ldots, M] \times [1, \ldots, M]$ the super-resolved one, we measure the difference between the super-resolved model reconstructed on the grid Σ and the predicted model obtained by reconstructing the face model on the original grid Ω and then increasing the resolution by resampling up to Σ and predicting values at the new grid points by bilinear interpolation. More formally, let F_ζ be the super-resolved model at a resolution $M = \zeta N$, and $\mathcal{R}(\cdot)$ the operator that resamples an image by bilinear interpolation, doubling the size of the input grid on both the x and

y axis. The ratio η measures the mean error between the predicted and the super-resolved model:

$$\eta(\zeta) = \frac{\sum_{i,j} |\mathcal{R}(F_{\zeta-1}) - F_\zeta|}{\zeta^2 N^2} . \tag{8}$$

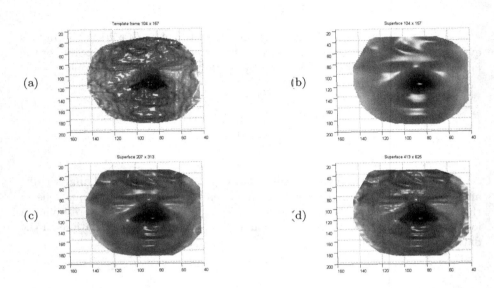

Fig. 3. (a) Reference frame of a sequence; (b)-(d) Three models reconstructed at resolutions, respectively, 104×157 (same resolution as the original, just denoising), 207×313, and 413×625

At the lowest value of the resolution gain, $\zeta = 2$, $F_{\zeta-1}$ is the reconstruction of the facial surface at the original resolution. Resampling this surface by bilinear interpolation yields $\mathcal{R}(F_{\zeta-1})$ whose resolution is twice the original. F_ζ is the output of the super-resolved facial surface at a resolution twice the original one. Values of $\eta(\zeta)$ are expected to decrease for increasing values of ζ. This is confirmed by the plot of Fig. 4, showing the values $\eta(\zeta)$ for $\zeta \in \{2, \ldots, 5\}$. For $\zeta = 2$ the error is computed between the bilinearly interpolated reference frame and the super-resolved model at a resolution twice the original one; For increasing values of ζ, the difference between the predicted and the reconstructed models decreases showing that the higher the resolution, the lower is the information truly added by the super-resolved model compared to the information predicted by interpolation.

4   Experimental Results

The proposed approach has been evaluated considering the accuracy of the super-resolution reconstruction, by computing the error between the super-resolved

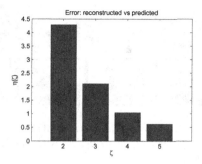

Fig. 4. Values of $\eta(\zeta)$ measure the error between the model reconstructed through the proposed super-resolution approach at the resolution gain ζ, and the prediction (by bilinear interpolation) based on the model reconstructed at the resolution gain ζ-1

models and the corresponding high-resolution scans (Sect. 4.1). In so doing, we also compared our approach against two alternative solutions (Sect. 4.2).

The study reported hereafter has been performed on the *The Florence face* dataset (UF-S) [24]. Some public datasets exist for face analysis from consumer cameras, like Kinect (see for example the EURECOM Kinect Face dataset [25], or the The 3D Mask Attack database specifically targeted to detect face spoofing attacks [26]). However, to the best of our knowledge the UF-S dataset is the only one providing sequences of low resolution face scans acquired with the Kinect camera and high resolution 3D scans, for the same subjects. This dataset enrolls 50 subjects, each with the following data:

- A 3D high-resolution face scan, with about 40,000 vertices. The geometry of the mesh is highly accurate with an average RMS error of about 0.2mm or lower, depending on the particular pre-calibration and configuration;
- A video sequence acquired with the *Kinect* camera. During acquisition the person sits in front of the sensor at an approximate distance of 80cm. The subject is also asked to rotate the head around the yaw axis, so that both the left and right side of the face are exposed to the camera. This results in video sequences lasting approximately 10 to 15 seconds on average, at 30fps.

The 3D high-resolution scans and the Kinect video sequences are provided in the form produced by the sensors, without any processing or annotation. Figure 5 shows samples of the raw data acquired for a subject (RGB frames of the sequence are also reported, but they are not used in our solution).

4.1   Reconstruction Accuracy

The first evaluation aims to show the error between the reconstructed 3D super-resolution model with respect to the 3D high-resolution scan of a same subject, also in comparison to the same measure of error computed between the first depth frame of a sequence (*reference frame*) and the 3D high-resolution scan.

Fig. 5. Sample of the *The Florence face* dataset: (a) 3D high-resolution scan; (b) RGB and depth frames from the Kinect video sequence, with the head pose changing from frontal to left and right side

Choosing the first frame of a sequence as *reference frame* is motivated by the fact that at the beginning of the acquired video sequences, persons sit in front of the camera looking at it, so that just small areas of the face are not visible to the sensor due to self-occlusion effects.

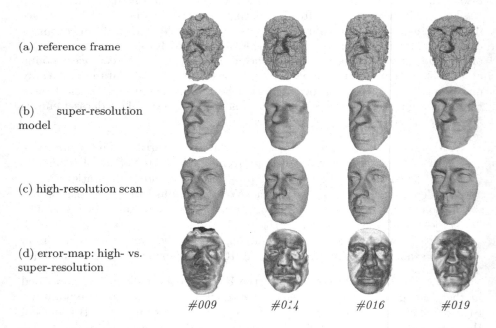

(a) reference frame

(b)   super-resolution model

(c) high-resolution scan

(d) error-map: high- vs. super-resolution

#009   #014   #016   #019

Fig. 6. Each column corresponds to a different subject and reports: (a) The low resolution 3D scan of the reference frame; (b) The super-resolution 3D model; (c) The high-resolution 3D scan. The error-map in (d) shows, for each point of the super-resolution model, the value of the distance to its closest point on the high-resolution scan after alignment (distance increases from red/yellow to green/blue).

All the subjects in the UF-S dataset have been used in the experiments, In particular, for each subject we considered: The high-resolution scan; The super-resolution (reconstructed) model; and the low-resolution scan (this latter obtained from the reference frame of the depth sequence). In all these cases, the 3D facial data are represented as a mesh and cropped using a sphere of radius $95mm$ centered at the nose tip (the approach in [27] is used to detect the nose tip). To measure the error between the high-resolution scan and the super-resolution model of the same subject, they are first aligned through ICP registration [28]. Then, for each point of the super-resolution model its distance to the closest point in the high-resolution scan is computed to build an error-map. As an example, Fig. 6 shows for some representative subjects (one column per subject), the cropped 3D mesh of the reference frame, the super-resolution model, the high-resolution scan and the error-map between the super-resolution model and the high-resolution scan (after alignment).

To represent the average error of the reconstructed models and reference frames with respect to high-resolution scans, the *Root Mean Square Error* (RMSE) between two surfaces S and S' is computed considering the vertex correspondences defined by the ICP registration, which associates each vertex $p \in S$ to the closest vertex $p' \in S'$:

$$RMSE(S, S') = \left(\frac{1}{N} \sum_{i=1}^{N} (p_i - p_i')^2 \right)^{1/2}, \tag{9}$$

being N the number of correspondent points in S and S'.

Table 1. The first two rows report the average RMSE between the 3D *high-resolution* scan and, respectively, the *super-resolution* model and the *reference* scan of *same subjects*. In the third row, the average RMSE between any two high-resolution scans of *different subjects* is reported. The rightmost column also evidences the relative variation of the intra-subjects distance values with respect to the inter-subject distance

	models	average $RMSE$	% variation
same subject	*reference* vs. high-res	1.48	+4.2%
	reconstructed vs. high-res	1.16	-18.3%
different subjects	*high-res* vs. high-res	1.42	–

Results obtained using this distance measure are summarized in Table 1. In particular, we reported the average values for the $RMSE$ computed between the high-resolution scan and, respectively, the super-resolution model and the reference scan. On the one hand, values in Table 1 measure the magnitude of the error between the super-resolution model and the high-resolution scan of same subjects; On the other, they give a quantitative evidence of the increased quality of the super-resolution model with respect to the reference scan. This latter result is indeed an expected achievement of the proposed approach, since the super-resolution models combine information of several frames of a sequence. However, it is interesting to note the substantial decrease of the error with respect to the reference frame (more than 20% decrease of the RMSE passing from the first to the second row). To better emphasize the actual improvement, the average inter-subject distance between any two high-resolution scans of different subjects is also reported in the last row of Table 1. The relative variation of the intra-subject distance values in the first two rows compared to the inter-subject high-resolution distance values is reported in the rightmost column in the Table. It can be noticed that compared to the average inter-subject distance, the accuracy of the super-resolution models is considerable higher than the accuracy of the reference scans. This supports the idea that 3D face recognition across scans with different resolutions can be performed.

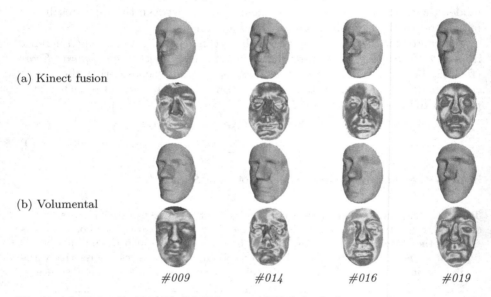

(a) Kinect fusion

(b) Volumental

#009   #014   #016   #019

Fig. 7. (a) *Kinect Fusion* [17]: (b) *Volumental* [29]. In both the cases, the reconstructed 3D models and the corresponding error-maps with respect to the high-resolution are reported in the top and bottom row.

4.2 Comparative Evaluation

The proposed approach has been compared against two solutions that permit fusion of multiple frames acquired with a Kinect sensor: The *Kinect Fusion* approach proposed in [17], which is released as part of the Kinect for Windows SDK; the commercial solution proposed by *Volumental*, which is given as an online service [29] (for the reported experiments, we used the data processing service available through the *Free account*). Both these methods use an acquisition protocol that requires the sensor to be moved around the object (supposed to be fixed) or across the environment to scan. In the proposed application, this protocol is implemented by asking the subject to sit still, and moving the sensor around his/her head at a distance of about 80 to 120cm, so as to maintain the best operating conditions for the camera and capture a large view of the face (i.e., the acquired sequence includes the frontal and the left/right side of the face). Compared to the protocol used for constructing super-resolved models, this paradigm is more general, not being constrained to faces, but it also requires substantial human intervention in the acquisition process and an even more constrained scenario, where the subject must remain still.

Figure 7(a) shows the reconstructed models obtained using the *Kinect Fusion* approach [17], and the corresponding error-maps computed with respect to the high-resolution scans. Compared to the super-resolution models obtained with our approach for the same subjects (see Fig. 6(b) and (d)), a general lower definition of face details can be observed. Results for the same subjects and for the *Volumental* approach [17] are reported in Fig. 7(b). The main facial traits (i.e., nose, eyebrows, chin) are reasonably defined in the reconstructed models, though finer details are roughly sketched, especially in the mouth and eyes regions.

Table 2. Average distance measure computed between the 3D high-resolution scans and the reconstructed models obtained, respectively, with the *Kinect Fusion*, *Volumental* and the super-resolution method proposed in this work

reconstructed vs. high-res	average $RMSE$
Kinect Fusion [17]	1.11
Volumental [29]	1.16
This work	0.84

Using the error measure defined in Sect. 4.1, we also evaluated quantitatively the distance between the models reconstructed with the *Kinect Fusion* and the *Volumental* approaches, and the corresponding high-resolution scans. Results are reported in Table 2, and compared with those obtained by our approach. It can be observed, the proposed approach scores the lowest error value.

5   Discussion and Conclusions

In this paper, we have defined an approach that permits the construction of a super-resolution face model starting from a sequence of low-resolution 3D scans acquired with a consumer depth camera. In particular, values of the points of the super-resolution model are constructed by iteratively aligning the low-resolution 3D frames to a reference frame (i.e., the first frame of the sequence) using the scaled ICP algorithm, and estimating an approximation function on the cumulated point cloud using Box-spline functions. Qualitative and quantitative experiments have been performed on the *The Florence face* dataset that includes, for each subject, a sequence of low-resolution 3D frames and one high-resolution

3D scan used as the ground truth data of a subject's face. In this way, results of the super-resolution process are evaluated by measuring the distance error between the super-resolved models and the ground truth. Results support the idea that constructing super-resolved models from consumer depth cameras can be a viable approach to make such devices deployable in real application contexts that also include identity recognition using 3D faces.

References

1. Passalis, G., Perakis, P., Theoharis, T., Kakadiaris, I.A.: Using facial symmetry to handle pose variations in real-world 3D face recognition. IEEE Trans. on Pattern Analysis and Machine Intelligence **33**(10), 1938–1951 (2011)
2. Drira, H., Ben Amor, B., Srivastava, A., Daouci, M., Slama, R.: 3D face recognition under expressions, occlusions, and pose variations. IEEE Trans. on Pattern Analysis and Machine Intelligence **35**(9), 2270–2283 (2013)
3. Pamplona Segundo, M., Silva, L., Bellon, O.: Real-time scale-invariant face detection on range images. In: Proc. IEEE Int. Conf. on Systems, Man, and Cybernetics (SMC), Anchorage, Alaska, USA, pp. 914–919 (2011)
4. Pamplona Segundo, M., Sarkar, S., Goldgof, D., Silva, L., Bellon, O.: Continuous 3D face authentication using RGB-D cameras. In: Proc. IEEE Work. on Biometrics, Portland, Oregon, USA, pp. 1–6 (June 2013)
5. Min, R., Choi, J., Medioni, G., Dugelay, J.L.: Real-time 3D face identification from a depth camera. In: Proc. Int. Conf. on Pattern Recognition (ICPR), Tsukuba, Japan, pp. 1739–1742 (November 2012)
6. Li, B.Y.L., Mian, A.S., Liu, W., Krishna, A.: Using kinect for face recognition under varying poses, expressions, illumination and disguise. In: Proc. IEEE Work. on Applications of Computer Vision (WACV), Clearwater, Florida, pp. 186–192 (January 2013)
7. Goswami, G., Bharadwaj, S., Vatsa, M., Singh, R.: On RGB-D face recognition using Kinect. In: Proc. IEEE Int. Conf. on Biometrics: Theory, Applications and Systems (BTAS), Washington DC, USA (September 2013)
8. Huang, T., Tsai, R.: Multi-frame image restoration and registration. Advances in Computer Vision and Image Processing **1**(10), 317–339 (1984)
9. Hardie, R., Barnard, K., Armstrong, E.: Joint map registration and high-resolution image estimation using a sequence of undersampled images. IEEE Trans. on Image Processing **6**(12), 1621–1633 (1997)
10. Baker, S., Kanade, T.: Limits on super-resolution and how to break them. IEEE Trans. on Pattern Analysis and Machine Intelligence **24**(9), 1167–1183 (2002)
11. Farsiu, S., Robinson, M., Elad, M., Milanfar, P.: Fast and robust multiframe super resolution. IEEE Trans. on Image Processing **13**(10), 1327–1344 (2004)
12. Ebrahimi, M., Vrscay, E.: Multi-frame super-resolution with no explicit motion estimation. In: Proc. Int. Conf. on Image Processing, Computer Vision, and Pattern Recognition (IPCV), Las Vegas, Nevada, USA, pp. 455–459 (July 2008)
13. Yang, Q., Yang, R., Davis, J., Nister, D.: Spatial-depth super resolution for range images. In: Proc. IEEE Int. Conf. on Computer Vision and Pattern Recognition (CVPR), Minneapolis, Minnesota, USA, pp. 1–8 (June 2007)
14. Schuon, S., Theobalt, C., Davis, J., Thrun, S.: Lidarboost: Depth superresolution for ToF 3D shape scanning. In: Proc. IEEE Int. Conf. Computer Vision and Pattern Recognition (CVPR), Miami, Florida, USA, pp. 343–350 (June 2009)

15. Peng, S., Pan, G., Wu, Z.: Learning-based super-resolution of 3D face model. In: Proc. IEEE Int. Conf. on Image Processing (ICIP), Genoa, Italy, vol. II, pp. 382–385 (September 2005)

16. Pan, G., Han, S., Wu, Z., Wang, Y.: Super-resolution of 3D face. In: Leonardis, A., Bischof, H., Pinz, A. (eds.) ECCV 2006. LNCS, vol. 3952, pp. 389–401. Springer, Heidelberg (2006)

17. Newcombe, R., Izadi, S., Hilliges, O., Molyneaux, D., Kim, D., Davison, A., Kohli, P., Shotton, J., Hodges, S., Fitzgibbon, A.: Kinectfusion: Real-time dense surface mapping and tracking. In: Proc. IEEE Int. Symposium on Mixed and Augmented Reality (ISMAR), Basel, Switzerland, pp. 1–10 (October 2011)

18. Hernandez, M., Choi, J., Medioni, G.: Laser scan quality 3-D face modeling using a low-cost depth camera. In: Proc. European Signal Processing Conf. (EUSIPCO), Bucharest, Romania, pp. 1995–1999 (August 2012)

19. Choi, J., Sharma, A., Medioni, G.: Comparing strategies for 3D face recognition from a 3D sensor. In: Proc. IEEE Int. Symposium on Robot and Human Interactive Communication (RO-MAN), Gyeongju, Korea, pp. 1–6 (August 2013)

20. Izadi, S., Newcombe, R., Kim, D., Hilliges, O., Molyneaux, D., Hodges, S., Kohli, P., Shotton, J., Davison, A., Fitzgibbon, A.:Kinectfusion: realtime dynamic 3D surface reconstruction and interaction. In: Proc. ACM SIGGRAPH, Vancouver, Canada, p. 1 (August 2011)

21. Berretti, S., Del Bimbo, A., Pala, P.: Superfaces: A super-resolution model for 3D faces. In: Fusiello, A., Murino, V., Cucchiara, R. (eds.) ECCV 2012 Ws/Demos, Part I. LNCS, vol. 7583, pp. 73–82. Springer, Heidelberg (2012)

22. Du, S., Zheng, N., Xiong, L., Ying, S., Xue, J.: Scaling iterative closest point algorithm for registration of m-D point sets. Journal of Visual Communication and Image Representation 21, 442–452 (2010)

23. Charina, M., Conti, C., Jetter, K., Zimmermann, G.: Scalar multivariate subdivision schemes and box splines. Computer Aided Geometric Design 28(5), 285–306 (2011)

24. The Florence face dataset (2013). http://www.micc.unifi.it/datasets/4d-faces/

25. Huynh, T., Min, R., Dugelay, J.-L.: An efficient LBP-based descriptor for facial depth images applied to gender recognition using RGB-D face data. In: Park, J.-I., Kim, J. (eds.) ACCV Workshops 2012, Part I. LNCS, vol. 7728, pp. 133–145. Springer, Heidelberg (2013)

26. Erdogmus, N., Marcel, S.: Spoofing in 2D face recognition with 3D masks and anti-spoofing with kinect. In: IEEE Int. Conf. on Biometrics: Theory, Applications and Systems, (BTAS), Washington DC, USA (September 2013)

27. Xu, C., Tan, T., Wang, Y., Quan, L.: Combining local features for robust nose location in 3D facial data. Pattern Recognition Letters 27(13), 1487–1494 (2006)

28. Rusinkiewicz, S., Levoy, M.: Efficient variants of the ICP algorithm. In: Proc. Int. Conf. on 3D Digital Imaging and Modeling (3DIM), Quebec City, Canada, pp. 145–152 (May 2001)

29. Volumental (2013). http://www.volumental.com/

Subspace Procrustes Analysis

Xavier Perez-Sala[1,3,4]($\boxtimes$), Fernando De la Torre[2], Laura Igual[3,5],
Sergio Escalera[3,5], and Cecilio Angulo[4]

[1] Fundació Privada Sant Antoni Abat, 08800 Vilanova i la Geltrú, Spain
xavier.perez-sala@upc.edu
[2] Robotics Institute, Carnegie Mellon University, Pittsburgh, PA 15213, USA
[3] Computer Vision Center, Universitat Autònoma de Barcelona, Bellaterra, Spain
[4] Universitat Politècnica de Catalunya, 08800 Vilanova i la Geltrú, Spain
[5] Universitat de Barcelona, 08007 Barcelona, Spain

Abstract. Procrustes Analysis (PA) has been a popular technique to align and build 2-D statistical models of shapes. Given a set of 2-D shapes PA is applied to remove rigid transformations. Then, a non-rigid 2-D model is computed by modeling (e.g., PCA) the residual. Although PA has been widely used, it has several limitations for modeling 2-D shapes: occluded landmarks and missing data can result in local minima solutions, and there is no guarantee that the 2-D shapes provide a uniform sampling of the 3-D space of rotations for the object. To address previous issues, this paper proposes Subspace PA (SPA). Given several instances of a 3-D object, SPA computes the mean and a 2-D subspace that can simultaneously model all rigid and non-rigid deformations of the 3-D object. We propose a discrete (DSPA) and continuous (CSPA) formulation for SPA, assuming that 3-D samples of an object are provided. DSPA extends the traditional PA, and produces unbiased 2-D models by uniformly sampling different views of the 3-D object. CSPA provides a continuous approach to uniformly sample the space of 3-D rotations, being more efficient in space and time. Experiments using SPA to learn 2-D models of bodies from motion capture data illustrate the benefits of our approach.

1 Introduction

In computer vision, Procrustes Analysis (PA) has been used extensively to align shapes (e.g., [4,19]) and appearance (e.g., [13,20]) as a pre-processing step to build 2-D models of shape variation. Usually, shape models are learned from a discrete set of 2-D landmarks through a two-step process [8]. Firstly, the rigid transformations are removed by aligning the training set w.r.t. the mean using PA; next, the remaining deformations are modeled using Principal Component Analysis (PCA) [5,18].

PA has been widely employed despite suffering from several limitations: (1) The 2-D training samples do not necessarily cover a uniform sampling of all 3-D rigid transformations of an object and this can result in a biased model (i.e., some poses are better represented than others). (2) It is computationally expensive

© Springer International Publishing Switzerland 2015
L. Agapito et al. (Eds.): ECCV 2014 Workshops, Part I, LNCS 8925, pp. 654–668, 2015.
DOI: 10.1007/978-3-319-16178-5_46

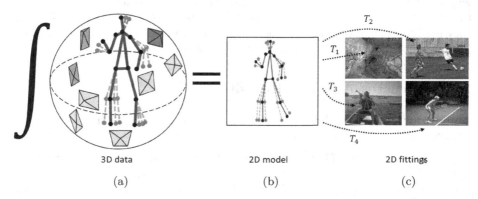

3D data   2D model   2D fittings

(a)   (b)   (c)

Fig. 1. Illustration of Continuous Subspace Procrustes Analysis (CSPA), which builds an unbiased 2-D model of human joints' variation (*b*) by integrating over all possible viewpoints of a 3-D motion capture data (*a*). This 2-D body shape model is used to reconstruct 2-D shapes from different viewpoints (*c*). Our CSPA model generalizes across poses and camera views because it is learned from a 3-D model.

to learn a shape model by sampling all possible 3-D rigid transformations of an object. (3) The models that are learned using only 2-D landmarks cannot model missing landmarks due to large pose changes. Moreover, PA methods can lead to local minima problems if there are missing components in the training data. (4) Finally, PA is computationally expensive, it scales linearly with the number of samples and landmarks and quadratically with the dimension of the data.

To address these issues, this paper proposes a discrete and a continuous formulation of Subspace Procrustes Analysis (SPA). SPA is able to efficiently compute the non-rigid subspace of possible 2-D projections given several 3-D samples of a deformable object. Note that our proposed work is the *inverse* problem of Non-Rigid Structure From Motion (NRSFM) [3,21,22]. The goal of NRSFM is to recover 3-D shape models from 2-D tracked landmarks, while SPA builds unbiased 2-D models from 3-D data. The learned 2-D model has the same representational power of a 3-D model but leads to faster fitting algorithms [15]. SPA uniformly samples the space of possible 3-D rigid transformations, and it is extremely efficient in space and time. The main idea of SPA is to combine functional data analysis with subspace estimation techniques.

Fig. 1 illustrates the main idea of this work. In Fig. 1 (*a*), we represent many samples of 3-D motion capture data of humans performing several activities. SPA simultaneously aligns all 3-D samples projections, while computing a 2-D subspace (Fig. 1 (*b*)) that can represent all possible projections of the 3-D motion capture samples under different camera views. Hence, SPA provides a simple, efficient and effective method to learn a 2-D subspace that accounts for non-rigid and 3-D geometric deformation of 3-D objects. These 2-D subspace models can be used for detection (i.e., constrain body parts, see Fig. 1 (*c*)), because the subspace models all 3-D rigid projections and non-rigid deformations. As we will show in the experimental validation, the models learned by SPA are able to generalize better than existing PA approaches across view-points (because they are built using 3-D models) and preserve expressive non-rigid deformations. Moreover, computing SPA is extremely efficient in space and time.

2 Procrustes Analysis Revisited

This section describes three different formulations of PA with a unified and enlightening matrix formulation.

Procrustes Analysis (PA): Given a set of m centered shapes (see footnote for notation[1]) composed by ℓ landmarks $\mathbf{D}_i \in \mathbb{R}^{d \times \ell}, \forall i = 1, \ldots, m$, PA [2,6,8–10] computes the d-dimensional reference shape $\mathbf{M} \in \mathbb{R}^{d \times \ell}$ and the m transformations $\mathbf{T}_i \in \mathbb{R}^{d \times d}$ (e.g., affine, Euclidean) that minimize the *reference-space model* [2,8,10] (see Fig. 2 (a)):

$$E_R(\mathbf{M}, \mathbf{T}) = \sum_{i=1}^{m} \|\mathbf{T}_i \mathbf{D}_i - \mathbf{M}\|_F^2, \tag{1}$$

where $\mathbf{T} = [\mathbf{T}_1^T, \cdots, \mathbf{T}_m^T]^T \in \mathbb{R}^{dm \times d}$. In the case of two-dimensional shapes $(d = 2)$, $\mathbf{D}_i = \begin{bmatrix} x_1 \ x_2 \cdots x_\ell \\ y_1 \ y_2 \cdots y_\ell \end{bmatrix}$. Alternatively, PA can be optimized using the *data-space model* [2] (see Fig. 2 (b)):

$$E_D(\mathbf{M}, \mathbf{A}) = \sum_{i=1}^{m} \|\mathbf{D}_i - \mathbf{A}_i \mathbf{M}\|_F^2, \tag{2}$$

where $\mathbf{A} = [\mathbf{A}_1^T, \cdots, \mathbf{A}_m^T]^T \in \mathbb{R}^{dm \times d}$. $\mathbf{A}_i = \mathbf{T}^{-1} \in \mathbb{R}^{d \times d}$ is the inverse transformation of $\mathbf{T}_i$ and corresponds to the rigid transformation for the reference shape $\mathbf{M}$.

The error function Eq. (1) of the reference-space model minimizes the difference between the reference shape and the registered shape data. In the data-space model, the error function Eq. (2) compares the observed shape points with the transformed reference shape, i.e., shape points predicted by the model and based on the notion of average shape [23]. This difference between the two models leads to different properties. Since the reference-space cost (E_R, Eq. (1)) is a sum of squares and it is convex in the optimization parameters, it can be optimized globally with Alternated Least Squares (ALS) methods. On the other hand, the data-space cost (E_D, Eq. (2)) is a bilinear problem and non-convex. If there is

---

[1] Bold capital letters denote a matrix $\mathbf{X}$, bold lower-case letters a column vector $\mathbf{x}$. $\mathbf{x}_i$ represents the ith column of the matrix $\mathbf{X}$. x_{ij} denotes the scalar in the ith row and j^{th} column of the matrix $\mathbf{X}$. All non-bold letters represent scalars. $\mathbf{I}_n \in \mathbb{R}^{n \times n}$ is an identity matrix. $\|\mathbf{x}\|_2 = \sqrt[2]{\sum_i |x_i|^2}$ and $\|\mathbf{X}\|_F = \sqrt{\sum_{ij} x_{ij}^2}$ denote the 2-norm for a vector and the Frobenius norm of a matrix, respectively. $\mathbf{X} \otimes \mathbf{Y}$ is the Kronecker product of matrices and $\mathbf{X}^{(p)}$ is the vec-transpose operator, detailed in Appendix A.

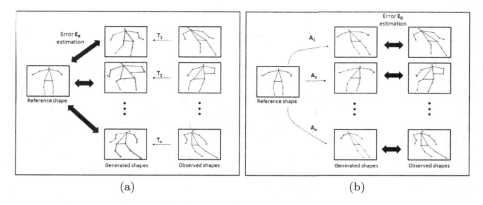

(a)   (b)

Fig. 2. (a): Reference-space model. (b): Data-space model. Note that $\mathbf{A}_i = \mathbf{T}_i^{-1}$.

no missing data, the data-space model can be solved using the Singular Value Decomposition (SVD). A major advantage of the data-space model is that it is *gauge invariant* (i.e., the cost does not depend on the coordinate frame in which the reference shape and the transformations are expressed) [2]. Benefits of both models are combined in [2]. Recently, Pizarro et al. [19] have proposed a convex approach for PA based on the reference-space model. In their case, the cost function is expressed with a quaternion parametrization which allows conversion to a Sum of Squares Program (SOSP). Finally, the equivalent semi-definite program of a SOSP relaxation is solved using convex optimization.

PA has also been applied to learn appearance models invariant to geometric transformations. When PA is applied to shapes, the geometric transformation (e.g., $\mathbf{T}_i$ or $\mathbf{A}_i$) can be directly applied to the image coordinates. However, to align appearance features the geometric transformations have to be composed with the image coordinates, and the process is a bit more complicated. This is the main difference when applying PA to align appearance and shape. Frey and Jojic [7] proposed a method for learning a factor analysis model that is invariant to geometric transformations. The computational cost of this method grows polynomially with the number of possible spatial transformations and it can be computationally intensive when working with high-dimensional motion models. To improve upon that, De la Torre and Black [20] proposed parameterized component analysis: a method that learns a subspace of appearance invariant to affine transformations. Miller et al. proposed the congealing method [13], which uses an entropy measure to align images with respect to the distribution of the data. Kookinos and Yuille [12] proposed a probabilistic framework and extended previous approaches to deal with articulated objects using a Markov Random Field (MRF) on top of Active Appearance Models (AAMs).

Projected Procrustes Analysis (PPA): Due to advances in 3-D capture systems, nowadays it is common to have access to 3-D shape models for a variety of objects. Given n 3-D shapes $\mathbf{D}_i \in \mathbb{R}^{3\times\ell}$, we can compute r projections $\mathbf{P}_j \in \mathbb{R}^{2\times3}$ for each of them (after removing translation) and minimize PPA:

$$E_{\text{PPA}}(\mathbf{M}, \mathbf{A}_{ij}) = \sum_{i=1}^{n} \sum_{j=1}^{r} \|\mathbf{P}_j \mathbf{D}_i - \mathbf{A}_{ij} \mathbf{M}\|_F^2, \tag{3}$$

where $\mathbf{P}_j$ is an orthographic projection of a 3-D rotation $\mathbf{R}(\boldsymbol{\omega})$ in a given domain $\boldsymbol{\Omega}$, defined by the rotation angles $\boldsymbol{\omega} = \{\phi, \theta, \psi\}$. Note that, while data and reference shapes are d-dimensional in Eq. (1) and Eq. (2), data $\mathbf{D}_i$ and reference $\mathbf{M} \in \mathbb{R}^{2 \times \ell}$ shapes in Eq. (3) are fixed to be 3-D and 2-D, respectively. Hence, $\mathbf{A}_{ij} \in \mathbb{R}^{2 \times 2}$ is a 2-D transformation mapping $\mathbf{M}$ to the 2-D projection of the 3-D data. ALS is a common method to minimize Eq. (2) and (3). ALS alternates between minimizing over $\mathbf{M}$ and $\mathbf{A}_{ij} \in \mathbb{R}^{2 \times 2}$ with the following expressions:

$$\mathbf{A}_{ij} = \mathbf{P}_j \mathbf{D}_i \mathbf{M}^T (\mathbf{M} \mathbf{M}^T)^{-1} \qquad \forall i, j, \tag{4}$$

$$\mathbf{M} = \left(\sum_{i=1}^{n} \sum_{j=1}^{r} \mathbf{A}_{ij}^T \mathbf{A}_{ij} \right)^{-1} \left(\sum_{i=1}^{n} \left(\sum_{j=1}^{r} \mathbf{A}_{ij}^T \mathbf{P}_j \right) \mathbf{D}_i \right). \tag{5}$$

Note that PPA and its extensions deal with missing data naturally. Since they use the whole 3-D shape of objects, the enhanced 2-D dataset resulting of projecting the data from different viewpoints can be constructed without occluded landmarks.

Continuous Procrustes Analysis (CPA): A major limitation of PPA is the difficulty to generate uniform distributions in the Special Orthogonal group $SO(3)$ [17]. Due to the topology of $SO(3)$, different angles should be sampled following different distributions, which becomes difficult when the rotation matrices must be confined in a specific region $\boldsymbol{\Omega}$ of $SO(3)$, restricted by rotation angles $\boldsymbol{\omega} = \{\phi, \theta, \psi\}$. Moreover, the computational complexity of PPA increases linearly with the number of projections (r) and 3-D objects (n).

In order to deal with these drawbacks, a continuous formulation (CPA) was proposed in [10] by formulating PPA within a functional analysis framework. CPA minimizes:

$$E_{\text{CPA}}(\mathbf{M}, \mathbf{A}(\boldsymbol{\omega})_i) = \sum_{i=1}^{n} \int_{\boldsymbol{\Omega}} \|\mathbf{P}(\boldsymbol{\omega}) \mathbf{D}_i - \mathbf{A}(\boldsymbol{\omega})_i \mathbf{M}\|_F^2 \, d\boldsymbol{\omega}, \tag{6}$$

where $d\boldsymbol{\omega} = \frac{1}{8\pi^2} \sin(\theta) d\phi d\theta d\psi$ ensures uniformity in $SO(3)$ [17]. This continuous formulation finds the optimal 2-D reference shape of a 3-D dataset, rotated and projected in a given domain $\boldsymbol{\Omega}$, by integrating over all possible rotations in that domain. The main difference between Eq. (3) and Eq. (6) is that the entries in $\mathbf{P}(\boldsymbol{\omega}) \in \mathbb{R}^{2 \times 3}$ and $\mathbf{A}(\boldsymbol{\omega})_i \in \mathbb{R}^{2 \times 2}$ are not scalars anymore, but functions of the integration angles $\boldsymbol{\omega} = \{\phi, \theta, \psi\}$. After some linear algebra and functional analysis, it is possible to find an equivalent expression to the discrete approach (Eq. (3)), where $\mathbf{A}(\boldsymbol{\omega})_i$ and $\mathbf{M}$ have the following expressions:

$$\mathbf{A}(\boldsymbol{\omega})_i = \mathbf{P}(\boldsymbol{\omega}) \mathbf{D}_i \mathbf{M}^T (\mathbf{M} \mathbf{M}^T)^{-1} \qquad \forall i, \tag{7}$$

$$\mathbf{M} = \left(\sum_{i=1}^{n} \int_{\boldsymbol{\Omega}} \mathbf{A}(\boldsymbol{\omega})_i^T \mathbf{A}(\boldsymbol{\omega})_i d\boldsymbol{\omega} \right)^{-1} \left(\sum_{i=1}^{n} \left(\int_{\boldsymbol{\Omega}} \mathbf{A}(\boldsymbol{\omega})_i^T \mathbf{P}(\boldsymbol{\omega}) d\boldsymbol{\omega} \right) \mathbf{D}_i \right). \tag{8}$$

It is important to notice that the 2-D projections are not explicitly computed in the continuous formulation. The solution of $\mathbf{M}$ is found using fixed-point iteration in Eq. (6):

$$\mathbf{M} = (\mathbf{Z}\mathbf{M}^T(\mathbf{M}\mathbf{M}^T)^{-1})^{-1}\mathbf{Z}, \tag{9}$$

where $\mathbf{X} = \int_{\Omega} \mathbf{P}(\boldsymbol{\omega})^T \mathbf{P}(\boldsymbol{\omega}) d\boldsymbol{\omega} \in \mathbb{R}^{3 \times 3}$ averages the rotation covariances and[2] $\mathbf{Z} = (\mathbf{M}\mathbf{M}^T)^{-1}\mathbf{M} \left(\sum_{i=1}^{n} (\mathbf{D}_i^T \otimes \mathbf{D}_i^T) \, \mathrm{vec}(\mathbf{X}) \right)^{(\ell)}$. Note that the definite integral $\mathbf{X}$ is not data dependent, and it can be computed off-line.

Our work builds on [10] but extends it in several ways. First, CPA only computes the reference shape of the dataset. In this paper, we add a subspace that is able to model non-rigid deformations of the object, as well as rigid 3-D transformations that the affine transformation cannot model. As we will describe later, adding a subspace to the PA formulation is not a trivial task. For instance, modeling a subspace following the standard methodology based on CPA would still require to generate r rotations for each 3-D sample. Hence, the CPA efficiency is limited to rigid models while our approach is not. Second, we provide a discrete and continuous formulation in order to provide a better understanding of the problem, and experimentally show that it converges to the same solution when the number of sampled rotations (r) increases. Finally, we evaluate the models in two challenging problems: pose estimation in still images and joints' modeling.

3   Subspace Procrustes Analysis (SPA)

This section proposes Discrete Subspace Procrustes Analysis (DSPA) and Continuous Subspace Procrustes Analysis (CSPA) to learn unbiased 2-D models from 3-D deformable objects.

Discrete Subspace Procrustes Analysis (DSPA): Given a set of r viewpoints $\mathbf{P}_j \in \mathbb{R}^{2 \times 3}$ of the n 3-D shapes, where $\mathbf{d}_i = \mathrm{vec}(\mathbf{D}_i) \in \mathbb{R}^{3\ell \times 1}$, DSPA extends PA by considering a subspace $\mathbf{B} \in \mathbb{R}^{2\ell \times k}$ and the weights $\mathbf{c}_{ij} \in \mathbb{R}^{k \times 1}$ which model the non-rigid deformations that the mean $\mathbf{M}$ and the transformation $\mathbf{A}_{ij}$ are not able to reconstruct. DSPA minimizes the following function:

$$E_{\mathrm{DSPA}}(\mathbf{M}, \mathbf{A}_{ij}, \mathbf{B}, \mathbf{c}_{ij}) = \sum_{i=1}^{n} \sum_{j=1}^{r} \left\| \mathbf{P}_j \mathbf{D}_i - \mathbf{A}_{ij}\mathbf{M} - (\mathbf{c}_{ij}^T \otimes \mathbf{I}_2)\mathbf{B}^{(2)} \right\|_F^2 = \tag{10}$$

$$\sum_{i=1}^{n} \sum_{j=1}^{r} \left\| (\mathbf{I}_\ell \otimes \mathbf{P}_j)\mathbf{d}_i - (\mathbf{I}_\ell \otimes \mathbf{A}_{ij})\boldsymbol{\mu} - \mathbf{B}\mathbf{c}_{ij} \right\|_2^2, \tag{11}$$

where $\mathbf{P}_j$ is a particular 3-D rotation, $\mathbf{R}(\boldsymbol{\omega})$, that is projected using an orthographic projection into 2-D, $\boldsymbol{\mu} = \mathrm{vec}(\mathbf{M}) \in \mathbb{R}^{2\ell \times 1}$ is the vectorized version of the reference shape, $\mathbf{c}_{ij}$ are the k weights of the subspace for each 2-D shape projection, and $\mathbf{B}^{(2)} \in \mathbb{R}^{2k \times \ell}$ is the reshaped subspace. Observe that the only

---

[2] See Appendix A for an explanation of the vec-transpose operator.

difference with Eq. (3) is that we have added a subspace. This subspace will compensate for the non-rigid components of the 3-D object and the rigid component (3-D rotation and projection to the image plane) that the affine transformation cannot model. Recall that a 3-D rigid object under orthographic projection can be recovered with a three-dimensional subspace (if the mean is removed), but PA cannot recover it because it is only rank two. Also, observe that the coefficient $\mathbf{c}_{ij}$ depends on two indexes, i for the object and j for the geometric projection. Dependency of $\mathbf{c}_{ij}$ on the geometric projection is a key point. If j index is not considered, the subspace would not be able to capture the variations in pose and its usefulness for our purposes would be unclear. Although Eq. (10) and the NRSFM problem follow similar formulation [3], the assumptions are different and variables have opposite meanings. For instance, the NRSFM assumptions about rigid transformations do not apply here, since $\mathbf{A}_{ij}$ are affine transformations in our case.

Given an initialization of $\mathbf{B} = 0$, DSPA is minimized by finding the transformations $\mathbf{A}_{ij}^*$ and reference shape $\mathbf{M}^*$ that minimize Eq. (3), using the same ALS framework as in PA. Then, we substitute $\mathbf{A}_{ij}^*$ and $\mathbf{M}^*$ in Eq. (11) that results in the expression:

$$E_{\text{DSPA}}(\mathbf{B}, \mathbf{c}_{ij}) = \sum_{i=1}^{n} \sum_{j=1}^{r} \left\| \widetilde{\mathbf{D}}_{ij} - (\mathbf{c}_{ij}^T \otimes \mathbf{I}_2)\mathbf{B}^{(2)} \right\|_F^2 = \tag{12}$$

$$\sum_{i=1}^{n} \sum_{j=1}^{r} \left\| \widetilde{\mathbf{d}}_{ij} - \mathbf{B}\mathbf{c}_{ij} \right\|_2^2 = \left\| \widetilde{\mathbf{D}} - \mathbf{B}\mathbf{C} \right\|_F^2, \tag{13}$$

where $\widetilde{\mathbf{D}}_{ij} = \mathbf{P}_j\mathbf{D}_i - \mathbf{A}_{ij}^*\mathbf{M}^* \in \mathbb{R}^{2\times\ell}$, $\widetilde{\mathbf{d}}_{ij} = \text{vec}(\widetilde{\mathbf{D}}_{ij}) \in \mathbb{R}^{2\ell\times 1}$, $\widetilde{\mathbf{D}} = [\widetilde{\mathbf{d}}_1 \ldots \widetilde{\mathbf{d}}_{nr}] \in \mathbb{R}^{2\ell\times nr}$, and $\mathbf{C} \in \mathbb{R}^{k\times nr}$. We can find the global optima of Eq. (13) by Singular Value Decomposition (SVD): $\mathbf{B} = \mathbf{U}$ and $\mathbf{C} = \mathbf{S}\mathbf{V}^T$, where $\widetilde{\mathbf{D}} = \mathbf{U}\mathbf{S}\mathbf{V}^T$.

Continuous Subspace Procrustes Analysis (CSPA): As it was discussed in the previous section, the discrete formulation is not efficient in space nor time, and might suffer from not uniform sampling of the original space. CSPA generalizes DSPA by re-writting it in a continuous formulation. CSPA minimizes the following functional:

$$E_{\text{CSPA}}(\mathbf{M}, \mathbf{A}(\boldsymbol{\omega})_i, \mathbf{B}, \mathbf{c}(\boldsymbol{\omega})_i) =$$

$$\sum_{i=1}^{n} \int_{\Omega} \left\| \mathbf{P}(\boldsymbol{\omega})\mathbf{D}_i - \mathbf{A}(\boldsymbol{\omega})_i\mathbf{M} - (\mathbf{c}(\boldsymbol{\omega})_i^T \otimes \mathbf{I}_2)\mathbf{B}^{(2)} \right\|_F^2 d\boldsymbol{\omega} = \tag{14}$$

$$\sum_{i=1}^{n} \int_{\Omega} \left\| (\mathbf{I}_\ell \otimes \mathbf{P}(\boldsymbol{\omega}))\mathbf{d}_i - (\mathbf{I}_\ell \otimes \mathbf{A}(\boldsymbol{\omega})_i)\boldsymbol{\mu} - \mathbf{B}\mathbf{c}(\boldsymbol{\omega})_i \right\|_2^2 d\boldsymbol{\omega}, \tag{15}$$

where $d\boldsymbol{\omega} = \frac{1}{8\pi^2} \sin(\theta)d\phi d\theta d\psi$. The main difference between Eq. (15) and Eq. (11) is that the entries in $\mathbf{c}(\boldsymbol{\omega})_i \in \mathbb{R}^{k\times 1}$, $\mathbf{P}(\boldsymbol{\omega}) \in \mathbb{R}^{2\times 3}$ and $\mathbf{A}(\boldsymbol{\omega})_i \in \mathbb{R}^{2\times 2}$ are not scalars anymore, but functions of integration angles $\boldsymbol{\omega} = \{\phi, \theta, \psi\}$.

Given an initialization of $\mathbf{B} = 0$, and similarly to the DSPA model, CSPA is minimized by finding the optimal reference shape $\mathbf{M}^*$ that minimizes Eq. (6). We used the same fixed-point framework as CPA. Given the value of $\mathbf{M}^*$ and the expression of $\mathbf{A}(\boldsymbol{\omega})_i^*$ from Eq. (7), we substitute them in Eq. (15) resulting in:

$$E_{\text{CSPA}}(\mathbf{B}, \mathbf{c}(\boldsymbol{\omega})_i) = \sum_{i=1}^{n} \int_{\boldsymbol{\Omega}} \left\| \mathbf{P}(\boldsymbol{\omega})\bar{\mathbf{D}}_i - (\mathbf{c}(\boldsymbol{\omega})_i^T \otimes \mathbf{I}_2)\mathbf{B}^{(2)} \right\|_F^2 d\boldsymbol{\omega} = \qquad (16)$$

$$\sum_{i=1}^{n} \int_{\boldsymbol{\Omega}} \left\| (\mathbf{I}_\ell \otimes \mathbf{P}(\boldsymbol{\omega}))\bar{\mathbf{d}}_i - \mathbf{B}\mathbf{c}(\boldsymbol{\omega})_i \right\|_2^2 d\boldsymbol{\omega}, \qquad (17)$$

where $\bar{\mathbf{D}}_i = \mathbf{D}_i(\mathbf{I}_\ell - (\mathbf{M}^{*T}(\mathbf{M}^*\mathbf{M}^{*T})^{-1}\mathbf{M}^*))$ and $\bar{\mathbf{d}}_i = \text{vec}(\bar{\mathbf{D}}_i)$. We can find the global optima of Eq. (17) by solving the eigenvalue problem, $\boldsymbol{\Sigma}\mathbf{B} = \mathbf{B}\boldsymbol{\Lambda}$, where $\boldsymbol{\Lambda}$ are the eigenvalues corresponding to columns of $\mathbf{B}$.

After some algebra (see Appendix B) we show that the covariance matrix $\boldsymbol{\Sigma} = ((\mathbf{I}_\ell \otimes \mathbf{Y})\text{vec}(\sum_{i=1}^{n} \sum_{j=1}^{r} \bar{\mathbf{d}}_{ij}\bar{\mathbf{d}}_{ij}^T))^{(2\ell)}$ where the definite integral $\mathbf{Y} = \int_{\boldsymbol{\Omega}} \mathbf{P}(\boldsymbol{\omega}) \otimes (\mathbf{I}_\ell \otimes \mathbf{P}(\boldsymbol{\omega}))d\boldsymbol{\omega} \in \mathbb{R}^{2\ell \times 2\ell}$ can be computed off-line, leading to an efficient optimization in space and time. Though the number of elements in matrix $\mathbf{Y}$ increase quadratically with the number of landmarks ℓ, note that the integration time is constant since $\mathbf{Y}$ has a sparse structure with only 36 different non-zero values (recall that $\mathbf{P}(\boldsymbol{\omega}) \in \mathbb{R}^{2 \times 3}$).

Although $\mathbf{A}(\boldsymbol{\omega})_i$ and $\mathbf{c}(\boldsymbol{\omega})_i$ are not explicitly computed during training, this is not a limitation compared to DSPA. During testing time, training values of $\mathbf{c}(\boldsymbol{\omega})_i$ are not needed. Only the deformation limits in each principal direction of $\mathbf{B}$ are required. These limits also depend on eigenvalues [4], which are computed with CSPA.

4   Experiments and Results

This section illustrates the benefits of DSPA and CSPA, and compares them with state-of-the-art PA methods to build 2-D shape models of human skeletons. First, we compare the performance of PA+PCA and SPA to build a 2-D shape model of Motion Capture (MoCap) bodies using the Carnegie Mellon University MoCap dataset [1]. Next, we compare our discrete and continuous approaches in a large scale experiment. Finally, we illustrate the generalization of our 2-D body model in the problem of human pose estimation using the Leeds Sport Dataset [11]. For all experiments, we report the Mean Squared Error (MSE) relative to the torso size.

4.1   Learning 2-D Joints Models

The aim of this experiment is to build a generic 2-D body model that can reconstruct non-rigid deformations under a large range of 3-D rotations. For training and testing, we used the Carnegie Mellon University MoCap dataset that is composed of 2605 sequences performed by 109 subjects. The sequences

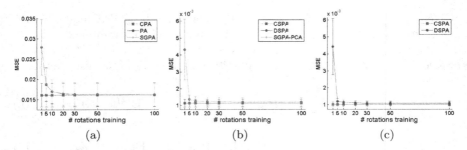

Fig. 3. Comparisons as a function of the number of training viewpoint projections. (*a*) Rigid and (*b*) Deformable models (using a subspace of 9 basis) from Experiment 1, respectively; (*c*) CSPA and DSPA deformable models (using a subspace of 12 basis) from Experiment 2.

cover a wide variety of daily human activities and sports. Skeletons with 31 joints are provided, as well as RGB video recordings for several sequences. We trained our models using the set of 14 landmarks as is common across several databases for human pose estimation.

Experiment 1: Comparison with State-of-the-Art PA Methods. This section compares DSPA, CSPA methods with the state-of-the-art Stratified Generalized Procrustes Analysis (SGPA) [2][3]. For training we randomly selected 3 sequences with 30 frames per sequence from the set of 11 running sequences of the user number 9 (this is due to the memory limitations of SGPA). For testing we randomly selected 2 sequences with 30 frames from the same set. We rotated the 3-D models in the yaw and pitch angles, within the ranges of $\phi, \theta \in [-\pi/2, \pi/2]$. The angles were uniformly selected and we report results varying the number of considered angles (i.e., rotations) between $1 \sim 100$ angles in training, and fixed 300 angles for testing.

There are several versions of SGPA. We selected the "Affine-factorization" with the data-space model to make a fair comparison with our method. Recall that under our assumption of non-missing data "Affine-All" and "Affine-factorization" achieve the same solution, with "Affine-factorization" being faster.

Fig. 3 shows the mean reconstruction error and 0.5 of the standard deviation for 100 realizations. Fig. 3 (a) reports the results comparing PA, CPA and SGPA. As expected, PA and SGPA converge to CPA as the number of training rotations increased. However, observe that CPA achieves the same performance, but it is much more efficient. Fig. 3 (b) compares DSPA, CSPA, and SGPA followed by PCA (we will refer to this method SGPA+PCA). From the figure we can observe that the mean error in the test for DSPA and SGPA+PCA decrease with the number of rotations in the training, and it converges to CSPA. CSPA provides a bound on the lower error. Observe, that we used 90 3-D bodies (3

---

[3] The code was downloaded from author's website (http://isit.u-clermont1.fr/~ab).

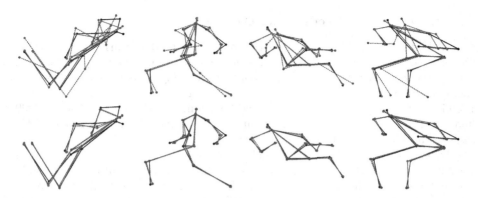

Fig. 4. Experiment 2 results with 1 (*top*), and 30 (*bottom*) rotations. Examples show skeleton reconstructions from continuous (*CSPA* in *solid red lines*) and discrete (*SPA* in *dashed blue lines*) models over ground truth (*solid black lines*).

sequences with 30 frames) within rotating angles $\phi, \theta \in [-\pi/2, \pi/2]$, and DSPA and SGPA+PCA needed about 30 angles to achieve similar result to CSPA. So, in this case, discrete methods need 30 times more space than the continuous one. The execution times with 30 rotations, on a 2.2GHz computer with 8Gb of RAM, were 1.44 sec. (DSPA), 0.03 sec. (CSPA) and 3.54 sec. (SGPA+PCA).

Experiment 2: Comparison between CSPA and DSPA. This experiment compares DSPA and CSPA in a large-scale problem as a function of the number of rotations. For training we randomly selected 20 sequences with 30 frames per sequence. For testing we randomly selected 5 sequences with 30 frames. We rotated the 3-D models in the yaw and pitch angles, within the ranges of $\phi, \theta \in [-\pi/2, \pi/2]$. The angles were uniformly selected and we report results varying the number of angles (i.e., rotations) between $1 \sim 100$ angles in training, and 300 angles for testing.

Fig. 3 (c) shows the mean reconstruction error and 0.5 of the standard deviation for 100 realizations, comparing DSPA and CSPA. As expected, DSPA converges to CSPA as the number of training rotations increases. However, observe that CSPA achieves the same performance, but it is much more efficient. In this experiment, with 6000 3-D training bodies (20 sequences with 30 frames) and domain: $\phi, \theta \in [-\pi/2, \pi/2]$ discrete method required, again, around 30 2-D viewpoint projections to achieve similar results to CSPA. Thus, discrete model DSPA needs 30 times more storage space than CSPA. The execution times with 30 rotations, on a 2.2GHz computer with 8Gb of RAM, were 14.75 sec. (DSPA) and 0.04 sec. (CSPA).

Qualitative results from CSPA and DSPA models trained with different number of rotations are shown in Fig. 4. Note that training DSPA model with 1 rotation (*top*) results in poor reconstruction. However, training it with 30 rotations (*bottom*) leads to reconstructions almost as accurate as made by CSPA.

4.2   Experiment 3. Leeds Sport Dataset

This section illustrates how to use the 2-D body models learned with CSPA to detect body configurations from images. We used the Leeds Sport Dataset (LSP) that contains 2000 images of people performing different sports, some of them including extreme poses or viewpoints (e.g., parkour images). The first 1000 images of the dataset are considered for training and the second set of 1000 images for testing. One skeleton manually labeled with 14 joints is provided for each training and test image.

We trained our 2-D CSPA model in the CMU MoCap dataset [1] using 1000 frames. From the 2605 sequences of the motion capture data, we randomly selected 1000 and the frame in the middle of sequence is selected as representative frame. Using this training data, we built the 2-D CSPA model using the following ranges for the pitch, roll and yaw angles: $\phi, \theta, \psi \in [-3/4\pi, 3/4\pi]$. We will refer to this model as CSPA-MoCap. For comparison, we used the 1000 2-D training skeletons provided by the LSP dataset and run SGPA+PCA to build an alternative 2-D model. We will refer to this model as SGPA+PCA-LSP. Observe, that this model was trained on similar data as the test set.

Table 1 reports MSE of reconstructing the test skeletons with rigid and deformable models. A subspace of 12 basis is used for both deformable models. Results show that CSPA-MoCap has less reconstruction error than the standard method SGPA+PCA-LSP, even trained in a different dataset (CMU MoCap) than the test. Qualitative results from CSPA-MoCap and SGPA+PCA-LSP models are shown in Fig. 5. Note that CSPA-MoCap provides more accurate reconstructions than SGPA+PCA-LSP because it is able to generalize to all possible 3-D rotations in the given interval.

Table 1. Experiment 3 results. MSE of our continuous model (*CSPA-MoCap*) trained with 3-D MoCap data, the discrete model trained in the LSP dataset (*SGPA+PCA-LSP*), and both rigid models (*CPA-MoCap, SGPA-LSP*).

Model	CPA-MoCap	SGPA-LSP	CSPA-MoCap	SGPA+PCA-LSP
MSE	0.16405	0.16231	**0.01046**	0.01366

Fig. 5. Experiment 3 examples, reconstructing ground truth skeletons of LSP dataset with *CSPA-MoCap* (*solid red lines*) and *SGPA+PCA-LSP* (*dashed blue lines*) models

5   Conclusions

This paper proposes an extension of PA to learn a 2-D subspace of rigid and non-rigid deformations of 3-D objects. We propose two models, one discrete (DSPA) that samples the 3-D rotation space, and one continuous (CSPA) that integrates over $SO(3)$. As the number of projections increases DPSA converges to CSPA. SPA has two advantages over traditional PA, PPA: (1) it generates unbiased models because it uniformly covers the space of projections, and (2) CSPA is much more efficient in space and time. Experiments comparing 2-D SPA models of bodies show improvements w.r.t. state-of-the-art PA methods. In particular, CSPA models trained with motion capture data outperformed 2-D models trained on the same database under the same conditions in the LSP database, showing how our 2-D models from 3-D data can generalize better to different viewpoints. In future work, we plan to explore other models that decouple the rigid and non-rigid deformation by providing two independent basis in the subspace.

Acknowledgments. This work is partly supported by the Spanish Ministry of Science and Innovation (projects TIN2012-38416-C03-01, TIN2012-38187-C03-01, TIN2013-43478-P), project 2014 SGR 1219, and the Comissionat per a Universitats i Recerca del Departament d'Innovació, Universitats i Empresa de la Generalitat de Catalunya.

A   Appendix. Vec-transpose

Vec-transpose $\mathbf{A}^{(p)}$ is a linear operator that generalizes vectorization and transposition operators [14,16]. It reshapes matrix $\mathbf{A} \in \mathbb{R}^{m \times n}$ by vectorizing each ith block of p rows, and rearranging it as the ith column of the reshaped matrix, such that $\mathbf{A}^{(p)} \in \mathbb{R}^{pn \times \frac{m}{p}}$,

$$
\begin{bmatrix} a_{11} & a_{12} & a_{13} \\ a_{21} & a_{22} & a_{23} \\ a_{31} & a_{32} & a_{33} \\ a_{41} & a_{42} & a_{43} \\ a_{51} & a_{52} & a_{53} \\ a_{61} & a_{62} & a_{63} \end{bmatrix}^{(3)} = \begin{bmatrix} a_{11} & a_{41} \\ a_{21} & a_{51} \\ a_{31} & a_{61} \\ a_{12} & a_{42} \\ a_{22} & a_{52} \\ a_{32} & a_{62} \\ a_{13} & a_{43} \\ a_{23} & a_{53} \\ a_{33} & a_{63} \end{bmatrix},
$$

$$
\begin{bmatrix} a_{11} & a_{12} & a_{13} \\ a_{21} & a_{22} & a_{23} \\ a_{31} & a_{32} & a_{33} \\ a_{41} & a_{42} & a_{43} \\ a_{51} & a_{52} & a_{53} \\ a_{61} & a_{62} & a_{63} \end{bmatrix}^{(2)} = \begin{bmatrix} a_{11} & a_{31} & a_{51} \\ a_{21} & a_{41} & a_{61} \\ a_{12} & a_{32} & a_{52} \\ a_{22} & a_{42} & a_{62} \\ a_{13} & a_{33} & a_{53} \\ a_{23} & a_{43} & a_{63} \end{bmatrix}.
$$

Note that $(\mathbf{A}^{(p)})^{(p)} = \mathbf{A}$ and $\mathbf{A}^{(m)} = \text{vec}(\mathbf{A})$. A useful rule for pulling a matrix out of nested Kronecker products is, $((\mathbf{BA})^{(p)}\mathbf{C})^{(p)} = (\mathbf{C}^T \otimes \mathbf{I}_p)\mathbf{BA} = (\mathbf{B}^{(p)}\mathbf{C})^{(p)}\mathbf{A}$, which leads to $(\mathbf{C}^T \otimes \mathbf{I}_2)\mathbf{B} = (\mathbf{B}^{(2)}\mathbf{C})^{(2)}$.

B   Appendix. CSPA formulation

In this Appendix, we detail the steps from Eq. (14) to Eq. (17), as well as the definition of the covariance matrix, introduced in Section 3.

Given the value of $\mathbf{M}^*$ and the optimal expression of $\mathbf{A}(\boldsymbol{\omega})_i^*$ from Eq. (7), we substitute them in Eq. (14) resulting in:

$$E_{\text{CSPA}}(\mathbf{B}, \mathbf{c}(\boldsymbol{\omega})_i) = \sum_{i=1}^{n} \int_{\Omega} \left\| \mathbf{P}(\boldsymbol{\omega})\mathbf{D}_i - \mathbf{P}(\boldsymbol{\omega})\mathbf{D}_i\mathbf{H} - (\mathbf{c}(\boldsymbol{\omega})_i^T \otimes \mathbf{I}_2)\mathbf{B}^{(2)} \right\|_F^2 d\boldsymbol{\omega}, \quad (18)$$

where $\mathbf{H} = \mathbf{M}^{*T}(\mathbf{M}^*\mathbf{M}^{*T})^{-1}\mathbf{M}^*$ and $\mathbf{D}_i \in \mathbb{R}^{3 \times \ell}$. Then,

$$E_{\text{CSPA}}(\mathbf{B}, \mathbf{c}(\boldsymbol{\omega})_i) = \sum_{i=1}^{n} \int_{\Omega} \left\| \mathbf{P}(\boldsymbol{\omega})\mathbf{D}_i(\mathbf{I}_\ell - \mathbf{H}) - (\mathbf{c}(\boldsymbol{\omega})_i^T \otimes \mathbf{I}_2)\mathbf{B}^{(2)} \right\|_F^2 d\boldsymbol{\omega} \quad (19)$$

leads us to Eq. (16) and Eq. (17), where $\bar{\mathbf{D}}_i = \mathbf{D}_i(\mathbf{I}_\ell - \mathbf{H})$ and $\bar{\mathbf{d}}_i = \text{vec}(\bar{\mathbf{D}}_i)$. From Eq. (17), solving $\frac{\partial E_{\text{CSPA}}}{\partial \mathbf{c}(\boldsymbol{\omega})_i} = 0$ we find:

$$\mathbf{c}(\boldsymbol{\omega})_i^* = (\mathbf{B}^T\mathbf{B})^{-1}\mathbf{B}^T(\mathbf{I}_\ell \otimes \mathbf{P}(\boldsymbol{\omega}))\bar{\mathbf{d}}_i. \quad (20)$$

The substitution of $\mathbf{c}(\boldsymbol{\omega})_i^*$ in Eq. (17) results in:

$$E_{\text{CSPA}}(\mathbf{B}) = \sum_{i=1}^{n} \int_{\Omega} \left\| (\mathbf{I}_\ell \otimes \mathbf{P}(\boldsymbol{\omega}))\bar{\mathbf{d}}_i - \mathbf{B}(\mathbf{B}^T\mathbf{B})^{-1}\mathbf{B}^T(\mathbf{I}_\ell \otimes \mathbf{P}(\boldsymbol{\omega}))\bar{\mathbf{d}}_i \right\|_2^2 d\boldsymbol{\omega} = \quad (21)$$

$$\sum_{i=1}^{n} \int_{\Omega} \left\| \left(\mathbf{I} - \mathbf{B}(\mathbf{B}^T\mathbf{B})^{-1}\mathbf{B}^T \right) (\mathbf{I}_\ell \otimes \mathbf{P}(\boldsymbol{\omega}))\bar{\mathbf{d}}_i \right\|_2^2 d\boldsymbol{\omega} = \quad (22)$$

$$\sum_{i=1}^{n} \int_{\Omega} \text{tr}\left[\left(\mathbf{I} - \mathbf{B}(\mathbf{B}^T\mathbf{B})^{-1}\mathbf{B}^T \right) (\mathbf{I}_\ell \otimes \mathbf{P}(\boldsymbol{\omega}))\bar{\mathbf{d}}_i \left((\mathbf{I}_\ell \otimes \mathbf{P}(\boldsymbol{\omega}))\bar{\mathbf{d}}_i \right)^T \right] d\boldsymbol{\omega} = \quad (23)$$

$$\text{tr}\left[\left(\mathbf{I} - \mathbf{B}(\mathbf{B}^T\mathbf{B})^{-1}\mathbf{B}^T \right) \boldsymbol{\Sigma} \right], \quad (24)$$

where:

$$\boldsymbol{\Sigma} = \int_{\Omega} (\mathbf{I}_\ell \otimes \mathbf{P}(\boldsymbol{\omega})) \left(\sum_{i=1}^{n} \bar{\mathbf{d}}_i \bar{\mathbf{d}}_i^T \right) (\mathbf{I}_\ell \otimes \mathbf{P}(\boldsymbol{\omega}))^T d\boldsymbol{\omega}. \quad (25)$$

We can find the global optima of Eq. (24) by solving the eigenvalue problem, $\boldsymbol{\Sigma}\mathbf{B} = \mathbf{B}\boldsymbol{\Lambda}$, where $\boldsymbol{\Sigma}$ is the covariance matrix and $\boldsymbol{\Lambda}$ are the eigenvalues corresponding to columns of $\mathbf{B}$. However, the definite integral in $\boldsymbol{\Sigma}$ is data dependent. To be able to compute the integral off-line, we need to rearrange the elements in $\boldsymbol{\Sigma}$. Using vectorization and vec-transpose operator[4]:

$$\boldsymbol{\Sigma} = (\text{vec}\,[\boldsymbol{\Sigma}])^{(2\ell)} = \tag{26}$$

$$\left(\text{vec}\left[\int_{\boldsymbol{\Omega}}(\mathbf{I}_\ell \otimes \mathbf{P}(\omega))\left(\sum_{i=1}^{n}\bar{\mathbf{d}}_i\bar{\mathbf{d}}_i^T\right)(\mathbf{I}_\ell \otimes \mathbf{P}(\omega))^T d\boldsymbol{\omega}\right]\right)^{(2\ell)} = \tag{27}$$

$$\left(\left(\int_{\boldsymbol{\Omega}}(\mathbf{I}_\ell \otimes \mathbf{P}(\omega)) \otimes (\mathbf{I}_\ell \otimes \mathbf{P}(\omega))d\boldsymbol{\omega}\right)\text{vec}\left[\sum_{i=1}^{n}\bar{\mathbf{d}}_i\bar{\mathbf{d}}_i^T\right]\right)^{(2\ell)}, \tag{28}$$

which finally leads to:

$$\boldsymbol{\Sigma} = \left((\mathbf{I}_\ell \otimes \mathbf{Y})\text{vec}\left[\sum_{i=1}^{n}\bar{\mathbf{d}}_{ij}\bar{\mathbf{d}}_{ij}^T\right]\right)^{(2\ell)}, \tag{29}$$

where the definite integral $\mathbf{Y} = \int_{\boldsymbol{\Omega}}\mathbf{P}(\omega) \otimes (\mathbf{I}_\ell \otimes \mathbf{P}(\omega))d\boldsymbol{\omega} \in \mathbb{R}^{4\ell \times 9\ell}$ can be computed off-line.

References

1. Carnegie mellon motion capture database. http://mocap.cs.cmu.edu
2. Bartoli, A., Pizarro, D., Loog, M.: Stratified generalized procrustes analysis. IJCV **101**(2), 227–253 (2013)
3. Brand, M.: Morphable 3D models from video. In: CVPR, vol. 2, pp. II-456. IEEE (2001)
4. Cootes, T.F., Edwards, G.J., Taylor, C.J., et al.: Active appearance models. PAMI **23**(6), 681–685 (2001)
5. De la Torre, F.: A least-squares framework for component analysis. PAMI **34**(6), 1041–1055 (2012)
6. Dryden, I.L., Mardia, K.V.: Statistical shape analysis, vol. 4. John Wiley & Sons New York (1998)
7. Frey, B.J., Jojic, N.: Transformation-invariant clustering using the em algorithm. PAMI **25**(1), 1–17 (2003)
8. Goodall, C.: Procrustes methods in the statistical analysis of shape. Journal of the Royal Statistical Society, Series B (Methodological), 285–339 (1991)
9. Gower, J.C., Dijksterhuis, G.B.: Procrustes problems, vol. 3. Oxford University Press, Oxford (2004)
10. Igual, L., Perez-Sala, X., Escalera, S., Angulo, C., De la Torre, F.: Continuous generalized procrustes analysis. PR **47**(2), 659–671 (2014)
11. Johnson, S., Everingham, M.: Clustered pose and nonlinear appearance models for human pose estimation. In: Proceedings of the British Machine Vision Conference (2010). doi:10.5244/C.24.12
12. Kokkinos, I., Yuille, A.: Unsupervised learning of object deformation models. In: ICCV, pp. 1–8. IEEE (2007)
13. Learned-Miller, E.G.: Data driven image models through continuous joint alignment. PAMI **28**(2), 236–250 (2006)
14. Marimont, D.H., Wandell, B.A.: Linear models of surface and illuminant spectra. JOSA A **9**(11), 1905–1913 (1992)

---

[4] See Appendix A for the vec-transpose operator.

15. Matthews, I., Xiao, J., Baker, S.: 2D vs. 3D deformable face models: Representational power, construction, and real-time fitting. IJCV **75**(1), 93–113 (2007)
16. Minka, T.P.: Old and new matrix algebra useful for statistics (2000). http://research.microsoft.com/en-us/um/people/minka/papers/matrix/
17. Naimark, M.A.: Linear representatives of the Lorentz group (translated from Russian). Macmillan, New York (1964)
18. Pearson, K.: On lines and planes of closest fit to systems of points in space. The London, Edinburgh, and Dublin Philosophical Magazine and Journal of Science **2**(11), 559–572 (1901)
19. Pizarro, D., Bartoli, A.: Global optimization for optimal generalized procrustes analysis. In: CVPR, pp. 2409–2415. IEEE (2011)
20. De la Torre, F., Black, M.J.: Robust parameterized component analysis: theory and applications to 2d facial appearance models. CVIU **91**(1), 53–71 (2003)
21. Torresani, L., Hertzmann, A., Bregler, C.: Nonrigid structure-from-motion: Estimating shape and motion with hierarchical pricrs. PAMI **30**(5), 878–892 (2008)
22. Xiao, J., Chai, J., Kanade, T.: A closed-form solution to non-rigid shape and motion recovery. IJCV **67**(2), 233–246 (2006)
23. Yezzi, A.J., Soatto, S.: Deformotion: Deforming motion, shape average and the joint registration and approximation of structures in images. IJCV **53**(2), 153–167 (2003)

Easy Minimax Estimation with Random Forests for Human Pose Estimation

P. Daphne Tsatsoulis[✉] and David Forsyth

Department of Computer Science, University of Illinois at Urbana-Champaign,
Champaign, USA
{tsatsou2,daf}@illinois.edu

Abstract. We describe a method for human parsing that is straight-forward and competes with state-of-the-art performance on standard datasets. Unlike the state-of-the-art, our method does not search for individual body parts or poselets. Instead, a regression forest is used to predict a body configuration in body-space. The output of this regression forest is then combined in a novel way. Instead of averaging the output of each tree in the forest we use minimax to calculate optimal weights for the trees. This optimal weighting improves performance on rare poses and improves the generalization of our method to different datasets. Our paper demonstrates the unique advantage of random forest representations: minimax estimation is straightforward with no significant retraining burden.

Keywords: Human pose estimation · Regression · Regression forests · Minimax

1 Introduction

In this paper, we address the problem of human pose estimation from a single RGB image. Pose estimation (or parsing) takes an image that is known to contain a person and reports locations of some body parts (typically head, torso, upper arms, lower arms, upper and lower legs). Parsing is a core vision problem with a long history. Despite much recent activity[1–6], it remains very difficult to produce fast, accurate parses.

All current parsers use local part models of some form to identify body layout. Unlike existing methods that require complex inference or search, we train a regression forest to predict multiple poses for a test image. This set of proposals, depicted in Figure 1, defines the problems of finding the best prediction for an example or of combining the predictions in an optimal way.

In our paper we apply a minimax optimization that improves our method's accuracy and generalizability. We explain how regression forests have a unique advantage over other methods since minimax estimation is easy to apply to their outputs without re-training. Our experiments show the sharp improvements made by the minimax optimization on rare poses and on different datasets.

© Springer International Publishing Switzerland 2015
L. Agapito et al. (Eds.): ECCV 2014 Workshops, Part I, LNCS 8925, pp. 669–684, 2015.
DOI: 10.1007/978-3-319-16178-5_47

Contributions: Our approach to pose estimation is simple and compares to state-of-the-art results. By applying the minimax optimization method to the output of regression forests we have presented a new approach to pose estimation that finds an optimal combination of pose predictions. This lets us significantly improve the accuracy and the generalization of our results on hard datasets.

Table 1. (top) By utilizing regression forests our system is able to make multiple predictions for a joint location in an image. Images in the top row are from the FLIC dataset and show the original predictions made by each tree in a 10-tree forest for right (magenta) and left (cyan) wrists. (bottom) The advantage to using regression forests is that their output is quickly and easily recombined to improve predictions. We present an optimization over the forests that predicts an alternative weighting for the trees. The uniformly-weighted prediction over the tree outputs have been marked in cyan and the optimally re-weighted predictions in magenta.

2   Background

For single images, it is usual to model body segments with rectangles. One then parses by solving an optimization problem to place these segments on the image.

Felzenszwalb and Huttenlocher showed how to produce highly efficient matchers for tree-structured models [7] (see also [8]). Most work since then assumes a tree-structured model (e.g. [6,9]). There have been efforts to build models beyond trees, e.g. loopy graphs [10–12], mixtures of trees [8,13], and fully connected graphs [3], and there is some evidence that the advantages due to such a model outweigh the disadvantages of approximate inference.

The key challenge of using full relational models is how to perform learning and inference efficiently. This has led to intense activity exploring pruning strategies [3,5,14–16]. All part-based parsers must manage a tradeoff: limb appearance models that are specialized to a particular image tend to yield better parses (for example, one can exploit the color of clothing), but obtaining such a specialized appearance model from a single image is hard to do. Various strategies have evolved, including re-estimation of the appearance model [9], strong priors on appearance [17], and using small, generic models [1].

One alternative is to look at the body on a longer spatial scale. Bourdev et al. [18] suggest that one should directly detect *poselets* — stylized structures on the body — then infer body configuration (respectively segmentation of the body [19]; body attributes [20]) from those poselets. One could produce a parse by directly decoding poselet response vectors [21], or by insisting on consistency between body segment detectors, local poselets, and long-scale poselets [2]. Another alternative is to look at small parts on a shorter spatial scale. This allows for the foreshortening of body segments, for example. Yang et al. show high accuracy parses derived from small parts [1]. There is some evidence that each method benefits from slightly different image information, so that a fused method could offer improved accuracy. Jammalamadaka et al. demonstrate that image based estimators can tell reliably whether a parser has succeeded or not [22].

Shotton et al. use regression forests in [23]. They construct 3 trees in order to predict pose from RGB-D data. In [24] regression trees were used as part of a tree-structured model to represent the unary potential. In neither of these cases was the output of a forest optimized to improve the generalization of the method as we have done. How well a method generalizes is a very important aspect of evaluation, as shown by the discussion in [25].

While image parsing itself is viewed as an important problem, there has been work demonstrating its applications. Ramanan et al. demonstrate a recipe for turning a parser into a tracker [26]. Ferrari et al. demonstrate search for human figures in video using pose as a search term [27]. Jammalamadaka et al. demonstrate improvements on this recipe, showing a variety of ways to query including a Kinect parse [22]. The parsing community has shown little interest in recovering 3D representations, though 3D estimates are known to be available from joint positions [28,29]. Ikizler and Forsyth show an application of such 3D representations in activity recognition [30]. When depth data is available, parsing is largely solved [23].

3 Method

We approach parsing with a unique construct. Our method has three steps. First, we register all images into a normalized coordinate system and extract image features. Second, we run a regression forest over the features to produce multiple joint-location predictions. Third, we propose a new way to combine the predictions that optimizes performance and generalizability.

3.1 Body-Space

The datasets we use provide an annotation of joint locations with each image. We consider the right and left shoulder, elbow, wrist, and hip joints in our method.

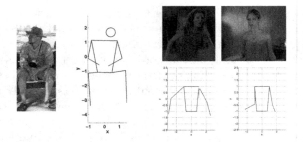

Fig. 1. (left) Example of joints projected into body-space. The torso is projected onto the xy-plane and aligned so that the shoulders are parallel to the x-axis. One unit in the x-dimension is equal to the distance between the neck and shoulders of the person. One unit in the y-dimension is equal to the distance between the shoulders and hips. (right) These two images have the right wrists in the same locations in the image, but in very different locations with respect to the body.

We want to be able to predict human pose in body-space rather than in an image. Body space is a normalized coordinate system that is centered at the torso and that is scale- and viewpoint-invarient.

We want to be able to predict pose in body-space because it is more interesting and informative to know what someone is doing relative to their body instead of at a specific pixel. With the number of monitoring/surveillance applications that want to know how people are interacting with scenes and with each other, it is more important to know where people's limbs are relative to objects (and themselves) than where in a picture their hands are located. Being able to do this in 3-dimensions is even more important but many current hardware systems only provide 2-dimensional images. By predicting joints in body-space we can construct a method gives real body poses in 2- or 3-dimensions.

We register the original joint locations (given as pixel coordinates) so that the origin lies at the center of the torso. One unit in the body-space's x-axis corresponds to the distance between the neck and a shoulder and one unit on the body-space's y-axis corresponds to the distance between the neck and center of the torso. An example of the effects of this projection can be seen in Figure 1. Images are registered by computing the rotation translation, and scale needed to project shoulders and hips in pixel-coordinates to a target torso in body-space.

When preprocessing 3-d annotated datasets, such as the H3D dataset, joints were projected into a 3-dimensional body-space by rotation, scale, and translation. In this space, the z-axis corresponds to the dimension going in front of and behind the body. Examples of these projections can be seen in Figure 6.

3.2   Regression Forests

Previous work in pose estimation has run inference over a tree-structured model or searched images for local patches. Our method does neither of these. It instead builds a regression forest to predict joint locations for an example image.

Unlike template-based methods that have to learn a unique representation for every joint configuration a tree can build-in unique visual representations automatically. For example, a hand can be turned in many different directions whilst being in the same location. Discriminative methods need to learn a template for each orientation of the hand in order to make a prediction. Since trees can have multiple leaves with the same output value they are able to capture the fact that visually different examples can map to the same output with no additional effort.

Regression forests are an ensemble of trees. Each of t trees is constructed using a random sampling, with replacement, of the training data. Trees split the training data on a feature dimension f_i until a leaf contains a minimum number of elements and is not split again. At each split, a subset of $\sqrt{d}$ features (where d is the dimensionality of the feature vector) is considered.

Let $\mathbf{y}_i \in \mathbb{R}^d$ be the vector representing the joint being predicted for example i. Note that $\mathbf{y}_i$ can take on any dimensionality so it can represent a 2- or 3-joint location or it can represent a number of joints such as the right wrist and elbow. Let $\mathbf{y}_{i,t}$ be the prediction for example i made by tree t. Our method makes a final prediction, $\mathbf{y}_i^*$ by calculating the summed weight of all tree predictions:

$$\mathbf{y}_i^* = \sum_{t=1}^{T} \frac{1}{w_t} \mathbf{y}_{i,t} \tag{1}$$

w_t is the weight of each tree. Initially we weight the trees uniformly, as is typically done in regression forests.

The regression forest predicts poses in body-space, we project (using rotation, translation, and scale) the images back into pixel-space for comparison. We do this by projecting our body-space torso onto a predicted torso in pixel-space. For each dataset we used torso predictions that were provided by the authors, please see the Experiments and Results section for more detail.

3.3 Minimax

There is good evidence that in most vision tasks training and test sets are not sampled from the same distribution [25]. This is a particular nuisance in human parsing, where performance falls off when a method is trained on one dataset and tested on another (eg [3]). One standard method for obtaining a well-behaved estimator in a situation like this is minimax. The recipe is as follows: Assume we have a model of the family of possible test distributions, parametrized by a parameter vector $\mathbf{l}$. Assume we have a parametric family of estimators, parametrized by a vector $\mathbf{w}$. We cannot know the true value of $\mathbf{l}$, because we do not know the true test distribution. However, we can assume that the true test distribution is "not too far" from the training distribution. We can then search the collection of distributions that are "not too far" and the estimator parameters for a pair $(\mathbf{l}, \mathbf{w})$ such that the error on the worst test distribution is best. One can visualize this as a problem with two players: the

Table 2. These are example images of the FLIC training set. Images on the left are images that were up-weighted during an iteration of minimax when optimizing for the right wrist (right-most wrist in the image). These are images that were difficult to solve, and therefore given more weight in the re-weighting. The set of images on the right are those that the optimization function found easy and down-weighted.

first chooses a test distribution l to make the performance as poor as possible, and the second then chooses a **w** to produce as good as possible performance on the worst test distribution. Write $\mathcal{E}_l$ for an expectation with respect to l. The search becomes $\min_{\mathbf{w}} (\max_l (\mathcal{E}_l [\text{Loss}(\mathbf{w})]))$ subject to an appropriate notion of "not too far" on the test distribution. This approach has not been used in detection or parsing to our knowledge. Although building a representation of a family of test distributions is straightforward (one reweights the training samples to get a different empirical training distribution), estimating **w** is hard because it creates a massive re-training burden. At each stage of the search, we would need to retrain the estimator to get the best loss on the current worst distribution. For most representations, this burden is unmanageable.

A unique feature of regression forests, not to our knowledge previously remarked, is that they make minimax estimation easy. Assume that the test distribution is "not too far" from the training distribution. Then the structure of the trees in the forest (which variables are split, etc.) is unlikely to be affected by the difference, because it is strongly random. We can then define a reasonable parametric family of estimators by simply reweighting the trees in the forest, so **w** is a non-negative weight vector. The appropriate notion of "not too far" is to bound above the k-l divergence of l from the uniform distribution; alternatively, one could bound the entropy of l below. Each generates unpleasant non-linear constraints. We relax these constraints by requiring $\frac{1}{kN} \leq l_i \leq \frac{k}{N}$ and $\sum_i l_i = 1$ for each component l_i of l and a parameter k. This prevents any example being over or under weighted. We define the loss of a particular weighting of a forest to be the squared error, so the objective function becomes $\min_{\mathbf{w}} \left(\max_{\mathbf{l}} \left(\sum_i l_i \left[(\mathbf{y}_i - \sum_j w_j T_j(\mathbf{x}))^2 \right] \right) \right)$ where $w_j \geq 0$. No retraining of trees is required, and the resulting optimization problem is straightforward to deal with (below). In practice, we show that minimax tends to weight up difficult examples and to weight down common ones (the dataset player is trying to make it difficult to predict good solutions; Figure 2). Minimax is known to be severely pessimistic for some problems; in this case, it offers real improvements in performance. We believe this is the result of constraining l. The constraints on l allow minimax to emphasize hard examples, but prevent it from putting all weight on the single most difficult example. As a result, the estimator is more willing to make risky predictions. This improves performance for lower arms, which move around a lot and where the distribution of configurations is poorly represented in training data.

Optimization Problem: Let $\mathbf{w} \in \mathbb{R}^t$ be the weighting over the t trees, $\mathbf{l} \in \mathbb{R}^n$ be the weighting over n training examples, $\mathbf{y} \in \mathbb{R}^{n \times d}$ be the correct location, and $\mathbf{M} \in \mathbb{R}^{t \times n \times d}$ be the predicted location made by each tree for every example.

$$\mathbf{w}^* = \underset{\mathbf{w}}{\operatorname{argmin}} \ \max_{\mathbf{l}} \sum_{i=1}^{n} l_i ||\mathbf{y}_i - \mathbf{w}^T \mathbf{M}_i||_2^2 \tag{2}$$

$$\text{s. t.} \ \sum_{i=1}^{n} l_i = 1 \tag{3}$$

$$\frac{1}{kn} \leq l_i \leq \frac{k}{n} \quad k \in \mathbb{R} \tag{4}$$

$$\mathbf{w} > 0$$

Where $\mathbf{M}_i \in \mathbb{R}^{t \times d}$ is the t tree predictions made for example i, $\mathbf{y}_i \in \mathbb{R}^{1 \times d}$ is the correct location for example i, and $l_i \in \mathbb{R}$ is the weight given to example i.

Solving the Optimization: Equation 2 is tractable in $\mathbf{w}$ and it is tractable in l. To solve the optimization we iteratively solved for each variable separately. We began by fixing l and $\mathbf{w}$ to be uniform weights and solved for an optimal $\mathbf{l}^*$. We then set $\mathbf{l} = \mathbf{l}^*$ and solved for $\mathbf{w}^*$. We iterate until $\mathbf{w}^*$ converges or until a maximum number of iterations has been reached.

This new weighting $\mathbf{w}^*$ is then applied in Equation 1.

4 Experiments and Results

Datasets. We evaluate our method on three datasets: Buffy Stickmen V3.01 [4], FLIC dataset (the smaller version of the dataset with approximately 5000 images) [31], and PASCAL Stickmen V1.11 [4]. The Buffy Stickmen and FLIC datasets were split into train and test sets as specified by the datasets and the PASCAL Stickmen was used in its entirety as a test set. For the PASCAL dataset we trained on the FLIC dataset. For all datasets, we evaluated our method on cropped images that contained a person.

Image Features. As image features we extract globalPb features [32] from the cropped images. We resized images uniformly and extracted the 8 per-pixel gPb features. We used all features when running our regressions. These features capture the overall contour of the individual in the image. This provides the global structure of a person's layout.

Joints Predicted. We built a separate forest for each of the four joints (right/left elbow and wrist). To grow these trees we regressed image features against joint positions that were projected into body-space. For evaluation, we project our predictions back into pixels for fair comparison. In order to do this we rotate, translate, and scale the body-space torso onto a predicted torso in pixels. For the FLIC dataset we use the torsos predicted by [31] for BUFFY and PASCAL we used the torsos provided with the datasets that were provided by [33].

4.1   Evaluation Metrics

We report our results in two formats. The first is the PCP evaluation metric used to evaluate the Buffy and Pascal Stickmen datasets. In this metric a prediction is correct if the average error (between ground truth and prediction) of the two endpoints of a body part is below a threshold. The second metric we use is a radial precision curve (Figure 3) as used in [31]. The radial precision curve is calculated based upon a predicted point's euclidean distance from the ground truth point. The prediction is normalized by the distance between the left hip and the right shoulder so that that distance is 100 pixels.

$$acc_i(r) = \frac{100}{n} \sum_{i=1}^{n} 1 \left(\frac{\|\mathbf{y}_i^* - \mathbf{y}_i\|_2}{(\text{torsoheight}_i)/100} \geq r \right)$$

n is the number of examples, $\mathbf{y}_i^*$ is the prediction for the joint of example i, and $\mathbf{y}_i$ is the ground truth location of the joint.

Evaluation is done after images have been projected into the pixel-coordinate system. We take our body-space predictions and project the torso into the image by using the shoulders and hips of a predicted pixel torso as a target.

4.2   Regression Forests: Average Prediction

For each training dataset we built four forests of 100 trees that were constrained to stop growing once a leaf had a minimum of 10 elements. Since a regression tree can have output of any dimension, we experimented with regressing to predict joints separately and jointly. In Figure 2 we compare performance on the FLIC dataset's elbows and wrist when we predict the four joints separately or the arms

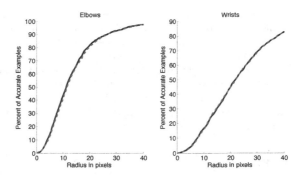

Fig. 2. The output of regression trees can be multidimensional. In this experiment we tested the performance of the regression forests when predicting each of the four joints (right/left elbows and wrists) separately (black curve) and when predicting the joints of each arm (wrist and elbow) jointly (red curve). Performance is not hurt by considering the full arm jointly, the advantage to predicting full arms is that you are insuring a real arm pose. The results shown here are the average prediction of the FLIC regression forest on the FLIC test dataset.

(one forest for the right elbow and wrist, one forest for the left elbow and wrist) as a whole.

We evaluate our method on three standard datasets. We present results for each dataset in the metrics used by other authors for those datasets. We present three different types of results for the datasets. First, we show the performance of the dataset when the test set is evaluated by forests grown by the same dataset, see Figure 3 and Table 4. Second, we show the performance of the dataset when the test set is evaluated by forests grown by another dataset, see Figure 3. Third, we show the results of regressing the images against 3-dimensional skeletons to predict a 3-dimensional results, see Figure 6. Since the PASCAL dataset does not have a training set it was evaluated using the regression forests learned from the FLIC dataset.

In order to regress images against 3-dimensional skeletons we trained the forests on the H3D dataset. We projected the 3-dimensional annotations of the H3D dataset into body-space by rotation, translation and scale. We then built regression forests in the same way as before but with each leaf output being a 3-dimensional joint location prediction. Examples of these predictions for the FLIC dataset can be seen in Figure 6.

The simple average of regression tree outputs produces results that are competitive with state-of-the-art results on elbows and comparable to state-of-the-art results on wrists. This is encouraging because state-of-the-art methods require complex inference or search. Our method provides the added benefit of being able to produce multiple predictions for the same data allowing us to recombine predictions in useful ways.

Table 3. Radial precision plots of elbow and wrist joint predictions. Radius (r) is reported for a normalized torso diagonal of 100 pixels. For all datasets we report our regression's prediction in black when projected onto a predicted torso. In 70 PASCAL images and 6 BUFFY images no torso was predicted, the result of the method when those rejected images are excluded from the test set are in red. In order to see how the method performs when the torso is known, we have projected our results onto the ground truth torso and reported results in blue. This image is best viewed in color. All test sets were evaluated on trees trained on the FLIC dataset, BUFFY was also evaluated on trees trained on the BUFFY dataset.

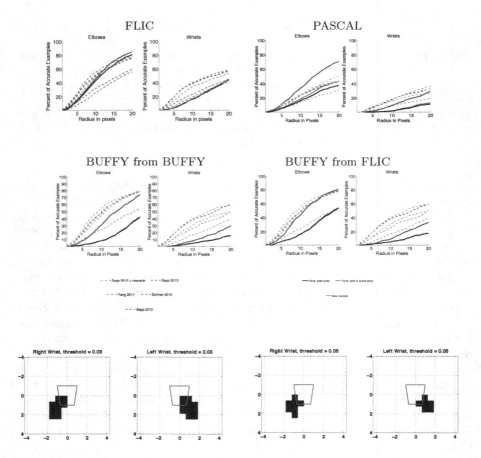

Fig. 3. This is a visualization of 'rare' and 'common' positions for wrists in the FLIC dataset relative to a torso in red. In black are marked locations that have more than 0.03 (left) and 0.05 (right) of the total data in them, these are considered common. For the right wrist, 65% of the data is common by a 0.05 threshold. For the left wrist, 62% of the data is common by a 0.05 threshold.

Table 4. PCP is the common evaluation metric for the Buffy Stickmen dataset, we report results with the standard threshold of 0.5. We report the performance of the BUFFY test set when evaluated on forests built using BUFFY data. These results were all projected onto predicted torsos in pixels for evaluation. In 6 BUFFY images no torso was predicted, the result of the method when those rejected images are excluded are labeled 'found predicted torso'. In order to see how the method performs when the torso is known, we have projected our results onto the ground truth torso and reported results as well.

Method	Torso	U. Arm	L. Arm
Andr. [6]	90.7	79.3	41.2
Eich. [4]	98.7	82.8	59.8
Sapp [34]	100	91.1	65.7
Sapp [5]	100	95.3	63.0
Yang [35]	98.8	97.8	68.6
Ours from BUFFY, predicted torso		80.6	18.5
Ours, found predicted torso		82.4	18.9
Ours, ground truth torso		96.1	45.3

Table 5. We report the performance of the BUFFY test set when evaluated on forests built using BUFFY or FLIC data. To report the performance of the test data when evaluated on FLIC forests with and without minimax optimization. We believe that the method performed better when trained on FLIC than when trained on BUFFY because of the size of the datasets. It is clear that applying the minimax optimization helps the performance of the wrists significantly.

Method	U. Arm	L. Arm
Trained on BUFFY, found predicted torso	82.4	18.9
Trained on FLIC, found predicted torso	79.7	26.0
Trained on FLIC with minimax, found predicted torso	79.7	34.1

4.3   Regression Forests: Minimax Optimization Predictions

Training: We trained our minimax optimization method on the FLIC dataset. We used a 100-tree forest for each wrist and applied the mimimax optimization to each wrist separately. We constrained the weighting of the training examples by $k = 10$ and number of maximum iterations of the optimization to 100. We then applied the learned weighting to the predictions made by the 100 trees (learned on FLIC) on the FLIC dataset and on the BUFFY and PASCAL datasets.

Figure 7 shows examples of the output of both the uniformly-weighted regression forests and the minimax-weighted regression forests. The minimax-weighting pulls original predictions to be longer or to change the direction of the limb.

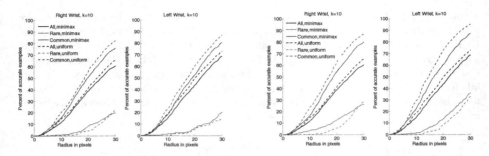

Fig. 4. For this experiment we separated the FLIC dataset into common and rare body-space locations (see Figure 3). Locations that were common by a threshold of 0.03 are evaluated on the left and results that were common by a threshold of 0.05 were evaluated on the right. The black curve represents the full FLIC test-set, the red curve represents rare pose locations, and the blue curve represents common pose locations. The dotted line is the result of uniformly weighting the tree outputs and the solid line is the result of using the minimax weights to predict a final output. Results were then projected onto predicted torsos for comparison. As expected, the minimax method improves performance on rare (and therefore often more difficult for this method) poses and loses accuracy on the common examples. The trade-off between the accuracies is made clear in the rare and common curves.

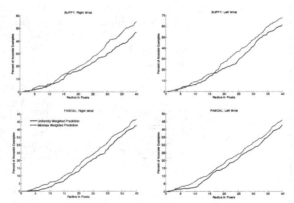

Fig. 5. The results of evaluating the BUFFY (top row) and PASCAL (bottom row) on the forests trained on FLIC. The black line is the average over the trees for the right and left wrists. The blue line is the result of the minimax re-weighting. The results were projected onto predicted torsos in pixel-space for evaluation (images in which no torso was found have been excluded from this evaluation). The minimax re-weighting has made our process more robust on datasets not trained on.

Performance on Same Dataset: For this experiment we define two types of pose, common and rare. In order to define these we gridded the space around the torso into bins as shown in Figure 3. We then classified a bin as common if more than a certain percentage of the data fell into this bin. As can be seen in Figure 4

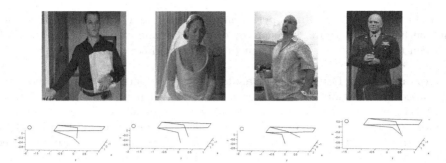

Fig. 6. Regression forests can predict multi-dimensional output. For this reason, when trained on the H3D dataset (that has 3-dimensional annotations) producing 3-dimensional output is easy. These are examples of the results obtained for the FLIC dataset when evaluated on the regression forests built by the H3D dataset. Skeletons are shown facing down and the x (across body), y (down body), and z (in-front of body) axes are marked.

Fig. 7. Examples of original uniformly-weighted predictions in cyan and the minimax-reweighted predictions in magenta. The minimax often produces results that are similar to the original prediction but that shift it in length or direction in attempt to correct the original prediction.

the minimax method improves performance on rare (and often more difficult for this method) poses and loses accuracy on the common examples. The trade-off between the accuracies is made clear in the rare and common curves.

Performance on Different Datasets: In this experiment we test how the mimimax optimization can improve performance when training on one dataset and testing on another. We trained two regression forests on the FLIC dataset, one for each wrist. We then evaluated the BUFFY and FLIC datasets using these forests and plotted their accuracies in Figure 5 when projected onto predicted torsos. When we used the weights calculated by the minimax optimization the accuracies improved on both wrists and on both datasets. The improvement can also be seen in Table 5. Using the minimax method has made our method more generalizable when evaluating on a different dataset than that which we trained on.

5   Conclusions

We present a radically different approach to the problem of human pose estimation from a single image. We have achieved accuracies comparable to state-of-the-art methods with a system that uses no inference or search techniques. Unlike current methods we use regression forests that provide multiple predictions for every example image. We have taken advantage of these many proposals by using the minimax optimization that quickly and easily improves the generalization of our method. We further utilize the regression forests to make predictions in 3-dimensions with no additional efforts.

We have presented the parsing problem in a new way. By producing multiple outputs we can now apply re-weighting techniques (such as minimax) or consider the problem of selecting the best of all proposals.

The method can be easily extended to lower body predictions. Because we do not search for localized parts we expect our method could be robust to occlusions, baggy clothing and motion blur.

References

1. Yang, Y., Ramanan, D.: Articulated pose estimation using flexible mixtures of parts. In: CVPR (2011)
2. Wang, Y., Tran, D., Liao, Z.: Learning hierarchical poselets for human parsing. In: CVPR (2011)
3. Tran, D., Forsyth, D.: Improved human parsing with a full relational model. In: Daniilidis, K., Maragos, P., Paragios, N. (eds.) ECCV 2010, Part IV. LNCS, vol. 6314, pp. 227–240. Springer, Heidelberg (2010)
4. Eichner, M., Ferrari, V.: Better appearance models for pictorial structures. In: IICCV (2009)
5. Sapp, B., Toshev, A., Taskar, B.: Cascaded models for articulated pose estimation. In: Daniilidis, K., Maragos, P., Paragios, N. (eds.) ECCV 2010, Part II. LNCS, vol. 6312, pp. 406–420. Springer, Heidelberg (2010)

6. Andriluka, M., Roth, S., Schiele, B.: Pictorial structures revisited: People detection and articulated pose estimation. In: CVPR (2009)
7. Felzenszwalb, P.F., Huttenlocher, D.P.: Pictorial structures for object recognition. IJCV **61**(1), 55–79 (2005)
8. Ioffe, S., Forsyth, D.: Human tracking with mixtures of trees. In: ICCV, pp. 690–695 (2001)
9. Ramanan, D.: Learning to parse images of articulated bodies. In: ANIPS, vol. 19, pp. 1129–1136 (2006)
10. Jiang, H., Martin, D.R.: Globel pose estimation using non-tree models. In: CVPR (2008)
11. Ren, X., Berg, A., Malik, J.: Recovering human body configurations using pairwise constraints between parts. In: IICCV, vol. 1, pp. 824–831 (2005)
12. Tian, T.P., Sclaroff, S.: Fast globally optimal 2D human detection with loopy graph models. In: CVPR (2010)
13. Wang, Y., Mori, G.: Multiple tree models for occlusion and spatial constraints in human pose estimation. In: Forsyth, D., Torr, P., Zisserman, A. (eds.) ECCV 2008, Part III. LNCS, vol. 5304, pp. 710–724. Springer, Heidelberg (2008)
14. Mori, G., Ren, X., Efros, A., Malik, J.: Recovering human body configuration: Combining segmentation and recognition. In: CVPR, vol. 2, pp. 326–333 (2004)
15. Ferrari, V., Marín-Jiménez, M., Zisserman, A.: Progressive search space reduction for human pose estimation. In: CVPR (2008)
16. Felzenszwalb, P.F., Girshick, R.B., McAllester, D.: Cascade object detection with deformable part models. In: CVPR (2010)
17. Eichner, M., Ferrari, V.: Better appearance models for pictorial structures. In: BMVC (2009)
18. Bourdev, L., Malik, J.: Poselets: Body part detectors training using 3D human pose annotations. In: IICCV (2009)
19. Brox, T., Bourdev, L., Maji, S., Malik, J.: Object segmentation by alignment of poselet activations to image contours. In: CVPR (2011)
20. Bourdev, L., Maji, S., Malik, J.: Describing people: Poselet-based attribute classification. In: ICCV (2011)
21. Gkioxari, G., Arbelaez, P., Bourdev, L.D., Malik, J.: Articulated pose estimation using discriminative armlet classifiers. In: CVPR, pp. 3342–3349 (2013)
22. Jammalamadaka, N., Zisserman, A., Eichner, M., Ferrari, V., Jawahar, C.V.: Video retrieval by mimicking poses. In: ACM ICMR (2012)
23. Shotton, J., Fitzgibbon, A., Cook, M., Sharp, T., Finocchio, M., Moore, R., Kipman, A., Blake, A.: Real-time human pose recognition in parts from single depth images. In: CVPR (2011)
24. Dantone, M., Gall, J., Leistner, C., van Gool, L.: Human pose estimation from still images using body parts dependent joint regressors. In: IEEE Conference on Computer Vision and Pattern Recognition (CVPR). IEEE (2013) (to appear)
25. Torralba, A., Efros, A.A.: Unbiased look at dataset bias. In: CVPR 2011 (June 2011)
26. Ramanan, D., Forsyth, D.: Finding and tracking people from the bottom up. In: Proc. CVPR (2003)
27. Ferrari, V., Marin, M., Zisserman, A.: Pose search: retrieving people using their pose. In: CVPR (2009)
28. Taylor, C.: Reconstruction of articulated objects from point correspondences in a single uncalibrated image. In: CVPR, pp. 677–684 (2000)
29. Kakadiaris, I., Metaxas, D.: Model-based estimation of 3D human motion with occlusion based on active multi-viewpoint selection. In: CVPR, pp. 81–87 (1996)

30. Ikizler, N., Forsyth, D.: Searching video for complex activities with finite state models. In: CVPR (2007)
31. Sapp, B., Taskar, B.: Modec: Multimodal decomposable models for human pose estimation. In: Proc. CVPR (2013)
32. Arbelaez, P., Maire, M., Fowlkes, C., Malik, J.: Contour detection and hierarchical image segmentation. IEEE Trans. Pattern Anal. Mach. Intell. **33**(5), 898–916 (2011)
33. Eichner, M., Marin-Jimenez, M., Zisserman, A., Ferrari, V.: 2D articulated human pose estimation and retrieval in (almost) unconstrained still images. In: ETH Zurich, D-ITET, BIWI, Technical Report No.272 (2010)
34. Sapp, B., Jordan, C., Taskar, B.: Adaptive pose priors for pictorial structures. In: CVPR (2010)
35. Yang, Y., Ramanan, D.: Articulated pose estimation using flexible mixtures of parts. In: IEEE PAMI (to appear)

Learning to Segment Humans
by Stacking Their Body Parts

E. Puertas[1,2]([envelope]), M.A. Bautista[1,2], D. Sanchez[1,2],
S. Escalera[1,2], and O. Pujol[1,2]

[1] Departament Matemàtica Aplicada i Anàlisi, Universitat de Barcelona,
Gran Via 585, 08007 Barcelona, Spain
[2] Computer Vision Center, Campus UAB, Edifici O, 08193 Bellaterra, Spain
{eloi,mabautista,oriol}@maia.ub.es

Abstract. Human segmentation in still images is a complex task due to the wide range of body poses and drastic changes in environmental conditions. Usually, human body segmentation is treated in a two-stage fashion. First, a human body part detection step is performed, and then, human part detections are used as prior knowledge to be optimized by segmentation strategies. In this paper, we present a two-stage scheme based on Multi-Scale Stacked Sequential Learning (MSSL). We define an extended feature set by stacking a multi-scale decomposition of body part likelihood maps. These likelihood maps are obtained in a first stage by means of a ECOC ensemble of soft body part detectors. In a second stage, contextual relations of part predictions are learnt by a binary classifier, obtaining an accurate body confidence map. The obtained confidence map is fed to a graph cut optimization procedure to obtain the final segmentation. Results show improved segmentation when MSSL is included in the human segmentation pipeline.

Keywords: Human body segmentation · Stacked Sequential Learning

1 Introduction

Human segmentation in RGB images is a challenging task due to the high variability of the human body, which includes a wide range of human poses, lighting conditions, cluttering, clothes, appearance, background, point of view, number of human body limbs, etc. In this particular problem, the goal is to provide a complete segmentation of the person/people appearing in an image. In literature, human body segmentation is usually treated in a two-stage fashion. First, a human body part detection step is performed, obtaining a large set of candidate body parts. These parts are used as prior knowledge by segmentation/inference optimization algorithms in order to obtain the final human body segmentation.

In the first stage, that is the detection of body parts, weak classifiers are trained in order to obtain a soft prior of body parts (which are often noisy and unreliable). Most works in literature have used edge detectors, convolutions with filters, linear SVM classifiers, Adaboost or Cascading classifiers [27].

© Springer International Publishing Switzerland 2015
L. Agapito et al. (Eds.): ECCV 2014 Workshops, Part I, LNCS 8925, pp. 685–697, 2015.
DOI: 10.1007/978-3-319-16178-5_48

For example, [18] used a tubular edge template as a detector, and convolved it with an image defining locally maximal responses above a threshold as detections. In [17], the authors used quadratic logistic regression on RGB features as the part detectors. Other works, have applied more robust part detectors such as SVM classifiers [4,14] or AdaBoost [15] trained on HOG features [6]. More recently, Dantone et. al used Random Forest as classifiers to learn body parts [7]. Although recently robust classifiers have been used, part detectors still involve false-positive and false-negatives problems given the similarity nature among body parts and the presence of background artifacts. Therefore, a second stage is usually required in order to provide an accurate segmentation.

In the second stage, soft part detections are jointly optimized taking into account the nature of the human body. However, standard segmentation techniques (*i.e.*region-growing, thresholding, edge detection, etc.) are not applicable in this context due to the huge variability of environmental factors (i.e lightning, clothing, cluttering, etc.) and the changing nature of body textures. In this sense, the most known models for the optimization/inference of soft part priors are Poselets [3,15] of Bourdev et. al. and Pictorial Structures [1,11,22] by Felzenszwalb et. al., both of which optimize the initial soft body part priors to obtain a more accurate estimation of the human pose, and provide with a multi-limb detection. In addition, there are some works in literature that tackle the problem of human body segmentation (segmenting the full body as one class) obtaining satisfying results. For instance, Vinet et al. [24] proposed to use Conditional Random Fields (CRF) based on body part detectors to obtain a complete person/background segmentation. Belief propagation, branch and bound or Graph Cut optimization are common approaches used to perform inference of the graphical models defined by human body [13,14,19]. Finally, methods like structured SVM or mixture of parts [28,29] can be use in order to take profit of the contextual relations of body parts.

In this paper, we present a novel two-stage human body segmentation method based on the discriminative Multi-Scale Stacked Sequential Learning (MSSL) framework [12]. Until now stacked sequential learning has been used in several domains, mainly in text sequences and time series [5,8] showing important computational and performance improvements when compared with other contextual inference methods such as CRF. Recently, the MSSL framework has been also successfully used on pixel wise classification problems [16]. To the best of our knowledge this is the first work that uses MSSL in order to find a context-aware feature set that encodes high order relations between body parts, which suffer non-rigid transformations, to obtain a robust human body segmentation. Fig. 1 shows the proposed human body segmentation approach. In the first stage of our method for human segmentation, a multi-class Error-Correcting Output Codes classifier (ECOC) is trained to detect body parts and to produce a soft likelihood map for each body part. In the second stage, a multi-scale decomposition of these maps and a neighborhood sampling is performed, resulting in a new set of features. The extended set of features encodes spatial, contextual and relational information among body parts. This extended set is then fed to the second classifier of MSSL, in this case a Random Forest binary classifier, which maps a multi-limb classification to a binary human classification problem. Finally, in order to obtain the resulting binary human segmentation, a post-processing step is performed by means of Graph Cuts optimization, which is applied to the output of the binary classifier.

The rest of the paper is organized as follows: Section 2 introduces the proposed method. Section 3 presents the experimental results. Finally, Section 4 concludes the paper.

2   Method

The proposed method for human body segmentation is based on the Multi-Scale Stacked Sequential Learning (MSSL)[12] pipeline. Generalized Stacked Sequential Learning was proposed as a method for solving the main problems of sequential learning, namely: (a) how to capture and exploit sequential correlations; (b) how to represent and incorporate complex loss functions in contextual learning; (c) how to identify long-distance interactions; and (d) how to make sequential learning computationally efficient. Fig. 1 (a) shows the abstract blocks of the process[1]. Consider a training set consisting of data pairs $\{(x_i, y_i)\}$, where $x_i \in \mathcal{R}^n$ is a feature vector and $y_i \in \mathcal{Y}$, $\mathcal{Y} = \{1, \ldots, K\}$ is the class label. The first block of MSSL consists of a classifier $H_1(x)$ trained with the input data set. Its output results are a set of predicted labels or confidence values Y'. The next block in the pipeline, defines the policy for taking into account the context and long range interactions. It is composed of two steps: first, a multi-resolution decomposition models the relationship among neighboring locations, and second, a neighborhood sampling proportional to the resolution scale defines the support lattice. This last step allows to model the interaction range. This block is represented by the function $z = J(x, \rho, \theta) : \mathcal{R} \rightarrow \mathcal{R}^w$, parameterized by the interaction range θ in a neighborhood ρ. The last step of the algorithm creates an extended data set by adding to the original data the new set of features resulting from the sampling of the multi resolution confidence maps which is the input of a second classifier $H_2(x)$.

2.1   Stage One: Body Parts Soft Detection

In this work, the first stage detector $H_1(x)$ in the MSSL pipeline is based on the soft body parts detectors defined in [21]. The work of Bautista *et al.* [21] is based on an ECOC ensemble of cascades of Adaboost classifiers. Each of the cascades focuses on a subset of body parts described using Haar-like features where regions have been previously rotated towards main orientation to make the recognition rotation invariant. Although any other part detector technique could be used in the first stage of our process, we also choose the same methodology. ECOC has

---

[1] The original formulation of MSSL also includes the input vector X as an additional feature in the extended set X'.

shown to be a powerful and general framework that allows the inclusion of any base classifier, involving error-correction capabilities and allowing to reduce the bias and variance errors of the ensemble [8,10]. As a case study, although any classifier can be included in the ECOC framework, here we considerer as base learner also the same ensemble of cascades given its fast computization.

Because of its properties, cascades of classifiers are usually trained to split one visual object from the rest of possible objects of an image. This means that the cascade of classifiers learns to detect a certain object (body part in our case), ignoring all other objects (all other body parts). However, some body parts have similar appearance, $i.e.$legs and arms, and thus, it makes sense to group them in the same visual category. Because of this, we learn a set of cascades of classifiers where a subset of limbs are included in the positive set of one cascade, and the remaining limbs are included as negative instances together with background images in the negative set of the cascade. In this sense, classifier H_1 is learned by grouping different cascades of classifiers in a tree-structure way and combining them in an Error-Correcting Output Codes (ECOC) framework [10]. Then, H_1 outputs correspond to a multi-limb classification prediction.

An example of the body part tree-structure defined taking into account the nature of human body parts is shown in Fig. 2(a). Notice that classes with similar visual appearance ($e.g.$upper-arm and lower-arm) are grouped in the same meta-class in most dichotomies. In addition, dichotomies that deal with difficult problems ($e.g.d^5$) are focused only in the difficult classes, without taking into account all other body parts. In this case, class c^7 denotes the background.

In the ECOC framework, given a set of K classes (body parts) to be learnt, m different bi-partitions (groups of classes or dichotomies) are formed, and n binary problems over the partitions are trained [2]. As a result, a codeword of length n is obtained for each class, where each position (bit) of the code corresponds to a response of a given classifier d (coded by $+1$ or -1 according to their class set membership, or 0 if a particular class is not considered for a given classifier). Arranging the codewords as rows of a matrix, we define a $coding\ matrix\ M$, where $M \in \{-1, 0, +1\}^{K \times n}$. During the $decoding$ (or testing) process, applying the n binary classifiers, a code c is obtained for each data sample x in the test set. This code is compared to the base codewords $(y^i, i \in \{1,..,K\}^2)$ of each class defined in the matrix M, and the data sample is assigned to the class with the $closest$ codeword [10].

We use the problem dependent coding matrix defined in [21] in order to allow the inclusion of cascade of classifiers and learn the body parts. In particular, each dichotomy is obtained from the body part tree-structure. Fig. 2(b) shows the coding matrix codification of the tree-structure in Fig. 2(a).

In the ECOC $decoding$ step an image is processed using a sliding windowing approach. Each image patch x, is described and tested. In our case, each patch is first rotated by main gradient orientation and tested using the ECOC ensemble

---

[2] Observe that we are overloading the notation of y so that y^i corresponds to the codeword of the matrix associated with class i, $i.e.$it is the i-th row of the matrix, $M(i,:)$.

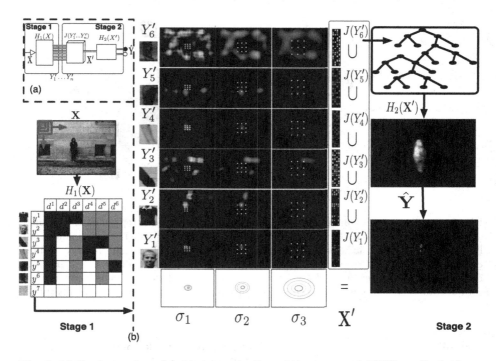

Fig. 1. Method overview. (a) Abstract pipeline of the proposed MSSL method where the outputs Y_i' of the first multi-class classifier $H_1(x)$ are fed to the multi-scale decomponsition and sampling function $J(x)$ and then used to train the second stacked classifier $H_2(x)$ which provides a binary output $\hat{Y}$. (b) Detailed pipeline for the MSSL approach used in the human segmentation context where $H_1(x)$ is a multi-class classifier that takes a vector $\mathbf{X}$ of images from a dataset. As a result, a set of likelihood maps $Y_1' \ldots Y_n'$ for each part is produced. Then a multi-scale decomposition with a neighborhood sampling function $J(x)$ is applied. The output $\mathbf{X}'$ produced is taken as the input of the second classifier $H_2(x)$, which produces the final likelihood map $\hat{Y}$, showing for each point the confidence of belonging to human body class.

with Haar-like features and cascade of classifier. In this sense, each classifier d outputs a prediction whether x belongs to one of the two previously learnt meta-classes. Once the set of predictions $c \in \{+1, -1\}^{1 \times n}$ is obtained, it is compared to the set of codewords of the classes y^i from M, using a decoding function $\delta(c, y^i)$ and the final prediction is the class with the codeword with minimum decoding, $i.e. \arg\min_i \delta(c, y^i)$. As a decoding function we use the Loss-Weighted approach with linear loss function defined in [10]. Then, a body-like probability map is built. This map contains, at each position the proportion of body part detections for each pixel over the total number of detections for the whole image. In other words, pixels belonging to the human body will show a higher

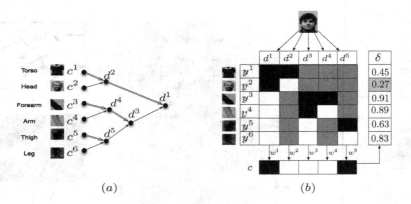

Fig. 2. (a) Tree-structure classifier of body parts, where nodes represent the defined dichotomies. Notice that the single or double lines indicate the meta-class defined. (b) ECOC decoding step, in which a head sample is classified. The coding matrix codifies the tree-structure of (a), where black and white positions are codified as +1 and −1, respectively. c, d, y, w, X, and δ correspond to a class category, a dichotomy, a class codeword, a dichotomy weight, a test codeword, and a decoding function, respectively.

body-like probability than the pixels belonging to the background. Additionally, we also construct a set of limb-like probability maps. Each map contains at each position (i, j) the probability of pixel at the entry (i, j) of belonging to the body part class. This probability is computed as the proportion of detections at point (i, j) over all detection for that class. Examples of probability maps obtained from ECOC outputs are shown in Fig. 3, which represents the $H_1(x)$ outputs $Y_1' \ldots Y_n'$ defined in Fig. 1 (a).

2.2 Stage Two: Fusing Limb Likelihood Maps Using MSSL

The goal of this stage is to fuse all partial body parts into a full human body like-lihood map (see Fig. 1 (b) second stage). The input data for the neighborhood modeling function $J(x)$ are the body parts likelihood maps obtained in the first stage $(Y_1' \ldots Y_n')$. In the first step of the modeling a set of different gaussian filters is applied on each map. All these multi-resolution decompositions give information about the influence of each body part at different scales along the space. Then, a 8-neighbor sampling is performed for each pixel with sampling distance proportional to its decomposition scale. This allows to take into account the different limbs influence and their context. The extended set X' is formed by stacking all the resulting samplings at each scale for each limb likelihood map (see the extended feature set X' in Fig. 1(b)). As a result, X' will have dimensionality equals to the number of samplings multiplied by the number of scales and the number of body parts. In our experiments we use eight neighbor sampling, three scales and six body parts. Notice that contrary to the MSSL traditional framework, we do not fed the second classifier H_2 with both the original X and extended X' features, and only the

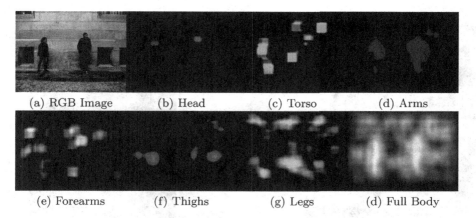

| (a) RGB Image | (b) Head | (c) Torso | (d) Arms |
| (e) Forearms | (f) Thighs | (g) Legs | (d) Full Body |

Fig. 3. Limb-like probability maps for the set of 6 limbs and body-like probability map. Image (a) shows the original RGB image. Images from (b) to (g) illustrate the limb-like probability maps and (h) shows the union of these maps.

extended set X' is provided. In this sense, the goal of H_2 is to learn spatial relations among body parts based on the confidences produced by first classifier. As a result, second classifier provides a likelihood of the membership of an image pixel to the class 'person'. Thus, the multiple spatial relations of body parts (obtained as a multi-class classifier in H_1), are labelled as a two-class problem (*person* vs *not person*) and trained by H_2. Consequently, the label set associated to the extended training data X' corresponds to the union of the ground truths of all human body parts. Although, within our method any binary classifier can be considerer for H_2, we use a Random Forest classifier to train 50 random trees that focus on different configurations of the data features. This strategy has shown robust results for human body segmentation in multi-modal data [23]. Fig. 4 shows a comparative between the union of the likelihood maps obtained by the first classifier and the final likelihoods obtained after the second stage. We can see that a naive fusion of the limb likelihoods produce noisy outputs in many body parts. The last column shows how second stage clearly detects the human body using the same data. For instance, Fig. 4 (f) shows how it works well also when two bodies are close one to other, splitting them accurately, preserving the poses. Notice that in Fig. 4 (f) a non zero probability zone exists between both silhouettes, denoting the existence of a handshaking. Finally in Fig. 4 (c) we can see how the foreground person is highlighted in the likelihood map, while in previous stage (Fig. 4 (b)) it was completely missed. This shows that the second stage is able to restore body objects at different scales. Finally, the output likelihood maps obtained after this stage are used as input of a post-process based on graph-cut to obtain final segmentation.

3   Experimental Results

Before present the experimental results, we first discuss the data, experimental settings, methods and validation protocol.

Original **H_1 joint output map** **H_2 maps**

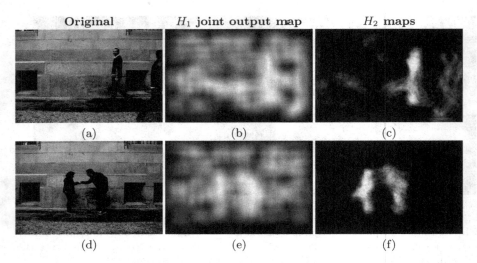

(a) (b) (c)

(d) (e) (f)

Fig. 4. Comparative between H_1 and H_2 output. First column are the original images. Second column are H_2 output likelihood maps. Last column are the union of all likelihood map of body parts.

3.1 Dataset

We used *HuPBA 8k+ dataset* described in [20]. This dataset contains more than 8000 labeled images at pixel precision, including more than 120000 manually labeled samples of 14 different limbs. The images are obtained from 9 videos (RGB sequences) and a total of 14 different actors appear in those 9 sequences. In concrete, each sequence has a main actor (9 in total) which during the sequence interacts with secondary actors portraying a wide range of poses. For our experiments, we reduced the number of limbs from the 14 available in the dataset to 6, grouping those that are similar by symmetry (right-left) as arms, forearms, thighs and legs. Thus, the set of limbs of our problem is composed by: *head, torso, forearms, arms, thighs* and *legs*. Although labeled within the dataset, we did not include hands and feet in our segmentation scheme. In Fig. 5 some samples of the *HuPBA 8k+* dataset are shown.

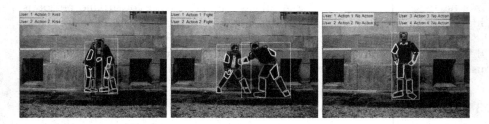

Fig. 5. Different samples of the HuPBA 8k+ dataset

3.2   Methods

We compare the following methods for Human Segmentation: **Soft Body Parts (SBP) detectors + MSSL + Graphcut.** The proposed method, where the body like confidence map obtained by each body part soft detector is learned by means of MSSL and the output is then fed to a GraphCut optimization to obtain the final segmentation. **SBP detectors + MSSL + GMM-Graphcut.** Variation of the proposed method, where the final GraphCut optimization also learns a GMM color model to obtain the final segmentation as in the GrabCut model [19]. **SBP detectors + GraphCut.** In this method the body like confidence map obtained by aggregating all body parts soft detectors outputs is fed to a GraphCut optimization to obtain the final segmentation. **SBP detectors + GMM-GraphCut.** We also use the GMM color modeling variant in the comparison.

3.3   Settings and Validation Protocol

In a preprocessing step, we resized all limb samples to a 32×32 pixels region. Regions are first rotated by main gradient orientation. In the first stage, we used the standard Cascade of Classifiers based on AdaBoost and Haar-like features [27] as our body part multi-class classifier H_1. As model parameters, we forced a 0.99 false positive rate and maximum of 0.4 false alarm rate during 8 stages. To detect limbs with trained cascades of classifiers, we applied a sliding window approach with an initial patch size of 32×32 pixels up to 60×60 pixels. As result of this stage, we obtained 6 likelihood maps for each image. In the second stage, we performed 3-scale gaussian decomposition with $\sigma \in [8, 16, 32]$ for each body part. Then, we generated a extended set selecting for each pixel its 8-neighbors with σ displacement. From this extended set, a sampling of 1500 selected points formed the input examples for the second classifier. As second classifier, we used a Random Forest with 50 decision trees. Finally, in a postprocessing stage, binary Graph Cuts with a GMM color modeling (we experimentally set 3 components) were applied to obtain the binary segmentation where the initialization seeds of foreground and background were tuned via cross-validation. For the binary Graph Cuts without a GMM color modeling we directly fed the body likelihood map to the optimization method. In order to assess our results, we used 9-fold cross-validation, where each fold correspond to images of a main actor sequence. As results measurement we used the Jaccard Index of overlapping ($J = \frac{A \bigcap B}{A \bigcup B}$) where A is the ground-truth and B is the corresponding prediction.

3.4   Quantitative Results

In Table 1 we show overlapping results for the *HuPBA 8K+* dataset. Specifically, we show the mean overlapping value obtained by the compared methods on 9 folds of the *HuPBA 8k+* dataset. We can see how our MSSL proposal consistently obtains a higher overlapping value on every fold.

Table 1. Overlapping results over the 9 folds of the *HupBA8K+* dataset for the proposed MSSL method and the Soft detectors post-processing their outputs with the Graph-Cuts method and GMM Graph-Cuts method

	GMM-GC		GC	
	MSSL	**Soft Detect.**	**MSSL**	**Soft Detect.**
Fold	**Overlap**	**Overlap**	**Overlap**	**Overlap**
1	**62.35**	60.35	**63.16**	60.53
2	**67.77**	63.72	**67.28**	63.75
3	**62.22**	60.72	**61.76**	60.67
4	**58.53**	55.69	**58.28**	55.42
5	**55.79**	51.60	**55.21**	51.53
6	**62.58**	56.56	**62.33**	55.83
7	**63.08**	60.67	**62.79**	60.62
8	**67.37**	64.84	**67.41**	65.41
9	**64.95**	59.83	**64.21**	59.90
Mean	**62,73**	59,33	**62,49**	59,29

Notice that MSSL proposal outperforms in the SBP+GC method in all folds (by at least a 3% difference), which is the state-of-the-art method for human segmentation in the HuPBA $8k+$ dataset [21].

3.5   Qualitative Results

In Fig. 6 some qualitative results of the compared methodologies for human segmentation are shown. It can be observed how in general SBP+MSSL+GMM-GC obtains a better segmentation of the human body than the SBP + GMM-GC method. This improvement is due to the contextual body part information encoded in the extended feature set. In particular, this performance difference is clearly visible in Fig. 6(f) where the human pose is completely extracted from the background. We also observe how the proposed method is able to detect a significant number of body parts at different scales. This is clearly appreciated in Fig. 6(c), where persons at different scales are segmented, while in Fig. 6(b) the SBP+GMM-GC fails to segment the rightmost person. Furthermore, Fig. 6(i) shows how the proposed method is able to recover the whole body pose by stacking all body parts, while in Fig. 6(h) the SBP+GMM-GC method just detected the head of the left most user. In this pair of images also we can see how our method is able to discriminate the different people appearing in an image, segmenting as background the interspace between them. Although, it may cause some loss, specially in the thinner body parts, like happens with the extended arm. Due to space restrictions, a table with more examples of segmentation results can be found in the supplementary material. Regards the dataset used, it is important to remark the large amount of segmented bodies (more than 10.000) and their high variability in terms of pose (performing different activities and interactions with different people), size and clothes. The scale variations are learnt by H_2 through spatial relationships of body parts. In addition, although

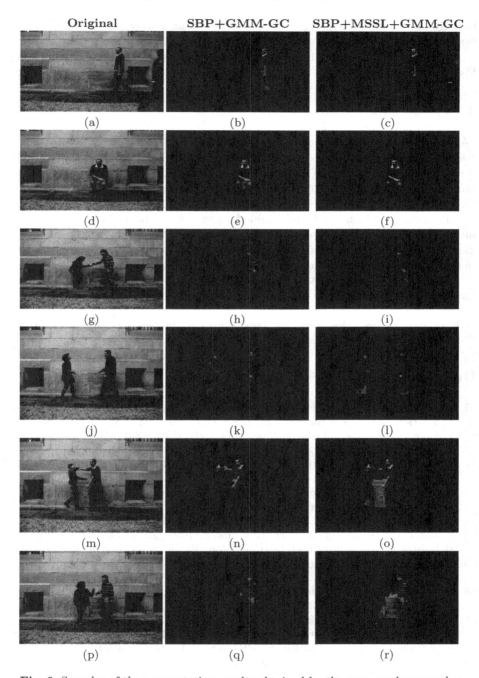

Fig. 6. Samples of the segmentation results obtained by the compared approaches

background is maintained across the data, H_2 is trained over the soft predictions from H_1 (see the large number of false positive predictions shown in Fig. 3), and our method considerably improves those person confidence maps, as shown in Fig. 4.

4   Conclusions

We presented a two-stage scheme based on the MSSL framework for the segmentation of the human body in still images. We defined an extended feature set by stacking a multi-scale decomposition of body part likelihood maps, which are learned by means of a multi-class classifier based on soft body part detectors. The extended set of features encodes spatial and contextual information of human limbs which combined enabled us to define features with high order information. We tested our proposal on a large dataset obtaining significant segmentation improvement over state-of-the-art methodologies. As future work we plan to extend the MSSL framework to the multi-limb case, in which two multi-class classifiers will be concatenated to obtain a multi-limb segmentation of the human body that takes into account contextual information of human parts.

Acknowledgments. This work has been supported in part by project TIN2013-43478-P.

References

1. Andriluka, M., Roth, S., Schiele, B.: Pictorial structures revisited: People detection and articulated pose estimation. In: IEEE Conference on Computer Vision and Pattern Recognition, CVPR 2009, pp. 1014–1021. IEEE (2009)
2. Bautista, M.A., Escalera, S., Baró, X., Radeva, P., Vitriá, J., Pujol, O.: Minimal design of error-correcting output codes. Pattern Recogn. Lett. **33**(6), 693–702 (2012)
3. Bourdev, L., Maji, S., Brox, T., Malik, J.: Detecting people using mutually consistent poselet activations. In: Daniilidis, K., Maragos, P., Paragios, N. (eds.) ECCV 2010, Part VI. LNCS, vol. 6316, pp. 168–181. Springer, Heidelberg (2010)
4. Chakraborty, B., Bagdanov, A.D., Gonzalez, J., Roca, X.: Human action recognition using an ensemble of body-part detectors. Expert Systems (2011)
5. Cohen, W.W., de Carvalho, V.R.: Stacked sequential learning. In: Proc. of IJCAI 2005, pp. 671–676 (2005)
6. Dalal, N., Triggs, B.: Histograms of oriented gradients for human detection. In: CVPR, vol. 1, pp. 886–893 (2005)
7. Dantone, M., Gall, J., Leistner, C., van Gool, L.: Human pose estimation using body parts dependent joint regressors. In: 2013 IEEE Conference on Computer Vision and Pattern Recognition (CVPR), pp. 3041–3048 (June 2013)
8. Dietterich, T., Bakiri, G.: Solving multiclass learning problems via error-correcting output codes. Journal of Artificial Intelligence Research **2**, 263–286 (1995)
9. Dietterich, T.G.: Machine learning for sequential data: A review. In: Caelli, T.M., Amin, A., Duin, R.P.W., Kamel, M.S., de Ridder, D. (eds.) SPR 2002 and SSPR 2002. LNCS, vol. 2396, pp. 15–30. Springer, Heidelberg (2002)

10. Escalera, S., Tax, D., Pujol, O., Radeva, P., Duin, R.: Subclass problem-dependent design of error-correcting output codes. PAMI **30**(6), 1–14 (2008)
11. Escalera, S., Pujol, O., Radeva, P.: On the decoding process in ternary error-correcting output codes. PAMI **32**, 120–134 (2010)
12. Felzenszwalb, P.F., Huttenlocher, D.P.: Efficient matching of pictorial structures. In: Proceedings of the IEEE Conference on Computer Vision and Pattern Recognition, vol. 2, pp. 66–73. IEEE (2000)
13. Gatta, C., Puertas, E., Pujol, O.: Multi-scale stacked sequential learning. Pattern Recognition **44**(10–11), 2414–2426 (2011)
14. Gkioxari, G., Arbelaez, P., Bourdev, L.D., Malik, J.: Articulated pose estimation using discriminative armlet classifiers. In: CVPR, pp. 3342–3349. IEEE (2013)
15. Hernández-Vela, A., Zlateva, N., Marinov, A., Reyes, M., Radeva, P., Dimov, D., Escalera, S.: Graph cuts optimization for multi-limb human segmentation in depth maps. In: CVPR, pp. 726–732 (2012)
16. Hernández-Vela, A., Reyes, M., Ponce, V., Escalera, S.: Grabcut-based human segmentation in video sequences. Sensors **12**(11), 15376–15393 (2012)
17. Pishchulin, L., Andriluka, M., Gehler, P., Schiele, B.: Poselet conditioned pictorial structures. In: 2013 IEEE Conference on Computer Vision and Pattern Recognition (CVPR), pp. 588–595. IEEE (2013)
18. Puertas, E., Escalera, S., Pujol, O.: Generalized multi-scale stacked sequential learning for multi-class classification. Pattern Analysis and Applications, 1–15 (2013)
19. Ramanan, D., Forsyth, D., Zisserman, A.: Strike a pose: tracking people by finding stylized poses. In: IEEE Computer Society Conference on Computer Vision and Pattern Recognition, CVPR 2005, vol. 1, pp. 271–278 (June 2005)
20. Ramanan, D., Forsyth, D., Zisserman, A.: Tracking people by learning their appearance. PAMI **29**(1), 65–81 (2007)
21. Rother, C., Kolmogorov, V., Blake, A.: "grabcut": interactive foreground extraction using iterated graph cuts. ACM Trans. Graph. **23**(3), 309–314 (2004)
22. Sánchez, D., Bautista, M.A., Escalera, S.: Hupba 8k+: Dataset and ecoc-graphcut based segmentation of human limbs. Neurocomputing (2014)
23. Sánchez, D., Ortega, J.C., Bautista, M.Á., Escalera, S.: Human body segmentation with multi-limb error-correcting output codes detection and graph cuts optimization. In: Sanches, J.M., Micó, L., Cardoso, J.S. (eds.) IbPRIA 2013. LNCS, vol. 7887, pp. 50–58. Springer, Heidelberg (2013)
24. Sapp, B., Jordan, C., Taskar, B.: Adaptive pose priors for pictorial structures. In: 2010 IEEE Conference on Computer Vision and Pattern Recognition (CVPR), pp. 422–429. IEEE (2010)
25. Shotton, J., Fitzgibbon, A., Cook, M., Sharp, T., Finocchio, M., Moore, R., Kipman, A., Blake, A.: Real-time human pose recognition in parts from single depth images. In: CVPR, p. 3 (2011)
26. Vineet, V., Warrell, J., Ladicky, L., Torr, P.: Human instance segmentation from video using detector-based conditional random fields. In: BMVC (2011)
27. Viola, P., Jones, M.: Rapid object detection using a boosted cascade of simple features. In: CVPR, vol. 1 (2001)
28. Yang, Y., Ramanan, D.: Articulated pose estimation with flexiblemixtures-of-parts. In: IEEE Conference on Computer Vision and PatternRecognition, pp. 1385–1392. IEEE (2011)
29. Yu, C.N.J., Joachims, T.: Learning structural svms with latentvariables. In: Proceedings of the 26th Annual International Conference on Machine Learning, pp. 1169–1176. ACM (2009)

G3Di: A Gaming Interaction Dataset with a Real Time Detection and Evaluation Framework

Victoria Bloom$^{(\boxtimes)}$, Vasileios Argyriou, and Dimitrios Makris

Kingston University, London, UK
{Victoria.Bloom,Vasileios.Argyriou,D.Makris}@kingston.ac.uk

Abstract. This paper presents a new, realistic and challenging human interaction dataset for multiplayer gaming, containing synchronised colour, depth and skeleton data. In contrast to existing datasets where the interactions are scripted, G3Di was captured using a novel game-sourcing method so the movements are more realistic. Our detection framework decomposes interactions into the actions of each person to infer the interaction in real time. This modular approach is applicable to a virtual environment where the interaction between people occurs through a computer interface. We also propose an evaluation metric for real time applications, which assesses both the accuracy and latency of the interactions. Experimental results indicate higher complexity of the new dataset in comparison to existing gaming datasets.

Keywords: Human interaction recognition · Multimodal dataset · Multiplayer gaming · Interaction evaluation metric

1 Introduction

Recognising human interaction is a very active research area in the field of computer vision and is key to a range of domains including security, entertainment and robotics. The goal of interaction recognition is to automatically detect human interactions in a sequence of observations. Conceptually, a two person interaction is composed of a pair of two single actions, an action and a counter action [14]. In traditional human interaction, people physically interact with each other like in a real boxing match. Recent technological developments, such as low cost depth sensors, have enabled a new form of interaction which is virtual, for example a full body boxing game illustrated in Fig. 1.

This new generation of games use the human body as the controller and have increased the appeal of gaming to family members of all ages. Multiplayer sports games encourage people to interact with other players across the globe or friends and family in the same living room. The interactions can be collaborative or competitive depending on the specific sport and game mode. Boxing is naturally a competitive sport but team sports can be played either collaboratively with friends on the same team or competitively with friends on the opposing team. For example, one can play table tennis alongside a friend in a doubles match

© Springer International Publishing Switzerland 2015
L. Agapito et al. (Eds.): ECCV 2014 Workshops, Part I, LNCS 8925, pp. 698–712, 2015.
DOI: 10.1007/978-3-319-16178-5_49

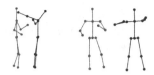

Fig. 1. Boxing interactions: A real attack (left) occurs when one person actually punches the other person, whereas a virtual attack (right) occurs when one person punches in the direction of the computer screen

or against a friend in a singles match. The players can act simultaneously or after a short delay depending on the sport. For example, in boxing the actions are concurrent but other sports such as table tennis have a delay between one person acting and the other reacting.

Past research has typically focused on recognising interactions from colour sequences but the recent release of low cost depth sensors combined with a real time pose estimation algorithm has seen the rapid growth of research on depth and skeleton data. Each modality has advantages and disadvantages: colour and depth data contain contextual information but are both dependent on the camera view and the persons' appearance. Depth and skeleton data are more robust than colour data when there are a lot of illumination changes and can even work in total darkness. Skeleton data is both invariant to the camera location and subject appearance, but lacks contextual information and does not work well when the player is not standing or sitting upright. Fusing colour and depth has overcome some limitations of the individual modalities but most current algorithms consider the depth and colour channels independently [2]. The new multimodal dataset presented in this paper with synchronised colour, depth and skeleton data can provide the opportunity to develop algorithms with improved fusion of the different modalities towards producing more robust algorithms that have a wider range of applications.

The contributions of this paper are a realistic and challenging human interaction 3D dataset with a real time detection and evaluation framework. G3Di is a novel multiplayer gaming dataset containing synchronised colour, depth and skeleton data. In contrast to existing datasets the movements are much more complex and realistic. Our new interaction framework recognises individual actions as they occur to infer the interaction in real time. We also propose an evaluation metric for real time applications which assesses both the accuracy and latency of the interactions.

2   Related Work

Human interactions are composed of actions therefore we review existing datasets, recognition algorithms and evaluation metrics at both the action and interaction levels of the activity hierarchy.

2.1   Datasets

Historically, human activity datasets were recorded with visible light cameras and consist only of colour data [9] [15] [16] . For a comprehensive review of these also see Aggarwal and Ryoo [1]. The major problem with colour data of human motion is that there is a considerable loss of information [2]. After the recent release of low cost depth sensors there has been a growth of 3D datasets that provide skeleton data with some also providing colour and/or depth data [4] [6] [7] [11] [12] [18] [20].

However, most 3D datasets are restricted to activities performed by a single human subject which subsequently limits the development of 3D recognition algorithms to a single person [2] [4] [7] [11] [18]. The problem with the existing 3D gaming datasets, MSRAction3D [11], MSRC-12 [7] and G3D [4] is that they are single player, whereas commercial games are often multiplayer.

Another major limitation of the existing gaming datasets is that the scenarios were scripted so the movements are not realistic. In scripted datasets, the participants were instructed beforehand on how and when to perform the actions. Furthermore, in the MSR Action3D and MSRC-12 datasets each sequence contains only a single action class and the transition between repetitions often includes the neutral position. The G3D dataset contains more realistic gaming scenarios as there are multiple action classes in a sequence, but as there is a delay between actions the subject often returns to the neutral position when changing action. In fast paced competitive games like boxing, players do not return to the neutral position between actions which creates complex action transitions.

The key features of the gaming 3D datasets are illustrated in Table 1. The table was ordered on the number of data sources provided which increases by row. G3D is the only existing gaming dataset to contain all three modalities (colour, depth and skeleton data). The SBU [20] and K3HI [10] traditional person to person interaction datasets contain all three modalities but in both of these datasets the people were captured from a side view and partially clipped, which created noisy and unreliable skeleton data.

To overcome the limitations of the current datasets we propose a new multiplayer gaming dataset, G3Di with synchronised colour, depth and skeleton. The people were captured from the front view and interacted indirectly with each other through a computer interface. Sports games introduced the element of competition between the players so the actions captured were more realistic and challenging in comparison to scripted actions.

Table 1. Comparison of 3D gaming datasets

Dataset	Classes	Subjects	Data sources	Instruction Modality	Scenario
MSRC-12 [7]	12	30	Skeleton	Scripted	Actions
MSRAction3D [11]	20	10	Depth+ Skeleton	Scripted	Actions
G3D [4]	20	10	Colour+ Depth+ Skeleton	Scripted	Actions
G3Di	18	12	Colour+ Depth+ Skeleton	Game-sourced	Actions+ Interactions

2.2 Recognition Algorithms

In human activity recognition there is a vast wealth of research on interaction recognition and traditionally approaches were appearance based as low level features could be quickly extracted from colour sequences. Recent work [2] [11] [12] suggests that human activity recognition accuracy can be improved by using features from 3D data. Pose based features from skeleton data are a very effective representation for human motion [3] [7] [10] [19] [20] so we focus on pose based approaches.

Due to the development of a real time pose estimation algorithm [17] from depth streams many recent activity recognition algorithms are based on skeletal joint information. In a recent review of human activity recognition from 3D data [2], the authors concluded that most current approaches only deal with a single human subject. Subsequently, the features are based on joints from a single skeleton such as the pairwise joint location difference feature [3] [7] [19].

These pose based features were extended to multiple skeletons by Yun et al. [20] to model human interactions. Their experiments showed that the distance between all pairs of joints was the optimum set of joint features for real time interaction. This feature measures the pairwise joint distance in each skeleton, as well as between the two skeletons. This feature set was specifically designed for person to person interaction where the distance between the joints of the people aids the classification. For example, the distance between two people can easily be used to differentiate between approaching and departing. However, this feature set is not so relevant in virtual human interaction where there is no physical interaction between the people.

Further research by Hu et al. [10] with pose based features from multiple skeletons discovered that an interaction can be represented by a positive and negative action. Their results showed that the positive action on its own was discriminative enough to classify the interactions in their dataset, so the interaction recognition was simplified to positive action recognition. This works for simple scenarios where there is only one outcome from an action, such as the punching in their dataset where the first person punches and the second person falls away from the hit. However, in more complex scenarios there are more than one possible reactions from a punch, for example, a hit as just described or a block where the second person defends themselves by raising their hands in front of their face. If the skeletal information from the second person is ignored it will be very difficult to differentiate between these two interactions.

To overcome these limitations, our framework decomposes the interaction into the actions of both people and infers the interaction from the action pair in real time. The pose based features are only extracted within a skeleton and not between skeletons so that our approach can be applied to virtual human interaction. Moreover, decoupling the action and counter action reduces the number of instances required for training and allows new interactions to be detected that are not in the training data.

2.3 Evaluation Metrics

A common performance measure used for activity recognition is classification accuracy which is applied to the entire sequence. For example, an interaction label is predicted for each frame in the sequence and a majority decision over all frames is taken to decide the interaction label for the complete sequence. However, this approach can only be applied to simple sequences containing the same action class which is not the case for the new dataset.

To overcome the limitations of sequence based evaluation, frame based evaluation metrics have been developed [6] [15]. Escalera et al. [6] introduced a Jaccard index that can evaluate sequences with multiple action/interaction classes with respect to time. Ryoo and Aggarwal [15] proposed spatial and temporal bounding boxes to evaluate sequences with multiple interactions with respect to both space and time. Both approaches are evaluated based on the overlap between the system detection and the ground truth labels. These application metrics include temporal constraints but do not evaluate the latency of the detection.

Low latency detection is critical for real world applications such as surveillance and gaming. Nowozin et al. [13] proposed a latency aware performance metric for online human action recognition. They introduced 'action points' as temporal anchors for the detection and evaluation of single person actions in real time. According to [13], an action label is correct if it is detected within a specific time window around the ground truth action point. We propose an interaction evaluation metric for real time applications which assesses both the accuracy and latency of the interactions by exploiting the generality of the action point metric.

3   G3Di Dataset

A new multimodal interaction dataset has been captured, for real time multiplayer gaming and is publicly available[1]. G3Di contains synchronised colour, depth and skeleton data. The dataset was captured using a novel gamesourcing approach where the users were recorded whilst playing computer games.

---

[1] G3Di can be downloaded from http://dipersec.kingston.ac.uk/G3D/

Fig. 2. Synchronised colour, depth and skeleton data from a boxing game

Our recording environment as illustrated in Fig. 3 allowed us to capture realistic gaming actions. The inherent competitive nature of the games resulted in the players putting more effort into their movements. The setup shows two players as the current generation of depth sensors are limited to full skeleton tracking of two people. However, the same setup could be used for up to six players when the next generation of depth sensors are released. The recording environment contains two overlapping depth sensors: one for playing full body games on a standard games console and the other to capture the colour, depth and skeleton data. The disadvantage of using two sensors with overlapping fields of view is that considerable noise is introduced to the depth data and consequently the skeleton data, due to infrared interference. Specifically, the depth sensor we used the Kinect, derives depth by projecting a structured light code onto the scene and comparing the reflected pattern with the stored pattern. To overcome this problem a motor was attached to one depth sensor to vibrate it and therefore reduce the interference between them as observed in experiments by Butler et al. [5].

Due to the formats selected, it is possible to view all the recorded data and metadata without any special software tools. The three streams were recorded at 30fps in a mirrored view. The depth and colour images were stored as 640x480 PNG files and the skeleton data in XML files. Each skeleton contains the player's position and pose: the pose comprises of 20 joints and the joint positions are given in X, Y and Z coordinates in meters. These positions are also mapped into the depth and colour coordinate spaces. The skeleton data includes a joint tracking state, displayed in Fig. 2 as tracked (green), inferred (yellow) and not tracked (red). The joint tracking state provides the confidence of the data for each joint. If the data is tracked, the confidence in the data is very high. Whereas, if the data is inferred by calculating it from other tracked joints, the confidence in the data is very low. This is important information for developers of multimodal algorithms fusing data between the skeleton data and other modalities.

To the best of our knowledge this is the first dataset comprised of virtual interactions, meaning that two players interact with each other through a computer interface. This dataset contains 12 people split into 6 pairs. Each pair performed 18 gaming actions, for six sports games: boxing (right punch, left punch, defend), volleyball (serve, overhand hit, underhand hit, jump hit, block

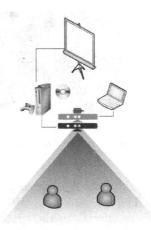

Fig. 3. Recording environment with 2 depth cameras for simultaneous gameplay and recording

and jump block), football (kick, block and save), table tennis (serve, forehand hit and backhand hit), sprint (run) and hurdles (run and jump). Most sequences contain multiple action classes in a controlled indoor environment with a fixed camera, a typical setup for gesture based gaming. The people played the game in a training mode to become familiar with the movements before they were recorded. The actual game was recorded and particular sections where several different actions were performed multiple times by each player were selected for the dataset.

4   Interaction Detection Framework

Our novel framework detects individual actions from multiple people, to infer the interaction between them. This modular approach is applicable for virtual interaction and enables interaction between people that are not in the same physical location. The three key stages of the interaction framework are: training, testing and evaluation, as illustrated in Fig. 4. The training phase is performed offline for each action and uses the training data to learn action models. The testing phase is executed for each frame in real time to provide online interaction recognition. Actions from different people are detected independently. At each frame, these detections are combined to infer the current interaction.

An existing approach for online action recognition is to represent each action by a reference point [3] [7] . An 'action point' is defined as a single time instance that an action is clear and can be uniquely identified for all instances of that action [13]. For example, the action point of a punch is defined as 'the time at which the arm is maximally extended'. An action point has no temporal duration which accurately represents some actions, for example a punch. However, this

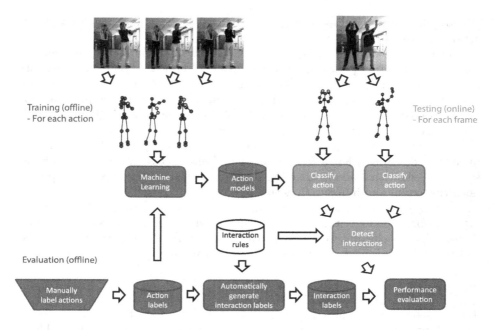

Fig. 4. The interaction framework comprising of three key stages: training, testing and evaluation

is not the case for all actions, such as the defend, which is defined as 'the time when two hands are positioned in front of the face' as in reality the hands remain in front of the face for a significant period of time.

To overcome the limitation of action points we propose action segments. In contrast to an action point, an action segment has temporal duration. The duration of the action segment is important for training action classifiers with consistent samples and should improve detection accuracy. It is also critical for recognising multiple interactions when one subject performs one long action and the other multiple short actions. An example is where one subject defends whilst the other subject punches him multiple times. These should all be detected as blocking interactions, but without considering the duration of the defend action, only the first would be detected as a block and the subsequent punches incorrectly as attacks.

4.1 Training

The training phase transpires offline and uses the data for each action to learn a model. The ground truth labels are used to select the frames and the subject within each frame that is performing the specific action. For each subject instance a feature vector is constructed and concatenated with all subject instances for the same action. The framework is generic so features from the colour, depth, skeleton or a fusion of these features can be used to train any classifier to learn action models.

In this work, we compare two approaches for training our action models, the first based on action points and the second based on action segments. Existing action recognition algorithms are based on action points, they use n frames before and after the action point to train their classifiers [3] [7] . This is appropriate for short actions but this new dataset confirms that under realistic gaming conditions some actions have a long duration. Therefore, we recommend that action classifiers should be trained with all the frames that are part of the action segment in addition to a few n frames before and after the segment. Our results in section 5.2 show that adopting action segments instead of action points improves both the action and interaction accuracy.

To assess the complexity of our realistic dataset we use an established online action recognition algorithm with published results for multiple existing gaming datasets [3]. Specifically, we use Adaptive Boosting (AdaBoost) [8] with the same parameters and skeleton based features as reported in [3].

4.2   Testing

Testing sequences are processed online for real time detection. Each frame is divided into different people, which are classified into individual actions. These classifications are then combined to infer the current interaction.

Action Recognition. For each subject, a feature vector is created containing the same features as used for training the action models. The action model with the highest response depicts the action label for the current subject to provide real time action classification. The action model responses for the subject are summed over a sliding window of w frames to smooth the results and increase accuracy. This temporal filtering prevents broken actions caused by individual bad frames and therefore reduces the number of false positives. After smoothing, the highest action result determines the action label for the current subject. A change in action label is the detected action point, which is also the start of the action segment. To incorporate the duration of the action we also record the end of the action.

Interaction Recognition. To detect interactions for multiple people we must identify the interaction rules between people. These rules are application specific and include the valid combinations of actions together with timing constraints. These rules can be tailored by the application designer to include any necessary additional constraints.

The interactions for the G3Di dataset are depicted in Table 2, for compactness just two scenarios are shown. The action a and counter action ca, are checked at each frame together with a timing constraint f to detect interactions in real time. The timing constraint depends on the scenario, for example all the interactions in boxing are instant ($f = 0$), the action and counter action co-occur.

Table 2. Gaming interactions for the boxing and table tennis scenarios in G3Di

Sport	Action	Counter Action	Interaction
Boxing	Right Punch	Defend	Block
	Left Punch	Defend	Block
	Right Punch	Other	Attack
	Left Punch	Other	Attack
	Right Punch	Right Punch	Attack
	Right Punch	Left Punch	Attack
	Left Punch	Left Punch	Attack
Table Tennis	Serve	Forehand hit	Rally
	Serve	Backhand hit	Rally
	Serve	Other	Miss
	Forehand hit	Forehand hit	Rally
	Forehand hit	Backhand hit	Rally
	Forehand hit	Other	Miss
	Backhand hit	Backhand hit	Rally
	Backhand hit	Other	Miss

However, other scenarios such as table tennis have a delay between the action and counter action ($f > 0$).

In this work we evaluate two approaches for detecting interactions, the first based on modelling actions as a single point in time and the second based on actions with temporal duration. In both cases, the detected interaction points can be compared with the ground truth interaction points to obtain a single F1 score. In the first case action points t, are used to represent the actions and interactions are detected if the action and counter action occur either at the same time or after a fixed delay, as described by Equation (1).

$$\phi\left(a_t, ca_t\right) = \begin{cases} 1 & ca_t - a_t = f \\ 0 & \text{otherwise} \end{cases} \tag{1}$$

In the second case action segments are used to represent the actions and interactions are detected if the action and counter segments overlap either at the same point in time or after a fixed delay, as described by Equation (2).

$$\psi\left(a_s, a_e, ca_s, ca_e\right) = \begin{cases} 1 & \text{if } (a_s + f \leq ca_e) \ \& \ (ca_s \leq a_e + f) \\ 0 & \text{otherwise} \end{cases} \tag{2}$$

Where s and e represent the start and end of the action segment respectively and $s \leq e$.

4.3 Interaction Evaluation Framework

To evaluate the performance of both action and interaction recognition algorithms on this new dataset, action and interaction online metrics and ground truth annotation are required. For action recognition, an existing evaluation

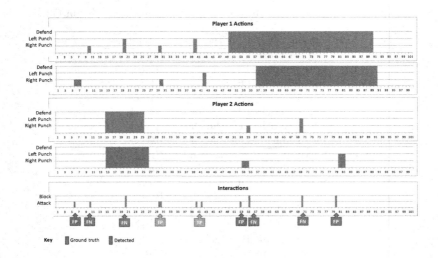

Fig. 5. An example timeline for a boxing game, showing the true positives (TP), false positives (FP) and false negatives (FN). A TP, is a correct interaction identified within Δ frames of the ground truth. A FN, is an undetected interaction on the ground truth. A FP, is an incorrect interaction detected.

metric is the action point metric [13]. Action points enable latency aware evaluation of online action recognition systems. This metric will be used to assess the timing of the action points with respect to the ground truth.

For interaction evaluation the existing frame based metrics [6] [15] include temporal constraints but do not evaluate the latency of the detection. To overcome these limitations we propose a new interaction point based evaluation metric that can evaluate both the accuracy and latency of the interactions. The interaction points can be evaluated in a similar manner to action points, to obtain a single F1 score for an easy comparison of different interaction algorithms.

Dataset Annotation. The ground truth for the action dataset was conventionally annotated by manually labelling each action point and each action segment. The interaction ground truth could have also been manually labelled but it was more efficient to automatically construct the interaction labels from the action ground truth labels. The ground truth interactions are automatically labelled based on the set of rules that govern the interactions for a particular game (as described in Section 4.2).

Interaction Evaluation Metric. To evaluate the timing accuracy of an interaction we adapt the existing action point metric [13] to assess the timing of the interaction points with respect to the ground truth. The interaction points are assessed for detection and timeliness and an F1 score is generated. The acceptable latency of the interaction is application specific and can be adjusted with the Δ parameter. To clarify the assessment of interaction points a dummy time-line for a boxing game has been created (Fig. 5), showing the ground truth and the detected points for actions and interactions. The precision and recall are measured for each interaction and both of these measures are combined to calculate a single interaction F1-score (F1). To measure accuracy for multiple interactions, the mean interaction F1-score is calculated over all interactions.

5   Real Time Results

The interaction framework proposed in Section 4 can be used with any classifier. To obtain our results we used a multiclass implementation of Gentle AdaBoost. Following [3] [7] we use a 'leave one person out' protocol. As there are 12 people, this process is repeated 12 times with different subsets to obtain the average performance.

5.1   Action Recognition Results

To evaluate the complexity of the actions in the new dataset G3Di in comparison with actions in existing gaming datasets we recreate experiments previously performed on those datasets. For a fair comparison, we use the same classifier, pose based features, parameters and action point evaluation metric as published in [3]. Specifically, a vector of 297 features is extracted for each skeleton in each frame which is a concatenation of 57 position difference features, 60 position velocity features, 20 position velocity magnitude features, 80 joint angle features and 80 angle velocity features. The latency parameter Δ was fixed at $330ms$ for consistency with previously published results [3] [7].

The previously published action recognition F1 results [3] for the G3D and MSRC-12 datasets and the new result for the G3Di dataset are shown in Table 3. The F1 for the new dataset is the lowest, indicating that G3Di is more challenging, especially as the actions in the G3Di boxing scenario are a subset of those actions found in the G3D fighting scenario.

Table 3. Gaming dataset action results highlighting the complexity of the new dataset

Datasets (Scenario)	G3D (Fighting)	MSRC-12 (FPS)	G3Di (Boxing)
Action F1	0.896	0.643	0.426

5.2   Interaction Recognition Results

To demonstrate our interaction detection framework on the new dataset G3Di we initally use action points for detection and the same experimental setup as described in the previous section to get a baseline result for the G3Di boxing dataset. We then incorporate action segments into our interaction detection framework and repeat the same experiments. We performed quantitative

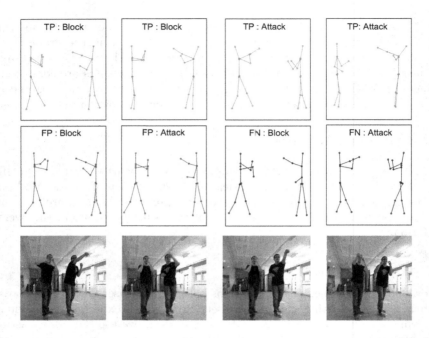

Fig. 6. Examples of real time interaction detection. Correct detections TP, are displayed in green and incorrect detections are shown in red for FP and blue for FN. The action detected by the system is displayed above each pair of skeletons. The colour images below each failure cases highlight the major sources of error, transition error between actions and noisy joints.

evaluation using the action point and interaction point metrics and qualitative evaluation by visually analysing our failure cases. The quantitative results are shown in Table 4, which highlight an increase in both the action recognition and interaction performance by 13%. This confirms that the duration is important for detecting actions and subsequently interactions in real time.

The qualitative results are displayed in Fig. 6, including examples of correct and incorrect detected interactions. The colour images below each failure cases highlight the major sources of error, which are transition error between actions and noisy joints. The transition errors occur when a player moves quickly from one action class directly to another without passing through a neutral state.

Table 4. Gaming dataset interaction detection results

Methods	Baseline (action points)	Proposed (action segments)
Action F1	0.426	0.561
Interaction F1	0.448	0.571

As Fig. 6 illustrates, when a player transition from a block to a punch it is difficult to infer from the skeleton data alone the current action. The colour images provide additional information to help differentiate the current action and suggest a fusion of colour and skeleton may improve detection in these cases. The transition errors support our claim that this new gaming dataset is more challenging than existing gaming datasets with simple transitions. Some of the failure cases were also related to noisy joints in our skeleton data but it is important to have some noise in a realistic gaming dataset as in a real home environment there may be noise caused by direct sunlight. The noisy joints endorse our inclusion of joint confidence and additional modalities (depth and colour) in our new dataset.

6   Conclusions

A novel, realistic and challenging human interaction dataset, G3Di for real time multiplayer gaming is introduced. It overcomes the limitations of existing 3D gaming datasets that only contain a single player with simple action sequences. Our interaction framework recognises individual actions with low latency for real time interaction detection. The incorporation of the action duration in our framework improved both the action and interaction performance. We also proposed an interaction evaluation metric for real time applications which assesses both the accuracy and latency of the interactions. Experimental results indicate higher complexity of the new dataset in comparison to the existing gaming datasets, highlighting the importance of this dataset for designing algorithms suitable for realistic interactive applications. Our future work is to develop an algorithm that fuses features from the depth or colour with the skeleton features to improve the performance of our interaction detection framework. Additionally, we will incorporate person to person features in the interaction framework to recognise traditional human interactions.

Acknowledgments. We would like to thank the staff, students and interns of Kingston University for participating in the gamesourcing. We would also like to thank Kevin Bottero and Nicolas Ferrand from Ecole Nationale Suprieure d'Ingnieurs de CAEN (ENSICAEN) for their assistance in collecting and annotating the new dataset.

References

1. Aggarwal, J.K., Ryoo, M.S.: Human activity analysis: A review. ACM Computing Surveys **43(3)**, 16:1–16:43 (2011)
2. Aggarwal, J., Xia, L.: Human Activity Recognition From 3D Data: A Review. Pattern Recognition Letters (2014)
3. Bloom, V., Argyriou, V., Makris, D.: Dynamic feature selection for online action recognition. In: Salah, A.A., Hung, H., Aran, O., Gunes, H. (eds.) HBU 2013. LNCS, vol. 8212, pp. 64–76. Springer, Heidelberg (2013)

4. Bloom, V., Makris, D., Argyriou, V.: G3D: A gaming action dataset and real time action recognition evaluation framework. In: Workshop on Computer Vision for Computer Games, IEEE Conference on Computer Vision and Pattern Recognition (CVPR Workshops), pp. 7–12 (2012)

5. Butler, A., Izadi, S., Hilliges, O., Molyneaux, D., Hodges, S., Kim, D.: Shake'n'Sense: reducing interference for overlapping structured light depth cameras. In: Human Factors in Computing Systems, pp. 1933–1936 (2012)

6. Escalera, S., Baró, X., Gonzàlez, J., Bautista, M.A., Madadi, M., Reyes, M., Ponce, V., Escalante, H.J., Shotton, J., Guyon, I.: ChaLearn Looking at People Challenge 2014: Dataset and Results. In: ECCV Workshop (2014)

7. Fothergill, S., Mentis, H., Kohli, P., Nowozin, S.: Instructing people for training gestural interactive systems. In: Proceedings of the SIGCHI Conference on Human Factors in Computing Systems, pp. 1737–1746 (2012)

8. Freund, Y., Schapire, R.E.: Experiments with a New Boosting Algorithm (1996)

9. Gorelick, L., Blank, M., Shechtman, E., Irani, M., Basri, R.: Actions as space-time shapes. IEEE Transactions on Pattern Analysis and Machine Intelligence (PAMI) **29**(12), 2247–2253 (2007)

10. Hu, T., Zhu, X., Guo, W., Su, K.: Efficient Interaction Recognition through Positive Action Representation. Mathematical Problems in Engineering **2013**, 1–11 (2013)

11. Li, W., Way, O.M.: Action Recognition Based on A Bag of 3D Points. In: IEEE Conference on Computer Vision and Pattern Recognition Workshop (CVPR Workshops), pp. 9–14 (2010)

12. Ni, B., Moulin, P.: RGBD-HuDaAct: A color-depth video database for human daily activity recognition. In: IEEE International Conference on Computer Vision Workshops (ICCV Workshops), pp. 1147–1153 (2011)

13. Nowozin, S., Shotton, J.: Action Points: A Representation for Low-latency Online Human Action Recognition. Tech. Rep. MSR-TR-2012-68, Microsoft Research Cambridge (2012)

14. Park, S., Aggarwal, J.: Event semantics in two-person interactions. In: IEEE Conference on International Conference on Pattern Recognition (ICPR), vol. 4, pp. 227–230 (2004)

15. Ryoo, M.S., Aggarwal, J.K.: UT-Interaction Dataset. In: ICPR contest on Semantic Description of Human Activities (SDHA) (2010)

16. Schuldt, C., Laptev, I., Caputo, B.: Recognizing human actions: a local SVM approach. In: IEEE Conference on International Conference on Pattern Recognition (ICPR), vol. 4, pp. 32–36 (2004)

17. Shotton, J., Fitzgibbon, A., Cook, M., Sharp, T., Finocchio, M., Moore, R., Kipman, A., Blake, A.: Real-time human pose recognition in parts from single depth images. In: IEEE Conference on Computer Vision and Pattern Recognition (CVPR), pp. 1297–1304 (2011)

18. Wang, J.: Mining actionlet ensemble for action recognition with depth cameras. In: IEEE Conference on Computer Vision and Pattern Recognition (CVPR), pp. 1290–1297 (2012)

19. Yao, A., Gall, J., Fanelli, G., Gool, L.V.: Does human action recognition benefit from pose estimation? In: Proceedings of the British Machine Vision Conference, pp. 67.1–67.11 (2011)

20. Yun, K., Honorio, J., Chattopadhyay, D., Berg, T.L., Samaras, D., Brook, S.: Two-person interaction detection using body-pose features and multiple instance learning. In: IEEE Conference on Computer Vision and Pattern Recognition Workshop (CVPR Workshops), pp. 28–35 (2012)

Three-Dimensional Hand Pointing Recognition Using Two Cameras by Interpolation and Integration of Classification Scores

Dai Fujita[✉] and Takashi Komuro

Graduate School of Science and Engineering, Saitama University, Saitama, Japan
fujita@is.ics.saitama-u.ac.jp

Abstract. In this paper, we propose a novel method of hand recognition for remote mid-air pointing operation. In the proposed method, classification scores are calculated in a sliding window for hand postures with different pointing directions. Detection of a pointing hand and estimation of the pointing direction is performed by interpolating the classification scores. Moreover, we introduce two cameras and improve the recognition accuracy by integrating the classification scores obtained from two camera images. In the experiment, the recognition rate was 73 % at around 1 FPPI when ±10° error was allowed. Though this result was still insufficient for practical applications, we confirmed that integration of two camera information greatly improved the recognition performance.

Keywords: Hand detection · Hand pose estimation · Multi-class classification

1 Introduction

Along with the progress of hardware performance and information processing technology, user interface (UI) applications using hand gestures recognized from camera images are being commercialized. Hand gesture UIs enable intuitive interaction with a computer.

However, existing hand gesture UIs have a problem that only limited kinds of input operations are possible compared to other conventional input interfaces. In addition, users have to move their hand largely and the users often get tired during operation. One of the reasons is that existing hand gesture systems cannot recognize subtle finger movement. Hand pointing is a gesture that uses subtle finger movement and that allows users to perform various types of input operations.

There have been studies that have investigated the effectiveness of the mid-air pointing operation [8,13]. These studies use a hand-worn device to recognize precise hand pointing. On the other hand, a hand gesture control device named Leap Motion that enables precise mid-air pointing operation without wearing a device has been commercialized [7]. Leap Motion has been paid attention as the next generation UIs, but it recognizes hands with a small sensor put on a

© Springer International Publishing Switzerland 2015
L. Agapito et al. (Eds.): ECCV 2014 Workshops, Part I, LNCS 8925, pp. 713–726, 2015.
DOI: 10.1007/978-3-319-16178-5_50

desk, and the operation space is limited within about $50\,cm^3$ above the sensor. Therefore, remote operation of a computer from a distance cannot be realized.

Some systems that realize remote hand pointing operation by putting several cameras on the environment have been developed [4, 10, 11], but the operation space is limited within a narrow area.

To realize mid-air remote pointing operation of a computer over a wide area, we have to put front-facing cameras for hand recognition on the display. However, it is difficult to recognize a hand that is pointing in the direction of the camera. A pointing hand towards the camera easily changes its appearance and lacks visual salient features in the images. Though much research which recognizes a hand by using color and/or shape information has been conducted [3, 10], such methods either lack robustness or require heuristics which use much prior knowledge to construct a recognition system. Meanwhile, research of recognizing a hand robustly based on machine learning using edge feature of images [1, 6, 12, 14], and estimating direction of a target object by using multi-class classification [5, 9] has been conducted.

The objective of this study is to realize robust hand pointing recognition in the three-dimensional (3-D) space with sufficient precision to enable remote pointing operation in a general indoor environment. To achieve this objective, we propose a method to detect a pointing hand and to estimate its direction using multi-class classification based on machine learning from images captured by two cameras.

In the proposed method, classification scores are calculated in a sliding window for hand postures with different pointing directions. Detection of a pointing hand and estimation of the pointing direction are performed by interpolating the classification scores. Then, the interpolated classification scores obtained from two camera images are integrated. By using two cameras, our method not only can obtain 3-D hand positions but also can improve its accuracy by utilizing the difference of hand appearances between two camera images. Since hand pointing has largely different appearances according to viewpoints and difference of camera positions reduces the effect of complex background, integration of two camera information can be more effective than just using doubled size of information.

2 Classification of Hands with Different Pointing Directions

The basic principle of the proposed method is to divide the angle space of hand pointing into some classes, and to recognize a pointing hand and its direction by interpolating classification scores for different classes. Interpolation of classification scores enables hand pointing direction recognition with higher resolution than just classification into one class. In the proposed method, pointing hands in an image are detected and their yaw and pitch angles are estimated. Figure 1 shows the overview of the proposed method.

The proposed method consists of two phases: classification and integration. In this section, we describe classification of hands with different pointing directions

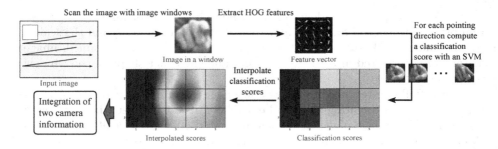

Fig. 1. Flow of the proposed method

and interpolation of classification scores. The integration phase will be described in Section 3.

2.1 Overview of Classification Score Computation

Classification score computation consists of the following four steps.

1. Scanning an image with sliding windows and correcting image distortion
2. Feature extraction
3. Computation of classification scores
4. Interpolation of classification scores and estimation of hand pointing direction

First, an input image is scanned with sliding image windows $W(x, y, s)$. The subsequent procedure will be performed per image in a window. Image distortion caused by perspective projection is corrected. Second, an input vector x is obtained by extracting Histograms of Oriented Gradient (HOG) features [2] from the image in the window. Third, a classification score $S(i, j)$ is computed for each pointing direction by using a classifier trained in advance. Fourth, classification scores are interpolated to improve the estimation resolution. Finally, if the maximum interpolated score is equal to or greater than a threshold λ, a pointing hand is detected and its direction (θ, ϕ) is estimated. We describe details of these steps in the rest of this section.

2.2 Scanning an Image with Sliding Windows and Correction of Image Distortion

To detect pointing hands over the input image, the whole input image is scanned by shifting a sliding window by a regular distance. To detect pointing hands regardless of individual variation of the size of a hand and distance to the hand, N different sizes of windows are used in scanning. The sizes of larger windows are determined by multiplying the size of the smallest window $N - 1$ times by a scale ratio a.

Since the shape of a window can vary due to image distortion on the projection plane, our method first determines the center position (x, y) and the scale s of the window while scanning. After the position and scale are obtained, image distortion is corrected around the position, and the exact shape of the window is determined.

Figure 2 illustrates an overview of how image distortion is corrected. Assuming the shape of a pointing hand to be a sphere, it looks larger when projected on a side of the image plane than when projected on the center of the plane as shown in Figure 2(a). Therefore, the distortion is corrected by projecting and rotating the window to the image center as shown in the Figure 2(b).

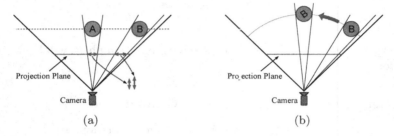

(a)   (b)

Fig. 2. Image distortion correction

2.3 Feature Extraction

A feature vector x is extracted from the image in the window $W(x, y, s)$. Here, HOG is used as a feature.

To equalize feature dimension, an image in a window is resized to a fixed size $w_p \times h_p$ pixels. Then a feature vector x is computed from the resized image.

2.4 Computation of Classification Scores

When a feature vector x in the window is obtained, classification of whether the vector belongs to each class with a different pointing direction is performed, and a classification score is computed for each direction.

First, we define classes for different hand pointing directions. The frontal direction is used as the origin in the angle space and the angle space is divided into $w_c \times h_c$ equal-sized rectangular regions. Columns of the classes are numbered $1, 2, \ldots, w_c$ from left to right. Likewise, rows of the classes are numbered $1, 2, \ldots, h_c$ from top to bottom. A class at i-th row and j-th column is denoted by $C_{i,j}$.

Let θ_{size} and ϕ_{size} be vertical and horizontal angle ranges included in a class. A class $C_{i,j}$ includes pointing hands with directions (θ, ϕ) satisfying the following constraints

$$\left(j - \frac{w_c}{2} - 1 \right) \theta_{\text{size}} \leq \theta < \left(j - \frac{w_c}{2} \right) \theta_{\text{size}}, \tag{1}$$

$$\left(i - \frac{h_c}{2} - 1 \right) \phi_{\text{size}} \leq \phi < \left(i - \frac{h_c}{2} \right) \phi_{\text{size}}, \tag{2}$$

where $\theta = 0°$ and $\phi = 0°$ mean a finger is pointing exactly to the center of a camera. θ increases when the hand rotates to the right, and ϕ increases when the hand rotates to the bottom.

We mention the parameters used in the experiment described later. In the integration phase, the angle difference caused by binocular disparity narrows an overlapping area of two cameras' fields of view. Therefore, $w_c > h_c$ is desirable to widen the view range. Moreover, $w_c h_c$ should be kept as small as possible to reduce the computation cost. From now on, we use $w_c = 5$, $h_c = 3$ in the example figures. Figure 3 shows an example of a class definition.

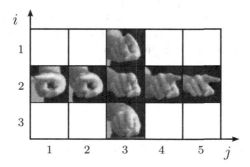

Fig. 3. An example of class definition. Example images are shown in several classes

Using the above-mentioned class definition, $w_c h_c$ classifiers, each of which classifies a feature vector into a class $C_{i,j}$ and the non-hand object class, are trained in advance. Linear support vector machines (SVMs) are used for training. The feature vector is classified by all those classifiers, and classification scores for all the classes are computed.

A classification score $S(i, j)$ for a class $C_{i,j}$ is defined as

$$S(i,j) = \frac{\boldsymbol{w}_{i,j}^{\mathsf{T}}\boldsymbol{x} + b_{i,j}}{||\boldsymbol{w}_{i,j}||}, \tag{3}$$

where $\boldsymbol{w}_{i,j}$ and $b_{i,j}$ are a weight vector and a bias parameter for $C_{i,j}$ respectively. $\boldsymbol{w}_{i,j}$ and $b_{i,j}$ are selected to satisfy $S(i,j) > 0$ if the feature vector $\boldsymbol{x}$ is in $C_{i,j}$. Thus the larger $S(i,j)$, the more the classifier is confident that $\boldsymbol{x}$ is of a pointing hand with the corresponding direction.

2.5   Interpolation of Classification Scores

If we classify the feature vector into the class with a maximum score, the resolution of hand pointing direction is limited to coarse and discrete values. Therefore, we improve the resolution by interpolating the classification scores.

Assuming the classification scores change smoothly, we use bicubic interpolation. Let k ($k > 1$) be a scale factor for interpolation, and $P(i', j')$ be an interpolated classification score using bicubic interpolation ($i' = 1, \ldots, kh_c, j' = 1, \ldots, kw_c$). A maximum score $\hat{S}$ of interpolated classification scores and its position $(\hat{i}, \hat{j})$ are obtained as

$$\hat{S} = \max \left\{ P(i', j'), i' = 1, \ldots, kh_c, j' = 1, \ldots, kw_c \right\}, \tag{4}$$

$$\hat{i} = \frac{\arg\max_{i'} \left\{ P(i', j'), i' = 1, \ldots, kh_c, j' = 1, \ldots, kw_c \right\}}{k}, \tag{5}$$

$$\hat{j} = \frac{\arg\max_{j'} \left\{ P(i', j'), i' = 1, \ldots, kh_c, j' = 1, \ldots, kw_c \right\}}{k}. \tag{6}$$

A pointing hand is detected in the window if the maximum interpolated score $\hat{S}$ is equal to or greater than a threshold λ. Otherwise the window is considered as a non-hand region. When the window is a hand pointing region, its horizontal and vertical directions (θ, ϕ) are estimated by

$$\theta = \left(\hat{j} - \frac{w_c}{2} \right) \theta_{\text{size}}, \tag{7}$$

$$\phi = \left(\hat{i} - \frac{h_c}{2} \right) \phi_{\text{size}}. \tag{8}$$

Figure 4 shows a typical example of classification score computation and interpolation.

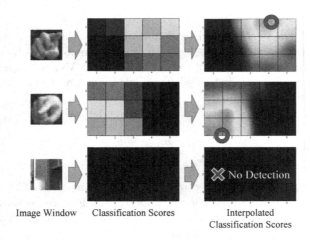

Image Window   Classification Scores   Interpolated
                                         Classification Scores

Fig. 4. A typical example of classification score computation and interpolation. Hand pointing direction is estimated using the position of the peak score drawn with a red circle

3   Three-Dimensional Hand Pointing Recognition Using Two Cameras

In the previous section, we described the algorithm for a single camera. In this section, we describe a method to improve the performance by using two cameras and integrating the classification scores.

It is obvious that the use of two cameras improves the accuracy because it doubles available sensor information. However, the accuracy may be further improved by using two cameras, for example, (i) when a hand is overlapping with a face and (ii) when a finger is pointing at around a camera.

When a hand is overlapping with a skin-colored region, gradients of a hand are weakened and unreliable as cues. In this situation hand recognition becomes difficult. However, even when a hand is overlapping with a skin-colored region from a camera, a non-overlapping hand can sometimes be seen from the other.

When a hand is pointing toward a camera, recognition is difficult because contours of an index finger (which has the most discriminative feature in hand pointing images) cannot be obtained. When using two camera information, such a problem can be alleviated by utilizing the angle difference from two cameras.

3.1   Layout of Two Cameras

Two cameras are horizontally placed as shown in Figure 5. Let b [mm] be a baseline length. b is set to be large enough to utilize the difference of hand appearances, and at the same time small enough to keep a wide field of view. Operation space of a user is where a hand can be captured with a sufficient size by both the cameras.

Fig. 5. Layout of two cameras

3.2   Classification and Interpolation for Each Camera

Before integration of two camera information, classification scores and their interpolation for both left and right camera images are calculated in advance.

The same algorithm described in Section 2 is applied to the two camera images independently.

3.3 Window Pair Selection Based on the Epipolar Constraint

To integrate two camera information, pairs of windows of left and right camera images which satisfy the epipolar constraint are selected. In this section, we describe a method to select pairs of windows considering the discreteness of window scale, image distortion correction and individual variation of the size of a hand. The procedure to select pairs of windows to be integrated is as follows:

1. Scan a left camera image with windows of all scales.
2. For each position and scale of the window for the left camera image, scan a right camera image with windows of appropriate scales
3. Select a pair of windows for left and right camera images

First, a left camera image is scanned with windows of all scales. Let (x_L, y_L) and s_L be the center position and scale of the window respectively. The scale s_L is a ratio of the size of the window to that of the smallest window.

Second, scales of windows for the right image are determined. Multiple scales for the right image are selected from $\{a^{-1}s_L, s_L, as_L\}$, where a is the scale ratio of window sizes, based on the difference between the distances from the left and right cameras to the position of the target point (the distances are transformed to depths in image distortion correction).

Third, the right camera image is scanned with windows of the selected scales. Let s_R be the current scale. The right camera image is scanned with windows which have the Y center equal to y_L. The scan range is calculated as follows. Let z_{s_R} [mm] be the optimal depth from a camera to a hand for the scale s_R. The depth for the smallest window z_1 is determined from the standard sizes of hands, and $z_{s_R} = z_1/s_R$ holds under the pinhole camera model. Here the scan range on the right image $[x_{\text{begin}}$ [pixel], x_{end} [pixel]) is written as

$$x_{\text{begin}} = x_L - \left\lfloor \frac{abf}{z_{s_R}} \right\rfloor, \tag{9}$$

$$x_{\text{end}} = x_L - \left\lfloor \frac{bf}{az_{s_R}} \right\rfloor, \tag{10}$$

where f [pixel] is the focal length and the origins of the images are at the center of the images.

Finally, a pair of windows for left and right camera images is selected. Let (x_R, y_R) be the center position of the window for the right image.

3.4 Integration of Two Camera Information

Integration of classification scores is performed on the selected pair of windows for the left and right images $W(x_L, y_L, s_L)$, $W(x_R, y_R, s_R)$. As a result of integration, the maximum classification score $\hat{S}$ and estimated direction (θ, ϕ) are obtained.

Let $P_L(i', j')$ and $P_R(i', j')$ be the interpolated classification scores calculated in the left and right windows respectively. Based on the centers of the windows, yaw angle difference $\Delta\theta$ between the windows is written as

$$\Delta\theta = \tan^{-1} \frac{(x_R - x_L)f}{x_L x_R + f^2}. \tag{11}$$

The sum of the interpolated scores is calculated considering the angle difference as

$$P(i', j') = \begin{cases} P_L(i', j' + \Delta j) + P_R(i', j') & (j' \le kw_c - 2\Delta j) \\ 0 & (\text{otherwise}) \end{cases}, \tag{12}$$

where k is a scale factor used in the interpolation, $i' = 1, 2, \ldots, kh_c$, $j' = 1, 2, \ldots, kw_c$ and

$$\Delta j = \text{round}\left(\frac{k\Delta\theta}{\theta_{\text{size}}}\right). \tag{13}$$

The maximum classification score $\hat{S}$ and estimated direction (θ, ϕ) are calculated from Equation (4), (5) and (6) in the same manner as that for a single camera. If the maximum integrated classification score is equal to or greater than a threshold λ, a pointing hand is detected in the pair of windows. When a pointing hand is detected, its direction is estimated as (θ, ϕ). Also, the 3-D position of the pointing hand is obtained as

$$X = \frac{b(x_L + x_R)}{x_L - x_R}, \ Y = \frac{by_L}{x_L - x_R}, \ Z = \frac{bf}{(x_L - x_R)}. \tag{14}$$

Figure 6 shows an overview of the integration process.

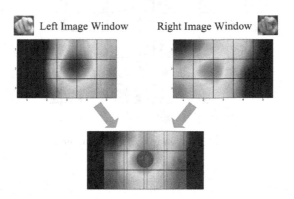
Left Image Window   Right Image Window

Fig. 6. An overview of integration of two camera information. Hand pointing direction is estimated using the peak classification score

4   Evaluation Experiment

We conducted an experiment to evaluate the performance of the proposed method. We evaluated recognition rates and false positives per image (FPPI) under various conditions for comparison. The experiment was conducted with two types of the numbers of cameras (single camera versus two cameras), two types of numbers of classes $((w_c, h_c) = (5, 3), (6, 4))$ and various peak threshold values λ.

4.1   Experimental Setup

The hand pointing training set consisted of pointing right hand images that were collected from four subjects of 21–22 years old students. Since our method does not support roll angles of hand pointing, subjects were asked to maintain pointing posture with their back of the hand facing upward. The test set consisted of 2,645 stereo images that were collected from the same four subjects as in the training set. The training set consisted of 66,825 positive hand images in total and 1,835 negative non-hand images. The number of the hand images were increased by translating 7,425 source images by one pixel in eight directions. When evaluating the performance for the images of a subject, the hand images of the subject were excluded from the training set (i.e. the training set for a subject did not contain any examples for the subject). An example of hand images in the training set is shown in Figure 7. The numbers of the hand images in the training set varied according to the subjects and the angle range. The number of the source images for each subject and number of classes is summarized in Table 1.

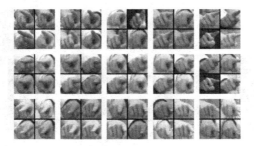

Fig. 7. An example of hand images

The hand images used in the training and test set were captured using a system specially made to obtain ground truth for hand pointing directions. The system consists of a rack and a Kinect sensor which is downwardly installed on top of the rack and can obtain direction of hand pointing.

This experiment was performed under the fluorescent lighting condition as in usual indoor environment. The baseline b was set to 400 mm. The horizontal

Table 1. The numbers of the source images in the training set. The subjects are identified as A, B, C and D.

$w_p \times h_p$	A	B	C	D
5×3	4827	4961	5026	4515
6×4	5586	5682	5760	5247

angle of view of cameras was 32.4°. The distance between the cameras and a user was around 2 m.

The size of the test set images were 640 × 480 pixels. The number of the sizes of sliding windows N was set to five. The scale ratio a was 1.2. Scaling of sliding windows is realized in a relative sense by resizing input images. The shift amount for window scanning was four pixels. Windows in which a pointing hand was detected were aggregated if they were largely overlapping and estimated directions were similar to each other. The image size for HOG feature extraction was 40 × 40 pixels (which was the same as the absolute fixed size of a sliding window). HOGs were computed with the cell size of 8 × 8 pixels and block size of 2 × 2 cells. The size of the feature dimension was 576. The angle range included in a class was $\theta_{\text{size}} = 10°$, $\phi_{\text{size}} = 13°$ when $(w_c, h_c) = (5, 3)$, $\theta_{\text{size}} = 9°$, and $\phi_{\text{size}} = 10°$ when $(w_c, h_c) = (6, 4)$.

We defined the evaluation criteria as follows. Recognition rates were defined as the ratio of a number of successful recognition to a number of hand pointing regions in the test set. Recognition was considered as successful if it satisfied the following conditions: (i) the relative error of the detected position was small and (ii) the error of the estimated direction was within α. The condition (i) can be written as follows:

$$|x - X| \leq \delta \wedge |y - Y| \leq \delta \wedge |x + w - X - W| \leq \delta \wedge |y + h - Y - H| \leq \delta \quad (15)$$

where (x, y), w and h denote the position, width and height of a detected window respectively, (X, Y), W and H denote those of the ground truth and $\delta = 0.3(\min(w, W) + \min(h, H))/2$. α was set to 10° unless otherwise specified. Unsuccessful recognition was considered as false detection.

Recognition was performed with several thresholds λ which were common to the data from all the subjects. Mean values of recognition rates and FPPIs for the data from each subject with the same threshold value were used as the overall recognition rates and FPPIs respectively.

Let λ^* be a threshold whose FPPI was nearest to 1. By using λ^* as a candidate threshold, we measured the recognition rates and FPPIs per subject when $\lambda = \lambda^*$. We also measured the recognition rates with varying angle error tolerances α when $\lambda = \lambda^*$.

4.2   Results and Discussion

Figure 9 shows some examples of recognition results. A rectangle represents the position of a detected pointing hand. An arrow drawn from a center of the rectangle represents the estimated pointing direction. From the results, we can see that the hand pointing was detected and its directions were estimated correctly.

Figure 9(a) shows Receiver Operating Characteristic (ROC) curves. Figure 9(b) shows the results with varying angle error tolerances α and the threshold of λ^*. Table 2 shows the result per subject with the threshold of λ^* and mean FPPIs was around 1.

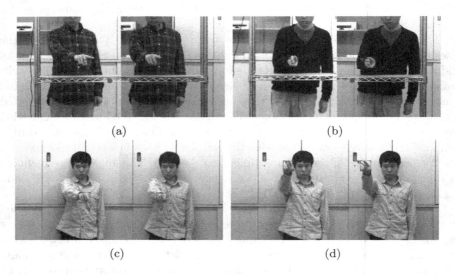

(a)   (b)

(c)   (d)

Fig. 8. Recognition result examples

The larger number of classes $((w_c, h_c) = (6, 4))$ gave better performance than the smaller one (5×3). Recognition rates were 42.83% when using a single camera and 72.80% when using two cameras, at around FPPI 1 with the number of classes 6×4. The accuracy was greatly improved by integrating two camera information.

Integration of two camera information improved the accuracy, but the recognition rate was still around 70%, which may be insufficient for the use in real applications. The accuracy will be improved by using information of multiple video frames. The detection rate, which is equal to the recognition rate regardless of the angle error tolerance α, was 79.03% when using two cameras and the number of classes 6×4. From Table 2, we can see that there were large gaps between the subjects. The reason may be that the number of subjects was small and thus sufficient variation could not be obtained. For reference, when the training set included the same data as in the test set, the recognition rate was 94.8% at around 1 FPPI when using two cameras and the number of classes 5×3. This result showed that the upper limit performance of the proposed method was much higher and therefore the accuracy may improve by increasing the variation of training data.

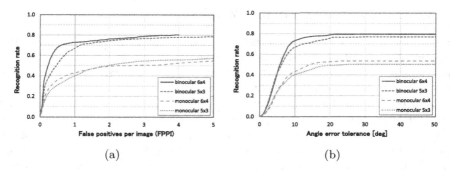

Fig. 9. (a) ROC curves with the angle error tolerance α of $10°$. (b) Recognition rates and angle error tolerances α with the threshold of λ^* (a threshold when FPPI was around 1). Numbers in legends denote the number of classes $(w_c \times h_c)$.

Table 2. Recognition rates and FPPIs with the threshold of λ^*

# of cameras	# of classes	Subject	Rec. rate [%]	FPPI
Single	5×3	A	27.51	2.00
		B	19.47	0.28
		C	38.12	0.42
		D	74.55	1.33
		Ave.	**39.91**	**1.01**
	6×4	A	36.11	1.72
		B	13.88	0.58
		C	49.39	0.75
		D	71.96	1.00
		Ave.	**42.83**	**1.01**
Two	5×3	A	86.60	1.02
		B	27.43	0.56
		C	62.53	0.68
		D	88.92	1.63
		Ave.	**66.37**	**0.97**
	6×4	A	94.09	1.23
		B	28.47	1.02
		C	84.24	0.75
		D	84.39	0.97
		Ave.	**72.80**	**0.99**

The mean execution time for one frame was 206 ms when $(w_c, h_c) = (5, 3)$ and 316 ms when $(w_c, h_c) = (6, 4)$. The computation was executed on a desktop PC with Intel Core-i5 2400 CPU with multiple threads. Though this execution time was not sufficient for real-time applications, it can be improved by using hand tracking as well as the accuracy.

5   Conclusions and Future Works

In this paper, we proposed a method for hand pointing recognition using two cameras. The result of the experiment showed that correct hand detection and direction estimation were realized, and that the accuracy was greatly improved by integrating two camera information.

Future works include accuracy improvement. The accuracy was still not sufficient to realize gesture UI applications using hand pointing operation. To improve it, we will increase the number of the training samples and use information of multiple consecutive frames by hand tracking. Furthermore, performance investigation in various environment is also needed. By training classifiers using a dataset including environmental variation, we should investigate whether or not our method can be used in various environment. In addition, to realize comfortable UI applications, operation space should be enlarged by using, for example, fish-eye lenses. Future works also include creation of a gesture UI application using hand pointing.

References

1. Athitsos, V., Sclaroff, S.: Estimating 3d hand pose from a cluttered image. In: CVPR, vol. 2, pp. 432–439 (2003)
2. Dalal, N., Triggs, B.: Histograms of oriented gradients for human detection. In: CVPR, pp. 886–893 (2005)
3. Dominguez, S., Keaton, T., Sayed, A.H.: A robust finger tracking method for multimodal wearable computer interfacing. IEEE Trans. on Multimedia 8(5), 956–972 (2006)
4. Hu, K., Canavan, S., Yin, L.: Hand pointing estimation for human computer interaction based on two orthogonal-views. In: ICPR, pp. 3760–3763 (2010)
5. Huang, C., Ding, X., Fang, C.: Head pose estimation based on random forests for multiclass classification. In: ICPR, pp. 934–937 (2010)
6. Huang, D.Y., Hu, W.C., Chang, S.H.: Gabor filter-based hand-pose angle estimation for hand gesture recognition under varying illumination. Expert Systems with Applications 38(5), 6031–6042 (2011)
7. Leap Motion. https://www.leapmotion.com/
8. Nakamura, T., Takahashi, S., Tanaka, J.: One-finger interaction for ubiquitous environment. In: ICIS, pp. 267–272 (2010)
9. Rogez, G., Rihan, J., Ramalingam, S., Orrite, C., Torr, P.H.S.: Randomized trees for human pose detection. In: CVPR, pp. 1–8 (2008)
10. Sato, Y., Saito, M., Koike, H.: Real-time input of 3d pose and gestures of a user's hand and its applications for hci. In: IEEE VR, pp. 79–86 (2001)
11. Schick, A., van de Camp, F., Ijsselmuiden, J., Stiefelhagen, R.: Extending touch: Towards interaction with large-scale surfaces. In: ITS, pp. 117–124 (2009)
12. Stenger, B., Thayananthan, A., Torr, P.H.S., Cipolla, R.: Model-based hand tracking using a hierarchical bayesian filter. IEEE Trans. on PAMI 28(9), 1372–1384 (2006)
13. Vogel, D., Balakrishnan, R.: Distant freehand pointing and clicking on very large, high resolution displays. In: UIST, pp. 33–42 (2005)
14. Yuan, Q., Thangali, A., Ablavsky, V., Sclaroff, S.: Parameter sensitive detectors. In: CVPR, pp. 1–6 (2007)

Video-Based Action Detection Using Multiple Wearable Cameras

Kang Zheng[(✉)], Yuewei Lin, Youjie Zhou, Dhaval Salvi, Xiaochuan Fan,
Dazhou Guo, Zibo Meng, and Song Wang

Department of Computer Science and Engineering, University of South Carolina,
Room 3D19, 315 Main Street, Columbia, SC 29208, USA
{zheng37,lin59,zhou42,salvi,fan23,guo22,mengz,songwang}@email.sc.edu,
songwang@cec.sc.edu

Abstract. This paper is focused on developing a new approach for
video-based action detection where a set of temporally synchronized
videos are taken by multiple wearable cameras from different and varying views and our goal is to accurately localize the starting and ending
time of each instance of the actions of interest in such videos. Compared
with traditional approaches based on fixed-camera videos, this new approach incorporates the visual attention of the camera wearers and allows
for the action detection in a larger area, although it brings in new challenges such as unconstrained motion of cameras. In this approach, we
leverage the multi-view information and the temporal synchronization
of the input videos for more reliable action detection. Specifically, we
detect and track the focal character in each video and conduct action
recognition only for the focal character in each temporal sliding window.
To more accurately localize the starting and ending time of actions, we
develop a strategy that may merge temporally adjacent sliding windows
when detecting durative actions, and non-maximally suppress temporally
adjacent sliding windows when detecting momentary actions. Finally we
propose a voting scheme to integrate the detection results from multiple videos for more accurate action detection. For the experiments, we
collect a new dataset of multiple wearable-camera videos that reflect the
complex scenarios in practice.

Keywords: Action detection · Multi-view videos · Focal character ·
Wearable cameras

1 Introduction

Video-based action detection, i.e., detecting the starting and ending time of
the actions of interest, plays an important role in video surveillance, monitoring, anomaly detection, human computer interaction and many other computer-
vision related applications. Traditionally, action detection in computer vision

---

K. Zheng and Y. Lin — Equal contribution.

© Springer International Publishing Switzerland 2015
L. Agapito et al. (Eds.): ECCV 2014 Workshops, Part I, LNCS 8925, pp. 727–741, 2015.
DOI: 10.1007/978-3-319-16178-5_51

is based on the videos collected from one or more fixed cameras, from which motion features are extracted and then fed to a trained classifier to determine the underlying action class [25,31,32,35]. However, using fixed-camera videos has two major limitations: 1) fixed cameras can only cover specific locations in a limited area, and 2) when multiple persons are present, it is difficult to decide the character of interest and his action from fixed-camera videos, especially with mutual occlusions in a crowded scene. In this paper, we consider a completely different approach where a set of temporally synchronized videos are collected from multiple wearable cameras and our main goal is to integrate the information from multiple wearable-camera videos for better action detection.

This new approach is applicable to many important scenarios. In a public crowded area, such as an airport, we can get all the security officers and other staff to wear a camera when they walk around for monitoring and detecting abnormal activities. In a prison, we can get each prisoner to wear a camera to collect videos, from which we may detect their individual activities, interactive activities, and group activities. Over a longer term, we may use these videos to infer the underlying social network among the prisoners to increase the security of the prison. In a kindergarten, we can get the teachers and the kids to wear a camera for recording what each of them sees daily, from which we can analyze kids' activities for finding kids with possible social difficulties, such as autism. We can see that, for some applications, camera wearers and action performers are different group of people, while for other applications, camera wearers and action performers can overlap. In our approach, we assume that the videos collected from multiple wearable cameras are temporally synchronized, which can be easily achieved by integrating a calibrated clock in each camera.

The proposed approach well addresses the limitation of the traditional approaches that use fixed cameras. 1) Camera wearers can move as he wants and therefore the videos can be collected in a much larger area; 2) Each collected video better reflects the attention of the wearer – the focal character is more likely to be located at the center of the view over a period of time and an abnormal activity may draw many camera-wearers' attention. However, this new approach also introduces new challenges compared to the approaches based on fixed cameras. For example, each camera is moving with the wearer and the view angle of the camera is totally unconstrained and time varying, while many available action recognition methods require the camera-view consistency between the training and testing data. In this paper, we leverage the multi-view information and the temporal synchronization of the input videos for more reliable action detection.

We adopt the temporal sliding-window technique to convert the action detection problem in long streaming videos to an action recognition problem over windowed short video clips. In each video clip, we first compensate the camera motions using the improved trajectories [32], followed by focal character detection by adapting the state-of-the-art detection and tracking algorithms [15,28]. After that, we extract the motion features around the focal character for action recognition. To more accurately localize the starting and ending time of an action, we develop a strategy that may merge temporally adjacent sliding windows when detecting durative actions, and non-maximally suppress temporally adjacent sliding windows when detecting momentary actions. Finally, we develop a majority-voting technique to integrate the action detection results from multiple videos. To evaluate the performance of the proposed method, we conduct experiments on a newly collected dataset consisting of multiple wearable-camera videos with temporal synchronization. The main contributions in this paper are: 1) a new approach for action detection based on multiple wearable-camera videos. 2) a new dataset consisting of multiple wearable-camera videos for performance evaluation.

2   Related Work

Video-based action detection can usually be reduced to an action recognition problem, when the starting and ending frames of the action are specified – an action classifier is usually used to decide whether these frames describe the action. Three techniques have been used for this reduction: the sliding-window technique [11], which divides a long streaming video into a sequence of temporally overlapped short video clips, the tracking-based technique [18,38], which localizes human actions by person tracking, and the voting-based technique [2,38], which uses local spatiotemporal features to vote for the location parameters of an action. The sliding-window technique could be improved by using more efficient search strategy [39].

Most of the existing work on action recognition uses a single-view video taken by fixed cameras. Many motion-based feature descriptors have been proposed [1] for action recognition, such as space time interest points (STIPs) [20] and dense trajectories [31]. Extended from 2D features, 3D-SIFT [29] and HOG3D [19] have also been used for action recognition. Local spatiotemporal features [10] have been shown to be successful for action recognition and dense trajectories achieve best performance on a variety of datasets [31]. However, many of these features are sensitive to viewpoint changes – if the test videos are taken from the views that are different from the training videos, these features may lead to poor action recognition performance.

To address this problem, many view invariant methods have been developed for action recognition [17,27,41]. Motion history volumes (MHV) [34], histograms of 3D joint locations (HOJ3D) [36] and hankelets [22] are view invariant features. Temporal self-similarity descriptors show high stability under view changes [17]. Liu *et al.* [23] developed an approach to extract bag-of-bilingual-words (BoBW) to recognize human actions from different views. Recent studies show that pose estimation can benefit action recognition [37], e.g., key poses are very useful for recognizing actions from various views [6,24]. In [33], an exemplar-based Hidden Markov Model (HMM) is proposed for free view action recognition.

In multi-view action recognition, a set of videos are taken from different views by different cameras. There are basically two types of fusion scheme to combine the multi-view videos for action recognition: feature-level fusion and decision-level fusion. Feature-level fusion generally employs bag-of-words model to combine features from multiple views [40]. Decision-level fusion simply combines the classification scores from all the views [26]. 3D action recognition approaches usually fuse the visual information by obtaining 3D body poses from 2D body poses in terms of binary silhouettes [5]. Most existing work on multi-view action recognition are based on videos taken by fixed cameras. As mentioned earlier, they suffer from the problems of limited spatial coverage and degraded performance in crowded scenes.

Also related to this paper is the egocentric video analysis and action recognition. For example, in [13,14] egocentric videos are used to recognize the daily actions and predict the gaze of the wearer. Similar to our work, they also take the videos from wearable cameras for action recognition. However, they are completely different from our work – in this paper, we recognize the actions of the performers present in the videos while the egocentric action recognition aims to recognize the actions of the camera wearers.

3   Proposed Method

3.1   Problem Description and Method Overview

We have a group of people, named *(camera) wearers*, each of whom wears a camera over head, such as Google Glasses or GoPro. Meanwhile, we have a group of people, named *performers*, each of whom performs actions over time. There may be overlap between wearers and performers, i.e., some wearers are also performers and vice versa. Over a period of time, each camera records a video that reflects what its wearer sees and the videos from all the cameras are temporally synchronized. We assume that at any time each wearer focuses his attention on at most one "focal character", who is one of the performers. The wearer may move as he wants during the video recording to target better to a performer or switch his attention to another performer. An example of such videos is shown in Fig. 1, where five videos from five wearers are shown in five rows respectively. For long streaming videos, the focal character in each video may change over time and the focal character may perform different actions at different time. Our goal of action detection is to accurately localize the starting and ending time of each instance of the actions of interest performed by a focal character by fusing the information from all the videos.

In this paper, we use the sliding-window technique to convert the action detection problem on a long streaming video into an action recognition problem on short video clips. Following sliding windows, a long-streaming video is temporally divided into a sequence of overlapped short video clips and the features from each clip are then fed into a trained classifier to determine whether a certain action occurs in the video clip. If yes, the action is detected with starting and ending frames aligned with the corresponding sliding window. However, in practice, instances of a same action or different actions may show substantially different duration time and it is impossible to exhaustively try different sliding-window lengths to match all possible action durations. In Section 3.4, we will introduce a new merging and suppression strategy to the temporally adjacent sliding windows to address this problem.

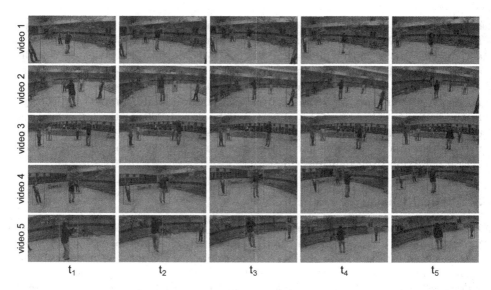

Fig. 1. An example of the videos taken by five wearable cameras from different views. Each row shows a sequence of frames from one video (i.e., from one wearer's camera) and each column shows the five frames with the same time stamp in the five videos respectively. In each frame, the focal character is highlighted in a red box and the blue boxes indicate the camera wearers, who wear a GoPro camera over the head to produce these five videos. Some wearers are out of the view, e.g., a wearer is not present in the video taken by his own camera. The same focal character is performing a *jump* action in these five videos.

When multiple temporally synchronized videos are taken for the same focal character, we can integrate the action detection results on all the videos for more reliable action detections. In this paper, we identify the focal character on each video, track its motion, extract its motion features, and feed the extracted features into trained classifiers for action detection on each video. In Section 3.5, we will introduce a voting scheme to integrate the action detection results from multiple synchronized videos.

Moving cameras pose new challenges in action recognition because the extracted features may mix the desired foreground (focal character) motion and undesired background (camera) motion. In this paper, we remove camera motions by following the idea in [32]. Specifically, we first extract the SURF features [3] and match them between neighboring frames using nearest neighbor search. Optical flow is also used to establish a dense correspondence between neighboring frames. Finally we estimate the homography between frames by RANSAC [16] and rectify each frame to remove camera motions.

After removing the camera motions, on each video clip we extract the dense trajectories and its corresponding descriptors using the algorithms introduced in [31,32]. Specifically, trajectories are built by tracking feature points detected in a dense optical flow field [12] and then the local motion descriptors HOG [7], HOF [21] and MBH [8] are computed and concatenated as the input for the action classifier for both training and testing. We only consider trajectories with a length of no less than 15 frames. We use the standard bag-of-feature-words approach to encode the extracted features – for each feature descriptor, we use K-means to construct a codebook from $100,000$ randomly sampled trajectory features. The number of entries in each codebook is $4,000$. In the following, we discuss in detail the major steps in the proposed method, i.e., focal character detection, temporal merging and suppression for action detection and integrated action detection from multiple videos.

3.2   Focal Character Detection

By detecting the focal character, we can focus only on his motion features for more reliable action recognition. As discussed earlier, videos taken by wearable cameras facilitate the focal character detection since the wearers usually focus their attentions on their respective focal characters. In this paper we take the following three steps to detect the focal character in each video clip constructed by the sliding windows.

1. Detecting the persons in each video frame using the state-of-the-art human detectors [15], for which we use a publicly available software package[1].
2. Tracking the motion of the detected persons along the video clip using the multiple-object tracking algorithm [28] for which we also use a publicly available software package[2]. Given missing detections on some frames (e.g., red dashed box in Fig. 2), we need to link short human tracklets (e.g., solid curves in Fig. 2) into longer tracks (e.g., the long red track in Fig. 2).
3. Ranking human tracks in terms of a proposed attention score function and selecting the track with the highest score as the focal character, e.g., the long red track in Fig. 2.

In the following, we elaborate on the tracklet linking and the attention score function.

Tracklet Linking Let $\{T_1, \cdots, T_N\}$ be the N tracklets obtained by the human detection/tracking. Each tracklet is a continuous sequence of detected bounding boxes, i.e., $T_i = \left\{B_t^i\right\}_{t=t_1}^{t_2}$ where B_t^i represents 2D coordinates of the 4 corners of the bounding box in frame t, and t_1 and t_2 indicate the starting and the ending frames of this tracklet. The tracklet linking task can be formulated as a Generalized Linear Assignment (GLA) problem [9]:

---

[1] http://www.cs.berkeley.edu/~rbg/latent/index.html
[2] http://people.csail.mit.edu/hpirsiav/

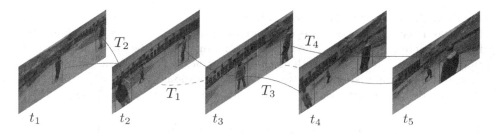

Fig. 2. An illustration of the focal character detection.

$$\min_{X} \sum_{i=1}^{N} \sum_{j=1}^{N} D_{ij} X_{ij}$$

$$s.t. \sum_{i=1}^{N} X_{ij} \leq 1; \sum_{j=1}^{N} X_{ij} \leq 1; X_{ij} \in \{0,1\} \tag{1}$$

where $X_{ij} = 1$ indicates the linking of the last frame of T_i to the first frame of T_j and D_{ij} is a distance measure between two tracklets T_i and T_j when $X_{ij} = 1$.

Specifically, we define $D_{ij} = D_P(T_i, T_j) \times D_A(T_i, T_j)$ where D_P and D_A are the location and appearance distances between T_i and T_j respectively. The location distance D_P is defined by the Euclidean distance between the spatiotemporal centers of T_i and T_j in terms of their bounding boxes. The appearance distance D_A is defined by the sum of χ^2 distances between their intensity histograms, over all three color channels inside all their bounding boxes.

The GLA problem defined in Eq. (1) is an NP-Complete problem [9] and in this paper, we use a greedy algorithm to find a locally optimal solution [9]. By tracklet linking, we can interpolate the missing bounding boxes and achieve longer human tracks along the windowed video clip.

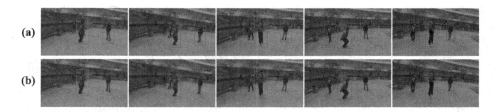

Fig. 3. An example of human detection and focal character detection. (a) Human detection results using Felzenszwalb detectors [15]. (b) Detected focal character.

Focal Character Detection. For each human track, we define an attention-score function to measure its likelihood of being the focal character for the wearer. Specifically, we quantify and integrate two attention principles here: 1) the focal character is usually located inside the view of the camera wearer and the wearer usually moves his eyes (therefore his camera) to keep tracking the focal character. Mapped to the detected human tracks, the track of the focal character tends to be longer than the other tracks; 2) the focal character is usually located at a similar location in the view along a video clip. Based on these, we define the attention score $A(T)$ for a human track $T = \{B_t\}_{t=t_1}^{t_2}$ as

$$A(T) = \sum_{t=t_1}^{t_2} \exp\left\{ -\left(\frac{(\bar{B}_{tx} - \mu_{Tx})^2}{\sigma_x^2} + \frac{(\bar{B}_{ty} - \mu_{Ty})^2}{\sigma_y^2} \right) \right\} \tag{2}$$

where (μ_{Tx}, μ_{Ty}) denotes the mean values of track T along the x and y axes, respectively, $(\bar{B}_{tx}, \bar{B}_{ty})$ denotes the center of the bounding box B_t in the track T at the frame t, and σ_x and σ_y control the level of the center bias, which we empirically set to $\frac{1}{12}$ and $\frac{1}{4}$ respectively in all our experiments. Given a set of human tracks in the video clip, we simply pick the one with the highest attention score as the track of the focal character, as shown in Fig. 3.

3.3   Action Recognition

In this section, we consider the action recognition on a short video clip generated by sliding windows. For both training and testing, we extract dense trajectory features only inside the bounding boxes of the focal character. This way, other irrelevant motion features in the background and associated to the non-focal characters will be excluded, with which we can achieve more accurate action recognition. Considering the large feature variation of a human action, we use a state-of-the-art sparse coding technique for action recognition [4]. In the training stage, we simply collect all the training instances of each action (actually their feature vectors) as the bases for the action class. In the testing stage, we extract the motion-feature vector of the focal character and sparsely reconstruct it using the bases of each action class. The smaller the reconstruction error, the higher the likelihood that this test video clip belongs to the action class. Specifically, let $\mathcal{T}$ be the feature vector extracted from a testing video clip. The likelihood of $\mathcal{T}$ belongs to action i is

$$L(i|\mathcal{T}) = \frac{1}{\sqrt{2\pi\sigma^2}} \exp\left(\frac{-\|\mathcal{T} - \tilde{\mathcal{T}}_i\|^2}{2\sigma^2} \right). \tag{3}$$

where $\tilde{\mathcal{T}}_i = \mathcal{A}_i \mathbf{x}^*$ denotes the sparse coding reconstruction of feature vector $\mathcal{T}$ using the bases $\mathcal{A}_i$ in action class i and $\mathbf{x}^*$ is the linear combination coefficients of the sparse coding representation which can be derived by solving the following minimization problem:

$$\mathbf{x}^* = \min_{\mathbf{x}}\{\|\mathcal{T} - \mathcal{A}_i\mathbf{x}\|^2 + \alpha\|\mathbf{x}\|_0\}. \tag{4}$$

3.4 Action Detection

As mentioned before, the video clips used for action recognition are produced by sliding windows. In the simplest case, when an action is recognized in a video clip, we can take the corresponding sliding window (with the starting and ending frames) as the action detection result. However, in practice, different actions, or even the same action, may show different duration time. In particular, some actions, such as "handwave", "jump", "run" and "walk", are usually durative, while other actions, such as "sitdown", "standup", and "pickup", are usually momentary. Clearly, it is impossible to try all possible length sliding windows to detect actions with different durations. In this paper we propose a new strategy that conducts further temporal window merging or non-maximal suppression to detect actions with different durations.

We propose a three-step algorithm to temporally localize the starting and ending frames of each instance of the actions of interest. First, to accommodate the duration variation of each action, we try sliding windows with different lengths. Different from a momentary action that is usually completed in a short or limited time, a durative action may be continuously performed for an indefinite time. Thus, it is difficult to pick a small number of sliding-window lengths to well cover all possible durations of a durative action. Fortunately, durative actions are usually made up of repetitive action periods and the duration of each period is short and limited. For example, a durative "walk" action contains a sequence of repeated "footsteps". For a durative action, we select sliding-window lengths to cover the duration of the action period instead of the whole action.

Second, for each considered action class, we combine its action likelihood estimated on the video clips resulting from sliding windows with different lengths, e.g., l_1, l_2 and l_3 in Fig. 4, where the value of the curve labeled "window-length l_1" at time t is the action likelihood estimated on the video clip in the time window $[t - \frac{l_1}{2}, t + \frac{l_1}{2}]$ (centered at t with length l_1), using the approach we introduced above. To estimate a unified action likelihood at time t, a basic principle is that we pick the largest value at time t among all the curves, as shown by the point A in Fig. 4. In this example, l_1 is the most likely length of this action (or action period) at t. As a result, we can obtain the unified action likelihood curve $(U(t), S(t))$, where $U(t)$ is the maximum action likelihood over all tested different-length sliding windows centered at t and $S(t)$ is the corresponding window length that leads to $U(t)$.

Finally, based on the unified action likelihood (U, S), we perform a temporal merging/suppression strategy to better localize the starting and ending frames of the considered action. For a durative action, each sliding window may correspond to one of its action period. Our basic idea is to merge adjacent sliding windows with high action likelihood for durative action detection. Specifically, this merging operation is implemented by filtering out all the sliding windows with $U(t) < T_h$, where T_h is a preset threshold. This filtering actually leads to a set of temporally disjoint intervals in which all the t satisfy $U(t) \geq T_h$. For each of these intervals, say $[t_1, t_2]$, we take the temporal interval $[t_1 - \frac{S(t_1)}{2}, t_2 + \frac{S(t_2)}{2}]$ as a detection of the action. For a momentary action, we expect that it does not

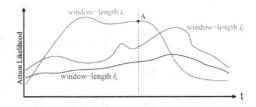

Fig. 4. An illustration of the estimated action likelihood using different-length sliding windows.

occur repetitively without any transition. We perform a temporal non-maximum suppression for detecting a momentary action – if $U(t) \geq T_h$ and $U(t)$ is a local maximum at t, we take the temporal interval $[t - \frac{S(t)}{2}, t + \frac{S(t)}{2}]$ as a detection of the action. This way, on each video, we detect actions of interest in the form of a set of temporal intervals, as illustrated in Fig. 5 where each detected action is labeled by red font.

3.5 Integrated Action Detection from Multiple Videos

In this section, we integrate the action detection results from multiple synchronized videos taken by different wearers to improve the accuracy of action detection. The basic idea is to use majority voting over all the videos to decide the underlying action class at each time. Note that here it is required that these videos are taken for a same focal character. As illustrated in Fig. 5, we take the following steps.

1. Temporally divide all the videos into uniform-length segments, e.g., segments (a) and (b) that are separated by the vertical dashed lines in Fig. 5. In this paper, we select the segment length to be 100 frames.
2. For each segment, e.g., segment (a) in Fig. 5, we examine its overlap with the temporal intervals of the detected actions in each video and label it with the corresponding action label or "no-action" when there is no overlap with any detected action intervals. For example, segment (a) is labeled "run" in Videos 1, 3, and 5, "walk" in Video 2, and "no-action" in Video 4.
3. For the considered segment, we perform a majority voting to update the action labels over all the videos. For example, on three out of five videos, segment (a) is labeled "run" in Fig. 5. We simply update the label of segment (a) to "run" on all the videos. When two or more actions are tied as majority, we pick the one with the maximum likelihood. For example, segment (c) is labeled "walk" on two videos and "run" on two other videos. We update the label of this segment to "run" on all the videos because "run" shows a higher likelihood.
4. After updating action labels for all the segments, update the action detection results by merging adjacent segments with the same labels, as shown in the last row of Fig. 5.

After these steps, the action detection results are the same for all the videos.

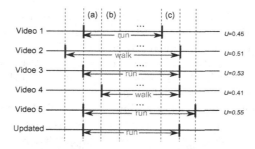

Fig. 5. An illustration of integrating action detection from multiple videos.

4 Experiments

We collect a new video dataset for evaluating the performance of the proposed method. In our experiment, we try two sliding-window lengths: 50 and 100 for computing the unified action likelihood. For comparison, we also try the traditional approach, where the motion features are extracted over the whole video without the focal character detection and the filtering of non-relevant features. Other than that, the comparison method is the same as the proposed method, including the type of the extracted features [31,32], camera motion compensation [32], and the application of sliding windows. For both the proposed method and the comparison method, we also examine the performance improvement by integrating the action detection results from multiple videos.

4.1 Data Collection

Popular video datasets that are currently used for evaluating action detection consist of either single-view videos with camera movement or multi-view videos taken by fixed cameras. In this work, we collect a new dataset that consists of temporally synchronized videos taken by multiple wearable cameras.

Specifically, we get 5 persons who are both performers and wearers and one more person who is only a performer. They perform 7 actions: *handwave, jump, pickup, run, sit-down, stand-up* and *walk* in an outdoor environment. Each of the 5 wearers mounts a GoPro camera over the head. We arrange the video recording in a way that the 6 performers alternately play as the focal character for the other people. As the focal character, each person plays the 7 actions once in the video recording. This way, we collected 5 temporally synchronized videos, each of which contains $5 \times 7 = 35$ instances of actions performed by 5 persons, excluding the wearer himself. The average duration of each action is about 18.4 seconds. We annotate these 5 videos for the focal characters and the starting and ending frames of each instance of the actions of interest, using the open video annotation tool of VATIC [30]. In our experiments, we use these 5 videos for testing the action detection method.

For training, we collect a set of video clips from two different views in a more controlled way. Each clip contains only one instance of the actions of interest.

Specifically, we get the same 6 persons to perform each of the 7 actions two or three times. In total we collected 204 video clips as the training data. The average length of the video clips in the training data is 11.5 seconds. The camera wearers are randomly selected from the five persons who are not the performer and the wearer may move his head to focus the attention on the performer in the recording. All the training videos (clips) are annotated with the focal characters for feature extraction and classifier training. Figure 6 shows sample frames of each action class from different cameras in our new dataset.

handwave   jump   pickup   run   sit-down   stand-up   walk

Fig. 6. Sample frames in the collected videos with annotated focal characters.

4.2   Independent Detection of Each Action

In this section, we conduct an experiment to detect each action independent of other actions. Specifically, we set the threshold T_h to 100 different values at the s-percentile of $U(t)$ over the entire video, i.e., $U(t) > T_h$ on $s\%$ of frames, where s continuously increases one by one from 1 to 100. Under each selected value of T_h, we perform temporal merging/suppression to detect each action independently. For each detected instance of an action (a temporal interval, e.g., D), if there exists an annotated ground-truth instance of the same action, e.g., G, with a temporal overlap $TO = \frac{|D \bigcap G|}{|D \bigcup G|}$, that is larger than $\frac{1}{8}$, we count this detection D to be a true positive. This way we can calculate the *precision*, *recall* and the *F-score* $= \frac{2 \times precision \times recall}{precision + recall}$. We pick the best *F-score* over all 100 selections of the threshold T_h for performance evaluation. From Table 1, we can see that the proposed method outperforms the comparison method on 6 out of 7 actions as well as the average performance. Note that in this experiment, the detected actions are allowed to temporally overlap with each other and therefore the integrated action detection technique proposed in Section 3.5 is not applicable. The performance reported in Table 1 is the average one over all the 5 videos.

4.3   Non-Overlap Action Detection

On the 5 collected long streaming videos, there is only one focal character at any time and the focal character can only perform one single action at any time. In this section, we enforce this constraint by keeping detecting at most one

Table 1. Performance (best *F-score*) of the proposed method and the comparison method when independently detecting each of the 7 actions on the collected multiple wearable-camera videos.

Methods	*handwave*	*jump*	*pickup*	*run*	*sitdown*	*standup*	*walk*	**Average**
Comparison	47.5%	48.0%	22.2%	48.4%	20.1%	13.1%	41.7%	35.5%
Proposed	55.0%	62.0%	19.6%	61.5%	22.2%	22.7%	60.7%	42.3%

action (the one with the highest action likelihood) at any time along the video. Specifically, we set the threshold T_h at the 99 percentile of $U(t)$. Then for each windowed short clip, we only consider it for the action with the highest action likelihood and the likelihood for the other actions is directly set to zero for this clip. After that, we follow the same temporal merging/suppression strategy to get the final action detection. Table 2 gives the *F-score* of the proposed method and the comparison method. It can be seen that the proposed method outperforms the comparison method in 3 out of 5 videos under two different definitions of the true positives – temporal overlap $TO > \frac{1}{4}$ and $TO > \frac{1}{8}$, respectively. We then further apply the technique developed in Section 3.5 to integrate the detection results from all 5 videos and the final detection performance is shown in the last column of Table 2. We can see that, by integrating detections from multiple videos, we achieve better action detection.

Table 2. Performance (*F-score*) of the proposed method and the comparison method when detecting all the 7 actions in a non-overlapping way on the collected multiple wearable-camera videos.

	Methods	Video1	Video2	Video3	Video4	Video5	**Average**	**Integrated**
$TO > \frac{1}{4}$	Comparison	25.4%	14.3%	4.1%	22.2%	16.7%	16.5%	28.6%
	Proposed	22.6%	28.9%	13.2%	22.2%	20.8%	21.5%	35.4%
$TO > \frac{1}{8}$	Comparison	32.3%	23.8%	8.2%	27.2%	19.4%	22.2%	28.6%
	Proposed	26.4%	30.9%	20.8%	26.7%	29.2%	26.8%	38.0%

5   Conclusions

In this paper, we developed a new approach for action detection – input videos are taken by multiple wearable cameras with temporal synchronization. We developed algorithms to identify focal characters from each video and combined the multiple videos to more accurately detect the actions of the focal character. We developed a novel temporal merging/suppression algorithm to localize starting and ending time of both the durative and momentary actions. Image frames were rectified before feature extraction for removing the camera motion. A voting technique was developed to integrate the action detection from multiple videos. We also collected a video dataset that contains synchronized videos taken by multiple wearable cameras for performance evaluation. In the future, we plan to enhance each of the steps of the proposed approach and develop algorithms to automatically identify subsets of videos with the same focal character.

Acknowledgement. This work was supported in part by AFOSR FA9550-11-1-0327 and NSF IIS-1017199.

References

1. Aggarwal, J., Ryoo, M.S.: Human activity analysis: A review. ACM Computing Surveys **43**(3), 16 (2011)
2. Bandla, S., Grauman, K.: Active learning of an action detector from untrimmed videos. In: ICCV (2013)
3. Bay, H., Tuytelaars, T., Van Gool, L.: SURF: speeded up robust features. In: Leonardis, A., Bischof, H., Pinz, A. (eds.) ECCV 2006, Part I. LNCS, vol. 3951, pp. 404–417. Springer, Heidelberg (2006)
4. Cao, Y., Barrett, D., Barbu, A., Narayanaswamy, S., Yu, H., Michaux, A., Lin, Y., Dickinson, S., Siskind, J., Wang, S.: Recognize human activities from partially observed videos. In: CVPR (2013)
5. Chaaraoui, A.A., Climent-Pérez, P., Flórez-Revuelta, F.: An efficient approach for multi-view human action recognition based on bag-of-key-poses. In: Salah, A.A., Ruiz-del-Solar, J., Meriçli, Ç., Oudeyer, P.-Y. (eds.) HBU 2012. LNCS, vol. 7559, pp. 29–40. Springer, Heidelberg (2012)
6. Cheema, S., Eweiwi, A., Thurau, C., Bauckhage, C.: Action recognition by learning discriminative key poses. In: ICCV Workshops (2011)
7. Dalal, N., Triggs, B.: Histograms of oriented gradients for human detection. In: CVPR (2005)
8. Dalal, N., Triggs, B., Schmid, C.: Human detection using oriented histograms of flow and appearance. In: Leonardis, A., Bischof, H., Pinz, A. (eds.) ECCV 2006. LNCS, vol. 3952, pp. 428–441. Springer, Heidelberg (2006)
9. Dicle, C., Sznaier, M., Camps, O.: The way they move: tracking multiple targets with similar appearance. In: ICCV (2013)
10. Dollár, P., Rabaud, V., Cottrell, G., Belongie, S.: Behavior recognition via sparse spatio-temporal features. In: VS-PETS (2005)
11. Duchenne, O., Laptev, I., Sivic, J., Bach, F., Ponce, J.: Automatic annotation of human actions in video. In: CVPR (2009)
12. Farnebäck, G.: Two-frame motion estimation based on polynomial expansion. In: Bigun, J., Gustavsson, T. (eds.) SCIA 2003. LNCS, vol. 2749, pp. 363–370. Springer, Heidelberg (2003)
13. Fathi, A., Farhadi, A., Rehg, J.M.: Understanding egocentric activities. In: ICCV (2011)
14. Fathi, A., Li, Y., Rehg, J.M.: Learning to recognize daily actions using gaze. In: Fitzgibbon, A., Lazebnik, S., Perona, P., Sato, Y., Schmid, C. (eds.) ECCV 2012, Part I. LNCS, vol. 7572, pp. 314–327. Springer, Heidelberg (2012)
15. Felzenszwalb, P.F., Girshick, R.B., McAllester, D., Ramanan, D.: Object detection with discriminatively trained part based models. TPAMI **32**, 1627–1645 (2010)
16. Fischler, M.A., Bolles, R.C.: Random sample consensus: a paradigm for model fitting with applications to image analysis and automated cartography. Communications of the ACM **24**(6), 381–395 (1981)

17. Junejo, I.N., Dexter, E., Laptev, I., Perez, P.: View-independent action recognition from temporal self-similarities. TPAMI **33**(1), 172–185 (2011)
18. Kläser, A., Marszałek, M., Schmid, C., Zisserman, A., et al.: Human focused action localization in video. In: SGA Workshop (2010)
19. Klaser, A., Marszałek, M., Schmid, C., et al.: A spatio-temporal descriptor based on 3D-gradients. In: BMVC (2008)
20. Laptev, I.: On space-time interest points. IJCV **64**(2–3), 107–123 (2005)
21. Laptev, I., Marszałek, M., Schmid, C., Rozenfeld, B.: Learning realistic human actions from movies. In: CVPR (2008)
22. Li, B., Camps, O.I., Sznaier, M.: Cross-view activity recognition using hankelets. In: CVPR (2012)
23. Liu, J., Shah, M., Kuipers, B., Savarese, S.: Cross-view action recognition via view knowledge transfer. In: CVPR (2011)
24. Lv, F., Nevatia, R.: Single view human action recognition using key pose matching and Viterbi path searching. In: CVPR (2007)
25. Matikainen, P., Hebert, M., Sukthankar, R.: Trajectons: Action recognition through the motion analysis of tracked features. In: ICCV Workshops (2009)
26. Naiel, M.A., Abdelwahab, M.M., El-Saban, M.: Multi-view human action recognition system employing 2DPCA. In: WACV (2011)
27. Parameswaran, V., Chellappa, R.: View invariance for human action recognition. IJCV **66**(1), 83–101 (2006)
28. Pirsiavash, H., Ramanan, D., Fowlkes, C.C.: Globally-optimal greedy algorithms for tracking a variable number of objects. In: CVPR (2011)
29. Scovanner, P., Ali, S., Shah, M.: A 3-dimensional SIFT descriptor and its application to action recognition. In: ACM Multimedia (2007)
30. Vondrick, C., Patterson, D., Ramanan, D.: Efficiently scaling up crowdsourced video annotation. IJCV **101**(1), 184–204 (2013)
31. Wang, H., Kläser, A., Schmid, C., Liu, C.L.: Action recognition by dense trajectories. In: CVPR (2011)
32. Wang, H., Schmid, C.: Action recognition with improved trajectories. In: ICCV (2013)
33. Weinland, D., Boyer, E., Ronfard, R.: Action recognition from arbitrary views using 3D exemplars. In: ICCV (2007)
34. Weinland, D., Ronfard, R., Boyer, E.: Free viewpoint action recognition using motion history volumes. CVIU **104**(2), 249–257 (2006)
35. Wu, S., Oreifej, O., Shah, M.: Action recognition in videos acquired by a moving camera using motion decomposition of Lagrangian particle trajectories. In: ICCV (2011)
36. Xia, L., Chen, C.C., Aggarwal, J.: View invariant human action recognition using histograms of 3D joints. In: CVPR Workshops (2012)
37. Yao, A., Gall, J., Fanelli, G., Van Gool, L.J.: Does human action recognition benefit from pose estimation?. In: BMVC (2011)
38. Yao, A., Gall, J., Van Gool, L.: A Hough transform-based voting framework for action recognition. In: CVPR (2010)
39. Yuan, J., Liu, Z., Wu, Y.: Discriminative subvolume search for efficient action detection. In: CVPR (2009)
40. Zhang, T., Liu, S., Xu, C., Lu, H.: Human action recognition via multi-view learning. In: Proceedings of the Second International Conference on Internet Multimedia Computing and Service (2010)
41. Zheng, J., Jiang, Z.: Learning view-invariant sparse representations for cross-view action recognition. In: ICCV (2013)

Multiple Human Pose Estimation with Temporally Consistent 3D Pictorial Structures

Vasileios Belagiannis[1]([✉]), Xinchao Wang[2], Bernt Schiele[3], Pascal Fua[2],
Slobodan Ilic[1,4], and Nassir Navab[1,5]

[1] Computer Aided Medical Procedures, Technische Universität München,
München, Germany
belagian@in.tum.de
[2] Computer Vision Laboratory, EPFL, Lausanne, Switzerland
{xinchao.wang,pascal.fua}@epfl.ch
[3] Max Planck Institute for Informatics, Saarbrücken, Germany
schiele@mpi-inf.mpg.de
[4] Siemens AG, Munich, Germany
slobodan.ilic@in.tum.de
[5] Computer Aided Medical Procedures, Johns Hopkins University, Baltimore, USA
nava@in.tum.deb

Abstract. Multiple human 3D pose estimation from multiple camera
views is a challenging task in unconstrained environments. Each individual has to be matched across each view and then the body pose has to
be estimated. Additionally, the body pose of every individual changes
in a consistent manner over time. To address these challenges, we propose a temporally consistent 3D Pictorial Structures model (3DPS) for
multiple human pose estimation from multiple camera views. Our model
builds on the 3D Pictorial Structures to introduce the notion of temporal
consistency between the inferred body poses. We derive this property by
relying on multi-view human tracking. Identifying each individual before
inference significantly reduces the size of the state space and positively
influences the performance as well. To evaluate our method, we use two
challenging multiple human datasets in unconstrained environments. We
compare our method with the state-of-the-art approaches and achieve
better results.

Keywords: Human pose estimation · 3D pictorial structures · Part-based pose estimation

1 Introduction

The problem of human pose estimation has drawn the attention of computer
vision researchers for many years. Determining the body pose of multiple human
has a wide range of potential applications such as motion capture, activity recognition and human interaction. In every application, the human motion remains
consistent over time. Different approaches have been proposed for multiple human

© Springer International Publishing Switzerland 2015
L. Agapito et al. (Eds.): ECCV 2014 Workshops, Part I, LNCS 8925, pp. 742–754, 2015.
DOI: 10.1007/978-3-319-16178-5_52

pose estimation on 2D [1,4,10,24] or 3D space [5,6,14,20,21]. Nevertheless, the utility of temporal consistency for pose estimation has not been sufficiently addressed yet.

Defining the body pose as a constellation of parts has become the standard model in human pose estimation using image data [4,24,25]. Pictorial structures is the most common part-based model for estimating the 2D body pose of single human [3,11,13]. The model has been extended to the 3D space, in order to cope with mutli-view camera setups as well [2,9,16]. Recently, pictorial structures have been successfully modelled for multiple human 3D pose estimation [6]. However, the temporal consistency, between the estimated body poses of different individuals among subsequent frames, has never been addressed within the framework of pictorial structures. This property is of high importance in multiple human pose estimation, where the trajectory of each individual is directly connected to the body pose.

In this work, we propose a temporally consistent 3D Pictorial Structures model (3DPS) for multiple human pose estimation from multiple camera views. We build our model on a Conditional Random Field (CRF), which is composed of unary, pairwise and ternary potential functions. The unary potentials incorporate the observation to our model, while the pairwise and ternary model the human body as a prior. In addition, we introduce the temporal function based on an additional potential that ensures temporal consistency between the human poses over time. In order to propagate the inferred poses with the correct identity, we rely on a multi-view state-of-the-art human tracker [7], which has been proven to work reliably and recently evolved to track interacting objects [28].

Our contributions are summarised as follows: We propose a temporally consistent 3DPS model which is applied to multiple human pose estimation. Our model takes input from a multi-object tracker, but it is not subjected to a particular one. Given the track of each individual, we signicantly reduce state space of each joint, which leads to much faster inference. On two challenging datasets for multiple human pose estimating from multiple views, we obtain the best results in comparison to previous work [6].

Camera 1   Camera 3   Camera 5

Fig. 1. Shelf dataset result: The 3D estimated body poses are projected across the camera views. The identity of each individual is derived by the tracker.

2   Related Work

The problem of multiple human pose estimation has been studied from a 2D and 3D perspective. Moreover, it has often been coupled with human tracking. We review the most related work and focus on multiple human pose estimation from multiple views. We refer the reader to [22, 26] for a more in-depth analysis of human pose estimation.

Part-based models have proved to be a powerful solution for 2D pose estimation [1, 4, 10, 24]. Among many of the proposed models, pictorial structures is the most widely used one [3, 11, 13]. In [24], the main focus has been articulated human tracking with manual initialization, based on the pictorial structures. Similarly in [4], pictorial structures have been integrated into a tracking-by-detection framework. More oriented towards pose estimation, the human interaction has been modelled using the pictorial structures framework in [10]. However, each frame has been treated independently without considering the temporal component. Recently, a segmentation approach has been combined with a part-based model for estimating the human pose from stereo data [1]. Despite the available 3D information, the final pose is in the 2D space.

In the 3D space, the problem of multiple human pose estimation has been addressed using monocular [5, 18, 29], stereo [14, 23] or multi-camera input information [20, 21]. In [29] and [18], the monocular 3D pose estimation has been combined with tracking. Both approaches rely on a blob detector, which can be unreliable for individuals with similar appearance. Richer appearance models have been introduced in [5] by building on the pictorial structures. Since the approach is monocular, the final 3D pose is inferred by 2D pose lifting. In [14], a two-stage algorithm is applied on stereo data for detecting human and recovering their pose. Similar to our framework, a multi-view system has been employed in [20, 21]. In [21], the proposed method can estimate the pose up to two people in a studio environment. Our model does not have such limitations and it is mainly applied to unconstrained environments. Finally, a model fitting approach has been proposed in [20]. The learned body model is fitted into a voxel representation.

The 3DPS model for multiple human pose estimation [6] is similar to our model. In this approach, a model for inferring multiple human body poses without knowing their identity has been proposed. However, keeping all the individuals in a common state space results in additional computations. Furthermore, the model does not consider the temporal consistency of the inferred poses and consequently cannot identify the individuals. In our method, we first recover the identity of each individual using tracking and afterwards infer the pose. Moreover, we introduce a temporal term for regularising our solution. This term keeps the inferred poses consistent over time. In the experiments we directly compare to [6] and observe that these differences lead not only to a significantly reduced state space and thus faster inference, but also to significantly improved performance. Finally, our model is advisable for multiple human pose estimation, where there are different individuals.

3   Method

In this section, we introduce the temporally consistent 3D pictorial structures (3DPS) model. We build our model on a Conditional Random Filed (CRF) that is composed of unary, pairwise and ternary potential functions. The unary potentials include geometric and appearance features, as well as temporal features that encode the identity and pose of the individuals. The pairwise and ternary potentials impose physical constrains and act as a body prior. In the following subsections, we present our model, the state space, the potential function (Subsection 3.1) and conclude with the inference of multiple human 3D poses (Subsection 3.2).

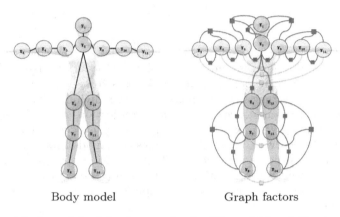

Body model   Graph factors

Fig. 2. Graphical model of the human body: We used 14 variables in our graph to represent the body joints. On the left, the undirected graphical model that corresponds to the human body is presented. On the right, the graph factors are illustrated with different colours. The kinematic constrains are presented with red (translation) and green (rotation) edges (factors). The collision constrains are represented with yellow edges.

3.1   Temporally Consistent 3DPS Model

In the temporally consistent 3D pictorial structure (3DPS) model, the body is represented as an undirected graphical model, wherein each node corresponds to a body joint (Figure 2). The edges of the graph denote relation between the body joints. In comparison to the original pictorial structure model, we have interchanged the notion of the body parts with the joints to avoid the foreshortening effect [2]. Let the random variable Y_i denote a joint location in the global 3D coordinate system, i.e., $Y_i = [\delta_i, \pi_i, \vartheta_i]^T \in \mathbb{R}^3$. The body pose is then defined by the configuration $\mathbf{Y} = (Y_1, Y_2, \ldots, Y_n)$, where n is the number of joints. Each random variable Y_i takes its values from a state space $\Lambda_i \in \Lambda$, where Λ is the global state space. We model the observations and interaction between the variables using a factor graph [17]. The factors are divided into unary, pairwise and ternary ones (Figure 2). The unary factors describe the relation between the state space and the random variables. The pairwise and ternary factors are categorized into kinematic and collision ones. The kinematic factors model the body prior, while the collision factors model the relation between symmetric body joints.

The posterior probability of the body configuration $\mathbf{y} \in \Lambda$ given an observation instance $\mathbf{x} \in \mathbf{X}$ and the temporal body pose $\mathbf{p} \in \mathbf{P}$ of an individual is defined as:

$$p(\mathbf{y} \mid \mathbf{x}, \mathbf{p}) = \frac{1}{Z(\mathbf{x})} \prod_i^n \phi_i^{conf}(y_i, \mathbf{x}) \cdot \prod_i^n \phi_i^{repr}(y_i, \mathbf{x}) \cdot \prod_i^n \phi_i^{vis}(y_i, \mathbf{x}) \cdot \prod_i^n \phi_i^{temp}(y_i, p_i) \cdot$$

$$\prod_{(i,j) \in E_{kin}} \psi_{i,j}^{tran}(y_i, y_j) \cdot \prod_{(i,j,k) \in E_{kin}} \psi_{i,j,k}^{rot}(y_i, y_j, y_k) \cdot \prod_{(i,j) \in E_{col}} \psi_{i,j}^{col}(y_i, y_j) \quad (1)$$

where $Z(\mathbf{x})$ is the partition function, E_{kin} and E_{col} are the edges corresponding to the kinematic factors and the collision factors, respectively. The temporal body pose $\mathbf{P}$ corresponds to inferred poses from a previous time step. A set of joints forms the temporal pose $\mathbf{P}$ of an individual. The unary terms include the detection confidence $\phi_i^{conf}(y_i, \mathbf{x})$, reprojection error $\phi_i^{repr}(y_i, \mathbf{x})$, joint multi-view visibility $\phi_i^{vis}(y_i, \mathbf{x})$ and the temporal consistence potential functions $\phi_i^{temp}(y_i, p_i)$. The pairwise potential functions are divided into the translation $\psi_{i,j}^{tran}(y_i, y_j)$ and collision $\psi_{i,j}^{col}(y_i, y_j)$, while the rotation $\psi_{i,j,k}^{rot}(y_i, y_j, y_k)$ is modelled as a ternary potential function. Next, we first define the state space Λ, then explain the potential functions and temporal consistency that we obtain by using tracking.

State space generation. The state space Λ_i of a variable Y_i comprises the values that correspond to a candidate joint location in a discretised 3D space. In order to be computationally efficient, we discretise the 3D space using 2D body joint detectors. We first sample 2D joint locations for each view using a body joint detector [2]. Next, we create the 3D locations by triangulation of the corresponding 2D body joints detected in all combinations of view pairs. Our only assumptions are that the camera system is calibrated and there is at least one true positive detection of each joint from a view pair. Finally, the global state space $\Lambda = \{\Lambda_1, \Lambda_2, \dots \Lambda_n\}$ includes locations which correspond either to true or false positive body joints. The false positive candidate locations usually occur by triangulating one or two false positive joint detections. Knowing the identity of each individual significantly reduces the cardinality of the state space in comparison to [6].

Unary potentials. Given the state space, we extract a set of features for each candidate joint 3D location. These features form the observation $\mathbf{X}$, which is provided to the unary potential functions. The first feature is the detection confidence, which is used by $\phi_i^{conf}(y_i, \mathbf{x})$. It corresponds to the mean confidence of the joint detector in the two views that have been used during triangulation.

Note here, we consider all combinations of two views. To account for the errors of triangulation between two views [15], we introduce the reprojection error function $\phi_i^{repr}(y_i, \mathbf{x})$, which is defined as follows:

$$\phi_i^{repr}(y_i, \mathbf{x}) = \frac{1}{1 + \exp(C(y_i))} \tag{2}$$

where $C(y_i)$ is the reprojection error in two views, which is computed using the Euclidean distance similar to [6]. The first two potential functions reason about combinations of two views. To also profit from the multi-view setup, the multi-view visibility function $\phi_i^{vis}(y_i, \mathbf{x})$ computes the number of views in which a candidate has been correctly detected. To that end, we project the candidate joint 3D location to each view and search for a detection instance in a small radius (5 pixels) around the projected location. We then accumulate the number of visible views and normalize the result with respect to the total number of cameras. Thus we obtain a score between 0 and 1, which we take as $\phi_i^{vis}(y_i, \mathbf{x})$. Note that, candidates that resulted from ambiguous views or false positive detections are implicitly penalised by obtaining a low visibility score.

Temporal consistency. The features of the observation are extracted from a single frame and thus do not account for temporal consistency. To assure consistency between the inferred joints, we introduce the temporal consistence function $\phi_i^{temp}(y_i, p_i)$. This is a potential that relies on a temporal body joint location p_i and acts as a regulariser. The aim of this function is to impose temporal consistency between the inferred poses. For this reason, it penalises candidates that geometrically differ significantly from the temporal joint. As temporal pose, we choose the inferred pose from the previous frame and assume small changes between two subsequent frames. However, the temporal poses can include wrongly inferred joints or identity. To address these problems, the geometric distance between the candidate and the temporal joint is not considered if it exceeds a threshold. The distance is expressed as a score using a sigmoid function and is given as follows:

$$\phi_i^{temp}(y_i, p_i) = \begin{cases} \frac{1}{1 + \exp(d(y_i, p_i))} & \text{if } d(y_i, p_i) < c \\ \epsilon & \text{otherwise} \end{cases} \tag{3}$$

where ϵ is a small constant for numerical stability and $d(y_i, p_i)$ is the Euclidean distance between the candidate 3D joint location and the temporal joint and c the distance threshold, which we set to $10cm$. The temporal prior is another observation in our posterior (1). We choose this computationally inexpensive formulation instead of formalising the problem using a dynamic CRF [27].

Pairwise and ternary potentials. The pairwise and ternary potential functions model the interaction between the random variables $\mathbf{Y} = (Y_1, Y_2, \ldots, Y_n)$ of our model. The interaction is interpreted as a body prior with kinematic and collision constraints. In the kinematic constraints, we impose physical constraints between the body joints. For that purpose, we define two types of transformation: translation and rotation. The collision constraints are introduced to mainly handle false positive detections. This phenomenon is usually observed in the symmetric joints where the classifier is occasionally triggered for the wrong joint.

The translation potential models a joint i in the local coordinate system of a joint j, which is defined using a multivariate Gaussian distribution:

$$\psi_{i,j}^{tran}(y_i, y_j) = \mathcal{N}(y_{ij}^T \mid \mu_{ij}^T, \Sigma_{ij}^T), \tag{4}$$

where μ_{ij}^T is the mean and Σ_{ij}^T is the covariance. We keep the covariance as a diagonal matrix for relaxing the computations.

The rotation transformation ternary potential denotes the rotation between two body parts. To model the transformation, a triad of joints is initially chosen. Then two vectors with the same origin are created. The origin corresponds to a hinge joint (1 DoF) and the vectors to body parts. Since a hinge joint allows the rotation only along one axis, we model the rotation potential using a univariate Gaussian distribution:

$$\psi_{i,j,k}^{rot}(y_i, y_j, y_k) = \mathcal{N}(y_{ijk}^R \mid \mu_{ijk}^R, \sigma_{ijk}^R), \tag{5}$$

where μ_{ijk}^R is the mean and σ_{ijk}^R the variance. The von Mises distribution is the actual distribution for the rotation but using a Gaussian has been proven to generalise well in [6]. For that reason, we follow the same formulation.

The collision constraints are introduced to ensure the spatial exclusion between joints. To force body joints not to collide and respect a minimum distance, we introduce the collision function $\psi_{i,j}^{col}(y_i, y_j)$. The joints are modelled as spheres and the collision function estimates if there is intersection between the spheres:

$$\psi_{i,j}^{col}(y_i, y_j) = \begin{cases} 1 \text{ if } inter(y_i, y_j) = 0 \\ \epsilon \text{ otherwise} \end{cases} \tag{6}$$

where ϵ is again a small constant for numerical stability and $inter(y_i, y_j) \in \{0, 1\}$ is the sphere-sphere intersection function [19]. This is a hard constraint, but in our experiments it functioned well.

In our model, we have cancelled the notion of the global coordinate system and express every variable relation in a local coordinate system. This is the principle of the original work on the pictorial structures [11, 13]. For this reason, our prior model is applicable to any multi-view setup independently of the system calibration. To learn the prior model, we have used ground-truth data from a single training dataset. Then in the experimental phase, we apply this prior model on different setups.

3.2   3D Pose Inference and Tracking

The last step for obtaining the pose of different individuals is the inference. We seek to maximize the posterior probability in (1) for each individual h, given as follows:

$$\mathbf{y_h}^* = \arg\max_{\mathbf{y}} p(\mathbf{y} \mid \mathbf{x_h}, \mathbf{p_h}) \tag{7}$$

where $\mathbf{y_h}^*$ are the configurations that maximize the posterior and h is the identity of each individual. To recover the identity, we introduce a human tracker in our framework. We rely on the work of [7] to derive the tracks of each individual. As as result, each individual has its own observation $\mathbf{x_h}$ and lies in its own state space using the tracking information. In addition, the identity of the inferred body poses $\mathbf{p_h}$ is propagated over time using the tracking output. Knowing the identity of each individual reduces the computations in the temporal consistence function. Theoretically, relying exclusively on the tracking information can result in drifts. Nevertheless, in practice the tracker performed very reliably in our experiments.

Our graphical model includes loops and thus the inference is performed with loopy belief propagation using the sum-product algorithm [8]. Finally, the MAP estimate for each individual gives the body pose. In addition, we profit from tracking and obtain the trajectory of each individual.

4 Experiments

Multiple human 3D pose estimation from multiple camera views in unconstrained environments is an active research topic, which is still growing. For that reason, the number of evaluation datasets is limited. To evaluate our method, we have used two challenging datasets [6], Campus and Shelf, which are the only available datasets for this problem to the best of our knowledge. The Campus dataset has 3 cameras and involves 3 individuals, while Shelf has 5 cameras and includes 4 individuals. Since one individual is mostly occluded and invisible from most of the views, we evaluate on the other three, as in [6].

Our model is composed of 14 body joints (Figure 2). We use the joint detector from [2] and learn the body prior using the ground-truth data from the KTH Multiview Football II dataset [9]. The evaluation is divided into three tasks: analysis of the state space, evaluation on the human detection and the body pose estimation. Since the method of [6] is closely related to our work, we compare our results with it for each experiment.

4.1 State Space Analysis

One of our main contributions is to impose the temporal consistence to the model. This is achieved by taking people tracking results as input. Given the identity of each individual, we can significantly reduce the number of candidates for each joint state space. This reduction results in faster inference. Our algorithms runs at 1 fps, given the tracks, for inferring up to 3 individuals in comparison to [6], which runs at 1 fps for single human pose estimation, given the detections. In Figure 3, we show the number of 3D candidates of a body joint versus the number of 2D joint detection samples.

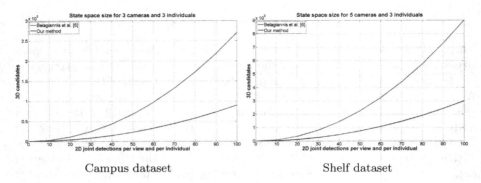

Campus dataset   Shelf dataset

Fig. 3. State space size: We show the number of recovered 3D candidates versus the number of 2D detection samples on both datasets. The number of 3D candidates is computed by summing up the triangulation instances of all combinations of all view pairs. The number of candidates is significantly lower than [6], because of the unknown identity of each individual.

The number of recovered 3D candidates is the aggregation of the triangulation instances of all combinations of view pairs, given different number of 2D body joint detection. In the case of [6], the triangulation is performed between all the individuals due to the unknown identity. This results in a much larger state space where inference is computationally more expensive.

4.2   People Detection

In our framework, we consider the task of people detection separately from pose estimation. Therefore, our model is dependent on the detection result. By taking the advantage of tracking, we not only improve the people detection results, but also obtain the identity of each individual in comparison to frame-by-frame detection [6]. To evaluate the people detection results, we employ the PCP evaluation score [12]. For each individual, we define a line in the centre of the ground-truth cube which is perpendicular to the ground. It corresponds to the height of each individual in the 3D space. In the evaluation stage, we derive the same line from the inferred pose by fitting a cube and estimate the PCP score. From our experiments, we have found that the results of this mean of evaluation is equivalent to cube intersection but the computation of the PCP score is way faster. The results are summarised in Table 1.

Table 1. Detection results: The detection recall is estimated using the PCP score. The threshold α is set to 0.5 for both methods.

	Campus		Shelf	
	Belagiannis et al. [6]	Our method	Belagiannis et al. [6]	Our method
Recall	98.05	99.30	90.50	97.82

In both datasets, the recall is quite high for both methods. However, the temporal consistence of our method gives an improvement of around 10% in the Shelf dataset over the frame-by-frame detection of [6]. The only failures that we have observed were small drifts over time. The precision of our method is totally corrected using the tracker information and thus we do not include it in the comparison.

Camera 1   Camera 2   Camera 3

Fig. 4. Campus dataset result: The 3D estimated body poses are projected across the camera views. The identity of each individual is derived by the tracker.

4.3 Body Pose Estimation

In our last task, we evaluate the final accuracy of pose estimation on the two datasets, both of which include several individuals and have been captured in unconstrained environments. We compare our results with the ones of a related work [6], which is a state-of-the-art approach. Unlike our model, the human model in [6] does not consider the temporal consistence over time. Furthermore, the unknown identity of each individual results in more false positive candidates. These differences between the two methods are reflected in their performance, presented in Tables 2. Below, we discuss the results for each dataset separately.

Table 2. Pose estimation results: The PCP score are presented for both datasets. The threshold α is set to 0.5 for both methods.

	Campus		Shelf	
	Belagiannis et al. [6]	Our method	Belagiannis et al. [6]	Our method
Actor 1	82	83	66	75
Actor 2	72	73	65	67
Actor 3	73	78	83	86
Average	75.6	78	71.3	76

Campus dataset: In this dataset, we achieve substantially better results for the Actor 3 and slightly better for the other two individuals. The results are demonstrated in Figure 4. The support of the tracker facilitates the pose recovery of the Actor 3 who often undergoes occlusions. For the same reason, there is a small predominance for the other two individuals. The reduced state space and the temporal consistence of our model improve the precision of the inferred poses, as it is depicted in Figure 5.

Shelf dataset: In this dataset, our method again achieves better results on all individuals. In particular, there is a big difference between our method and [6] in the result of Actor 1, thanks to the temporal consistence. False positive candidates are penalised by the temporal potential function, and therefore the performance is improved. Qualitative results are presented in Figure 1 and Figure 5.

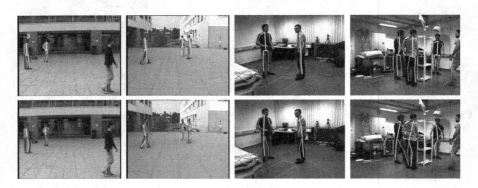

Fig. 5. Qualitative comparison: We show the results of our method on the top row, and those from [6] on the bottom row. We have chosen different frames and camera views from the Campus and Shelf datasets to illustrate the advances of our model. In all cases, the inferred poses of our model are more precise due to the regularisation of the temporal potential function and the reduced state space.

5   Conclusion

We have presented a temporally consistent 3D pictorial structures model. Our model applies to unconstrained environments for multiple human pose estimation from multiple views. We have introduced tracking and temporal consistency to our formulation for recovering the 3D human pose. Knowing the identity of each individual results in a small state space which allows efficient inference. Moreover, the temporal consistency helps to penalise false positive candidates of the state space. To demonstrate the advances of our model, we have evaluated on two challenging datasets and achieved state-of-the-art results.

References

1. Alahari, K., Seguin, G., Sivic, J., Laptev, I.: Pose estimation and segmentation of people in 3d movies. In: ICCV (2013)
2. Amin, S., Andriluka, M., Rohrbach, M., Schiele, B.: Multi-view pictorial structures for 3d human pose estimation. In: BMVC (2013)

3. Andriluka, M., Roth, S., Schiele, B.: Pictorial structures revisited: People detection and articulated pose estimation. In: CVPR (2009)
4. Andriluka, M., Roth, S., Schiele, B.: People-tracking-by-detection and people-detection-by-tracking. In: CVPR, pp. 1–8. IEEE (2008)
5. Andriluka, M., Roth, S., Schiele, B.: Monocular 3d pose estimation and tracking by detection. In: CVPR (2010)
6. Belagiannis, V., Amin, S., Andriluka, M., Schiele, B., Navab, N., Ilic, S.: 3D pictorial structures for multiple human pose estimation. In: CVPR. IEEE (2014)
7. Berclaz, J., Fleuret, F., Turetken, E., Fua, P.: Multiple object tracking using k-shortest paths optimization. TPAMI (2011)
8. Bishop, C.M., et al.: Pattern Recognition and Machine Learning. Springer, New York (2006)
9. Burenius, M., Sullivan, J., Carlsson, S.: 3d pictorial structures for multiple view articulated pose estimation. In: CVPR (2013)
10. Eichner, M., Ferrari, V.: We are family: joint pose estimation of multiple persons. In: Daniilidis, K., Maragos, P., Paragios, N. (eds.) ECCV 2010, Part I. LNCS, vol. 6311, pp. 228–242. Springer, Heidelberg (2010)
11. Felzenszwalb, P., Huttenlocher, D.: Pictorial structures for object recognition. IJCV (2005)
12. Ferrari, V., Marin-Jimenez, M., Zisserman, A.: Progressive search space reduction for human pose estimation. In: CVPR (2008)
13. Fischler, M.A., Elschlager, R.A.: The representation and matching of pictorial structures. IEEE Transactions on Computers (1973)
14. Gammeter, S., Ess, A., Jäggli, T., Schindler, K., Leibe, B., Van Gool, L.: Articulated multi-body tracking under egomotion. In: Forsyth, D., Torr, P., Zisserman, A. (eds.) ECCV 2008, Part II. LNCS, vol. 5303, pp. 816–830. Springer, Heidelberg (2008)
15. Hartley, R., Zisserman, A.: Multiple view geometry in computer vision, vol. 2. Cambridge Univ Press (2000)
16. Kazemi, V., Burenius, M., Azizpour, H., Sullivan, J.: Multi-view body part recognition with random forests. In: BMVC (2013)
17. Kschischang, F.R., Frey, B.J., Loeliger, H.A.: Factor graphs and the sum-product algorithm. IEEE Transactions on Information Theory 47(2), 498–519 (2001)
18. Lee, M.W., Nevatia, R.: Human pose tracking using multi-level structured models. In: Leonardis, A., Bischof, H., Pinz, A. (eds.) ECCV 2006. LNCS, vol. 3953, pp. 368–381. Springer, Heidelberg (2006)
19. Lin, M., Gottschalk, S.: Collision detection between geometric models: A survey. In: Proc. of IMA Conference on Mathematics of Surfaces (1998)
20. Luo, X., Berendsen, B., Tan, R.T., Veltkamp, R.C.: Human pose estimation for multiple persons based on volume reconstruction. In: ICPR. pp. 3591–3594. IEEE (2010)
21. Mitchelson, J.R., Hilton, A.: Simultaneous pose estimation of multiple people using multiple-view cues with hierarchical sampling. In: BMVC, pp. 1–10 (2003)
22. Moeslund, T.B., Hilton, A., Krüger, V.: A survey of advances in vision-based human motion capture and analysis. Computer vision and image understanding (2006)
23. Plankers, R., Fua, P.: Articulated soft objects for multi-view shape and motion capture. IEEE PAMI 25(10) (2003)
24. Ramanan, D., Forsyth, D.A.: Finding and tracking people from the bottom up. In: CVPR. IEEE (2003)

25. Sigal, L., Isard, M., Haussecker, H., Black, M.: Loose-limbed people: Estimating 3d human pose and motion using non-parametric belief propagation. IJCV (2011)
26. Sigal, L., Black, M.J.: Guest editorial: state of the art in image-and video-based human pose and motion estimation. IJCV (2010)
27. Sutton, C., McCallum, A., Rohanimanesh, K.: Dynamic conditional random fields: Factorized probabilistic models for labeling and segmenting sequence data. The Journal of Machine Learning Research **8**, 693–723 (2007)
28. Wang, X., Türetken, E., Fleuret, F., Fua, P.: Tracking interacting objects optimally using integer programming. In: Fleet, D., Pajdla, T., Schiele, B., Tuytelaars, T. (eds.) ECCV 2014, Part I. LNCS, vol. 8689, pp. 17–32. Springer, Heidelberg (2014)
29. Zhao, T., Nevatia, R.: Tracking multiple humans in complex situations. TPAMI (2004)

W06 - Video Event Categorization, Tagging and Retrieval towards Big Data

Camera Calibration and Shape Recovery from Videos of Two Mirrors

Quanxin Chen[✉] and Hui Zhang

Department of Computer Science, United International College, 28, Jinfeng Road,
Tangjiawan, Zhuhai, Guangdong, China
cqxooo1988@gmail.com, amyzhang@uic.edu.hk

Abstract. This paper addresses the problem of motion and shape recovery from a two-mirror system which is able to generate five views of an object. Different from existing methods, this paper uses a short video instead of static snapshots so that it can help with action recognition once the 3D visual hull model is reconstructed. In order to solve the problem, this paper shows the geometry relationship between the two-mirror system and circular motion, so that the two-mirror system can be solved as circular motions. Different from the approach of Zhang et al. [22], we avoid using the vanishing point of X-axis which would cause accumulate error when calculating the epipoles of two views. Results of comparative experiments and the 3D visual hull of model show the feasibility and the accuracy of the proposed approach.

Keywords: Video · Motion and shape recovery · Camera calibration · Two-mirror system · Circular motion

1 Introduction

In recent years, videos have been studied to recover the shape and motion of models in different aspects. Guillemaut et al. [5] proposed an approach based on view-dependent segmentation and reconstruction which is used in challenging outdoor environments with moving cameras. Plänkers et al. [14] developed an interesting approach for motion and shape recovery of articulated deformable objects from silhouettes by using trinocular video sequence of complex 3D motions. Similarly, we also use articulated deformable objects but using normal video camera and only analyze single frame alone. Moreover, self-calibration is another important aspect in video study. Camera Calibration in video can be used as a pre-processing step for many later video analysis and event recognition applications [10][17][18]. Lv et al. [12] calibrated the video camera from three vanishing points in the image. This paper also calibrates the camera but in a more flexible way. Sinha et al. [19] calibrated the video camera from dynamic silhouettes by camera network. However, this approach should keep synchronizing for every video camera.

A system consisting of refracting (lens) and reflecting (mirror) elements are called catadioptric systems [8]. This system is used to be studied because it

© Springer International Publishing Switzerland 2015
L. Agapito et al. (Eds.): ECCV 2014 Workshops, Part I, LNCS 8925, pp. 757–768, 2015.
DOI: 10.1007/978-3-319-16178-5_53

provides symmetric relationships for object and its reflections which enable us to use only a single camera. Therefore, we do not need to consider camera synchronization any more. Martin et al. [13] studied camera calibration and 3D reconstruction by one mirror. However, one-mirror system provide only two views for object which is not enough for 3D reconstruction. Gluckman et al. [4] exploited the geometry of the two-mirror system and recover the focal length via corresponding points of two views. Different from [4], Forbes et al. [3] introduced an approach based on silhouettes alone which avoid exacting corresponding points of views in image. However, both this two papers should figure out the reflection matrix of mirror which is in a traditional way but difficult for every situation. Zhang et al. [22] and Ying et al. [20] recovered the geometry relationship between the two-mirror system and the circular motion which makes the calibration easier.

Inspired by [3][20][22], this paper aims to recover the motion and shape of object from video other than static snapshots with two-mirror system because the reconstructed 3D model can help to boost the accuracy of action recognition and avoid processing large dataset. A novel approach which is cross-view action recognition without body part tracking was proposed in [6]. However, it still required a large collection of mocap data. Lu et al. [11] proposed binary range-sample feature in depth for action recognition which is robust to occlusion and data corruption. In this paper, two equal but unknown angles could be figured out from the two-mirror system so that they can be used to recover the image of circular points [9]. The rotation axis of circular motion is initialized from the intersections of epipolar bitangent lines of two views. Once the camera is calibrated, the projection matrices of views can be obtained. Therefore, the 3D visual hull model is recovered.

This paper is organized as follows. §2 gives the notation and geometry of the two-mirror system and the relationship between it and circular motion. This section also presents several image invariants which play important roles in our approach. §3 and §4 present the details of the camera calibration and motion recovery. §5 and §6 show the experimental results and the conclusion of this approach.

2   Notation and Geometry

2.1   Geometry of Two Mirror Setup

Considering a two-mirror setup for picturing five views of an object in a single image (see Fig. 1(a)). Note there is a real object O and its four mirror reflections O_1, O_2, O_{12} and O_{21}. The virtual object O_1 is the reflection of O in Mirror M_1; O_2 is the reflection of O in Mirror M_2; O_{12} is the reflection of O_2 in Mirror M_1; and O_{21} is the reflection of O_1 in Mirror M_2. Note there are two virtual mirrors M_{12} and M_{21} which reflect O_1 to O_{12} and O_2 to O_{21}, respectively. There are also several virtual cameras C_1, C_2, C_{21}, C_{12} can be similarly formed as the way of the virtual objects.

According to the lines joining corresponding points between O and O_1 are perpendicular to the mirror M_1 and those between O and O_2 are perpendicular to the mirror M_2, we can easily find that the three objects O, O_1 and O_2 lie on a plane Π which is perpendicular to both the mirror plane M_1 and M_2, and the intersection line of the mirror M1 and M_2. Similarly, O_{21} and O_{12} also lie on the plane Π. Therefore, the two virtual mirrors M_{21} and M_{12} are both perpendicular to the plane Π. Similarly, the five camera centers should all lie on a plane parallel to the plane Π. More importantly, the plane Π is generally not the desk plane where the real object O lying on.

Let's denote the vanishing line of Π as l_h (see Fig. 1(b)), then we will show how to get l_h according to vanishing points of the directions perpendicular to all four mirror planes. For the mirror M_1, four outer bitangents (two between the object O and O_1, two between the object O_2 and O_{12}) intersect at the vanishing point v_1, which is their vanishing point on the l_h. Similarly, for the

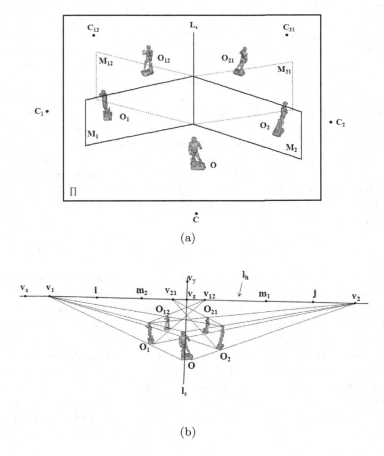

(a)

(b)

Fig. 1. Geometry of the two mirrors. (a) Two mirror setup. (b) The image invariants of the two mirror setup.

mirror M_2, we can get vanishing point v_2 which the four outer bitangents (two between the object O and O_2, two between the object O_1 and O_{21}) intersect at; for the mirror M_{12}, the two outer bitangents between the object O_1 and O_{12} intersect with the l_h at the vanishing point v_{12}; for the mirror M_{21}, the two outer bitangents between the object O_2 and O_{21} intersect with the l_h at the vanishing point v_{21}. Hence the horizon l_h passes through vanishing points v_1, v_2, v_{12}, v_{21}.

Moreover, the plane Π intersects mirror M_1 and M_2 at two lines which intersect with vanishing line l_h at point m_1 and m_2 respectively(see fig. 1(b)).

2.2 Relationship between the Two Mirror System and the Turntable Motion

Considering the top view of the real and virtual objects on the plane Π and let the real camera C lying on the positive Z-axis of the world coordinate system (see Fig. 2). Let the mirrors be M_1, M_2, M_{12} and M_{21}, and Y-axis intersects Π at point O. Then the real camera C has its reflections C_1, C_2, C_{12} and C_{21} with respect to the M_1, M_2, M_{12} and M_{21} respectively. Let's denote the angle between C and the mirror M_1 as α, denote the angle between C and the mirror M_2 as β. Hence, the angle between M_1 and M_2 is $\theta = \alpha + \beta$. Since all the views are generated by mirrors, it can be easily found that the length $|OC_1| = |OC_2| = |OC_{12}| = |OC_{21}| = |OC|$ and the angle $\angle COC_1 = \angle C_2OC_{21} = 2\alpha$, $\angle COC_2 = \angle C_1OC_{12} = 2\beta$. According to the symmetric relationship of mirrors, we can easily divide the five views into two turntable motions based on the image direction. By thinking of this, we can find that C_{21}, C and C_{12} are in similar direction, and C_2 and C_1 are in another similar direction. Hence, we can get two turntable motions: one is C_{12} rotates to C about the Y-axis with angle of 2θ and then rotates to C_{21} with the same angle of 2θ. Another one is the C_2 rotates to C_1 with the angle of 2θ. Note it can be observed from the Figure 2 that the angles:

$$\angle CC_1C_{12} = \angle C_1CC_2 = \angle CC_2C_{21} = \pi - \theta \qquad (1)$$

Turntable motion is always regarded as a scene that a camera rotating about a fixed axis. The invariants related to the geometry of turntable motion have been well established in [1] (see Fig. 1(b)). l_h is the vanishing line of the turntable plane. l_s is both the image of rotation axis and the vanishing line of the Y-axis. v_z is the vanishing point of the Z-axis. v_x is the vanishing point of the X-axis and v_y is the vanishing point of the Y-axis. v_x lies on l_h, v_y lies on l_s, and v_z is the intersection point of l_h and l_s. Note v_x and l_s form a pole-polar relationship with respect to the image of the absolute conic [2]. The pair of imaged circular points i and j for the turntable plane Π also lie on l_h. i.e., $l_h = i \times j$. All the aforementioned image entities will be fixed if the camera intrinsics are invariants.

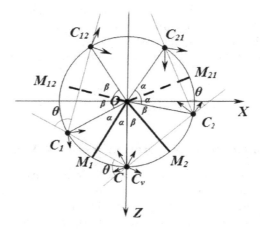

Fig. 2. Top view of the two-mirror setup

3   Camera Calibration

3.1   Recovery of the Imaged Circular Points and the Angle between Two Mirrors

In order to rectify the five-view image to affine, we should construct a "pure projective" transformation matrix P [9] by use the vanishing line $l_h = [\,l_1\ l_2\ l_3\,]^T$.

$$P = \begin{bmatrix} 1 & 0 & 0 \\ 0 & 1 & 0 \\ l_1 & l_2 & l_3 \end{bmatrix} \tag{2}$$

Denotes the circular points on the affine space as $[\,\alpha \mp \beta i\ 1\ 0\,]^T$. The five-view image can be further rectified from affine to metric by another transformation matrix A [9].

$$A = \begin{bmatrix} \frac{1}{\beta} & -\frac{\alpha}{\beta} & 0 \\ 0 & 1 & 0 \\ 0 & 0 & 1 \end{bmatrix} \tag{3}$$

From section 2.2, we can know there are equal unknown angles on the world plane and according to [9]. We can find α and β both lie on a circle with center(c_α, c_β).

$$(c_\alpha, c_\beta) = \left(\frac{a_1 b_2 - a_2 b_1}{a_1 - b_1 - a_2 + b_2}, 0\right) \tag{4}$$

and squared radius

$$r^2 = \left(\frac{a_1 b_2 - a_2 b_1}{a_1 - b_1 - a_2 + b_2}\right)^2 + \frac{(a_1 - b_1)(a_1 b_1 - a_2 b_2)}{a_1 - b_1 - a_2 + b_2} - a_1 b_1 \tag{5}$$

where the angle between two lines imaged with directions a_1, b_1 is the same as that between lines imaged with directions a_2, b_2. Hence the circular points are imaged on the vanishing line at $i, j = [(\alpha \mp \beta i) l_3 \; l_3 \; -\alpha l_1 - l_2 \pm \beta l_1 i]^T$.

The angle θ can be directly obtained from the rectified metric image by Laguerre Formula [16]:

$$\theta = \frac{1}{2j} log\{l_1, l_2; i, j\} \qquad (6)$$

3.2 Recovery of the Imaged Rotation Axis and Vanishing Point v_x

In order to initialize l_s accurately, [20] propose an effective method to guess l_s. Inspired by it, we induce a formula to compute epipoles for two views under circular motion. Let's denote e_{v_1} and e_{v_2} as the epipoles for $\{C, C_{12}\}$ and $\{C, C_{21}\}$. From section 3.1, we know that the angle between C and C_{12} is 2θ, so is C and C_{21}. It is easy to get that the angle between OC and CC_{21} is $\frac{\pi}{2} - \theta$, and the angle between OC and CC_{12} is $-\frac{\pi}{2} + \theta$(see Fig. 3(a)). From (6), we can get

$$\frac{\pi}{2} - \theta = \frac{1}{2j} log\{v_z, e_{v_2}; i, j\}, \qquad (7)$$

and

$$-\frac{\pi}{2} + \theta = \frac{1}{2j} log\{v_z, e_{v_1}; i, j\} \qquad (8)$$

Similarly, denote $e_{v_{12}}$ and $e_{v_{21}}$ as the epipoles for $\{C_{21}, C_{12}\}$(see Fig. 3(b)). We can get

$$\frac{\pi}{2} - 2\theta = \frac{1}{2j} log\{v_z, e_{v_{21}}; i, j\} \qquad (9)$$

and

$$-\frac{\pi}{2} + 2\theta = \frac{1}{2j} log\{v_z, e_{v_{12}}; i, j\} \qquad (10)$$

Since v_1 and v_2 are the vanishing points of tangent lines which are perpendicular to mirrors. Obviously, we can get

$$\frac{\pi}{2} = \frac{1}{2j} log\{v_1, m_1; i, j\} \qquad (11)$$

and

$$\frac{\pi}{2} = \frac{1}{2j} log\{v_2, m_2; i, j\} \qquad (12)$$

From (11) (12), we can easily get m_1 and m_2, so that we can search for v_z by using Golden Section search [15] between m_1 and m_2.

Therefore, the epipoles e_{v_1} and e_{v_2} for $\{C, C_{12}\}$, $\{C, C_{21}\}$ and $\{C_1, C_2\}$; and the epipoles $e_{v_{12}}$ and $e_{v_{21}}$ for $\{C_{21}, C_{12}\}$ can be recovered by (9) (10) (11) (12). Draw bitangent lines on corresponding silhouettes from this epipoles, so that we can get 8 intersection points. Adding v_z, a hypothesis $\overline{l_s}$ is fitted by 9 points.

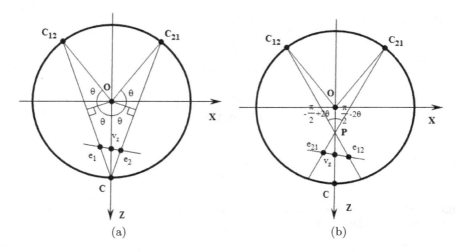

Fig. 3. Epipoles of two views in circular motion. (a) Rotation with 2θ. (b) Rotation with 4θ.

Using the sum of the distances between the 9 points and $\overline{l_s}$ to be the cost for Golden Section method can obtain a better rotation axis l_s.

After the initialized imaged rotation axis l_s is recovered, then the vanishing point v_z can be obtained as the intersection between l_s and l_h. The vanishing point v_x can also be easily recovered from the cross ratio $\{i, j; v_x, v_z\} = -1$.

And the optimization of the imaged rotation axis l_s may be carried out as two dimensional optimization problem by minimizing the distance from the transformed line $l'_i = W^{-T} l_i$ to the profile in the second image(see fig. 4). Where W is harmonic homology:

$$W = I - 2\frac{v_x l_s^T}{v_x^T l_s} \tag{13}$$

l_s and v_x can be further optimized by minimizing the transformation error of the silhouette brought about by the harmonic homology W.

3.3 Recovery of the Intrinsics

From section 3.2, the obtained imaged circular points can be used to find the camera intrinsics since they lie on the image of the absolute conic (IAC)ω. Besides, the imaged rotation axis l_s and the vanishing point v_x define a pole-polar relationship respect to ω [7]. It can then be estimated from the following constraints:

$$\begin{cases} i^T \omega i = 0 \quad \text{and} \quad j^T \omega j = 0 \\ l_s = \omega v_x \end{cases} \tag{14}$$

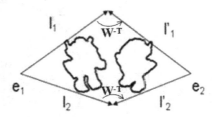

Fig. 4. The overlapping of two silhouettes and their epipolar tangents. l_1, l'_1, l_2 and l'_2 are the outer epipolar tangent lines.

At last, the intrinsics K can be obtained by Chloesky decomposition of IAC ω,

$$\omega^{-1} \sim KK^T \qquad (15)$$

4   Shape Recovery

In mathematical expression, the camera projection matrix P can be written as:

$$P = KR[R_y(\theta)| - T], \qquad (16)$$

where K is camera intrinsic parameter, R is the camera pose, $R_y(\theta)$ is the rotation matrix about rotation axis with angle θ and $T = \begin{bmatrix} 0 & 0 & 1 \end{bmatrix}^T$.

In order to unify the two different directions of turntable motions, let's image that there is a virtual mirror which passes through O and C. Let C_v be the reflection of C according to the virtual mirror(see fig. 2). The camera projection matrices for C and C_v can be written as:

$$P_C = KR[R_y(\theta)\Sigma| - T], \qquad (17)$$

$$P_{C_v} = KR[R_y(\theta)| - T] \qquad (18)$$

where $\Sigma = diag(\begin{bmatrix} -1 & 1 & 1 \end{bmatrix})$. The projection matrices for C_{21} and C_{12} can be derive easily in a similar way. So far, we have obtained all the parameters except camera pose. Zhang et al. [21] introduced a traditional method to obtain camera pose(see fig. 5).

According to this method, we firstly rotate the camera respect to Y-axis of so that the principal point x_0 can lie on rotation axis l_s. Secondly, we rotate the camera respect to Z-axis to enable rotation axis l_s to be perpendicular. At last, we rotate the camera respect to X-axis to enable the principal point x_0 to be the intersection of vanishing line l_h and rotation axis l_s.

Finally, we can use the projection matrix P to get a visual hull of a model.

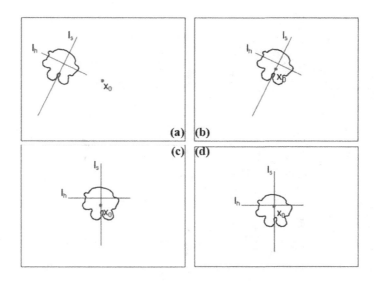

Fig. 5. Three steps of rectification. (a)Before rectification. (b)After rotated the camera with respect to Y-axis. (c)After rotated the camera with respect to Z-axis. (d)After rotated the camera with respect to X-axis.

5   Experimental Result

In this part, we show three experimental results of applying the approach to reconstruct 3D object models from three frames of video which contain three different motions of robot. The video had a resolution of 640 × 425. The natural camera was assumed to be zero-skew and unit aspect ratio when calibrated. The angle between the mirrors was computed to be 72.2 degrees. Table 1 shows the differences of results between our method and Zhang's checkerboard calibration method [23]. It can be told that focal length f and the u_0 coordinate of the principal point were both estimated with around 5% error compared to Zhang's method while v_0 was larger. It results from the accumulative error in the estimated v_x. Figure 6 shows the frames of video we used and the visual hull model of robot.

Table 1. Comparative results of the intrinsics between Zhang's method and our method

	f	u_0	v_0
Zhang's method	507.85	319.5	212
Proposed method	488.21	301.40	230.92
Error to Zhang's method	3.87%	5.67%	8.92%

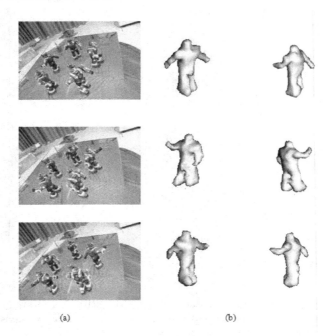

(a)   (b)

Fig. 6. Experimental result. (a) Three frames from video. (b) Visual hull models for corresponding frame.

6   Conclusion

In this paper, we have introduced a novel approach which transforms five views generated by two mirrors to turntable motion. Difference from previous silhouette-based methods, the approach requires a short video instead of a static snapshot. This can allow us to build a moving 3D model based on the motions of object. We used a simple formulation of the imaged circular points to obtain the image of absolute conic. A closed-form solution for the image invariants, the mirror angle and the camera intrinsics is obtained. After calibration, a visual hull of the objet can be obtained from the silhouettes. Experimental results demonstrated the performance of our approach.

Acknowledgments. This work is supported by the National Natural Science Foundation of China (Project no. 61005038) and an internal funding from United International College (Project no. R201312).

References

1. Fitzgibbon, A.W., Cross, G., Zisserman, A.: Automatic 3D model construction for turn-table sequences. In: Koch, R., Van Gool, L. (eds.) SMILE 1998. LNCS, vol. 1506, p. 155. Springer, Heidelberg (1998)

2. Faugeras, O., Luong, Q., Maybank, S.: Camera self-calibration: Theory and experiments. In: Proc. 2nd European Conf. on Computer Vision, pp. 321–334 (1992)
3. Forbes, K., Nicolls, F., de Jager, G., Voigt, A.: Shape-from-Silhouette with two mirrors and an uncalibrated camera. ECCV 2006. LNCS, vol. 3952, pp. 165–178. Springer, Heidelberg (2006)
4. Gluckman, J., Nayar, S.K.: Planar catadioptric stereo: Geometry and calibration. In: IEEE Computer Society Conference on Computer Vision and Pattern Recognition, vol. 1 (1999)
5. Guillemaut, J.Y., Kilner, J., Hilton, A.: Robust graph-cut scene segmentation and reconstruction for free-viewpoint video of complex dynamic scenes. In: 12th International Conference on Computer Vision, pp. 809–816 (2009)
6. Gupta, A., Martinez, J., Little, J.J., Woodham, R.J.: 3d pose from motion for cross-view action recognition via non-linear circulant temporal encoding. In: Proc. Conf. Computer Vision and Pattern Recognition (2014)
7. Hartley, R.I., Zisserman, A.: Multiple View Geometry in Computer Vision. Cambridge University Press, Cambridge (2000)
8. Hecht, E., Zajac, A.: Optics. Addison-Wesley (1974)
9. Liebowitz, D., Zisserman, A.: Metric rectification for perspective images of planes. In: Proc. Conf. Computer Vision and Pattern Recognition, pp. 482–488 (1998)
10. Liu, L., Shao, L., Rockett, P.: Boosted key-frame selection and correlated pyramidal motion-feature representation for human action recognition. Pattern Recognition 46(7), 1810–1818 (2013)
11. Lu, C., Jia, J., Tang, C.K.: Range-sample depth feature for action recognition. In: Proc. Conf. Computer Vision and Pattern Recognition (2014)
12. Lv, F., Zhao, T.: Self-calibration of a camera from video of a walking human. In: 16th International Conference on Pattern Recognition, vol. 1, pp. 562–567 (2002)
13. Martins, N., Dias, J.: Camera calibration using reflections in planar mirrors and object reconstruction using volume carving method. The Imaging Science Journal 52, 117–130 (2004)
14. Plänkers, R., Fua, P.: Articulated soft objects for multi-view shape and motion capture. IEEE Transactions on Pattern Analysis and Machine Intelligence 25(9), 1182–1187 (2003)
15. Press, W.H., Teukolsky, S.A., Vetterling, W.T., Flannery, B.P.: Numerical Recipes 3rd Edition: The Art of Scientific Computing. Cambridge University Press, New York (2007)
16. Semple, J., Kneebone, G.: Algebraic Projective Geometry. Oxford University Press, USA (1952)
17. Shao, L., Jones, S., Li, X.: Efficient search and localization of human actions in video databases. IEEE Transactions on Circuits and Systems for Video Technology 24(3), 504–512 (2014)
18. Shao, L., Zhen, X., Tao, D., Li, X.: Spatio-temporal laplacian pyramid coding for action recognition. IEEE Transactions on Cybernetics 44(6), 817–827 (2014)
19. Sinha, S.N., Pollefeys, M., McMillan, L.: Camera network calibration from dynamic silhouettes. In: CVPR, vol. 1, pp. 195–202 (2004)
20. Ying, X., Peng, K., Y.B. Hou, S.G., J. Kong, H.Z.: Self-Calibration of Catadioptric Camera with Two Planar Mirrors from Silhouettes. IEEE Trans. on Pattern Analysis and Machine Intelligence (2012)

21. Zhang, H., Mendonça, P.R.S., Wong, K.Y.K.: Reconstruction of surface of revolution from multiple uncalibrated views: A bundle-adjustment approach. In: Proc. Asian Conference on Computer Vision (ACCV2004), pp. 378–383. Jeju Island, Korea, January 2004
22. Zhang, H., Shao, L., Wong, K.-Y.K.: Self-calibration and motion recovery from silhouettes with two mirrors. In: Lee, K.M., Matsushita, Y., Rehg, J.M., Hu, Z. (eds.) ACCV 2012, Part IV. LNCS, vol. 7727, pp. 1–12. Springer, Heidelberg (2013)
23. Zhang, Z.: A flexible new technique for camera calibration. IEEE Trans. Pattern Anal. Mach. Intell. **22**(11), 1330–1334 (2000)

Efficient Online Spatio-Temporal Filtering for Video Event Detection

Xinchen Yan[1,2,3], Junsong Yuan[2]([⊠]), and Hui Liang[2]

[1] Department of Computer Science and Engineering,
Shanghai Jiao Tong University, Shanghai 200240, China
skywalkeryxc@gmail.com
[2] School of Electrical and Electronic Engineering,
Nanyang Technological University, Singapore 639798, Singapore
jsyuan@ntu.edu.sg, hliang1@e.ntu.edu.sg
[3] Computer Science and Engineering Division,
Electrical Engineering and Computer Science Department, University of Michigan,
Ann Arbor, MI 48105, USA

Abstract. We propose a novel spatio-temporal filtering technique to improve the per-pixel prediction map, by leveraging the spatio-temporal smoothness of the video signal. Different from previous techniques that perform spatio-temporal filtering in an offline/batch mode, e.g., through graphical model, our filtering can be implemented online and in real-time, with provable lowest computational complexity. Moreover, it is compatible to any image analysis module that can produce per-pixel map of detection scores or multi-class prediction distributions. For each pixel, our filtering finds the optimal spatio-temporal trajectory in the past frames that has the maximum accumulated detection score. Pixels with small accumulated detection score will be treated as false alarm thus suppressed. To demonstrate the effectiveness of our online spatio-temporal filtering, we perform three video event tasks: salient action discovery, walking pedestrian detection, and sports event detection, all in an online/causal way. The experimental results on the three datasets demonstrate the excellent performances of our filtering scheme when compared with the state-of-the-art methods.

1 Introduction

Despite the success of object/event detection in images, it remains a challenging task to extend state-of-the-art image analysis techniques to streaming videos. It is not uncommon that the generated per-pixel prediction map becomes more noisy and unreliable due to the low quality of video data, e.g., illumination variations, motion blur, low resolution, not to mention the challenges caused by moving camera.

Instead of performing image analysis on each video frame independently, enforcing consistent labels among pixels over space and time has shown great improvement of the prediction map and avoids the "flickering" prediction in streaming videos [20,22,26]. Many existing spatio-temporal filtering methods

L. Agapito et al. (Eds.): ECCV 2014 Workshops, Part I, LNCS 8925, pp. 769–785, 2015.
DOI: 10.1007/978-3-319-16178-5_54

[4, 10, 20, 23, 26, 35], only works in an offline/batch mode where the whole video is required to perform the spatio-temporal smoothing of prediction maps. In streaming video applications, however, we need to refine the prediction map by only using the previous detections without accessing future frames. As a result, offline filtering methods are not directly applicable. Therefore, we still lack efficient online spatio-temporal filtering schemes for video event detection.

Motivated by classic linear causal filtering, we propose a novel online spatio-temporal filtering method to improve the per-pixel prediction map of streaming videos. Suppose the image analysis module can produce a per-pixel discriminative detection map for each video frame, e.g. positive value for positive class while negative value for negative class. For each pixel at the detection map, we search for its optimal spatio-temporal trajectory in the previous frames with maximum accumulated detection score, as illustrated in Figure 1. Pixel with small accumulated detection score will be treated as false alarm thus filtered. Pixel that miss detected can be retrieved if one can find a historical trajectory of high accumulated scores to support itself. Compared to classic linear causal filters, our proposed filtering method can adaptively choose the temporal window size to perform temporal filtering. Our spatio-temporal filtering can be easily extended to handle per-pixel prediction map where each pixel is associated with a multi-class probability distribution rather than a single discriminative score. It can also easily incorporate appearance modeling to improve detection results. The proposed filtering method is general enough for video event/object detection applications.

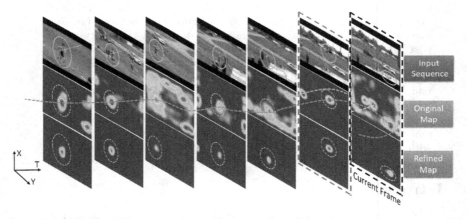

Fig. 1. Overview of our proposed spatio-temporal filtering, which refines the current prediction map by accumulating prediction score at previous frames

In order to search for optimal spatio-temporal trajectories of each pixel with high efficiency, we further design an online dynamic programming algorithm that can achieve the goal with lowest time complexity and small memory cost. Instead of searching for the optimal trajectory per pixel, we propagate the accumulated score from one frame to another, with optimality guarantee. In practice, our online spatio-temporal filtering algorithm can run 67 frames per second for video of size 320×240, given that per-pixel detection map is available and parameters have been set.

To evaluate the effectiveness of our online spatio-temporal filtering, we perform three video event tasks: salient action discovery, walking pedestrian detection, and sports event detection. The excellent performances compared with the state-of-the-art methods validate the effectiveness and efficiency of the proposed spatio-temporal filtering method.

2 Related Work

Omniscient Spatio-Temporal Filtering. Omniscient approaches [1,2,4,7, 11,23,26,30,32,33,35,38,39] take both past and future data into consideration. Andriluka et al. [1] introduced a hierarchical Gaussian process latent variable model to improve people-detection by people-tracklet detection in frames. Berclaz et al. [4] formulated multi-target tracking as a k-shortest node-disjoint paths problem and utilized disjoint path algorithm in calculation. Pirsiavash et al. [26] formulated multi-target tracking as a "spatio-temporal grouping" problem and proposed a near-optimal algorithm based on dynamic programming. Lan et al. [18] built a figure-centered model for joint action localization and categorization based on statistical scene context and structural representation of individual person. Tran et al. [35] formulated video event detection as a spatio-temporal path discovery problem. They proposed an OPD algorithm that searches the global optimal path that connects a sequence of regions with efficiency. Tran et al. [34] and Nataliya et al. [23] implemented structured output learning combined with spatio-temporal smoothing over entire video sequences.

Causal Spatio-Temporal Filtering. Causal approaches [6,8,12–14,17,19,22, 24,25,29,42] perform online spatio-temporal filtering relying on past data only. Kalman filtering had been used to aggregate data over time by Kim and Woods [17], and Patti et al. [25]. Paris et al. [24] derived the equivalent tool of mean-shift image segmentation for video streams based on ubiquitous use of the Gaussian kernel. Leibe et al. [19] introduced a non-Markovian hypothesis selection framework that searches globally optimal set of spatio-temporal trajectories for object detection. Grundmann et al. [12] proposed a hierarchical graph-based algorithm to segment long video sequences. Chen and Corso [6] introduced a Video Graph-Shifts approach for efficiently incorporating temporal consistency into MRF energy minimization framework. Hernández et al. [13] proposed a generic framework for object segmentation using depth maps based on Random Forests and Graph-cuts theory. Miksik et al. [22] designed a filtering algorithm to improve scene analysis by learning visual similarities across frames.

3 Online Spatio-Temporal Filtering

3.1 Problem Formulation

For each frame I_t of a video sequence S, we denote its per-pixel prediction map as M_t. For each pixel $\mathbf{p} = (x, y)$, let $M_t(\mathbf{p})$ denote the corresponding detection score. Without loss of generality, we assume the prediction map is discriminative, where $M_t(\mathbf{p}) \in [-1, 1]$. A positive score of $M_t(\mathbf{p})$ indicates a strong response at pixel $\mathbf{p}$ of the t−th frame, while a negative score stands for weak response.

As the prediction map M_t is generated independently per image, temporal consistency of pixel labels among video frames is not considered. Thus, it is necessary to avoid the "flickering" prediction issue by enforcing consistent labels among pixels over time. To denoise the prediction map, we believe the online spatio-temporal filtering should be able to achieve the following three goals.

1. it can suppress false alarm prediction of M_t based on previous prediction maps;
2. it can recover missing prediction of M_t based on previous prediction maps;
3. it can be performed online and implemented in real-time.

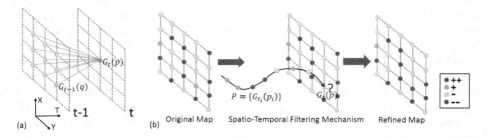

(a)

(b)   Original Map   Spatio-Temporal Filtering Mechanism   Refined Map

Fig. 2. Online Spatio-Temporal Filtering by refining prediction score of each pixel through finding a spaito-temporal path that has the maximum accumulated score. (a) spatio-temporal trellis. (b) our spatio-temporal filtering mechanism.

For the above three requirements, classic linear causal filters such as temporal mean filter may not provide satisfactory result as the prediction noise can be abrupt and non-Gaussian. To provide a better filtering, we design a novel non-linear filtering criterion. To help better explain our idea, we introduce a 3-dimensional trellis $W \times H \times T$ denoted by $\mathcal{G}$, where $W \times H$ is the frame size and T is the length of sequence. We denote each pixel $\mathbf{p}$ of the t−th frame as a vertex $\mathcal{G}_t(\mathbf{p})$. As shown in Figure 2, in the trellis, each vertex is connected to the spatial neighbors, e.g., 9-neighborhood in the previous frame. In general, we measure the distance between two pixels $\mathbf{p}$ and $\mathbf{q}$ by $\|\mathbf{p} - \mathbf{q}\|_\infty$, where $\|\mathbf{x}\|_\infty = \max\{|x_1|, |x_2|, \cdots, |x_d|\}$. For simplicity, $\|\mathbf{p} - \mathbf{q}\|_\infty$ is denoted as $\|\mathbf{p} - \mathbf{q}\|$. We define a spatio-temporal trajectory as a path $\mathcal{P}$, which connects a sequence of vertices $\mathcal{P} = \{\mathcal{G}_{t_i}(\mathbf{p}_i)\}$ in consecutive frames.

For each vertex $\mathcal{G}_t(\mathbf{p})$, we search for the maximum path in the past prediction maps that can generate the overall accumulated score. For each pixel, its maximum path score is denoted by $U_t(\mathbf{p})$. As the length of our path is adaptive (e.g. $1 \leq s \leq t$), we actually perform adaptive temporal filtering rather than performing temporal filtering with a fixed length window. For each pixel, its refined prediction map is the multiplication of the original prediction score and its maximum path score. Formally, the following definition explains how to obtain the refined prediction map from the original map.

$$U_t(\mathbf{p}) = \max_{s\,:\,1\leq s\leq t}\left\{\max_{\mathbf{p}_i:\|\mathbf{p}_i-\mathbf{p}_{i+1}\|\leq R}\sum_{t_i=s}^{t-1}M_{t_i}(\mathbf{p}_i)\right\} + M_t(\mathbf{p})$$

$$M_t'(\mathbf{p}) = M_t(\mathbf{p}) \times U_t(\mathbf{p})$$

(1)

From Eq. 1, we can see that the accumulated detection score $U_t(\cdot)$ serves as the confidence weight that strengths or weakens original prediction score $M_t(\cdot)$. For example, the prediction $M_t(\mathbf{p})$ will be enhanced if there exists a spatio-temporal trajectory $\mathcal{P} = \{\mathcal{G}_{t_i}(\mathbf{p}_i)\}$ ending at $\mathcal{G}_t(\mathbf{p})$ with large enough accumulated score. On the other hand, even if the pixel has a strong positive detection at the current location, if it is an isolated one and cannot find a historical path to support itself, the detection at that location will be treated as false alarm thus suppressed.

To verify the effectiveness of our filtering scheme, we simulate a video sequence of prediction maps $\{M_t\}$. The noise ϵ is generated first, in which the noise follows a Gaussian distribution $\mathcal{N}(\mu_\epsilon, \sigma_\epsilon^2)$. On top of the noise map, the object is generated as a sequence of bounding boxes centered at pixel $\mathbf{p}_t$ in the t−th frame. To incorporate the slow motion constraint, we require $\|\mathbf{p}_i - \mathbf{p}_{i+1}\| \leq R$ (R is an upper bound on spatial-temporal consistency). For each frame, pixels in the object bounding box are treated as the target and the values also follow Gaussian distribution $\mathcal{N}(\mu, \sigma^2)$. Finally, by following Eq 1, we visualize the simulated prediction map, filtered map (mean) and our refined map in Figure 3. The mean filter refers to averaged score over fixed number of frames (10) for each pixel at the same location. It is worth noting that mean filter addresses short-term temporal consistency well but fails to take long-term temporal consistency into consideration (shown in Figure 3). Detailed configuration of the simulation has been included in supplementary materials.

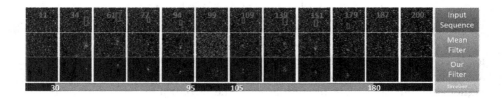

Fig. 3. Visualized snapshots of a simulated video sequence. The top row shows the groundtruth and frame number, in which the target exists from 30th frame to 180th frame and is temporally overwhelmed by noise from 95th frame to 105th frame. The second row and the third row compares results of mean filter and our filter. It is clear that our filter achieves better refined prediction map. More importantly, mean filter fails to recover the signal from 95th frame to 105th frame when signal is overwhelmed by noise.

From the simulation result, it shows that our filtering can suppress false alarm predictions. Since a false alarm prediction $M_t(\mathbf{p})$ is usually not supported by a high accumulated detection score $U_t(\mathbf{p})$ and hence will be suppressed. Similarly, the filtering criterion can address miss predictions. A missing prediction at pixel $\mathbf{p}$ is often featured by $0 < M_t(\mathbf{p}) < M_t(\mathbf{q})$, where $\mathbf{q}$ is another pixel with much lower accumulated detection score $U_t(\mathbf{q})$ compared to $U_t(\mathbf{p})$. Since refined prediction map is generated by multiplying M_t and U_t, it is likely $0 < M_t(\mathbf{q}) \times U_t(\mathbf{q}) < M_t(\mathbf{p}) \times U_t(\mathbf{p})$. Thus, the missing prediction in M_t will be recovered in the refined prediction map M_t' with high chance. In our formulation, we do not recover missing prediction when $M_t(\mathbf{p}) \le 0$, since it may lead to false alarm prediction again.

3.2   Online Filtering Algorithm

Despite the effectiveness of our online spatio-temporal filtering, its implementation is a non-trivial issue. The search space of the spatio-temporal path for each pixels is $O(c^T)$, where c denotes the number of spatial neighbors. Following the idea of using dynamic programming, [35] and [26], we can reduce the cost of finding one path to $O(T)$, thus the cost of a whole frame is $O(W \times H \times T)$ as there are $W \times H$ pixels. Considering that we have in total T frames, the computational cost will be $O(W \times H \times T^2)$.

In order to provide real-time implementation, we propose an efficient online filtering algorithm that further reduces the complexity to obtain the accumulated map U_t. Instead of finding spatio-temporal path for each pixel separately, dynamic programming helps to avoid redundant calculation of subproblems (e.g. $U_{t-1}(\mathbf{p})$ and $U_{t-1}(\mathbf{q})$). The idea of our algorithm can be explained in the following Lemma.

Lemma 1. $U_t(\mathbf{p})$ *resulted from Eq. 2 is the maximum accumulated detection score tracing back from* $\mathcal{G}_t(\mathbf{p})$.

$$U_t(\mathbf{p}) = \max\left\{ \max_{\|\mathbf{p}-\mathbf{q}\| \le R} U_{t-1}(\mathbf{q}), 0 \right\} + M_t(\mathbf{p}) \tag{2}$$

The correctness of Lemma 1 is proved in supplementary material. Intuitively, for $U_{t-1}(\mathbf{q}) < 0$, it cannot bring higher accumulated detection score in the future and hence will be neglected. On the contrary, for $U_{t-1}(\mathbf{q}) > 0$, we can obtain a higher accumulation score by adding it to the next frame. Our online filtering algorithm achieves the lowest time complexity $O(W \times H)$ for one step, and so it has an overall complexity $O(W \times H \times T)$ for the whole video. Based on the observation that calculation of $U_t(\mathbf{p})$ in Eq. 2 only relies on input $M_t(\mathbf{p})$ and accumulated detection score in previous frame $U_{t-1}(\mathbf{q})$, we then implement an iterative filtering algorithm with the memory cost $O(W \times H)$.

To ensure that $M_t' \in [-1, 1]$, accumulated map U_t will be normalized to $\widetilde{U}_t$ that satisfying $\widetilde{U}_t \in [0, 1]$. The technical details will be discussed in experiments. The radius R can be chosen by users to satisfy different requirements.

Algorithm 1. Online Filtering Algorithm

1: Calculate $M_1(\mathbf{p})$ based on input I_1;
2: $U_1(\mathbf{p}) \leftarrow M_1(\mathbf{p}), \forall \mathbf{p}$;
3: **for** $t \leftarrow 2$ to n **do**
4:     Calculate $M_t(\mathbf{p})$ based on input I_t;
5:     **for all** $\mathbf{p} \in [1, W] \times [1, H]$ **do**
6:         $\mathbf{q}' \leftarrow \mathrm{argmax}_{\|\mathbf{p}-\mathbf{q}\| \leq R} U_{t-1}(\mathbf{q})$;
7:         $U_t(\mathbf{p}) \leftarrow \max\{U_{t-1}(\mathbf{q}'), 0\} + M_t(\mathbf{p})$;
8:     **end for**
9:     Release the space of $U_{t-1}(\cdot)$ and $M_{t-1}(\cdot)$;
10:    Calculate $\widetilde{U}_t(\cdot)$ based on $U_i(\cdot)$;
11:    **for all** $\mathbf{p} \in [1, W] \times [1, H]$ **do**
12:        $M_t'(\mathbf{p}) \leftarrow M_t(\mathbf{p}) \times \widetilde{U}_t(\mathbf{p})$;
13:    **end for**
14: **end for**

When slow motion constraint can be satisfied, a smaller R is preferred. Otherwise, larger R is utilized to handle the effect of fast camera motion.

Multi-class label prediction. Our proposed method can be easily applied to multi-class pixel labeling. In such a case, each pixel has a prediction of multi-class distribution. Instead of working on a single prediction map, we can separate K different prediction maps $M_t(\cdot, k)$ for different classes, where K is the number of classes. Similarly, we accumulate detection scores separately via K different accumulated maps $U_t(\cdot, k)$.

3.3 Spatio-Temporal Filtering by Appearance Tracking

One limitation of our spatio-temporal filtering in Sec. 3.2 is that it only takes the prediction map into consideration while does not leverage extra information such as the appearance of the target. To mitigate this problem, we can incorporate tracking into our framework by adding the weight of the edge in the trellis. By measuring the visual similarity between two neighboring vertices in the trellis, we define $\mathcal{W}_{t_i}(\mathbf{p}_i, \mathbf{p}_{i+1})$ as the weight of the edge connecting two vertices.

Instead of only summing up vertex scores in a path, the accumulated score now sums all the edge scores and vertex scores. For each spatio-temporal trajectory $\mathcal{P} = \{\mathcal{G}_{t_i}(\mathbf{p}_i)\}$, we introduce an energy function $\mathcal{E}(\mathcal{P})$ that accumulates not only the detection scores, but also the tracking scores.

$$\mathcal{E}(\mathcal{P}) = -U(\mathcal{P}) - \lambda \cdot \mathcal{E}_a(\mathcal{P}) \qquad (3)$$

The first term $U(\mathcal{P}) = \sum_{t_i=1}^{T} M_{t_i}(\mathbf{p}_i)$ represents the accumulated detection score while the second term $\mathcal{E}_a(P) = \sum_{t_i=1}^{T-1} \mathcal{W}_{t_i}(\mathbf{p}_i, \mathbf{p}_{i+1})$ stands for the accumulated visual similarity measure thus is the tracking score. Intuitively, the energy $\mathcal{E}(P)$ is minimized with presence of higher accumulated detection and appearance score, where λ is referred as *appearance weight* which will be further discussed in the experiments.

Lemma 2. $\mathcal{E}_t(\mathbf{p})$ *resulted from Eq. 4 is the minimum accumulated energy tracing back from* $\mathcal{G}_t(\mathbf{p})$.

$$\mathcal{E}_t(\mathbf{p}) = \begin{cases} -M_t(\mathbf{p}) & t = 1 \\ \min\left\{\min_{\|\mathbf{p}-\mathbf{q}\| \leq R}\{\mathcal{E}_{t-1}(\mathbf{q}) - \lambda \cdot \mathcal{W}_t(\mathbf{q}, \mathbf{p})\}, 0\right\} - M_t(\mathbf{p}) & t > 1 \end{cases} \quad (4)$$

In order to calculate the minimum energy *tracing back from* $\mathcal{G}_t(\mathbf{p})$ (denoted by $\mathcal{E}_t(\mathbf{p})$) with high efficiency, we design a similar algorithm, as shown in Algorithm 2.

The correctness of Lemma 2 and Algorithm 2 have been proved in supplementary materials. In our implementation, we set $\mathcal{W}_{t_i}(\mathbf{p}_i, \mathbf{p}_{i+1}) = K(h_{t_i}(\mathbf{p}_i),$ $h_{t_i}(\mathbf{p}_{i+1}))$, where $h_t(\mathbf{p})$ is intensity histogram of local patch centered at $\mathbf{p}$ at the t–th frame I_t. The similarity is measured by $K(h, h_*) = b - \|h - h_*\|$. Here, the bias b is to ensure discriminative score of appearance similarity, where histograms h and h_* should be normalized before calculation.

Algorithm 2. Energy Minimization

1: Calculate $M_1(\mathbf{p})$ and $h_1(\mathbf{p})$ based on input I_1;
2: $\mathcal{E}_1(\mathbf{p}) \leftarrow -M_1(\mathbf{p}), \forall \mathbf{p}$;
3: **for** $t \leftarrow 2$ to n **do**
4:     Calculate $M_t(\mathbf{p})$ and $h_t(\mathbf{p})$ based on input I_t;
5:     **for all** $\mathbf{p} \in [1, W] \times [1, H]$ **do**
6:         $\mathbf{q}' \leftarrow \text{argmin}_{\|\mathbf{q}-\mathbf{p}\| \leq R}\{\mathcal{E}_{t-1}(\mathbf{q}) - \lambda \cdot K(h_{t-1}(\mathbf{q}), h_t(\mathbf{p}))\}$;
7:         $\mathcal{E}_t(\mathbf{p}) \leftarrow \mathcal{E}_{t-1}(\mathbf{q}') - \lambda \cdot K(h_{t-1}(\mathbf{q}'), h_t(\mathbf{p})) - M_t(\mathbf{p})$;
8:     **end for**
9:     Release the space of $\mathcal{E}_{t-1}(\cdot)$, $h_{t-1}(\cdot)$, and $M_{t-1}(\cdot)$;
10: **end for**

---

4 Experiments

The evaluation of our online filtering algorithm is composed of three different experiments. In Sec. 4.1, we show temporal consistency of video saliency can be utilized to discover video event in an unsupervised way. This helps to detect salient object in videos, which achieves higher accuracy in UCF101 Dataset[1] [31]. In Sec. 4.2, we illustrate that our appearance tracking version achieves superior performance when detecting actions (walking pedestrians) at UIUC-NTU Youtube Walking Dataset[2] [35]. In Sec. 4.3, we demonstrate that when combined with Exemplar-SVMs, our spatio-temporal filter can achieve excellent performances when localizing complex actions with large intra-class variations.

---

[1] http://crcv.ucf.edu/data/UCF101.php
[2] http://www.cs.dartmouth.edu/~dutran/projects/event/

4.1   Unsupervised Video Event Discovery via Saliency Map Filtering

In this experiment, we show that video saliency maps can be improved by proposed filtering algorithm. In addition, the refined saliency map can be utilized to discover video event in an unsupervised way. Discovering events based on accumulated saliency parallels the theory that selective visual attention results from competition among multiple responses in visual cortex [5,36].

Method. We leverage a Phase Discrepancy method [43] to generate motion saliency map. This method works well with slow moving background, but will output noisy saliency map when applied to fast moving background, changes in lighting condition, and camera zooming. Since values of saliency map ranges from 0 to 1, we therefore introduce a further step to generate discriminative prediction scores M_t. That is, M_t is normalized by $M_t \sim \mathcal{N}(0,1)$. In this experiment, we fix the radius to $R = 3$ pixels.

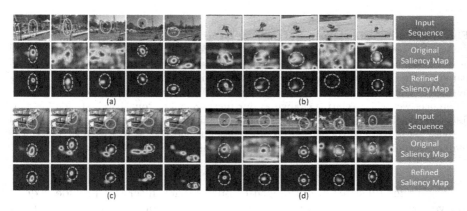

Fig. 4. Qualitative results on UCF101 Dataset. Four sequences are (a) "pole vault", (b) "skiing", (c) "diving", and (d) "long jump". In general, the four sequences represent four challenges in saliency map generation: (a) fast movement, (b) noisy saliency map, (b) several saliency regions, and (d) fast camera motion. For each video sequence, we visualize original saliency map as well as refined map obtained from our spatio-temporal filter. Note our filter is able to refine saliency map via long-term temporal consistency.

We use UCF101 Dataset [31] for test, which provides fully annotated bounding boxes for 25 action categories. For this experiment, more than 2000 video sequences from 15 categories have been tested.

Results. We provide qualitative results of our filtering method first, as shown in Figure 4. The video sequences are quite challenging: saliency maps generated by baseline method [43] are frequently overwhelmed by noise. In such situations, existing causal linear filters cannot work well, since their performance are largely determined by few previous frames. However, our filter deals with this difficulty by treating all previous frames equally and selectively accumulating scores. The refined saliency maps, are shown to have higher quality.

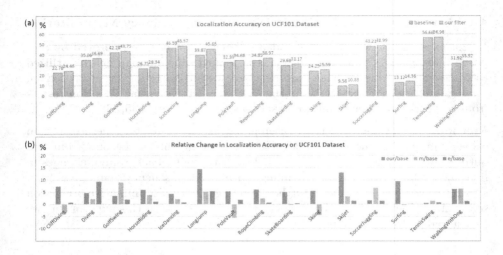

Fig. 5. Quantitative comparison of localization accuracy on UCF101 Dataset. (a) Comparison between our filter and baseline method. We use Phase Discrepancy method [43] as our baseline. On average, our filter improves about 2% of absolute accuracy compared to the baseline method. (b) Comparison in localization accuracy (%) among our filter, (temporal) mean filter, and (temporal) exponential filter. To highlight the difference, we utilize relative change as our measurement ("our/base" stands for "our filter vs. baseline method", "m/base" stands for "mean filter vs. baseline method", and "e/base" stands for "exponential filter vs. baseline method"). In this test, we fix the temporal window of size 10 for both mean filter and exponential filter.

To further illustrate the strength of our saliency filter, we provide a qualitative comparison. Since this dataset does not provide groundtruth mask for motion saliency, we take a further step to localize salient object in videos. That is, we evaluate the saliency of a region Ω by summing up the discriminative scores at every pixel: $\sum_{\mathbf{p} \in \Omega} M_t(\mathbf{p})$.

We evaluate the localization accuracy in each frame by PASCAL metric (shown in Figure 5(a)). On average, our filter achieves 1.76% improvements in accuracy (6.20% of relative improvements). To show the difference between our filter and classic linear causal filters (e.g. mean filter and exponential filter), we also compare the relative change of localization accuracy (shown in Figure 5(b)). Although the quantitative evaluation of saliency filtering is conducted indirectly (via localization accuracy), improvements in localization accuracy still illustrate effectiveness of our filtering method to some extent. Note that performance of salient object detector varies between different action categories. For actions like "long jump" and "diving", in which actor moves horizontally or vertically, baseline detector is able to output valid saliency map. But actor's tiny scale in "cliff diving" and actor's fast movement in "pole vault" greatly affect the quality of saliency map. Even in such scenarios, our proposed filtering algorithm still contributes to accuracy improvements.

Finally, our online filtering algorithm can run at 67 fps with binary classification setting when input size is 320×240 pixels, radius is 3 using C++ Implementation, where the experiments are conducted on a computer with Intel(R) Core(TM) i5-4570 CPU and 8GB RAM. Note that we do not take into account I/O delays and the time for generating baseline saliency map.

4.2 Walking Pedestrian Detection

In this experiment, we show that our online spatio-temporal filtering can benefit object/action localization in video sequences by appearance modeling and tracking.

Method. Following [35], a walking pedestrian detector was previously trained by SVM with TUD-Motion Pairs [40] Dataset, while features of HOG [9], IMHd2, and Self-Similarity [37] are combined in the training step. We use UIUC-NTU Youtube Walking Dataset for testing, which consists of 27 video sequences (25 short videos of 100-150 frames and 2 long videos of 800-900 frames) of catwalk models. This data-set is challenging since catwalk models are frequently exposed to occlusions, changes in lighting conditions and cluttered background.

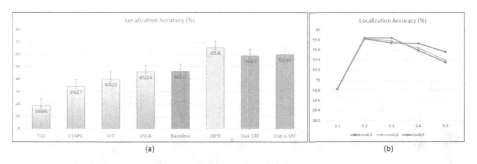

Fig. 6. Quantitative comparison on NTU-UIUC Youtube Walking Dataset. (a) Comparison of four online tracking algorithms, detection baseline, OPD algorithm and our spatio-temporal filtering method ("STF" for original version and "a-STF" for appearance tracking version). Our proposed filtering method improves 12-14% of accuracy compared to baseline detector and achieves superior performance over online tracking algorithms. (b) Averaged localization accuracy (%) of appearance tracking version over different *appearance weights* λ. The y-coordinate is localization accuracy, while the x-coordinate represents *appearance weight* λ. Three different *appearance adaptation ratios* r_u are used in the test.

We first generate dense detection maps using our SVM classifier on 15 different scales. Then, we take detection maps as input for our spatio-temporal filtering. To localize walking pedestrian, we report our filtering result by the region $\Omega(\mathbf{p})$ centered at pixel $\mathbf{p}$ with maximum refined prediction score in each frame. To take scale changes into consideration, we modify the distance metric a little: $\|\mathbf{p} - \mathbf{q}\| + \|\delta_{\mathbf{p}} - \delta_{\mathbf{q}}\| \leq R$, where $\delta_{\mathbf{p}}$ corresponds to the scale order of region $\Omega(\mathbf{p})$. For our appearance tracking version, a simple color histogram h is used to calculate appearance score and we fix radius R to 2. In addition, we introduce a ratio r_u in Eq. 5 to set appearance score dynamically for *appearance adaptation* and better tracking.

$$\mathcal{W}_{t_i}(\mathbf{p}_i, \mathbf{p}_{i+1}) = K(\overline{H}_{t_i}(\mathbf{p}_i), h_{t_i}(\mathbf{p}_{i+1}))$$
$$\overline{H}_{t_{i+1}}(\mathbf{p}_{i+1}) = r_u \cdot \overline{H}_{t_i}(\mathbf{p}_i) + (1 - r_u) \cdot h_{t_{i+1}}(\mathbf{p}_{i+1}) \tag{5}$$

Such a strategy brings certain improvements in our test. However, achieving minimum energy $\min_{\mathbf{p}} \mathcal{E}_t(\mathbf{p})$ under Eq. 5 turns out to be intractable in polynomial time. We attempt to minimize the energy by updating dynamic appearance $\overline{H}_t$.

For comparison, detection baseline, OPD algorithm [35] as well as four online tracking algorithms (L1APG [3], ASLA [15], TLD [16], and IVT [28]) are utilized. We report the region with maximum prediction score in each frame as baseline detection result. Note that OPD algorithm utilizes both past and future prediction maps to localize walking pedestrian, which is an omniscient (non-causal) method. For each of four trackers, we report tracking accuracy based on maximum score under *SRE* defined in [41], so the result is comparatively independent of initialized bounding box.

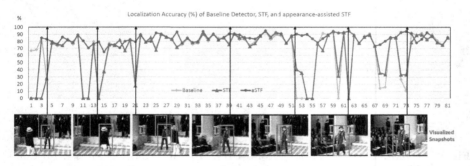

Fig. 7. Plots of localization accuracy of baseline detector, our spatio-temporal filtering method, and appearance tracking version with visualized snapshots. In the visualized snapshots, localization results are represented by bounding boxes of different colors ("orange" for groundtruth, "green" for baseline, "blue" for our filter, and "red" for our appearance tracking version).

Results. The evaluation is based on averaged localization accuracy of each frame under PASCAL metric. Figure 6(a) compares localization accuracy of four online tracking algorithms, baseline detector, OPD algorithm [35], and two versions of our spatio-temporal filtering method. In general, baseline detector fails to localize walking pedestrian due to challenging testing sequences with cluttered background. By utilizing temporal consistency, our filter can improve localization to about 12-14% compared to baseline result For roughly one-third of video sequences, tracking algorithms fail to capture the target even in the first 30 frames due to catwalk models' fast walking. It is worth noting that OPD [35] achieves higher accuracy by taking both past and future data, while our filter is a causal method and can be implemented in real-time.

Figure 6(b) illustrates the performance of proposed filtering method with different λ, the parameter to balance between detection score and visual similarity. When baseline detector outputs reasonable detection map, small λ is enough to refine detection map. But when baseline detector fails frequently to provide valid detection results, larger weight λ is preferred as appearance tracking can help throughout filtering process. For all 27 video sequences, our appearance tracking achieves better performance compared to our original version that does not utilize appearance tracking (shown in Figure 7).

4.3   UCF Sports Action Detection

In this experiment, we show that our filtering with Exemplar-SVMs [21] can beat state-of-the-art action detection approaches on more complex actions (with large intra-class variations).

Method. We evaluate our action detection method on the UCF Sports dataset, which consists of 150 video clips from broadcast television channels with 10 different action categories (e.g., "diving", "golf swinging", "kicking"). Two action categories, "diving" and "horse riding", are evaluated, since they are representative. For action "diving", athlete is moving fast vertically with various shapes and poses. But for all athletes, appearances are quite similar. For action "horse riding", athlete is moving horizontally with various appearances and poses.

Following the training-testing splits proposed by [18], we train our Exemplar-SVMs for each category using two-thirds of video frames and test on remaining one-third frames. TUD MotionPairs [40] is chosen as negative set, which consists of 196 image pairs taken from city district. To better adapt this negative set to our action detection task, we add 40 examples from Google search engine with similar background configuration as our positive samples. Intuitively, these additional negative samples enhance the generalization of our trained model. Half of training frames are used to train individual exemplar while remaining frames are utilized for calibration. In total, 270 exemplars are trained for action "diving" and 240 for action "horse riding" with HOG feature.

Action detection is based on the localization scheme. For each frame, the maximum score corresponded region is selected as our action detection results. For our filtering framework, we generate a collection of prediction maps with different aspect ratios and scales with interpolated discriminative scores based on sparse outputs of Exemplar-SVMs.

We compare our method with three state-of-the-art approaches. [18] implemented figure-centered model trained by latent SVM with HOG feature. [34] and [23] implemented structured output learning with both static feature HOG and motion feature HOF and HOMB [27] and both results are smoothed in a spatio-temporal scheme over entire video.

Table 1. Quantitative comparison of action localization accuracy on UCF Sports Dataset. The averaged localization accuracy is evaluated based on PASCAL metric (intersection divided by the union of detection and ground truth). The five columns are methods of [18], [34], [23], our Exemplar-based action detection, and our Exemplar-based action detection with online spatio-temporal refinement. In both categories, our final version (corresponding to the rightmost column) shows excellent performances when performin action localization.

Method / Category	Lan [18]	Tran [34]	Nataliya [23]	Exemplar	Exemplar+OSTF
Horse Riding	21.75	68.06	20.30	**73.59**	**73.59**
Diving	42.67	36.54	**52.37**	48.33	**50.19**

Results. As shown in Table 1, our method achieves more than 5% accuracy over Lan's and Tran's methods on two categories of UCF Sports Dataset and also approximates Nataliya's method when detecting "diving" action.

Note that [18] built a figure-centered model for each action, while [34] and [23] utilized motion feature like HOF and implemented spatio-temporal smoothing over entire video. However, our method filters the detection map with only HOG feature in use. We attribute the improved localization results to the unique training mechanism and our filtering method. More specifically, the Exemplar-SVMs help to address large intra-class variations in sports actions. When Exemplar-SVMs fail to work well, online spatio-temporal filtering can still improve the localization results a little bit (see Table 1).

As illustrated in Figure 8, our detection method performs better localization results compared to current localization methods. Note that [18] tends to miss detect target action and leads to false alarm detections due to background clut-

Fig. 8. Visualization of action localization of our Exemplar-based method, methods of [18] and [34]. In the visualized snapshots, localization results are represented by bounding boxes of different colors ("green" for groundtruth, "yellow" for Lan's method, "white" for Tran's method, and "red" for our Exemplar-based version (without online spatio-temporal filtering).

ter. Also, the temporal consistency is not well addressed by its figure-centered model. Compared to Lan's method, [34] produces more stable detection results temporally. However, the bounding boxes produced by Tran's method are generally much smaller than the groundtruth bounding boxes. This can be contributed to its smoothing mechanism via maximum path algorithm. When smoothing in the spatio-temporal domain, only very confident regions are selected. Our method, however, is more robust to background clutter and intra-class variations due to our unique training mechanism. In the "horse riding" sequence, the target is never lost while in the "diving" sequence, the target is only temporally miss detected.

5 Conclusions

In this paper, we have introduced a novel spatio-temporal filtering method to improve per-pixel prediction map by accumulating detection score along spatio-temporal trajectories. To search maximum accumulated detection score, we have proposed an online filtering algorithm with the lowest time complexity and small memory cost. We have extended the online filtering algorithm to enable multi-channel processing and incorporate appearance information. With refined prediction map, we have shown that our method can benefit streaming video analysis tasks like human body recognition, saliency detection, and specific action detection.

Our online filtering algorithm only assumes the temporal dependence between video frames, with which many real-world video sequences share. As our filtering can perform in real-time, the refined prediction map can benefit other tasks like multiple object detection and tracking, which will be our future work.

Acknowledgments. The authors would like to thank Prof. Liqing Zhang for valuable discussions and thoughtful comments. This work was carried out at the Rapid-Rich Object Search (ROSE) Lab at the Nanyang Technological University, Singapore. The ROSE Lab is supported by a grant from the Singapore National Research Foundation. This grant is administered by the Interactive & Digital Media Programme Office at the Media Development Authority, Singapore.

References

1. Andriluka, M., Roth, S., Schiele, B.: People-tracking-by-detection and people-detection-by-tracking. In: CVPR (2008)
2. Badrinarayanan, V., Budvytis, I., Cipolla, R.: Semi-supervised video segmentation using tree structured graphical models. IEEE Transactions on Pattern Analysis and Machine Intelligence **35**(11), 2751–2764 (2013)
3. Bao, C., Wu, Y., Ling, H., Ji, H.: Real time robust l1 tracker using accelerated proximal gradient approach. In: CVPR (2012)
4. Berclaz, J., Fleuret, F., Turetken, E., Fua, P.: Multiple object tracking using k-shortest paths optimization. PAMI **33**(9), 1806–1819 (2011)

5. Borji, A., Itti, L.: State-of-the-art in visual attention modeling. PAMI **35**(1), 185–207 (2013)
6. Chen, A.Y., Corso, J.J.: Temporally consistent multi-class video-object segmentation with the video graph-shifts algorithm. In: WACV (2011)
7. Choi, W., Pantofaru, C., Savarese, S.: A general framework for tracking multiple people from a moving camera. PAMI **35**(7), 1577–1591 (2013)
8. Couprie, C., Farabet, C., LeCun, Y.: Causal graph-based video segmentation (2013)
9. Dalal, N., Triggs, B.: Histograms of oriented gradients for human detection. In: CVPR (2005)
10. Efros, A.A., Berg, A.C., Mori, G., Malik, J.: Recognizing action at a distance. In: ICCV (2003)
11. Floros, G., Leibe, B.: Joint 2d–3d temporally consistent semantic segmentation of street scenes. In: CVPR (2012)
12. Grundmann, M., Kwatra, V., Han, M., Essa, I.: Efficient hierarchical graph-based video segmentation. In: CVPR (2010)
13. Hernández-Vela, A., Zlateva, N., Marinov, A., Reyes, M., Radeva, P., Dimov, D., Escalera, S.: Graph cuts optimization for multi-limb human segmentation in depth maps. In: CVPR (2012)
14. Hoai, M., De la Torre, F.: Max-margin early event detectors. In: CVPR (2012)
15. Jia, X., Lu, H., Yang, M.H.: Visual tracking via adaptive structural local sparse appearance model. In: CVPR (2012)
16. Kalal, Z., Mikolajczyk, K., Matas, J.: Tracking-learning-detection. PAMI **34**(7), 1409–1422 (2012)
17. Kim, J., Woods, J.W.: Spatio-temporal adaptive 3-d kalman filter for video. IEEE Trans. on Image Processing **6**(3), 414–424 (1997)
18. Lan, T., Wang, Y., Mori, G.: Discriminative figure-centric models for joint action localization and recognition. In: ICCV (2011)
19. Leibe, B., Schindler, K., Cornelis, N., Van Gool, L.: Coupled object detection and tracking from static cameras and moving vehicles. PAMI **30**(10), 1683–1698 (2008)
20. Lezama, J., Alahari, K., Sivic, J., Laptev, I.: Track to the future: Spatio-temporal video segmentation with long-range motion cues. In: CVPR (2011
21. Malisiewicz, T., Gupta, A., Efros, A.A.: Ensemble of exemplar-svms for object detection and beyond. In: ICCV (2011)
22. Miksik, O., Munoz, D., Bagnell, J.A., Hebert, M.: Efficient temporal consistency for streaming video scene analysis. In: ICRA (2013)
23. Nataliya, S., Michalis, R., Leonid, S., Greg, M.: Action is in the eye of the beholder: Eye-gaze driven model for spatio-temporal action localization. In: NIPS (2013)
24. Paris, S.: Edge-preserving smoothing and mean-shift segmentation of video streams. In: Forsyth, D., Torr, P., Zisserman, A. (eds.) ECCV 2008, Part II. LNCS, vol. 5303, pp. 460–473. Springer, Heidelberg (2008)
25. Patti, A.J., Tekalp, A.M., Sezan, M.I.: A new motion-compensated reduced-order model kalman filter for space-varying restoration of progressive and interlaced video. IEEE Trans. on Image Processing **7**(4), 543–554 (1998)
26. Pirsiavash, H., Ramanan, D., Fowlkes, C.C.: Globally-optimal greedy algorithms for tracking a variable number of objects. In: CVPR (2011)
27. Raptis, M., Kokkinos, I., Soatto, S.: Discovering discriminative action parts from mid-level video representations. In: CVPR (2012)
28. Ross, D.A., Lim, J., Lin, R.S., Yang, M.H.: Incremental learning for robust visual tracking. IJCV **77**(1–3), 125–141 (2008)

29. S. Hussain, R., Matthias, G., Irfan, E.: Geometric context from video
30. Sharma, P., Huang, C., Nevatia, R.: Unsupervised incremental learning for improved object detection in a video. In: CVPR (2012)
31. Soomro, K., Zamir, A.R., Shah, M.: Ucf101: A dataset of 101 human actions classes from videos in the wild (2012)
32. Supancic III, J.S., Ramanan, D.: Self-paced learning for long-term tracking. In: CVPR (2013)
33. Tang, K., Ramanathan, V., Fei-Fei, L., Koller, D.: Shifting weights: adapting object detectors from image to video. In: NIPS (2012)
34. Tran, D., Yuan, J.: Max-margin structured output regression for spatio-temporal action localization. In: NIPS (2012)
35. Tran, D., Yuan, J., Forsyth, D.: Video event detection: From subvolume localization to spatio-temporal path search. PAMI (2013)
36. Kastner, S., Ungerleider, G.L.: Mechanisms of visual attention in the human cortex. Annual review of neuroscience 23(1), 315–341 (2000)
37. Walk, S., Majer, N., Schindler, K., Schiele, B.: New features and insights for pedestrian detection. In: CVPR (2010)
38. Wang, X., Hua, G., Han, T.X.: Detection by detections: non-parametric detector adaptation for a video. In: CVPR (2012)
39. Wojek, C., Schiele, B.: A dynamic conditional random field model for joint labeling of object and scene classes. In: Forsyth, D., Torr, P., Zisserman, A. (eds.) ECCV 2008, Part IV. LNCS, vol. 5305, pp. 733–747. Springer, Heidelberg (2008)
40. Wojek, C., Walk, S., Schiele, B.: Multi-cue onboard pedestrian detection. In: CVPR (2009)
41. Wu, Y., Lim, J., Yang, M.H.: Online object tracking: a benchmark. In: CVPR (2013)
42. Zhang, L., Tong, M.H., Cottrell, G.W.: Sunday: saliency using natural statistics for dynamic analysis of scenes. In: Proceedings of the 31st Annual Cognitive Science Conference (2009)
43. Zhou, B., Hou, X., Zhang, L.: A phase discrepancy analysis of object motion. In: Kimmel, R., Klette, R., Sugimoto, A. (eds.) ACCV 2010, Part III. LNCS, vol. 6494, pp. 225–238. Springer, Heidelberg (2011)

Learning Spatio-Temporal Features
for Action Recognition with Modified Hidden
Conditional Random Field

Wanru Xu[1(✉)], Zhenjiang Miao[1], Jian Zhang[2], and Yi Tian[1]

[1] Institute of Information Science, Beijing Jiaotong University, Beijing, China
11112063@bjtu.edu.cn
[2] School of Software, Advanced Analytics Institute, University of Technology,
Sydney, Australia

Abstract. Previous work on human action analysis mainly focuses on designing hand-crafted local features and combining their context information. In this paper, we propose using supervised feature learning as a way to learn spatio-temporal features. More specifically, a modified hidden conditional random field is applied to learn two high-level features conditioned on a certain action label. Among them, the individual features can describe the appearance of local parts and the interaction features can capture their spatial constraints. In order to make the best of what have been learned, a new categorization model is proposed for action matching. It is inspired by the Deformable Part Model and the intuition is that actions can be modeled by local features in a changeable spatial and temporal dependency. Experimental result shows that our algorithm can successfully recognize human actions with high accuracies both on the simple atomic action database (KTH and Weizmann) and complex interaction activity database (CASIA).

Keywords: Human action recognition · Spatio-temporal features · HCRF · Changeable spatial-temporal constraint model (CSTCM) · Feature learning

1 Introduction

For human action recognition, there are two important issues: feature extraction and efficient classification. The former is to extract discriminative and robust features to describe actions. The latter is to choose the best category model that uses such type features for corresponding classification. In this paper, we solve the two problems with a unified framework.

In recent years, some "conceptually weaker" models such as applying spatio-temporal descriptors [1] to "bag-of-features" (BOF) [2] have achieved promising results on object detection and even human action recognition. However, one obvious limitation is that interactional information of local features is neglected in such model. An interest point is not isolated but surrounded by its spatio-temporal context. Nowadays, several methods aim to integrate some hand-designed contextual features into it. Bregonzio [3] treats the interest points in a sub-volume as point "cloud".

© Springer International Publishing Switzerland 2015
L. Agapito et al. (Eds.): ECCV 2014 Workshops, Part I, LNCS 8925, pp. 786–801, 2015.
DOI: 10.1007/978-3-319-16178-5_55

A histogram in [4] which is called "featuretype×featuretype×relationship" is proposed to capture both appearance and relationship between pairwise visual words. A hierarchical model [5] including three context levels: point-level, intra-trajectory and inter-trajectory, is present to structure the spatio-temporal constraint of interest points. A video is modeled using a collection of both global and segment-level features in [20]. A weakness of such approaches is they must apply specific features, so that it is difficult to extend these features to other datasets. Another disadvantage is that after extracting the designed features, no suitable algorithm is proposed for corresponding classification. The common way is just to concatenate these multiple features to generate a new feature vector for action matching. Such simple concatenation may make them submerge each other. Therefore, in this paper we not only replace the hand-crafted features by learned features with a supervised feature learning algorithm, but also propose a new changeable spatial-temporal constraint categorization model (CSTCM) to make the utmost of what have been learned. We also provide evidence that our feature learning method generalizes to different domains and achieves promising results both on atomic action dataset and multi-persons activity dataset.

Hidden conditional random field (HCRF) is allowed to relax the assumption of conditional independence of the observed data, so any flexible spatial constraints among local features can be modeled. Due to its strong capability of description to spatial interaction, HCRF is widely used to build the structure of local patches in object detection. For action recognition, Wang Y et al. [6, 7] use HCRF to model each frame in the video sequence independently and then obtain the class label for the whole video by majority voting of the labels of its frames. Because action is a natural and continuous process, it is certainly not desirable to describe the action with only one frame. Instead of making a decision for the whole video, a modified HCRF is just applied to learn two compact and semantic representations called individual features and interaction features.

Deformable Part Model (DPM) [8] is now treated as the best method for object detection, which can achieve a two-fold improvement in average to the state-of-the-art. The intuition that objects can be modeled by parts in a deformable configuration provides an elegant framework for representing object categories. Inspired by it, a new categorization model (CSTCM) is proposed which can make use of the two high-level features without submerging each of them. Similar to objects, actions are modeled by local features in a changeable spatial-temporal constraint in this paper. Therefore, our classification model measures not only how similar the appearances of local parts are, but also how much their dependencies change.

The overview of our approach is illustrated in Fig.1. For the atomic action, space-time interest point [1] with HOG\HOF [2] is as the original descriptor. For the interactional activity, five trajectory based motion features [9] are extracted. In the training stage, two high-level features are learned by a modified HCRF. In the testing stage, the individual features are used to measure the similarity of appearance, while the interaction features are applied to estimate the change of constraint through the CSTCM. Both the changes in spatial and temporal domain are calculated for the final action matching.

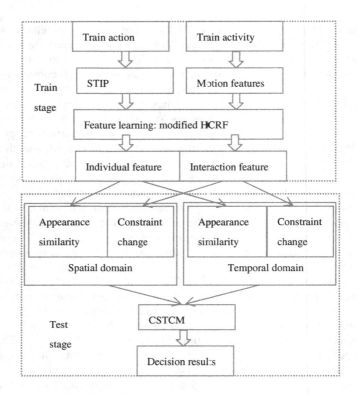

Fig. 1. Overview of our approach

2   Feature Learning

Hidden conditional random field was first proposed for speech classification and then has been applied to gesture [11] and object recognition [10]. In this section, a feature learning algorithm is introduced. By the means of a modified-HCRF, we convert the hand-designed features to data-adaptive descriptors which are more structured and semantic. But most of all, the learned features have the fixed dimension which is convenient for action matching.

Now we describe how to model the *t-th* video frame. $\mathbf{x}$ is the original feature vector of the *t-th* frame and y be the corresponding frame label which is a member of a finite possible action label set Y. Our task is not to get a mapping from $\mathbf{x}$ to y, but to learn a series of high-level representations conditioned on the class label y. For atomic action recognition, the feature vector $\mathbf{x}$ composes of a set of local observations $\{x_1, x_2, ..., x_N\}$. When the task is to analysis interaction activity, it contains motion features of N persons. For any frame $\mathbf{x}$, we also define a vector of hidden states $\mathbf{h} = \{h_1, h_2, ..., h_N\}$ corresponding to the N local patches, where each h_i takes values from a finite possible state set H. These variables are not observed, and each of them will assign a state label to the corresponding x_i in training stage. The hidden variables can capture certain underlying spatial structure of these local parts, so they are used as the basic elements to generate two sets of high-level feature descriptors $\{O_1^1, O_2^1, \dots, O_n^1\}$ and $\{O_1^2, O_2^2, \dots, O_m^2\}$.

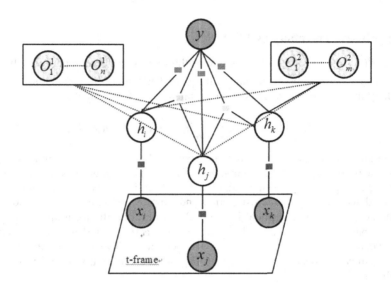

Fig. 2. Illustration of the modified-HCRF

The new modified-HCRF is illustrated in Fig.2. Each circle denotes a variable and each square represents a potential factor. The circles with white are hidden variables, the blacks mean they can be observed and the grays are the high-level features which can be learned from the model. In the graph $G = (E, V)$, $\{h_1, h_2, \dots, h_N\}$ are considered to be vertices and edge $(i, j) \in E$ represents the constraint between h_i and h_j. Given $\{\mathbf{x}, y\}$ of *t-th* frame, the modified- HCRF is defined as:

$$p(y \mid \mathbf{x}; \theta) = \sum_{h \in H} p(y, h \mid \mathbf{x}; \theta) = \frac{\sum_{h \in H} e^{\Phi(y, h, \mathbf{x}; \theta)}}{\sum_{y \in Y, h \in H} e^{\Phi(y, h, \mathbf{x}; \theta)}}$$

(1)

Where θ is a set of model parameters and $\Phi(y, h, \mathbf{x}; \theta)$ refers to potential function which can measure the compatibility among a class label, a set of observations and a configuration of hidden variables.

2.1 Potential Function

In this paper, the potential function is defined in Eq. (2) which is similar to [6, 7]. Note that the potential is linear in the model parameters $\theta = \{\theta(\mathbf{x}_i, h_i), \theta(y, h_i), \theta(y, h_i, h_j)\}$. $f(x_i)$ refers to original feature of the node i; $f(h_i)$ is the feature corresponding to the hidden node i; $f(h_i, h_j)$ denotes the feature depending on the edge between node i and j. The details are described in the following.

$$\Phi(y,h,x;\theta) = \sum_{i \in V} f(x_i) \cdot \theta(x_i, h_i) + \sum_{i \in V} f(h_i) \cdot \theta(y, h_i) + \sum_{i,j \in E} f(h_i, h_j) \cdot \theta(y, h_i, h_j) \tag{2}$$

Feature-Hidden Potential $f(x_i) \cdot \theta(x_i, h_i)$

We use $\theta(x_i, h_i)$ to refer to the parameter that measures the compatibility between a hidden state h_i and an observational feature $f(x_i)$. The feature-hidden potential describes how likely the local patch x_i is assigned as state h_i. It is formulated as:

$$f(x_i) \cdot \theta(x_i, h_i) = \sum_{\mu \in H} f(x_i) \cdot 1_{\{h_i = \mu\}} \cdot \theta(x_i, h_i) \tag{3}$$

Different types of original features are extracted to represent atomic action and interaction activity separately. For simple atomic action, $f(x_i)$ denotes the feature vector describing the appearance of the local patch x_i. Like in [2], we use the Harris 3D detector to detect the local interest points and employ histograms of oriented gradient (HOG) and histograms of optical flow (HOF) to describe the local appearance. Some trajectory based features are applied for complex activity, and now $f(x_i)$ denotes the feature vector describing the motion of the person x_i. Two features in [9] are used here. The moving speed is calculated by Eq. (4) and the motion intensity can be got through Eq. (5).

$$v = \frac{\| L_1(x, y) - L_2(x, y) \|}{|t_2 - t_1|} \tag{4}$$

$$I = | v_{opticalflow} - v | \tag{5}$$

Where $L_1(x, y)$ and $L_2(x, y)$ refer to the locations of one person at time t_1 and t_2. We use the optical flow to represent the whole motion in the rectangle box of a person, which is defined as the magnitude of the average optical flow speed. It includes two parts, global moving and local motion. The motion intensity I in Eq. (5) is defined as only induced by strong local motions, so we need minus the global moving from the whole motion.

Hidden-label potential $f(h_i) \cdot \theta(y, h_i)$:

We use $\theta(y, h_i)$ to denote the parameter that measures the compatibility between a hidden state h_i and an action label y. The hidden-label potential represents how likely the t-th frame contains a local patch with state h_i conditioned on action label y. It can be formulated as:

$$f(h_i) \cdot \theta(y, h_i) = \sum_{\mu \in H, \upsilon \in Y} 1_{\{h_i = \mu\}} \cdot 1_{\{y = \upsilon\}} \cdot \theta(y, h_i) \tag{6}$$

Edge-Label Potential $f(h_i, h_j) \cdot \theta(y, h_i, h_j)$

As the same, $\theta(y, h_i, h_j)$ corresponds to the parameter for modeling the compatibility between action label y and the edge between nodes i and j. The edge-label potential represents how likely the t-th frame contains a pair of local patches with states h_i and h_j conditioned on action label y. It is formulated as:

$$f(h_i, h_j) \cdot \theta(y, h_i, h_j) = \sum_{\mu \in H, \omega \in H, \upsilon \in Y} f(h_i, h_j) \cdot 1_{\{h_i = \mu\}} \cdot 1_{\{h_j = \omega\}} \cdot 1_{\{y = \upsilon\}} \cdot \theta(y, h_i, h_j) \quad (7)$$

Similarly, atomic action and interaction activity have different pairwise features. For the atomic action, if $(i, j) \in E$, $f(h_i, h_j)$ is set to 1; otherwise it is set to 0. For complex activity, three pairwise features are extracted, including distance, intersection angle of moving orientations and difference of moving speeds between the two persons.

2.2   Two High-Level Features

The output of this modified-HCRF is two sets of high-level features conditioned on a certain action label rather than a decision made only by this one frame. The spatial constraints among local patches can be completely captured by the two features. The learned hidden state $\{h_1, h_2 ... h_N\}$ is used as the basic elements to generate these high-level representations due to its compact and semantic. The individual features and the interaction features are defined as follows.

Individual Features:

$$O^1_{index(\mu)} = \sum_{i \in V} p(h_i = \mu | y, \mathbf{x}, \theta) = \sum_{i \in V} \sum_{h_i = \mu} p(h | y, \mathbf{x}, \theta) = \frac{\sum_{i \in V} \sum_{h_i = \mu} e^{\Phi(y, h, \mathbf{x}; \theta)}}{\sum_{y \in Y, h \in H} e^{\Phi(y, h, \mathbf{x}; \theta)}} \quad (8)$$

Interaction Features:

$$O^2_{index(\mu, \omega)} = \sum_{i, j \in E} p(h_i = \mu, h_j = \omega | y, \mathbf{x}, \theta) = \sum_{i, j \in E} \sum_{h_i = \mu, h_j = \omega} p(h | y, \mathbf{x}, \theta)$$

$$= \frac{\sum_{i, j \in E} \sum_{h_i = \mu, h_j = \omega} e^{\Phi(y, h, \mathbf{x}; \theta)}}{\sum_{y \in Y, h \in H} e^{\Phi(y, h, \mathbf{x}; \theta)}} \quad (9)$$

Where $\mu, \omega \in H$ refer to the hidden states. The $index(\mu)$ and $index(\mu, \omega)$ are the indexes of individual features and interaction features separately which are according to the hidden states. In Eq. (8) and Eq. (9), the two marginal probabilities $p(h_i = \mu | y, \mathbf{x}, \theta)$ and $p(h_i = \mu, h_j = \omega | y, \mathbf{x}, \theta)$ can be calculated by belief propagation. No matter how the number of local patches or persons changes among different frames, dimension of the two features is fixed. It is only related to the number of hidden states.

Intuitively, the individual features are achieved by clustering similar features into a group. For example, to the action "walk", these individual features may be used to characterize the movement patterns of the left and right legs. The interaction features capture certain spatial constraints between pairs of these individual parts. In the case of "walk", two local patches at the left legs might have strong constraint that they tend to have the same state label, since both of them are characterized by the movement of the left leg. The two features cumulate the occurrence probability of each state and each interactional edge in a frame separately. Fig. 3 shows the visualization of the two high-level features in the KTH dataset.

3   Changeable Spatial-temporal Constraint Model

After feature learning, a new changeable spatial-temporal constraint model (CSTCM) is proposed for action classification which can make the utmost of these learned features. Our classification strategy specifies a local part filter and a changeable constraint model. The filter measures the similarity of appearance of local parts contained in a video sequence or a frame. The constraint model calculates the changeable cost of context for each local part. Because human actions appear in the three-dimensional space, both the dependencies in spatial and temporal domain should be concerned.

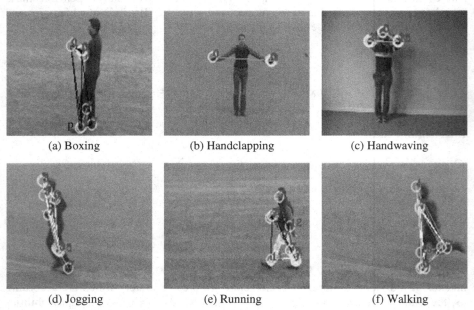

| (a) Boxing | (b) Handclapping | (c) Handwaving |
| (d) Jogging | (e) Running | (f) Walking |

Fig. 3. Images show the high-level individual features and interaction features learned from the modified-HCRF in the KTH action dataset. Each circle corresponds to a local individual feature with a red number which is the assignment of hidden states. Each line corresponds to an interaction feature between two individual features and different grayscales of the line represent different labels of interaction features.

For two video sequences v_i and v_j, the matching score $L(v_i, v_j)$ is the spatial score $S(v_i, v_j)$ of the whole video sequence plus the sum of temporal score $T(v_i^{t_1}, v_j^{t_2})$ over frames. Due to varying in time or speed, dynamic time warping (DTW) is used to measure their temporal similarity. Specially, T_i and T_j are frame numbers of the two videos which can be unequal in Eq. (10).

$$L(v_i, v_j) = S(v_i, v_j) + \sum_{\max(T_i, T_j)} \underset{t_1 \in T_i, t_2 \in T_j}{DTW} T(v_i^{t_1}, v_j^{t_2}) \tag{10}$$

Each of the scores includes two parts to describe the similarity of appearance and the change of constraint respectively. First, we define the spatial score between the two whole videos in Eq. (11).

$$S(v_i, v_j) = \sum_{\mu \in H} m_\mu(i, j) + \sum_{\mu, \omega \in H} d_{\mu, \omega}(i, j) \tag{11}$$

$$m_\mu(i, j) = (\sum_{t=1}^{T_i} O^1_{\text{index}(\mu_t^i)} - \sum_{t=1}^{T_j} O^1_{\text{index}(\mu_t^j)})^2 \tag{12}$$

$$d_{\mu, \omega}(i, j) = (\sum_{t=1}^{T_i} O^2_{\text{index}(\mu_t^i, \omega_t^i)} - \sum_{t=1}^{T_j} O^2_{\text{index}(\mu_t^j, \omega_t^j)})^2 \tag{13}$$

$m_\mu(i, j)$ is defined as a local part filter to measure the similarity of each individual features. It is something like the traditional BOF method, but we apply a feature learning algorithm to cluster local features. We all know that a local feature is not isolated but surrounded by its context. For example, when a local state occurs, another corresponding state always occurs as the same time. However, this relation may have some slight changes. Therefore, a constraint model $d_{\mu, \omega}(i, j)$ is used to calculate the changeable cost of interactional information for pair-wise local parts. $\sum_{\omega \in H} d_{\mu, \omega}(i, j)$ represents the whole cost of contextual change for a local part μ. Because only the spatial constraint is model here, the individual features and interaction features are cumulated over the whole video sequence.

Next, we define the temporal score with the same form that the first term denotes the local part filter and the second term refers to the constraint model. Unlike the spatial score, the temporal score is computed on each frame rather than the whole video to describe the temporal dependencies.

$$T(v_i^{t_1}, v_j^{t_2}) = T_1(v_i^{t_1}, v_j^{t_2}) + T_2(v_i^{t_1}, v_j^{t_2})$$
$$= \sum_{\mu \in H} (O^1_{\text{index}(\mu_{t_1}^i)} - O^1_{\text{index}(\mu_{t_2}^j)})^2 + \sum_{\mu, \omega \in H} (O^2_{\text{index}(\mu_{t_1}^i, \omega_{t_1}^i)} - O^2_{\text{index}(\mu_{t_2}^j, \omega_{t_2}^j)})^2 \tag{14}$$

There are three advantages in this classification model. Firstly, it takes the two key elements of human action into account, which are spatial and temporal constraints. Secondly, separating of the individual features from the interaction features in Eq. (12) and Eq. (13) makes the model easy to use the two high-level features independently and avoid them submerge each other. Through combining them in Eq. (11), the mutual influence of the two different features can be completely represented as well. Thirdly, rather than simple rigid matching, our CSTCM can tolerate some changes of local parts both on the spatial and temporal domain which is more adaptive to recognize action. Finally, the total matching score is employed in KNN for action matching.

4   Experiments

In this section, we evaluate our model both on the simple atomic action database and complex interaction activity database. To evaluate its effectiveness, we compare our algorithm with some other similar action recognition methods and some well-designed contrast experiments.

4.1   Databases

To test our proposed method, we use three well-known benchmark action recognition databases including both simple atomic action and complex interaction activity. For the simple atomic action, the public dataset KTH [12] and Weizmann [17] are used. The KTH contains 6 types of actions that are boxing, handwaving, running, handclapping, walking and jogging, under four different scenarios. Each video is captured at 25HZ with a size of 160×120. The Weizmann contains 93 video clips from 9 different actors. There are 10 different action categories: wave1, wave2, run, bend, walk, jump, side, jack, skip and pjump. Each video is captured at 25HZ with a size of 180×144. In these two datasets, each video contains only one actor performing a single action.

For the complex interaction activity, a two-person activity datasets CASIA [13] is adopted. It contains 84 video clips from three different views: angle view, horizontal view and top down view. There are 7 different activity categories: fight, followalways, followtogether, meetapart, meettogether, overtake and rob. So each activity has 12 clips and each view has 4 clips. The meaning of each activity is illustrated as follows and Fig.4 shows some example frames of two-person activities in the CASIA dataset.

Fight: Two persons are close to and then fight each other.

Followalways: One person follows another person and is behind him at a distance all the time.

Followtogether: One person follows another person and then they walk together.

Meetapart: Two persons are close to, then meet each other and depart at last.

Meettogether: Two persons are close to, then meet each other and walk together at last.

Overtake: One person is behind another person and then he overtakes.

Rob: One person follows another person, then robs him and runs away at last.

| (1) Rob | (2) Fight | (3) Follow | (4) Follow and gather | (5) Meet and part | (6) Meet and gather | (7) Overtake |

Fig. 4. Example frames of two-person activities in the CASIA dataset

4.2   Details of Our Model

For our model, the original input is the features directly extracted in videos. A 162 dimension vector including HOG (72) and HOF (90) around a local interested point is treated as the descriptor for the atomic action. For the interactional activity, five trajectory based features are applied. The size of possible hidden states in our modified-HCRF is 20, so we can learn 20 individual features and 400 interaction features. Then, these learned high-level features are applied in CSTCM for action classification, and the parameter K in KNN is set to 1 for simply.

A leave-one-out cross-validation strategy is used for Weizmann and CASIA. For KTH dataset, we use 16 actors for training and other 9 actors for testing like other papers' setup.

4.3   Recognition Results

Our proposal includes two parts: feature learning and CSTCM categorization. To evaluate the model completely, we test each of them separately.

Evaluate Feature Learning

Three contrast experiments are designed to evaluate our feature learning process, where the same descriptor is used as the original feature. Firstly, we classify every frame in a video sequence which is the standard HCRF method (per-frame recognition). Secondly, through the majority voting of the labels of its frames, the class label for the whole video sequence can be achieved (per-video recognition). Lastly, we use the two high-level features learned from the modified-HCRF to calculate histogram in the whole video sequence for action matching (histogram based method). Fig. 5 shows the visualization of the histogram based method in the CASIA dataset. Table 1 lists the recognition results of the three approaches on the KTH and CASIA dataset. It shows the following point:

- The accuracy of per-frame approach is lower than the per-video method. Because action is a continuous process, it is not enough to represent the whole action with only one frame. For example, the frame with the pose of "stand" may occur in all kinds of actions.

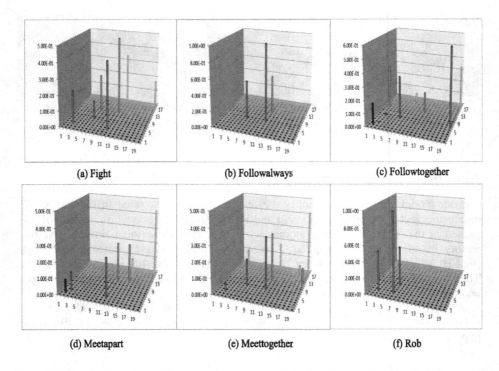

Fig. 5. Visualization of the histogram based method in the CASIA dataset. The histogram is cumulated by the high-level features learned from the whole video sequence. Elements on the primary diagonal are individual features and others denote the interaction features.

- The performance of the high-level features based approach (histogram based approach) is better than another two methods with low-level features (per-frame and per-video). It evidences that there is no much information lost and these learned features become more compact and semantic for action representation.

Table 1. A comparison of the three methods in feature learning part test on the KTH and CASIA dataset (%)

	Per-frame	Per-video	Histogram based
KTH	34.35	37.17	93.17
CASIA	58.98	84.52	91.67

Evaluate CSTCM

There are a local part filter and a changeable constraint model in the CSTCM. And both the *spatial and* temporal dependencies are modeled. For evaluating the model completely, we design some contrast experiments to test each of them separately. Table 2 lists their recognition results on the KTH, CASIA and the meaning of each variant is illustrated as follows.

Temporal score: the method only using temporal score to calculate the difference between two videos in the temporal domain.

Spatial score: the method only using *spatial* score to calculate the difference between two videos in the *spatial* domain and it is just the histogram based approach in Table 1.

Spatial score1: the method only using the local part filter in the *spatial* domain to measure similarity of appearance of local parts contained in the two whole video sequences. It is something like the traditional BOF method.

Spatial score2: the method only using the changeable constraint model in the *spatial* domain to calculate the changeable cost of context in the two whole video sequences.

CSTCM1: the method using the local part filter both in the *spatial*-temporal domain which can completely evaluate contribution of the local part filter.

CSTCM2: the method using the changeable constraint model both in the *spatial*-temporal domain which can completely evaluate contribution of the changeable constraint model.

CSTCM: the whole model proposed in this paper which contains the local part filter and changeable constraint model and both the differences in *spatial*-temporal domain are measured.

Table 2. A comparison of some variants with our proposal test on the KTH, CASIA dataset (%) and the mathematically definition of their matching scores

	Matching score ($L(v_i, v_j) =$)	KTH	CASIA
Spatial score1	$\sum_{\mu \in H} m_\mu(i,j)$	82.33	89.29
Spatial score2	$\sum_{\mu,\omega \in H} d_{\mu,\omega}(i,j)$	92	90.48
Spatial score	$S(v_i, v_j)$	93.17	91.67
Temporal score	$\sum_{\max(T_i,T_j)} DTW_{t_1 \in T_i, t_2 \in T_j} T(v_i^{t_1}, v_j^{t_2})$	78	45.24
CSTCM	$S(v_i, v_j) + \sum_{\max(T_i,T_j)} DTW_{t_1 \in T_i, t_2 \in T_j} T(v_i^{t_1}, v_j^{t_2})$	96.17	92.86
CSTCM1	$\sum_{\mu \in H} m_\mu(i,j) + \sum_{\max(T_i,T_j)} DTW_{t_1 \in T_i, t_2 \in T_j} T_1(v_i^{t_1}, v_j^{t_2})$	88.67	90.48
CSTCM2	$\sum_{\mu,\omega \in H} d_{\mu,\omega}(i,j) + + \sum_{\max(T_i,T_j)} DTW_{t_1 \in T_i, t_2 \in T_j} T_2(v_i^{t_1}, v_j^{t_2})$	92.17	91.67

Note that when we evaluate contribution of the local part filter, only the individual features are used. While when the constraint model is test, only the interaction features are applied. From the table, it indicates following points.

- The performance of changeable constraint model is better than local part filter no matter in the spatial or temporal domain. Because changeable constraint model allows some non-rigid matching and the interaction features also contain more information for classification.
- The methods combining local part filter and changeable constraint model achieve a higher accuracy than using the two independently. Because when only using local part filter, the interactional constraint is lack and vice versa. It proves that each part can play a complementary role in most cases.
- No matter for the local part filter or changeable constraint model, when calculating both in the spatial and temporal domain, it can reach a better recognition result. It illustrates that human action has the characteristics of space and time. Both of them should be modeled.

Compare with Other Methods

Finally, we compare our proposal with some other similar algorithms and it is summarized in Table 3. These similar approaches contain HCRF based methods (eg. [6], [7]); graphical model based methods for activity recognition (eg. [9], [14]); hand-designed contextual features methods (eg. [3], [15], [16], [19]); unsupervised feature learning approach [18]; and specially [2] is the traditional BOF. Note that the original local features and motion features adopted in our model are the same as [2, 15, 9], where it can fully evidence the effectiveness of our feature learning. From this table, we can find our recognition accuracy outperforms or is similar to all previous published results. Though the best result on Weizmann is just slightly higher than ours, the performance of our model on KTH and CASIA is much better. The results obtained by our proposed method on the KTH, Weizmann and CASIA dataset are reported in Fig.6 in detail which are the confusion matrixes for action classification.

Table 3. A comparison of our proposal with other algorithms test on the KTH, Weizmann and CASIA dataset (%)

Algorithm	Weizmann	KTH	CASIA
Wang et al.[6]	97.22	87.6	—
Wang et al.[7]	100	92.51	—
Guo et al. [9]	—	—	83.28
Brand et al. [14]	—	—	76.14
Bregonzio al.[3]	96.6	93.17	—
Jiang et al. [15]	—	93.8	—
Wu et al. [16]	—	94.5	—
Fathi et al.[19]	100	90.5	—
Dollar et al. [2]	—	Over 80	—
Quoc et al. [18]	—	93.9	—
Our model	98.89	96.17	92.86

It is significantly inspired that through replacing hand-designed features by learned features and adopting a corresponding classification model CSTCM, we achieve a huge improvement both on simple atomic action database and complex interaction activity database. That is to say, our model not only proposes an effective feature leaning method, but also finds a way to make the best of what have been learned.

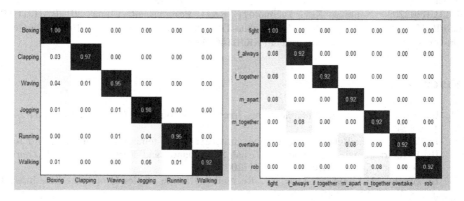

(a) The confusion matrix of KTH dataset   (b) The confusion matrice of CASIA dataset.

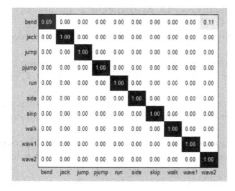

(c) The confusion matrice of Weizmann dataset.

Fig. 6. The confusion matrices for action classification on KTH (a), CASIA (b) and Weizmann (c)

5   Conclusions

The paper proposes a unified framework for human atomic action and interaction activity recognition. A supervised way is introduced to replace traditional hand-designed features by high-level learned features with the modified-HCRF. A new categorization model is used for corresponding classification which can make the utmost of the individual features and interaction features. The CSTCM specifies a local part filter and a changeable constraint model. In the spatial and temporal domain, the similarity of local appearance is measured by the former, while the change of dependency is estimated by the latter.   Therefore in this paper, actions can be modeled by local features in a changeable spatial-temporal constraint. Our method is evaluated on the KTH, Weizmann and CASIA dataset with significant improvement results.

Acknowledgements. This work is supported by the NSFC 61273274, 973 Program 2011CB302203, National Key Technology R&D Program of China 2012BAH01F03, NSFB4123104, Z131110001913143, Tsinghua-Tencent Joint Lab for IIT and Beijing Jiaotong University Research Foundation Program KKJB14029536.

References

1. Laptev, I.: On space-time interest points. International Journal of Computer Vision **64**(2–3), 107–123 (2005)
2. Dollár, P., et al.: Behavior recognition via sparse spatio-temporal features. In: 2nd Joint IEEE International Workshop on Visual Surveillance and Performance Evaluation of Tracking and Surveillance, 2005. IEEE (2005)
3. Bregonzio, M., Gong, S., Xiang, T.: Recognising action as clouds of space-time interest points. In: CVPR (2009)
4. Ryoo, M., Aggarwal, J.: Spatio-temporal relationship match: video structure comparison for recognition of complex human activities. In: ICCV (2009)
5. Sun, J., Wu, X., Yan, S., Cheong, L.F., Chua, T.-S., Li, J.: Hierarchical spatio-temporal context modeling for action recognition. In: CVPR (2009)
6. Wang, Y., Mori, G.: Learning a discriminative hidden part model for human action recognition. In: NIPS, vol. 8 (2008)
7. Wang, Y., Mori, G.: Max-margin hidden conditional random fields for human action recognition. In: IEEE Conference on Computer Vision and Pattern Recognition, 2009, CVPR 2009. IEEE (2009)
8. Felzenszwalb, P., McAllester, D., Ramanan, D.: A discriminatively trained, multiscale, deformable part model. In: IEEE Conference on Computer Vision and Pattern Recognition, 2008, CVPR 2008. IEEE (2008)
9. Guo, P., et al.: Coupled Observation Decomposed Hidden Markov Model for Multiperson Activity Recognition. IEEE Transactions on Circuits and Systems for Video Technology **22**(9), 1306–1320 (2012)
10. Quattoni, A., Collins, M. , Darrell, T.: Conditional random fields for object recognition (2004)
11. Wang, S.B., et al.: Hidden conditional random fields for gesture recognition. In: 2006 IEEE Computer Society Conference on Computer Vision and Pattern Recognition, vol. 2. IEEE (2006)
12. Schuldt, C., Laptev, I., Caputo, B.: Recognizing human actions: a local SVM approach. In: ICPR (2004)
13. CASIA Action Database. http://www.cbsr.ia.ac.cn/english/Action%20Databases%20EN.asp
14. Brand, M., Oliver, N., Pentland, A.: Coupled hidden markov models for complex action recognition. In: Proc. IEEE Conf. Comput. Vis. Pattern Recognit., pp. 994–999 (1997)
15. Wang, J., Chen, Z., Wu, Y.: Action recognition with multiscale spatio-temporal contexts. In: CVPR (2011)
16. Wu, X., Xu, D., Duan, L., Luo, J.: Action recognition using context and appearance distribution features. In: CVPR (2011)
17. Blank, M., Gorelick, L., Shechtman, E., Irani, M., Basri, R.: Actions as space-time shapes. In: ICCV (2005)

18. Le, Q.V., Zou, W.Y., Yeung, S.Y., Ng, A.Y.: Learning hierarchical invariant spatio-temporal features for action recognition with independent subspace analysis. In: CVPR (2011)
19. Fathi, A., Mori, G.: Action recognition by learning mid-level motion features. In: CVPR (2008)
20. Vahdat, A., Cannons, K., Mori, G., et al.: Compositional models for video event detection: a multiple kernel learning latent variable approach [C]. In: 2013 IEEE International Conference on Computer Vision (ICCV), pp. 1185–1192. IEEE (2013)

Activity Recognition in Still Images with Transductive Non-negative Matrix Factorization

Naiyang Guan[1](✉), Dacheng Tao[2], Long Lan[1], Zhigang Luo[1],
and Xuejun Yang[3]

[1] Science and Technology on Parallel and Distributed Processing Laboratory,
College of Computer, National University of Defense Technology,
Changsha, People's Republic of China
{ny_guan,zgluo}@nudt.edu.cn, lan19901@126.com
[2] Centre for Quantum Computation and Intelligent Systems and the Faculty
of Engineering and Information Technology, University of Technology,
Sydney, Australia
dacheng.tao@uts.edu.au
[3] State Key Laboratory of High Performance Computing,
National University of Defense Technology, Changsha, People's Republic of China
xjyang@nudt.edu.cn

Abstract. Still image based activity recognition is a challenging problem due to changes in appearance of persons, articulation in poses, cluttered backgrounds, and absence of temporal features. In this paper, we proposed a novel method to recognize activities from still images based on transductive non-negative matrix factorization (TNMF). TNMF clusters the visual descriptors of each human action in the training images into fixed number of groups meanwhile learns to represent the visual descriptor of test image on the concatenated bases. Since TNMF learns these bases on both training images and test image simultaneously, it learns a more discriminative representation than standard NMF based methods. We developed a multiplicative update rule to solve TNMF and proved its convergence. Experimental results on both laboratory and real-world datasets demonstrate that TNMF consistently outperforms NMF.

Keywords: Still image based action recognition · Non-negative matrix factorization · Transductive learning

1 Introduction

Activity recognition aims to recognize actions and goals of one or more individuals from a series of observations on the individuals' actions and the environmental conditions. It has found many applications in human-computer interaction [29], human interaction recognition [28], robot trajectory planning [30], and video surveillance [31] thanks to the convenience of capturing videos through cameras [1–3,13,27]. Until now, activity recognition is an open and challenging problem due to changes in appearance of persons, articulation in poses, cluttered backgrounds, and camera movements.

© Springer International Publishing Switzerland 2015
L. Agapito et al. (Eds.): ECCV 2014 Workshops, Part I, LNCS 8925, pp. 802–817, 2015.
DOI: 10.1007/978-3-319-16178-5_56

Recognizing actions from benchmark videos has achieved promising performance because of the dynamic features, but it is difficult to recognize actions recorded in still wild images, e.g., images collected from Internet, because the dynamic features cannot be extracted from still images. To recognize actions from still images, it is important to extract representative cues including both high-level and low-level cues. Traditional video-based activity recognition can directly use the low-level cues such as the spatiotemporal interest point [23] extracted from space-time volume, but the still image-based activity recognition usually cannot because only the spatial information is available on single images [35]. The high-level cues can be characterized by various low-level features, e.g., color names [21], and different high-level cues can be combined to enhance the performance, e.g., combining pose and context information [20]. Interested readers can refer to [24] for a systematic survey.

To construct high-level cues, it is an important pre-processing step to detect human bodies, body parts and objects. However, it is quite challenging because existing object detection methods usually work unsatisfactorily. Liu et al. [11] proposed to represent actions by selecting key poses from video sequences. Zhang and Tao [12] proposed the slow-feature analysis (SFA) framework to recognizing human actions from video sequences by incorporating discriminative information with SFA and spatial relationship of body components. Although these methods have achieved great successes by utilizing human poses, they are not direct for action recognition in still images due to the difficulty to extract body components. In this paper, we constructed a high-level cues by clustering human poses with non-negative matrix factorization (NMF, [7]) to avoid explicitly reasoning about the body components [22]. Non-negative matrix factorization is a popular data representation method which can extract intrinsic structure of dataset and boost the performance of subsequent processing. Different from conventional data representation methods, e.g., principal component analysis (PCA, [14]) and Fisher's linear discriminative analysis (FLDA, [15]), which learns holistic representation, NMF can learn parts-based representations from non-negative datasets. For example, it can extract several versions of facial components such as 'noses', 'eyes', and 'mouth' from frontal face image datasets. It is therefore reasonable to believe that NMF can automatically extract body poses from bounding boxes.

Thurau and Hlavac [4] proposed static histogram of oriented gradient (HOG)-based features for activity recognition on still images by clustering a set of training human poses with NMF and utilizing histograms of the clustered poses to represent each action. At the classification stage, they concatenated the pose clusters of all actions and features of background, and calculated the histogram of each test image on concatenated features and determined the label by classification. Since then, many works utilize NMF in activity recognition. Agarwal and Xia [5] applied NMF to 3D poses recovery problem since NMF can effectively represents local features of human body. According to [5], background usually has a negative influence on action recovery because its changes are usually misunderstood as human actions. NMF is suitable for recovering poses from single image because it can significantly separate background from action poses. Waltner *et al.* [6] utilized NMF to recognize actions from a small amount of video frames. Different from [4] and [5], their method considers HOG of both appearances and motions. The discriminative power of the learned poses is improved by motions, but it is far from enough because aforementioned methods [4–6] ignore test samples during training.

In this paper, we propose a novel method to recognize actions from still images by using transductive NMF (TNMF). TNMF jointly learns a dictionary of features on both training images from different actions and the test image to be recognized. In particular, TNMF has two types of objectives: 1) it minimizes the distance between the visual descriptors of the training poses of each action and the product of its features and encodings, and 2) it minimizes the distance between the visual descriptor of test image and the product of dictionary concatenated by those features of all actions and an encoding vector. Intuitively, since the dictionary of features learned by TNMF contains the visual features from both training images and test image, it can more accurately recover the pose in single still image, and thus boost the recognition performance. TNMF balances both objectives by a positive parameter and utilizes a multiplicative update rule (MUR) to learn all features and the corresponding encodings. In this paper, we proved the convergence of the MUR-based algorithm for TNMF. Experiment results on both laboratory datasets and real-life datasets confirm that TNMF significantly outperforms NMF in still image-based activity recognition.

This paper is organized as follows: Section 2 surveys both NMF and its application in activity recognition; we introduce the TNMF model and its MUR based algorithm in Section 3; Section 4 verifies the method on both laboratory and real-world datasets and Section 5 concludes this paper.

2   Related Works

2.1   Non-negative Matrix Factorization

Given a non-negative dataset, i.e., $V \in \mathbb{R}_+^{m \times n}$, non-negative matrix factorization (NMF, [7]) decomposes it into the product of two lower-rank matrices, i.e., $W \in \mathbb{R}_+^{m \times r}$ and $H \in \mathbb{R}_+^{r \times n}$, where $r \ll \min\{m, n\}$, by solving the following problem

$$\min_{W \geq 0, H \geq 0} ||V - WH||_F^2. \tag{1}$$

Usually, W and H can be considered as features and encodings, respectively. It is obvious that NMF represents each sample by only additive, non-subtractive combination of features. Therefore, NMF yields parts-based features representation.

Since such parts-based representation has strong evidence in human brain, NMF has been widely applied in many real-world applications such as text mining [8–10,14] and hyper-spectral imaging [10,15].

2.2 Transductive NMF

Recently, Guan *et al.* [16] have proposed transductive NMF (TNMF) to simultaneously learn from multiple tasks, i.e., V_k, where $1 \leq k \leq K$. TNMF combines both training stage and test stage together to simultaneously learn single features for each task and coefficient of test sample on concatenated dictionary.

The objective function of TNMF is

$$\min_{\forall 1 \leq k \leq K, W_k \geq 0, H_k \geq 0, \overline{H} \geq 0} \{\sum\nolimits_{k=1}^{K} ||V_k - W_k H_k||_F^2 + \lambda ||\overline{V} - \overline{W}\overline{H}||_F^2\}, \quad (2)$$

where $\overline{W} = [W_1, \cdots, W_K]$, and $\lambda \in [0, 1]$ is a positive tradeoff parameter. When $\lambda = 0$, TNMF reduces to NMF on each task separately.

2.3 NMF-Based Activity Recognition

Taking the advantage of clustering ability the parts-based representation of NMF, Thurau and Hlavac [4,6] proposed a static HOG-based NMF method for activity recognition on still images since the HOG-descriptor of any an image is non-negative. Given training HOG-descriptors of all actions, i.e., V_k for the k-th action of totally K actions, they utilized NMF to learn features W_k and encodings H_k, i.e., by

$$\min_{W_k \geq 0, H_k \geq 0} ||V_k - W_k H_k||_F^2. \quad (3)$$

By concatenating features of all actions together, they constructed a dictionary of features, i.e., $\overline{W} = [W_1, \cdots, W_K]$, and projected the HOG-descriptors of test image, i.e., $\overline{V}$, onto $\overline{W}$ to calculate its encoding, i.e.,by

$$\overline{H} = \arg\min_{\overline{H} \geq 0} ||\overline{V} - \overline{W}H||_F^2, \quad (4)$$

where $\overline{H}$ is the encodings of $\overline{V}$.

At the classification stage, they calculated the histogram of each action based on $\{H_1, \cdots, H_K\}$, and the histogram of the test image based on $\overline{H}$, followed by classification with the nearest neighbor (NN) classifier. Since the training stage of learning the features of each action (see the formula (3)) and the classification stage of learning the encodings on the dictionary of concatenated features (see the formula (4)) are separate, NMF usually suffers from overfitting problem.

3   TNMF-Based Activity Recognition in Still Images

In still image-based activity recognition, most actions have sufficient training images but some actions has rare training images because the training images are collected from different sources and the activities are performed separately by different individuals. Therefore, NMF cannot accurately learn features on limited training images due to the overfitting problem in this situation.

Since TNMF leverages the test set to enhance representing the training samples, it learns more representative dictionary and reduces the influence of overfitting by jointly learning the dictionary from both training and test sets. In other words, TNMF has better generalization ability than NMF. In this paper, we taken this advantage of TNMF to solve the overfitting problem in still image-based activity recognition [4]. In particular, we applied TNMF to jointly learns a dictionary on both training samples V_k, e.g., HOG-descriptors, from different actions and the test samples $\overline{V}$, e.g., HOG-descriptors, of the probe image to be recognized. Since TNMF transduces the training poses to the learned dictionary by incorporating the second term in (4), it represents the test data more accurately and overcomes the deficiency of NMF. Experimental results confirm that TNMF greatly boosts the activity recognition performance.

Although the objective function of TNMF is jointly non-convex with respect to all variables, i.e., $\{W_1, \cdots, W_K, H_1, \cdots, H_K, \overline{H}\}$, it is convex with respect to each of them separately. According to [17, 20], we utilized the majorization minimization (MM) method to derive a multiplicative update rule (MUR, [16]) for solving TNMF (2). MUR updates W_k, H_k, and $\overline{H}$, respectively, by

$$W_k \leftarrow W_k \circ \frac{(V_k H_k^T + \lambda \overline{V} \overline{H}_k^T)}{(W_k H_k H_k^T + \lambda \overline{W} \overline{H} \overline{H}_k^T)}, \tag{5}$$

$$H_k \leftarrow H_k \circ \frac{W_k^T V_k}{W_k^T W_k H_k}, \tag{6}$$

and

$$\overline{H} \leftarrow \overline{H} \circ \frac{\overline{W}^T \overline{V}}{\overline{W}^T \overline{W} \overline{H}}, \tag{7}$$

where $\circ$ signifies the element-wise multiplication operator, and $\overline{H}_k$ is the k-th component of $\overline{H}$ that corresponds to W_k, i.e., $\overline{H} = [\overline{H}_1^T, \cdots, \overline{H}_K^T]^T$. MUR alternatively updates all variables until they do not change the objective value of (2).

Distinguished from our previous work, we proved the convergence of the MURs (5)(6)(7) by using the majorization minimization (MM, [17]) technique. MM builds an auxiliary function whose curve lies above that of the original objective function everywhere and both curves are tangent at a certain point. When calculating the gradient of the original function is non-trival, MM instead updates the current variable by using the minimum of the constructed auxiliary function. The auxiliary function is defined in **Definition 1** and has the property shown **Lemma 1**.

Definition 1. Given x^t, the function $g(x, x^t)$ is an auxiliary function of $f(x)$, if $g(x, x^t) \geq f(x)$ and $g(x^t, x^t) = f(x^t)$.

Lemma 1. If $g(x, x^t)$ is an auxiliary function of $f(x)$, then $f(x)$ is non-increasing under the update rule $x^{(t+1)} = \arg\min_x g(x, x^t)$.

Proof. $f(x^{t+1}) \leq g(x^{t+1}, x^t) \leq g(x^t, x^t) = f(x^t)$. ∎

It is easy to verify that (6) and (7) decrease the objective function because they are same as the MURs in [17]. It is remaining to prove that (5) decreases the objective function (see **Proposition 1**).

Proposition 1. The multiplicative update rule (5) decreases the objective function of (2).

Proof. At the t-th iteration round, we expect to prove that the update of W_k can decrease the objective function

$$f_t = \sum_{l \neq k}^{K} ||V_l - W_l^t H_l^t||_F^2 + ||V_k - W_k H_k^t||_F^2 + \lambda ||\overline{V} - \overline{W}^t \overline{H}^t + W_k \overline{H}_k^t - W_k \overline{H}_k^t||_F^2,$$

with all variables except W_k fixed. Since the first term does not influence f_t, it is only necessary to prove that (5) decreases the following objective function

$$f(W_k) = ||V_k - W_k H_k^t||_F^2 + \lambda ||\overline{V} - \overline{W}^t \overline{H}^t + W_k \overline{H}_k^t - W_k \overline{H}_k^t||_F^2. \quad (8)$$

To this end, we constructed its auxiliary function as follows:

$$g(W_k, W_k^t) = f(W_k^t) + \langle \nabla f(W_k^t), W_k - W_k^t \rangle$$
$$+ \langle \frac{W_k^t H_k^t H_k^{t^T} + \lambda \overline{W}^t \overline{H}^t \overline{H}_k^{t^T}}{(W_k^t)}), [W_k - W_k^t]^2 \rangle, \quad (9)$$

where $\nabla f(W_k^t) = (W_k H_k^t - V_k) H_k^{t^T} + \lambda (\overline{W}^t \overline{H}^t - \overline{V}) H_k^{t^T}$ and $[\cdot]^2$ signifies the element-wise square of a matrix. Since it is obvious that $g(W_k^t, W_k^t) = f(W_k^t)$, we only need to show $f(W_k) \leq g(W_k, W_k^t)$ for any W_k.

To do this, we have the Taylor series expansion of $f(W_k)$ at W_k^t, and the objective function with respect to the (i, j)-th element of W_k is

$$f([W_k]_{ij}) = f([W_k^t]_{ij}) + [\nabla f(W_k^t)]_{ij}([W_k]_{ij} - [W_k^t]_{ij})$$
$$+ ([H_k^t H_k^{t^T}]_{jj} + \lambda [\overline{H}_k^t \overline{H}_k^{t^T}]_{jj})([W_k]_{ij} - [W_k^t]_{ij})^2. \quad (10)$$

Since $H_k^t \leq 0$ and $W_k^t \leq 0$, we have

$$[H_k^t H_k^{t^T}]_{jj} \leq \frac{\sum_l [W_k^t]_{il} [H_k^t H_k^{t^T}]_{lj}}{[W_k^t]_{ij}} = \frac{[W_k^t H_k^t H_k^{t^T}]_{ij}}{[W_k^t]_{ij}}. \quad (11)$$

Since $\overline{H}_k^t \leq 0$ and $W_k^t \leq 0$, we have

$$[\overline{H}_k^t \overline{H}_k^{t^T}]_{jj} \leq \frac{\sum_l [W_k^t]_{il} [\overline{H}_k^t \overline{H}_k^{t^T}]_{lj}}{[W_k^t]_{ij}} = \frac{[W_k^t \overline{H}_k^t \overline{H}_k^{t^T}]_{ij}}{[W_k^t]_{ij}} \leq \frac{[\overline{W}_k^t \overline{H}_k^t \overline{H}_k^{t^T}]_{ij}}{[W_k^t]_{ij}}, \quad (12)$$

where the last inequality comes from the fact that $\bar{W}^t \bar{H}^t = \sum_{l \neq k}^{K} W_l^t \bar{H}_l^t + W_k^t \overline{H}_k^t$ and $\sum_{l \neq k}^{K} W_l^t \overline{H}_l^t \geq 0$.

By substituting (11) and (12) into (10), we can easily verify that $f(W_k) \leq g(W_k, W_k^t)$, and thus $g(W_k, W_k^t)$ is an auxiliary function of $f(W_k)$ according to

Definition 1. By setting $\frac{\partial g(W_k, W_k^t)}{\partial [W_k]_{ij}} = 0$ and substituting $\nabla f(W_k^t) = (W_k H_k^t - V_k) H_k^{t^T} + \lambda (\overline{W}^t \overline{H}^t - \overline{V}) \overline{H}_k^{t^T}$, we have

$$[W_k^t H_k^t H_k^{t^T}]_{ij} - [V_k H_k^{t^T}]_{ij} + \lambda [\overline{W}^t \overline{H}^t \overline{H}_k^{t^T}]_{ij} - \lambda [\overline{V H}_k^{t^T}]_{ij}$$

$$\frac{[W_k^t H_k^t H_k^{t^T}]_{ij} + \lambda [\overline{W}^t \overline{H}^t \overline{H}_k^{t^T}]_{ij}}{[W_k^t]_{ij}} ([W_k]_{ij} - [W_k^t]_{ij}) = 0.$$

It is equivalent to

$$-[V_k H_k^{t^T}]_{ij} - \lambda [\overline{V H}_k^{t^T}]_{ij} + \frac{[W_k^t H_k^t H_k^{t^T}]_{ij} + \lambda [\overline{W}^t \overline{H}^t \overline{H}_k^{t^T}]_{ij}}{[W_k^t]_{ij}} [W_k]_{ij} = 0. \quad (13)$$

From (14), we have the minimum of $g(W_k, W_k^t)$ with respect to the (i, j)-th element of W_k as follows:

$$[W_k^*]_{ij} = [W_k^t]_{ij} \frac{([V_k H_k^{t^T}]_{ij} + \lambda [\overline{V H}_k^{t^T}]_{ij})}{[W_k^t H_k^t H_k^{t^T}]_{ij} + \lambda [\overline{W}^t \overline{H}^t \overline{H}_k^{t^T}]_{ij}}. \quad (14)$$

By rewriting (14) in a matrix form, we have

$$W_k^* = W_k^t \circ \frac{V_k H_k^{t^T} + \lambda \overline{V H}_k^{t^T}}{W_k^t H_k^t H_k^{t^T} + \lambda \overline{W}^t \overline{H}^t \overline{H}_k^{t^T}}.$$

By setting $W_k^{t+1} = W_k^*$, we know that $f(W_k^{t+1}) \leq f(W_k^t)$ according to **Lemma 1**. This completes the proof. ∎

Interestedly, the above proof procedure suggest the generalization ability of TNMF. By simple algebra, the formula (9) is equivalent to the following minimization:

$$\min_{W_k \geq 0} ||X_k - W_k Y_k|_F^2,$$

where $X_k = [V_k, \sqrt{\lambda}(\overline{V} - \overline{W}^t \overline{H}^t + W_k^t \overline{H}_k^t)]$ and $Y_k = [H_k^t, \sqrt{\lambda} \overline{H}_k^t]$. It means that TNMF learns dictionary both from training examples and test examples. In other words, TNMF achieves better generalization ability than the standard NMF only on training examples.

Since MURs decrease the objective function of TNMF, the objective function gets more and more close to the minimum, and gets farther and farther from the initial point, on its fly. We therefore gave the following stopping condition of MUR like [25,26]:

$$\frac{|f_t - f_{t-1}|}{|f_t - f_0|} \leq \varepsilon, \tag{15}$$

where $f_t = \sum_{k=1}^{K} ||V_k - W_k^t H_k^t||_F^2 + \lambda ||\overline{V} - \overline{W}^t \overline{H}^t||_F^2$ signifies the objective value at the t-th iteration round ($t \leq 1$), and ε signifies the tolerance, i.e., $\varepsilon = 10^{-3}$. We summarized the total procedure of MUR for TNMF in **Algorithm 1**.

Algorithm 1. MUR for Optimizing TNMF

    Input: $\{V_1, \cdots, V_K\}$, $\overline{V}$, and r
    Output: $\{W_1, \cdots, W_K\}$, $\{H_1, \cdots, H_K\}$, and $\overline{H}$
1.   Initialize $\{W_1, \cdots, W_K\}$, $\{H_1, \cdots, H_K\}$, and $\overline{H}$ with random matrices
2.   Set $W^t = [W_1, \cdots, W_K]$ and $t = 1$
    Repeat
      For $k = 1, \cdots, K$
3.   Update W_k^{t+1} with $W_k^{t+1} = W_k^t \circ \frac{V_k H_k^{t\,T} + \lambda \overline{V} \overline{H}_k^{t+1\,T}}{W_k^t H_k^t H_k^{t\,T} + \lambda \overline{W}^t \overline{H}^t \overline{H}_k^{t\,T}}$
4.   Update H_k^{t+1} with $H_k^{t+1} = H_k^t \circ \frac{W_k^{t+1\,T} V_k}{W_k^{t+1\,T} W_k^{t+1} H_k^t}$
      End For
5.   Update $\overline{W}^{t+1} = [W_1^{t+1}, \cdots, W_k^{t+1}]$
6.   Split $\overline{H}^{t+1}$ into $\overline{H}^{t+1} = [\overline{H}_1^{t+1\,T}, \cdots, \overline{H}_k^{t+1\,T}]^T$
7.   Update $t \leftarrow t + 1$
    Until {The stopping condition (15) is satisfied.}
8.   **Return** $\{W_1, \cdots, W_K\}$, $\{H_1, \cdots, H_K\}$, and $\overline{H}$

TNMF provides a flexible framework for transductive NMF learning and various algorithms can be easily developed by replacing the Frobenious norm in (2) with other losses, e.g., Kullback Leibler divergence. **Algorithm 1** can be easily modified for optimizing TNMF variants and can be accelerated by utilizing the line search strategy introduced in [25,26]. In addition, the Frobenius norm based TNMF can be optimized by using the efficient NeNMF [33] method. We omit these studies due to the limit of space.

In summary, TNMF presents a friendly way of recognizing actions from still image due to the simplicity and flexibility of TNMF. We can easily construct the histograms of training actions and test image according to [4] and recognizing the action of the test image by the nearest neighbor (NN) classifier. By further incorporating constraints or regularizations on either features or encodings, interesting readers can easily extend this method for their own purposes in the future.

4   Experiments

Although the NMF-based method performs well on laboratory video frames [4], it is difficult to be applied to some tasks especially when some actions have insufficient examples, e.g., web images. This is because the pose clusters learned for some actions containing rare examples may be ill-posed.

4.1   Laboratory Datasets

For each collected images, we used an effective human detector [18] to detect people in different poses and aligned the detection rectangle by positioning the human head in its top-middle. Each of the detected human images is cropped and resized to a 78×42 color image. Based on the same image retrieval procedure for eight actions, we obtained a set of web images and extracted the HOG-descriptor for each cropped image. The HOG-descriptor for each image of each action is reshaped to a 1296-dimensional long vector and treated as a pose example [4].

Table 1. Statistics of the Google and Weizmann dataset, and 'tr/ts' means that the numbers of training poses and test poses are tr and ts, respectively

Action Name	'run'	'walk'	'skip'	'jump'	'pjump'	'wave'	'jack'	'bend'	'side'
Google	201/202	285/286	67/68	118/119	109/109	52/53	43/44	30/30	-
Weizmann	30/165	129/238	30/184	30/140	103/167	283/326	90/206	97/84	96/124

Google Search Images. Figure 1(a) depicts some web images collected by using Google image search engine corresponding to human actions 'run', 'walk', 'skip', 'jump', 'pjump', 'wave', 'jack', and 'bend'. For each action, e.g., 'run', we searched images on Google image search engine by using the keywords 'run people', 'running people', 'run person', and 'running person', and manually filtered all irrelevant images. Figure 1(b) shows the flow chart of generating the HOG descriptors of the Google web images. We constructed the Google dataset to include all the collected pose examples of web images.

Weizmann Video Frames. We conducted the same procedure on Weizmann video frames [1] which contains nine actions and formed another Weizmann pose dataset (or simply Weizmann dataset). Figure 2 gives examples of four actions including 'run', 'walk', 'jump', and 'bend' in the Weizmann dataset. It shows that video frames have more static backgrounds, and are therefore easier than the Google dataset.

Table 1 summarizes both datasets. It shows that actions 'bend' and 'jack' of the Google dataset contain a small number of training examples, and actions 'run', 'skip', and 'jump' of the Weizmann dataset contain a small number of training examples. Thus, the numbers of training examples for all actions are

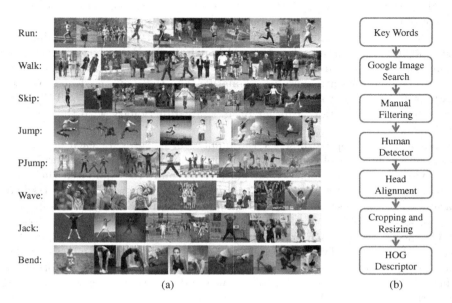

Run:

Walk:

Skip:

Jump:

PJump:

Wave:

Jack:

Bend:

(a)

Key Words
↓
Google Image
Search
↓
Manual
Filtering
↓
Human
Detector
↓
Head
Alignment
↓
Cropping and
Resizing
↓
HOG
Descriptor

(b)

Fig. 1. Examples of web images returned by Google image search, where the action names from top to bottom are 'run', 'walk', 'skip', 'jump', 'pjump', 'wave', 'jack', and 'bend' (a), and (b) the flow chart of generating the HOG descriptor

Run:

Walk:

Jump:

Bend:

Fig. 2. Examples of video frames extracted from Weizmann dataset, where the action names from top to bottom are 'run', 'walk', 'jump', and 'bend'

imbalanced and performing NMF on the training examples of individual actions cannot obtain 'effective' primitive poses. In this experiment, we employed TNMF to overcome this deficiency by jointly learning dictionary from both training samples and test samples of each action. Although some actions have rare training examples, the dictionary obtained by simultaneously learning from both training and test samples are more discriminative than those obtained by separately learning from training samples [4]. To evaluate the effectiveness of TNMF, we compared the recognition accuracy of its learned dictionary with those learned by NMF.

According to [19], we first set the number of features for each action to 5 based on the number of common viewpoints for each action (2 for lateral views, 2 for views $\pm 45°$ and 1 for frontal/back view), and cross-validated the trade-off parameter on a set $\lambda \in \{0.1, 0.3, 0.5, 0.7, 0.9\}$. Then we fixed the trade-off parameter to the best one, and cross-validated the number of features on a set $r \in \{5, 30, 50, 70, 90\}$. To evaluate the effectiveness of TNMF, Figure 3 gives the highest accuracies of NMF and TNMF obtained by cross-validation. Figure 3(a) and (b) show that TNMF outperforms NMF on Google dataset when varying r and λ in wide ranges of [50,90] and [0.1,0.7]. It shows that TNMF performs best when $\lambda = 0.7$ and $r = 50$. From Figure 3(c) and (d), we can see that MT-NMF outperforms NMF on Weizmann dataset when varying r and λ in wide ranges of [5,90] and [0.1,0.5], and it performs best when $\lambda = 0.1$ and $r = 70$.

Table 2. Accuracy (%) of NMF and TNMF on the Google and Weizmann dataset

Algorithms	NMF	TNMF
Google	74.66	**78.09**
Weizmann	88.30	**91.17**

Table 2 depicts the average accuracy of NMF and TNMF on both Google and Weizmann datasets. It shows that TNMF outperforms NMF on the Google dataset because it leverages the datasets across actions and learns better pose clusters for actions whose training examples are insufficient. The experimental results on the Weizmann dataset are consistent with this observation. It confirms the effectiveness of TNMF in action recognition from still images.

4.2   Willows Dataset

The Willow dataset[1] [22] contains totally 913 images for 7 activities including 'interacting with computer', 'photographing', 'playing music', 'riding bike', 'riding horse', 'running', and 'walking' (see Figure 4 for some examples of each action). Khan et al. [21] have demonstrated that fusing color and shape information can

---

[1] The Willow dataset is available at: http://www.di.ens.fr/willow/research/ stillactions/.

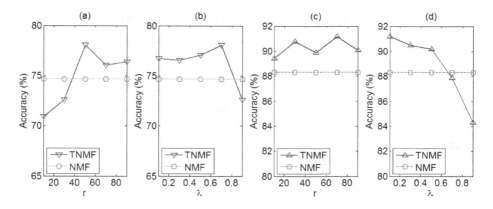

Fig. 3. Cross-validation of the number of features r and trade-off parameter λ of TNMF on the Google and Weizmann datasets, (a) accuracy versus r when $\lambda = 0.7$ and (b) accuracy versus λ when $r = 5$ on the Google dataset; (c) accuracy versus r when $\lambda = 0.1$ and (b) accuracy versus λ when $r = 70$ on the Weizmann dataset. The highest accuracies of NMF are included for comparison.

produce promising results of action recognition in still images. Along this direction, we extracted the shape cues by SIFT descriptors [32] and color cues by color names [34] separately, from each image, and fused them to construct the feature vector. The SIFT descriptor has 289 dimensionality and the color names has 11

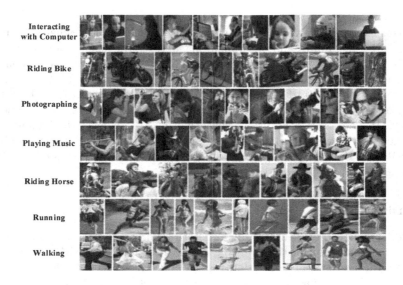

Fig. 4. Example images of different actions in the Willow dataset

dimensionality, and thus we constructed a 300-dimensional feature vector for each image.

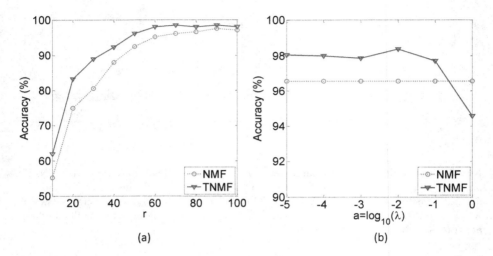

Fig. 5. Cross-validation of the reduced dimensionality r and trade-off parameter λ of TNMF on the Willow dataset: (a) accuracy when varying the reduced dimensionality r from 10 to 100 and fixing $\lambda = 0.1$, and the highest accuracy appears at $r = 70$; (b) accuracy when varying the trade-off parameter λ from 10^{-5} to 1 and fixing $r = 70$, and the highest accuracy appears at $\lambda = 10^{-2}$

In this experiment, we selected 100 images for each action, where 70 images are utilized for training and the remaining images are utilized for testing. To filter the influence of hyper-parameters of TNMF, i.e., the reduced dimensionality r and the trade-off parameter λ, to the final results, we varied the reduced dimensionality from 10 to 100 with a step size 10, and varied λ from 10^{-5} to 1. Such trial was repeated ten times for eliminate the influence of initialization of both TNMF and TNMF. Figure 5 shows that TNMF achieves the highest accuracy when $r = 70$ and $\lambda = 10^{-2}$, and that TNMF consistently outperforms NMF on the Willow dataset. This observation confirms the effectiveness of TNMF in still image based activity recognition.

4.3   Discussion

In summary, the experimental results on both laboratory dataset and real-world dataset demonstrate that the transductive learning trick in TNMF significantly improves the performance of action recognition still images. It should be honest that the TNMF based activity recognition method performs not very well when the number of actions are quite large, e.g., Stanford 40 [36] dataset. That is because the concatenation operator in TNMF (2) might lead to cancellation

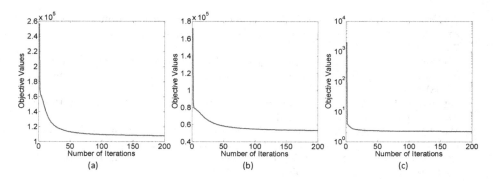

Fig. 6. The objective values versus number of iterations of TNMF on the Google (a), Weizmann (b), and Willow (c) datasets

among dictionaries of actions in this situation, and thus reduces the discriminative ability of the learned dictionary.

In this paper, we have theoretically proved the convergence of the MUR algorithm for TNMF. To verify this point, Figure 6 depicts the objective values versus number of iterations on the Google, Weizmann, and Willow datasets. They show that the MUR algorithm converges quite quickly, e.g., within 50 iteration rounds.

5   Conclusion

This paper proposes a novel method for activity recognition in still images based on transductive non-negative matrix factorization (TNMF). TNMF can transduce the visual features from training images to the learned encoding of test image. Therefore, TNMF boosts the performance of NMF based activity recognition especially on the datasets that contain insufficient training images for some actions. Experiments on both laboratory and real-world datasets demonstrate the effectiveness of TNMF.

Acknowledgments. This work is partially supported by Research Fund for the Doctoral Program of Higher Eduction of China, SRFDP (under grant No. 2034307110017) and Australian Research Council Projects (under grant No. FT-130101457 and DP-120103730).

References

1. Blank, M., Gorelick, L., Shechtman, E., Irani, M., Basri, R.: Actions as space-time shapes. In: International Conference on Computer Vision, vol. 2, pp. 1395–1402 (2005)
2. Laptev, I., Perez, P.: Retrieving actions in movies. In: Proceedings of International Conference on Computer Vision, pp. 1–8 (2007)

3. Niebles, J.C., Wang, H., Fei-Fei, L.: Unsupervised Learning of Human Action Categories Using Spatial-Temporal Words. International Journal of Computer Vision **79**(3), 299–318 (2008)
4. Thurau, C., Hlavac, V.: Pose primitive based human action recognition in videos or still images. In: IEEE Conference on Computer Vision and Pattern Recognition (2008)
5. Aggarwal, J.K., Xia, L.: Human Activity Recognition from 3DData: A Review. Pattern Recognition Letters (2014)
6. Waltner, G., Mauthner, T., Bischof, H.: Indoor Activity Detection and Recognition for Sport Games Analysis. arXiv preprint arXiv:1404.6413 (2014)
7. Lee, D.D., Seung, H.S.: Learning the Parts of Objects with Non-negative Matrix Factorization. Nature **401**(6755), 788–791 (1999)
8. Xu, W., Liu, X., Gong, Y.: Document clustering based on nonnegative matrix factorization. In: ACM Special Interest Group on Information Retrieval, pp. 167–273 (2014)
9. Huang, X., Zheng, X., Yuan, W., Wang, F., Zhu, S.: Enhanced Clustering of Biomedical Documents Using Ensemble Nonnegative Matrix Factorization. Information Sciences **181**(11), 2293–2302 (2011)
10. Pauca, V., Piper, J., Plemmons, R.: Nonnegative Matrix Factorization for Spectral Data Analysis. Linear Algebra and its Applications **416**(1), 29–47 (2006)
11. Liu, L., Shao, L., Zhen, X., Li, X.: Learning Discriminative Key Poses for Action Recognition. IEEE Transactions on Cybernetics **43**(6), 1860–1870 (2013)
12. Zhang, Z., Tao, D.: Slow Feature Analysis for Human Action Recognition. IEEE Transactions on Pattern Analysis and Machine Intelligence **34**(3), 436–450 (2012)
13. Liu, L., Shao, L., Zheng, F., Li, X.: Realistic Action Recognition via Sparsely-constructed Gaussian Processes. Pattern Recognition **47**, 3819–3827 (2014)
14. Hotelling, H.: Analysis of a Complex of Statistical Variables into Principal Components. Journal of Educational Psychology **24**, 417–441 (1933)
15. Fisher, R.A.: The Use of Multiple Measurements in Taxonomic Problems. Annals of Eugenics **7**, 179–188 (1936)
16. Guan, N., Lan, L., Tao, D., Luo, Z., Yang, X.: Transductive nonnegative matrix factorizationfor semi-supervised high-performance speech separation. In: Proceedings of IEEE International Conference on Acoustics, Speech, and Signal Processing, pp. 2553–2557 (2014)
17. Lee, D.D., Seung, H.S.: Algorithms for Non-negative matrix factorization. In: Proceedings of Advances in Neural Information and Processing Systems, pp. 556–562 (2000)
18. Felzenszwalb, P., McAllester, D., Ramanan, D.: A discriminatively trained, multiscale, deformable part model. In: Proceedings of IEEE Conference on Computer Vision and Pattern Recognition, vol. 7, pp. 1–8 (2008)
19. Ikizler-Cinbis, N., Cinbis, R.G., Sclaroff, S.: Learning actions from the web. In: IEEE International Conference on Computer Vision, pp. 995–1002 (2009)
20. Zheng, Y., Zhang, Y.J., Li, X., Liu, B.D.: Action recognition in still images using a combination of human pose and context information. In: International Conference on Image Processing (2012)
21. Khan, F.S., Anwer, R.M., van deWeijer, J., Bagdanov, A.D., Lopez, A.M., Felsberg, M.: Coloring Action Recognition in Still Images. International Journal of Computer Vision **105**, 205–221 (2013)
22. Delaitre, V., Laptev, I., Sivic, J.: Recognizing human actions in still images: astudy of bag-of-features and part-based representations. In: British Machine Vision Conference (2010)

23. Laptev, I.: On Space-time Interest Points. International Journal of Computer Vision **64**, 107–123 (2005)
24. Guo, G., Lai, A.: A Survey on Still Image Based Human Action Recognition. Pattern Recognition **47**, 3343–3361 (2014)
25. Guan, N., Tao, D., Luo, Z., Yuan, B.: Manifold Regularized Discriminative Non-negative Matrix Factorization with Fast Gradient Descent. IEEE Transactions on Image Processing **20**(7), 2030–2048 (2011)
26. Guan, N., Tao, D., Luo, Z., Yuan, B.: Non-negative Patch Alignment Framework. IEEE Transactions on Neural Networks **22**(8), 1218–1230 (2011)
27. Li, K., Fu, Y.: Prediction of Human Activity by Discovering Temporal Sequence Patterns. IEEE Transactions on Pattern Analysis and Machine Intelligence **36**(8), 1644–1657 (2014)
28. Kong, Y., Jia, Y., Fu, Y.: Interactive Phrases: Semantic Descriptions for Human Interaction Recognition. IEEE Transactions on Pattern Analysis and Machine Intelligence **36**(9), 1775–1788 (2014)
29. Poppe, R.: A survey on vision-based human action recognition. Image and Vision Computing **28**(6), 976–990 (2010)
30. Lambrecht, J., Kleinsorge, M., Rosenstrauch, M., Krger, J.: Spatial Programming for Industrial Robots Through Task Demonstration. International Journal of Advanced Robotic Systems 10(254) (2013)
31. Danafar, S., Gheissari, N.: Action recognition for surveillance applications using optic flow and SVM. In: Asian Conference on Computer Vision, pp. 457–466 (2007)
32. Lowe, D.G.: Distinctive Image Features from Scale-invariant Points. International Journal of Computer Vision **60**(2), 91–110 (2004)
33. Guan, N., Tao, D., Luo, Z., Yuan, B.: NeNMF: An Optimal Gradient Method for Non-negative Matrix Factorization. IEEE Transactions on Signal Processing **60**(6), 2882–2898 (2012)
34. van de Seijer, J., Schmid, C., Verbeek, J.J., Larlus, D.: Learning Color Names for Real-world Applications. IEEE Transactions on Image Processing **18**(7), 1512–1524 (2009)
35. Guo, G., Lai, A.: A survey on still image based human action recognition. Pattern Recognition **47**(10), 3343–3361 (2014)
36. Yao, B., Jiang, X., Khosla, A., Lin, A.L., Guibas, L.J., Fei-Fei, L.: Human action recognition by learning bases of action attributes and parts. In: International Conference on Computer Vision, Barcelona, Spain, 6–13 November 2011

Mode-Driven Volume Analysis
Based on Correlation of Time Series

Chengcheng Jia[1]([⊠]), Wei Pang[3], and Yun Fu[1,2]

[1] Electrical and Computer Engineering, Northeastern University, Boston, USA
cjia@coe.neu.edu
[2] Computer and Information Science, Northeastern University, Boston, USA
yunfu@ece.neu.edu
[3] School of Natural and Computing Sciences, University of Aberdeen, Aberdeen, UK
pang.wei@abdn.ac.uk

Abstract. Tensor analysis is widely used for face recognition and action recognition. In this paper, a mode-driven discriminant analysis (MDA) in tensor subspace is proposed for visual recognition. For training, we treat each sample as an N-order tensor, of which the first N-1 modes capture the spatial information of images while the N-th mode captures the sequential patterns of images. We employ Fisher criteria on the first N-1 modes to extract discriminative features of the visual information. After that, considering the correlation of adjacent frames in the sequence, i.e., the current frame and its former and latter ones, we update the sequence by calculating the correlation of triple adjacent frames, then perform discriminant analysis on the N-th mode. The alternating projection procedure of MDA converges and is convex with different initial values of the transformation matrices. Such hybrid tensor subspace learning scheme may sufficiently preserve both discrete and continuous distributions information of action videos in lower dimensional spaces to boost discriminant power. Experiments on the MSR action 3D database, KTH database and ETH database showed that our algorithm MDA outperformed other tensor-based methods in terms of accuracy and is competitive considering the time efficiency. Besides, it is robust to deal with the damaged and self-occluded action silhouettes and RGB object images in various viewing angles.

1 Introduction

Tensor discriminant analysis (TDA) [1,11,32] has been successfully applied to various recognition related problems, such as action recognition [9,19,23], face recognition [4,10,30], and gait recognition [7,17,31]. TDA is essentially the extension of vector or matrix analysis to higher-order tensor analysis. In the tensor subspace, the discriminant projection matrix of each mode [16] is calculated alternately by fixing the other modes.

However, most tensor-based methods have been performed directly on samples [10] [7], which may decrease the accuracy in situations where image occlusion or damage exist. Considering the variations of an object due to different angles

© Springer International Publishing Switzerland 2015
L. Agapito et al. (Eds.): ECCV 2014 Workshops, Part I, LNCS 8925, pp. 818–833, 2015.
DOI: 10.1007/978-3-319-16178-5_57

and illuminated conditions, canonical correlation analysis (CCA) [6,12,22,27] is often used for computing the similarity of two data sets to overcome this problem. Kim *et al.* [15] proposed the tensor canonical correlation analysis (TCCA) by calculating the correlation of two tensor samples for action detection and recognition. TCCA improves the accuracy compared with CCA and is time efficient for action detection. In our previous work [13], a CCA-based discriminant analysis in multi-linear subspace (MDCC) is proposed for action recognition. In that work, we took an action image sequence as a *3-order* tensor, and calculated the discriminant projection matrices using canonical correlations between any pairwise of tensors. MDCC with discriminant information obtained better accuracy than TCCA. However, all the above mentioned methods perform Fisher criteria [2] or canonical correlation analysis on an action tensor individually, irrespective of the different realistic meanings of each mode, *e.g.*, the pixel character of the image mode and the correlation of the sequence mode.

Since an action image sequence can be seen as a *3-order* tensor, of which *mode-1* and *mode-2* represent the action image information and *mode-3* describes the temporal information [15], in a similar way, a RGB object images can also be represented as a *3-order* tensor, of which the first and second modes stand for image, while the third mode indicates lateral illumination or RGB color. In this case Fisher criteria is usually used to extract image features for classification. It is also noted that the correlations among the images can reflect the temporal ordering of an action or among various RGB colors of an object caused by multi-view and illumination, thus by considering the correlations among images we can improve the performance of the subsequent recognition task [5,21,28]. Motivated by these insights, in this paper we explore a mode alignment method with different criteria which employs Fisher criteria on the image modes and discriminant correlation analysis on the sequence mode, called mode-driven discriminant analysis (MDA). The reason we use different discriminant criteria in different mode is that different modes have different visual distributions, *i.e.*, the discrete distribution means the image subspaces in the first N-1 modes, while the continuous distribution means the sequential patterns in the N-th mode. The proposed framework is shown in Figure 1.

In this framework, there are m samples in the whole dataset, and we dig out the *mode-1,2* spatial information of an action by discriminant criterion. Suppose an action is composed of I_3 frames, we re-organized the dataset to be I_3 subsets, each of which contains m frames. We call this **frame-to-frame** reconstruction of the action sequence, *i.e.*, we update the *mode-3* tensor by calculating the correlation of their adjacent frames, then, we use the discriminant analysis on the updated *mode-3*. We propose to make full and reasonable use of different representation of data, *i.e.*, for the spatial pattern, we extract feature directly from raw data represented by pixels, while for the sequential pattern, we want to extract the feature by digging out the intrinsic correlation between the adjacent frames. This idea can be generalized to other representation of data with various factors, such as pose, illumination, multi-view, expression, color for face recognition, and multi-view, subject diversity, depth for action recognition. We let the

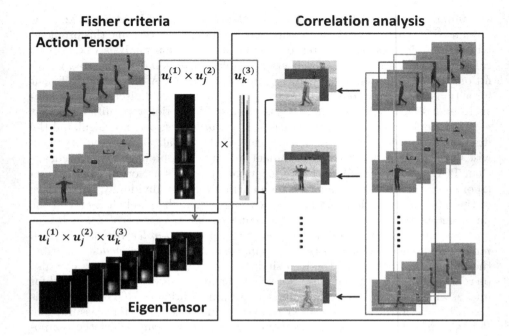

Fisher criteria   **Correlation analysis**

Fig. 1. Framework of MDA. The left is *mode-1, 2* aligned by Fisher criteria, while the right is frame alignment along *mode-3*, containing I_3 subsets (each is shown in red, blue, green boxes). We update the action sequence by using the correlation between three adjacent subsets, then perform the Fisher criteria on *mode-3*.

iterative learning subject to a plausible convergence condition. The projection is both discriminant and canonical correlated, in contrast to traditional ones [10] [15]. Hence we achieve good accuracy and performance on action and object recognition even with a simple nearest neighbor classifier (NNC). We summarize the advantages of the proposed MDA as follows.

1. MDA employs a mode alignment method with specific discriminant criteria on different modes of one tensor.

2. MDA considers the correlation between adjacent frames in the temporal sequence or RGB pattern by the **frame-to-frame** reconstruction.

3. MDA converges as proved in Section 3 and discussed in Section 4.

The rest of this paper is organized as follows: Section 2 introduces fundamentals of tensor and canonical correlation analysis. Section 3 describes in detail the MDA algorithm for dimensional reduction. Experiments on action recognition and object recognition using the proposed method and other compared methods are presented in Section 4. Then, conclusions are given in Section 5.

2   Fundamentals

A multi-dimensional array $\mathcal{A} \in \mathbb{R}^{I_1 \times \cdots \times I_n \times \cdots \times I_N}$, is called an *N-order* tensor, where I_n is the dimension of *mode-n*. $\mathcal{A}_{i_1 \ldots i_N}$ is an element of $\mathcal{A}$. A tensor can usually be unfolded, which means one mode is fixed, while other modes are stretched to form a huge matrix $\mathbf{A}^{(n)}$ [16].

Definition 1. Tucker decomposition [16] $\mathcal{A} \in \mathbb{R}^{I_1 \times \cdots \times I_N}$ *is an N-order tensor and* $\mathbf{U}_n \in \mathbb{R}^{I_n \times J_n} (1 \leqslant n \leqslant N)$ *is used for decomposition, we have the following equation:*

$$\mathcal{S} = \mathcal{A} \times_1 \mathbf{U}_1^{\mathrm{T}} \times_2 \mathbf{U}_2^{\mathrm{T}} \ldots \times_n \mathbf{U}_n^{\mathrm{T}} \ldots \times_N \mathbf{U}_N^{\mathrm{T}} \tag{1}$$

The above equation indicates the procedure of dimensional reduction of a tensor, and $\mathcal{S}$ is called the core tensor, $\times_n$ is mode-n *product.*

Definition 2. Canonical correlation [22] *Given two vectors $x \in \mathbb{R}^m$, $y \in \mathbb{R}^n$, and two coefficient vectors $\alpha \in \mathbb{R}^m$, $\beta \in \mathbb{R}^n$, the correlation of x and y is calculated by*

$$\rho(u, v) = \underset{u,v}{\arg\max} \frac{\mathrm{Cov}(u, v)}{\sqrt{\mathrm{Var}(u)}\sqrt{\mathrm{Var}(v)}}, \tag{2}$$

subject to variance $\mathrm{Var}(u) = 1$ *and* $\mathrm{Var}(v) = 1$, *where $u = \alpha^T x$ and $v = \beta^T y$, $\rho(u, v)$ and $\mathrm{Cov}(u,v)$ are the canonical correlation and covariance matrix, respectively.*

3   Mode Alignment with Different Discriminant Criteria in Tensor Subspace

It has been reported in several publications that the discriminant analysis on an action image sequence can extract more effective information which reflects the properties of images [29] [25]. For temporal space, discriminant correlations among the images can reflect the temporal ordering of an action in subsequent recognition methods [5]. The proposed MDA uses Fisher criteria to transform the image information and uses discriminant canonical correlation analysis to transform the temporal information.

In MDA, an action sample is represented as a *3-order* tensor. The *mode-1,2* represent spatial dimension and the *mode-3* represents temporal information. Suppose there are m tensor samples in C classes, of which $\mathcal{A} \in \mathbb{R}^{I_1 \times I_2 \times I_3}$ is a tensor sample. Our purpose is to find the transformed matrices $\mathbf{U}_n \in \mathbb{R}^{I_n \times J_n}$ $(1 \leqslant n \leqslant 3)$ for projection in tensor space to achieve dimension reduction. $\mathbf{U}_n$ is calculated alternately by fixing the other modes. $\mathbf{U}_n$ is defined with the *mode-n* discriminant function $\boldsymbol{F_n}$ by

$$\begin{aligned} \mathbf{U}_n &= \underset{\mathbf{U}_n}{\arg\max} \; \boldsymbol{F_n} \\ &= \underset{\mathbf{U}_n}{\arg\max} \; tr\left(\mathbf{U}_n^T(\mathbf{S}_b^{(n)} - \alpha \mathbf{S}_w^{(n)})\mathbf{U}_n\right), \end{aligned} \tag{3}$$

where tr is the sum of diagonal elements of matrix $\left(\mathbf{U}_n^T (\mathbf{S}_b^{(n)} - \alpha \mathbf{S}_w^{(n)}) \mathbf{U}_n\right)$, α is a tuning parameter.

3.1   Fisher Analysis on Image Mode

Given a tensor set with m samples, each of which $\mathcal{A}_{ij} \in \mathbb{R}^{I_1 \times \cdots \times I_N}$ indicates the j-th sample belongs to the i-th class.

In the case of $1 \leq n \leq N-1$, $\mathbf{S}_b^{(n)}$ is the inter-class scatter matrix calculated by

$$\mathbf{S}_b^{(n)} = \frac{1}{m} \sum_{i=1}^{C} m_i (\bar{\mathbf{A}}_i^{(n)} - \bar{\mathbf{A}}^{(n)})(\bar{\mathbf{A}}_i^{(n)} - \bar{\mathbf{A}}^{(n)})^T, \tag{4}$$

and $\mathbf{S}_w^{(n)}$ is the intra-class scatter matrix calculated by

$$\mathbf{S}_w^{(n)} = \frac{1}{m} \sum_{i=1}^{C} \sum_{j=1}^{m_i} (\mathbf{A}_{ij}^{(n)} - \bar{\mathbf{A}}_i^{(n)})(\mathbf{A}_{ij}^{(n)} - \bar{\mathbf{A}}_i^{(n)})^T, \tag{5}$$

where m_i is the number of the i-th class; $\bar{\mathbf{A}}^{(n)}$ is the mean of training samples of $mode\text{-}n$; $\bar{\mathbf{A}}_i^{(n)}$ is the mean of i-th class (C_i) of $mode\text{-}n$; and $\mathbf{A}_{ij}^{(n)}$ is the j-th sample of C_i. In the end, $\mathbf{U}_n$ composed of the eigenvectors corresponding to the largest J_n eigenvalues of $(\mathbf{S}_b^{(n)} - \alpha \mathbf{S}_w^{(n)})$.

In Fisher criteria, the discriminant function $\boldsymbol{F}_n$ is calculated by the original data. While in discriminant canonical correlation analysis, $\boldsymbol{F}_n$ is calculated by the canonical tensor, which is detailed in Section 3.2.

3.2   Correlation of Time Series

An action sequence is actually a time series of frames, ranking orderly. We want to make use of the correlations between two adjacent frames, which can reflect the variation of an action as time elapses. So, we want to update the dataset by exploring the correlations between the time series.

In the tensor set, we re-organized the the new subsets by collecting the k-th $(1 \leq k \leq I_N)$ frame of the samples, so there are I_N subsets in the dataset. What we want to do is updating the new subsets then re-organizing them to form a new dataset, then performing discriminant criterion.

We consider a sample $\mathcal{A}_{ij}$ as a action sequence $\{f_1, \ldots, f_k, \ldots, f_{I_N}\}$, and we organized a new sub-set $\mathcal{A}_k$ by extracting each k-th frame from all the samples, then we calculate the correlation between $(k-1)$-th, k-th, and $(k+1)$-th sub-sets, which is indicated as $\rho_{k-1,k,k+1}$, as shown in Figure 2. Our goal is to decompose the whole tensor set into I_N subsets, then update the whole tensor sequence by the correlations of the sub-sets. So, the new dataset has explored the correlation in the time series, which accords with the real situation and can describe the time series more precisely. The procedure is detailed as follows.

In the case of mode $n = N$ (here $N = 3$), we organized the k-th subset by collecting the k-th frames of the dataset as $A_k \in \mathbb{R}^{(I_1 I_2) \times m}$. The singular value decomposition (SVD) [16] is performed on $\mathbf{A}_k \mathbf{A}_k^{\mathrm{T}}$ as shown below:

$$\mathbf{A}_k \mathbf{A}_k^{\mathrm{T}} = \mathbf{P} \Lambda \mathbf{P}^{\mathrm{T}}, \tag{6}$$

where Λ is the diagonal matrix and $\mathbf{P} \in \mathbb{R}^{(I_1 I_2) \times J_N}$ is the matrix composed by the eigenvectors of the J_N largest eigenvalues, J_N is the subspace dimension. We perform CCA on the $k - 1$, k, and $k + 1$ sets as follows:

$$\mathbf{P}_{k-1}^{\mathrm{T}} \mathbf{P}_k = \mathbf{Q}_{k-1,k} \Lambda \mathbf{Q}_{k,k-1}^{\mathrm{T}}, \quad \mathbf{P}_k^{\mathrm{T}} \mathbf{P}_{k+1} = \mathbf{Q}_{k,k+1} \Lambda \mathbf{Q}_{k+1,k}^{\mathrm{T}}, \tag{7}$$

where Λ is the diagonal matrix and $\mathbf{Q}_{k-1,k}$, $\mathbf{Q}_{k,k+1} \in \mathbb{R}^{J_N \times J_N}$ are orthogonal rotation matrices. The k-th subset $\mathbf{P}_k$ is updated as follows:

$$\mathbf{P}_{k-1,k,k+1} \leftarrow \mathrm{SVD}(\mathbf{P}_k \mathbf{Q}_{k,k+1}^{\mathrm{T}} \mathbf{P}_k^{\mathrm{T}} \mathbf{P}_k \mathbf{Q}_{k,k-1}). \tag{8}$$

Then, we update the dataset by the new sub-sets $\mathbf{A}_k = \{\mathbf{P}_{k-1,k,k+1} | k = 1, \ldots, I_N\}$. Then perform discriminant analysis on the *mode-N* samples by Eqs. (4,5).

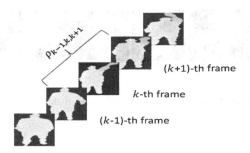

Fig. 2. Illustration of correlation analysis on the time series subspace

MDA is different from TCCA [15] when calculating the transformation matrix (TM). In TCCA, all the TMs are composed of the coefficients vectors of data by CCA, and there is no discriminant analysis; while in MDA, all the TM is calculated by discriminant analysis of data. What's more, TCCA calculates the TM by pairwise tensors; while MDA calculates the inter-class and intra-class scatter matrices by making use of the correlation of multi-sets.

Definition 3. Similarity *The similarity of two tensors, which is actually the mode-N correlation between two tensors, is defined as follows:*

$$S = (\mathbf{P}_i^{(N)} \mathbf{Q}_{ik}^{(N)})^T (\mathbf{P}_k^{(N)} \mathbf{Q}_{ki}^{(N)}), \tag{9}$$

where i, k indicate a pair of tensors. S is called the similarity matrix.

Algorithm 1. Mode-driven discriminant analysis (MDA)

INPUT: m N-order tensors $\Gamma_m = \{\mathcal{A}_i^{C_i}\}$, with label $\{C_i\}$, $(1 \leq i \leq m)$, the tuning parameter α, and the maximum iterations t_{max}.
OUTPUT: Updated $U_n^{(t)}$, $1 \leqslant n \leqslant$ N.

1: Initialize $\mathbf{U}_n$ by eigen-decomp of $\mathcal{A}_i^{C_i}$, $1 \leqslant i \leqslant m$.
2: **for** $t = 1$ to t_{max} **do**
3:    **for** $n = 1$ to N **do**
4:       $\mathcal{A}_i^{C_i} \leftarrow \mathcal{A}_i^{C_i} \times_1 (\mathbf{U}_1^{(t-1)})^{\mathrm{T}} \cdots \times_{n-1} (\mathbf{U}_{n-1}^{(t-1)})^{\mathrm{T}} \times_{n+1} (\mathbf{U}_{n+1}^{(t-1)})^{\mathrm{T}} \cdots \times_{\mathrm{N}} (\mathbf{U}_{\mathrm{N}}^{(t-1)})^{\mathrm{T}}.$
5:       **if** $n =$ N **then**
6:          Update $\mathcal{A}_i$ via Eqs. (6, 7, 8).
7:       **end if**
8:       Calculate $\mathbf{S}_b^{(n)}$ and $\mathbf{S}_w^{(n)}$ by Eqs. (4) and (5).
9:       Update $\mathbf{U}_n^{(t)}$ by eig-decomp $\left(\mathbf{S}_b^{(n)} - \alpha \mathbf{S}_w^{(n)}\right)$.
10:      Convergence condition: $\boldsymbol{F}^{(t)}(\mathbf{U}_n) = \sum_{n=1}^{N} tr\left[(\mathbf{U}_n^{(t)})^{\mathrm{T}}[\mathbf{S}_b^{(n)} - \alpha \mathbf{S}_w^{(n)}]\mathbf{U}_n^{(t)}\right]$,
        if $\|\boldsymbol{F}^{(t)}(\mathbf{U}_n) - \boldsymbol{F}^{(t-1)}(\mathbf{U}_n)\| \leqslant \varepsilon$, return.
11:    **end for**
12:    $\mathbf{U}_n^{(t-1)} = \mathbf{U}_n^{(t)}$, $1 \leqslant n \leqslant$ N.
13: **end for**

Fig. 3. Actions of MSR 3D action database

4 Experiments

In this section, we have three experiments, including depth action recognition, silhouette action recognition, and RGB object recognition. We aim to test the performance of discriminant correlation analysis in action sequence and RGB pattern, and show the effectiveness of the proposed method.

4.1 Experiments on the MSR 3D Action Database

This database[1] contains 20 categories of depth actions, which are *arm waving, horizontal waving, hammer, hand catching, punching, throwing, drawing x, drawing circle, clapping, two hands waving, sideboxing, bending, forward kicking, side kicking, jogging, tennis swing, golf swing,* and *picking up and throwing.* There are total 567 samples from 10 subjects, and each sample is performed 2-3 trials. Each action is composed by a series of frames. In order to align the image sequence

---

[1] http://research.microsoft.com/en-us/um/people/zliu/ActionRecoRsrc/

with one another, we first cropped and resized each frame to be 80×80, then subsampled each action sequence to be in the size of $80 \times 80 \times 10$. The key frames are shown in Figure 3.

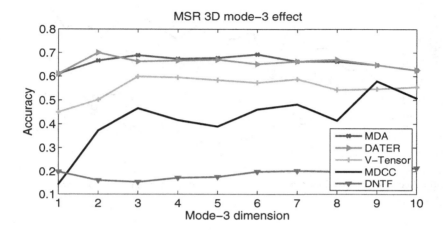

Fig. 4. Recognition of different methods versus different dimensions on MSR 3D action database

We used DATER [29], MDCC [13], DNTF [33], V-TensorFace [26] (renamed as V-Tensor for simplicity) for comparison. All of them except V-tensor are discriminant tensor methods. V-Tensor is a kind of mode-driven method, which finds the *mode-3* neighbors of tensor, while *mode-1,2* do not. DATER applied Fisher criteria on each mode of a tensor sample directly. MDCC performs discriminant CCA in the tensor subspace. DNTF employs discriminant non-negative matrix factorization in tensor subspace, and the key is iteratively calculating the non-negative transformation matrices.

Here, the effect of dimensional reduction on the time series is tested. Fig. 4 indicates the accuracy under various *mode-3* dimension while the dimensions of *mode-1,2* are fixed to be 10. We can see the proposed MDA is compatible with DATER, which reflects the less influence of *mode-3* correlation of frame series. Besides, the V-Tensor performs worse than both MDA and DATER, which also indicates that *mode-3* manifold does not work better than Fisher criterion. Here, MDCC performs worse than MDA and V-Tensor, *i.e.*, the similarity of *mode-1,2* plays a negative role because of different levels of distortion by the previous cropping. Fig. 5 shows the recognition accuracies of different methods under various dimensions. As Fig. 4 shows, we select the *mode-3* dimension to be 3, while the dimensions of *mode-1,2* is increased from 1 to 20. We can see that the results of our method are comparable to the accuracy of DATER in average, which means the correlation analysis is feasible on the time series. All the results

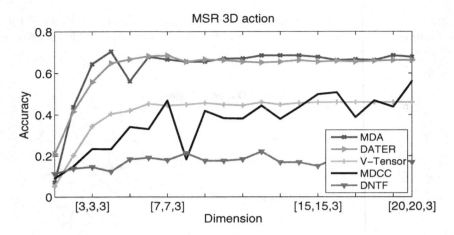

Fig. 5. Accuracies of different methods versus different dimensions on MSR 3D action database

do not improve much when the dimensions are small, which indicate the best subspace dimension.

4.2   Experiments on the KTH Database

KTH database [24] is employed in this experiment, containing six different action classes: running, boxing, waving, jogging, walking and clapping. There are 90 videos with 9 people, and each person performs 10 class actions. We took the outdoor scenario in this experiment. From the videos 1310 samples are distilled, and each sample is in the size of $90 \times 50 \times 20$ pixels. 10-fold cross-validation is used for the dataset. Each time 101 samples are used for training, and 30 for testing.

Figure 6(a) shows the silhouettes processed in the procedure, and these silhouettes are generated from the raw gray images. In order to highlight the performance of *mode-3* transformation matrix, Figures 6(b) $\sim$ 6(f) are used to illustrate the projected actions of different methods. Note that most of the projected actions concentrate the main energy in a few significant eigenvectors, which indicates that our discrimination of $\mathbf{U}_3$ is competitive with that of Fisher-based performance. The convergence character of MDA is demonstrated in Figure 7, from which we can see that each experiment for learning uses a different training data set and starts with the initial value of $\mathbf{U}_n$, which is composed of eigenvectors. The value of the discriminant function $\boldsymbol{F}$ (calculated as the sum of $\boldsymbol{F}_n$) becomes stable after first few iterations. This fast and stable convergence property is very suitable for keeping the learning cost low. Furthermore, as shown in Figure 7(b), MDA converged to the same point irrespective of different initial values of $\mathbf{U}_n$, which means that MDA is convex.

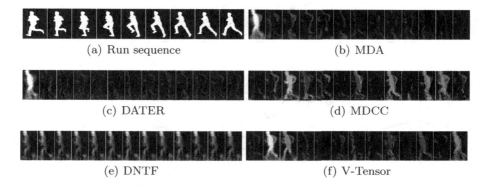

(a) Run sequence (b) MDA

(c) DATER (d) MDCC

(e) DNTF (f) V-Tensor

Fig. 6. The projected actions from the KTH database. Projected actions in (e) are due to all the nonnegative elements of transformation matrices.

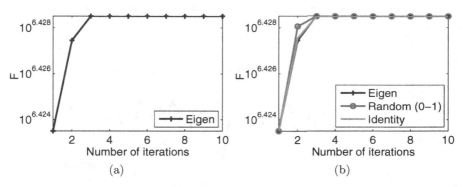

Fig. 7. Convergence characteristics of the optimization in MDA. (a) is the F value of total modes varies with the iterations. (b) shows the convergence to a unique maximum value with different initial values of U. This sub-figure indicates that MDA is convex.

Fig. 8 shows the effect of dimensional reduction on *mode-3* data. We can see the accuracy is increased along with the increase of dimensions. So, next step we will test the effect of the *mode-1,2* dimension by fixing the *mode-3*. In Fig. 9, the dimensions of *mode-3* is fixed to be 20, and we can see the MDA gets the best result within dimensions of [15,15,20], which indicates the best subspace dimension of *mode-1,2*. MDA performs better than DATER, which means the *mode-3* correlation plays an important role in the action silhouette sequence. V-Tensor also performs better than DATER in this database, which indicates the effectiveness of the action sequence by *mode-3* manifold learning. MDCC gets better results than DATER most of time, which is another evidence of the effectiveness of *mode-3* correlation. DNTF is suitable for dealing with images with rich information, like face, *etc.* While for silhouette with 0 and 1 value, the preserved energy is too little to perform well. The training time of all the

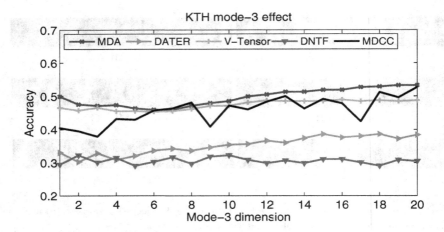

Fig. 8. Recognition rates *w.r.t.* dimension of different methods

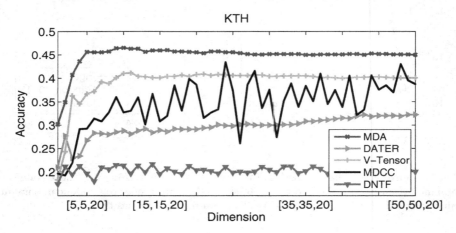

Fig. 9. Recognition rates *w.r.t.* dimension of different methods

Table 1. Training time (second) on the KTH database

Method	DATER [29]	MDCC [13]	DNTF [33]	V-Tensor [26]	MDA [Ours]
Time (s)	∼10	∼10	∼5	∼5	∼5

methods are shown in Table 1. The time complexity of MDA is also competitive with others.

Fig. 10. ETH dataset. The objects from left to right are apple, car, cow, cup, dog, horse, pear, and tomato, respectively.

4.3 Experiments on the ETH Database

In this experiment, we use a RGB object database to testify the proposed method by generalizing its application besides action sequence. In this experiment we employed the ETH dataset [18], which is an ideal simple dataset, to test the performance of our method. There are 3280 RGB images within 8 classes, each of which has 10 subjects. Fig. 10 shows the samples of each class. Leave-one-out cross validation was used, and each time one subject was selected for testing, and the rest for training.

The recognition results are shown in Fig. 11, in which the projected dimensions are selected from [1,1,1] to [32,32,3]. MDA performs well even when the

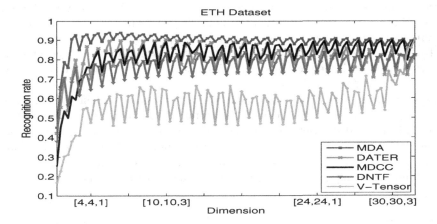

Fig. 11. The recognition rate of different methods versus different dimensions

image dimension is small, which demonstrates that the *mode-1,2* rank is small, and the discriminant correlations of *mode-3* is effective. DNTF performs well in the common ETH object dataset, while poorly in the KTH dataset. This is reasonable because the pixel-based input data, the unoccluded and undamaged RGB object contains much more information than an action silhouette, which contains 0 and 1 value merely.

Table 2. Recognition rate (%) on the ETH database

Method	DATER [29]	MDCC [13]	DNTF [33]	V-Tensor [26]	MDA [Ours]
Apple	94.39±6.23	95.00±7.04	91.20±5.73	87.59±14.61	**95.24±4.57**
Car	70.40±22.90	74.30±14.53	65.41±19.59	35.63±27.70	**84.64±8.90**
Cow	62.87±24.53	67.63±20.29	65.74±20.98	29.59±21.30	**80.32±11.82**
Cup	89.04±14.15	83.85±20.31	80.58±18.55	47.30±41.06	**94.23±7.08**
Dog	70.96±24.58	77.93±16.61	67.38±16.87	43.38±25.26	**87.80±9.10**
Horse	67.26±25.67	72.19±18.18	66.06±16.82	43.22±27.18	**81.82±8.77**
Pear	92.57±8.72	93.08±8.45	84.83±15.90	89.02±11.90	**95.32±3.55**
Tomato	**95.90±6.41**	91.16±15.91	91.13±12.61	82.08±29.16	95.78±6.91
Overall	80.42±16.65	81.89±15.16	76.54±15.88	57.23±24.77	**89.39±7.59**

Fig. 12 shows the similarity matrices of samples from the same and different classes. The *mode-3* reduced dimension is 2. The corresponding correlations in the similarity matrices are ρ_1 and ρ_2, and $diag(\rho_1) = [1, 0.9812]$, $diag(\rho_2) = [1, 0.1372]$. Fig. 12 illustrates that the correlation value of the same class is larger than that of different classes, which indicates that the *mode-3* discriminant performance of MDA is reliable.

Table 2 shows the recognition rates of each class. Obviously we can see that the performance of our method is better than others. Because ETH is an ideal pixel-based dataset, all the methods performed well under each class, compared to the last experiment. The results demonstrated the fact that, the same algorithm may perform diversely on various datasets, due to complicated background, changing views, lateral illumination, or partial occlusion, and so on.

5   Conclusions

In this paper we proposed a novel mode alignment method with different discriminant criteria in tensor subspace, and we name this method mode-driven discriminant analysis (MDA). MDA is used to perform the dimension reduction tasks on different tensorial modes; MDA employs Fisher criteria on the first (N-1) feature modes of all the tensors to extract image features, then it updates the whole tensor sequence by considering the correlations of $(k − 1)$-th, k-th, and $(k+1)$-th subsets, and finally it performs discriminant analysis on the N-th mode to calculate *mode-3* projection matrix. The proposed MDA outperforms other tensor-based methods in two commonly used action databases: MSR action 3D

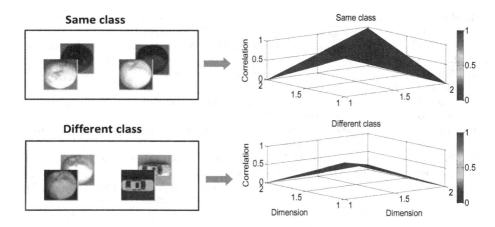

Fig. 12. Similarity matrices for MDA on ETH dataset. The upper left upper part indicates projected tensors from the same class, whose correlations illustrated in the similarity matrix shown in the upper right. The lower part shows the situation from different class. It can be intuitively seen the correlation on the second mode is smaller than that of the upper.

database, KTH action database, and one object ETH database. The time cost of MDA is competitive with others, therefore is suitable for large-scale computing. MDA can deal well with damaged action silhouettes and RGB object images in various view angles, which demonstrates its robustness. Moreover, the alternating projection procedure of MDA converges, as proved theoretically and confirmed by experiments, and finally, MDA is convex with different initial values of the transformation matrices.

Our future work will involve applying the sparse representation [3,20] to MDA, so that we can eliminate those trivial variables while keeping the important ones in the transformation matrices, thus improving the tensor's interpretation ability. We can also work on the low-rank tensor approximation [8,14], which can be used for denoising and occlusion elimination, and for image recovery.

Acknowledgments. This research is supported in part by the NSF CNS award 1314484, ONR award N00014-12-1-1028, ONR Young Investigator Award N00014-14-1-0484, and U.S. Army Research Office Young Investigator Award W911NF-14-1-0218.

References

1. Ballani, J., Grasedyck, L.: A projection method to solve linear systems in tensor format. Numerical Linear Algebra with Applications **20**(1), 27–43 (2013)
2. Belhumeur, P., Hespanha, J., Kriegman, D.: Eigenfaces vs. fisherfaces: Recognition using class specific linear projection. IEEE TPAMI **19**(7), 711–720 (1997)
3. Birnbaum, A., Johnstone, I.M., Nadler, B., Paul, D., et al.: Minimax bounds for sparse pca with noisy high-dimensional data. The Annals of Statistics **41**(3), 1055–1084 (2013)

4. Biswas, S., Aggarwal, G., Flynn, P.J., Bowyer, K.W.: Pose-robust recognition of low-resolution face images. TPAMI **35**(12), 3037–3049 (2013)
5. Fukunaga, K.: Introduction to statistical pattern recognition. Pattern Recognition **22**(7), 833–834 (1990)
6. Gong, D., Medioni, G.: Dynamic manifold warping for view invariant action recognition. In: ICCV, pp. 571–578. IEEE (2011)
7. Gong, W., Sapienza, M., Cuzzolin, F.: Fisher tensor decomposition for unconstrained gait recognition. Training **2**, 3 (2013)
8. Grasedyck, L., Kressner, D., Tobler, C.: A literature survey of low-rank tensor approximation techniques. GAMM-Mitteilungen **36**(1), 53–78 (2013)
9. Guo, K., Ishwar, P., Konrad, J.: Action recognition from video using feature covariance matrices. IEEE TIP **22**(6), 2479–2494 (2013)
10. Ho, H.T., Gopalan, R.: Model-driven domain adaptation on product manifolds for unconstrained face recognition. IJCV **109**(1–2), 110–125 (2014)
11. Hu, H.: Enhanced gabor feature based classification using a regularized locally tensor discriminant model for multiview gait recognition. IEEE Transactions on Circuits and Systems for Video Technology **23**(7), 1274–1286 (2013)
12. Huang, C.-H., Yeh, Y.-R., Wang, Y.-C.F.: Recognizing actions across cameras by exploring the correlated subspace. In: Fusiello, A., Murino, V., Cucchiara, R. (eds.) ECCV 2012 Ws/Demos, Part I. LNCS, vol. 7583, pp. 342–351. Springer, Heidelberg (2012)
13. Jia, C., Wang, S., Peng, X., Pang, W., Zhang, C., Zhou, C., Yu, Z.: Incremental multi-linear discriminant analysis using canonical correlations for action recognition. Neurocomputing **83**, 56–63 (2012)
14. Jia, C., Zhong, G., Fu, Y.: Low-rank tensor learning with discriminant analysis for action classification and image recovery. In: AAAI (2014)
15. Kim, T., Cipolla, R.: Canonical correlation analysis of video volume tensors for action categorization and detection. IEEE T. Pattern Anal. 1415–1428 (2008)
16. Kolda, T., Bader, B.: Tensor decompositions and applications. SIAM Review **51**(3), 455–500 (2009)
17. de Laat, K.F., van Norden, A.G., Gons, R.A., van Oudheusden, L.J., van Uden, I.W., Norris, D.G., Zwiers, M.P., de Leeuw, F.E.: Diffusion tensor imaging and gait in elderly persons with cerebral small vessel disease. Stroke **42**(2), 373–379 (2011)
18. Leibe, B., Schiele, B.: Analyzing appearance and contour based methods for object categorization. In: CVPR, vol. 2, pp. II-409 (2003)
19. Lui, Y.M., Beveridge, J.R.: Tangent bundle for human action recognition. In: FG, pp. 97–102. IEEE (2011)
20. Lykou, A., Whittaker, J.: Sparse cca using a lasso with positivity constraints. Computational Statistics & Data Analysis **54**(12), 3144–3157 (2010)
21. Miyamoto, K., Adachi, Y., Osada, T., Watanabe, T., Kimura, H.M., Setsuie, R., Miyashita, Y.: Dissociable memory traces within the macaque medial temporal lobe predict subsequent recognition performance. The Journal of Neuroscience **34**(5), 1988–1997 (2014)
22. Goud Tandarpally, M., Nagendar, G., Ganesh Bandiatmakuri, S., Jawahar, C.V.: Action recognition using canonical correlation kernels. In: Lee, K.M., Matsushita, Y., Rehg, J.M., Hu, Z. (eds.) ACCV 2012, Part III. LNCS, vol. 7726, pp. 479–492. Springer, Heidelberg (2013)
23. Perez, E.A., Mota, V.F., Maciel, L.M., Sad, D., Vieira, M.B.: Combining gradient histograms using orientation tensors for human action recognition. In: ICPR, pp. 3460–3463. IEEE (2012)

24. Schuldt, C., Laptev, I., Caputo, B.: Recognizing human actions: a local SVM approach. In: ICPR, vol. 3, pp. 32–36 (2004)
25. Tao, D., Li, X., Wu, X., Maybank, S.: General tensor discriminant analysis and gabor features for gait recognition. IEEE T. Pattern Anal. **29**, 1700–1715 (2007)
26. Tian, C., Fan, G., Gao, X., Tian, Q.: Multiview face recognition: From tensorface to v-tensorface and k-tensorface. IEEE T. Syst. Man Cy. B **42**(2), 320–333 (2012)
27. Wu, X., Wang, H., Liu, C., Jia, Y.: Cross-view action recognition over heterogeneous feature spaces. In: ICCV, pp. 609–616 (2013)
28. Xue, G., Mei, L., Chen, C., Lu, Z.L., Poldrack, R., Dong, Q.: Spaced learning enhances subsequent recognition memory by reducing neural repetition suppression. Journal of Cognitive Neuroscience **23**(7), 1624–1633 (2011)
29. Yan, S., Xu, D., Yang, Q., Zhang, L., Tang, X., Zhang, H.: Discriminant analysis with tensor representation. In: CVPR, vol. 1, pp. 526–532 (2005)
30. Yang, F., Bourdev, L., Shechtman, E., Wang, J., Metaxas, D.: Facial expression editing in video using a temporally-smooth factorization. In: CVPR, pp. 861–868. IEEE (2012)
31. Youn, J., Cho, J.W., Lee, W.Y., Kim, G.M., Kim, S.T., Kim, H.T.: Diffusion tensor imaging of freezing of gait in patients with white matter changes. Movement Disorders **27**(6), 760–764 (2012)
32. Yu, Z.Z., Jia, C.C., Pang, W., Zhang, C.Y., Zhong, L.H.: Tensor discriminant analysis with multiscale features for action modeling and categorization. IEEE Signal Processing Letters **19**(2), 95–98 (2012)
33. Zafeiriou, S.: Discriminant nonnegative tensor factorization algorithms. IEEE TNN **20**(2), 217–235 (2009)

Author Index

Printed in the United States
By Bookmasters